Most Recent Episode Manic
Most Recent Episode Mixed
Most Recent Episode Depressed
Bipolar II Disorder (Recurrent major depressive episodes with hypomania)
Cyclothymic Disorder
Mood Disorder due to a General Medical Condition

Substance-Induced Mood Disorder

ANXIETY DISORDERS

Panic Disorder

Without Agoraphobia

With Agoraphobia

Agoraphobia Without History of Panic Disorder

Specific Phobia

Social Phobia (Social Anxiety Disorder)

Obsessive-Compulsive Disorder

Posttraumatic Stress Disorder

Acute Stress Disorder

Generalized Anxiety Disorder

Anxiety Disorder Due to a General Medical Condition

Substance-Induced Anxiety Disorder

SOMATOFORM DISORDERS

Somatization Disorder

Conversion Disorder

Hypochondriasis

Body Dysmorphic Disorder

Pain Disorder

Undifferentiated Somatoform Disorder

FACTITIOUS DISORDERS

Factitious Disorder

DISSOCIATIVE DISORDERS

Dissociative Amnesia

Dissociative Fugue

Dissociative Identity Disorder

Depersonalization Disorder

SEXUAL AND GENDER IDENTITY DISORDERS

Sexual Dysfunctions
Sexual Desire Disorders
Hypoactive Sexual Desire Disorder

Sexual Aversion Disorder
Sexual Arousal Disorders
Female Sexual Arousal Disorder
Male Erectile Disorder
Orgasm Disorders
Female Orgasmic Disorder
Male Orgasmic Disorder
Premature Ejaculation
Sexual Pain Disorders
Dyspareunia
Vaginismus
Sexual Dysfunctions due to a General Medical Condition
Substance-Induced Sexual Dysfunction

Paraphilias
Exhibitionism
Fetishism
Frotteurism
Pedophilia
Sexual Masochism
Sexual Sadism
Voyeurism
Transvestic Fetishism

Gender Identity Disorders
Gender Identity Disorder

EATING DISORDERS

Anorexia Nervosa

Bulimia Nervosa

SLEEP DISORDERS

Primary Sleep Disorders
Dyssomnias
Primary Insomnia
Primary Hypersomnia
Narcolepsy
Breathing-Related Sleep Disorder
Circadian Rhythm Sleep Disorder
Parasomnias
Nightmare Disorder
Sleep Terror Disorder
Sleepwalking Disorder

Sleep Disorders Related to Another Mental Disorder

Other Sleep Disorders

Sleep Disorder due to a General Medical Condition

Substance-Induced Sleep Disorder

IMPULSE CONTROL DISORDERS NOT ELSEWHERE CLASSIFIED

Intermittent Explosive Disorder

Kleptomania

Pyromania

Pathological Gambling

Trichotillomania

ADJUSTMENT DISORDERS

Adjustment Disorder with Anxiety

Adjustment Disorder with Depressed Mood

Adjustment Disorder with Disturbance of Conduct

Adjustment Disorder with Mixed Disturbance of Emotions and Conduct

Adjustment Disorder with Mixed Anxiety and Depressed Mood

AXIS II: PERSONALITY DISORDERS

PERSONALITY DISORDERS

Paranoid Personality Disorder

Schizoid Personality Disorder

Schizotypal Personality Disorder

Antisocial Personality Disorder

Borderline Personality Disorder

Histrionic Personality Disorder

Narcissistic Personality Disorder

Avoidant Personality Disorder

Dependent Personality Disorder

Obsessive-Compulsive Personality Disorder

AXIS III: GENERAL MEDICAL CONDITIONS

AXIS IV: PSYCHOSOCIAL AND ENVIRONMENTAL PROBLEMS

AXIS V: GLOBAL ASSESSMENT OF FUNCTIONING

ABNORMAL PSYCHOLOGY

IN A CHANGING WORLD

SECOND EDITION

JEFFREY S. NEVID

SPENCER A. RATHUS

BEVERLY GREENE

St. John's University

PRENTICE HALL, Englewood Cliffs, New Jersey 07632

Library of Congress Cataloging-in-Publication Data

Nevid, Jeffrey S.
    Abnormal psychology in a changing world / Jeffrey S. Nevid,
Spencer A. Rathus, Beverly Greene.—2nd ed.
        p. cm.
    Rev. ed. of: Abnormal psychology / Spencer A. Rathus, Jeffrey S.
Nevid. ©1991.
    Includes bibliographical references and index.
    ISBN 0-13-044918-0 (c)
    1. Psychology. Pathological.   2. Psychiatry.   I. Rathus, Spencer
A.   II. Greene, Beverly,   III. Rathus, Spencer A. Abnormal
psychology.   IV. Title.
    [DNLM: 1. Mental Disorders.   2. Psychopathology.   WM 100 N521a
1994]
RC454.N488   1994
616.89—dc20
DNLM/DLC
for Library of Congress   93-13056
                                                                    CIP

Executive editor: *Peter Janzow*
Editorial/production and supervision: *Margaret Antonini*
Interior and cover design: *Thomas Nery*
Production coordinators: *Herb Klein and Tricia Kenny*
Photo editor: *Lorinda Morris-Nantz*
Photo research: *Ilene Cherna Bellovin and Joelle Burrows*
Managing editor: *Heidi Freund*
Senior marketing manager: *Bill Hendee*
Editorial assistant: *Marilyn Coco*
Cover photo: *Self Portrait* by Marisol, 1961–62.
    Wood, plaster, marker, paint, graphite, human teeth,
    gold and plastic, 43 1/2 × 45 5/8 inches.
    Museum of Contemporary Art, Chicago, gift of Joseph & Jory Shapiro.
    © Marisol/VAGA, New York, 1993.

 © 1994, 1991 by Prentice-Hall, Inc.
A Simon & Schuster Company
Englewood Cliffs, New Jersey 07632

Printed in the United States of America
10 9 8 7 6 5 4 3 2

ISBN   0-13-044918-0

Prentice-Hall International (UK) Limited, *London*
Prentice-Hall of Australia Pty. Limited, *Sydney*
Prentice-Hall Canada Inc., *Toronto*
Prentice-Hall Hispanoamericana, S.A., *Mexico*
Prentice-Hall of India Private Limited, *New Delhi*
Prentice-Hall of Japan, Inc., *Tokyo*
Simon & Schuster Asia Pte. Ltd., *Singapore*
Editora Prentice-Hall do Brasil, Ltda., *Rio de Janeiro*

Contents

1

WHAT IS ABNORMAL PSYCHOLOGY? 1

2

THEORETICAL PERSPECTIVES 39

3

CLASSIFICATION AND ASSESSMENT OF ABNORMAL BEHAVIOR 85

4

STRESS, PSYCHOLOGICAL FACTORS, AND HEALTH 125

5

ANXIETY DISORDERS
171

6

DISSOCIATIVE AND SOMATOFORM DISORDERS
211

7

MOOD DISORDERS AND SUICIDE
239

8

DISORDERS OF PERSONALITY AND IMPULSE CONTROL 283

9

SUBSTANCE-RELATED DISORDERS 319

10

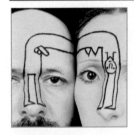

SEXUAL AND GENDER IDENTITY DISORDERS AND VARIATIONS IN SEXUAL BEHAVIOR 365

11

SCHIZOPHRENIA AND OTHER PSYCHOTIC DISORDERS
407

12

DELIRIUM, DEMENTIA, AMNESTIC, AND OTHER COGNITIVE DISORDERS
453

13

ABNORMAL BEHAVIOR IN CHILDHOOD AND ADOLESCENCE
483

14

METHODS OF THERAPY AND TREATMENT
531

15

CONTEMPORARY AND LEGAL ISSUES 575

Preface

The field of abnormal psychology is a moving target. Anyone who attempts a portrait risks grasping at its coattails. Authors of textbooks in abnormal psychology face the challenges of keeping current with the literature and of integrating the research findings that shape our understandings of abnormal behavior and its treatment. We hope that you found the first edition to have met these challenges and will hold us accountable for continuing to remain current and relevant in this and future editions.

A textbook is more than a compendium of recent developments in a field of study. It is more than a repository of accumulated knowledge and thought that has defined and shaped a field of study. A textbook is also a teaching device—a means of presenting material to students in a way that motivates them and fosters understanding and critical thinking. We strived to make this book a teaching device by adopting a style of writing that speaks to the reader in a clear expository style. We sought to explain complex material in understandable terms and to provide numerous case examples to illustrate the concepts in the text. We went a step further toward stimulating student involvement by incorporating two time-tested pedagogical features—"Truth-or-Fiction?" items and learning objectives—and by including such high-interest features as self-scoring questionnaires,

thought-provoking boxed inserts, and resource materials that highlight special concerns and applications (for example, "Rape Prevention," "Suicide Prevention," "Ways of Decreasing Type A Behavior," and "Controlling a Panic Attack").

WHAT'S NEW IN THIS EDITION

We wrote this second edition with the recognition that professors who use the book would expect us to take a fresh look at each topic and to incorporate new research findings to maintain currency with the latest developments in the field. The second edition contains a comprehensive updating of the research literature in abnormal psychology, including more than 600 citations to scientific findings reported in the past three years, for example:

- Ross's large-scale study of 236 cases of multiple personality in Canada
- Implantation in mouse embryos of genes linked to Alzheimer's disease
- Effectiveness of tacrine in treating Alzheimer's disease

- Fetal tissue brain implants in treating Parkinson's disease
- New findings on genetic factors and brain abnormalities in schizophrenia
- Effectiveness of newer psychotropic drugs, including Prozac and Clozaril
- New findings of MRI studies of autism
- Evidence of familial transmission of autism based on the Utah epidemiological study
- Coverage of the Fragile X syndrome
- Evidence of brain abnormalities in the visual pathways of dyslexics
- Evidence on stimulant therapy and growth retardation in children with ADHD
- New evidence of possible genetic factors in suicide risk
- Emerging evidence of relationships between immune system and stress
- New studies of relationships between optimism and physical and mental health
- New evidence on genetic factors in obesity
- New evidence of prevalences of sexual dysfunction in community samples
- Biological factors in sexual dysfunctions
- New evidence on genetic factors in various mental disorders, including several major twin studies on anxiety disorders, depression, and alcohol abuse
- New evidence of structural differences in the brains of gay males and heterosexual men
- Prevalences of dual diagnoses of substance abuse and other mental disorders
- Latest findings on effectiveness of antidepressants in treating obsessive-compulsive disorder, eating disorders, as well as depression
- Effects of antidrug education programs
- Changes in drug use among young people in the United States from 1981 to 1991
- Recent research on use of gateway drugs among adolescents

Other highlights of the second edition include:

- Extensive coverage of the NIMH ECA study and its findings that bear on ethnic and gender differences in mental disorders
- Comprehensive and up-to-date evaluation of deinstitutionalization, with special emphasis on the problems of the psychiatric homeless
- Recent developments in integrative approaches in psychotherapy

- Development of a multifactorial view of health and illness
- Expanded coverage of interpersonal psychotherapy
- New features that focus on current issues in the field, such as *Do Rose-Colored Glasses Keep Us Mentally Healthy?* or, *Does Survival in Today's World Require Distortion of Reality?*

INCORPORATION OF A MULTICULTURAL PERSPECTIVE

Those who are familiar with the first edition of the text will notice several changes on the book cover of the second edition. The order of authorship has been changed to reflect a realignment of responsibilities. There is also the inclusion of a new coauthor, Beverly A. Greene, and a change in title from *Abnormal Psychology* to *Abnormal Psychology in a Changing World*. Professor Greene draws upon her research on issues relating to diversity in psychology and clinical practice to expand coverage of multicultural material in the text. We adopted the new title to place abnormal psychology within the larger context of culture and society in a changing world. We seek to expand the student's understanding of cultural variations in psychopathology and the importance of taking into account cultural factors in diagnosis and treatment. *Abnormal Psychology in a Changing World* breaks new ground by incorporating a multicultural perspective throughout the text. Students will see how behavior that is deemed normal in one culture may be labeled abnormal in another; how states of psychological distress, like anxiety and depression, may be experienced differently in different cultures; how some abnormal behavior patterns are culture-bound or culture-related; and how therapists can incorporate sensitivity to cultural factors in psychotherapy.

Sensitivity to issues of diversity in psychology embraces more than a respect for cultural variations. It extends to differences relating to gender, sexual orientation, and physical ability. We were excited by the opportunity to bring issues of diversity such as the following to the attention of students who are embarking on their first study of abnormal psychology:

- Cultural differences in explanations of abnormal behavior
- Cultural differences in how states of psychological distress are experienced

- Culture-bound and culture-related syndromes
- Ethnic differences in our own society in the prevalences of various mental health problems
- Cultural factors in the assessment of abnormal behavior in other cultures, with special emphases on linguistic issues
- Relationships between acculturation and mental health problems of immigrant groups, with special emphasis on Hispanic Americans
- Perspectives on gender differences and gender-role stereotypes in the diagnosis of depression
- Culturally sensitive approaches to psychotherapy, including a special feature on cultural and linguistic issues in treating African Americans, Asian Americans, Hispanic Americans, and Native Americans
- Ethnic differences in utilization of mental health services
- Ethnic differences in response to psychotropic medication
- Ethnicity and diagnosis of schizophrenia
- Gender, ethnicity, and antisocial personality disorder
- Cultural variations in sexual behavior
- Gender and ethnic differences in suicide rates
- Feminist therapy

INCORPORATION OF DSM-IV

The field of abnormal psychology is indeed a moving target, as those of us trying to keep abreast of the developments with the DSM-IV can attest. The DSM-IV is expected to be published in late 1993 or early 1994, about the time of publication of this new edition. Many textbooks lag behind developments in the field by a couple of years because of the time it takes to produce and publish a book. We are grateful to the publishing professionals at Prentice-Hall who literally kept the presses waiting to permit us the time needed to incorporate the latest developments on the DSM-IV. As a result, we were able to incorporate the diagnostic criteria contained in the 3/1/93 version of the DSM-IV draft criteria that was to be submitted to the APA Assembly of District Branches and Board of Trustees for approval. The DSM-IV Task Force offered this draft as a "likely near-final version" of the DSM-IV diagnostic criteria. We expect to inform you of any substantive changes that may be incorporated in the final version.

FEATURES OF THE TEXTBOOK

Textbooks walk balance beams, as it were, and they can fall off in three directions, not just two. They must do justice to their subject matter while also meeting the needs of instructors and students. In subject matter, this textbook is comprehensive, providing depth and breadth. It contains full coverage of the history of societal responses to abnormal behavior, historic and contemporary models of abnormal behaviors, methods of assessment, psychological and biological models of treatment, contemporary issues, the comprehensive range of problem behaviors set forth in the DSM, and a number of other behavioral problems that entail psychological factors—most notably in the interfaces between psychology and health.

This book also contains a number of features that are intended to keep it on the beam as a vehicle for instruction and learning:

A 15-CHAPTER FORMAT

Although our coverage is as comprehensive as that of other abnormal psychology textbooks, we organize the subject matter into 15 chapters to meet the needs of instructors who prefer to be able to teach one chapter a week during the course of a semester.

TRUTH-OR-FICTION? ITEMS

Each chapter begins with a number of Truth-or-Fiction? items that are intended to whet students' appetites for the subject matter within the chapter. We have used such items in our other textbooks for many years, and instructors and students have repeatedly reported that they are effective ways of stimulating and challenging students. Some of the items are intended to be generally motivating ("Innocent people were drowned in medieval times as a way of certifying that they were not possessed by the devil") or to highlight interesting research findings ("Cycles of dieting and regaining lost weight make it progressively more difficult to take off extra pounds"). Others are designed to encourage students to take a scientific look at the subject matter by questioning folklore and preconceptions ("People can recognize when their blood pressure is high").

LEARNING OBJECTIVES

On the third page of each chapter is a list of learning objectives that provide students with concrete educational goals for the chapter.

TRUTH-OR-FICTION-REVISITED SECTIONS

The Truth-or-Fiction? items are revisited in these sections where the topics are discussed in the text. Students are thus given feedback concerning the accuracy of their preconceptions in the light of the material being addressed.

"A CLOSER LOOK" INSERTS

These sections include applications, focused discussions on controversial issues (e.g., "AIDS and the Duty to Warn") and information on state-of-the-art techniques of assessment (e.g., advances in brain-imaging techniques and in biological markers for depression).

MULTICULTURAL PERSPECTIVES

These boxed features, interspersed throughout the text, focus on multicultural issues relating to the chapter material. These features include the following:

- Mental Health Problems Among Native Americans—Loss of a Special Relationship with Nature?
- Mediators of the Effects of Stress Among African Americans
- Treatment of Alcoholism Among Ethnic Minority Groups
- Effects of Childhood Sexual Abuse on African-American and White Women
- *Schizophrenia* or *Nervios*? What's in a Name?— Quite a Lot, Apparently
- Families of Schizophrenics: Roles for Cultural Factors
- Treatment of Schizophrenia Among Asian Americans
- Multicultural Influences on Judgments of Children's Behavior as Normal or Abnormal
- Risk of Suicide Among Native American Youth
- Culturally Sensitive Therapies for Hispanic Children
- Ethnic Matching of Clients and Therapists
- Ethnic Differences Between Native Americans and Euro-Americans in Psychological Adjustment Following the Exxon *Valdez* Disaster
- Anxiety Disorders in Ethnic Minorities
- Socioeconomic, Sociocultural, and Ethnic Factors in Obesity

SELF-SCORING QUESTIONNAIRES

Self-scoring questionnaires (for example, "Are you a Type A or Type B?" and the "Temple Fear Survey Inventory") involve students in the discussion at hand and permit them to evaluate their own behavior. In some cases, students may become more aware of troubling concerns, such as phobias or states of depression, that they may wish to bring to the attention of a professional. We have screened the questionnaires to ensure that they will provide students with useful information to reflect on as well as serve as a springboard for class discussion.

CHAPTER SUMMARIES

Chapter summaries are organized according to the major heads of the chapters. Students who use the SQ3R method may be advised by their instructors to read them before the chapters as a way of surveying the material and helping form questions to guide their reading.

GLOSSARY

Key terms are boldfaced in the text and defined in a glossary.

ANCILLARIES

No matter how comprehensive a textbook is, today's instructors and students require a complete teaching package to advance teaching and comprehension. Nevid, Rathus, and Greene's *Abnormal Psychology in a Changing World* is accompanied by the following teaching and learning tools:

■ **INSTRUCTOR'S MANUAL.** Designed to provide you with maximal assistance in preparing your lectures, each chapter of the Instructor's Manual includes chapter and lecture outlines, teaching suggestions, class activities and discussion questions, suggested additional readings, key terms, film and video descriptions, and a list of film and video distributors.

■ **TEST ITEM FILE.** A Test Item File containing over 1500 page-referenced conceptual and applied questions is also available for your convenience. Multiple choice, short answer, true-false, and essay questions span a range of difficulty levels.

■ **PRENTICE HALL TEST MANAGER 2.0.**
—3.5″ IBM 0-13-044934-2
—5.25″ IBM 0-13-044942-3
—Macintosh 0-13-045060-5
The new release of Prentice Hall's exclusive computerized testing package now features full control over printing, print preview, complete mouse support, on-screen VGA graphics, import capabilities for .TIFF and .PCX file formats, and the ability to export your files to WordPerfect, Word, and ASCII. Context-sensitive help is available at all times and Prentice Hall also offers toll-free technical support.

■ **TELEPHONE TEST PREPARATION SERVICE.** Select up to 200 questions from the Test Item File and call Prentice Hall toll free at (800) 842-2958. They prepare the test (and an alternate version if requested) on bond paper or ditto master within 48 hours and mail it together with a separate answer key directly to you.

■ **PRENTICE HALL TRANSPARENCIES FOR ABNORMAL PSYCHOLOGY, SERIES I.** This series of thirty full-color transparencies covering the major topics in the course adds visual impact to both learning and lectures.

■ **HANDOUTS AND TRANSPARENCY MASTERS.** Involve your students and stimulate classroom discussion! These versatile questionnaires and activities can be handed out in class or turned into overhead transparencies.

 ABC NEWS/PRENTICE HALL VIDEO LIBRARY FOR ABNORMAL PSYCHOLOGY (0-13-044975-X). The result of an exclusive arrangement between ABC News and Prentice Hall, this video library contains relevant feature- and documentary-style segments from award-winning ABC News programs including Nightline, 20/20, Prime Time Live, and American Agenda. A summary of each segment and suggestions on how to incorporate the video into your classroom are included in the Instructor's Manual.

■ **VIDEO CASES IN ABNORMAL PSYCHOLOGY: PATIENTS AS EDUCATORS.** This is an exclusive video series of 10 patient interviews with a range of disorders (depression, schizophrenia, OCD among others). Each interview is preceded by a brief history of the patient and a synopsis of some major symptoms of the disorder. Each interview ends with a summary and a brief analysis.

FOR THE STUDENT

 The New York Times and Prentice Hall are sponsoring **Themes of the Times:** a program designed to enhance student access to current information of relevance in the classroom.

Through this program, the core subject matter provided in the text is supplemented by a collection of time-sensitive articles from one of the world's most distinguished newspapers, **The New York Times.** These articles demonstrate the vital, ongoing connection between what is learned in the classroom and what is happening in the world around us.

To enjoy the wealth of information of **The New York Times** daily, a reduced subscription rate is available. For information, call toll-free: 1-800-631-1222.

Prentice Hall and **The New York Times** are proud to co-sponsor **Themes of the Times.** We hope it will make the reading of both textbooks and newspapers a more dynamic, involving process.

■ **STUDENT STUDY GUIDE AND WORKBOOK (0-13-04499-1).** The Study Guide and Workbook provides a chapter review, learning objectives, key concepts/terms with definitions, self-tests including multiple choice, true-false questions, and activities for each chapter of the text.

■ **STILL LIFE: CLINICAL PORTRAITS IN PSYCHOPATHOLOGY, CHRISTOPHER F. MONTE, MANHATTANVILLE COLLEGE (0-13-137217-3).** Still Life is a unique casebook featuring fourteen extended case histories which provide students with the diagnostic data on which each case is based. Students are then invited to interpret the same clues that the diagnostician used to formulate their own hypotheses.

■ **ASKING THE RIGHT QUESTIONS ABOUT ABNORMAL PSYCHOLOGY, STUART KEELEY, BOWLING GREEN STATE UNIVERSITY** Asking the Right Questions About Abnormal Psychology teaches students to actively interact with their abnormal psychology textbooks by asking critical thinking questions. The book helps students practice their critical thinking skills by applying core critical thinking questions to research studies that are "classics" in the field of abnormal psychology. Research topics selected for critical questioning integrate nicely with major topics in abnormal psychology texts.

ACKNOWLEDGMENTS

We noted that the field of abnormal psychology is a moving target. We are deeply indebted to a number of talented individuals who helped us hold our camera steady, focus in on the salient features of our subject matter, and develop our snapshots through prose.

First, our professional colleagues, who reviewed our manuscript through the first two editions and continue to help us refine and strengthen the material:

Bernard S. Gorman, Ph.D.
Nassau Community College
and Hofstra University Doctoral Programs

William G. Iacono
University of Minnesota

Robert Lavallee, Ph.D.
St. Michael's College

Robin J. Lewis, Ph.D.
Old Dominion University

Elinor MacDonald
Quinebaug Valley Community College

Richard D. McAnulty
University of North Carolina at Charlotte

Robert J. McMahon, Ph.D.
University of Washington

Kathryn K. Rileigh
Pembroke State University

Caton F. Roberts, Ph.D.
State University of New York, Buffalo

Norman R. Simonson
University of Massachusetts

Jerome Small, Ph.D.
Youngstown State University

Robert M. Tipton, Ph.D.
Virginia Commonwealth University

Max Zwanziger
Central Washington University

Second, but by no means second rate, are the publishing professionals at Prentice Hall: Margaret Antonini, Bill Hendee, Phil Miller, Tracy Augustine, Jan Stephan, Pete Janzow, and Heidi Freund.

Third, we wish to thank graduate research assistants Sharon Sorrentino, Christina Corsello, Warren Bush, and John Moulton III for their assistance with the library research for this edition that helped make this book as comprehensive in its coverage of recent scientific findings as possible.

Finally, we especially wish to thank the two people without whose inspiration and loving support this effort would never have materialized or been carried through to completion, Judith Wolf-Nevid and Lois Fichner-Rathus.

J.S.N
New York, New York

S.A.R.
Short Hills, New Jersey

B.A.G.
Brooklyn, New York

ABOUT THE AUTHORS

Jeffrey S. Nevid is professor of psychology at St. John's University in New York, where he also directs the doctoral program in clinical psychology. He earned his Ph.D. in clinical psychology from the State University of New York at Albany and was awarded an NIMH postdoctoral fellowship in mental health evaluation research at Northwestern University. He has published numerous articles in the areas of clinical and community psychology, health psychology, training models in clinical psychology, and methodological issues in clinical research. He holds a Diplomate in Clinical Psychology from the American Board of Professional Psychology, has served on the editorial board of the **Journal of Consulting and Clinical Psychology,** has coauthored several books with Spencer Rathus, and is author of **A Student's Guide to AIDS and Other Sexually Trans-**

mitted Diseases. His current research on smoking cessation with Hispanic smokers is supported by a research grant from the National Heart, Lung, and Blood Institute of the National Institutes of Health.

Spencer A. Rathus received his Ph.D. from the State University of New York at Albany. He is on the psychology faculty at St. John's University, where he has taught courses in behavior therapy and supervised doctoral trainees in psychotherapy. He has published numerous articles in the areas of psychological assessment, cognitive behavior therapy, and deviant behavior. He is the author of the Rathus Assertiveness Schedule and has written many books, including **Psychology, Essentials of Psychology,** and **Understanding Child Development.** He has coauthored **Making the Most of College** with Lois Fichner-Rathus; **AIDS—What Every Student Needs to Know** with Susan Boughn; **Adjustment and Growth: The Challenges of Life** and **Behavior Therapy** with Jeffrey S. Nevid; and **Human Sexuality in a World of Diversity** with Jeffrey S. Nevid and Lois Fichner-Rathus.

Beverly A. Greene is associate professor of psychology at St. John's University, where she teaches courses in the area of ethics and professional issues and supervises doctoral trainees in psychotherapy. She was awarded a Ph.D. in clinical psychology from the Gordon Derner Institute of Advanced Psychological Studies at Adelphi University and was a supervising psychologist at the University of Medicine and Dentistry of New Jersey before joining the St. John's faculty. An active contributor to the professional literature on ethnic minority issues and diversity in psychology, she is an editor of the books **Women of Color: Integrating Ethnic and Gender Identities in Treatment** and **Psychological Perspectives on Lesbian and Gay Issues,** and is a member of the editorial board of the journal **Women & Therapy.** In 1992 she was honored with the Distinguished Professional Contributions to Ethnic Minority Issues Award of Division 44 of the American Psychological Association.

NEVID, RATHUS, GREENE MEDIA GUIDE

TOPIC	VIDEO SEGMENT	THE NEW YORK TIMES ARTICLES
STRESS	Case #1, Ann, Bulimia*	"How Dangerous to the Heart is Anger? Perhaps Not Very." "For Blast Survivors, Shock Waves of Stress" "Where the Unorthodox Gets a Hearing at N.I.H."
ANXIETY DISORDERS	Case #8, Jerry, Panic Disorder* Case #7, Ed, Obsessive-Compulsive Disorder*	"Early Onset Found for Panic Attacks" "Postal Officials Examine System After 2 Killings" "Strategies for Lifting Spirits are Emerging from Studies"
MOOD DISORDERS	Case #3, Helen, Major Depression* Case #10, Craig, Bipolar Disorder* Depression: Beyond the Darkness+ Desperate for Light+ What Made Them do It (Prozac)+	"Myriad Masks Hide an Epidemic of Depression" "Scientists Now Say They Can't Find a Gene for Manic Depressive Illness" "Doctors Urged to Look for Signs of Depression" "Teen-age Accidents and Suicides"
PERSONALITY DISORDERS	Case #2, Paul, Antisocial Personality*	
SUBSTANCE ABUSE AND DEPENDENCE	Alcoholism+ Drugs and the Brain+	"For Children of Cocaine, Fresh Reasons for Hope"
SEXUAL AND GENDER IDENTITY DISORDERS	Case #9, Denise, Transsexual* Case #4, Karen, Adult Survivor of Abuse*	"How to Outwit a Rapist: Rehearse"
SCHIZOPHRENIA	Case #6, Georgiana, Schizophrenia*	
DELIRIUM, DEMENTIA, AMNESTIC, AND OTHER COGNITIVE DISORDERS	New Life for Andrew (Epilepsy)+ Desperate for Anything (Alzheimer's)+	"Study Backs Theory on a Cause of Alzheimer's"
ABNORMAL BEHAVIOR IN CHILDHOOD AND ADOLESCENCE	Free From Silence (Autism)+ Case #5, Billy, Autism* Motivation: What Causes Crime?+	"Growing Up Under Koresh: Cult Children Tell of Abuses" "Teen agers Called Shrewd Judges of Risk" "Troubled Marriage: Relations may be at Fault" "Studies Reveal Suggestibility of Very Young as Witnesses"
METHODS OF THERAPY	Pushed to the Edge (Battered Women Fight Back)+	"PriceTag: Psychotherapy" "Helping Mentally Ill Find a Niche, to the Admiration of Japanese" "When a Long Therapy Goes a Little Way"
CONTEMPORARY AND LEGAL ISSUES		"Danger of Mentally Ill Homeless to be Reevaluated in New York" "More Than 1 in 4 U.S. Adults Suffers a Mental Disorder Each Year" "Report is Critical of Mental Clinics"

* "Patients As Educators" Video Series
\+ ABC News/Prentice Hall Video Library

ABNORMAL
PSYCHOLOGY
IN A CHANGING WORLD

Marisol, Self-Portrait, 1961–62. Wood, plaster, marker, paint, graphite, human teeth, gold, and plastic; 43½ × 45¼ × 75⅝ inches. Museum of Contemporary Art, Chicago. Gift of Joseph and Jory Shapiro. © Marisol/VAGA, New York, 1993.

CHAPTER OUTLINE

1

What Is Abnormal Psychology?

TRUTH OR FICTION?

___ Abnormal behavior affects virtually everyone.

___ Unusual behavior is abnormal.

___ Behavior that is normal in one culture may be regarded as abnormal in another.

___ Many Native Americans claim to hear the spirits of people who have recently died calling to them as they ascend to the afterlife.

___ Innocent people were drowned in medieval times as a way of certifying that they were not possessed by the devil.

___ Many of the nation's homeless people are discharged mental patients.

___ Native Hawaiians lead a carefree existence.

___ In order to carry out valid research, it may be necessary to keep people unaware of the treatments they receive.

___ Surveys of several million Americans may not represent the general population.

___ Case studies have been conducted on people who have been dead for hundreds of years.

Abnormal behavior might seem the concern of a few. After all, only a minority of the population will ever be admitted to a psychiatric hospital. Most people never seek the help of a **psychologist** or **psychiatrist**. Only a few people plead not guilty to crimes on grounds of insanity. Many of us have an "eccentric" relative, but few of us have relatives we would consider truly bizarre.

The truth of the matter is that abnormal behavior affects everyone in one way or another. If we confine our definition of abnormal behavior to traditional mental disorders—anxiety, depression, schizophrenia, abuse of alcohol and other drugs, and the like—perhaps one in three of us have been affected (Robins et al., 1984). If we include sexual dysfunctions and difficulties adjusting to the demands of adult life, many more are added. If we extend our definition to include maladaptive or self-defeating behavior patterns like compulsive gambling and dependence on nicotine, a clear majority of us are affected.

Contemporary professionals tend to include these and other categories that broaden the traditional definitions of abnormal behavior. Moreover, if we expand the sense of "being affected" by these problems to family members, friends, and co-workers of those who are afflicted—along with those who foot the bill for treatment in the form of taxes and health insurance premiums—virtually none of us remains uninvolved.

 It is true that virtually everyone is affected by abnormal behavior, even if only a minority display traditional disorders such as anxiety, depression, and schizophrenia.

Abnormal psychology is the branch of the science of psychology that addresses the description, causes, and treatment of abnormal behavior.

In this chapter we first address the task of defining abnormal behavior. We see that throughout history, and prehistory, abnormal behavior has been viewed from different perspectives, or models. We chronicle the development of concepts of abnormal behavior and its treatment. We see that historically speaking, "treatment" usually referred to what was done *to*, rather than *for*, people with abnormal behavior. Finally, we describe the ways in which psychologists and other scholars study abnormal behavior today.

WHAT IS ABNORMAL BEHAVIOR?

There are diverse patterns of abnormal behavior. Some are typified by anxiety or depression, but most of us become anxious or depressed from time to time, and our behavior is not deemed abnormal. It is normal to become anxious in anticipation of an important job interview or a final examination. It is appropriate to feel depressed when you have lost someone close to you or when you have failed at a test or on the job.

When are emotions like anxiety and depression thus judged abnormal? One answer is that these feelings may be appraised as abnormal when they are not appropriate to the situation. It is normal to feel blue because of failure on a test, but not when one's grades are good or excellent. It is normal to feel anxious during a college admissions interview, but not whenever one enters a department store or boards a crowded elevator.

Abnormal behavior may also be suggested by the magnitude of the problem. Although some anxiety is normal enough before a job interview, feeling that one's heart is hammering away so relentlessly that it might leap from one's chest—and consequently cancelling the interview—are not. Nor is it normal to feel so anxious in this situation that your clothing becomes soaked with perspiration.

Psychologists generally concur that behavior may be deemed abnormal when it meets some combination of these criteria:

1. *Behavior is unusual.* Behavior that is unusual is often considered abnormal. Only a few of us report seeing or hearing things that are not really there; "seeing things" and "hearing things" are almost always considered abnormal in our culture, except, perhaps, in cases of religious experience (see Chapter 11). Yet we shall see that hallucinations are not deemed unusual in some non-Western cultures. Becoming overcome with feelings of panic when entering a department store or when standing in a crowded elevator is also uncommon and considered abnormal. But uncommon behavior is not in itself abnormal. Only one person can hold the record for swimming or running the fastest 100 meters. The record-holding athlete differs from you and us but, again, is not considered abnormal.

(A)

(B)

When is anxiety abnormal? Negative emotions such as anxiety are considered abnormal when they are judged to be excessive or inappropriate to the situation. Anxiety is generally regarded as normal when it is experienced during a job interview (A), so long as it is not so severe that it prevents the interviewee from performing adequately. Anxiety is deemed to be abnormal if it is experienced whenever one boards an elevator (B).

 Unusual or statistically deviant behavior is not necessarily abnormal. Exceptional behavior, for example, also deviates from the norm.

Thus rarity or statistical deviance is not a sufficient basis for labeling behavior as abnormal; nevertheless, it is one yardstick often used to judge abnormality.

2. *Behavior is socially unacceptable or violates social norms.* All societies have standards or norms that define the kinds of behaviors which are acceptable in given contexts. In our society, standing on a soapbox in a park and repeatedly shouting "Kill!" to passersby would be labeled abnormal; shouting "Kill!" in the grandstands at an important football game is usually within normal bounds, however tasteless it may seem. Although the use of norms remains one of the important standards for defining abnormal behavior, we should be aware of some limitations of this definition.

One implication of basing the definition of abnormal behavior on social norms is that norms reflect relative standards, not universal truths. What is normal in one culture may be abnormal in another. For example, Americans who assume that strangers are devious and try to take advantage are usually regarded as distrustful, perhaps even **paranoid**. But such suspicions were justified among the Mundu-gumor, a tribe of cannibals studied by anthropologist Margaret Mead (1935). Within that culture, male strangers, even the male members of one's own family, *were* typically malevolent toward others.

 Behavior that is deemed normal in one culture may in fact be viewed as abnormal in another.

Clinicians need to weigh cultural differences in determining what is normal and abnormal (American Psychological Association, 1993). In the case of the Mundugumor, this need is more or less obvious. Sometimes, however, differences are more subtle. For example, what is seen as healthful outspoken behavior by most American women might be interpreted as brazen behavior within some traditional Hispanic cultures. Although many clinicians appear to consider a client's culture in evaluating abnormal behavior, little research has been conducted into the relationships between cultural factors and clinical judgments (López & Hernandez, 1986).

Moreover, what strikes one generation as abnormal may be considered by others to fall within the normal spectrum. For example, until the mid-1970s homosexuality was classified as a mental disorder by the psychiatric profession (see Chapter 10). Today, however, the psychiatric profession no longer considers homosexuality a mental disorder, and many people argue that contemporary societal norms should include homosexuality as a normal variation in behavior.

Another implication of basing normality on compliance with social norms is the tendency to brand nonconformists as mentally disturbed. We may come to brand behavior we do not like or understand as "sick," rather than accept that behavior may be normal even if it offends or puzzles us.

3. *Perception or interpretation of reality is faulty.* Normally speaking, our sensory systems and cognitive processes permit us to form accurate mental representations of the environment. But seeing things and hearing voices that are not present are considered **hallucinations**, which in our culture are often taken as signs of mental disorder. Similarly, holding unfounded ideas or **delusions**, such as **ideas of persecution** that the CIA or the mafia are "out to get" one may be regarded as signs of mental disturbance—unless, of course, they *are*. (A former secretary of state is credited with having remarked that he might, indeed, be paranoid; his paranoia, however, did not mean that he was without enemies.)

It is normal in the United States to say that one "talks" to God through prayer. If, however, a person claims to have literally seen God or heard the voice of God—as opposed to, say, being divinely inspired—we may come to regard her or him as mentally disturbed.

4. *The person is in severe personal distress.* States of personal distress caused by troublesome emotions, such as anxiety, fear, or depression, may be considered abnormal. As noted earlier, however, anxiety and depression are sometimes appropriate responses to one's situation. Real threats and losses occur from time to time, and *lack* of emotional response to them would be regarded as abnormal. Appropriate feelings of distress are not considered abnormal unless they become prolonged or persist long after the source of anguish has been removed (after most people would have adjusted) or if they are so intense that they impair the individual's ability to function.

5. *Behavior is maladaptive or self-defeating.* Behavior that leads to unhappiness rather than self-fulfillment can be regarded as abnormal. Behavior that limits our ability to function in expected roles, or to adapt to our environments, may also be considered abnormal. According to these criteria, persistent alcohol consumption that impairs one's health or social and occupational functioning may be viewed as abnormal.

Agoraphobic behavior, characterized by intense fear of venturing into public places, is abnormal in that it is uncommon. But people who show such behavior may also be unable to fulfill their work and family responsibilities; so agoraphobia is maladaptive as well. People with faulty perceptions of reality may also be unable to meet day-to-day responsibilities to their employers and families. Hallucinations or delusions may preoccupy or confuse them when they should be focusing on their jobs or family responsibilities.

6. *Behavior is dangerous.* Behavior that is dangerous to oneself or other people may be considered abnormal. Here, too, the social context is crucial. In wartime, people who sacrifice themselves or charge the enemy with little apparent concern for their own safety may be characterized as courageous, heroic,

and patriotic. But people who threaten or attempt suicide because of the pressures of civilian life are usually considered abnormal.

Football and hockey players, even adolescent boys who occasionally get into altercations, may be normal enough. Given the cultural demands of the sports, unaggressive football and hockey players would not last long in the college or professional ranks. But individuals who are involved in frequent unsanctioned fights may be regarded as abnormal. Physically aggressive behavior is most often maladaptive in modern life. Moreover, outside the contexts of sports and warfare, physical aggression is discouraged as a way of resolving interpersonal conflicts—although it is by no means uncommon.

Abnormal behavior thus has multiple definitions. In most cases, a combination of these criteria is used to define abnormality. Some criteria may be weighed more heavily than others, depending on the situation. Let us consider some **cases** and see how they can advance our understanding of the kinds of behaviors that are considered abnormal:

It was about 2 A.M. when the police brought Margaret to the Emergency Room. She looked to be about 45, her hair was matted and uncombed, her clothing disheveled. Her face was expressionless, fixed in a blank stare. She clutched a clove of garlic in her right hand. She did not respond to the interviewer's questions: "Do you know where you are? Can you tell me your name? Can you tell me if anything is bothering you?"

The police officers filled in the details. Margaret had been found meandering along the painted line that divided the main street through town, apparently oblivious to the cars which swerved around her. She was waving the clove of garlic in front of her. She said nothing to the officers when they arrived on the scene, but she offered no resistance.

Margaret was admitted to the hospital and brought to the psychiatric ward. The next morning, she was brought before the day staff, still clutching the clove of garlic, and interviewed by the chief psychiatrist. She said little but her intentions could be pieced together from mumbled fragments. Margaret said something about "devils" who were trying to "rob" her mind. The garlic was meant to protect her. She had decided that the only way to rid the town of the "devils" that hounded her was to walk down the main street, waving the garlic in front of her.

Margaret would become well known to the hospital. This was but one of a series of **psychotic** *episodes.*

■ *The Authors' Files*

Margaret's behavior met several of the criteria for abnormality. It is statistically deviant—rare!—for a person to be ambling along the divider in a busy main street, sweeping the area of supernatural forces. Margaret's behavior was socially unacceptable or deviant, and indeed unlawful. It was also maladaptive—dangerous to herself and to those who swerved to avoid her. Moreover, she showed faulty perception of reality. It is normal within various religious perspectives to believe that a devil may be waging a cosmic conflict with God—with humankind in the middle. But it is generally deemed abnormal in contemporary Western society to believe that one is personally besieged by devils. Moreover, her thoughts were jumbled and confused, impairing her ability to sift through and evaluate the welter of frightening beliefs and perceptions. Margaret came to be diagnosed as schizophrenic (see Chapter 11).

Phil, unlike Margaret, was not out of touch with reality. Still, his behavior may be considered abnormal:

*Phil was 42, a police photographer. It was his job to take pictures at crime scenes. "Pretty grisly stuff," he admitted, "corpses and all." Phil was married and had two teenage sons. He sought a psychological consultation because he was bothered by fears of being confined in enclosed spaces—***claustrophobia.*** Many situations evoked his fears. He was terrified of becoming trapped in an elevator, and took the stairs whenever possible. He felt uncomfortable sitting in the back seat of a car. He had lately become fearful of flying, although in the past he had worked as a news cameraperson and would often fly to scenes of news events at a moment's notice—usually by helicopter.*

"I guess I was younger then and more daring," he related. "Sometimes I would hang out of the helicopter to shoot pictures with no fear at all. But now, just thinking about flying makes my heart race. It's not that I'm afraid the plane will crash. I just start trembling when I think of them closing that door, trapping us inside. I can't tell you why."

■ *The Authors' Files*

Phil recognized that his fears exceeded a realistic appraisal of danger in the situations that evoked his fears. Although he was not hampered by faulty perceptions of reality, his behavior could be considered abnormal on the basis of several other criteria listed earlier. Of primary concern were Phil's feelings of personal distress—his fear of enclosed spaces and the resulting limitations on his behavior. His fears also impaired his ability to carry out his occupational and familial responsibilities. The criterion of statistical infrequency might also be employed. Most people are not so fearful of confinement that they avoid flying or taking elevators.

Jessica, a 20-year-old communications major, engaged in a pattern of maladaptive, self-defeating behavior:

Jessica was engaged to be married in three months. There was one problem, she told the psychologist, "I have to stop bingeing and throwing up."

Jessica had kept a personal secret for the past three years. "I would go on binges, and then throw it all up. It made me feel like I was in control, but really I wasn't." To conceal her secret, she would lock herself in the bathroom, run the water in the sink to mask the sounds, and induce vomiting. She would then clean up after herself and spray an air deodorant to mask any telltale odors.

"The only one who suspects," she said with embarrassment, "is my dentist. He said my teeth were beginning to decay from stomach acid."

Jessica was diagnosed as showing **bulimia nervosa***, an eating disorder characterized by recurrent cycles of bingeing and purging. Jessica decided that she wanted to overcome her problem before her marriage. "I don't want Ken [her fiancé] to find out," she explained. "I don't want to bring this into the marriage."*

■ *The Authors' Files*

Jessica, like Phil, was personally distressed about her behavior. Her behavior was also self-defeating and physically harmful or dangerous: It was decaying her teeth and may have led to other, more serious health consequences (see Chapter 13). She also anticipated that her cycles of bingeing and purging would impair her forthcoming marriage.

Several criteria thus lead professionals to label behavior as abnormal. It is one thing to recognize and label behavior as abnormal; it is another to understand and explain it. Philosophers, physicians, natural scientists, and psychologists have used various approaches, or **models**, in the effort to explain abnormal behavior. Some approaches have been based on superstition; others have invoked religious explanations. Some current views are predominantly biological; others, psychological. We consider various historical and contemporary approaches to understanding abnormal behavior. First let us look further at the importance of cultural beliefs and expectations in determining which behavior patterns are deemed abnormal.

CULTURAL BASES OF ABNORMAL BEHAVIOR

Behavior that is considered normal in one culture may be deemed abnormal in another. Hallucinations (hearing voices or seeing things that are not in fact present) is a common experience among Australian aborigines (Spencer, 1983) but is generally taken as a sign of abnormality in our culture. Aborigines also believe that they can communicate with the spirits of their ancestors and that dreams are shared among people, especially close relatives. Such beliefs may be regarded in Western culture as delusions (fixed false beliefs). Hallucinations and delusions are taken to be common features of schizophrenia in Western culture. Should we thus conclude that aborigines are schizophrenic or seriously disturbed? What standards should be applied in judging abnormal behavior in other cultures? Even aborigines perceive "madness" in some members of their community, although the criteria used to label someone as mentally disturbed may differ from those used by health professionals in Western society.

Kleinman (1987) offers an example of "hearing voices" among Native Americans to underscore the ways in which judgments about abnormal behavior are embedded within a cultural context:

Ten psychiatrists trained in the same assessment technique and diagnostic criteria who are asked to examine 100 American Indians shortly after the latter have experienced the death of a spouse, a parent or a child may determine with close to 100% consistency that those individuals report hearing, in the first month of grieving, the voice of the dead person calling to them as the spirit ascends to the afterworld. . . . [While such judgments may be consistent across observers] the determination of whether such reports are a sign of an abnormal mental state is an interpretation based on knowledge of this group's behavioural norms and range of normal experiences of bereavement. (p. 453)

Kleinman's example leads us to recognize that behavior should not be regarded as falling within an abnormal spectrum when it is normative in the cultural setting in which it occurs.

 Many Native Americans do indeed report that they hear the spirits of people who have recently died calling to them as they ascend to the afterlife. Such behavior is normal within their cultural setting.

Concepts of health and illness may also have different meanings in different cultures. Many tradi-

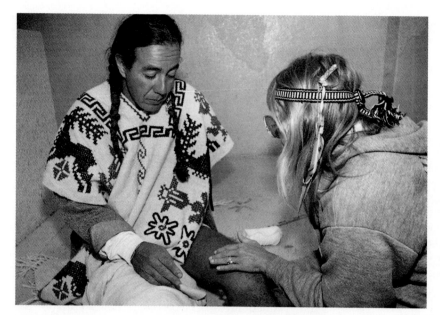

A traditional Native American healer. Many traditional Native Americans distinguish between illnesses that are believed to arise from influences external to their own culture ("white man's sicknesses") and those that emanate from a lack of harmony with traditional tribal life and thought ("Indian sicknesses"). Traditional healers such as the one shown here may be called on to treat "Indian sickness," whereas "white man's medicine" may be sought to help people deal with problems whose causes are seen as lying outside the community, such as alcoholism and drug addiction.

tional Native-American cultures distinguish illnesses that are believed to arise from influences outside the culture ("white man's sicknesses"), such as alcoholism and drug addition, from those that emanate from a lack of harmony with traditional tribal life and thought ("Indian sicknesses") (Trimble, 1991). Traditional healers, shamans, and medicine men and women are called on to treat and cure "Indian sickness." When the problem is thought to have its cause outside the community, help may be sought from "white man's medicine."

The very words that Western cultures use to describe mental disorders—words like depression or even mental health—may have very different meanings in other cultures, or no equivalent meaning at all. In many non-Western societies, depression may be best represented by indigenous concepts of "soul loss" rather than by Western concepts involving a sense of loss of purpose and meaning in life (Shweder, 1985). Western health professionals should not apply Western concepts of abnormal behavior to other peoples without determining that the concepts are valid within those cultures (Kleinman, 1987). The reverse is also true. The concept of "soul loss" may characterize psychological distress in some non-Western societies but have little or no relevance to middle-class North Americans (Kleinman, 1987).

Abnormal behavior patterns may also take different forms in different cultures. Westerners may experience anxiety, for example, in the form of excessive worrying about paying the mortgage, losing a job, and so on. Yet " . . . in a number of African cultures, anxiety is expressed as fears of failure in procreation, in dreams and complaints about witchcraft" (Kleinman, 1987). Some Australian aborigines

develop intense fears of sorcery, which may be accompanied by the belief that one is in mortal danger from evil spirits (Spencer, 1983). Trancelike states in which young aboriginal women are mute, immobile, and unresponsive are also quite common. If women do not recover from the trance within hours or, at most, a few days, they may be brought to a sacred site for healing.

Societal views of abnormal behavior or mental illness also vary across cultures. In our culture, models based on medical disease and psychological factors have achieved prominence in explaining abnormal behavior. "In traditional cultures, mental disorder is frequently perceived in terms of supernatural causation or possession" (Lefley, 1990). The notion of supernatural causation, or **demonology**, held prominence in Western society until the Age of Enlightenment.

HISTORICAL PERSPECTIVES ON ABNORMAL BEHAVIOR

Throughout the history of Western culture, concepts of abnormal behavior have been shaped, to some degree, by the prevailing **worldview** of the time. Throughout much of history, beliefs in supernatural forces, demons, and evil spirits held sway. Abnormal behavior was often taken as a sign of **possession.** In more modern times, the predominant—but by no means universal!—worldview has shifted toward beliefs in science and reason. Abnormal behavior has

MULTICULTURAL PERSPECTIVES

Ethnicity[1] and Mental Health

When Europeans first arrived on America's shores, the land was populated solely by Native Americans. By the time the United States achieved nationhood, the numbers of people of European descent were approaching those of Native Americans. During the 19th century, the nation became predominantly populated by white people. Although white people remain in the majority today, the nation is showing increasing diversity, both as a result of an excess of births over deaths among various U.S. ethnic groups and contemporary trends in immigration.

Table 1.1 shows how the percentages of cultural and ethnic minorities have been increasing in some major metropolitan areas. According to the Bureau of the Census, in New York City and the surrounding region, the percentages of all ethnic minority groups rose between 1980 and 1990. In 1990, nearly one metropolitan New Yorker in five was foreign born. African Americans comprised 18.2% of the total; Hispanic Americans, 15.4%; and Asian Americans, 4.8%. Texas's "Metroplex," the Dallas-Fort Worth area, similarly showed increases for every ethnic minority group, with the numbers of the foreign born mushrooming in particular. As of 1990, one-third of the metropolitan Miami, Florida, area was Hispanic, and a third foreign born. By 1990, nearly 15% of the population of San Francisco, which tends to attract many immigrants from across the Pacific, was Asian, and one resident in five was foreign born. If present trends continue, non-Hispanic white Americans[2] may be in the minority in California by the year 2000 or shortly thereafter, and in the United States at large sometime during the next century.

Asian Americans—whose backgrounds and ancestries include peoples from areas as diverse as China, Japan, Korea, Indochina, Thailand, the Philippines, India, and Pakistan—are now the fastest growing ethnic group in the United States (Zane & Sue, 1991). At current growth rates, their population will have doubled between the years 1980 and 2000. Hispanic Americans, too, are a fast-growing minority group. During the 1980s, the Hispanic-American population grew by nearly 40% because of immigration

Table 1.1 Changes in the Ethnic Composition of U.S. Metropolitan Regions, 1980–1990		
Population	**1980**	**1990**
NEW YORK (including Long Island, northern New Jersey, southwestern Connecticut, and the lower Hudson Valley)		
TOTAL	16,121,297	18,087,251
Asian American	2.3%	4.8%
African American	17.1%	18.2%
Hispanic American	12.4%	15.4%
Native American	0.1%	0.3%
Foreign born	16.9%	19.7%
DALLAS-FORT WORTH		
TOTAL	2,974,805	3,885,415
Asian American	0.8%	2.5%
African American	14.1%	14.3%
Hispanic American	8.4%	13.4%
Native American	0.3%	0.5%
Foreign born	4.2%	18.1%
MIAMI-FORT LAUDERDALE		
TOTAL	2,643,981	3,192,582
Asian American	0.7%	1.4%
African American	14.9%	18.5%
Hispanic American	23.5%	33.3%
Native American	0.1%	0.2%
Foreign born	26.1%	33.6%
SAN FRANCISCO-OAKLAND-SAN JOSE		
TOTAL	5,179,784	6,253,311
Asian American	8.7%	14.8%
African American	9.0%	8.6%
Hispanic American	12.2%	15.5%
Native American	0.6%	0.7%
Foreign born	14.2%	20.0%

Source of data: "Census Reveals Changes as it Paints a Picture of Metropolitan America" by F. Barringer. Copyright © 1992, by the New York Times Company. Reprinted by permission.

[1]The word *ethnicity* is derived from the Greek word *ethnikos*, meaning people or nation.

[2]The use of the term *non-Hispanic white Americans* reflects the fact that many white Americans are Hispanic. The term *Hispanic American* includes people from diverse racial backgrounds who trace their cultural heritage to the Spanish-speaking countries of Latin America. We use the term *Hispanic American* because it is the term favored by the U.S. Census Bureau. However, we recognize that many "Hispanics" prefer the term Latino. Others prefer to identify themselves by the use of national origin labels, such as Puerto Rican American, Cuban American, or Mexican American.

and an excess of births over deaths. We must also add in an unknown number of undocumented migrants and the population of Puerto Rico (Rogler et al., 1991). The largest Hispanic-American population groups are Mexican Americans, Puerto Ricans, and Cubans. Mexican Americans number over 10 million in the United States (De La Cancela & Guzman, 1991). Puerto Ricans number about 2.5 million in the United States; Cubans number slightly more than 1 million. Overall, Hispanic Americans numbered about 22 million according to the 1990 census (Gonzalez, 1992).

Hispanic Americans differ in their cultural back-

The increasing diversity of the United States. Because of trends in reproduction and immigration, the numbers of African Americans, Hispanic Americans, and Asian Americans in the United States are growing more rapidly than those of non-Hispanic white Americans. Researchers are investigating whether ethnic groups vary from one another with respect to prevalence of abnormal behavior patterns. Researchers also focus on intercultural differences among ethnic groups. For example, researchers find higher levels of depression among Hispanic-American immigrants from Central America than from Mexico.

grounds. Hispanic Americans who immigrated from the Caribbean share a cultural tradition that was largely influenced by African and native Carib Indian cultures. The cultural backgrounds of Hispanic Americans from Mexico, Central America, and the northern parts of South America show a strong influence of indigenous native peoples from those regions. Those who immigrated from central and southern parts of South America, especially Argentina, show a strong European influence (Javier, 1993).

Given the increasing ethnic diversity in the United States, researchers have attempted to determine whether ethnic groups vary from one another with respect to prevalence of abnormal behavior patterns. Researchers recognize that socioeconomic level needs to be considered in comparing the rates of a given diagnosis across ethnic groups. Researchers also concur on the need to focus on intercultural differences among ethnic groups, such as among the various subgroups that comprise the Hispanic-American and Asian-American populations. For example, researchers have found higher levels of depression among immigrants to the United States from Central America than from Mexico, even when they consider differences in educational backgrounds (Salgado de Snyder et al., 1990).

Some minority groups have been underrepresented in previous research. For example, no major studies have been conducted on the prevalence of psychiatric disorders within the Asian-American community (Zane & Sue, 1991). Existing knowledge from smaller scale surveys, however, shows a generally high rate of mental health problems among Asian Americans (Zane & Sue, 1991). Asian Americans in these surveys were found to have high rates of both depression and psychosis (a severe form of abnormal behavior characterized by a break with reality, the major form of which is schizophrenia—see Chapter 11) (Sue, 1988; Ying, 1988). There is also a dearth of evidence concerning the effectiveness of psychological and psychopharmacological therapies with Asian-American groups (Zane & Sue, 1991).

In a major study of ethnicity and mental health, researchers in Los Angeles (Flaskerud & Hu, 1992) examined differences in rates of psychiatric diagnoses across ethnic groups for people treated within the entire Los Angeles County mental health system between January 1983 and August 1988. The investigators took socioeconomic differences into consideration and still found significant and consistent relationships between ethnicity and psychiatric diagnoses (see Table 1.2). African Americans and Asian Americans were more likely to receive diagnoses of schizophrenia than were non-Hispanic white Americans. Hispanic Americans, however, were less likely than non-Hispanic white Americans to be diagnosed as schizophrenics. Non-Hispanic white Americans and Asian Americans were more likely to receive diagnoses of major affective (mood) disorder than African Americans or Hispanic Americans. (Major affective disorders include major depression and bipolar disorder, formerly called manic-depression—see Chapter 7.)

Why might these ethnic groups differ in their rates of psychiatric diagnoses? Might differences reflect differential vulnerabilities to particular mental disorders? Would such vulnerabilities reflect genetic factors, sociocultural factors, or an interaction of these and other factors? Do diagnostic patterns reflect a bias on the part of mental health providers to assign diagnoses on the basis of racial and ethnic stereotypes? Moreover, might the differences in diagnostic patterns among ethnic groups that receive treatment from mental health facilities reflect their distribution in the general population—not just among those who receive treatment? These questions and others about the diagnosis of abnormal behaviors among various ethnic groups remain to be answered.

We need to be careful not to overgeneralize the findings from the L.A. study. Generally speaking, research on the relationship between mental disorders and ethnicity has

(continued)

Table 1.2 Ethnicity and Specific Diagnoses—The Los Angeles Study

Type of Disorder	Non-Hispanic White American	African American	Hispanic American	Asian American
Outpatients (N = 19,688)	(n = 5322) 27%	(n = 4976) 25.3%	(n = 4146) 21%	(n = 5244) 26.7%
Substance abuse	25.7%	30.9%	28%	15.4%
Schizophrenia	21.3%	35.2%	14.5%	28.9%
Major affective disorder	31.7%	20.6%	16.8%	30.9%
Inpatients (N = 6,662)	(n = 1783) 26.8%	(n = 2095) 31.5%	(n = 1137) 17%	(n = 1647) 24.7%
Substance abuse	20.3%	48.9%	25.1%	5.7%
Schizophrenia	23.7%	36.8%	14.1%	25.4%
Major affective disorder	30.5%	27.5%	15.3%	24.8%

Source: Flaskerud, J. U., & Hu, L. Relationship of ethnicity to psychiatric diagnosis. Journal of Nervous and Mental Disease, 180, 296–303. Copyright © Williams & Wilkins, 1992.

yielded inconsistent findings (Flaskerud & Hu, 1992). Some studies find no differences in the prevalences of diagnoses such as schizophrenia, depression, and personality disorders across ethnic groups. Others report some differences. Still others find the evidence so conflicting that no conclusions can be drawn. Consider some of the findings of the largest community study to date, the National Institute of Mental Health's Epidemiologic Catchment Area (ECA) Study. In this study, nearly 20,000 residents in five U.S. communities (New Haven, CT; Baltimore, MD; St. Louis, MO; Durham, NC; and Los Angeles, CA) were interviewed to determine the prevalences of various mental disorders. Researchers in this survey found that African Americans overall showed a higher rate of schizophrenia than non-Hispanic white Americans (Keith et al., 1991). Yet this difference disappeared when researchers controlled for differences between non-Hispanic white Americans and African Americans in socioeconomic level and other factors such as age and mari-

tal status. We should caution, however, that the sites selected in the ECA study, and the respondents in each site who participated, were not randomly drawn. Thus the prevalences reported are not necessarily representative of the U.S. population at large. Clearly more research is needed to examine the complex relationships between ethnicity and mental health status.

Whatever the underlying differences in psychopathology between ethnic groups may be, some ethnic minorities, such as Mexican Americans (Griffith, 1985; Hough et al., 1987) and Asian Americans (Zane & Sue, 1991) underutilize mental health services in relation to non-Hispanic white Americans. Those who do seek services are more likely to drop out prematurely from treatment. In Chapter 14 we consider barriers that may limit the utilization of mental health services by ethnic minorities in our society.

come to be viewed in our culture as the product of physical and psychosocial factors, not demonic possession.

The Demonological Model

Let us begin our journey with an example from prehistory. Archaeologists have unearthed human skeletons from the Stone Age with egg-sized cavities in the skull. One interpretation of these holes is that our prehistoric ancestors believed that abnormal behavior reflected the invasion of evil spirits. Perhaps they

used the harsh method—called **trephining**—of creating a pathway through the skull to provide an outlet for those irascible spirits. Fresh bone growth indicates that some people managed to survive the ordeal.

Most of the time, however, trephining put an end to the person as well as any disturbing behavior. Threat of trephining may have persuaded people to comply with group or tribal norms to the best of their abilities. Since no written records or accounts of the purposes of trephination exist, other explanations are possible. Perhaps trephination was actually used as a primitive form of surgery to remove shattered pieces

Origins of the Medical Model: In "Ill Humor"

Not all ancient Greeks believed in the demonological model. Hippocrates (ca. 460–377 B.C.), the celebrated physician of the golden age of Greece, attempted to challenge the prevailing beliefs of his time by arguing that illnesses of the body and mind were the result of natural causes, not possession by supernatural spirits. Hippocrates believed that the health of the body and mind depended on the balance of **humors**, or vital fluids, in the body: phlegm, black bile, blood, and yellow bile. An imbalance of humors, he thought, accounted for abnormal behavior. A lethargic or sluggish person was believed to have an excess of phlegm, from which we derive the word **phlegmatic.** An overabundance of black bile was believed to cause depression, or **melancholia.** An excess of blood created a **sanguine** disposition: cheerful, confident, and optimistic. An excess of yellow bile made people "bilious" and **choleric**—quick-tempered, that is.

Hippocrates's concept of humors attained much currency. The adjectives *phlegmatic, melancholy, sanguine,* and *choleric* have remained in use over the millennia. Two thousand years later, Shakespeare wrote of the brooding Hamlet as that "melancholy Dane." Today Hippocrates's views on bodily humors is known to be without physiological merit, but it was of historic importance because of its break from demonology.

Hippocrates's view that abnormal behavior could result from biological imbalances formed the basis of the modern **medical model.** Also called the disease model, the medical model seeks to explain abnormal behavior as rooted in underlying biological or biochemical abnormalities. Hippocrates made many contributions to modern thought and, indeed, to modern medical practice. Medical schools continue to pay homage to Hippocrates by having new physicians swear the Hippocratic oath.

There were other physicians in ancient times who adopted and expanded on the teachings of Hippocrates. One was Galen (ca. A.D. 130–200), a Greek who attended the Roman emperor-philosopher Marcus Aurelius. Among Galen's contributions was the discovery that arteries carried blood, not air, as had been formerly believed.

The seeds of naturalistic explanations of abnormal behavior were thus sown by Hippocrates and developed by other physicians, especially Galen. Hippocrates had even begun to classify abnormal behavior patterns, using three main categories: *melancholia* to characterize excessive depression, *mania* to refer to exceptional excitement, and *phrenitis* (from the Greek meaning "inflammation of the brain") to characterize

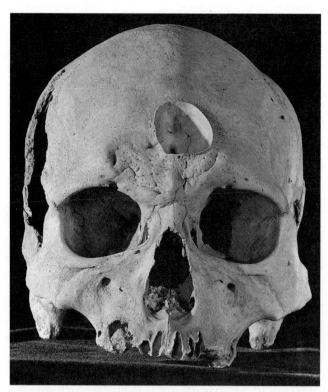

Trephining Trephining refers to a practice of some prehistoric cultures in which a hole was chipped into a person's skull. Some investigators speculate that the practice represented an ancient form of surgery. Perhaps trephining was intended to release demons that were believed responsible for abnormal behavior.

of bone or blood clots that resulted from head injuries (Maher & Maher, 1985).

Explanation of abnormal behavior in terms of supernatural or divine causes is termed the *demonological model.* The ancients explained natural forces in terms of divine will and spirits. The ancient Babylonians believed that the movements of the stars and the planets were fashioned by the adventures and conflicts of the gods (Boorstin, 1983). The ancient Greeks believed that their gods toyed with humans; when aroused to wrath, they could unleash forces of nature to wreak havoc on disrespectful or arrogant humans, even cloud their minds with madness. In the time of Homer (ca. 800 B.C.), author of the epics *The Iliad* and *The Odyssey,* it was widely believed that strange or bizarre behavior signified punishment of insolent humans by the gods.

In ancient Greece, people who behaved abnormally were often sent to temples dedicated to Asclepius, the god of healing. Priests believed that Asclepius would visit the afflicted persons while they slept in the temple and offer them restorative advice through dreams. Rest, a nutritious diet, and exercise were also believed to contribute to treatment. Incurables might be driven from the temple by stoning.

Exorcism. This medieval woodcut illustrates the practice of exorcism, which was used to expel evil spirits who had possessed people. Although exorcism was in its heyday in the Europe of the Middle Ages, one occasionally hears of exorcisms being conducted in the United States today.

the bizarre kinds of behavior that might today typify schizophrenia, a severe type of mental disorder that is characterized by bizarre behavior, strange thoughts, and auditory or visual hallucinations (that is, "hearing voices" or seeing things that are not present).

Medieval Times

The Middle Ages, or medieval times, cover the millennium of European history from about A.D. 476 through A.D. 1450. The Middle Ages are also sometimes referred to as the Dark Ages because some historians view them as a time of intellectual and cultural decline and stagnation.

After the passing of Galen, belief in supernatural causes, especially the doctrine of possession, increased in influence and eventually dominated medieval thought. The doctrine of possession held that abnormal behaviors were a sign of possession by evil spirits of the devil. This belief was embodied within the teachings of the Christian church, which became the unifying force in western Europe following the decline of the Roman Empire. Although belief in possession antedated the Christian church and is found in ancient Egyptian and Greek writings, the Church revitalized it. The treatment of choice for abnormal behavior was **exorcism**. Exorcists were employed to persuade evil spirits that the bodies of their intended

victims were basically uninhabitable. Methods included prayer, waving a cross at the victim, beating and flogging, even starving the victim. If the victim still displayed unseemly behavior, there were yet more powerful remedies, such as the rack, a device of torture. It seems clear that recipients of these "remedies" would be motivated to conform their behavior to social expectations as best they could.

The Renaissance—the great European revival in learning, art, and literature—began in Italy in the 1400s and spread gradually throughout Europe. The Renaissance is considered the transition from the medieval world to the modern. Therefore, it is ironic that fear of witches also reached its height during the Renaissance.

Witchcraft

The late 15th through the late 17th centuries were especially dangerous times to be unpopular with your neighbors. These were times of massive persecutions of people, particularly women, who were accused of witchcraft. Church officials believed that witches made pacts with the devil, practiced satanic rituals, and committed heinous acts, such as eating babies and poisoning crops. In 1484, Pope Innocent VIII decreed that witches be executed. Two Dominican priests compiled a manual for witch-hunting, called the *Malleus Maleficarum* ("The Witches' Hammer"), to help inquisitors identify suspected witches. Over 100,000 accused witches were killed in the next two centuries.

There were also creative "diagnostic" tests for detecting possession and witchcraft. One was a water-float test. It was based on the principle that pure metals settle to the bottom during smelting, whereas impurities bob up to the surface. Suspects who sank and were drowned were ruled pure. Suspects who were able to keep their heads above water were regarded as being in league with the devil. Then they were in "real" trouble. This trial is the fount of the phrase, "Damned if you do and damned if you don't."

 Innocent people were in fact drowned in medieval times as a way of certifying that they were not possessed by the devil.

Modern scholars once believed that the "witches" of the Middle Ages and the Renaissance were actually people with mental disorders. They were believed to be persecuted because their abnormal behavior was taken as evidence that they were in league with the devil. It is true that many suspected

The water-float test. This test was one way in which medieval authorities sought to detect possession and witchcraft. Managing to float above the water line was deemed a sign of impurity. In the lower right-hand corner, you can see the bound hands and feet of one poor unfortunate who failed to remain afloat, but whose drowning would have cleared any suspicions of possession.

witches confessed to impossible behaviors, such as flying or engaging in sexual intercourse with the devil. At face value such confessions might suggest disturbances in thinking and perception that are consistent with a modern diagnosis of mental disorders, such as schizophrenia. Most of these confessions can be discounted, however, because they were extracted under torture by inquisitors who were bent on finding evidence to support accusations of witchcraft (Spanos, 1978). In other cases, the threat of torture and other forms of intimidation were sufficient to extract false confessions. Although some of those who were persecuted as witches probably did show abnormal behavior patterns, most did not (Schoeneman, 1977). Rather, accusations of witchcraft

appeared to be a convenient means of disposing of social nuisances and political rivals, of seizing property, and of suppressing heresy (Spanos, 1978). In English villages, many of the accused were poor, unmarried elderly women who were forced to beg their neighbors for food. If misfortune befell people who declined to help, the beggar might be accused of causing the misery by having cast a curse on the uncharitable family (Spanos, 1978). If the woman was generally unpopular, accusations of witchcraft were more likely to be followed up.

Although demons were believed to play roles both in abnormal behavior and witchcraft, there was a difference between the two. Victims of possession might have been afflicted as retribution for wrongdoing, but it was allowed that some people who showed abnormal behavior might be totally innocent victims of demonic possession. Witches, on the other hand, were believed to have voluntarily entered into a pact with the devil and renounced God. Witches were generally seen as more deserving of torture and execution (Spanos, 1978).

Historic trends do not follow straight lines. Although the demonological model held sway during the Middle Ages and much of the Renaissance, it did not universally supplant belief in naturalistic causes (Schoeneman, 1977). In medieval England, for example, demonic possession was only rarely invoked as the cause of abnormal behavior in cases in which a person was held to be insane by legal authorities (Neugebauer, 1979). Most explanations involved natural causes for unusual behavior, such as illness or trauma to the brain. In England, in fact, some disturbed people were kept in hospitals until they were restored to sanity (Alleridge, 1979).

The Renaissance Belgian physician, Johann Weyer (1515–1588), also took up the cause of Hippocrates and Galen by arguing that abnormal behavior and thought patterns were caused by physical problems.

■ **ASYLUMS** By the late 15th and early 16th centuries, **asylums**, or "madhouses," began to crop up throughout Europe. Many were former leprosariums, which were no longer needed because of a decline in leprosy that occurred during the late Middle Ages. Asylums often gave refuge to beggars as well as the disturbed, and conditions were generally appalling. Residents were often chained to their beds and left to lie in their own waste or wander about unassisted. Some asylums became public spectacles. In one asylum in London, Bethlehem Hospital—from which the word *bedlam* is derived—the public could buy tickets to observe the bizarre antics of the inmates, much as they would view a sideshow in a circus or animals at a zoo.

"Bedlam."   The bizarre antics of the patients at Bethlehem Hospital in London in the 18th century were a source
of entertainment for the well-heeled gentry of the town,
such as the two well-dressed women in the middle of the
painting. The word *bedlam* derives from the name of this
hospital.

The Rise of Modern Thought

By the late 17th century, now called the Age of Reason, and the 18th century, the Age of Enlightenment,
society at large began to turn from religious dogma to
reason and science to explain natural phenomena and
human behavior. The nascent sciences of biology,
chemistry, physics, and astronomy offered promise
that knowledge could be derived from scientific methods of observation and experimentation.

■ **ADVANCES IN MEDICINE**   The 18th and 19th
centuries witnessed rapid developments in medical
science. Scientific discoveries uncovered the microbial
causes of some kinds of diseases and gave rise to preventive measures. In 1796, the smallpox vaccine was
developed by the English physician Edward Jenner.
By 1864, Frenchman Louis Pasteur devised the
process of pasteurization. In 1865, an English surgeon, Joseph Lister, performed the first antiseptic
surgery, using carbolic acid on a wound. In the same
year, Gregor Mendel published his theory of genetics.
By 1871, the bacterium that causes leprosy was discovered by G. A. Hansen. Robert Koch discovered the
bacterium that causes anthrax in 1876. In 1883, he
developed a vaccine for the disease.

Against this backdrop the German physician
Wilhelm Griesinger (1817–1868) argued that abnormal behavior was rooted in diseases of the brain.
Griesinger's views influenced another German physician, Emil Kraepelin (1856–1926), who wrote an
influential textbook on psychiatry in 1883 in which
he likened mental disorders to physical diseases.
Griesinger and Kraepelin paved the way for the

development of the modern medical model which
attempts to explain abnormal behavior on the basis of
underlying biological defects or abnormalities, not
evil spirits. According to the medical model, people
behaving abnormally suffer from mental illnesses or
disorders that can be classified, like physical illnesses,
according to their distinctive causes and symptoms.
Not all adopters of the medical model believe that
every pattern of abnormal behavior is a product of
defective biology, but they maintain that patterns of
abnormal behavior can be likened to physical illnesses in that their features can be conceptualized as
symptoms of underlying disorders.

■ **EMIL KRAEPELIN**   Kraepelin specified two
main groups of mental disorders or diseases: **dementia praecox** (from roots meaning "precocious [pre-
mature] insanity"), which we now call schizophrenia,
and manic-depressive psychosis, which is now
labeled **bipolar disorder**. Kraepelin believed that
dementia praecox was caused by a biochemical
imbalance and manic-depressive psychosis by an
abnormality in body metabolism. But his major contribution was the development of a classification system that forms the cornerstone for current diagnostic
systems.

The medical model was supported by evidence
that a form of derangement called **general paresis**
represented an advanced stage of syphilis in which
the syphilis bacterium directly invaded brain tissue.
Scientists grew optimistic that other biological causes,
and, as important, treatments, would soon be discovered for other so-called mental disorders. This early
optimism has remained largely unfulfilled, since the
causes of most patterns of abnormal behavior remain
obscure.

The Reform Movement
and Moral Therapy

The modern era of treatment can be traced to the
efforts of individuals like the Frenchmen Jean-Baptiste Pussin and Philippe Pinel in the late 18th and
early 19th centuries. They argued that people who
behaved abnormally suffered from disease and should
be treated humanely. This view was not popular at
the time. Deranged people were generally regarded
by the public as threats to society, not as sick people
in need of treatment.

From 1784 to 1802, Pussin, a layman, was
placed in charge of a ward for people considered
"incurably insane" at La Bicêtre, a large mental hospital in Paris. Although Pinel is often given credit for
freeing the inmates of La Bicêtre from their chains,
Pussin was actually the first official to unchain a

The unchaining of inmates at La Bicêtre by 18th-century French reformer Philippe Pinel. Continuing the work of Jean-Baptiste Pussin, Pinel stopped harsh practices, such as bleeding and purging, and moved inmates from darkened dungeons to sunny, airy rooms. Pinel also took the time to converse with inmates, in the belief that understanding and concern would help restore them to normal functioning.

group of the "incurably insane." These unfortunates had been considered too dangerous and unpredictable to be left unchained. But Pussin believed that if they were treated with kindness, there would be no need for chains. As he predicted, most of the shut-ins became manageable and calm when their chains were removed. They could walk the hospital grounds and take in fresh air. Pussin also forbade the staff from treating the residents harshly, and he discharged employees who disregarded his directives.

Pinel (1745–1826) became medical director for the incurables' ward at La Bicêtre in 1793 and continued the humane treatment that Pussin had begun. He stopped harsh practices, such as bleeding and purging, and moved patients from darkened dungeons to well-ventilated, sunny rooms. Pinel also spent hours talking to inmates, in the belief that showing understanding and concern would help restore them to normal functioning.

The philosophy of treatment that emerged from these efforts was labeled **moral therapy**. It was based on the belief that functioning could be restored by providing humane treatment in a relaxed and decent environment. Similar reforms were instituted at about this time in England by William Tuke and later in the United States by Dorothea Dix. Another influential figure was the American physician Benjamin Rush (1745–1813)—also a signatory to the Declaration of Independence. Rush, considered the "father of American psychiatry," penned the first American textbook on psychiatry in 1812: *Medical Inquiries and Observations upon the Diseases of the Mind.* Rush believed that madness was caused by engorgement of the blood vessels of the brain. To relieve pressure, he recommended bloodletting and other harsh treatments like purging and ice-cold baths. On

the other hand, he advanced humane treatment by encouraging the staff of his Philadelphia Hospital to treat patients with kindness and understanding. His hospital became the first in the United States to admit patients for mental disorders.

Dorothea Dix (1802–1887), a Boston schoolteacher, traveled about the country decrying the deplorable conditions in the jails and almshouses where deranged people were often placed. As a direct result of her efforts, 32 mental hospitals were established throughout the United States.

■ **A STEP BACKWARD** In the latter half of the 19th century, however, the belief that abnormal behaviors could be successfully treated or cured by moral therapy fell into disfavor. A period of apathy ensued in which patterns of abnormal behavior were deemed incurable (Grob, 1983). American mental institutions grew in size and came to provide little more than custodial care. Conditions deteriorated. Mental hospitals became frightening places. It was not uncommon to find residents "wallowing in their own excrements," in the words of a New York State official of the time (Grob, 1983). Straitjackets, handcuffs, cribs, straps, and other devices were used to restrain excitable or violent patients.

Deplorable hospital conditions remained commonplace through the middle of the 20th century, when public attention began to focus on revamping the mental health system. By the mid-1950s, the population in mental hospitals had risen to half a million patients. Although some good state hospitals provided decent and humane care (Grob, 1983), many were described as little more than *human snakepits.* Residents were crowded into wards that lacked even rudimentary sanitation. Inhabitants were literally locked up for indefinite stays and received little more than custodial care. By the mid-20th century, the appalling conditions that many mental patients were forced to endure led to increasing calls for reforms of the mental health system in the United States.

■ **THE CONTEMPORARY EXODUS FROM STATE HOSPITALS** Two major factors led to a mass exodus from mental hospitals in the post–World War II era: the advent of a new class of drugs—the *phenothiazines*—and the community mental health centers act of 1963. The 1950s ushered in the **phenothiazines**—a group of "major tranquilizers" that quelled the most flagrant behavior patterns associated with schizophrenia. Phenothiazines reduced the need for indefinite hospital stays and permitted many schizophrenics to be discharged to less restrictive living quarters in the community, such as halfway houses, group homes, and independent living.

In response to the growing call for reform of the mental health system, Congress established in 1963 a nationwide system of community mental health centers that was intended to offer continuing support and care to former hospital residents. It was hoped that these centers would help patients return to their communities and assume more independent and fulfilling lives. This policy of **deinstitutionalization** caused a steady decline in the mental hospital census. The mental hospital population across the United States declined from about 560,000 in 1955 to about 125,000 by 1981 (Kiesler & Sibulkin, 1987). By 1983, it was estimated that 93% of those who would otherwise be hospitalized were living in the community (Goldman et al., 1983).

Critics contend that the exodus from state hospitals abandoned tens of thousands of marginally functioning people to communities that lacked adequate housing and other forms of support. Many of the homeless people we see wandering city streets and sleeping in bus terminals and train stations are discharged mental patients.

 Many of the nation's homeless are in fact former residents of mental hospitals who have been discharged into the community.

Although deplorable conditions may persist in some institutions, most contemporary mental hospitals are better managed and provide more humane care than those of the 19th and early 20th centuries. The daily life of today's mental hospital is more treatment oriented. It focuses on preparing residents to return to the community. For younger and intensely disturbed people, the hospital stay is usually brief, lasting only until their condition allows them to reenter society. To elderly chronic clients, however, the mental hospital may be the only stable home they have known as adults. They find themselves unprepared to handle basic tasks of independent life such as shopping, cooking, and cleaning.

Contemporary Concepts of Abnormal Behavior

Today many scholars of abnormal behavior adhere to the medical model, although research into the biological and biochemical factors in abnormal behavior is by no means limited to medical personnel. Psychologists, biologists, and others are also intensely involved in such work. A number of psychological models of abnormal behavior have also attained prominence, including psychodynamic, learning, cognitive, and existential-humanistic perspectives.

■ **THE MEDICAL MODEL AND BIOLOGICAL PERSPECTIVES** The medical model, inspired by physicians from Hippocrates through Kraepelin, remains a powerful force in contemporary psychology. Much of the terminology in current use reflects the influence of the medical model. Because of the medical model, many professionals and laypeople speak of people whose behavior is deemed abnormal as being mentally *ill* or mentally *disordered*. It is because of the medical model that so many speak of the *symptoms* of abnormal behavior, rather than the features or characteristics of abnormal behavior. Other terms spawned by the medical model include *mental health, syndrome, diagnosis, patient, mental patient, mental hospital, prognosis, treatment, therapy, cure, relapse,* and *remission.*[1]

The medical model is a major advance over demonology. It inspired the idea that abnormal behavior should be treated by learned professionals and not be punished. Compassion supplanted hatred, fear, and persecution.

The medical model has its shortcomings. For one, biological causes for most forms of abnormal behavior have not yet been (and may never be)

---

[1]Because the medical model is not the only way of viewing abnormal behavior patterns, we adopt a more neutral language in this text in describing abnormal behavior patterns. For example, we often refer to "features" or "characteristics" of abnormal behavior patterns or psychological disorders, rather than "symptoms." But our adoption of nonmedical jargon is not an absolute rule. In some cases, there may be no handy substitutes for terms that derive from the medical model, such as the term "remission" or the reference to patients in "mental hospitals" as "mental patients." In other cases we may use terms like "disorder," "therapy," and "treatment" because they are commonly used by psychologists who "treat" "mental disorders" with psychological "therapies."

unearthed. The model implies that people with "mental illnesses," like those with physical illnesses, are not responsible for their difficulties. In the past, this belief often led to lengthy hospitalization and suspension of occupational and family responsibilities among people with abnormal behavior problems. Removed from the real world, their abilities to function often showed further decline rather than return to normal. Today, however, even most devotees of the medical model recognize the value of encouraging people to remain in the community and maintain whatever responsibility they can.

Within the medical model, treatment of abnormal behavior involves the application by medical personnel of biological therapies that seek to control or correct the assumed underlying biological or biochemical abnormalities. Treatments derived from other models have also been shown to be of help with many types of abnormal behavior, however.

The medical model represents a biological perspective on abnormal behavior. We prefer to use the term *biological perspectives* rather than *medical model* to refer to approaches that emphasize the role of biological factors in explaining abnormal behavior and the use of biologically based treatments in treating abnormal behavior. One can speak of biological perspectives without adopting the tenets of the medical model, which treat abnormal behavior patterns as *disorders* and their features as *symptoms*. For example, certain behavior patterns (shyness or a lack of musical ability) may reflect biological factors, such as genetics, but not be considered "symptoms" of underlying "disorders."

Many sources of evidence support the role of biological factors in explaining and treating abnormal behavior patterns. For example, genetics may play a prominent role in the transmission of many abnormal behavior patterns that tend to run in families. Yet biology alone cannot fully account for abnormal behavior patterns. The best available data support roles for both genetic and environmental factors as causal influences in abnormal behavior (Weiss et al., 1991). Researchers have also found links between certain abnormal behavior patterns, like severe depression and schizophrenia, and chemical imbalances in the brain. In addition, biological treatments, such as drug therapies, have been effective in treating various forms of abnormal behavior.

■ **PSYCHODYNAMIC PERSPECTIVES** Although the medical model was gaining influence in the 19th century, there were those who believed that organic factors alone could not explain the many forms of abnormal behavior. The contributions of a French neurologist, Jean-Martin Charcot (1825–1893), and a Viennese physician, Joseph Breuer (1842–1925), excited the interest of a young physician, Sigmund Freud (1856–1938), who went on to develop the first major psychological theory of abnormal behavior. Before discussing Freud's contributions, we need to set the stage.

Earlier, the Austrian physician Friedrich Mesmer (1734–1815), from whose name the term *mesmerism* is derived (we still sometimes speak of people being "mesmerized" by things), had become quite a controversial figure on the basis of his experiments

A teaching clinic held by the Parisian neurologist Jean-Martin Charcot. Here, Charcot presents a woman patient who exhibits the highly dramatic behavior associated with hysteria, such as becoming faint at a moment's notice. Charcot was an important influence on the young Sigmund Freud.

into "animal magnetism." Mesmer focused on so-called **hysterics**, or people with hysteria, who have physical complaints without any identifiable physical cause. Hysterical complaints may involve feelings of numbness or pain, paralysis of the arms or limbs, even blindness. Mesmer believed that hysteria was caused by an underlying imbalance in the distribution of a magnetic fluid in the body. To effect a cure, Mesmer had persons with hysterical complaints sit around a covered tub that held bottles of chemicals and protrusions of metal rods. The lights were dimmed, and Mesmer made his entrance with much flourish and fanfare. Then he prodded afflicted parts of clients' bodies with his hands and the rods. Mesmer maintained that the rods transmitted animal magnetism to clients' bodies, correcting the distribution of magnetic fluid and curing afflictions. A scientific commission dismissed Mesmer's claims for animal magnetism as charlatanism, but the astonishing aspect of his treatment—recognized even by the commission—was that it often produced relief. Today, Mesmer's "cures" are largely attributed to the power of suggestion. His method is recognized as perhaps the first medical use of the technique we now call **hypnosis**.

Although Mesmer's views were debunked, interest in hypnosis began to grow in the latter part of the 19th century, especially in France. A highly respected Parisian neurologist, Jean-Martin Charcot, experimented with the hypnotic induction of hysterical symptoms in normal people. Charcot had once discounted the importance of psychological factors in explaining states of abnormal behavior, like hysteria. But experiments with hypnosis eventually persuaded him otherwise. Charcot demonstrated that hysterical behaviors, like paralysis or numbness in the arms, could be induced in normal subjects under hypnosis through the use of suggestions. Hypnotically induced hysterical behavior was indistinguishable from "genuine" hysterical behavior. Even more startling, Charcot and others who experimented with hypnosis demonstrated that hysterical behavior could often be eliminated, at least temporarily, by suggesting to hypnotized clients that their "symptoms" would vanish when they awoke.

Among the young physicians who observed Charcot's work was Sigmund Freud. Charcot's work with hypnosis had a profound impact on Freud, since it demonstrated that hysterical behavior—which could be treated or abolished by the suggestion of "ideas"—was psychological in origin (Jones, 1953). Freud was also influenced by his association with Joseph Breuer, a prominent Viennese physician, 14 years Freud's senior. Breuer too had used hypnosis to treat a woman—"Anna O."—with hysterical complaints. The case of "Anna O." figured prominently in

Sigmund Freud at about the age of 30. Sigmund Freud was influenced by Charcot, Breuer, and others to believe that unusual patterns of behavior, such as hysteria, could be attributed to psychological problems rather than physical problems.

Freud's eventual development of **psychoanalysis** (Spitzer et al., 1989). For this reason we take a closer look at the case.

The Case of Anna O. When Anna was 21, she assumed the responsibilities of night nurse for her father, who lay dying with tuberculosis. Anna was very much attached to her father and sat with him every night, watching him gradually deteriorate in pain. Soon she began to be troubled by problems with no apparent physical basis—"hysterical symptoms." She complained of paralysis in her limbs, numbness, and disturbances of vision and hearing (Jones, 1953). A "paralyzed" muscle in her neck prevented her from turning her head. Immobilization of the fingers of her left hand made it all but impossible for her to feed herself. Breuer believed there was a strong psychological component to the symptoms. He treated her by encouraging her to talk about them, sometimes under hypnosis. Recalling and talking about events connected with the appearance of the symptoms—especially events that evoked feelings of fear, anxiety, or guilt—appeared to provide symptom relief.

The hysterical symptoms apparently represented the transformation of these blocked-up emotions, forgotten but not lost, into physical complaints. In

Bertha Pappenheim. Pappenheim (1859–1936) is known more widely in the psychological literature as "Anna O." Freud believed that her hysterical symptoms represented the transformation of blocked-up emotions into physical complaints.

Anna's case, the symptoms seemed to disappear once the emotions were brought to the surface and "discharged." Breuer labeled the therapeutic effect **catharsis**, a Greek term meaning purgation or purification of feelings. Anna referred to the treatment as the "talking cure" or, when joking, as "chimney sweeping." After 18 months of treatment, she seemed well enough that Breuer told her she no longer needed to see him. But that very night Breuer was summoned to Anna's house, where he found her thrashing about in her bed, as if delivering a child, and insisting that the baby was his. Breuer managed to calm Anna with hypnosis, but he left the house in a cold sweat and never saw her again.

Breuer and Freud published the case of Anna O. in their classic *Studies in Hysteria*. Cases of hysteria, like that of Anna O., seemed to have been a common occurrence in the later Victorian period, but are relatively rare today (Spitzer et al., 1989). After Breuer's departure from her life, Anna had intermittent episodes for several years and spent considerable lengths of time in a sanatorium. She completely recovered by the age of 30, however, and went on to become the first social worker in Germany and an early feminist leader. Anna, whose real name was Bertha Pappenheim, became a popular speaker and apparently had no recurrences of hysteria. She developed very negative attitudes toward "the talking cure," however, and at one point refused to allow one of the residents of a home she ran for "wayward girls" to be psychoanalyzed. In 1936, at the age of 77, she died of abdominal cancer (Spitzer et al., 1989).

His own case experiences led Freud to the belief that psychological problems, such as hysteria, are derived from unconscious conflicts of childhood origin. Such conflicts involve the opposition of primitive sexual and aggressive drives and the effort to keep these drives from being expressed in action or brought into direct awareness. According to **psychoanalytic theory**, which Freud developed, abnormal behavior patterns reflect the dynamic struggle within the mind between opposing psychic forces. Freud viewed abnormal behavior patterns as "symptoms" of these conflicts. In the case of hysteria, the "symptom" represented the *conversion* of an unconscious psychological conflict into a physical problem.

Freud's psychoanalytic theory represents a **psychodynamic model**, or perspective, of abnormal behavior. But psychodynamic perspectives also incorporate the views of Freud's followers who differed with Freud in some respects but still retained the central belief that unconscious dynamic conflicts are at the root of abnormal behavior patterns. Psychodynamic theorists believe that psychological disorders require resolution of the unconscious conflicts that underlie them. Freud initially followed Breuer's example and experimented with hypnosis as a means of unearthing conflicts. He eventually became disillusioned with the technique, however, because not every client could be hypnotized and the *cures* he attained were not lasting (Brill, 1938). Freud came to believe that many of the beneficial effects of hypnosis were fleeting because they largely represented the client's attempt to please the hypnotist (Jones, 1953). Once the hypnotist was gone, the symptoms might return. Freud developed the method of psychoanalysis to replace hypnosis. Psychoanalysis uses techniques like **free association** and dream analysis (see Chapter 14).

■ **LEARNING PERSPECTIVES** Psychodynamic models of Freud and his followers were the first major psychological theories of abnormal behavior, but other relevant psychologies were also taking shape early in the 20th century. Among the most important was the behavioral perspective, which is identified with contributions by the Russian physiologist Ivan Pavlov (1849–1936), the discoverer of the conditioned reflex, and the American psychologist John B. Watson (1878–1958), the father of **behaviorism**. The behavioral perspective focuses on the

John B. Watson.   Watson and other behaviorists argued that human behavior—normal and abnormal—is basically the product of genetic endowment and environmental or situational influences.

role of learning in explaining both normal and abnormal behavior. From the behavioral perspective, abnormal behavior represents the learning of inappropriate, maladaptive behaviors.

From the medical and psychodynamic perspectives, abnormal behavior is *symptomatic,* respectively, of underlying biological or psychological problems. From the behavioral perspective, however, abnormal behavior need not be symptomatic of anything. The abnormal behavior itself is the problem. Abnormal behavior is regarded as learned in much the same way as normal behavior. Why, then, do some people behave abnormally? One reason is found in situational factors: Their learning histories, that is, might differ from most people's. For example, harsh punishment for early exploratory behavior, such as childhood sexual exploration in the form of masturbation, might give rise to adult anxieties over autonomy or sexuality. Inconsistent discipline, as shown in haphazard rewards for good behavior and capricious punishment of misconduct, might give rise to antisocial behavior. Then, too, children with abusive or neglectful parents might learn to pay more attention to inner fantasies than the world outside, giving rise, at worst, to difficulty in separating reality from fantasy.

Watson and other behaviorists, such as Harvard University psychologist B. F. Skinner (1904–1990), believed that human behavior is basically the product of genetic endowment and environmental or situational influences. The behavioral perspective has given rise to a treatment approach called **behavior therapy**, which applies principles of learning to help people overcome psychological problems and develop more effective behaviors.

In Chapter 2 we see that other learning theorists have called for an expanded model, called **social-learning theory**, which focuses on the roles that our personal values, expectancies, and observations of others play in explaining the development and maintenance of behavior.

■ HUMANISTIC-EXISTENTIAL PERSPECTIVES

A "third force" in modern psychology emerged during the mid-20th century—humanistic psychology. Humanistic theorists such as American psychologists Carl Rogers (1902–1987) and Abraham Maslow (1908–1970) believed that human behavior was nei-

(A)

(B)

Carl Rogers (A) and Abraham Maslow (B), two of the principal forces in humanistic psychology.   Humanists reject the determinism implicit in psychodynamic and learning theories. They viewed people as *actors* in the drama of life, not as *reactors* to instincts (as psychodynamic theorists saw them) or to environmental stimuli (as behaviorists saw them).

Mental Health Problems Among Native Americans— Loss of a Special Relationship with Nature?

Native Americans—American Indians and Alaskan Natives—constitute one of the smallest ethnic minority groups in the United States (Trimble, 1991). According to the 1990 censuses, nearly 2 million people describe themselves as either American Indian or Alaskan Native (Aleut Eskimo, or Indian). Native American populations are found in virtually every state but are largely concentrated in states west of the Mississippi River. On the whole, the Native-American population is among the most impoverished ethnic groups in the country. Like other groups who are socially and economically disadvantaged, Native Americans suffer from a disproportionate incidence of mental health problems, such as alcoholism, depression, drug abuse, and delinquency (Westermeyer et al., 1981). In one study, the death rate for cirrhosis of the liver (a liver disease caused primarily by chronic alcoholism) was four times greater among Native Alaskans (Indians, Eskimos, Aleuts) than among white Alaskans (Kraus & Buffler, 1979). The death rate due to suicide among Native Alaskans was three times the national average (Kraus & Buffler, 1979).

When you envision hula dancing, luaus, and wide tropical beaches, you may assume that Native Hawaiians are a carefree people. Research shows, however, that Native Hawaiians also suffer a disproportionate share of physical diseases and mental health problems. The death rate for Native Hawaiians is 34% higher than that of the general U.S. population, largely because of an increased rate of serious diseases including cancer and heart disease (Mokuau, 1990). Native Hawaiians also have a 5- to 10-year lower life expectancy than other groups in Hawaii (Hammond, 1988). Compared to other Hawaiians, Native Hawaiians have also experienced heightened rates of mental health problems, including higher suicide rates among males, higher rates of alcoholism and drug abuse, and higher rates of antisocial disorders (Mokuau, 1990). Depression and associated feelings of despair and a sense of hopelessness and self-doubt are also common among the native Hawaiian population.

Native Hawaiians do not lead a carefree existence. They have a higher death rate than the general U.S. population and show greater-than-average incidences of suicide, drug abuse, and antisocial behavior in relation to other Hawaiians. Another reason for studying the relationships between ethnicity and abnormal behavior is to debunk erroneous stereotypes.

Mental health problems among Native Americans and Native Hawaiians may at least partly reflect the alienation and disenfranchisement from the land and a way of life that resulted from colonization by European cultures. Native peoples often attribute mental health problems, especially depression and alcoholism, to the collapse of their traditional culture brought about by colonization (Timpson et al., 1988). Here some researchers describe how a Native Canadian elder in northwestern Ontario explained depression in his people:

> Before the White Man came into our world we had our own way of worshipping the Creator. We had our own church and rituals. When hunting was good, people would gather together to give gratitude. This gave us close contact with the Creator. There were many different rituals depending on the tribe. People would dance in the hills and play drums to give recognition to the Great Spirit. It was like talking to the Creator and living daily with its spirit. Now people have lost this. They can't use these methods and have lost conscious contact with this high power. . . . The more distant we are from the Creator the more complex things are because we have no sense of direction. We don't recognize where life is from.
> Timpson et al., 1988, p. 6

The depression that is so common among indigenous or native peoples apparently reflects the loss of a relationship with the world that was based on maintaining harmony with nature (Timpson et al., 1988). The description of the loss of this special relationship reminds one of the Western concept of alienation, as put forward by humanistic-existential psychologists.

ther a product of unconscious conflicts nor simple conditioning. Rejecting the determinism implicit in these theories, they saw people as *actors* in the drama of life, not *reactors* to instinctual or environmental presses. Humanistic psychology is closely linked with the school of European philosophy called *existentialism*. The existentialists, notably the philosophers Martin Heidegger (1889–1976) and Jean-Paul Sartre

(1905–1980), focused on the search for meaning and the importance of choice in human existence. Existentialists believe that our humanness makes us responsible for the directions that our lives will take.

The humanists maintain that people have an inborn tendency toward *self-actualization*—to strive to become all that they are capable of being. Each of us possesses a singular cluster of traits and talents that gives rise to an individual set of feelings and needs and grants us a unique perspective on life. Despite the finality of death, we can each imbue our lives with meaning and purpose if we recognize and accept our genuine needs and feelings. By being true to ourselves, we live *authentically*. We may not decide to act out every wish and fancy, but self-awareness of authentic feelings and subjective experiences can help us to make more meaningful choices.

To understand abnormal behavior, in the humanist's view, we need to understand the roadblocks that people encounter in striving for self-actualization and authenticity. To accomplish this, psychologists must learn to view the world from clients' own perspectives, since their views of their world lead them to interpret and evaluate their experiences in self-enhancing or self-defeating ways. The humanistic-existential viewpoint is sometimes called the *phenomenological* perspective because it involves the attempt to understand the subjective or phenomenological experience of others.

■ **COGNITIVE PERSPECTIVES** The word *cognitive* derives from the Latin *cognito*, meaning "knowledge." Cognitive theorists study the cognitions—the thoughts, expectations, and attitudes—that accompany and may underlie abnormal behavior. They focus on how reality is colored by our expectations, attitudes, and so forth, and how inaccurate or biased processing of information about the world—and our places within it—can give rise to abnormal behavior. Researchers have learned that the cognitions we hold about ourselves and the world around us are important aspects of our behavioral and emotional adjustment.

One cognitive approach to explaining abnormal behavior has been strongly influenced by computer science, or information processing. Information-processing theorists relate the functions of the mind to those of the computer and describe human cognition on the basis of cycles of sensory input, storage, retrieval, manipulation, and output of information. They perceive abnormal thought processes as disturbances in the cycle. Such disturbance might reflect the distortion or blocking of input, or the faulty storage, retrieval, or manipulation of information. These may lead, in turn, to impoverished output (lack of behavior) or distorted output (i.e., outlandish behavior). Schizophrenic people, for example, often jump from topic to topic in a chaotic manner, which information-processing theorists may explain in terms of problems in manipulating stored information.

Other cognitive theorists focus on the effects of self-defeating beliefs and attitudes. Albert Ellis (1977a, 1987), for example, views excessive anxiety

as frequently stemming from overwhelming irrational desires for social approval and perfectionism. Psychiatrist Aaron Beck suggests that depression may result from "cognitive errors" such as judging oneself entirely on the basis of one's flaws or failures, and interpreting events in a negative light (sort of wearing blue-colored glasses) (Beck et al., 1979). Many behavior therapists today identify with an expanded model of therapy, *cognitive* behavior therapy, which focuses on modifying self-defeating beliefs in addition to overt behaviors.

■ **SOCIOCULTURAL PERSPECTIVES** Does abnormal behavior arise from forces within the person as the psychodynamic theorists propose, or from the learning of maladaptive behaviors, as the learning theorists suggest? To the sociocultural theorists, abnormal behavior is not the product of conflicts within the person or of faulty learning. Sociocultural theorists look for the causes of abnormal behavior in the failures of society, rather than in the person. Within this view, abnormal behavior is rooted in societal ills, such as poverty, social decay, discrimination, and lack of opportunity. Some of the more radical psychosocial theorists even deny the existence of mental illness, believing that abnormal behavior is merely a label that society attaches to people who act differently in order to stigmatize and subjugate them. The sociocultural theorists have focused much needed attention on the social stressors that may lead to abnormal behavior. As we see in Chapter 2, evidence shows that people from lower socioeconomic levels are more likely to be institutionalized for abnormal behavior. But does this suggest that abnormal behavior is caused by poverty and other social ills, or that it is a label used by the establishment to discredit behavior of people of lesser means and social power? Or might there be other explanations linking abnormal behavior and social class?

■ **ECLECTIC MODELS** Many researchers and clinicians are **eclectic**. They make use of multiple models in explaining and treating abnormal behavior. Many learning theorists, for example, regard some abnormal behavior problems as arising from biochemical factors or the interaction of biochemistry and experience. They are willing to use a combination of drugs and behavior therapy to deal with problems like bipolar disorder and schizophrenia. Or they might make use of psychodynamic concepts to help explain the development of long-standing personality problems.

Clinicians trained in psychodynamic approaches may also be eclectic. They may believe that extreme fears or phobias symbolize unconscious childhood conflicts that carry over into adulthood. Still, they may employ behavior therapy techniques to help clients overcome their fears directly, even as they attempt more probing analysis of the childhood roots of the fears in long-term therapy.

Models of abnormal behavior not only provide perspectives for understanding and treatment but they also suggest various kinds of research into abnormal behavior. The medical model, for example, fosters inquiry into genetic and biochemical research. Learning models encourage inquiries into the situational determinants of abnormal behavior. In the following section we consider the types of research conducted by investigators of abnormal behavior.

RESEARCH METHODS IN ABNORMAL PSYCHOLOGY

Imagine that you are a brand-new graduate student in psychology and are sitting in your research methods course on the first day of the term. The professor, a distinguished woman of about 50, enters the class. She is carrying a small wire-mesh cage with a white rat. She smiles and sets the cage on her desk.

The professor removes the rat from the cage and places it on the desk. She asks the class to observe its behavior. As a serious student, you attend closely. The animal moves to the edge of the desk, pauses, peers over the edge, and seems to jiggle its whiskers at the floor below. It maneuvers along the edge of the desk, tracking the perimeter. Now and then it pauses and vibrates its whiskers downward in the direction of the floor.

The professor picks up the rat and returns it to the cage. She asks the class to describe the animal's *behavior.*

A student responds, "The rat seems to be looking for a way to escape."

Another student: "It is reconnoitering its environment, examining it." Reconnoitering? you think. That student has seen too many war movies.

The professor writes each response on the blackboard. Another student raises her hand. "The rat is making a visual search of the environment," she says. "Maybe it's looking for food."

The professor prompts other students for their descriptions.

"It's looking around," says one.

"Trying to escape," says another.

Your turn arrives. Trying to be scientific, you say, "We can't say what its motivation might be. All we know is that it's scanning its environment."

"How so?" the professor asks.

"Visually," you reply, confidently.

The professor writes the response and then turns to the class, shaking her head. "Each of you observed the rat," she said, "but none of you described its *behavior.* Each of you made certain *inferences,* that the rat was 'looking for a way down' or 'scanning its environment' or 'looking for food' and the like. These are not unreasonable inferences, but they are inferences, not descriptions. They also happen to be wrong. You see, the rat is blind. It's been blind since birth. It couldn't possibly be looking around, at least not in a visual sense."

Description, Explanation, Prediction, and Control: The Objectives of Science

Description is one of the primary objectives of science. To understand abnormal behavior, we must first learn to describe it. Description allows us to recognize abnormal behavior and provides the basis for explaining it.

Descriptions should be clear, unbiased, and based on careful observation. Our anecdote about the blind rat illustrates the point that our observations and our attempts to describe them can be influenced by our expectations, or biased. Our expectations reflect our models of behavior, and they may incline us to perceive events—such as the rat's movements and other people's behavior—in certain ways. Describing the rat in the classroom as "scanning" and "looking" for something is **inferential** and is based on our models of how animals explore their environments. It would be more descriptive to simply chart its movements around the desk, measuring how far in each direction it moves, how long it pauses, how it bobs its head from side to side, and so on.

Inference is also important in science, however. Inference allows us to jump from the particular to the general—to suggest laws and principles of behavior that can be woven into models and **theories** of behavior, such as psychodynamic and learning models. Without a way of organizing our descriptions of phenomena in terms of models and theories, we would be left with a buzzing confusion of unconnected observations. The crucial issue is to distinguish between description and inference—to recognize when one jumps from a description of events to an inference based on an interpretation of events. For example, one does not *describe* a person's behavior as "schizophrenic," but rather one *interprets* behavior as schizophrenic on the basis of one's model of schizophrenia. To do otherwise, we would affix ourselves to a given label or model and lose the intellectual flexibility that is needed to revise our inferences in the light of new evidence or ways of conceptualizing information.

Theories help scientists explain puzzling behavior and predict future behavior. Prediction entails the discovery of factors that anticipate the occurrence of events. Geology, for example, seeks clues in the forces affecting the earth that can forecast natural events such as earthquakes and volcanic eruptions. Scientists who study abnormal behavior seek clues in overt behavior, biological processes, family interactions, and so forth, that predict the development of abnormal behaviors as well as factors that might predict response to various treatments. It is not sufficient for theoretical models such as psychodynamic or learning models to help us explain or make sense of events or behaviors that have already occurred. Useful theories must allow us to make predictions. So one test of psychodynamic and learning models is whether or not they lead us to predict the occurrence of particular behaviors.

The idea of controlling human behavior—especially the behavior of people with serious problems—is controversial. The history of societal response to abnormal behaviors—including abuses such as exorcism and cruel forms of physical restraint—render the idea particularly distressing. Within science, however, the word *control* need not imply that people are coerced into doing the bidding of others—like puppets dangling on strings. Psychologists, for example, are committed to the dignity of the individual, and the concept of human dignity requires that people be free to make decisions and exercise choices. Within this context, *controlling behavior* means using scientific knowledge to help people shape their own goals and more efficiently use their resources to accomplish them. Today, in the United States, even when helping professionals restrain people who are violently disturbed, their goal is to assist them to overcome their agitation and regain the ability to exercise meaningful choices in their lives.[2] Ethical standards prohibit the use of injurious techniques in research or practice.

Psychologists and other scientists use the *scientific method* to advance the description, explanation, prediction, and control of abnormal behavior.

---

[2]Here we are talking about violently confused and disordered behavior, not criminal behavior. Criminals and disturbed people may both be dangerous to others, but with criminals the intention of restraint is usually limited to protecting society.

The Scientific Method

The scientific method is an approach to testing theoretical assumptions through empirical research. It has four basic steps:

1. *Formulating a research question.* Scientists derive research questions from their observations and theories of events and behavior. For instance, observations of dietary habits or theories about nutrition–behavior relationships might motivate psychologists to conduct research into whether or not the ingestion of sugar exacerbates **hyperactivity** among hyperactive children.

2. *Framing the research question in the form of a hypothesis.* A **hypothesis** is a precise prediction about behavior that is examined through research. The specific hypothesis regarding sugar and hyperactivity might be that the administration of so many ounces of a sugar-sweetened drink in the morning would produce greater disruption of behavior among hyperactive children than a sweet-tasting drink flavored with a sugar substitute. (We describe such research in Chapter 13.)

Or consider this hypothesis about depression: Depressed people hold more negative beliefs about themselves and their lives than normal people. (Research along these lines is described in Chapter 7.) Or one might hypothesize that **antisocial personality disorder**, which is characterized by social conflict and disregard of the rights of other people, is transmitted genetically. (See Chapter 8.)

3. *Testing the hypothesis.* Scientists test hypotheses through carefully controlled observation and experimentation. The hypothesis about sugar and hyperactivity might be tested by randomly assigning hyperactive children to experimental conditions in which, for several mornings, they consume either (1) a sugared drink or (2) a drink containing an artificial sweetener. After ingesting these beverages, the children would be carefully observed at school or at play by trained observers for evidence of disturbed behavior.

The hypothesis concerning attitudinal differences between depressed and nondepressed people might be tested by the administration of questionnaires that measure negative beliefs. The hypothesis about genetic contributions to antisocial personality disorder might be tested by sorting out genetic and environmental influences on behavior, as described more fully in Chapter 2.

4. *Drawing conclusions about the hypothesis.* In the final step, scientists draw conclusions from their find-

ings about the correctness of their hypotheses. Psychologists use statistical methods to determine the likelihood that differences between groups are **significant** as opposed to chance fluctuations. Psychologists are reasonably confident that group differences are significant—that is, not due to chance—when the probability that chance alone can explain the difference is less than 5%. When well-designed research findings fail to bear out hypotheses, scientists can modify the theories from which the hypotheses are derived. Research findings often lead to modifications in theory, new hypotheses, and, in turn, subsequent research.

The findings regarding depression confirm that depressed people tend to hold more negative beliefs than nondepressed people. However, a question remains as to whether negative beliefs lead to depression or are a result of depression. The "sugar challenge" described in Chapter 13 did not exacerbate the behavior problems of hyperactive boys. The findings regarding genetic contributions to antisocial behavior are more complex, but they suggest that genetic and environmental factors both contribute to antisocial personality disorder.

Let us now consider the major research methods used by psychologists and others to study abnormal behavior: the naturalistic-observation, correlational, experimental, quasi-experimental, epidemiological, and case-study methods.

The Naturalistic-Observation Method

The **naturalistic-observation method** is used to observe behavior in the field, where it happens. Anthropologists have lived among primitive tribes throughout the world in order to study human diversity. Sociologists have followed the activities of adolescent gangs in inner cities. Psychologists have spent weeks observing the behavior of the homeless in city train stations and bus terminals. They have even observed the eating habits of slender and overweight people in fast-food restaurants, searching for clues to obesity.

Scientists take every precaution to ensure that their naturalistic observations are **unobtrusive**, so as to prevent any interference with the behavior they observe. Otherwise, the presence of the observer may distort the behavior that is observed. Over the years naturalistic observers have sometimes found themselves in controversial situations. For example, they have allowed sick or injured apes to die when medicine could have saved them. Observers of substance abuse and other criminal behavior have allowed illicit behavior to go unreported to authorities. In such cases, the ethical trade-off is that unobtrusive observation can yield information which will be of benefit to all.

■ **SAMPLES AND POPULATIONS** The subjects or individuals who are observed or who participate in the research are said to comprise a research **sample**. A sample is a segment or part of a **population** of interest, and researchers need to ensure that the subjects in the research sample *represent* the target population. For example, the population of interest might be the student population of your college or university. Selecting your research sample from one particular dormitory or class is unlikely to constitute a representative sample, unless the dormitory or class in question was truly representative of the student body at large.

Naturalistic observation provides a good deal of information as to how subjects behave, but it does not necessarily reveal why they do so. Men who frequent bars and drink, for example, are more likely to get into fights than men who do not. But such observations do not show that alcohol *causes* aggression. As we see in the following pages, questions of cause and effect are best approached by means of controlled experiments.

Correlation

Correlation is a statistical measure of the relationships between two factors, or **variables**. In the naturalistic-observation study that occurred in the fast-food restaurant, eating behaviors were related—or correlated—to patrons' weights. They were not directly manipulated. In other words, the investigators did not manipulate the weights or eating rates of their subjects, but merely measured the two variables in some fashion and examined whether they were statistically related to each other. When one variable (weight level) increases as the second variable (rate of eating) increases, there is a **positive correlation** between them. If one variable decreases (for example, incidence of heart disease) as the other variable increases (level of physical activity), however, the correlation between the variables is said to be **negative**. In Chapter 4 we see that the correlation between activity levels and incidence of heart disease is generally negative, but somewhat more complex.

Although correlational research reveals whether or not there are connections between variables, it does not show cause-and-effect relationships. Consider the research that links cigarette smoking to cardiovascular disorders and cancer. In Chapter 4 we report correlational evidence that shows that people who smoke run higher risks of heart attacks and certain kinds of cancer, such as lung cancer. But correlation does not, in itself, rule out rival hypotheses concerning causation. Rather than smoking causing disease, people who experience more stress in their lives may be more likely to turn to smoking to help them cope as well as eventually becoming physically ill as the result of prolonged stress. But more direct experimental evidence exists that directly supports the causal link between cigarette smoking and health problems, including cancer.

Causal connections sometimes work in unexpected directions, and sometimes there is no causal

Does smoking cause cancer?   Correlational research reveals connections between smoking and physical disorders in human beings, but does not show cause-and-effect relationships. We know from correlational research that people who smoke run higher risks of disorders such as heart attacks and cancer, but the smokers in these studies have *chosen* to smoke. From this avenue of research, we therefore cannot say whether smoking itself or the factors (such as stress) that might have led these people to choose to smoke are responsible for the illnesses. Experimental research with lower animals—in which subjects are assigned at random to exposure to cigarette smoke—provides supportive evidence of the causal links between cigarette smoke and such physical disorders, however.

connection between variables that are correlated. There are correlations between depression and negative thoughts, and it may seem logical that depression is caused by such thoughts. However, it is also possible that feelings of depression give rise to negative thoughts. Moreover, depression and negative thinking may both reflect a common causative factor, such as stress, and not be causally related to each other at all.

Although correlational research does not reveal cause and effect, it can be used to serve the scientific objective of prediction. When two variables are correlated, we can use one to predict the other. In other words, even if questions concerning causality remain, we can still predict that smokers are more likely than nonsmokers to incur various kinds of diseases. Knowledge of correlations among alcoholism, family history, and attitudes toward drinking helps us predict which adolescents are at great risk of developing problems with alcohol, although causal connections are complex and somewhat nebulous. But knowing which factors predict future problems may help us direct prevention efforts toward these high-risk groups to help prevent these problems from developing.

Although correlational research does not in itself demonstrate cause and effect, it can be an early step in a research program that leads to controlled experiments which more directly address cause and effect. Experiments do a better job of ruling out rival hypotheses, for the variables in controlled experiments are directly manipulated.

■ **THE LONGITUDINAL STUDY**   One type of correlational study is the *longitudinal study*, in which subjects are studied at periodic intervals over lengthy periods, perhaps for decades. By studying people over time, researchers can investigate the events that are associated with the onset of abnormal behavior and, perhaps, learn to identify factors that predict the development of such behavior. However, such research is time consuming and costly. It requires a commitment that may literally outlive the original investigators. Therefore, long-term longitudinal studies are relatively uncommon.

Perhaps the best known example of longitudinal research in abnormal psychology is the work of Sarnoff Mednick and his colleagues. Since 1962 they have been following 207 offspring of Danish schizophrenic mothers. When the study began, the children averaged about 15 years of age and were matched with a reference group of children of normal mothers. In 1967, when the children were about 20, they were examined closely (Mednick & Schulsinger, 1968). The researchers found that the schizophrenic mothers of offspring who developed abnormal behavior—though not necessarily schizophrenic behavior—had experienced a relatively high rate of complications during pregnancy or childbirth. Schizophrenic mothers of children who had not developed abnormal behavior had experienced easier pregnancies and deliveries. These findings raised the possibility that a combination of genetic factors and complications in pregnancy or childbirth play a causal role in the development of severe forms of abnormal behavior. Again, however, causal interpretations must be tempered by the fact that the longitudinal data were correlated and not necessarily causally connected. One rival hypothesis would be that complications of pregnancy or childbirth and eventual abnormal behaviors are both effects of genetic defects in the fetus. If that were so, then the pregnancy and birth complications would play no direct role in the development of abnormal behavior. Still, longitudinal research provides clues to possible causal factors.

A combination of genetic factors and pregnancy or birth complications may thus help us *predict* the later occurrence of abnormal behavior in the offspring, even though causal connections remain open to rival hypotheses. Prediction is based on the *correlation* between events or factors that are separated in time. But we must be careful not to infer *causation* from *prediction*. A **causal relationship** between two events involves a time-ordered relationship in which the second event is the direct result of the first. We need to meet two strict conditions to posit a causal relationship between two factors:

1. The effect must follow the cause in a time-ordered sequence of events.
2. Other plausible causes of the observed effects (rival hypotheses) must be eliminated.

Through the experimental method, scientists seek to demonstrate causal relationships by first manipulating the causal factor and then measuring its effects under controlled conditions that minimize the risk of possible rival hypotheses.

The Experimental Method

The term *experiment* can cause some confusion. Broadly speaking, an "experiment" is a trial or test of a hypothesis. From this vantage point, any method that actually seeks to test a hypothesis could be considered "experimental"—including naturalistic observation and correlational studies. But investigators usually limit the use of the term **experimental method** to refer to studies in which researchers seek to uncover cause-and-effect relationships by directly manipulating possible causal factors. By using an experimental manipulation, sometimes called a treatment, researchers can come closer to answering questions such as whether or not alcohol causes aggression, cigarette smoking causes cancer, or psychotherapy relieves anxiety.

The factors or variables that are hypothesized to play a causal role are manipulated or controlled by the investigator in experimental research. These are called the **independent variables**. The observed effects are labeled **dependent variables**, since changes in them are believed to depend on the independent or manipulated variable. Dependent variables are observed and measured, not manipulated, by the experimenter. Examples of independent and dependent variables of interest to investigators of abnormal behavior are shown in Table 1.3.

In an experiment, subjects are exposed to an *independent variable,* for example, the type of beverage (alcoholic vs. nonalcoholic) they consume in a laboratory setting. They are then observed or examined to determine whether the independent variable makes a difference in their behavior, or, more precisely, whether the independent variable affects the depen-

Table 1.3 Examples of Independent and Dependent Variables in Experimental Research	
Independent Variables	**Dependent Variables**
Type of treatment: for example, different types of drug treatments or psychological treatments	Behavioral variables: for example, measures of adjustment, activity levels, eating behavior, smoking behavior
Treatment factors: for example, brief vs. long-term treatment, inpatient vs. outpatient treatment	Physiological variables: for example, measures of physiological responses such as heart rate, blood pressure, and brain wave activity
Experimental manipulations: for example, type of beverage consumed (alcoholic vs. nonalcoholic)	Self-report variables: for example, measures of anxiety, mood, or marital or life satisfaction

dent variable—in this case, whether they behave more aggressively if they consume alcohol.

■ EXPERIMENTAL AND CONTROL SUBJECTS

Model experiments assign subjects to experimental and control groups at random. **Experimental subjects** are given the experimental treatment. **Control subjects** are not. Care is taken to hold other conditions constant for each group. By using random assignment and holding other conditions constant, experimenters can be reasonably confident that the experimental treatment, and not uncontrolled factors such as room temperature or differences between the types of subjects in the experimental and control groups, brought about the outcome.

■ RANDOM ASSIGNMENT

Why should experimenters assign subjects to experimental and control groups at random? Consider a study intended to investigate the effects of alcohol on behavior. If we allowed subjects to decide whether or not they wanted to be in a group that drank alcohol, a **selection factor**, rather than the independent variable, might be responsible for the results. In this example, subjects who chose to drink might differ in important ways from those who preferred not to drink. One of their differences might lie in their aggressiveness. Therefore, we would not know whether the experimental manipulation (giving them or not giving them alcohol) or the selection factor was ultimately responsible for observed differences in behavior. Moreover, knowledge of which treatment they were receiving might also affect the experimental outcome—in this case by shaping subjects' expectations.

■ CONTROLLING FOR SUBJECTS' EXPECTATIONS

Apparent treatment effects may stem from subjects' expectations regarding their effects rather than from treatments themselves. Thus researchers also try to control for subjects' expectations about the treatments. In order to do so, they may have to render subjects **blind** as to what treatment they are receiving. For example, the taste of an alcoholic beverage like vodka may be masked by mixing it with tonic water in certain amounts, so as to keep subjects blind as to whether the drinks they receive contain alcohol or tonic water only.

■ PLACEBO-CONTROL STUDIES

Drug treatment studies are often designed to control for subjects' expectations by keeping subjects in the dark or blind as to whether they are receiving the experimental drug or an *inert placebo* control. The term **placebo** derives from the Latin meaning "I shall please," referring to the fact that belief in the effectiveness of a treatment (its pleasing qualities) may inspire hopeful expectations that help people mobilize themselves to overcome their problems—regardless of whether the substance they receive is chemically active or inert. In medical research on chemotherapy, a placebo—also referred to as a "sugar pill"—is an inert substance that physically resembles an active drug. By comparing the effects of the active drug with those of the placebo, the experimenter can determine whether or not the drug has specific effects beyond those accounted for by expectations.

In a *single-blind placebo-control study,* subjects are randomly assigned to treatment conditions in which they receive an active drug (experimental condition) or a placebo (placebo-control condition), but they are kept blind or uninformed about which drug they are receiving. It is also helpful to keep the dispensing researchers blind as to which substances the subjects are receiving, lest the researchers' expectations come to affect the results. So in the case of a *double-blind placebo design,* neither the researcher nor the subject is told whether an active drug or a placebo is being administered. Of course, this approach assumes that the subjects and the experimenters cannot "see through" the blind. In some cases, however, telltale side effects or obvious drug effects may break the blind. Still, the double-blind placebo control is among the strongest and most popular experimental design, especially in drug treatment research.

Placebo-control groups have also been used in psychotherapy research in order to control for subject expectancies. Assume that you were to study the effects of therapy method A on mood. It would be inadequate to randomly assign the experimental group to therapy A and the control group to a no-treatment waiting list. The experimental group might show improvement because of group participation, not because of therapy method A. Participation might raise expectations of success, and these expectations might be sufficient to engender improvement. Changes in control subjects placed on the "waiting list" would help to account for effects that were due to the passage of time, but they would not account for placebo effects, such as the benefits of therapy that result from instilling a sense of hope.

An *attention-placebo* control group is often used to separate the effects of a particular form of psychotherapy from placebo effects. In an attention-placebo group, subjects are exposed to a believable or credible treatment that contains the nonspecific factors that therapies share—such as the attention and emotional support of a therapist—but not the specific ingredients of therapy represented in the active treatment. Attention-placebo treatments commonly substitute general discussions of participants' problems for the specific ingredients of therapy that are contained in the experimental treatment. Unfortunately, although attention-placebo subjects may be kept blind as to whether or not they are receiving the experimental treatment, the therapists themselves are generally aware of which treatment is being administered. Therefore, the attention-placebo method may not control for therapists' expectations.

 In order to carry out experimental research, it may in fact be necessary to keep participants blind as to whether or not they are receiving the experimental treatment or a placebo. Otherwise, we may not be able to control for the effects of expectations.

■ **EXPERIMENTAL VALIDITY** Experimental studies are judged as to whether or not they are valid, or sound. The concept of experimental validity has multiple meanings and we consider three of them: *internal validity, external validity,* and *construct validity.*

Experiments are said to have **internal validity** when the observed changes in the dependent variable(s) can be causally related to the independent or treatment variable. Assume that a group of depressed subjects is treated with a new antidepressant medication (the independent variable), and changes in their mood and behavior (the dependent variables) are tracked over time. After several weeks of treatment, the researcher finds that most subjects have improved and claims that the new drug is an effective treatment for depression. "Not so fast," you think to yourself, "how does the experimenter know that the independent variable and not some other factor was causally responsible for the improvement? Perhaps the subjects improved naturally as time passed, or perhaps they were exposed to other events that were responsible for their improvement." Experiments lack internal validity to the extent that they fail to control for other factors (called confounds, or threats to validity) that might pose rival hypotheses for the results.

Experimenters randomly assign subjects to treatment and control groups to help control for such rival hypotheses. Random assignment helps ensure that subjects' attributes—intelligence, motivation, age, race, and so on—and presumably life events are randomly distributed across the groups and are not likely to favor one group over the other. Through the random assignment to groups, researchers can be reasonably confident that significant differences between the treatment and control groups reflect the effects of

independent (treatment) variables and not confounding selection factors.

External validity refers to the generalizability or applicability of the results of an experimental study to other subjects and settings, and at other times. In most cases, researchers are interested in generalizing the results of a specific study (for example, effects of a new antidepressant medication on a sample of depressed subjects) to a larger population (depressives in general). The external validity of a study is strengthened to the degree that the sample is representative of the target population. In studying the problems of the urban homeless, it is essential to make the effort to recruit a representative sample of the homeless population, rather than focusing on a few homeless people who happen to be available. One way of obtaining a representative sample is by means of random sampling. In a **random sample**, every member of the target population has an equal chance of being selected.

Researchers may seek to extend the results of a particular study by replication, which refers to the process of repeating the experiment in other settings, with samples drawn from other populations, or at other times. A treatment for hyperactivity may be helpful with economically deprived children in an inner-city classroom but not with children in affluent suburbs or rural areas. The external validity of the treatment may be limited if its effects do not generalize to other samples or settings. That does not mean that the treatment is less effective, but that its range of effectiveness is limited to certain populations or situations.

Analogue Studies One method of research that gives rise to many questions of external validity is the **analogue study**. Analogue studies usually take place in laboratory settings that are designed to simulate **in vivo** (real-life) behaviors or events. In the laboratory, however, the experimenter has the ability to investigate the behavior of interest under more tightly controlled conditions. In Chapter 5 we see that subjects with panic disorders who receive infusions of certain substances in the laboratory are more likely than normal people to report feelings of panic. Since it may not be feasible to monitor panic attacks in the natural setting, the induction of panicky sensations under laboratory conditions allows researchers to explore the factors that may give rise to attacks in the natural environment. But the external validity of such experimental analogues can be challenged. Abnormal behaviors or feeling states (in this case, "panicky" feelings) that are induced in the laboratory are not necessarily similar to naturally occurring experiences.

Researchers have also conducted analogue experiments on animals, such as in research into the effects of smoking. For example, rodents and other animals have been randomly assigned to smoking and nonsmoking conditions in which the amount of smoke that is introduced into their environments is precisely controlled in order to investigate the long-term effects of inhaling cigarette smoke. Such studies, for obvious ethical reasons, could not be conducted with humans.

To the extent that experimental arrangements for analogue studies are reasonable counterparts of natural settings, we can have confidence in their applicability to real-life settings. To the extent that we share physiological processes with other species, animal experiments may have much to teach us about ourselves. We have learned much from animal studies about the relationships between stress and development of physical disorders or diseases such as ulcers and cancer, and about the harmful effects of cigarette smoke on health. Animal experiments may also inform us about processes of learning that are shared by humans and animals. We should be careful, however, in conjecturing about whether or not animals can become "depressed" or "anxious" or suffer loss of problem-solving ability in ways that mirror these experiences among humans.

Construct (pronounced CON-struct) **validity** represents a conceptually higher level of validity—the degree to which treatment effects can be accounted for by the theoretical mechanisms or constructs that are represented in the independent variables. A drug, for example, may have predictable effects but not for the theoretical reasons assumed by the researchers.

Consider a hypothetical experimental study of a new antidepressant medication. The research may have internal validity in the form of solid controls and external validity in the form of generalizability across samples of seriously depressed people. However, it may lack construct validity if the drug does not work for the reasons proposed by the researchers. Perhaps the researchers assumed that the drug would work by raising the levels of certain chemicals in the nervous system, whereas the drug actually works by increasing the sensitivity of receptors for those chemicals. So what? you may think. After all, the drug still works. True enough—in terms of immediate clinical applications. However, a better understanding of why the drug works can advance theoretical knowledge of depression and give rise to the development of yet more effective treatments.

We can never be certain about the construct validity of research. Scientists recognize that current theories may eventually be toppled by theories that better account for research findings.

Quasi-Experimental Methods

The major features of true experiments are random assignment of subjects to experimental and control groups and manipulation of the independent variables. However, randomization is not always possible or ethically responsible. It would be irresponsible, for the sake of methodological rigor, to assign people who are suicidally depressed to a group discussion placebo control at random in an effort to determine the benefits of a suicide prevention program. Or we may be interested in whether or not children who watch the television show *Sesame Street* are better prepared for school than those who don't, but may not be able to control experimentally which preschoolers watch the show at home.

So-called **quasi-experiments** (*quasi* is a Latin word meaning "as if") contain some but not all of the features of a true experiment. When experimenters cannot directly assign subjects randomly to treatment or control conditions, quasi-experiments may yet offer valuable information about the relationship between the independent and dependent variables. Unlike a correlational study, a quasi-experiment is concerned with investigating the causal effects of the independent variable on the dependent variables of interest. However, they do not provide the degree of confidence we associate with true experiments. Having noted this drawback, some quasi-experiments are nearly as powerful as true experiments in controlling for possible confounds (Campbell & Stanley, 1963; Cook & Campbell, 1979).

The basic problem with quasi-experimental designs is the lack of random assignment of subjects to experimental conditions. Lacking random assignment, the researcher may be unable to account for possible differences in the types of subjects that make up the experimental and control groups. Thus differences in outcomes between treatment and control groups may have more to do with differences in the types of people making up the groups than to the treatment itself. Although experimenters may be able to control for certain subject characteristics, such as by ensuring that both treatment and control groups have equal numbers of males and females, only random assignment is likely to balance the groups on many other characteristics that the experimenter was unable to control.

Constraints on the use of random assignment in conducting research in various field settings challenges researchers to design quasi-experiments that provide a reasonable degree of confidence in the results. Consider a quasi-experiment on the effectiveness of inpatient versus outpatient behavioral treatment for **obsessive-compulsive disorder** (van den

Hout et al., 1988). Obsessive-compulsive people are bothered by nagging thoughts (obsessions) and by urges to repeat certain behaviors (compulsions), such as repeated hand washing or checking that appliances are turned off. In this particular study, the researchers could not control which subjects received inpatient treatment and which received outpatient care. The study found significant decreases in obsessive-compulsive behavior among subjects in both treatment settings but no significant differences in outcomes between the two settings. However, the finding of no differences between settings does not demonstrate that both treatment settings were equally effective because subjects in the two settings may have differed from each other in important ways. For instance, subjects admitted to the hospital setting might have been more severely disturbed. That is, a selection factor could have masked *true* differences in treatment effectiveness. Still, the value of this study is that it suggests that outpatient treatment may yield similar benefits as the much more costly inpatient form of treatment. But more definitive conclusions must await experiments in which subjects are randomly assigned to inpatient or outpatient treatment settings.

Epidemiological Method

The **epidemiological method** studies the rates of occurrence of abnormal behavior in various settings or population groups. One type of epidemiological study is the **survey** method, which relies on interviews or questionnaires. Survey methods, for example, have shown that rates of alcoholism vary among diverse ethnic groups (see Chapter 9), in part because ethnic groups have different attitudes toward alcohol and regulate alcohol consumption in different ways.

Like other samples used in research, survey samples need to reflect accurately the population they are intended to represent. A researcher who sets out to study smoking rates in a local community by interviewing people drinking coffee in late-night cafés will probably overestimate its true prevalence.

One method of obtaining a representative sample is random sampling. A random sample is drawn in such a way that each member of the population of interest has an equal probability of selection. Researchers also use **stratified random samples**, which are drawn so that known subgroups in the population are randomly selected in proportion to their numbers. For example, African Americans constitute about 12% of the population in the United States. Thus a racially stratified sample of the United States would be approximately 12% African Ameri-

can. Practically speaking, large randomly selected samples show reasonably proportionate stratification. Scientists use randomly drawn nationwide samples of about 1,500 people to gain an accurate picture of the voting patterns of the general U.S. population. But a sample of several million that was haphazardly drawn might not provide an accurate picture.

In one famous example of this error, *Literary Digest* magazine polled millions of readers in 1936 and predicted that Alf Landon, the Republican candidate for president, would defeat the incumbent Franklin D. Roosevelt in a landslide. Actually, the landslide victory went in the opposite direction. The *Literary Digest* readership, you see, contained a higher proportion of conservative voters than the nation at large.

It is true that a sample of several million people might not represent the population of the United States. A large sample size does not guarantee that members of the target population have an equal chance of being selected.

The epidemiologist must also determine whether people who participate in a study differ in important ways from those who refuse to participate, or else the conclusions might only represent the types of people who are willing to participate rather than the general population. This can be a vital issue in population surveys of the prevalence of abnormal behavior. For one thing, persons who show abnormal behavior are to some degree stigmatized by society, and may thus be reluctant to come forth. For another, people with some patterns of abnormal behavior shun social contacts and for that reason may be unwilling to participate.

Epidemiologists also rely on public health records and records of hospital admissions to track prevalences of disorders. But the survey method may be the only means of measuring certain behaviors that are not included in public records, such as rates of alcohol intake.

Epidemiological studies may point to potential causal factors in illness and disorders, even though they lack the power of experiments. By finding that illnesses or disorders "cluster" in certain groups or locations, researchers may be able to identify underlying causal factors that place these groups or regions at higher risk. For example, the Japanese who live in Japan eat low-fat diets and have low rates of colorectal cancer. However, Americans of Japanese descent eat higher fat diets and have relatively higher rates of colorectal cancer, suggesting that the ingestion of fats is connected with the development of this kind of cancer. Of course, such epidemiological studies cannot control for selection factors—that is, they cannot rule out rival hypotheses concerning other differences between Japanese and Japanese Americans that may play a causal role. Therefore, they must be considered suggestive of possible causal influences that must be further tested in experimental studies.

The Case-Study Method

Case studies have been important influences in the development of theories and treatment of abnormal behavior. Psychodynamic theory, originated by Sigmund Freud, was developed primarily on the basis of case studies, such as that of Anna O. Although learning theories focus more on laboratory research, learning theorists have also compiled a number of model cases, such as that of Little Albert (see Chapter 2).

■ **TYPES OF CASE STUDIES** There are many kinds of case studies. Generally speaking, **case studies** are carefully sketched biographies of the lives of individuals. Some case studies are basically historical and aim to divulge the factors that cause or contribute to abnormal behavior patterns. These case studies may be based on clinical interviews with subjects, interviews with persons who were close to the subjects, or writings by or about the subjects. Freud, for example, carried out such a case study on the Renaissance artist and inventor Leonardo da Vinci.

 Case studies have in fact been conducted on people who have been dead for hundreds of years, such as Freud's study of Leonardo. Such studies rely on historic records rather than interviews with subjects and their contemporaries.

Other case studies reflect an in-depth analysis of an individual's course of treatment. Such case studies typically include detailed histories of the subject's background and response to treatment. The therapist attempts to glean information from a particular client's experience in therapy that may be of help to other therapists treating similar clients.

Despite the richness of clinical material that case studies can provide, they are much less rigorous as research designs than experiments. There are bound to be gaps in memory when people discuss historic events, especially those of their childhoods. Many of us have the impression that we have vivid recollections of events from the first two or three years of life, but studies attempting to verify these memories

through interviews with older, independent witnesses show they are riddled with inaccuracies (Sheingold & Tenney, 1982). Freud himself was aware of this problem and labeled it *childhood amnesia*.[3] Moreover, again as noted by Freud, people may distort their pasts, even to themselves, in the effort to avoid painful memories. Then, too, some clients purposefully color events in such a way as to make a favorable impression on the interviewer; others aim to shock the interviewer with exaggerated or fabricated recollections.

Interviewers themselves may unintentionally encourage subjects to slant their histories in ways that are compatible with their theoretical perspectives. Psychoanalysts have been reproached, for example, for directing clients into viewing their personal histories from the psychodynamic perspective (for example, Bandura, 1986). But clinicians and interviewers who hold other theoretical perspectives also run the risk of subtly guiding subjects into uttering what they expect to hear. Then, too, clinicians and interviewers may unintentionally slant subjects' reports when they jot them down—again, subtly shaping them in ways that are more consistent with their own outlooks. And, in his case study of Leonardo, Freud had never met the subject. (Freud was also aware of this limitation.)

So the remembrance of things past, as recounted in case studies, is subject to many distortions. Case reports of treatment effectiveness also have certain problems. When clinicians try out a treatment with a client in the course of practice, they are manipulating treatment as the independent variable. However, they are doing so with one or a small number of people who are hardly representative of the general population. For example, they have sought (or been placed in) professional treatment. Another weakness of the treatment-oriented case study is the lack of a control group. There is usually one client ("subject"), and he or she receives the treatment. In the absence of a control group, it is difficult to tell whether beneficial changes in behavior that are observed over the course of treatment are due to

1. Specific treatment techniques,
2. Nonspecific therapeutic factors such as raising clients' expectations or giving them time to talk

---

[3]Freud attributed childhood amnesia to the repression ("motivated forgetting") of primitive sexual and aggressive impulses, but contemporary theorists note that the status of neurological and language developments during the first few years provide a more likely explanation (Rathus, 1993).

about their problems with a supportive therapist,

3. Naturally occurring ("spontaneous") improvement over time, or

4. External factors such as advice from loved ones,
   winning the lottery, and so forth.

Like many of us, therapists sometimes engage in self-
serving explanations of therapy outcomes: They tend
to accept credit for treatment successes but to blame
treatment failures on other factors, such as lack of full
cooperation on the part of the client.

■ THE SINGLE-CASE EXPERIMENTAL DESIGN

The limitations of traditional treatment-oriented case
studies have led researchers to develop more sophisticated methods, called **single-case experimental
designs**, in which subjects are used as their own controls. One of the most common forms of the single-
case experimental design is the A-B-A-B or so-called
reversal design (see Figure 1.1). The reversal design
consists of the repeated measurement of clients'
behavior across four successive phases:

1. A baseline phase (A). The baseline phase occurs
   prior to the inception of treatment and is characterized by repeated measurement of the target
   problem behaviors at periodic intervals. This
   measurement allows the experimenter to establish a **baseline** rate for the behavior before
   treatment begins;

2. A treatment phase (B). Now the target behaviors are measured as the client undergoes treatment;

3. A second baseline phase (A, again). Treatment is
   now temporarily withdrawn or suspended. This
   is the reversal in the reversal design, and it is
   expected that the positive effects of treatment
   should now be reversed since the treatment has
   been withdrawn; and

4. A second treatment phase (B, again). Treatment
   is reinstated and the target behaviors are
   assessed yet again.

Clients' target behaviors or response patterns are
compared from one phase to the next in order to
determine the effects of treatment. The experimenter
looks for evidence of a correspondence between the
subject's behavior and the particular phase of the
design to determine whether or not the independent
variable (that is, the treatment) has produced the
intended effects. If the behavior improves whenever
treatment is introduced (during the first and second
treatment phases) but returns (or is reversed) to baseline levels during the reversal phase, the experimenter can be reasonably confident that the treatment had the intended effect.

The method is illustrated by a case in which
Azrin and Peterson (1989) used a controlled blinking
treatment to eliminate a severe eye tic—a form of
squinting in which her eyes shut tightly for a fraction
of a second—in a 9-year-old girl. The tic occurred
about 20 times a minute when the girl was at home.
In the clinic, the rate of eye tics or squinting was
measured for 5 minutes during a baseline period (A).
Then the girl was prompted to softly blink her eyes
every five seconds (B). The experimenters reasoned
that voluntary "soft" blinking would activate motor
(muscle) responses which were incompatible with
those producing the tic, thereby suppressing the tic.
As you can see in Figure 1.2, the tic was virtually
eliminated in but a few minutes of practicing the
incompatible, or competing, response ("soft" blinking) but returned to near baseline levels during the
reversal phase (A) when the competing response was
withdrawn. The positive effects were quickly reinstated during the second treatment period (B). The
child was also taught to practice the blinking
response at home during scheduled 3-minute practice
periods and whenever the tic occurred or she felt an
urge to squint. The tic was completely eliminated
during the first 6 weeks of the treatment program
and remained absent at a follow-up evaluation 2
years later.

Although reversal designs offer better controls
than traditional treatment case studies, it is not
always possible or ethical to reverse certain behaviors

Figure 1.1 Diagram of an A-B-A-B reversal design.

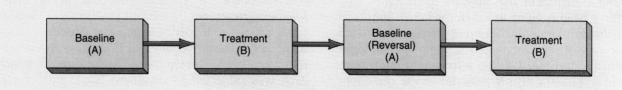

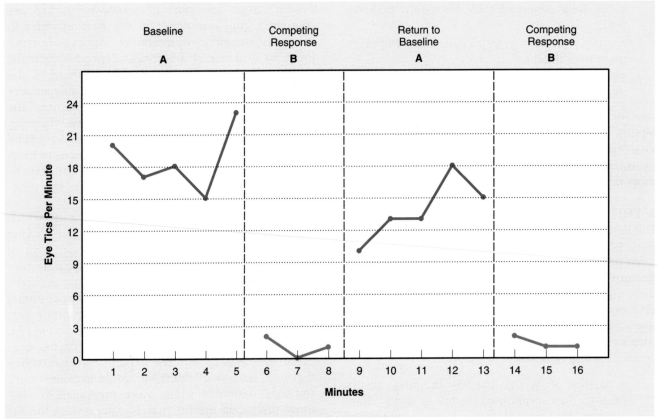

Figure 1.2 Treatment results from the Azrin and Peterson study.
Notice how the target response, eye tics per minute, decreased when the competing
response was introduced in the first "B" phase. It then increased to near baseline levels
when the competing response was withdrawn during the second "A" phase. It decreased
again when the competing response was reinstated in the second "B" phase.

or treatment effects. Clients in programs aimed at quitting smoking, for example, may reduce their rate of smoking during treatment but not revert to baseline rates when treatment is temporarily withdrawn. Such "failure to reverse" can have various explanations. One possibility is simply that the treatment had a desired *and lasting* positive effect. Or perhaps such clients learn that they can cut down their cigarette consumption and are not about to return to baseline levels when treatment is suspended.

It may also be unethical to withdraw a treatment program, even briefly, merely to demonstrate that the treatment was effective in maintaining the improvement. We would hardly encourage withdrawing a treatment that appears to be controlling repetitive head banging in a disturbed child simply to meet the requirements of a more scientific approach to the case study. Nor would a school psychologist who helps a teacher develop a treatment strategy to control a student's unruly behavior in the classroom

be willing to reverse treatment in order to demonstrate that the student's behavior during "reversal" will return to baseline levels. (Or if the psychologist were willing to do so, the classroom teacher might decide to become "unruly" and "reverse" the behavior of the psychologist.) Nor are most therapists pleased at the thought of attempting to restore clients' behaviors to baseline levels once improvement has been achieved. Thus the utility of the reversal design is generally limited to situations in which behavior can be readily reversed without undesirable consequences.

The *multiple-baseline design* is a type of single-case experimental design that does not require a reversal phase. In a multiple-baseline design *across behaviors,* treatment is applied, in turn, to two or more behaviors following a baseline period. A treatment effect would be inferred if changes in each of these behaviors corresponded to the time at which each was subjected to treatment. Since no reversal phase is required, many of the ethical and practical problems associated with reversal designs are avoided.

A multiple-baseline design was used to evaluate the effects of a social-skills training program in the treatment of the case of a shy, unassertive 7-year-old girl named Jane (Bornstein et al., 1977). The program taught Jane to maintain eye contact, speak more loudly, and make requests of other people through **modeling** (therapist demonstration of the target behavior), **rehearsal** (practice), and therapist **feedback** regarding the effectiveness of practice. However, the behaviors were taught sequentially, not simultaneously. Measurement of each behavior, and an overall rating of assertiveness, were obtained during a baseline period from observations of Jane's role playing of social situations with other children, such as playing social games at school and conversing in class. As shown in Figure 1.3, Jane's performance of each behavior improved following treatment. The rating of overall assertiveness showed more gradual improvement as the number of behaviors included in the program increased. Treatment gains were generally maintained at a follow-up evaluation.

To show a clear-cut treatment effect, changes in target behaviors should occur only when they are subjected to treatment. In some cases, however, changes in the treated behaviors may lead to changes in the yet untreated behaviors, apparently because of generalization. Multiple-baseline designs may not be too useful in situations in which generalization occurs, since it may be unclear whether the changes that occur in either the treated or untreated behaviors were due to the treatment itself or to some external factor. Fortunately, though, generalization effects have tended to be the exception, rather than the rule, in experimental research (Kazdin, 1992).

No matter how tightly controlled the design, or how impressive the results, single-case designs suffer from weak external validity because they do not show whether a treatment that is effective for one person is effective for others. Replication with other individuals can help strengthen external validity. Encouraging results in replication studies may also lead to controlled experiments.

Scientists are generally agreed that experiments are the research designs of choice. Other forms of research are generally conducted in order to pave the way for controlled experiments, or because such experiments would be impractical or unethical.

In this chapter we have defined abnormal behavior and considered historic and contemporary ways of conceptualizing abnormal behavior. We have also reviewed methods of research that investigators use to learn more about the causes of abnormal behavior and to determine effective treatments. In Chapter 2 we expand on contemporary models of abnormal behavior.

Figure 1.3 **Treatment results from the study by Bornstein, Bellack, and Hersen.**

The red dotted line shows the point at which social skills training was applied to each of the targeted behaviors. Here we see that the targeted behaviors (eye contact, loudness of speech, and number of requests) improved only when they were subject to the treatment approach (social skills training). We thus have evidence that the treatment—and not another, unidentified factor—accounted for the results. The section on the bottom shows ratings of Jane's overall level of assertiveness during the baseline assessment period, the social skills training program, and the follow-up period.

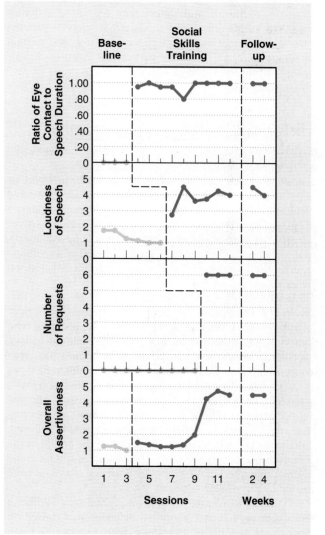

SUMMARY

What Is Abnormal Behavior?

Various criteria are used to define abnormal behavior. Psychologists generally consider behavior abnormal when it meets some combination of the following criteria: (1) unusual or statistically infrequent; (2) socially unacceptable or in violation of social norms; (3) fraught with misperceptions or misinterpretations of reality; (4) associated with states of severe personal distress; (5) maladaptive or self-defeating; or (6) dangerous.

Cultural Bases of Abnormal Behavior

The determination of which behavior patterns are deemed abnormal depends on cultural beliefs and expectations. Concepts of health and illness may also have different meanings in different cultures. Abnormal behavior patterns may take different forms in different cultures, and societal views of abnormal behavior vary across cultures. Ethnic groups within the United States differ in their rates of psychiatric diagnoses.

Historical Perspectives on Abnormal Behavior

Ancient societies attributed abnormal behavior to divine or supernatural forces. Prehistoric peoples may have practiced trephining as a form of treatment, although recent evidence suggests that this practice may represent an ancient form of surgery. In ancient Greece, people who behaved abnormally were sometimes sent to special temples where divine intervention was sought to effect a cure. In medieval times, belief in possession held sway, and exorcists were used to rid people who behaved abnormally of the evil spirits that were believed to possess them. There were some authorities in ancient times, like the Greek physician Hippocrates, who believed that abnormal behavior reflected natural causes, specifically imbalances in bodily fluids or humors. Different concentrations of these humors resulted in different types of abnormal behavior. Galen, a Greek physician who attended the Roman emperor Marcus Aurelius, adopted Hippocrates's teachings and is credited with discovering that arteries carried blood, not air, as was formerly believed. Johann Weyer, a Belgian physician during the period of the Renaissance, took up the cause of Hippocrates and Galen by arguing that abnormal behavior and thought patterns were caused by physical problems.

The 19th-century German physician Wilhelm Griesinger argued that abnormal behavior was caused by diseases of the brain. He, along with another German physician who followed him, Emil Kraepelin, were influential in the development of the modern medical model, which likens abnormal behavior patterns to physical illnesses. Kraepelin's categorization of mental disorders set the stage for the development of modern systems of classification.

Asylums, or "madhouses," began to crop up throughout Europe in the late 15th and early 16th centuries, often on the site of former leprosariums. Conditions in these asylums were dreadful and in some, such as Bethlehem Hospital in England, a circus atmosphere prevailed. With the rise of moral therapy in the 19th century, largely spearheaded by the Frenchmen Jean-Baptiste Pussin and Philippe Pinel, conditions in mental hospitals improved. Proponents of moral therapy believed that mental patients could be restored to functioning if they were treated with dignity and understanding. The cause of humane treatment was advanced in the United States by such figures as Benjamin Rush, the "father of American psychiatry," and the schoolteacher Dorothea Dix. But Rush also used certain harsh treatments that are now discredited, such as purging and ice-cold baths. Dix, who traveled widely throughout the United States advocating more humane treatment for people with mental disorders, was credited with the establishment of some 32 mental hospitals across the country. The decline of moral therapy in the latter part of the 19th century led to a period of apathy and to the belief that the "insane" could not be successfully treated. Conditions in mental hospitals deteriorated, and they offered little more than custodial care.

Not until the middle of the 20th century did public outrage and concern about the plight of mental patients mobilize legislative efforts toward the development of community mental health centers as alternatives to long-term hospitalization. This movement toward deinstitutionalization was spurred by the introduction of psychoactive drugs, called phenothiazines, which curbed the more flagrant features of schizophrenia.

Abnormal behavior may be viewed from various contemporary perspectives. The medical model conceptualizes abnormal behavior patterns, like physical diseases, in terms of clusters of symptoms, called syndromes, which have distinctive causes that are presumed to be biological in nature. Biological perspectives incorporate the medical model but refer more broadly to approaches that relate abnormal behavior to biological processes and apply biologically based treatments. Psychodynamic perspectives reflect the views of Freud and his followers, who believed that abnormal behavior stemmed from psychological causes involving underlying psychic forces. After abandoning hypnosis as a form of treatment, Freud developed psychoanalysis as a means of uncovering the unconscious conflicts dating back to childhood that he believed were at the root of mental disorders such as hysteria. Also arising in the early 20th century were learning perspectives that flowered from the work of the physiologist Ivan Pavlov and the contributions of behaviorists like John Watson and B.F. Skinner. Learning theorists posit that the principles of learning can be used to explain both abnormal and normal behavior. Behavior therapy is an outgrowth of the learning model. Humanistic-existential perspectives reject the determinism of psychodynamic theory and behaviorism. Humanistic and existential theorists believe that it is important to understand the obstacles that people encounter as they strive toward self-actualization and authenticity. Cognitive theorists focus on the role of distorted and self-defeating thinking in explaining abnormal behavior. Some adopt an information-processing model to explain abnormal behavior. Sociocultural theorists believe that abnormal behavior is rooted in social ills, such as poverty, not in the individual. Eclectic models attempt to integrate the contributions of various models.

Research Methods in Abnormal Psychology

The scientific approach focuses on four general objectives: description, explanation, prediction, and control. There are four steps to the scientific method: formulating a research question, framing the research question in the form of a hypothesis, testing the hypothesis, and drawing conclusions about the correctness of the hypothesis.

Research samples need to be representative of the target population. Understanding of abnormal behavior is approached from various types of research strategies or designs. The naturalistic-observation method allows scientists to measure behavior under naturally occurring conditions. Correlational research explores the relationship between variables, which may help predict future behavior and suggest possible underlying causes of behavior. But correlational research does not directly test cause-and-effect relationships. Longitudinal research is a type of correlational design that involves the study of selected subjects at periodic intervals over long periods of time, sometimes spanning decades.

In the experimental method, the investigator directly controls or manipulates the independent variable under controlled conditions in order to demonstrate cause-and-effect relationships. Experiments use random assignment as the basis for determining which subjects (called experimental subjects) receive an experimental treatment, and which others (called control subjects) do not. By using random assignment and holding other conditions constant, experimenters can be reasonably confident that the independent variable (experimental treatment), and not uncontrolled factors or differences between the types of subjects in the experimental and control groups, was causally related to the outcome.

Researchers use various methods to attempt to control for subjects' and researchers' expectations. In a *single-blind placebo-control study,* subjects are randomly assigned to treatment conditions in which they receive an active drug (experimental condition) or a placebo (placebo-control condition), but they are kept blind, or uninformed, about which drug they are receiving. *Double-blind placebo designs* seek to control both subjects' and researchers' expectations by keeping both researchers and subjects uninformed about whether an active drug or a placebo is being administered. *Attention-placebo* control groups are sometimes used in psychotherapy research to control for expectancy effects.

Experiments are evaluated in terms of their experimental validity. Internal validity refers to the ability of an experimental study to justify a cause-and-effect relationship between the independent and dependent variables. Internally valid studies control for possible confounds, or rival hypotheses. External validity refers to the degree to which experimental results can be generalized to other subjects, settings, and at other times. Construct validity refers to the degree to which treatment effects can be accounted for by the theoretical mechanisms or constructs that are represented by the independent variables.

Quasi-experiments are sometimes used when random assignment to treatment or control conditions is not possible. However, the lack of direct control over the types of people who compose the treatment and control groups places serious limitations on the ability to justify cause-and-effect relationships between the independent and dependent variables (that is, internal validity).

The epidemiological method examines the rates of occurrence of abnormal behavior in various population groups or settings. Evidence of how disorders cluster in certain groups or geographic areas may reveal underlying causes. But nonrepresentativeness of survey samples, volunteer biases, and selection factors represent possible sources of error.

Case-study methods can provide a richness of clinical material, but they are limited by difficulties of obtaining accurate and unbiased client histories, by possible therapist biases, and by the lack of control groups. Single-case experimental designs are intended to help researchers overcome some of the limitations of the case-study method.

Lucero Isaac, Confined to Silence, 1990. Mixed media: 21⅓ × 27¼ × 4 inches. Gerald Peters Gallery, Sante Fe, New Mexico.

CHAPTER OUTLINE

2

Theoretical Perspectives

TRUTH  FICTION?

___ According to psychodynamic theory, the mind is analogous to an immense iceberg: Only the tip of it emerges into conscious awareness.

___ Fingernail biting and cigarette smoking as an adult are signs of early childhood conflict.

___ A woman was expelled from the New York Psychoanalytic Institute for arguing that little girls are not envious of boys' penises.

___ Researchers conditioned a young boy to fear rats by clanging steel bars behind his head while he played with a rat.

___ Punishment does not work.

___ People are more motivated to tackle arduous tasks if they believe they will succeed at them.

___ People make themselves miserable by the ways in which they interpret events.

___ Hispanic-American women who are well acculturated (e.g., who are comfortable with English and who have tastes similar to those of non-Hispanic white women) are more likely than less well-acculturated Hispanic-American women to be heavy drinkers.

___ Abnormal behavior is connected with chemical imbalances in the brain.

___ Anxiety can give you indigestion.

___ Abnormal behavior patterns run in families.

Since earliest times humans have sought explanations for strange or deviant behavior. In ancient times and through the Middle Ages, beliefs about abnormal behavior centered on the role of demons and other supernatural forces. But even in ancient times, there were some scholars, such as Hippocrates and Galen, who sought natural explanations of abnormal behavior. In contemporary times, the understanding of abnormal behavior has been largely approached from psychological, sociocultural, and biological perspectives.

Although models of abnormal behavior can be traced to earliest times, the scientific study of abnormal psychology is still relatively young. We are only beginning to understand many disorders. As we do so, our earlier beliefs are modified or replaced by new ones. Each perspective has led to the development of theories about why we behave normally, and why we do not. Each has something to offer to our understanding of abnormal behavior, but none have been universally accepted. This is not surprising, given the range and complexity of human behavior in general, and abnormal behavior in particular. Some perspectives have more to offer our understanding of certain abnormal behavior patterns than they do of others.

PSYCHODYNAMIC PERSPECTIVES

Psychodynamic theory is based on the contributions of Sigmund Freud and his followers. There are differences among psychodynamic theorists, but they have a number of things in common. Each endorses the principle of **psychic determinism**, the view that our behavior—normal and abnormal—is determined by the outcome of dynamic processes and conflicts within the mind. Inner drives such as sex and aggression are seen as conflicting with social rules and moral codes. The social rules and moral codes become internalized. We make them parts of ourselves. After doing so, the dynamic struggle becomes a clashing of opposing *inner* forces. At a given moment our observable behaviors, as well as our thoughts and emotions, represent the outcome of these inner clashes.

Psychodynamic theories also agree that many of the motivating forces within us are fully or partially unconscious. We do not fully recognize them, even when they seem intense. These theories also focus on the importance of early childhood experience. The seed of psychological disorders are planted during our early, "formative" years.

Each psychodynamic theory owes its origin to the thinking of Sigmund Freud. Our coverage thus begins with his contributions.

Sigmund Freud's Theory of Psychosexual Development

The year was 1856. In a small Czechoslovakian village, an elderly woman prophesized that a newborn child would become a great man. The child, Sigmund Freud (1856–1939), was reared with great expectations. As a man, Freud himself would be skeptical of this belief. Soothsayers, after all, earn larger favors by forecasting good news than bad. The revelation about Freud proved prescient, however. Few people have had such an enormous impact on our contemplations of human nature.

Trained as a physician, Freud was intrigued by patients who appeared to suffer the loss of feeling in parts of their bodies or paralysis of their arms or legs without a medical disorder that could explain their symptoms. These symptoms, which were taken as signs of hysteria, often disappeared once the patients, under hypnosis, recalled and discussed upsetting events and feelings of anxiety and guilt that appeared to be connected with them. Although the patients' feelings and experiences had remained hidden for many years, they had the capacity to influence their behavior.

This clinical evidence led Freud to conclude that the mind is like an iceberg (Figure 2.1). Only the tip of an iceberg is visible above the surface of the water. The great mass of the iceberg lies below the surface, darkening the deep. Freud came to believe that people, similarly, perceive but a few of the ideas, wishes, and impulses that dwell within them and determine their behavior. Freud held that the larger part of the mind, which includes our deepest wishes, fears, and urges, remains below the surface of consciousness.

 Freud's psychodynamic theory does consider the mind as analogous to an immense iceberg, with only the tip rising into conscious awareness.

■ CONSCIOUS, PRECONSCIOUS, UNCONSCIOUS: THE GEOGRAPHY OF THE MIND
Freud labeled the region that corresponds to one's present awareness the **conscious** part of the mind. The regions that lay beneath the surface of awareness were labeled the *preconscious* and the *unconscious.*

In the **preconscious** mind are found memories of experience that are not in awareness, but which

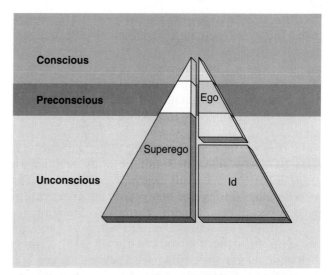

Figure 2.1 The parts of the mind, according to Sigmund Freud.
According to psychodynamic theory, the mind is akin to an iceberg in that only a small part of it rises to conscious awareness at any moment in time. Although material in the preconscious mind may be brought into consciousness by focusing our attention on it, the impulses and ideas in the unconscious tend to remain veiled in mystery.

can be brought into awareness by focusing on them. Your telephone number, for example, remains in the preconscious until you focus on it. The **unconscious** mind, the largest part of the mind, remains shrouded in mystery. Its contents can only be brought to awareness with great difficulty, if at all. Freud believed that the unconscious is the repository of biological drives, or instincts, such as sex and aggression. He posited the existence of **defense mechanisms**, such as **repression**, which protect us from recognizing wishes or impulses that would be inconsistent with our moral values and social requirements. Repression, or motivated forgetting, is the automatic ejection of anxiety-evoking ideas and desires from conscious awareness. Through repression, people can remain outwardly calm and controlled while they inwardly harbor murderous or lustful impulses of which they are unaware.

■ THE STRUCTURE OF PERSONALITY
Freud also put forth the **structural hypothesis**, which divides the clashing forces of personality into three mental or **psychic** structures: the *id, ego,* and *superego.* Psychic structures cannot be seen or measured directly, but their presence is suggested by observable behavior and expressed thoughts and emotions.

The **id** is the only psychic structure present at birth. The id represents the biological drives and is completely unconscious. It is, in Freud's view, "a chaos, a cauldron of seething excitations" (1964, p.

73). The id follows what Freud termed the **pleasure principle**. It demands instant gratification of instincts without consideration of social custom or the needs of others. One way of achieving rapid gratification is by **primary process thinking**, or the conjuring up of mental images of the objects of desire. The id, that is, operates in a world of desire and fantasy.

During the first year of life, the child discovers that its every demand is not instantly gratified. It must learn to cope with delay of gratification. The **ego** develops during this first year to organize reasonable ways of coping with frustration. Standing for "reason and good sense" (Freud, 1964, p. 76), the ego seeks to curb the demands of the id and to direct behavior that is in keeping with social customs and expectations. Gratification can thus be achieved, but not at the expense of social disapproval. The id floods your consciousness with hunger pangs. Were it to have its way, the id might also prompt you to inhale any food at hand or even to swipe someone else's plate. But the ego creates the ideas of walking to the refrigerator, making yourself a sandwich, and pouring a glass of milk.

The ego is governed by the **reality principle**. It considers what is practical and possible, as well as the urgings of the id. The ego also engenders the conscious sense of self. The ego engages in **secondary process thinking**—the remembering, planning, and weighing of circumstances that permits a compromise between the fantasies of the id and the realities of the world outside.

During middle childhood, the **superego** develops. The moral standards and values of parents and other key people become internalized through **identification**. The superego operates according to the **moral principle**; it demands strict adherence to moral standards. The superego represents the moral values of an ideal self, called the **ego ideal**. It also serves as a conscience, or internal moral guardian, that monitors the ego and passes judgment on right and wrong. It metes out punishment in the form of guilt and shame when it finds that ego has failed to adhere to superego's moral standards. Ego stands between the id and the superego. It endeavors to satisfy the cravings of the id without offending the moral standards of the superego.

■ **DEFENSE MECHANISMS** While part of the ego rises to consciousness, some of its activity is carried out unconsciously. In the unconscious, the ego serves as a kind of watchdog, or censor, that screens impulses from the id. The ego makes use of psychological defenses to prevent socially unacceptable impulses from rising into consciousness. If it were not for these defenses, or defense mechanisms, the dark-

Denial? Denial is a defense mechanism in which the ego fends off anxiety by preventing recognition of the true nature of a threat. Failing to take seriously the warnings of health risks from cigarette smoking can be considered a form of denial.

est sins of our childhoods, the primitive demands of our ids, and the censures of our superegos might disable us psychologically. Repression is considered the most basic of the defense mechanisms. Others are described in Table 2.1.

A dynamic unconscious struggle thus takes place between the id and the ego. It pits biological drives that strive for expression (the id) against the ego, which seeks to restrain them or channel them into socially acceptable outlets. The conflict can give rise to psychological disorders and behavioral problems.

Since we cannot view the unconscious mind directly, Freud developed a method of mental detective work called **psychoanalysis**. In psychoanalysis clients are encouraged to talk about anything that comes to mind, a process called **free association**. People may achieve **self-insight** through this process of pursuing the thoughts that pop into awareness. Defense mechanisms resist full disclosure of disturbing material, however.

The use of defense mechanisms to cope with feelings like anxiety, guilt, and shame is considered normal. These mechanisms enable us to constrain impulses from the id as we go about our daily business. In his work *The Psychopathology of Everyday Life*, Freud noted how slips of the tongue and forgetfulness represent hidden motives or ways of keeping them repressed. If a friend means to say, "I hear what you're saying," but it comes out, "I hate what you're saying," are her unconscious feelings revealed? If a lover storms out in anger but forgets his umbrella, is he unconsciously creating an excuse for returning?

Defense mechanisms may also give rise to abnormal behavior, however. For example, Freud hypothesized that hysterical behavior *symbolizes* and

Table 2.1 Some Defense Mechanisms of the Ego, According to Psychodynamic Theory

Defense Mechanism	Definition	Theoretical Examples of Defense Mechanisms in Normal Behavior	Theoretical Examples of Defense Mechanisms in Abnormal Behavior
Repression	The ejection of anxiety-evoking ideas from awareness.	A student forgets that a difficult term paper is due. A client in psychoanalysis forgets an appointment when anxiety-evoking material is about to be brought up.	A person who has hurt people close to him cannot recall his identity or the facts concerning his personal life.
Regression	The return, under stress, to a form of behavior characteristic of an earlier stage of development.	An adolescent cries when forbidden to use the family car. An adult becomes highly dependent on his parents following the breakup of his marriage.	Under extreme stress a person regresses to the first months of life, where she is ruled by impulses and cannot distinguish between fantasy and reality.
Rationalization	The use of self-deceiving justifications for unacceptable behavior.	A student blames her cheating on her teacher for leaving the room during a test. A man explains his cheating on his income tax by saying, "Everyone does it."	A man justifies raping a woman by claiming that she was dressed provocatively.
Displacement	The transfer of ideas and impulses from threatening or unsuitable objects onto less threatening objects.	A worker picks a fight with her spouse after being criticized sharply by her supervisor.	A man who is frustrated at work kills his family.
Projection	The thrusting of one's own unacceptable impulses onto others so that others are assumed to harbor them.	A hostile person perceives the world as being a dangerous place. A sexually frustrated person interprets innocent gestures of others as sexual advances.	A hostile person develops delusions that others are attempting to destroy him.
Reaction formation	Assumption of behavior in opposition to one's genuine impulses in order to keep impulses repressed.	A person who is angry with a relative behaves in a "sickly sweet" manner toward that relative.	A conservative woman who cannot accept her sexual desires goes on a compulsive "holy crusade" to ban pornography.
Denial	Refusal to accept the true nature of a threat.	A college student in academic difficulty refuses to accept the possibility of failure.	A person with a heart condition denies the seriousness of recurring symptoms, placing himself at greater risk by refusing to seek medical attention.
Sublimation	The channeling of primitive impulses into positive, constructive efforts.	A person paints nudes for the sake of "beauty" and "art." A hostile person directs aggressive energies into competitive sports.	(Sublimation is not usually associated with abnormal behavior.)

defends against unbearable memories or wishes. Hysterical paralysis of an arm may prevent the acting out of unconscious aggressive wishes. The symptom symbolizes or represents the unconscious dynamic struggle between the unacceptable or threatening urges that seek expression and the counterforces that seek to restrain or rechannel them into acceptable outlets. Freud's observations on hysteria provided much of the impetus for the development of psychoanalytic theory.

■ **STAGES OF PSYCHOSEXUAL DEVELOPMENT** Freud aroused heated controversy in the medical establishment of his time by arguing that sexual drives are dominant factors in the development of personality, even among children. Freud believed that the child's basic relationship to the world in its first several years of life is organized in terms of its pursuit of sexual pleasures that take the form of sucking their mothers' breasts and moving their bowels. (In Freud's view, all activities that are physically pleasurable, such as eating or moving one's bowels, are in essence sexual.)

The drive for sexual pleasure represents, in Freud's view, the expression of a major life instinct, which he called **Eros**—the basic drive to preserve and perpetuate life. The energy contained in Eros that allows it to fulfill its function was termed **libido**, or sexual energy. Freud believed that libidinal energy is expressed through sexual pleasure in different body parts, called **erogenous zones**, as the child progresses through development. In Freud's view, the stages of human development are **psychosexual** in nature, since they correspond to the transfer of libidinal energy from one erogenous zone to another. Freud proposed the existence of five psychosexual stages of development: oral, anal, phallic, latency, and genital. Let us briefly review these stages.

During its first year, the child's encounters with the world are mostly experienced through its mouth. Anything that fits into the mouth, goes into the mouth. Freud labeled this period the **oral stage** and argued that oral stimulation, in the form of sucking and biting, is a source of both sexual gratification and nourishment.

One of Freud's central beliefs is that the child may encounter conflict during each of the psychosexual stages of development. Conflict during the oral stage centers around the issue of whether or not the infant receives adequate oral gratification. Too much gratification could lead the infant to expect that everything in life is given with little or no effort on its part. In contrast, early **weaning** might lead to frustration. Too little or too much gratification at any stage could lead to **fixation** in that stage, which leads to the development of personality traits characteristic

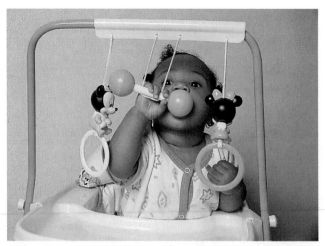

The oral state of psychosexual development? According to Freud, children get the flavor of the world during the oral stage. Children's early encounters with the world are largely experienced through the mouth, that is.

of that stage. Oral fixations could include an exaggerated desire for "oral activities," which could become expressed in later life in smoking, alcohol abuse, overeating, and nail biting. Like the infant who is dependent on the mother's breast for survival and gratification of oral pleasure, orally fixated adults may also become clinging and dependent in their interpersonal relationships.

 Within psychodynamic theory, fingernail biting and cigarette smoking as an adult may be considered signs of early childhood conflict.

During the **anal stage** of psychosexual development, the child experiences sexual gratification through contraction and relaxation of the sphincter muscles that control elimination of bodily waste. Although elimination had been controlled reflexively during much of the first year of life, the child now learns that she or he is able, though perhaps not reliably at first, to exercise voluntary muscular control over elimination.

Now the child begins to learn that she or he can delay gratification of the need to eliminate when the urge is felt. During toilet training, the issue of self-control may become a source of conflict between the parent and the child. **Anal fixations** that derive from this conflict are associated with two sets of traits. Harsh toilet training may lead to the development of **anal retentive** traits, which involve excessive needs for self-control. These include perfectionism and extreme needs for orderliness, cleanliness, and neatness. By contrast, excessive gratification during the anal period might lead to **anal-expulsive** traits, which include carelessness and messiness.

The next stage of psychosexual development, the **phallic stage**, generally begins during the third year of life. The major erogenous zone during the stage is the phallic region (the penis in boys, the clitoris in girls). Conflict between parent and child may occur over masturbation—the rubbing of the phallic areas for sexual pleasure—which parents may react to with threats and punishments. Perhaps the most controversial of Freud's beliefs was his suggestion that phallic stage children develop incestuous wishes for the parent of the opposite gender and begin to view the parent of the same sex as a rival for the affections of the parent they wish to possess.

■ THE OEDIPUS AND ELECTRA COMPLEXES

Conflict at the phallic stage is believed to have far-reaching consequences in determining later development and assumption of **sex roles**. Freud believed that **castration anxiety** played an important role in resolving the conflict for boys. Adults sometimes threaten boys with castration to try to get them to stop touching themselves. Freud documented such castration threats from parents or nurses in several case studies. At some point boys discover that girls are different—they do not have penises. Freud conjectured that boys might imagine that girls had lost their penises as a form of punishment. Going further, Freud hypothesized that boys develop castration anxiety, based on the fantasy that their rivals for their

Are young children interested in sex? According to Freud, even young children have sexual impulses. Freud's view of childhood sexuality shocked the scientific establishment of his day, and many of Freud's own followers believe that Freud placed too much emphasis on sexual motivation.

mother's affections, namely their fathers, would seek to punish them for their incestuous wishes by removing the organ that has become connected with sexual pleasure. To prevent castration, Freud argued, boys repress their incestuous wishes for their mothers and identify with their fathers. Keep in mind that Freudian theory posits that these developments are quite normal, and ordinarily lead to the boy's development of the aggressive, independent characteristics associated with the traditional masculine sex role. The conflict in boys was labeled the **Oedipus complex**, after Oedipus, the legendary Greek king who unwittingly slew his father and married his mother.

The female counterpart to the Oedipal conflict has been called by some the **Electra complex** after the character of Electra, who, according to Greek legend, avenged the death of her father, King Agamemnon, by slaying her father's murderers—her own mother and her mother's lover. The Electra complex is like a mirror image of the Oedipus complex in boys. When resolved successfully, in Freud's view, it leads girls to identify with their mothers and acquire the more passive, dependent characteristics traditionally associated with the feminine sex role. Freud believed that little girls become envious of boys' penises. This jealousy leads them to become resentful toward their mothers, whom they blame for bringing them into the world so "ill-equipped," as Freud wrote in his *New Introductory Lectures on Psychoanalysis*. Girls then desire to possess their fathers, in a way substituting their fathers' penises for their own missing ones. But the rivalry with their mothers for their fathers' affection places them in peril of losing their mothers' love and protection.

The crisis resolves with girls forsaking their incestuous desires for their fathers and identifying with their mothers. Eventually the wish for a penis is transformed into the desire to marry a man and bear children, which represents the ultimate adjustment of surrendering the wish "to be a man" by accepting a baby as a form of penis substitute. Freud hypothesized that, in adulthood, women who retain the wish for a penis of their own ("to be a man") can become maladjusted and develop masculine-typed characteristics such as competitiveness, dominance, and even female homosexuality.

Freud's views of female psychosexual development have been roundly attacked by women and by modern-day psychoanalysts. One of the most prominent critics, the psychoanalyst Karen Horney (1885–1952), for example, argued that evidence of penis envy was not confirmed by observations of children and that Freud's view reflected the cultural prejudice in Western society against women. To Horney, cultural expectations played a great role in shaping women's self-images, not penis envy. Interestingly, Horney's outspoken opposition to the manner in which the psychoanalytic establishment of her time conceptualized and treated women led to her expulsion from the staid New York Psychoanalytic Institute (Quinn, 1987).

A woman was indeed expelled from the New York Psychoanalytic Institute for arguing that traditional psychodynamic views of personality development—such as the penis-envy hypothesis—were degrading to women. Her name was Karen Horney.

We should also note that Freud's psychodynamic theory was a product of its day. In Freud's day, motherhood and family life were, by and large, the only socially proper avenues of fulfillment for women. Today, the choices available to women are more varied, and normality is not conceived in terms of rigidly defined gender roles.

The Oedipus and Electra complexes come to a point of resolution by about the age of 5 or 6 with the repression of incestuous wishes for the parent of the opposite gender and the identification with the parent of the same sex. From this identification comes the internalization of parental values in the form of the superego. Children then enter the **latency stage**

Karen Horney. Psychoanalyst Karen Horney took issue with Freud's belief that women's personalities are shaped by penis envy. Horney argued that Freud's view reflects a cultural prejudice against women. Horney believed cultural expectations and not penis envy largely shape women's self-images.

of psychosexual development, a period of late childhood during which sexual impulses remain in a latent state. Interests become directed toward school and play activities. But sexual drives are once again aroused with the **genital stage**, beginning with puberty, which reaches fruition in mature sexuality, marriage, and the bearing of children. The sexual feelings toward the parent of the opposite gender that had remained repressed during the latency period emerge during adolescence, but are displaced, or transferred, onto socially appropriate members of the opposite gender. Boys might still look for girls "just like the girl that married dear old dad." And girls might still be attracted to boys who resemble their "dear old dads."

In Freud's view, successful adjustment during the genital stage involves the attainment of sexual gratification through sexual intercourse with someone of the opposite gender, presumably within the context of marriage. Other forms of sexual expression, such as oral or anal stimulation, masturbation, and homosexual activity are considered **pregenital** fixations, or immature forms of sexual conduct.

Other Psychodynamic Theorists

Freud left a rich intellectual legacy that has stimulated the thinking of many theorists. Psychodynamic theory has been shaped over the years by the contributions of psychodynamic theorists who shared certain central tenets in common with Freud, such as the belief that behavior reflects unconscious motivation, inner conflict, and the operation of defensive responses to anxiety (Wachtel, 1982). They tended to deemphasize the roles of basic instincts such as sex and aggression, however, and to place greater emphasis on roles for conscious choice, self-direction, and creativity. These theorists also differed from each other in various ways.

One of the most prominent of the early psychodynamic theorists was Carl Jung (1875–1961), a Swiss psychiatrist who was formerly a member of Freud's inner circle. His break with Freud came when he developed his own psychodynamic theory, which he called **analytical psychology**. Like Freud, Jung believed that unconscious processes are important in explaining behavior. Jung believed that an understanding of human behavior must incorporate the facts of self-awareness and self-direction as well as the impulses of the id and the mechanisms of defense. He believed that not only do we have a *personal* unconscious, a repository of repressed memories and impulses, but we also inherit a **collective unconscious**. To Jung, the collective unconscious represents the accumulated experience of humankind, which he believed is passed down genetically through the generations. The collective unconscious is believed to contain primitive images, or **archetypes**, which reflect upon the history of our species, including vague, mysterious mythical images like the all-powerful God, the fertile and nurturing mother, the young hero, the wise old man, and themes of rebirth or resurrection. Although archetypes remain unconscious, in Jung's view, they influence our thoughts, dreams, and emotions and render us responsive to cultural themes in stories and films.

Alfred Adler (1870–1937), like Jung, had held a place in Freud's inner circle, but broke away as he developed his own beliefs that people are basically driven by an **inferiority complex**, not by the sexual instinct as Freud had maintained. For some people, feelings of inferiority are based on physical problems and the resulting need to compensate for them. But all of us, because of our small size during childhood, encounter feelings of inferiority to some degree. These feelings lead to a powerful **drive for superiority**, which motivates us to achieve prominence and social dominance. In the healthy personality, however, strivings for dominance are tempered by devotion to helping other people.

Consider the example of the English poet Lord Byron, who had a crippled leg yet became a champion swimmer. Beethoven's encroaching deafness may have spurred him on to greater musical accomplishments. Adler as a child was crippled by rickets and suffered from pneumonia, and it may be that his

Carl Gustav Jung. Jung agreed with Freud that unconscious processes influence behavior, but Jung also believed in the importance of self-awareness and self-direction. Jung wrote that people inherit a collective unconscious mind that represents the accumulated experience of humankind and contains certain primitive images, or archetypes.

theory developed in part from his own childhood striving to overcome repeated bouts of illness. However, there is no empirical support for the view that all of us harbor feelings of inferiority.

Adler, like Jung, believed that self-awareness plays a major role in the formation of personality. Adler spoke of a **creative self**, a self-aware aspect of personality that strives to overcome obstacles and develop the individual's potential. With the hypothesis of the creative self, Adler shifted the emphasis of psychodynamic theory from the id to the ego. Because our potentials are uniquely individual, Adler's views have been termed **individual psychology**.

There are many other psychodynamic models that have arisen with the work of Freud's followers, who are sometimes referred to collectively as **neo-Freudians**. Some psychodynamic theorists, such as Karen Horney and Harry Stack Sullivan (1892–1949), focused on the social context of psychological problems and stressed the importance of child-parent relationships in determining the nature of later interpersonal relationships. Sullivan, for example, maintained that children of rejecting parents tend to become self-doubting and anxious. These personality features persist and impede the development of close relationships in adult life.

More recent psychodynamic models also place a greater emphasis on the self or the ego, and less emphasis on the sexual instinct, than Freud. Today, most psychoanalysts see people as motivated on two tiers: by the growth-oriented, conscious pursuits of the ego as well as by the more primitive, conflict-ridden drives of the id. Heinz Hartmann (1894–1970) was one of the originators of **ego psychology**, which posits that the ego has energy and motives of its own. Freud, remember, believed that ego functions are fueled by the id, are largely defensive, and are perpetually threatened by the irrational. Hartmann and other ego analysts find Freud's views of the ego—and of people in general—too pessimistic and ignoble. Hartmann argued that the cognitive functions of the ego could be free of conflict. The choices to seek an education, dedicate oneself to art and poetry, and further humanity are not merely defensive forms of sublimation, as Freud had seen them.

Another ego analyst, Erik Erikson (b. 1902), attributed more importance to children's social relationships than to unconscious processes. Whereas Freud viewed development as psychosexual, Erikson saw it as **psychosocial**. Erikson posited eight stages of psychosocial development (see Table 2.2). Each stage is named according to the possible outcomes, which are polar opposites.

Whereas Freud's developmental theory ends with the genital stage, beginning in early adolescence,

Table 2.2   Erik Erikson's Stages of Development

Time Period	Life Crisis	The Developmental Task
Infancy (0–1)	Trust versus mistrust	Coming to trust the mother and the environment—to associate surroundings with feelings of inner goodness
Early childhood (2–3)	Autonomy versus shame and doubt	Developing the wish to make choices and the self-control to exercise choice
Preschool years (4–5)	Initiative versus guilt	Adding planning to choice, becoming active and on the move
Elementary school years (6–12)	Industry versus inferiority	Becoming eagerly absorbed in mastering the fundamentals of technology
Adolescence	Identity versus role diffusion	Connecting skills and social roles to the formation of career objectives
Young adulthood	Intimacy versus isolation	Committing the self to another in an intimate relationship
Middle adulthood	Generativity versus stagnation	Needing to be needed; guiding and encouraging the younger generation; striving to be creative
Late adulthood	Integrity versus despair	Accepting one's place in the life cycle; achieving wisdom and dignity

Source: Adapted from Erikson (1963), pp. 247–269.

Erikson focuses on continued developmental processes throughout adulthood. The goal of adolescence, in Erikson's view, is not genital sexuality, but rather the attainment of **ego identity**. Adolescents who achieve ego identity develop a clearly defined and firm sense of who they are and what they believe in. Adolescents who drift without purpose or clarity of self remain in a state of **role diffusion** and are especially subject to negative peer influences.

One popular contemporary psychodynamic approach is termed **object-relations theory**, which focuses on how children come to develop symbolic representations of important others in their lives, especially their parents. One of the major contributors to object-relations theory was Margaret Mahler (1897–1985), who saw the process of separating from the mother during the first three years of life as crucial to personality development.

According to psychodynamic theory, we **introject**, or incorporate, into our own personalities, elements of major figures in our lives. Introjection is more powerful when we fear losing others to death or rejection of us. Thus we might be particularly apt to incorporate elements of people who *disapprove* of us or who see things differently.

Margaret Mahler.   Margaret Mahler saw the process of separating from one's mother early as crucial to personality development. She believed we experience internal conflict as the attitudes of introjected people battle with our own. Because of such conflict, we may not be able to tell where the influences of other people end and our own selves begin.

In Mahler's view, these symbolic representations, which are formed from images and memories of others, come to influence our perceptions and behavior. We experience internal conflict as the attitudes of introjected people battle with our own. Some of our perceptions may be distorted or seem unreal to us. Some of our impulses and behavior may seem unlike us, as if they come out of the blue. With such conflict, we may not be able to tell where the influences of other people end and our "real selves" begin. The aim of Mahler's therapeutic approach was to help clients separate their own ideas and feelings from those of the introjected objects so that they could develop as individuals—as their own persons.

Psychodynamic Perspectives on Normality and Abnormality

Psychodynamic theorists account for abnormal behavior in various ways. According to Freud, there is a thin line between the normal and the abnormal. Normal as well as abnormal people are motivated or driven by the irrational drives of the id. The difference between normal and abnormal people may be largely a matter of degree.

■ **THE CONTINUUM OF NORMALITY, NEUROSIS, AND PSYCHOSIS** Normality is a matter of the balance of energy among the psychic structures of id, ego, and superego. Freud believed that we may all be capable of becoming neurotic or even psychotic when these mental structures become unbalanced. Among normal people, the ego has the strength to control the instincts of the id and to withstand the condemnation of the superego. The presence of acceptable outlets for the expression of some primitive impulses, such as the expression of mature sexuality in marriage, decreases the pressures within the id, and, at the same time, lessens the burdens of the ego in repressing the remaining impulses. Being reared by reasonably tolerant parents might prevent the superego from becoming overly harsh and condemnatory.

Among neurotic and psychotic people, the balance of energy is lopsided. Neurotic people spend a great deal of energy attempting to keep threatening impulses tamped down. As a result, they may feel weak, drained of energy. Yet some impulses may "leak," producing anxiety, or lead to the development of neurotic behavior patterns, or symptoms, such as hysteria and phobias. An overly powerful superego can create excessive feelings of guilt and lead to depression. An underdeveloped superego is believed to play a role in explaining the antisocial tendencies of people who intentionally hurt others without feelings of guilt.

In Freud's theory, **neuroses** develop as ways of trying to stem the leakage of unacceptable impulses from the id. Neuroses refer to maladaptive behavior patterns, such as hysteria or **phobia**, which Freud believed represented or symbolized these inner conflicts. **Neurotic anxiety** occurs when the ego senses that unacceptable impulses might break through to consciousness. Neurotic anxiety, then, is a fear of one's own forbidden impulses, in contrast to **reality anxiety**, which represents fear of external dangers or threats (for example, feeling afraid if you were awakened at night by sounds of an intruder). Neurotic symptoms such as hysterical paralysis or phobias are believed to serve a purpose of shielding the self from awareness of these unconscious promptings.

Freud believed that the underlying conflicts in neuroses have childhood origins that are buried in the depths of the unconscious. Through psychoanalysis, he sought to help people uncover and learn to deal with these underlying conflicts to free themselves of the need to maintain the overt symptom.

Perpetual vigilance and defense takes its toll. The ego can weaken and, in extreme cases, lose the ability to keep a lid on the id. **Psychosis** results when the urges of the id spill forth, untempered by an ego that has either been weakened or is underdeveloped. The fortress of the ego is overrun, and the person loses the ability to distinguish between fantasy and reality. Behavior becomes detached from reality. Primary process thinking and bizarre behavior rule the day. Psychoses are characterized, in general, by more severe disturbances of functioning than neuroses, by the appearance of bizarre behavior and thoughts, and by faulty perceptions of reality, such as hallucinations ("hearing voices" or seeing things that are not present). Speech may become incoherent and there may be bizarre posturing and gestures. The most prominent form of psychosis is schizophrenia, which is discussed in Chapter 11.

■ **THE ABILITIES TO LOVE AND TO WORK** Freud equated psychological health with the abilities to love and to work. The normal person can care deeply for other people, find sexual gratification in an intimate relationship, and engage in productive work. To accomplish these ends, there must be an opportunity for sexual impulses to be expressed in a relationship with a partner of the opposite gender. Other impulses must be channeled (sublimated) into socially productive pursuits, such as work, enjoyment of art or music, or creative expression. When some impulses are expressed directly and others are sublimated, the ego has a relatively easy time of it repressing those that remain in the boiling cauldron.

■ **DIFFERENTIATION OF THE SELF**   For Jung and Adler, normality depends, in part, on the differentiation of a self—the unifying force that provides direction to behavior and helps develop a person's potential. For Mahler, similarly, abnormal behavior derives from failure to separate ourselves from those we have psychologically brought within us. The notion of a guiding self provides bridges between psychodynamic theories and other theories, such as humanistic-existential theories (which also speak of a self and the fulfillment of inner potential) and social-learning theory (which speaks in terms of self-regulatory processes).

■ **COMPENSATION FOR FEELINGS OF INFERIORITY**   None of us can expect to be good at everything. In Adler's view, normal people compensate for feelings of inferiority by striving to excel in one or more of the arenas of human endeavor. So choosing how best to apply ourselves, by examining our abilities and developing our talents, constitutes healthful behavior.

■ **ERIKSON'S POSITIVE OUTCOMES**   A positive outcome within each of Erik Erikson's psychosocial stages also contributes to the healthy personality. That is, it is healthful to develop a basic sense of trust during infancy, to develop a sense of industry during the elementary school years, to develop a sense of who we are and what we stand for during adolescence, to develop intimate relationships during young adulthood, to be productive during middle adulthood, and so on.

Evaluating Psychodynamic Perspectives

In evaluating psychodynamic theory, we must first note its pervasive influence. Psychodynamic theory has changed the Western world. It has focused attention on our inner lives—our dreams, our fantasies, our hidden motives. People unschooled in Freud per se nevertheless look for the symbolic meanings of each other's slips of the tongue and assume that abnormalities can be traced to early childhood. Terms like *ego* and *repression* have become commonplace, although their everyday meanings do not fully overlap with those intended by Freud.

Psychodynamic theories are popular in part because they are rich theories. They incorporate many concepts in attempting to explain the many

varieties of human behavior, both normal and abnormal. People who wish to explore the hidden recesses of themselves often turn to psychoanalysis.

One of the major contributions of the psychodynamic model was the increased awareness that people may be motivated by hidden drives and impulses of a sexual or aggressive nature. Freud's beliefs about childhood sexuality were both illuminating and controversial. Before Freud, children were perceived as *pure innocents,* free of sexual desire. That is why they were so often depicted in paintings of the Renaissance period without clothing. Without lust, there was no need for shame. Freud recognized, however, that young children, even infants, seek pleasure through stimulation of the oral and anal cavities and the phallic region. Yet his beliefs that primitive drives give rise to incestuous desires, intrafamily rivalries and conflicts, and castration anxiety and penis envy remain sources of controversy, even within psychodynamic circles. The stages of psychosexual development have also been subject to criticism. Many observers have noted that children may begin to masturbate in their first year, not in the "phallic stage." And masturbation may continue through the so-called latency period when sexual drives are believed to remain dormant. Still, a strength of the psychodynamic model is its attention to the importance of childhood experiences in shaping personality and abnormal behavior.

Another major contribution was the recognition that defensive processes may distort people's perceptions of their feelings, needs, and desires. The concept of defense mechanisms has become part of everyday parlance. Whether or not we attribute such cognitive distortions to unconscious processes, it seems that our thoughts can become slanted by our attempts to defend ourselves against anxiety and guilt.

Despite their richness, psychodynamic theories have met with criticism. Many critics, including some of Freud's followers, believe that he placed too much emphasis on sexual and aggressive impulses and underemphasized social relationships. Critics have also argued that the psychic structures—the id, ego, and superego—may be little more than useful fictions, poetic ways to represent inner conflict. Sir Karl Popper (1985) argued that Freud's hypothetical mental processes are not scientific concepts because they cannot be directly observed or tested. Therapists can speculate, for example, that a client "forgot" about an appointment because "unconsciously" she or he did not want to attend the session. Such unconscious motivation is not subject to scientific verification, however.

Popper argued that scientific propositions must be subject to tests that can show them to be false. Popper held that Freud's propositions about mental structures are unscientific because no imaginable evidence can disprove them. Any behavior (e.g., showing up or not showing up for an appointment) can be explained in terms of the interactions of these hypothesized (but unobservable) mental structures. In contrast, the belief that anxiety suppresses the functioning of the immune system *can* be falsified. That is, we can induce anxiety experimentally and measure the resultant functioning of the immune system (see Chapter 4).

In science, we speak of disproving theories, not proving them. Theories are not truth in themselves. Rather, they approximate truth, and scientists should stand ready to revise or discard favored theories when disconfirming evidence comes along. Freud's critics contend that many of his concepts do not lend themselves to disconfirmation through scientific tests.

Freud formulated his views of normal development on the basis of case studies of troubled people in Victorian Vienna, mostly white, upper-middle-class women aged 20 to 44 (Fisher & Greenberg, 1977). How can they be said to represent African Americans in Detroit, Hispanic Americans in Dade County, Native Americans in the Southwest, Asian Americans in Silicon Valley, or contemporary American non-Hispanic white suburbanites? Persons seeking psychotherapy are also unlikely to represent the general population. (They are likely to have more psychological problems than the population at large.) Freud carried out his work in an era of culturally repressed sexuality but nevertheless concluded that all people undergo similar sexual conflicts. Can his findings generalize to contemporary young people who have been repeatedly exposed to sexually provocative films and TV programs?

Also, as the philosopher Adolph Grünbaum (1985) took note, Freud's method of gathering evidence from the therapy session may be suspect. Freud based his views of childhood on the recollections of his clients, not on direct observation. Therapists may influence their clients in subtle ways to produce material that they expect to find. Therapists may also be negligent in separating the information reported by their clients from their own interpretations.

LEARNING PERSPECTIVES

The existence of abnormal behavior provided the wellsprings of psychodynamic theory. Without psychological problems, and troubled clients, there probably would have been no psychodynamic theory. Learning theory would certainly exist in the absence

of abnormal behavior, however. It focuses largely on the normal processes of learning from experience. Learning theorists have also attempted to explain abnormal behavior. Broadly speaking, learning theorists assume that the principles of learning that account for normal (adaptive) behavior also account for many kinds of abnormal (maladaptive) behavior. In this section we focus on two broad learning perspectives: behaviorism and social-learning theory.

Behaviorism

> Give me a dozen healthy infants, well-formed, and my own specified world to bring them up in and I'll guarantee to take any one at random and train him to become any type of specialist I might suggest—doctor, lawyer, merchant-chief and, yes, even beggarman and thief, regardless of his talents, penchants, tendencies, abilities, vocations, and the race of his ancestors.
>
> John B. Watson, 1924, p. 82

Thus did Johns Hopkins University psychologist John B. Watson sound the battle cry of the **behaviorist** movement. Watson argued that environmental influences—not spirits, demons, or intrapsychic forces—shape our behavior. If psychology were to be accepted as a science, unseen, undetectable mental structures must be rejected in favor of behavior that can be detected and measured by scientific instruments—behaviors such as pressing a lever; turning left or right; eating and mating; or even involuntary body functions such as heart rate, dilation of the pupils of the eyes, blood pressure, or emission of brain waves. All these behaviors and functions can be made public by observation or measurement by laboratory instruments. Even brain waves are made public by scientific instruments, and separate observers readily agree about their reality and qualities. In the 1930s, Watson's hue and cry was taken up by B. F. Skinner, who argued that scientists should focus on the impact of reinforcers on behavior.

Like Freud, Watson and Skinner discarded concepts of personal freedom, choice, and self-direction. But whereas Freud saw us as driven by irrational forces, behaviorists see us as products of environmental influences that shape and manipulate our behavior. To Watson and Skinner, even the belief that we have free will is determined by the environment as surely as our learning to raise our hands in class before speaking.

Behaviorists focus on two basic types of learning: classical conditioning and operant conditioning.

■ **CLASSICAL CONDITIONING** Classical conditioning was discovered by chance. The Russian physiologist Ivan Pavlov was exploring the biological

Ivan Pavlov. Here Russian physiologist Ivan Pavlov (the bearded man in the center) demonstrates his apparatus for classical conditioning to students. Can classical conditioning explain the acquisition of excessive irrational fears that we refer to as phobias?

pathways of dogs' salivary glands, but the animals fouled up his results by salivating apparently arbitrarily. Upon inquiry, Pavlov noted that the animals were in fact salivating not arbitrarily, but in response to his assistants' coming into the lab or to the accidental clanging of metal on metal. So Pavlov undertook a clever experimental program to show that the dogs salivated to these events because the events were *associated* with feeding.

When you put meat on a dog's tongue, the dog salivates. Salivation in response to meat is a reflex—a simple kind of unlearned behavior. People also have many reflexes, such as blinking the eye in response to a puff of air and jerking the knee in response to a tap beneath.

A change in the environment, like putting meat on a dog's tongue or tapping beneath the knee, is referred to as a **stimulus**. A reflex is one type of **response** to a stimulus. Reflexes are not learned, but they can be *conditioned* to, or associated with, various stimuli.

To demonstrate the power of classical conditioning, Pavlov (1927) strapped dogs into harnesses (see Figure 2.2). He then placed meat powder on their tongues, and they salivated. He repeated the procedure a number of times, with one difference. He rang a bell before presenting the meat. After numerous

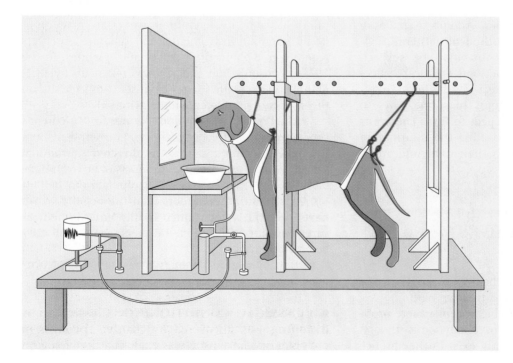

Figure 2.2 The apparatus used in Ivan Pavlov's experiments on conditioning.
Pavlov used an apparatus such as this to demonstrate the process of conditioning. To the left is a two-way mirror, behind which a researcher rings a bell. After ringing the bell, meat is placed on the dog's tongue. Following several pairings of the bell and the meat, the dog learns to salivate in response to the bell. The animal's saliva passes through the tube to a vial, where its quantity may be taken as a measure of the strength of the conditioned response.

pairings of the bell and the food, Pavlov rang the bell but did not follow it with the meat. The dog salivated anyway. The dog had learned to salivate when the bell was rung because the bell had been repeatedly presented just prior to the meat.

In this classic demonstration, meat is an **unconditioned stimulus** (US). Salivation in response to meat is termed an **unconditioned response** (UR) (see Figure 2.3). "Unconditioned" means unlearned. Originally, the bell is a neutral or meaningless stimulus. But after being associated repeatedly with the US (meat), the bell becomes a learned, or **conditioned stimulus** (CS). The bell is then capable of eliciting salivation. Salivation in response to the bell is termed a learned, or **conditioned response** (CR).

Conditioning of Fears Can you recognize classical conditioning in your everyday life? Do you flinch in the waiting room at the sound of the dentist's drill? The drill sounds may be conditioned stimuli for conditioned responses of fear and muscle tension. John Watson and Rosalie Rayner (1920), his future wife, showed that fears can be conditioned by showing "Little Albert," an 11-month-old boy who has become a celebrity in the psychological literature, a laboratory rat and then banging steel bars together behind his head. Before conditioning, Albert reached out to play with the rat. After numerous pairings of the rat and the clanging, however, Albert cried when the rat was brought in and tried to avoid it. Through classical conditioning we come to associate stimuli, so that a response elicited by one is then elicited by the other. With Little Albert, jarring clanging was associated with a rat, so that the rodent came to evoke the fear elicited by the noise.

Figure 2.3 Schematic diagram of the process of classical conditioning.
Before conditioning, food (an unconditioned stimulus, or US) that is placed on a dog's tongue will naturally elicit salivation (an unconditioned response, or UR). The bell, however, is a neutral stimulus that may elicit an orienting response but not salivation. During conditioning, the bell (the conditioned stimulus, CS) is rung while food (the US) is placed on the dog's tongue. After several conditioning trials have occurred, the bell (the CS) will elicit salivation (the conditioned response, or CR) when it is rung, even though it is not accompanied by food (the US). The dog is said to have been conditioned, or to have learned, to display the conditioned response (CR) in response to the conditioned stimulus (CS). Learning theorists have suggested that irrational excessive fears of harmless stimuli may be acquired through principles of classical conditioning.

 Researchers did condition a young boy to fear rats by clanging steel bars behind his head while he played with a rat. His name was "Little Albert," and the researchers were John B. Watson and Rosalie Rayner.

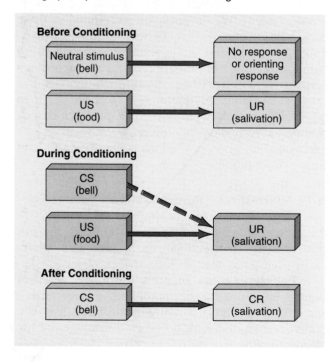

From the behaviorist perspective, normal behavior involves responding adaptively to stimuli—including conditioned stimuli. After all, if we do not learn to be afraid of touching a hot stove after one or two pairings of the sight of the crimson burner and blistering pain, we shall suffer unnecessary burns. If we do not learn to abstain from eating food that nauseates us, we may become poisoned. On the other hand, acquiring inappropriate and maladaptive fears may cripple our efforts to function in the world. Chapter 5 explains how conditioning may help to explain anxiety disorders such as phobias and **posttraumatic stress disorder**.

Extinction and Spontaneous Recovery Researchers **extinguish** conditioned responses (CRs) by presenting conditioned stimuli (CSs) repeatedly in the absence of the unconditioned stimuli (USs). Pavlov found that salivation to the bell could be extinguished by presenting the bell (CS) repeatedly and not following it with the meat (US). Extinction can be adaptive. If your dentist becomes more adroit or uses an effective painkiller, why should the sound of the drill persist in making you cringe? If you acquire solid social skills, why should you persist in experiencing anxiety at the prospect of meeting people or asking them out on dates?

Extinguished responses may recur simply as a function of the passage of time. Such recurrence is termed **spontaneous recovery**. After Pavlov had extinguished salivation in response to a bell, his dogs would salivate again if the bell were presented a few days later. You might cower again in your dentist's office if a year has passed between checkups, even though you remained calm throughout your last (painless) procedure. If you haven't dated for several months, the thought of asking someone out might again elicit anxiety, even if your most recent efforts were successful.

■ **OPERANT CONDITIONING** Classical conditioning is also referred to as respondent conditioning, because organisms learn responses that are largely respondent to, or *elicited* by, certain stimuli. In **operant conditioning**, organisms learn to *emit* learned behaviors because of the behavior's effects. Operant behavior is so called because it operates upon, or manipulates, the environment to produce certain effects.

Operant conditioning can occur mechanically with lower animals. Skinner (1938) showed that food-deprived pigeons will learn to peck buttons when food pellets drop into their cages as a result. It takes a while for the birds to happen on the first peck, but after a few repetitions of the button pecking–food association, pecking becomes fast and furious until the pigeons have had their fill. Food-deprived rats similarly learn to press levers to obtain food.

In operant conditioning, organisms acquire responses or skills that lead to **reinforcement**. Reinforcers are changes in the environment (stimuli) that increase the frequency of the preceding behavior. A **reward** is a *pleasant* stimulus that increases the frequency of behavior, and so it is a type of reinforcer.

B. F. Skinner.   Skinner demonstrated that if pigeons such as these are deprived of food, they will learn to peck buttons—apparently mechanically—when food pellets fall into their cages as a result. The food pellets are said to positively reinforce pecking.

But Skinner found the concept of reinforcement to be preferable to that of reward because it is defined in terms of relationships between observed behaviors and environmental effects. In contrast to *reward,* the meaning of reinforcement does not depend on "mentalistic" conjectures about what is pleasant to another person or lower animal. Many psychologists use the words *reinforcement* and *reward* interchangeably, however.

Types of Reinforcers   Psychologists talk about various types of reinforcers, and we need to be able to differentiate them as well.

Positive reinforcers boost the frequency of behavior when they are presented. Food, money, social approval, and the opportunity to mate are examples of positive reinforcers. **Negative reinforcers** increase the frequency of behavior when they are removed. Fear, pain, and social disapproval are examples of negative reinforcers. We usually learn to do what leads to the removal or abatement of fear, pain, or censure of others.

Adaptive, normal behavior involves learning responses or skills that permit us to obtain positive reinforcers and avoid or remove negative reinforcers. In the preceding examples, adaptive behavior involves developing skills that permit us to obtain money, food, and social approval, and to avoid fear, pain, and social condemnation. But if our early learning environments do not provide opportunities for learning new skills, we might be hampered in our efforts to obtain reinforcers.

We can also differentiate primary and secondary, or conditioned, reinforcers. **Primary reinforcers** influence behavior because they satisfy basic physical needs. We do not learn to respond to these basic reinforcers; we are born with that capacity. Food, water, sexual stimulation, and escape from pain are examples of primary reinforcers. **Secondary reinforcers** influence behavior through their association with established reinforcers. Thus we learn to respond to secondary reinforcers. People learn to seek money—a secondary reinforcer—because it can be exchanged for primary reinforcers like food and heat (or air conditioning).

■ **PUNISHMENT**   Punishments are painful, aversive events that decrease or suppress the frequency of the preceding behavior. Negative reinforcers, by contrast, increase the frequency of the preceding behavior by their removal.

Punishment can suppress unsuitable behavior rapidly. So its use may be appropriate in emergencies, such as when a child is trying to run into the street. Many learning theorists, however, discourage the use of punishment, particularly in rearing children. They point out that punishment does not in itself suggest alternate, permissible kinds of behavior. For punishment to be effective, the recipient must have skills available to perform alternate behaviors. Punishment only suppresses unwanted behavior in circumstances in which it is used reliably, but does not eliminate the behavior. It may also encourage people to withdraw from such learning situations. Punished children may cut classes, drop out of school, or run away. Punishment may generate anger and hostility, rather than constructive learning. Finally, since people also learn by observation, punishment may become imitated as a means for solving interpersonal problems.

Rewarding desirable behavior is thus generally preferable to punishing misbehavior. But rewarding good behavior requires paying attention to it, not just to misbehavior. Some children who develop conduct problems can only gain the attention of other people by misbehaving. They learn that by acting out others will pay attention to them. To them punishment may actually serve as a positive reinforcer, increasing the rate of response of the behavior it follows. Learning theorists point out that it is not sufficient to expect good conduct from children. Instead, adults need to teach children proper behavior and regularly reinforce them for emitting it.

> Actually, punishment *does* work. That is, severe enough punishment suppresses the behavior it follows. However, psychologists generally favor the use of positive reinforcers because of problems associated with the use of punishment.

Classical and operant conditioning stress the importance of environmental factors, which are also called situation variables, in explaining behavior. Let us now consider a contemporary model of learning, called social-learning theory, which broadens the focus of traditional learning theory by considering how both situation and person variables affect human behavior.

Social-Learning Theory

Social-learning theory represents the contributions of learning theorists such as Albert Bandura, Julian B. Rotter, and Walter Mischel. Social-learning theorists emphasize the roles of cognitive activity and learning by observation in human behavior. Social-learning theorists view people as impacting upon their environments, just as the environment impacts upon them. Social-learning theorists concur with more traditional behaviorists that theories of human nature should be tied to observable behavior. They

assert, however, that factors *within* the person—**person variables**—must be considered in explaining human behavior.

Social-learning theorists see people as self-aware and purposeful learners who seek information about their environments, not just respond automatically to the stimuli that impinge upon them. Rotter (1972) argues that behavior cannot be predicted from situational factors alone. Whether or not people behave in certain ways also depends on their **expectancies** about the outcomes of their behavior and the **subjective values** of those outcomes.

■ **OBSERVATIONAL LEARNING** Observational learning, or learning through **modeling**, refers to the

Observational learning. According to social-learning theory, much human behavior is acquired through modeling, or observational learning. In contrast to operant conditioning, observational learning can occur even when the observer does not engage in the behavior or is not directly reinforced for doing so. Here children acquire some stereotypical gender-role behaviors through observational learning.

process of acquiring new behaviors and knowledge by observing others. Operant conditioning occurs when an organism (1) engages in a response and (2) that response is reinforced. Observational learning takes place even when the observer does not engage in the behavior or is not directly reinforced. Observational learning can occur while observing the behaviors of others firsthand or by observing models in films or television, or by reading about others. Both normal and abnormal behavior patterns can be acquired vicariously, by observation. For example, Albert Bandura and his colleagues (1963) showed in a classic study that children will imitate aggressive models they observe in films, whether the film models are real people or cartoons.

■ **PERSON VARIABLES** Social-learning theorists believe that behavior stems from a fluid, continuous interaction between person and **situation variables**. Situation variables refer to the external determinants of behavior, such as rewards and punishments. Person variables incorporate such characteristics of the person as competencies, encoding strategies, expectancies, subjective values, and self-regulatory systems and plans (Mischel, 1993; see Figure 2.4). We focused on the role of situation variables in learning in the context of classical and operant conditioning.

Figure 2.4 Person and situational variables in social-learning theory.
Social-learning theorists believe our behavior is influenced by the interaction of internal, or person variables, and external, or situational variables.

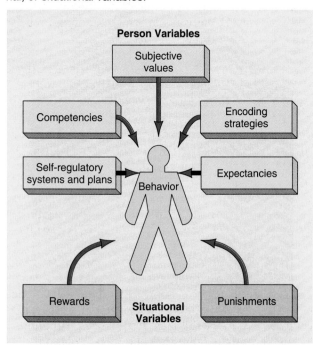

Now let us consider such person variables as competencies, encoding strategies, expectancies, subjective values, and self-regulatory systems.

Competencies Academic skills such as reading, writing, and arithmetic; athletic skills such as hitting a tennis serve or tossing a football properly; social skills such as knowing what to say or how to dress on a job interview or how to ask someone out on a date—all are examples of **competencies**, or skills and knowledge that have been acquired from past learning. Competencies include knowledge about ourselves and others, knowledge of the physical world, of cultural codes of conduct, and of the behavior patterns expected in certain situations. Our capacity to use information to plan behavior depends on our competencies.

Encoding Strategies Encoding refers to the process of symbolizing or representing stimuli. People may encode the same stimuli in different ways. Some people encode a tennis game as an opportunity to relax and have some fun. Others encode the game as a demand to prove their mettle or perfect their serves and volleys. Some people encode unsuccessful dates as signs of their social ineptitude. Others encode failed dates as evidence that people sometimes are not "meant for each other." Encoding strategies may help to explain why some people become depressed and withdrawn following setbacks and disappointments while others shrug them off and remain unperturbed. In Chapter 7, we see that the ways in which people interpret or *encode* events may play an important role in determining their proneness toward depression.

Expectancies

> . . . if one advances confidently in the direction of his dreams, and endeavors to live the life which he has imagined, he will meet with a success unexpected in common hours.
>
> Henry David Thoreau, *Walden*

Expectancies are personal predictions about the outcomes (or potential for reinforcement) of engaging in particular responses. Expectancies can be represented as "if-then" statements: If I do "A" then I expect "B" to follow. Bandura (1982) distinguishes between two types of expectations: outcome and efficacy expectations. Outcome expectations are anticipations that certain behavior patterns will have certain effects. For example, you may expect that by diligently studying the material in the textbook, you are more likely to do well on the course examinations. (Outcome expectations may or may not prove true, of course.)

The value of positive self-efficacy expectancies. We are more likely to attempt challenging tasks when we judge ourselves capable of performing successfully. With a strong sense of self-efficacy, we are more likely to approach tasks with vigor and sustained effort.

Self-efficacy expectations concern beliefs that one will be able to execute behavior successfully. Taking the example further, believing that you can acquire the information in the textbook if you put your mind to it would represent a high level of self-efficacy. Believing that you couldn't possibly learn this material despite your best efforts would be an example of low self-efficacy. Efficacy expectancies are based in part on our competencies and on our own experiences in similar situations. Competencies affect expectancies and expectancies, in turn, affect motivation to perform. People who think that they are competent are more likely to attempt arduous tasks than those who doubt that they can master them.

 People are in fact more likely to tackle arduous tasks if they believe they will succeed at them. Positive self-efficacy expectancies foster striving and persistence.

Bandura suggests that one of the common beneficial features of psychotherapy is the changing of clients' self-efficacy expectations from "I can't" to "I can." For this reason, clients are inspired to attempt new, more adaptive, patterns of behavior.

Subjective Values   The same events or stimuli tend to be valued differently by different people. What frightens one person may attract another. What inter-

ests one may repel another. Social-learning theorists, in contrast to behaviorists, do not see us as controlled by external events and stimuli. Rather, they believe we imbue events with meaning and value, and the meanings we give them affect our behavior. If your grades have little value to you, then your mood is unlikely to be affected if you do poorly in your courses. You will also be little motivated to apply yourself to obtain good grades. By contrast, if your grades are very important to you, then you are more likely to work harder and your emotional responses are more likely to reflect the outcomes.

Self-Regulatory Systems and Plans   Social-learning theorists note that people regulate their own behavior, even when observers and external constraints are not present. People set their own goals and standards, make plans for attaining them, and applaud or reprimand themselves, according to their progress. In fact, social-learning theorists see self-rewards ("Hey, I'm doing fine!") and self-punishments ("I'm such a jerk! I'll never get this right.") as equally potent to or more potent than external rewards and punishments.

Learning Perspectives on Abnormal Behavior

Learning theorists largely see abnormal behavior patterns as largely learned according to the same principles, such as conditioning and observational learning, that govern normal behavior. Although learning theorists admit that genetic inheritance plays a part in determining behavior, they focus on the ways in which we learn to adapt to our environments. Let us consider some of the ways in which learning models account for abnormal behavior.

■ **ACQUISITION OF ABNORMAL BEHAVIOR** Some abnormal behaviors, such as phobias, may be conditioned. The conditioning explanation of phobias suggests that a previously neutral stimulus may become phobic by virtue of being paired or associated with a painful or aversive stimulus. An individual may develop a phobia for riding on elevators following a traumatic experience while riding on an elevator. Social-learning theorists suggest that such fears may also be learned vicariously, by observing the phobic reactions of others in real life or in the media.

■ **LACK OF SKILLS** Abnormal behavior may reflect a lack of adequate knowledge and skills, such as social skills. Lack of social skills can reduce the opportunities for social reinforcement, especially when a person withdraws from social situations, leading perhaps to depression and social isolation.

QUESTIONNAIRE

The Expectancy for Success Scale

What do you do when faced with an arduous challenge? Do you rise to the occasion, or do you back off?

Social-learning theorists note that our outcome and efficacy expectancies influence our behavior. When we think that we can realize great achievements through our own endeavors, we marshal our resources and dedicate ourselves. When we believe that our exertion will pay off, we are likely to persevere.

The following scale, developed by Hale and Fibel (1978) offers insight as to whether or not you expect that your efforts will be successful. Compare your expectancies to those of other undergraduates taking psychology courses by filling out the questionnaire and referring to the answer key at the end of the chapter.

Directions: Indicate the degree to which each item applies to you by circling the appropriate number, according to this key:

1 = highly improbable
2 = improbable
3 = equally improbable and probable, not sure
4 = probable
5 = highly probable

In the Future I Expect That I Will:

1. Find that people don't seem to understand what I'm trying to say   1 2 3 4 5
2. Be discouraged about my ability to gain the respect of others   1 2 3 4 5
3. Be a good parent   1 2 3 4 5
4. Be unable to accomplish my goals   1 2 3 4 5
5. Have a stressful marital relationship   1 2 3 4 5
6. Deal poorly with emergency situations   1 2 3 4 5
7. Find my efforts to change situations I don't like are ineffective   1 2 3 4 5
8. Not be very good at learning new skills   1 2 3 4 5
9. Carry through my responsibilities successfully   1 2 3 4 5
10. Discover that the good in life outweighs the bad   1 2 3 4 5
11. Handle unexpected problems successfully   1 2 3 4 5
12. Get the promotions I deserve   1 2 3 4 5
13. Succeed in the projects I undertake   1 2 3 4 5
14. Not make any significant contributions to society   1 2 3 4 5
15. Discover that my life is not getting much better   1 2 3 4 5
16. Be listened to when I speak   1 2 3 4 5
17. Discover that my plans don't work out too well   1 2 3 4 5
18. Find that no matter how hard I try, things just don't turn out the way I would like   1 2 3 4 5
19. Handle myself well in whatever situation I'm in   1 2 3 4 5
20. Be able to solve my own problems   1 2 3 4 5
21. Succeed at most things I try   1 2 3 4 5
22. Be successful in my endeavors in the long run   1 2 3 4 5
23. Be very successful working out my personal life   1 2 3 4 5
24. Experience many failures in my life   1 2 3 4 5
25. Make a good first impression on people I meet for the first time   1 2 3 4 5
26. Attain the career goals I have set for myself   1 2 3 4 5
27. Have difficulty dealing with my superiors   1 2 3 4 5
28. Have problems working with others   1 2 3 4 5
29. Be a good judge of what it takes to get ahead   1 2 3 4 5
30. Achieve recognition in my profession   1 2 3 4 5

Source: Fibel, B., & Hale, W. D. (1978). The generalized expectancy for success scale: A new measure. Journal of Consulting and Clinical Psychology, 46, 924–931. Copyright © 1978 by the American Psychological Association. Reprinted by permission.

■ INAPPROPRIATE OR INADEQUATE REINFORCEMENT Most people are positively reinforced by the praise of their family members, teachers, and employers. Children with conduct disorders, on the other hand, may find teacher *disapproval* positively reinforcing. Inadequate levels of reinforcement may also be involved in explaining abnormal behavior patterns. In Chapter 7 we explore learning models that relate changes in the level of reinforcement to the development of depression.

■ SELF-DEFEATING EXPECTANCIES, ENCODING, AND SELF-REGULATORY SYSTEMS People who believe that their efforts will meet with failure may develop feelings of helplessness and hopelessness that can set the stage for depression. Positive self-efficacy expectancies encourage us to persist at challenges.

Some people become socially withdrawn and depressed because they encode one or two social failures as emblematic of their worthlessness and of the futility of social interaction. Some people become hostile and engage in violent behavior because they encode social provocations as injuries that must be avenged, not as social problems that need to be solved. Still other people fail to develop or apply self-regulatory systems that enable them to reinforce themselves for achieving incremental steps toward desired goals.

Evaluating the Learning Perspectives

Learning theorists have made substantial contributions to the understanding of normal and abnormal behavior. One of the principal values of learning models is their emphasis on observable behavior and environmental factors. Psychodynamic theorists focus on hypothesized internal variables, such as psychic structures and unconscious conflicts, that may not be available to scientific study. Learning theorists emphasize the significance of environmental or situational variables, such as rewards and punishments, which can be systematically varied and whose effects on behavior can be measured. Social-learning theorists have broadened the scope of conditioning models of learning by considering how person and situation variables affect human behavior and learning.

Learning theories have had a broad impact on psychology. They deal with issues ranging from learning per se, animal behavior, and motivation to child development, abnormal behavior, therapy methods, even attitude formation and change. Learning models have spawned the development of behavior therapy, which has become a prominent method of treatment for many forms of abnormal behavior.

Critics contend that learning models, especially behaviorism, cannot explain the richness of human behavior and that human experience cannot be reduced to observable responses. Many learning theorists, too—especially social-learning theorists—have been dissatisfied with the behavioristic view that environmental conditions mechanically control our behavior. Humans experience thoughts and dreams, formulate goals and aspirations, and behaviorism seems not to address much of what it means to be human. Behaviorism also seems at a loss to explain how many people will strive, despite hardships, to realize remote inner visions. If people only repeat reinforced behaviors, how do they struggle—without external reinforcers—to invent new ideas and works? How do composers and mathematicians sit still for hours, then all at once pen new concertos and equations?

Social-learning theorists see human beings as active seekers of information, however, not as passive reactors to environmental stimuli. Social-learning theory has evolved so far from its behaviorist forebears that its overlap with cognitive theories and models is striking. Critics of social-learning theory do not accuse it of denying the value or role of cognitive activity. They might contend, however, that social-learning theory has not derived satisfying statements about the development of personality traits or accounted for self-awareness. In addition, social-learning theory—like its intellectual progenitor, behaviorism—does not always pay adequate attention to genetic variation in explaining individual differences in behavior or in accounting for abnormal behavior patterns.

Now let us turn our attention to cognitive perspectives, which focus on processes of thinking and cognition in explaining human behavior.

COGNITIVE PERSPECTIVES

Psychological perspectives continue to evolve. They draw on the philosophies and technologies of the day. Sigmund Freud was impressed by the internal combustion engine. Perhaps this suggested to him a way of viewing people as containing seething inner energies—as needing to vent some of their "steam" (by verbalizing feelings and finding acceptable ways of partially gratifying impulses) if they were to avert an explosion in the personality. One of the great technologies of the modern day is computer science, or information processing. So it is not surprising that many cognitive psychologists conceptualize human behavior and **cognition** in terms of information-processing models. Others, such as George Kelly, Albert Ellis, and Aaron Beck, focus on how people interpret events that they experience, and how these interpretations affect their moods and behavior.

Information Processing

Many cognitive psychologists are influenced by concepts of computer science. Computers process information to solve problems. Information is fed into the computer (encoded so that it can be accepted by the computer as input). Then it is placed in *memory* while it is manipulated. You can also place the information permanently in *storage*, on a floppy disk, a hard disk, or another device. Information-processing theorists thus think in terms such as the *input* (based on perception), *storage, retrieval, manipulation,* and *output* of information. They view psychological disorders as disturbances in these processes. Disturbances might be caused by the blocking or distortion of input or by faulty storage, retrieval, or manipulation of information. Any of these can lead to lack of output or distorted output (e.g., bizarre behavior). Schizophrenics, for example, frequently jump from topic to topic in a disorganized fashion, which may reflect problems in retrieving and manipulating information. They also seem to have difficulty focusing their attention and filtering out extraneous stimuli, like distracting noises. This may represent problems relating to initial processing of input from their senses.

Some theorists focus on the ways in which social information is encoded. It has been found, for example, that aggressive boys and adolescents are likely to incorrectly encode other people's behavior as threatening (Dodge, 1985; Lochman, 1987). They assume other people intend them ill when they do not (Dodge & Frame, 1982; Jurkovic, 1980). Similarly, some rapists, particularly date rapists, misread women's expressed wishes. They may wrongly assume, for example, that dates who say "no" really mean yes and are merely playing "hard to get" (e.g., Lipton et al., 1987).

George Kelly

According to George Kelly (1955, 1958), people function much like scientists. This does not mean that all people have a bent for astronomy, math, or biology. It means that people strive to understand, anticipate, and control the events in their own lives.

George Kelly. Kelly believed that people function much like scientists; that is, they strive to understand, anticipate, and control the events in their lives. To understand people, we must understand the ways in which they categorize and interpret (*construe*) events.

To understand people, we must discern the ways in which they categorize and interpret experience—the ways in which they *construe* events. People construe similar events in diverse ways. Consider an example offered by Walter Mischel:

> A boy drops his mother's favorite vase. What does it mean? The event is simply that the vase has been broken. Yet ask the child's psychoanalyst and he may point to the boy's unconscious hostility. Ask the mother and she tells you how "mean" he is. His father says he is "spoiled." The child's teacher may see the event as evidence of the child's "laziness" and chronic "clumsiness." Grandmother calls it just an "accident." And the child himself may construe the event as reflecting his "stupidity." (1986, pp. 207–208)

People try to understand the world around them by employing **personal constructs** that allow them to anticipate events. Personal constructs are psychological dimensions or axes according to which we categorize ourselves, others, and the events we experience. For example, people may appraise certain experiences by employing such constructs as "good–bad," "dull–stimulating," and "safe–dangerous." For example, a certain event, like swimming in deep water, may be construed by some as "good" and also "stimulating" and "safe." An inexperienced swimmer might construe the same event as "bad," "dangerous," but also "stimulating." Kelly reminds us that these qualities are not intrinsic properties of the events themselves but are imposed on the events by the person who construes them. People come to predict or anticipate events by means of these personal constructions. The inexperienced swimmer, for example, will come to predict that swimming in deep water is dangerous and is to be avoided. The experienced swimmer may predict that it's fun.

Various ways of construing an event—alternate constructions of an event—give rise to different emotional responses and, perhaps, different courses of action. The boy construed the event in terms of a smart–stupid construct, in such a way that might engender self-loathing. Over time, such patterns of negative self-appraisal might lead to depression. Kelly argued that there may be no absolutely true way of construing events. Instead, when our constructions of events make us anxious or depressed and prevent adaptive behavior, we might be better off by changing how we construe events. His approach to therapy focused on helping people develop more adjustive constructions of events.

Kelly was optimistic about human behavior. He saw people as capable of continuous change, of enacting different roles and forming different constructions in life. If our life roles and patterns of construing events are making us miserable, we can make broad sweeping changes in our constructions of experience and our day-to-day behavior.

Albert Ellis

Psychologist Albert Ellis (1977a, 1977b, 1985), the developer of **rational-emotive therapy**, also focuses on the ways in which people process information or encode experience. Ellis points out that people's beliefs about events, as well as the events themselves, can make them miserable and foster maladaptive behavior. Consider an example in which someone loses a job and is anxious and despondent about it. It may seem that being fired is the direct cause of the person's misery, but the misery actually stems from the person's beliefs about the loss, and not directly from the loss itself.

Ellis uses an "A→B→C approach" to explain the causes of the misery. Being fired is an *activating event* (A). The ultimate outcome, or *consequence* (C), is emotional distress. But the activating event (A) and the consequences (C) are mediated by various *beliefs* (B). Some of these beliefs might include "That job was the major thing in my life," "What a useless washout I am," "My family will go hungry," "I'll never be able to find another job as good," "I can't do a thing about it." Beliefs like these compound depression, nurture helplessness, and distract us from evaluating what to do. For instance, the belief "I can't do a thing about it" promotes helplessness. The belief "What a useless washout I am" internalizes blame and is an exaggeration that is, perhaps, based on perfectionism. The belief "My family will go hungry" may also be an exaggeration.

The situation can be diagrammed like this:

Activating events → Beliefs → Consequences

Ellis points out that apprehension about the future and feelings of disappointment are perfectly normal when people face losses. However, the adoption of irrational beliefs can lead people to **catastrophize** the magnitude of losses and contribute to profound distress and depression. By intensifying emotional responses and nurturing feelings of helplessness, such beliefs impair coping ability. Such beliefs also lower self-efficacy expectations and distract people from trying to solve their problems. Rational-emotive therapists help clients dispute these irrational beliefs and substitute more rational ones.

Ellis submits that irrational beliefs, such as those listed here, are obstacles to happiness in themselves and may intensify the impact of negative events.

1. You must have love and approval nearly all the time from people who are important to you.
2. You must be completely competent in all your endeavors. Or you must have real expertise or talent in something important.
3. Life must go the way you want it to go. Things are awful when you don't get your first choices.
4. Other people should treat everyone fairly. When people are unfair or unethical, they are horrible and rotten and should be punished or avoided.
5. People and things should turn out better than they do. It's awful and terrible when quick solutions to life's hassles are not forthcoming.
6. Your past is a strong influence on your behavior and must continue to affect you and determine your behavior.
7. You can find happiness by inertia, inactivity, or passivity.

Ellis notes that the desire for others' approval is understandable, but it is irrational to assume you

Seeing the world through blue-colored glasses? Cognitive theorists believe the ways in which we interpret events play an important role in shaping our emotional responses and behavior. This young woman is seeing the world through blue-colored glasses; that is, she interpreted her failure on a single quiz as evidence she was generally incapable of succeeding in college. Cognitive theorists believe such catastrophic self-appraisals can set the stage for depression.

cannot survive without it. It would be marvelous to excel in everything we do, but it's absurd to demand it of oneself. Sure, in tennis it would be great to serve and volley like a pro, but most people haven't the leisure or aptitude to perfect the game. Insisting on perfection deters people from playing simply for fun.

Ellis admits that childhood experiences are involved in the origins of irrational beliefs, but cognitive appraisal—the here and now—causes people misery. For most people who are anxious and depressed, the ticket to greater happiness does not lie in discovering and liberating deep-seated conflicts, but in recognizing and modifying irrational self-demands.

Aaron Beck

Psychiatrist Aaron Beck (Beck, 1976; Beck et al., 1979, 1985) also focuses on how cognitive distortions contribute to misery. He encourages therapy clients to see the irrationality of their thought patterns. For example, minimizing accomplishments and assuming that the worst will come to pass intensifies feelings of despondency. Cognitive errors or distortions—such as minimization and pessimism—can occur so quickly and routinely that they are difficult for the person to detect. Beck's approach to therapy, called **cognitive therapy**, helps clients identify and correct these cognitive errors.

Beck stresses the pervasive roles of four basic types of cognitive errors that contribute to emotional distress:

1. *Selective abstraction.* People may *selectively abstract* the parts of their experiences that reflect upon their flaws and ignore evidence of their competencies.
2. *Overgeneralization.* People may *overgeneralize* from a few isolated experiences. For example, they may see their futures as hopeless because they were laid off or believe that they will never marry because they were rejected by a dating partner.
3. *Magnification.* People may blow out of proportion, or *magnify,* the importance of unfortunate events. Students may catastrophize a bad test grade by jumping to the conclusion that they will flunk out of college and their lives will be ruined.
4. *Absolutist thinking.* Absolutist thinking is seeing the world in black and white terms, rather than in shades of gray. Absolutist thinkers may assume that any grade less than a perfect "A," or a work evaluation less than a rave, is a total failure.

 People can indeed make themselves miserable by the ways in which they interpret events.

Aaron T. Beck. Beck theorizes that cognitive errors or distortions such as selective abstraction, overgeneralization, magnification, and absolutist thinking can give rise to emotional distress. His form of psychotherapy aims to help clients identify and correct such cognitive errors.

Evaluating the Cognitive Perspectives

Cognitive perspectives have had an enormous impact on the development of contemporary therapeutic approaches. We note these many contributions of cognitive therapists to the treatment of various emotional disorders throughout the course of this text. The cognitive approaches to therapy, like the behavioral, focus on making changes in the *here and now,* rather than probing the distant past in great depth, like therapists who adopt a traditional psychodynamic approach. The overlap between the behavioral and cognitive approaches is best represented by the emergence of cognitive behavior therapy, a form of therapy that integrates behavioral and cognitive techniques.

The contributions of cognitive theorists have also had a major impact on theories of emotional disorders. Cognitive theorists believe that the ways in which we construe our failures and shortcomings are linked to our emotional responses. We examine how cognitive theories have been applied to various emotional disorders and evaluate the research evidence that supports the role of cognitive factors.

A major issue concerning cognitive perspectives is their range of applicability. Cognitive therapists have largely focused on emotional disorders relating to anxiety and depression, but have had less impact on the development of treatment approaches, or conceptual models, of more severe forms of disturbed behavior, such as schizophrenia. Moreover, in the case of depression, it remains unclear, as we see in Chapter 7, whether distorted thinking patterns are causes of depression or merely effects of depression. We next turn our attention to humanistic-existential perspectives, which, like the cognitive perspective, focus on the importance of conscious experience.

HUMANISTIC-EXISTENTIAL PERSPECTIVES

My experience in therapy and in groups makes it impossible for me to deny the reality and significance of human choice. To me it is not an illusion that man is to some degree the architect of himself.

Carl Rogers, 1974, p. 119

Man . . . is the particular being who has to be aware of himself, be responsible for himself, if he is to become himself. He also is that particular being who knows that at some future moment he will not be; he is the being who is always in a dialectical relation with non-being, death. And he not only knows he will sometime not be, but he can, in his own choices, slough off and forfeit his being.

Rollo May, 1958, p. 42

Technology, science, automation, artificial intelligence—these are some of the artifacts of 20th-century life. World war and genocide are others. In the midst of modern upheaval, humanists and existentialists have chosen to dwell on the ultimate meaning of life. Intensely aware of their own consciousness, of their transient existence on the third planet out from Sol, personal awareness of being in the world becomes the focus of the humanistic-existential quest for meaning.

The term *humanism* has existed for hundreds of years and has had different meanings. Humanism emerged as a third force in American psychology in the 1950s and 1960s, in part as a reaction to the prevailing psychodynamic and behavioral models. But humanistic thought was also in reaction to the increasing industrialization and automation of modern society. Terms like *rat race* were current, and

humanists contested the placement of people on the gray anonymous treadmills of industry. *Alienation* became a buzz word. People complained of feeling alienated in a society that was becoming increasingly technological and divorced from inner sources of meaning. It was against this backdrop that humanistic theories of psychologists Abraham Maslow and Carl Rogers gained prominence.

Existentialism is more European in origin. Although its roots recede into past centuries, contemporary existentialism refers to some degree to the horrors of World War II and the Holocaust. This philosophy is termed *existentialism* because it concerns the larger questions of existence that confront us all as we come to terms with our mortality and our experience of being in the world.

The 20th-century existential philosophers Jean-Paul Sartre (in France) and Martin Heidegger (in Germany) saw human existence as meaningless within the grand scheme of things, and they wrote about our consequent feelings of alienation. The Swiss psychiatrists Ludwig Binswanger (1963) and Medard Boss (1977) translated these philosophical views into the more personal world of psychology. They argued that this worldview could give rise to abnormal behavior patterns related to philosophical alienation—withdrawal and apathy, for example. To them, salvation is personal and psychological, when it occurs at all, and is based on making personal choices because of the personal meanings we implant on things. Although there is pain in life—in our being in the world—and life ends ultimately in death, we are at least capable of seeing the world as it is and of making real, **authentic** choices. It is the role of psychotherapy to respond to clients' feelings of alienation and help them make the choices that may imbue their lives with some meaning.

Freud's psychodynamic theory argued, in contrast, that unconscious irrational motives and defensive distortions of reality prevent us from even perceiving the world as it is, much less make free choices. Behaviorists like Watson and Skinner saw freedom as an illusion that is determined from without, just as our wants and fears are. If behaviorists saw a "meaning" in life, it was whatever "meaning" people were conditioned to believe in and talk about. Even social-learning theorists focus on the combination of situation and person variables that govern behavior. To existentialists we are truly, painfully free to do what we will with life.

Humanistic and existential theorists have much in common, most notably (1) their focus on the search for meaning and purpose in life and (2) their belief that personal freedom and responsibility for one's choices are part and parcel of being human. Although there is much that the various theorists have in common, each has a unique vision of human nature. Our focus centers on the existential theorist Viktor Frankl and two American humanistic theorists, Abraham Maslow and Carl Rogers.

Viktor Frankl

The Austrian psychiatrist Viktor Frankl (1959) suffered the horrors of the Nazi concentration camps—the brutality, the labor, the starvation, the bitter cold, the typhus, the apathy, the ultimate question about whether any of his family remained alive. Throughout it all, he tried to find some meaning in life, despite the awful situation he faced every day. Occasionally he made a joke. Now and then he gazed at the sunrise. He came to believe this: Death is omnipresent, but while one is alive, one is free to choose one's own attitudes toward the situations one encounters.

Frankl survived the camps. He thought he did so because he had found some meaning in life. When suffering has meaning, it can be endured. People, he believed, have basic wills to find meaning and to love. Frankl's meaning of love is not Freud's biologically based sex drive; it is a psychologically based, generous love.

Frankl devised a form of therapy called **logotherapy**, which derives from the Greek *logos*, meaning "a word" and is used to refer to the ways in which we talk about things. *Logos* is usually used at the end of words, as in psycho*logy* and bio*logy*, fields of science that provide ways of talking about their phenomena. Logotherapy was created as a way of helping patients find meaningful ways of talking about, or organizing, their lives. In essence, Frankl confronts clients with their responsibility for their own lives, with their need to clarify or construct their own meanings and values, and their capacity to make their own choices. By discovering or creating meaning, Frankl believed that people could gain control over their own lives. Without meaning, people experience existential frustration and are prone to abnormal behavior. Frankl, like other humanistic and existential theorists, believed that human beings are all unique. For him to understand the world through another's eyes, he would have to have patience and develop a strong sense of empathy. Notions about empathy and clients' frames of references were also adopted by the American humanistic psychologist Carl Rogers.

Frankl did not set forth a crisp list of axioms and theorems about human nature. His writings, however, seem to make the following points. These points also summarize much of general humanistic-existential thought.

1. *People are capable of perceiving the world as it is. The individual person's consciousness is the real center of his or her universe.* The personal, or subjective, experiencing of events is the most meaningful aspect of human nature.

2. *People have distinctive potentials within them that can be recognized and used to guide their behavior.* People are, or can be, the conscious architects of their own personalities. Moreover, people as

The Living Dead of Buchenwald. This Bourke-White photo, taken following the liberation of Buchenwald, suggests the horrors of the Nazi concentration camp. His experience of the atrocities of the camps influenced Viktor Frankl to write that people are better able to endure suffering that is meaningful to them.

individuals are their own best experts on themselves, when they choose to look within.

3. *People are in the world, and what they do in it is up to them.* People make real choices and are responsible for themselves, whether they make choices that help them develop as individuals or defensive choices that deny their real natures but allow them to take the easy path.

4. *People are hard working when their labors have meaning for them.*

5. *People are capable of being caring, loving beings when their lives are filled with meaning.*

6. *People need to behave authentically.* There are many pressures to adapt and conform, pressures Frankl believe were felt by the Nazi storm trooper as well as by the death camp inmate. People feel fulfilled when they live authentically. When outer constraints prevent people from acting authentically—just as external constraints prevented Frankl from leaving the camps—people must at least recognize the presence and reality of their own values and impulses.

7. *People are alienated, estranged, withdrawn, and apathetic when life circumstances prevent them from striving to fulfill their potentials.*

8. *People can bring their negative life experiences inward and behave in ways that run counter to their genuine feelings, as did concentration camp inmates who acted as Capos, or watchdogs over their fellow inmates.* Then their sense of self becomes distorted and their lives feel basically wrong.

9. *Therapists must find empathic ways of responding to the uniqueness of each client.*

10. *Therapy involves helping clients construct meanings and clarify values so they can make authentic choices and get on with their lives, despite current and eventual constraints.*

We should note that survivors of the Holocaust, like Elie Wiesel, believe that the Holocaust was too horrendous and too extraordinary to serve as a metaphor for anything else—much less for the constraints and sorrows of everyday life. Our reference to the Holocaust is only intended to describe the circumstances under which Viktor Frankl crystallized his thinking.

Abraham Maslow and the Challenge of Self-Actualization

To humanists, Freud was preoccupied with the "basement" of the human condition. He believed that people are primarily motivated to gratify defensive, life-sustaining biological drives. American psychologist Abraham Maslow argued that people also have powerful growth-oriented needs for **self-actualization**—to become whatever they are capable of being. Because of their uniqueness, people must follow their own paths of self-actualization. People can only actualize themselves if they set out on their own and take risks. If they stick to the tried and true, their lives may degenerate into monotony and predictability. The self-actualized person experiences life in the present—in the here and now.

Maslow attributed the characteristics shown in Table 2.3 to self-actualizing individuals. We have added the flip side of the coin—that is, the kinds of adjustment problems encountered by people who are not self-actualizing.

■ **THE HIERARCHY OF NEEDS: WHAT DO YOU DO WHEN YOU'RE NO LONGER HUNGRY?** Maslow is perhaps best known for his theoretical **hierarchy of needs**, which ranges from basic biological needs, like hunger and thirst, to self-actualization needs (see Figure 2.5).

Freud saw all motivation as arising from the id. He contended that our pursuit of higher ideals of art, literature, and creative expression are defensive—forms of sublimation. Maslow viewed all levels of needs as authentic in their own right. Once we had fulfilled lower-level needs, we would strive to satisfy higher-level needs for personal growth. We would not sleep away the hours until lower-level needs stirred us to act once more. Some of us, moreover,

Self-actualization. Humanistic theorists believe that there exists in each of us a drive toward self-actualization—to become all that we are capable of being. In the humanistic view, each of us, like artist—Betye Saar—is unique. No two people follow quite the same pathway toward self-actualization.

Table 2.3   Characteristics of Self-Actualizing Persons and Adjustment Problems of Individuals Who Are Not Self-Actualizing

Characteristics of Self-Actualizing Persons	Adjustment Problems of Persons Who Are Not Self-Actualizing
Fully experiencing life in the present—the here and now. Self-actualizers do not focus excessively on the past or wait to start their lives as they pursue distant goals.	Forgoing daily opportunities for pleasure and self-fulfillment. Ruminating about the past or obsessing about the future.
Making growth choices rather than fear choices. Self-actualizers are willing to take reasonable risks in developing their unique potentials. They do not accept the status quo as the only possible reality. They do not "settle."	Avoiding risks. Taking tried and tested routes that earn the approval of others. Accepting a dull, safe life. "Settling."
Acquiring self-knowledge. Self-actualizers look within and search themselves for values, talents, and sense of meaningfulness.	Not bothering to look inward and search for one's unique talents and authentic values.
Striving toward honesty in interpersonal relationships by stripping away the social facades and gamesmanship that prevent self-disclosure and the formation of intimate relationships.	Accepting superficial relationships. Playing games that allow one to avoid true intimacy.
Becoming self-assertive and expressing one's own ideas and feelings, even if at the risk of occasional disapproval from others.	Keeping one's genuine feelings bottled up in an effort to be a nice person and avoid social disapproval.
Striving toward new goals and striving to become the best in one's chosen life role. Self-actualizers do not live in the memories of their past accomplishments; nor do they give second-rate efforts.	Accepting mediocrity. Meeting the requirements of jobs and social relationships, but not bothering to give one's best.
Becoming involved in meaningful and rewarding life activities that might lead to brief moments of actualization identified as **peak experiences.** For example, completing a painting, having a baby, falling in love, redesigning a machine tool, writing a poem, or suddenly solving a challenging problem in math or physics.*	Being involved in humdrum, dulling activities. Valuing a consistent, dependable life over a creative, stimulating life.
Remaining open to new experiences. Self-actualizers are not held back by fear that new experiences might shake their perceptions of the world or of right and wrong. They are willing to revise their perceptions, values, and opinions.	Accepting the religious, political, and scientific views of authority figures. Avoiding people and experiences that have the potential of challenging one's world outlook. Being prejudiced against people who are different in background and outlook.

*Since individuals differ, one person's peak experience might be a total bore to another.

like the cliché of the struggling artist, would even sacrifice basic comforts to apply ourselves to higher-order needs.

Maslow's hierarchy of needs includes the following:

1. *Biological needs.* Water, food, warmth, elimination, rest, avoidance of pain, sex, and so on.
2. *Safety needs.* Protection from physical exposure by means of adequate clothing and housing; protection from the social environment by ensuring one's security from crime and financial hardship.
3. *Love and belongingness needs.* Love and acceptance through the formation of friendships and intimate relationships, and by participation in social groups. Maslow suggested that the principal source of maladjustment in a well-fed and securely housed society would be in the frustration of love and belongingness needs. When children's environments are loveless or harsh, they as adults may focus on gratifying the unfulfilled needs of childhood and be incapable of further progress.
4. *Esteem needs.* Competence, achievement, approval, recognition, status, prestige.
5. *Self-actualization.* The development of our

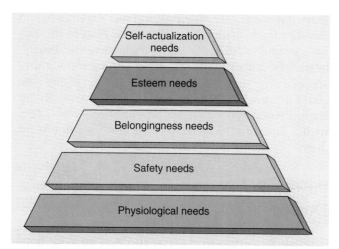

Figure 2.5 Maslow's hierarchy of needs.
Maslow's need hierarchy can be likened to a pyramid. Basic physiological or biological needs (hunger, thirst, sexual release) are found at the bottom of the pyramid. Self-actualization resides at the pinnacle. Maslow maintained that once basic survival needs are met, people progress toward higher psychological needs. The frustration of needs can give rise to abnormal behavior.

unique potentials and personal growth. Also at the highest level are needs for cognitive understanding (novelty, exploration, and pursuit of knowledge) and aesthetic experience (order, music, art, and poetry).

Humanists accuse traditional psychodynamic and behavioral theorists of focusing on deficiencies at the lower end of the psychological spectrum. Humanists do not merely aim to foster adjustment to inner and outer forces. They believe that being human means being creative, and that psychology must aim to help people live more creative lives.

Carl Rogers's Self Theory

Carl Rogers was a minister before he was a psychologist. Like other humanistic psychologists, he believed that people tend to shape themselves through freedom of choice and action.

Rogers's views are termed *self theory* because of his interest in the self as the executive of personality. To Rogers the sense of self is inborn, or innate. It is an "organized, consistent, conceptual gestalt composed of perceptions of the characteristics of the 'I' or 'me' and the perceptions of the relationships of the 'I' or 'me' to others and to various aspects of life, together with the values attached to these perceptions" (1959, p. 200). The self is the center of experience. The self provides the experience of being human in the world. It is the continuing sense of who we are, our sense of

how and why we react to the environment, and how we elect to act upon the environment. Rogers believed that choices are conscious and based on personal values. Values are also parts of the self. The self is at the heart of Rogers's theory, but remember that many psychoanalysts, including Jung, Adler, and Sullivan, also found important roles for a concept of a self.

Rogers believed that people have unique ways of seeing themselves and the world—unique **frames of reference**. We define ourselves in different ways and judge ourselves according to different sets of values. Rogers assumed we all develop a need for self-regard or **self-esteem**, and our self-esteem is wrapped up in how we live up to our ideals.

When our ideals are genuine and authentic—when they come from within—we have the opportunity to actualize ourselves. When our ideals are based purely on what others expect of us, we will have a hard time trying to live up to them, and our self-esteem may plummet. Parents help children develop self-esteem and actualize themselves when they show them **unconditional positive regard**—accept them as having intrinsic merit regardless of their behavior at the particular moment in time.

The power of unconditional positive regard. Rogers believed that parents can help their children develop self-esteem and set them on the road toward self-actualization by showing them unconditional positive regard—prizing them on the basis of their inner worth, regardless of their behavior of the moment.

When parents show children **conditional positive regard**—accept them only when they behave in an approved manner—the children may learn to disown the thoughts, feelings, and behaviors their parents have rejected. With conditional positive regard, children may learn to develop **conditions of worth**, to think of themselves as worthwhile only if they behave in certain approved ways. For example, children who are valued by their parents only when they are compliant may deny to themselves ever having feelings of anger. Children in some families learn that it is unacceptable to hold their own ideas, lest they depart from their parents' views. Parental disapproval causes them to see themselves as rebels and their feelings as wrong, selfish, or evil. If they wish to retain self-esteem, they may have to deny or mask many of their genuine feelings, or disown parts of themselves. In this way their self-concepts, or views of themselves, also grow distorted. According to Rogers, anxiety often arises from the partial perceptions of feelings and ideas that are inconsistent with one's distorted self-concept. Since anxiety is unpleasant, we may deny to ourselves that these feelings and ideas even exist. And so the actualization of our authentic self is bridled by the denial of important ideas and emotions. Psychological energy is channeled toward continued denial and self-defense, not growth. Under such conditions, we cannot hope to perceive our genuine values or personal talents, leading to frustration and setting the stage for abnormal behavior.

So we cannot fulfill all of the wishes of others and remain true to ourselves. This does not mean that self-actualization invariably leads to conflict. Rogers was more optimistic about human nature than Freud. Rogers believed that people hurt one another or become antisocial in their behavior only when they are frustrated in their endeavors to reach their unique potentials. But when parents and others treat children with love and tolerance for their differences, children, too, grow to be loving—even if some of their values and preferences differ from their parents'.

In Rogers's view, the pathway to self-actualization involves a process of self-discovery and self-awareness, of getting in touch with our true feelings, accepting them as our own, and acting in ways that genuinely reflect them. These are the goals of Rogers's method of psychotherapy, called person-centered therapy.

Rogers also believed that people have mental images of what they are capable of becoming, or **self-ideals**. People strive to reduce the discrepancy between their self-concepts and their self-ideals. But as they actualize themselves, their self-ideals may grow more intricate. Their aspirations may change in magnitude or quality. The self-ideal is akin to the carrot suspended from the stick strapped to the burro's head. The burro labors to grasp the carrot without appreciating that its own advancement causes the carrot to move ahead. Progress creates more distant goals. People may be happiest when their goals seem within grasp and they are striving confidently toward them.

Evaluating Humanistic-Existential Perspectives

Humanistic perspectives have also had an enormous impact on society at large. They were responsible in part for the human potential movement of the 1960s and 1970s. They have underscored ways in which technological advances threaten to leave humanity behind. Humanistic thought has spawned popular slogans, such as "doing your own thing," as well as the common assumption that we should trust ourselves: "If it feels right, go with it." Certainly the notion of free will—and the debate over it—has been with humankind for millennia. The humanistic-existential movement put concepts of free choice, inherent goodness, responsibility, and authenticity back on center stage and brought them into a psychology that had been dominated by psychodynamic and behavioral perspectives earlier in the century.

The strengths of humanistic-existential perspectives to the understanding of abnormal behavior lie largely in their focus on conscious experience and their innovation of therapy methods that assist people along pathways of self-discovery and self-acceptance. As individuals, we treasure our conscious experiences (our "selves"). For lower organisms (or so we presume), life means movement, food processing, exchanging oxygen and carbon dioxide, and reproduction. For people, life also means conscious experience—the bittersweet sense of the self progressing through space and time. Humanistic-existential perspectives capture these aspects of life through their blending of philosophy and psychology.

Unlike the psychodynamic and behavioral theorists, the humanistic-existential theorists see us as being free to make authentic choices that give meaning to our lives. Psychodynamic theorists and behaviorists suspect that the sense of freedom may be an illusion. For humanistic-existential psychologists, genuine personal freedom is axiomatic.

Many of the theorists we have discussed have made important innovations in the practice of psychotherapy, especially Carl Rogers. According to a survey of clinical and counseling psychologists

(Smith, 1982), Rogers is the single most influential psychotherapist of recent years. This is an astounding tribute not only to Rogers's prominence, but also to the hunger for a humanistic approach to psychological thought.

Ironically, the primary strength of the humanistic-existential approaches—their focus on conscious experience—may also be their primary weakness. Conscious experience is private and subjective. Therefore, the validity of formulating theories in terms of consciousness has been questioned. How can psychologists be certain that they are accurately perceiving the world through the eyes of their clients?

Nor can the concept of self-actualization—which is so basic to Maslow and Rogers—be proved or disproved. Like a psychic structure, a self-actualizing force is not directly measurable or observable. It is inferred from its supposed effects. Self-actualization also yields circular explanations for behavior. When someone is observed engaging in striving, what do we learn by attributing striving to a self-actualizing tendency? The source of the tendency remains a mystery. And when someone is observed not to be striving, what do we gain by attributing the lack of endeavor to a blocked or frustrated self-actualizing tendency? We must still determine the source of frustration or blockage.

SOCIOCULTURAL PERSPECTIVES

Proponents of the **sociocultural perspective** focus on socioeconomic, sociocultural, and ethnic factors in abnormal behavior. There are many approaches within this perspective, but we consider two of them. One is so-called **sociocultural theory**, as propounded by writers such as Szasz, Scheff, and Laing. The other addresses issues of acculturation—for example, whether personal adjustment is fostered by "melting" in the pot, or by becoming bicultural.

Sociocultural Theory

Sociocultural theorists propose that the causes of abnormal behavior are found not in the individual but in society. People develop psychological problems when they are subjected to the stresses of poverty, social decay, discrimination, and lack of opportunity. According to the more radical sociocultural theorists, such as the psychiatrist Thomas Szasz, mental illness is no more than a myth—a label used to stigmatize and subjugate people whose behavior is socially deviant. Szasz argues that so-called mental illnesses are really "problems in living," not diseases in the sense that influenza, hypertension, and cancer are diseases. Szasz argues that people who offend others or engage in socially deviant behavior are perceived as threats by the establishment. Labeling them as sick allows others to deny the validity of their problems and to put them away in institutions.

Sociocultural theorists maintain that once the label of "mental illness" is applied, it is very difficult to remove. The label also affects other people's responses to the "patient." Mental patients are stigmatized and socially degraded. Job opportunities may be denied, friendships may dissolve, and the "patient" may become increasingly alienated from society. Szasz argues that treating people as mentally ill strips them of their dignity, since it denies them responsibility for their own behavior and choices. Szasz argues that troubled people should be encouraged to take more responsibility for managing their lives and solving their problems.

Mental patients may be viewed as playing a stereotypical social role (Scheff, 1966, 1975). They are expected to conform to the role of "mental patient" by acting in a helpless and dependent manner, especially in institutional settings such as mental hospitals. Since sick people are expected to obey doctors' orders, labeling people with problems as "sick" bestows a great deal of power on mental health professionals (Szasz, 1984). Behaviors that are contrary to the prescribed role—independence, self-assertiveness, noncompliance—are either ignored, discouraged, or punished by hospital staff. In time, the mental patient responds to these rewards and punishments by conforming to the prescribed role. This passive and dependent "sick role" may make it more difficult for the mental patient to readjust to the more independent roles associated with life outside the mental hospital.

Another prominent contributor to the sociocultural perspective is the British psychiatrist R. D. Laing (1979). Laing shares with the humanists a concern for various social ills in contemporary society. But, generally speaking, he takes a more critical stance, accusing society of being basically unjust, striving to keep the underclasses in "their place." Laing also eyes modern communication critically, especially family patterns of communication. Children are given double messages, such as "Stop being such a child!" and "What do you mean, you want to drive the car?" Or, "You've got to go out there and beat the other guys!" and "Why can't you be more sharing?" Double messages and confused social mores provide conflicting, meaningless goals and urge us to suppress authentic behavior. By adulthood, believes Laing, we are cut off

R. D. Laing. According to sociocultural theorist R. D. Laing, psychological problems originate within the society and the culture, not within the individual. Laing viewed schizophrenia as "a special strategy that a person invents in order to live in an unlivable situation."

from our true selves. We develop, instead, false selves that interface with the social world. Even those of us who do not develop obviously disturbed patterns of behavior feel alienated within.

Laing is probably best known for his claim that psychological disturbances originate within the society and the culture, not within the individual. According to Laing, even so severe a disturbance as schizophrenia is not a disorder in the person; instead, it is "a special strategy that a person invents in order to live in an unlivable situation" (1979, p. 110). Schizophrenics can no longer maintain the false face demanded by society. They withdraw into their personal world of fantasy. To others their behavior looks disordered. Schizophrenics, however, have created an inner sanctuary within which they try to reconcile their inner and outer selves, to determine what is authentic and what is sham. They are not "sick" and inferior to others; instead, they aim to grow beyond "normal" people who continue to live out their meaningless, false lives. From Laing's perspective, schizophrenics do not need conventional therapy that aims at helping people "adjust" to the "realities" of their everyday lives. Rather, they need a warm, supportive environment within which to conduct their inner exploration, even though such an environment tolerates disorganized, even primitive behavior. By undertaking such voyages of probing self-discovery, schizophrenics may eventually find the remnants of their true selves and emerge as more creative and genuine people. Schizophrenics, to Laing, are romantic rebels.

Evaluating Sociocultural Perspectives

Some evidence for sociocultural theory is found in studies of social class and mental illness. Classic research in New Haven, Connecticut, showed that people from the lower socioeconomic classes are more likely to be institutionalized for abnormal behavior (Hollingshead & Redlich, 1958; Myers & Bean, 1968). One reason is that they have less access to private outpatient care. Hollingshead and Redlich (1958) and Myers and Bean (1968) also suggest that persons from lower socioeconomic groups are more likely to express their problems through aggressive behavior. This interpretation, however, mirrors the prevailing cultural bias against people of low income and members of minority groups. This bias may play a significant role in creating this perception.

There are competing explanations as to why people of lower socioeconomic status may have more severe behavior problems. For example, problem behaviors, such as excessive drinking, can lead people to drift downward in social status. Genetic factors may also be associated both with lowered socioeconomic status and the incidence of various kinds of abnormal behavior patterns.

Certainly it is valuable for sociocultural theorists to focus on the social stressors that may contribute to abnormal behavior. Certainly it is desirable for social critics like Szasz to rivet our attention on the political implications of our responses to deviance. The views of Szasz and other critics of the mental health establishment have been influential in bringing about changes to better protect the rights of mental patients in institutions.

Theories of Acculturation

Should Hindu women who emigrate to the United States give up the sari in favor of California Casuals? Should Soviet immigrants continue to teach their children Russian in the home? Should African-American children be acquainted with the music and art of African peoples? Should women from traditional Islamic societies remove the veil and enter the workplace alongside American Murphy Browns? How do the stresses of acculturation affect the psychological well-being of immigrants and their families?

Sociocultural theorists have alerted us to the importance of accounting for social stressors in explaining abnormal behavior. One of the primary sources of stress imposed on immigrant groups, or on native groups adapting to living in the larger mainstream culture, is the need to adapt to a new culture.

How does acculturation affect the psychological well-being of immigrants? The melting pot theory holds that acculturation helps people adjust to living in the host culture. From this perspective, Hispanic Americans might adjust better by replacing Spanish with English and adopting the values and customs of the mainstream U.S. culture. According to bicultural theory, adjustment is fostered by identification with both traditional and host cultures—that is, maintaining a supportive cultural tradition while adapting to the ways of the new society.

The term **acculturation** refers to the process of adaptation in which immigrants and native groups identify with the new culture through making behavioral and attitudinal changes (Rogler et al., 1991).

Consider the challenges faced by Hispanic Americans. There are two general theories of the relationships between acculturation and adjustment (Griffith, 1983). One theory, dubbed the melting pot theory, holds that acculturation helps people adjust to living in the host culture. From this perspective, Hispanic Americans might adjust better by replacing Spanish with English and adopting the values and customs associated with mainstream American culture. A competing theory, the **bicultural theory**, holds that psychosocial adjustment is fostered by identification with both traditional and host cultures. That is, ability to adapt to the ways of the new society combined with a supportive cultural tradition and a sense of ethnic identity may predict good adjustment. From a bicultural perspective, immigrants maintain their ethnic identity and traditional values while learning to adapt to the language and customs of the host culture.

We first must be able to measure acculturation if we are to investigate its relationship to mental health among immigrant and native groups. Measures of acculturation vary. In assessing acculturation among Hispanic Americans, for example, researchers assess variables such as the degree to which people favor English or Spanish in social situations, when reading, or watching media such as TV; preferences for types of food and styles of clothing; and self-perceptions of ethnic identity. Using such measures, the relationships between acculturation and adjustment are complex.

Let us summarize some of the findings concerning the relationships between acculturation and psychological disorders among Hispanic Americans:

- According to a study of a nationwide probability sample of Hispanic Americans, highly acculturated Hispanic-American women were nine times more likely than relatively unacculturated women to be heavy drinkers (Caetano, 1987). In Latin American cultures, men tend to drink much more alcohol than women, largely because gender-based cultural prohibitions against drinking constrain women. These constraints appear to have loosened among Hispanic-American women who adopt "mainstream" U.S. attitudes and values.

 It is true that Hispanic-American women who are well acculturated are more likely than less well-acculturated Hispanic-American women to be heavy drinkers. Perhaps they are less likely to accept traditional Hispanic constraints against drinking in women.

- Third-generation Mexican-American male adolescents—who are more likely to be acculturated than first- or second-generation Mexican Americans—were at higher risk of delinquency (Buriel et al., 1982).
- Acculturated, U.S.-born Mexican Americans showed greater evidence of depression, phobias, drug and alcohol abuse (Burnam et al., 1987), and suicidal thinking (Sorenson & Golding, 1988) than people born in Mexico.
- Highly acculturated Hispanic-American high school girls were more likely than their less acculturated counterparts to show test scores associated with anorexia [an eating disorder characterized by excessive weight loss and fears of becoming fat—see Chapter 13] on an eating attitudes questionnaire (Pumariega, 1986). Acculturation apparently made these girls more vulnerable to the demands of striving toward the contemporary American ideal of the (very!) slender woman.
- Despite these associations of acculturation with mental health problems, studies have also found that Mexican Americans who are *less* proficient in English show *more* signs of depression and anxiety than those who are more proficient (Salgado de Snyder, 1987; Warheit et al., 1985).

reduced-personality syndrome

Are these Mexican Americans depressed because they remain more invested in Mexican culture, because they have lower language proficiency, or because third factors—such as economic problems—can be connected both to acculturation and language proficiency? Mexican-American women who remain more invested in Mexican culture also show generally lower levels of self-esteem and encounter more stress in adapting to living in the United States (Salgado de Snyder, 1987).

Some studies thus suggest that acculturation is associated with a greater risk of psychological problems. Others link increased risk with failure to become acculturated. Still other researchers have found that *bicultural* Hispanic Americans—those who identify both with their traditional culture and their host society (Lang et al., 1982)—are best adjusted. Yet another study of 259 Mexican-American adults in Southern California failed to show clear support for either the melting pot or bicultural theory (Griffith, 1983). Overall, approximately equal numbers of studies show positive and negative relationships between mental health status among immigrant and native groups and the level of acculturation (Rogler et al., 1991).

Researchers suspect that inconsistencies in results may partly reflect differences in the indices by which mental health is measured and the complexities of acculturative processes. Adjustment to a host society may depend on such factors as economic opportunity, language proficiency, and the availability of a supportive network of acculturated individuals of similar cultural background. Moreover, some outcomes need careful interpretation. For example, does the finding that highly acculturated Hispanic-American women are more likely to drink heavily argue in favor of the placing of greater social constraints on women? The point would seem to be that a loosening of restraint is a double-edged sword, and that all people—male and female, Hispanic and non-Hispanic—may encounter adjustment problems when they gain new freedoms.

Other research appears to bear out this point. There is a strong relationship in Hispanic immigrants between the stress of adapting to a new culture and environment and states of psychological distress. In one study, female immigrants showed higher levels of depression than male immigrants (Salgado de Snyder, Cervantes, & Padilla, 1990). The depression may be linked to the greater level of stress women encountered in adjusting to changes in family and personal issues, such as the greater freedom of gender roles for men and women in U.S. society. Because they were reared in cultures in which men are expected to be breadwinners and women homemakers, immigrant women may encounter more family and internal conflict when they enter the work force, regardless of whether their entry results from economic necessity or personal choice.

BIOLOGICAL PERSPECTIVES

Many researchers today are investigating the roles of biological structures and processes in abnormal behavior. In some cases, as with **Alzheimer's disease** (discussed in Chapter 12), biological abnormalities are implicated as direct causes of abnormal behavior. In other cases, there is apparently an interaction between psychological and biological processes.

Let us consider biological structures and processes that are involved with abnormal behavior. They include the nervous system, the endocrine system, and heredity.

The Nervous System

Perhaps you would not be nervous if you did not have a nervous system, but even calm people have nervous systems. The nervous system is intimately involved in anxiety reactions, but it also has divisions that are responsible for perception, muscle movement, automatic functions like breathing and secreting hormones, and psychological events like thoughts and feelings.

The nervous system is made up of nerve cells called **neurons**. We are born with about 12 billion neurons, and that is all we shall ever have. Neurons communicate with one another, or transmit "messages." These messages somehow account for events as diverse as sensing an itch from a bug bite, coordinating a figure skater's vision and muscles, composing a symphony, solving an architectural equation, and, in the case of hallucinations, hearing or seeing things that are not really there.

Every neuron has a cell body, or **soma**, dendrites, and an axon (see Figure 2.6). The cell body contains the nucleus of the cell. The cell body metabolizes oxygen to carry out the work of the cell. Short fibers called **dendrites** project from the cell body to receive messages from adjoining neurons. Each neuron has a single **axon** that projects trunklike from the cell body. Axons are microscopic because they are thin. However, they are the part of the neuron that extends for several feet if they are conveying messages between the toes and the spinal cord. Axons

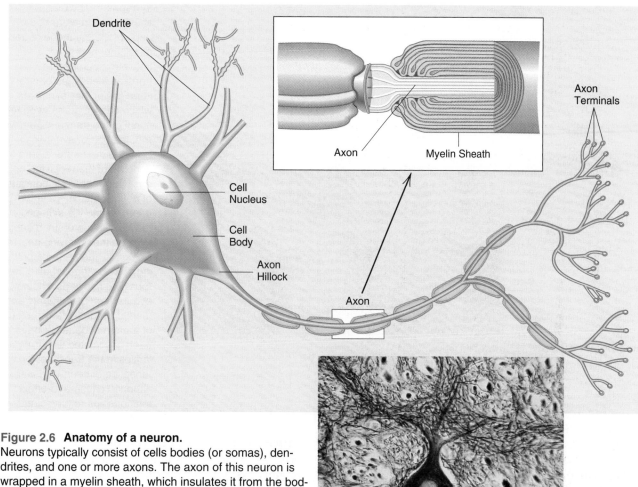

Figure 2.6 Anatomy of a neuron.
Neurons typically consist of cells bodies (or somas), dendrites, and one or more axons. The axon of this neuron is wrapped in a myelin sheath, which insulates it from the bodily fluids surrounding the neuron and facilitates transmission of neural impulses (messages that travel within the neuron).

may branch and project in various directions. Axons terminate in small branching structures that are aptly termed **terminals**. Swellings called **knobs** occupy the tips of axon terminals. Neurons convey messages in one direction, from the dendrites or cell body along the axon to the axon terminals. The messages are then conveyed from terminal knobs to other neurons, muscles, or glands.

Neurons transmit messages to other neurons by means of chemical substances called **neurotransmitters**. Neurotransmitters induce chemical changes in receiving neurons. These changes cause axons to conduct the messages in electrical form.

The junction between a transmitting neuron and a receiving neuron is termed a **synapse**. A transmitting neuron is termed *presynaptic*. A receiving neuron is said to be *postsynaptic*. A synapse consists of an axon terminal from a transmitting neuron, a dendrite of a receiving neuron, and a small fluid-filled gap between the two that is called the synaptic cleft. The message does not jump the synaptic cleft like a spark. Instead, axon terminals release neurotransmitters

into the cleft like myriad ships casting off into the seas (Figure 2.7).

Each kind of neurotransmitter has a distinctive chemical structure. It will fit only into one kind of harbor, or **receptor site**, on the receiving neuron. Consider the analogy of a lock and key. Only the right key (neurotransmitter) operates the lock, causing the postsynaptic neuron to forward the message.

Once released, some molecules of a neurotransmitter reach port at receptor sites of other neurons. "Loose" neurotransmitters may be broken down in the synaptic clefts by enzymes or be reabsorbed by the axon terminal (a process termed *reuptake*), so as to prevent the receiving cell from continuing to fire.

Excesses or deficiencies of neurotransmitters have been linked to diseases and some kinds of abnormal behavior. Alzheimer's disease, which involves the progressive loss of memory and cognitive functioning, has been associated with reductions in the levels of the neurotransmitter **acetylcholine** in the brain. Another neurotransmitter, **dopamine**, has been linked to schizophrenia. Schizophrenics may

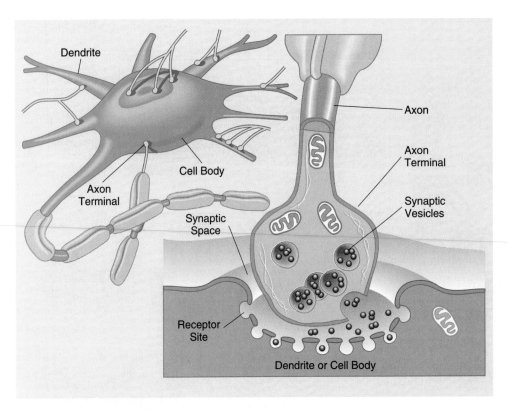

Figure 2.7 Transmission of neural impulses across the synapse. The diagram shows the structure of the neuron and the mode of transmission of neural impulses between neurons. Neurons transmit messages or neural impulses across synapses, which consist of the axon terminal of the transmitting neuron, the gap or synaptic cleft between the neurons, and the dendrite of the receiving neuron. The "message" consists of neurotransmitters that are released into the synaptic cleft and taken up by receptor sites on the receiving neuron. Somehow the patterns of firing of many thousands of neurons give rise to psychological events such as thoughts and mental images. Many patterns of abnormal behavior have been associated with irregularities in the transmission or reception of neural messages, although cause-and-effect relationships remain clouded.

Labels in figure: Dendrite; Axon; Cell Body; Axon Terminal; Axon Terminal; Synaptic Vesicles; Synaptic Space; Receptor Site; Dendrite or Cell Body

use more of the dopamine that is available in the brain than others. (see Chapter 11). The result may be hallucinations, emotional disturbances, and incoherence. The phenothiazines, a class of drugs used to treat schizophrenia, may work by locking some dopamine out of its receptor sites (Snyder, 1984).

Norepinephrine is manufactured mostly by neurons in the brain stem. It is chemically akin to the hormone epinephrine (also known as adrenaline), which we discuss later in the chapter. Norepinephrine acts as a neurotransmitter and a hormone. Like epinephrine, norepinephrine accelerates the heart rate and other body processes. Norepinephrine is involved in learning and memory, eating, and general emotional arousal. Excesses and deficiencies of norepinephrine have been connected with mood disorders (see Chapter 7) and eating disorders (see Chapter 13).

Serotonin, another neurotransmitter, may be linked to anxiety, insomnia, and mood disorders. Although neurotransmitters play a role in psychological disorders, precise causal relationships have not been determined.

 Many kinds of abnormal behavior patterns are connected with chemical imbalances in the level of neurotransmitters in the brain. Researchers, however, have not yet unearthed the precise causal relationships.

■ **PARTS OF THE NERVOUS SYSTEM** The parts of the nervous system are made up of neurons. The nervous system consists of the central and peripheral divisions (see Figure 2.8). These parts are further divided. The **central nervous system** consists of the brain and spinal cord. The **peripheral nervous system** is made up of nerves that receive and transmit sensory messages to the brain and spinal cord, and of nerves that transmit messages from the brain or spinal cord to the muscles, causing them to contract, and to glands, causing them to secrete hormones.

Let us review the nature and functions of the parts of the nervous system. We begin with the back of the head, where the spinal cord meets the brain, and work forward (see Figure 2.9). The lower part of the brain, or hindbrain, consists of the medulla, pons, and cerebellum. Many nerves that link the spinal cord to higher brain levels pass through the **medulla**. The medulla plays roles in such vital functions as heart rate, respiration, and blood pressure, and also in sleep, sneezing, and coughing. The **pons** transmits information about body movement and is involved in functions related to attention, sleep, and respiration.

Behind the pons is the **cerebellum**, or "little brain" in Latin. The cerebellum is involved in balance and motor (muscle) behavior. Injury to the cerebellum may impair motor coordination and cause stumbling and loss of muscle tone.

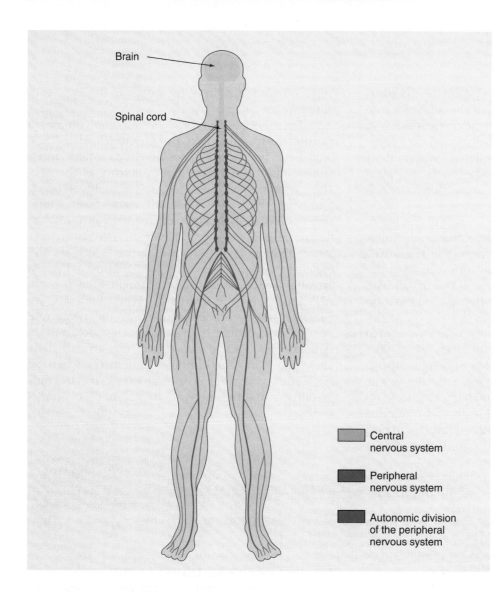

Brain

Spinal cord

Central
nervous system

Peripheral
nervous system

Autonomic division
of the peripheral
nervous system

Figure 2.8 The central nervous system and the peripheral nervous system. The central nervous system consists of the brain and spinal cord. Parts of the peripheral nervous system inform the brain of the nature of the world outside and provide the means for acting on the world. The functioning of the autonomic nervous system is intimately connected with the experiencing of emotions.

Figure 2.9 The geography of the brain.
Part a shows parts of the hindbrain, midbrain, and forebrain. Part b shows the four lobes of the cerebral cortex: frontal, parietal, temporal, and occipital. In part b, the sensory (tactile) and motor areas lie across the central fissure from one another. Researchers are investigating the potential relationships between various patterns of abnormal behavior and irregularities in the formation or functioning of the structures of the brain.

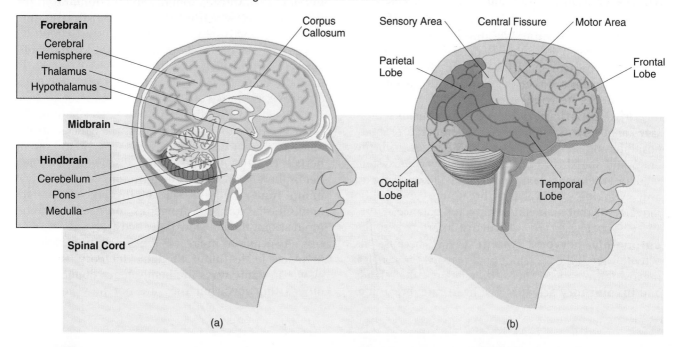

Forebrain
Cerebral Hemisphere
Thalamus
Hypothalamus

Midbrain

Hindbrain
Cerebellum
Pons
Medulla

Spinal Cord

Corpus Callosum

Sensory Area   Central Fissure   Motor Area

Parietal Lobe

Frontal Lobe

Occipital Lobe

Temporal Lobe

(a)   (b)

The **reticular activating system** (RAS) starts in the hindbrain and rises through the midbrain into the lower forebrain. The RAS plays vital roles in sleep, attention, and arousal. RAS injury may leave an animal **comatose**. RAS stimulation triggers messages to the cortex that heighten alertness. So-called central nervous system depressants, like alcohol, lower RAS activity.

Important areas in the frontal part of the brain, or forebrain, are the thalamus, hypothalamus, limbic system, basal ganglia, and cerebrum. The **thalamus** relays sensory information to the cortex, as from the eyes to the visual areas of the cortex. The thalamus is also involved in sleep and attention in coordination with other structures, like the RAS.

The **hypothalamus** is a tiny structure located between the thalamus and the pituitary gland. The hypothalamus is vital in regulation of body temperature, concentration of fluids, storage of nutrients, and motivation and emotion. By implanting electrodes in parts of the hypothalamus of animals and observing the effects when a current is switched on, researchers have found that the hypothalamus is involved in hunger, thirst, sex, and aggression.

The hypothalamus, along with parts of the thalamus and other structures, make up the **limbic system**. The limbic system is involved in memory and in the drives of hunger, sex, and aggression. The **basal ganglia** lie under the cortex in front of the thalamus and help to regulate postural movements and coordination.

The **cerebrum** is your crowning glory. It is responsible for the shape of your delightfully rounded head. The surface of the cerebrum is convoluted with ridges and valleys. This surface is called the **cerebral cortex.** The hemispheres of the cerebral cortex are connected by the **corpus callosum**, a thick fiber bundle.

The peripheral nervous system connects the brain to the outer world. Without the peripheral nervous system, people could not perceive the world or act on it. The two main divisions of the peripheral nervous system are the somatic nervous system and the autonomic nervous system.

The **somatic nervous system** transmits messages about sights, sounds, smells, temperature, body position, and so on, to the brain. Messages from the brain and spinal cord to the somatic nervous system regulate intentional body movements, like raising an arm, winking, or walking; breathing; and subtle movements that maintain posture and balance.

Psychologists are particularly interested in the **autonomic nervous system** (ANS) because its activities are linked to emotional response. *Autonomic* means "automatic." The ANS regulates the glands and **involuntary** activities like heart rate, breathing, digestion, and dilation of the pupils of the eyes, even when we are asleep.

The ANS has two branches or subdivisions, the **sympathetic** and the **parasympathetic**. These branches have mostly opposing effects. Many organs and glands are served by both branches of the ANS. The sympathetic division is most involved in processes that draw body energy from stored reserves, which helps prepare the person to fend off threats or dangers (see Chapter 4). The parasympathetic division is most active during processes that replenish energy reserves, like digestion. When we are afraid or anxious, the sympathetic branch of the ANS accelerates the heart rate. When we relax, the parasympathetic branch decelerates the heart rate. The parasympathetic branch incites digestion, but the sympathetic branch constrains digestive activity. Since the sympathetic branch dominates when we are fearful or anxious, fear or anxiety can cause indigestion by interfering with digestion of consumed food.

Anxiety can certainly give you indigestion. A threat heightens activity of the sympathetic branch of the ANS, giving rise to biological aspects of anxiety and, at the same time, interfering with parasympathetic activities like digestion.

■ **THE CEREBRAL CORTEX** The human activities of thought and language involve the two hemispheres of the cerebrum. Each hemisphere is divided into four parts, or lobes, as shown in Figure 2.9.

When light stimulates the retinas of the eyes, neurons in the occipital lobe are activated, creating the sense of sight. The auditory area of the cortex lies in the temporal lobe. Sounds induce structures in the ear to vibrate, which relay messages to the auditory area. When activated, neurons in this area produce our experience of sound or hearing. The **somatosensory cortex** receives messages from skin senses all over the body. When neurons in the **motor cortex** are active, we move certain parts of our bodies.

Patients with injuries to one hemisphere of the brain usually show sensory or motor deficits on the opposite side of the body because sensory and motor nerves cross in the brain and elsewhere. The left hemisphere controls functions on, and receives inputs from, the right side of the body. The right hemisphere controls functions on, and receives inputs from, the left side of the body.

Association areas of the cerebral cortex are involved in learning, thought, memory, and language. In many ways the hemispheres duplicate each other's functions, but they are not fully equal. For most people, the left hemisphere contains language functions and is dominant (Rasmussen & Milner, 1975).

The Endocrine System

The body has two kinds of glands: glands that carry their secretions to specific locations by means of ducts, and ductless glands that pour their secretions directly into the bloodstream. Saliva, tears, and sweat reach their destinations by way of a system of ducts. Psychologists are particularly interested in the chemicals secreted by ductless glands because of their behavioral effects. The ductless glands make up the **endocrine system**, and they secrete chemicals called **hormones**.

Although they are discharged into the bloodstream and circulate throughout the body, hormones act on receptors in specific locations. Certain hormones released by the hypothalamus influence the pituitary gland, for example. Some hormones

secreted by the pituitary affect the adrenal cortex, others affect the testes and ovaries, and so on. Some endocrine glands are shown in Figure 2.10.

The hypothalamus produces various releasing hormones, or "factors," that induce the pituitary gland to release corresponding hormones. The pituitary gland is so vital that it has been referred to as the "master gland." The anterior (front) and posterior (back) lobes of the pituitary secrete many hormones. Growth hormone regulates development of muscles, bones, and glands. Prolactin, another pituitary hormone, regulates maternal behavior in lower mammals, like rats, and stimulates milk production in women. Still another pituitary hormone, adrenocorticotrophic hormone (ACTH), causes the adrenal cortex to release several steroids (cortisol is one) that help the body manage stress by countering inflammation and allergic reactions.

The pancreas regulates the blood sugar level through the hormones insulin and glucagon. Diabetes mellitus is characterized by excess sugar in the blood (hyperglycemia) and urine; it can cause coma and

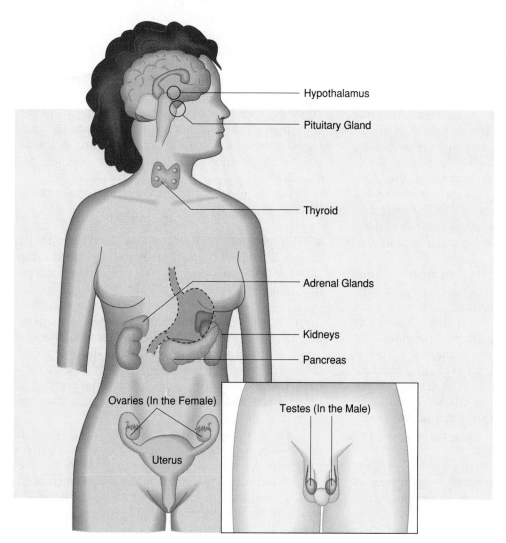

Hypothalamus

Pituitary Gland

Thyroid

Adrenal Glands

Kidneys

Pancreas

Ovaries (In the Female)

Uterus

Testes (In the Male)

Figure 2.10 Major glands of the endocrine system. The glands of the endocrine system pour their secretions—called *hormones*—directly into the bloodstream. Although hormones may travel throughout the body, they act only on specific receptor sites. Many hormones are implicated in stress reactions and various patterns of abnormal behavior.

death. Diabetes is caused by deficient secretion or utilization of insulin. The biological disorder **hypoglycemia** is characterized by a deficient blood sugar level. Symptoms of hypoglycemia include shakiness, lack of energy, and dizziness—a syndrome easily mistaken for anxiety. Many people seek help for anxiety and learn by means of blood tests that they actually have hypoglycemia. Hypoglycemia is usually controlled by diet.

The thyroid gland produces **thyroxin**, which affects the metabolic rate. Thyroxin deficiency can cause **cretinism** in children, a disorder characterized by mental retardation and stunted growth. Adults deficient in thyroxin are said to have **hypothyroidism**. They may feel sluggish and put on weight. Excess thyroxin can cause **hyperthyroidism**, which is characterized by excitability, insomnia, and weight loss.

The adrenal glands, situated above the kidneys, have an exterior layer, or cortex, and an interior core, or medulla. The adrenal cortex is regulated by ACTH. The cortex secretes many **corticosteroids**, or cortical **steroids** (a class of steroidal hormones produced by the adrenal cortex). Cortical steroids boost resistance to stress, foster muscle development, and induce the liver to release sugar, providing energy for emergencies. They may bolster self-esteem, stimulate the sex drive, and increase one's energy level.

The **catecholamines** adrenaline and noradrenaline are released by the adrenal medulla. **Adrenaline** (also called epinephrine) is secreted solely by the adrenal glands. Noradrenaline (norepinephrine), however, is also manufactured elsewhere in the body. Under stress, the sympathetic branch of the ANS prompts the adrenal medulla to secrete a mixture of epinephrine and norepinephrine that prepares the body to cope. Norepinephrine raises the blood pressure. In the nervous system, it functions as a neurotransmitter.

The male sex hormone **testosterone** is produced by the testes. A few weeks following conception, testosterone prompts prenatal development of male sex organs. During puberty it fosters growth of muscle and bone and the ripening of **primary** and **secondary sex characteristics**. Primary sex characteristics differentiate females from males and are directly involved in reproduction. The sex organs are prime examples. Secondary sex characteristics, such as deepening of the voice and growth of the beard, also differentiate males and females but are not directly involved in reproduction.

The ovaries secrete **estrogen** and **progesterone**. Estrogen is a collective name for numerous female sex hormones that spur development of female reproductive capacity and secondary sex characteristics. They account for accumulation of fatty deposits in the breasts and hips. Progesterone also has many functions. It induces growth of the female reproductive organs and preserves pregnancy.

Genetics and Behavior Genetics

Heredity plays a critical role in the determination of our traits. The structures we inherit make our behavior possible (humans can walk and run) and at the same time place limits on us (humans cannot fly without artificial equipment). The branch of biology that studies heredity is called **genetics. Behavior genetics** is a specialty that bridges the sciences of psychology and biology. It is concerned with the genetic transmission of structures and traits that give rise to patterns of behavior.

Genetics are fundamental in the transmission of physical traits such as height, race, and eye color. Genetic factors also appear to play roles in the origins of psychological traits like intelligence (Plomin, 1989), **extraversion**, and **neuroticism** (McCartney et al., 1990; Pedersen et al., 1988; Tellegen et al., 1988), shyness (Kagan, 1984; Plomin, 1989), social dominance, and aggressiveness (Goldsmith, 1983).

Genetic influences are also implicated in abnormal behavior patterns such as schizophrenia (Gottesman, 1991), bipolar (manic-depression) disorder (Vandenberg et al., 1986), alcoholism (Newlin & Thomson, 1990), and antisocial personality (DiLalla & Gottesman, 1991; Mednick et al., 1987). In the coming chapters we examine the evidence regarding genetic contributions to these and other psychological disorders.

Let us review the biological mechanisms of heredity.

■ **GENES AND CHROMOSOMES** **Genes** are the basic building blocks of heredity. They are the biochemical materials that regulate the development of traits. Some traits, such as blood type, are transmitted by a single pair of genes—one of which is derived from each parent. Other traits, referred to as **polygenic**, are determined by complex combinations of genes. **Chromosomes** are the rod-shaped genetic structures found in the nuclei of the body's cells. Each consists of more than 1,000 genes. A normal human cell contains 46 chromosomes, which are organized into 23 pairs.

There are about 100,000 genes in every cell in our bodies. Chromosomes consist of large complex molecules of deoxyribonucleic acid (DNA). Genes occupy various segments along the length of chromosomes. The form of DNA was first described in the 1950s by the team of James Watson and Francis Crick (1958). In all living things, DNA takes the form of a double helix, similar in appearance to a twisting ladder (see Figure 2.11). The sequence of our genes is referred to as our genetic code.

The set of traits specified by our genetic code is referred to as our **genotype**. Our appearance and behavior are not determined by our genotype alone. We are also influenced by environmental factors such as nutrition, exercise, accident and illness, learning, and culture. The constellation of our actual or expressed traits is called our **phenotype**. Our phenotype represents the interaction of genetic and environmental influences. A genetic predisposition toward, say, shyness may be enhanced or reversed by social influences. So, too, with psychological problems ranging from schizophrenia to obesity (Brownell & Wadden, 1992). In the view of behavior geneticists, we may not develop certain psychological disorders such as depression or schizophrenia unless we possess a particular genotype and are exposed to certain environmental stresses (e.g., birth complications, family conflict, loss of loved ones, etc.) that foster the emergence of the problem. In the parlance of behavior geneticists, individuals who possess genotypes for particular psychological disorders are said to have a *genetic predisposition* that makes them more likely to develop the disorder in response to stress.

The interaction between genetics and environment in determining the development of psychological disorders is expressed in the **diathesis–stress** hypothesis. According to this model, the genotype provides a vulnerability (or diathesis) within the person that interacts with stress to produce the disorder (which is part of the phenotype). Not all susceptible offspring develop the disorder. Many environmental, behavioral, and psychological factors may also be involved, ranging from situational sources of stress (such as the loss of a job or of a loved one) to learning experiences to ways of mentally representing the world. In some cases, however, the diathesis (the biological predisposition, or vulnerability) may be so potent that the person will develop the disorder even in the most benign of environments. The diathesis–stress hypothesis may apply to a number of disorders, especially schizophrenia.

The biological perspective seeks evidence of genetic transmission in abnormal behavior patterns through various types of studies, such as kinship studies, including twin studies, and adoptee studies.

■ **KINSHIP STUDIES** The more closely people are related, the more genes they have in common. Children receive half their genes from each parent. There is thus a 50% overlap in genetic heritage between each parent and his or her offspring. Siblings (brothers and sisters) similarly share half their genetic heritage. Aunts and uncles who are related by blood to their nephews and nieces have a 25% overlap; first cousins, a 12.5% overlap (see Figure 2.12).

In order to determine whether a pattern of abnormal behavior has a genetic basis, researchers locate one case of a person with the disorder and then study how the disorder is distributed among the person's family members. The case first diagnosed is referred to as the index case, or *proband*. If the distribution of the disorder among family members approximates their degree of kinship, there may be genetic involvement. However, the closer their kinship, the more likely people also are to share environmental backgrounds. For this reason, adoptee studies are of particular value.

Figure 2.11 The double-helix structure of DNA.
Chromosomes are made up of large molecules of deoxyribonucleic acid (DNA). Genes consist of segments of chromosomes. Genetic contributions to abnormal behavior involve our genetic codes—the sequences of chemicals in our genes.

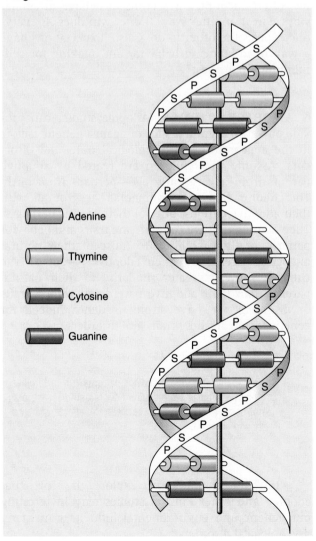

Adenine

Thymine

Cytosine

Guanine

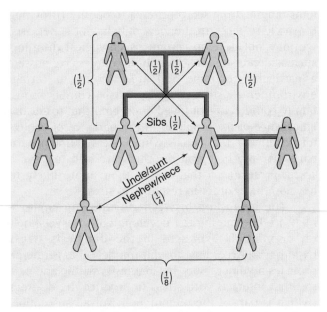

Figure 2.12 A family tree showing the proportion of shared inheritance among relatives.
The more closely people are related, the more genes they have in common. Kinship studies, including twin studies and adoptee studies, afford researchers insight into the heritability of various patterns of abnormal behavior.

■ **TWIN STUDIES** Sometimes a fertilized egg cell (or zygote) divides into two cells that separate, so that each develops into a separate person. In such cases, there is a 100% overlap in genetic makeup, and the couple are known as identical twins, or **monozy-**

Identical twins. Identical twins, like those shown here, develop from a single zygote, and are thus referred to as *monozygotic*, or MZ twins. Fraternal twins develop from separate zygotes and are thus called *dizygotic*, or DZ twins. Because the genetic heritage of MZ twins is identical, it is assumed that differences between them in appearance and behavior reflect environmental influences. Studies of MZ twins who have been reared apart suggest that genetic factors are involved in the development of some patterns of abnormal behavior.

gotic (MZ) twins. Sometimes a woman releases two egg cells, or ova, in the same month, and they are both fertilized. In such cases, the zygotes (fertilized egg cells) develop into fraternal twins, or **dizygotic** (DZ) twins. DZ twins overlap 50% in their genetic heritage, just as other siblings do.

Identical, or MZ, twins are important in the study of the relative influences of heredity and environment because differences between MZ twins are the result of environmental rather than genetic influences. MZ twins look more alike and are closer in height than DZ twins. In twin studies, researchers identify disordered people who are members of MZ or DZ twin pairs and then study the other twins in the pairs. A role for genetic factors is suggested when MZ twins are significantly more likely than DZ twins to share a disorder. In later chapters, we examine the differences in the rates of **concordance** for MZ versus DZ twins for particular forms of abnormal behavior, such as schizophrenia and bipolar disorder. Even among MZ twins, though, environmental influences cannot be ruled out. Parents and teachers, for example, often encourage MZ twins to behave in similar ways. Put it another way: If one twin does X, everyone expects the other to do X also. Expectations have a way of influencing behavior and making for self-fulfilling prophecies.

■ **ADOPTEE STUDIES** Adoptee studies can provide powerful arguments for or against genetic factors in the appearance of psychological traits and disorders. Assume that children are reared by adoptive parents from a very early age—perhaps from birth. The children share environmental backgrounds with their adoptive parents, but not their genetic heritages. Then assume that we compare the traits and behavior patterns of these children to those of their natural biological parents and their adoptive parents. If the children show a greater similarity to their natural parents than their adoptive parents on certain traits or disorders, we have strong evidence indeed for genetic factors in these traits and disorders.

 Yes, many abnormal behavior patterns run in families. However, unless we examine adoptee studies, we may not be able to distinguish between the effects of heredity and environment.

In later chapters we explore the role that adoptee and other kinship studies play in ferreting out genetic and environmental influences in many psychological disorders.

Evaluating Biological Perspectives

Biological perspectives have had much to offer to our understanding of abnormal behavior. Biological research is replete with current successes and future promise. Drugs for some disorders are synthesized on the basis of knowledge of the actions of neurotransmitters and hormones. Drugs have been developed that quell the more flagrant features of schizophrenia although they do not bring about a "cure." Drugs alone do not prepare institutionalized patients for reentry into society, however. Hospitalized patients may acquire dependent "sick roles" in institutional settings. Acquiring social and vocational skills that will permit them to assume more independent communal roles requires psychosocial or psychoeducational training.

Drugs are used in the treatment of a wide variety of other psychological disorders, including anxiety and mood disorders. In some cases, researchers are finding that the combination of psychotherapy and **chemotherapy** may be more effective than either approach alone. In other cases, one or the other approach may be more effective.

Genetic engineering remains a future promise that may someday be realized. Perhaps someday a number of disorders that are connected with certain genetic defects may be corrected in the womb or by direct manipulation of parental sperm and egg cells.

There is also no question that biological structures and processes are involved in many patterns of abnormal behavior. In some cases, as in Alzheimer's disease, biological processes play the causative role. Even then, however, the precise causes remain unknown. In other cases, as is the case with schizophrenia, biological factors, especially genetics, appear to interact with stressful environmental factors in the development of the disorder.

Today, no single theoretical perspective accounts fully for all kinds of abnormal behavior or offers the final word on treatment. As rounded human beings, we can extract what is of value from each of them. Even the most controversial sociocultural ideas at least remind us to keep an eye on the sociopolitical aspects of our assumptions. The differential incidences of psychological disorders among various cultural and ethnic groups also alerts us to remain aware of possible roles for cultural factors. In many ways the main theories overlap, as in the nearly universal concept of a self and the nearly universal notion that our interpretations of events influence our emotional and behavior reactions. Nor would any scientist deny that mental experience is dependent on the brain. As we learn more about people and about abnormal behavior, our theories may focus on subtler and more complex interactions.

SUMMARY

Psychodynamic Perspectives

The psychodynamic perspectives include the contributions of Freud and his followers. Although there are differences among psychodynamic theorists, they all share certain tenets in common, such as beliefs in psychic determinism, unconscious motivation, and the importance of childhood experiences in shaping personality and behavior.

Freud believed that the mind is composed of three regions: the conscious, the preconscious, and the unconscious. Freud posited the existence of three mental or psychic structures: the id, the ego, and the superego. Defense mechanisms, such as repression, protect the ego from anxiety by keeping unacceptable impulses out of awareness. Although the use of defense mechanisms is quite normal, it can lead to abnormal behavior patterns.

Abnormal behavior patterns occur from imbalances among the mental structures. Neurotic anxiety occurs when the ego senses that unacceptable impulses may break through to consciousness. Neuroses are means of stemming the leakage of these impulses and are characterized by maladaptive behavior patterns that represent or symbolize the inner conflict. In contrast, reality anxiety represents a fear of external danger. In psychoses, such as schizophrenia, the id completely breaks through and primary process thinking and bizarre behavior become dominant.

Freud charted five stages of psychosexual development that correspond to changes in the transfer of sexual energy, or libido, from one erogenous zone to another. The stages are oral, anal, phallic, latency, and genital. Undergratification or overgratification at particular stages can lead to fixation, which is characterized by the development of traits associated with the particular stage.

Other psychodynamic theorists placed lesser importance on primitive drives, such as sex and aggression, and greater importance on the functions of the ego, especially the development of concepts of the self.

Learning Perspectives

Learning theorists attempt to account for both normal and abnormal behavior on the basis of principles of learning, rather than on unconscious mental processes. Behaviorists focus on classical and operant conditioning, in which learning is believed to be shaped by the environment. Social-learning theorists focus on the importance of cognitive variables in learning and the process of learning by observation. They believe that situational variables, like rewards and punishments, are not sufficient to account for learned behavior. Person variables also need to be considered. These include competencies, encoding strategies, expectancies such as outcome expectancies and self-efficacy expectations, subjective values, and self-regulatory systems and plans.

Learning theorists see abnormal behavior as largely learned by means of the same principles of learning as normal behavior. Behavior therapy represents the application of principles of learning to help people overcome abnormal behavior patterns and develop more adjusted behaviors.

Cognitive Perspectives

Cognitive theorists focus on the roles of thinking and information processing in explaining human behavior. Information-processing models liken the human organism to the computer in terms of processes relating to input, storage, retrieval, manipulation, and output of information.

Kelly views people as personal scientists who seek to understand and predict events through the use of personal constructs, or dimensions for categorizing events. To understand people, we need to understand how they construe events. Kelly's approach to therapy focused on helping people make more adjustive constructions of events.

Ellis believes that people endure emotional misery because of the ways they interpret events, rather than from the events themselves. By exaggerating the importance of negative events, people can turn disappointment into despair. He proposed an A-B-C model for analyzing the relationships between activating events (A's), intervening beliefs (B's), and emotional consequences (C's). Ellis's rational-emotive therapy attempts to help clients dispute their irrational beliefs and substitute more rational alternative beliefs.

Beck also focuses on tendencies of people to exaggerate negative consequences of upsetting events, which he calls cognitive distortions or errors in thinking. Beck's approach to therapy, namely cognitive therapy, focuses on helping clients identify and correct such cognitive errors as selective abstraction, overgeneralization, magnification, and absolutist thinking.

Cognitive theorists focus on how maladaptive thoughts or cognitions may lead to emotional problems. Cognitive theorists have helped spawn the development of cognitive behavior therapy, a model of treatment that integrates behavioral and cognitive techniques, as well as developing their own particular methods of therapy. Cognitive theorists have had less impact on our understanding or treatment of certain disorders like schizophrenia. Questions remain about whether distorted cognitions cause emotional problems like depression or merely result from these problems.

Humanistic-Existential Perspectives

Humanistic and existential theorists focus on the importance of conscious awareness and the uniqueness of the individual. They also believe in free choice and personal responsibility for one's actions. Humanists emphasize self-actualization, the inner drive to achieve one's potential. Existentialists focus on the importance of authenticity, living according to the dictates of one's own values and goals.

Frankl focused on the person's pursuit of meaning in life, and he developed a model of therapy, called logotherapy, that helps people find meaningful ways of talking about and organizing their lives. Maslow believed we are all motivated by the inner drive of self-actualization and that there is a hierarchy of needs traversing the basic biological needs to the highest levels of self-actualization. Rogers developed self theory, which views the self, the center of experience, as the innate, organized, and consistent basis by which people relate to others and to the world. The self strives to develop its unique potential but may be fettered by conditional positive regard, which leads to denial or disownment of parts of the self that meet with rebuke from others.

Sociocultural Perspectives

Proponents of the sociocultural perspective focus on socioeconomic, sociocultural, and ethnic factors in abnormal behavior.

Sociocultural theorists look for causes of abnormal behavior in society rather than the individual. People become disturbed when they are subjected to extreme social pressures, such as poverty, prolonged unemployment, discrimination, and social decay. The more radical psychosocial theorists, such as Szasz, dispute the existence of mental illness, believing mental illness is merely a label that society uses to stigmatize people whose behavior is socially deviant.

Psychological theories may not focus adequately on the challenges faced by immigrants—and native groups who become ethnic minorities—in adapting to their new societies. Theories of the relationships between acculturation and adjustment include the melting pot theory and bicultural theory.

Biological Perspectives

Biological perspectives focus on biological factors in abnormal behavior. In some cases, most notably Alzheimer's disease, biological factors are implicated as direct causes. Other cases reflect an interaction of biological, psychological, and other factors.

The nervous system is composed of neurons that communicate with one another through means of chemical messengers, called neurotransmitters, that transmit nervous impulses across the gaps, or synapses, between neurons. The balance of neurotransmitters in the brain is believed to play an important role in various mental disorders, but the precise role is not yet determined. The biological aspects of anxiety involve the activity of the autonomic nervous system, especially the sympathetic branch of the system.

Behavior geneticists use various types of studies, including kinship studies, twin studies, and adoption studies, to explore the influence of genetics on abnormal behavior patterns.

Biological perspectives have had an important influence on conceptions and treatment of abnormal behavior. Abnormal behavior may reflect, in many cases, the interaction of biological, psychological, and other factors. The diathesis–stress hypothesis posits roles for genetic vulnerability (the diathesis) and stress in the development of abnormal behavior.

SCORING KEY FOR THE EXPECTANCY-FOR-SUCCESS SCALE

To calculate your total score for the expectancy-for-success scale, first reverse the scores for the following items: 1, 2, 4, 6, 7, 8, 14, 15, 17, 18, 24, 27, and 28. In other words, change a 1 to a 5; a 2 to a 4; leave a 3 as is; change a 4 to a 2; and a 5 to a 1. Now add up the scores.

The higher your score, the greater your expectancy for success in the future—and, presumably, the more motivated you will be to accept and meet challenges.

Fibel and Hale administered their test to psychology students. Women's scores ranged from 65 to 143. Men's scores ranged from 81 to 138. The average score for both genders was 112 (112.32 for women and 112.15 for men).

Barbara Dixon Drewa, Hindsight, 1988. Fischbach Gallery. New York.

CHAPTER OUTLINE

3

Classification and Assessment of Abnormal Behavior

LEARNING OBJECTIVES

When you have completed your study of Chapter 3, you should be able to:

1. Discuss historical origins of modern diagnostic systems.

2. Define the concept of "mental disorders" in the DSM system and show how the diagnostic system adheres to the medical model.

3. Describe the features of the DSM system.

4. Explain the multiaxial feature of the DSM system.

5. Describe the strengths and weaknesses of the DSM.

6. Discuss sociocultural and ethnic factors in the classification of abnormal behavior.

7. Explain three approaches to demonstrating the reliability of methods of assessment.

8. Explain three approaches to demonstrating the validity of methods of assessment.

9. Discuss sociocultural and ethnic factors in the assessment of abnormal behavior.

10. Describe what is meant by a structured interview.

11. Describe the elements of the mental status examination.

12. Describe the use of standardized interview techniques.

13. Discuss the nature and value of psychological tests.

14. Discuss the history and features of the Stanford-Binet Intelligence Scale.

15. Describe the features of the Wechsler Scales.

16. Distinguish between self-report and projective personality assessment techniques.

17. Discuss the history, features, reliability, and validity of personality tests, focusing on the MMPI and the Rorschach.

18. Explain how various response sets can distort test results.

19. Describe the use of psychological tests in the assessment of neuropsychological functioning.

20. Discuss the advantages and limitations of behavioral assessment.

21. Describe the following techniques: the behavioral interview, self-monitoring, use of contrived measures, direct observation, and behavioral rating scales.

22. Discuss the use of thought diaries and questionnaires that assess automatic thoughts and dysfunctional attitudes.

23. Explain the relationships between emotional states and physiological measurement.

24. Describe contemporary brain-imaging techniques.

S ystems of classification of abnormal behavior date to ancient times. Hippocrates classified abnormal behaviors on the basis of his theory of humors. Although his theory proved to be flawed, he arrived at some diagnostic categories that generally correspond to those in modern diagnostic systems. His description of melancholia, for example, is similar to present conceptions of depression; his description of "mania" resembles what is now called a manic episode. Hippocrates's conception of phrenitis describes behaviors that today would roughly correspond to schizophrenia.

It is true that the most widely used contemporary system for classifying abnormal behaviors can trace some of its roots to a system of classification proposed more than 2,000 years ago. Hippocrates, the physician of the golden age of Greece, proposed a number of categories that have since been revised but remain in use.

During the Middle Ages some "authorities" classified abnormal behaviors according to those that represented possession and those that represented natural causes. The 19th-century German psychiatrist Emil Kraepelin is generally considered the first modern theorist to develop a comprehensive model of classification based on the distinctive features, or "symptoms," associated with abnormal behavior patterns. The most commonly used classification system today is largely an outgrowth and extension of Kraepelin's work: the *Diagnostic and Statistical Manual of Mental Disorders* (DSM), which is published by the American Psychiatric Association. The DSM system classifies abnormal behavior patterns as mental disorders on the basis of specified diagnostic criteria.

Why is it important to classify abnormal behavior? Classification is the core of science (Barlow, 1991). Without labeling and organizing patterns of abnormal behavior, researchers could not communicate with one another, and progress toward understanding these disorders would come to a halt. Moreover, important decisions are made on the basis of classification. For example, treatment techniques vary according to the kinds of problems shown by clients. Certain patterns of abnormal behavior respond better to one therapy than another. Classification also helps clinicians predict behavior. Some patterns of abnormal behavior, such as schizophrenia, follow more or less predictable courses of development. Classification also helps researchers identify populations with similar patterns of abnormal behavior. By classifying groups of people as depressed, for example, researchers might be able to identify common factors that help to explain the origins of depression.

This chapter reviews the classification and assessment of abnormal behavior. First we examine the DSM system. We then consider the basic requirements for methods of assessment—that they be reliable and valid. Next we explore methods of assessment that clinicians use to arrive at diagnostic impressions, including interviews, psychological testing, self-report questionnaires, behavioral measures, and physiological measures. The role of assessment, however, goes further than classification. A careful assessment provides a wealth of information about clients' personalities and cognitive functioning. This information helps clinicians acquire a broader understanding of their clients' problems and recommend appropriate treatment.

CLASSIFICATION OF ABNORMAL BEHAVIOR

The DSM was introduced in 1952 and has been revised several times. The present version is the fourth edition of the DSM, which is called DSM-IV. Another common system of classification, published by the World Health Organization, is used mainly for compiling statistics on the worldwide occurrence of disorders: the *International Classification of Diseases* (ICD). The DSM was designed to be compatible with the ICD. DSM diagnoses can be easily coded in the ICD system as well.

We focus on the DSM because of its widespread adoption by mental health professionals. However, many psychologists and other professionals criticize the DSM on several grounds, such as relying too strongly on the medical model. Our focus on the DSM reflects recognition of its widespread use, not an endorsement.

In the DSM, people are regarded as exhibiting *psychopathology* or abnormal behavior patterns—or, in the medical jargon of the manual, as having "mental disorders"—if they experience emotional distress or show significant impairment in functioning. Impaired functioning involves difficulties in meeting responsibilities at work, within the family, or within society at large. It also includes behavior that places people at risk for personal suffering, pain, or death.

Diagnosis of mental disorders within the DSM system also requires that the behavior pattern not represent an expected or culturally appropriate response to a stressful event, such as the loss of a loved one. People who show signs of bereavement or grief following the death of loved ones are not considered disordered, even if their behavior is signifi-

cantly impaired. If their behavior remains significantly impaired over an extended period of time, however, a diagnosis of a mental disorder might be appropriate.

The DSM and Models of Abnormal Behavior

The DSM system adheres in some important respects to the medical model. It treats abnormal behaviors as signs or symptoms of underlying pathologies called mental disorders. Unlike the strictest form of the medical model, however, the manual does not assume that abnormal behaviors necessarily reflect biological causes or defects. It recognizes that the causes of most mental disorders remain uncertain: Some disorders may have purely biological causes. Some may have psychological causes. Still others are likely to reflect a multifactorial model that reflects the interaction of biological, psychological, social (socioeconomic, sociocultural, and ethnic), and physical environmental factors.

Nor does the DSM subscribe to a particular theory of abnormal behavior. With the introduction in 1980 of the third edition of the DSM, the DSM-III, terms linked to specific theories (such as **neurosis**, which was originally a psychoanalytic term) were deemphasized in favor of atheoretical descriptive terms like "anxiety disorders" and "mood disorders." Disorders are now classified on the basis of their clinical features and behavior patterns, not on the basis of inferences about underlying theoretical mechanisms. Because the DSM does not endorse particular theoretical models unless evidence of causal factors is overwhelming, it can be used by practitioners of diverse theoretical persuasions, who can agree on what constitutes anxiety disorders, mood disorders, and schizophrenic disorders, even if they disagree on their causes and proper treatments.

Features of the DSM

The DSM is descriptive, not explanatory. It describes the diagnostic features—or, in medical terms, symptoms—of abnormal behaviors rather than attempting to explain their origins. Let us consider a number of features of the DSM classification system.

Specific diagnostic criteria are used. The clinician arrives at a diagnosis by matching clients' behaviors with the criteria that define particular patterns of abnormal behavior ("mental disorders"). Diagnostic categories are described in terms of *essential features* (criteria that must be present for the diagnosis to be made) and *associated features* (criteria that are often associated with the disorder but not essential to making a diagnosis). An example of diagnostic criteria for Conduct Disorder, a disorder of childhood or adolescence, is shown in Table 3.1. The diagnostic criteria in the text are based upon the draft criteria for the DSM-IV that were available at the time of this writing and that had been submitted to the governing board of the American Psychiatric Association for final approval. It was expected that any changes between the draft criteria and the final criteria would be minimal.

Abnormal behavior patterns that share clinical features are grouped together. Abnormal behavior patterns are categorized according to their shared clinical features, not theoretical speculation about their causes. Abnormal behavior patterns that are chiefly characterized by anxiety are classified as anxiety disorders. Behaviors chiefly characterized by disruptions in mood are categorized as mood disorders.

The system is "multiaxial." The DSM employs a multiaxial, or multidimensional, system of assessment that provides a broad range of information about the individual's functioning, not just a diagnosis. The system contains the following axes:

1. *Axis I includes a classification of Clinical **Syndromes**,* which incorporates a wide range of diagnostic classes such as anxiety disorders, mood disorders, schizophrenia and other psychotic disorders, adjustment disorders, and disorders usually first diagnosed during infancy, childhood, or adolescence. Axis I also includes a classification of *Other Conditions That May Be a Focus of Clinical Attention.* These are conditions or problems that may be the focus of diagnosis and treatment, such as relationship problems, academic or occupational problems, or uncomplicated bereavement, but do not constitute definable mental disorders. These conditions also include a category of psychological factors that affect medical conditions, such as anxiety that exacerbates an asthmatic condition, or depressive symptoms that delay recovery from surgery.

2. *Axis II, Personality Disorders,* includes the more enduring or chronic patterns of maladaptive behavior that generally impair interpersonal relationships and social adaptation, including antisocial, paranoid, narcissistic, and borderline personality disorders.

Separating the diagnostic categories into two axes provides greater flexibility in reaching diagnostic impressions. People may be given either Axis I or Axis II diagnoses, or a combination of the two when both apply. A person may receive a diagnosis of an anxiety disorder (Axis I) and a second diagnosis of a personality disorder (Axis II) if the diagnostic criteria for both are met, for example. When multiple diagnoses are given, the *principal diagnosis* is the condition that apparently precipitated the evaluation and that in most cases is the main focus of treatment.

Clients may also receive multiple diagnoses within axes. For example, they may be given Axis I diagnoses for a substance abuse disorder and a mood disorder, if both apply. When evaluating children, the separation between the axes allows the clinician to distinguish between disorders involving difficulties in developing social, cognitive, and motor skills (Axis II) and those involving other developmental problems (Axis I).

3. *Axis III, General Medical Conditions,* lists medical conditions and diseases that may be important to the understanding or treatment of the individual's mental disorder. For example, if *hypothyroidism* is a direct cause of an individual's mood disorder (such as major depression), it would be coded under Axis III. Medical condi-

---

Table 3.1   Sample Diagnostic Criteria for Conduct Disorder

A. A persistent and repeated pattern of disturbed conduct involving behaviors which violate other's basic rights or social norms and rules appropriate to the individual's age, lasting for at least 6 months, which is characterized by at least three behaviors from a listing of 15 behaviors that include the following:

1. Bullying, threatening or intimidating others
2. Starting physical fights
3. Using a weapon, such as a bat, gun, or knife, that could harm others
4. Stealing with confrontation of the victim, as in a mugging, purse-snatching, armed robbery, or extortion
5. Showing physical cruelty to people
6. Showing physical cruelty to animals
7. Forcing another person into sexual activity with him or herself
8. Frequent lying or breaking of promises in the attempt to "con" others to acquire desired goods or favors or to avoid fullfilling obligations
9. Frequently violates parental prohibitions about staying out at night, beginning before age 13
10. Stealing property without actually confronting the victim, such as by shoplifting, burglary or forgery

B. If age 18 or older, person does not meet diagnostic criteria for Antisocial Personality Disorder.

Source: Adapted from DSM-IV Draft Criteria (American Psychiatric Association, 1993), p. E: 10.

tions which affect the understanding or treatment of a mental disorder but are not direct causes of the disorder are also listed on Axis III. For instance, the presence of a heart condition may determine whether a particular course of pharmacotherapy would be used with a depressed person.

4. *Axis IV, Psychosocial and Environmental Problems,* is used for listing psychosocial and environmental problems that are believed to affect the diagnosis, treatment or outcome of a mental disorder. Psychosocial and environmental problems include negative life events (such as a job termination or a marital separation or divorce), homelessness or inadequate housing, lack of social support, the death or loss of a friend, or exposure to war or disasters. Some positive life events may also be listed, such as a job promotion, but only when they create problems for the individual, such as difficulties adapting to a new job. A listing of these types of problems is found in Table 3.2.

5. *Axis V, Global Assessment of Functioning,* refers to the clinician's overall judgment of clients' psy-

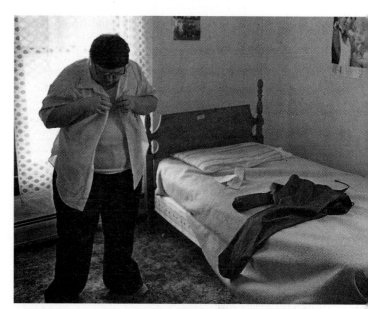

Assessment of level of functioning. The assessment of functioning takes into account the individual's ability to manage the responsibilities of daily living, such as personal hygiene and self-maintenance. Here a young retarded man is able to meet the responsibilities of living in a group home for retarded men.

Table 3.2 Psychosocial and Environmental Problems	
Problem Categories	**Examples**
Problems with Primary Support Group	Death of family members; health problems of family members; marital disruption in the form of separation, divorce, or estrangement; sexual or physical abuse within the family; child neglect; birth of a sibling
Problems Related to the Social Environment	Death or loss of a friend; social isolation or living alone; difficulties adjusting to a new culture (acculturation); discrimination; adjustment to transitions occurring during the life cycle, such as retirement
Educational Problems	Illiteracy; academic difficulties; problems with teachers or classmates; inadequate or impoverished school environment
Occupational Problems	Work-related problems including stressful work loads and problems with bosses or coworkers; changes in employment; job dissatisfaction; threat of loss of job; unemployment
Housing Problems	Inadequate housing or homelessness; living in an unsafe neighborhood; problems with neighbors or landlord
Economic Problems	Financial hardships or extreme poverty; inadequate welfare support
Problems with Access to Health Care Services	Inadequate health care services or availability of health insurance; difficulties with transportation to health care facilities
Problems Related to Interaction with the Legal System/Crime	Arrest or imprisonment; becoming involved in a lawsuit or trial; being a victim of crime
Other Psychosocial Problems	Natural or human-made disasters; war or other hostilities; problems with caregivers outside the family, such as counselors, social workers and physicians; lack of availability of social service agencies

Source: Adapted from DSM-IV Draft Criteria (American Psychiatric Association, 1993), p. D: 5.

chological, social, and occupational functioning. Using a scale similar to that shown in Table 3.3, the clinician rates clients' current functioning and highest level of previous functioning. The level of current functioning is taken to indicate the current need for treatment or intensity of care. The level of highest functioning is suggestive of the level of functioning that might be restored.

An overview of the multiaxial system is shown in Table 3.4. Table 3.5 provides an example of a multiaxial diagnosis using the system.

Evaluation of the DSM System

Two basic criteria used in evaluating the value of a diagnostic system such as the DSM are its reliability and validity. A diagnostic system may be considered **reliable**, or consistent, if various diagnosticians using the system are likely to arrive at the same diagnoses when they evaluate the same cases. Versions of the DSM system that preceded the 1980 introduction of the DSM-III generally suffered from poor reliability. Skilled diagnosticians often disagreed on the correct diagnoses for clients, largely because the diagnostic criteria were often fuzzy or ambiguous.

The DSM-III was based on more specific ("tighter") diagnostic criteria than the DSM-II and showed greater interrater reliability (i.e., agreement among diagnosticians). The DSM-III showed weak reliability in the diagnosis of the Axis II personality disorders, however (Drake & Vaillant, 1985). We await further evidence to determine the reliability of the DSM-IV in diagnosing the personality disorders.

The issue of **validity**, or accuracy, of diagnostic categories is more complex. How are we to know whether a diagnosis is valid or accurate? A physician

Table 3.3	Global Assessment of Functioning Scale (GAF)	
Code	**Severity of Symptoms**	**Examples**
91-100	Superior functioning across a wide variety of activities of daily life	Lacks symptoms Handles life problems without them "getting out of hand"
81–90	Absent or minimal symptoms, no more than everyday problems or concerns	Mild anxiety before exams Occasional argument with family members
71–80	Transient and predictable reactions to stressful events, OR no more than slight impairment in functioning	Difficulty concentrating after argument with family Temporarily falls behind in schoolwork
61–70	Some mild symptoms, OR some difficulty in social, occupational, or school functioning, but functioning pretty well	Feels down, mild insomnia Occasional truancy or theft within household
51–60	Moderate symptoms, OR moderate difficulties in social, occupational, or school functioning	Occasional panic attacks Few friends, conflicts with co-workers
41–50	Serious symptoms, OR any serious impairment in social, occupational, or school functioning	Suicidal thoughts, frequent shoplifting Unable to hold job, has no friends
31–40	Some impairment in reality testing or communication, OR major impairment in several areas	Speech illogical Depressed man unable to work, neglects family, and avoids friends
21–30	Strong influence on behavior of delusions or hallucinations, OR serious impairment in communication or judgment, OR inability to function in almost all areas	Grossly inappropriate behavior, speech sometimes incoherent Stays in bed all day, no job, home, or friends
11–20	Some danger of hurting self or others, OR occasionally fails to maintain personal hygiene, OR gross impairment in communication	Suicidal gestures, frequently violent Smears feces
1–10	Persistent danger of severely hurting self or others, OR persistent inability to maintain minimal personal hygiene, OR seriously suicidal act	Largely incoherent or mute Serious suicidal attempt, recurrent violence

Source: American Psychiatric Association: Diagnostic and Statistical Manual of Mental Disorders, Third Edition, Revised. *Washington, DC: American Psychiatric Association, 1987.*

Table 3.4   The Multiaxial Classification System of the DSM-IV

Axis	Type of Information	Brief Description
Axis I	Clinical Syndromes	The patterns of abnormal behavior ("mental disorders") that impair functioning and are stressful to the individual
	Other Conditions That May Be a Focus of Clinical Attention	Other problems that may be the focus of diagnosis or treatment but do not constitute mental disorders, such as academic, vocational, or social problems, and psychological factors that affect medical conditions (such as delayed recovery from surgery due to depressive symptoms)
Axis II	Personality Disorders	Deeply ingrained, maladaptive ways of perceiving others and behavior that are stressful to the individual or those who relate to the individual. Notable personality traits can be listed here, even when no personality disorder per se is diagnosed.
Axis III	General Medical Conditions	Chronic and acute illnesses and medical conditions that are important to the understanding or treatment of the mental disorder or that play a direct role in causing the mental disorder
Axis IV	Psychosocial and Environmental Problems	Problems in the social or physical environment that affect the diagnosis, treatment, and outcome of mental disorders
Axis V	Global Assessment of Functioning	Overall judgment of current functioning with respect to psychological, social, and occupational functioning; clinician may also rate the highest level of functioning occurring for at least a few months during the past year

Source: Adapted from DSM-IV Draft Criteria *(American Psychiatric Association, 1993).*

may seek to confirm the validity of a diagnosis of a physical disorder through a laboratory test. If blood samples are taken and the suspected microbe is found, the diagnosis may be confirmed. No such laboratory tests exist for psychological disorders.

The discovery of **biological markers** for psychological disorders would bolster the disease model

Table 3.5   Example of a Diagnosis in the Multiaxial DSM-IV System

Axis	
Axis I	Generalized Anxiety Disorder
Axis II	Dependent Personality Disorder
Axis III	Hypertension
Axis IV	Problem with Primary Support Group (marital separation); Occupational Problem (unemployment)
Axis V	GAF = 62

Source: Table from Psychology, *Fourth Edition by Spencer A. Rathus, copyright © 1990 by Holt, Rinehart, and Winston, Inc., reproduced by permission of the publisher.*

of abnormal behavior. Today the most appropriate test of the validity of the diagnostic system is its correspondence with behavioral observations, not biochemical analysis. Researchers generally approach the question of validity in terms of whether or not the behavior of people who are given particular diagnoses differs in predictable ways from that of people given other diagnoses. Certain DSM classes, such as anxiety disorders, appear to have generally good validity in terms of grouping people with similar behaviors (Turner et al., 1986). The validity of some other diagnostic classes remains to be demonstrated.

The predictive validity of the DSM system may be tested by determining whether or not it is useful in *predicting* the course the disorder is likely to follow or response to treatment. Evidence is accumulating that persons classified in certain categories respond better to certain types of medication. Persons with bipolar disorder, for example, respond reasonably well to lithium (see Chapter 7). Specific forms of psychological treatment may also be more effective with certain diagnostic groupings. For example, persons who are classified as *specific phobics* are generally highly responsive to behavioral techniques for reducing fears (see Chapter 5).

Another yardstick by which a diagnostic system is evaluated is its degree of coverage, or its ability to place cases of abnormal behavior into suitable categories (Blashfield & Draguns, 1976). A system with low coverage essentially "dumps" or sweeps aside a large number of cases that don't precisely fit existing categories into a catchall or so-called wastebasket category like "unspecified disorder." Attempts to increase the coverage of the system may occur at the expense of reducing the "purity" of the diagnostic categories, however. Think of it this way: The more cases with slightly varying patterns you try to squeeze into a given category, the less similar the cases assigned to the particular category are likely to be.

The DSM-III contained tighter diagnostic criteria than its predecessors, thereby increasing the diagnostic purity of the categories but at the expense of reduced coverage. In contrast, coverage of Axis II personality disorders apparently increased with revised criteria in the DSM-III-R, such that there were fewer unspecified cases of personality disorders, but at the expense of increasing the number of cases that seem to fit two or more diagnostic categories, which reduces purity (Morey, 1988). It is too early to tell how diagnostic coverage and purity will be affected under the DSM-IV.

Advantages and Disadvantages of the DSM System

Many consider the major advantage of the DSM to be its designation of specific diagnostic criteria. The DSM permits the clinician to readily match a client's complaints and associated features with specific standards to see which diagnosis fits the case. The multiaxial system paints a comprehensive picture of clients by integrating information concerning abnormal behaviors, medical conditions that affect abnormal behaviors, psychosocial and environmental problems that may be stressful to the individual, and level of functioning. The possibility of multiple diagnoses prompts clinicians to consider presenting problems (Axis I) along with the relatively long-standing personality problems (Axis II) that may contribute to them.

Criticisms have also been leveled against the DSM system. Questions remain about the system's reliability and validity. Other challenges have been posed as well.

The DSM system is based on a medical approach to classification: Problem behaviors are viewed as symptoms of underlying psychological disorders in much the same way that physical symptoms are signs of underlying physical disorders. The very use of the term *diagnosis* presumes that the medical model is an appropriate basis for classifying abnormal behaviors. Some clinicians feel that behavior, abnormal or otherwise, is too complex and meaningful to be treated merely as symptomatic. They assert that the medical model focuses too much on what may happen within the individual and not enough on external influences on behavior, such as social factors (socioeconomic, sociocultural, and ethnic) and physical environmental factors.

Another concern is that the medical model focuses on categorizing mental disorders rather than describing people's behavioral strengths and weaknesses. The DSM aims to determine what "disorders" people "have"—not what they can "do" in particular situations. An alternative model of assessment, the behavioral model, focuses more on behaviors than on underlying processes—more on what people "do" than on what they "are" or "have." Behaviorists and behavior therapists also use the DSM, of course, in part because mental health centers and health insurance carriers require the use of a diagnostic code, in part because they want to communicate in a common language with practitioners of other theoretical persuasions. Many behavior therapists view the DSM diagnostic code as a convenient means of labeling patterns of abnormal behavior, a shorthand for a more extensive behavioral analysis of the problem.

Sociocultural and Ethnic Factors in the Classification of Abnormal Behavior

The DSM aims to be atheoretical, but the very designation of behaviors as normal or abnormal rests on cultural and professional assumptions. Many observers (e.g., Eisenbruch, 1992; Fabrega, 1992) have argued that the DSM should become more sensitive to diversity in culture and ethnicity. The behaviors that are included as diagnostic criteria in the DSM are determined by consensus of mostly U.S.-trained psychiatrists, psychologists, and social workers. Had the American Psychiatric Association asked Asian-trained or Latin American-trained professionals to develop their diagnostic manual, for example, there might have been some different or some revised diagnostic categories.

In fairness to the DSM, however, the latest edition—the DSM-IV—does place greater emphasis than did earlier editions on weighing cultural factors when assessing abnormal behavior. It recognizes that clinicians who are unfamiliar with an individual's cultural background may incorrectly classify the individual's behavior as abnormal when in fact it falls within the normal spectrum in the individual's culture. In Chapter 1 we noted that the same behavior may be deemed normal in one culture but abnormal in another. As an example (see Chapter 1), certain cultures may deem the experiencing of hallucinations (for example, hearing the voice of a deceased relative) in the context of bereavement as normal rather than a feature of abnormal behavior. The DSM-IV also recognizes the abnormal behaviors may take different forms in different cultures and that some abnormal behavior patterns are culturally-specific (see feature, "Culture-Bound Syndromes").

To explore cultural variations in diagnostic practices, Baskin (1984) asked mental health professionals in Europe, Asia, Oceania, and North America to indicate whether the people described in several case vignettes were mentally ill and, if so, to fix an appropriate diagnosis. His results showed wide variation among respondents from country to country and

Ataques de Nervios.   Researchers in Puerto Rico have identified a local syndrome termed *ataques de nervios* ("attack of nerves"), which is similar in some ways to the DSM concept of panic attacks. Unlike panic attacks, however, *ataques de nervios* follow social stresses and do not seem to come out of the blue.

MULTICULTURAL PERSPECTIVES

Culture-Bound Syndromes

There are more things in heaven and earth, Horatio,
Than are dreamt of in your philosophy.

Shakespeare, *Hamlet*

There are also more patterns of abnormal behavior than those described in the *Diagnostic and Statistical Manual* of the American Psychiatric Association— even more than are found in the *International Classification of Diseases* of the World Health Organization.

Some patterns of psychological distress are limited to just one, or a few, cultures (American Psychiatric Association, 1993). These **culture-bound** disorders are believed to be a manifestation, however exaggerated, of common superstitions and belief patterns within the particular culture or cultures. For example, the psychiatric syndrome **taijin-kyofu-sho**, or TKS, is common in Japan but rare elsewhere. TKS is characterized by excessive fear that one may behave in ways that will embarrass or offend other people (McNally et al., 1990). People with TKS may dread blushing in front of others for fear of causing them embarrassment, not for fear of embarrassing themselves. In our culture, an excessive fear of social embarrassment is called a *social phobia* (see Chapter 5). Unlike people with TKS, however, social phobics have excessive concern they will be rejected by, or embarrassed in front of, others, not that they will embarrass other people. People with TKS may also fear

mumbling thoughts aloud, lest they inadvertently offend others (Prince & Tcheng-Laroche, 1987). The syndrome primarily affects young Japanese men and is believed to be related to the Japanese cultural emphasis on not embarrassing others (McNally et al., 1990). Chang (1984) reports that TKS is diagnosed in 7 to 36% of the people who are treated by psychiatrists in Japan.

Taijin-Kyofu-Sho.   TKS is a psychiatric syndrome that is common in Japan but rare elsewhere. It is characterized by excessive fear that one may embarrass or offend other people. The syndrome primarily affects young Japanese men and is apparently connected with the Japanese cultural emphasis on avoiding embarrassing other people.

within countries in terms of whether or not behavior patterns were considered normal or abnormal, and in terms of the diagnostic categories that were used to classify people deemed abnormal. If a diagnostic system is to be used with people from other cultures than the one in which it was developed, evidence should be gathered that it too is reliable and valid with the culture to which it is applied. Some categories in the DSM may be valid in other cultures; others may not (Fabrega, 1990; Good & Good, 1985; Rogler et al., 1991).

Psychological distress may also be experienced differently in different cultures (Rubio-Stipec et al., 1989). For example, researchers in Puerto Rico have examined a culture-bound or locally identified syndrome—*ataques de nervios* ("attack of nerves") (Guarnaccia et al., 1989). Although similar in some ways to the DSM concept of panic attacks (discussed in Chapter 5), unlike panic attacks, *ataques de nervios* do not come out of the blue. Instead, they follow particular social stresses (Fabrega, 1990).

Some critics argue that recent editions of the DSM have been overzealous in the removal of concepts of abnormal behavior that are derived from particular theories, such as the concept of neurosis. Some would like to see a return to a diagnostic system that focuses more on the causes of abnormal behaviors. Description alone, such critics claim, is too superficial. Many critics likewise claim that the DSM focuses too much on current behaviors and not enough on history or childhood experiences.

The DSM system, despite its critics, has become part and parcel of the everyday practice of most U.S. mental health professionals. It may be the one reference manual that is found on the bookshelves of nearly all professionals and dog-eared from repeated use. Perhaps the DSM is best considered a work in progress, not a final product.

Now let us consider various ways of assessing abnormal behavior. We begin with a discussion of the characteristics of useful methods of assessment: reliability and validity.

CHARACTERISTICS OF METHODS OF ASSESSMENT

Important decisions are made on the basis of classification and assessment. For example, recommendations for specific treatment techniques vary according to our assessment of the problems that clients exhibit. Therefore, methods of assessment, like diagnostic categories, must be *reliable* and *valid*.

Reliability

The reliability of a method of assessment, like that of a diagnostic system, refers to its consistency. A gauge of height would be unreliable if people looked taller or shorter at every measurement. A reliable measure of abnormal behavior must also yield comparable results on different occasions. Also, different people should be able to check the yardstick and agree on the measured height of the subject. A yardstick that shrinks and expands markedly with the slightest change in temperature will be unreliable. So will one that is difficult to read.

There are three main approaches for demonstrating the reliability of assessment techniques.

■ **INTERNAL CONSISTENCY** Correlational techniques are used to show whether the different parts or items of an assessment instrument, such as a psychological test, yield results that are consistent with one another and with the technique or test as a whole. **Internal consistency** is crucial for tests that are intended to measure single traits or construct dimensions. When the individual items or parts of a test are highly correlated with each other, we can assume that they are measuring a common trait or construct. For example, a self-administered depression inventory may measure various aspects of depression. If the responses to the items are not highly correlated with each other, there is no basis for assuming that the items measure a single, common dimension or construct—in this case, depression.

One commonly used method of assessing internal consistency, **coefficient alpha**, is based on a statistical computation of the average intercorrelations (interrelationships) of all the items making up the particular test. The higher the coefficient alpha, the greater the internal consistency of the test.

Some tests are multidimensional in content. They contain subscales or factors that measure different construct dimensions. One such test is the Minnesota *Multiphasic* Personality Inventory (MMPI), which assesses various dimensions of abnormal behavior. In such cases, subscales within the test that are intended to measure individual traits, such as the hypochondriasis and depression subscales, are expected to show internal consistency. Items from one subscale need not correlate with items from other subscales, however, unless the traits they are presumed to measure are interrelated.

■ **TEMPORAL STABILITY** Reliable methods of assessment have **temporal stability** (stability over time). They yield similar results on separate occasions. We would not trust a bathroom scale that yielded different results each time we weighed ourselves—unless we had stuffed or starved ourselves between weighings. The same principle applies to psychological tests. In the case of tests, temporal stability is measured by means of **test–retest reliability**. Correlational methods compare scores obtained on different testing occasions. The higher the correlation, the greater the temporal stability or test–retest reliability of the test.

Assessment of test–retest reliability is most important in the measurement of traits that are assumed to remain stable over time, such as intelligence and aptitude. Yet measures of test–retest reliability on intelligence and aptitude tests can be compromised because of a "warm-up effect"; that is, scores can improve due to familiarity with the test.

■ **INTERRATER RELIABILITY Interrater reliability**—also referred to as **interjudge reliability**—is usually of greatest importance in making diagnostic decisions and for measures requiring ratings of behavior. A diagnostic system is not reliable unless expert raters agree as to their diagnoses on the basis of the system. Two teachers may be asked to use a behavioral rating scale to evaluate a child's aggressiveness, hyperactivity, and sociability. The level of agreement between the raters would be an index of the reliability of the scale.

Validity

The validity of assessment techniques or measures refers to the degree to which the instruments in question measure what they are intended to measure. There are various kinds of validity, such as *content, construct,* and *criterion validity.*

■ **CONTENT VALIDITY** The **content validity** of an assessment technique is the degree to which its content covers a representative sample of the behaviors associated with the construct dimension or trait in question. For example, depression includes features such as sadness and lack of participation in previously enjoyed activities. To have content validity, techniques that assess depression should thus have features or items that address these areas. One type of content validity, called **face validity**, is the degree to which questions or test items bear an apparent relationship to the constructs or traits they purport to measure. A face-valid item on a test of assertiveness could be, "I have little difficulty standing up for my rights." An item that lacks face validity as a measure of assertiveness could read, "I usually subscribe to magazines that contain features about world events."

The limitation of face validity is its reliance on subjective judgment in determining whether or not the test measures what it is supposed to measure. The apparent or face validity of an assessment technique is not sufficient to establish its scientific value. A scientific test may also be valid if its results relate to some standard or criterion, even though the items themselves do not have high face validity. This brings us to criterion validity.

■ **CRITERION VALIDITY** The **criterion validity** of an assessment technique is the degree to which responses correlate with an independent, external criterion (standard) of what the technique is intended to assess. There are two general types of criterion validity: concurrent validity and predictive validity.

Concurrent validity is the degree to which test responses predict scores on criterion measures taken at about the same time. Most psychologists presume that intelligence is in part responsible for academic success. The concurrent validity of intelligence test scores is thus frequently studied by correlating test scores with criteria such as school grades and teacher ratings of cognitive abilities. A self-report scale of depression might be validated against judgments of experts based on concurrent interviews.

Predictive validity is the ability of a diagnostic technique or test to predict future behavior. A test of academic aptitude may be validated in terms of its ability to predict school performance in that particular area. General intelligence tests taken during childhood should predict school grades in general. They turn out to be correlated at a high enough level to be acceptable in demonstrating predictive validity (Sattler, 1988). The correlation is less than perfect, however, because the measures are not perfectly reliable and factors other than intelligence, such as motivation to succeed and level of adjustment, also affect school performance (Anastasi, 1983; Hrncir et al., 1985; Scarr, 1981).

■ **CONSTRUCT VALIDITY** **Construct validity** is the degree to which a test or assessment technique corresponds to the theoretical model of the underlying construct or trait it purports to measure. Consider problems in determining the construct validity of a test that purports to measure anxiety. Anxiety is not a concrete object or phenomenon. Anxiety cannot be measured directly, counted, weighed, or touched. Anxiety is a theoretical construct that helps to explain phenomena like a pounding heart or sudden inability to speak when you ask an attractive person out on a date. Anxiety may be indirectly measured by means such as self-report (rating one's own level of anxiety) and physiological measures (measuring the level of sweat on the palms of one's hands).

The construct validity of a test or measure of anxiety requires that the test response correlate with other aspects of behavior that are theoretically associated with the construct of anxiety. Let us assume that your theoretical model predicts that highly anxious college students should experience greater difficulties than low-anxious students in speaking coherently when asking someone for a date, but not when they are merely rehearsing the invitation in private. The degree to which the speech behavior of high and low scorers on a test of anxiety fit these predicted patterns would provide a measure of the construct validity of the test.

Assessment techniques can be highly reliable but invalid. Nineteenth-century **phrenologists** believed that they could gauge people's personalities by measuring the bumps on their heads. Their calipers provided reliable measures of their subjects' bumps

and protrusions; the measurements, however, did not provide valid estimates of subjects' psychological traits. The phrenologists were bumping in the dark, so to speak. A test of musical aptitude might have excellent reliability but be invalid as a measure of general intelligence.

 A psychological test can indeed be highly reliable yet also invalid. A test of musical aptitude may have superb reliability but be invalid as a measure of general intelligence or of height.

Sociocultural and Ethnic Factors in the Assessment of Abnormal Behavior

Researchers and clinicians also need to be aware of sociocultural and ethnic factors when they assess personality and psychological disorders. Information-gathering techniques may be reliable and valid within one culture but not within another, even when they are translated accurately (Kleinman, 1987).

For example, do standard measures of psychological functioning in our own culture apply to people around the world and to people from cultural and ethnic minorities within the United States? In one study, Chan (1991) administered a Chinese-language version of the Beck Depression Inventory (BDI), a widely used inventory of depression in the United States, to a sample of Chinese students and psychiatric patients in Hong Kong. The Chinese BDI met tests of reliability, as judged by internal consistency, and of validity, as judged by its ability to distinguish depressives from nondepressives among a small sample of Chinese psychiatric patients. Yet other investigators found that Chinese people in both Hong Kong and the People's Republic of China tended to achieve higher scores on the Chinese MMPI's F subscale (Cheung et al., 1991), which includes items infrequently endorsed by U.S. samples that are suggestive of deviant responses (Cheung et al., 1991). The higher F-scale scores of Chinese subjects appeared to reflect cultural differences, however, rather than greater psychopathology.

Other investigators found a greater prevalence of depression among Mexican Americans than among non-Hispanic white Americans in Los Angeles, as measured by the CES-D, a commonly used measure of depression (Garcia & Marks, 1989). Here again the meaning of this difference was unclear. The difference may have reflected semantic or sociocultural factors rather than differences in the prevalences of

Phrenology. In the 19th century, some people believed mental faculties and abilities were based in certain parts of the brain and that people's acumen in such faculties could be assessed by gauging the protrusions and indentations of the skull.

depression (Fabrega, 1990). Researchers thus need to disentangle psychopathology from sociocultural factors (Fabrega, 1992).

A review of widely used diagnostic instruments for assessing abnormal behavior revealed that most (8 of 11) made references to cultural factors in helping evaluators make diagnostic judgments (López & Núñez, 1987). For example, 6 of 10 instruments for diagnosing schizophrenia require the user to determine that beliefs and perceptions which may be judged as delusional or hallucinatory are not shared by other members of the person's cultural group. In some Native-American cultures, hallucinations during tribal rituals are common and are not indicative of schizophrenia. Similarly, speech or thought patterns deemed abnormal within our culture might be considered normal in others. As an example, pressured speech (speaking so fast that it seems as if the brain is racing ahead of the person's ability to form

Are hallucinations features of abnormal behavior? In some Native American cultures, hallucinations during tribal rituals are common and are not indicative of schizophrenia or other patterns of abnormal behavior. Perceptions are usually not regarded as hallucinatory when they are shared by other members of the individual's cultural group.

words) may be taken as a sign of manic behavior in the United States at large, but may represent normative speaking patterns among certain sociocultural groups, such as the Amish (Egeland et al., 1983).

Most diagnostic schedules consider culture to some degree, but researchers believe that they fail to provide adequate norms for different cultural and ethnic groups. Translations of instruments should not only translate words; they should also provide instructions that encourage examiners to address the importance of cultural beliefs, norms, and values, so that diagnosticians and interviewers will be prompted to consider the individual's background seriously when making assessments of abnormal behavior patterns.

Interviewers need also to be sensitized to problems that can arise when interviews are conducted in a language other than the client's mother tongue (Fabrega, 1990). Hispanic-American schizophrenics, for example, appeared more severely disturbed when they were interviewed in English than in Spanish (Marcos et al., 1973). Problems can also arise when interviewers who use a second language fail to appreciate the idioms and subtleties of the language. The first author recalls a case in a U.S. mental hospital in which the interviewer, a foreign-born and trained psychiatrist, reported that a patient exhibited the delusional belief that he was outside his body. This assessment was based on the patient's response to a question posed by the psychiatrist. The psychiatrist had asked the patient if he was feeling anxious and the patient replied, "Yes, Doc, I feel like I'm jumping out of my skin at times."

THE CLINICAL INTERVIEW

The interview is the most widely used means of assessment. It is employed by all helping professionals and paraprofessionals. The interview, moreover, is usually the client's first face-to-face contact with a clinician.

The interview is usually initiated by a phone call made by the client or someone who is concerned about the client's behavior—perhaps a family member, a member of the clergy, or a social service agency. A telephone screening might be used to determine whether it seems appropriate to schedule the client for a face-to-face interview, or whether another agency might be better suited to evaluate the problem.

A client who would apparently profit from the services offered by the agency is scheduled for an

intake interview. The intake provides the clinician an opportunity to learn more about the client's **presenting problem** and history. On the basis of this information, the interviewer may arrive at an initial diagnostic impression and recommend treatment or further evaluation.

The primary means of obtaining clinically useful information is a **structured interview**. The interviewer asks a fairly standard series of questions to gather information about the client's presenting problems, psychological state, life circumstances, and history. The interview may cover a wide range of topics and vary in structure from client to client, but it usually follows a plan and is designed to gather essential information. Most interviewers are reasonably flexible, however, because no two clients are alike. Some clients are cooperative; others are stubborn or reticent. Some are insightful; others offer little insight. Some need immediate reassurance; others show little interest in their problems or the proceedings.

Clinicians often begin by asking clients to describe the presenting complaint in their own words. They may say something like, "Can you describe to me the problems you've been having lately?" (Therapists learn not to ask, "What brings you here?" to avoid receiving answers like, "A car," "A bus," or "My social worker.") The clinician will then usually probe aspects of the presenting complaint, such as behavioral abnormalities and feelings of discomfort, the circumstances regarding the onset of the problem, history of past episodes, and how the problem affects the client's daily functioning. The clinician may explore possible precipitating events, such as changes in life circumstances, social relationships, employment, or schooling.

The interviewer encourages the client to describe the problem in her or his own words in order to understand it from the client's point of view. If the client is a child, the parent usually describes the problem and its history. The therapist may still interview the child to ascertain how the child views the problem.

The interview is also influenced by the interviewer's theoretical framework. A behaviorally oriented interviewer might seek detailed information about the events that precede and follow the occurrence of the problem behavior—searching for stimuli that trigger the problem behavior and for reinforcements that maintain it.

Consider the case of Pamela:

A young woman of 19, Pamela, is seen for an initial evaluation. She complains of fear of driving her car across a bridge on a route that she must take to attend college. She reports that she fears "freezing up" at the wheel and causing an accident if she were to drive across the bridge. Upon interview, she reports that the problem began 6 months earlier, shortly after she experienced intense anxiety driving across a different bridge. It nearly caused her to lose control of the car. Now she takes three buses to make the trip, increasing her commutation by more than an hour each way. But she has heard that the bus company may terminate her route, so she would have to take another local bus to make connections, adding another half hour or more to the trip. She wonders whether she should transfer to a community college nearer home, even though it doesn't offer the program of study that most interests her.

■ *The Authors' Files*

Pamela's behavioral interviewer might try to determine the stimulus cues that evoke a fear response. For example, is the fear greater or lesser depending on the height of the bridge? The depth of the ground or water below? The steepness of the incline? The narrowing of the road? Can the client quantify the fear she encounters at the inclines, overpasses, and bridges in the roadways she uses? Such information might help the therapist map out a strategy of gradual exposure to these stimuli (see Chapter 5).

The psychodynamically oriented interviewer might focus on Pamela's early childhood experiences, seeking clues as to how her fear of driving over bridges may symbolize unconscious conflicts. Might the crossing of a bridge symbolically represent separation from her parents and signify conflict concerning issues of independence and separation? Did Pamela experience separation anxiety as a child that might be reactivated in her current travel? Does her travel phobia protect her from facing adult challenges that require more independence and self-confidence than she can muster—such as attending a college outside her immediate community and pursuing the more demanding career opportunities that the college offers?

Whatever the theoretical orientation of the interviewer, interviewing skills and techniques have some features in common. Psychologists and other professionals are trained to establish **rapport** and feelings of trust with the client. These feelings help put the client at ease and encourage candid communication. Effective interviewers do not pressure clients to disclose sensitive information. Clients are generally more willing to disclose their personal feelings and experiences to someone who shows concern and understanding, someone they feel they can trust. When the interviewer is skillful, clients are less likely to fear that they will be criticized or judged for revealing sensitive information.

Although the format of the intake process may vary from clinician to clinician, most interviews cover topics such as these:

1. *Identifying Data.* Information regarding the client's sociodemographic characteristics: address and telephone number, marital status, age, gender, racial/ethnic characteristics, religion, employment, family composition, and so on.

2. *Description of the Presenting Problem(s).* How does the client perceive the problem? What troubling behaviors, thoughts, or feelings are reported? How do they affect the client's functioning? When did they begin?

3. *Psychosocial History.* Information describing the client's developmental history: educational, social, and occupational history; early family relationships.

4. *Medical/Psychiatric History.* History of medical and psychiatric treatment and hospitalizations. Is the present problem a recurrent episode of a previous problem? How was the problem handled in the past? Was treatment successful? Why or why not?

5. *Medical Problems/Medication.* Description of present medical problems and present treatment, including medication. The clinician is alert to ways in which medical problems may affect the presenting psychological problem. For example, drugs for certain medical conditions can affect people's moods and general levels of arousal.

In the course of the interview, the clinician may also conduct a formal assessment of the client's cognitive functioning through what the psychiatric community usually refers to as a **mental status examination**. A diagnostic impression is usually based on an assessment of the client's presenting problems, history, and apparent cognitive functioning.

Mental Status Examination

The mental status examination is based on observation of the client's behavior and self-presentation, and the client's response to questions that probe various aspects of cognitive functioning. The specifics of the mental status exam may vary from clinician to clinician, but the following factors are usually assessed:

1. *Appearance.* The examiner describes the appropriateness of the client's general appearance, grooming, and dress or attire.

2. *Behavioral Observations.* The examiner notes signs of psychological disturbance in the client's verbal and nonverbal behavior. Does the client maintain eye contact? (Avoidance can indicate shyness, depression, or other problems.) Do facial expressions or general posture suggest underlying emotional states? How does the client relate to the interviewer? Is she or he cooperative and friendly, or hostile and evasive? Are there signs of serious disturbance, such as bizarre behavior, inappropriate laughter, or giggling? Is the client's manner of speech pressured, controlled, or hesitant?

A client who squirms in the seat may be experiencing anxiety or backache. Nonverbal cues are interpreted according to their context. Grimacing and clenching jaws throughout an interview may express general discomfort or anxiety. If these behaviors occur only in response to questions about one's spouse, they may reflect more specific feelings.

The tone of voice and style of speech are important sources of information. Pressured or rapid speech may suggest stress or a manic episode. Slow, halting speech is more characteristic of depression or brain damage.

The client's body movement and posture, facial expressions, and gestures are clues to the client's emotions. The interviewer looks for subtle changes in the client's nonverbal behavior throughout the interview, connecting nonverbal cues that accompany discussion of particular topics to become better aware of the emotions that these issues may evoke.

3. *Orientation.* Normally speaking, we know who we and our relations are, where we are, and what time it is—although your authors are usually off by a day or two. The clinician notes whether the client shows lapses in *orientation* and, if there is any doubt, questions the client about who she or he is, who other people present are, where they are (where the interview is taking place), and what time it is (year, day, time of day). An elderly woman who had suffered brain damage told the authors that her hospital room was "some kind of spaceship" and that "Nixon" was president (at the time, Ronald Reagan was president). Disorientation may be associated with problems such as degeneration of the brain, drug intoxication, or schizophrenia.

4. *Memory.* Is the client's memory intact for recent events and remote events? Can the client recall last night's dinner (recent memory) or when and where she or he was married (remote

memory)? In some conditions associated with advanced age, people can recall events 30 years in the past but have difficulty forming new memories. As a result, they may not be able to recall the name of a new grandchild or whether they have taken their medication.

5. *Sensorium.* Sensorium derives from the Latin *sensus,* meaning "sense," and *-ium,* a suffix used to form the names of biological structures. The term *sensorium* is defined as the individual's entire sensory apparatus and is used by clinicians to refer to the client's focusing of attention, capacity for concentration, and level of awareness of the world. Clients whose attention or concentration drifts in and out during the interview, or who are generally unresponsive, may have difficulties processing information from the external world, perhaps due to brain damage. Clinicians may write that the client's "sensorium is clear" to indicate apparently accurate sensing of the external world.

6. *Perceptual Processes.* Perception is a psychological process by which people interpret the information provided by the senses. Sometimes, as in the case of hallucinations, perceptions may occur in the absence of external sensory input, and the client may not be able to distinguish them from reality. The clinician notes whether or not the client appears to be responding to hallucinations, such as attending to voices or seeing things that are not there. In the case of schizophrenia, the senses may be flooded with false perceptions (hallucinations).

7. *Mood and Affect.* These terms are often used interchangeably, but have a slightly different meaning. The noun **affect** (pronounced AFF-ect) refers to the emotions or feelings that the client attaches to objects or ideas. The central issue is whether or not the affect is *appropriate* to the client's life situation and the ideas being expressed. Inappropriateness of affect (such as laughing while discussing tragic events) or impoverished emotional reactivity (described as blunted or flat affect) is often connected with severe problems such as schizophrenia. **Mood** refers to the prevailing emotions displayed during the interview, such as sadness, anxiety, or anger.

8. *Intelligence.* The clinician usually judges the client's general level of intellectual functioning on the basis of the client's speech (level of vocabulary and ability to formulate and express ideas clearly), apparent level of sophistication (general knowledge), and achieved socioeco-

nomic status (educational and employment history). If questions arise as to the client's cognitive abilities, the interviewer may direct questions that test the client's ability to interpret proverbs, to name officeholders like the local mayor or governor, or to compute simple arithmetic tasks—questions that assess the client's capacities for acquiring and manipulating information.

9. *Thought Processes.* This category refers to the form and content of thought. Concerning the form of thought, the clinician notes whether or not the client's thought processes appear logical and coherent. Is there perhaps a loosening of associations—an apparent stringing together of loosely connected or disconnected thoughts or ideas that is suggestive of disordered thinking processes that often occur in schizophrenia? Is there evidence of thought blocking—a gap or pause in the client's speech when a troubling topic is touched on? Is there evidence of flight of ideas—a tendency to jump from topic to topic that may prevent the examiner from following the connections, as might occur during manic episodes? Does the client speak very little, perhaps because of impoverishment of thought? Description of the client's thought content touches on any evidence of troubling belief patterns such as delusional beliefs (false ideas) or obsessions (nagging, repetitious thoughts).

10. *Insight.* Does the client recognize a problem exists, as is usually the case with anxiety and depression? Has the client developed a reasonable understanding of the factors that might account for the problem? Does the client deny the existence of the problem or blame others for it, as may occur in personality disorders?

   The interviewer takes note of apparent discrepancies between the client's verbal and nonverbal behavior. Nonverbal cues may be more accurate reflections of emotional state than verbal reports. Clients may lack insight into feelings of anger toward their parents but raise their voices when they discuss them. Clients may deny problems at work but tightly grasp the arms of their chairs when they talk about work.

11. *Judgment.* Does the client apply sound and reasonable judgments in making life decisions? Does the client approach problems thoughtfully and rationally? Or does the client act in a rash or impulsive manner, failing to consider the consequences of his or her actions, as may happen, for example, in manic episodes, personality disorders, or substance abuse?

Standardized Interview Techniques

Standardized interview techniques increase the consistency or reliability of diagnostic judgments. **Standardized interview** techniques based on the DSM system and other diagnostic schemes enable clinicians to pose similar sets of questions. Examples include the National Institute of Mental Health's Diagnostic Interview Schedule (DIS; Robins et al., 1981) and the Structured Clinical Interview for DSM-III-R (SCID; Spitzer et al., 1992b).

The DIS uses prearranged questions that can be administered by a clinician or a lay interviewer (see Table 3.6). The interview responses are fed into a computer that determines the most appropriate diagnostic category. In addition to specifying the behaviors exhibited and reported by the client, the DIS outlines the history of the problems and the life experiences associated with them.

The clinician or layperson must be well trained in administering the interview. The DIS, for example, requires a 1- to 2-week training course. The DIS shows high interjudge reliability; it produces high rates of agreement in diagnostic judgments among professional clinicians (Helzer et al., 1985). Evidence is mixed concerning the reliability of information attained by nonprofessional interviewers, however, even when they are well trained (Erdman et al., 1987).

Although the DIS provides information that a computer can analyze to make diagnoses, it more closely resembles a symptom checklist or questionnaire than an interview, which is why it can be administered by a lay interviewer. The SCID, on the other hand, is intended for professionals who are experienced interviewers and familiar with the DSM system. The SCID includes **closed-ended questions** to determine the presence of behavior patterns that suggest specific diagnostic categories and **open-ended questions** that allow clients to elaborate their problems and feelings. The SCID guides the clinician in testing diagnostic hypotheses as the interview progresses. Recent research supports the reliability of the SCID across various clinical settings (Williams et al., 1992).

Several standard interview schedules, such as the SCID, caution the interviewer to consider clients' cultural backgrounds when they are assessing the deviance of their beliefs or perceptual experiences (López & Núñez, 1987). An experience that may be foreign to the interviewer, such as an hallucination occurring in the context of a religious rite, may not be deviant for some cultural groups.

Table 3.6 A Section of the DIS Relevant to Panic Disorder

61. Have you ever considered yourself a nervous person?

62. Have you ever had a spell or attack when all of a sudden you felt frightened, anxious, or very uneasy in situations when most people would not be afraid?

For those answering yes to Q. 62, the following questions would be asked. If the answer is no, the interviewer skips to the next series of questions.

A. During one of your worst spells of suddenly feeling frightened or anxious or uneasy, did you ever notice that you had any of the following problems?

During this spell—

   (1) were you short of breath—having trouble catching your breath?
   (2) did your heart pound?
   (3) were you dizzy or light-headed?
   (4) did your fingers or face tingle?
   (5) did you have tightness or pain in your chest?
   (6) did you feel like you were choking or smothering?
   (7) did you feel faint?
   (8) did you sweat?
   (9) did you tremble or shake?
   (10) did you feel hot or cold flashes?
   (11) did things around you seem unreal?
   (12) were you afraid either that you might die or that you might act in a crazy way?

B. How old were you the first time you had one of these sudden spells of feeling frightened or anxious? Age _____

   Whole Life = code 02
   If don't know and age under 40, code 01
   If don't know and age 40 or more, ask: "Would you say it was before or after you were 40?"

C. Have you ever had 3 spells like this close together—say within a 3-week period?

D. Have spells like this occurred during at least 6 different weeks of your life?

E. Have you had a spell like this within the last 2 weeks?

Note: A panic disorder is a type of anxiety disorder characterized by recurrent panic attacks (see Chapter 5).

Source: Archives of General Psychiatry, 41, *1981, 949–958. Copyright 1981, American Medical Association.*

A CLOSER LOOK

Would You Tell Your Problems to a Computer?

Picture yourself seated before a computer screen in the not-too-distant future. The message on the screen asks you to type in your name and press the return key. Not wanting to offend, you comply. This message then comes on the screen: "Hello, my name is Sigmund. I'm programmed to ask you a set of questions to learn more about you. May I begin?" You nod your head yes, momentarily forgetting that the computer can only "perceive" key strokes. You type "yes" and the interview begins.

The future, as the saying goes, is now. Computerized clinical interviews have been used for more than 20 years. Computers offer some advantages over us traditional human interviewers (Farrell et al., 1987):

1. Computers can be programmed to ask a specific set of questions in a predetermined order, whereas human beings may omit critical items or steer the interview toward less important topics.

2. The client may be less embarrassed about relating personal matters to the computer because computers do not show emotional responses to clients' responses.

3. Computerized interviews can free clinicians to spend more time providing direct clinical services.

Consider a computerized interview system named CASPER, which includes interview and update functions. The interview component takes about 30 minutes and contains 127 questions that cover 62 target problems. The questions cover a wide range of topics, such as demographic information, family relations, social activities, sex, life satisfaction, and behavioral problems related to physical and mental disorders. The interview questions and

Interview by computer.   Would you be more likely, or less likely, to tell your problems to a computer than to a person? Computerized clinical interviews have been used for more than 20 years, and some research suggests the computer may be more sensitive than its human counterpart in teasing out problems.

response options, such as the following, are presented on the screen:

> "About how many days in the past month did you have difficulty falling asleep, staying asleep, or waking too early (include sleep disturbed by bad dreams)?"
>
> "During the past month, how have you been getting along with your spouse/partner? (1) Very satisfactory; (2) Mostly satisfactory; (3) Sometimes satisfactory, sometimes unsatisfactory; (4) Mostly unsatisfactory; (5) Very unsatisfactory"
>
> Farrell et al., 1987, p. 692

PSYCHOLOGICAL TESTS

Psychological tests are structured methods of assessment which are used to evaluate reasonably stable traits such as intelligence and personality. Tests are usually standardized on large numbers of subjects and provide norms that compare clients' scores to the average. Comparisons of test results from normal and abnormal populations suggest response patterns indicative of abnormal behavior.

Tests are more structured than interviews. The instructions are precise. Tests can therefore be interpreted more objectively than even most structured interviews. Moreover, test responses can often be readily quantified, facilitating assessment of their reliability and validity. The tests used in clinical settings include tests of intelligence, personality, and neuropsychological functioning.

The subject presses a numeric key to respond to each item. CASPER is a branching program that follows up on problems suggested by clients' responses. For example, if the client indicates difficulty in falling or remaining asleep, CASPER asks whether or not sleep has become a major problem—"something causing you great personal distress or interfering with your daily functioning" (p. 693). If the client indicates yes, the computer will return to the problem after other items have been presented and ask the client to rate the duration and intensity of the problem. Clients may also add or drop complaints—change their minds, that is.

In one study, 103 outpatients compared the results of an interview "by CASPER" with those obtained by means of a clinical interview and a self-report symptom checklist. The results supported the utility of the computer as a means of assessing complaints. Clients were generally able to complete the computer interview with little difficulty, and most rated the procedure favorably. Moreover, it appeared that clients reported a greater number of problems to CASPER than to a flesh-and-blood clinician (Angle et al., 1979). Perhaps the computer interview is especially helpful in identifying problems that the client is embarrassed or unwilling to report to a human. Perhaps the computer seems more willing to take the time to note all complaints.

 Research shows that clients are generally more willing to admit to problems when interviewed by computers than by humans. Perhaps people are less concerned about being "judged" by computers.

A review of research suggests that some computer programs are as capable as skilled clinicians at obtaining information from a client and reaching an accurate diagnosis (Bloom, 1992). It seems that most of the resistance to using computer interviews for this purpose comes from clinicians rather than clients (Bloom, 1992).

INTELLIGENCE TESTS

The assessment of abnormal behavior often includes evaluation of intelligence. Formal tests of intelligence are used to help diagnose mental retardation. They evaluate the intellectual impairment that may be caused by other disorders, such as organic mental disorders caused by damage to the brain. They also pro-vide a profile of the client's intellectual strengths and weaknesses to help develop a treatment plan that is suited to the client's competencies.

Intelligence is a controversial concept in psychology, however. Even attempts at definition stir debate. David Wechsler, the originator of a widely used series of intelligence tests, defined intelligence as "capacity . . . to understand the world . . . and . . . resourcefulness to cope with its challenges" (1975). From his perspective, intelligence has to do with the ways in which we (1) mentally represent the world and (2) adapt to its demands. There are various intelligence tests, including group tests and those that are administered individually, such as the Stanford-Binet and Wechsler scales. Individual tests allow examiners to observe the behavior of the respondent as well as record answers. Examiners can thus gain insight as to whether factors such as testing conditions, language problems, illness, or level of motivation contribute to a given test performance.

The Stanford-Binet Intelligence Scale (SBIS)

The SBIS was originated by the Frenchmen Alfred Binet and Theodore Simon in 1905 in response to the French public school system's quest for a test that could identify children who might profit from special education. The initial Binet-Simon scale yielded a score called a **mental age** (MA) that represented the child's overall level of intellectual functioning. The child who received an MA of 8 was functioning like the typical 8-year-old. Children received "months" of credit for correct answers, and their MAs were determined by adding them up. Binet assumed that intelligence grew as children developed so that older children would obtain more correct answers. He thus age-graded his questions, as in Table 3.7, and arranged them according to difficulty.

Louis Terman of Stanford University adapted the Binet-Simon test for American children in 1916, which is why it is now called the *Stanford*-Binet Intelligence Scale (SBIS). The SBIS also yielded an **intelligence quotient** (IQ), not an MA, which reflected the relationship between a child's MA and chronological age (CA), according to this formula:

$$IQ = \frac{MA}{CA} \times 100$$

Examination of this formula shows that children who received identical mental-age scores might differ markedly in IQ, with the younger child attaining the higher IQ.

Table 3.7   Items Similar to Those on the Stanford-Binet Intelligence Scale

Level (Years)	Item
2 years	1. Children show knowledge of basic vocabulary words by identifying parts of a doll such as the mouth, ears, and hair. 2. Children show counting and spatial skills along with visual-motor coordination by building a tower of four blocks to match a model.
4 years	1. Children show word fluency and categorical thinking by filling in the missing words when they are asked questions such as: "Father is a man; mother is a _____?" "Hamburgers are hot; ice cream is _____?" 2. Children show comprehension by answering correctly when they are asked questions such as: "Why do people have automobiles?" "Why do people have medicine?"
9 years	1. Children can point out verbal absurdities, as in this question: "In an old cemetery, scientists unearthed a skull which they think was that of George Washington when he was only five years of age. What is silly about that?" 2. Children show fluency with words, as shown by answering the questions: "Can you tell me a number that rhymes with snore?" "Can you tell me a color that rhymes with glue?"
Adult	1. Adults show knowledge of the meanings of words and conceptual thinking by correctly explaining the differences between word pairs like "sickness and misery," "house and home," and "integrity and prestige." 2. Adults show spatial skills by correctly answering questions like "If a car turned to the right to head north, in what direction was it heading before it turned?"

Source: Archives of General Psychiatry, 41, *949–958. Copyright © 1981,* American Medical Association.

 It is true that children who answer intelligence test items identically may differ markedly in intelligence. The younger child (that is, the child with the lower *CA*) will receive the higher IQ score.

Today, the SBIS is used with children and adults, and test takers' IQ scores are based on their deviation from the norms of their age group. A score of 100 is defined as the mean. People who answer more items correctly than the average obtain IQ scores above 100; those who answer fewer items correctly obtain scores of less than 100.

The so-called **deviation IQ** was developed by psychologist David Wechsler, who also originated various intelligence tests of his own.

The Wechsler Scales

Wechsler developed several intelligence scales for children and adults. The Wechsler scales group questions into subtests like those shown in Table 3.8, each of which measures a different intellectual task. The Wechsler scales are thus designed to offer insight into respondents' relative strengths and weaknesses, and not simply yield an overall score.

Wechsler's scales describe so-called *verbal* and *performance* subtests. Verbal subtests generally require knowledge of verbal concepts; performance subtests rely more on spatial relations skills. (Figure 3.1 shows items like those on performance scales of the Wechsler scales.) Wechsler's scales allow for computation of verbal and performance IQs.

Students from various backgrounds yield different profiles. College students, generally speaking, perform better on verbal subtests than on performance subtests. Australian Aboriginal children outperform white Australian children on performance-type tasks that involve visual-spatial skills (Kearins, 1981). Such skills are likely to foster survival in the harsh Australian outback. Intellectual attainments, like psychological adjustment, are connected with the demands of particular sociocultural (Helms, 1992) and physical-environmental settings.

Wechsler IQ scores are based on how respondents' answers deviate from those attained by their age-mates. The mean whole test score at any age is defined as 100. Wechsler distributed IQ scores so that 50% of the scores of the population would lie within a "broad average" range of 90 to 110.

Most IQ scores cluster around the mean (see Figure 3.2). Just 5% of them are above 130 or below 70. Wechsler labeled people who attained scores of 130 or above as "very superior," those with scores below 70 as "intellectually deficient." IQ scores below 70 are one of the criteria used in diagnosing mental retardation.

Table 3.8 Subtests from the Wechsler Adult Intelligence Scale-Revised (WAIS-R)	
Verbal Subtest	**Performance Subtests**
1. *Information:* "What is the capital of the United States?"	7. *Digit Symbol:* Learning and drawing meaningless figures that are associated with numbers.
2. *Comprehension:* "Why do we have zip codes?" "What does 'A stitch in time saves 9' mean?"	8. *Picture Completion:* Pointing to the missing part of a picture.
3. *Arithmetic:* "If 3 candy bars cost 25 cents, how much do 18 candy bars cost?"	9. *Block Design:* Copying pictures of geometric designs using multicolored blocks.
4. *Similarities:* "How are good and bad alike?" "How are peanut butter and jelly alike?"	10. *Picture Arrangement:* Arranging cartoon pictures in sequence so that they tell a meaningful story.
5. *Digit Span:* Repeating a series of numbers forward and backward.	11. *Object Assembly:* Putting pieces of a puzzle together so that they form a meaningful object.
6. *Vocabulary:* "What does canal mean?"	

Items for verbal subtests 1, 2, 3, 4, and 6 are similar but not identical to actual test items on the WISC.

Source: Table from Psychology, *Fourth Edition by Spencer A. Rathus, copyright © 1990 by Holt, Rinehart, and Winston, Inc., reproduced by permission of the publisher.*

Figure 3.1 Items similar to those found on the performance subtests of the Wechsler Intelligence Scale.
The Wechsler scales yield verbal and performance IQs that are based on the extent to which an individual's test scores deviate from the norm for her or his age group.

PICTURE ARRANGEMENT
These pictures tell a story but they are in the wrong order. Put them in the right order so that they tell a story.

PICTURE COMPLETION
What part is missing from this picture?

BLOCK DESIGN
Put the blocks together to make this picture.

OBJECT ASSEMBLY
Put the pieces together as quickly as you can.

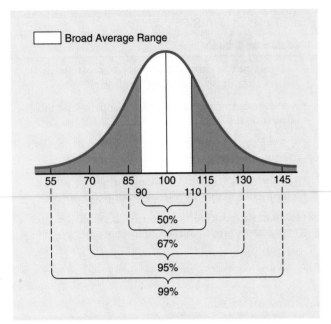

Figure 3.2 An idealized distribution of IQ scores.
The distribution of IQ scores is based on a bell-shaped
curve, which is referred to by psychologists as a normal
curve. Wechsler defined the deviation IQ in such a way that
50% of the scores fall within the broad average range of 90
to 110.

PERSONALITY TESTS

Clinicians use various formal tests to assess personality. We consider two types of personality tests: *self-
report* and *projective* tests.

Self-Report Personality Inventories

Do you like automobile magazines? Are you easily
startled by noises in the night? Are you bothered by
periods of anxiety or shakiness? Self-report inventories use structured items, similar to these, to measure
personality traits like anxiety, depression, emotionality, hypomania, masculinity–femininity, and introversion. Comparison of clients' responses on scales measuring these traits to those of a normative sample
reveals their relative standing.

Self-report personality inventories are also
called **objective tests**. They are objective in that the
range of possible responses to items is limited. Empirical objective standards—rather than psychological
theory—are also used to derive test items. Tests might
ask respondents to check adjectives that apply to
them, to mark statements as true or false, to select

preferred activities from lists, or to indicate whether
items apply to them "always," "sometimes," or
"never." Tests with **forced-choice formats** require
respondents to mark which of a group of statements
is truest for them, or to select their most preferred
activity from a list. They cannot answer "none of the
above." Forced-choice formats are commonly used in
interest inventories, as in this item:

I would rather

a. be a forester.

b. work in an office setting.

c. play in a band.

In some tests, as with the most widely
researched self-report inventory, the Minnesota Multiphasic Personality Inventory (MMPI), items are
selected empirically—according to whether or not
they differentiate clinical diagnostic groups from normal people.

■ MINNESOTA MULTIPHASIC PERSONALITY
INVENTORY (MMPI)   The MMPI contains several
hundred true-false statements that assess interest patterns, habits, family relationships, somatic complaints, attitudes, beliefs, and behaviors characteristic
of psychological disorders. Although it is also used
widely in personality research (Costa et al., 1985),
the MMPI was intended to help diagnose abnormal
behavior.

The MMPI permits psychologists to compare the
response patterns of clients to those of people with
diagnosed problems. A similar pattern of responses to
the test is suggestive of comparable problems. Psychologists can send completed test records to computerized scoring agencies or score them by hand. Computers can generate MMPI reports by interpreting
responses according to rules or by comparing them to
test records held in memory (Fowler, 1985).

In the 1930s, the developers of the MMPI—
Starke Hathaway, a psychologist, and Charles McKin-
ley, a psychiatrist—constructed the MMPI scales on
the basis of clinical data. This was an innovation
because most personality tests at the time were based
on a theoretical approach, in which the developer
derives test items according to her or his theoretical
belief that a given item measures a certain psychological attribute (Graham, 1988). The meaning given to
responses to the Rorschach inkblot test, in contrast, is
usually based on psychodynamic theory. Items were
assigned to particular MMPI scales according to the
way different clinical groups and normal groups
answered them, not on the basis of theory.

Consider a hypothetical item: "I often read
detective novels." If groups of depressed people
tended to answer the item in a direction different

from normal groups, the item would be placed on the depression scale—regardless of whether or not the item had face validity. Many items that discriminate normal people from clinical groups are transparent in meaning, such as "I feel down much of the time." Some items are more subtle in meaning or bear no manifest relationship to the measured trait.

 Test items can be used to measure traits even when they bear no apparent relationship to the trait. Such items may lack face validity, but they are of use if they are shown to have criterion validity.

Derivation of scales on the basis of their ability to distinguish the response patterns of comparison groups such as clinical and normal groups is called the **contrasted groups approach**. The contrasted groups technique establishes concurrent validity; group membership is the criterion by which the validity of the test is measured.

The MMPI was standardized by comparing the responses of normal groups, composed primarily of relatives and visitors of patients in the University of Minnesota hospitals, to those of carefully selected diagnostic groups, such as depressives, schizophrenics, and paranoids. Eight clinical scales were derived through the contrasted groups approach. Two additional clinical scales were developed by using nonclinical comparison groups: a scale measuring masculine–feminine interest patterns and one measuring social introversion. The clinical scales are described in Table 3.9.

The MMPI also has **validity scales** that assess tendencies to distort test responses in a favorable ("faking good") or unfavorable ("faking bad") direction. Many items on objective tests like the MMPI are obvious testimony of disturbed thoughts and feelings, as in items of the type, "I frequently hear things that are not there." The transparency of these items makes them fertile ground for faking. MMPI validity scales include the L (Lie) scale, the F scale (for *Frequency*), and the K (correction) scale among others. The L scale contains items that refer to minor foibles or flaws in character that nearly all of us possess and admit to readily. An example of a similar item would be, "I sometimes do not answer the phone in a cheerful manner." People who disavow these foibles may also deny items with more serious clinical implications. The F scale contains items that were endorsed by less than 10% of the normal sample. A high F score may suggest random or careless responding, difficulty in reading or comprehending the test items, or an effort to "fake bad" to exaggerate complaints. An

irony that clouds interpretation of the MMPI is that abnormal validity scale scores do *not* necessarily invalidate the test for highly disturbed respondents such as schizophrenics. The K scale measures a more subtle form of distortion, called psychological defensiveness or guardedness—respondents' tendency to conceal genuine feelings about sensitive issues in order to create a favorable impression. The K scale is used as a correction factor; scores on clinical scales that may be biased by defensive tendencies are augmented (corrected) by a fraction of the K scale score.

The respondent's raw score for each MMPI scale is simply the number of items scored in a clinical direction. Raw scores are converted into **standard scores** with a mean of 50 and a standard deviation of 10. A standard score of 65 or higher on a particular scale places an individual at approximately the 92nd percentile or higher of the revised normative sample, and is considered to be clinically significant.

The MMPI is interpreted according to individual scale elevations and interrelationships among scales. For example, a "2–7 profile," which is commonly found among people seeking therapy, refers to a test pattern in which scores for scales 2 ("Depression") and 7 ("Psychasthenia") are clinically elevated. Clinicians may refer to "atlases," or descriptions, of people who usually attain various profiles.

MMPI scales are regarded as reflecting continua of personality traits associated with the diagnostic categories represented by the test. For example, a high score on psychopathic deviation suggests the respondent holds a higher-than-average number of nonconformist beliefs and may be rebellious, but it does not establish a diagnosis of psychopathic deviation or antisocial personality. Although the MMPI was originally intended as a diagnostic instrument, it has frequently been criticized for its failure to diagnose respondents accurately. One reason for its diagnostic shortcoming is that the clinical scales are not pure measures of the diagnostic categories. Respondents may score high on several scales because many of them are interrelated (Graham, 1990). Intercorrelations among the scales stem in part from the fact that many of them share items. It is difficult for the clinician to use the test to pinpoint a diagnosis when a respondent attains several high-scale scores. In addition, clients with clinically diagnosable disorders may score within the normal range on the test and normals may score in the elevated range (Graham, 1990).

Perhaps it is unfair to expect that the MMPI, which was developed under a largely outmoded diagnostic system, should provide diagnostic judgments that are consistent with the current version of the DSM system. Even so, MMPI profiles may suggest

Table 3.9   Clinical Scales of the MMPI

Scale Number	Scale Label	Items Similar to Those Found on MMPI Scale	Sample Traits of High Scorers
1	Hypochondriasis	My stomach frequently bothers me. At times, my body seems to ache all over.	Many physical complaints, cynical defeatist attitudes, often perceived as whiny, demanding
2	Depression	Nothing seems to interest me anymore. My sleep is often disturbed by worrisome thoughts.	Depressed mood; pessimistic, worrisome, despondent, lethargic
3	Hysteria	I sometimes become flushed for no apparent reason. I tend to take people at their word when they're trying to be nice to me.	Naive, egocentric, little insight into problems, immature; develops physical complaints in response to stress
4	Psychopathic Deviate	My parents often disliked my friends. My behavior sometimes got me into trouble at school.	Difficulties incorporating values of society, rebellious, impulsive, antisocial tendencies; strained family relationships; poor work and school history
5	Masculinity–Femininity	I like reading about electronics. (M) I would like to work in the theater. (F)	Males endorsing feminine attributes: have cultural and artistic interests, effeminate, sensitive, passive Females endorsing male interests: Aggressive, masculine, self-confident, active, assertive, vigorous
6	Paranoia	I would have been more successful in life but people didn't give me a fair break. It's not safe to trust anyone these days.	Suspicious, guarded, blames others, resentful, aloof, may have paranoid delusions
7	Psychasthenia	I'm one of those people who have to have something to worry about. I seem to have more fears than most people I know.	Anxious, fearful, tense, worried, insecure, difficulties concentrating, obsessional, self-doubting
8	Schizophrenia	Things seem unreal to me at times. I sometimes hear things that other people can't hear.	Confused and illogical thinking, feels alienated and misunderstood, socially isolated or withdrawn, may have blatant psychotic symptoms such as hallucinations or delusional beliefs, or may lead detached, schizoid lifestyle
9	Hypomania	I sometimes take on more tasks than I can possibly get done. People have noticed that my speech is sometimes pressured or rushed.	Energetic, possibly manic, impulsive, optimistic, sociable, active, flighty, irritable, may have overly inflated or grandiose self-image or unrealistic plans
0	Social introversion	I don't like loud parties. I was not very active in school activities.	Shy, inhibited, withdrawn, introverted, lacks self-confidence, reserved, anxious in social situations

Is this for real?!?

Source: Table from Psychology, *Fifth Edition by Spencer A. Rathus, copyright © 1993, by Holt, Rinehart, and Winston, Inc., reproduced by permission of the publisher.*

possible diagnoses that can be considered in the light of other evidence. Moreover, many clinicians use the MMPI to gain general information about respondents' personality traits and attributes rather than a diagnosis per se.

The MMPI has been recently revised and contains additional scales that provide assessors with information which goes beyond that provided by the clinical scales. These new scales, called *content scales,* assess an individual's specific complaints and concerns, such as anxiety, anger, family problems, and problems of low self-esteem. These content scales may increase the ability of the test to distinguish among different diagnostic categories (Ben-Porath et al., 1991). It is too early to tell how well the revised MMPI, called the MMPI-2, will perform as a diagnostic instrument, however.

The MMPI-2 was also restandardized on a nationwide sample of some 2,600 normal adults (Butcher et al., 1989; Graham, 1990), including a proportionate number of African Americans (the original normative group was all white). In addition to the incorporation of new content scales and some additional validity scales, the wording of a number of items has been updated to reflect modern usage. Some items in the original test that referred to 1930s customs that are all but unknown today (such as "dropping the handkerchief") were dropped. (P.S. Ask your grandparents.) There is also a new adolescent version.

■ THE MILLON CLINICAL MULTIAXIAL INVENTORY (MCMI)

The MCMI (Millon, 1982) was developed to help the clinician make diagnostic judgments within the multiaxial DSM system, especially in the personality disorders found on Axis II. The MCMI consists of 175 true-false items that yield scores for 20 clinical scales that are associated with DSM categories.

The MCMI is the only objective personality test that focuses on personality style and disorders (Antoni et al., 1986). The MMPI, in contrast, focuses on personality patterns associated with Axis I diagnoses, such as mood disorders, anxiety disorders, and schizophrenic disorders. Using the MCMI and MMPI in combination may help the clinician make more subtle diagnostic distinctions than are possible with either test alone because they assess different patterns of psychopathology (Antoni et al., 1985, 1986).

Some self-report inventories are oriented toward assessing the clinical features of specific abnormal behavior patterns, such as anxiety or depression. One prominent example is the Beck Depression Inventory (BDI) (Beck et al., 1961).

■ THE BECK DEPRESSION INVENTORY (BDI)

Some inventories such as the Beck Depression Inventory (BDI) assess a single trait or dimension. The BDI was developed by Aaron Beck, who is known for his cognitive approach to treatment of depression, and his colleagues (Beck et al., 1961). The 21 BDI items measure various features of depression, such as downcast mood and changes in appetite and sleeping patterns. Each presents four response options that vary in level of severity. Subjects select the response that represents their feelings during the preceding week. The items are summed to yield a total score that can range between 0 and 63. The higher the score, the more severe the depression. The BDI has been used extensively in research on depression and as a clinical measure of outcome in the treatment of depression. It correlates highly with clinician ratings of depression (Bumberry et al., 1978; Metcalfe & Goldman, 1965; Schwab et al., 1967), which is a common way of assessing the validity of such scales.

■ EVALUATION OF SELF-REPORT INVENTORIES

Self-report tests have the benefits of relative ease and economy of administration. Once the examiner has read the instructions to clients, and ascertained that they can read and comprehend the items, clients can complete the tests unattended. Because the tests permit limited response options, such as marking items either true or false, they can be scored with high interrater reliability. Moreover, the accumulation of research findings on respondents provides a quantified basis for interpreting test responses.

A disadvantage of self-rating tests is that they rely on clients as the source of data. Test responses may therefore reflect underlying response biases rather than accurate self-perceptions.

Tests are also only as valid as the criteria that were used to validate them. The original MMPI was limited in its role as a diagnostic instrument by virtue of the obsolete diagnostic categories that were used to classify the clinical groups. Moreover, if a test does nothing more than identify people who are likely to belong to a particular diagnostic category, its utility is usurped by more economical means of arriving at diagnoses, such as the structured clinical interview. We expect more from personality tests than diagnostic classification, and the MMPI has shown its value in generating research into the relationships between personality characteristics and specific response patterns. Psychodynamically oriented critics suggest that self-report instruments tell us little about possible unconscious processes. The use of such tests may also be limited to relatively high functioning individuals who can read well, respond to verbal material, and focus on a potentially tedious task. Clients who are disorganized, unstable, or confused may not be able to complete tests.

Projective Personality Tests

Projective tests, unlike objective tests, offer no clear, specified answers. Clients are presented with ambiguous stimuli, such as vague drawings or inkblots, and are usually asked to describe what the stimuli look like or to relate stories about them. The tests are called projective because they were derived from the psychodynamic projective hypothesis—the belief that people impose, or "project," their psychological needs, drives, and motives, much of which may lie in the unconscious, onto their interpretations of unstructured stimuli. Ambiguous stimuli can be interpreted in diverse ways, and people are free to draw on their own psychological processes as well as stimulus cues in determining their responses.

The psychodynamic model holds that potentially disturbing impulses and wishes, often of a sexual or aggressive nature, are often hidden from consciousness by defense mechanisms. Defense mechanisms may thwart direct probing of threatening material. Indirect methods of assessment, however, such as projective tests, may offer clues to unconscious processes. More behaviorally oriented critics contend, however, that the results of projective tests are based more on clinicians' subjective interpretations of test responses than on empirical evidence.

The two most prominent projective techniques are the Rorschach inkblot test and the Thematic Apperception Test (TAT).

■ **RORSCHACH INKBLOT TEST** The Renaissance artist and inventor Leonardo da Vinci suggested that individual differences could be studied by means of people's interpretations of cloud formations. A century later, Shakespeare's Hamlet toyed with Polonius by suggesting alternately that a cloud formation resembled a camel, a hunched weasel, or a whale. Polonius showed more political savvy than integrity because he agreed with each suggestion. Hamlet saw through him, of course.

Hermann Rorschach (1884–1922), a Swiss psychiatrist, also believed that ambiguous figures could be used to help clinicians "see through"—or better understand—people with psychological problems. Rorschach turned to inkblots and not clouds, however. As a child, Rorschach was intrigued by the game of dripping ink on paper and folding the paper to make symmetrical figures. He noted that people saw different things in the same blot, and he believed that

their "percepts" reflected their personalities as well as the stimulus cues provided by the blot. In high school his fellows gave him the nickname *Klecks*, which means "inkblot" in German. As a psychiatrist, Rorschach experimented with hundreds of blots to identify those that could help in the diagnosis of psychological problems. He finally found a group of 15 blots that seemed to do the job and could be administered in a single session. Ten blots are used today because Rorschach's publisher did not have the funds to reproduce all 15 blots in the first edition of the text on the subject. Rorschach never had the opportunity to learn how popular and influential his inkblot test would become. The year following its publication, at the age of 38, he died of complications from a ruptured appendix.

Some clinicians do use psychological tests made up of inkblots to help them arrive at diagnostic impressions. The most widely used of these is the Rorschach inkblot test.

Five of the inkblots are black and white and the other five have color (see Figure 3.3). Each inkblot is printed on a separate card, which is handed to subjects in sequence. Subjects are asked to tell the examiner what the blot might be or what it reminds them of.

Figure 3.3 An inkblot similar to those found on the Rorschach inkblot test.
What does the blot look like to you? What could it be? Rorschach assumed that people project their personalities into their responses to ambiguous inkblots as well as respond to the stimulus characteristics of the blot.

Most systems for scoring responses refer to the *location, determinants, content,* and *form level* of responses. After the subject has responded to all cards, the examiner conducts an **inquiry** to clarify which aspects of the blot gave rise to the responses. If the subject says that a card looks like "two dancing bears," the examiner might ask, "What was it about the card that reminded you of dancing bears?" The examiner does *not* say, "Was it the shape of these areas or their shagginess that led you to see bears?" That would be leading the witness.

The location is the area of the blot selected—the whole card or a prominent or minor detail. **Determinants** include properties of the blot such as form, shading, texture, or color that inspire the response, and features of the percept that the respondent imposes upon, or reads into, the blot, such as **movement**—perceiving figures as animated, as running, dancing, or flying. The content is the *what* of the percept, for instance a winged creature, a jack-o'-lantern, or a torso. **Form level** signifies (1) the consistency of a response with the shape of the blot and (2) the complexity of the response.

Clinicians who use the Rorschach tend to interpret responses in the following ways. Clients who use the entire blot in their responses show ability to perceive part–whole relationships and integrate events in meaningful ways. People whose responses are based solely on minor details may have obsessive-compulsive tendencies that, in psychodynamic theory, protect them from having to cope with the larger issues in their lives. Clients who respond to the negative (white) spaces tend to see things in their own way, suggestive of negativism or stubbornness.

Relationships between form and color are suggestive of clients' capacity to control impulses. When clients use color but are primarily guided by the form of the blots, they are believed capable of feeling deeply but also of holding their feelings in check. When color predominates—as in perceiving any reddened area as "blood"—clients may not be able to exercise control over impulses. A response that is consistent with the form or contours of the blot is suggestive of adequate **reality testing**. People who see movement in the blots may be revealing intelligence and creativity. Content analysis may shed light on underlying conflicts. For example, adult clients who see animals but no people may have problems relating to people. Clients who appear confused about whether or not percepts of people are male or female may, according to psychodynamic theory, be in conflict over their own gender.

Evaluation of the Rorschach The validity of the Rorschach has been the subject of extensive debate.

One problem with the Rorschach is that the interpretation of clients' responses is not objective; it depends to some degree on the subjective judgment of the examiner. Two examiners may interpret the same Rorschach response differently. Another problem is lack of a standard scoring procedure. There are several scoring systems; even within systems, the scoring of responses has met with questionable interrater reliability. Recent attempts to develop a comprehensive scoring approach, such as the Exner system (Exner, 1978; Exner & Weiner, 1982), have advanced the effort to standardize scoring of responses. Evidence suggests that the Exner system may have greater clinical validity for testing schizophrenics than depressives or people with personality disorders, however (Vincent & Harman, 1991).

Even if a Rorschach response can be scored reliably, the interpretation of the response—what it means—remains an open question. Critics and even some proponents of the Rorschach technique (Hertz, 1986) suggest that there is a lack of empirical research to support the interpretation of some particular responses. On the whole, though, the test may have adequate reliability and validity, as judged by a review of research studies conducted between 1971 and 1980 (Parker et al., 1988). Although these results are encouraging for Rorschach proponents, more carefully conceived Rorschach research needs to be carried out. Many psychologists view the Rorschach not only as a diagnostic tool but also as an experimental means of discovering how people construct meaning from unstructured or ambiguous situations (Blatt, 1986).

■ THE THEMATIC APPERCEPTION TEST (TAT)

The Thematic Apperception Test (TAT) was developed by psychologist Henry Murray (1943) at Harvard University in the 1930s. *Apperception* is a French word that can be translated as "interpreting (new ideas or impressions) on the basis of existing ideas (cognitive structures) and past experience." The TAT consists of a series of cards, like that shown in Figure 3.4, each of which depicts an ambiguous scene. Respondents are asked to construct stories about the cards. It is assumed that their tales reflect their experiences and outlooks on life—and, perhaps, also shed light on deep-seated needs and conflicts.

Respondents are asked to describe what is happening in each scene, what led up to it, what the characters are thinking and feeling, and what will happen next. Psychodynamically oriented clinicians assume that respondents identify with the protagonists in their stories and project their psychological needs and conflicts into the events that they *apperceive.* On a more superficial level, the stories also sug-

Figure 3.4 A drawing similar to those found on the Thematic Apperception Test (TAT).
Psychologists ask test takers to provide their impressions of what is happening in the scene depicted in the drawing. They ask test takers what led up to the scene and how it will turn out. How might your responses reveal aspects of your own personality?

gest how respondents might interpret or behave in similar situations in their own lives. TAT results are also suggestive of clients' attitudes toward others, particularly family members and lovers.

The TAT has been used extensively in research on motivation as well as in clinical practice. For example, psychologist David McClelland (1958, 1982), also of Harvard University, helped pioneer the TAT assessment of social motives such as the needs for achievement and power. The rationales for this research are that we are likely to be somewhat preoccupied with our needs, and that our needs are projected into our reactions to ambiguous stimuli and situations.

Evaluation of the TAT One criticism of the TAT is that the stimulus properties of some of the cards, such as cues depicting sadness or anger, may exert too strong a "stimulus pull" on the subject (Goldfried & Zax, 1965). If so, clients' responses may represent reactions to the stimulus cues rather than projections of their personalities. The TAT, like the Rorschach, is open to criticism that the scoring and interpretation of responses is largely dependent on the clinician's subjective impressions. The validity of the TAT in eliciting deep-seated material also remains to be demonstrated.

Proponents of projective testing argue that in skilled hands tests like the TAT and the Rorschach can yield meaningful material which might not be revealed in interviews or by self-rating inventories. Moreover, allowing subjects freedom of expression through projective testing reduces the tendency of individuals to offer socially desirable responses. Despite the lack of direct evidence for the projective hypothesis, the appeal of projective tests among clinicians remains high (Lubin et al., 1984; Lubin et al., 1985).

NEUROPSYCHOLOGICAL ASSESSMENT

Various methods of **neuropsychological** assessment help researchers and clinicians evaluate whether or not behavioral problems reflect underlying organic conditions. Such methods run the gamut from psychological tests to innovative ways of producing images of the brain.

When neurological impairment is suspected, a neurological evaluation may be requested from a *neurologist*—a medical doctor who specializes in disorders of the nervous system. A clinical **neuropsychologist** may also be consulted to administer neuropsychological assessment techniques. Clinical neuropsychologists use behavioral observation and psychological testing to reveal signs of possible brain damage. Neuropsychological tests not only suggest whether or not clients are suffering from brain damage, but may also suggest which parts of the brain may be involved.

The Bender Visual Motor Gestalt Test

One of the first neuropsychological tests to be developed was the Bender Visual Motor Gestalt test (Bender, 1938). "The Bender" consists of geometric figures that illustrate various Gestalt principles of perception. The client is asked to copy nine geometric designs (see Figure 3.5). Signs of possible brain damage include rotation of the figures, distortions in shape, and incorrect sizing of the figures in relation to one

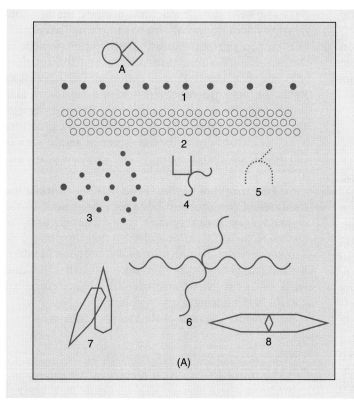
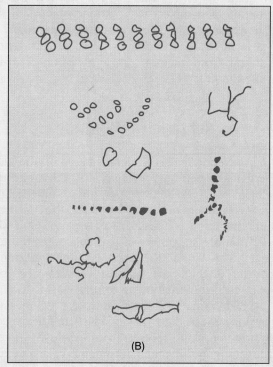

Figure 3.5 The Bender Gestalt test.
The Bender is intended to assess organic impairment. Part A shows the series of figures respondents are asked to copy. Part B shows the drawings of a person who is known to be brain damaged.

another. The examiner then asks the client to reproduce the designs from memory because neurological damage can impair memory functioning.

Although the Bender remains a convenient and economical means of uncovering possible organic impairment, it has been criticized for producing too many **false negatives**—that is, persons with neurological impairment who make satisfactory drawings (Bigler & Ehrenfurth, 1981). In recent years, more sophisticated tests have been developed.

The Halstead-Reitan Neuropsychological Battery

The Halstead-Reitan Neuropsychological Battery may be the most widely used neuropsychological battery. Psychologist Ralph Reitan developed the battery by adapting tests used by his mentor, Ward Halstead, an experimental psychologist, to study brain–behavior relationships among organically impaired individuals. The battery contains tests that measure perceptual, intellectual, and motor skills and performance. A battery of tests permits the psychologist to observe patterns of results, and various patterns of performance

deficits are suggestive of certain kinds of organic defects. The tests in the battery include the following:

1. *The Category Test.* This test measures abstract thinking ability, as indicated by the individual's proficiency at forming principles or categories that relate different stimuli to one another. A series of groups of stimuli that vary in shape, size, location, color, and other characteristics are flashed on a screen. The subject's task is to discern the principle that links them, such as shape or size, and to indicate which stimuli in each grouping represent the correct category by pressing a key. A correct response is signaled by a bell, an incorrect choice by a buzzer. By analyzing the patterns of correct and incorrect choices, the subject normally learns to identify the principles that determine the correct choice. Performance on the test is believed to reflect functioning in the frontal lobe of the brain.

2. *The Rhythm Test.* This is a test of concentration and attention. The subject listens to 30 pairs of tape-recorded rhythmic beats and indicates whether the beats in each pair are the same or different. Performance deficits are associated with damage to the right temporal area of the brain.

3. *The Tactual Performance Test.* This test requires the blindfolded subject to fit wooden blocks of different shapes into corresponding depressions on a form board. Afterward, the subject draws the board from memory as a measure of visual memory.

The Luria Nebraska Test Battery

The Luria Nebraska Test Battery is based on the work of the Russian neuropsychologist A.R. Luria and was developed by psychologists at the University of Nebraska (Golden et al., 1980). Like the Halstead-Reitan, the Luria Nebraska reveals patterns of skill deficits that are suggestive of particular sites of brain damage. The Luria Nebraska is more efficiently administered than the Halstead-Reitan, requiring about one-third of the time to complete.

A wide range of skills is assessed. Tests measure tactile, kinesthetic, and spatial skills; complex motor skills; auditory skills; receptive and expressive speech skills; reading, writing, and arithmetic skills; and general intelligence and memory functioning. Although the Luria Nebraska is promising, more research is needed to substantiate its reliability and validity.

Neuropsychological tests attempt to reveal brain dysfunctions without surgical procedures. We later consider other contemporary techniques that figuratively and literally allow us to see inside the brain without surgery.

BEHAVIORAL ASSESSMENT

The traditional model of assessment, or **psychometric approach**, holds that psychological tests reveal *signs* of reasonably stable traits or dispositions that largely determine people's behavior. The psychometric approach aims to classify people in terms of personality types according to traits such as anxiety, introversion–extraversion, obsessiveness, hostility, impulsivity, and aggressiveness. This model inspired development of trait-based tests such as the Rorschach, TAT, and the MMPI.

The alternative model of **behavioral assessment** treats test results as samples of behavior that occur in specific situations rather than signs of underlying personality types or traits. According to the behavioral approach, behavior is primarily determined by environmental or situational factors, such as stimulus cues and reinforcements.

The behavioral model has inspired the development of techniques that aim to sample an individual's behavior in settings that are as similar as possible to the real-life situation, thus maximizing the relationship between the testing situation and the criterion. Behavior may be observed and measured in such settings as the home, school, or work environment. The examiner may also try to simulate situations in the clinic or laboratory that serve as **analogues** of the problems that the individual confronts in daily life.

The examiner may conduct a **functional analysis** of the problem behavior—relating it to the *antecedents*, or stimulus cues that trigger it, and the *consequences*, or reinforcements that maintain it. Knowledge of the environmental conditions in which a problem behavior occurs may help the therapist work with the client and the family to change the conditions that trigger and maintain it.

Consider the case of Kerry:

A 7-year-old boy, Kerry, is brought by his parents for evaluation. His mother describes him as a "royal terror." His father complains that he won't listen to anyone. Kerry throws temper tantrums in the supermarket, screaming and stomping his feet if his parents refuse to buy him what he wants. At home, he breaks his toys by throwing them against the wall and demands new ones. Sometimes, though, he appears sullen and won't talk to anyone for hours. At school he appears inhibited and has difficulty concentrating. His progress at school is slow and he has difficulty reading. His teachers complain that he has a limited attention span and doesn't seem motivated.

■ *The Authors' Files*

The psychologist may use direct home observation to assess the interactions between Kerry and his parents. Alternately, the psychologist may observe Kerry and his parents through a one-way mirror in the clinic. Such observations may suggest interactions that explain the child's noncompliance. For example, Kerry's noncompliance may follow parental requests that are vague (e.g., a parent says, "Play nicely now," and Kerry responds by throwing toys) or inconsistent (e.g., a parent says, "Go play with your toys but don't make a mess," to which Kerry responds by scattering the toys). Observation may suggest ways in which Kerry's parents can improve communication and cue and reinforce desirable behaviors.

Clinicians may directly observe children's school behavior in the classroom or ask teachers to complete behavior rating scales that highlight problem behaviors which can be targeted for treatment. Clinicians can also observe children performing school tasks, such as math problems, in the clinic to evaluate their approach to problem solving and possible deficits in attention or concentration.

Behavioral clinicians may supplement behavioral observations with traditional forms of assessment, such as the MMPI, or even with projective tests, such as the Rorschach or TAT. However, they are likely to interpret test data as samples of clients' behavior at a particular point in time, and not as signs of stable traits. Trait-oriented clinicians may similarly employ behavioral assessment to learn how personality "traits" are "revealed" in different settings and to see how particular traits affect clients' daily functioning.

Let us consider some of the techniques of behavioral assessment and the issues that they raise.

The Behavioral Interview

The **behavioral interview** poses questions to learn more about the history and situational aspects of problem behavior. Like other interviewers, the behavioral interviewer establishes rapport with clients and evaluates clients' nonverbal behaviors. She or he seeks discrepancies between verbal and nonverbal behaviors and notes movements, gestures, or facial expressions that reflect emotional reactions to topics under discussion.

The behavioral interview more so than the general clinical interview focuses on the situational factors that relate to the problem behavior. If a client seeks help for feelings of panic, the behavioral interviewer might ask how the client experiences panic attacks—when, where, how often, under what circumstances. The interviewer looks for precipitating cues, such as thought patterns (e.g., thoughts of dying or losing control) or situational factors (e.g., entering a department store) that may provoke an attack. The interviewer also seeks information about reinforcers that may maintain the panic. Does the client flee the situation when an attack occurs? Is escape reinforced by relief from anxiety? Has the client learned to lessen anticipatory anxiety by avoiding exposure to situations in which attacks have occurred?

How have other aspects of the client's life been affected by the problem behavior? Do family members treat the client differently? (Have they changed patterns of reinforcement?) For example, have family members assumed added responsibilities to relieve the client of stress, thereby reinforcing dependent behavior? Does the client possess behavioral competencies or skills—such as self-relaxation skills—for coping with the problem? Do skill deficits such as communication or social skills deficits impede progress in coping?

The behavioral interviewer may also assess cognitive factors that affect the problem behavior. The interviewer may ask the client to relate any thoughts that she or he can associate with an attack. The interviewer might probe the client's attitudes and beliefs to ascertain whether dysfunctional beliefs (such as mislabeling a minor bodily sensation as a sign of an impending heart attack) are present in the chain of events that lead to a panic attack.

Self-Monitoring

Training clients to record or monitor the problem behavior in their daily lives is a direct method of relating problem behavior to the settings in which it occurs. In **self-monitoring**, clients assume the primary responsibility for assessing the problem behavior.

An early example of self-monitoring was described by Benjamin Franklin. He kept records of the daily frequency of 13 "virtues" that he attempted to increase:

> I made a book, in which I allotted a page for each of the virtues. I ruled each page with red ink, so as to have seven columns, one for each day of the week, marking each column with a letter for the day. I crossed these columns with thirteen red lines, marking the beginning of each line with the first letter of one of the virtues, on which line, and in its proper column, I might mark by a little black spot every fault I found upon examination to have been committed respecting that virtue upon that day. (Cited in Thoresen & Mahoney, 1974, p. 41)

Franklin's diary is akin to contemporary self-monitoring of "nonvirtuous" behaviors such as cigarette smoking or overeating. Self-monitoring permits direct measurement of the problem behavior when and where it occurs. Behaviors that can be easily counted, such as food intake, cigarette smoking, nail-biting, hair-pulling, study periods, dating occasions, or other social interactions, are well suited for self-monitoring. Clients are usually best aware of the frequency of these behaviors and their situational contexts. Self-monitoring can also produce highly accurate measurement because the behavior is recorded as it occurs, and not reconstructed from memory.

There are various devices for keeping track of the targeted behavior. A behavioral diary or log, like Franklin's, is a handy way to record calories ingested or cigarettes smoked. Such logs are organized in columns and rows to track the frequency of occurrence of the problem behavior and the situations in which it occurs (time, setting, feeling state, etc.). A record of eating may include entries for the type of food eaten, the number of calories, the location in which the eating occurred, the feeling states associated with eating, and the consequences of eating (e.g., how the client felt afterward). In reviewing an eating diary with the clinician, a client can identify problematic eating patterns, such as eating when feeling bored or in response to TV food commercials, and devise better ways of handling these challenges.

Behavioral diaries can also help clients increase desirable but low-frequency behaviors, such as self-assertive or dating behaviors. Unassertive clients might track occasions that seem to warrant an assertive response and jot down their actual responses to each occasion. Clients and clinicians then review the log to highlight problematic situations and rehearse assertive responses. A client who is anxious about dating might record social contacts with the opposite gender. To measure the effects of treatment, clinicians may encourage clients to engage in a **baseline** period of self-monitoring before treatment is begun.

Another popular device for counting troubling behaviors that occur frequently throughout the day such as nail-biting is the wrist or golf counter. In one case, a boy who was treated for **trichotillomania** (hair-pulling) was instructed to record every hair pull with a wrist counter (Anthony, 1978).

Self-monitoring, though, is not without its disadvantages. Some clients are unreliable and do not keep accurate records. They become forgetful or sloppy, or they underreport undesirable behaviors, such as overeating or smoking, because of embarrassment or fear of criticism. To offset these biases, clinicians may, with clients' consent, corroborate the accuracy of self-monitoring by gathering information from other parties, such as clients' spouses. Private behaviors such as eating or smoking alone cannot be corroborated in this way, however. Sometimes other means of corroboration, such as physiological measures, are available. For example, biochemical analysis of the carbon monoxide in clients' breath samples or of nicotine metabolites in their saliva or blood can be used to corroborate reports of abstinence from smoking.

Another issue in self-monitoring is *reactivity*, or changes in measured behavior that stem from the act of measurement. Some clients may change undesirable behaviors merely as a consequence of focusing on or recording them. When reactivity leads to more adaptive behavior, it renders the measurement process an effective therapeutic tool, although it can make it difficult to tease out the effects due to measurement from those due to treatment. In actual practice, however, self-monitoring tends to have only modest lasting effects on behavior.

Analogue or Contrived Measures

Analogue or contrived measures are intended to simulate the setting in which the behavior naturally takes place but are carried out in laboratory or controlled settings. Role-playing exercises are common analogue measures. Clinicians cannot follow clients who have difficulty expressing dissatisfaction to authority figures throughout the day. Instead, clinicians may rely on role-playing exercises, such as having the clients enact challenging an unfair grade. A scene might be described to the client as follows: "You've worked very hard on a term paper and received a very poor grade, say a D or an F. You approach the professor, who asks, 'Is there some problem?' What do you do now?" The client's enactment of the scene may reveal deficits in self-expression that can be addressed in therapy or assertiveness training.

Behavioral approach task. One form of behavioral assessment of phobia involves the measurement of the degree to which the phobic person can approach or interact with the phobic stimulus. Here we see a snake-phobic woman tentatively reaching out to touch the phobic object. Other snake phobics would not be able to touch the snake or even remain in its presence unless it was securely caged.

*betrays bias of. heterosexually-oriented assumptions, and further needed assessment of issues of sensitivity + awareness

The Behavioral Approach Task, or BAT (Lang & Lazovik, 1963), is a popular analogue measure of a phobic person's approach to a feared object, such as a snake. Approach behavior is broken down into levels of response, such as looking in the direction of the snake from about 20 feet, touching the box holding the snake, and touching the snake. The BAT provides direct measurement of a response to a stimulus in a controlled situation. The subject's approach behavior can be quantified by assigning a score to each level of approach.

Direct Observation

Direct observation, or behavioral observation, is the hallmark of behavioral assessment. Through behavioral observation, clinicians can quantify performance of bad habits in real-life and analogue settings, examine the antecedents and consequences of abrasive interpersonal behaviors, study hyperactive children in the classroom, and so on. Observations may be videotaped to permit subsequent analysis of behavioral patterns. Observers are trained to identify and record targeted patterns of behavior. Behavior coding systems have been developed that enhance the reliability of recording.

There are advantages and disadvantages to direct observation. One advantage is that direct observation does not rely on the client's self-reports, which may be distorted by efforts to make a favorable or unfavorable impression. In addition to providing accurate measurements of problem behavior, behavioral observation can suggest strategies for intervention. A mother might report that her son is so hyperactive that he cannot sit still long enough to complete homework assignments. By using a one-way mirror, the clinician may discover that the boy becomes restless only when he encounters a problem that he cannot solve right away. The child may thus be helped by being taught ways of coping with frustration and of solving certain kinds of academic problems.

Direct observation also has its drawbacks. One issue is the possible lack of consensus in defining problems in behavioral terms. In coding the child's behavior for hyperactivity, clinicians must agree on which aspects of the child's behavior represent hyperactivity. Another potential problem is a lack of reliability, or inconsistency, of measurement across time or between observers. Reliability is reduced when an observer is inconsistent in the coding of specific behaviors or when two or more observers code behavior inconsistently.

Observers may also show response biases. An observer who has been sensitized to expect that a child is hyperactive may perceive normal variations in behavior as subtle cues of hyperactivity and erroneously record them as instances of hyperactive behavior. Such expectations are less likely to affect behavioral ratings when the target behaviors are defined concretely (Foster & Cone, 1986).

Reactivity is a potential problem. People may put their best feet forward when they know they are being observed. Reactivity may be reduced by using covert observation techniques, such as hidden cameras or one-way mirrors. Covert observation may not be feasible, however, because of ethical concerns or practical constraints. Another approach is to accustom subjects to observation by watching them a number of times before collecting data (Foster & Cone, 1986).

Another potential problem is *observer drift*—the tendency of observers, or groups of raters, to deviate from the coding system in which they were trained as time elapses. One suggestion to help control this problem is to retrain observers regularly to ensure continued compliance with the coding system (Kazdin, 1992). As time elapses, observers may also become fatigued or distracted. It may be helpful to limit the duration of observations and to provide frequent breaks.

Behavioral observation is limited to measuring overt behaviors. Many clinicians also wish to assess subjective or private experiences—for example, feelings of depression and anxiety or distorted thought patterns. Such clinicians may combine direct observation with forms of assessment that permit clients to reveal internal experiences. Staunch behavioral clinicians tend to consider self-reports unreliable and to limit their data to direct observation.

Behavioral Rating Scales

A **behavioral rating scale** is a checklist that provides information about the frequency, intensity, and range of problem behaviors. Behavioral rating scales differ from self-report personality inventories, in that items assess specific behaviors rather than personality characteristics, interests, or attitudes.

Behavioral rating scales are often used by parents to assess children's problem behaviors. The Child Behavior Problem Checklist (CBCL) (Achenbach, 1978; Achenbach & Edelbrock, 1979), for example, asks parents to rate their children on more than 100 specific problem behaviors, including the following:

___ refuses to eat	___ is uncooperative
___ is disobedient	___ destroys own things
___ hits	

The scale yields an overall problem behavior score and subscale scores on dimensions such as delinquency, aggressiveness, and physical problems. The clinician can compare the child's score on these dimensions with norms based on samples of age-mates.

COGNITIVE ASSESSMENT

Cognitive assessment is used most frequently by cognitive behavior therapists and involves the measurement of thoughts, beliefs, and attitudes. Therapists then attempt to replace self-defeating or distorted thought patterns with self-enhancing, rational thought patterns.

Several methods of cognitive assessment have been developed. One of the most straightforward is the thought record or diary. Depressed clients may carry such diaries to record dysfunctional thoughts as they arise. Aaron Beck (Beck et al., 1979) designed a thought diary or "Daily Record of Dysfunctional Thoughts" to help clients identify thought patterns that are connected with troubling emotional states. Each time the client experiences a negative emotion such as anger or sadness, entries are made to identify

1. The situation in which the emotional state occurred,
2. The automatic or disruptive thoughts that passed through the client's mind,
3. The type or category of disordered thinking that the automatic thought(s) represented (e.g., selective perception, overgeneralization, magnification, or absolutist thinking—see Chapter 2),
4. A rational response to the troublesome thought,
5. The emotional outcome or final emotional response.

A thought diary can become part of a treatment program in which the client learns to replace dysfunctional thoughts with rational alternatives.

Cognitive assessment of Pamela (see p. 98), the travel phobic, might ask her to describe the thoughts that passed through her mind when she imagined herself approaching the fearful situation. Pamela might also be asked to keep a diary of the thoughts she experienced while preparing for a drive, or while driving toward a phobic stimulus like a bridge or an overpass. By examining her imagined and **in-vivo** thoughts, the therapist can help Pamela identify styles of thinking that are linked to phobic episodes,

such as catastrophizing ("I'm going to lose control of the car") and self-deprecation ("I'm just a jerk. I can't handle anything").

A rating scale provides a more structured approach to cognitive assessment. The Automatic Thoughts Questionnaire (ATQ-30; Hollon & Kendall, 1980), for example, has clients rate the weekly frequency and degree of conviction associated with 30 apparently automatic negative thoughts. (Automatic thoughts seem to just pop into our minds.) Sample items include the following:

- I don't think I can go on.
- I hate myself.
- I've let people down.

A total score is obtained by summing the frequencies of occurrence of each item. Higher scores are considered typical of depressive thought patterns. The scale discriminates between college students who attain high or low scores on the Beck Depression Inventory (Hollon & Kendall, 1980) and between depressed psychiatric outpatients, nondepressed psychiatric patients, and normal people (Harrel & Ryon, 1983). The 30-item ATQ has been statistically sorted into four categories or factors of related thoughts (Hollon & Kendall, 1980; see Table 3.10).

Another cognitive measure, the Dysfunctional Attitudes Scale (DAS; Weissman & Beck, 1978), consists of 40 beliefs or attitudes associated with depression. Examples include "I feel like I'm nothing if someone I love doesn't love me back." Subjects rate the conviction with which they hold each belief on a 7-point scale ranging from "not at all" (1) to "totally" (7). Scores can range from 40 to 280. Higher scores are suggestive of depressive styles of thinking; one study found that hospitalized depressed patients attained significantly higher DAS scores than patients hospitalized for reasons other than depression (Hamilton & Abramson, 1983).

■ EVALUATION OF COGNITIVE ASSESSMENT

Cognitive assessment opens a new domain to the psychologist in understanding how disruptive thoughts are related to abnormal behavior. It is too early to tell whether or not cognitive assessment will have lasting value for clinical practice, however. Many behavior therapists prefer to assess and treat observable behaviors only. Historically, psychodynamic and humanistic-existential therapists have probed the workings of clients' minds. Only in the past two decades or so have cognitive and cognitive-behavioral therapists begun to explore what Skinner labeled the "black box"—people's internal states—to learn how thoughts and attitudes influence emotional states and behavior.

Table 3.10 Items Defining Factors on the Automatic Thoughts Questionnaire

Factor 1: Personal Maladjustment and Desire for Change	Something has to change. What's the matter with me? I wish I were a better person. What's wrong with me? I'm so disappointed in myself.
Factor 2: Negative Self-Concept and Negative Expectations	My future is bleak. I'm a failure. I'll never make it. My life's not going the way I wanted it to. I'm a loser. Why can't I ever succeed? I'm no good.
Factor 3: Low Self-Esteem	I'm worthless. I hate myself.
Factor 4: Giving Up/Helplessness	I can't finish anything. It's just not worth it.

Source: Hollon, S. D., & Kendall, P. C. (1980). Cognitive self-statements in depression: Development of an automatic thoughts questionnaire. Cognitive Therapy and Research, 4, 383–395. Copyright © 1980 by Plenum Publishing Corporation.

The behavioral objection to cognitive techniques is that clinicians have no direct means of verifying clients' subjective experiences—their thoughts and beliefs. These are private experiences that can be reported but not observed and measured directly. Even though thoughts remain private experiences, their written or spoken report constitutes behaviors that can be quantified.

PHYSIOLOGICAL MEASUREMENT

We can also learn about abnormal behavior by studying people's physiological responses. Anxiety, for example, is associated with arousal of the sympathetic division of the autonomic nervous system (see Chapter 2). Anxious people therefore show elevated heart rates and blood pressure, which can be measured directly by means of the pulse and a blood pressure cuff. People also sweat more heavily when they are anxious. When we sweat, our skin becomes wet, increasing its ability to conduct electricity. Sweating can be measured by means of the **electrodermal response** or **galvanic skin response** (GSR). (*Electrodermal* contains the Greek word *derma*, meaning "skin." *Galvanic* is named after the Italian physicist and physician, Luigi Galvani, who was a pioneer in research in electricity.) Measures of the GSR assess the amount of electricity that passes through two points on the skin—usually of the hand. We assume the person's anxiety level correlates with

the amount of electricity that is conducted across the skin.

The GSR is just one example of a physiological response that is measured through probes or sensors that are connected to the body. The **electroencephalograph** (EEG) measures brain waves by attaching electrodes to the scalp (see feature "How Researchers and Clinicians Study the Functions of the Brain").

Changes in muscle tension are also often associated with states of anxiety or tension. They can be detected through the **electromyograph** (EMG), which monitors muscle tension through sensors attached to targeted muscle groups. (*Myo-* derives from the Greek *mys*, meaning "mouse" or "muscle." The Greeks observed that muscles moved mouselike beneath the skin.) Placement of EMG probes on the forehead can indicate muscle tension associated with tension headaches. Other probes are used to assess sexual arousal (see Chapter 10).

Ambulatory blood pressure devices allow clinicians to monitor clients' blood pressure at intervals throughout the day. Clients may log their concurrent activities or feeling states to reveal how changes in blood pressure are connected with stress.

 Clients can be fitted with equipment that allows psychologists to measure *physiological markers* of their emotional responses as they go about their daily lives.

■ **RESPONSE SYSTEMS** Lang (1968) suggested that fear or anxiety consists of three different

[handwritten note:] # It would seem necessary to be very cautious with such a measure, as sweating can vary greatly at times depending on their genetic propensity for this physiological response.

A CLOSER LOOK

How Researchers and Clinicians Study the Functions of the Brain

Researchers and clinicians use various techniques to study the structure and function of the brain. One of the most common is the electroencephalograph (EEG), which is a record of the electrical activity of the brain (Figure 3.6). The EEG detects minute amounts of electrical activity in the brain, or brain waves, that are conducted between electrodes. Certain brain waves are connected with feelings of relaxation and stages of sleep. Schizophrenics and persons with brain damage produce patterns of brain waves that differ in recognizable ways from those of normal people. The EEG is used to study various abnormal behavior patterns. The EEG is also used by medical personnel to reveal brain abnormalities, such as tumors.

Today computers are used to generate images of parts of the brain. In **computerized axial tomography** (CAT scan), a narrow X-ray beam is aimed at the head (Figure 3.7). The radiation that passes through is measured from multiple angles. The CAT scan reveals abnormalities in shape and structure that may be suggestive of lesions, blood clots, or tumors. The computer enables scientists to integrate the measurements into a three-dimensional picture of the brain. Evidence of brain damage that was once detectable only by surgery may now be displayed on a monitor.

Another imaging method, **positron emission tomography** (the PET scan), is used to study the functioning of various parts of the brain (Figure 3.8). In this method, a small amount of a radioactive compound or tracer is mixed with glucose and injected into the bloodstream. When it reaches the brain, patterns of neural activity are revealed by measurement of the positrons—positively charged particles—emitted by the tracer. The glucose metabolized by parts of the brain generates a computer

Figure 3.6 The Electroencephalogram (EEG).
The EEG is a record of brain wave activity as recorded by an electroencephalograph. The EEG can be used to study differences in brain waves between groups of normal people and people with problems such as schizophrenia or organic brain damage.

Figure 3.7 The Computerized Axial Tomography (CAT) Scan.
The CAT scan aims a narrow X-ray beam at the head, and the resultant radiation is measured from multiple angles as it passes through. The computer enables researchers to consolidate the measurements into a three-dimensional image of the brain. The CAT scan reveals structural abnormalities in the brain that may be implicated in various patterns of abnormal behavior.

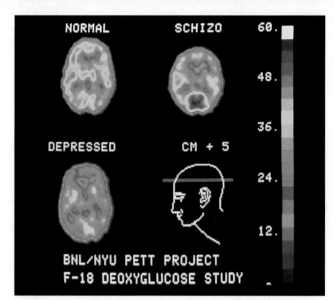

Figure 3.8 Positron Emission Tomography (the PET Scan).
In the PET scan, a small amount of a radioactive tracer is mixed with glucose and injected into the bloodstream. When it reaches the brain, patterns of neural activity are revealed by measurement of the positively charged particles that are emitted by the tracer. The glucose metabolized by parts of the brain generates a computer image of neural activity. Areas of greater activity metabolize more glucose. These PET scan images suggest differences in the metabolic processes of the brains of normal, schizophrenic, and depressed individuals.

image of neural activity. Areas of greater activity metabolize more glucose. The PET scan has been used to learn which parts of the brain are most active (metabolize more glucose) when we are listening to music, solving a math problem, or using language (Petersen et al., 1988). Patterns of neural activity also differ in the brains of normal and schizophrenic people.

A third imaging technique is **magnetic resonance imaging** (MRI) (Figure 3.9). In MRI, the person is placed in a donut-shaped tunnel that generates a strong magnetic field. Radio waves of certain frequencies are directed at the person. As a result, parts of the brain emit signals that are measured from several angles. As with the CAT scan, the signals are integrated into a computer-generated image of the brain.

Brain electrical activity mapping (BEAM), a type of EEG, uses the computer to analyze brain wave patterns to reveal areas of relative activity and inactivity from moment to moment (Figure 3.10). Twenty or more electrodes are attached to the scalp and simultaneously feed information about brain activity to a computer. The computer analyzes the signals and displays the pattern of brain activity on a color monitor, providing a vivid image of the electrical activity of the brain at work. BEAM technology has been helpful in identifying brain tumors (Duffy, 1982), epilepsy (Lombroso & Duffy, 1982), and dyslexia (Duffy et

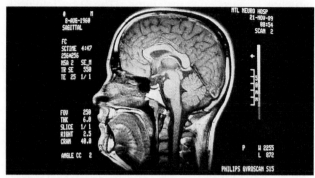

Figure 3.9 Magnetic Resonance Imaging (MRI).
In MRI, the person is placed in a donut-shaped tunnel that generates a strong magnetic field. Radio waves are directed at the brain, which emit signals that are measured from several angles and integrated into a computer-generated image of the brain.

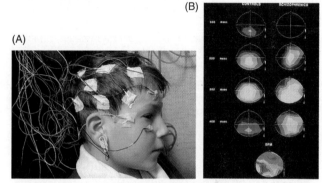

Figure 3.10 Brain Electrical Activity Mapping (BEAM).
BEAM is a type of EEG in which electrodes are attached to the scalp (Part A) to measure electrical activity in various regions of the brain. The left column of Part B shows the average level of electrical activity in the brains of 10 normal people ("controls") at 4 time intervals. The column to the right shows the average level of activity of schizophrenic subjects during the same intervals. Higher activity levels are represented in increasing order by yellows, reds, and whites. The computer-generated image in the bottom center summarizes differences in activity levels between the brains of normal and schizophrenic subjects. Areas of the brain depicted in blue show small differences between the groups. White areas represent larger differences.

al., 1980); and for examining differences in brain activity between schizophrenics and nonschizophrenics (Morihisa et al., 1983).

 Imaging techniques such as the CAT scan, the PET scan, MRI, and BEAM do allow us to form inner images of the brain without surgery.

In later chapters we see how modern imaging techniques are furthering our understanding of various patterns of abnormal behavior.

response systems—behavioral, physiological, and verbal. The behavioral response is avoidance of fear-inducing objects or situations. The physiological response can be measured in terms of changes in heart rate, GSR, or other bodily responses. The verbal system involves measurement of the subjective experience of anxiety. These response systems may act independently, however, so that changes in one may not be generalized to another (Rachman & Hodgson, 1974). For example, people may report they feel progressively less anxious when they confront a fearful situation, but their hearts may continue to pound. Or people may be able to approach a phobic situation—such as blood tests or surgery—even though they report lingering anxiety or fear. Because response systems can be independent, most researchers recommend that investigations include multiple measures of anxiety or fear across response domains (Holden & Barlow, 1986), such as self-report of subjective feelings, behavioral approach measures, and physiological measurement.

People's psychological problems, which are no less complex than people themselves, are thus assessed in many ways. Clients are generally asked to explain their problems as best they can, and sometimes a computer does the asking. Psychologists can also draw on batteries of tests that assess intelligence, personality, and neuropsychological integrity. Many psychologists prefer to observe people's behavior directly when possible, and sometimes the observations are recorded by devices that assess physiological markers of emotional states. The methods of assessment selected by clinicians reflect the problems of their clients, the clinicians' theoretical orientations, and the clinicians' mastery of specialized technologies.

As we survey abnormal behavior patterns in the following chapters, we see that our expanding ability to assess people's problems has led to new insights and raised a host of new questions.

SUMMARY

Classification of Abnormal Behavior

The modern diagnostic system may be traced to Hippocrates, who classified such disorders as melancholia, mania, and phrenitis, which generally correspond to several modern diagnostic categories. The modern era of diagnosis of psychological disorders was ushered in by Kraepelin in the late 19th century. His classification system influenced the development of the *Diagnostic and Statistical Manual of Mental Disorders* (DSM), which is the most widely accepted diagnostic system.

The DSM uses specific diagnostic criteria to group patterns of abnormal behaviors that share common clinical features and a multiaxial system of evaluation. Strengths of the DSM include its use of specified diagnostic criteria and a multiaxial system to provide a comprehensive picture of the person's functioning. Weaknesses include questions about reliability and validity, and about the medical model framework.

Characteristics of Methods of Assessment

Methods of assessment must be reliable and valid. Reliability of assessment techniques is shown in various ways, including internal consistency, temporal stability, and interrater reliability. Validity is measured by means of content validity, criterion validity, and construct validity.

The Clinical Interview

The most widely used method of assessment, the clinical interview involves the use of a set of questions designed to elicit relevant information from people seeking treatment. Clinicians generally use a structured interview, which consists of a fairly standard series of questions to gather a wide range of information concerning presenting problems or complaints, present circumstances, and history.

Psychological Tests

Psychological tests are structured methods of assessment that are used to evaluate reasonably stable traits such as intelligence and personality.

Intelligence Tests

Tests of intelligence, like the Stanford-Binet and the Wechsler scales, are used for various purposes in clinical assessment, including determining evidence of mental retardation or cognitive impairment, and assessing strengths and weaknesses. Intelligence is expressed in the form of an intelligence quotient (IQ).

Personality Tests

Self-report personality inventories, like the MMPI, MCMI, and Beck Depression Inventory use structured items to measure various personality traits, such as anxiety, depression, and masculinity–femininity. These tests are considered *objective* in the sense that they make use of a limited range of possible responses to items and an empirical, or objective, method of test construction.

Projective personality tests ask subjects to interpret ambiguous stimuli in the belief that their answers may shed light on the unconscious processes. In the Rorschach inkblot test, subjects are presented with ten inkblots and are asked to say what the inkblots look like to them and how they formed their responses. The Thematic Apperception Test (TAT) presents subjects with a series of cards that depict ambiguous scenes.

Neuropsychological Assessment

Methods of neuropsychological assessment help determine organic bases for impaired behavior and psychological functioning. The Bender Visual Motor Gestalt Test requires subjects to reproduce nine geometric designs on a piece of paper. The Halstead-Reitan Neuropsychological Battery and Luria Nebraska Test Battery are more sophisticated batteries of tests measuring various perceptual, intellectual, and motor skills and performance.

Behavioral Assessment

In behavioral assessment, test responses are taken as samples of behavior rather than as signs of underlying traits or dispositions. The behavioral examiner may conduct a functional assessment, which relates the problem behavior to its antecedents and consequents. Methods of behavioral assessment include behavioral interviewing, self-monitoring, use of analogue or contrived measures, direct observation, and behavioral rating scales.

Cognitive Assessment

Cognitive assessment focuses on the measurement of thoughts, beliefs, and attitudes in order to help identify distorted thinking patterns. Specific methods of assessment include the use of a thought record or diary and the use of rating scales such as the Automatic Thoughts Questionnaire (ATQ) and the Dysfunctional Attitudes Scale (DAS).

Physiological Measurement

Measures of physiological function include heart rate, blood pressure, galvanic skin response (GSR), muscle tension, and brain wave activity. Brain-imaging techniques such as EEG, CAT scans, PET scans, MRI, and BEAM probe the workings of the brain.

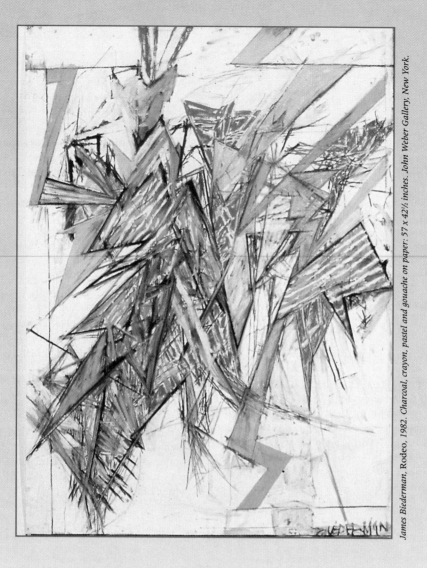

James Biederman, Rodeo, 1982. Charcoal, crayon, pastel and gouache on paper: 57 x 42½ inches. John Weber Gallery, New York.

CHAPTER OUTLINE

4

Stress, Psychological Factors, and Health

TRUTH  FICTION?

—— Trouble concentrating on your schoolwork because of the breakup of a recent romance could result in your being labeled as having a "mental disorder."

—— As you read this page, millions of microscopic warriors in your body are engaged in search-and-destroy missions against invading hordes.

—— Stress places people at greater risk for forming dental cavities.

—— Optimistic people recover more rapidly than pessimistic people from coronary artery bypass surgery.

—— A sense of humor may buffer the impact of stress.

—— African Americans are more likely than non-Hispanic white Americans to die from cancer.

—— Japanese-American men who reside in California and Hawaii are more likely than Japanese men who reside in Japan to become obese.

—— Single men tend to live longer than married men.

—— People have relieved migraine headaches by raising the temperature in a finger.

—— People recognize when their blood pressure is high.

—— Cycles of dieting and regaining lost weight make it progressively more difficult to take extra pounds off.

—— Dieting has become the normal way of eating for American women.

—— Stress can affect the course of cancer.

LEARNING OBJECTIVES

When you have completed your study of Chapter 4, you should be able to:

1. Describe the features of adjustment disorders.

2. Explain how labeling an adjustment disorder a "mental disorder" may blur the line between what is normal and what is abnormal.

3. Explain what is meant by a multifactorial view of health and illness.

4. Explain the significance of biological factors in health and illness, paying special attention to the role of the immune system.

5. Explain the significance of psychological factors in health and illness.

6. Explain the significance of socioeconomic, sociocultural, and ethnic factors in health and illness.

7. Explain the significance of natural environmental factors in health and illness.

8. Explain the significance of technological factors in health and illness.

9. Discuss the origins and treatment of headaches.

10. Discuss the origins, risk factors, and treatment of cardiovascular disorders.

11. Discuss the origins and treatment of gastrointestinal disorders.

12. Discuss the origins and treatment of asthma.

13. Discuss the origins and treatment of obesity.

14. Discuss the origins, risk factors, and treatment of cancer.

15. Explain why a discussion of AIDS is included in an abnormal psychology textbook.

16. Discuss the origins and prevention of AIDS.

*T*here is an age-old debate concerning the relationships between the mind and the body. Mental functioning is certainly dependent on the brain, but because the workings of the mind are of a different quality than biological processes, there is continuing temptation to regard them separately. The 17th-century French philosopher René Descartes (1596–1650) influenced modern thinking with his belief in dualism, or separateness, between the mind and body. Today scientists and clinicians have come to recognize that mind and body are more closely intertwined than would be suggested by a dualistic model—that psychological factors influence physical functioning while the physical condition of the body affects mental functioning. Psychologists who study the interrelationships between psychology and health are called **health psychologists**.

We begin this chapter by focusing on the role of stress in both mental and physical functioning. **Stress** is a general term that refers to any demand made upon an organism to adapt or adjust. Sources of stress include life changes, such as the death of a loved one or a job termination; psychosocial factors, like problems in social relationships; or physical environmental factors, such as exposure to extreme temperatures or noise levels. There is increasing evidence that stress plays a role in physical and psychological problems. Researchers find, for instance, that people exposed to numerous stressful events in the recent past are at increased risk for depression and anxiety (Noshpitz & Coddington, 1990). We examine a group of psychological disorders—*adjustment disorders*—in which people have difficulty adapting to stress. We also consider the interrelationships between stress and illness and the multiple factors that help account for health and illness including the roles played by psychological and sociocultural factors in various physical disorders.

ADJUSTMENT DISORDERS

Adjustment disorders are the first psychological disorders we discuss in this book, and they are among the mildest. Adjustment disorders are maladaptive reactions in adapting to an identified stressor that develop within a few months of the onset of the stressor. These maladaptive reactions are characterized by significant impairment in social, occupational, or academic functioning, or by states of emotional distress that exceed those normally induced by the stressor. For the diagnosis to apply, the stress-related reaction must not be sufficient to meet the diagnostic criteria for other clinical syndromes, such as anxiety disorders or mood disorders. The maladaptive reaction may be resolved if the stressor is removed or the individual learns to cope with it. If the

Difficulty in concentrating or adjustment disorder? An adjustment disorder is a maladaptive reaction to a stressful event that may take the form of impaired functioning at school or at work, such as having difficulties keeping one's mind on one's studies.

maladaptive reaction lasts for more than six months after the stressor or its consequences have been removed, the diagnosis may be changed.

If your relationship with someone comes to an end (an identified stressor) and your grades are falling off because you are unable to keep your mind on schoolwork, you may fit the bill for an adjustment disorder. If Uncle Harry has been feeling down and pessimistic since his divorce from Aunt Jane, he too may be diagnosed with an adjustment disorder. So too might Cousin Billy if he has been cutting classes and spraying obscene words on the school walls or showing other signs of disturbed conduct.

The concept of "adjustment disorder" as a *mental disorder* highlights some of the difficulties in attempting to define what is normal and what is not. When something important goes wrong in life, we should feel bad about it. If there is a crisis in business, if we are victimized by a crime, if there is a flood or a devastating hurricane, it is understandable that we might become anxious or depressed. There might, in fact, be something more seriously wrong with us if we did not react in a "maladaptive" way—at least temporarily.

Consider the student who leaves home to attend college for the first time—another identified stressor. Brief reactions such as loneliness and a mildly depressed mood following separation from family and friends, or anxiety over meeting new people or completing academic assignments, may represent a normal adjustment to the stressor. The clinician tries to gauge whether or not the individual's emotional complaints exceed an expectable level, or whether or not the individual's ability to function is impaired. In the example, an adjustment disorder might involve evidence of impaired functioning (for example, avoidance of social interactions, difficulty

getting out of bed or attending classes) or emotional features such as anxious or depressed mood that the clinician considers excessive under the circumstances. This is a judgment call. There are no precise boundaries between an "expectable reaction" and an "adjustment disorder."

 If you are having trouble concentrating on your schoolwork because of the breakup of a recent romance, you may have a mild form of "mental disorder" called an *adjustment disorder.*

In some cases of adjustment disorder, the stressor is severe enough to distress most people. The diagnosis of adjustment disorder may still apply if distress impairs the ability to function in occupational or social roles. The stressor in the following case, learning that one is infected with HIV, typically generates strong feelings of anxiety and depression (Kelly & Murphy, 1992). Yet a diagnosis of adjustment disorder was made because of impairment in occupational functioning.

Marvin was a 35-year-old journalist who tested positive for [HIV] in his system, but he was presently in good health, except for some bothersome allergies which produced sore throat and other physical symptoms. He worries that his symptoms might represent the first signs of AIDS, and has been bothered by frequent and intrusive thoughts about dying and recurrent fantasies of becoming seriously ill and dependent on others. His anxiety has become so severe that he finds it difficult to concentrate at work and is worried that exposure to job-related stress may weaken his body's immune system, leaving him more vulnerable to the disease. He is considering quitting his job and retiring to a country home, where he could lead a simpler life. His anxiety was heightened in the past week in hearing that two acquaintances were diagnosed as having AIDS. He now avoids reading anything about AIDS in the newspaper or attending social situations in which AIDS may be discussed. Marvin had never contacted a mental health professional before and always regarded himself, until now, as a happy person who was fulfilled in his work and personal relationships.

■ *Adapted from Spitzer et al., 1989, pp. 5–7*

Stress and Illness

Stressful life events can not only diminish our capacity for adjustment, they may also have detrimental effects on our health. One of the ways in which stress may affect our health is by impairing the functioning of our **immune system**, our body's line of defense against diseases. Before discussing links between stress and illness, let us take a closer look at the workings of the immune system.

■ **THE IMMUNE SYSTEM**   Given the intricacies of the human body and the rapid advance of scientific knowledge, we tend to consider ourselves dependent on highly trained medical specialists to contend with illness. Actually we cope with most diseases by ourselves, through the functioning of our immune systems.

The immune system combats disease in a number of ways. It produces white blood cells that systematically envelop and kill pathogens like bacteria, viruses, and fungi; worn-out body cells; and cells that have become cancerous. White blood cells are

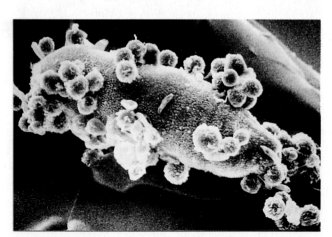

White blood cells attacking and engulfing pathogens.
White blood cells—or *leukocytes*—form part of the body's immune system.

referred to as **leukocytes**. Leukocytes sustain microscopic warfare. They undertake search-and-destroy missions; they identify and eradicate foreign agents and infirmed cells.

Leukocytes recognize invading pathogens by their surface fragments, called **antigens**, literally *anti*body *gen*erators. Some leukocytes produce **antibodies**, kinds of specialized proteins, that attach to these foreign bodies, inactivate them, and mark them for destruction.

Special "memory lymphocytes" (lymphocytes are a type of leukocyte) are held in reserve, rather than marking foreign bodies for destruction or going to war against them. They can remain in the bloodstream, sometimes for several years, and they form the basis for a quick immune response to an invader the second time around. **Vaccination** is the placement of a weakened form of an antigen in the body, which activates the creation of antibodies and memory lymphocytes. Many diseases, including smallpox, have been all but annihilated by vaccination, and researchers are trying to develop a vaccine against HIV (*human immunodeficiency virus*, the virus that causes *acquired immunodeficiency syndrome*—AIDS).

Another function of the immune system is **inflammation**. When we are injured, blood vessels in the region initially contract to check bleeding. Then they dilate. Dilation expands blood flow to the injured region, causing the redness and warmth that identify inflammation. The elevated blood supply also brings in an army of leukocytes to combat invading microscopic life forms, like bacteria, that would otherwise use the local injury as a beachhead into the body.

 It is true that millions of microscopic warriors in your body are engaged in search-and-destroy missions against invading microbes as you read this page. They are leukocytes, and they form the basis for the body's immune response.

■ **PSYCHONEUROIMMUNOLOGY AND THE IMMUNE SYSTEM**   The field of **psychoneuroimmunology** studies relationships among stressors, the endocrine system, the nervous system, and the immune system (Kiecolt-Glaser & Glaser, 1992). Although evidence is still being marshaled, what is available suggests that stress (for example, chronic unemployment) dampens immunological functioning (O'Leary, 1990). Let us consider the results of some recent experiments examining connections between stress and the immune system.

In one study with dental students (Jemmott et al., 1983), saliva levels of immunoglobulin A, an antibody that combats a kind of bacteria which causes respiratory infection and dental cavities, were measured during stressful school periods and right after relaxing vacations. The students showed a weaker immune response, in terms of lowered immunoglobulin A levels, during stressful school periods.

 Stress can contribute to dental cavities by suppressing levels of antibodies that fight the bacteria which cause cavities.

Medical students, similarly, show poorer immune functioning during exam time than they do a month before exams, when their lives are relatively less stressful (Glaser et al., 1985, 1986, 1987). Medical and dental students with larger numbers of friends show better immune functioning than students with fewer friends (Jemmott et al., 1983; Kiecolt-Glaser et al., 1984). Social support thus appears to moderate the stresses of school life as well as other stresses (McClelland, 1989). In another study, undergraduates were encouraged to think about selfless love by watching a film in which Mother Teresa of Calcutta cared for abandoned babies and sick people. The students showed significantly higher immunoglobulin A levels after viewing the film (McClelland & Kirshnit, 1988), but these levels returned to normal in about an hour. In a follow-up study, however, students were able to maintain enhanced immune system functioning, as assessed by immunoglobulin A levels, by thinking about loving experiences. McClelland (1989) speculates that people "who chronically think a lot about loving . . . might develop higher stable levels" of immunoglobulin A (p. 678).

Another study with college students found that the stress produced by examinations suppressed the immune response to the Epstein-Barr virus, a non-lethal pathogen which causes fatigue and related problems (Glaser et al., 1991). Consistent with the previously described study, lonely students showed greater suppression of the immune response than students with greater social support. Newly separated and divorced people also show evidence of suppressed immune response, especially those who remain more attached to their ex-partners (Kiecolt-Glaser et al., 1987, 1988).

Research in the field of psychoneuroimmunology remains mostly correlational. Most studies consider immunological functioning in relation to certain sources or times of stress, such as loneliness or examination periods, and among certain groups of people who may be subject to particular stresses, such as newly separated or divorced people. Correlational research helps researchers understand relationships

Stress and the functioning of the immune system. Students show evidence of lower immunological response—as measured, for example, by levels of antibodies such as immunoglobulin A in the saliva—during periods when they are under stress, like during exams. People may thus be more susceptible to illness at times when they are under stress.

between variables but does not establish causation. Yet there is some evidence showing the causal effects of psychological treatment on immune functioning. One experiment with elderly people demonstrated that a combination of relaxation training and training in coping skills *enhanced* the functioning of the immune system (Kiecolt-Glaser et al., 1985). Immunological functioning declines with age. Efforts to help improve immune function in the elderly could potentially increase their resistance to disease and prolong life.

In another study, a broad-based psychological intervention consisting of stress management techniques (such as relaxation training) and psychological support led to improved immunological response in (postsurgical) patients with malignant skin cancer (Fawzy et al., 1990).

Investigators have also found that writing about the traumatic events that one has experienced also improves immunological functioning (Pennebaker et al., 1988). Inhibiting thoughts or feelings about traumatic events may place a stressful burden on the autonomic nervous system, contributing to the development of stress-related disorders. Facing trauma by talking or writing about it may free people from the need to inhibit such thoughts and feelings.

Although evidence has accumulated that psychological interventions can bolster immune functioning, it is too early to tell whether such effects will translate into concrete improvements in health. Still, the research findings to date are promising (Kiecolt-Glaser & Glaser, 1992).

Stress and Life Changes

Another way in which researchers have investigated the stress–illness connection is by quantifying life stress in terms of **life changes.** Holmes and Rahe (1967) assembled a scale to gauge the effect of life changes. They calibrated the scale by assigning marriage a weight of 50 "life-change units." (Both positive events, like marriage, and negative events, like a job termination, can be stressful because the changes they involve impose demands on us to adjust.) Then, using marriage as a reference point, subjects from various walks of life assigned units to additional life changes. Most changes were considered less stressful than marriage. A few, however, were rated as more stressful, including death of a spouse (100 units) and divorce (73 units). Other items are listed in Table 4.1.

Researchers have investigated links between life changes and proneness to illness. Holmes and Rahe (1967) reported that about 80% of the people who chalked up 300 or more life-change units during a year developed medical problems. By contrast, only about 30% of those who "earned" fewer than 150 units within a year developed medical difficulties. Other investigators have also reported a link between other sources of life stress, such as hassles (daily annoyances like commuting in traffic) and physical illness (for example, Kanner et al., 1981). Still others found that marital disruption in the form of separation or divorce was linked to higher rates of physical illnesses such as cancer and emotional problems (Ernster et al., 1979; Somers, 1979). High numbers of life-change units amassed within a year have also

Life changes.   Life changes such as marriage and the death of loved ones are sources of stress that require adjustment. People identified the death of a spouse as the most stressful life change on Holmes and Rahe's scale of life-change units.

been linked to problems ranging from heart disease to accidents, school failure, and relapses among persons with schizophrenia (Lloyd et al., 1980; Perkins, 1982; Rabkin, 1980; Thoits, 1983).

Despite these findings, we need to be cautious in our interpretations. For one thing, the links are correlational and not experimental (Dohrenwend et al., 1984; Monroe, 1982). In other words, researchers did not (and would not!) assign subjects to conditions in which they would be exposed to either high or low levels of hassles and life changes to see what effects these conditions might have on the subjects' health over time. Rather, the existing data are based on observations of relationships between hassles and life changes, on the one hand, and psychological and

Table 4.1 Scale of Life-Change Units

Life Event	Life-Change Units	Life Event	Life-Change Units
Death of one's spouse	100	Son or daughter leaving home	29
Divorce	73	Trouble with in-laws	29
Marital separation	65	Outstanding personal achievement	28
Jail term	63	Wife beginning or stopping work	26
Death of a close family member	63	Beginning or ending school	26
Personal injury or illness	53	Change in living conditions	25
Marriage	50	Revision of personal habits	24
Being fired at work	47	Trouble with one's boss	23
Marital reconciliation	45	Change in work hours or conditions	20
Retirement	45		
Change in the health of a family member	44	Change in residence	20
		Change in schools	20
Pregnancy	40	Change in recreation	19
Sex difficulties	39	Change in church activities	19
Gain of a new family member	39	Change in social activities	18
Business readjustment	39	Mortgage or loan of less than $10,000	17
Change in one's financial state	38		
Death of a close friend	37	Change in sleeping habits	16
Change to a different line of work	36	Change in number of family get-togethers	15
Change in number of arguments with one's spouse	35	Change in eating habits	15
Mortgage over $10,000*	31	Vacation	13
Foreclosure of a mortgage or loan	30	Christmas	12
Change in responsibilities at work	29	Minor violations of the law	11

*This figure seemed appropriate in 1967, when the scale was constructed. Today, inflation and advances in real estate prices probably balloon this figure to at least $100,000.

Source: Holmes and Rahe (1967).

physical problems on the other. These relationships are open to other interpretations. It could be that people who are predisposed to physical or psychological difficulties face more hassles and accumulate more life-change units. For example, physical illness may contribute to more life disruptions involving hassles and life changes, such as quarrels with one's family, changes in housing and sleeping patterns, and so forth. Hence, in many cases the causal direction may be reversed: Physical and psychological problems may give rise to, rather than stem from, daily hassles and life changes (Dohrenwend et al., 1984; Dohrenwend & Shrout, 1985; Monroe, 1983).

Although both positive and negative life changes can be stressful, positive life changes seem to be less disruptive than daily hassles and negative life changes (Lefcourt et al., 1981; Perkins, 1982; Thoits, 1983). In other words, marriage tends to be less stressful than divorce or separation. Or to put it another way: A change for the better may be a change, but it is less of a hassle.

■ THE GENERAL ADAPTATION SYNDROME

Stress researcher Hans Selye (1976) coined the term **general adaptation syndrome** (GAS) to describe a common biological response pattern to prolonged or excessive stress. Selye pointed out that our bodies respond similarly to many kinds of stressors, whether the source of stress is an invasion of microscopic disease organisms, a divorce, or the aftermath of a flood. The GAS model suggests that our bodies, under stress, are like clocks with alarm systems that do not shut off until their energy is perilously depleted.

The GAS includes three stages: the alarm reaction, the resistance stage, and the exhaustion stage. Perception of an immediate stressor (for example, a car that swerves in front of your own on the highway) triggers the **alarm reaction**. The alarm reaction mobilizes the body for defense. It is initiated by the brain and regulated by the endocrine system and the sympathetic branch of the autonomic nervous system (ANS). In 1929, Harvard University physiologist Walter Cannon called the initial mobilization of the body's defenses the **fight-or-flight reaction**. Some of the components of the alarm reaction are shown in Table 4.2.

The fight-or-flight reaction most probably helped our early ancestors cope with the many perils they faced. The reaction may have been provoked by the sight of a predator or by a rustling sound in the undergrowth. But our ancestors usually did not experience prolonged activation of the alarm reaction. Once a threat was eliminated, the body reinstates a lower level of arousal. Our ancestors fought off predators or they fled quickly; if not, they failed to contribute their genes to the genetic pools of their groups. In short, they died. Sensitive alarm reactions bestowed survival. Yet our ancestors did not invest years in the academic grind, carry 30-year adjustable mortgages, struggle to balance the budget each month, or face any of the myriad prolonged stressors that contemporary men and women endure. Modern stressors can excite our alarm systems for hours, days, or weeks at a time, or longer.

If the alarm reaction is aroused and the stressor persists, we progress to the **resistance stage**, or adaptation stage, of the GAS. Endocrine and sympathetic activities remain at high levels, but not quite as high as during the alarm reaction. During this stage the body tries to renew spent energy and repair damage. When stressors continue to persist, we may advance to the final, or **exhaustion stage** of the GAS. Although there are individual differences in capacity to resist stress, all of us will eventually exhaust or deplete our bodily resources. The exhaustion stage is characterized by dominance of the parasympathetic branch of the ANS. Consequently, our heart and respiration rates decelerate. Do we benefit from the respite? Not necessarily. If the source of stress persists, we may develop what Selye termed "diseases of adaptation." These range from allergic reactions to ulcers and coronary heart disease—and, at times, even death.

Stress has a domino effect on the endocrine system. First, the hypothalamus secretes corticotrophin-releasing hormone (CRH), which causes the pituitary gland to secrete adrenocorticotrophic hormone (ACTH). ACTH, in turn, stimulates the adrenal cortex to release cortisol and other corticosteroids (discussed in Chapter 2). Corticosteroids—steroidal hormones produced by the adrenal cortex—help defend the body by fighting allergic reactions (like difficulty breathing) and inflammation.

Under conditions of stress, the sympathetic branch of the ANS activates the adrenal medulla, causing the release of a mixture of catecholamines—epinephrine (adrenaline) and norepinephrine (noradrenaline). The mixture mobilizes the body by accelerating the heart rate and stimulating the liver to release stored glucose (sugar), making more energy available where it can be of use. Table 4.2 summarizes bodily changes that take place when people are under stress.

Table 4.2 Stress-Related Changes in the Body	
Corticosteroids are released	Muscles tense
Adrenaline is released	Blood shifts from the internal organs to the skeletal muscles
Norepinephrine is released	Digestion is inhibited
Respiration rate escalates	Sugar is released by the liver
Heart rate escalates	Blood coagulability elevates
Blood pressure escalates	

Stress triggers the alarm reaction. The reaction is defined by secretion of corticosteroids, catecholamines, and activity of the sympathetic branch of the ANS. The alarm reaction mobilizes the body for combat or flight.

Cortical steroids are perhaps one reason that persistent stress eventually exhausts our capacities to cope. Although cortical steroids in some ways help the body cope with stress, persistent secretion of these steroids ironically suppresses the activity of the immune system. Cortical steroids have negligible effects when they are only periodically released. Continuous secretion, however, decreases inflammation and weakens the immune system by disrupting the production of antibodies. As a result, we grow more vulnerable to various diseases, even the common cold (Cohen et al., 1991).

Although Selye's model speaks to the general response pattern of the body under stress, different biological processes may be involved in response to particular kinds of stressors. For example, persistent exposure to excessive noise may invoke different bodily processes than other sources of stress, such as overcrowding, or psychological sources of stress, such as divorce or separation.

Individuals, too, may react differently to stress depending on psychological factors such as cognitive appraisal. For example, the impact of a stressful event reflects the individual's appraisal of the event in terms of its positive and negative features. For example, whether pregnancy is a positive or negative life change depends on a couple's desire for a child and their readiness to care for a child. In social-learning theory terms, the stress of pregnancy is moderated by the subjective value of children in a couple's eyes and their self-efficacy expectancies concerning child rearing. We evaluate hassles and life changes cognitively (Lazarus et al., 1985). The same event is less taxing for people who appraise it as meaningful and believe they can cope with it. Other psychological factors, like hardiness and humor, may also mediate or buffer the effects of stress.

A MULTIFACTORIAL VIEW OF HEALTH AND ILLNESS

Although some people inherit predispositions toward certain illnesses, health professionals no longer see people as simply "lucky" enough to have rugged constitutions, or as "unlucky" enough to have certain disorders run in their families. Research has shown that many factors interact to determine whether or not people will incur various physical disorders (Blanchard, 1992a; Kiecolt-Glaser & Glaser, 1992; Stokols, 1992). Biological variables such as family history of an illness, exposure to disease-causing agents (**pathogens**), the ability of the immune system to fight them off, and inoculations may strike us as the most likely causes or deterrents of physical illnesses.

Yet as shown in Table 4.3, the causes of physical illness are best viewed as *multifactorial*. Psychological, social, technological, and natural environmental factors are also involved. Even though our heredity may work against us in certain ways, biology may not be destiny and we may be able to change other factors to maintain or restore health. In later chapters we see that a multifactorial approach may also best explain the origins of many psychological disorders.

A multifactorial view of health and illness provides insight into causation and also suggests multiple pathways of prevention and treatment involving psychosocial and medical approaches. Let us consider some of the multiple factors that are connected with physical health and illness.

Biological Factors

Biology plays key roles in health and illness. We are generally healthier when we are younger, when we receive inoculations for common illnesses, and when we control physiological conditions such as hypertension and serum cholesterol levels. It has been clearly established that people with family histories of some disorders, such as cardiovascular disease and certain types of cancer, are at greater risk of developing these problems. In some cases the genetic predisposition may be so powerful that prevention and treatment efforts are either futile or can only forestall the inevitable. In other cases, such as obesity (Brownell & Wadden, 1992) and many cases of cancer (Andersen, 1992), genetic predispositions interact with dietary and other factors either to bring on or prevent the problem.

Psychological Factors

Psychological factors include our behavior patterns and personalities. Our behavior patterns are fundamental factors in health and illness. For example, diet and exercise are two facets of behavior that figure prominently in proneness to health problems such as obesity and coronary heart disease. Our personalities are reasonably stable patterns of emotions, motives, attitudes, and psychological traits that distinguish people from one another (Prigatano, 1992). Many personality features, such as self-efficacy expectancies, psychological hardiness, optimism, and a sense of humor, are believed to have positive effects on our health, by means of buffering the effects of stress. The so-called Type A personality and chronic feelings of hostility may increase our susceptibility to coronary heart disease, however. Our style of coping with illness may also play a large role in recovery, as we explore in the feature "Styles of Coping with Illness."

Table 4.3 Factors in Health and Illness: Biological, Psychological, Social, Technological, and Natural Environmental

Biological	Psychological		Social: Socioeconomic, Sociocultural, and Ethnic	Technological	Natural Environmental
	Personality	Behavioral			
Family history of illness	Self-efficacy expectancies	Diet (intake of calories, fats, fiber, vitamins, etc.)	Socioeconomic status	Adequacy of available health care	Natural disasters (earthquakes, floods, hurricanes, drought, extremes of temperature, tornados)
Exposure to infectious pathogens (e.g., bacteria and viruses)	Psychological hardiness	Consumption of alcohol	Availability and use of social support	Vehicular safety	Radon
Functioning of the immune system	Health locus of control (belief that one is in charge of one's own health)	Cigarette smoking	Social climate in the home environment and in the workplace	Architectural features (e.g., injury-resistant design, nontoxic construction materials, aesthetic design, air quality, noise insulation)	
Inoculations	Optimism/pessimism	Level of physical activity	Major life changes such as death of a spouse or divorce		
Medication history	Sense of humor	Sleep patterns	Health-related cultural and religious beliefs and practices	Aesthetics of residential, workplace, and communal architecture and landscape architecture	
Congenital disabilities	Attributional style (how one explains one's failures to oneself)	Safety practices (e.g., driving with seat belts; careful driving; practice of sexual abstinence, monogamy, or "safe sex"; attaining of comprehensive prenatal care)	Major economic changes (e.g., taking out of a large mortgage, losing one's job)	Water quality	
Physiological conditions (e.g., obesity, hypertension, serum cholesterol level)	Introversion/extraversion	Health-care utilization; e.g., regular medical and dental checkups	Health promotion programs in the workplace or the community	Solid waste treatment and sanitation	
Reactivity of the cardiovascular system (e.g., "hot reactor")	Coronary-prone (Type A) personality	Compliance with medical and dental advice	Ethnicity	Pollution	
Age	Depression/anxiety	Interpersonal/social skills	Prejudice and discrimination	Radiation	
Gender	Hostility/suspiciousness	Type A behavior pattern (TABP)	Health-related legislation	Global warming	
	Tendencies to express or deny feelings of frustration and anger		Availability of health insurance	Ozone depletion	

This table incorporates elements from Table 2, p. 13 in Stokols, D. (1992), Establishing and maintaining healthy environments: Toward a social ecology of health promotion, *American Psychologist, 47,* 6–22. Copyright 1992 by the American Psychological Association. Adapted by permission.

A CLOSER LOOK

Styles of Coping with Illness

What do you do when faced with a serious problem? Do you pretend that it does not exist? Like Scarlett O'Hara in *Gone with the Wind,* do you say to yourself, "I'll think about it tomorrow" and then banish it from your mind? Or do you take charge and confront it squarely?

Pretending that problems do not exist is a form of denial. Denial is an example of **emotion-focused coping** (Lazarus & Folkman, 1984). In emotion-focused coping, people take measures that immediately reduce the impact of the stressor, such as denying its existence or withdrawing from the situation. Emotion-focused coping, however, does not eliminate the stressor or help the individual develop better ways of managing the stressor. In **problem-focused coping,** by contrast, people examine the stressors they face and do what they can to change them or modify their own reactions to render stressors less harmful. These basic styles of coping—emotion-focused and problem-focused—have been applied to ways in which people respond to illness.

Emotion-Focused Coping: Reducing Awareness of Physical Trauma Denial is one of the principal ways of passively coping with illness. It can take various forms, including the following:

1. Failure to recognize the seriousness of the illness,
2. Minimization of the emotional distress that the illness causes,
3. Misattribution of symptoms to other causes (for example, assuming that the appearance of blood in the stool represents nothing more than a local abrasion), and
4. Ignoring of threatening information about the illness (Levine et al., 1987).

Some researchers speculate that denial may actually improve the chances of surviving a heart attack—at least on a short-term basis (Hackett et al., 1968). The idea is that the use of denial protects the heart by shielding it from the physiological effects of anxiety or heightened arousal (Byrne et al., 1981). Research, however, has failed to confirm that the chances of recovery from a heart attack are improved by the use of denial (Krantz, 1980). Regardless of whether or not denial offers short-term benefits in the acute phase of an illness, denial is connected with poorer recovery over the long haul (Krantz, 1980; Mullen & Suls, 1982). Persistent denial apparently impedes compliance with appropriate medical treatment (Levine, 1987).

Another form of emotion-focused coping, the use of wish-fulfillment fantasies, has also been linked to poorer adjustment in coping with serious illness. Examples of wish-fulfillment fantasies include ruminating about what might have been had the illness not occurred and longing

for better times. Wish-fulfillment fantasy offers the patient no means of coping with life's difficulties other than an imaginary escape (Felton & Revenson, 1984).

Does this mean that people are invariably better off when they face their illnesses squarely? Not necessarily. Whether or not you will be better off handling the facts of an illness may depend on your preferred style of coping. A mismatch between the individual's style of coping and the amount of information provided may hamper recovery. In one study, cardiac patients with a repressive style of coping (relying on denial) who received information about their condition showed a higher incidence of medical complications than repressors who were kept in the dark (Shaw et al., 1985). Sometimes ignorance helps people manage stress—at least temporarily.

Imparting medical information when patients cannot make use of it can be an empty and possibly harmful gesture. In one study, patients were given either high or low amounts of information about their conditions, and were or were not provided with ways of controlling certain aspects of their treatment (Cromwell et al., 1977). Patients in the high information/high control condition were found to have shorter stays in the hospital. But the provision of information in the absence of ways of exercising control was associated with prolonged stays.

Problem-Focused Coping: Confronting the Trauma of Serious Illness Problem-focused coping involves strategies to deal directly with the source of stress, like seeking information about the illness through self-study and medical consultation. Information seeking may help the individual maintain a more optimistic frame of mind by creating an expectancy that the information will prove to be useful, an approach that has been shown to be adaptive among cancer patients (Weisman & Worden, 1976).

The ways in which we come to terms with serious illness affect our emotional adjustment and, perhaps, our survival. Finding a silver lining in a dark cloud is apparently healthful. One study interviewed heart attack victims seven weeks after they were stricken. Victims who were able to cite benefits of their attacks were less likely to suffer recurrent attacks and were more likely to have survived at an 8-year follow-up than patients who were unable to recognize benefits associated with the attack (Affleck et al., 1987). The types of benefits connected with subsequent health are shown in Table 4.4. Blaming others for the initial heart attacks and attributing them to stress responses (for example, excessive worrying or anxiety) were associated with increased mortality at the 8-year follow-up. Patients who saw their heart attacks as caused by factors they could control, like diet and smoking, more often followed through on behavioral programs that modified these risk behaviors.

(continued)

Table 4.4 Examples of Perceived Benefits Following Heart Attacks Associated with Increased Rates of Survival

Type of Perceived Benefit	Life Changes Associated with Perceived Benefits
Helped victim recognize the benefits of preventative health behaviors	Smoking cessation Regular exercise Proper diet
Helped lead or expected it would lead to positive life changes	Taking life easier Taking more vacations Slowing down the pace of daily life
Helped produce changes in "philosophy of life," personal values, and religious view	Becoming more content with accepting one's lot in life Taking each day as it comes Valuing home life more Renewing religious faith

Source: Stokols, D. (1992). Establishing and maintaining healthy environments: Toward a social ecology of health promotion. American Psychologist, 47, 6–22. Copyright © 1992 by the American Psychological Association. Reprinted by permission.

■ **SELF-EFFICACY EXPECTANCIES** Self-efficacy expectancies refer to one's perceived ability to cope, to perform certain behaviors, or to effect change (Bandura, 1982, 1986; Bandura et al., 1985). We may be better able to manage stress if we feel confident in our ability to cope. Research by Bandura and his colleagues (Bandura et al., 1985) showed that spider-phobic women who doubted their ability to cope with tasks that required them to interact with spiders, such as letting a spider crawl on their laps, showed high levels of the stress hormones adrenaline and

Psychological hardiness. Psychological hardiness is a psychological factor that moderates the effects of stress. Psychologically hardy business executives resist illness despite heavy stress loads. Psychologically hardy executives are committed to their work (they believe in what they are doing), seek challenges, and perceive themselves as in control of their lives.

noradrenaline in the bloodstream. As their confidence or self-efficacy expectancies for coping with these tasks increased, the levels of these hormones declined. Adrenaline and noradrenaline arouse the body by way of the sympathetic branch of the ANS. As a consequence, we are likely to feel shaky, to have "butterflies in the stomach" and general feelings of nervousness. Since high self-efficacy expectancies appear to be associated with lower secretion of catecholamines, people who believe that they can cope with their problems may be less likely to feel nervous. Interestingly, subjects in the Bandura study who said they could not handle a performance task with the phobic object and then refused to attempt it showed sudden drops in the levels of these hormones. In other words, avoiding a frightening task may reduce the secretion of these stress hormones and be reinforced by immediate reductions in fear arousal.

■ **PSYCHOLOGICAL HARDINESS** Psychological hardiness refers to a cluster of traits that may help people manage stress. Research on the subject is largely indebted to Suzanne Kobasa (1979) and her colleagues who investigated business executives who resisted illness despite heavy burdens of stress. Three key traits distinguished the psychologically hardy executives (Kobasa et al., 1982, pp. 169–170):

1. The hardy executives were high in *commitment*. Rather than feeling alienated from their tasks and situations, they involved themselves fully. That is, they believed in what they were doing.

2. The hardy executives were high in *challenge*. They believed that change was the normal state of things, not sterile sameness or stability for the sake of stability.

3. The hardy executives were also high in perceived *control* over their lives (Maddi & Kobasa, 1984). They believed and acted as though they were effectual rather than powerless in controlling the rewards and punishments of life. In terms suggested by social-learning theorist Julian Rotter (1966), psychologically hardy individuals have an internal **locus of control**.

Research evidence has shown relationships between proneness to illness and psychological hardiness in people with behavior patterns that may place them at risk of cardiovascular illness, such as the **Type A behavior pattern** (TABP). Type A people are highly driven, impatient, competitive, and hostile (Thoresen & Powell, 1992). Psychologically hardy Type A people have been shown to be more resistant to coronary heart disease than nonhardy Type A people (Booth-Kewley & Friedman, 1987; Friedman & Booth-Kewley, 1987; Kobasa et al., 1983; Rhodewalt & Agustsdottir, 1984). Kobasa suggests that hardy people are better able to handle stress because they perceive themselves as *choosing* their stress-creating situations. They encode stress as rendering life interesting, not as intensifying the pressures on them. A sense of control is a key factor in psychological hardiness.

■ **OPTIMISM** Research suggests that seeing the glass as half full is healthier than seeing it as half empty (Scheier & Carver, 1992). In one study on the relationships between optimism and health, Scheier and Carver (1985) administered a measure of optimism, the Life Orientation Test (LOT), to college students. The students also tracked their physical symptoms for 1 month. It turned out that students who received higher optimism scores reported fewer symptoms such as fatigue, dizziness, muscle soreness, and blurry vision. (Subjects' symptoms at the beginning of the study were statistically taken into account, so that it could not be argued that the study simply shows that healthier people are more optimistic.)

Optimism is related to a number of health concerns (Peterson & Bossio, 1991). In a study of 185 adults who were suffering from pain of various origins, patients who reported more pessimistic thoughts during flare-ups of pain also reported more severe pain and distress (Gil et al., 1990). The pessimistic thoughts included, "I can no longer do anything," "No one cares about my pain," and "It isn't fair I have to live this way."

Optimistic women are less likely than pessimistic women to experience postpartum depression (a type of depression that affects some women following childbirth) (Carver & Gaines, 1987). Optimistic cardiac patients even recover relatively more rapidly from coronary artery bypass surgery (Scheier et al., 1989). The optimistic patients are up and about their rooms more rapidly after surgery. They have fewer postoperative complications and return sooner to their preoperative routines (including their work and exercise routines).

Research to date shows only correlational links between optimism and health. Perhaps we shall soon learn whether learning to alter one's attitude—to learn to see the glass as half-filled—plays a role in maintaining or restoring health.

 It is true that optimistic people tend to recover more rapidly than pessimistic people from coronary artery bypass surgery.

You can complete the nearby Life Orientation Test to evaluate your own level of optimism.

■ **HUMOR: DOES "A MERRY HEART DOETH GOOD LIKE A MEDICINE"?** The notion that humor eases the burdens of the day has been with humankind for millennia (Lefcourt & Martin, 1986). Ponder the biblical adage, "A merry heart doeth good like a medicine" (Proverbs 17:22).

Research evidence buttresses the biblical maxim by suggesting that humor may indeed play a stress-buffering role. In one study, the investigators (Martin & Lefcourt, 1983) administered a measure of mood disturbance and a checklist of stressful events to college subjects. The mood disturbance measure also provided a stress score. Moreover, students filled out scales about their sense of humor, and behavioral measures of their capacity to produce humor under stress were taken. Overall, there was a significant correlation between stressful events and stress scores. But stressful events had less of an impact on students with better senses of humor and on students who were better able to produce humor under adversity. Humor may thus play a stress-buffering role. But we should be careful about drawing causal inferences from such correlational relationships. Persons with a better developed sense of humor may also possess other qualities that buffer the impact of stress.

 A sense of humor may buffer or moderate the impact of stress, but more research needs to be done to determine whether it plays a causal role.

QUESTIONNAIRE

The Life Orientation Test

Do you see the glass as half full or half empty? Do you expect bad things to happen or do you find the silver lining in every cloud? The Life Orientation Test can afford you insight as to how optimistic or pessimistic you are.

Directions: Indicate whether or not each of the items represents your feelings by writing a number in the black space according to the following code. Then turn to the scoring key at the end of the chapter.

4 = strongly agree
3 = agree
2 = neutral
1 = *dis*agree
0 = strongly *dis*agree

___ 1. In uncertain times, I usually expect the best.
___ 2. It's easy for me to relax.
___ 3. If something can go wrong for me, it will.
___ 4. I always look on the bright side of things.
___ 5. I'm always optimistic about my future.
___ 6. I enjoy my friends a lot.
___ 7. It's important for me to keep busy.
___ 8. I hardly ever expect things to go my way.
___ 9. Things never work out the way I want them to.
___ 10. I don't get upset too easily.
___ 11. I'm a believer in the idea that "every cloud has a silver lining."
___ 12. I rarely count on good things happening to me.

Source: Scheier, M. F., & Carver, C. S. (1985). Optimism, coping, and health: Assessment and implications of generalized outcome expectancies. Health Psychology, 4, pp. 219–247.

Socioeconomic, Sociocultural, and Ethnic Factors

Social factors in health include economic realities, cultural issues, and ethnic and racial differences. One economic reality is that many poor people do not have access to health insurance or cannot afford to carry health insurance on their own. They thus have more limited access to health care, which can jeopardize their health by preventing them from receiving the care they need. There is also an interaction between health-care utilization and cultural values. Within some groups, as among Christian Scientists and some native peoples, mainstream health-care utilization may be essentially nil because of preference for religious or spiritual practices.

Health problems have differential impacts on various cultural and ethnic groups around the world and within the United States. In some cases, genetic factors may interact with cultural and ethnic factors. In others, poverty, prejudice and discrimination, lack of education, and lack of accessibility of health care may play the predominant roles. Consider the following examples:

- African Americans are more prone to suffer from hypertension than non-Hispanic white Americans (Leary, 1991). They are also more apt to have hypertension than Black Africans are, which leads many health professionals to conclude that particular features of U.S. life such as the stresses of poverty and prejudice, unhealthful diets, and smoking contribute to hypertension in Black people who are genetically vulnerable (Leary, 1991).

- Cases of severe uncontrolled hypertension among African Americans and Hispanic Americans are found predominantly among those with lower levels of education and limited access to medical care (Shea et al., 1992).

- The incidence of most kinds of cancer is also higher among African Americans than non-Hispanic white Americans. Cancer is also more likely to be lethal to African Americans than to non-Hispanic white Americans (Andersen, 1991; Bal, 1992). The dismaying cancer mortality for African Americans may be attributed mainly to their lower socioeconomic status (SES) (Baquet et al., 1991). A lower SES makes it more difficult to gain access to high-quality medical care.

 African Americans are in fact more likely than non-Hispanic white Americans to die from cancer. The reasons probably have more to do with the relatively lower socioeconomic status of African Americans than with genetic factors.

MULTICULTURAL PERSPECTIVES

Mediators of the Effects of Stress Among African Americans

African Americans are at greater risk than non-Hispanic white Americans of incurring various health problems such as obesity (Van Italie, 1985), hypertension (Leary, 1991), heart disease, diabetes, and certain types of cancer (Andersen, 1991). Researchers suspect that the particular stressors that African Americans in our society often face, such as racism, poverty, violence, and overcrowding, may play an important role in explaining the heightened health risks they face (Anderson, 1991).

There is no one-to-one connection between stress and such disorders among African Americans, however. Factors such as the availability of social support from family and friends, beliefs in one's ability to handle stress (self-efficacy), coping skills, and awareness of one's ethnic identity may mediate the effects of stress. Yet African Americans who may be in the greatest need of support, such as the elderly and single parents, are often the most reluctant to seek support from family members (Anderson, 1991).

Among African Americans, as among other groups, self-esteem is tied to racial or ethnic identity. Acquiring and maintaining pride in one's racial identity and cultural heritage may help African Americans—and other ethnic minorities—withstand the stresses imposed by racism. Although more research is needed to elucidate the links between racial identity, self-esteem, and tolerance of stress, the available evidence shows that African Americans who become alienated from their culture develop more negative self-images and stand a greater risk of developing not only physical and psychological disorders, but also academic underachievement and marital conflicts (Anderson, 1991).

Ethnic pride as a moderator of the effects of stress. Among African Americans and other minority groups, pride in one's racial and cultural heritage may help one withstand the stresses imposed by racism.

- Death rates from cancer are higher in nations where the population consumes large quantities of fat, such as England, the Netherlands, Denmark, the United States, and Canada (Cohen, 1987). Cancer takes fewer lives in nations such as Thailand, the Philippines, and Japan, where people consume lower levels of fat.

- Ingestion of fatty foods is also connected with obesity. Japanese-American men who reside in California and Hawaii are two to three times more likely than Japanese men who reside in Japan to become obese (Curb & Marcus, 1991).

 Japanese-American men who reside in California and Hawaii are in fact much more likely than Japanese men who reside in Japan to become obese. Dietary differences are the apparent culprit.

- Hispanic Americans utilize health care less regularly than African Americans and non-Hispanic white Americans do, largely because of lack of health insurance, language obstacles, qualms about medical intervention, and—for illegal aliens—concern about possible deportation (Perez-Stable, 1991; Thompson, 1991).

Social Support   Researchers are finding that the support of other people apparently buffers the impact of stress (Cohen & Wills, 1985; Pagel & Becker, 1987; Rook & Dooley, 1985) and has a positive impact on health. People with more social support may actually live longer, as suggested by studies of Alameda County, California (Berkman & Breslow, 1983; Berkman & Syme, 1979) and Tecumseh, Michigan (House et al., 1982). During the 12 years the Tecumseh study followed 2,754 adults, the mortality rate was significantly lower for men who were married, who attended meetings of voluntary associations regularly, and who participated frequently in social leisure activities. It may be tempting to conclude that marriage saves lives, but keep in mind that these findings are correlational. Men who get married may also be generally more stable or more apt to take care of themselves.

 Actually, married men tend to live longer than single men.

Natural Environmental Factors

Some say the world will end in fire,
Some say in ice.

Robert Frost

Hurricanes, blizzards, monsoons, floods, tornadoes, wind storms, ice storms, earthquakes, avalanches, mudslides, and volcanic eruptions provide a sampling of the natural disasters humankind has faced. Sometimes we are warned of natural disasters. We may be aware of living in earthquake- or flood-prone areas. When warned, we may be able to evade or avert disaster. Otherwise, we are dazed by the abruptness of a disaster and left numb.

Natural disasters are dangerous as they occur and also create lingering problems. Like Hurricane Andrew, which ripped the Florida and Louisiana coastlines in 1992, they can kill our loved ones, destroy our property, and disrupt our communities (Wilkerson, 1992). They are thus among the most stressful types of experiences. Electric power, water, and other services that had been taken for granted may be disrupted. Hurricane Andrew left 250,000 Floridians homeless and disrupted electric power to some communities for weeks. Disasters that involve many casualties also lead to more severe adjustment

problems (Rubonis & Bickman, 1991). Disasters, whether natural or human-made, can deprive us of our sense of control over things, compromising our psychological hardiness (Davidson et al., 1982).

Technological Factors

We owe our dominion over nature to technological advances. Through technology we build and power our communication, transportation, and other systems. Advances in medical technology have enabled us to overcome many of the health problems posed by nature.

Sometimes technology fails, however, or fails to reach all those who need it. Many people, especially those from cultural and ethnic minorities, do not have available access to the latest technological advances in health care. Sometimes technology leads to disaster. Consider the leakage of poisonous gas at Bhopal, India, in 1984; the collapse of a bridge along the Connecticut Turnpike in 1983; the nuclear accident at Three Mile Island in 1979; the Buffalo Creek dam collapse in 1976; the fire at the Beverly Hills Supper Club in 1977 (Green et al., 1983); the Exxon *Valdez* oil spill; blackouts, airplane disasters, and the leakage of toxic wastes. These are but a sampling of the human-made disasters that befall us and can have profound effects on the psychological and physical functioning of survivors.

The Buffalo Creek dam collapse inundated the town of Saunders, West Virginia, with thousands of tons of water. The flood lasted 15 minutes but killed 125 people and left over 5,000 homeless. Reactions included anxiety, emotional numbness, depression, physical complaints, unfocused feelings of anger (Hargreaves, 1980), regression among children, and sleep disturbances, including nightmares (Gleser et al., 1981). Many victims experienced **survivor guilt** that they had been spared the deluge while family members and friends had drowned (Titchener & Kapp, 1976). Fourteen years after the collapse, a study of 120 adult survivors revealed that nearly 3 in 10 (28%) showed continuing evidence of stress reactions (Green et al., 1990a).

Not surprisingly, people with social support tend to adjust better to disasters. Residents of the Three Mile Island nuclear accident who had solid networks of social support—friends and relatives with whom they could share the ordeal—reported less stress than residents who had to go it alone (Fleming et al., 1982).

MULTICULTURAL PERSPECTIVES

Ethnic Differences in Psychological Adjustment Following the Exxon Valdez Disaster

On March 24, 1989, the supertanker Exxon *Valdez* ran aground, spilling millions of gallons of crude oil into the waters of pristine Prince William Sound in Alaska. It was the largest oil spill in U.S. history. In addition to fouling beaches and killing thousands of shorebirds, the fishing industry in the sound was shattered. Americans followed the legal proceedings against the ship captain and Exxon in the media, but what of the effects on the people in the region? How did they cope with the stress wrought by the disaster? What did the destruction of the fishing industry mean to them? What of the stress of the cleanup?

The affected area, populated largely by people of Native Alaskan and Euro-American backgrounds, provided researchers with an opportunity to examine the role of cultural factors in coping with disasters. A year after the disaster, researchers conducted a survey of adults in 596 households in area communities, about one-third of which were populated by Native Alaskans.

Researchers found that both Alaskan Natives and Euro-Americans were affected by the oil spill. Reports of depression, a key indicator of adjustment, were associated with the level of exposure to the effects of the oil spill and to the cleanup efforts that followed. Other psychological problems also varied with the level of exposure, including alcohol and drug abuse, domestic violence, and anxiety disorders (Palinkas et al., in press). The results were generally consistent with those of researchers who studied people exposed to natural and technological disasters such as the Three Mile Island nuclear accident (Baum et al., 1983), the Mount St. Helens eruption (Shore et al., 1986), and Hurricane Andrew (Wilkerson, 1992).

Cultural differences appeared to play a role in determining the impact of the Exxon *Valdez* disaster, however. Participation in the cleanup activities was associated with greater depression among Native Alaskans, but not among Euro-Americans. Native Americans who participated in the cleanup, and who benefited economically from the income they received, reported higher levels of depression than those who continued to work in the traditional industries, which mostly revolved around commercial fishing. Researchers suspect that depression was linked to the sudden shift from working in the traditional subsistence industries to the cleanup. Unequal participation in the cleanup among households in the native community may also have created divisions within the extended families of this close-knit society. Perhaps those who opted to participate in the cleanup were ostracized for failing to do their share to maintain the traditional industries.

Euro-Americans may not have been as dependent on the extended family or on traditional industries for their economic subsistence. Perhaps their participation in the cleanup did not subject them to these sorts of social conflicts.

After the spill. In 1989, the supertanker Exxon *Valdez* ran aground and spilled millions of gallons of oil into Alaska's Prince William Sound, shattering the local fishing industry. Of people who were paid to participate in the cleanup, Native Alaskans appeared to become depressed, but not Euro-Americans. Perhaps Native Alaskans were suffering from social ostracism because they were not perceived as doing their share to maintain the traditional fishing industry of the region.

PSYCHOLOGICAL FACTORS AND PHYSICAL DISORDERS

We noted at the start of the chapter that psychological factors can influence physical functioning, while physical factors can influence mental functioning. In these next sections we take a look at the role of psychological factors in various physical disorders. Physical disorders in which psychological factors are believed to play a causal or contributing role have traditionally been termed **psychosomatic** or **psychophysiological**. These disorders include certain cardiovascular disorders, ulcers, asthma, obesity, and headaches. The field of psychosomatic medicine was developed to explore the possible health-related connections between the mind and the body. The term *psychosomatic* is derived from the Greek roots *psyche*, meaning "soul" or "intellect," and *soma*, which means "body." Today, evidence points to the importance of psychological factors in a much wider range of physical disorders than those traditionally identified as psychosomatic. In this section we discuss several of the traditionally identified psychosomatic disorders as well as two other diseases in which psychological factors may play a role in the course or treatment of the disease—cancer and AIDS.

Headaches

Headaches are symptomatic of many medical disorders. When they occur in the absence of other symptoms, however, they may be classified as stress-related. Severe headaches affect about 1 American in 5 (Bonica, 1980).

The single most frequent kind of headache is the muscle-tension headache. Persistent stress can lead to persistent contractions of the muscles of the scalp, face, neck, and shoulders, giving rise to chronic muscle-tension headaches. Such headaches develop gradually and are generally characterized by dull, steady pain on both sides of the head and feelings of pressure or tightness.

Most other headaches, including the severe migraine headache, are believed to involve changes in the blood flow to the brain. Migraine headaches affect perhaps as many as 18 million Americans (Brody, 1988). Typical migraines last for hours or days. They may occur as often as daily or as seldom as every other month. Piercing or throbbing sensations may become so intense that they seem intolerable. Sleep, mood, and thinking processes may be affected as the individual's mental state becomes dominated by the misery of a brutal migraine. The so-called common migraine headache is identified by sudden onset and throbbing on one side of the head. Migraine attacks are frequently accompanied by exquisite sensitivity to light; loss of appetite, nausea, and vomiting; sensory and motor disturbances, such as loss of balance; and mood changes.

In the so-called classic migraine, an aura, or cluster of warning sensations, precedes the attacks of about 1 migraine sufferer in 5. Auras are typified by perceptual distortions, such as flashing lights, bizarre images, or blind spots. These sensations are apparently connected with fluctuations of the serotonin and norepinephrine available to the brain.

■ **THEORETICAL PERSPECTIVES** Why, under stress, do some people develop tension headaches? One possible answer is found in the principle of **individual response specificity**, which holds that people may respond to a stressor in idiosyncratic ways. Differences in response may reflect a combination of genetic influences, histories of learning, and ways of encoding experience. In classic research, Malmo and Shagass (1949) induced pain in patients with muscular complaints (backaches) and patients with hypertension. The hypertensive patients responded to the stimulus with larger changes in the heart rate, whereas the backache group showed greater muscle contractions. Tension-headache sufferers may thus be more likely to respond to stress by tensing the muscles of the forehead, shoulders, and neck.

According to the vascular model formulated by Harold Wolff in 1938, migraine attacks reflect stress-related changes in the blood vessels supplying the head. Under stress, the blood vessels in some parts of the brain become constricted while vessels in other parts of the brain dilate, producing throbbing, piercing sensations. Today, many theorists have replaced the vascular theory with the view that people who are prone to migraines may have a genetic dysfunction in the brain mechanisms responsible for regulating the amount of serotonin in the brain (Brody, 1988c). Disregulation of other neurotransmitters, such as norepinephrine, may also be involved. From this perspective, changes in blood flow to the brain may be an effect of serotonin disregulation rather than the direct cause of the migraine headache. Drugs that are most helpful with migraine attacks, such as ergotamine, appear to affect serotonin levels in the brain (Brody, 1988c), lending some support to the disregulation theory.

Given a genetic predisposition to migraines, many other factors are implicated in attacks. These include stress; stimuli like bright lights; barometric pressure; pollen; certain drugs; the chemical monosodium glutamate (MSG), which is often used to enhance the flavor of food; and red wine. Hormonal changes of the sort that affect women prior to and during menstruation can also trigger attacks, and the incidence of migraines among women is about twice that among men.

■ **TREATMENT** Aspirin and ibuprofen (brand names Medipren, Nuprin, Advil, etc.) frequently decrease pain, including headache pain, by inhibiting the production of hormones (*prostaglandins*) that incite transmission of pain messages to the brain. Ergotamine also helps many migraine sufferers, perhaps by regulating serotonin levels in the brain.

Behavioral methods of relaxation training and biofeedback are also of help (Blanchard, 1992b). Progressive relaxation, which reduces muscle tension, is particularly helpful in relieving tension-headache pain (Blanchard et al., 1990a, 1991). **Biofeedback training** (BFT) helps people gain control over various bodily functions, such as muscle tension and brain waves, by giving them information (feedback) about these functions in the form of auditory signals (e.g., "bleeps") or visual displays. People learn to attend to ways of making the signal change in the desired direction. Relaxation training combined with biofeedback has also been shown to be effective.

Electromyographic (EMG) biofeedback relays information about muscle tension in the forehead. EMG biofeedback thus heightens awareness of muscle tension in this region and helps people learn to reduce it. Blanchard and his colleagues (1985a, 1987) have successfully treated between 50 to 60% of tension-headache sufferers with relaxation training, or with relaxation and EMG biofeedback when relaxation alone does not do the job. Tension-headache patients treated with biofeedback and relaxation maintained initial reductions of headache pain for four years following treatment (Blanchard et al., 1987).

Thermal BFT for migraine headaches alters the blood supply to the head (Blanchard et al., 1985a, 1985b, 1987, 1990b). One way of providing thermal feedback is by attaching a **thermistor** to a finger. A console "bleeps" more slowly[1] as the temperature rises. The temperature rises because more blood is flowing into the limb—away from the head. The client can imagine the finger growing warmer to facilitate the change in the body's distribution of blood. In one study, relaxation training combined with thermal BFT led to improvement in 52% of

migraine and combined migraine/tension-headache subjects (Blanchard et al., 1985b).

Some people have in fact relieved migraine headaches by raising the temperature in a finger. This biofeedback technique modifies patterns of blood flow throughout the body.

A combination of relaxation training and cognitive-behavioral methods which help clients cope with stressors that prompt muscle-tension headaches was also shown to reduce headache pain in many sufferers (Holroyd et al., 1991). Cognitive approaches may be of greater benefit in treating tension headache than migraine headache (Blanchard, 1992b).

Cardiovascular Disorders

Cardiovascular disorders are the leading cause of death in the United States (USDHHS, 1991). Cardiovascular disorders include heart disease and disorders of the circulatory system, the most common of which is stroke.

Coronary heart disease (CHD), also called arteriosclerotic heart disease, accounts for more than 1.5 million deaths per year. The death rate from heart disease for African-American adults aged 45 to 64 is about 75% higher than for non-Hispanic white Americans. Within the same age range, the death rate from heart disease for Native Americans is slightly higher (8% higher) than the rate for non-Hispanic white Americans. The comparable death rate for Hispanic Americans is about 23% lower than the rate for non-Hispanic white Americans, and the rate for Asian Americans is lowest, about half that of non-Hispanic white Americans (USDHHS, 1991). We see that the incidences of hypertension and obesity, which are key risk factors for CHD, follow similar ethnic patterns.

The disease process in CHD is **arteriosclerosis**, or thickening of the walls of the blood vessels, which impedes the passage of blood. A major cause of arteriosclerosis is **atherosclerosis**, or buildup of fatty deposits in the blood vessels, which clogs them and causes them to lose their elasticity. Clogging of the blood vessels that serve the heart obstructs the flow of blood to the heart. Insufficient blood supply leads to the destruction of muscular tissue of the heart—causing a **myocardial infarction**, or heart attack.

Researchers have identified several risk factors for CHD.

---

[1]Or more rapidly. The choice of direction is decided by the therapist or therapist and client.

A CLOSER LOOK

Psychological Methods for Lowering Arousal

Stress induces bodily responses such as excessive levels of sympathetic nervous system arousal, which if persistent may impair our ability to function optimally and possibly increase the risk of stress-related illnesses. Psychological treatments have been shown to lower states of bodily arousal that may be prompted by stress. In this feature, we consider two widely used psychological methods of lowering arousal; meditation and progressive relaxation.

Meditation   Meditation comprises several ways of narrowing consciousness to moderate the stressors of the outer world. Yogis study the design on a vase or a mandala. The ancient Egyptians riveted their attention on an oil-burning lamp, which is the inspiration for the tale of Aladdin's lamp. Islamic mystics of Turkey, so-called whirling dervishes, fix on their movements and the cadences of their breathing.

There are many meditation methods, but they share the common thread of narrowing one's attention by focus-ing on repetitive stimuli. Through passive observation, the regular person–environment connection is transformed. Problem solving, worry, planning, and routine concerns are suspended, and consequently, levels of sympathetic arousal are reduced.

Thousands of Americans regularly practice **transcendental meditation** (TM), a simplified kind of Indian meditation brought to the United States in 1959 by Maharishi Mahesh Yogi. Practitioners of TM repeat **mantras**—relaxing sounds like *ieng* and *om*.

Benson (1975) studied TM practitioners aged 17 to 41—students, businesspeople, artists. His subjects included relative novices and veterans of 9 years of practice. Benson found that TM yields a so-called relaxation response in many people. This response decreases the metabolic rate, as gauged by oxygen consumption, and the blood pressure of people with high blood pressure (hypertension). Regular meditators showed normalized blood pressure through the day (Benson et al., 1973). Meditators also produced more alpha waves—brain waves that are connected with relaxation.

Other researchers concur that meditation lowers arousal but contend that similar effects can be attained by other relaxing activities (West, 1985), or simply by resting silently for an equal amount of time (Holmes et al., 1983; Holmes, 1984, 1985). The Holmes group (1983) reported no differences between veteran meditators and subjects who simply sat quietly in heart or respiration rate, blood pressure, and galvanic skin response (GSR). Critics of meditation do not hold that meditation is without value; they suggest, instead, that meditation may have no distinct effects when compared to a restful break from a stressful routine.

Although there are differences among meditative techniques, the following suggestions illustrate some general guidelines:

1. Try meditation once or twice a day for 10 to 20 minutes at a time.
2. Keep in mind that when you're meditating, what you *don't* do is more important than what you do. So embrace a passive attitude: Tell yourself, "What happens, happens." In meditation, you take what you get. You don't *strive* for more. Striving of any kind hinders meditation.
3. Place yourself in a hushed, calming environment. For example, don't face a light directly.
4. Avoid eating for an hour before you meditate. Avoid caffeine (found in coffee, tea, many soft drinks, and chocolate) for at least 2 hours.

Going with the flow.   Meditation is a popular method of managing the stresses of the outside world by reducing states of bodily arousal. This young woman practices yoga, a form of meditation. She "goes with the flow," allowing the distractions of her environment to sort of "pass through." Contrast her meditative state with the apparently stressful features of the young man sitting behind her.

5. Get into a relaxed position. Modify it as needed. You can scratch or yawn if you feel the urge.

6. For a focusing device, you can concentrate on your breathing or sit in front of a serene object like a plant or incense. Benson suggests "perceiving" (not "mentally saying") the word *one* each time you breathe out. That is, think the word, but "less actively" than you normally would. Other researchers suggest thinking the word *in* as you breathe in and *out*, or *ah-h-h*, as you breathe out. They also suggest mantras like *ah-nam, rah-mah*, and *shi-rim*.

7. When preparing for meditation, repeat your mantra aloud many times—if you're using a mantra. Enjoy it. Then say it progressively more softly. Close your eyes. Focus on the mantra. Allow thinking the mantra to become more and more "passive" so that you "perceive" rather than think it. Again, embrace your "what happens, happens" attitude. Keep on focusing on the mantra. It may become softer or louder, or fade and then reappear.

8. If unsettling thoughts drift while you're meditating, allow them to sort of "pass through." Don't worry about squelching them, or you may become tense.

9. Remember to take what comes. Meditation and relaxation cannot be forced. You cannot force the relaxing effects of meditation. Like sleep, you can only set the stage for it and then permit it to happen.

10. Let yourself drift. (You won't get lost.) What happens, happens.

Progressive Relaxation Progressive relaxation was originated by University of Chicago physician Edmund Jacobson in 1938. Jacobson noticed that people tense their muscles under stress, intensifying their uneasiness. They tend to be unaware of these contractions, however. Jacobson reasoned that if muscle contractions contributed to tension, muscle relaxation might reduce tension. But clients who were asked to focus on relaxing muscles often had no idea what to do.

Jacobson's method of progressive relaxation teaches people how to monitor muscle tension and relaxation. With this method, people first tense, then relax, selected muscle groups in the arms; facial area; the chest, stomach, and lower back muscles; the hips, thighs, and calves; and so on. The sequence heightens awareness of muscle tensions and helps people differentiate feelings of tension from relaxation. The method is progressive, in that people progress from one group of muscles to another in practicing the technique. Since the 1930s, progressive relaxation has been used by a number of behavior therapists, including Joseph Wolpe and Arnold Lazarus (1966).

The following instructions from Wolpe and Lazarus (1966, pp. 177–178) illustrate how the technique is applied to relaxing the arms. Relaxation should be practiced in a favorable setting. Settle back on a recliner, couch, or a bed with a pillow. Select a place and time when you're unlikely to be disturbed. Make the room warm and comfortable. Dim sources of light. Loosen tight clothing. Tighten muscles about two-thirds as hard as you could if you were trying your hardest. If you sense that a muscle could have a spasm, you are tightening too much. After tensing, let go of tensions completely.

Relaxation of Arms (time: 4–5 minutes) Settle back as comfortably as you can. Let yourself relax to the best of your ability. . . . Now, as you relax like that, clench your right fist, just clench your fist tighter and tighter, and study the tension as you do so. Keep it clenched and feel the tension in your right fist, hand, forearm . . . and now relax. Let the fingers of your right hand become loose, and observe the contrast in your feelings. . . . Now, let yourself go and try to become more relaxed all over. . . . Once more, clench your right fist really tight . . . hold it, and notice the tension again. . . . Now let go, relax; your fingers straighten out, and you notice the difference once more. . . . Now repeat that with your left fist. Clench your left fist while the rest of your body relaxes; clench that fist tighter and feel the tension . . . and now relax. Again enjoy the contrast. . . . Repeat that once more, clench the left fist, tight and tense. . . . Now do the opposite of tension—relax and feel the difference. Continue relaxing like that for a while. . . . Clench both fists tighter and together, both fists tense, forearms tense, study the sensations . . . and relax; straighten out your fingers and feel that relaxation. Continue relaxing your hands and forearms more and more. . . . Now bend your elbows and tense your biceps, tense them harder and study the tension feelings . . . all right, straighten out your arms, let them relax and feel that difference again. Let the relaxation develop. . . . Once more, tense your biceps; hold the tension and observe it carefully. . . . Straighten the arms and relax; relax to the best of your ability. . . . Each time, pay close attention to your feelings when you tense up and when you relax. Now straighten your arms, straighten them so that you feel most tension in the triceps muscles along the back of your arms; stretch your arms and feel that tension. . . . And now relax. Get your arms back into a comfortable position. Let the relaxation proceed on its own. The arms should feel comfortably heavy as you allow them to relax. . . . Straighten the arms once more so that you feel the tension in the triceps muscles; straighten them. Feel that tension . . . and relax. Now let's concentrate on pure relaxation in the arms without any tension. Get your arms comfortable and let them relax further and further. Continue relaxing your arms even further. Even when your arms seem fully relaxed, try to go that extra bit further; try to achieve deeper and deeper levels of relaxation.

■ **AGE** The risk of CHD increases sharply with age from about 40 upward. For men, the rate of increase is steady. For women, it is slow until menopause and then increases rapidly (USDHHS, 1991).

■ **GENDER** Men are victimized by CHD twice as frequently as women. The mortality rate among women approximates that of men 15 years younger. A 65-year-old woman has about the same risk of dying from a heart attack as a man of 50 (Jenkins, 1988).

■ **FAMILY HISTORY** People whose families show a history of CHD are more likely to develop CHD themselves.

■ **SOCIOECONOMIC STATUS (SES)** Persons of low SES are at greater risk for CHD than persons higher in SES. Persons of lower SES are more likely to smoke, less likely to watch their diets, and more likely to encounter various stresses and strains, all of which may contribute to CHD (Jenkins, 1988).

■ **OBESITY** Obesity is a major risk factor for CHD (Brownell & Wadden, 1992; Jenkins, 1988). Obesity may raise bodily accumulation of fat, cholesterol levels, and blood pressure (USDHHS, 1991).

One frequently cited study of the obesity–CHD relationship followed 2,252 men and 2,818 women in Framingham, Massachusetts (Dawber, 1980; Haynes et al., 1980, 1983). Participants were first assessed between 1948 and 1950, then reexamined every 2 years for a period of 26 years. Initial levels of obesity predicted CHD throughout the duration of the study. Later weight gains were also linked to CHD.

Risk. What's wrong with this picture? How many risk factors for cardiovascular disorders can you identify in this photograph?

The incidence of CHD might have been reduced by 25% if everyone had maintained an optimal weight.

■ **HYPERTENSION** About 20% of Americans are reported to have **hypertension**, or high blood pressure (USDHHS, 1991). As shown by Figure 4.1, non-Hispanic African Americans are more likely than non-Hispanic white Americans to have hypertension, and non-Hispanic white Americans are more likely to have hypertension than Hispanic Americans (USDHHS, 1991). Except in the case of non-Hispanic African Americans, men aged 20 to 74 are more likely to have hypertension than women in the same age group.

Contractions (beats) of the heart expel blood from the heart through blood vessels, causing them to dilate. The blood vessels also dilate and constrict according to internal biological factors and external factors, like stress. Your blood pressure (BP) is the pressure that blood exerts on the walls of your blood vessels. BP varies according to the degree of constriction of the blood vessels. The more constricted the blood vessels, the harder it is for the blood to squeeze through, and the higher the BP. In most people, when the BP rises beyond normal limits, baroreceptors (*baro* derives from the Greek *baros,* meaning "weight" or "pressure") signal the brain which, in turn, relaxes the walls of the blood vessels.

In hypertensive people the system works inadequately, leaving the vessel walls constricted. Some people have high BP because of known organic problems, such as kidney malfunction (Shapiro & Goldstein, 1982). High BP in the absence of identifiable organic causes is termed *essential hypertension.* Hypertension predisposes people to cardiovascular disorders like arteriosclerosis, heart attacks, and strokes (USDHHS, 1991). Because elevated blood pressure can damage the cardiovascular system for years without noticeable symptoms, it is crucial to have our BP checked periodically.

> **T or F** People actually tend *not* to recognize their own high blood pressure.

Stressors like high levels of noise can raise the blood pressure. In an industrial setting, workers over age 55 who had suffered hearing loss, presumably from prolonged exposure to workplace noise, showed significantly higher BP than age-mates who had not suffered hearing loss (Talbott et al., 1985). BP also becomes elevated in situations requiring continuous vigilance, whether people are in combat, in the workplace, at home, or commuting on congested highways (Stokols & Novaco, 1981).

*Has anybody considered that Fam. Hist. and CHD might be a product of a common SES? (i.e. not necessarily primarily genetically related?)

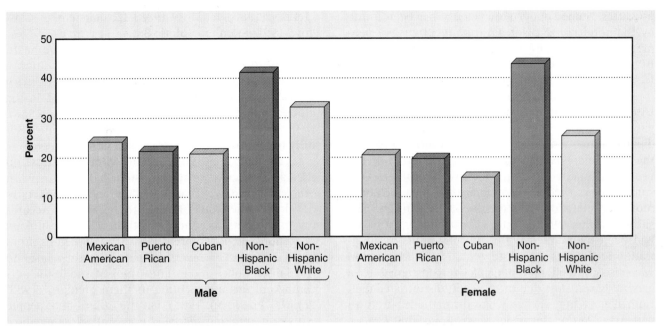

Figure 4.1 Hypertension among people aged 20 to 74, according to race/ethnicity.
Non-Hispanic African Americans are more likely than non-Hispanic white Americans to have
high blood pressure, and non-Hispanic white Americans are more likely to have high blood
pressure than Hispanic Americans. Except in the case of non-Hispanic African Americans, men
aged 20 to 74 are more likely than women in the same age group to have high blood pressure.
Source: USDHHS, Public Health Service (1991), Health United States 1990. DHHS Pub. No. (PHS) 91-1232.

From the biological perspective, essential hypertension may reflect overresponsiveness of the cardiovascular system to stress (Steptoe et al., 1984). So-called **hot reactors**, for example, respond to stress with quickened heart rate and constriction of blood vessels in peripheral areas of the body, whereas others do not (Eliot & Buell, 1983).

Because African Americans are more likely than non-Hispanic white Americans to suffer from hypertension, some researchers suggest that cardiovascular responsiveness to stress may have genetic origins. If so, African Americans of darker skin color should be more prone to hypertension because they have a higher percentage of black ancestors. However, the shade-of-skin–hypertension connection holds only for African Americans of lower socioeconomic status. For this reason, Klag (1991) suggests that stress is the key culprit. He argues that African Americans of darker color are subjected to greater discrimination—a socioeconomic and sociocultural stressor. Better educated, more affluent African Americans encounter relatively less discrimination and have better dietary and exercise habits, all of which lessen the stress load they bear.

The prevailing psychodynamic perspective on hypertension has been that hypertensive people have difficulty expressing pent-up anger (Alexander, 1939). Pent-up feelings press against a biological barrier—the walls of blood vessels—increasing blood

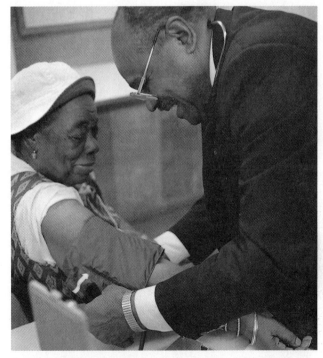

Assessing blood pressure.   About 20% of Americans are reported to have hypertension, or high blood pressure. African Americans are more likely than non-Hispanic white Americans to suffer from hypertension, but it is unclear whether genetic factors or stress play more crucial causal roles. Because we cannot directly sense our own blood pressure, it is advisable to have it checked regularly.

pressures. Some supportive evidence has been found by Diamond (1982): Normal (nonhypertensive) people show elevated BP when they are angered. Their BP remains elevated so long as they suppress their feelings, but returns to normal if they vent them.

High BP is frequently controlled by medicine. Unfortunately, because of lack of symptoms, many patients do not take medication reliably. Obesity and dietary components such as sodium (salt) can elevate the BP. Dietary restrictions are therefore part of the usual treatment program for hypertensives. One study underscored the potential of dietary behavior modification in the treatment of hypertension. The subjects were 496 hypertension patients whose BP had been maintained within normal limits by medication for 5 years (Langford et al., 1985). Medication was discontinued and patients were assigned to a general weight-loss diet or to a sodium-restricted diet. Both dietary approaches worked for the majority of patients: 72% of the weight-loss group and 78% of the sodium-restricted group maintained normal BP without medication.

Behavioral methods like meditation and relaxation training have also shown to be of value in supplementing the medical treatment of high BP (Agras et al., 1983; Benson et al., 1983; Hoelscher et al., 1987).

■ **SERUM CHOLESTEROL** A study of 2,541 middle-aged men who had suffered heart attacks showed that men with high **serum cholesterol** levels were more likely than men with normal cholesterol levels to die from heart disease (Pekkanen et al., 1990).

We can distinguish between so-called bad cholesterol (low-density lipoprotein, or LDL) and good cholesterol (high-density lipoprotein, or HDL). LDL increases the risk for CHD, whereas HDL lowers it (Jenkins, 1988). LDL is found in animal fats (including the fat in whole milk). The body also converts saturated fats to cholesterol. Even cholesterol-free vegetable matter may thus be dangerous if it is high in saturated fats. Coconut and palm oils and cashew nuts are examples of plant foods high in saturated fats. Regular exercise also appears to lower the level of harmful (LDL) cholesterol in the blood.

Evidence shows that among people who have previously suffered a heart attack but whose hearts still function normally, deaths from subsequent heart attacks and incidence of nonfatal heart attacks are lowered by substantially reducing the level of serum cholesterol (Buchwald et al., 1990; Kolata, 1990b).

■ **PATTERNS OF CONSUMPTION** Such patterns include heavy drinking, smoking, overeating, and eating food high in cholesterol or saturated fats

(Jeffery, 1988; Jenkins, 1988; Lichtenstein & Glasgow, 1992; Stamler et al., 1986).

High levels of alcohol are harmful to the heart, but low to moderate levels (for example, a drink a day) may actually reduce the risk of CHD and certain kinds of strokes by lowering the level of LDL in the blood (Jenkins, 1988; Stampfer & Hennekens, 1988). Researchers do not suggest that abstainers purposefully imbibe to reduce their risks of CHD, however.

Smoking may intensify the effects of stress on the cardiovascular system (Epstein & Perkins, 1988). Smokers are about twice as likely as nonsmokers to develop or die from CHD (USDHHS, 1983). According to the National Cancer Institute (1991), smoking is responsible for more than 20% of deaths from heart disease. The level of risk is directly related to the daily number of cigarettes smoked and to the percentage of tar and nicotine in them (Jenkins, 1988; Pettiti & Friedman, 1985). On the other hand, people who quit smoking before the age of 65 can reduce the risk of CHD by as much as 50% (Kannel et al., 1984). The longer an ex-smoker remains abstinent, the lower the risk of CHD (USDHHS, 1983).

■ **TYPE A BEHAVIOR** Studies carried out in the 1970s generally showed that Type A behavior contributed to coronary heart disease (CHD) and risk of recurrent heart attacks (for example, Rosenman et al., 1975), although some more recent studies have found no link between these variables (for example, Shekelle et al., 1985). Nonetheless, Miller's (1991) reanalysis of the conflicting data suggests there is a modest connection between the TABP and CHD when the TABP is assessed by means of a standardized interview.

The questionnaire "Are You Type A or Type B?" will help you assess whether or not you manifest the Type A behavior pattern (TABP). The feature "Ways of Decreasing Type A Behavior" describes methods that have been used successfully to reduce the TABP and help prevent recurrent heart attacks.

■ **ANGER** Anger and hostility are components of the TABP, and research indicates that chronic anger may be as prominent a risk factor for CHD as cigarette smoking, obesity, and a high-fat diet (Angier, 1990b). Hostility is also associated with an increased risk of recurrent heart attacks among men who have suffered an earlier attack (Blakeslee, 1990). People who are chronically angry produce excessive amounts of stress-related hormones like adrenaline and noradrenaline (which increase the heart rate and blood pressure). Their bodies thus remain aroused for prolonged periods of time by these adrenal hormones, increasing the wear and tear on their cardiovascular systems.

■ **SOCIAL ENVIRONMENTAL STRESS** Social environmental stress also appears to heighten the risk of CHD (Krantz, 1988). Overtime work, assembly-line labor, and exposure to conflicting demands all appear to make their contributions (Jenkins, 1988).

The stress–CHD connection is not straightforward, however. For example, the effects of demanding occupations are apparently moderated by factors such as psychological hardiness and whether or not people find their work meaningful (Cohen et al., 1986; Krantz, 1988).

One model relates the demands of an occupation to the degree of control afforded the individual worker. As suggested by Figure 4.2, waiters and waitresses, store managers, and fire fighters have highly demanding jobs. Architects, scientists, physicians, and some others have occupations in which they exert a good deal of control over their job-related activity. **High-strain** jobs are high in demand and low in the amount of personal control they afford. High-strain jobs apparently place workers at highest risk for CHD (Karasek et al., 1981, 1982; Krantz et al., 1988). Workers in high-strain occupations were found to

have about 1½ times the risk of CHD as workers in low-strain occupations (LaCroix & Haynes, 1987). Working women in general have not been found to incur a greater risk of CHD as compared to home-makers and to men. However, women are at greater risk for CHD when they hold clerical (low-control) jobs, when they have nonsupportive bosses (high stress), and when they have children and incur high family demands (Haynes & Feinleib, 1980; Krantz et al., 1988).

■ **SEDENTARY LIFESTYLE** The heart is built of muscle tissue. Exercise has a healthful effect on the heart, as it does on other muscles. The sedentary life, in contrast, weakens the capacity of the heart, just as it saps the power of the large skeletal muscles.

Many health professionals recommend **aerobic** exercise as part of the overall treatment plan for people who are at risk for CHD and for people who have had a heart attack (Dubbert, 1992). A review of the evidence suggests that exercise prolongs the lives of CHD patients, with an overall reduction of about 20% in the mortality rate (Blumenthal & Emery,

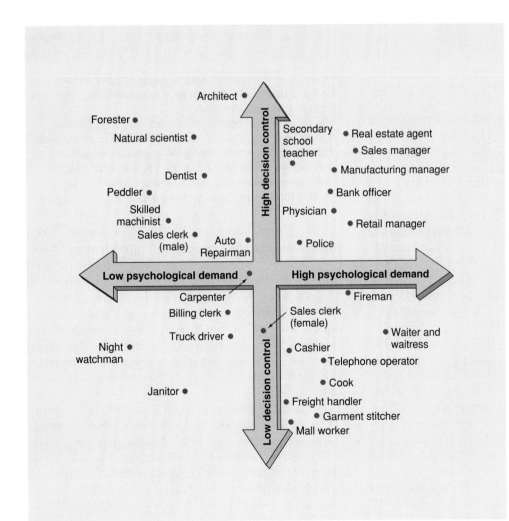

Figure 4.2 The job strain model.
The job strain model shows the relationship of various occupations to two dimensions of job strain: decision control and psychological demand. Occupations characterized by both *low* control and *high* demand (the lower right quadrant) have been associated with greater risk of cardiovascular disease.

Source: "Bosses Face Less Risk Than the Bossed," April 3, 1983. New York Times. *Copyright 1983 by the New York Times Company. Reprinted by permission.*

Aerobic exercise. These women are stretching as part of their running routine. Many health professionals recommend aerobic exercise as part of the treatment plan for people who are at risk for CHD. Evidence suggests that exercise prolongs the lives of CHD patients.

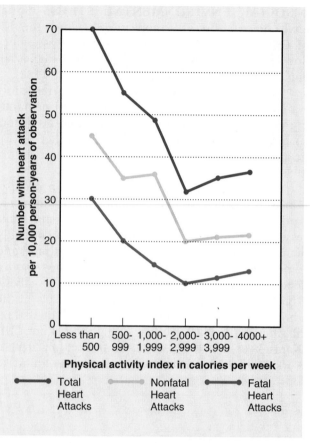

Figure 4.3 The frequencies of heart attacks among Harvard University Alumni as a function of the exertion level of physical exercise.
The probability of heart attacks declines as the physical activity level increases up to about 2,000 calories per week. Then the frequency of heart attacks increases gradually with increases in physical activity. You can expend about 2,000 calories a week by jogging about 3 miles a day or by walking for approximately an hour a day.

1988; O'Connor et al., 1989). Aerobic exercise requires a sustained increase in the consumption of oxygen. Aerobic exercises include but are not limited to running and jogging, running in place, walking (at more than a leisurely pace), aerobic dancing, jump rope, swimming, bicycle riding, basketball, racquetball, and cross-country skiing. Health professionals usually provide warm-up and cool-down periods, in addition to intervals of vigorous exercise. **Anaerobic exercises**, by contrast, involve short bursts of muscle activity, as in weight training and sports like baseball. The cardiovascular benefits of exercise are obtained from aerobic exercise.

Studies by Ralph Paffenbarger and his colleagues have supported the connection between exercise and cardiovascular health. In one study, Paffenbarger and his associates (1972) surveyed 3,700 San Francisco longshoremen. Longshoremen who handled cargo continuously suffered about 60% as many heart attacks as those who engaged in less exhausting activity. The Paffenbarger group (1978, 1984, 1986) have also tracked 17,000 Harvard University alumni through university records and questionnaires and correlated their incidence of heart attacks with their physical activity levels. The incidence of heart attacks decreased as activity levels

increased to a level of exertion equivalent to "burning" about 2,000 calories per week (see Figure 4.3). This is the exercise equivalent of running about 20 miles a week. Above 2,000 calories a week, however, the incidence of heart attacks gradually climbed again, but not steeply. Inactive alumni incurred the greatest risks of heart attacks. Alumni who burned up at least 2,000 calories per week through exercise lived an average of 2 years longer than less active alumni.

The Paffenbarger studies are limited because they are correlational and not experimental. Persons who are already in better health may elect, and enjoy, higher activity levels. Thus better health would account for both higher rates of physical activity and a lower incidence of heart attacks.

QUESTIONNAIRE

Are You Type A or Type B?

People with the Type A behavior pattern are impatient, competitive, and aggressive. They feel rushed, under pressure; they keep one eye glued to the clock. They are prompt and often early for appointments. They walk, talk, and eat rapidly. They grow restless when others work slowly.

Type A people don't just stroll out on the tennis court to bat the ball around. They scrutinize their form, polish their strokes, and demand consistent self-improvement.

Are you Type A? The following questionnaire may afford you insight.

Directions: Write a checkmark under the Yes if the behavior pattern described is typical of you. Place one under the No if it is not. Work rapidly and answer all items. Then check the scoring key at the end of the chapter.

Do You: **Yes No**

1. Strongly emphasize important words in your ordinary speech? — —
2. Walk briskly from place to place or meeting to meeting? — —
3. Think that life is by nature dog-eat-dog? — —
4. Get fidgety when you see someone complete a job slowly? — —
5. Urge others to complete what they're trying to express? — —
6. Find it exceptionally annoying to get stuck in line? — —
7. Envision all the things you have to do even when someone is talking to you? — —
8. Eat while you're getting dressed, or jot notes down while you're driving? — —
9. Catch up on work during vacations? — —

Do You: **Yes No**

10. Direct the conversation to things that interest you? — —
11. Feel as if things are going to pot because you're relaxing for a few minutes? — —
12. Get so wrapped up in your work that you fail to notice beautiful scenery passing by? — —
13. Get so wrapped up in money, promotions, and awards that you neglect expressing your creativity? — —
14. Schedule appointments and meetings back to back? — —
15. Arrive early for appointments and meetings? — —
16. Make fists or clench your jaws to drill home your views? — —
17. Think that you have achieved what you have because of your ability to work fast? — —
18. Have the feeling that uncompleted work must be done *now* and fast? — —
19. Try to find more efficient ways to get things done? — —
20. Struggle always to win games instead of having fun? — —
21. Interrupt people who are talking? — —
22. Lose patience with people who are late for appointments and meetings? — —
23. Get back to work right after lunch? — —
24. Find that there's never enough time? — —
25. Believe that you're getting too little done, even when other people tell you that you're doing fine? — —

We finish this section with encouraging news. Risk factors for cardiovascular disorders, especially smoking and high-fat diets, have been known for 25 years or more. The American public has apparently responded to this knowledge by making changes in their lifestyles, so that the incidence of CHD has declined (Pell & Fayerweather, 1985; Stamler, 1985a, 1985b). Better educated people are also more likely to modify unhealthful behavior patterns and reap the benefits of change (Stamler, 1985a, 1985b). Is there a message in there for you?

Gastrointestinal Disorders

Gastrointestinal disorders are problems of the digestive system. (*Gastro-* derives from the Greek *gaster*, meaning "stomach.") There are some clear connections between stress, emotional response, and gastrointestinal problems. Diarrhea, for example, is a nearly universal feature of anxiety and can beset people before important job interviews, during examinations, or before delivering a speech. Acid stomach and indigestion are also related to stress. The symptoms of

Ways of Decreasing Type A Behavior

Psychologists and other health professionals have investigated reduction of the TABP through anxiety reduction techniques, cognitive behavior therapy techniques (Haaga, 1987), and rational-emotive therapy (Thurman, 1985a, 1985b). Successful interventions have been found to reduce the TABP on self-administered inventories and directly observed behaviors (Blumenthal et al., 1987; Roskies et al., 1986). Cardiac patients in such programs have shown favorable changes in blood pressure, serum cholesterol, perceptions of time urgency (Roskies et al., 1979), and physiological reactivity to stress (Razin et al., 1986). Questions remain about whether or not modifying the TABP reduces health risks, however (Haaga, 1987). Methodological concerns have been expressed about such issues as the lack of consistency in the measurement of Type A behavior in TABP reduction programs, the lack of no-treatment control groups in a number of studies, and a need for replication of findings (Blumenthal & Emery, 1988).

The largest and best controlled study in changing the TABP is the Recurrent Coronary Prevention Program (RCPP). RCPP focused on men who had suffered a heart attack in hopes of preventing recurrence. Of the 868 men who participated, 98% were classified as Type A. Each had suffered a heart attack at least 6 months earlier and was under 65 years of age. The study used a controlled comparison of two types of treatment and a waiting list control group (Friedman et al., 1984; Powell et al., 1984). Subjects were divided into three groups:

1. A health information condition that provided exercise, diet and medical information,

2. A multimodal (comprehensive) treatment condition that combined health information and cognitive behavior techniques, and

3. A no-treatment condition.

The multimodal treatment incorporated training in relaxation and lifestyle changes designed to change the pace of daily life and reduce the sense of time urgency. Men who participated in multimodal therapy showed greater TABP reductions than men in the health information condition. The rate of recurrence of cardiac events (defined as heart attacks and other cardiovascular incidents) among the men who received the multimodal treatment was significantly lower than among men in the other two groups (see Figure 4.4). After 3 years, subjects in the multimodal group had one-third as many recurrent heart attacks as subjects in the control group (Friedman & Ulmer, 1984; Friedman et al., 1986). As promising as the RCPP is, there were so many facets to the multimodal treatment that it may be impossible to ferret out which were most beneficial.

Following are broad guidelines and some specifics of the RCPP program. The three broad guidelines were alleviating men's sense of time urgency, hostility, and such self-destructive tendencies as gorging on high-fat foods, drinking heavily, smoking, and working excessively. The buffering effects of humor were noted also. Some specific suggestions follow that were offered for helping participants alleviate the sense of time urgency and reduce hostility.

Alleviating the Sense of Time Urgency For Type A people, the day begins urgently and never lets up. The initial step in handling time urgency is to confront and alter the self-defeating beliefs that support it, such as "I can't do

Decreasing Type A behavior. Decreasing Type A behavior involves reducing one's sense of time urgency and alleviating feelings of hostility. How are the people in these photographs accomplishing these goals?

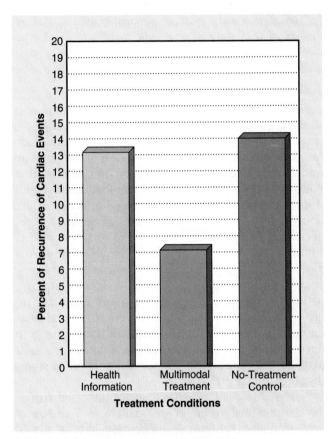

Figure 4.4 Results of the Recurrent Coronary Prevention Program (RCPP).
Men who received the multimodal treatment were less likely to experience a recurrent cardiac event than men who received only health information or who were placed in a no-treatment control condition.

4. Visit art galleries and museums. Consider works for their aesthetic value, not their prices.

5. Go to the movies, theater, concerts, ballet.

6. Write letters to family and old friends.

7. Take an art course; start violin or piano lessons.

8. Keep in mind that life is by nature unfinished. You needn't have all your projects finished by a certain date.

9. Ask family members what they did during the day. *Listen* to the answer.

Alleviating Hostility Some researchers believe that hostility is the most harmful feature of the TABP. Friedman and Ulmer (1984) write that hostility (like time urgency) is supported by irrational beliefs. It is helpful to recognize maladaptive, irrational beliefs and substitute adaptive beliefs. Some of the irrational beliefs they identified that support hostility include, "I need a certain amount of hostility to get ahead in the world" (p. 222), "Giving and receiving love is a sign of weakness" (p. 228), and "I can't do anything about my hostility" (p. 222). Countering beliefs include the recognition that instant irritation, aggravation, and anger do not contribute to success, that giving and receiving love is not a sign of weakness, and behavior change can occur at any age.

In addition to challenging irrational ideas, Friedman and Ulmer (1984) offer suggestions like these for alleviating hostility:

1. Tell your family that you love them.

2. Make new friends.

3. Let friends know that you are available to help them.

4. Get a pet and care for it.

5. Don't get involved in discussions that you know lead to pointless arguments.

6. When others do things that disappoint you, consider situational factors like education and cultural background that affect their behavior. Don't jump to the conclusion that they intend to get you upset.

7. Focus on the beauty and pleasure in things.

8. Don't curse as much.

9. Express appreciation to people for their support and assistance.

10. Play to lose, at least occasionally.

11. Say "Good morning" cheerfully.

12. Check out your face in the mirror from time to time. Look for signs of anger and aggravation; ask yourself if you really need to look like that.

anything about it" (p. 182) or "My sense of time urgency has helped me gain social and economic success" (p. 179).

Friedman and Ulmer counter that maladaptive habits can be changed even in later adulthood and that impatience and irritation do not contribute to success. They also offer the following suggestions to reduce the sense of time urgency:

1. Increase social activity with family and friends.

2. Each day, spend a few minutes recalling distant events. Peruse photos of family and old friends.

3. Read books—biographies, literature, drama, politics, nature, science, science fiction. (Books on business and on climbing the corporate ladder are not recommended!)

indigestion can be so severe that people believe that they are experiencing a heart attack. Whereas diarrhea and acid stomach can come and go according to whether or not we experience anxiety, ulcers are a more enduring gastrointestinal disorder.

■ **ULCERS** Ulcers may afflict 1 person in 10 and cause as many as 10,000 deaths each year in the United States (Whitehead & Bosmajian, 1982). Ulcers are open sores on the lining of the stomach or the small intestine. So-called peptic ulcers are related to, or caused by, *pepsin,* an enzyme found in gastric juices that helps break down proteins into digestive form. Persons with ulcers tend to have high levels of pepsinogen, a gastric secretion that is converted into pepsin by hydrochloric acid.

Concepts of *stimulus specificity* and *individual response specificity* may help to explain the development of ulcers. Certain stimulus situations involving stress (stimulus specificity) may be connected with vulnerability to ulcers. Also, certain people (individual response specificity) may be at greater risk to the effects of stress by virtue of their characteristic response patterns.

The following case example connects stress with the development of ulcers:

*M*r. M was a 30-year-old electronics engineer who designed supersonic aircraft in an aerospace company. He was given the enormous responsibility of preparing designs to be submitted to the government in an effort to attain government contracts. He appeared to delight in the challenge and saw it as a major opportunity for career advancement. The first symptom of gastric problems was burning, gnawing sensations following a dinner. The sensations returned periodically after eating and were diagnosed as revealing a peptic ulcer.

M had been hard-working and independent since adolescence. M was the oldest child in a large family. He worked during high school because his parents had turned their attention to his younger siblings. College was a great burden, but M saw it through. He married and had a family. He moved from firm to firm in an effort to attain more responsible and remunerative positions. His family lived on a careful budget so that they could take advantage of property investments that came along from time to time. Just before being assigned the government project, M was subjected to multiple decision-making pressures: decisions whether or not to buy a new house, to move his oldest son to a new school, to go on a long vacation, and to sell an investment property.

The ulcer was controlled by diet and lifestyle changes that reduced the pressures assailing him. He

retained the government project but was counseled to declare a moratorium on making the other decisions. He took up some recreational activities and worked on ways of reducing family and occupational pressures. Ulcer pain lessened within a few months.

■ *Adapted from Suinn, 1975, p. 360*

The view that the body responds to different stimuli, or different sources of stress, in different ways has been supported by some fascinating historic case histories. Consider the classic case of "Tom," who underwent gastrointestinal surgery in 1947 (Wolf & Wolff, 1947). A plastic window was installed over his stomach, making it possible to observe its operation. It turned out that Tom's flow of gastric juices decreased when he was exposed to anxiety-evoking stimuli—a sign of sympathetic activity, which inhibits digestion. The juices increased when he was provoked by anger-inducing stimuli—a sign of parasympathetic activity. Now, when copious quantities of digestive juices are secreted and there is no food matter to digest, the gastrointestinal tract may begin to devour itself. This is one reason a link may exist between ulcers and long-term exposure to stressors that provoke anger.

Loss of social support is also implicated in the development of ulcers. For example, a number of adolescents with high pepsinogen levels have developed ulcers following separation from, or loss of, loved ones (Ackerman et al., 1981).

People may also differ in their characteristic response patterns to stress. Some individuals may be "gastric reactors," in the sense of secreting greater levels of pepsinogen under conditions of stress. In social-learning theory terms, the situational variables (exposure to stressful, anger-provoking stimuli) and person variables (differences in individual response patterns) interact to create conditions that may foster the development of ulcers. But why might some individuals be more prone to produce gastric secretions under conditions of stress?

The psychodynamic approach speculates that an individual's physiological response to stress can reflect disturbances in psychosexual development. The somatic expression of the conflict (for example, increased secretion of gastric juices such as pepsinogen) would be symbolic of the character of the underlying conflict (Alexander, 1950). For example, because food may symbolize parental love, adults with unfulfilled but repressed wishes for parental love may experience a persistent "hunger" that leads to overactivation of the stomach. The stomach, in effect, continuously prepares itself for food, the symbolic equivalent of love. Evidence of the psychodynamic perspective is drawn largely from case studies of clients whose histories appear to be consistent with the theory (Fann et al., 1982). But uncontrolled case studies may be open to other interpretations.

According to the biological perspective, heredity largely determines levels of pepsinogen (Mirsky, 1958). There are numerous kinship studies in which pepsinogen levels, and incidence of ulcers, appear to follow genetic patterns. In one of them, the concordance rate for ulcers among 34 pairs of monozygotic twins was 50%, as compared to 14% among 78 pairs of dizygotic twins (Eberhard, 1968). These results are consistent with a genetic explanation because monozygotic twins share 100% genetic similarity, compared to 50% genetic overlap between dizygotic twins. Still, although genetic endowment may create a predisposition (or diathesis) for the development of ulcers, other factors, such as the level of stress and the individual's reactions to stress, may determine whether or not ulcers actually develop.

Asthma

Asthma is a respiratory disorder in which the main tubes of the windpipe—the bronchi—constrict and become inflamed, and large amounts of mucus are secreted (Israel et al., 1990). As a result, people wheeze, cough, and struggle to breathe in enough air. They may feel as though they are suffocating. Asthma afflicts about 3% of the American population. About one-third of the sufferers are children under 16. Attacks can last from a few minutes to several hours and vary notably in intensity. Series of attacks can harm the bronchial system, causing mucus to collect and muscles to lose their elasticity. Sometimes the bronchial system is weakened to the point where a subsequent attack is lethal. Few sufferers die from asthma, however.

■ **THEORETICAL PERSPECTIVES** Asthma attacks can be triggered by allergic reactions, cold, dry air, emotional responses such as anger, even laughing too hard (Brody, 1988a). Some researchers suggest that there are two kinds of asthma: allergic and non-allergic. Allergic individuals may have attacks in response to pollen, mold spores, and animal dander. Nonallergic types could stem from a variety of causes, including respiratory infections such as bronchitis and pneumonia (Alexander, 1981) and maternal smoking during pregnancy (Martinez et al., 1992). Regardless of the original cause, stress can apparently heighten the frequency and severity of attacks. Asthma, moreover, has psychological consequences. Some sufferers avoid strenuous activity, including exercise, for fear

of increasing their demand for oxygen and tripping attacks.

■ **TREATMENT** Treatment for asthma often consists of medications, including the use of bronchodilators. Recent reports also show that asthma sufferers can improve their breathing by muscle relaxation training (Lehrer et al., 1992), biofeedback that focuses on relaxing facial muscles (Klotses et al., 1991), and family therapy that reduces the stresses on asthmatic children (Lehrer et al., 1992).

Obesity

There is no sincerer love than the love of food.
George Bernard Shaw

The two biggest sellers in any bookstore are the cookbooks and the diet books. The cookbooks tell you how to prepare the food and the diet books tell you how not to eat any of it.

Andy Rooney

Food is essential to survival, but food means much more to many of us. Food symbolizes family life and caring. We connect food with the warmth of the parent–child relationship, with visits home on the holidays. Hosts offer food when we visit, and saying no can be construed as a personal rejection. Bacon and eggs, coffee and cream, red meat and potatoes mashed in butter—all seem inextricably interwoven with American values and agricultural abundance.

Yet many Americans are paying the price of plenty—**obesity**:

- One American in four is obese (weighs more than 20% above her or his recommended weight) (Kuczmarski, 1992).
- Forty percent of Americans label themselves overweight (Burros, 1988).
- Americans consume 815 billion calories of food each day, which is 200 billion calories more than necessary to maintain their weight at moderate levels of activity (Jenkins, 1988). The extra calories are enough to sustain a country of 80 million people (Jenkins, 1988).
- Some 65 million Americans diet every year and use nearly 30,000 approaches (Blumenthal, 1988).
- More than 90% of dieters fail to keep pounds off permanently. Whether they drop 15 pounds or 50, most dieters put almost all the pounds back on within a year (Brody, 1992a).
- Although food can be expensive, the incidence of obesity is highest among people of lower socioeconomic status (Ernst & Harlan, 1991).

Why is obesity included in an abnormal psychology textbook? There are at least four reasons:

1. Psychological factors contribute to obesity or impair dieting efforts. These include negative emotions like depression (Baucom & Aiken, 1981; Ruderman, 1985) and anxiety (Herman et al., 1987).

2. Obesity is a risk factor for many health problems, including coronary heart disease and diabetes (Brownell & Wadden, 1992).

3. Obesity has negative psychological repercussions, such as low self-esteem (Rosen et al., 1987; Smith & Fremouw, 1987).

4. Psychological approaches have been shown to help obese people take off pounds and keep them off (Brownell & Wadden, 1992).

Extreme thinness is at least as unhealthful as obesity, and extreme thinness has become fairly common, especially among young women. In Chapter 13 we discuss the eating disorders of anorexia nervosa and bulimia nervosa, each of which involves maladaptive methods of keeping weight down.

■ **THEORETICAL PERSPECTIVES** Why are so many people overweight? Is obesity a biological problem or a multifactorial problem? Research suggests that multiple factors contribute to obesity.

Heredity Obesity clearly runs in families. The question is *why?* It was once assumed that obese parents encouraged their children to become heavy by setting poor examples. Studies of Scandinavian adoptees by Stunkard and his colleagues (1986, 1990) strongly suggest a key role for heredity, however. They reveal that children's weight is more

All in the family? Obesity tends to run in families. The question is, *Why?*

closely related to the weight of their biological parents than to that of their adoptive parents. Perhaps the strongest evidence for the role of genetics comes from a study of identical twins which showed that regardless of whether or not the twins were reared together or apart, they wound up weighing virtually the same as adults (Stunkard et al., 1990). The researchers also studied fraternal (DZ) twins, who share only 50% genetic overlap, as compared with 100% genetic similarity among identical (MZ) twins. Consistent with the genetic hypothesis, fraternal twins varied much more in body weight (corrected for height) than MZ twins.

Heredity can influence body weight through transmission of tendencies toward higher or lower **metabolic rates,** the rates at which food is processed, or "burned," in the body (Ravussin et al., 1988). In a study of 126 southwestern Native Americans, metabolic rates predicted weight gains 4 years into the future (Ravussin et al., 1988).

Does the genetic role in obesity mean that biology is destiny? Not necessarily. Although there appears to be a genetic predisposition toward obesity, people may be able to control their weight within some broad limits by following a sensible (not drastic) diet and adopting a more active lifestyle. Still, there are limits to what a person can accomplish in attempting to sculpt their bodies to some idealized form (Brownell, 1991). Even people whose heredity is working against them can affect their weight through diet and exercise, although the contemporary slim ideal may be an unrealistic goal for many people (Brownell & Wadden, 1992).

Behavioral Factors Evidence is lacking to support the commonly held belief that overweight people, as a group, have a different style of eating than normal weight people, one that is characterized by taking larger bites and eating more quickly (Brownell & Wadden, 1992). Yet evidence does show that periodic binge eating (consuming massive amounts of food in a short time) is a particular problem for a large subgroup of obese people, perhaps 25 to 45%. Evidence also shows that obese people tend to be less physically active than normal weight people (Brownell & Wadden, 1992). Although correlational evidence is insufficient to establish causality, it is conceivable that inactivity may play a causal role in some cases of obesity, whereas it may result from obesity in others.

Fat Cells The efforts of heavy people to keep a slender profile may be sabotaged by cells within their own bodies termed **fat cells.** No, fat cells are not corpulent cells. They are adipose tissue—cells that store fat. Hunger is related to the quantity of stored fat. As time passes after eating, the blood sugar level declines, drawing fat from these cells to supply more nourishment. At some point—termed the **set point**—the hypothalamus in the brain detects the depletion of fat in these cells. The hypothalamus, in turn, signals the cerebral cortex, triggering the hunger drive.

People with higher levels of adipose tissue send more signals of depletion to the brain than people who are equal in weight but who have fewer fat cells. As a result, they feel food-deprived sooner. Markedly obese individuals usually have more adipose tissue than people who are of normal weight or mildly obese (Brownell & Wadden, 1992). Sad to say, dieters do not expel fat cells; instead, they shrink them. Many dieters who are markedly obese, even successful dieters, thus complain that they are constantly hungry as they struggle to maintain normal weights.

How is the number of fat cells in our bodies determined? Unfortunately, heredity seems to play a role. Excessive food intake in early childhood may also have an influence, however (Brownell & Wadden, 1992).

Adipose Tissue and Metabolism People with high levels of adipose tissue are doubly beset because adipose tissue metabolizes food more sluggishly than muscle. People with high fat-to-muscle ratios metabolize food more slowly than people of the same weight with lower fat-to-muscle ratios. As a result, they find it harder to lose weight and easier to gain weight at a given level of food consumption than people with lower fat-to-muscle ratios.

The standard distribution of adipose tissue is "sexist." The average man is composed of 40% muscle and 15% fat. The average woman is composed of 23% muscle and 25% fat. These differences may account for much of the sex appeal of the opposite gender. If men and women with typical distributions of fat and muscle are equal in weight, however, the woman—with relatively more adipose tissue—will have to consume fewer calories to maintain the same weight.

Compensating Metabolic Forces That Affect Dieters The body is a wondrous thing. It adjusts to all sorts of conditions, including deprivation. Sad to say, this capacity for adjustment can backfire on dieters. Dieters and people who have lost notable amounts of weight usually do not consume enough calories to satisfy their set points (Keesey, 1980). As a result, the body compensates by burning fewer calories.

The Yo-Yo Syndrome Repeated cycles of dieting and regaining weight—the yo-yo syndrome—may especially disturb the set point. Such cycles apparently "teach" the body that it will be episodically

deprived of food. As a result, repeated cycles of losing and regaining weight—the yo-yo syndrome—may contribute to obesity by slowing down the person's body metabolism (Brownell & Wadden, 1992; Garner & Wooley, 1991). To maintain weight loss, formerly overweight people who were yo-yo dieters must usually consume fewer calories than people of equal weight who were always thin.

As suggested by the case of Christine, changes in the body's fat-to-muscle ratio also frustrate yo-yo dieters:

> Christine . . . drops from 140 pounds down to 120 pounds. She might lose 15 pounds of fat and 5 pounds of muscle. If she regains the 20 pounds, will she replace all 5 pounds of muscle? [Animal studies] suggest that she won't, so Christine may replace 18 pounds of fat and only 2 pounds of muscle. She may be the same weight before and after this cycle, but her metabolic rate would be lower after the cycle because she has more fat, which is less metabolically active than muscle. (Brownell, 1988, p. 22)

It is harder for Christine just to maintain her 140 pounds the second time around. If she consumes as many calories as she had when she was previously 140 pounds, her weight will rise above 140. Now that she has increased her fat-to-muscle ratio, her body is "less metabolically active." It is thus more difficult for her to shed the same 20 pounds again.

 Cycles of dieting and regaining lost weight (the yo-yo syndrome) do make it progressively more difficult to take extra pounds off. During each cycle, some muscle tissue is replaced by adipose tissue, which metabolizes food more slowly.

In addition to sabotaging future dieting efforts, yo-yo dieting may also have injurious effects on the heart and cardiovascular system (Garner & Wooley, 1991). For example, a study of 21,000 middle-aged men carried out by the University of Texas School of Public Health found a higher rate of death due to CHD among men whose weights fluctuated markedly (Blumenthal, 1988). Repeated dieting and weight regain may also lead to psychological problems such as depression, anxiety and even personality changes (Garner & Wooley, 1991).

In any event, one way dieters may avoid slowing metabolism is to take weight off gradually (Blumenthal, 1988). Another is regular exercise.

Psychological Factors According to psychodynamic theory, eating is the cardinal oral activity. Under stress, people who were fixated in the oral stage by conflicts concerning dependence and independence are likely to regress in times of stress to excessive oral activities such as overeating.

Other psychological factors connected with overeating and obesity include low self-esteem, lack of self-efficacy expectancies, family conflicts, and negative emotions. Although the connections between these factors and obesity affect both genders, women most frequently seek assistance from professionals and diet centers, largely because of the pressures imposed on them by society to adhere to expectations of thinness. Consider the cases of Joan and Terry:

*J*oan was trapped in the yo-yo syndrome, repeatedly dropping 20 pounds, then regaining it. Whenever Joan got stuck at a certain weight plateau, or started to regain weight, her self-esteem plummeted. She'd hear herself muttering, "Who am I kidding? I'm not worthy of being thin. I should just accept being fat."

An incident with her mother revealed how her negative thinking was often triggered. Joan had lost 24 pounds from an original weight of 174 and was beginning to feel good about herself. Most other people reinforced her by complimenting her on her weight loss. She called her mother, who lived in another state, to share the good news. Instead of jumping on the bandwagon, her mother cautioned her not to expect too much from her success. After all, her mother pointed out, she had been repeatedly disappointed in the past. The message came through loud and clear: Don't get your hopes up because you will only be more disappointed in the end. Joan's mother may have only meant to protect Joan from eventual disappointment, but the message she conveyed reinforced the negative view that Joan held of herself: You're a loser. Don't expect too much of yourself. Accept your reality. Don't try to change. You're a hopeless case.

As soon as she hung up the receiver, Joan rushed to the pantry. Without hesitation she devoured three packages of Famous Amos Chocolate Chip Cookies in a frenzied binge on the stairway. The next day she told her psychologist that the binge had reactivated memories of childhood bingeing on Oreos while hiding under the stairwell. ■

*F*or years Terry's husband had scrutinized every morsel she consumed. "Haven't you had enough?" he would ask derisively. The more he harped on her weight, the more anger she felt, although she did not express her feelings directly. The criticism did not apply only to her weight. She also heard, "You're not smart enough. . . . Why don't you take better care of yourself? . . . How come you're not sexy?" After years of assault on her self-esteem, Terry petitioned for divorce, convinced that the single life could be no worse than her marriage.

While separated and awaiting the final divorce decree, Terry felt free to be herself for the first time in her adult life. However, she had not expected the effect freedom would have on her weight. She ballooned from 155 pounds to 186 pounds within a few months. She identified leftover resentment from her marriage as the driving factor. "There's no one to make me diet anymore," she said. Her overeating was like saying, "See, I can eat if I want to." Without her husband, she could express her anger and outrage toward him by eating to excess. Unfortunately, her mode of expressing anger was self-defeating. Terry's lingering resentments encouraged her to act spitefully rather than constructively.

■ *The Authors' Files*

In some cases, people who seek help in losing weight may profit from counseling that helps them recognize that they are not as heavy as they think (Brownell, 1991). Women, all in all, appear to be burdened by nearly impossible standards—so much so that the "normal" (that is, typical) eating pattern for American women today *is* dieting (Polivy & Herman, 1987)! Four of five women in our country diet by the time they are 18 ("Women," 1991). This excessive concern in our society about body weight and adhering to idealized images of slenderness underlies the development of eating disorders such as bulimia and anorexia (see Chapter 13). About 1 high school senior in 10 has already developed an eating disorder ("Women," 1991). Dieters also need to be made aware of the perils of yo-yo dieting. When losing weight appears to be a losing battle, health professionals may consider helping the client develop an improved self-concept and adopt a generally healthful lifestyle, rather than focusing all efforts on weight loss per se (Smith & Fremouw, 1987).

 Dieting has indeed become the "normal" way of eating for American women. The great majority of women go on weight-loss diets at some time in their lives, about 4 of 5 by the time they are 18.

■ **METHODS OF WEIGHT CONTROL** Literally thousands of methods of weight control have been offered in recent years. Some, like surgery and diet pills, involve biological interventions. Others, like modifying eating habits and exercising, involve changes in behavior. Still other methods combine biological and behavioral approaches. Because our attitudes and expectations—including our self-

MULTICULTURAL PERSPECTIVES

Socioeconomic, Sociocultural, and Ethnic Factors in Obesity

There is a gender gap in obesity. The average woman has a higher percentage of body fat than the average man, meaning that when a man and woman have the same weight, the metabolism of the woman tends to be slower.

There is also a racial gap in weight. African Americans are more likely than non-Hispanic white Americans to be obese. In fact, some 60% of African-American women aged 45 to 75 are considered obese (Van Italie, 1985). The incidence of obesity also increases with age, particularly in women (Williamson et al., 1990).

Perceptions of ideal weight are also culturally related. In the mainstream American culture, slenderness has become idealized in recent years and dieting has become a way of life for many, especially women. However, in some cultural groups, such as among some Haitian (Laguerre, 1981) and Puerto Rican groups (Harwood, 1981), the fuller body form is connected with happiness and good health.

Obesity is also related to socioeconomic status (SES) in our society. Obesity is more prevalent among people who are lower in socioeconomic status (SES) (Ernst & Harlan, 1991). Dietary customs may play a part in explaining the connections between race and SES and obesity. For example, African Americans are more likely than non-Hispanic white Americans to be low in SES, and more likely to consume a diet heavy in high-fat, high-cholesterol foods that are linked to coronary heart disease and cancer

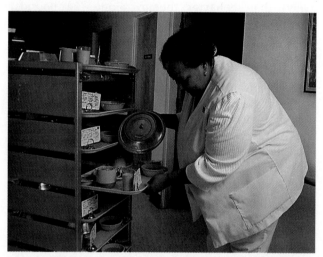

The racial gap in weight. More than half of middle-aged and elderly African-American women are obese. Obesity is connected with a complex web of cultural factors, socioeconomic status, and dietary customs that may place African-American women at distinct risk.

as well as obesity. Many African Americans of lower socioeconomic status who reside in inner-city neighborhoods may also turn to food as a way of coping with the combined stresses of poverty, discrimination, crowding, and crime (Freeman, 1991).

---

efficacy expectancies—influence our adherence to weight-loss regimens, cognitive factors play a part in behavioral programs.

Very Low-Calorie Diet (VLCD) Programs Very low-calorie diet (VLCD) programs replace regular foods with a liquid protein mixture that provides 300 to 600 calories per day. The diet is based on dairy protein and is nutritionally balanced with respect to amino acids and nutrients. (Liquid protein formulas sold over the counter in the 1970s were often nutritionally inadequate, resulting in a number of deaths [Backburn et al., 1986].) VLCD programs are associated with rapid weight losses that average about 45 pounds over a 12-week period and appear to be safe when properly medically supervised (Brownell & Wadden, 1992). Today, liquid protein diets are dispensed only by a physician, and the patient's health is closely monitored.

Although liquid protein diets lead to initial rapid, large weight losses, many dieters do not maintain their weight losses once they resume eating regular food. One study of 517 people at 18 hospitals across the country (Wadden et al., 1992) showed that the long-term results of a liquid diet program, Optifast, were no better than those of a moderate low-calorie program featuring regular foods and a focus on behavior change (Brody, 1992d). Only 1 in 5 participants who completed the program kept off all the weight they had lost for at least a year. Moreover, 45% of subjects who started the program dropped out before completion.

Appetite-Suppressing Drugs The effects of appetite suppressant medication for treating obesity are at best modest and temporary (Craighead & Agras, 1991). Although appetite suppressants may suppress hunger cues, they do not prepare dieters to handle cues of hunger once medication is terminated, leading to rebound weight gains.

In one study, the use of an appetite suppressant (fenfluramine hydrochloride), taken alone or in combination with behavior therapy that focused on changing maladaptive eating habits, initially led to more rapid weight losses (32 and 34 pounds, respectively) than behavior therapy alone (24 pounds) (Craighead et al., 1981). At a 1-year follow-up, however, subjects treated with the drug alone had regained 18 pounds, and those treated with both the drug and behavior therapy had regained 24 pounds. In sharp contrast, subjects treated with behavior therapy alone had regained an average of only 4 pounds. Helping subjects change their eating habits apparently had more enduring effects than handing out diet pills. People who use appetite suppressants may attribute their successes to the drug rather than to their own efforts, so they bounce back upward in weight once they discontinue the drug (Craighead, 1984).

Behavioral Approaches Successful behavioral approaches to weight loss involve changes in lifestyle that include enhancing nutritional knowledge, lessening calorie intake, increasing exercise, and changing eating habits through behavior modification (Brownell & Wadden, 1992).

Dieters need nutritional knowledge to ensure they do not deprive themselves of basic food elements. Ingesting fewer calories does not only mean taking smaller portions. It also means switching to lower-calorie nutritious foods, such as fresh fruits and vegetables (apples, not apple pie); lean meats; poultry and fish; and skim milk and cheeses. Eliminating or cutting down on butter and polysaturated oils is good for the heart and also helps take off pounds. Generally speaking, the same foods that help control weight are also high in vitamins and fiber and low in cholesterol and saturated fats. They may thus lower the risk of CHD, cancer, and other diseases as well as the numbers on the scale.

Exercise fosters weight loss (Brownell & Wadden, 1992; Dubbert, 1992; Foreyt & Goodrick, 1991). In one classic study, obese women who walked 30 minutes or longer a day lost about 20 pounds in one year, whereas women who walked less than 30 minutes failed to show significant weight loss (Gwinup, 1975). Unfortunately, many obese people who start an exercise program drop out within a few months. People are more likely to adhere to exercise programs when they are convenient, not overly stressful, and conducted in a group setting—which provides social support (Stern & Lowney, 1986).

Dieting combined with exercise is more effective than dieting alone (Brownell & Wadden, 1992; Dub-

bert, 1992; Foreyt & Goodrick, 1991). When people restrict calories, their metabolic rates compensate by decreasing. Exercise burns calories in itself and increases the metabolic rate by replacing some fatty tissue with muscle.

Behavior modification tends to focus on the "ABCs" of eating. The A's are the *antecedents* of eating—cues or stimuli that may "trigger" eating. These include environmental stimuli such as the sight and aromas of food, and internal stimuli such as sensations of hunger, or emotional states like anxiety, fatigue, anger, depression, and boredom. Controlling the A's of eating involves redesigning the environment so that people are not continuously bombarded by food-related cues.

The B's of eating refer to eating *behaviors* themselves. People who eat too quickly prevent their brains from "catching up" to their stomachs because it takes about 15 minutes or so for feelings of satiety to register in the brain after food reaches the stomach. The B's of eating extend to preparatory behaviors such as shopping, food storage habits, and so on.

The C's of eating are the *consequences*. The immediate pleasure of overeating often overshadows the long-term negative consequences of obesity and risk to health. Food is also connected to other reward systems. Food can become a substitute friend or lover. When people feel depressed, they can lift their spirits with food, if only temporarily. Because food activates the parasympathetic branch of the autonomic nervous system (through digestive processes), food also acts as a natural sedative or tranquilizer, quelling feelings of anxiety or tension and helping people relax or get to sleep. In helping people cope with the C's of eating, psychologists make the long-term benefits of sensible eating more immediate. Methods commonly used to address the ABCs of eating are shown in Table 4.5.

A recent review of behavioral studies found that the average participant loses about 1⅓ pounds a week, or nearly 21 pounds on the average through the course of a 16-week program or nearly 27 pounds in a 20-week program (Brownell & Wadden, 1992). About 60 to 70% of the weight loss, on the average, is maintained for at least a year following the treatment program. Generally speaking, the longer the treatment and the greater number of therapy hours, the greater the weight loss. Regular exercise and adhering to a rigorous diet are also connected with greater weight losses (Bennett, 1986).

Cancer

The various forms of cancer are caused by the development of aberrant, or mutant, cells that breed briskly and plunder the body of nutrients. Cancerous

Table 4.5 Behavioral Techniques of Modifying the ABCs of Eating to Foster Weight Loss

Changing the A's of Overeating

Changing the Environmental A's	Avoid settings that trigger overeating. (Eat at The Celery Stalk, not The Chocolate Gourmet.) Don't leave tempting treats around the house. Serve food on smaller plates. Use a lunch plate rather than a dinner plate. Don't leave seconds on the table. Serve preplanned portions. Do not leave open casseroles on the table. Immediately freeze leftovers. Don't keep them warm on the stove. Avoid the kitchen as much as possible. Disconnect eating from other stimuli, such as watching television, talking on the telephone, or reading. Establish food-free zones in your home. Imagine there is a barrier at the entrance to your bedroom that prevents the passage of food.
Controlling the Internal A's	Don't bury disturbing feelings in a box of cookies or a carton of mocha delight ice cream. Relabel feelings of hunger as signals that you're burning calories. Say to yourself, "It's okay to feel hungry. It doesn't mean I'm going to die or pass out. Each minute I delay eating, more calories are burned."

Changing the B's of Overeating

Slow Down the Pace of Eating	Put down utensils between bites. Take smaller bites. Chew thoroughly. Savor each bite. Don't wolf bites down to make room for the next. Take a break during the meal. Put down your utensils and converse with your family or guests for a few minutes. (Give your rising blood sugar level a chance to signal your brain.) When you resume eating, ask yourself whether you need to finish every bite. Leave something over to be thrown away or enjoyed later.
Modify Shopping Behavior	Shop from a list. Don't browse through the supermarket. Shop quickly. Don't make shopping the high point of your day. Treat the supermarket like enemy territory. Avoid the aisles containing junk food and snacks. If you must walk down these aisles, put on mental blinders and look straight ahead. Never shop when hungry. Shop after meals, not before.
Practice Competing Responses	Substitute nonfood activities for food-related activities. When tempted to overeat, leave the house, take a bath, walk the dog, call a friend, or walk around the block. Substitute low-calorie foods for high-calorie foods. Keep lettuce, celery, or carrots in the middle of the refrigerator so that they are available when you want a snack. Fill spare time with nonfood-related activities: volunteer at the local hospital, play golf or tennis, join exercise groups, read in the library (rather than the kitchen), take long walks.
Chain Breaking	Stretch the overeating chain. Before allowing yourself to snack, wait 10 minutes. Next time wait 15 minutes, etc. Break the eating chain at its weakest link. It's easier to interrupt the eating chain by taking a route home that bypasses the bakery than to exercise self-control when you're placing your order.

Changing the C's of Overeating

Reward Yourself For Meeting Calorie/Diet Goals	One pound of body weight is equivalent to 3,500 calories. To lose 1 pound per week, you need to cut 3,500 calories per week, or 500 calories per day, from your typical calorie intake level, assuming your weight has been stable. Reward yourself for meeting weekly calorie goals. Reward yourself with gifts that you would not otherwise purchase for yourself, such as a special gift for yourself, like a cashmere sweater or tickets to a show. Repeat the reward program from week to week. If during some weeks you miss your calorie goals, don't lose heart. Get back on track next week.
Use Self-Punishment	Charge yourself for deviating from your diet. Send one dollar to a political candidate you despise, or to a hated cause, each time the chocolate cake wins.

cells can take root anywhere—the blood, the bones, lungs, digestive tract, and genital organs. When they are not contained early, cancer may metastasize, or establish colonies throughout the body, leading to death.

■ **RISK FACTORS**   As with cardiovascular and many other disorders, people appear to inherit dispositions toward developing cancer (Eysenck, 1991; USDHHS, 1991). The risk of cancer also increases with age.

In the case of cancer, sociocultural and ethnic groups within the United States show great diversity in risk and survival rates (USDHHS, 1991). African-American men have greater risks of contracting lung cancer and prostate cancer than men from other U.S. ethnic groups. Japanese Americans and white Americans have relatively high rates of colorectal cancer, apparently connected with their dietary practices. White women have relatively higher incidences of breast cancer than women from other ethnic groups. Non-Hispanic white Americans and Asian Americans have higher 5-year survival rates for cancers of the lung, colon, rectum, and prostate gland than African Americans, Native Americans, and Mexican Americans, apparently because of earlier detection and treatment. For example, although the incidences of cancers of the colon and rectum are about 25% lower among Mexican-American men than among non-Hispanic white men, non-Hispanic white men who contract these cancers are more likely to survive (USDHHS, 1991).

Many behavior patterns clearly heighten the risk for cancer, such as dietary practices, alcohol, smoking, and sunbathing (ultraviolet light causes skin cancer). Food preservatives, high levels of fat intake (Willett et al., 1990), and vitamin deficiencies pose particular risks. On the other hand, regular intake of vitamins, calcium, fruits and vegetables, and nonfatty fish (Kromhaut et al., 1985) may reduce the risk of some forms of cancer. Death rates from cancer are lower in Japan than in the United States, where people ingest more fat, especially animal fats (Cohen, 1987). The difference is not genetic or racial, however, because Japanese Americans whose fat intake approximates that of other Americans show similar death rates from cancer. Cigarette smoking is implicated in 87% of the deaths from lung cancer (USDHHS, 1991).

Health psychologists are investigating whether personality factors and stress pose risks for cancer.

■ **PERSONALITY, STRESS, AND CANCER**
Researchers have found links between psychosocial factors such as feelings of helplessness and hopeless-

ness, depression, loss of social support, and stress and the development or course of cancer.

Evidence has implicated the immune system as playing a role in susceptibility to cancer. For example, researchers find that people whose immune systems are weakened are more likely to develop tumors (Antoni, 1987; Greenberg, 1987). The immune system may fail for many reasons. One is advanced age. External irritants like cigarette smoke compromise the immune system. The immune system is also affected by stress, and studies reveal relationships between various stressors and the development of cancer. Le Shan (1966), for example, found that 72% of 400 cancer patients had experienced the loss of a significant person within 8 years preceding the diagnosis of cancer, as compared to 10% of a reference group. A study of children with cancer by Jacob and Charles (1980) disclosed that a significant percentage had encountered severe life changes within a year of the diagnosis. As in the Le Shan study, these changes often involved the death of a loved one or the loss of a close relationship.

Such studies are weakened by the fact that they are retrospective (Krantz et al., 1985). Patients are studied *after* cancer has been diagnosed, that is. Only then are events preceding the diagnoses explored. Self-reports of personal histories may be confounded by memory problems and other sources of error. Causal connections in such research are also clouded. For example, development of the cancer may precipitate stressful events rather than result from them.

As in other areas of psychology, experimental research has been conducted with lower animals that could not be carried out with people. In one type of study, animals are injected with cancerous cells or carcinogenic viruses and then exposed to various conditions, enabling us to determine whether or not these conditions affect the probability that the animals' immune systems will be able to repulse the invading antigens. Experiments like these with rats suggest that stress can influence the course of cancer. In one study, small numbers of cancer cells were implanted in rats so that the animals' immune systems would have a chance of successfully fending them off (Visintainer et al., 1982). Some rats were then exposed to inescapable shocks. Others were exposed to escapable shocks or to no shock. The rats in the most stressful condition—the inescapable shock—were only half as likely as rats in the other conditions to repel the cancer, and two times as apt to die from it.

In a similar study with mice, Riley (1981) analyzed the effects of a carcinogenic virus that can be transmitted from mothers to offspring via nursing. This virus normally produces breast cancer in 80% of the female progeny by 400 days of age. Riley set one group of at-risk female offspring in a stressful environment with blaring noises and repulsive odors. Another group was placed in a more congenial environment. At 400 days of age, 92% of the stressed mice developed breast cancer, as compared with 7% of the controls. The high-stress mice also showed higher levels of stress hormones (corticosteroids), which suppress immune system functioning and lower blood levels of antibodies. After another 200 days went by, the "low-stress" mice nearly caught up to their "high-stress" counterparts in incidence of cancer, however. Stress seems to have accelerated the inevitable for most mice, but the eventual outcomes for at-risk mice were not strongly affected by stress.

Perhaps stress affects the timing of the onset of some disorders, like cancer, but genetic predispositions toward disease and powerful antigens eventually do their damage. We await further research before we draw firm conclusions about the relationship between stress and cancer.

Stress does appear to affect the course of cancer. It has not been shown, however, that stress affects the eventual outcome.

■ PSYCHOLOGICAL FACTORS IN TREATMENT AND RECOVERY

Cancer is a physical disorder that is treated medically through means such as surgery, radiation, and chemotherapy. Health psychologists have also found key roles for psychological factors and interventions, however (Andersen, 1992).

Feelings of hopelessness and helplessness that often attend the diagnosis of cancer can apparently hinder recovery (Andersen, 1992), perhaps by depressing the patient's immune system. Evidence also shows that cancer patients who maintain a "fighting spirit" experience better outcomes than those who resign themselves to their illness (O'Leary, 1990). For example, a 10-year follow-up of breast cancer patients found that patients who met their diagnosis with anger and a fighting spirit rather than stoic acceptance showed significantly higher survival rates (Pettingale et al., 1985). The will to fight the illness may help to increase survival.

Social support may also be of help. Women with metastatic breast cancer who participated in one group support program survived a year and half longer on the average than women assigned to a no-treatment control group (Spiegel et al., 1989). How psychological approaches affect the course of cancer is unclear, however. One possible mode of action is enhancement of the functioning of the immune system (Andersen, 1992).

Psychologists are also investigating the value of training cancer patients to use coping skills (e.g., relaxation, stress management, restructuring of maladaptive cognitions, problem solving, assertive communication, and pleasant activities) to relieve the stress and pain of coping with cancer (Keefe et al., 1992). In one study, such training was found superior to supportive group therapy and to a no-treatment control condition in reducing distress, helping patients meet the demands of daily life, and restoring feelings of control (Telch & Telch, 1986). It remains to be seen whether such an approach prolongs life.

Cognitive and cognitive-behavioral interventions help cancer patients who receive chemotherapy, which has side effects such as inducing nausea and vomiting. One cognitive program, which provided information about chemotherapy and a tour of chemotherapy facilities, was effective in reducing the distress associated with chemotherapy, either by itself or combined with relaxation training (Burish et al., 1991). Cognitive-behavioral interventions also help chemotherapy patients cope with aversive side effects through relaxation, guided imagery, and distraction strategies (Burish et al., 1987; Keefe et al., 1992). In one study, chemotherapy patients who received relaxation training and guided imagery techniques showed significantly less nausea and vomiting than untreated patients (Burish et al., 1987). Their blood pressures and pulse rates were lower and their moods were less negative than those of control subjects. Investigators also find that distraction through playing video games lessens the discomfort of chemotherapy in children (Kolko & Rickard-Figueroa, 1985; Redd et al., 1987). The children concentrate on vying with computer-generated opponents, and not on the upsetting effects of chemotherapy.

Acquired Immunodeficiency Syndrome (AIDS)

*L**ily was not supposed to get AIDS. She was an heiress to a cosmetics fortune. She had received her bachelor's degree from Wellesley and had been enrolled in a graduate program in art history when she came down with intractable flu-like symptoms and was eventually diagnosed as having AIDS.*

"No one believed it," she said. "I was never a gay male in San Francisco. I never shot up crack in the alleys of The Bronx. My boyfriends didn't shoot up either. There was just Matthew . . ." Now Lily was 24. At 17, in her senior year in high school, she had had a brief affair with Matthew. Later she learned that Matthew was bisexual. Five years ago, Matthew died from AIDS.

"I haven't exactly been a whore," Lily said ironically. "You can count my boyfriends on the fingers of one hand. None of them caught it from me; I guess I was just lucky." Her face twisted in anger. "You may think this is awful," she said, "but there are times when I wish Jerry and Russ had gotten it from me. Why should they get off?"

Lily's family was fully supportive, emotionally and, of course, financially. Lily had been to fine clinics. Physicians from Europe had been brought in. She was on a regimen of three medicines: two antiviral drugs, which singly and in combination had shown some ability to slow the progress of AIDS, and an antibiotic intended to prevent bacterial infections from taking hold. She took some vitamins—not megavitamin therapy. She exercised almost daily when she felt up to it, and she was doing reasonably well. In fact, there were times when she thought she might get over her illness.

"Sometimes I find myself thinking about children or grandchildren. Or sometimes I find myself looking at all these old pictures [of grandparents and other relatives] and thinking that I'll have silver in my hair, too. Sometimes I really think this is the day the doctors will call me about the new wonder drug that's been discovered in France or Germany."

"I want to tell you about Russ," she said once. "After we found out about me, he went for testing, and he was clear [of antibodies indicative of infection by the AIDS virus]. He stayed with me, you know. When I wanted to do it, we used condoms. A couple of months later, he went for a second test and he was still clear. Then maybe he had second thoughts, because he became impotent—with me. We'd try, but he couldn't do anything. Still he stayed with me, but I felt us drifting apart. After a while, he was just doing the right thing by staying with me, and I'll be damned if anyone is going to be with me because he's doing the right thing."

Lily looked the [interviewer] directly in the eye. "What sane man wants to play Russian roulette with AIDS for the sake of looking like a caring person? And I'll tell you why I eventually sent him away," she added, tears welling, "the one thing I've learned is that you die alone. I don't even feel that close to my parents anymore. Everyone loves you and wishes they could trade places with you, but they can't. You're suddenly older than everyone around you and you're going to go alone. I can't tell you how many times I thought about killing myself, just so that I could be the one who determines exactly where and when I die—how I would be dressed and how I would feel on the final day."

Lily died in 1992.

■ *The Authors' Files*

Acquired immunodeficiency syndrome—AIDS—is a lethal viral condition that is caused by the **human immunodeficiency virus** (HIV). Psychologists have become involved in the fight against AIDS because behavior is the major determinant of the risk of contracting the deadly virus and because AIDS, like cancer, has devastating psychological effects on the persons affected by the disease, their families and friends, and society at large.

HIV is abundant in blood, semen, and vaginal secretions. Infection by HIV may be determined by examining the blood for the presence of specific HIV antibodies. Unfortunately, these antibodies are unable to eradicate the infection.

HIV is most likely to be transmitted by sexual contact (vaginal and anal intercourse; oral-genital contact); direct infusion of contaminated blood, as in transfusions of contaminated blood or sharing hypodermic needles when a group shoots up a drug; and from an infected mother to a child during pregnancy or childbirth or through breast-feeding (USDHHS, 1991). You cannot get HIV from donating blood, as syringes are used only once. Blood supplies have been routinely screened for HIV since 1985, greatly reducing, though not eliminating entirely, the risks of infection from blood transfusions. (Tennis great Arthur Ashe, who died of complications from AIDS in 1993, believed he had contracted HIV from a blood transfusion he received during an operation performed before routine blood screening for the virus went into effect.) Estimates are that the chances today of contracting the virus from a single transfusion are about 1 in 75,000 (Altman, 1992).

AIDS is not contracted by airborne germs or by casual contact, such as using public toilets, holding or hugging infected people, sharing eating utensils with them, or living or going to school with them.

By late 1992, more than 250,000 Americans had been diagnosed with AIDS and more than 150,000 had died of complications from the disease since the epidemic began (Centers for Disease Control, 1992). By 1990, one death from AIDS-related illnesses was occurring every 12 minutes in the United States (Kramer, 1990). By the beginning of the 1990s it was estimated that 1 million Americans and 10 million people around the world were infected with HIV. The World Health Organization (WHO) estimates that by the year 2000, 40 million people worldwide will be infected with HIV, and 10 million people will develop AIDS (Altman, 1991). A Harvard University research group offered even more dire predictions in estimating that as many as 110 million people worldwide will be infected with HIV by 2000 (Mann et al., 1992).

Magic Johnson.   Magic Johnson's public announcement that he was infected with HIV (left photo) brought home the fact that healthy heterosexual people are vulnerable to HIV infection and AIDS. Johnson went on to star at the 1992 Olympic Games in Barcelona (right photo), but he retired from basketball a few months afterward. Research suggests that an average of 10½ years may pass between becoming infected with HIV and developing a full-blown case of AIDS.

Heterosexual transmission accounts for 75% of cases of HIV infection worldwide (Novello, 1991). Although many Americans such as Magic Johnson, who reported in 1991 that he was infected with HIV, reportedly contracted the virus through heterosexual sex, sex between men and needle sharing among substance abusers continue to account for most cases in the United States—56% and 24% of cases, respectively (Centers for Disease Control, 1990). Heterosexual transmission accounted for slightly less than 6% of cases by the early 1990s (Kolata, 1991a) and was largely concentrated among the population of injecting drug users (IDUs) and their sex partners. Yet HIV infection and AIDS cut across all boundaries of race, ethnicity, income level, gender, sexual orientation, and drug use classification.

Transmission patterns vary across racial and ethnic groups. Sex between gay men accounts for 70 to 80% of cases of AIDS among non-Hispanic white American men and Asian-American men (USDHHS, 1991), and 40 to 60% of cases among Hispanic-, Native-, and African-American men. Anal intercourse is a key factor in transmission of HIV among gay men. The proportion of new cases among gay men has been decreasing, however, due in large part to the adoption of safer sex practices, including increased use of latex condoms (Centers for Disease Control, 1990).

People who inject (shoot up) drugs account for less than 10% of cases of AIDS among non-Hispanic white men and Asian-American men, but for 30 to 40% of cases among Hispanic-American and African-

American men (USDHHS, 1991). Shooting up drugs is the single largest contributor to cases of AIDS among Hispanic-, African-, and non-Hispanic white American women (USDHHS, 1991). Shooting up drugs is also the greatest contributor to the spread of AIDS among heterosexuals in the United States. The spread of AIDS in the United States is therefore intertwined with the poverty and other sociocultural problems of the inner cities, which are beset with drug addiction and the attendant problem of prostitution. Kelly and Murphy (1992) argue that prevention strategies need to especially target gay men and people who shoot up drugs, particularly among poor, urban minority populations.

■ **AIDS AND THE IMMUNE SYSTEM** HIV invades and destroys a particular type of white blood cell, the T_4 lymphocyte. The T_4 cell has been called the "quarterback" of the immune system (Shilts, 1988). T_4 cells recognize invading pathogens and direct other white blood cells to manufacture antibodies and others to destroy infected cells. The depletion of T_4 cells renders the body vulnerable to so-called opportunistic diseases—diseases that stand little chance of taking hold in people with intact immune systems. Opportunistic diseases include some forms of cancer, such as Kaposi's sarcoma, a cancer of the blood cells that produces purplish spots on the body, and a rare type of pneumonia, *Pneumocystis carinii pneumonia* (PCP). HIV may also attack the central nervous system, leading to a form of mental deterioration or dementia (see Chapter 12).

The average length of time between HIV infection and the development of full-blown AIDS is 10.5 years (Kolata, 1991b). Shortly following HIV infection, the person may experience passing flu-like symptoms. During the first few years of HIV infection the person may look and feel well, or may develop symptoms that do not yet merit a diagnosis of AIDS. People infected with HIV are capable of passing along the virus to others, even if they have no symptoms themselves and are unaware of being infected. The development of AIDS is denoted by the appearance of opportunistic diseases and by such symptoms as night sweats, diarrhea, unexplained weight loss, excessive fatigue, and swollen glands.

Although there is no cure or vaccine for HIV infection or AIDS, antiviral drugs, such as zidovudine (AZT), have shown promise in slowing the progress of AIDS (Graham et al., 1992; McKinney et al., 1991; Moore et al., 1991).

■ **ADJUSTMENT OF PEOPLE WITH HIV AND AIDS** Given the nature of AIDS and the stigma suffered by people with HIV and AIDS, many HIV/AIDS patients have feelings of anxiety, depression (Hays et al., 1992), and guilt, even though these emotional states may not be severe enough to constitute a clinical diagnosis of an anxiety or depressive disorder (Williams et al., 1991). They also frequently incur problems such as poor self-esteem, suicidal thoughts, and anger. Anger is often directed toward medical caregivers (there is no cure and no vaccine) and social discrimination. Although it has been speculated that distress may weaken the immune system and spur the development of AIDS among people infected with HIV, researchers (Kessler et al., 1991; Rabkin et al., 1991) to date have not been able to demonstrate relationships between stressful life events and immune system functioning or symptomatology of HIV infection among samples of infected gay men. On the other hand, psychological and behavioral interventions that seek to boost the immune system, such as stress-management programs, are being tested with people infected with HIV to determine whether they can prolong life (Antoni et al., 1990, 1991; LaPerriere et al., 1990, 1991).

■ **PSYCHOLOGICAL INTERVENTIONS** Psychologists have been involved in developing behavior change programs that focus on reducing risky sexual and injection practices. In one study, Kelly and his colleagues (1988) assigned 104 seemingly healthy, sexually active gay men who engaged in high-risk activities with multiple partners to one of two groups—an experimental group that received 12 group counseling sessions or a control group. The counseling program provided information about high-risk behavior. It suggested steps for averting risky behavior, such as avoiding excessive use of drugs and casual sex. Social skills training imparted skills that clients could use to refuse high-risk sex and to develop low-risk stable relationships. The program decreased the experimental group's incidence of unprotected sex and increased their adoption of safer sex practices and knowledge about risky behaviors. A 16-month follow-up evaluation showed that the majority of counseling subjects who could be followed up reported no resumption of high-risk sexual behaviors, such as unprotected anal intercourse (Kelly et al., 1991).

Reducing the risk of AIDS depends not only on providing people with information about the risk of transmission but also on increasing their motivation to reduce the risks they face and helping them acquire behavioral skills for practicing AIDS-preventive behavior, such as the ability to communicate with their sexual partners and act assertively in practicing safer sex behaviors (Fisher & Fisher, 1992). Safer sex practices in both gay males and heterosexual college students are also linked to the avoidance of drinking and drug use before sex.

Research also shows that psychological interventions can help improve the quality of life of people with HIV and AIDS. Support groups, self-help groups, and organized therapy groups provide help for AIDS patients, their families, and friends. Relaxation training, positive mental imagery, and other stress management techniques help individuals develop better ways of handling stress. Intrusive thoughts and preoccupations that interfere with everyday functioning may be controlled through cognitive therapy. The acquisition of coping skills can help heighten the sense of control over one's own life. Reducing alcohol and illicit drugs and following a proper diet and sensible exercise program may all help the immune system ward off opportunistic infections. A study in which AIDS patients used stress management techniques, developed good health habits, and built new social support systems led to reductions in anxiety, depression, and high-risk sexual behavior, and to improved immunological functioning (McKusick et al., 1987).

The advent of AIDS presents the mental health community an unparalleled challenge to help prevent the spread of AIDS and to treat people who have been infected with HIV and who have developed AIDS. As frightening as AIDS may be, it is preventable, as noted in the feature "Preventing AIDS."

A CLOSER LOOK

Preventing AIDS

 For the first time, a generation of college students is coming of age at a time when the threat of AIDS hangs over every sexual encounter. People may decrease the risk of being infected by HIV and other sexually transmitted diseases (STDs) by taking the following measures. Only the first two are sure paths to avoiding the sexual transmission of HIV. The others reduce the risk of infection, but cannot be certified as perfectly safe. If we are going to be sexually active without knowing (not guessing) whether we or our partners are infected with HIV or some other STD, we can speak only of safe(r) sex—not of perfectly safe sex.

1. Maintaining lifelong celibacy.
2. Remaining in a lifelong monogamous relationship with an uninfected person who is doing the same thing. Although these first two sexual careers paths guarantee safety, they are not followed by the majority of students or other Americans.
3. *Being discerning in one's choice of sex partners.* Get to know another person before engaging in sexual activity. Still, getting to know a person is no guarantee the person is uninfected with HIV. Avoid contact with multiple partners, or with people who are likely to have multiple partners.
4. *Being assertive with sex partners.* It is important to communicate concerns about AIDS clearly and assertively with sex partners (Fisher & Fisher, 1992).
5. *Inspecting one's partner's sex organs.* There are usually no local telltale signs of HIV infection, but people who are infected with HIV are often infected by other sexually transmitted diseases as well. It may be feasi-

ble to visually inspect your partner's sex organs for rashes, chancres, blisters, discharges, warts, and lice during foreplay. Consider any disagreeable odor a warning sign.

6. *Using latex condoms.* Condoms protect men from infected vaginal fluids and stop semen from entering women. All condoms act as barriers to sperm, but only latex condoms can prevent transmission of HIV.
7. *Using spermicides.* Spermicides (chemicals that kill sperm) are used as a means of birth control. Spermicides containing the ingredient nonoxynol-9 also kill HIV. Spermicides are no substitute for use of latex condoms, however, in preventing transmission of HIV and other microbes. It is still more effective to combine condoms with spermicides.
8. *Consulting a physician following suspected exposure to a sexually transmitted disease.* Antibiotics following unprotected sex may guard against bacterial infections, but they are of no avail against viral diseases such as genital herpes and AIDS. Also, routine use of antibiotics renders them less effective when you need them.
9. *Seeking regular medical checkups.* Checkups and appropriate laboratory tests enable you to learn about and treat disorders that might have gone unnoticed. Early diagnosis of HIV infection may prolong life through a combination of antiviral drugs and drugs that combat the opportunistic infections which afflict people with weakened immune systems. Even so, these drugs do not eradicate HIV infection or cure AIDS.
10. *Avoiding sexual activity if there are doubts about safety.* None of the safer sex practices listed guarantees protection. Why not avoid sexual activity when doubts of safety exist?

In this chapter we have focused on relationships between stress and mental and physical health, and on the psychological factors involved in physical health and illness. Psychology has much to offer to the understanding and treatment of physical illness. Psychological approaches may help in the treatment of such physical disorders as headaches, hyperten-

sion, and coronary heart disease. Psychologists also help people reduce the risks of contracting health problems such as cardiovascular disorders, cancer, and AIDS. Emerging fields like psychoneuroimmunology promise to further enhance our knowledge of the intricate relationships between mind and body.

Summary

Adjustment Disorders

Adjustment disorders are maladaptive reactions to identified stressors. Impairment usually takes the form of problems at work or in social relationships or activities, or by signs of personal distress that are greater than expected given the circumstances.

A Multifactorial View of Health and Illness

Many factors interact to determine physical health and illness. Health is not a matter of luck.

Biological variables such as family history of an illness, exposure to pathogens, the ability of the immune system to fight them off, and inoculations are common causes or deterrents of physical illnesses. The immune system combats disease by producing white blood cells that systematically envelop and kill pathogens, worn-out body cells, and cancerous cells.

Psychological factors that affect our health include our personalities and our behavior patterns. Many personality features, such as self-efficacy expectancies, psychological hardiness, optimism, and a sense of humor, are believed to have positive effects on our health. The stress imposed by social, biological, and physical environmental factors reflects people's psychological appraisal of these factors. Persistent stress eventually exhausts our capacities to cope by compromising our immune systems.

Social factors that affect our health include economic realities, cultural issues, and ethnic variables. Health problems have differential impacts on diverse cultural and ethnic groups. In some cases, genetic factors may interact with cultural and ethnic factors. In others, poverty, prejudice and discrimination, education, and the accessibility of health care play predominant roles. Social support helps buffer the impact of stress.

Natural and technological disasters are dangerous as they occur and also create lingering problems. Technological advances create methods for correcting many health problems.

Psychological Factors and Physical Disorders

Psychological factors are involved in the origins, course, and treatment of many physical health problems. The principle of individual response specificity holds that people respond to stress in idiosyncratic ways, giving rise to particular health problems.

The most common headache is the muscle-tension headache, which is often stress related. Behavioral methods of relaxation training and biofeedback are of help in treating headaches.

Risk factors in cardiovascular disorders include age, gender, family history, socioeconomic status, obesity, hypertension, serum cholesterol, patterns of consumption, Type A behavior, anger, stress, and a sedentary lifestyle. Health psychologists help people vary the risk factors that are modifiable.

There are clear connections between stress, emotional response, and some gastrointestinal problems, such as diarrhea and ulcers.

Asthma attacks can be tripped by allergic reactions; cold, dry air; emotional responses such as anger; and stress. Treatment for asthma often consists of medications, including bronchodilators, but asthma sufferers can improve their breathing by muscle relaxation training and family therapy that reduces the stresses on asthmatic children.

Psychological factors such as anxiety, depression, and low self-efficacy expectancies contribute to obesity or impair dieting efforts. Heredity is implicated in obesity, but so are dietary habits. Successful weight-control programs foster enduring changes in dietary behavior patterns and physical activity.

Risk factors for cancer include family history, dietary practices (especially high fat intake and vitamin deficiencies), alcohol, smoking, sunbathing, and lingering depression, which can compromise the immune system. Research shows that a fighting spirit may help people recover from cancer. Cognitive-behavioral interventions help cancer patients who receive chemotherapy tolerate side effects such as nausea.

Our behavior patterns influence our risk for contracting AIDS. AIDS is caused by HIV, which is abundant in blood, semen, and vaginal secretions. Psychologists have become involved in the prevention and treatment of AIDS because AIDS, like cancer, has devastating psychological effects on victims, their families and friends, and society at large, and because AIDS can be prevented through behavior modification.

Scoring Key for "The Life Orientation Test"

In order to arrive at your total score for the test, first *reverse* your score on items 3, 8, 9, and 12. That is,

- 4 is changed to 0
- 3 is changed to 1
- 2 remains the same
- 1 is changed to 3
- 0 is changed to 4

Now add the numbers of items 1, 3, 4, 5, 8, 9, 11, and 12. (Items 2, 6, 7, and 10 are "fillers"; that is, your responses are not scored as part of the test.) Your total score can vary from 0 to 32.

Scheier and Carver (1985) provide the following norms for the test, based on administration to 357 undergraduate men and 267 undergraduate women. The average (mean) score for men was 21.03 (standard deviation = 4.56), and the mean score for women was 21.41 (standard deviation = 5.22). All in all, approximately 2 out of 3 undergraduates obtained scores between 16 and 26. Scores above 26 may be considered quite optimistic, and scores below 16, quite pessimistic. Scores between 16 and 26 are within a broad average range, and higher scores within this range are relatively more optimistic.

Answer Key for "Are You Type A or Type B?"

Yesses are suggestive of the Type A behavior pattern (TABP). In appraising whether or not you show the TABP, you need not be concerned with the precise number of "yes" answers. We have no normative data for you. As Freidman and Rosenman (1974, p. 85) note, however, you should have little trouble spotting yourself as "hard core" or "moderately afflicted"—that is, if you are honest with yourself.

Tom Nakashima, Cage, 1990. Oil and guilding on canvas: 96 × 115 inches. Courtesy of the artist.

Chapter Outline

5

Anxiety Disorders

TRUTH **or** FICTION?

___ Some people are suddenly overtaken by feelings of panic, even though there is no external threat.

___ Some people live in dread of receiving injections even though the potential pain doesn't bother them a bit.

___ Some people feel compelled to check and recheck that they have locked the doors and windows, so much so that they are delayed in leaving the house for an hour or more.

___ Victims of post-traumatic stress disorder may develop problems years after their disturbing experiences.

___ Misinterpretations of feelings of anxiety can trigger panic attacks.

___ Relaxing in a recliner and fantasizing can be an effective way of reducing fears.

___ You may be able to deter a panic attack by breathing into a paper bag.

*A*nxiety is a generalized state of apprehension or foreboding. There is much to be anxious about—our health, social relationships, examinations, careers, international relations, and the condition of the environment are but a few sources of possible concern. It is normal, even adaptive, to be somewhat anxious about these aspects of life. Anxiety serves us when it prompts us to seek regular medical checkups or motivates us to study for tests. Anxiety is an appropriate response to threats, but anxiety can be abnormal when its level is out of proportion to a threat, or when it seems to come out of the blue—that is, when it is not in response to environmental changes. In extreme forms, anxiety can impair our daily functioning. Consider the case of Dick:

*S*lowly the trains snake their way through the maze of tunnels that lie beneath the city, carrying the Dashing Dans and Danielles on their way to work each morning. Most commuters pass the time by reading the morning newspapers, sipping coffee, or catching a few last winks. For Dick, the morning commute became an exercise in terror on an ordinary day in July. At first, Dick noticed the perspiration clinging to his shirt. The air conditioning seemed to be working fine, for a change. How then was he to account for the sweat? As the train entered the tunnel and darkness shrouded the windows, Dick was gripped by terror. He sensed his heart beating faster, the muscles in his neck tightening. Queasiness soured his stomach. He felt as though he might pass out. Other commuters, engrossed in their morning papers or their private thoughts, paid no heed to Dick, nor did they seem concerned about the darkness that enveloped the train.

Dick had known these feelings all too well before. But now the terror was worse. Other days he could bear it. This time, it seemed to start earlier than usual, before the train entered the tunnel. "Just don't think about it," he told himself, hoping it would pass. "I must think of something to distract myself." He tried humming a song, but the panic grew worse. He tried telling himself that it would be all right, that at any moment the train would enter the station and the doors would open. Not this day, however. On this day, the train came to a screeching halt. The conductor announced a "signaling problem." Dick tried to calm himself: "It's only a short delay. We'll be moving soon." But the train did not start moving soon. More apologies were announced by the conductor. A train had broken down further ahead in the tunnel. Dick realized it could be a long delay, hours perhaps. Suddenly he felt the urgent desire to escape. But how? he wondered. There was barely room for a crawlspace outside the train. Then again, could he even break the window and crawl out of the train, if he had to?

He felt as though he were losing control. Wild imaginings flooded his mind. He saw himself bolting down the aisles in a futile attempt to escape, bowling people over, trying vainly to pry open the doors. He was charged with a sense of doom. Something terrible was about to happen to him. "Is this the first sign of a heart attack?" he wondered anxiously. By now, the perspiration had soaked his clothes. His once neat tie hung awry. He felt his breathing become heavy and labored, drawing attention from other passengers. "What do they think of me?" he thought. "Will they help me if I need them?"

The train jerked into motion. He realized he would soon be free. "I'm going to be okay," he told himself, "the feelings will pass. I'm going to be myself again." The train pulled slowly into the station, twenty minutes late. The doors opened and the passengers hurried off. Stepping out himself, Dick adjusted his tie and readied himself to start the day. He felt as though he'd been in combat. Nothing that his boss could fire at him could hold a candle to the 7:30 train.

■ *The Authors' Files*

Dick had suffered a panic attack, one of many he had experienced before seeking treatment. The attacks varied in frequency. Sometimes they occurred daily, sometimes once a week or so. He never knew whether an attack would occur on a particular day. He knew, however, that he couldn't go on living like this. He feared that one day he would suffer a heart attack on the train. He pictured some passengers trying vainly to revive him while others stared at him in the detached distant way that people stare at traffic accidents. He pictured emergency workers rushing to the train, bearing him on a stretcher through the dismal tunnels to an ambulance.

For a while he considered changing jobs, accepting a less remunerative job closer to home—one that would free him from the train. He also considered driving to work, but the roads were too thick with traffic. No choice, he figured; either commute by train or switch jobs. His wife, Jill, was unaware of his panic attacks. She wondered why his shirts were heavily stained with perspiration and why Dick was talking about changing jobs. She worried about making ends meet on a lower income. She had no idea that it was the train ride, and not his job, that Dick was desperate to avoid.

Panic attacks, like that suffered by Dick, are a feature of **panic disorder,** a type of **anxiety disorder.** During a panic attack, one's level of anxiety can rise to terror. A host of anxiety-related physical fea-

tures, cognitions, and behaviors are shown in Table 5.1. Although anxious people do not often experience all of them, it is easy to see why anxiety is distressing.

HISTORIC PERSPECTIVES ON ANXIETY DISORDERS

The anxiety disorders, along with dissociative disorders and somatoform disorders (see Chapter 6), were classified as **neuroses** throughout most of the 19th century. The term *neurosis* derives from roots meaning "an abnormal or diseased condition of the nervous system." It was coined by the Scottish physician William Cullen in the 18th century. As the derivation implies, it was assumed that neurosis had biological origins. It was seen as an affliction of the nervous system.

At the beginning of the 20th century, Cullen's organic assumptions were largely replaced by Sigmund Freud's psychodynamic views. Freud maintained that neurotic behavior stems from the threatened emergence of unacceptable anxiety-evoking ideas into conscious awareness. Various neurotic behavior patterns—anxiety disorders, somatoform disorders, and dissociative disorders—might look different enough on the surface. According to Freud, however, they all represent ways in which the ego attempts to defend itself against anxiety. Freud's **etiological** assumption, in other words, united the disorders as neuroses. Freud's concepts were so widely accepted in the early 1900s that they formed the basis for the classification systems found in the first two editions of the *Diagnostic and Statistical Manual of Mental Disorders* (DSM).

Since 1980, the DSM has not contained a category termed *neuroses*. The present DSM is based on similarities in observable behavior and distinctive features rather than on causal assumptions. Many clinicians continue to use the terms *neurosis* and *neurotic* in the manner in which Freud described them, however. Many clinicians also use "neuroses" as a convenient means of grouping milder behavioral problems in which people maintain relatively good contact with reality. **"Psychoses"** such as schizophrenia are generally more severe than neuroses. *Psychoses* involve loss of touch with reality and are typified by bizarre behavior, beliefs, and hallucinations. Signs of anxiety are not limited to categories traditionally

Table 5.1 Some Features of Anxiety

Physical Features of Anxiety	Cognitive Features of Anxiety
Jumpiness, jitteriness	Worrying about something
Trembling or shaking of the hands or limbs	A nagging sense of dread or apprehension about the future
Sensations of a tight band around the forehead	
Tightness in the pit of the stomach or chest	Belief that something dreadful is going to happen, with no clear cause
Heavy perspiration	Preoccupation with bodily sensations
Sweaty palms	Keen awareness of bodily sensations
Light-headedness or faintness	Feeling threatened by people or events that are normally of little or no concern
Dryness in the mouth or throat	
Difficulty talking	Fear of losing control
Difficulty catching one's breath	Fear of inability to cope with one's problems
Shortness of breath or shallow breathing	Thinking that one's world is caving in
Heart pounding or racing	Thinking that things are getting out of hand
Tremulousness in one's voice	Thinking that things are swimming by too rapidly to take charge of them
Cold fingers or limbs	
Dizziness	Worrying about every little thing
Weakness or numbness	Thinking the same disturbing thought over and over
Difficulty swallowing	Thinking that one must flee crowded places or else pass out
A "lump in the throat"	
Stiffness of the neck or back	Finding one's thoughts jumbled or confused
Choking or smothering sensations	Not being able to shake off nagging thoughts
Cold, clammy hands	Thinking that one is going to die, even when one's doctor finds nothing medically wrong
Upset stomach or nausea	
Hot or cold spells	Worrying that one is going to be left alone
Frequent urination	Difficulty concentrating or focusing one's thoughts
Feeling flushed	The feeling that the world or oneself is unreal
Diarrhea	The sense that one is observing oneself or one's thoughts from outside
Feeling irritable or "on edge"	

Behavioral Features of Anxiety

Avoidance behavior

Clinging, dependent behavior

Agitated behavior

termed "neuroses," moreover. People with adjustment problems, depression, and psychotic disorders can exhibit anxiety.

In this chapter we review various anxiety disorders: panic, phobias, generalized anxiety, obsessive-compulsive disorder, and post-traumatic stress disor- der. The anxiety disorders are not mutually exclusive. People frequently meet diagnostic criteria for more than one of them (Turner & Beidel, 1989). A social phobic may also be agoraphobic; a person with a specific phobia may also show evidence of obsessive-compulsive disorder.

MULTICULTURAL PERSPECTIVES

Anxiety Disorders in Ethnic Minorities

Despite extensive research on the anxiety disorders in the past 20 years, little attention has been paid to anxiety disorders among ethnic minorities (Friedman, Hatch, & Paradis, 1992; Neal & Turner, 1991). The Epidemiologic Catchment Area (ECA) study of five different locales in the United States did find anxiety disorders overall to be more prevalent among African Americans than among other groups (Robins et al., 1984). Yet African Americans and Hispanic Americans were less likely than non-Hispanic white Americans to develop panic disorder in their lifetimes. They were more likely to have or to have had phobic disorders (Eaton et al., 1991). The samples of African Americans contained overrepresentations of poor, elderly, and female respondents, however (Neal & Turner, 1991). They may therefore be more reflective of the variables of socioeconomic status, age, and gender than of race or ethnicity per se.

More research is needed that focuses on problems of anxiety within the African-American community. On the one hand, the stressors faced by African Americans, such as racism, economic hardship, and violence might be expected to contribute to maladaptive anxiety (Neal & Turner, 1991). On the other, it is possible that African Americans, by dint of having to cope with hardships early in life, may develop a resiliency in the face of stress that shields them from anxiety disorders.

Panic. This man was walking to his car when he was suddenly overcome by a panic attack. He thought he might be having a heart attack because his heart was pounding and he felt dizzy and short of breath. Panic attacks have stronger physical components—especially cardiovascular symptoms—than other types of anxiety reactions. They are apparently qualitatively different from other forms of anxiety, and not just more intense. According to the ECA study, African Americans and Hispanic Americans are less likely than non-Hispanic white Americans to develop panic disorder.

PANIC DISORDER

The essential feature of a **panic disorder,** according to the DSM, is recurrent panic attacks. Panic attacks are intense anxiety reactions with oppressive physical features such as a pounding heart; rapid respiration, shortness of breath, or difficulty breathing; heavy perspiration; and weakness or dizziness. There is a stronger bodily component to panic attacks than to other forms of anxiety. Panic sufferers tend to be keenly aware of their cardiac (heart) sensations (Ehlers & Breuer, 1992) and often believe they are having a heart attack. A German study found that panic sufferers are more likely than others to associate anxiety with cardiac sensations (Pauli et al., 1991).

Panic attacks are more intense and may differ

qualitatively from other forms of anxiety (McNally, 1990; Rapee, 1987). The physical features are often accompanied by feelings of terror and of losing control, going crazy, or dying. Attacks usually last for several minutes, but can extend to hours. Initially the attacks occur unexpectedly and are not triggered by specific objects or situations that evoke fear. They seem to come out of the blue.

Victims feel exhausted afterward, as if they have survived a truly traumatic experience, as in the following case:

"I was inside a very busy shopping precinct and all of a sudden it happened; in a matter of seconds I was like a mad woman. It was like a nightmare, only I was awake; everything went black and sweat poured out of me—my body, my hands, and even my hair got wet through. All

of the blood seemed to drain out of me; I went white as a ghost. I felt as if I was going to collapse; it was as if I had no control over my limbs; my back and legs were very weak and I felt as though it were impossible to move. It was as if I had been taken over by some stronger force. I saw all of the people looking at me—just faces, no bodies; all merged into one. My heart started pounding in my head and my ears; I thought that my heart was going to stop. I could see black and yellow lights. I could hear the voices of the people but from a long way off. I could not think of anything except the way I was feeling and that I had to get out and run quickly or I would die. I must escape and get into fresh air. Outside it subsided a little but I felt limp and weak; my legs were like jelly as though I had run a race and lost; I had a lump in my throat like a golf ball. The incident seemed to me to have lasted hours. I was absolutely drained when I got home and I just broke down and cried; it took until the next day to feel normal again."

■ *Adapted from Hawkrigg, 1975, pp. 1280–1282*

may be perceived as unpredictable because the subtle cues are not readily detected (Barlow et al., 1985). If panic sufferers are unable to identify the actual triggers, they may attribute their sensations to more serious events, such as an impending heart attack or "going crazy."

 Some people who suffer from panic disorder are in fact suddenly overtaken by feelings of panic in the absence of an external threat. Other panic sufferers are aware of certain situations that heighten the probability of an attack.

The DSM lists the features shown in Table 5.2 as indicative of panic attacks. Not all of these features need be present in an attack. People may be diagnosed with panic disorder if (1) they encounter repeated unexpected panic attacks and (2) at least one of the attacks is followed by at least a month of

People often describe panic attacks as the worst experiences of their lives. Their coping abilities are overwhelmed. They may feel that they must flee. If flight seems useless, they may freeze. There is a tendency to cling to others for help or support. Some people with panic attacks fear going out alone. Recurrent panic attacks may become so difficult to cope with that sufferers may become suicidal. A study of community residents who suffered panic attacks found that 12% had attempted suicide (Weissman et al., 1989).

People with panic disorder first experience spontaneous or unexpected panic attacks. Later, however, the attacks may be cued by certain situations, such as driving a car, entering a confined space, or as in the case of Dick, boarding a train. Sufferers whose attacks seem to come out of the blue tend to report more severe distress than those whose attacks are more predictable (Barlow et al., 1985). Unpredictable panic may involve different biological processes than situationally cued attacks. Sometimes, however, it is difficult to distinguish between predictable and unpredictable attacks. Panic sufferers may be unaware of more subtle cues that precipitate attacks, such as cues concerning making decisions, even minor decisions such as those involved in making a grocery list. Panic may also be triggered by imperceptible physiological changes that are brought about by stress, sexual arousal, vigorous exercise, or sudden temperature changes (Barlow et al., 1985). The panic

---

Table 5.2 Features of Panic Attacks

A panic attack involves an episode of intense fear or discomfort in which at least four of the following features develop suddenly and reach a peak within 10 minutes:

1. Heart palpitations, pounding heart, tachycardia (rapid heart rate)
2. Sweating
3. Trembling or shaking
4. Shortness of breath or smothering sensations
5. Choking sensations
6. Chest pains or discomfort
7. Feelings of nausea or other signs of abdominal distress
8. Feelings of dizziness, unsteadiness, lightheadedness, or faintness
9. Feelings of strangeness or unreality about one's surroundings (derealization) or detachment from oneself (depersonalization)
10. Fear of losing control or going crazy
11. Fear of dying
12. Numbness or tingling sensations
13. Chills or hot flushes

Source: Adapted from DSM-IV Draft Criteria (American Psychiatric Association, 1993), p. K: 1.

persistent fear of subsequent attacks, or worry about the implications or consequences of the attack (e.g., fear of losing one's mind or "going crazy" or having a heart attack), or significant change in behavior (e.g., refusing to leave the house or venture into public for fear of having another attack) (American Psychiatric Association, 1993).

In many cases, panic sufferers limit their activities to avoid places in which they fear attacks may occur or they are cut off from their usual supports (Cox et al., 1992). Panic disorder is thus often associated with agoraphobia—fear of being in public places.

People with other types of phobias may become panicky when they are exposed to fear-evoking stimuli. Claustrophobics (persons with fears of enclosed spaces) may experience panic when they are confined to a crowded elevator. A social phobic may panic when asking someone for a date. Persons with panic disorder are reasonably accurate in predicting the likelihood of an attack (Rachman & Bichard, 1988; Rachman & Levitt, 1985; Rachman et al., 1988); they are never certain if or when an attack will occur, however.

Panic disorder usually begins in late adolescence or early adulthood. Panicky sensations occasionally afflict one-third to one-half of the general population (Norton & Rhodes, 1983; Norton et al., 1985), and 5 out of 6 people who are diagnosed as having other anxiety disorders (Barlow et al., 1985). Although reports of panic attacks are common among college samples and other nonclinical samples, these "panic attacks" tend to be milder than those experienced by people with diagnosable panic disorder (Wilson et al., 1992). Yet, in one college sample of more than 1,600 students, 7 to 8% of the respondents reported experiencing panic attacks that were similar in severity to those experienced by people with panic disorder (Wilson et al., 1992). However, the largest community study of its kind, the Epidemiologic Catchment Area (ECA) Study found that only 1 to 2% of the adult population could be diagnosed as having met criteria for panic disorder at some point during their lives (Robins et al., 1991). Women are about twice as likely as men to have panic attacks (National Institute of Mental Health, 1992).

GENERALIZED ANXIETY DISORDER

Generalized anxiety disorder (GAD) is characterized by a persistent, diffused sense of anxiety that is not triggered by any specific object, situation, or activity, but rather seems to be what Freud labeled "free-floating." Excessive worrying is the keynote feature of GAD (Rapee, 1991). People with generalized anxiety may be excessively worried about life circumstances such as finances, the well-being of their children, or social relationships. Nine of ten of them, according to one study, reported worrying excessively about even minor things (Sanderson & Barlow, 1990). Children with generalized anxiety are more likely to be worried about academics, athletics, and other social aspects of school life. According to the DSM, the anxiety and worry that characterize generalized anxiety disorder are associated with such features as restlessness, feeling "keyed up" or "on edge," becoming easily fatigued, having difficulty concentrating or finding one's mind going blank, irritability, muscle tension, and disturbances of sleep, such as difficulty falling asleep, staying asleep, or having restless and unsatisfying sleep (American Psychiatric Association, 1993). The features of generalized anxiety—anxiety, worry, and physical symptoms—cause a significant level of emotional distress or impaired functioning (American Psychiatric Association, 1993).

Generalized anxiety disorder is about equally common in women and men. It tends to be a stable disorder that initially arises in the mid-teens to mid-twenties and then follows a lifelong course (Rapee, 1991). According to the Epidemiologic Catchment Area (ECA) study, the disorder was found to affect 8.5% of the adult population at some point during their lives (Robins et al., 1991).

Although panic disorder and generalized anxiety disorder are both considered anxiety disorders, they differ in quality. Generalized anxiety is more pervasive and generally not as intense or impairing. The physical aspects of panic are much more potent, like the pounding of the heart and the heaviness of the sweating that accompany panic attacks. Intentional **hyperventilation** is unlikely to intensify the anxiety experienced by people with generalized anxiety, but it may elicit panic attacks in people with panic disorder (Rapee, 1990; Rapee et al., 1992). It may be that the biological correlates of the disorders thus differ in quality as well as intensity (McNally, 1990; Rapee et al., 1992).

People with generalized anxiety are often depressed. Sometimes the anxiety follows a depressive episode, but chronic anxiety can become depressing in its own right. The diagnosis of generalized anxiety is applied only when other possible sources of anxiety—such as anxieties over physical problems, leaving the house, or panic attacks—are ruled out. A sizable percentage of individuals with other anxiety disorders, such as agoraphobia and obsessive-compulsive disorder, also meet the diagnostic criteria for generalized anxiety disorder (Barlow et al., 1986). This raises the question, which continues to be debated, as to whether or not generalized anxiety disorder is a distinct diagnostic category.

In the following case example we find a number of features of generalized anxiety disorder:

Earl was a 52-year-old supervisor at the automobile plant. His hands trembled as he spoke. His cheeks were pale. His face was somewhat boyish, making his hair seem grayed with worry.

He was reasonably successful in his work, although he noted that he was not a "star." His marriage of nearly three decades was in "reasonably good shape," although sexual relations were "less than exciting—I shake so much that it isn't easy to get involved." The mortgage on the house was not a burden and would be paid off within 5 years, but "I don't know what it is; I think about money all the time." The three children were doing well. One was employed, one was in college, and one was in high school. But "With everything going on these days, how can you help worrying about them? I'm up for hours worrying about them."

"But it's the strangest thing," Earl shook his head. "I swear I'll find myself worrying when there's nothing in my head. I don't know how to describe it. It's like I'm worrying first and then there's something in my head to worry about. It's not like I start thinking about this or that and I see it's bad and then I worry. And then the shakes come, and then, of course, I'm worrying about worrying, if you know what I mean. I want to run away; I don't want anyone to see me. You can't direct workers when you're shaking."

Going to work had become a major chore. "I can't stand the noises of the assembly lines. I just feel jumpy all the time. It's like I expect something awful to happen. When it gets bad like that I'll be out of work for a day or two with shakes."

Earl had been worked up "for everything; my doctor took blood, saliva, urine, you name it. He listened to everything, he put things inside me. He had other people look at me. He told me to stay away from coffee and alcohol. Then from tea. Then from chocolate and Coca-Cola, because there's a little bit of caffeine [in them]. He gave me Valium [a minor tranquilizer] and I thought I was in heaven for a while. Then it stopped working, and he switched me to something else. Then that stopped working, and he switched me back. Then he said he was 'out of chemical miracles' and I better see a shrink or something. Maybe it was something from my childhood."

■ *The Authors' Files*

PHOBIC DISORDERS

The word *phobia* derives from the Greek *phobos,* meaning "fear." The concepts of fear and anxiety are closely related. **Fear** is the feeling of anxiety and agitation in response to a threat. Phobic disorders are persistent fears of objects or situations that are disproportionate to the threat posed by them. The onset of gripping fear when one's car is about to go out of control is normal because there is objective jeopardy in the situation. In phobic disorders, however, the fear exceeds any reasonable appraisal of danger. People with a phobia for cars, for example, might become fearful even when the vehicle is traveling well below the speed limit on a sunny, uncrowded highway. Or they might be so afraid that they will not drive or even ride in a car.

Phobias may interfere with people's normal routines, impairing their occupational or social functioning, even though sufferers generally realize that their fears are excessive or unreasonable. Their cognitive functioning is not so distorted that they are out of touch with reality. Put it this way: A person with a phobia for elevators may refuse to enter one at all costs, but she or he usually realizes that the fear is overblown.

Phobias usually involve fears of the ordinary events in life, not the extraordinary. Phobics become fearful of ordinary experiences that most people take for granted, such as taking an elevator or driving on a highway. Phobias become disabling when they interfere with daily tasks like taking buses, planes, or trains, driving, shopping, or leaving the house.

Phobias are quite common. The Epidemiologic Catchment Area (ECA) Study found that phobic disorders were the most frequently experienced type of mental disorder, affecting 14.3% of adults during their lives (Robins et al., 1991). Different kinds of phobias tend to appear at different ages, as noted in Table 5.3. The ages of onset appear to reflect factors such as cognitive development and life experiences. Animals are frequent subjects of children's fantasies, for example. The kinds of experiences that may relate to fears of leaving the house, as in agoraphobia, may follow the development of panic attacks that begin in early adulthood.

Phobic disorders are often categorized as *specific phobias, social phobias,* or *agoraphobia.*

Specific Phobias

Specific phobias are persistent, excessive fears of specific objects or situations. These fears prompt

Table 5.3   Typical Age of Onset for Various Phobias

	N	**Mean Age of Onset**
Animal phobia	50	7
Blood phobia	40	9
Injection phobia	59	8
Dental phobia	60	12
Social phobia	80	16
Claustrophobia	40	20
Agoraphobia	100	28

Source: Adapted from Öst (1987, 1992).

strong tendencies to avoid contact with the feared stimulus (Lang, 1985). When they imagine the fear-inducing stimuli, specific phobics tend to show greater arousal, as measured by changes in heart rate and skin conductance, than social phobics or agoraphobics (Cook et al., 1988). Unpleasant arousal helps mobilize the individual to escape or avoid the feared stimulus (Cook et al., 1988).

One specific phobia is fear of elevators. Some phobics will not enter elevators despite hardships such as walking six or more flights of stairs (Rathus, 1993). True, the cable *could* break. Yes, the ventilation *could* fail. One *could* get caught in midair waiting for repairs. These calamities are uncommon, however, and most people would find it unreasonable to walk up many flights of stairs to avoid them, or to reject an attractive job offer because the office is located on an upper floor. Persons with specific phobias for hypodermic syringes may similarly refuse injections, even when their health suffers as a result. Injections are sometimes painful, but many injection phobics would be willing to endure equally painful pinches in the arm if they would improve their health, as suggested by the case of a 28-year-old high school English teacher:

"This will sound crazy, but I wouldn't get married because I couldn't stand the idea of getting the blood test. [Blood tests for syphilis were required at the time.] I finally worked up the courage to ask my doctor if he would put me out with ether or barbiturates—taken by pills—so that I could have the blood test. At first he was incredulous. Then he became sort of sympathetic but said that he couldn't risk putting me under any kind of general anesthesia just to draw some blood. I asked him if he would consider faking the report, but he said that 'administrative procedures' made that impossible.

"Then he got me really going. He said that getting tested for marriage was likely to be one of my small life problems. He told me about minor medical problems that could arise and make it necessary for blood to be drawn, or to have an IV in my arm, so his message was I should try to come to grips with my fear. I nearly fainted while he was talking about these things, so he gave it up.

(A)

(B)

(C)

Three types of phobic disorders.   The woman in photo A has such severe agoraphobia that she resists leaving her house, even when her daughter offers to accompany her. The young man sitting by himself in photo B is a social phobic. He would like to form relationships with his peers but keeps largely to himself because of fears of social criticism and rejection. The woman in photo C has a specific phobia for injections. She does not fear the potential pain of the injection; she cannot tolerate the idea of the needle sticking her.

QUESTIONNAIRE

The Temple Fear Survey Inventory

Thunder? Cars? Being alone? Tests? Blood? Needles and knives? Illness? High or tight places? Making a speech? Creepy-crawlies? What objects or situations do you fear? What stimuli do you strive to avoid?

To compare your fears with those of undergraduate students at Temple University, use this code to signify the amount of fear you encounter when faced with each of these stimuli:

1 = None
2 = Some
3 = Much
4 = Very Much
5 = Terror

Then check the answer key at the end of the chapter.

____ 1. Noise of vacuum cleaners
____ 2. Being cut
____ 3. Being alone
____ 4. Speaking before a group
____ 5. Dead bodies
____ 6. Loud noises
____ 7. Being a passenger in a car
____ 8. Driving a car
____ 9. Auto accidents
____ 10. People with deformities
____ 11. Being in a strange place
____ 12. Riding a roller coaster
____ 13. Being in closed places
____ 14. Thunder
____ 15. Falling down
____ 16. One person bullying another
____ 17. Being bullied by someone
____ 18. Loud sirens
____ 19. Doctors
____ 20. High places
____ 21. Being teased
____ 22. Dentists
____ 23. Cemeteries
____ 24. Strangers
____ 25. Being physically assaulted
____ 26. Failing a test
____ 27. Not being a success
____ 28. Losing a job
____ 29. Making mistakes
____ 30. Sharp objects (knives, razor blades, scissors)
____ 31. Death
____ 32. Death of a loved one
____ 33. Worms
____ 34. Imaginary creatures
____ 35. Dark places
____ 36. Strange dogs
____ 37. Receiving injections
____ 38. Seeing other people injected
____ 39. Illness
____ 40. Angry people
____ 41. Mice and rats
____ 42. Fire
____ 43. Ugly people
____ 44. Snakes

"The story has half a happy ending. We finally got married in [a state] where we found out they no longer insisted on blood tests. But if I develop one of those problems the doctor was talking about, or if I need a blood test for some other reason, even if it's life threatening, I really don't know what I'll do. But maybe if I faint when they're going to [draw blood], I won't know about it anyway, right? . . .

"People have me wrong, you know. They think I'm scared of the pain. I don't like pain—I'm not a masochist—but pain has nothing to do with it. You could pinch my arm till I turned black and blue and I'd tolerate it. I wouldn't like it, but I wouldn't start shaking and sweating and faint on you. But even if I didn't feel the *needle at all—just the knowledge that it was in me is what I couldn't take."*

■ *The Authors' Files*

 Some people do live in dread of receiving injections, although they are not bothered by the pain. It is the injection itself that they fear.

Other specific phobias include **claustrophobia** (fear of tight or enclosed places), **acrophobia** (fear of heights), and fears of snakes, mice, and various other "creepy-crawlies."

___ 45. Lightning
___ 46. Sudden noises
___ 47. Swimming alone
___ 48. Witnessing surgical operations
___ 49. Prospects of a surgical operation
___ 50. Deep water
___ 51. Dead animals
___ 52. Blood
___ 53. Seeing a fight
___ 54. Being in a fight
___ 55. Being criticized
___ 56. Suffocating
___ 57. Looking foolish
___ 58. Being a passenger in an airplane
___ 59. Arguing with parents
___ 60. Meeting someone for the first time
___ 61. Being misunderstood
___ 62. Crowded places
___ 63. Being a leader
___ 64. Losing control
___ 65. Being with drunks
___ 66. Being self-conscious
___ 67. People in authority
___ 68. People who seem insane
___ 69. Boating
___ 70. God
___ 71. Being with a member of the opposite sex
___ 72. Stinging insects
___ 73. Crawling insects

___ 74. Flying insects
___ 75. Crossing streets
___ 76. Entering a room where other people are already seated
___ 77. Bats
___ 78. Journeys by train
___ 79. Journeys by bus
___ 80. Feeling angry
___ 81. Dull weather
___ 82. Large open spaces
___ 83. Cuts
___ 84. Tough-looking people
___ 85. Birds
___ 86. Being watched while working
___ 87. Guns
___ 88. Dirt
___ 89. Being in an elevator
___ 90. Parting from friends
___ 91. Feeling rejected by others
___ 92. Odors
___ 93. Feeling disapproved of
___ 94. Being ignored
___ 95. Premature heartbeats
___ 96. Nude men
___ 97. Nude women
___ 98. Unclean silverware in restaurants
___ 99. Dirty restrooms
___ 100. Becoming mentally ill

Fear survey inventory reprinted from "A factor analysis of a 100-item fear survey inventory" by P. R. Braun and D. J. Reynolds, 1969, Behaviour Research and Therapy, 7, pp. 399–402.

Social Phobia

Many of us have mild fears of social situations, such as dating, parties, and social gatherings. A **social phobia** is an intense fear of social situations arising from concerns of being judged negatively by others. Social phobics have persistent fears of doing something humiliating or embarrassing. They tend to be overly critical of their own performance, fear negative evaluations by other people, and experience excessive bodily arousal in social interactions (Turner et al., 1986). Social phobics may feel as if a thousand eyes are scrutinizing them. Stage fright and speech anxiety are common social phobias. The Epidemio-logic Catchment Area (ECA) survey revealed a lifetime prevalence of social phobias in the United States of 2.7% (Eaton et al., 1991).

Social phobics may find excuses for declining social invitations. They may lunch at their desks to avoid socializing with co-workers. Or they may find themselves in social situations and attempt a quick escape at the first sign of anxiety. Escape behavior is reinforced by relief from anxiety, but escape prevents phobic people from learning to cope with fear-evoking situations more adaptively. Leaving the scene before the anxiety dissipates only strengthens the association between the social situation and anxiety.

Some anxiety in unfamiliar social situations is

normal and adaptive. It prompts us to pay some attention to what we wear, say, and do. Simple shyness also occurs often enough. Many shy people and social phobics seem capable of handling themselves in social situations, but set unrealistically high expectations of themselves. They judge themselves harshly in comparison to more socially skillful people. Although shy people and social phobics may share such features in common as fear of criticism, social phobics are more likely to suffer impairment in their daily functioning, such as avoiding social contacts (Turner & Beidel, 1989). Yet it remains unclear whether social phobia is an extreme form of shyness or a qualitatively different phenomenon (Turner et al., 1990).

Social phobias can produce serious emotional distress and impair social and vocational functioning (Turner et al., 1986). Social phobias may prevent people from completing educational goals, advancing in their careers, or even holding a job in which they interact with others (Liebowitz et al., 1985). Social phobics often turn to tranquilizers or try to "medicate" themselves with alcohol in preparing for social interactions (see Figure 5.1). In extreme cases, social phobics may become so fearful of interacting with others that they become essentially housebound (Turner & Beidel, 1989).

Some social phobics are unable to order food in a restaurant for fear that the waiter or their companions might make jest of the foods they order or how they pronounce them. Others fear meeting new people and dating. Still others cannot sign their signatures in public, as in this case:

Estelle, 37, was a signature phobic. She was literally terrified of signing her name in public. She had arranged her life to avoid situations requiring her signature. She paid for purchases in cash rather than by credit card. She filed documents by mail rather than in person. She even registered her car in her husband's name so that he would be responsible for signing the motor vehicle forms. Like many phobics, Estelle cleverly structured her life to avoid exposure to fearful situations. She had even kept her phobia a secret from her husband for 15 years.

Underlying her signature phobia was a fear of social embarrassment. She feared being ridiculed for having an illegible or sloppy signature, or being accused of committing a forgery by bank officers or other officials. Estelle knew that she could prove her identity by other means than her signature. She also recognized that no one really cared whether or not her signature was neatly written. But she had become a victim of a vicious cycle of anxiety. The more she tried to prevent her hands from shaking in order to write legibly, the stronger her anxiety became and the more her hands shook, making it even more difficult for her to sign her name legibly.

■ *The Authors' Files*

Figure 5.1 Percentages of social phobics reporting specific difficulties associated with their fears of social situations.
More than 90% of social phobics feel handicapped by anxiety in their jobs.
Source: Adapted from Turner & Beidel, 1989.

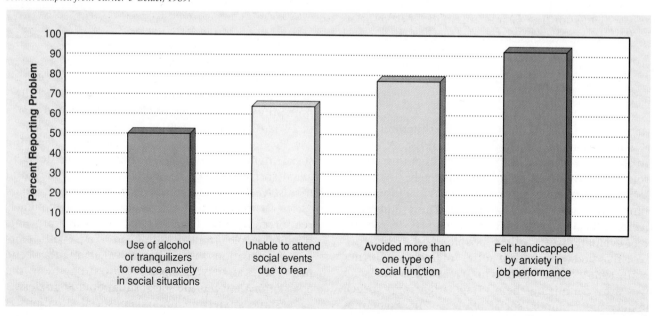

Social phobia is believed to affect women and men in about equal numbers and to have an earlier age of onset than most other anxiety disorders, generally beginning in adolescence (Liebowitz et al., 1985; Turner & Beidel, 1989). Social phobias tend to follow a chronic and persistent course (Liebowitz et al., 1985).

Agoraphobia

The word *agoraphobia* is derived from Greek words meaning "fear of the marketplace," which is suggestive of a fear of being out in open busy areas. Agoraphobia involves fear of places and situations from which it might be difficult or embarrassing to escape in case of an anxiety or panic attack, or of situations in which help may be unavailable if such an attack should occur. Agoraphobics may fear shopping in crowded stores, walking through crowded streets, eating in restaurants, crossing a bridge, traveling on a bus, train, or car or even leaving the house. They may structure their lives to avoid exposure to fearful situations and in some cases become housebound, making agoraphobia potentially the most incapacitating type of phobia.

Agoraphobia is more common in women than men. It frequently begins in late adolescence or early adulthood. The ECA study found that 5.6% of adult Americans suffered from agoraphobia at some point during their lifetimes (Eaton et al., 1991). Agoraphobia may occur with or without an accompanying panic disorder. In panic disorder with agoraphobia, sufferers may live in fear of recurrent attacks and avoid situations in which attacks have occurred or might occur (Franklin, 1987). Because panic attacks can descend from nowhere, some sufferers restrict their activities for fear of making public spectacles of themselves or finding themselves without help. Others venture outside only with a companion. Still others forge ahead despite anxiety. The following case illustrates panic disorder with agoraphobia:

> *A 30-year-old-accountant experienced recurrent panic attacks through a six-month period. The attacks occurred unexpectedly several times a week in a variety of situations, which led him to avoid driving by himself or shopping in department stores, lest he suffer an attack in such situations in which help might not be immediately available. He persuaded his wife to accompany him on errands and eventually became so fearful of leaving the house that he took a medical leave from work.*
>
> ■ *Adapted from Spitzer et al., 1989, pp. 213–214*

A study of 60 agoraphobics with a history of panic attacks found that many had other diagnosable disorders, such as depression, alcohol abuse, and other anxiety disorders (Breier et al., 1986). Agoraphobia usually developed within a year of the onset of the panic attacks. The panic sufferers thus apparently learned to avoid situations in which they feared an attack.

Panic attacks have also been associated with other anxiety disorders, such as specific phobia and social phobia (Barlow et al., 1985). However, people diagnosed as having panic disorder or panic disorder with or without agoraphobia reported that their panic attacks included more distressing features, such as dizziness and fears of losing control or of going crazy, than did specific phobics or social phobics who experienced panic attacks (Barlow et al., 1985).

Agoraphobics without a history of panic disorder are also anxious about being caught in public situations in which escape would be difficult or help would be unavailable in the event of anxiety attacks or panic-like symptoms such as feelings of dizziness. They too may become dependent on nonphobic companions. The following case of agoraphobia without a history of panic disorder illustrates the dependencies of agoraphobics:

> *A 32-year-old housewife complains that she is terrified of leaving home for fear of losing her balance and falling or fainting, although she has never fallen or fainted. She began having problems shortly after she and her family moved further away from her mother. Before the move she was able to walk to her mother's and sister's homes, but afterwards the greater distance between them prevented them from immediately coming over if she felt that she needed them. In addition, her husband started his own business, keeping him away from home for much of the time. While at first she avoided leaving her home, she eventually was able to shop on her own in the neighborhood stores when they were not crowded. But then a friend of hers, a 41-year-old man, died of a brain cyst. She then became continually anxious, was unable to leave the house, and only felt comfortable at home when her husband was with her. While no history of panic attacks is reported, the woman did experience similar agoraphobic symptoms 12 years earlier, immediately following her marriage, another point of separation from her family on whom she was dependent.*
>
> ■ *Adapted from Spitzer et al., 1989, pp. 134–135*

OBSESSIVE-COMPULSIVE DISORDER

An **obsession** is an intrusive and recurrent thought or idea that seems beyond the person's ability to control (Foa, 1990). Obsessions can be potent and persistent enough to interfere with daily life and can engender significant distress and anxiety. They include doubts, impulses, and mental images. One may wonder endlessly whether or not one has locked the doors and shut the windows, for example. One may be obsessed with the impulse to do harm to one's spouse. One can harbor images, such as one mother's recurrent fantasy that her children had been run over by traffic on the way home from school. Some people complain that they cannot get the lyrics to songs "out of my head," but most of the time the lyrics "pass through" and do not reach obsessional proportions.

The line between obsessions and the firmly held but patently false beliefs that are called **delusions,** which are found in schizophrenia, is sometimes less than clear. Obsessions, such as the belief that one is contaminating other people, can, like delusions, become almost unshakable. People with obsessions

An obsessive thought?   One type of obsession involves recurrent, intrusive images of a calamity occurring as the result of carelessness. For example, one may not be able to shake the image of the house catching fire due to an electrical short in an appliance left on.

will eventually concede that their concerns are groundless or excessive however, whereas true delusions fail to be shaken.

A **compulsion** is a seemingly irresistible, repetitious urge to engage in an act, such as lengthy, elaborate washing after using the bathroom. The impulse can occur frequently and forcefully enough to interfere with daily life. A compulsive hand-washer, Corinne, engaged in elaborate hand-washing rituals. She spent 3 to 4 hours daily at the sink and complained, "My hands look like lobster claws." Some people literally take hours checking and rechecking that all the appliances are off before they leave home, and then doubts still remain.

 Some obsessive-compulsive people are in fact delayed in leaving the house for an hour or more as they carry out their checking rituals.

Most compulsions fall into two categories: checking rituals and cleaning rituals (Rachman & Hodgson, 1980). Rituals apparently reduce anxieties that would occur if they were prevented from occurring (Foa, 1990). Rituals can become the focal point of life. Checking rituals, like repeatedly checking that the gas jets are turned off or that the doors are securely locked before leaving the house, cause delays and annoy companions; cleaning can occupy several hours a day. Table 5.4 shows some relatively common obsessions and compulsions.

Compulsions often accompany obsessions and appear to at least partially relieve the anxiety that is created by obsessive thinking (Steketee & Foa, 1985). Compulsive rituals apparently also reduce the anxiety that would occur if they were prevented from being carried out (Foa, 1990).

The DSM diagnoses obsessive-compulsive disorder when people are troubled by recurrent obsessions, compulsions, or both such that they cause marked distress, occupy more than an hour a day, or significantly interfere with occupational or social functioning (American Psychiatric Association, 1993). Adults with obsessive-compulsive disorder are capable of recognizing at some point during the course of the disorder the unreasonableness or excessiveness of their obsessions or compulsions; children with this disorder may not (American Psychiatric Association, 1993).

Obsessive-compulsive disorder is believed to affect 2 to 3% of adult Americans during their lifetimes, according to the results of the ECA study (Robins et al., 1991). The disorder seems to afflict women and men in about equal numbers (Karno et al., 1988).

Table 5.4   Examples of Obsessive Thoughts and Compulsive Behaviors

Obsessive Thought Patterns	Compulsive Behavior Patterns
Thinking that one's hands remain dirty despite repeated washing.	Rechecking one's work time and time again.
Difficulty shaking the thought that a loved one has been hurt or killed.	Rechecking the doors or gas jets before leaving home.
Repeatedly thinking that one has left the door to the house unlocked.	Constantly washing one's hands to keep them clean and germ-free.
Worrying constantly that the gas jets in the house were not turned off.	
Repeatedly thinking that one has done terrible things to loved ones.	

The case of Jack illustrates a checking compulsion:

Jack, a successful chemical engineer, was urged by his wife Mary, a pharmacist, to seek help for "his little behavioral quirks," which she had found increasingly annoying. Jack was a compulsive checker. When they left the apartment, he would insist on returning to check that the lights or gas jets were off, or that the refrigerator doors were shut. Sometimes he would apologize at the elevator and return to the apartment to carry out his rituals. Sometimes the compulsion to check struck him in the garage. He would return to the apartment, leaving Mary fuming. Going on vacation was especially difficult for Jack. The rituals occupied the better part of the morning of their departure. Even then, he remained plagued by doubts.

Mary had also tried to adjust to Jack's nightly routine of bolting out of bed to recheck the doors and windows. Her patience was running thin. Jack realized that his behavior was impairing their relationship as well as causing himself distress. Yet he was reluctant to enter treatment. He gave lip service to wanting to be rid of his compulsive habits. However, he also feared that surrendering his compulsions would leave him defenseless against the anxieties they helped ease.

■ *The Authors' Files*

ACUTE AND POST-TRAUMATIC STRESS DISORDERS

In adjustment disorders (discussed in Chapter 4), people have difficulty adjusting to life stressors—business or marital problems, chronic illness, or bereavement over a loss. Here we focus on stress-related disorders that arise from exposure to *traumatic* events. Exposure to traumatic events can produce both acute or prolonged stress-related disorders that are labeled, respectively, **acute stress disorder** and **post-traumatic stress disorder** (PTSD). In these disorders, the traumatic event involved either actual or threatened death or serious physical injury, or a threat to one's own or other's physical safety (American Psychiatric Association, 1993). The person's response to the threat involved feelings of intense fear, helplessness, or a sense of horror. Children with PTSD may have experienced the threat differently, such as by showing disorganized or agitated behavior. Both types of stress disorders have occurred among soldiers exposed to combat, rape victims, and people who have witnessed the destruction of their homes and communities by natural disasters like floods or tornadoes, or technological disasters like railroad or airplane crashes.

Some of the basic features of these traumatic stress reactions are reexperiencing of the traumatic event; avoidance of cues or stimuli connected with the event; a numbing of general or emotional responsiveness; heightened states of bodily arousal; and significant emotional distress or impairment of functioning, or in the case of an acute stress reaction, an inability to perform necessary tasks, such as obtaining needed medical or legal assistance, or failing to mobilize one's resources to obtain support from family by failing to inform family members about the traumatic experience (American Psychiatric Association, 1993). Acute stress disorder is further characterized by extreme anxiety and by **dissociation** or feelings of detachment from oneself or one's environment (American Psychiatric Association, 1993). People with an acute stress disorder may feel that they are "in a daze" or that the world seems unreal.

The diagnosis of acute stress disorder applies to

a stress reaction that is limited to the days and weeks immediately following a traumatic experience. By contrast, a post-traumatic stress disorder persists for months or even years or decades and may not develop until many months or years after exposure to the stressor.

 Victims of post-traumatic stress disorder may in fact develop problems years after their disturbing experiences.

Acute stress disorders frequently occur in the context of combat or exposure to natural or technological disasters. A soldier may come through a horrific battle not remembering important features of the battle, and feeling numb and detached from the environment. People who are injured or who nearly lose their lives in a hurricane may walk around "in a fog" for days or weeks afterwards, be bothered by intrusive images, flashbacks and dreams of the disaster, or relive the experience as though it were happening again.

The traumatic event may be reexperienced in various ways. There can be intrusive memories, recurrent disturbing dreams (Wood et al., 1992), and the feeling that the event is indeed recurring (as in "flashbacks" to the event). Exposure to events that resemble the traumatic experience can cause intense psychological distress. People with traumatic stress reactions tend to avoid stimuli that evoke recollections of the trauma. For example, they may not be able to handle a television account of it or a friend's wish to talk about it. People with PTSD often report feelings of detachment or estrangement from other people. They may show less responsiveness to the external world after the traumatic event, losing the ability to enjoy previously preferred activities or to have loving feelings (Litz, 1992).

Have you ever been awakened by a nightmare and been reluctant to return to sleep for fear of reentering the orb of the dream? Nightmares in traumatic stress reactions often involve the reexperiencing of the traumatic event, which can lead to abrupt awakenings and difficulty falling back to sleep—because of fear associated with the nightmare and elevated levels of arousal. Other features of heightened arousal include difficulty falling or staying asleep, or irritability or anger outbursts, hypervigilance (being continuously on guard), difficulty concentrating, and an exaggerated startle response (jumping in response to

sudden noises or other stimuli) (American Psychiatric Association, 1993).

Sutker and her colleagues (1991) estimate that 1 to 2% of the general population could be diagnosed as having PTSD at any given time. The diagnostic category of acute stress disorder was introduced recently with the publication of the DSM-IV and we know little about its prevalence. Much of the previous work on traumatic stress disorders has focused on post-traumatic stress disorder among combat veterans, especially the Vietnam veteran.

PTSD Among Combat Veterans

Combat and psychological distress go hand in hand (Solomon et al., 1987). Soldiers (and local civilians) can face numerous brushes with death. Civilians may witness the annihilation of their neighborhoods and ways of life. Soldiers may face cold, rain, and filth, along with the threat of death. Even if they escape personal harm, their fellows may be killed and wounded.

Although PTSD entered the popular vocabulary after the Vietnam conflict, World War II and Korean veterans are estimated to account for some 30% of the total number of combat-related cases (Gelman, 1988). Some aging veterans of Korea and the battlefields of World War II have complained of recurrent dreams of battlefield dismemberments and deaths for more than 40 years. It remains unclear why some soldiers are affected by the disorder and others are not (Gelman, 1988). In one study, 188 World War II prisoners of war were evaluated for 40 years following their return to the United States to evaluate lifetime prevalences of PTSD (Kluznik et al., 1986). Two out of three of the men (67%) showed evidence of having suffered PTSD at some time or another. Signs of PTSD usually did not occur during the men's captivity, but shortly following their return home. Their problems (e.g., insomnia, nightmares, heightened startle response) typically persisted for some years, then gradually declined. Yet some problems persisted for four decades among nearly half of the PTSD sufferers.

The effects of combat may adversely affect the soldiers' adjustment long after the cannons of battle have been silenced. Combat veterans are at greater risk for developing PTSD in civilian life than nonveterans or veterans who did not see combat. Many PTSD sufferers abuse alcohol and drugs and are violent or socially withdrawn (Sutker et al., 1991). PTSD

The trauma of combat.
The stresses of combat can lead to intense anxiety and impaired functioning. Stress-related problems may continue for years afterward in the form of post-traumatic stress disorder (PTSD).

can develop many years after discharge and affect adjustment into later adulthood.

■ **PTSD AND THE VIETNAM VETERAN** Numerous studies have illuminated the plight of the Vietnam veteran (e.g., Green et al., 1990b; Hendin & Haas, 1991; Yehuda et al., 1992). A survey of 2.7 million Vietnam veterans found that 20 to 25% had PTSD or PTSD-like problems (Walker & Cavenar, 1982). Another study found the incidence of PTSD to be 19% among 36-year-old Vietnam veterans, as compared to 12% among 36-year-old veterans who did not serve in Vietnam (Card, 1987). The severity of PTSD was also greater among Vietnam veterans than non-Vietnam veterans diagnosed with the disorder. Among Card's respondents, 27% of the men who had been in heavy combat developed PTSD. In another study, 60% of wounded Vietnam combat veterans reported at least one feature of PTSD (Foy et al., 1987). Twenty percent met the criteria for a diagnosis of PTSD. All in all, PTSD has been estimated to have affected about 470,000 male Vietnam veterans, or 15% of the 3.14 million men who served there (Gelman, 1988).

Postwar stress factors also seem to play a role. Being part of a supportive social network appears to lessen the impact of traumatic events like combat (Stretch, 1985, 1987). The incidence of PTSD was thus greater among combat veterans who lived alone (whether divorced, separated, or never married), as compared to married veterans (Card, 1987). PTSD was also more common among men who regularly used tranquilizers and other prescription drugs, and among men who used illicit drugs such as stimulants and narcotics. PTSD sufferers were more frequently arrested and convicted for major crimes. They were more likely to have sought treatment or hospitalization for abnormal behavior, drug- or alcohol-related problems, or marital- or job-related stress (Card, 1987).

Vietnam-era combat veterans who develop PTSD-like problems have been found to be less capable of solving problems and using active coping skills, as compared to well-adjusted Vietnam-era veterans (Nezu & Carnevale, 1987). People with PTSD may also have difficulty developing and using social supports to moderate the effects of stress. For example, veterans with PTSD have more trouble disclosing their intimate feelings and are less well adjusted in marital and cohabiting relationships than are veterans without PTSD (Carroll et al., 1985). Church groups and the availability of a spouse similarly may reduce the risk of PTSD (Card, 1987). These studies tend to be correlational, however, so it may be that veterans who have trouble expressing their feelings and participating in groups are also at greater risk for developing PTSD. Coping deficits may make it more difficult for the PTSD sufferer to handle various life stressors when they arise, such as marital or employment problems, adding to the "cycle of distress" that may help perpetuate the symptoms of PTSD (Nezu & Carnevale, 1987).

PTSD can persist. Some surveys found that 40 to 50% of Vietnam combat veterans were suffering from PTSD-like problems 10 years later (Frye & Stockton, 1982; Wilson, 1977).

■ **WHY VIETNAM WAS WORSE** Humanistic-existential theorists note that people can endure much when their suffering is meaningful. In the Vietnam conflict, however, the goals were muddy, the war seemed unwinnable, and some of "the folks back home" blamed U.S. soldiers for fighting a war they saw as immoral. The justifications for World War II were much clearer. Unlike earlier veterans and those who returned from the Persian Gulf War, the Vietnam veteran was not welcomed home with ticker tape parades. The Vietnam conflict was also fought by younger combatants (who averaged 19.2 years of age) than those who fought in World War II (whose average age was 26) (Gelman, 1988). Adolescence can be difficult enough at home, let alone in jungles halfway around the world. The nature of the battlefield also differed from most of those encountered in World War II. The terrain of Europe and North Africa was more familiar than the jungles of Southeast Asia, and the enemy usually wore a uniform. Combat soldiers in Vietnam faced an unseen enemy in the jungles and villagers who might be friend or foe. Their encounters with hostile civilian populations occasionally led to atrocities that ran counter to basic human rights as well as military codes of conduct:

> *O*ne Vietnam veteran with PTSD recounted an experience in which he saw a frail old man walking along a dike and bearing an agricultural tool. The soldier killed him with a single shot. What had flashed through his mind? the grieving soldier wondered later. Had he been primed to shoot at any figure with an object that resembled a weapon? Had he mistaken the old man for an enemy in disguise? He would probably never unearth his motives. "No one said anything [about the shooting]," the soldier recalled. In fact, his lieutenant, who had witnessed the shooting, promptly recorded it as his own kill to elevate his body count.
>
> ■ *Adapted from Gelman, 1988*

Even when soldiers succeed in their missions, they must come to terms with the devastation they unleash on others. Many Vietnam veterans bear unresolved feelings of guilt, however, especially those who were involved in killings of civilians who they believed, mistakenly or not, to be enemies in disguise. Hendin and Haas (1991) examined the factors that predicted suicide attempts among a sample of 100 Vietnam veterans with PTSD, 19 of whom had attempted suicide after discharge, and 15 more of whom were preoccupied with suicide. Several factors distinguished the suicide attempters, including guilt about their combat actions, survivor guilt, depression, anxiety, and the severity of PTSD itself. Combat guilt was the strongest predictor of suicide attempts and suicidal thoughts.

THEORETICAL PERSPECTIVES

The anxiety disorders offer something of a theoretical laboratory. Many theories of abnormal behavior were developed with these disorders in mind. Classic case studies and experiments have been carried out to affirm or disprove various points of view. Let us consider how the anxiety disorders have been conceptualized from the psychological and biological perspectives.

Psychodynamic Perspectives

From the psychodynamic perspective, anxiety disorders are viewed as neuroses. The anxiety experienced in neuroses reflects (1) the efforts of unacceptable, repressed impulses to break into consciousness and (2) fear as to what might happen if they do. Feelings of anxiety represent danger signals that threatening impulses are nearing the level of awareness. To fend off these threatening impulses, the ego tries to stem or divert the tide through defense mechanisms.

Phobias develop through the use of the defense mechanisms of **projection** and **displacement.** A phobic reaction is believed to represent the projection of the person's own threatening impulses onto the phobic object. For instance, persons who are excessively fearful of knives and other sharp instruments may harbor unconscious desires to use these implements on themselves or others. Avoiding contact with sharp instruments prevents these destructive wishes from becoming consciously realized or acted upon. Similarly, acrophobic people may harbor unconscious

Do phobias represent the operation of unconscious defense mechanisms?   Psychodynamic theorists suggest that phobias represent the operation of unconscious defense mechanisms such as projection and displacement. In their view, a fear of heights, or acrophobia, may represent the ego's attempt to defend itself against the emergence of threatening self-destructive impulses, such as an impulse to jump from a dangerous height. By avoiding heights, the person can maintain a safe distance from such threatening impulses. Because this process occurs unconsciously, the person may be only aware of the phobia, not of the unconscious impulses it symbolizes.

wishes to jump that are controlled by avoiding heights. Freud believed that phobias help both to contain threatening impulses and to keep them out of awareness by motivating the person to keep away from the phobic object or situation. The phobic object or situation symbolizes or represents these unconscious wishes or desires. The person is aware of the phobia, but not of the unconscious impulses that it symbolizes.

Freud believed that most of our motives are unconscious and that we repress socially unacceptable ideas. Then we can ignore their existence and need not fear punishment or self-condemnation. Impulses seek expression, however, and are often

expressed as symbols. These conflicts are believed to have childhood origins. Consider Freud's (1909/1959) historic case of "Little Hans," a 5-year-old boy who feared that he would be bitten by a horse if he left his house. Freud suggested that Hans feared horses because of what horses symbolized to him. Hans's fear of horses represented the displacement of an unconscious fear of his father. According to Freud's conception of the Oedipus complex, boys have unconscious incestuous desires to possess their mothers and fears of retribution from their fathers, whom they see as rivals in love. Hans's fear of being bitten by horses thus symbolized underlying fear of castration.

Learning theorists view Hans's childhood fears as a case of classical conditioning (Bandura, 1969; Wolpe & Rachman, 1960). They argue that Hans's fear had been learned from his being frightened by an accident involving a horse and a transport vehicle, which generalized to fears of horses. The story of Little Hans is one of the great cases in the psychoanalytic literature. The interpretation of the case has sparked a fascinating debate.

Let us consider how various anxiety disorders may be conceptualized within the psychodynamic model. In generalized anxiety disorder, unconscious conflicts remain hidden, but anxiety leaks through to the level of awareness. The person is unable to account for the anxiety because its source remains shrouded in unconsciousness, however. In panic disorder, unacceptable sexual or aggressive impulses approach the boundaries of consciousness and the ego strives desperately to repress them, generating high levels of conflict that bring on a full-fledged panic attack. Panic dissipates when the impulse has been safely repressed.

Within the psychodynamic model, obsessions represent the leakage of unconscious impulses into consciousness, and compulsions are acts that help to keep these impulses repressed. For instance, obsessive thoughts about contamination by dirt or germs may represent the threatened emergence of unconscious infantile wishes to soil oneself and play with feces. The compulsion (in this case, cleanliness rituals) helps keep such wishes at bay or partly repressed.

People who become obsessed with thoughts of harming the people they love may harbor unconscious aggressive impulses that intrude into consciousness. The aggressive impulses may be clearly expressed, as in the case of a man who becomes obsessed with thoughts of killing his wife. The aggressive impulses may also be indirectly expressed, in the form of obsessions or repeated fantasies of one's children or spouse being struck by a car or involved in a terrible accident. Consider, for example, the case of Bonnie:

---

*B*onnie, 29, complained of being obsessed by fantasies that her 8- and 11-year-old children were run over on their way home from school. It was April and the fantasies had begun in September, gradually occupying more time during the day.

　　"I'm usually all right for most of the morning," she explained. "But after lunch the pictures come back to me. There's nothing I can do about it. The pictures are in my head. I see them walking home and crossing the street, and I know what's going to happen and I think 'Why can't I do something to stop it?' but I can't. They're walking into the street and a car is coming along speeding, or a truck, and then it happens again, and they're lying there, and it's a horrible mess." She broke into tears. "And I can't function. I can't do anything. I can't get it out of my head.

　　"Then sometimes it bothers me at night and [my husband] says 'What's wrong?' He says I'm shaking and white as a ghost and 'What's wrong?' I can't tell him what's going on because he'll think I'm crazy. And then I'm in and out of [the children's] bedrooms, checking that they're all right, tucking them in, kissing them, making sure I can see that they're breathing. And sometimes I wake [the 11-year-old] up with my kissing and he says 'Mommy' and I start crying as soon as I get out of the room."

　　Through discussions with the psychologist, it appeared that Bonnie was generally dissatisfied with her life. She had gotten married at a young age because of an unplanned pregnancy and had remained largely housebound. Her daytime companion was her television set. Her husband was generally good to her, but he did not understand why Bonnie might be unhappy, "especially when so many women have to work these days to make ends meet." Within a few weeks Bonnie came to the conclusion that it was "all right" for her to feel resentments toward being thrown into the role of mother at an early age. Her resentment at never having made decisions about the course her life would take did not mean that she was a bad mother. Open discussion of her frustrations was connected with a marked decrease in her report of obsessive thoughts.

■ *The Authors' Files*

Bonnie's case is of the type that may lend support to psychodynamic views. It suggests that obsessions and other anxious behavior patterns can reflect hostilities that we (psychologically) "sweep under the rug" or do not think about (that is, no "good mother" should have hostile feelings toward her children). On the other hand, Bonnie's case does not offer direct evidence of the existence of such unconscious impulses or conflicts.

Learning Perspectives

From the behavioral perspective, anxiety disorders are acquired through conditioning. According to O. Hobart Mowrer's (1948) **two-factor model,** both classical and operant conditioning are involved in phobias. The fear component of phobia is assumed to be acquired by means of classical conditioning. As with Little Albert, the boy who was conditioned to fear rats by John Watson and Rosalie Rayner (see Chapter 2), it is assumed that neutral objects and situations gain the capacity to evoke fear by being paired with aversive stimuli. A child who is frightened by a barking dog may acquire a phobia for dogs. A child who receives a painful injection may develop a phobia for hypodermic syringes. Studies suggest prominent roles for specific aversive experiences in the development of many cases of acrophobia, claustrophobia, and blood and injection phobias (Kendler et al., 1992c; Merckelbach et al., 1991). Phobic avoidance behavior is acquired and maintained by means of operant conditioning. That is, the avoidance of fear-inducing stimuli is negatively reinforced by relief from anxiety. Successful avoidance of the phobic stimuli prevents the person from *un*learning the fear (through extinction) by experiencing the phobic stimulus in the absence of the aversive event.

From the behavioral perspective, generalized anxiety is precisely that: a product of stimulus generalization. People who are concerned about broad life themes, such as finances, health, and family matters, are likely to experience their apprehensions in a variety of settings. Anxiety would thus become connected with almost any environment or situation. Similarly, agoraphobia would represent a kind of generalized anxiety. Anxiety would become triggered by cues associated with various social or vocational situations outside of the home in which the individual is expected to perform independently, as in traveling, going to work, even shopping. Some learning theorists similarly assume that panic attacks which appear to descend out of nowhere are triggered by cues that are not readily identified.

There are many challenges to these behaviorist notions. For example, many people with phobias insist that they cannot recall painful exposures to the dreaded stimuli. Behaviorists may assume that such memory failures are understandable because many phobias are acquired in early childhood. Yet many phobias, such as social phobias and agoraphobia, develop at later ages and appear to reflect cognitive processes relating to the appraisal of threat in social situations (excessive fears of embarrassment or criticism) or public places (perceptions of helplessness or fears of panic attacks).

■ THE "VALUE" OF AVOIDING FEAR-EVOKING STIMULI

There is strong evidence for the idea that avoiding phobic stimuli brings fast relief from anxiety. In an experiment by Bandura and his colleagues (1985), women who feared spiders were given tasks such as allowing a spider to crawl on them. Blood samples were collected while the women confronted the spiders and were analyzed for concentrations of the catecholamines adrenaline and noradrenaline. The catecholamines arouse the body by way of the sympathetic branch of the ANS. As a result, we feel shaky, have "butterflies in the stomach," and other signs of anxiety. In the study, women who said they could not manage facing the spider *and who then refused to try to do so* showed sudden drops in catecholamine levels. Avoidance of a fear-inducing stimulus was thus reinforced by immediate reductions in arousal associated with fear. The Bandura study adds to the body of evidence that suggests that people may learn to avoid fear-evoking stimuli because avoidance reduces anxiety.

On the other hand, Bandura (1982) points out that there is no mechanical one-to-one relationship between one's anxiety level and willingness to confront fear-evoking stimuli. Beliefs as to whether or not one can manage fear-inducing stimuli—that is, self-efficacy expectancies—can be more powerful predictors of behavior than one's anxiety level. Many women in the study with spiders tackled the spiders when they believed they could manage them, regardless of their catecholamine levels (Bandura et al., 1985).

Although there are immediate anxiety-reduction benefits to avoiding feared stimuli, there is a long-term price. Avoidance of fearful stimuli prevents people from extinguishing fear of them. Behavioral treatments of phobias thus employ some kind of exposure to fear-inducing stimuli.

■ REINFORCEMENT OF OBSESSIVE-COMPULSIVE BEHAVIOR

From the learning perspective, compulsive behaviors are operant responses that are reinforced by relief of the anxiety that is engendered by obsessional thoughts. If a person obsesses that other people's hands are contaminated by dirt or foreign bodies, shaking hands or turning a doorknob may evoke powerful anxiety. Compulsive hand washing following exposure to a possible contaminant provides some relief from anxiety. People thus become more likely to repeat the obsessive-compulsive cycle the next time they are exposed to anxiety-evoking cues, such as shaking hands or touching doorknobs.

The question remains as to why some people develop obsessive thoughts whereas others do not. Some theorists look to an interaction of learning and biological factors for answers. Perhaps people who develop obsessive-compulsive disorder are physiologically sensitized to overreact to minor cues of danger (Steketee & Foa, 1985).

■ PREPARED CONDITIONING

Some investigators suggest that people may be genetically prepared to acquire phobic responses to certain classes of stimuli (McNally, 1987; Mineka, 1991; Seligman & Rosenhan, 1984). For this reason, this model is often referred to as **prepared conditioning.** The model suggests that evolutionary forces would have favored the survival of human ancestors who were genetically predisposed to acquire fears of large animals, snakes, heights, entrapment, sharp objects, and strangers. Humans who were not so genetically endowed, and who did not readily acquire these fears, would have been less likely to survive and to pass along their genetic dispositions. Therefore, people may have inherited a tendency to develop phobias that had survival value in the past, even if they no longer do today.

Subjects in laboratory experiments have received electric shock while being shown photographs of various stimuli (Hugdahl & Ohman, 1977; Ohman et al., 1976). The subjects typically acquire fear reactions to some stimuli (e.g., spiders and snakes) more readily than to others (e.g., flowers and houses), as measured by galvanic skin response to subsequent photos. People are also relatively more resistant to attempts to extinguish fears of snakes and spiders (McNally, 1987). All in all, subjects seem more *prepared* to acquire and maintain fear responses to stimuli like snakes and spiders. These experiments do not demonstrate that the subjects are *genetically* prepared to develop their fear responses, however. Keep in mind that subjects were reared in a society in which many people react negatively to these creepy-crawlies. People might therefore be culturally and cognitively prepared—not genetically prepared—to acquire fear responses to snakes, spiders, and other stimuli generally perceived as repugnant in our society.

■ A CONDITIONING MODEL OF POST-TRAU-MATIC STRESS DISORDER (PTSD)

From a classical conditioning perspective, traumatic experiences function as unconditioned stimuli that become paired with neutral (conditioned) stimuli such as the sights, sounds, and smells associated with the trauma scene—for example, the battlefield or the neighborhood in which a person has been raped or assaulted (Foy et al., 1987; Wirtz & Harrell, 1987). Subsequent exposure to similar stimuli evoke the anxiety (a conditioned emotional response) associated with PTSD. The conditioned stimuli that reactivate the conditioned response include memories or dream images of the trauma, or visits to the scene of the trauma. Research supporting the conditioning model of PTSD shows that PTSD subjects whose problems are combat-related show greater arousal (as measured by heart rate and GSR) than control subjects do when they are exposed to slides or recordings of the sounds of combat (Blanchard et al., 1982; Malloy et al., 1983).

PTSD is likely to persist when sufferers avoid exposure to conditioned stimuli—as in refusing to think or talk about painful memories (Foy et al., 1987). Avoidance of combat- or assault-related stimuli can be viewed as an operant response that is reinforced by reduction of the anxiety produced by the stimuli (Fairbank & Nicholson, 1987). Avoidance prolongs PTSD because sufferers do not have the opportunity to learn to manage their conditioned reactions. Extinction of conditioned anxiety may only occur when conditioned stimuli (e.g., the cues related to combat or the traumatic setting) are presented in the absence of the troubling unconditioned stimuli. That is, the fear may extinguish when the person is able to gradually encounter the conditioned stimuli without incident.

■ OBSERVATIONAL LEARNING

Learning theorists have also noted a role of observational learning in acquiring fears. In one study of 42 people with severe phobias for spiders, observational learning apparently played a more prominent role than conditioning in fear acquisition (Merckelbach et al., 1991).

In a classic study, Bandura and Rosenthal (1966) hooked up a confederate to an ominous array of electrical equipment. A buzzer was sounded, and the confederate's arm shot up as though he had been stung with shock. He also yowled and grimaced convincingly, but no shock was actually given. The true subjects in the study watched the confederate while their own physiological responses were being monitored. After a few repetitions, the subjects showed higher autonomic reactivity when the buzzer was sounded, even though they were in no danger of receiving shock. Similarly, if parents squirm, grimace, and shudder at mice, blood, or dirt on the kitchen floor, children may learn to respond to them with fear and avoidance behavior.

Cognitive Perspectives

Cognitive theorists and researchers have identified various patterns of thinking, or cognitive factors, that are associated with anxiety disorders. These include overprediction of fear, irrational beliefs, oversensivity to threats, self-efficacy expectancies, self-defeating thoughts, and attributional styles.

■ OVERPREDICTION OF FEAR

Anxious people tend to overpredict the fear they will experience when they encounter a fear-evoking object or situation (Rachman & Bichard, 1988). In one study, snake phobic subjects overpredicted the fear that would be induced by exposure to snakes (Rachman & Lopatka, 1986). In another, 3 out of 4 panic patients (76%) overestimated the fear they would encounter when exposed to fear-inducing situations (Rachman et al., 1988).

Overprediction of fear may have survival value because it encourages people to keep their distance from fear-evoking situations (Rachman & Bichard, 1988). From the cognitive perspective, however, avoidance of fear-inducing situations prevents people from gaining experience that can promote a more benign appraisal of the stimuli. Research has shown that fearful subjects become more accurate in predicting their level of fear following exposure to the fearful situation (Rachman & Bichard, 1988). A clinical implication is that with repeated exposure, phobic clients may become more accurate in predicting their responses to fear-inducing stimuli. Clients can be informed that anticipated fear often exceeds actual fear, and that exposure can therefore reduce expectancies of fear.

■ IRRATIONAL BELIEFS

Phobics have been found to hold more of the sorts of irrational beliefs catalogued by Albert Ellis than nonfearful people do. Such beliefs often center around exaggerated needs to be approved of by everyone one meets and to avoid any situation in which problems might arise (Mizes et al., 1987). Consider these beliefs: "I couldn't stand it if people saw me having an attack. What would they think of me? They might think I was crazy. I couldn't stand it if they looked at me that way." In one study, 65% of the anxious subjects, as compared to only 2% of nonanxious subjects, endorsed the belief that one must be loved by, and earn the approval of, practically everyone (Newmark et al., 1973). Results of another study may hit closer to home: College men who believe that it is awful to be turned down when requesting a date show more social anxiety than men who are less likely to catastrophize rejection (Gormally et al., 1981).

Cognitive theorists relate obsessive-compulsive disorder to tendencies to exaggerate the risk of negative outcomes and to adopt irrational beliefs, especially perfectionistic beliefs (Steketee & Foa, 1986). Because they expect bad things to happen, obsessive-compulsive people engage in rituals to prevent them. An accountant who imagines terrible consequences for slight mistakes on a client's tax forms may feel compelled to repeatedly check her or his work. The perfectionist exaggerates the consequences of turning in less than perfect work, and may feel compelled to redo his or her efforts until every detail is flawless.

■ **OVERSENSITIVITY TO THREATS** People's appraisals of the magnitude of threatening events influence whether or not the events are traumatic and may lead to PTSD (Creamer et al., 1992). Phobic people may likewise harbor cognitions that prompt them to perceive danger in situations most people consider safe. In comparison to normal people, agoraphobics more often perceive ambiguous physical sensations and internal states of arousal as threatening (McNally & Foa, 1987). People with panic disorder are more attentive than normal reference subjects to cardiac sensations (McNally et al., 1990).

Anxious people apparently pay special attention to threatening information and construe unclear events in an ominous way (Mathews, 1990; Rapee, 1991). Oversensitivity to threats often reflects exaggerated perceptions of external dangers (as in, "The bridge might collapse," or "The elevator cables may break"). They may refer to internal cues that function as signs of danger (as in "I think I'm going to fall apart," or "I feel like I'm about to lose control"). Sometimes the cognitions involve themes of social embarrassment or rejection (as in "What if they think I'm stupid? That would be awful," or "I'm afraid of making a scene"). Phobic people may dwell on vari-

ous combinations of self-defeating cognitions. Fear of flying may involve perceptions of the plane as unsafe ("What's that vibration? It feels like the plane is about to come apart"), perceptions of personal vulnerability ("What if I have an anxiety attack? There's no escape at 35,000 feet!") and threats of social embarrassment ("Everybody will notice that I'm shaking. They'll think I'm a fool").

■ **LOW SELF-EFFICACY EXPECTANCIES** Beliefs that we will not be able to manage a threat (low or negative self-efficacy expectancies) tend to heighten anxiety (Bandura, 1981; Bandura et al., 1982). When people feel capable of performing a task—playing the piano, giving a speech in public, riding on a train without panicking, or touching a small rodent or

How do self-doubts affect our performance? According to the self-efficiency model, we are likely to feel more anxious in situations in which we doubt our ability to perform competently. Anxiety may hamper our performance, making it more difficult for us to perform successfully. Even accomplished athletes may be seized with anxiety when they are under extreme pressure, as during slumps or in championship games.

insect—they are less likely to be troubled by anxiety or fear when they attempt it.

When people rivet their attention on perceived incapacities, they may fail to seek out personal resources that might be used to cope with stressful situations, as in the case of Brenda:

Brenda, a 19-year-old sophomore, was plagued by anxiety almost from the moment she began her college studies. She had enrolled in a college several hundred miles away from home. While she had been away from home before—at sleep-away camp and on a teen tour through Europe—college life presented various challenges and stresses which she felt a lack of ability to handle. She seemed to be most anxious when meeting new friends and when sitting in class, especially the small seminar classes in which she expected to be called on by the professor. She found herself becoming tongue tied and dripping with perspiration whenever she confronted these situations. What was more surprising and perplexing to her was that she had never had any trouble before either making new friends or talking in class.

In both situations, Brenda lost confidence in her ability to express herself. The ideas she wished to express were blocked by anxiety, which impaired her ability to think and speak clearly. The anxiety was maintained by an erroneous perception of herself as incapable of saying the right thing when called upon in class or when meeting new people. Brenda reported that she hadn't had any problems in high school either speaking up in class or making new friends. College, however, was a different experience. At college there were people she hadn't grown up with, and there were professors who had no tolerance, or so she believed, for any student who wasn't a budding genius. Her whole mental set had shifted into a defensive attitude in which self-doubts replaced self-confidence.

Brenda's history of social and academic success couldn't shield her from the nagging self-doubts she began to experience as she confronted the more demanding stresses of college life. Brenda was not any less capable of coping with these challenges in college than she was in high school. She didn't suddenly lose her wits or her social skills when she entered college. What was different was that she began to perceive herself as unable to cope with the demands of a new environment that seemed both unsupportive and threatening. Appraising herself this way, it was little wonder that she experienced anxiety in class and social situations, which impaired her efforts to speak clearly. She then interpreted her speech difficulties as evidence of her inadequacies, feeding the vicious cycle of anxiety in which self-doubt leads to anxiety, which hampers performance, which occasions more self-doubts and anxiety, and so on.

■ *The Authors' Files*

■ **SELF-DEFEATING THOUGHTS** People with anxiety disorders may not encounter more anxiety-evoking events than other people. They may, instead, interpret events in more self-defeating ways (Rapee et al., 1990). Self-defeating thoughts can heighten and perpetuate anxiety and phobic disorders. When faced with fear-evoking stimuli, many anxious people think, "I've got to get out of here," or "My heart is going to leap out of my chest" (Meichenbaum & Deffenbacher, 1988). Thoughts like these intensify autonomic arousal, disrupt planning, magnify the aversiveness of stimuli, prompt avoidance behavior, and decrease self-efficacy expectancies concerning capacity to control the situation.

Schwartz and Michelson (1987) found that agoraphobics tend to produce self-defeating thoughts prior to treatment and more adaptive thoughts during and immediately following treatment. Those who show the most improvement with treatment also make the greatest shifts from self-defeating to adaptive thoughts.

■ **MISATTRIBUTIONS FOR PANIC SENSATIONS** Cognitive models of panic disorders generally assume that panic attacks involve catastrophic misinterpretations of bodily sensations (Clark, 1986). Unless people are psychologically and biologically sophisticated, they are likely to misread the sensations of a panic attack. Victims are likely to attribute the sensations to threatening events, such as an impending heart attack or "going crazy." People who suffer from other kinds of anxiety, which are less physically traumatic, tend to recognize their sensations for what they are and not to confuse them with physical illness (Rapee, 1985). Clark (1986) offers these examples of the misinterpretations of panic sufferers:

1. A physically healthy person perceives palpitations or tachycardia as evidence of an impending heart attack.

2. A physically healthy person perceives slight breathlessness and dizziness as evidence of impending cessation of breathing and death.

3. The person perceives a shaky feeling as evidence of impending loss of control or insanity.

The triggering stimuli for panic attacks may be external—such as entering a supermarket in which a previous attack has occurred. Often, however, the precipitating stimuli are internal cues like minor changes in physical sensations, thoughts, and images. If the internal cues are perceived as threatening, mild anxiety or apprehension may develop, which compounds the bodily sensations. When these secondary anxiety signals are "blown out of proportion" or catastrophized, anxiety is exacerbated and further intensifies bodily sensations and subsequent fear. There can thus be a vicious cycle that culminates in a full-blown panic attack.

Some people may have such a *fear of anxiety* that they encode sensations of anxiety as awful and thereby heighten them (see Figure 5.2), setting the stage for a vicious cycle that leads to panic. Fears of anxiety may arise from various factors, such as biological predispositions, psychological factors such as excessive fears of embarrassment and loss of control, and a history of frightening anxiety attacks that may have sensitized the individual to anxiety cues (Reiss et al., 1987).

Recent studies shed light on cognitive factors. In one, agoraphobics with panic were asked to describe their thoughts about their first panic attacks (Breier et al., 1986). Most attributed the attack to grave origins such as a heart attack, stroke, brain tumor, or

"going crazy." Those who perceived their first attacks as life threatening were more likely to develop agoraphobia than those who attributed them to anxiety. Also, people whose initial attacks seemed spontaneous or out of the blue were more likely to progress to agoraphobia than people whose attacks seemed connected with specific stimuli. Spontaneous attacks may instill the belief that outside activities must be avoided because attacks might occur during them.

 Such factors as catastrophic misinterpretations of anxiety cues, and fear of anxiety, apparently can set a vicious cycle into motion that brings on panic attacks in some people.

In another study, 25 persons diagnosed as having panic disorder and 25 control subjects were connected with an electrocardiograph that provided false feedback about their heart rates (Ehlers et al., 1988). The machine falsely indicated that heart rates were increasing when they were not, so that researchers could assess subjects' responses to the *belief* that they were becoming aroused. Persons with panic disorder reported more anxiety and a heightened level of excitement on the basis of the false feedback. They also showed objectively measured autonomic arousal in the form of increased heart rate, blood pressure, and galvanic skin response. The control subjects, in contrast, reported no changes in anxiety or excitement, and showed *decreased* levels of autonomic activity in response to the false feedback. The control subjects apparently encoded the false feedback as a signal to relax, whereas people with panic disorder may have been so fearful of their own bodily arousal that they tensed up, raising their physiological arousal and feelings of anxiety.

More support for the view that cognitive factors may play an important role in panic attacks is provided by a study in which normal student volunteers received **sodium lactate** infusions under very different sets of expectations (van der Molen et al., 1986). Infusions of sodium lactate induce panicky feelings or panic attacks in some people, especially people with panic disorder. Some students were led to expect that the lactate infusion would produce unpleasant bodily sensations similar to those of anxiety. Others were told to expect feelings of pleasant tension, similar to what they might feel at an exciting sporting event or while watching an adventure film. The volunteers were then administered a lactate infusion or a placebo (glucose) infusion (see Figure 5.3). At a second session, they received the alternate infusion. The placebo infusion produced no significant changes in

Figure 5.2 A cognitive model of panic disorder
This model involves the interaction of cognitive and physiological factors. In panic-prone people, perceptions of threat from internal or external cues lead to feelings of apprehension or anxiety, which lead to changes in body sensations (for example, cardiovascular symptoms). These changes lead, in turn, to catastrophic interpretations, thereby intensifying the perception of threat, which further heightens anxiety, and so on in a vicious circle that may culminate in a full-blown panic attack.
Source: Adapted from Clark, 1986.

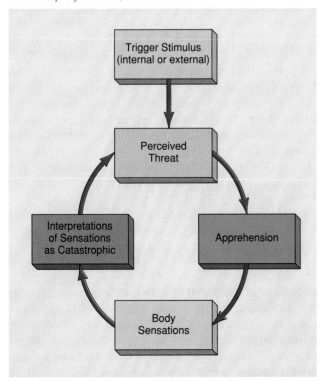

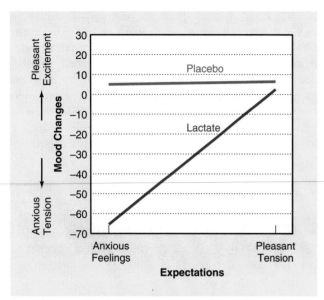

Figure 5.3 Effects of physiological arousal in combination with various expectations.
The figure shows the mood changes of normal subjects in the van der Molen study who were infused with a placebo solution or with sodium lactate and were led to believe the infusion would either produce sensations similar to anxiety or "pleasant tension." Subjects were asked to rate their mood changes following infusion on a 100-point scale ranging from +100 ("very pleasant excitement") to −100 ("very anxious tension"). The zero point was to represent their baseline mood state. The effects of sodium lactate on mood were apparently influenced by the expectations given the subjects. Yet subjects' expectations did not affect their mood in the placebo condition. It appears that negative mood changes resulted from the combination of the physiological arousal caused by lactate infusion and the expectation that subjects would become anxious.
Source: Adapted from van der Molen et al., 1986.

mood, regardless of expectation. However, the effects of sodium lactate on mood were mediated by the expectations the subjects received prior to the infusion. Those who were given the "anxious feelings" expectation reported significantly more anxious tension after the infusion. Lactate subjects given the "pleasant tension" expectation showed a slight, but nonsignificant, *increase* in positive excitement. It appears that negative mood changes reflected the interaction of physiological arousal and the expectation of anxiety. Cognitive factors may thus affect people's responses to physiological arousal.

Biological Perspectives

Biological factors play roles in anxiety disorders. Many questions remain concerning the interactions of biological and other factors, however.

■ **GENETIC FACTORS** Anxiety and anxiety disorders tend to run in families (Turner et al., 1987). In a study of genetic contributions to personality traits, Sandra Scarr and her colleagues (1981) compared the **neuroticism** (a personality trait characterized by anxiety, a sense of foreboding, and the tendency to avoid fear-inducing stimuli) test scores of adopted adolescents to those of their natural and adoptive parents. The scores of parents and their natural children correlated more highly than those of parents and adopted children.

Twin studies have also been reported. The results of one carefully thought out study examined the monozygotic (MZ) and dizygotic (DZ) twins of people identified as having anxiety disorders (Torgersen, 1983). Overall, the concordance rate (i.e., the percentage of co-twins who had the disorder) for anxiety disorders was twice as high for MZ twins (34%) as for DZ twins (17%). This 2:1 ratio supports a genetic contribution because MZ twins share twice as many (100%) of their genes as DZ twins, who share 50%.

An analysis of 2,163 female twin pairs supported a moderate role for a genetic contribution to the development of phobias in women. Genetic factors were most prominent in agoraphobia and least prominent in specific phobias (Kendler et al., 1992c). A study of 1,033 female twin pairs showed that genetic factors also play a modest role in generalized anxiety disorder in women (Kendler et al., 1992c).

Genetics apparently plays less of a role in specific phobias than in agoraphobia because specific aversive experiences are more likely to contribute to the development of specific phobias, such as nearly falling out of a window or being locked in a closet (Kendler et al., 1992c). Although there is evidence for genetic factors in panic disorder (Horwath, 1992; Noyes et al., 1986), environmental factors also play a role. For example, people with panic disorders are more likely than reference groups to have experienced major life changes in the year preceding the onset of the disorder, and to have perceived the changes as more uncontrollable, undesirable, and damaging to their self-esteem (Roy-Byrne et al., 1986).

Research suggests that genetics may play only a small role in obsessive-compulsive disorder (Steketee & Foa, 1985).

■ **NEUROTRANSMITTERS** The neurotransmitter **gamma-aminobutyric acid** (GABA) is implicated in many cases of anxiety. GABA is an *inhibitory* neurotransmitter found throughout the gray matter of the central nervous system. That is, GABA regulates nervous activity by preventing neurons from overly exciting their neighbors. When the action of GABA is inadequate, neurons can fire excessively, bringing about seizures. In less dramatic cases, inadequate action of GABA apparently contributes to anxiety. This view of the role of GABA is supported by the action of the family of antianxiety drugs referred to as **benzodiazepines,** which include the well-known Valium and Librium. Benzodiazepines make GABA receptors more sensitive, thus enhancing GABA's calming (inhibitory) effects (Zorumski & Isenberg, 1991).

Interestingly, generalized anxiety is more responsive to the benzodiazepines than panic disorder. Perhaps different biochemical mechanisms are connected with the disorders. Panic disorder is apparently more responsive to antidepressant medication than benzodiazepines (Margraf et al., 1986). Because antidepressants affect the action of the neurotransmitters serotonin and norepinephrine, it may be that these neurotransmitters—and not GABA—are more closely connected with panic disorder.

■ **BIOLOGICAL ASPECTS OF PANIC DISORDER** Panic attacks can be experimentally induced in people who are prone to them by biological challenges such as the infusion of sodium lactate. Hyperventilation can also trigger attacks in people with panic disorder (Halloway & McNally, 1987).

Lactate infusions often induce responses that resemble panic attacks in some 50 to 70% of people with a history of attacks (Liebowitz et al., 1984), but only rarely among normal controls (van Hout, 1987). Such differences in response to a biological challenge lead some researchers to attribute panic disorder to biological causes, even if they are not yet well understood (McNally, 1990; Rapee, 1990; Rapee et al., 1992; van Hout, 1987). Because only a small minority of persons with social phobias (Liebowitz et al., 1985) or obsessive-compulsive disorder (Gorman et al., 1985) appear to respond to lactate infusion with panic, different biological mechanisms may distinguish panic disorder from these other anxiety disorders. It is also possible, however, that a history of panic attacks makes victims overly sensitive to physical sensations, such as those induced by lactate infusion. Thus cognitive rather than biological differences could also account for panic sufferers' relatively greater sensitivity to lactate infusion.

The fact that panic attacks often seem to come out of the blue would also seem to support the role of internal biochemical triggers of disorders. It remains possible, however, that people with panic disorder overreact to slight changes in physical sensations because of prior exposure to traumatic attacks. Some researchers (e.g., Clark, 1986) suggest that the ten-dency of panic sufferers to catastrophize or misattribute physical changes—even minor changes in heart rate—as signs of an impending attack may help explain the development of panic disorder. Perceptions that panic attacks come out of the blue may thus arise from lack of understanding of internal bodily cues and catastrophizing cognitions about the cues. Others suggest that specific classes of cognitions that involve themes of death, loss of control, and misattributions for arousal may precede the onset of panic attacks (Beck et al., 1974; Hibbert, 1984).

Researchers have begun to develop integrative models that combine cognitive and biological factors in explaining panic disorders, as represented in the model depicted in Figure 5.2 and in a model relating hyperventilation to panic.

■ **HYPERVENTILATION AND PANIC** Proper cardiovascular functioning requires a balance of oxygen and carbon dioxide. Buildup of carbon dioxide triggers the breathing reflex, so that we exchange some carbon dioxide for oxygen. However, we need to retain a certain amount of carbon dioxide to maintain the proper balance.

Hyperventilation is a pattern of shallow, rapid breathing that causes us to breathe off too much carbon dioxide. Hyperventilation often accompanies and compounds feelings of anxiety. When we hyperventilate, we often breathe excessively from the chest, rather than more deeply from the diaphragm (Fried & Golden, 1989). Hyperventilation reduces the levels of carbon dioxide in the blood, interferes with body metabolism, and is accompanied by sensations like dizziness, numbness, coldness, tingling, anxiety, and, in some cases, panic (Fried & Golden, 1989). All in all, it may feel very much as if one is about to suffer a heart attack or suffocate. Many people who hyperventilate are unaware of any unusual breathing pattern, however. Their irregular breathing may be so subtle that neither they nor trained observers can detect it without physiological monitoring equipment (Fried & Golden, 1989).

Hyperventilation appears to be involved in many naturally occurring panic attacks (Hibbert, 1986; Salkovskis et al., 1986). In laboratory settings, hyperventilation has been used to induce panic attacks in people with panic disorder (Bonn et al., 1984; Clark, 1986; Clark et al., 1985). Such evidence has prompted some theorists to propose that hyperventilation *in combination with catastrophic thinking* can prompt the development of panic attacks and agoraphobia (Ley, 1985; Rapee, 1987). According to this model, a stressful event leads to a period of hyperventilation, which produces cardiovascular symptoms. Panic-prone people are especially sensitive to these bodily sensations and misattribute them to dire causes, such as a heart attack. Their anxiety prompts further hyperventilation, which intensifies bodily sensations, yet they remain unaware that their symptoms stem from hyperventilation. A vicious cycle can ensue in which hyperventilation and catastrophic thoughts escalate anxiety to a full-blown panic attack. Still, the causal role of hyperventilation in naturally occurring panic attacks remains unclear. Hyperventilation may merely accompany panic attacks in some people with panic disorder, rather than act as a causal factor in producing such attacks (Garssen et al., 1992). Whatever its causal role, clinicians are finding that breathing retraining, which helps panic sufferers restore a proper balance of carbon dioxide in the blood by means of such techniques as slow, deep (abdominal) breathing, is proving helpful in the treatment of panic disorder (Garssen et al., 1992; Ley, 1991).

Sometimes breathing into a paper bag may help restore a more optimal balance between oxygen and carbon dioxide. Accurate knowledge may also help panic sufferers develop more realistic appraisals of their cardiovascular sensations. Gradual exposure to such sensations may also help them learn to tolerate them without overreacting (Barlow, 1986; Rapee, 1987).

TREATMENT OF ANXIETY DISORDERS

Each of the major theoretical perspectives has spawned approaches for treating anxiety disorders. Psychological approaches may differ from one another in their techniques and expressed aims, but they seem to have one thing in common: In one way or another, they encourage clients to face rather than avoid the sources of their anxieties. The biological perspective, by contrast, has focused largely on drugs that quell anxiety.

Psychodynamic Approaches

From the psychodynamic perspective, anxieties reflect the energies attached to early childhood conflicts and the ego's efforts to keep them repressed. Traditional psychoanalysis fosters awareness of how clients' anxiety disorders symbolize their inner conflicts, so that the ego can be freed from expending its energy on repression. The ego can thus attend to more creative and enhancing tasks.

More modern psychodynamic therapies also foster clients' awareness of inner sources of conflict. They focus more so than traditional approaches on exploring sources of anxiety that arise from current rather than past relationships, however, and they encourage clients to assume more adaptive behavior. Such therapies are briefer and more directive than traditional psychoanalysis.

Humanistic-Existential Approaches

Humanistic-existential theories posit that many of our anxieties stem from social repression of our genuine selves. Anxiety occurs when the incongruity between one's true inner self and one's social facade draws closer to the level of awareness. The person senses that something bad will happen, but is unable to say what it is because the disowned parts of oneself are not directly expressed in consciousness. Because of the disapproval of others, people may fail to develop their individual talents and recognize their authentic feelings. Humanistic-existential therapies thus aim at helping people get in touch with and express their genuine talents and feelings. As a result, clients become free to discover and accept their true selves, rather than reacting with anxiety whenever their true feelings and needs begin to surface.

Biological Approaches

Pharmaceutical houses earn large shares of their income from minor tranquilizers, the drugs that are most often used to treat tension and anxiety. For many years, the benzodiazepine Valium (generic name, diazepam) was the most widely prescribed drug in the world. Other commonly used benzodiazepines include Tranxene (clorazepate), Librium (chlordiazepoxide), and Xanax (alprazolam).

Although the therapeutic use of benzodiazepines is usually limited to 60 days, an American Psychiatric Association (1991) task force estimates that as many as 2 million Americans have taken them for many years because of chronic insomnia, lingering depression, or other long-standing problems. Physical dependence on benzodiazepines can develop with chronic use, however (American Psychiatric Association, 1991). Physically dependent patients may experience rebound symptoms such as heightened anxiety, insomnia, and restlessness shortly after they stop using benzodiazepines (American Psychiatric Association, 1991; Noyes et al., 1991).

These symptoms prompt many patients to return to benzodiazepines.

Drugs which are primarily used to treat depression, *antidepressants*, also show some promise in treating panic disorder (Michelson & Marchione, 1991). Some investigators have reported troublesome side effects from antidepressant medication, however (Marks, 1987). In one study on panic disorder, half of the subjects could not tolerate a commonly used antidepressant, imipramine (brand name Tofranil), mainly because of amphetamine-like side affects (Aronson, 1987).

Although investigators report some success in treating panic disorder and agoraphobia with the benzodiazepine alprazolam (Xanax), the evidence suggests that claims of effectiveness are premature and require further support from controlled trials of the drug versus placebo (Marks et al., 1989). A recent drug–placebo trial failed to show alprazolam to be clinically superior to placebo medication (Klosko et al., 1990). People who experience relief from troubling problems like panic attacks when taking medication may be responding to a placebo effect rather than the medication itself.

One potential problem with drug therapy is that users may attribute improvements in their conditions to the drugs and not their own resources. Nor do such drugs effect cures. People with panic disorder frequently report reemergence of panic after they discontinue chemotherapy, for example (*"Treatment,"* 1988, November; Rapee, 1987). Reemergence of panic may be likely unless the treatment incorporates cognitive techniques that help sufferers modify their overreactions to bodily sensations (Clark, 1986). Imipramine has also shown some promise in the treatment of agoraphobia, at least when it is combined with behavioral exposure treatments (Mavissakalian & Perel, 1985). The mode of action of antidepressants on panic and agoraphobia remains unclear.

Researchers report some promising findings in using antidepressant medication to treat social phobia (Gelernter et al., 1991; Levin et al., 1989; Liebowitz et al., 1985b, 1992) and obsessive-compulsive disorder (Goodman et al., 1990; Jenike et al., 1990; Pato et al., 1991; Pigott et al., 1990). Other research suggests that alprazolam may also be of help in treating social phobia (Reich & Yates, 1988).

Obsessive-compulsive disorder (OCD) appears to be especially responsive to a class of antidepressant drugs called serotonin re-uptake inhibitors (such as fluoxetine—brand name Prozac, and clomipramine—brand name Anafranil) (Hollander, 1992). These drugs act by inhibiting the re-uptake (reabsorption by the transmitting neuron) of the neurotransmitter serotonin, thereby increasing the concentration of serotonin available along these pathways in the brain (Goodman et al., 1990; Jenike et al., 1990; Pato et al., 1991; Pigott et al., 1990). These findings lead researchers to suspect that a dysregulation of serotonin transmission in the brain may be involved in the development of OCD in at least some people with the disorder (e.g., Hollander, 1992; Pigott et al., 1990). Still, many people with OCD fail to respond to serotonin re-uptake inhibitors, and those who do respond generally achieve only modest benefits (Goodman et al., 1989). As with the chemotherapeutic treatment of other anxiety disorders, there may be high relapse rates following withdrawal of medication.

Learning-Based Approaches

Behavioral treatments based on learning approaches include a variety of techniques aimed at helping individuals confront the objects or situations that elicit their fears and anxieties (Öst et al., 1991).

■ SYSTEMATIC DESENSITIZATION

Adam has a phobia for receiving injections. His behavior therapist treats him as he reclines in a comfortable padded chair. In a state of deep muscle relaxation, Adam observes slides projected on a screen. A slide of a nurse holding a needle has just been shown three times, 30 seconds at a time. Each time Adam has shown no anxiety. So now a slightly more discomforting slide is shown: one of the nurse aiming the needle toward someone's bare arm. After 15 seconds, our armchair adventurer notices twinges of discomfort and raises a finger as a signal (speaking might disturb his relaxation). The projector operator turns off the light, and Adam spends two minutes imagining his "safe scene"—lying on a beach beneath the tropical sun. Then the slide is shown again. This time Adam views it for 30 seconds before feeling anxiety.

■ *Rathus, 1993, p. 596*

Adam is undergoing systematic desensitization, a fear-reduction procedure originated by psychiatrist Joseph Wolpe (1958, 1973) in the 1950s. Systematic desensitization is a gradual process. Clients learn to handle progressively more disturbing stimuli while they remain relaxed. About 10 to 20 stimuli are

Systematic desensitization. In systematic desensitization, clients practice deep muscle relaxation while the therapist presents an ordered series or hierarchy of fear-evoking stimuli. Although systematic desensitization has been demonstrated to be of theraputic value, psychologists of different theoretical persuasions account for its efficacy in diverse ways.

arranged in a sequence or hierarchy—called a **fear-stimulus hierarchy**—according to their capacity to evoke anxiety. By using their imagination or by viewing photos, clients are exposed to the items in the hierarchy, gradually imagining themselves approaching the target behavior—be it ability to receive an injection or the capacity to remain in a room without windows—without undue anxiety.

 In the method of systematic desensitization, relaxing in a recliner and fantasizing *traveling up a fear-stimulus hierarchy* can be an effective way of reducing fears.

Joseph Wolpe developed systematic desensitization on the assumption that maladaptive anxiety responses, like other behaviors, are learned or conditioned. He assumed that they can be unlearned by counterconditioning. In counterconditioning, a response that is incompatible with anxiety is made to appear under conditions that usually elicit anxiety. Muscle relaxation is generally used as the incompatible response, and followers of Wolpe usually use the method of progressive relaxation (described in Chapter 4) to help clients acquire relaxation skills. For this reason Adam's therapist is teaching Adam to experience relaxation in the presence of (otherwise) anxiety-evoking slides of needles.

Behaviorally oriented therapists, like Wolpe, explain the benefits of systematic desensitization and similar therapies in terms of principles of counterconditioning, or extinction. Cognitively oriented therapists note, however, that remaining in the presence of phobic imagery, rather than running from it, is also likely to enhance self-efficacy expectancies (i.e., self-perceptions of being able to manage the phobic stimuli without anxiety) (Galassi, 1988). Positive self-efficacy expectancies are negatively (inversely) correlated with catecholamine levels in the bloodstream (Bandura et al., 1985). A treatment that raises clients' self-efficacy expectancies may thus lower their catecholamine levels, which may counteract feelings of nervousness and relieve the physical aspects of anxiety.

■ **GRADUAL EXPOSURE** This method helps people overcome phobias through a stepwise approach of actual exposure to the phobic stimuli, as in the following case example:

Kevin was a claustrophobic with intense fear of riding on elevators. Ironically, Kevin's occupation was that of an elevator mechanic. Kevin spent his work days repairing elevators. Unless it was absolutely necessary, however, Kevin managed to complete the repairs without riding in the elevator. Like many other phobics, Kevin had become adept at arranging his life to meet his responsibilities while avoiding exposure to phobic stimuli. Basically, Kevin would climb the stairs to the floor where an eleva-

tor was stuck, make repairs, and hit the down button. He would then race downstairs to see that the elevator had operated correctly. When his work required an elevator ride, panic would seize him as the doors closed. Kevin tried to cope by praying for divine intervention to prevent him from passing out before the doors opened.

Kevin related the origin of his phobia to an accident three years earlier in which he had been pinned in his overturned car for nearly an hour. He remembered feelings of helplessness and of suffocation. Kevin developed claustrophobia—a fear of situations from which he could not escape, such as flying on an airplane, driving through a tunnel, taking public transportation, and, of course, riding in an elevator. Kevin's fear had become so incapacitating that he was seriously considering switching careers, although the change would require financial sacrifice. Each night he lay awake wondering whether he would be able to cope the next day if he were required to test ride an elevator.

Kevin's therapy involved gradual exposure. Gradual exposure, like systematic desensitization, is a step-by-step procedure that involves a fear-stimulus hierarchy. In gradual exposure, however, the target behavior is approached in actuality rather than symbolically. Moreover, the individual is active rather than relaxed in a recliner.

A typical hierarchy for overcoming a fear of riding on an elevator might include the following steps:

1. Standing outside the elevator.
2. Standing in the elevator with the door open.
3. Standing in the elevator with the door closed.
4. Taking the elevator down one floor.
5. Taking the elevator up one floor.
6. Taking the elevator down two floors.
7. Taking the elevator up two floors.
8. Taking the elevator down two floors and then up two floors.
9. Taking the elevator down to the basement.
10. Taking the elevator up to the highest floor.
11. Taking the elevator all the way down and then all the way up.

Clients begin at step 1 and do not progress to step 2 until they are able to maintain a state of calmness on the first. If anxiety intrudes, the client removes herself or himself from the situation and regains calmness by muscle relaxation or focusing on soothing mental imagery. The encounter is then repeated as often as necessary to reach and sustain feelings of calmness. The individual then proceeds to the next step, repeating the process.

Kevin was also trained to practice self-relaxation and talk calmly and rationally to himself to help himself remain calm during his exposure trials. Whenever he began to feel even slightly anxious, he would tell himself to calm down and relax. He was able to counter the disruptive belief that he was going to fall apart if he were trapped in an elevator with rational self-statements such as "Just relax. I may experience some anxiety, but it's nothing that I haven't been through before. In a few moments I'll feel relieved."

Kevin gradually overcame his phobia but still occasionally experienced some anxiety, which he interpreted as a reminder of his former phobia. He did not exaggerate the importance of these feelings. Now and then it dawned on him that an elevator he was servicing had once occasioned fear. One day following his treatment, Kevin was repairing an elevator which serviced a bank vault 100 feet underground. The experience of moving deeper and deeper underground aroused fear, but Kevin did not panic. He repeated to himself, "It's only a couple of seconds and I'll be out." By the time he took his second trip down, he was much calmer.

■ *The Authors' Files*

Exposure has also emerged as an effective form of treatment of social phobia (Marks, 1985; Wlazlo et al., 1990). In exposure therapy, social phobics are instructed to enter increasingly stressful social situations and to remain in those situations until their urge to escape has lessened. The therapist may help guide social phobics through these exposure situations, gradually withdrawing direct support so that clients grow capable of negotiating the situations on their own. Exposure treatment is often combined with cognitive techniques that help phobics monitor their thoughts during exposure and replace upsetting thoughts with more rational alternatives. In the case of social phobia, distressing beliefs often involve excessive fears of embarrassment or criticism. One research study showed that the combination of guided exposure and cognitive techniques produced greater reductions in social phobia than exposure alone (Butler, 1989). Subjects who succeeded in modifying their attitudes about the importance of other people's opinions were generally more successful than subjects who maintained more fixed beliefs.

■ BEHAVIORAL TREATMENT OF AGORAPHOBIA

Gradual exposure is also helpful in the treatment of agoraphobia (Jacobson et al., 1988). People with agoraphobia may gradually expose themselves to increasingly disturbing stimulus situations, such as walking through congested streets or shopping in department stores. They may do so on their own or with a companion, even the therapist. The goal is to be able to remain alone indefinitely in each situation, without discomfort, without the urge to escape. The benefits of gradual exposure have been found to persist at follow-ups of up to 7 years (Mavissakalian & Michelson, 1986). Overall, researchers find that about 6 in 10 agoraphobics show clinically meaningful improvement following exposure-based treatment (Jacobson et al., 1988). Only 27% are no longer agoraphobic by the end of treatment, however.

The companion is of help in managing agoraphobia. A 2-year follow-up of the effects of exposure therapy with 56 agoraphobic women showed that treatment was more effective when the spouse was involved (Cerny et al., 1987). As a side effect, marital satisfaction was also enhanced. Involving the spouse in treatment can provide social support and convert a spouse from a sideline critic into a helpmate (Kleiner & Marshall, 1985).

Gradual exposure.   In gradual exposure, the phobic person is exposed to a fear-stimulus hierarchy in real-life situations, often with a therapist or companion serving in a supportive role. The therapist or companion gradually withdraws direct support, so as to encourage the person to accomplish the exposure tasks increasingly on his or her own. Gradual exposure is often combined with cognitive techniques that focus on helping the phobic person replace anxiety-producing thoughts and beliefs with calming, rational alternatives.

■ BEHAVIORAL TREATMENT OF POST-TRAUMATIC STRESS DISORDER

Behavioral treatment for PTSD similarly involves progressive exposure to the cues related to the trauma. Exposure may be accomplished through talking about the trauma, viewing related slides or films, or visiting the scene of the event. It is assumed that exposure to anxiety-producing cues, in the absence of aversive experiences, will extinguish anxiety. Stress management skills, such as self-relaxation, enhance the client's ability to cope with the features of PTSD, such as heightened arousal (Fairbank & Nicoholson, 1987) and the desire to run away from trauma-related stimuli.

A study of 165 victims of violent assault, including rape victims, supported the value of exposing the victim to trauma-related stimuli without incident (Wirtz & Harrell, 1987). Six months after their traumatic experiences, subjects who repeatedly encountered stimuli reminiscent of their attacks—such as continuing to live in or pass by the sites of their attacks—showed less distress than those who were not exposed to them.

The U.S. government has established hundreds of storefront centers to provide counseling and outreach services to Vietnam veterans. Most therapists encourage patients to confront their traumatic memories and work through their feelings in the therapeutic environment.

Counseling a Vietnam veteran with post-traumatic stress disorder.   Storefront counseling centers have been established across the country to provide supportive services to Vietnam veterans suffering from PTSD. Here we see a Vietnam veteran discussing his experiences in the war and afterward with a counselor at a government-sponsored veterans' center in Chicago.

The following case is supportive of the use of exposure to traumatic stimuli in a civilian disaster. It also shows how therapy can be approached from various perspectives:

Margaret was a 54-year-old woman who lived with her husband Travis in a small village in the hills to the east of the Hudson River. Two winters earlier, in the middle of the night, a fuel truck had skidded down one of the icy inclines that led into the village center. Two blocks away, Margaret was shaken from her bed by the explosion ("I thought the world was coming to an end. My husband said the Russians must've dropped the H-bomb.") when the truck slammed into the general store. The store and the apartments above were immediately engulfed in flames. The fire spread to the church next door. Margaret's first and most enduring visual impression was of shards of red and black that rose into the air in an eerie ballet. On their way down, they bathed the centuries-old tombstones in the church graveyard in hellish light. A dozen people died, mostly those who had lived above and in back of the general store. The old caretaker of the church and the truck driver were lost as well.

Margaret shared the village's loss, took in the temporarily homeless, and did her share of what had to be done. Months later, after the general store had been leveled to a memorial park and the church was on the way toward being restored, Margaret started to feel that life was becoming strange, that the world outside was becoming a little unreal. She began to withdraw from her friends and scenes of the night of the fire would fill her mind. At night she now and then dreamt the scene. Her physician prescribed a sleeping pill which she discontinued because "I couldn't wake up out of the dream." Her physician turned to Valium, a minor tranquilizer, to help her get through the day. The pills helped for a while, but "I quit them because I needed more and more of the things and you can't take drugs forever, can you?"

Over the next year and a half, Margaret tried her best not to think about the disaster, but the intrusive recollections and the dreams came and went, apparently on their own. By the time Margaret visited the community mental health center, her sleep had been seriously distressed for nearly two months and the recollections were as vivid as ever.

After the initial interview, Margaret's case was discussed by an interdisciplinary treatment team representing a variety of perspectives. John, one of the social workers, had a psychodynamic perspective. John believed that Margaret had deep-seated concerns or conflicts about her "empty nest" (the children had left home) and about her womanhood, now that childbearing and child rearing were behind her. When asked to formulate a treatment approach, John responded, "I think she's got to do some talking about her feelings, to help her identify the underlying conflicts she faces. But the main thing for her to do is get involved with things that will substitute for the gratification of raising a family. This woman was fully invested in her children. Her husband is still out working every day, and she sits alone in the house. That's no life."

Myrna, a psychologist who had an **eclectic** *orientation, agreed that talking about the incident would help because it would reexpose Margaret to the distressing stimuli in a warm, therapeutic environment. "It will help Margaret gain a sense of control or mastery over the thing. Now she's a victim of intrusive images. By talking about it she will put these images in perspective. I also agree with John that she should be encouraged to do something during the day. This woman has got no life."*

A behaviorally oriented social worker concurred. "By talking about the fire while she remains relatively relaxed, the fear associated with the fire will gradually become extinguished. I'd also like to see her take some classes, do some volunteer work, maybe get a job. The outside stimulation will compete for attention with the memories [of the fire]."

"What about something to help her sleep better?" asked a nurse.

"I don't think so," the team psychiatrist said. "She doesn't like medicine and she hasn't asked for it. She may doze away half the day, anyway. I agree with John and Myrna. Margaret doesn't need a night of sleep; she needs a life."

John, the social worker, saw Margaret once a week. During that time Margaret talked about the incident and John encouraged her to find activities to fill her days. Margaret and Travis did not have enough money for a second car, so Travis brought her into the city with him when he went to work. Margaret got a part-time job at the cash register in a hospital coffee shop, and she took a crafts course at the YWCA.

After 6 months Margaret still thought about the fire, but her mental imagery did not seem intrusive or beyond her control and her sleeping was improved.

■ *The Authors' Files*

■ BEHAVIORAL TREATMENT OF OBSESSIVE-COMPULSIVE DISORDER

Behavior therapy for obsessive-compulsive disorder usually involves a combination of exposure and response prevention (Foa et al., 1985). Exposure involves the purposeful placement of the individual in situations that evoke obsessive thoughts. For many people, such situations are hard to avoid. Leaving the house, for example, can trigger obsessional thoughts about whether or not the gas jets are turned off or the windows and doors are locked. Response prevention means physically preventing the compulsive behavior. Exposure with response prevention helps obsessive-compulsives learn to tolerate the anxiety they experience when they are prevented from performing their compulsive rituals. With repeated exposure, the anxiety eventually subsides and the person feels less compelled to perform the ritual.

Exposure with response prevention may be used, for example, in the cases of people with obsessions that their hands are contaminated by germs and who feel compelled to repeatedly wash their hands. The treatment plan may call for the client to be exposed to sources of contamination such as digging in the dirt with bare hands and to be prevented washing immediately afterward. Clients who complain of checking rituals may be exposed to situations in which they experience checking urges, such as leaving their homes, and prevented from rechecking the appliances or the lock. Exposure trials are usually structured in a hierarchy of increasingly stressful situations. In one study, exposure and response prevention resulted in improvement in 65 to 75% of approximately 200 obsessive-compulsive clients (Skeketee & Foa, 1986).

■ **RELAXATION TRAINING IN TREATING GENERALIZED ANXIETY** Behavior therapists often treat generalized anxiety with relaxation training (Rapee, 1991). Such training usually involves some variation of progressive relaxation, biofeedback, or breathing exercises. A combination of progressive relaxation and cognitive techniques that counter self-defeating thoughts has been found helpful to college undergraduates with milder forms of generalized anxiety disorder (Borkovec et al., 1987) and to older clients with more severe generalized anxiety and panic disorders (Borkovec & Mathews, 1988).

Behavioral treatments are frequently combined with cognitive techniques. People with generalized anxiety may use calming, rational thoughts to counter irrational, catastrophizing ideas. In a study of the factors that contributed to improvement among 45 clients with generalized anxiety, one factor was basically behavioral (exposure to anxiety-related cues), but two were primarily cognitive: modification of anxiety-related thoughts and the enhancement of self-efficacy expectancies (Butler et al., 1987). Another experiment with people with generalized anxiety disorder compared a behavioral treatment program, consisting of relaxation training and gradual exposure to anxiety situations with a cognitive-behavioral treatment program, in which attention

was also focused on changing anxiety-producing thoughts (Butler et al., 1991). Results showed that cognitive behavior therapy generally proved more effective than behavior therapy alone. Let us now consider cognitive approaches in more detail.

Cognitive Approaches

Cognitive methods help clients identify and modify self-defeating and distorted thoughts and beliefs that contribute to anxiety. Cognitive treatment of social phobia, for example, generally involves helping clients learn to identify, challenge, and correct dysfunctional cognitions, such as beliefs that it is horrible to be rejected or that one cannot tolerate rejection (Heimberg et al., 1990). Role playing of social encounters (e.g., approaching someone for a date) is often used to ferret out and correct problem cognitions.

Two of the more important cognitive theorists are Albert Ellis, the developer of rational-emotive therapy, and Aaron Beck, the originator of cognitive therapy.

■ **RATIONAL-EMOTIVE THERAPY AND COGNITIVE THERAPY** Through his rational-emotive approach, Ellis might show social phobics how irrational needs for social approval and perfectionism engender unnecessary anxiety in social interactions. Lessening social phobics' exaggerated needs for social approval is apparently a key therapeutic factor (Butler, 1989). Through his cognitive therapy methods, Beck might point out how cognitive errors such as dwelling on perceived weaknesses, catastrophizing disappointments, and anticipating failure in all social endeavors give rise to social fears and avoidance (Beck & Emery, 1985).

Beck's cognitive therapy seeks to identify and correct dysfunctional or distorted beliefs. For example, social phobics might think that no one at a party will want to talk with them and that they will wind up lonely and isolated for the rest of their lives (Butler, 1989). Cognitive therapists help clients recognize the logical flaws in their thinking and view situations differently. Clients may be asked to consider whether their beliefs are logical or assume the worst. Therapists may encourage clients to test their beliefs by attending a party, initiating conversations, and monitoring other people's reactions as "homework." Therapists may also help clients develop social skills and teach them how to handle social rejection without catastrophizing.

■ **COGNITIVE RESTRUCTURING** In the method of **cognitive restructuring,** therapists help clients pinpoint their self-defeating thoughts and generate rational alternatives to help them cope with anxiety and other negative emotions. Consider the case of Phyllis:

Phyllis, a 32-year-old writer and mother of two sons, had not been on an elevator in 16 years. Her life revolved around finding ways to avoid appointments and social events on high floors. She had suffered from fear of elevators since the age of 8, when she had been stuck between floors with her grandmother.

To help overcome her fear of elevators, Phyllis imagined herself getting stuck in an elevator and countering the self-defeating thoughts she might experience with rational statements. She closed her eyes and reported the thoughts that would come to mind. The psychologist encouraged her to create a rational counterpoint to each of them. She then repeated the exercise in imagination and practiced replacing the self-defeating thoughts with rational alternatives, as in the following examples:

Self-Defeating Thought	Rational Alternative
Oh, oh, I'm stuck. I'm going to lose control.	*Relax. Just think coolly, what do I have to do next?*
I can't take it. I'm going to pass out.	*Okay, practice your deep breathing. Help will be coming shortly.*
I'm having a panic attack. I can't stand it.	*You've experienced all these feelings before. Just let them pass through.*
If it takes hours, that would be horrible.	*That would be annoying, but it wouldn't necessarily be horrible. I've gotten stuck in traffic longer than that.*
I've got to get out of here.	*Stay calm. There's no real danger. I can sit down and imagine I'm somewhere else until someone comes to help.*

■ *The Authors' Files*

■ **COGNITIVE FACTORS IN THE TREATMENT OF PANIC DISORDER** According to the cognitive model of panic, people who are susceptible to panic disorder are likely to react to cardiovascular sensations as signs that a catastrophe, like having a heart attack, is about to happen. By catastrophizing their symptoms, panic sufferers set the stage for a vicious cycle in which anxiety spirals to the point that a full-blown panic attack ensues. Cognitive therapists help panic sufferers think differently about their physical symptoms, such as passing sensations of dizziness or heart palpitations. Receiving corrective information that these sensations will subside naturally and are not signs of an impending catastrophe helps clients to reattribute the unpleasant sensations of panic to less threatening sources (Beck et al., 1992; Salkovskis et al., 1991). (Persons who complain of cardiovascular symptoms should also be evaluated medically to ensure they are physically healthy.)

Clinicians are finding that breathing retraining is also proving helpful in the treatment of panic disorder (Garssen et al., 1992; Ley, 1991). Breathing retraining techniques focus on restoring a normal level of carbon dioxide in the blood by means of such techniques as slow, deep (abdominal) breathing (Garssen et al., 1992). Clients are taught to breathe slowly and deeply (to avoid the shallow, rapid breathing that characterizes hyperventilation) and—on a cognitive level—to replace catastrophizing thoughts with calming, rational thoughts. In some treatment programs (for example, Clark et al., 1985), people with panic disorder purposefully hyperventilate to produce cardiovascular symptoms and discover for themselves the relationship between breathing off too much carbon dioxide and panic. In this way, clients build tolerance for such sensations and learn that they do not lead to dire consequences.

Evidence suggests that multifaceted cognitive-behavioral programs can be helpful in treating panic disorder (Craske et al., 1991; Klosko et al., 1990; Michelson et al., 1990). Such programs employ treatment elements such as relaxation training; deep, regular breathing; cognitive restructuring; corrective information about the import of cardiovascular symptoms; and in vivo (actual) and imaginary exposure to cardiovascular symptoms. Elements of cognitive-behavioral programs are shown in Table 5.5.

A review of behavioral, cognitive, and pharmacological treatments of panic disorder with agoraphobia found compelling evidence that both cognitive-behavioral therapy and antidepressant medication are effective treatments (Michelson & Marchione, 1991). The reviewers found that the treatment of choice for panic disorder without accompanying avoidance (agoraphobia) is cognitive-behavioral therapy, consisting of training in skills relating to handling panic attacks without catastrophizing, breathing retraining,

A CLOSER LOOK

Controlling a Panic Attack

People who have panic attacks usually feel their hearts pounding such that they are overwhelmed and unable to cope. They typically feel an urge to flee the situation as quickly as possible. If escape is impossible, they may become immobilized and "freeze" until the attack dissipates.

What can you do if you suffer a panic attack or an intense anxiety reaction? Let us suggest a few coping responses:

- Don't let your breathing get out of hand. Breathe slowly and deeply.
- Try breathing into a paper bag. The carbon dioxide in the bag may help you calm down by reversing the effects of hyperventilation.

 When hyperventilation is contributing to the onset of a panic attack, one may in fact be able to avert or shorten the attack by breathing into a paper bag.

- "Talk yourself down." Tell yourself to relax. Tell yourself that you're not going to die. Tell yourself that no matter how painful the attack is, it is likely to pass soon.
- Find someone to help you through the attack. Telephone someone you know and trust. Talk about anything at all until you regain control.
- Don't fall into the trap of making yourself housebound to avert future attacks.
- If you are uncertain as to whether or not sensations such as pain or tightness in the chest have physical causes, seek immediate medical assistance. Even if you suspect that your attack may "only" be one of anxiety, it is safer to have a medical evaluation than to diagnose yourself.

You need not suffer recurrent panic attacks and fears about loss of control. If attacks are persistent or frightening, consult a professional. When in doubt, see a professional.

Table 5.5	Elements of Cognitive-Behavioral Programs for Treatment of Panic Disorder
Self-Monitoring	Keeping a log of panic attacks to help determine situational stimuli that might trigger them.
Exposure	Some form of direct exposure to the triggering events helps panic clients learn to tone down their anxiety before it spirals out of control, leading to a full-blown attack.
Development of Coping Responses	Developing coping skills to interrupt the vicious cycle in which overreactions to anxiety cues or cardiovascular sensations culminate in panic attacks. Behavioral methods focus on deep, regular breathing and relaxation training. Cognitive methods focus on cognitive restructuring of anxiety cues and cardiovascular sensations.

Sources: Adapted from Beitman, 1987; Rapee, 1987.

exposure to bodily cues associated with panic, and training in relaxation skills. For panic disorder with agoraphobia, additional behavioral treatment in the form of gradual exposure to anxiety-evoking situations, perhaps assisted by the therapist, is advised. Clients who fail to respond to these treatments, or who are also depressed, may benefit from a combination of antidepressant medication and cognitive-behavioral therapy.

In this chapter we have explored the diagnostic class of anxiety disorders. In the next chapter we examine dissociative and somatoform disorders, which have been historically linked to the anxiety disorders as neuroses.

SUMMARY

Anxiety, a generalized sense of apprehension or fear, is normal and desirable under some conditions, but it can become abnormal when it is excessive or inappropriate. Anxiety may be experienced with a range of physical features, cognitions, and behaviors.

Historical Perspectives on Anxiety Disorders

Disorders involving anxiety were historically classified as neuroses, which were originally believed to be organic in nature. Psychodynamic theory posited that the origins of neurosis lay in psychological factors, that neuroses reflected the threat of the conscious emergence of repressed unacceptable impulses. Freud believed that the different kinds of neuroses reflected the different ways in which the ego defended itself from anxiety. This etiological hypothesis united current anxiety, dissociative, and somatoform disorders as neuroses.

Panic Disorder

Panic disorder is characterized by repeated panic attacks, which involve intense physical features, notably cardiovascular symptoms, that may be accompanied by sheer terror and fears of losing control, losing one's mind, or dying. Etiological speculation focuses on biological causes or interactions between biological and cognitive factors. Panic attack sufferers often limit their outside activity in fear of recurrent attacks. This can lead to agoraphobia, the fear of venturing into public places.

Generalized Anxiety Disorder

Generalized anxiety disorder involves persistent anxiety that seems to be "free-floating." Persons with other anxiety disorders often meet diagnostic criteria for generalized anxiety disorder, so questions persist about whether it is a distinct diagnostic category.

Phobic Disorders

Phobias are excessive irrational fears of specific objects or situations. Phobias involve a behavioral component, avoidance of the phobic stimulus, in addition to physical and cognitive features. There are different types of phobias. Specific phobias are excessive fears of particular objects or situations, such as mice, spiders, tight places, or heights. Social phobia involves an intense fear of being judged negatively by others. Agoraphobia involves fears of venturing into public places. In severe cases, agoraphobics can become literally housebound or venture out only with assistance. Agoraphobia may occur with or in the absence of panic disorder.

Obsessive-Compulsive Disorder

Obsessive-compulsive disorder involves recurrent patterns of obsessions, compulsions, or a combination of the two. Obsessions are nagging, persistent thoughts that create anxiety and seem beyond the person's ability to control. Compulsions are apparently irresistible repetitious urges to perform certain behaviors, such as repeated elaborate washing after using the bathroom.

Acute and Post-Traumatic Stress Disorders

In acute and post-traumatic stress disorder (PTSD), people develop stress reactions that follow exposure to traumatic events. Acute stress disorder occurs in the days and weeks following exposure to a traumatic event. Post-traumatic stress disorder persists for months or even years or decades after the traumatic experience and may not begin until months or years after the event. Many Vietnam veterans have been affected by PTSD long after returning from the battlefield. Vietnam veterans who suffer from PTSD may be less able to use problem-solving or coping skills or to draw on social support in handling stress, which may compound their difficulties.

Theoretical Perspectives

Psychodynamic theorists view anxiety disorders as attempts by the ego to control the conscious emergence of threatening impulses. Feelings of anxiety are warning signals that threatening impulses are nearing awareness. The ego mobilizes defense mechanisms to divert the impulses, thus leading to different anxiety disorders. Phobic objects symbolize aspects of unconscious conflicts, for example.

Learning theorists explain anxiety disorders through conditioning and observational learning. Mowrer's two-factor model incorporates classical and operant conditioning in the explanation of phobias. Phobias, however, appear to be moderated by cognitive factors, such as self-efficacy expectancies. The principles of reinforcement may help to explain patterns of obsessive-compulsive behavior. People may be genetically predisposed to acquire certain types of phobias that may have had survival value for our prehistoric ancestors. Cognitive factors may also play a role in the anxiety disorders, such as overpredictions of fear, irrational beliefs, self-efficacy expectancies, self-defeating thoughts, and attributions for panic attacks.

Biological perspectives have sought explanations of anxiety disorders on the basis of studies of genetic factors, neurotransmitters, and the induction of panic by biological means. Kinship studies provide evidence that genetic factors may play a role in generalized anxiety disorder and panic disorder.

Treatment of Anxiety Disorders

Each theoretical perspective is connected with methods of treating anxiety disorders. Traditional psychoanalysis helps people work through unconscious conflicts that are thought to underlie anxiety disorders. Modern psychodynamic approaches also focus on current disturbed relationships and encourage clients to assume more adaptive behavior patterns. The biological perspectives have spawned the development of various drugs to treat anxiety.

Learning perspectives encompass a broad range of behavioral and cognitive-behavioral techniques to help people overcome anxiety-related problems. Exposure methods help phobics overcome fears through gradual exposure to phobic stimuli under nonarousing circumstances. Obsessive-compulsive disorder is often treated with a combination of exposure and response prevention. Relaxation training is often used to help people with generalized anxiety learn skills of self-relaxation. Behavioral treatment of PTSD incorporates progressive exposure to trauma-related cues and training in stress management skills, such as self-relaxation.

Cognitive approaches, such as rational-emotive therapy and cognitive therapy, help people identify and correct cognitive errors that give rise to or maintain anxiety disorders. Cognitive restructuring helps clients pinpoint self-defeating thoughts and substitute rational alternatives. Cognitive approaches to the treatment of panic disorder help panic-prone people learn to cope more effectively with cardiovascular and other bodily sensations.

NORMATIVE DATA FOR THE TEMPLE FEAR SURVEY INVENTORY

You may compare your responses on the Temple Fear Survey Inventory to those of 435 introductory psychology students at Temple University by using the following table. Some items tend to evoke little fear, such as vacuum cleaner noise (item 1) and dull weather (81). Others such as the death of a loved one (32) or an anticipated surgical operation (49) elicit more intense fears. How do your fears compare to the fears of this student sample?

Item	Mean Score Male	Female	Item	Mean Score Male	Female	Item	Mean Score Male	Female
1	1.1	1.0	35	1.5	2.0	68	2.1	2.3
2	2.2	2.2	36	1.8	2.0	69	1.3	1.5
3	1.5	1.7	37	1.8	1.9	70	1.6	1.5
4	2.4	2.6	38	1.5	1.7	71	1.4	2.1
5	2.0	2.8	39	1.8	1.9	72	2.0	2.4
6	1.5	1.7	40	1.7	1.9	73	1.7	2.3
7	1.3	1.2	41	1.6	2.6	74	1.6	2.1
8	1.2	1.5	42	1.8	2.7	75	1.1	1.1
9	2.5	2.9	43	1.3	1.3	76	1.6	1.7
10	1.5	1.6	44	2.0	2.8	77	1.9	2.7
11	1.6	1.8	45	1.4	1.9	78	1.1	1.1
12	2.0	2.1	46	1.8	2.1	79	1.1	1.1
13	1.5	1.6	47	1.6	1.8	80	1.4	1.4
14	1.1	1.5	48	1.9	2.7	81	1.1	1.1
15	1.6	1.8	49	2.5	2.7	82	1.1	1.1
16	1.7	1.8	50	1.7	2.1	83	1.7	1.8
17	2.0	2.0	51	1.4	2.0	84	1.7	2.0
18	1.3	1.7	52	1.6	1.8	85	1.1	1.2
19	1.5	1.6	53	1.5	1.9	86	1.8	1.9
20	2.0	2.1	54	2.2	2.6	87	1.6	2.2
21	1.6	1.6	55	2.0	2.1	88	1.1	1.2
22	1.9	2.1	56	2.5	2.6	89	1.1	1.4
23	1.4	1.7	57	2.3	2.3	90	1.7	1.9
24	1.4	1.6	58	1.5	1.7	91	2.2	2.4
25	2.2	3.1	59	1.6	1.6	92	1.4	1.3
26	2.6	2.7	60	1.6	1.7	93	2.3	2.3
27	2.7	2.4	61	1.7	1.9	94	2.0	2.1
28	2.1	2.0	62	1.4	1.4	95	1.6	1.5
29	2.2	2.1	63	1.5	1.7	96	1.1	1.7
30	1.7	1.7	64	1.7	1.7	97	1.1	1.2
31	2.4	2.7	65	1.7	2.2	98	1.8	1.9
32	3.0	3.4	66	1.9	2.1	99	1.9	2.1
33	1.2	1.8	67	1.4	1.5	100	2.1	2.0
34	1.2	1.4						

Paul Giovanopoulos, Mona Lisa, 1988. Acrylic and mixed media on canvas: 72×54 inches. Lois K. Meisel Gallery. New York.

Chapter Outline

6

Dissociative and Somatoform Disorders

TRUTH or FICTION?

___ Some people have several personalities, and each personality may have its own allergies and eye-glass prescription.

___ Experienced clinicians can determine whether or not people are faking amnesia for their misdeeds.

___ At some time or another, the majority of young adults feel that they are detached from their own bodies or thought processes.

___ The great majority of people with multiple personalities were physically or sexually abused as children.

___ College students can be cued to adopt the role of a multiple personality.

___ People have lost all feeling in their hands and legs, although nothing has been medically wrong with them.

___ In China, 2,000 people recently fell prey to the belief that their genitals were shrinking and retracting into their bodies.

___ Some people show up repeatedly at hospital emergency rooms, feigning illness and seeking treatment for no apparent reason.

*I*n the Middle Ages, the clergy exorcised the possessed to bring forth demons. Curious incantations were heard during the contests for victims' souls.

Curious phrasings were also heard recently in 20th-century Los Angeles. They were intended to evoke another sort of demon from a suspect in a police inquest—Kenneth Bianchi. At one point, the question was put to Bianchi, "Part, are you the same thing as Ken or are you different?" The question was styled not by the clergy but by a police psychiatrist. The interviewee had been dubbed the "Hillside strangler" by the press. He had terrorized the city, leaving prostitutes dead in the mountains that bank the metropolis.

Under hypnosis—not religious incantations—Bianchi claimed that a hidden personality named "Steve" had committed the murders. "Ken" knew nothing of them. Bianchi claimed to be suffering from multiple personality disorder, one of the intriguing but perplexing diagnostic categories we explore in this chapter.

In Chapter 5, we reviewed the anxiety disorders, which were classified as neuroses in the first and second editions of the *Diagnostic and Statistical Manual* (DSM) and conceptualized according to the psychodynamic model. The writers of the earlier editions of the DSM were heavily influenced by psychodynamic theory in their conceptualizations and categorization of disorders. Neuroses were chiefly characterized by anxiety. More recent editions of the DSM classify disorders more on the basis of descriptive criteria and observable behavior than on theoretical formulations. The DSM now includes a category of anxiety disorders to refer to abnormal behavior patterns in which anxiety either causes distress or interferes with functioning.

In this chapter, we focus on two classes of disorders, the dissociative and somatoform disorders, which were also categorized as neuroses in early editions of the DSM. They were related to anxiety in theory, however, not in terms of observable behavior. Unlike the other forms of neuroses, the role of anxiety in the dissociative and somatoform disorders was inferred rather than expressed in behavior. Persons with *dissociative disorders* may show no signs of overt anxiety, in fact. However, they manifest other psychological problems, such as loss of memory or changes in identity, that are theorized within the psychodynamic model to serve the purpose of keeping the underlying sources of anxiety out of awareness. Persons with *somatoform disorders* complain of physical symptoms that have no apparent organic basis. They often manifest a queer indifference to physical ailments that would concern most of us. Here, too, it is theorized that the "symptoms" mask unconscious sources of anxiety. Some theorists interpret indifference to symptoms to mean that there is an underlying benefit to them; that is, they help prevent anxiety from intruding into consciousness.

The DSM now separates the anxiety disorders from the other categories of neuroses—the dissociative and somatoform disorders—with which they were historically linked. Yet many practitioners continue to use the broad conceptualization of neuroses as a useful framework for classifying the anxiety, dissociative, and somatoform disorders.

Billy Milligan

DISSOCIATIVE DISORDERS

The key feature of the **dissociative disorders** is a change or disturbance in the functions of self-identity, memory, or consciousness that make the personality whole. Normally speaking, we know who we are. We may not be certain of ourselves in an existential, philosophical sense, but we know our names, where we live, and what we do for a living. We also tend to remember the salient events of our lives. We may not recall every detail, and we may confuse what we ate for dinner on Tuesday with what we had on Monday, but we generally know what we have been doing for the past days, weeks, and years. Normally speaking, there is a unity to consciousness that gives rise to a sense of self. We perceive ourselves as progressing through space and time. In the dissociative disorders, one or more of these aspects of daily living is disturbed—sometimes bizarrely so.

The major dissociative disorders include *dissociative identity disorder, dissociative amnesia, dissociative fugue,* and *depersonalization disorder.* In each case there is a disruption or dissociation (splitting-off) of the functions of identity, memory, or consciousness that normally make us whole.

Dissociative Identity Disorder

*T*he Ohio State campus dwelled in terror as four college women were seized, coerced to cash checks or get money from automatic teller machines, then raped. A cryptic phone call led to the capture of Billy Milligan, a 23-year-old drifter who had been dishonorably discharged from the Navy.

Billy wasn't quite the boy next door.

He tried twice to commit suicide while he was awaiting trial, so his lawyers requested a psychiatric evaluation. The psychologists and psychiatrists who examined Billy deduced that ten personalities dwelled inside of him. Eight were male and two were female. Billy's personality had been fractured by a brutal childhood. The personalities displayed diverse facial expressions, memories, and vocal patterns. They performed in dissimilar ways on personality and intelligence tests.

Arthur, a sensible but phlegmatic personality, conversed with a British accent. Danny, 14, was a painter of still lifes. Christopher, 13, was normal enough, but somewhat anxious. A 3-year-old English girl went by the name of Christine. Tommy, a 16-year-old, was an antisocial personality and escape artist. It was Tommy who had enlisted in the Navy. Allen was an 18-year-old con artist. Allen also smoked. Adelena was a 19-year-old introverted lesbian. It was she who had committed the rapes. It was probably David who had made the mysterious phone call. David was an anxious 9-year-old who wore the anguish of early childhood trauma on his sleeve. After his second suicide attempt, Billy had been placed in a straitjacket. When the guards checked his cell, however, he was sleeping with the straitjacket as a pillow. Tommy later explained that he had effected Billy's escape.

The defense argued that Billy was afflicted with multiple personality disorder. Several alternate personalities resided within him. The alternate personalities knew about Billy, but Billy was unaware of them. Billy, the core or dominant personality, had learned as a child that he could sleep as a way of avoiding the sexual and physical abuse of his father. A psychiatrist claimed that Billy had likewise been "asleep"—in a sort of "psychological coma"—when the crimes were committed. Therefore, Billy should be judged innocent by reason of insanity.

Billy was decreed not guilty by reason of insanity. He was committed to a mental institution. In the institution, 14 additional personalities emerged. Thirteen were rebellious and labeled "undesirables" by Arthur. The fourteenth was the "Teacher," who was competent and supposedly represented the integration of all the other personalities. Billy was released six years later.

■ *Adapted from Keyes, 1982*

Billy was adjudged to be suffering from multiple personality disorder, which is now called **dissociative identity disorder**. In dissociative identity disorder, which is sometimes referred to as "split personality," two or more personalities—each with well-defined traits and memories—"occupy" one person. They may or may not be aware of one another. Various personalities may even require different eyeglass prescriptions (Miller et al., 1991).

Braun (1986) reports cases in which different personalities display different allergic reactions. In one person, a personality called Timmy was not susceptible to orange juice. When other personalities took control and drank orange juice, they would erupt in hives. Hives would also break out when Timmy drank orange juice if another personality appeared while the juice was being digested. Moreover, if Timmy reemerged when the allergic reaction was in full sway, the hives at once would cease to itch, and the blisters—filled with water—would begin to recede. In other cases, different personalities in the same person show different responses to the same medicine. Or one personality is color blind, whereas others have sound color vision (Braun, 1986). If fascinating cases such as these stand up to further scientific scrutiny, they would offer a remarkable illustration of the diversity of perceptions and somatic patterns that are possible within the same person.

 People with multiple personality disorder (MPD) are considered to have several personalities, and some evidence suggests that each personality may in fact have its own allergies and eyeglass prescription.

Celebrated cases of multiple personality have been depicted in the popular media. One became the subject of the film *The Three Faces of Eve*. In the film Eve White is a timid housewife who harbors two other personalities: Eve Black, a libidinous antisocial personality, and Jane, a balanced, developing personality who could accept her primitive urges but still engage in socially appropriate behavior (see Figure 6.1). The three faces eventually merged into one—Jane, providing a "happy ending." In real life, however, Eve was Chris Sizemore. After Sizemore's personality was apparently integrated, it reportedly split into 22 subsequent personalities. A second well-known case is that of Sybil. Sybil was played by Sally Field in the film of the name and reportedly had 16 personalities.

In one of the largest studies on multiple personality to date, Ross and his colleagues (1989) collected 236 case reports of people with the disorder from 203 health professionals in Canada. Unlike reports of multiple personality in the 19th and early 20th centuries, in which most cases involved dual personalities, cases in the Canadian sample averaged 15 to 16 alter personalities each (Ross et al., 1989).

There are many variations of multiple personality. Sometimes two personalities vie for control of the person. Sometimes there is one dominant or core personality and several subordinate personalities. Some of the more common alternate personalities (or "alter personalities") include children of various ages, including one whose emotions were shaped by parental abuse; adolescents of the opposite gender; prostitutes; and homosexuals. In the Canadian study of 236 cases of multiple personality, a child personality was present in 86% of cases; a personality of a different age in 85% of cases; a protector personality, in 84%; and a persecutor personality, also in 84% of cases (Ross et al., 1989). Some of the personalities may appear psychotic.

All in all, the clusters of alter personalities serve as something of a microcosm of conflicting urges and cultural themes. Themes of sexual ambivalence and ambiguity are particularly common. It is as if conflicting internal impulses cannot coexist or achieve dominance. As a result, each is expressed as the cardinal or steering trait of an alternate personality. The clinician can sometimes elicit alternate personalities by inviting them to make themselves known, as in asking, "Is there another part of you that wants to say something to me?"

The case of Margaret illustrates the emergence of an alternate personality:

*[M*argaret explained that] she often "heard a voice telling her to say things and do things." It was, she said, "a terrible voice" that sometimes threatened to "take over completely." When it was finally suggested to [Margaret] that she let the voice "take over," she closed her eyes, clenched her fists, and grimaced for a few moments dur-*

(A)   (B)   (C)

Figure 6.1 *The Three Faces of Eve.*
In the film *The Three Faces of Eve*, a timid housewife, Eve White (A), harbors two alter
personalities: Eve Black (B), a libidinous antisocial personality, and Jane (C), an integrated
personality who can accept her sexual and aggressive urges but still engage in socially
appropriate behavior. In real life, however, the person depicted in the film reportedly split
into 22 personalities later in life.

*ing which she was out of contact with those around her.
Suddenly she opened her eyes and one was in the presence of another person. Her name, she said, was "Harriet." Whereas Margaret had been paralyzed, and complained of fatigue, headache and backache, Harriet felt
well, and she at once proceeded to walk unaided around
the interviewing room. She spoke scornfully of Margaret's religiousness, her invalidism, and her puritanical
life, professing that she herself liked to drink and "go
partying" but that Margaret was always going to church
and reading the Bible. "But," she said impishly and
proudly, "I make her miserable—I make her say and do
things she doesn't want to." At length, at the interviewer's suggestion, Harriet reluctantly agreed to "bring
Margaret back," and after more grimacing and fist
clenching, Margaret reappeared, paralyzed, complaining
of her headache and backache, and completely amnesiac
for the brief period of Harriet's release from prison.*

■ *Nemiah, 1978, pp. 179–180*

As with Billy Milligan, Chris Sizemore, and
Margaret, the dominant personality is often unaware
of the existence of the alternate personalities. It thus
seems that the mechanism of dissociation is controlled by unconscious processes. Although the dominant personality lacks insight into the existence of
the other personalities, she or he may vaguely sense

that something is amiss. There may even be "inter-
personality rivalry" in which one personality aspires
to do away with another, usually in blissful ignorance
of the fact that conferring the *coup de grace* on an
alternate would result in the death of all. The diagnostic features of dissociative identity disorder are
listed in Table 6.1.

Although multiple personality is generally considered to be rare, its prevalence is a topic of debate.

**Table 6.1: Diagnostic Features of Dissociative
Identity Disorder (Multiple Personality Disorder)**

1. At least two distinct personalities exist within the
   person, with each having a relatively enduring and
   distinct pattern of perceiving, thinking about, and
   relating to the environment and the self.

2. Two or more of these personalities repeatedly take
   complete control of the individual's behavior.

3. Failure to recall important personal information that
   is too substantial to be accounted for by ordinary forgetfulness.

4. The disorder cannot be accounted for by the effects of
   a psychoactive substance or a general medical condition.

*Source: Adapted from DSM-IV Draft Criteria (American Psychiatric
Association, 1993), p. N: 1.*

It is difficult to acquire reliable information about how frequently it occurs. Few psychologists have ever encountered a case of multiple personality. The first case was reported in 1817 (Boor, 1982). The majority of cases involve women (Kluft, 1984a; Ross et al., 1989; Schafer, 1986). Some practitioners have suggested that multiple personality is more common than is generally believed (Bliss & Jeppsen, 1985; Schafer, 1986). Others believe that the research evidence does not clearly demonstrate greater prevalence (Ludolph, 1985). One problem with determining the prevalence of multiple personality is that estimates are often obtained from clinicians who specialize in treating the disorder and who may see more cases of multiple personality than other clinicians do (Ludolph, 1985). Increased public attention paid to the disorder in recent years may also account for the perception that its prevalence is greater than is commonly believed.

In any event, multiple personality may not be all that unusual among some subgroups in the population, such as among psychiatric inpatients. In one study of 484 adult psychiatric inpatients, at least 5% showed evidence of multiple personality (Ross et al., 1991). Your authors have noted a tendency for *claims* of multiple personality to spread on inpatient units. In one case, Susan, a prostitute admitted for depression and suicidal thoughts, claimed that she could only exchange sex for money when "another person" inside her emerged and took control. (Suicidal behavior is common among people with multiple personalities. Seventy-two percent of the cases in the Canadian study [Ross et al., 1989] had attempted suicide, and about 2% had succeeded.) Upon hearing this, another woman, Ginny—a child abuser who had been admitted for depression after her daughter had been removed from her home by social service—later claimed that she only abused her daughter when another person inside of her assumed control of her personality. Susan's chart recommended that she be evaluated further for multiple personality disorder (the term used at the time for the disorder), but Ginny was diagnosed with a depressive disorder and a personality disorder, not with multiple personality disorder.

Multiple personality, which is often called "split personality" by laypeople, should not be confused with schizophrenia. Schizophrenia (which comes from roots that mean "split brain") occurs much more commonly than multiple personality, and involves the "splitting" of cognition, affect, and behavior. There may thus be little agreement between the thoughts and the emotions, or between the individual's perception of reality and what is truly happening. The schizophrenic, for example, may become giddy when told of disturbing events, or may experience hallucinations or delusions. In people with multiple personalities, the personality apparently divides into two or more personalities, but each of them usually shows more integrated functioning on cognitive, affective, and behavioral levels than is true of people with schizophrenia.

Clouding the issue of diagnosis, however, is the finding that some people with multiple personalities also show behaviors associated with schizophrenia, such as auditory and visual hallucinations (Kluft, 1987). Although dissociative identity disorder is not considered a form of schizophrenia, the dominant personalities of people with the disorder may report auditory hallucinations like two voices arguing about them. One of the voices may be threatening and the other protective. Another common auditory hallucination involves voices that provide a running commentary on the dominant personality's behavior, often derogatory. (The subordinate personalities typically comment on the dominant personality.)

Some people with the disorder complain of being "possessed" but are actually experiencing the influence of an alter personality. Many clinicians, however, are likely to take a claim of being possessed as a type of schizophrenic delusion. Perhaps more cases of dissociative identity disorder would be diagnosed if the competing diagnosis of schizophrenia were not so common (Putnam et al., 1986). Clinicians may also be reluctant to report a case of multiple personality for fear that others might believe that they had been duped by clients who faked their symptoms. Some clinicians have been accused of being in collusion with their clients to protect them from, say, criminal charges, by providing them with a basis for a pleading of "not guilty by reason of insanity."

Clinicians may also be reluctant to make a diagnosis of dissociative identity disorder because it is considered rare and its features can overlap those of other diagnoses. People with the disorder may thus go unrecognized or receive other diagnoses for years after their initial evaluations (Schafer, 1986). In a study of 100 persons with multiple personalities, the mean length of time between initial assessment and ultimate diagnosis of the disorder was nearly 7 years (Putnam et al., 1986). These people averaged 3.6 alternative diagnoses in the process. These alternative diagnoses may also reflect the finding that persons with multiple personalities display a wide range of abnormal behaviors, including physical complaints with no known organic basis; amnesia; depression and suicidal behavior; anxiety and panic attacks; and other disturbances in states of consciousness, such as depersonalization and **derealization** (Bliss, 1984).

Several features may alert the clinician to the possible presence of a multiple personality:

1. Amnesic periods ("blackouts") in the dominant personality (Schafer, 1986).
2. Severe physical or sexual abuse in childhood.
3. A stormy or turbulent history of psychiatric or psychological treatment (Schafer, 1986).
4. A nickname that does not fit the individual's dominant personality. Perhaps an alter personality is known by that name to others (Schafer, 1986).
5. High hypnotizability (ability to be hypnotized) (Bliss, 1984). Braun (1986) suggests that hypnotizability may be used as a diagnostic criterion when it is necessary to distinguish between various diagnostic possibilities.

Some persons with multiple personalities lead surprisingly accomplished lives, in fact. Three such cases, two physicians and a research scientist, were recently reported (Kluft, 1986). High-functioning multiple personalities often elude diagnosis because clinicians are not likely to probe for evidence of the disorder among functional clients. Accomplished people with multiple personalities also may have developed elaborate strategies to cloak their alter personalities. Sometimes alter personalities apparently cooperate with the effort to keep them out of the limelight. The careers of such individuals are stabilizing influences, and they may maintain a veneer of normality for fear of losing them.

Dissociative Amnesia

Amnesia derives from the Greek roots *a-*, meaning "not," and *mnasthai,* meaning "to remember." In **dissociative amnesia**, (formerly called *psychogenic amnesia*) there is sudden inability to recall important personal information usually involving material relating to traumatic or stressful experiences, that cannot be accounted for by simple forgetfulness. Nor can the memory loss be attributed to a particular organic cause, such as a blow to the head or a particular medical condition, or to the direct effects of drugs or alcohol. Dissociative amnesia may last for hours or years. Termination of amnesia tends to occur suddenly and spontaneously.

There are four types of dissociative amnesia: localized, selective, generalized, and continuous:

1. **Localized amnesia**. In this most common type, events that occur during a specific time period are lost to memory. For example, the person cannot recall events for a number of hours after a stressful or traumatic incident, as in warfare or as in the case of the uninjured survivor of an accident.
2. **Selective amnesia**. In this form of amnesia, people forget only the disturbing particulars that take place during a certain time period. A person may recall the period of life during which he conducted an extramarital affair, but not the guilt-arousing affair itself. The soldier may recall most of the battle, but not the death of his buddy.
3. **Generalized amnesia**. In generalized amnesia, people forget their entire lives—who they are, what they do, where they live, whom they live with. This form of amnesia is rare, but it is the one most likely to be depicted in daytime soap operas and other fictional accounts. Persons with generalized amnesia cannot recall personal information, but they tend to retain their habits, tastes, and skills. If you had generalized amnesia, you would still know how to read, although you would not recall your elementary school teachers. You would still prefer French fries to baked potatoes—or vice versa.
4. **Continuous amnesia**. In this form of amnesia, people forget all events that take place after the problem begins. Everything from that time through to the present is lost, and, of course, the present keeps moving ahead. If you had continuous amnesia since the time you began college, all of your college experiences would be lost to you. You would not be able to recall what you are reading; all new information would go in one ear and out the other. Continuous amnesia is a rare form of *dissociative amnesia*.

Although only one type of dissociative amnesia is labeled selective, most instances of amnesia are selective. That is, people usually forget events or periods of life that were traumatic—that generated strong negative emotions such as horror or guilt. Consider the case of Rutger:

*H*e was brought to the emergency room of a hospital by a stranger. He was dazed and claimed not to know who he was or where he lived, and the stranger had found him wandering in the streets. Despite his confusion, it did not appear that he had been drinking or abusing drugs or that his amnesia could be attributed to physical trauma. After staying in the hospital for a few days, he awoke in distress. His memory had returned. His name was Rutger and he had urgent business to attend to. He *wanted to know why he had been hospitalized and demanded to leave. At time of admission, Rutger appeared to be suffering from general amnesia: He could not recall his identity or the personal events of his life. But now that he was requesting discharge, Rutger showed localized amnesia for the period between entering the emergency room and the morning he regained his memory for prior events.*

Rutger provided information about the events prior to his hospitalization that was confirmed by the police. On the day when his amnesia began, Rutger had killed a pedestrian with his automobile. There had been witnesses, and the police had voiced the opinion that Rutger—although emotionally devastated—was blameless in the incident. Rutger was instructed, however, to fill out an accident report and to appear at the inquest. Still nonplussed, Rutger filled out the form at a friend's home. He accidentally left his wallet and his identification there. After placing the form in a mailbox, Rutger became dazed and lost his memory.

Although Rutger was not responsible for the accident, he felt awful about the pedestrian's death. His amnesia was probably connected with feelings of guilt, the stress of the accident, and concerns about the inquest.

■ *Adapted from Cameron, 1963, pp. 355–356*

Amnesiacs seem less concerned about their memory problems than their family, friends, and the people who are trying to help them. This relative lack of concern has inspired hypotheses that the memory loss serves the adaptive function of relieving anxiety or some other kind of psychological pain associated with past trauma. Sometimes the painful circumstances can be recalled under hypnosis.

People sometimes claim that they cannot recall certain events of their lives: engaging in socially unacceptable behavior, making promises, and so forth. Falsely claiming amnesia as a way of escaping responsibility is **malingering**, an attempt to fabricate symptoms or make false claims for personal gain. Current research methods cannot guarantee that we can ferret out all malingerers.

 Experienced clinicians can *not* invariably differentiate the true amnesiac from the malingerer.

But experienced clinicians can make reasonably well-educated guesses.

Dissociative Fugue

Fugue derives from the Latin *fugere,* meaning "flight." The word *fugitive* has the same origin. Fugue is like amnesia "on the run." In **dissociative fugue** (formerly called *psychogenic fugue*), the person travels suddenly from his or her home or place of work, shows a loss of memory for past personal information, and either becomes confused about his or her identity or assumes a new identity (either partially or completely) (American Psychiatric Association, 1993). The person may not think about the past, or may report a past filled with bogus memories that are not recognized as false.

Whereas people with amnesia appear to wander aimlessly, people in a fugue state act more purposefully. Some people in a fugue state stick close to home. They spend the afternoon in the park or in a theater, or they spend the night at a hotel under another name, usually having little if any contact with others during the fugue state. But the new identity is incomplete and fleeting and the individual's former sense of self soon returns in a matter of hours or a few days. More uncommon is a pattern in which the fugue state lasts for months or years, involving travel to distant cities or foreign lands. These individuals may create new identities and pasts for themselves. They often assume an identity that is more spontaneous and sociable than their former selves, which were typically "quiet" and "ordinary." They may establish new families and successful businesses. Although these events may sound rather bizarre, the fugue state is not considered psychotic because people with the disorder can think and behave quite normally—in their new lives, that is. Then one day, quite suddenly, their awareness of their past identity returns to them, and they are flooded with old memories. Now they typically do not recall the events that occurred during the fugue state. The new identity, the new life—including all its involvements and responsibilities—vanish from memory.

Fugue, like amnesia, is rare. It is most likely to occur in wartime (Loewenstein, 1991) or in the wake of another kind of disaster. The underlying notion is that dissociation in the fugue state protects one from traumatic memories or other sources of psychological pain.

Fugue can also be difficult to distinguish from malingering. That is, a number of persons who were dissatisfied with their former lives could claim to be amnesic when they are uncovered in their new locations and new identities.

Consider the following case, in which the evidence supports a diagnosis of dissociative fugue (Spitzer et al., 1989):

*T*he man told the police that his name was Burt Tate. "Burt," a 42-year-old white male, had gotten into a fight at the diner where he worked. When the police arrived, they found that he carried no identification. He told them he had drifted into town a few weeks earlier, but could not recall where he had lived or worked before arriving in town. While no charges were pressed against him, the police prevailed upon him to come to the emergency room for evaluation. "Burt" knew the town he was in and the current date, and recognized that it was somewhat unusual that he couldn't remember his past, but didn't seem to be concerned about it. There was no evidence of any physical injuries or head trauma, or of drug or alcohol abuse. The police made some inquiries and discovered that "Burt" fit the profile of a missing person, Gene Saunders, who had disappeared a month earlier from a city some 2,000 miles away. Mrs. Saunders was called in and confirmed that "Burt" was indeed her husband. She reported that her husband, who had worked in middle-level management in a manufacturing company, had been having difficulty at work before his disappearance. He was passed over for promotion and his supervisor was highly critical of his work. The job stress apparently affected his behavior at home. Once easygoing and sociable, he withdrew into himself and began to criticize his wife and children. Then, just before his disappearance, he had a violent argument with his 18-year-old son. His son called him a "failure" and stormed out the door. Two days later, the man disappeared. When he came face to face with his wife again, he claimed he didn't recognize her, but appeared visibly nervous.

■ *Adapted from Spitzer et al., 1989, pp. 215–216*

Although the presenting evidence supported a diagnosis of psychogenic fugue, clinicians can find it difficult to distinguish true amnesia from amnesia that is faked to allow a person to get a new start in life.

Depersonalization Disorder

Depersonalization involves a temporary loss or change in the usual sense of our own reality. In a state of depersonalization, people may feel detached from their minds or bodies. They may have the sense of not being able to believe that they are where they are or that they are doing what they are doing. They may feel as though they are observing themselves or their thought processes from outside. They may feel like robots, as if they are functioning on automatic pilot. They may feel as if their movements are impaired, as if they are walking underwater or in a dream. **Derealization**—strange changes in perception of surroundings, or in the sense of the passage of time—may also be present. People and objects may seem to change in size or shape; they may sound different. All these feelings can be associated with feelings of anxiety, including dizziness and fears of going insane, or with depression.

Although these sensations are strange, people with depersonalization maintain contact with reality. They can distinguish reality from unreality, even during the depersonalization episode. In contrast with generalized amnesia and fugue, they know who they are. Their memories are intact and they know where they are—even if they do not like their present state.

Depersonalization.
Episodes of depersonalization are characterized by feelings of detachment from oneself. During an episode, it may feel as if one were walking through a dream or observing the environment or oneself from outside one's body.

Feelings of depersonalization usually come on suddenly and fade gradually.

What is even more unusual about all this is that we have thus far described only normal *feelings of depersonalization. According to the DSM, single brief episodes of depersonalization are experienced by the majority of young adults!*

 According to the DSM, the majority of young adults will at some time encounter the feeling that they are detached from their own bodies or mental processes.

Consider Richie's experience:

"*We* went to Orlando with the children after school let out. I had also been driving myself hard, and it was time to let go. We spent three days 'doing' Disneyworld, and it got to the point where we were all wearing shirts with mice and ducks on them and singing Disney songs like 'Yo ho, yo ho, a pirate's life for me.' On the third day I began to feel unreal and ill at ease while we were watching these middle-American Ivory-soap teenagers singing and dancing in front of Cinderella's Castle. The day was finally cooling down, but I broke into a sweat. I became shaky and dizzy and sat down on the cement next to the 4-year-old's stroller without giving [my wife] an explanation. There were strollers and kids and [adults'] legs all around me, and for some strange reason I became fixated on the pieces of popcorn strewn on the ground. All of a sudden it was like the people around me were all silly mechanical creatures, like the dolls in the 'It's a Small World' [exhibit] or the animals on the 'Jungle Cruise.' Things sort of seemed to slow down, the way they do when you've smoked marijuana, and there was this invisible wall of cotton between me and everyone else.

"Then the concert was over and my wife was like 'What's the matter?' and did I want to stay for the Electrical Parade and the fireworks or was I sick? Now I was beginning to wonder if I was going crazy and I said I was sick, that my wife would have to take me by the hand and drive us back to the Sonesta Village [motel]. Somehow we got back to the monorail and turned in the strollers. I waited in the herd [of people] at the station like a dead person, my eyes glazed over, looking out over kids with Mickey Mouse ears and Mickey Mouse balloons. The mechanical voice on the monorail almost did me in and I got really shaky.

"I refused to go back to the Magic Kingdom. I went with the family to Sea World, and on another day I dropped [my wife] and the kids off at the Magic Kingdom and picked them up that night. My wife thought I was goldbricking or something, and we had a helluva fight about it, but we had a life to get back to and my sanity had to come first."

■ *The Authors' Files*

Richie's depersonalization experience was limited to the one episode and would not qualify for a diagnosis of **depersonalization disorder**. Depersonalization disorder is diagnosed only when such experiences are persistent or recurrent and cause marked distress (Steinberg, 1991). The DSM diagnoses depersonalization according to the criteria shown in Table 6.2. Note the following case example:

A 20-year-old college student feared that he was going insane. For two years, he had increasingly frequent experiences of feeling "outside" himself. During these episodes, he experienced a sense of "deadness" in his body, and felt wobbly, frequently bumping into furniture. He was more apt to lose his balance during episodes which occurred when he was out in public, especially when he was feeling anxious. During these episodes, his thoughts seemed "foggy," reminding him of his state of mind when he was given shots of a pain-killing drug for an appendectomy five years earlier. He tried to fight off these episodes when they occurred, by saying "stop" to himself and by shaking his head. This would temporarily clear his head, but the feeling of being outside himself and the sense of deadness would shortly return. The dis-

Table 6.2: Diagnostic Features of Depersonalization Disorder

1. Recurrent or persistent experiences of depersonalization, which are characterized by feelings of detachment from one's mental processes or body, as if one were an outside observer of oneself. The experience may have a dream-like quality.

2. The individual is able to maintain reality testing (i.e., distinguish reality from unreality) during the depersonalization state.

3. The depersonalization experiences cause significant personal distress or impairment in one or more important areas of functioning, such as social or occupational functioning.

4. Depersonalization experiences cannot be attributed to other disorders or to the direct effects of drugs, alcohol, or medical conditions.

Source: Adapted from DSM-IV Draft Criteria (American Psychiatric Association, 1993), p. N: 2.

turbing feelings would gradually fade away over a period of hours. By the time he sought treatment, he was experiencing these episodes about twice a week, each one lasting from three to four hours. His grades remained unimpaired, and had even improved in the past several months, since he was spending more time studying. However, his girlfriend, in whom he had confided his problem, felt that he had become totally absorbed in himself and threatened to break off their relationship if he didn't change. She had also begun to date other men.

■ *Adapted from Spitzer et al., 1989, pp. 234–235*

Inclusion of depersonalization disorder as a dissociative disorder is controversial. One reason is that in contrast to the other three major dissociative disorders, there is no disturbance in memory. Another is that in multiple personality, amnesia, and fugue, dissociation seems to *protect* the individual from anxiety. In depersonalization, however, dissociation—and the resultant sense that things are unreal—frequently *generate* anxiety. Note, too, that depersonalization involves some cardiovascular sensations (e.g., dizziness) that can be blown out of proportion and generate further cycles of anxiety. Richie, for example, was motivated to avoid another visit to the Magic King-

---

QUESTIONNAIRE

The Dissociative Experiences Scale

Many of us experience brief dissociative experiences from time to time, such as transient feelings of depersonalization. Recently, researchers randomly sampled 1,055 adults in Winnipeg, Canada, and found that dissociative experiences were quite common in the general population, although they tended to decline with age (Ross et al., 1990). Dissociative disorders, by comparison, involve the occurrence of more persistent and severe dissociative experiences. Researchers have recently developed a measure, the Dissociative Experiences Scale (DES) (Bernstein & Putnam, 1986) to offer clinicians a means of measuring dissociative experiences that occur among both normal and abnormal populations. Normals tend to report fewer, and less varied, dissociative experiences than people with dissociative disorders, such as multiple personalities, but they still often report some such experiences. Following is a listing of some of the types of dissociative experiences drawn from the Dissociative Experiences Scale. Bear in mind that transient experiences such as these tend to be reported by both normal and abnormal populations in varying frequencies.

How Often Have You Experienced the Following?

1. Suddenly realizing, when you are driving the car, that you don't remember what has happened during all or part of the trip.
2. Suddenly realizing, when you are listening to someone talk, that you did not hear part or all of what the person said.
3. Finding yourself in a place and having no idea how you got there.
4. Finding yourself dressed in clothes that you don't remember putting on.
5. Being approached by other people you do not know who call you by another name and insist that they know you.
6. Experiencing a feeling that seemed as if you were standing next to yourself or watching yourself do something and actually seeing yourself as if you were looking at another person.
7. Losing the memories of important events in your life, such as your wedding or graduation.
8. Looking in a mirror and not recognizing yourself.
9. Feeling sometimes that other people, objects, and the world around you are not real.
10. Feeling sometimes that your body does not seem to belong to you.
11. Remembering a past event so vividly that it seems like you are reliving it in the present.
12. Having the experience of being in a familiar place but finding it strange and unfamiliar.
13. Becoming so absorbed in watching television or a movie that you are unaware of other events happening around you.
14. Becoming so absorbed in a fantasy or daydream that it feels as though it were really happening to you.
15. Talking out loud to yourself when you are alone.
16. Finding that you act so differently in a particular situation compared with another that it feels almost as if you were two different people.
17. Finding that you cannot remember whether or not you have just done something or perhaps had just thought about doing it (for example, not knowing whether you have just mailed a letter or have just thought about mailing it.)
18. Feeling sometimes as if you were looking at the world through a fog so that people and objects appear faraway or unclear.

Source: Bernstein, E. M., & Putnam, F. W. (1986). Development, reliability, and validity of a dissociation scale. Journal of Nervous and Mental Disease, 174, 727–735. Copyright © Williams & Wilkins, 1986.

dom at Disneyworld. He also arranged to be elsewhere when the children watched the Disney Channel.

In terms of observable behavior and associated features, depersonalization may be more closely related to disorders such as phobias and panic than to dissociative disorders. Depersonalization can motivate avoidance behavior, and our reactions to the sensations of depersonalization can generate cycles of anxiety.

Theoretical Perspectives

Exposure to psychological trauma apparently plays a preeminent role in many cases of dissociative disorders. The literature on these disorders shows overwhelming evidence of traumatic experiences. Child abuse, often sexual in nature, is especially common in the backgrounds of people with multiple personalities (Baldwin, 1990; Spiegel & Cardena, 1991; Terr, 1991). Researchers report that 83% of people with multiple personalities in one sample had been sexually abused in childhood (Putnam et al., 1986). Others had been physically abused, and 2 of 3 (68%) had been both physically and sexually abused. Incest was also reported by 2 out of 3 people with the disorder (68%). Another survey found that 95% of 102 people with multiple personalities had suffered childhood physical or sexual abuse (Ross et al., 1990). Rape was reported in 2 cases out of 3. These results indicate that dissociative identity disorder (multiple personality) is linked more closely than any other psychological disorder to a history of childhood abuse, lending support to the view that this disorder typically represents a dissociative strategy for coping with and surviving abuse in childhood (Ross et al., 1990).

 The great majority of people with multiple personalities do in fact report being physically or sexually abused as children. For this reason, many theoreticians view the disorder as developing as a defense against such abuse.

A study of psychogenic (dissociative) amnesia also underscored the role of childhood abuse: 82% of people who were diagnosed with psychogenic amnesia reported physical, sexual, or verbal abuse or neglect in their childhoods (Coons et al., 1989). Exposure to the trauma of warfare among both civilians and soldiers plays a part in some cases of fugue as well as psychogenic amnesia. In dissociative fugue, the stress of combat and the secondary gain of leaving the battlefield seem to be cardinal contributors (Loewenstein, 1991). The stress of coping with severe financial problems and the wish to avert punishment for socially unacceptable behavior are other possible antecedents to episodes of fugue (Riether & Stoudemire, 1988). Exposure to high levels of stress may also be linked to depersonalization disorder (Kluft, 1988).

Many or most instances of dissociative disorders thus apparently represent ways of surviving childhood abuse or other traumatic experiences. Psychological theories may help us understand *how* such experiences become translated into dissociative disorders.

■ **PSYCHODYNAMIC PERSPECTIVES** According to the psychodynamic model, dissociation and dissociative disorders represent psychological defenses that help people block out troubling memories and unacceptable impulses. Some children who are severely abused may retreat into alter personalities to escape their suffering psychologically. In the face of repeated abuse, alter personalities may become stabilized so that people cannot maintain a unified personality, leading to the development of multiple personalities. People with multiple personalities may be blocking out traumatic childhood memories and their emotional reactions to them—wiping the slate clean and beginning life anew in the guise of alter personalities (Schafer, 1986).

Children with more creative imaginations and richer fantasy lives may be prone to construct alter personalities as a defense against unbearable abuse. As children, people with multiple personalities showed evidence of a rich fantasy life, inventing imaginary playmates and frequently enacting games of "make believe" (Spanos et al., 1985). Adults with multiple personalities are also highly hypnotizable, which suggests that they possess the knack of disconnecting or dissociating various aspects of consciousness from others (Bliss, 1984; Wilbur, 1986). There may also be a link between self-hypnosis and multiple personality. Multiple personalities may be hypnotizing themselves into trancelike states when they enact their alter personalities (Bliss, 1984).

Dissociative disorders are theorized to involve massive use of repression to prevent recognition of unacceptable impulses. In dissociative amnesia and in fugue, the ego protects itself from becoming flooded with anxiety by blotting out disturbing memories or dissociating threatening impulses. In multiple personality, people may express unacceptable impulses through alternate personalities. In depersonalization, people stand outside themselves—safely distanced from the turmoil within.

Friends? It is normal for children to have imaginary playmates. In the case of many multiple personalities, however, games of "make-believe" and the invention of imaginary playmates may be used as psychological defenses against abuse. Research suggests that the majority of people who develop multiple personalities were abused as children.

Because of their dissociative capacities, people who develop multiple personalities may handle the intense anger and hatred that is generated by abuse by forming alter personalities to express their negative feelings. The core or dominant personality thus finds it easier to keep such feelings repressed, easing the burden of the ego to censor them. Wilbur (1986) notes that sometimes during therapy, an angry, violent subordinate personality may emerge who threatens or attacks the analyst. Persons with multiple personalities may also have phobic reactions to stimuli that are connected with early traumatic experiences. Alter personalities may emerge who can confront and manage these phobic objects and situations.

Kluft (1984b) integrates and expands on these views to advance a four-factor theory of the development of a multiple personality:

- *Factor 1:* The internal capacity to dissociate from one's surroundings, which may be a genetic trait. This genetic capacity brings in biological factors.
- *Factor 2:* The occurrence of overwhelming trauma, such as physical or sexual abuse perpetrated by a parent, which prompts the use of dissociation as a defense mechanism. Braun (1986) notes that abused children are generally placed in a bind because they are discouraged from discussing the abuse both by the perpetrator of the abuse and by the other parent, who usually does not want to hear about it.
- *Factor 3:* The development of the personality around an imaginary companion, ego states, or

other such phenomena, which prevents the personality from achieving a cohesive self.
- *Factor 4:* The failure of other people to protect the child from further trauma or to provide nurturance that might help the child endure the trauma and develop normally. For example, a daughter who tells her mother that her father is sexually abusing her may be accused of lying and told that she is bad for making such outlandish accusations. The child may adapt to this bind by adopting two conflicting personalities—the dependent child who is eager to please, and the hostile, noncompliant child (Braun, 1986).

Despite its rarity, much theoretical attention has been paid to multiple personality—partly because the phenomenon is fascinating, partly because it serves as sort of inspiration to theorists of various persuasions. Early theoretical work by Janet (1889) and Prince (1906) outlined psychological mechanisms believed responsible for splitting the personality. They also connected the fracturing of consciousness with childhood trauma.

■ **LEARNING AND COGNITIVE PERSPECTIVES** Learning and cognitive theorists generally regard dissociative disorders as conditions in which people learn *not to think* about disturbing acts or thoughts in order to avoid feelings of guilt and shame. Technically speaking, *not thinking about these matters* is negatively reinforced by relief from anxiety, or by removal of feelings of guilt or shame.

Social-learning and cognitive theorists also suggest that people can learn to enact the role of a multi-

A CLOSER LOOK

Did Clinicians Create Personalities for the Hillside Strangler?

"**P**art, are you the same thing as Ken or are you different?" This was the question the Los Angeles police psychiatrist put to Kenneth Bianchi when he sought to elicit another personality within him. Bianchi, the so-called Hillside strangler, claimed under hypnosis that a hidden personality named "Steve" had murdered the string of prostitutes in the hills overlooking the city. "Ken" was innocent and knew nothing.

Was this a true case of multiple personality, or was Bianchi's performance staged to evade responsibility for his behavior? Perhaps so-called true cases of multiple personality can also be explained as a form of role-playing behavior.

Psychologist Nicholas Spanos and his colleagues (Spanos et al., 1985) argue that multiple personality can indeed be explained through a social psychological model of role-playing behavior. People learn to enact the role of a multiple personality by picking up on cues from therapists and other people that guide their performance. Perhaps the interrogation methods used with Bianchi had cued him to enact the role of a person with multiple personality.

In order to determine whether certain interviewing techniques could give rise to enactment of multiple personality-related behaviors, Spanos and his colleagues performed an experiment with college students that was modeled after the Bianchi interrogation. They asked normal college students to enact the role of an accused murderer in an interview with an experimenter playing the part of a police psychiatrist. There were three conditions:

1. *The Bianchi Condition.* This group of "accused murderers" was exposed to cues that paralleled the Bianchi interrogation. They were told that hypnosis would be used to uncover hidden aspects of their personalities, and perhaps another part of themselves would want to talk to a psychiatrist. These "Bianchi" subjects were then hypnotized and the "other part" was encouraged to reveal itself to the interviewer by reporting its name. The precise question that had been asked of Bianchi under hypnosis was put to the hypnotized students: "Part, are you the same thing as [student's name] or are you different?"

2. *The Hidden-Part Condition.* Another group of "accused murderers," a "hidden-part" group, was also told that hypnosis would be used to help the psychiatrist talk to a hidden part of themselves. They were not asked the question posed to Bianchi and to students in the Bianchi condition, however.

3. *The Control Group.* The third group of "accused murderers" was neither hypnotized during the interview

Kenneth Bianchi. Bianchi was dubbed the *Hillside strangler* by the press. Did the police psychiatrist who interviewed Bianchi suggest to him that he could role-play a person with multiple personalities?

nor told that the psychiatrist would ask to talk to a hidden part of themselves.

It turned out that 81% of the students in the Bianchi condition revealed a second name during the interview, compared to 31% of the hidden-part subjects and none of the control subjects. After they were "awakened" from their "trances," the majority (63%) of the Bianchi and hidden-part subjects claimed amnesia for the events that took place under hypnosis, denying knowledge of the alternate personality they had enacted. The control group stood firm in denying guilt for the crimes of which they were accused. The Bianchi and hidden-part subjects were more likely to admit guilt, but to ascribe it to the alternate personality.

 When appropriately cued in a laboratory experiment, college students did in fact enact a multiple personality role and have the alternate personality take the blame for a murder that they were accused of committing.

With the proper cues, it was a relatively simple matter for students to enact the multiple personality role. The student "multiples" readily picked up the cues that encouraged the enactment of a "hidden part" in their personalities. The hidden part had its own name and showed a unique pattern of psychological test responses. The hidden part, moreover, could be assigned the blame for wrongdoing. The core personality could safely claim ignorance of the alternate personality and of the alternate's crimes.

The Spanos experiment is only a laboratory simulation of a Bianchi-type interrogation. It did not study persons diagnosed as having a multiple personality or dissociative identity disorder. Nevertheless, it prompts consideration of whether or not normal people can be induced to enact the multiple personality role when they are tipped off as to how to do so and given the right incentives. Perhaps the manner in which the Bianchi interrogation was conducted had cued Bianchi to enact the multiple personality role.

Relatively few cases of people with multiple personalities involve criminal behavior, in which enactment of the multiple personality role may be connected with clear expectations of gain. But even in more typical cases, there may be subtle incentives for enacting the role of a multiple personality. Such incentives include the therapist's expression of interest and excitement at the possibility of discovering a multiple personality. People who seek help for problems may be ready to accept their clinicians' interpretations of their distressing behavior patterns—even when unusual possibilities such as multiple personality are raised. People with multiple personalities were often highly imaginative during childhood. Accustomed to playing games of "make believe," they may readily adopt alternate identities—especially if they learn how to enact the multiple personality role and there are external sources of validation—such as a clinician's interest and concern. This is not to suggest that people with multiple personalities are "faking" any more than to suggest that you are faking your behavior when you perform daily roles as student, spouse, or worker. You may enact the role of a student (e.g., sitting attentively in class, raising your hand when you wish to talk, etc.) because you have learned to organize your behavior according to the nature of the role and because you have been rewarded for doing so. So, too, people with multiple personalities may have learned to identify with the multiple personality role through cuing and repeated reinforcement to such an extent that they no longer realize that they are "playing a role."

The social reinforcement model may help to explain why some clinicians seem to "discover" many more cases of multiple personality than others. These clinicians may be "multiple personality magnets." They may unknowingly cue clients to enact the multiple personality role and reinforce the performance with extra attention and concern. With the right set of cues, certain clients may adopt the role of a multiple personality to please their clinicians. Yet it remains to be seen how many cases of the disorder in clinical practice can be accounted for by role playing.

ple personality by means of observational learning and reinforcement. This is not quite the same as pretending or malingering; people can honestly come to organize their behavior patterns according to particular roles that they have observed. They might also become so absorbed in role playing that they "forget" they are enacting a role.

Many reinforcers may become contingent on the enactment of the role of a multiple personality: Receiving attention from others and evading accountability for unacceptable behavior are two (Spanos et al., 1985; Thigpen & Cleckley, 1984). According to Nicholas Spanos and his colleagues (1985), films and TV shows like *The Three Faces of Eve* and *Sybil* have given the public detailed examples of the behaviors that characterize multiple personalities. That is, people may learn how to enact the role of persons with the disorder by watching others enacting the role on television and in the movies.

Perhaps most of us can divide our consciousness so that we become unaware of—at least temporarily—those events that we normally focus on. Perhaps most of us can thrust the unpleasant from our minds and enact various roles—parent, child, lover, businessperson, soldier—that help us meet the requirements of our situations. Perhaps the marvel is *not* that attention can be splintered, but that human consciousness is normally integrated into a meaningful whole.

Treatment of Dissociative Disorders

Dissociative amnesia and fugue are usually transient and terminate abruptly. Episodes of depersonalization can be recurrent and persistent, and they are most likely to occur when people are undergoing periods of mild anxiety or depression. In such cases, clinicians usually focus on managing the anxiety or the depression.

Theorists and clinicians have developed some interesting approaches to treatment of multiple personalities, which are the focus of this section.

■ **PSYCHODYNAMIC APPROACHES** Traditional psychoanalysis is relevant in the treatment of multiple personalities because it aims to help clients uncover and learn to cope with early childhood traumas. Wilbur (1986) offers some variations on the theme in her discussion of the psychoanalytic treatment of people with multiple personalities.

First, Wilbur points out that the analyst can work with whatever personality is in ascendance during the therapy session. Any and all personalities can be asked to talk about their memories and dreams as best they can. Any and all personalities can be assured that the therapist will help them make sense of their anxieties and to safely "relive" traumatic experiences so that they can be made conscious and they can free the psychic energy that is trapped by them. Wilbur enjoins therapists to keep in mind that anxiety experienced during a therapy session may lead to a switch in personalities because alternate personalities were presumably developed as a means to cope with intense anxiety. Eventually, however, sufficient early experience may be brought to light so that reintegration of the personality becomes possible.

Wilbur describes the formation of another treatment goal in the case of a woman with a multiple personality:

A 45-year-old woman had suffered from a multiple personality disorder throughout her life. Her dominant personality was timid and self-conscious, rather reticent about herself. But soon after she entered treatment, a group of "little ones" emerged, who cried profusely. The therapist asked to speak with someone in the personality system who could clarify the personalities that were present. It turned out that they included several children, all of whom were under 9 years of age and had suffered severe, painful sexual abuse at the hands of an uncle, a great-aunt, and a grandmother. The great-aunt was a lesbian with several voyeuristic lesbian friends. They would watch the sexual abuse, generating fear, pain, rage, humiliation, and shame.

It was essential in therapy for the "children" to come to understand that they should not feel ashamed because they had been helpless to resist the abuse.

■ *Adapted from Wilbur, 1986, pp. 138–139*

By and large, reports of the effectiveness of psychoanalytic psychotherapy rely on case studies. The relative infrequency of the disorder has hampered efforts to conduct controlled experiments that compare different forms of treatment with each other and with control groups. In one of the few reports of case studies of multiple personalities, Coons (1986) followed 20 "multiples" aged from 14 to 47 at time of intake for an average of 3¼ years. They were treated primarily by means of psychoanalytically-oriented psychotherapy and hypnosis. Only five of the subjects showed a complete reintegration of their personali-

ties. Therapy was reportedly hampered by continuation of mechanisms of repression and denial and the use of secrecy—a pattern that had begun during childhood. Reflecting the difficulties in working therapeutically with such clients, therapists often reported feelings of anger, emotional exhaustion, and exasperation.

■ **BIOLOGICAL APPROACHES** No drugs have been developed to integrate alter personalities in people with multiple personalities. However, persons with multiple personalities frequently suffer from depression, anxiety, and other problems that may be treated with drugs such as antidepressants and antianxiety agents. Drugs tend to be most readily prescribed when the different personalities "agree" in the problems they present—whether anxiety, depression, or other problems (Barkin et al., 1986). However, more research is needed to investigate biological approaches that may help clinicians foster integration of the various personalities.

■ **BEHAVIORAL APPROACHES** Behavioral techniques have been applied to the treatment of people with multiple personalities. Here as well, we are limited to the isolated case study. Kohlenberg (1973), for example, reported a case in which token reinforcers (poker chips that could be exchanged for tangible rewards) were used to increase the frequency of response of the best adjusted of three alternate personalities in a 51-year-old institutionalized person. Any time the preferred personality emitted a response, the subject earned a token and a pat on the hand. During reinforced trials, the preferred personality "appeared" significantly more often. During extinction trials, however, when reinforcement was withheld, the preferred personality dropped to a response level below the original baseline, and alternate personalities spent more time out in the open.

Kohlenberg concluded that multiple personality is a learned response pattern whose performance is connected with reinforcement contingencies. In the case of multiple personality, as noted by Spanos and his colleagues (1985), reinforcement can take the form of extra attention from therapists who consider cases of multiple personality to be glamorous and exotic. There is too little evidence to conclude that people with multiple personalities will generally respond to selective reinforcement of the most adaptive personality. This form of therapy also raises the ethical issue as to whether or not therapists have the right to determine which personality should be selectively reinforced.

SOMATOFORM DISORDERS

The word *somatoform* derives from the Greek *soma*, meaning "body." In the **somatoform disorders**, people show or complain of physical symptoms suggestive of physical disorders, but no organic abnormalities can be found to account for them. Moreover, there is evidence, or some reason to believe, that the symptoms reflect psychological factors or conflict. Some people complain of problems in breathing or swallowing, or of a "lump in the throat." Problems such as these can reflect overactivity of the sympathetic branch of the autonomic nervous system (dryness in the mouth that is related to anxiety can impair swallowing). Sometimes the symptoms take more unusual forms, as in a "paralysis" of a hand or leg that is inconsistent with the workings of the nervous system. In yet other cases, people are preoccupied with the belief that they have a serious disease, yet no evidence of a physical abnormality can be found. We consider several forms of somatoform disorders, including *conversion disorder, hypochondriasis,* and *somatization disorder.* We also consider *Münchausen's syndrome,* which is a form of feigned illness, or **factitious disorder**, that seems to be motivated by a desire to be hospitalized and treated for a feigned illness.

Conversion Disorder

Conversion disorder is characterized by a major change in or loss of physical functioning, although there are no medical findings to support the physical symptoms or deficits (see Table 6.3). The symptoms are not intentionally produced. The person is not malingering. The physical symptoms usually come on suddenly in stressful situations. A soldier's hand may become "paralyzed" during intense combat, for example. The fact that conversion symptoms first appear in the context of, or are aggravated by, conflicts or stressors that the individual encounters gives credence to the view that they related to psychological factors (American Psychiatric Association, 1993).

Conversion disorder is so named because of the psychodynamic belief that it represents the channeling or *conversion* of repressed sexual or aggressive energies into physical symptoms. Conversion disorder was formerly called *hysteria* or *hysterical neurosis.* Investigations of cases of hysterical neurosis played a prominent role in the development of psychoanalysis.

Table 6.3: Diagnostic Features of Conversion Disorder

1. At least one symptom or deficit involving voluntary motor or sensory functions that suggests the presence of a physical disorder.

2. Psychological factors are judged to be associated with the disorder because the onset or exacerbation of the physical symptom is linked to the occurrence of psychosocial stressors or conflict situations.

3. The person does not purposefully produce or fake the physical symptom.

4. The symptom cannot be explained as a cultural ritual or response pattern, nor can it be explained by any known physical disorder on the basis of appropriate testing.

5. The symptom causes significant emotional distress, impairment in one or more important areas of functioning, such as social or occupational functioning, or is sufficient to warrant medical attention.

6. The symptom is not restricted to complaints of pain or problems in sexual functioning, nor can it be accounted for by another mental disorder.

Source: Adapted from DSM-IV Draft Criteria (American Psychiatric Association, 1993), pp. L: 1-2.

In one of the classic cases in the annals of abnormal behavior, Anna O., a young woman who complained of numerous physical problems that fit the pattern of conversion disorder, received psychoanalytic treatment. Hysterical or conversion disorders seem to have been common in Freud's day but are relatively rare today.

According to the DSM, conversion symptoms mimic neurological or general medical conditions involving problems with voluntary motor (movement) or sensory functions. Some of the "classic" symptom patterns involve paralysis, epilepsy, problems in coordination, blindness and tunnel vision, loss of the sense of hearing or of smell, or loss of feeling in a limb (anesthesia).

The bodily symptoms found in conversion disorders often do not match the medical conditions they suggest. For example, conversion epileptics, unlike true epileptic patients, may maintain control over their bladders during an attack. People whose vision is supposedly impaired may wend their ways through the physician's office without bumping into the furniture. People who become "incapable" of standing or walking may nevertheless perform other leg movements normally.

If you suddenly lost your vision, or if your legs no longer supported your weight, you would probably show understandable concern. But some people with conversion disorders, like those with dissociative amnesia, show a remarkable indifference to their symptoms, a phenomenon termed **la belle indifférence** ("beautiful indifference"). The DSM advises against relying on indifference to symptoms in making the diagnosis, however, because many people cope with real physical disorders by denying their pain or concern, which provides the semblance of indifference and relieves anxieties—at least temporarily.

Labels of hysteria or conversion disorder are now and then applied erroneously to people with underlying medical conditions that go unrecognized and untreated, as in the case of Gladys:

*G*ladys *was a 57-year-old housewife who complained to her physician of a "lump in the throat." The physician found no organic basis for the complaint and referred her to a psychiatrist who informed her that her symptom was a common neurotic symptom and probably reflected her unwillingness to "swallow" her lot in life, now that the children were grown and she sat alone in the house much of the day. Several months later, the symptom persisted and Gladys visited a psychologist at a community mental health center. Before treating the "hysterical symptom," the psychologist referred her to medical specialists in Boston so that an organic basis for the disorder could be ruled out. Throat cancer was diagnosed, but the cancer had metastasized and it was too late to save Gladys's life.*

■ *The Authors' Files*

Gladys's case is not unique. One study compared the subsequent medical histories of 56 psychiatric clients who had been diagnosed as having conversion disorder with those of 56 clients who had been diagnosed as suffering from anxiety or depression. Thirty-five (62.5%) of the clients diagnosed with conversion disorder later developed organic brain disorders as compared with only 3 (5.3%) of those diagnosed as having anxiety or depressive disorders (Whitlock, 1967).

Another study took a very different approach. It examined 30 consecutively admitted patients, each of whom had documented neurological problems, to a hospital neurology unit. Most of them showed some features of conversion disorder, such as la belle indifférence and sensory losses that were inconsistent with recognized organic patterns of pathology (Gould

et al., 1986). In the opinion of these researchers, certain classes of people, including women and gay men, are at greater risk of being misdiagnosed as hysterical because of stereotypes held by clinicians that they are more prone to such disorders. Perhaps as many as 80% of individuals given the diagnosis of conversion disorder have real neurological problems that go undiagnosed (Gould et al., 1986).

Persons with conversion disorder do lose sensory and motor functions without evidence of organic pathology. (However, some people who are assumed to have conversion disorders have organic involvements that go undiagnosed.)

Hypochondriasis

The term **hypochondriasis** is derived from the Greek *hypochondrion*, which refers to the abdomen, the soft part of the body below (*hypo-*) the cartilage (*chondrion*) of the breastbone. This area is the site of many—but not all—of the physical complaints of the hypochondriac. Based on their interpretation of bodily signs (for example, sores) or sensations (for example, "heaviness in the chest"), hypochondriacs are preoccupied with the fear that their symptoms are due to an underlying serious illness, such as cancer or a heart defect. No organic basis can be found for the complaints, however. Fear of serious illness persists despite medical reassurance (see Table 6.4).

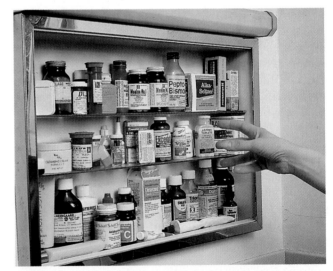

What to take?   Hypochondriacs are preoccupied with the persistent fear they are seriously ill. They frequently medicate themselves with over-the-counter medications and find little if any reassurance in doctors' assertions that their health is not in jeopardy.

Table 6.4: Diagnostic Features of Hypochondriasis

1. The person is preoccupied with a fear of having a serious illness, or with the belief that one has a serious illness. The person interprets bodily sensations or physical signs as evidence of physical illness.

2. Fears of physical illness, or beliefs of having a physical illness, persist despite medical reassurances.

3. The preoccupations are not of a delusional intensity (the person recognizes the possibility that these fears and beliefs may be exaggerated or unfounded) and are not restricted to concerns about appearance.

4. The preoccupations cause significant emotional distress or interfere with one or more important areas of functioning, such as social or occupational functioning.

5. The disturbance has persisted for 6 months or longer.

6. The preoccupations do not occur exclusively within the context of another mental disorder.

Source: Adapted from DSM-IV Draft Criteria (American Psychiatric Association, 1993), p. L: 2.

Hypochondriacs are not faking their symptoms. They believe they suffer from a serious disease and they experience their reported discomfort. Unlike conversion disorder, hypochondriasis does not involve the loss or distortion of physical function. Unlike the attitude of indifference toward one's symptoms that are sometimes found in conversion disorders, hypochondriacs express apprehension about their symptoms. The disorder is about equally common in men and women and most often begins between the ages of 20 and 30, although it can begin at any age.

Hypochondriacs may focus on slight changes in heartbeat and minor aches and pains. Anxiety about one's physical status produces its own physical sensations, however—for example, heavy sweating, dizziness, even fainting. Hypochondriacs may be incredulous and resentful when the doctor explains how their own fears may be plaguing them. They frequently go "doctor shopping" in the hope that a competent and sympathetic physician will heed them before it is too late. Physicians, too, can be hypochondriacs, as we see in the following case example:

A 38-year-old radiologist has just returned from a 10-day stay at a famous diagnostic center where he has undergone extensive testing of his entire gastrointestinal tract. The evaluation proved negative for any significant physical illness, but rather than feel relieved, the radiologist appeared resentful and disappointed with the findings. The radiologist has been bothered for several months with various physical symptoms, which he describes as symptoms of mild abdominal pain, feelings of "fullness," "bowel rumblings," and a feeling of a "firm abdominal mass." He has become convinced that his symptoms are due to colon cancer and has become accustomed to testing his stool for blood on a weekly basis and carefully palpating his abdomen for "masses" while lying in bed every several days. He has also secretly performed X-ray studies on himself after regular hours. There is a history of a heart murmur that was detected when he was 13 and his younger brother died of congenital heart disease in early childhood. When the evaluation of his murmur proved to be benign, he nonetheless began to worry that something might have been overlooked. He developed a fear that something was actually wrong with his heart, and while the fear eventually subsided, it has never entirely left him. In medical school he worried about the diseases that he learned about in pathology. Since graduating, he has repeatedly experienced concerns about his health that follow a typical pattern: noticing certain symptoms, becoming preoccupied with what the symptoms might mean, and undergoing physical evaluations that proved negative. His decision to seek a psychiatric consultation was prompted by an incident with his 9-year-old son. His son accidentally walked in on him while he was palpating his abdomen and asked, "What do you think it is this time, Dad?" He becomes tearful as he relates this incident, describing his feelings of shame and anger—mostly at himself.

■ *Adapted from Spitzer et al., 1989, pp. 16–18*

Hypochondriasis is generally considered to be more common among elderly people. As noted by Paul Costa and Robert McCrae (1985) of the National Institute on Aging, however, authentic age-related health changes do occur, and most "hypochondriacal" complaints probably reflect these changes.

Researchers found that a great majority (88%) of the hypochondriacs in one sample also had other psychological disorders, especially depression and anxiety disorders (Barsky et al., 1992).

Somatization Disorder

Somatization disorder, formerly known as Briquet's syndrome, is characterized by multiple and recurrent somatic complaints that began prior to the

MULTICULTURAL PERSPECTIVES

Koro and Dhat Syndromes: Far Eastern Somatoform Disorders?

In the United States, it is common for hypochondriacs to be troubled by the idea that they have serious illnesses, such as cancer. The Koro and Dhat syndromes of the Far East share some clinical features with hypochondriasis. Although these syndromes may seem, well, foreign to most American readers, they are each connected with folklore within their Far Eastern cultures.

Koro Syndrome Koro syndrome is a culture-related syndrome that is found primarily in China and some other Far Eastern countries. People with Koro syndrome fear that their genitals are shrinking and retracting into the body, which they believe will result in death (Fabian, 1991; Tseng et al., 1992). Because cases of Koro have been reported outside China and the Far East (Kennedy & Flick, 1991), Koro may be considered a culture-related syndrome rather than a culture-bound syndrome (Fishbain, 1991; Sajjad, 1991). Koro syndrome has been identified mainly in young men, although some cases have also been reported in women (Tseng et al., 1992). Koro syndrome tends to be short-lived and to involve episodes of acute anxiety that one's genitals are retracting. Physiological signs of anxiety that approach panic proportions are common, including profuse sweating, breathlessness, and heart palpitations (Devan, 1987; Tseng et al., 1992). Men who suffer from Koro have been known to use mechanical devices, such as chopsticks, to try to prevent the penis from retracting into the body (Devan, 1987).

Koro syndrome. Koro is a culture-related syndrome that is found primarily in China and mainly afflicts young men. People with the disorder fear their genitals are retracting into the body, which they believe will lead to death. Sufferers may show signs of anxiety that approach panic proportions, such as profuse sweating, breathlessness, and heart palpitations. Koro has been traced within Chinese culture as far back as 3000 B.C. Medical reassurance that the genitals do not retract into the body often allays sufferers' fears.

age of 30 (but usually during the teen years) and have persisted for at least several years and that result in the seeking of medical attention or significant impairment in fulfilling social or occupational roles. Complaints usually involve different organ systems (Spitzer et al., 1989). There is seldom a year that passes without some physical complaint that prompts a trip to the doctor. People with somatization disorder are heavy users of medical services. Community surveys show that virtually all (95%) of the people with somatization disorder had visited a doctor during the past year, and nearly half (45%) had been hospitalized (Swartz et al., 1991). The complaints cannot be explained by physical causes or exceed what would be expected from a known physical problem. Com-

plaints seem vague or exaggerated, and the person frequently receives medical care from a number of physicians, sometimes at the same time.

The DSM provides groups of symptoms and specifies that the diagnosis of somatization disorder requires that the individual have a history of complaints involving four separate symptom groups (American Psychiatric Association, 1993). The groups of symptoms are categorized as pain involving multiple sites (e.g., head, abdomen, back or joints) or functions (e.g., during sexual intercourse, menstruation, or urination); gastrointestinal (e.g., vomiting or diarrhea); sexual other than pain (e.g., loss of sexual interest, erectile or ejaculatory problems, excessive menstrual bleeding or irregular menses); and

The **Koro syndrome** has been traced within Chinese culture as far back as 3000 B.C.. (Devan, 1987). Epidemics involving hundreds or thousands of people have been reported in parts of Asia such as China, Singapore, Thailand, and India (Tseng et al., 1992). In Guangdong Province in China, an epidemic involving more than 2,000 persons occurred during the 1980s (Tseng et al., 1992). Guangdong residents who did not fall victim to Koro tended to be less superstitious, higher in intelligence, and less accepting of Koro-related folk beliefs (such as the belief that shrinkage of the penis will be lethal) than those who fell victim to the epidemic (Tseng et al., 1992). Medical reassurance that such fears are unfounded often quell Koro episodes (Devan, 1987). Medical reassurance generally fails to dent the concerns of hypochondriacs in Western cultures, however. Koro episodes among those who do not receive corrective information tend to pass with time but may recur.

In China, 2,000 people did recently fall prey to the belief that their genitals were shrinking and retracting into their bodies. The syndrome is known as *Koro* and can be said to serve as an example of a culture-related somatoform disorder.

A number of investigators (Bernstein & Gaw, 1990; Fishbain, 1991) would like to see the Koro syndrome incorporated into the DSM as a somatoform disorder.

Dhat Syndrome *Dhat*[1] syndrome is found among young Asian-Indian males and involves excessive fears over the loss of seminal fluid during nocturnal emissions (Akhtar,

---

[1]The word *Dhat* can be loosely translated as the elixir of life.

1988). Some men with this syndrome also believe (incorrectly) that semen mixes with urine and is excreted through urination. Men with *Dhat* syndrome may roam from physician to physician seeking help to prevent nocturnal emissions or the imagined loss of semen mixed with excreted urine. There is a widespread belief within Indian culture (and other Near and Far Eastern cultures) that the loss of semen is harmful because it depletes the body of physical and mental energy (Chadda & Ahuja, 1990). Like other culture-bound or culture-related syndromes, *Dhat* must be understood within its cultural context:

> In India, attitudes toward semen and its loss constitute an organized, deep-seated belief system that can be traced back to the scriptures of the land . . . [even as far back as the classic Indian sex manual, the Kama Sutra, which was believed to be written by the sage Vatsayana between the third and fifth centuries A.D.] . . . Semen is considered to be the elixir of life, in both a physical and mystical sense. Its preservation is supposed to guarantee health and longevity.
>
> Akhtar, 1988, p. 71

It is a commonly held Hindu belief that it takes "forty meals to form one drop of blood; forty drops of blood to fuse and form one drop of bone marrow, and forty drops of this to produce one drop of semen" (Akhtar, 1988, p. 71). Based on the cultural belief in the life-preserving nature of semen, it is not surprising that some Indian males experience extreme anxiety over the involuntary loss of the fluid through nocturnal emissions (Akhtar, 1988). Dhat syndrome has also been associated with difficulty in achieving or maintaining erection, apparently due to excessive concern about loss of seminal fluid through ejaculation (Singh, 1985).

---

pseudoneurological (e.g., symptoms suggesting a neurological disorder such as conversion symptoms like blindness, difficulty swallowing, blurry vision, paralysis, or weakness, or dissociative symptoms such as loss of memory for personal events). The Epidemiologic Catchment Area (ECA) study revealed that somatization disorder was relatively uncommon, affecting about 1 American in 1,000 (Swartz et al., 1991). The ECA study found that the disorder was 10 times more likely to occur among women than men and 4 times more likely to occur among African Americans than other ethnic or racial groups (Swartz et al., 1991). Moreover, the ECA study revealed that somatization disorder tends to occur within the context of other abnormal behavior patterns. All of the

people with somatization disorder experienced at least one other psychiatric disorder at some point in their lives, most commonly phobic disorders (69%) or major depression (55%) (Swartz et al., 1991).

Although not much is known of the childhood background of people with somatization disorder, a recent study found that women with the disorder were significantly more likely to report sexual molestation in childhood than a matched comparison group of women with mood disorders (Morrison, 1989).

The essential feature of hypochondriasis is fear of disease, of what bodily symptoms may portend. Persons with somatization disorder, by contrast, are pestered by the symptoms themselves. Both diagnoses may be given to the same individual if the diagnostic criteria for both disorders are met. Somatization disorder is rarely diagnosed in males, whereas hypochondriasis is believed to affect women and men equally.

Emil Kraepelin, one of the founders of modern psychiatry, presented a case in the 19th century that closely parallels somatization disorder (Spitzer et al., 1989). It involved a 30-year-old woman who complained of many physical problems that dated to adolescence and for which no physical cause could be determined: seizures, difficulty walking, muscle weakness, abdominal pain, diarrhea, menstrual problems, chest pain, and urinary problems, among others. Like many others with the disorder, the woman also presented with genuine physical problems, but her physical condition could not account for the range of complaints. Every type of treatment available at the time was tried, but with temporary benefits or none. They included therapeutic baths, stays on the Riviera and in the country, even mild electric currents.

Theoretical Perspectives

Conversion disorder, or "hysteria," was known to Hippocrates, who attributed the strange bodily symptoms to a wandering uterus, which created internal chaos. The term *hysterical* derives from the Greek *hystera*, meaning "uterus." Hippocrates noticed that these complaints were less common among married women. He prescribed marriage as a "cure" on the basis of these observations, and also on the theoretical assumption that pregnancy would satisfy uterine needs and fix the organ in place. Pregnancy fosters hormonal and structural changes that are of benefit to some women with menstrual complaints, but Hippocrates's beliefs in the "wandering uterus" has contributed to degrading interpretations of complaints by women of physical problems throughout the centuries. Despite Hippocrates's beliefs that hysteria was exclusively a female concern, it also occurs in men.

Modern theoretical accounts of the somatoform disorders, like those of the dissociative disorders, have most often sprung from psychodynamic and learning theories. Hysterical disorders provided an arena for some of the debate between the psychological and biological theories of the 19th century. The alleviation—albeit often temporarily—of hysterical symptoms through hypnosis by Charcot, Breuer, and Freud contributed to the belief that hysteria was rooted in psychological rather than physical causes and led Freud to the development of a theory of the unconscious mind. Freud held that the ego manages

to control unacceptable or threatening sexual and aggressive impulses arising from the id through defense mechanisms such as repression. Such control prevents the outbreak of anxiety that would occur if the person were to become aware of them. In some cases, the leftover emotion or energy that is "strangulated," or cut off, from the threatening impulses becomes *converted* into a physical symptom, such as hysterical paralysis or blindness.

According to psychodynamic theory, hysterical symptoms are functional: They allow the person to achieve **primary gains** and **secondary gains**. The primary gains consist of allowing the individual to keep internal conflicts repressed. The person is aware of the physical symptom, but not of the conflict it represents. In such cases, the "symptom" is symbolic of, and provides the person with a "partial solution" of, the underlying conflict. For example, the hysterical paralysis of an arm might symbolize and also prevent the individual from acting out on repressed unacceptable sexual (e.g., masturbatory) or aggressive (e.g., murderous) impulses. Repression occurs automatically, so that the individual remains unaware of the underlying conflicts. The secondary gains may allow the individual to avoid burdensome responsibilities and to gain the support—rather than condemnation—of those around them. For example, soldiers sometimes experience sudden "paralysis" of their hands, which prevents them from firing their guns in battle. They may then be sent to recuperate at a hospital, rather than face enemy fire. The symptoms in such cases are not considered contrived, as would be the case in malingering. A number of bomber pilots during World War II suffered hysterical "night blindness" that prevented them from carrying out dangerous nighttime missions. In the psychodynamic view, their "blindness" may have achieved a primary gain of shielding them from guilt associated with dropping bombs on civilian areas. It may also have achieved a secondary purpose of helping them avoid dangerous missions. *La belle indifférence,* first noted by Charcot, is believed to occur because the physical symptoms help relieve rather than cause anxiety. From the psychodynamic perspective, conversion disorders, like dissociative disorders, serve a purpose.

Although the early psychodynamic formulation of hysteria is still widely held, empirical evidence has been lacking (Miller, 1987). One problem with the Freudian view is that it does not explain how energies left over from unconscious conflicts become transformed into physical symptoms (Miller, 1987). Because of these limitations, learning theories have gained some favor. Before exploring the learning perspectives, however, let us consider a classic case reported by the influential learning theorists John

B-29 bombers on a bombing mission over Japan during World War II. Some World War II pilots were reported to have suffered from hysterical night blindness, which prevented them from carrying out dangerous nighttime missions. Their night blindness may have served the psychological purpose of shielding them from guilt over dropping bombs on civilian areas—a type of primary gain. It may also have served the secondary purpose of helping them avoid dangerous combat missions.

Dollard and Neal E. Miller in 1950. It permits a variety of interpretations:

*M*rs. *C was a 35-year-old married woman whose legs were "paralyzed." Mrs. C was reared by a stern mother who "belted" her repeatedly so that she would remain a "good" girl. As a girl, Mrs. C swore that she would never get married, and her resolve changed only later in life. Marriage was apparently a means for escaping the punishment of home life. Ignorant of sex and conception, Mrs. C reported that she "felt nausea every time my husband touched me."*

During 15 years of marriage, Mrs. C became pregnant four times and had three surviving children. Her sexual aversion became stronger after her most recent, painful pregnancy. She allowed her husband to engage in intercourse only once or twice a month, and only after extensive pleading. She gave in only because of "pity."

After the fourth pregnancy, Mrs. C developed a morbid fear of pregnancy. She connected the fear to feelings of "doom" related to the fact that a paternal aunt had been hospitalized for a mental disorder. The fear was not sufficient to put off her husband, and Mrs. C next developed symptoms in her legs, which felt "weak, wobbly and trembled." Soon afterward she was brought to

the hospital, unable to flex her knees, walk, or stand. Although her symptoms might reflect serious pathology, her anxiety level was low, which was attributed to la belle indifférence.

Physicians showed that the symptoms were not organic. Organic signs of paralysis were lacking, and Mrs. C's legs were freely movable under the influence of sodium pentothal—a barbiturate that relieves anxiety and alters one's state of consciousness. (It has also been referred to as "truth serum.") Mrs. C was unwilling to try psychotherapy, so the doctors resorted to forcing Mrs. C to try walking. They helped her stand and used pressure to bend her knees. In short, they proved to her that she could stand and walk. Rather than showing relief and gratitude that her disorder was not severe, Mrs. C became enraged, expressing her hostility toward the doctors and nurses.

Upon returning home, Mrs. C contemplated divorce and spent some time living with a sister. Conflict with the sister's family forced a return home. Mrs. C refused intercourse with her husband, heightening the conflict between them. Eventually she received contraceptive advice, but she did not use it, apparently because her aversion to sex extended beyond fears of pregnancy. There was no happy ending.

■ *Adapted from Dollard and Miller, 1950, pp. 168–170*

Mrs. C's weakness in the legs seemed to have clear primary and secondary gains. They relieved her of having to deal more directly with her deep-seated aversion to sex and pregnancy. Her symptom also provided her with perhaps more than a "partial solution" to her problem. With weak, wobbly legs, she could not be expected to care for her family or engage in intercourse with her husband. On the other hand, there was no evidence that Mrs. C's complaint was the symbolic expression of unconscious conflicts involving the banishment of unacceptable impulses to the unconscious. Within a learning-theory perspective, then, conversion symptoms may serve the purpose of helping the individual avoid or escape from stressful situations without confronting them directly.

Dollard and Miller explained the "gains" associated with her complaints in learning-theory terms. A transient weakness in the legs might have prompted the passing thought, "This will prevent intercourse" (1950, p. 169). The thought would relieve anxiety over sex and thus reinforce the symptom. Dollard and Miller do not suggest that Mrs. C consciously seized her opportunity by purposefully faking the symptom, but rather that the reinforcer of anxiety relief heightened the probability of its occurrence.

Dollard and Miller explain Mrs. C's indifference to her symptom as evidence of its anxiety-relieving role. They interpret her rage at being deprived of her symptom as further evidence of its crucial functions.

Psychodynamic theory and learning theory concur that the symptoms in conversion disorders relieve anxiety. Psychodynamic theorists, however, seek the causes of anxiety in unconscious conflicts. Learning theorists focus on the more direct reinforcing properties of the symptom.

From the learning perspective, the symptoms in conversion and other somatoform disorders may also carry the benefits, or reinforcing properties of, the "sick role" (Kendell, 1983). Persons with conversion disorders may be relieved of chores and responsibilities like going to work or performing household tasks (Miller, 1987). Being sick also usually earns sympathy and support. People who received such reinforcers during past illnesses are likely to learn to adopt a sick role even when they are not ill (Kendell, 1983).

Differences in learning experiences may explain why conversion disorders were historically more often reported among women. It may be that women in our culture have been socialized, more so than men, to react to stress by enacting a sick role (Miller, 1987). We are not suggesting that people with conversion disorders are fakers. We are merely pointing out that people may learn to adopt roles that lead to reinforcing consequences, regardless of whether or not they deliberately seek to enact these roles.

Most theorists distinguish between malingering, or consciously making false claims to achieve various gains, and conversion disorder, in which the symptoms are not seen as being consciously directed (Miller, 1987). Malingerers fake or exaggerate symptoms to obtain external rewards or incentives, such as avoiding military service or obtaining better living conditions. If persons with conversion disorders fake their symptoms, they do not appear to be consciously aware of it. One might even say that they are deceiving *themselves* as well as others about the legitimacy of their complaints.

Some learning theorists see the hypochondriac's repeated seeking of medical consultations and reassurance as a form of obsessive-compulsive behavior (Salvoskis & Warwick, 1986). Obsessive-compulsive behavior involves a pattern of persistent, disturbing thoughts (obsessions) that are followed by urges to perform certain behaviors (compulsions). Obsessional thoughts and compulsions are experienced as being beyond the individual's control. Hypochondriacs are bothered by obsessive, anxiety-inducing thoughts that something terrible is wrong with their health. The urge to run from doctor to doctor may be seen as a compulsion that is reinforced by the temporary, partial relief from anxiety they experience when reassured by their doctors that their fears are unwarranted. The troublesome thoughts eventually return, prompting repeated consultations. The cycle may then repeat.

Cognitive theorists have speculated that some hypochondriacs use their complaints as a type of self-handicapping strategy (Smith et al., 1983). That is, they may complain of physical symptoms in situations in which sickness can serve as a reasonable excuse for poor performance. In other cases, diverting attention to physical complaints can serve as a means of avoiding thinking about other life problems.

Treatment of Somatoform Disorders

The treatment approach that Freud pioneered, psychoanalysis, began with the treatment of hysteria, which is now termed conversion disorder. Psychoanalysis seeks to uncover and bring unconscious conflicts that originated in childhood into conscious awareness. Once the conflict is aired and worked through, the symptom is no longer needed as a "partial solution" to the conflict and should disappear. The psychoanalytic method is supported by case studies, some reported by Freud and others by his followers. However, the infrequency of conversion disorders in contemporary times has made it difficult to mount controlled studies of the psychoanalytic technique.

The behavioral approach to treating conversion disorders, and other somatoform disorders, may focus on removing sources of secondary reinforcement (or secondary gain) that may become connected with physical complaints. Individuals with somatization disorder, for example, are often perceived by family members and others as sickly and infirm, as incapable of carrying normal responsibilities. Other people may be unaware of how they reinforce dependent and complaining behaviors when they relieve the sick person of responsibilities. The behavior therapist may teach family members to reward attempts to assume responsibility and ignore nagging and complaining. The behavior therapist may also work more directly with the person with a somatoform disorder, helping the person learn more adaptive ways of handling stress or anxiety through relaxation and cognitive restructuring, for example. Here again, the absence of controlled studies in the treatment of somatoform disorders prevents a fair assessment of relative efficacy of different approaches.

The dissociative and somatoform disorders are among the most intriguing and least well understood patterns of abnormal behavior.

Münchausen Syndrome

A woman staggered into the emergency room of a New York City hospital bleeding from the mouth, clutching her stomach and wailing with pain. It was some entrance. Even in that setting, forever serving bleeders and clutchers and wailers, there was something about her, some terrible star quality that held stage center. Her pain was larger than life.

She told a harrowing story: A man had seduced her, then tied her up, beaten her, forced her to surrender money and jewelry on threat of death. She had severe pain in her lower left side, and an unbearable headache.

She was admitted, and exhaustively tested. Nothing could be found; no reason for the bleeding or the pain; the specialists were left scratching their heads.

Then, one day, a hospital aide came upon these items in her bedside table: a needle, syringe, and a blood thinner called heparin. Eureka. Inject yourself with enough blood thinner and you, too, can take stage center in an emergency room.

Confronted, she denied all charges. The stuff was not hers; someone was trying to frame her; if nobody believed her, she would check out of the place and find doctors who really cared. And off she went. Later, it was learned that she had recently been in two other hospitals: the same story, same symptom and same sequence of events.

Diagnosis: Münchausen syndrome.

Source: "Mad Malady," by M. W. Lear. Copyright © 1988 by The New York Times Company, reprinted by permission.

Münchausen Syndrome Münchausen syndrome was named after Baron Karl von Münchausen, one of history's great fibbers. The good baron, an 18th-century German army officer, entertained friends with tales of outrageous adventures. In the vernacular, *Münchausenism* describes tellers of tall tales. In abnormal psychology, **Münchausen syndrome** refers to patients who tell tall tales or outrageous lies to their doctors. The baron was a jolly man, but patients who carry his name usually suffer deep anguish as they bounce from hospital to hospital and subject themselves to unnecessary, painful, and, sometimes, risky medical treatments (Schoenfeld et al., 1987).

Factitious Disorders Although there may be gains in having physical symptoms, individuals with somatoform disorders do not purposefully produce them. Even if there is no medical basis to their symptoms, they do not set out to deceive others. Thus Münchausen syndrome is not a somatoform disorder. It is a kind of factitious disorder. Factitious disorders involve the deliberate fabrication of physical or psychological complaints. Münchausen syndrome, in particular, refers to a chronic pattern of deliberate fabrication of seemingly plausible physical complaints.

In factitious disorders, as with malingering (faking), physical or psychological symptoms are consciously and deliberately produced. The malingerer also invents a complaint, but for obvious gain. Perhaps the malingerer wishes to be relieved of military or jury duty or wants to take a day off. Because malingering is motivated by external incentives, it is not considered a mental disorder, according to the DSM. In factitious disorders, the symptoms are not

Tall tales. The Baron Münchausen, who regaled his friends with tales of his incredible feats. In one of his tall tales, depicted here, he had fallen asleep inside a cannon and was inadvertently shot across the Thames River.

connected with obvious gains. The absence of external incentives suggests that factitious disorder serves a psychological need; hence, it is considered a mental disorder. Factitious disorders are maladaptive. Persons with factitious disorders seem compelled to feign illness, even though their fakery may subject them to painful or dangerous medical procedures (Schretlen, 1988).

Persons with Münchausen syndrome may travel widely, visiting emergency rooms in one city after another, where they present themselves as suffering from acute, dramatic symptoms.

 People with Münchausen syndrome may in fact show up repeatedly at emergency rooms, feigning illness and demanding treatment. Their motives remain a mystery.

People with Münchausen syndrome weave tales of illness for no apparent reason other than gaining admission to the hospital. The syndrome may be seen as a form of compulsive behavior, perhaps even a form of "addiction" to hospitals, in which people crave the sick role (Lear, 1988). They may go to great lengths to seek a confirmatory diagnosis, such as agreeing to exploratory surgery. They may acquire sophisticated medical knowledge to feign complaints or manufacture plausible symptoms. For example, they may inject themselves with certain drugs to produce skin rashes. When confronted with evidence of their deception, they may turn nasty and stick to their guns. They are also skillful enough actors to convince others that their

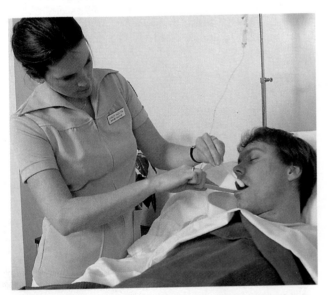

Is this patient telling the truth? Münchausen syndrome is characterized by the fabrication of medical complaints for no other apparent purpose than to gain admission to hospitals. Some Münchausen patients may produce life-threatening symptoms in their attempts to deceive doctors.

complaints are genuine (Sutherland & Rodin, 1990). Unlike malingerers, people with Münchausen disorders are often unaware of the motives for their behavior (Schoenfeld et al., 1987).

Why Fake Symptoms? The psychological needs served by Münchausen syndrome are conjectural. It has been suggested that people with Münchausen disorder may be trying to expunge guilt for felt misdeeds by subjecting themselves to painful medical procedures. Perhaps they hold grudges against doctors or hospitals for perceived injustices at the hands of the medical establishment (Lear, 1988) and delight in their ability to "put one over on the doctors." Methods of inducing symptoms can be dangerous and have sometimes been interpreted as expressing suicidal wishes (Schoenfeld et al., 1987).

Some conjectures focus on the early childhood experiences of Münchausen patients. Perhaps they learned to garner attention from parents by "playing sick," and this childhood pattern is reactivated when they need attention as adults (Lear, 1988). Their childhoods were often characterized by parental rejection or deprivation, family instability and foster homes, parental illness, or childhood hospitalizations (Schoenfeld et al., 1987). Somehow they learn what being sick means. Perhaps enacting the sick role in the protected hospital environment provides a sense of security that was lacking in childhood. Perhaps the hospital becomes a stage on which they can act out resentments against doctors and parents that have been brewing since childhood. Perhaps they are trying to identify with a parent who was often sick.

Münchausen Syndrome by Proxy: A New Mental Disorder? Writers and health professionals have speculated that a new mental disorder might have recently emerged, one in which people induce symptoms *in others* rather than themselves—"Münchausen Syndrome by Proxy."

Whereas people who have Münchausen syndrome itself may appropriately elicit our sympathy and concern, Münchausen Syndrome by Proxy has been connected with heinous crimes against children—with as many as 200 cases of child abuse since 1977 (Balleza, 1992). Parents or caregivers induce illnesses in their children or foster children, perhaps to gain the sympathy of outsiders or to experience the sense of control made possible by attending to a sick child. In a California case, a foster mother is alleged to have brought about the deaths of three children by giving them overdoses of medicines containing potassium and sodium. The chemicals induced suffocation or heart attacks. In 1992, the FBI's *Law Enforcement Bulletin* carried articles which noted that cases of Münchausen Syndrome by Proxy are suggested by mysterious high fevers in children, seizures of unknown origin, and similar symptoms. Doctors typically find the illnesses to be unusual, prolonged, and unexplained (Balleza, 1992). They require some medical sophistication on the part of the perpetrator.

Speculations abound as researchers explore the meanings and variations of Münchausen syndrome.

SUMMARY

The dissociative and somatoform disorders were historically linked with the anxiety disorders as forms of neuroses. The various forms of neurosis were theorized to be related to anxiety in different ways. Anxiety is expressed directly in different forms in the anxiety disorders, but its role in the dissociative and somatoform disorders is inferred.

Dissociative Disorders

Dissociative disorders involve changes or disturbance in identity, memory, or consciousness that affect the ability to maintain an integrated sense of self. Dissociative disorders include dissociative identity disorder, dissociative amnesia, dissociative fugue, and depersonalization disorder.

In dissociative identity disorder, two or more distinct personalities, each possessing well-defined traits and memories, exist within the person and repeatedly take control of the person's behavior. Dissociative amnesia involves loss of memory for personal information. There are four types of dissociative amnesia: localized, selective, generalized, and continuous. In dissociative fugue, the person travels suddenly away from home or place of work, shows a loss of memory for his or her personal past, and experiences identity confusion or takes on a new identity. Depersonalization disorders involve persistent or recurrent episodes of depersonalization that are of sufficient severity to cause significant distress or impairment in functioning. Still, the person can distinguish reality from unreality during these depersonalization experiences.

Psychodynamic theorists view dissociative experiences as a form of psychological defense by which the ego defends itself against troubling memories and unacceptable impulses by blotting them out of consciousness. There is increasing documentation of a link between dissociative disorders, especially multiple personality, and early childhood trauma, which lends support to the view that dissociation may serve to protect the self from troubling memories.

To learning and cognitive theorists, dissociative experiences involve ways of learning not to think about certain troubling behaviors or thoughts that might lead to feelings of guilt or shame. Relief from anxiety negatively reinforces this pattern of dissociation. Social-learning theorists and cognitive theorists suggest that multiple personality may represent a form of role-playing behavior.

Some dissociative states, like dissociative amnesia and fugue, may be transient and terminate abruptly. More persistent dissociative disorders, like depersonalization disorder, may occur more frequently during periods of anxiety or depression. In such cases, treatment may be directed at managing anxiety or depression. Treatment of dissociative identity disorder (multiple personality) is approached from several theoretical perspectives. Psychodynamic approaches help the individual uncover and cope with dissociated painful experiences from childhood. Biological approaches focus on the use of drugs to treat the anxiety and depression often associated with the disorder, but drugs have not been able to bring about reintegration of the personality. Learning perspectives focus on the use of behavioral methods of reinforcement of the most well-adjusted personality.

Somatoform Disorders

In somatoform disorders, there are physical complaints for which no organic basis can be found. Thus the symptoms are theorized to reflect psychological rather than organic factors. Three types of somatoform disorders are considered: conversion disorder, hypochondriasis, and somatization disorder.

In conversion disorder, symptoms or deficits in voluntary motor or sensory functions occur which suggest an underlying physical disorder but no apparent medical basis for the condition can be found. Hypochondriasis is a preoccupation with the fear of having, or the belief that one has, a serious medical illness, but no medical basis for the complaints can be found and fears of illness persist despite medical reassurances. Formerly known as Briquet's syndrome, somatization disorder involves multiple and recurrent complaints of physical symptoms that have persisted for many years and began prior to the age of 30, but most typically during adolescence.

Freud's belief that hysterical complaints (now called conversion disorders) were rooted in psychological, rather than physical, causes led to his development of a theory of the unconscious mind. The psychodynamic view holds that conversion disorders represent the conversion into physical symptoms of the leftover emotion or energy that is cut off from unacceptable or threatening impulses that the ego has prevented from reaching awareness. The symptom is functional, allowing the person to achieve both primary and secondary gains.

Learning theorists focus on the reinforcements that are associated with conversion disorders, such as the reinforcing effects of adopting a "sick role." A learning-theory view likens hypochondriasis to obsessive-compulsive behavior. Cognitive theorists propose that hypochondriacal complaints may represent a type of self-handicapping strategy.

Münchausen syndrome is a form of factitious disorder involving the conscious fabrication of medical complaints for no apparent cause other than to gain admission to a hospital. Malingering, by contrast, involves the fabrication of physical or psychological symptoms for obvious external gain.

Psychoanalysis seeks to uncover and bring to the level of awareness the unconscious conflicts, originating in childhood, that are believed to be at the root of the problem. Once the conflict is uncovered and worked through, the hysterical symptom should disappear because it is no longer needed as a partial solution to the underlying conflict. Behavioral approaches focus on removing sources of reinforcement that may be maintaining the abnormal behavior pattern. Behavior therapists may also work more directly to help people with somatoform disorders learn to handle stressful or anxiety-arousing situations more effectively.

Pablo Picasso, Sleeping Woman, 1936.

CHAPTER OUTLINE

7

Mood Disorders and Suicide

TRUTH  FICTION?

___ It is abnormal to feel depressed.

___ Bleak winter light casts some people into a diagnosable state of depression.

___ Some people ride an emotional roller coaster, swinging from the heights of elation to the depths of depression without external cause.

___ In some ways, many "mentally healthy" people see things *less* realistically than depressed people do.

___ There is a blood test for diagnosing depression.

___ The ancient Greeks and Romans used a contemporary form of chemotherapy to treat turbulent mood swings.

___ Suicide is a sign of insanity.

___ People who threaten to commit suicide are only seeking attention.

*L*ife has its ups and downs. Most of us feel elated when we have earned high grades, a promotion, or the affections of Ms. or Mr. Right. Most of us feel down or depressed when we are rejected by a date, flunk a test, or suffer financial reverses. It is normal and appropriate to be happy about uplifting events. It is just as normal, just as appropriate, to feel depressed by dismal events. It might very well be "abnormal" if one were *not* depressed by life's miseries.

 Feeling depressed is *not* abnormal when we have encountered depressing events or circumstances.

Personal ups and downs are appropriate responses to the ups and downs of life. Some people, however, experience emotional extremes in mood that seem divorced from events or are unusually prolonged or profound. Illness or the loss of a loved one may trigger depression that seems abnormal because of its extent and duration. Some people become severely depressed when things appear to be doing well, or when they encounter mildly upsetting events that most people take in stride. Still other people experience mood swings. They ride an emotional roller coaster with dizzying heights and abysmal depths when the world around them remains largely on an even keel.

MOOD DISORDERS

Our **moods** are enduring states of feeling that color our psychological lives. When we are in a "good mood," many of the insults of daily life roll off our backs. When our moods are depressed, however, even delightful events may do little to cheer us. **Mood disorders** are disturbances in mood that are serious enough to impair daily functioning. Mood disorders are relatively common, affecting 8% of the adult population at some point in their lives, according to the Epidemiologic Catchment Area (ECA) Study (Weissman et al., 1991).

In this chapter we focus on several mood disorders, including two kinds of depressive disorders, major depression and dysthymic disorder, and two kinds of disorders that involve mood swings, bipolar disorder and cyclothymic disorder (see Table 7.1). The depressive disorders are considered **unipolar** because the disturbance lies in only one emotional direction or pole. Disorders that involve mood swings are **bipolar**. They involve excesses of both depression and elation, usually in an alternating pattern.

Table 7.1 Types of Mood Disorders

Depressive Disorders (Unipolar Disorders)

Major Depression (Major Depressive Disorder)	Occurrence of one or more periods or episodes (called major depressive episodes) of depression without a history of naturally occurring manic or hypomanic episodes. People may have one major depressive episode, followed by a return to normal functioning. The majority of people with a major depressive episode have recurrences that are separated by periods of normal or perhaps impaired functioning.
Dysthymic Disorder	A pattern of mild depression (but perhaps an irritable mood in children or adolescents) that occurs for an extended period of time—in adults, typically for many years.

Bipolar Disorders

Bipolar Disorder	Disorders with one or more manic or hypomanic episodes (episodes of inflated mood and hyperactivity in which judgment and behavior are often impaired). Manic or hypomanic episodes often alternate with major depressive episodes with intervening periods of normal mood.
Cyclothymic Disorder	A chronic mood disturbance involving numerous hypomanic episodes (episodes with manic features of a lesser degree of severity than manic episodes) and numerous periods of depressed mood or loss of interest or pleasure in activities, but not of the severity to meet the criteria of major depressive episodes.

Source: Adapted from the DSM-IV Draft Criteria (American Psychiatric Association, 1993) pp. J:1–11.

Depression has been referred to as the "common cold" of psychological problems (Seligman, 1973). It is often the most frequent complaint prompting outpatient psychiatric visits (Woodruff et al., 1975). Depressive disorders are characterized by features such as those shown in Table 7.2.

When are changes in mood considered abnormal? Although changes in mood in response to the ups and downs of everyday life may be quite normal, persistent or severe changes in mood, or cycles of extreme elation and depression, may suggest the presence of a mood disorder.

Table 7.2 Common Features of Depression

Changes in Emotional States	Changes in mood (persistent periods of feeling down, depressed, sad or blue) Tearfulness or crying Increased irritability, jumpiness, or loss of temper
Changes in Motivation	Feeling unmotivated, or having difficulty getting going in the morning or even getting out of bed Reduced level of social participation or interest in social activities Loss of enjoyment or interest in pleasurable activities Reduced interest in sex Failure to respond to praise or rewards
Changes in Functioning and Motor Behavior	Moving about or talking or moving about more slowly than usual Changes in sleep habits (sleeping too much or too little, awakening earlier than usual and having trouble getting back to sleep in early morning hours—so-called early morning awakening) Changes in appetite (eating too much or too little) Changes in weight (gaining or losing weight) Functioning less effectively than usual at work or school
Cognitive Changes	Difficulty concentrating or thinking clearly Thinking negatively about oneself and one's future Feeling guilty or remorseful about past misdeeds Lack of self-esteem or feelings of inadequacy Thinking of death or suicide

MAJOR DEPRESSION (MAJOR DEPRESSIVE DISORDER)

Many, if not most of us, are sad from time to time. We may feel down in the dumps, cry, lose interest in things, find it hard to concentrate, expect the worst to happen, or even consider suicide. For most of us, these mood changes pass quickly and do not prevent us from functioning. Among people with **major depression**, however, mood changes are more severe and affect daily functioning. People with major depression may also have poor appetite and lose substantial weight. They may be physically agitated or—at the other extreme—slow down in motor activity. They may lose interest in most of their usual activities and pursuits, have difficulty concentrating and making decisions, and have pressing thoughts of death or attempt suicide.

People with major depression may have faulty perceptions of reality. In this case, depression may have psychotic features, such as delusions of unworthiness or guilt for assumed wrongdoings, or delusions that one's body is rotting from illness. Severely depressed people may also experience hallucinations, such as "hearing" the voices of others, or of demons, condemning one for perceived misdeeds.

The most prominent feature of depression is downcast mood. Depressed people also may be unable to find pleasure in activities and events enjoyed by others (Miller, R.E., 1987). An ebbing capacity for pleasure (**anhedonia**) discourages them from participating in normally pleasant activities, such as sports or family barbecues.

Major depression is diagnosed on the basis of one or more major depressive episodes in the absence of a history of **manic** or **hypomanic** episodes. (Major depression is a *unipolar* disorder, not a *bipolar*, or manic-depressive, disorder.) Major depression is the most common type of diagnosable mood disorder, affecting about 5% of the adult population at some point in their lives (Weissman et al., 1991). Some of the clinical features of a major depressive episode are listed in Table 7.3. To be diagnosed, a major depressive disorder cannot be accounted for by another mental disorder, an organic factor, such as a tumor or other physical illness, or by the use of drugs or medications. Nor can it represent a normal grief reaction to the death of a loved one—that is, **bereavement**.

The following case illustrates the range of features connected with major depression:

A 38-year-old female clerical worker has suffered from recurrent bouts of depression since she was about 13 years of age. Most recently, she has been troubled by cry-

ing spells at work, sometimes occurring so suddenly she wouldn't have enough time to run to the ladies room to hide her tears from others. She has difficulty concentrating at work and feels a lack of enjoyment from work she used to enjoy. She harbors severe pessimistic and angry feelings, which have been more severe lately since she has been recently putting on weight and has been neglectful in taking care of her diabetes. She feels guilty that she may be slowly killing herself by not taking better care of her health. She sometimes feels that she deserves to be dead. She has been bothered by excessive sleepiness for the past year and a half, and her driving license has been suspended due to an incident the previous month in which she fell asleep while driving, causing her car to hit a telephone pole. She wakes up most days feeling groggy

Table 7.3 Clinical Features of a Major Depressive Episode

A major depressive episode is denoted by the occurrence of five or more of the following features or symptoms during a two-week period and represents a change from previous functioning. At least one of the features must involve either (1) depressed mood or (2) loss of interest or pleasure in activities. Moreover, the symptoms must cause either clinically significant levels of distress or impairment in at least one important area of functioning, such as social or occupational functioning, and must not be due directly to the use of drugs or medications, or to a medical condition.*

1. Depressed mood during most of the day, nearly every day. Can be irritable mood in children or adolescents.

2. Greatly reduced sense of pleasure or interest in all or almost all activities, nearly every day for most of the day.

3. A significant loss or gain of weight (more than 5% of body weight in a month) without any attempt to diet, or an increase or decrease in appetite.

4. Daily (or nearly daily) insomnia or hypersomnia.

5. Excessive agitation or slowing down of movement responses nearly every day.

6. Feelings of fatigue or loss of energy nearly every day.

7. Feelings of worthlessness or misplaced or excessive or inappropriate guilt nearly every day.

8. Reduced ability to concentrate or think clearly or make decisions nearly every day.

9. Recurrent thoughts of death or suicide without a specific plan, or occurrence of a suicidal attempt or specific plan for committing suicide.

* Note: The DSM includes separate diagnostic categories for mood disorders due to medical conditions or use of substances such as drugs of abuse.

Source: Adapted from DSM-IV Draft Criteria (American Psychiatric Association, 1993), p. J: 1.

Major depression versus bereavement Major depression should be distinguished from a normal grief reaction to the death of a loved one, which is termed *bereavement*. But major depression may occur in people whose bereavement becomes prolonged or seriously interferes with normal functioning.

and just "out of it," and remains sleepy throughout the day. She has never had a steady boyfriend, and lives quietly at home with her mother, with no close friends outside of her family. During the interview, she cried frequently and answered questions in a low monotone, staring downward continuously.

■ *Adapted from Spitzer et al., 1989, pp. 59–62*

The course of major depression is variable. Some people experience a single episode with full return to previous levels of functioning. Other people have repeated episodes, with only partial restoration of earlier functioning between episodes. More than half of those who suffer a major depressive episode will have another. The highest rates of recurrence are found in the first months following recovery (Maj et al., 1992). The longer a person who overcomes an episode remains functioning normally, the lower the likelihood of recurrence (Belsher & Costello, 1988). Most recurrences occur within a year of the first episode. The recurrence rate then tapers off.

More than half of the 3,000 adult respondents to a large community-based survey who experienced a major depressive disorder reported a first episode

---

A CLOSER LOOK

Gender Differences and Gender Role Stereotypes in the Diagnosis of Depression: A Commentary

Women are at greater risk than men of developing depression (Coryell et al., 1992a; Weissman et al., 1991). The ECA survey of residents of five U.S. communities showed that, over the lifetime, major depression affected 7% of the women surveyed, as compared to 2.6% of the men (Weissman et al., 1991).

The reasons that women are more likely to encounter major depressive episodes than men remain unclear, although biological gender differences may be involved. A panel convened by the American Psychological Association (APA) attributed the increased rate of depression among women to the greater stress that women encounter in contemporary life (McGrath et al., 1990). Based on their review of recent research, the panel concluded that women are more likely than men to be subjected to socioeconomic and sociocultural factors such as physical and sexual abuse, impoverishment, single parenthood, and sexism. Women are also more frequent victims of violence and poverty and the stress that accompanies these conditions (McGrath et al., 1990). The APA panel acknowledged that hormonal changes during the menstrual cycle, childbirth, and unhappy marriages may also contribute to increased rates of depression among women. Yet the chairperson of the committee, Ellen McGrath, primarily attributed the gender difference to the stressors imposed on women in the United States today (Goleman, 1990c). Women are also more likely than men to be support-givers, which may compound the stress they encounter by heaping additional caregiving burdens on them and by exposing them to the problems that others face (Shumaker & Hill, 1991).

(continued)

They were never promised a rose garden Women are more likely to suffer from major depression than men. A panel convened by the American Psychological Association (APA) attributed the higher rates of depression among women to factors such as unhappy marriages, physical and sexual abuse, impoverishment, single parenthood, sexism, hormonal changes, childbirth, and excessive caregiving burdens. APA panel member Bonnie Strickland expressed surprise that even more women were not clinically depressed, since they are treated as second-class citizens.

Another APA panel member, Bonnie Strickland, expressed surprise that still greater numbers of women are not clinically depressed, given that they are treated as second-class citizens and are more likely than men to fall beneath the poverty line in socioeconomic status (Goleman, 1990c).

Differences in coping styles may also help explain women's greater proneness toward depression. Nolen-Hoeksema (1991; Nolen-Hoeksema et al., 1992) proposes a psychological explanation for the gender difference. Men, according to this hypothesis, are more likely to distract themselves when they are depressed, whereas women are more likely to amplify depression by ruminating about their feelings and their possible causes. Regardless of whether or not the initial precipitants of depression are biological, psychological, or social, one's responses may exacerbate or reduce the severity and duration of depressive episodes. On the other hand, men often distract themselves by turning to alcohol, which can lead to another set of psychological and social problems (Nolen-Hoeksema, 1991; Nolen-Hoeksema et al., 1992).

In considering gender differences for depressive disorders, it is also important to attend to gender role stereotypes and their effect on the client and therapist in the diagnosis of such disorders. Gender role stereotypes are sociocultural beliefs about what women and men are like and the things they are supposed to do or want to do. Gender roles are often attributed to presumed natural or biological gender differences, but they are sociocultural constructs that often say more about cultural values than biology. Mental health professions are institutions of the dominant culture, and despite attempts at academic rigor, many gender role stereotypes pervade apparently scientific definitions of mental health as well as diagnosis and treatment. Adherence to gender role stereotypes and cultural assumptions about psychological normalcy that accompany them can produce double standards in diagnosis of depression among women and men. Although there are no gender differences in the formal diagnostic criteria for depression, Loring and Powell (1988) found that the gender and race of the therapist and the client affect the likelihood of making the diagnosis, even when therapists are provided with clear diagnostic criteria.

Gender role stereotypes of women may bear closer similarity than stereotypes of men to features of depression. Descriptions of healthy adults usually emphasize assertiveness, competence, and rationality (Rothblum, 1983). Conversely, healthy women are generally perceived as warm, emotionally expressive, dependent, and demure (that is, passive). These expectations render the woman who conforms to gender role stereotypes closer in behavior to a depressive pattern. Men, moreover, are expected, like cowboys, to be rugged and independent. This expectation may also discourage many depressed men from seeking help for depressive symptoms (Basow, 1992). The reason that men are more likely than women to respond to inner hurt by turning to alcohol or other drugs, or by aggressive acting out, may also have a lot to do with gender role stereotypes. Because of stereotypical response patterns to depression, however, some men who are primarily depressed may receive a diagnosis of substance abuse or antisocial personality if they are brought to the attention of mental health professionals. Women, however, who are expected to be emotionally expressive and dependent, are likely to be more comfortable in admitting to depressive symptoms and seeking help for them.

Social restrictiveness and institutionalized gender biases lead to and reinforce the social inequalities between women and men. Moreover, the biased gender role expectations of many mental health professionals influence them to encourage women and men who are depressed, or who show other psychological problems, to conform to cultural stereotypes as part and parcel of coping with these problems (Basow, 1992). People's options may thus be restricted rather than expanded by culturally insensitive therapists.

by age 25 (Sorenson, et al., 1991). The ECA study reported an average age of onset of major depression of 27 (Weissman et al., 1991). One of four reported a first episode prior to age 18 (Sorenson et al., 1991). Women tend to report earlier ages of onset than men do. Although the initial onset of depression can occur in childhood (see Chapter 13), the risks are very low through age 14 (Lewinsohn et al., 1986). The risks of developing depression increase in late adolescence and early adulthood, peaking between ages 45 to 55. The likelihood of initial onset of depression falls off sharply with advancing age. People in their 70s who have never experienced a depressive episode are unlikely to become initially depressed at that advanced age. Still, depression can occur or recur at any age.

A review of studies reported between 1978 and 1987 showed that major depression may have decreased in frequency among the elderly during this period, but increased among segments of the population born since the end of World War II—among so-called baby boomers (Klerman et al., 1989). Researchers speculate that baby boomers may be more susceptible to depression because of factors such as unfulfilled economic expectations, increased urbanization, increased relocation from town to town (destroying networks for social support), and the pressures of adjusting to changing roles for men and women in the home, the marketplace, and society at large (Klerman et al., 1989).

The ECA study reported that lifetime prevalences of major depression were lower among African Americans (3.1%) than among non-Hispanic white Americans (5%) or Hispanic Americans (4.4%) (Weissman et al., 1991). It appears that African Americans report more depressive complaints, perhaps because they encounter greater stress, but they are less likely to suffer from the clinical syndrome of major depression (Somervell et al., 1989; Weissman et al., 1991).

A CLOSER LOOK

Seasonal Affective Disorder

Are you glum on gloomy days? Is your temper short during the brief days of winter? Are you dismal during the dark of long winter nights? Are you up when the sun is high in the sky?

Many people report that their moods vary with the weather, especially with the amount of direct sunlight. People who suffer from a repeated pattern of severe fall and winter depressions, but who bounce back during the spring and summer, are said to be afflicted with a type of major depression termed *seasonal affective (mood) disorder*—SAD (Rosenthal et al., 1984).

 The changing of the seasons apparently does produce a depressive disorder in some people.

The features of SAD include fatigue, excessive sleep, craving for carbohydrates, and weight gain (Jacobsen et al., 1987). SAD tends to lift with the early buds of spring. SAD affects women more often than men, and is most common among young adults. Nearly half of those who are afflicted report that SAD episodes began during childhood or adolescence (Murray, 1989b).

Although the causes of SAD remain unknown, many sufferers gain relief from 2 to 3 hours of bright artificial light a day, which apparently augments the meager sunlight they otherwise receive (Jacobsen et al., 1987; Lewy, 1987; Rosenthal et al., 1984, 1985). Patients usually carry out some of their daily activities (for example, eating, reading, writing) in comfortable proximity to the source of arti-

SAD in winter? Some people complain of depression during the fall and winter seasons but bounce back during the spring and summer. This pattern of depression has been called seasonal affective disorder—SAD—and is associated with changes in climate, especially seasonal changes in the amount of sunlight. Artificial phototherapy is helpful with many SAD sufferers. Would natural phototherapy in the Caribbean also be of benefit?

ficial light (Murray, 1989b). Light directed at the eyes tends to be more successful than light directed at the skin (Wehr et al., 1987). Improvement generally occurs within several days of phototherapy, but treatment is apparently required throughout the course of the winter season (Murray, 1989b). Although different theories have emerged to explain the effectiveness of phototherapy, the mechanisms of therapeutic action remain unclear (Murray, 1989b). However, subjects' expectations of improvement may be connected with phototherapy's effectiveness, suggesting that at least part of the benefit may be due to a placebo effect (Wehr et al., 1987). Because phototherapy does not help all SAD sufferers, research is needed to optimize its effectiveness (Murray, 1989b).

Reactive Versus Endogenous Depression

Some depressive episodes are apparently connected with external events or stressors, such as the loss of a loved one or failure to achieve a professional goal. Changes that affect intimate relationships are promi-nently connected with depression, especially "exit events," which involve the departure or loss of significant others through death, divorce, or academic or military obligations (Slater & Depue, 1981).

We expect people to be depressed following the loss of a loved one. Major depression persists beyond what is considered a normal time period or is signifi-

---

A CLOSER LOOK

Postpartum Depression

Many, perhaps most, new mothers experience mood changes, periods of tearfulness, and irritability following the birth of a child. These mood changes (Harding, 1989) are commonly called the "maternity blues," "postpartum blues," or "baby blues." The blues usually last for a couple of days and are believed to be a normal response to hormonal changes that attend childbirth (Harding, 1989). Given these turbulent hormonal shifts, it would be "abnormal" for most women *not* to experience some changes in feeling states shortly following childbirth.

Some mothers, however, undergo severe mood changes that may persist for months or even a year or more. Such problems in mood are referred to as **postpartum depression** (PPD). *Postpartum* derives from the Latin roots *post,* meaning "after," and *papere,* meaning "to bring forth." PPD is often accompanied by disturbances in appetite and sleep, low self-esteem, and difficulties in maintaining concentration or attention. Between 8 and 15% of mothers have been found to have a diagnosable depressive disorder of moderate severity in the months following childbirth (Campbell & Cohn, 1991; Gitlin et al., 1989). Questions remain as to whether these rates are greater among postpartum women than among women similar in age and social background in the general population, however (Campbell & Cohn, 1991; Gitlin et al., 1989; O'Hara et al., 1990). If they are not, it might be that the diagnostic category of PPD, as a distinct form of depression linked to the period following childbirth, is invalid (Gitlin et al., 1989).

Whiffen (1992) is one who argues for a distinct diagnostic category for PPD. Postpartum depressions tend to fall in a mild range of severity and to resolve more quickly than depressive disorders in the general population (Whiffen, 1992). Perhaps they represent a type of adjustment disorder that affects women (especially first-time mothers) who encounter difficulties adapting to the demands of caring for a new baby as well as a consequence of the birth itself (Whiffen, 1992).

Although PPD may involve biological factors, psychological and social factors such as financial problems, a troubled marriage, a history of depression, or an unwanted or

What are the origins of postpartum depression? Many or most new mothers experience transient periods of tearfulness and irritability following childbirth, which are commonly given such names as the "baby blues." The blues are considered a normal response to the hormonal changes that attend childbirth. More severe and enduring mood changes are referred to as *postpartum depression* (PPD). The origins of PPD are more uncertain, although psychosocial factors such as financial problems, a troubled marriage, a history of depression, or an unwanted or sick baby all appear to increase a woman's vulnerability to PPD.

sick baby may all increase a woman's vulnerability to PPD (Gitlin et al., 1989; Gotlib et al., 1991; Hopkins et al., 1987; O'Hara et al., 1991). PPD also appears to increase the risk of future depression (Philipps & O'Hara, 1991). Mothers who appear to be most at risk of PPD include first-time mothers, single mothers, and mothers who lack social support from their partners or other family members (Gitlin et al., 1989).

A study of 124 women carrying their firstborns showed that PPD could be predicted on the basis of factors such as depressed mood and marital stress during pregnancy (Whiffen, 1988). About 1 in 6 women in this sample (16.5%) met the criteria for diagnosable depression 8 weeks following delivery. PPD was also related to the mother's perceptions of the infant as temperamentally difficult and as crying excessively. Caring for a difficult, temperamental infant heightens the mother's level of stress and can contribute to feelings of maternal inadequacy, which may, in turn, both contribute to depression.

QUESTIONNAIRE

Are You Depressed?

This test, offered by the organizers of the National Depression Screening Day (October 8, 1992), can help you assess whether you are suffering from a serious depression. It is not intended for you to diagnose yourself, but rather to raise your awareness of concerns you may want to discuss with a professional.

Rating your responses: If you agree with at least five of the statements, including either item 1 or 2, and if you have had these complaints for at least 2 weeks, professional help is strongly recommended. If you answered "yes" to statement 3, seek consultation with a professional immediately. If you don't know to whom to turn, contact your college counseling center, neighborhood mental health center, or health provider.

YES NO

___ ___ 1. I feel downhearted, blue, and sad.

___ ___ 2. I don't enjoy the things that I used to.

___ ___ 3. I feel that others would be better off if I were dead.

___ ___ 4. I feel that I am not useful or needed.

___ ___ 5. I notice that I am losing weight.

___ ___ 6. I have trouble sleeping through the night.

___ ___ 7. I am restless and can't keep still.

___ ___ 8. My mind isn't as clear as it used to be.

___ ___ 9. I get tired for no reason.

___ ___ 10. I feel hopeless about the future.

Source: "Myriad Masks Hide an Epidemic of Depression," by J. E. Brody. Copyright © 1992 by The New York Times Company, reprinted by permission.

cantly more intense than "uncomplicated" bereavement or grief. In contrast to uncomplicated bereavement, major depression may entail feelings of worthlessness, suicidal thoughts, profound impairment in functioning, or sluggish psychological activity and movements (**psychomotor retardation**).

Depressive episodes that are linked to negative events are often called *reactive* depressions. It is believed that they are responsive to external precipitants. Many depressive episodes seem to occur in the absence of clear external events, however. Such depressive episodes are often labeled **endogenous** (deriving from Greek roots meaning "born" from "within"). Endogenous depression is often seen as biologically based because its occurrence is presumably linked to inner causes rather than to external changes (Heiby et al., 1987). In contrast, reactive depressions (also referred to as neurotic or *exogenous* depressions) are more likely to reflect psychological, social, and physical environmental factors.

There are problems in distinguishing reactive from endogenous depressions on the basis of precipitants, however. For one, depressed people may be forgetful or confused and be unable to recall external precipitants. Their friends and loved ones may also be unaware of precipitating factors. Depressed people may also report problems that actually occur coincidentally with the onset of the depressive episode rather than causing it. Our clinical experience has

suggested that it is nearly always possible to find some apparent precipitant of a depressive episode, even when things are apparently going well in general. It is useful to remain cautious in labeling events as precipitants of depression, as it is useful to remain cautious in any endeavor that attempts to ferret out cause and effect.

Because of such problems, the distinction between reactive and endogenous depressions typically rests more on manifest behaviors than on the presence or absence of potential precipitants. Depressions labeled endogenous are more likely to be characterized by the "vegetative" or physical features of depression, such as loss of weight or appetite, early morning awakening, apathy, and psychomotor retardation. These physical features appear to be less prominent in reactive depressions.

DYSTHYMIC DISORDER

Major depression is severe and marked by a relatively abrupt change from one's preexisting state. A milder form of depression seems to follow a chronic course of development that often begins in childhood or adolescence (Klein et al., 1988). Earlier diagnostic formulations had characterized this type of depression as "neurotic" or as a "depressive neurosis." It was so labeled in an effort to account for several features that are traditionally connected with neurosis, such as early childhood origins, a chronic course, and generally mild levels of severity. The DSM labels this form of depression **dysthymic disorder** (from Greek roots *dys-*, meaning "bad" or "hard" and *thymos*, meaning "spirit"). It was diagnosed in 3% of the adult population in the five U.S. communities surveyed in the ECA study (Weissman et al., 1991). Dysthymic disorder occurred about twice as often among women (4.1%) as among men (2.2%) but did not vary in prevalence across ethnic groups.

Dysthymic persons do feel "bad spirited" or "down in the dumps" most of the time and for most of the day, but they are not so severely depressed as those with major depression. Dysthymic disorder may develop in childhood, adolescence, or adulthood. Whereas major depression tends to be severe and time limited, dysthymic disorder is relatively mild and nagging, typically lasting for a period of years in adults. The average duration of the disorder is estimated to be about 5 years (Keller, 1990).

In dysthymics, complaints of depression may become such a fixture of people's lives that it seems to be intertwined with their personality structures (Klein et al., 1988). The persistence of complaints may lead others to perceive depressed people as whining (Akiskal, 1983). Although the disorder is less severe than major depression, persistent depressed mood and low self-esteem can affect the person's occupational and social functioning, as we see in the following case:

*T*he woman, a 28-year-old junior executive, complained of chronic feelings of depression since the age of 16 or 17. Despite doing well in college, she brooded about how other people were "genuinely intelligent." She felt she could never pursue a man she might be interested in dating because she felt inferior and intimidated. While she had extensive therapy through college and graduate school, she could never recall a time during those years when she did not feel somewhat depressed. She got married shortly after college graduation to the man she was dating at the time, although she didn't think that he was anything "special." She just felt she needed to have a husband for companionship and he was available. But they soon began to quarrel and she's lately begun to feel that marrying him was a mistake. She has had difficulties at work, turning in "slipshod" work and never seeking anything more than what is basically required of her, showing no initiative. While she dreams of acquiring status and money, she doesn't expect that she or her hus-

band will rise in their professions because they lack "connections." Her social life is dominated by her husband's friends and their spouses and she doesn't think that other women would find her interesting or impressive. She lacks interest in life in general and expresses dissatisfaction with all facets of her life—her marriage, her job, her social life.

■ *Adapted from Spitzer et al., 1989, pp. 37–39*

Dysthymic disorder often occurs together with a major depressive episode (Klein et al., 1988; Weissman et al., 1991). Some clinicians use the term **double depression** to describe people who have a major depressive episode superimposed upon a dysthymic disorder (Miller et al., 1986). Major depressive episodes tend to occur more frequently and to be longer in duration among these so-called double depressives than among "pure" major depressives.

Prior to the publication of the DSM-IV, James McCullough and his colleagues (1992) reported the results of a field study of the diagnostic criteria for major depression and dysthymic disorder to a symposium at a meeting of the American Psychological Association. The investigators assessed 526 subjects who met the diagnostic criteria for various forms of depression in five different clinical settings. On the basis of a structured clinical interview, symptom checklists, and other measures, the most prominent symptoms of dysthymic disorder were pessimism and self-pity, inactivity, and feelings of inadequacy and low self-esteem. Yet the investigators in the field trial concluded that the features of both disorders—major depression and dysthymic disorder—were very similar. They stated that further research was needed to determine whether the patterns of features associated with these disorders (see Table 7.4), or the frequency of occurrence of these features, might reliably differentiate them.

BIPOLAR DISORDER

Most of us have our ups and downs, but people with bipolar disorder have severe mood swings from extreme elation to severe depression. The initial episode is usually manic, although some bipolar disorders begin with a depressive episode. Manic episodes are usually shorter in duration and end more abruptly than depressive episodes. Some people with recurrent bipolar disorder attempt suicide "on

Table 7.4 Prevalence of Various Diagnostic Features Among Cases of Dysthymic Disorder and Recurrent Episodes of Major Depression in the DSM-IV Field Trial

Prevalence of the diagnostic feature	Major Depression (*N* = 59) (%)	Dysthymic Disorder (*N* = 39) (%)	Probability that difference is due to chance fluctuation
Loss of interest, loss of pleasure	95	54	.0000
Loss of appetite, loss of weight	51	5	.0000
Trouble thinking, concentrating, making decisions	89	41	.0000
Reduced level of activity	88	59	.0020
Feelings of worthlessness	73	41	.0033
Worsening of depression in the morning	32	5	.0035
Inability to cope	64	33	.0049
Talking or moving more slowly	81	54	.0071
Fatigue, loss of energy	86	62	.0092
Sleep-onset insomnia	59	31	.0104
Feelings of hopelessness	64	36	.0104

Based on samples of "pure" subjects—subjects, that is, not considered to have a history of the other depressive disorder.

Adapted from J. P. McCullough, D. N. Klein, M. T. Shea, I. Miller, & A. L. Kaye (1992, August 17). DSM-IV field trials for major depression, dysthymia, and minor depressions. Paper presented to the Symposium on DSM-IV Field Trials: Part One. Centennial Convention of the American Psychological Association, Washington, D.C.

the way down" from the manic phase. They report they would do nearly anything to escape the depths of depression that lie ahead.

Bipolar disorder affects perhaps ½ to 1% of the adult population at some point during their lives (Weissman et al., 1991). Unlike major depression, bipolar disorder is believed to affect men and women in about equal numbers (Weissman et al., 1991). The DSM distinguishes between two general types of bipolar disorders, *bipolar I disorder* and *bipolar II disorder* (American Psychiatric Association, 1993). The essential feature of bipolar I disorder is the occurrence of one or more manic episodes. A disorder can thus be labeled "bipolar" even if it consists of manic episodes wihtout any past or present major depressive episodes. In such cases, it is possible that a major depression will eventually appear or has been overlooked. In a few cases of bipolar I disorder, called the mixed type, both a manic episode and a major depressive episode occur simultaneously. More frequently, though, cycles of elated and depressed mood states alternate with intervening periods of normal mood. In bipolar II disorder, the person has experienced one or more major depressive episodes and at

least one hypomanic episode, but has never had a full-blown manic episode. Whether bipolar I and bipolar II disorders represent qualitatively different disorders or different points along a continuum of severity of bipolar disorder remains to be determined.

Sometimes there are periods of "rapid cycling" in which the individual experiences two or more full cycles of mania and depression within a year without intervening normal periods. Rapid cycling is relatively rare and typically limited to a year or less. Rapid cycling is associated with greater impairment in vocational and social functioning while it lasts, however. A study of 45 rapid cyclers showed that rapid cycling was most likely to occur during the first year of a 5-year follow-up period (Coryell et al., 1992b). Over the long term, rapid cycling was not associated with a more negative outcome than nonrapid cycling.

 Some people do ride an emotional roller coaster, swinging from the heights of elation to the depths of depression without external cause. They are said to have bipolar disorder.

Manic Episode

Bipolar I disorders are recognized by the presence of **manic episodes**, or periods of mania. Manic episodes typically begin in the early 20s but may first occur at age 50 or beyond. Such episodes typically begin abruptly, gathering force within days, and tend to last from a week to a few months. Manic episodes are relatively uncommon, affecting 8 persons in 1,000 (0.8%) in the ECA survey (Weissman et al., 1991).

The manic person experiences a sudden elevation or expansion of mood and feels unusually cheerful, euphoric, or optimistic. In stark contrast to the depressed state, persons in a manic phase seem to have boundless energy and are extremely sociable, although they tend to become demanding and overbearing toward others. Other people recognize the sudden shift in mood to be excessive in light of the person's circumstances. It is one thing to feel elated if one has just won the state lottery. It is another to feel euphoric "because" it's Wednesday.

Manic people are excited and may strike others as silly, by carrying jokes too far, for example. They tend to show poor judgment and to become argumentative, sometimes going so far as destroying property (Depue et al., 1981). Roommates may find them abrasive and avoid them. People in a manic phase often speak very rapidly (show **pressured speech**). Their thoughts and speech may jump from topic to topic (in a **rapid flight of ideas**). Others find it difficult to get a word in edgewise. People in a manic state may be extremely generous. They may make huge charitable contributions or give away costly possessions. They may not be able to sit still or sleep restfully. They almost always show less need for sleep. They tend to awaken early yet feel well rested and full of energy. Manics sometimes go for days without sleep and without feeling tired. Although persons in a manic episode may have abundant stores of energy, they seem unable to organize their efforts constructively. Their elation impairs their ability to work and maintain normal relationships.

People in a manic episode generally experience an inflated sense of self-esteem that may range from extreme self-confidence to wholesale delusions of grandeur. They may feel capable of solving the world's problems or of composing symphonies, despite a lack of special knowledge or talent. Manic persons may spout off about matters on which they know little, such as how to solve world hunger or create a new world order. It soon becomes clear that they are disorganized and incapable of completing their projects. They become highly distractible. Their attention is easily diverted by irrelevant stimuli like

the sounds of a ticking clock or of people talking in the next room. They tend to take on multiple tasks, biting off more than they can chew. Manic people may suddenly quit their jobs to enroll in law school, wait tables at night, organize charity drives on weekends, and work on the great American novel in their "spare time." Manic people tend to exercise poor judgment. They fail to weigh the consequences of their actions and may get into trouble as a result of lavish spending, reckless driving, or sexual escapades. In severe cases, manics may experience disorders of thinking similar to those of schizophrenics. They may experience hallucinations or become grossly delusional, believing, for example, that they have a special relationship with God.

The following case provides a firsthand account of a manic episode. The early stages are dominated by euphoria, boundless energy, and an inflated sense of self. As mania intensifies, the individual may become confused:

When I start going into a high, I no longer feel like an ordinary housewife. Instead I feel organized and accomplished and I begin to feel I am my most creative self. I can write poetry easily. I can compose melodies without effort. I can paint. My mind feels facile and absorbs everything. I have countless ideas about improving the conditions of mentally retarded children, of how a hospital for these children should be run, what they should have around them to keep them happy and calm and unafraid. I see myself as being able to accomplish a great deal for the good of people. I have countless ideas about how the environment problem could inspire a crusade for the health and betterment of everyone. I feel able to accomplish a great deal for the good of my family and others. I feel pleasure, a sense of euphoria or elation. I want it to last forever. I don't seem to need much sleep. I've lost weight and feel healthy and I like myself. I've just bought six new dresses, in fact, and they look quite good on me. I feel sexy and men stare at me. Maybe I'll have an affair, or perhaps several. I feel capable of speaking and doing good in politics. I would like to help people with problems similar to mine so they won't feel hopeless.

It's wonderful when you feel like this. . . . The feeling of exhilaration—the high mood—makes me feel light and full of the joy of living. However, when I go beyond this stage, I become manic, and the creativeness becomes so magnified I begin to see things in my mind that aren't real. For instance, one night I created an entire movie, complete with cast, that I still think would be terrific. I saw the people as clearly as if watching them in real life. I also experienced complete terror, as if it were actually happening, when I knew that an assassination scene was about to take place. I cowered under the covers and became a complete shaking wreck. As you know, I went into a manic psychosis at that point. My screams awakened my husband, who tried to reassure me that we were in our bedroom and everything was the same. There was nothing to be afraid of. Nevertheless, I was admitted to the hospital the next day.

■ *Fieve, 1975, pp. 12–18*

CYCLOTHYMIC DISORDER

The word **cyclothymic** is derived from the Greek *kyklos,* which means "circle," and *thymos* ("spirit"). The notion of a circular-moving spirit is an apt description because this disorder involves a chronic cyclical pattern of mood disturbance characterized by mild mood swings of at least 2 years (one year for children and adolescents). Cyclothymic disorder usually begins in late adolescence or early adulthood and persists for years. Few, if any, periods of normal mood last for more than a month or two. Neither the periods of elevated or depressed mood are severe enough to warrant a diagnosis of bipolar disorder.

The periods of elevated mood are called **hypomanic episodes**, from the Greek prefix *hypo-,* meaning "under" or "less than." *Hypo* manic episodes are less severe than manic episodes. People are more restless and irritable than normal during them, however. Hypomanic episodes also occur without the severe social or occupational problems that are engendered by full-blown manic episodes. In the hypomanic phase, the person may have an inflated sence of self-esteem and feel unusually charged with energy and alert. They may be able to work long hours with little fatigue or need for sleep. Their projects may be left unfinished when their moods reverse, however. Then they enter a mildly depressed mood and find it difficult to summon the energy or interest to persevere. They feel lethargic and depressed, but not to the extent that is typical of a major depressive episode.

Social relationships may become strained by shifting moods, and work may suffer. Social invitations, eagerly sought during hypomanic periods, may be declined during depressed periods. Phone calls may not be returned as the mood slumps. Sexual interest waxes and wanes.

The boundaries between bipolar disorder and cyclothymic disorder are not yet clearly established. Cyclothymic disorder may represent a milder form of bipolar disorder. Although cyclothymic disorder is chronic and can last a lifetime, it also frequently progresses to bipolar disorder.

The following case presents an example of the mild mood swings that typify cyclothymic disorder:

The man, a 29-year-old car salesman, reports that since the age of 14 he has experienced alternating periods of "good times and bad times." During his "bad" periods, which generally last between 4 and 7 days, he sleeps excessively and feels a lack of confidence, energy, and motivation, as if he were "just vegetating." Then his moods abruptly shift for a period of three or four days, usually upon awakening in the morning, and he feels aflush with confidence and sharpened mental ability. During these "good periods" he engages in promiscuous sex and uses alcohol, in part to enhance his good feelings and in part to help him sleep at night. The good periods may last upwards of 7–10 days at times, before shifting back into the "bad" periods, generally following a hostile or irritable outburst.

■ *Adapted from Spitzer et al., 1989, pp. 96–97*

THEORETICAL PERSPECTIVES

Multiple factors—biological, psychological, social, and physical environmental—apparently contribute to vulnerability to various emotional and physical disorders. In this section we first consider the relationships between stress and the mood disorders. Then we consider psychological and biological perspectives on depression.

Stress and Mood Disorders

Stressors such as the loss of a loved one, unemployment, physical illness, marital discord, poverty, pressure at work, prejudice and discrimination, may all contribute to or maintain depression (Billings et al., 1983; Coyne et al., 1987; Eckenrode, 1984; Folkman & Lazarus, 1986; Stone & Neale, 1984; Weissman, 1987). Unemployed people are more likely to suffer a mood disorder, especially major depression, than are people who are employed, especially when unemployment is prolonged (Weissman et al., 1991). People who lose a spouse are at greater risk of suffering a depressive disorder. In one study, about 23% of widows and widowers met diagnosable criteria for a depressive disorder when evaluated 7 months following the loss, as compared to 4% of a comparison group whose spouses were still alive (Zisook & Schuchter, 1991). We may be most likely to feel depressed when we assume responsibility for undesirable events, such as school-related problems, financial difficulties, unwanted pregnancy, interpersonal problems, and problems with the law (Hammen & Mayol, 1982). Stressors of various kinds may also make it more difficult to overcome depressive episodes, especially recurrent episodes (Monroe et al., 1992).

Stressful life events that bear on people's core concerns may be relatively more powerful precipitants of recurrent depression. In one study (Segal et al., 1992), depressed people who were highly concerned about personal failure were more likely to relapse into depression following a stressful achievement-related event (for example, failing in school or being demoted at work) than they were following exposure to interpersonal stressors such as a broken engagement, divorce, or death of a spouse. Stressful events also apparently contribute to the recurrence of bipolar disorder, if not necessarily to its initial appearance (Ellicott et al., 1990).

Some people seem better able to withstand stress or recover from losses than others. Researchers have found that the relationships between stress and depression may be moderated by such psychosocial factors as coping styles and social support. For example, depressed people are less likely than nondepressed persons to use active problem-solving strategies to alleviate stress (Asarnow et al., 1987; Nezu & Ronan, 1985; Pagel & Becker, 1987; Schotte & Clum, 1987). Depressed people tend to be deficient in skills needed to solve personal problems, such as problems with friends or at work (Marx et al., 1992).

Evidence supports the role of social support as a buffer against depression. People who are divorced or separated have the highest rates of depression; married people have the lowest. Major depression occurs twice as often among people who live alone than among others (Weissman et al., 1991). A strong marital relationship may provide a source of support during times of stress (Weissman et al., 1991). In one study, people assessed as having poor marital relationships reported more signs of depression 4 years later than did people with better relationships, even when the initial level of depression was taken into consideration (Menaghan & Lieberman, 1986). In another study, wives who rated their husbands as more supportive were less likely than wives who rated their husbands as less supportive to be depressed a year later (Monroe et al., 1986).

Research also shows that people with poor social integration (people who lack important relationships and who rarely join in social activities) are more likely to suffer depression (Barnett & Gotlib, 1988). Depressed people who perceive that social support is available also tend to recover relatively more quickly from a major depressive episode than people who do not (McLeod et al., 1992).

Although there are links between mood disorders and stress, the directionality of the connections are not perfectly clear. It seems obvious that external events can precipitate or moderate disturbances in

Social support as a buffer against depression. People who are divorced or separated have much higher rates of depression than married people, and major depression occurs twice as often among people who live alone. Wives who rate their husbands as supportive are less likely than wives who rate their husbands as unsupportive to be depressed. People who lack important relationships and who rarely join in social activities are more likely to suffer from depression.

mood, but preexisting psychological problems and strategies for coping may figure into whether people encounter stress and how they respond to it.

Psychodynamic Perspectives

Psychodynamic theorists suggest various explanations for mood disorders. Each involves inner, unconscious sources.

■ **TRADITIONAL PSYCHODYNAMIC THEORY** The classic psychodynamic theory of depression of Freud (1957/1917) and his followers (e.g., Abraham, 1948/1916) holds that depression represents anger directed inward rather than against others. Anger may become directed against the self following the actual or threatened loss of important others.

Freud believed that **mourning**, or normal bereavement, is a healthful process by which one eventually comes to separate from a person who is lost through death, separation, divorce, or another avenue. Pathological mourning, however, does not promote separation and could foster lingering depression. Pathological mourning is likely to occur in people who held powerful **ambivalent** feelings— a combination of positive (love) and negative (anger, hostility) feelings—toward the person who has departed or whose departure is feared. Freud theorized that when people lose, or fear losing, an important figure about whom they are ambivalent, their feelings of anger toward the other person turn to rage. Rage triggers conscious and unconscious imagery of harm, producing guilt. Guilt, in turn, prevents the person from venting anger directly at the lost person ("object").

To preserve the lost object, people **introject**, or bring inward, their mental representations of the object. They thus incorporate the other person into their selves. Now anger is further turned inward, against the part of the self that represents the inward representation of the lost person, producing self-loathing and associated feelings of depression.

From the psychodynamic viewpoint, bipolar disorder represents shifting dominance of the individual's personality by the ego and superego. In the depressive phase, the superego is dominant, producing exaggerated notions of wrongdoing and flooding the individual with feelings of guilt and worthlessness. After a time, the ego rebounds and asserts supremacy, producing feelings of elation and self-confidence that come to characterize the manic phase. The excessive display of ego eventually triggers a return of guilt, once again plunging the individual into depression.

■ **THE SELF-FOCUSING MODEL** More recent psychodynamic models of depression have focused on the effects of loss on the individual's sense of self-worth or self-esteem. According to the self-focusing model, for example, depression may occur when an individual pursues love objects or goals that it would be more adaptive to surrender (Pyszczynski & Greenberg, 1987). The self-focusing model considers how people allocate their attentional processes after the loss. It is thus a type of psychodynamic-cognitive model. The self-focusing model shares with the traditional psychodynamic model an emphasis on the depressed individual's reaction to loss. The emphasis, however, is on how the loss of an important person or occupational goal can lower self-esteem.

When depression-prone people suffer major losses or disappointments, they undergo a period of intense self-examination or self-focus to try to reconcile the discrepancy between what they have and what they want. Inability to surrender hope of retrieving the person or goal leads to self-absorption. Fruitless focus on restoring the lost object or goal triggers self-blame, diminishing self-esteem and depressing mood. The disappointments of the day may rekindle self-criticism for past disappointments, such as failed relationships, which exacerbates negative feelings. People may become so trapped in negative self-focusing that they cannot accept success experiences as reasons to reevaluate their self-concepts. They may attribute negative events to personal shortcomings, but explain away positive events as "good fortune." They come to expect the worst in relationships, an expectation that may become a self-fulfilling prophecy.

Consider a person who must cope with the termination of a failed romantic relationship. It may be clear to all concerned that the relationship is beyond hope of revival. The self-focusing model proposes, however, that the depression-prone individual persists in focusing attention on restoring the relationship, rather than recognizing the futility of the effort and getting on with life. Moreover, the self-focusing model proposes that the lost partner provided emotional support which helped the depression-prone individual maintain feelings of self-esteem. Following the loss, the depression-prone individual feels stripped of hope and optimism because these positive feelings had depended on the other person, now lost. The loss of feelings of self-esteem and security, not of the relationship per se, precipitates depression. If depression-prone people peg their self-worth to a specific occupational goal, such as success in a modeling career, failure triggers self-focusing and consequent depression. Only by surrendering the object or lost goal and fostering alternate sources of identity and self-worth can the cycle be broken.

■ **RESEARCH EVIDENCE** Psychodynamic theorists focus on the role of loss in depression. Research does show that the losses of significant others (through death or divorce, for example) are often associated with the onset of depression (Paykel, 1982). Such losses may also lead to other psychological disorders, however. There is yet a lack of research to support Freud's view that repressed anger toward the departed loved one is turned inward in depression.

Research on the utility of the self-focusing model has been mixed. On one hand, depressed people have been shown to engage in higher levels of self-focusing than normal people following failures, and in relatively lower levels of self-focusing following successes (Pyszczynski & Greenberg, 1985, 1986). On the other hand, self-focused attention has been linked to disorders other than depression, including anxiety disorders, alcoholism, mania, and schizophrenia (Ingram, 1990, 1991). The general linkage between self-focused attention and psychopathology may limit the model's value as an explanation of depression (Ingram, 1991).

What happens when we lose our sense of direction? According to the humanistic-existential perspective, depression may result from the inability to find meaning and purpose in one's life.

Humanistic-Existential Perspectives

From the humanistic-existential perspective, people become depressed when they cannot imbue their existence with meaning and make authentic choices that lead to self-fulfillment. The world is then a drab place. People's search for meaning gives color and substance to their lives. Guilt may arise when people believe that they have not lived up to their potentials. Humanistic psychologists challenge us to take a long hard look at our lives. Are they worthwhile and enriching? Or are they drab and routine? If the latter, it may be that we have frustrated our needs for self-actualization. We may be settling, coasting through life. Settling can give rise to a sense of dreariness that becomes expressed in depressive behavior—lethargy, sullen mood, and withdrawal.

Like psychodynamic theorists, humanistic theorists also focus on the loss of self-esteem that can arise when people lose friends or family members, or suffer occupational setbacks or losses. We tend to connect our personal identity and sense of self-worth with our social roles as parents, spouses, students, or workers. When these role identities are lost, through the death of a spouse, the departure of children to

college, or loss of a job, our sense of purpose and self-worth can be shattered. Depression is a frequent consequence of such losses. It is especially likely when we base our self-esteem on our occupational role or success. The loss of a job, a demotion, or a failure to achieve a promotion are common precipitants of depression, especially when we are reared to value ourselves on the basis of occupational success.

Learning Perspectives

Whereas psychodynamic perspectives focus on inner, often unconscious, determinants of mood disorders, learning perspectives dwell more on situational factors, such as the loss of positive reinforcement. We perform best when levels of reinforcement are commensurate with our efforts. Changes in the frequency or effectiveness of reinforcement can shift the balance so that life becomes unrewarding.

■ **REINFORCEMENT AND DEPRESSION** Peter Lewinsohn (1974) suggests that depression may result when a person's behavior receives too little reinforcement from the environment. Lack of reinforcement can sap motivation and induce feelings of depression. A vicious cycle may ensue: Inactivity and social withdrawal deplete opportunities for reinforcement; lesser reinforcement exacerbates withdrawal. The low rate of activity which is typical of depression may also be a source of secondary gain or secondary reinforcement. Family members and other people may rally around depressed people and release them from their responsibilities. Rather than help depressed people regain normal levels of instrumental behavior, sympathy may thus backfire and maintain depressed behavior.

Reduction in reinforcement levels can occur for many reasons. A person who is recuperating at home from illness may find little that is reinforcing to do. Social reinforcement may plummet when people close to us, who were suppliers of reinforcement, die or leave us. People who suffer social losses are more likely to become depressed when they lack the social skills to form new relationships. Some first-year college students are homesick and depressed because they lack the skills to form rewarding new relationships. Widows and widowers may be at a loss as to how to ask someone for a date or start a new relationship.

Changes in life circumstances may also alter the balance of effort and reinforcement. A prolonged layoff may reduce financial reinforcements, which may in turn force painful cutbacks in lifestyle. A disability or an extended illness may also impair one's ability to ensure a steady flow of reinforcements.

Lewinsohn's model is supported by research findings that connect depression to a low level of positive reinforcement. For example, Lewinsohn and Libet (1972) noted a correspondence between depressed moods and lower rates of participation in potentially reinforcing activities. People with depressive disorders were found to report fewer pleasant activities than nondepressed people (MacPhillamy & Lewinsohn, 1974). It remains unclear, however, whether depression precedes or follows a decline in the level of reinforcement (Williams, J. M., 1984). It may be that depressed people lose interest in pleasant activities or withdraw from potentially reinforcing social interactions, and not that inactivity leads to depression. Regardless of the causes of depression, behavioral treatment approaches that encourage depressed people to increase their levels of pleasant activities and provide them with the skills to do so show promise in alleviating depression.

■ **INTERACTIONAL THEORY** The interactions between depressed persons and other people may help to explain the former group's shortfall in positive reinforcement. Interactional theory, developed by James Coyne (1976), proposes that the adjustment to living with a depressed person can become so stressful that the partner or family member becomes

progressively less reinforcing toward the depressed person.

Interactional theory is based on the concept of reciprocal interaction. People's behavior influences, and is influenced by, the behavior of others. The theory holds that depression-prone people react to stress by demanding greater social support and reassurance. At first depressed people may succeed in garnering support. Over time, however, their demands and behavior begin to elicit anger or annoyance. Although loved ones may keep negative feelings to themselves, so as not to further upset the depressed person, the feelings may surface in subtle ways that spell rejection. The depressed person may react to rejection with deeper depression and greater demands, triggering a vicious cycle of further rejection and more profound depression. Depressed people may also feel guilty about distressing family members, which can exacerbate negative feelings about themselves.

Evidence shows that depressed people do tend to experience rejection in long-term relationships (Marcus & Nardone, 1992). Living with a depressed spouse also tends to heighten marital strains (Haas et al., 1985). Family members may find it stressful to adjust to depressed people's behavior, especially their withdrawal, lethargy, fretfulness, and despair. In one study, 40% of the family members of people who were currently depressed showed signs of emotional distress that seemed significant enough to warrant psychological intervention. This percentage was significantly higher than that among the family members of formerly depressed people (Coyne et al., 1987). In another study, spouses whose partners were formerly depressed were often as distressed as spouses whose partners remained currently depressed, suggesting that family distress can often linger even as the partner's depression lifts (Krantz & Moos, 1987).

The links between depression, the seeking of reassurance, and social rejection may be moderated by traditional gender role expectations. A study of mildly depressed college students supported Coyne's prediction that depressed people seek reassurance from others (in this case, college roommates of the same gender) to relieve their doubts about whether others really care about them (Joiner et al., 1992). Depressed men, but not women, encountered rejection by roommates when they strongly sought such reassurance. Perhaps depressed men who "suffer in silence" and "take it like a man" are more valued by their peers. Depressed women may not be perceived as violating a gender stereotype when they seek emotional reassurance, and thus may be less likely to be rejected.

The Pleasant Events Schedule

Psychologist Peter Lewinsohn of the University of Oregon has suggested that depression results from a low rate of positive reinforcement. To keep our moods on an even keel, we need positive feedback from our environments. Engaging in pleasant events provides a number of opportunities for reinforcement.

Lewinsohn and his colleagues have developed a number of Pleasant Events Schedules that list activities such as watching a sports event and taking a long hot bath. Which of the activities in the following list are pleasant for you?

You can run a personal experiment on the connection between your moods and your activities. Track your daily moods by use of a scale from 1 to 10 (1 = "severely depressed . . . down in the dumps"; 10 = "best possible mood . . . feel wonderful"). Rate your mood at the same time each day (before retiring for bed, for example). Select and engage in several events you find pleasurable each week. Average your daily mood ratings for each week and see whether or not your average daily mood is related to the number or kinds of pleasant activities you engaged in that week.

____ 1. Being in the country
____ 2. Wearing expensive or formal clothes
____ 3. Making contributions to religious, charitable, or political groups
____ 4. Talking about sports
____ 5. Meeting someone new
____ 6. Going to a rock concert
____ 7. Playing baseball, softball, football, or basketball
____ 8. Planning trips or vacations
____ 9. Buying things for yourself
____ 10. Being at the beach
____ 11. Doing artwork (painting, sculpture, drawing, moviemaking, etc.)
____ 12. Rock climbing or mountaineering
____ 13. Reading the Scriptures
____ 14. Playing golf
____ 15. Rearranging or redecorating your room or house
____ 16. Going naked
____ 17. Going to a sports event
____ 18. Going to the races
____ 19. Reading stories, novels, poems, plays, magazines, newspapers
____ 20. Going to a bar, tavern, club
____ 21. Going to lectures or talks
____ 22. Creating or arranging songs or music
____ 23. Boating
____ 24. Restoring antiques, refinishing furniture
____ 25. Watching television or listening to the radio
____ 26. Camping

Does participation in pleasant events help keep our moods on an even keel?
According to psychologist Peter Lewinsohn, participation in reward-producing activities, such as pleasant events, can contribute to feelings of happiness and well-being.

___ 27. Working in politics

___ 28. Working on machines (cars, bikes, radios, television sets)

___ 29. Playing cards or board games

___ 30. Doing puzzles or math games

___ 31. Having lunch with friends or associates

___ 32. Playing tennis

___ 33. Driving long distances

___ 34. Woodworking, carpentry

___ 35. Writing stories, novels, poems, plays, articles

___ 36. Being with animals

___ 37. Riding in an airplane

___ 38. Exploring (hiking away from known routes, spelunking, etc.)

___ 39. Singing

___ 40. Going to a party

___ 41. Going to church functions

___ 42. Playing a musical instrument

___ 43. Snow skiing, ice skating

___ 44. Wearing informal clothes, "dressing down"

___ 45. Acting

___ 46. Being in the city, downtown

___ 47. Taking a long hot bath

___ 48. Playing pool or billiards

___ 49. Bowling

___ 50. Watching wild animals

___ 51. Gardening, landscaping

___ 52. Wearing new clothes

___ 53. Dancing

___ 54. Sitting or lying in the sun

___ 55. Riding a motorcycle

___ 56. Just sitting and thinking

___ 57. Going to a fair, carnival, circus, zoo, amusement park

___ 58. Talking about philosophy or religion

___ 59. Gambling

___ 60. Listening to sounds of nature

___ 61. Dating, courting

___ 62. Having friends come to visit

___ 63. Going out to visit friends

___ 64. Giving gifts

___ 65. Getting massages or backrubs

___ 66. Photography

___ 67. Collecting stamps, coins, rocks, etc.

___ 68. Seeing beautiful scenery

___ 69. Eating good meals

___ 70. Improving your health (having teeth fixed, changing diet, having a checkup, etc.)

___ 71. Wrestling or boxing

___ 72. Fishing

___ 73. Going to a health club, sauna

___ 74. Horseback riding

___ 75. Protesting social, political, or environmental conditions

___ 76. Going to the movies

___ 77. Cooking meals

___ 78. Washing your hair

___ 79. Going to a restaurant

___ 80. Using cologne, perfume

___ 81. Getting up early in the morning

___ 82. Writing a diary

___ 83. Giving massages or backrubs

___ 84. Meditating or doing yoga

___ 85. Doing heavy outdoor work

___ 86. Snowmobiling, dune buggying

___ 87. Being in a body awareness, encounter, or "rap" group

___ 88. Swimming

___ 89. Running, jogging

___ 90. Walking barefoot

___ 91. Playing Frisbee or catch

___ 92. Doing housework or laundry, cleaning things

___ 93. Listening to music

___ 94. Knitting, crocheting

___ 95. Making love

___ 96. Petting, necking

___ 97. Going to a barber or beautician

___ 98. Being with someone you love

___ 99. Going to the library

___ 100. Shopping

___ 101. Preparing a new or special dish

___ 102. Watching people

___ 103. Bicycling

___ 104. Writing letters, cards, or notes

___ 105. Talking about politics or public affairs

___ 106. Watching attractive women or men

___ 107. Caring for houseplants

___ 108. Having coffee, tea, or Coke, etc., with friends

___ 109. Beachcombing

___ 110. Going to auctions, garage sales, etc.

___ 111. Water skiing, surfing, diving

___ 112. Traveling

___ 113. Attending the opera, ballet, or a play

___ 114. Looking at the stars or the moon

Source: Adapted from D. J. MacPhillamy & P. M. Lewinsohn, Pleasant Events Schedule, Form III-S, *University of Oregon, Mimeograph, 1971.*

Cognitive Perspectives

Cognitive theorists relate the origin and maintenance of depression to ways in which people see themselves and the world.

■ **AARON BECK'S COGNITIVE THEORY** One of the most influential cognitive theorists, psychiatrist Aaron Beck (Beck, 1976; Beck et al., 1979; Beck & Young, 1986), relates the development of depression to the adoption of an habitual style of negative thinking—the **cognitive triad of depression** (see Table 7.5). The cognitive triad includes negative beliefs about oneself (e.g., "I'm no good"), the environment or the world at large (e.g., "This school is awful"), and the future (e.g., "Nothing will ever turn out right for me"). Such negative concepts, or *schemas,* are believed to be adopted in childhood and later to be activated by negative events such as a poor grade or loss of a job.

Children's early learning experiences are thought to shape negative attitudes. Children may find, for example, that nothing they do is good enough to please their parents or teachers. As a result, they may come to regard themselves as basically incompetent and to perceive their prospects as dim. These beliefs sensitize them later in life to interpret any failure or disappointment as a crushing blow or a total defeat, leading to depression. Minor disappointments and personal shortcomings become blown out of proportion. Beck considers such magnification of the importance of minor failures to be an error in thinking, or "cognitive distortion."

David Burns (1979) summarized a number of these cognitive distortions:

1. *All-or-Nothing Thinking.* Seeing events in all-or-none terms, as either all good or all bad. For example,

one may perceive a relationship that ended in disappointment as a totally negative experience, despite any positive feelings or experiences that occurred along the way. Perfectionism is an example of all-or-nothing thinking. Perfectionists may judge any outcome other than perfect success to be complete failure. Perfectionists may consider a grade of B+ or even an A− to be tantamount to an F. They may feel like abject failures if they fall a few dollars short of their sales quotas or receive a very fine (but less than perfect) performance evaluation.

2. *Overgeneralization.* Believing that if a negative event occurs, it is likely to recur in similar situations. One thus interprets a single negative event as foreshadowing an endless series of negative events. For example, one receives a letter of rejection from a potential employer and assumes that all other job applications will be rejected.

3. *Mental Filter.* Focusing only on negative details of events, thereby rejecting the positive features of one's experiences. Like a droplet of ink that spreads to discolor an entire beaker of water, focusing only on a single negative detail can darken one's vision of reality. Beck called this cognitive distortion **selective abstraction**, meaning that the individual selectively abstracts the negative details from events and ignores their positive features. One thus bases one's self-esteem on perceived weaknesses and failures, rather than on positive features, or on a balance of accomplishments and shortcomings. For example, one receives a job evaluation that contains positive and negative comments but focuses only on the negative.

4. *Disqualifying the Positive.* Converting neutral or positive events into negative events. An example is dismissal of congratulations for a job well done by thinking and saying, "Oh, it's no big deal. Anyone could have done it." One thus snatches defeat from

Table 7.5 The Cognitive Triad of Depression	
Negative view of oneself	Perceiving oneself as worthless, deficient, inadequate, unlovable, and as lacking the skills necessary to achieve happiness.
Negative view of the environment	Perceiving the environment as imposing excessive demands and/or presenting obstacles that are impossible to overcome, leading continually to failure and loss.
Negative view of the future	Perceiving the future as hopeless and believing that one is powerless to change things for the better. All that one expects of the future is continuing failure and unrelenting misery and hardship.

According to Aaron Beck, depression involves the adoption of an habitual style of negative thinking—the so-called cognitive triad of depression.

Sources: Adapted from Beck et al., 1979; Beck & Young, 1986.

the jaws of victory. By contrast, taking credit where credit is due may help people overcome depression by increasing their belief that they can make changes that will lead to a positive future (Needles & Abramson, 1990).

5. *Jumping to Conclusions.* Forming a negative interpretation of events, despite a lack of evidence. Two examples of this style of thinking are "mind reading" and "the fortune teller error." In *mind reading*, one arbitrarily jumps to the conclusion that others don't like or respect one, as in interpreting a friend's not calling for a while as a rejection. The *fortune teller error* is the prediction that something bad is always about to happen, which one takes as factual in the absence of evidence. For example, one concludes that chest pain *must* signify an impending heart attack, even though other causes are possible.

6. *Magnification and Minimization.* Magnification, or **catastrophizing**, refers to making mountains out of molehills, or exaggerating the importance of negative events, personal flaws, fears, or mistakes. Minimization is the mirror image—a type of cognitive distortion in which one minimizes or underestimates one's good points.

7. *Emotional Reasoning.* Basing reasoning on emotions—thinking, for example, "If I feel guilty, it must be because I've done something really wrong." One interprets feelings and events on the basis of emotions rather than dispassionate evaluation.

8. *Should Statements.* Creating personal imperatives or self-commandments—"shoulds" or "musts." For example, "I *should* always get my first serve in!" or, "I *must* make Chris like me!" By creating unrealistic expectations, **musterbation**—the label given this form of thinking by Albert Ellis—can lead one to become depressed when one falls short.

9. *Labeling and Mislabeling.* Explaining behavior by attaching negative labels to oneself and others. One may, for example, explain a poor grade on a test by thinking that one is a "lazy" or "stupid" person rather than unprepared for the specific exam or, perhaps, ill. Labeling other people as "stupid" or "insensitive" can engender hostility toward them. Mislabeling is the use of labels that are emotionally charged and inaccurate, such as calling oneself a "pig" because one ate a food forbidden by one's diet.

10. *Personalization.* Assuming that one is responsible for other people's problems and behavior. For example, one may assume that her or his spouse is crying because of something she or he has done.

Consider the errors in thinking illustrated in the following case:

How could he have missed that tackle?   This football player missed a crucial tackle and is rehashing it. He is putting himself down and telling himself there is nothing he can do to improve his performance. Cognitive theorists believe that a person's self-defeating or distorted interpretations of negative events can set the stage for depression.

*C*hristie *was a 33-year-old real estate sales agent who suffered from frequent episodes of depression. Whenever a deal fell through, she would blame herself: "If only I had worked harder . . . negotiated better . . . talked more persuasively . . . the deal would have been done." After several successive disappointments, each one followed by self-recriminations, she felt like quitting altogether. Her thinking became increasingly dominated by negative thoughts, which further depressed her mood and lowered her self-esteem: "I'm a loser. . . . I'll never succeed. . . . It's all my fault. . . . I'm no good and I'm never going to succeed at anything."*

Christie's thinking included cognitive errors such as the following: (1) personalization (believing herself to be the sole cause of negative events), (2) labeling and mislabeling (regarding herself to be a loser); (3) overgeneralization (predicting a dismal future on the basis of a present disappointment); and (4) mental filter (judging her personality entirely on the basis of her disappointments). In therapy, Christie was helped to think more realistically about events and not to jump to conclusions that she was automatically at fault whenever a deal fell through, or to judge her whole personality on the basis of disappointments or perceived flaws within herself. In place of this self-defeating style of thinking, she began to think more realistically when disappointments occurred, like telling herself, "Okay, I'm disappointed. I'm frustrated. I feel lousy. So what? It doesn't mean I'll never succeed. Let me discover what went wrong and try to correct it the next time. I have to look ahead, not dwell on disappointments in the past."

■ *The Authors' Files*

Distorted thinking tends to be experienced as automatic, as if the thoughts had just popped into one's head. So-called **automatic thoughts** are likely to be accepted as statements of fact rather than opinions or habitual ways of interpreting events.

Beck and his colleagues (1976) formulated a **cognitive-specificity hypothesis**, which proposes that different disorders, anxiety disorders and depressive disorders in particular, are characterized by different types of automatic thoughts. The results of one study (Beck et al., 1987) showed some interesting differences in the types of automatic thoughts reported by people with depressive and anxiety disorders (see Table 7.6). Depressed people more often reported thoughts concerning themes of loss, self-depreciation, and pessimism. Anxious people more often reported thoughts concerning physical danger and other threats.

A CLOSER LOOK

Do Rose-Colored Glasses Keep Us Mentally Healthy? or, Does Survival in Today's World Require Distortion of Reality?

 "The human world, it's a mess." Do you recognize Sebastian the crab's introduction to the song "Under the Sea" from the Disney film *The Little Mermaid*? Sebastian's reasons for his generalization are based on his viewpoint as a cartoon creature, but the human world in many ways is a mess. Even though the menace of a nuclear exchange with the nations that made up the former Soviet Union has waned, many nations continue to possess and develop the bomb. Much of the world lives in poverty, and famine regularly plagues parts of Asia and Africa. In many places, rose-colored glasses would just give the smog a threatening ruddy cast.

Is it then so distorted to see the human world, and one's prospects in it, as a mess? Perhaps not. According to Alloy and Abramson (1988), the judgments and perceptions of many depressed people are not distorted at all, but rather quite realistic. In contrast, note Alloy and Clements (1992), it is people who are *not* depressed who show "systematic optimistic biases and distortions." Although we usually equate good mental health with accurate reality testing, and mental illness with illogic and cognitive distortions, many depressed people may actually be showing rather good reality testing. It may be, in fact, that many people keep themselves out of the dumps by maintaining persistently rosy outlooks despite evidence to the contrary. Perhaps optimistic illusions and biases are psychologically adaptive! Perhaps we need to have some illusions if we are to maintain high self-esteem and belief in our own coping

ability (Alloy & Clements, 1992). Such positive biases may reduce vulnerability to depression and other psychological disorders.

Researchers managed to devise a research project to test this hypothesis. In essence, they created a laboratory situation in which subjects had no control over a laboratory task so that they could assess which subjects nevertheless managed to maintain an *illusion of control*. The results showed that subjects who maintained an illusion of control showed less evidence of depression following exposure to stressful experiences afterward (Alloy & Clements, 1992). Perhaps people who continue to think they are in charge of their destinies decrease their susceptibility to depression, even when they are wrong.

 Research suggests that "mentally healthy" people may in some ways view the world less realistically than depressed people do. Many depressed people may be more accurate in their assessment of the extent to which they can exercise control over events.

Only 3 in 10 first-year U.S. college students agreed with the statement that an individual can do little to bring about changes in society, by the way (*Chronicle of Higher Education* 1992, March 18). Is the optimism of the other 7 in 10 realistic or illusory?

Table 7.6 Automatic Thoughts Associated with Depression and Anxiety

Common Automatic Thoughts Associated with Depression:

1. I'm worthless.
2. I'm not worthy of other people's attention or affection.
3. I'll never be as good as other people are.
4. I'm a social failure.
5. I don't deserve to be loved.
6. People don't respect me anymore.
7. I will never overcome my problems.
8. I've lost the only friends I've had.
9. Life isn't worth living.
10. I'm worse off than they are.
11. There's no one left to help me.
12. No one cares whether I live or die.
13. Nothing ever works out for me anymore.
14. I have become physically unattractive.

Common Automatic Thoughts Associated with Anxiety:

1. What if I get sick and become an invalid?
2. I am going to be injured.
3. What if no one reaches me in time to help?
4. I might be trapped.
5. I am not a healthy person.
6. I'm going to have an accident.
7. Something will happen that will ruin my appearance.
8. I am going to have a heart attack.
9. Something awful is going to happen.
10. Something will happen to someone I care about.
11. I'm losing my mind.

Source: Beck, A. T., Brown, G., Steer, R. A., Eidelson, J. I., & Reskind, J. H. (1987). Differentiating anxiety and depression: A test of the cognitive content-specificity hypothesis. Journal of Abnormal Psychology, 96, 179–183. Copyright © 1987 by the American Psychological Association. Reprinted by permission.

Evidence has accumulated that depressed people tend to think more negatively than other people. For example, groups of depressed college students (Dobson & Breiter, 1983; Michael & Funabiki, 1985) and depressed clients at clinics (Eaves & Rush, 1984) show greater incidence of distorted, negative thoughts than nondepressed reference groups. Students with more distorted thoughts tend to be more depressed and to perceive their lives as more stressful (Olinger et al., 1987). They also become more depressed in response to negative life events such as illness, relocation, or death of loved ones than students with more productive outlooks (Wise & Barnes, 1986). Depressed people also tend to hold more pessimistic views of the future (Alloy & Ahrens, 1987; Pyszczynski; et al., 1987) and are more critical of themselves (Zurott & Mongrain, 1987) than nondepressives.

The presence of negative thoughts is not necessarily destructive, so long as the thoughts are balanced by positive thoughts. Research using a thought counting method has found that psychologically functional people produce one and a half to two times as many positive thoughts as negative thoughts (Schwartz, 1986). Mildly dysfunctional people, by contrast, produce about equal numbers of positive and negative thoughts.

Research does support Beck's view that depressed people magnify their shortcomings. In one study, college students were given a test that supposedly measured the presence of a personality trait and were asked to indicate the value of the trait to them. Normal students inflated the value of the trait when they were told they possessed a great deal of it. Depressed students, by contrast, exaggerated the importance of the trait when they were informed that they had done poorly on the test (Wenzlaff & Grozier, 1988). Whereas depressed students accentuated the negative, nondepressed students were more self-enhancing; they emphasized the importance of a quality they believed themselves to have.

Although distorted negative thinking is more common among depressed people, the causal pathways remain unclear. Some research suggests that distorted cognitions accompany rather than precede depression, in which case distorted thinking would be a consequence rather than a cause of depression (Lewinsohn et al., 1981). More research is needed into cause–effect relationships.

Even if distorted cognitions do not cause depression, they may help maintain depression (Dent & Teasdale, 1988). The presence of negative cognitive distortions among formerly depressed people also seems to predict recurrences of depressive episodes (Rush et al., 1986). On the other hand, taking credit where credit is due—rather than denying one's achievements—may help people overcome depression by increasing their sense that they can make their futures more positive (Needles & Abramson, 1990).

A recent review of Beck's cognitive theory of depression finds broad support for many aspects of the theory, including Beck's concept of the cognitive triad of depression, and his view that depressed people think more negatively than nondepressed people about themselves, the future, and the world in general. Yet the central theme of cognitive theory, that distorted negative thinking is causally related to depression, remains unsubstantiated and requires further study (Haaga et al., 1991).

■ LEARNED HELPLESSNESS (ATTRIBUTIONAL) THEORY

The **learned helplessness** model proposes that people may become depressed because they learn to view themselves as helpless to control the reinforcements in their environments—or to change their lives for the better. The originator of the learned helplessness concept, Martin Seligman (1974, 1975), believes that people learn to perceive themselves as helpless because of their experiences. The learned helplessness model thus straddles the behavioral and the cognitive: Situational factors foster attitudes that lead to depression.

The learned helplessness model is based on laboratory studies of animals by Seligman and his colleagues. In early studies, dogs exposed to an inescapable electric shock later failed to learn to escape when the shock was made escapable (Overmier & Seligman, 1967; Seligman & Maier, 1967). Exposure to uncontrollable forces apparently teaches organisms that they are helpless. Animals who developed learned helplessness showed behaviors reminiscent of those of depressed people, including lethargy, lack of motivation, and difficulty acquiring new skills (Maier & Seligman, 1976).

Seligman (1975) proposed that some forms of depression in humans might result from exposure to apparently uncontrollable situations. Such experiences can instill the expectation that future reinforcements will also be beyond the individual's control. A cruel vicious cycle may come into play with many depressed people. A few failures may produce feelings of helplessness and expectations of further failure. Perhaps you know people who have failed certain subjects, such as mathematics. They may come to believe themselves incapable of succeeding in math. They may thus decide that studying for the quantitative section of the Graduate Record Exam is a waste of time. They then do poorly, completing the self-fulfilling prophecy by confirming their expectations, which further intensifies feelings of helplessness, leading to lowered expectations, and so on, in a vicious cycle.

Although it stimulated much interest, Seligman's model failed to account for the low self-esteem that is typical of depressed people. Nor did it explain variations in the persistence of depression. Seligman and his colleagues (Abramson et al., 1978) offered a reformulation of the theory to meet such shortcomings. The revised theory held that perception of lack of control over reinforcement alone did not explain the persistence and severity of depression. It was also necessary to consider cognitive factors—especially the ways in which people explain their failures and disappointments to themselves.

Seligman and his colleagues recast helplessness theory in terms of the social psychology concept of **attributional style**. An attributional style is a personal style of explanation. When disappointments or failures occur, we may explain them in various characteristic ways. We may blame ourselves (an **internal attribution**) or our circumstances (an **external attribution**). We may see bad experiences as typical events (a **stable attribution**) or as isolated events (an **unstable attribution**). We may see them as evidence of broader problems (a **global attribution**) or as evidence of precise and limited shortcomings (a **specific attribution**). The revised helplessness theory—called the reformulated helplessness theory—holds that people who explain the causes of negative events (like failure in work, school, or romantic relationships) according to these three types of attributions are most vulnerable to depression:

1. Internal factors, or beliefs that failures reflect their personal inadequacies, rather than external factors, or beliefs that failures are caused by environmental factors;
2. Global factors, or beliefs that failures reflect sweeping flaws in personality rather than specific factors, or beliefs that failures reflect limited areas of functioning; and
3. Stable factors, or beliefs that failures reflect fixed personality factors rather than unstable factors, or beliefs that the factors leading to failures are changeable.

Let us illustrate these attributional styles with the example of a first-year student who goes on a disastrous date. Afterward he shakes his head in wonder and tries to make sense of his experience. An internal attribution for the calamity would involve self-blame, as in "I really messed it up." An external attribution would place the blame elsewhere, as in "Some couples just don't hit it off," or, "She must have been in a bad mood." A stable attribution would suggest a problem that cannot be changed, as in "It's my personality." An unstable attribution, on the other hand, would suggest a transient condition, as in "It was probably the head cold." A global attribution for failure magnifies the extent of the problem, as in "I really have no idea what I'm doing when I'm with people." A specific attribution, in contrast, chops the problem down to size, as in "My problem is how to make small talk to get a relationship going."

The revised theory holds that each attributional dimension makes a specific contribution to feelings of helplessness. Internal attributions are linked to diminished self-esteem. Stable attributions help explain the persistence—or, in medical terms, the chronicity—of signs of depression. Global attributions are associated with the generality or pervasiveness of feelings of helplessness following negative events.

Research is generally but not completely supportive of the reformulated helplessness (attributional) model. Many studies have found that depressed people are more likely than nondepressed people to attribute the causes of failures to internal, stable, and global factors (Blumberg & Izard, 1985; Heimberg et al., 1987; Miller et al., 1982; Peterson et al., 1981; Pyszczynski & Greenberg, 1985; Raps et al., 1982; Seligman et al., 1984, 1988; Sweeney, 1986).

Despite the weight of these studies, it must be mentioned that some researchers have not found the predicted relationships between depression and attributional style (e.g., Devins et al., 1981; Hammen & de Mayo, 1982). This inconsistency has not been clearly explained (Peterson et al., 1985). It also remains to be seen whether attributional style is a cause or an effect of depression. Some researchers argue that there is not yet enough evidence to demonstrate that depressive attributional styles precede rather than follow depression (Beidel & Turner, 1986).

Biological Perspectives

Although psychological factors have been linked to mood disorders, biological factors are also involved. Researchers suspect that biological factors are principally responsible for some mood disorders, such as bipolar disorder (Klein & Depue, 1985), and play important roles in others.

■ **GENETIC FACTORS** Mood disorders tend to run in families. Families, however, share environmental similarities as well as genes. Family members may share blue eyes (an inherited attribute) but also a common religion (a cultural attribute). Evidence from twin and adoptee studies sheds light on the possible genetic contribution.

A higher concordance rate among monozygotic (MZ) twins than dizygotic (DZ) twins is taken as evidence of genetic factors. Both types of twins share common environments, but MZ twins share 100% of their genes as compared to 50% for DZ twins. Although there are inconsistencies in the research evidence, it appears overall that genetics plays a sig-

nificant role in the transmission of major affective disorders, such as major depression and bipolar disorder (Faraone et al., 1990). The closer the genetic relationship one shares with a person with a major affective disorder, the greater the likelihood that one will also suffer from a major affective disorder. The concordance rate between MZ twins for major affective disorders is 70%, which is about triple the concordance rate for DZ twins.

Kendler and his colleagues conducted a large-scale twin study in which they evaluated more than 1,000 pairs of twin women for the presence of depression (Kendler et al., 1992a). By comparing differences in the concordance rates of major depression between MZ and DZ twin pairs, the researchers concluded that between 33 and 45% of the risk for major depression in women was due to genetic factors. Although this genetic component is substantial, psychosocial and environmental factors, especially stressful life events, apparently play an even greater role. There is also a higher concordance rate for bipolar disorder among MZ than DZ twins (Bertelsen et al., 1977; Klein et al., 1985; Smith & Winokur, 1983). Researchers report an overall concordance rate of 72% among MZ twins for bipolar disorder, as compared to only 14% among DZ twins (Allen, 1976).

Evidence from adoptee studies appears consistent with a genetic means of transmission in mood disorders (McGuffin & Katz, 1986). In one study of 29 adoptees who had bipolar disorder, researchers found more than double the rate of mood disorders of all types in their biological parents than in their adoptive parents—28 versus 12%, respectively (Mendlewicz & Rainer, 1977). One estimate is that perhaps 80% of the risk of developing bipolar disorder is accounted for by genetic factors (McGuffin & Katz, 1986). However, the mode of genetic transmission in bipolar disorder remains unclear (Blehar et al., 1988). Although genetic factors are likely to create a predisposition for bipolar disorder, they do not, in themselves, determine whether it will occur. Psychological, social, and environmental stresses are also involved (Hirschfeld & Cross, 1982).

In sum, genetics appears to account for a substantial amount of the risk in mood disorders, particularly in major depression and in bipolar disorder. Yet genetic factors alone do not determine risk of mood disorders. Psychosocial and environmental factors play a part, as do the interactions among these factors. Genetics is believed to play a relatively greater role in explaining bipolar mood disorders than unipolar depression (Faraone et al., 1990; Kendler et al., 1992; McGuffin & Katz, 1986). Data from twin studies suggest that dysthymic disorder may be relatively less influenced by genetic factors (Torgersen, 1986).

■ BIOCHEMICAL FACTORS IN DEPRESSION

If there is a genetic component to depression, just what is inherited? Perhaps the genetic vulnerability expresses itself in abnormalities in neurotransmitter actions. The dominant biological model of depression during the past 30 years—the **catecholamine hypothesis** (Schildkraut, 1965)—has focused on the role of norepinephrine. Catecholamines include the neurotransmitters norepinephrine (noradrenaline), epinephrine (adrenaline), and dopamine.

The catecholamine theory proposes that depression results from deficiencies in norepinephrine, whereas excessive levels of norepinephrine produce manic behavior. Other researchers believe that the neurotransmitter serotonin, which belongs to the indoleamine class, also plays an important role in mood disorders (e.g., Berger, 1978). Neurotransmit-

ters of both the catecholamine and indoleamine class are monoamines—organic compounds that have nitrogen in one amino acid group. Still other researchers argue for roles for acetylcholine deficiencies (Nadi et al., 1984) or for excessive production of thyroid hormones (Whybrow & Prange, 1981) in mood disorders.

Evidence for the role of neurotransmitters was first found in the 1950s through two lines of research. One focused on findings that hypertensive patients who were taking the drug *reserpine* often reported feelings of depression. Reserpine is known to reduce the supplies of various neurotransmitters in the brain, including norepinephrine and serotonin. The second line of research focused on the discovery that drugs which increase the brain levels of neurotransmitters such as norepinephrine and serotonin in

A CLOSER LOOK

In Search of Biological Markers of Depression

Imagine this. You feel down and moody and consult your doctor to see if you're depressed or perhaps physically run-down. After a brief examination, your doctor says, "Please roll up your sleeves. We'll take a sample of blood and see whether or not you're depressed." Sound farfetched? After all, depression concerns *feelings,* and feelings are psychological events. What, then, can be revealed by examining your blood?

Quite a bit, perhaps. Researchers have been searching for a *biological marker* of depression that might be revealed by a simple biological test—such as a blood test. Although it remains experimental, one such test exists: the dexamethasone suppression test, or DST. The DST has become the most extensively studied biological test in psychiatry (American Psychiatric Association, 1987b), although questions remain about its validity.

The DST requires swallowing a synthetic steroid, dexamethasone. In normal people, dexamethasone suppresses release of the hormone cortisol from the adrenal gland for about 24 hours. Low levels of cortisol in the blood following the administration of dexamethasone are indicative of a normal (nondepressed) response. High levels of cortisol suggest nonsuppression, which is thought to indicate the presence of clinical depression.

For such a test to be valid, it must demonstrate high levels of sensitivity (as measured by the percentage of actual cases who yield positive test results) and specificity

(as measured by the percentage of normal subjects who yield negative test results). Research shows that the sensitivity of the DST procedure is modest at best—yielding positive test results for about one-third to one-half of the depressed people who take the test (American Psychiatric Association, 1987b; Belsher & Costello, 1988; Heiby et al.,

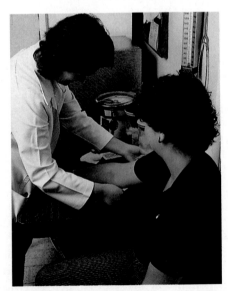

Is there a blood test for depression? The dexamethasone test (DST) has been proposed as a possible biological marker of depression, but its validity remains questionable.

laboratory animals also help relieve depression in humans. These drugs, called antidepressants, consist of **tricyclics**, such as imipramine (trade name Tofranil) and amitriptyline (trade name Elavil); **monoamine oxidase (MAO) inhibitors**, such as phenelzine (trade name Nardil); and **serotonin-reuptake inhibitors**, such as fluoxetine (trade name Prozac).

On the other hand, research based on examination of the biological fluids (such as urine or blood) of depressed people, and on autopsies of depressed people (Cooper, S. J., et al., 1986; Deakin & Crow, 1986) does not consistently indicate reduced levels of norepinephrine or serotonin in brain tissue. Moreover, although antidepressant drugs may boost the brain levels of neurotransmitters in laboratory animals,

1987). Neuroendocrine function, as revealed by nonsuppression of cortisol release following ingestion of dexamethasone, may thus be a marker for some but not all cases of depression.

Specificity of the test appears to be higher, with over 90% of normals showing negative (nondepressed) test results. This means that the test is relatively unlikely to suggest that you're depressed if you're not. A positive DST might thus help confirm a diagnosis of a depressive disorder, but a negative test result would not necessarily contraindicate depression (American Psychiatric Association, 1987b).

Another problem with the DST is that positive test results in actual depressives may be confounded by factors such as the use of psychotropic medications, the chemical effects of drug withdrawal, and by use of drugs such as caffeine (Krauss & Brown, 1988). Moreover, the test has not been able to predict the likelihood of response to antidepressant medications or to hospitalization (Nelson et al., 1990). Still, the test may help researchers predict the course of depression. Some research suggests that failure to convert to normal suppression of cortisol with apparent remission of depression may suggest an increased risk of recurrence (Arana et al., 1985; Braddock, 1986). However, determination of the utility of the test as a prognostic indicator also requires further study (American Psychiatric Association, 1987b).

**T   It is true there is a blood test for the diagnosis of
OR
F   depression. It is called the DST. However, the validity of
    the test has been questioned.**

questions remain as to whether these effects in animals explain the therapeutic effectiveness of antidepressant drugs in people (Green & Goodwin, 1986). It must also be considered that antidepressant drugs increase the availability of neurotransmitters in the brain within hours, but the depression-relieving effects of the drugs take 2 to 3 weeks to develop (Katona et al., 1986). Therefore, it is unlikely that the therapeutic effects rely solely on increased supply of neurotransmitters. Perhaps the heightened presence of these neurotransmitters gradually increases the sensitivity of neural receptor sites to these chemicals. Antidepressant drugs appear to have more complex effects on the brain than was originally thought (Deakin & Crow, 1986).

In sum, most researchers believe that neurotransmitter imbalances play some role in mood disorders. However, the causal pathways relating neurotransmitters and depression remain unclear (Cooper, S.J., et al., 1986; Deakin & Crow, 1986).

In sum, depression may reflect the interaction of biological factors (levels or actions of neurotransmitters), psychological factors (such as cognitive distortions or learned helplessness), and social and environmental stressors (such as divorce or loss of a job). Consider a speculative example of a possible causal pathway: A stressor such as loss of a job or the effects of a hurricane might be catastrophized. The person might see herself or himself as helpless to change the situation. The stressful event and its overly negative interpretation might lead to feelings of depression. Some combination of the stressor, its interpretation, and feelings of depression may lower the action of catecholamines in the brain. Such biochemical effects would be more likely to occur among people with a genetic predisposition for depression. Biochemical changes in the brain might then intensify one's depressive mood and behavior, making it more difficult to cope effectively and bounce back. Lingering biochemical changes and feelings of depression may exacerbate feelings of helplessness, compound the effects of the initial stressor, and so on. Such potential causal pathways require further study.

TREATMENT

Just as theoretical perspectives suggest that many factors may interact to produce mood disorders, there are multiple approaches to their treatment. In this section we review psychological and biological treatments of the mood disorders.

Psychodynamic Approaches

Traditional psychoanalysis aims to help depressed people understand their ambivalent feelings toward the lost object. By working through feelings of anger toward the lost object, depressed people can turn anger outward—through verbal expression of feelings, for example—rather than leave it to fester and turn inward.

Traditional psychoanalysis can take years to uncover and deal with unconscious conflicts. Modern psychoanalytic approaches also focus on unconscious conflicts, but they are more direct, relatively brief, and focus on present as well as past conflicted relationships. Consistent with the self-focusing model, for example, clients would be encouraged to surrender pursuit of the lost object or frustrating goal and to build self-worth through developing new goals and relationships. Eclectic psychodynamic therapists may also use behavioral methods to help clients acquire the social skills they need to develop a broader social network.

■ **INTERPERSONAL PSYCHOTHERAPY** Newer models of psychotherapy for depression have emerged from the interpersonal school of psychodynamic therapy derived initially from the work of Harry Stack Sullivan (see Chapter 2) and other neo-Freudians, such as Karen Horney. One contemporary example is interpersonal psychotherapy (IPT) (Klerman et al., 1984). IPT is a brief form of therapy (usually no more than 9 to 12 months) that focuses on the client's current interpersonal relationships. The developers of ITP believe that depression occurs

Interpersonal psychotherapy (IPT) Depression occurs within interpersonal contexts that are addressed through IPT, a brief form of psychodynamic therapy. Like traditional psychodynamic approaches, IPT assumes that early life experiences are key issues in adjustment, but IPT focuses on the present—the here and now.

within an interpersonal context and that relationship issues need to be emphasized in treatment.

Although IPT shares some features with traditional psychodynamic approaches (principally the belief that early life experiences and persistent personality features are important issues in psychological adjustment), it differs from traditional psychodynamic therapy by focusing primarily on clients' current relationships, rather than helping them acquire insight into unconscious internal conflicts of childhood origins. Although unconscious factors and early childhood experiences are recognized, therapy focuses on the present—the here and now.

IPT helps clients learn to identify areas of conflict in their relationships, understand the issues that underlie them, and change their relationships for the better. IPT therapists do not aim to preserve relationships that are essentially unworkable, however. Attention is also focused on helping clients come to terms with the loss of loved ones in their lives.

In the case of Sal D., a 31-year-old TV repairman's assistant, depression was associated with marital conflict:

*S*al began to explore his marital problems in the fifth therapy session, becoming tearful as he recounted his difficulty expressing his feelings to his wife because of feelings of being "numb." He felt that he had been "holding on" to his feelings, which was causing him to become estranged from his wife. The next session zeroed in on the similarities between himself and his father, in particular how he was distancing himself from his wife in a similar way to how his father had kept a distance from him. By session 7, a turning point had been reached. Sal expressed how he and his wife had become "emotional" and closer to one another during the previous week and how he was able to talk more openly about his feelings, and how he and his wife had been able to make a joint decision concerning a financial matter that had been worrying them for some time. When later he was laid off from his job, he sought his wife's opinion, rather than picking a fight with her as a way of thrusting his job problems on her. To his surprise he found that his wife responded positively—not "violently" as he had expected—to times when he expressed his feelings. In his last therapy session (session 12), Sal expressed how therapy had led to a "reawakening" within himself with respect to the feelings he had been keeping to himself—an openness that he hoped to create in his relationship with his wife.

■ *Adapted from Klerman et al., 1984, pp. 111–113*

Humanistic-Existential Approaches

Humanistic and existential therapists aim to help clients grow aware of their authentic feelings and their needs for self-actualization and self-fulfillment. They teach clients that authenticity requires living according to one's own values and choices, not submerging one's needs to the will of others. Fulfillment and self-esteem derive from instilling life with meaning and purpose. The sadness and depression that attend upsets and losses are authentic and are not to be shunned, but people can then go on to find or create new meaning in life.

Abraham Maslow, a foremost humanistic theorist, focused on self-actualization as a path toward meaning. Maslow (1963) described his treatment approach in the case of a woman who complained of depressive features such as boredom, apathy, insomnia, and physical complaints. The woman had been a brilliant psychology student. She was forced to leave graduate school for economic reasons during the Great Depression, however, and take a job as a personnel officer in a factory. Maslow writes:

Half-consciously then she saw a whole lifetime of greyness stretching out ahead of her. I suggested that she might be feeling profoundly frustrated and angry simply because she was not being her own very intelligent self, that she was not using her intelligence and her talent for psychology and that this might well be a major reason for her boredom with life and her body's boredom with the normal pleasures of life. Any talent, any capacity, I thought, was also a motivation, a need, an impulse. With this she agreed, and I suggested that she could continue her graduate studies at night after her work. In brief, she was able to arrange this and it worked well. She became more alive, more happy, and zestful, and most of her physical symptoms had disappeared at my last contact with her.

■ *Maslow, 1963, pp. 43–44*

Behavioral Approaches

Behavioral approaches to treatment presume that depressive behaviors are learned and can be unlearned. Behavior therapists aim to modify depressive behaviors directly rather than to foster client awareness of possible unconscious causes of these behaviors.

Lewinsohn and his colleagues (Lewinsohn et al., 1984) have designed a group treatment approach for depression that consists of a 12-session, 8-week course—the *Coping with Depression Course*. The course helps depressed clients acquire relaxation skills, engage in pleasant activities, and build social skills that enable them to obtain social reinforcement. For example, students learn how to accept rather than deny compliments and how to ask friends to join them in activities to raise the frequency and quality of their social interactions. Participants are taught to generate a self-change plan, to think more constructively, and to develop a lifetime plan for maintaining treatment gains and preventing recurrent depression. The therapist is considered a teacher; the client, a student; the session, a class. No one is considered sick or "crazy." Each participant is treated as a responsible adult who is capable of learning. The structure involves lectures, activities, and homework. Each session has a lesson plan that begins with a review of homework and continues with a presentation of a new topic. Cognitive-behavioral treatment, based on an adaptation of the Coping with Depression Course used in treating adult depressives, has been shown to produce favorable results in the treatment of depression in adolescents (Lewinsohn et al., 1991).

The following case illustrates how this course helped one participant:

Liz Foster, a 27-year-old woman diagnosed as suffering from major depression, participated in an eight-member Coping with Depression Course. Prior to therapy, Liz had been feeling depressed for two months, eating poorly, sleeping excessively, and experiencing suicidal thoughts. She had had similar bouts of depression during the previous eight years. When she was depressed, she would spend most of her time alone at home—watching TV, reading, or just sitting. She engaged in a low rate of pleasant activities.

Liz had been laid off from work eleven months earlier and had few social contacts other than her boyfriend. She rarely saw her family, and two of her closest friends had moved away. Her remaining friends rarely visited, and she made no effort to see them.

With the eight other women in her class, Liz learned to focus on behaviors that she could change to increase her level of pleasant activities. At first she complained, "I don't feel like doing anything." The group instructors acknowledged that it would be hard, at first, to select desired reinforcers. Group members were encouraged to try out activities they had formerly enjoyed to see if they still found pleasure in them. Group members were instructed to identify stressful situations or hassles that increased their level of daily stress and were trained in relaxation techniques that they could use to cope with these stresses. They were given Pleasant Events Schedules to complete and encouraged to increase their frequency of pleasant activities.

Liz and the other group members plotted on a graph their level of pleasant activities from week to week and rated their mood levels on a daily basis. Most group members, including Liz, noticed a relationship between their moods and pleasant activities. Liz, whose initial rate of pleasant activities was about 8 per day, decided to increase her rate to 15–20 activities a day, and devised a plan to reinforce herself with rewards of 25 cents for each activity she completed over 13, pooling her rewards until she had earned $8.00, which she then used to buy a record album. Liz was able to increase her rate to 20 and noticed that her mood had improved.

The course also exposed participants to various techniques for controlling their thoughts. Liz selected the technique of self-reward/self-punishment: She rewarded herself with money for positive thoughts and charged herself (a nickel a thought) for negative thoughts. In tracking her thoughts, Liz found that she was able to increase her daily average of positive thoughts from 6 to 11 and decrease her negative thoughts from 7 to 2. By the eighth session, Liz was reporting that she was no longer depressed and felt more in control of her thoughts and feelings.

In later class sessions, group members learned assertive techniques for handling conflicts, such as dealing with aggressive salespeople, and for starting conversations with strangers. In later sessions, group members prepared life plans which they could use to deal with major life events and maintain the progress they had made. Liz recognized that she needed to maintain her frequency of pleasant activities at a high level, and she continued to monitor these activities to ensure that the frequency remained above a critical level. At a class-reunion six months following the course, she reported that she continued to use the techniques she had learned. Follow-up evaluations through a period of one and one half years showed that Liz had maintained her gains.

■ *Adapted from Lewinsohn et al., 1983, pp. 94–101*

Cognitive Approaches

Cognitive theorists attribute depression to cognitive errors and suggest that treatment of depression should aim to help clients correct them. Aaron Beck and his colleagues have developed a multicomponent treatment approach to depression, called **cognitive therapy**, that centers on helping depressed clients identify distorted, self-defeating thoughts and substitute more rational thoughts. Depressed people tend to focus on their feelings of fatigue, lethargy, sadness, and hopelessness rather than on the thoughts that may give rise to them. Depressed people, that is, usually pay more attention to how bad they feel than to the thoughts that may trigger or maintain the feelings.

Cognitive therapy, like behavior therapy, entails a relatively brief therapy format, frequently 15 to 20 weekly sessions. Therapy employs behavioral and cognitive techniques to help clients identify and change dysfunctional thoughts and develop more adaptive behavior.

To help clients connect distorted thoughts and negative moods, clients are taught to monitor their automatic negative thoughts through a thought diary or daily record. They note when and where the thoughts occur and how they feel at the time. Once disruptive thoughts are identified, the therapist helps the client challenge the validity of these thoughts. For example, a depressed person might react to the termination of a relationship by thinking, "I'll never find anyone to love." The therapist might challenge the validity of this thought by having the client consider whether there was another time when she or he was not dating but had held a more positive attitude about the future. Or the therapist might ask whether the future can truly be predicted with such certainty. The client may thus begin to doubt the validity of distorted thoughts, even if they are not fully rejected. Homework assignments are also designed to help clients evaluate preconceived (and often false) ideas.

The following case shows how a cognitive therapist uses logic to dispute the validity of the cognitive distortion called selective abstraction (the tendency to judge oneself entirely on the basis of specific weaknesses or flaws in character). In this case, the client judged herself to be completely lacking in self-control because she ate a piece of candy while she was on a diet.

CLIENT: I don't have any self-control at all.

THERAPIST: On what basis do you say that?

C: Somebody offered me candy and I couldn't refuse it.

T: Were you eating candy every day?

C: No, I just ate it this once.

T: Did you do anything constructive during the past week to adhere to your diet?

C: Well, I didn't give in to the temptation to buy candy every time I saw it at the store. . . . Also, I did not eat any candy except that one time when it was offered to me and I felt I couldn't refuse it.

T: If you counted up the number of times you controlled yourself versus the number of times you gave in, what ratio would you get?

C: About 100 to 1.

T: So if you controlled yourself 100 times and did not control yourself just once, would that be a sign that you are weak through and through?

C: I guess not—not *through* and *through* (smiles).

Adapted from Beck et al., 1979, p. 68

Or consider the case of Cliff, a 22-year-old stock clerk who worked in an auto parts store:

Cliff became depressed in the course of a romantic relationship that followed a seesaw pattern of breakups and brief reconciliations. Most of the time a breakup would follow an incident in which Cliff had reacted excessively and angrily when he perceived—or rather misperceived—his girlfriend as acting distant or aloof, even in trivial matters such as how far away from him she sat in the front seat of the car. Cliff needed constant reassurance of love and was acutely sensitive to verbal criticism and nonverbal cues of emotional distance. His girlfriend would say to him, "You must really want this relationship, since you're always badgering me to tell you that I love you."

Cliff's thinking was patterned by a set of underlying beliefs that helped undermine his relationships. These beliefs included musterbation ("This relationship must work out . . . or else"), personalizing ("If she's in a bad mood it's because she doesn't really love me"), and catastrophizing ("I won't be able to survive if this relationship breaks up"). In therapy, Cliff began to see that his way of viewing himself and the world limited possibilities for growth. Cliff was a quick study and readily learned to monitor his thoughts and replace self-defeating thoughts with rational alternatives. Instead of responding automatically to a perception that his girlfriend was rejecting him, he stopped and asked himself, "Where's the evidence for that? Might there be another explanation for her behavior?" When she wasn't available to see him on a particular night, he was able to attribute it to her feeling fatigued rather than misconstrue it as a sign of rejection. When problems arose in the relationship, Cliff learned to distinguish disappointment from disaster. He began to ease his expectations, seeing the relationship less as a "do or die" situation and more as a growth experience.

■ *The Authors' Files*

In one study, reductions in dysfunctional thinking early in cognitive therapy predicted alleviation of depression later in therapy, lending support to the view that cognitive change underlies the success of cognitive therapy (DeRubeis et al., 1990). A review of the research literature concluded that psychotherapy for depression is more effective than no treatment at all. Moreover, behavioral, cognitive, and cognitive-behavioral techniques of psychotherapy were found to produce stronger effects than insight-oriented forms of therapy, such as psychodynamic therapy (Robinson et al., 1990). However, the reviewers cautioned that experimenter biases (expectations that one's preferred method of treatment would produce better results) may have confounded the direct comparison of one form of therapy with another. Results from the large-scale National Institute of Mental Health (NIMH) Treatment of Depression Collaborative Research Program (TDCRP), which was conducted at various sites across the United States, showed a comparable level of therapeutic benefit from interpersonal psychotherapy and cognitive therapy (Elkin et al., 1989; Imber et al., 1990). Perhaps more attention should be focused on discovering the factors common to various forms of therapy that are responsible for improvement.

Biological Approaches

The most common biological treatments of the mood disorders are antidepressant drugs and electroconvulsive therapy for depression and the metal lithium for bipolar disorder.

A CLOSER LOOK

Correcting Cognitive Distortions with Rational Alternatives

 Cognitive theorists suggest that cognitive errors can lead to depression if they are left to rummage around unchallenged in the individual's mind. Cognitive therapists thus help clients to recognize cognitive distortions and to replace them with more rational alternative thoughts.

Table 7.7 shows some common examples of automatic thoughts, the types of cognitive distortions they represent, and some rational alternative responses.

(continued)

Table 7.7   Cognitive Distortions and Rational Responses

Automatic Thought	Kind of Cognitive Distortion	Rational Response
I'm all alone in the world.	All-or-Nothing Thinking	It may feel like I'm all alone, but there are some people who care about me.
Nothing will ever work out for me.	Overgeneralization	No one can look into the future. Concentrate on the present.
My looks are hopeless.	Magnification	I may not be perfect looking, but I'm far from hopeless.
I'm falling apart. I can't handle this.	Magnification	Sometimes I just feel overwhelmed. But I've handled things like this before. Just take it a step at a time and I'll be okay.
I guess I'm just a born loser.	Labeling and Mislabeling	Nobody is destined to be loser. Stop talking yourself down.
I've only lost 8 pounds on this diet. I should just forget it. I can't succeed.	Negative Focusing/Minimization/Disqualifying the Positive/Jumping to Conclusions/All-or-Nothing Thinking	Eight pounds is a good start. I didn't gain all this weight overnight, and I have to expect that it will take time to lose it.
I know things must really be bad for me to feel this awful.	Emotional Reasoning	Feeling something doesn't make it so. If I'm not seeing things clearly, my emotions will be distorted too.
I know I'm going to flunk this course.	Fortune Teller Error	Give me a break! Just focus your thoughts on getting through this course, not on jumping to negative conclusions.
I know John's problems are really my fault.	Personalization	Stop blaming yourself for everyone else's problems. There are many reasons why John has these problems that have nothing to do with me.

■ **ANTIDEPRESSANT DRUGS** The drugs that are used to treat depression include tricyclics, monoamine oxidase (MAO) inhibitors, and serotonin-reuptake inhibitors, all of which affect the brain levels and, perhaps, the actions of neurotransmitters. These drugs appear to increase the availability of neurotransmitters in different ways (see Figure 7.1). The tricyclics, so named because of their three-ringed molecular structure, are believed to interfere with the reuptake (the return to the storage vesicles) of norepinephrine and serotonin. The serotonin-reuptake inhibitor fluoxetine hydrochloride (trade name Prozac) works in similar fashion to increase levels of serotonin. As a result, the concentration of these chemical messengers at the synapse is increased, which can induce the receiving cell to continue to fire. The MAO inhibitors increase the availability of neurotransmitters by inhibiting the action of monoamine oxidase, an enzyme that normally breaks down or degrades neurotransmitters in the synaptic cleft. In both cases, the increased availability of key neurotransmitters in the synaptic clefts may enhance the sensitivity of postsynaptic neurons to the transmitters.

The most frequently prescribed antidepressant medication is fluoxetine hydrochloride—Prozac (Touchette, 1991). Other commonly used antidepressants are the tricyclics imipramine (trade name

Automatic Thought	Kind of Cognitive Distortion	Rational Response
Someone my age should be doing better than I am.	Should Statements	Stop comparing yourself to others. All anyone can be expected to do is their best. What good does it do to compare myself to others? It only leads me to get down on myself, rather than get motivated.
I just don't have the brains for college.	Labeling and Mislabeling	Stop calling yourself names like stupid. I can accomplish a lot more than I give myself credit for.
Everything is my fault.	Personalization	There you go again. Stop playing this game of pointing blame at yourself. There's enough blame to go around. Better yet, forget placing blame and try to think through how to solve this problem.
It would be awful if Sue turns me down.	Magnification	It might be upsetting. But it needn't be awful unless I make it so.
If people really knew me, they would hate me.	Mind Reader	What evidence is there for that? More people who get to know me like me than don't like me.
If something doesn't get better soon, I'll go crazy.	Jumping to Conclusions/Magnification	I've dealt with these problems this long without falling apart. I just have to hang in there. Things are not as bad as they seem.
I can't believe I got another pimple on my face. This is going to ruin my whole weekend.	Mental Filter	Take it easy. A pimple is not the end of the world. It doesn't have to spoil my whole weekend. Other people get pimples and seem to have a good time.

Tofranil), amitriptyline (Elavil), desipramine (Norpramin), and doxepin (Sinequan). The potential side effects of tricyclics and MAO inhibitors include psychomotor retardation, dry mouth, constipation, blurred vision, and, less frequently, urinary retention, paralytic ileus (a paralysis of the intestines, which impairs the passage of intestinal contents), confusion, delirium, and cardiovascular complications, such as reduced blood pressure. Prozac is connected with a different constellation of potential side effects, including upset stomach, headaches, agitation, insomnia, and sexual problems, such as sexual apathy and delayed orgasm (Miller, 1992).

Another problem associated with the use of flu-oxetine and tricyclics is the delayed onset of therapeutic effects. Amelioration of depression may require weeks of treatment, when it occurs at all. Tricyclics are highly toxic, moreover, raising the prospect of suicidal overdoses if the drugs are used without close supervision.

MAO inhibitors were commonly used in the treatment of depression prior to the advent of the tricyclics and fluoxetine. Some of the more popular MAO inhibitors include isocarboxazid (trade name Marplan), tranylcypromine (Parnate), and phenelzine (Nardil). They play a smaller role in treatment of depression today because of potentially serious interactions with certain foods and alcoholic beverages,

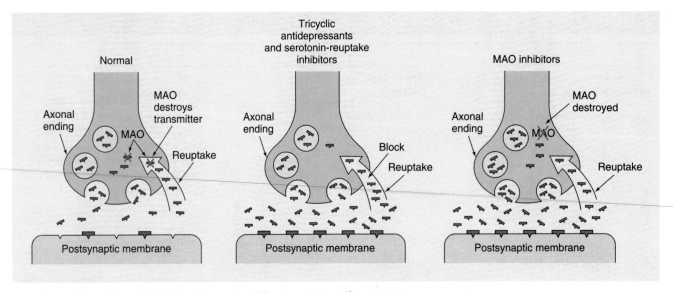

Figure 7.1 The action of various types of antidepressants at the synapse.
Tricyclic antidepressants and serotonin-reuptake inhibitors both increase the availability of neurotransmitters by preventing their reuptake by the presynaptic neuron. Tricyclic antidepressants impede the reuptake of both norepinephrine and serotonin. MAO inhibitors work by inhibiting the action of monoamine oxidase, an enzyme that normally breaks down neurotransmitters in the synaptic cleft.

Source: Schneider & Tarshis (1986), p. 173.

and because of doubts regarding their effectiveness (Paykel & Hale, 1986). Drug–placebo comparisons have also failed to consistently demonstrate the efficacy of MAO inhibitors (Paykel, 1979; Paykel & Hale, 1986). The most serious side effect of MAO inhibitors is a sudden, potentially life-threatening rise in blood pressure that can occur when a user consumes foods that contain tyramine, which is found in cheeses, chocolate, beer, and red wines.

Fluoxetine and the tricyclics clearly help alleviate depression in many cases. Yet questions remain as to whether antidepressant drugs are as effective or more effective than psychotherapy, or whether a combination of antidepressant drugs and psychotherapy is more effective than either treatment approach alone. Evidence shows that psychotherapy—cognitive therapy, behavior therapy, or interpersonal therapy—is roughly comparable in effectiveness to antidepressants in treating depression (Hollon et al., 1991; Imber et al., 1990; Robinson et al., 1990), or perhaps even superior to antidepressants alone (Burns & Nolen-Hoeksema, 1992; Robinson et al., 1990; Wexler & Cicchetti, 1992). Reviewers also find that the combination of psychotherapy and medication offers no overall advantage to either medication or psychotherapy alone (Burns & Nolen-Hoeksema, 1992; Robinson et al., 1990; Wexler & Cicchetti, 1992). Psychotherapy also appears to have more lasting benefits than treatment with antidepressant medication (McLean & Hakstian, 1990; Shelton et al.,

1991; Wexler & Cicchetti, 1992). Yet some depressives who fail to respond to psychological approaches may respond to antidepressant medication, and vice versa. Antidepressant medication may be most appropriate for depressed people who do not respond to psychotherapy alone (Steward et al., 1990), as in some acute and severe cases of depression.

Relapse following discontinuance of antidepressant medication remains a vexing problem, however. A review of drug withdrawal studies showed relapse rates of up to 69% when antidepressants were terminated within 2 months of a treatment response. This is at least double the rate among depressives who were continued on the medication for periods of 6 months to 1 year (Paykel & Hale, 1986). It remains unclear, however, whether or not eventual recurrence of depression would become less likely with longer periods of use.

We also need to note a controversy about fluoxetine (Prozac). Although Prozac was hailed as a miracle drug by some investigators and quickly achieved great popularity as an antidepressant following its introduction in 1988, there have been suggestions that the drug instigates suicidal thoughts and spurs violent behavior in the form of suicide attempts, self-mutilation, assault, and even murder (Masand & Mantosh, 1991; Touchette, 1991). The concerns were raised by a 1990 article in the *American Journal of Psychiatry* by Martin Teicher and his colleagues of the Harvard University Medical School. The Teicher group reported intense suicidal preoccupations among six patients that followed the initiation of Prozac and stopped shortly following discontinuation. Other researchers and clinicians, however, claim that the underlying depression for which these people were being treated with the drug, and not Prozac, was responsible for their suicidal thoughts and aggressive behavior (Touchette, 1991). Other studies with much larger samples have failed to link the use of Prozac with increased suicidal thinking or aggression (Beal et al., 1991; Fava, 1991; Touchette, 1991).

■ **LITHIUM** Bipolar disorder is most commonly treated with the metal lithium (Crammer et al., 1982). It could be said that the ancient Greeks and Romans were among the first to use lithium as a form of chemotherapy. They prescribed mineral water that contained lithium for people with turbulent mood swings.

The ancient Greeks and Romans did use a contemporary form of chemotherapy to treat turbulent mood swings. That chemical is lithium.

Lithium has been found to be effective in treating both the manic and depressive phases of the disorder, and has **prophylactic** value when taken regularly in reducing both the frequency and severity of subsequent recurrences (Janicak & Boshes, 1987; Johnson,

1975; Prien, 1977). People with bipolar disorder may need to use lithium indefinitely to control their mood swings, just as medical patients with diabetes use insulin continuously to control their illness. Lithium is given orally in the form of a natural mineral salt, lithium carbonate. Lithium appears to be most effective in treating manic episodes, with success rates reported of about 67% (Janicak & Boshes, 1987). Some cases of unipolar depression also seem to respond to lithium, especially in people with no personal history of manic episodes but with a family history of bipolar disorder (Fieve, 1977).

Lithium treatment must be closely monitored because of potential toxic effects. There are also side effects. Lithium seems to impair the memory and to slow people down (Shaw et al., 1987). Memory impairment is the primary reason that people who are prescribed preventive regimens of lithium stop taking it (Jamison & Akiskal, 1983).

■ **ELECTROCONVULSIVE THERAPY** Early in the century, electroconvulsive therapy (ECT) was used for many psychological disorders, including major depression, schizophrenia, and bipolar disorder. Because of the advent of chemotherapy, the American Psychiatric Association (1990) now recommends that ECT be used to treat major depression in people who do not respond to antidepressant medication. However, ECT is still used with some schizophrenic and manic patients who fail to respond to chemotherapy (Goleman, 1990a).

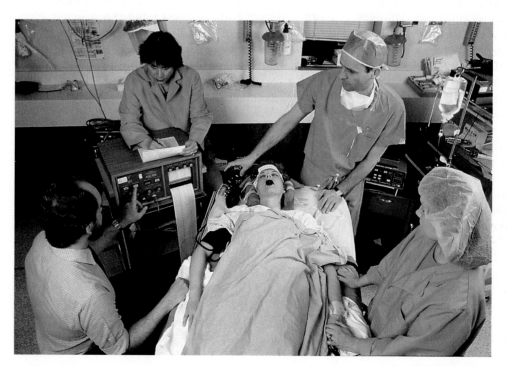

Electroconvulsive therapy (ECT) In ECT, an electric current is passed through the head to induce a convulsive seizure. ECT is effective in lifting the mood of many severely depressed people who do not respond to psychotherapy or to antidepressant medication. Although many professionals regard ECT as a safe and effective treatment for depression, questions remain concerning its side effects, such as memory loss.

ECT involves the administration of an electrical current to the head. A current of between 70 to 130 volts is used to induce a convulsion that is similar to a grand mal epileptic seizure. ECT, or "shock therapy" as it is more commonly known, is usually administered in a series of 6 to 12 treatments over a period of several weeks. The ECT patient is put to sleep with a brief-acting general anesthetic and given a muscle relaxant to avoid wild convulsions and injury. As a result, spasms may be barely perceptible to onlookers. The patient awakens soon after the procedure and generally remembers nothing.

Although ECT often leads to dramatic relief from severe depression, no one knows exactly how ECT works. ECT produces such mammoth chemical and electrical changes in the body that it is difficult to pinpoint the mechanism of therapeutic action. It is suspected, however, that ECT may work by affecting brain levels of neurotransmitters (Coffey & Weiner, 1990).

The effectiveness of ECT remains a matter of debate. ECT is regarded by many professionals as an effective form of treatment for depression, especially for more severe or endogenous forms of depression (National Institute of Mental Health, 1985). One review of the literature estimated that ECT leads to significant improvement in at least 80% of cases of major depression (Coffey & Weiner, 1990). An averaging of results from various studies comparing real ECT treatment to simulated or sham ECT treatment (i.e., treatment that follows the same procedure as ECT but does not deliver shock) showed evidence of superiority of real ECT. The overall improvement rate for real ECT was 72% as compared to 40% for sham ECT (Janicak et al., 1985). Yet we must be cautious in interpreting these results because 4 of the 6 studies that were analyzed were at least 20 years old. Newer, more methodologically sound studies were not included in the analysis (Uebersax, 1987). Newer studies apparently suggest that real ECT produces superior immediate benefits when compared to sham ECT, but *not* superior long-term benefits (Uebersax, 1987). Moreover, the relative effectiveness of ECT as compared to antidepressant medications is even less clear: Some studies show superior results for ECT (Coffey & Weiner, 1990), whereas others show no differences (Janicak et al., 1985).

ECT may be administered to either both sides of the head (*bilateral ECT*) or to one side of the head (*unilateral ECT*). Unilateral ECT is applied to the non-dominant hemisphere of the brain, which, for most people, is the right side. There is disagreement in the research literature concerning the relative effectiveness of these approaches. Some studies show clear advantages for bilateral ECT (Abrams et al., 1983;

Persad, 1990), whereas others show only marginal superiority for bilateral treatment (D'Elia & Raotma, 1975). A review of the research literature suggested that bilateral and unilateral ECT are about equal in effectiveness (Janicak et al., 1985).

There is also controversy as to whether ECT induces memory loss in patients. Although some researchers fail to find any memory impairment in ECT patients (for example, Devannand et al., 1991), critics of ECT have argued that memory loss—especially for recent events—is a frequent side effect (Breggin, 1990). Although memory functioning appears about normal for most people a few months following ECT, some people appear to suffer more lasting memory impairment (Roueche, 1980). It is possible, however, that the profound memory losses that are apparently associated with ECT may actually reflect the severe depression that led to treatment rather than the treatment (Squire & Slater, 1983). In any event, it seems that unilateral ECT is associated with less memory loss than bilateral ECT (American Psychiatric Association, 1978; Janicak et al., 1985; Squire, 1982; Squire & Zouzounis, 1986). Because it may reduce memory loss, unilateral ECT is often tried first, followed by bilateral ECT only in people who fail to respond (Abrams & Fink, 1984; Paykel & Hale, 1986).

Some research suggests that briefer pulses of electricity than those usually applied in ECT may be as therapeutically effective but less likely to impair memory (Coffey & Weiner, 1990). However, these findings have not been consistent (Persad, 1990; Squire & Zouzounis, 1986). Breggin (1990) also argues that ECT works by generally blunting emotional responsiveness, not simply the negative emotion of depression. In sum, many questions remain about the effectiveness and side effects of ECT. For reasons such as these, many professionals view ECT as a treatment of last resort, to be used only after other treatment approaches have been tried and failed. Evidence suggests that about 50% of depressives who fail to respond to antidepressants show significant improvement following ECT (Sackheim et al., 1990).

SUICIDE

Suicidal thoughts are common enough. Under great stress, many, if not most, people have considered suicide. More than half (54%) of one sample of 694 college first-year students reported that they had contemplated suicide on at least one occasion (Meehan et al., 1991). It is fortunate that most people who entertain such thoughts do not act on them. Among the college first-year students who had considered suicide, fewer than 1 in 5 had attempted suicide (Meehan et al., 1991). Still, nearly one-quarter of a million Americans try to commit suicide each year (Blumenthal, 1985). About 30,000 of them succeed (U.S. Bureau of the Census, 1989).

■ **WHO COMMITS SUICIDE** Who is most likely to commit suicide? As you can see in Figure 7.2, white Americans are more likely than African Americans to commit suicide. Although more women in the United States attempt suicide, more men "succeed." Men actually commit between 2.5 and 4 times as many suicides as women (Centers for Disease Control, 1985; Rich et al., 1988). It appears that more males succeed because they choose quicker acting and more lethal means (Carlson & Miller, 1981; Morris et al., 1974). A study of 204 San Diego County suicides that took place in the early 1980s found that males who committed suicide were more likely to use guns (60% of the males versus 28% of the females) (Rich et al., 1988). Females who committed suicide more often used drugs or poisons (44% of the females versus 11% of the males).

Although teenage suicides tend to receive the media spotlight, government statistics show that the elderly are much more likely to commit suicide (see Figure 7.3). The suicide rate among the elderly is 21.6 cases per 100,000 people, nearly twice the national rate of 12.8 cases. The rate of suicide among older people increased in the 1980s, reversing the trend of a half century of decline (Tolchin, 1989). This increase is somewhat surprising because the rate of major depression among the elderly appears to have declined in recent years (Klerman et al., 1989).

Today's elderly are generally healthier and more financially secure than in earlier years, which leaves professionals perplexed about their suicide rate. Several possible causes have been suggested for the high suicide rate among those aged 65 and above (Tolchin, 1989). With longer life, older people are more susceptible to diseases such as Alzheimer's, which can leave them feeling helpless. Some suicides may thus stem from fear of impending helplessness. Or perhaps society's increased tolerance of suicide as a means of "solving" problems makes it a more attractive alternative. Despite life-extending advances in medical care, some elderly people may find that the quality of their lives is less than satisfactory. Many elderly people also suffer a mounting accumulation of losses as time pro-

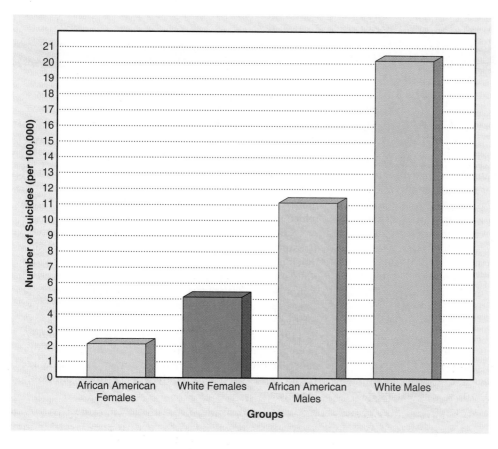

Figure 7.2 Suicide rates according to gender and ethnicity.
Males are significantly more likely than females to commit suicide, and white Americans are significantly more likely than African Americans to do so.
Source: U.S. Bureau of the Census (1989).

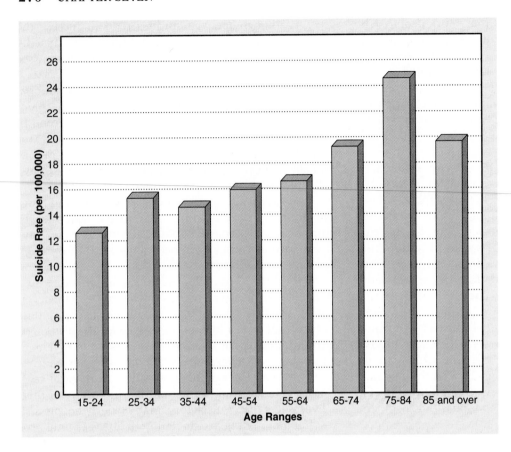

Figure 7.3 Suicide rates according to age.
Although adolescent suicides may be more highly publicized, adults, especially the elderly, have significantly higher suicide rates.
Source: U.S. Bureau of the Census (1989).

MULTICULTURAL PERSPECTIVES

Risk of Suicide Among Native American Youth

Native Americans are at greater than expected risk for suicide attempts and completed suicides. Among young people aged 15 to 24, for example, the suicide rate for Native Americans is nearly twice that for non-Hispanic white youth: 26 per 100,000 as compared with 14 per 100,000 (USDHHS, 1991). The suicide rates for Hispanic, African, and Asian Americans of the same age group are 30 to 60% *lower* than that of non-Hispanic white youth (USDHHS, 1991).

One in six Native American teenagers overall has attempted suicide—a rate that is four times higher than that of other U.S. teenagers (Resnick et al., 1992). A recent study of 83 Native American Zuni adolescents 15 to 16 years of age showed an even higher rate of suicide attempts of 30%, as compared to rates of 4 to 13% reported in stud-

ies of adolescents in the general population (Howard-Pitney et al., 1992). Native-American girls were two to three times more likely than boys to have attempted suicide, a finding which mirrors that of the general population.

Hopelessness and exposure to other people who have attempted or completed suicide would appear to explain much of the risk of suicide among Native American youth. Native American youth at greatest risk tend to be reared in communities that are largely isolated from the benefits of U.S. society at large. They perceive themselves as having relatively few opportunities to gain the skills necessary to join the work force in the larger society and are also relatively more prone to substance abuse, including alcohol abuse. Knowledge that peers have attempted or completed suicide renders suicide a highly visible escape from psychological pain.

gresses. The losses of a spouse, friends, and family members and of good health and a responsible role in the community may wear down the will to live. Whatever the causes, suicide has become an increased risk for elderly people. Perhaps society should focus its attention as much on the quality of life that is afforded our elderly and not simply on providing them the medical care that helps make longer life possible.

Why Do People Commit Suicide?

Why do people commit suicide? To many lay observers, suicide seems so extreme an act that they believe that only "insane" people (meaning people who are out of touch with reality) would commit suicide. However, suicidal thinking does not necessarily imply loss of touch with reality, deep-seated unconscious conflict, or a personality disorder. The contemplation of suicide, instead, generally reflects a narrowing of the range of options people think are available to them (Rotheram-Borus et al., 1990; Schotte et al., 1990). That is, they are discouraged by their problems and see no other way out.

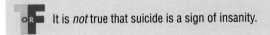 It is *not* true that suicide is a sign of insanity.

The majority of suicides are apparently connected with depression (Beck et al., 1990; Marttunen et al., 1991; Schotte & Clum, 1982), which is why we include the topic in this chapter. Although suicide is most closely linked to mood disorders, many people who take their lives have other problems such as alcoholism, schizophrenia, or panic disorder (Fawcett et al., 1987; Marttunen et al., 1991).

Stress also appears to play an important role in many suicides. Suicide attempts occur more frequently following exposure to highly stressful life events, especially "exit events" such as the death of a spouse, close friend, or relative; divorce or separation; a family member's leaving home; or the loss of a close friend (Slater & Depue, 1981). People who consider taking their lives in response to stressful events have been found to have poorer problem-solving skills than those who did not consider suicide (Schotte & Clum, 1987). It appears that people who consider suicide in times of stress may be less able to find alternative ways of coping with the stressors they face.

Theoretical Perspectives on Suicide

The classic psychodynamic model views depression as the turning inward of anger against the internal representation of a lost love object. Suicide then represents inward-directed anger that turns murderous. Suicidal people, then, do not seek to destroy themselves. Instead, they seek to vent their rage against the internalized representation of the love object. In so doing, they destroy themselves as well, of course. In his later writings, Freud speculated that suicide may be motivated by the "death instinct"—a tendency to return to the tension-free state that preceded birth.

Existential and humanistic theorists relate suicide to the perception that life is meaningless and hopeless. Suicidal people report that they find life duller, emptier, and more boring than nonsuicidal people (Mehrabian & Weinstein, 1985; Neuringer, 1982).

In the last century, social thinker Emile Durkheim (1958) noted that people who experienced *anomie*—who felt lost, without identity, rootless— were more likely to commit suicide. Sociocultural theorists likewise believe that alienation in today's society may play a role in suicide. In our modern mobile society, people frequently move hundreds or thousands of miles to school and jobs. Executives and their families may be relocated every 2 years or so. Military personnel and their families may be shifted about yet more rapidly. Many people are thus socially isolated or cut off from their support groups. Moreover, city dwellers tend to limit or discourage informal social contacts because of crowding, overstimulation, and fear of crime. It is thus understandable that many people find few sources of support in times of crisis.

Moreover, the availability of a "close" family does not guarantee that they will be helpful. In a Boston University study, college women who had attempted suicide were more likely than nonsuicidal peers to implicate their parents as a source of their troubles (Cantor, 1976). The suicidal students were also less likely to feel able to ask their parents or others for help when they were in crisis. "Close" relations are sometimes perceived as part of the problem, not part of the solution.

Learning theorists point to the reinforcing effects of prior suicide threats and attempts, and to the effects of stress, especially when combined with inability to solve personal problems. According to Shneidman (1985), suicide attempters usually wish to escape unbearable psychological pain. People who threaten or attempt suicide may also receive sympathy and support from loved ones and others, perhaps making future—and more lethal—attempts more likely. This is not to suggest that suicide attempts or gestures should be ignored. The majority of people who commit suicide provide clues concerning their intentions beforehand (Cordes, 1985).

 It is *not* true that people who threaten to commit suicide are only seeking attention. Most people who commit suicide have informed others of their intentions.

Social-learning and cognitive theorists suggest that suicide may be motivated by positive outcome expectancies. People who kill themselves may expect that they will be missed or eulogized after death, or that survivors will feel guilty for mistreating them. Suicidal psychiatric patients have been shown to hold more positive expectancies concerning suicide than nonsuicidal psychiatric samples. They more often expressed the belief that suicide would solve their problems, for example (Linehan et al., 1987). Suicide may represent a desperate attempt to deal with one's problems in one fell swoop rather than piecemeal.

Social-learning theory also focuses on the potential modeling effects of observing suicidal behavior in others, especially among teenagers who feel overwhelmed by academic and social stressors. A *social contagion*, or spreading of suicide in a community, may occur in the wake of suicides that receive widespread publicity. Teenagers, who seem to be especially vulnerable to these modeling effects, may even romanticize the suicidal act as one of heroic courage. The incidence of suicide among teenagers sometimes rises markedly in the period following news reports about suicide (Kessler et al., 1990; Phillips & Carstensen, 1986). Copycat suicides may be more likely to occur when reports of suicides are sensationalized such that other teenagers expect their demises to have broad impacts on their communities (Kessler et al., 1990).

Suicide, like other psychological problems, also tends to run in families. There are hints of genetic factors: For example, one twin study showed that among nine twin pairs in which both twins committed suicide, seven were MZ twins and two were DZ twins (Roy et al., 1991). All in all, about one suicide attempter in four has a family member who has committed suicide (Sorensen & Rutter, 1991). The presence of various psychological disorders among family members is also apparently connected with suicide (Sorensen & Rutter, 1991). But what are the causal connections? Do people who attempt suicide inherit vulnerabilities to disorders that are connected with suicide? Does the family atmosphere subject its members to feelings of hopelessness? Does the suicide of one family member give others the idea of doing the same thing? Does one suicide create the impression that other family members are destined to kill themselves?

Suicide is connected with a complex web of factors, and its prediction is no simpler.

Predicting Suicide

"I don't believe it. I just saw him last week and he looked fine."

"She sat here just the other day, laughing with the rest of us. How were we to know what was going on inside her?"

"I knew he was depressed, but I never thought he'd do something like this. I didn't have a clue."

"Why didn't she just call me?"

Friends and family members often respond to news of a suicide with disbelief or guilt that they failed to pick up signs of the impending act. Yet even trained professionals find it difficult to predict who is likely to commit suicide.

Researchers report evidence that hopelessness is an important predictor of eventual suicide among psychiatric outpatients. Among one sample of 1,958 psychiatric outpatients, 16 of 17 people who committed suicide had obtained high scores on a measure of hopelessness (Beck et al., 1990). Outpatients whose scores exceeded a particular cutoff score were 11 times more likely to commit suicide than those whose scores fell below the cutoff. But *when* does hopelessness lead to suicide?

Many people who commit suicide signal their intentions, often quite explicitly. Others attempt to cloak their intentions. Behavioral clues may still reveal suicidal intent, however. People contemplating suicide, for example, may suddenly try to sort out their affairs, as in drafting a will or buying a cemetery plot. They may purchase guns despite lack of prior interest in firearms. When troubled people decide to commit suicide, they may seem to be suddenly at peace; they feel relieved of having to contend with life problems. This sudden calm may be misinterpreted as a sign of hope.

The prediction of suicide is not an exact science, even for experienced professionals. Many observable factors, such as hopelessness, do seem to be connected with suicide, but we cannot predict *when* a hopeless person will attempt suicide, if at all.

A CLOSER LOOK

Suicide Prevention

Imagine yourself having an intimate conversation with a close campus friend, Chris. You know that things have not been good. Chris's grandfather died 6 weeks ago, and the two were very close. Chris's grades have been going downhill, and Chris's romantic relationship also seems to be coming apart at the seams. Still, you are unprepared when Chris says very deliberately, "I just can't take it anymore. Life is just too painful. I don't feel like I want to live anymore. I've decided that the only thing I can do is to kill myself."

When somebody discloses that he or she is contemplating suicide, you may feel bewildered and frightened, as if a great burden has been placed on your shoulders. It has. If someone confides suicidal thoughts to you, your goal should be to persuade him or her to see a professional, or to get the advice of a professional yourself as soon as you can. But if the suicidal person declines to talk to another person and you sense that you can't break away for such a conference, there are some things you can do then and there:

1. Draw the person out. Shneidman advises framing questions like, "What's going on?" "Where do you

A suicide hotline. Suicide hotlines have been established on many college campuses and in most communities. If you or someone you know is entertaining suicidal thoughts, why not speak to a mental health professional or call a hotline for advice?

hurt?" "What would you like to see happen?" (1985, p. 11). Such questions may prompt people to verbalize thwarted psychological needs and offer some relief. They also grant you the time to appraise the risk and contemplate your next move.

2. Be sympathetic. Show that you fathom how troubled the person is. Don't say something like, "You're just being silly."

3. Suggest that means other than suicide can be discovered to work out the person's problems, even if they are not apparent at the time. Shneidman (1985) notes that suicidal people can usually see only two solutions to their predicaments—either suicide or some kind of magical resolution. Professionals try to broaden the available alternatives of people who are suicidal.

4. Inquire as to *how* the person expects to commit suicide. People with explicit methods who also possess the means (for example, a gun or drugs) are at greater risk. Ask if you may hold on to the gun, drugs, or whatever for a while. Sometimes the person agrees.

5. Propose that the person accompany you to consult a professional right *now*. Many campuses have hot lines that you or the suicidal individual can call. Many towns and cities have such hot lines and they can be called anonymously. Other possibilities include the emergency room of a general hospital, a campus health center or counseling center, or the campus or local police. If you are unable to maintain contact with the suicidal person, get professional assistance as soon as you separate.

6. Don't say something like, "You're talking crazy." Such comments are degrading and injurious to the individual's self-esteem. Don't press the suicidal person to contact specific people, such as parents or a spouse. Conflict with them may have given rise to the suicidal thoughts.

Above all, keep in mind that your primary goal is to confer with a helping professional. Don't go it alone any longer than you have to.

SUMMARY

Mood Disorders

Mood disorders are disturbances in mood that are serious enough to impair daily functioning. There are various kinds of mood disorders, including depressive (unipolar) disorders such as major depression and dysthymic disorder, and disorders involving mood swings, such as bipolar disorder and cyclothymic disorder.

Major Depression

People with major depression experience profound changes in mood that impair their ability to function. There are many associated features of major depression, including depressed mood, changes in appetite, difficulty sleeping, reduced sense of pleasure in formerly enjoyable activities, feelings of fatigue or loss of energy, sense of worthlessness, excessive or misplaced guilt, difficulties concentrating, thinking clearly or making decisions, repeated thoughts of death or suicide, attempts at suicide, or even psychotic behaviors (hallucinations and delusions).

The course of major depression is variable. Some people experience one episode; others have recurrent episodes. About twice as many women as men seem to be affected by major depression, but the reasons for this gender difference remain unclear. Depression can begin or recur at any age, but the risk of initial onset of depression is age-related. Major depression may have declined in recent years among the elderly, but increased among the so-called baby boomers.

Depressions that appear to be precipitated by stressful events, such as the loss of a loved one, are termed reactive. Depressions that are not linked to any clear precipitating events are often called endogenous.

Whereas mood changes in the mother shortly following childbirth are quite normal, and probably reflect hormonal changes, more persistent mood changes in the following weeks and months may be signs of a type of depression called postpartum depression (PPD). Various factors may increase risk, especially lack of support from others and first-time or single motherhood.

Dysthymic Disorder

Dysthymic disorder is a form of chronic depression that is milder than major depression but may nevertheless be associated with impaired functioning in social and occupational roles.

Bipolar Disorder

There are two general types of bipolar disorders, bipolar I and bipolar II. Bipolar I disorder is identified by the occurrence of one or more manic episodes, which generally but not necessarily occur in persons who have experienced major depressive episodes. In bipolar II disorder, depressive episodes occur along with hypomanic episodes, but without the occurrence of a full-blown manic episode.

Manic episodes usually begin abruptly and tend to last from a few days to perhaps a few months. They are characterized by sudden elevation or expansion of mood and sense of self-importance, feelings of almost boundless energy, hyperactivity, and extreme sociability, which often takes a demanding and overbearing form. Manic people tend to exhibit pressured or rapid speech, rapid "flight of ideas," and decreased need for sleep.

Cyclothymic Disorder

Cyclothymic disorder is a type of bipolar disorder that is characterized by a chronic pattern of mild mood swings and sometimes progresses to bipolar disorder.

Theoretical Perspectives

In classic psychodynamic theory, depression is viewed in terms of inward-directed anger. People who hold strongly ambivalent feelings toward people they have lost, or whose loss is threatened, may direct unresolved anger toward the inward representations of these people that they have incorporated or introjected within themselves, producing self-loathing and depression. Bipolar disorder is understood within psychodynamic theory in terms of the shifting balances between the ego and superego. More recent psychodynamic models, such as the self-focusing model, incorporate both psychodynamic and cognitive aspects in explaining depression in terms of the continued pursuit of lost love objects or goals that would be more adaptive to surrender.

In the existential-humanistic framework, feelings of depression reflect the lack of meaning and authenticity in the person's life.

Learning perspectives focus on situational factors in explaining depression, such as changes in the level of reinforcement. When reinforcement is reduced, the person may feel unmotivated and depressed, which can occasion inactivity and further reduces opportunities for reinforcement. Coyne's interactional theory focuses on the negative family interactions that can lead the family members of depressed people to become less reinforcing toward them.

Beck's cognitive theory focuses on the role of negative or distorted thinking in depression. Depression-prone people hold negative beliefs toward themselves, the environment, and the future. This cognitive triad of depression leads to specific errors in thinking, or cognitive distortions, in response to negative events, that in turn lead to depression.

The learned helplessness model is based on the belief that people may become depressed when they come to view themselves as helpless to control the reinforcements in their environment or to change their lives for the better. A reformulated version of the theory held that the ways in which a people explain events—their attributions—determine their proneness toward depression in the face of negative events. The combination of internal, global, and stable attributions for negative events renders one most vulnerable to depression.

Genetics appears to play a role in mood disorders, especially in explaining major depression and bipolar disorder. The dominant biological model of depression in the past 25 years has been the catecholamine hypothesis, which links depression to reductions in the levels of norepinephrine and mania to excesses of norepinephrine.

Treatment

Psychodynamic treatment of depression has traditionally focused on helping the depressed person uncover and work through ambivalent feelings toward the lost object, thereby lessening the anger directed inward. Modern psychodynamic approaches tend to be more direct and briefer and focus on developing more adaptive means of achieving self-worth and resolving interpersonal conflicts. Humanistic and existential therapists focus on helping depressed clients become better aware of their true feelings and needs for self-actualization and personal fulfillment. Increased self-worth and happiness comes from being true to oneself and finding avenues of personal fulfillment that give life meaning and purpose.

Learning-theory approaches have focused on helping depressed people increase the frequency of reinforcement in their lives through such means as helping them increase the rates of pleasant activities in which they participate and assisting them in developing more effective social skills to increase their ability to obtain social reinforcements from others. Cognitive therapists focus on helping depressed people identify and correct distorted or dysfunctional thoughts and learn more adaptive behaviors. Biological approaches have focused on the use of drugs and other biological treatments, such as electroconvulsive therapy (ECT), in the treatment of mood disorders. Antidepressant drugs appear to increase the levels of neurotransmitters in the brain in different ways. Bipolar disorder is commonly treated with lithium.

Suicide

Mood disorders are often linked to suicide. Although women are more likely to attempt suicide, more men actually succeed, perhaps because they select more lethal means. The elderly—not the young—are more likely to commit suicide, and the rate of suicide among the elderly appears to be increasing. People who attempt suicide are often depressed, but they are generally in touch with reality. They may, however, lack effective problem-solving skills and see no way to deal with their life stress other than suicide.

Roy Lichenstein, *Woman with Flowered Hat, 1963. Acrylic on canvas: 50 × 40 inches.*

CHAPTER OUTLINE

8

Disorders of Personality and Impulse Control

TRUTH  FICTION?

___ Some people can intentionally injure others without experiencing feelings of guilt or remorse.

___ It can be difficult to draw the line between normal variations in behavior and personality disorders.

___ The concept of certain types of personality disorders may be sexist.

___ Gamblers Anonymous groups, modeled after Alcoholics Anonymous, have been established to help pathological gamblers.

___ Kleptomania is usually motivated by poverty.

*A*ll of us have particular styles of behavior and ways of relating to others. Some of us are orderly, others sloppy. Some of us prefer solitary pursuits, others are more social. Some of us are followers; others, leaders. Some of us seem immune to rejection by others, whereas others avoid social initiatives for fear of getting shot down. When behavior patterns become so inflexible or maladaptive that they cause significant personal distress or impair people's social or occupational functioning, they may be diagnosed as personality disorders.

PERSONALITY DISORDERS

In most of us by the age of thirty, the character has set like plaster, and will never soften again.

William James

Personality disorders are excessively rigid patterns of behavior, or ways of relating to others. Their rigidity prevents people from adjusting to external demands; thus they ultimately become self-defeating. The disordered personality traits usually become evident by adolescence or early adulthood and continue through much of adult life, becoming so deeply ingrained that they are highly resistant to change.

Despite the self-defeating consequences of their behavior, people with personality disorders do not generally perceive a need to change. In psychodynamic terms, people with personality disorders tend to perceive their traits as **ego syntonic**—as natural parts of themselves. As a result, persons with personality disorders are more likely to be brought to the attention of mental health professionals by others than to seek services themselves. In contrast, persons with anxiety disorders or mood disorders tend to view their disturbed behaviors as **ego dystonic**. They do not see their behaviors as parts of their self-identities and are thus more likely to seek help to relieve the distress caused by them.

The DSM groups clinical syndromes on Axis I and personality disorders on Axis II. Both clinical syndromes and personality disorders may thus be diagnosed in clients whose behavior meets the criteria for both classes of disorders. A person may have an Axis I mood disorder, for example, like major depression, and also show the characteristics associated with an Axis II personality disorder.

Types of Personality Disorders

The DSM groups personality disorders into three clusters:

Cluster A: People who are perceived as odd or eccentric. This cluster includes paranoid, schizoid, and schizotypal personality disorders.

Cluster B: People whose behavior is overly dramatic, emotional, or erratic. This grouping consists of antisocial, borderline, histrionic, and narcissistic personality disorders.

Cluster C: People who often appear anxious or fearful. This cluster includes avoidant, dependent, and obsessive-compulsive personality disorders.

In this chapter we consider each of these personality disorders, organized according to cluster. We also discuss disorders of impulse control which, like personality disorders, are maladaptive and often self-defeating patterns of behavior.

An 85-year-old retired businessman was interviewed by a social worker to determine the health-care needs for himself and his infirm wife. The man had no history of treatment for a mental disorder. He appeared to be in good health and mentally alert. He and his wife had been married for 60 years, and it appeared that his wife was the only person he'd ever really trusted. He had always been suspicious of others. He would not reveal personal information to anyone but his wife, believing that others were out to take advantage of him. He had refused offers of help from other acquaintances because he suspected their motives. When called on the telephone, he would refuse to give out his name until he determined the nature of the caller's business. He'd always involved himself in "useful work" to occupy his time, even during the 20 years of his retirement. He spends a good deal of time monitoring his investments and has had altercations with his stock broker when errors on his monthly statement prompted suspicion that his broker was attempting to cover up fraudulent transactions.

■ *Adapted from Spitzer et al., 1989, pp. 163–164*

PERSONALITY DISORDERS CHARACTERIZED BY ODD OR ECCENTRIC BEHAVIOR

This group of personality disorders includes paranoid, schizoid, and schizotypal disorders. People with these disorders often have difficulty relating to others, or they may show little or no interest in developing social relationships.

Paranoid Personality Disorder

The defining trait of the **paranoid personality disorder** is pervasive suspiciousness—the tendency to interpret other people's behavior as deliberately threatening or demeaning. People with the disorder are excessively mistrustful of others, and their relationships suffer for it. They may be suspicious of co-workers and supervisors but can generally hold on to jobs.

The following case illustrates the unwarranted suspicion and reluctance to confide in others that typifies people with paranoid personalities:

Paranoid personalities tend to be overly sensitive to criticism, whether real or imagined. They take offense at the smallest slight. They are readily angered and hold grudges when they think they have been mistreated. They are unlikely to confide in others because they believe that personal information may be used against them. They question the sincerity and trustworthiness of friends and associates. A smile or a glance may be viewed with suspicion. As a result, they have few friends and intimate relationships. When they do form an intimate relationship, they may suspect infidelity in the absence of evidence. They tend to remain hypervigilant, as if they must be on the lookout against harm. They deny blame for misdeeds, even when warranted, and are perceived by others as cold, aloof, scheming, devious, and humorless. They tend to be argumentative and may launch repeated lawsuits against those who they believe have mistreated them.

Although the suspicions of the paranoid personality are exaggerated and unwarranted, there is an absence of the paranoid delusions that characterize the thought patterns of paranoid schizophrenics (for example, believing that the FBI is out to get them). Paranoid personalities are unlikely to seek treatment for themselves; they see others as causing their problems.

Schizoid Personality Disorder

Social isolation is the cardinal feature of **schizoid personality disorder**. Often described as a loner or an eccentric, the schizoid individual lacks interest in social relationships. The emotions of persons with schizoid personalities appear shallow or blunted, but not to the degree found in schizophrenia (see Chapter 11). People with this disorder seem rarely, if ever, to experience strong anger, joy, or sadness. They look distant and aloof. Their faces rarely show emotional expression, and they rarely exchange social smiles or nods. They seem indifferent to criticism or praise and appear to be wrapped up in abstract ideas rather than in thoughts about people. Although they prefer to remain distant from others, they maintain better contact with reality than schizophrenics do.

The schizoid personality pattern is usually recognized by early adulthood. Men with this disorder rarely date or marry. Schizoid women are more likely to accept romantic advances passively and marry, but they seldom initiate relationships or develop strong attachments to their partners.

Akhtar (1987) claims that there may be discrepancies between outer appearances and the inner lives of schizoid personalities. Although they may appear to have little appetite for sex, for example, schizoid personalities may harbor voyeuristic wishes and become attracted to pornography. Akhtar also suggests that the distance and social aloofness of schizoid personalities may be somewhat superficial. They may also harbor exquisite sensitivity, deep curiosities about people, and wishes for love that they cannot express. In some cases, sensitivity is expressed in deep feelings for animals rather than people:

> *John, a 50-year-old retired police officer, sought treatment a few weeks after his dog was hit by a car and died. Since the dog's death, John has felt sad and tired. He has had difficulty concentrating and sleeping. John lives alone and prefers to be by himself, limiting his contacts with others to a passing "Hello" or "How are you?" He feels that social conversation is a waste of time and feels awkward when others try to initiate a friendship. Although he avidly reads newspapers and keeps abreast of current events, he has no real interest in people. He works as a security guard and is described by his co-workers as a "loner" and a "cold fish." The only relationship he had was with his dog, with whom he felt he could exchange more sensitive and loving feelings than he could share with people. At Christmas, he would "exchange gifts" with his dog, buying presents for the dog and wrapping a bottle of Scotch for himself as a gift from the animal. The only event that ever saddened him was the loss of his dog. In contrast, the loss of his parents failed to evoke an emotional response. He considers himself to be different from other people and is bewildered by the displays of emotionality that he sees in others.*
>
> ■ *Adapted from Spitzer et al., 1989, pp. 249–250*

Schizotypal Personality Disorder

Schizotypal personality disorder usually becomes evident in early adulthood. The diagnosis refers to people whose behavior, mannerisms, and thought patterns are peculiar or odd, but not disturbed enough to merit a diagnosis of schizophrenia. In the DSM-II, the behavior pattern was considered a type of schizophrenia labeled *simple schizophrenia*. Simple schizophrenia was characterized by persistent oddities in behavior that did not include the gross disorganization which typified other types of schizophrenia. With the advent of the DSM-III in 1980, the label of schizo*typal* personality disorder was initiated to help distinguish between schizophrenic disorders and behavior patterns that were similar and persistent but not as severe.

The eccentricity of the schizoid personality is limited to lack of interest in social relationships. Schizotypal personality disorder refers to a wider range of odd behaviors, beliefs, and perceptions. Persons with the disorder may experience unusual perceptions or illusions, such as feeling the presence of a deceased family member in the room. They may become unduly suspicious of others or paranoid in

Schizoid personality. It is normal to be reserved about displaying one's feelings, especially when one is among strangers. But people with schizoid personalities rarely express emotions and are distant and aloof. Yet the emotions of persons with schizoid personalities are not shallow or blunted to the degree found in schizophrenia.

their thinking. They may develop **ideas of reference**, such as the belief that other people are talking about them. They may engage in "magical thinking"—such as believing that they possess a "sixth sense" (i.e., can foretell the future) or that others can sense their feelings. They may attach unusual meanings to words. Their own speech may be vague or unusually abstract but not so that it becomes incoherent or filled with the loose associations that characterize schizophrenia. They may appear unkempt, display unusual mannerisms, and engage in unusual behaviors such as talking to themselves in the presence of others. Their faces may register little emotion. Like schizoid personalities, they may fail to exchange smiles with, or nod at, others. Or they may appear silly, and smile and laugh at the wrong times. They tend to be socially withdrawn and aloof, with few if any close friends or confidants. They seem to be especially anxious around unfamiliar people.

Some of these features are found in the case of Jonathan:

> *Jonathan, a 27-year-old auto mechanic, had few friends and preferred science fiction novels to socializing with other people. He seldom joined in conversations. At times, he seemed to be lost in his thoughts, and his co-workers would have to whistle to get his attention when he was working on a car. He often showed a "queer" expression on his face. Perhaps the most unusual feature of his behavior was his reported intermittent experience of "feeling" his deceased mother standing nearby. These illusions were reassuring to him, and he looked forward to their occurrence. Jonathan realized that they were not real. He never tried to reach out to touch the apparition, knowing that it would disappear as soon as he drew closer. It was enough, he said, to feel her presence.*
>
> ■ *The Authors' Files*

Despite the DSM's grouping of "schizotypal" behaviors with personality disorders, the behavior pattern may represent a milder form of schizophrenia (Siever et al., 1991) or fall within a spectrum of schizophrenia-related disorders that includes such disorders as paranoid, schizoid, and schizotypal personality disorders and schizoaffective disorder (discussed in Chapter 11), as well as schizophrenia. There is some evidence that schizophrenia and schizotypal personality disorder have a common genetic basis (Burman et al., 1987; Spitzer et al., 1979). In a Danish adoption study, for example, 14.3% of the biological relatives of adoptees who became schizophrenic showed schizotypal personality disorder, as compared with *none* of the relatives of adoptees who did not become schizophrenic (Kendler & Gruenberg, 1984). Re-

searchers have also found that close relatives of people with schizotypal personality disorder are more likely than relatives of patients with nonschizophrenic-related personality disorders (for example, histrionic, borderline, o narcissistic disorders) to be diagnosed as suffering from a schizophrenia-spectrum disorder (Siever et al., 1990b).

Perhaps the emergence of schizophrenia in persons with this shared genetic predisposition is determined by such factors as stressful early family relationships. Schizophrenics have been found to report poorer childhood relationships with their parents than do those who develop schizotypal personalities (Burman et al., 1987).

PERSONALITY DISORDERS CHARACTERIZED BY DRAMATIC, EMOTIONAL, OR ERRATIC BEHAVIOR

This cluster of personality disorders includes the antisocial, borderline, histrionic, and narcissistic types. The behavior patterns of these types are excessive, unpredictable, or self-centered. People with these disorders have difficulty forming and maintaining relationships.

Antisocial Personality Disorder

People with **antisocial personality disorders** persistently violate the rights of others and often break the law. They disregard social norms and conventions, are impulsive, and fail to live up to interpersonal and vocational commitments (Hare et al., 1988). Cleckley (1976) notes that these people often show a superficial charm and are at least average in intelligence. Perhaps the features that are most striking about them, given their antisocial behavior, are their low levels of anxiety and lack of guilt. Punishment seems to have little if any effect on their behavior. Although they have usually been punished by parents and others for their misdeeds, they persist in leading irresponsible and impulsive lives. Researchers estimate that 4% of adults in the United States could be classified as having met diagnostic criteria for antisocial personality disorder at some point in their lives (Robins et al., 1991).

The terms *psychopath* and *sociopath* also refer to people with antisocial personality disorder. Both terms describe people whose behavior is amoral and asocial, impulsive, and lacking in remorse and shame. The roots of *psychopath* focus on the idea that there is

(A)

(B)

Antisocial personalities. Some antisocial personalities fit the common stereotype of the violent, amoral career criminal. Gary Gilmore (A), for example, was convicted of two murders and executed for his crimes. Gilmore displayed many characteristics of the antisocial personality. He was unable to follow rules at home or at school. He began abusing alcohol and drugs during adolescence. He was repeatedly in trouble with the law for crimes that included armed robberies and murder. He had no remorse or guilt for his crimes, had never held a job or maintained a steady relationship, and was intentionally abusive and cruel. Some antisocial personalities, however, are charming and unlikely to engage in violent behavior. The fictional character Gordon Gekko (B), played by Michael Douglas in the movie *Wall Street,* was a charismatic figure with many antisocial characteristics: self-centeredness; lying, conning, and manipulation of others in the pursuit of personal gain; and lack of remorse for misdeeds.

something amiss (pathological) in the individual's psychological functioning. The roots of *sociopath* center on the person's social deviance. As we see, use of these terms reflected popular beliefs of the times in which they arose.

■ HISTORICAL PERSPECTIVES ON ANTISOCIAL PERSONALITY

In the 18th century, some thinkers proposed that moral depravity might represent mental defects which impaired the person's ability to conform to common standards of decency. The French reformer Philippe Pinel, who called for more humane treatment of mental patients, regarded moral depravity as a form of mania *without* insanity. In 1835, the English psychiatrist J. R. Prichard reconceptualized the disorder as "moral insanity." He considered the problem to be a form of mental derangement in which the intellectual functions remained relatively intact but the

> . . . moral and active principles of the mind were strongly perverted or depraved . . . and the individual is found to be incapable not of talking or reasoning on any subject proposed to him, but of conducting himself with decency and propriety in the business of his life. (Prichard, 1835, p. 15)

Pinel argued that people with abnormal behavior need a kind and gentle form of treatment that became known as moral therapy. Moral therapy was based on the belief that abnormal behaviors, including morally depraved behaviors, reflect oppressive or deprived childhoods. It was hoped that a nurturant and supportive therapeutic environment would steer depraved people in the right direction (Smith, R.J., 1978).

Later in the 19th century, discoveries of the causes of various physical diseases and some abnormal behavior patterns (e.g., general paresis) inspired hope that organic causes would eventually be discovered for all abnormal behaviors, including antisocial behavior. The medical model suggested that psychopaths—as they were labeled at the time—suffered from a biological defect, presumably hereditary, that predisposed them to criminal or antisocial conduct.

The rise of interest in sociology and social work in the early and mid-20th century led to the view that deviant behavior is rooted in the person's alienation from society. Recognition that social problems such as poverty, unemployment, and antisocial models are related to deviant behavior led many to substitute the label of sociopathy for psychopathy. Remember a delinquent's discovery in the 1960s musical *West Side Story:* "Hey, I've got a social disease!"

■ DIAGNOSTIC FEATURES OF ANTISOCIAL PERSONALITY

The DSM states that in order for the diagnosis of antisocial personality disorder to be applied, the person must be at least 18 years old. The alternate diagnosis of conduct disorder is used with children (see Chapter 13). Many conduct-disordered children do not continue to show antisocial behavior as adults. Although there is apparently a strong relationship between antisocial personality traits and criminal behavior (Hare, 1986), only about half of prison inmates could be diagnosed with antisocial personality disorder (Robins et al., 1991). The criminal behavior of the professional thief or drug pusher, although antisocial, does not in itself justify a diagnosis of antisocial personality disorder.

Conversely, fewer than half of the people with antisocial personalities run afoul of the law (Robins et al., 1991). Hervey Cleckley (1941) showed that the characteristics defining the antisocial personality—self-centeredness, irresponsibility, impulsivity, and insensitivity to the needs of others—exist not only among criminals but also among many respected members of the community, including doctors, lawyers, politicians, and business executives. The clinical features of antisocial personality disorder, as defined in the DSM, are shown in Table 8.1.

■ **GENDER, RACE, AND ANTISOCIAL PERSONALITY DISORDER** Whereas women are more likely than men to have anxiety and depressive

Table 8.1 Diagnostic Features of Antisocial Personality Disorder

(a) The person is at least 18 years old.

(b) There is evidence of a conduct disorder prior to the age of 15 as shown by such behavior patterns as truancy, running away, initiating physical fights, use of weapons, forcing someone into sexual activities, physical cruelty to people or animals, deliberate destruction of property or fire setting, lying, stealing, or mugging.

(c) Since the age of 15, there has been general indifference to and violation of the rights of other people, as shown by several of the following:

   (1) Lack of conformity to social norms and legal codes, as shown by law-breaking behavior that may or may not result in arrest, such as destruction of property, engaging in unlawful occupations, stealing, or harrassing others

   (2) Aggressive and highly irritable style of relating to others, as shown by repeated physical fights and assaults with others, possibly involving abuse of one's spouse or children

   (3) Consistent irresponsibility, as shown by failure to maintain employment due to chronic absences, lateness, abandonment of job opportunities or extended periods of unemployment despite available work; and/or by failure to honor financial obligations, such as failing to maintain child support or defaulting on debts; and/or by lack of a sustained monogamous relationship

   (4) Failure to plan ahead or impulsivity, as shown by traveling around without prearranged employment or clear goals

   (5) Disregard for the truth, evidenced by repeated lying, conning others, or use of aliases for personal gain or pleasure

   (6) Recklessness with regard to personal safety or the safety of other people, as shown by driving while intoxicated or repeated speeding

   (7) Lack of remorse for misdeeds, as shown by indifference to the harm done to others, and/or by rationalizing that harm

Source: Adapted from DSM-IV Draft Criteria (American Psychiatric Association, 1993), p. T:4.

disorders, men are more likely to exhibit antisocial personality disorder (Russo, 1990). The ECA study of the residents of five U.S. communities found antisocial personality disorder to be more than five times more common among men than among women (Robins et al., 1991). The prevalence of the disorder has been rising for both genders in recent years, and more sharply among women. The disorder is more common among the lower socioeconomic classes, in part because antisocial personalities tend to drift downward occupationally and in part because many antisocial personalities were reared by antisocial parents who presumably served as models.

The ECA study found no ethnic differences in the rates of antisocial personality disorder (Robins et al., 1991). Kosson and his colleagues (1990) provide evidence of some similarities and differences between African Americans and white Americans with antisocial personality disorder. Prison inmates of both ethnic groups with antisocial personality disorder had histories of greater criminality than other inmates in these ethnic groups. Moreover, the measures used to classify antisocial personality disorder among white Americans appear generalizable to African Americans.

■ **ANTISOCIAL BEHAVIOR AND CRIMINALITY** Although infamous crimes have been committed by people who apparently fit the diagnosis of antisocial personality disorder, criminal and aggressive behavior has multiple causes and represents many personality styles (Siegel, 1992; Smith, R.J., 1978). Some people become criminals or delinquents not because of a disordered personality but because they were reared in environments or subcultures that encouraged and rewarded criminal behavior (Hare, 1970). Although their behavior is deviant to society at large, it is normal by the standards of their subcultures. We should also recognize that lack of remorse, which is a cardinal feature of antisocial personality disorder, does not typify all criminals. Some criminals regret their crimes, and evidence of remorse is considered when sentence is passed.

■ **PROFILE OF ANTISOCIAL PERSONALITY DISORDER** Common features of antisocial personality disorder include failure to conform to social norms, outright lawlessness, violence, chronic unemployment, marital problems, substance abuse, a history of alcoholism (Robins et al., 1991; Smith & Newman, 1990), and disregard for the truth. Consider the following case:

The 19-year-old male is brought by ambulance to the hospital emergency room in a state of cocaine intoxication. He's wearing a T-shirt with the imprint "Twisted

Sister" on the front, and he sports a punk-style haircut. His mother is called and sounds groggy and confused on the phone; the doctors must coax her to come to the hospital. She later tells the doctors that her son has arrests for shoplifting and for driving while intoxicated. She suspects that he takes drugs, although she has no direct evidence. She believes that he is performing fairly well at school and has been a star member of the basketball team.

It turns out that her son has been lying to her. In actuality, he never completed high school and never played on the basketball team. A day later, his head cleared, the patient tells his doctors, almost boastfully, that his drug and alcohol use started at the age of 13, and that by the time he was 17, he was regularly using a variety of psychoactive substances, including alcohol, speed, marijuana, and cocaine. Lately, however, he has preferred cocaine. He and his friends frequently participate in drug and alcohol binges. At times they each drink a case of beer in a day along with downing other drugs. They have adopted a nickname for these group binges— "The André-the-Giant Club." He steals car radios from parked cars and money from his mother to support his drug habit, which he justifies by adopting a (partial) "Robin Hood" attitude—that is, taking money only from people who have lots of it.

■ *Adapted from Spitzer, 1989, pp. 9–12*

Although this case is suggestive of antisocial personality disorder, the diagnosis was maintained as provisional because the interviewer could not determine that the deviant behavior (lying, stealing, skipping school) began before the age of 15.

We base our profile of the antisocial personality on the criteria listed by Cleckley in describing this personality type in his classic book *The Mask of Sanity,* which was first published in 1941 and has continued, in subsequent editions, to influence conceptions of the disorder. Although there is much overlap between Cleckley's characterization and the DSM concept of antisocial personality disorder, we should note some differences. The DSM places a greater emphasis on specific undesirable behaviors, such as a history of lying, cheating, or criminal behavior, or inability to maintain steady employment or meet family or financial responsibilities. Although he recognized specific antisocial behaviors as part of his overall profile, Cleckley emphasized interpersonal and subjective aspects of the antisocial personality, such as superficial charm and lack of capacity for love, along with inability to profit from experience. By focusing more on behavior, the DSM may improve the reliability of diagnostic judgments of antisocial personality. Cleckley's clinical profile, how-

ever, provides researchers and clinicians a richer understanding of its psychological features:

1. *Superficial charm and intelligence.* The antisocial personality may be superficially charming, even while committing cruel or murderous actions. The antisocial personality may appear friendly and easy to talk to, giving no impression of being fraudulent or manipulative.

2. *Absence of anxiety in stressful situations.* The antisocial personality may be poised and cool under pressure, not displaying nervousness in stressful situations that might cause others to feel embarrassed or anxious.

3. *Insincerity and lack of truthfulness.* The antisocial personality is able to speak convincingly of feelings toward loved ones and appears to be sensitive to the needs of others, even while taking advantage.

4. *Lack of remorse and shame.* The antisocial personality feels no pangs of guilt or remorse, no feelings of shame for misdeeds and injurious behavior.

 Antisocial personalities can intentionally injure others without experiencing feelings of guilt or remorse.

5. *Inability to experience love or genuine emotion.* Although the antisocial personality may profess feelings of love, often convincingly so, the feelings are not genuine. The antisocial personality is egocentric, lacking the capacity to love and often hurting the purported objects of love. Lack of empathy and deep feelings may facilitate the callous mistreatment of "loved ones."

6. *Unreliability and irresponsibility.* Antisocial personalities lack a sense of obligation, duty, or responsibility. They may walk away from jobs or desert their families, leaving a pile of unpaid bills.

7. *Impulsivity and disregard for socially acceptable behavior.* Antisocial personalities tend to act on the spur of the moment. They drift from place to place without concrete goals or destinations in mind. They may commit impulsive antisocial acts with little or no planning, such as stealing a car because they "felt like it," using illicit drugs, or passing bad checks when money runs out. The aimlessness with which they break the law often separates them from committed criminals whose crimes are planned and rehearsed. Antisocial personalities seem unable to tolerate frustration or delay gratification. They demand to have (or take) what they want when they want it, even if it means stealing or otherwise breaking the law.

8. *Absence of delusions or irrational thinking.* Antisocial personalities seem to be clearheaded. Others may

The Pause That Reflects

Persons with antisocial personalities are notoriously undeterred by punishment. They may repeatedly engage in self-defeating patterns of behavior, such as gambling or coming in late to work, despite negative consequences. Perhaps one reason that they fail to profit from experience is that they find it difficult to switch gears (change their behavior) in the face of changing reinforcement contingencies. They may once have won at gambling or been able to sneak late into work without getting caught. But gambling losses eventually exceed winnings, and latenesses eventually put them on the unemployment line. Nonetheless, antisocial personalities are apparently stuck in maladaptive patterns of behavior—a response deficit that psychologists label **perseveration.**

Perseveration (and what might be done about it) was demonstrated in a card-playing experiment with antisocial personalities and normal control subjects (Newman et al., 1987). Subjects could win or lose money by playing repeated hands of cards. The odds of winning were stacked, however, so that subjects were likely to win in the early rounds and lose in the later rounds. Both groups of subjects, people with antisocial personality disorder and normals, were free to stop at any time. Normals tended to play as long as they were winning and to quit when they started to lose as frequently as they won. They apparently recognized that the odds had turned against them and chose to take their winnings and leave. Antisocial personalities tended to play on when their "luck" changed, however, until they lost all their money or were out of cards.

In another experimental condition, a forced delay of a few seconds was introduced between rounds. The antisocial personalities who had to pause terminated their playing when the odds changed just as the normal control subjects did. Giving antisocial personalities time to think about punishment apparently disrupted their perseveration and helped them to benefit from experience. Perhaps antisocial personalities would benefit from other treatments that focus on teaching them to stop and think about the consequences before they act.

perceive them as holding firm rational convictions and being capable of warm responses toward their families and loved ones.

9. *Inability to profit from experience.* Antisocial personalities may commit the same misdeeds repeatedly, despite a history of punishment. Punishment has little effect on their behavior; despite promises to "go straight," they eventually return to impulsive antisocial behavior.

10. *Lack of insight.* Antisocial personalities are unable to see themselves as others do. They are more likely to blame others for their difficulties than to recognize that they have brought their problems on themselves.

Borderline Personality Disorder

People with borderline personality disorder are characterized as failing to develop a stable or coherent self-image. They tend to be uncertain about their values, goals, loyalties, careers, choices of friends, perhaps even their sexual orientations. This instability in self-image or identity leaves them with persistent feelings of emptiness and boredom. They cannot tolerate being alone and will make desperate attempts to avoid feelings of abandonment. Fear of abandonment renders them clinging and demanding in their social relationships, but their clinging often pushes away the people on whom they depend. Signs of rejection may enrage them, straining their relationships further. Their feelings toward others are consequently intense and shifting. They alternate between extremes of adulation (when their needs are met) and loathing (when they feel scorned). They tend to view other people as all good or all bad, shifting abruptly from one extreme to the other. As a result, they may flit from partner to partner in a series of brief and stormy relationships. People whom they had idealized are treated with contempt when relationships end (Gunderson & Singer, 1986).

The label of borderline personality has been applied to people as diverse as Marilyn Monroe, Lawrence of Arabia, Adolf Hitler, and the philosopher Sören Kierkegaard (Sass, 1982). According to the DSM, the primary feature of **borderline personality disorder** is instability in relationships, self-image, mood, and control over impulses. Borderline personality disorder was first recognized as a diagnostic category in 1980 with the publication of the DSM-III. It is estimated to occur in perhaps 3 to 5% of the general population and has become one of the most commonly applied diagnoses in mental health settings, with about 20% of psychiatric patients having received the diagnosis (Frances & Widiger, 1986). Some theorists believe we live in highly fragmented and alienating times that tend to create the problems in forming cohesive identities and stable relationships which characterize borderline personalities (Sass, 1982). "Living on the edge," or border, can be seen as a metaphor for an unstable society (Sass, 1982).

The term *borderline personality* was originally used to refer to individuals whose behavior appeared on the border between neuroses and psychoses. Borderline personalities generally maintain better contact with reality than psychotic people do, although they

Two famous people thought to have had borderline personalities. A number of famous people, such as Marilyn Monroe and Lawrence of Arabia, have been described as having personality characteristics associated with borderline personality disorder.

may show transient psychotic behaviors during times of stress. Generally speaking, they seem to be more severely impaired than most neurotics but not as dysfunctional as psychotics. It now seems, however, that borderline personality is closer to the mood disorders. Some researchers find that nearly half of those diagnosed as borderline personalities also meet the diagnostic criteria for major depression or bipolar disorder (Pope et al., 1983). Others, however, find a weaker link between borderline personality and depression (Gunderson & Phillips, 1991). Many borderline personalities also meet the criteria for other personality disorders, such as histrionic, narcissistic, and antisocial personality disorders. Although questions remain about the diagnostic category, the evidence supports the belief that borderline personality is a distinct disorder (Zalewski & Archer, 1991).

Instability of moods is a central characteristic of borderline personality disorder. Moods run the gamut from anger and irritability to depression and anxiety, with each lasting from a few hours to a few days. Borderline personalities have difficulty controlling anger and are prone to fights or smashing things. They often act on impulse, like eloping with someone they have just met. This impulsive and unpredictable behavior is often self-destructive. It may involve spending sprees, drug abuse, sexual promiscuity, reckless driving, binge eating, or shoplifting. Suicidal threats or gestures and acts of self-mutilation, such as scratching their wrists or burning cigarettes on their arms, may be seen in extreme cases:

CLIENT: I've got such repressed anger in me; what happens is . . . I can't *feel* it; I get anxiety attacks. I get very nervous, smoke too many cigarettes. So what happens to me is I tend to *explode*. Into tears or hurting myself or whatever . . .

because I don't know how to contend with all those mixed up feelings.

INTERVIEWER: What was the more recent example of such an "explosion"?

CLIENT: I was alone at home a few months ago; I was frightened! I was trying to get in touch with my boyfriend and I couldn't. . . . He was nowhere to be found. All my friends seemed to be busy that night and I had no one to talk to . . . I just got more and more nervous and more and more agitated. Finally, *bang!*—I took out a cigarette and lit it and stuck it into my forearm. I don't know why I did it because I didn't really care for him all that much. I guess I felt I had to do something dramatic. . . ."

Adapted from Stone, 1980, p. 400

Self-mutilation is sometimes carried out as an expression of anger or a means of manipulating others. Such acts may be intended to counteract self-reported feelings of "numbness," particularly in times of stress.

Borderline personalities are difficult to work with in psychotherapy. They demand a great deal of support from therapists, calling them at all hours or acting suicidally to elicit help. They tend to drop out early from psychotherapy and those who improve seem more the exception than the rule (Aronson, 1989), except for people who have a coexisting mood disorder that is more amenable to treatment (Pope et al., 1983). Their feelings toward therapists, as toward other people, undergo rapid alterations between idealization and outrage. These abrupt shifts in feelings are interpreted by psychoanalysts as signs of "splitting," or inability to reconcile the positive and negative aspects of one's experience of oneself and others. From the modern psychodynamic perspective, borderline individuals cannot synthesize positive and negative elements of personality into complete wholes. They therefore fail to achieve fixed self-identities or images of others. Rather than viewing important figures in their lives as sometimes loving and as sometimes rejecting, borderline personalities shift back and forth between viewing them as all good or all bad (Abend et al., 1983), between idealization and abhorrence. The psychoanalyst Otto Kernberg, a leading authority on borderline personality, tells of a woman in her thirties whose attitude toward him vacillated in such a way:

> In one session, the patient may experience me as the most helpful, loving, understanding human being and may feel totally relieved and happy, and all the problems are solved. Three sessions later, she may berate me as the most ruthless, indifferent, manipulative person she has ever met. Total unhappiness about the treatment, ready to drop it and never come back. (Source: Cited in "The Borderline Personality," by L. Sass. Copyright © 1982 by The New York Times Company. Reprinted by permission.)

Borderline personality disorder remains a perplexing and frustrating problem.

Histrionic Personality Disorder

Histrionic personality disorder refers to individuals with excessive emotionality and needs to be the center of attention. The term is derived from the Latin *histrio*, which means "actor." People with histrionic personality disorder tend to be dramatic and emotional, but their emotions seem shallow, exaggerated, and volatile. The disorder was formerly called *hysterical* personality. The supplanting of *hysterical* with *histrionic* and the associated exchange of the roots *hystera* (meaning "uterus") and *histrio* allow professionals to distance themselves from the notion that the disorder is intricately bound up with being female. The disorder is diagnosed more frequently in women than men, however (Pfohl, 1991). Whether this gender discrepancy reflects the true prevalence of the disorder, diagnostic biases, or other factors remains an open question.

People with histrionic personalities may become unusually upset by news of a sad event and cancel plans for the evening, inconveniencing their friends. They may exude exaggerated delight when they meet someone or become enraged when someone fails to notice their new hairstyle. They may faint at the sight of blood or blush at a slight faux pax. They tend to demand that others meet their needs for praise and attention and play the victim when others fall short. If they feel a touch of fever, they may insist that others drop everything to rush them to the doctor. They tend to be self-centered and intolerant of delays of gratification; they want what they want when they want it. They grow quickly restless with routine and crave novelty and stimulation. They are drawn to fads. Others may see them as putting on airs or play-acting, although they may evince a certain charm. They may enter a room with a flourish. They embellish their experiences with flair. When pressed for details, however, they fail to color in the specifics of their tales. They tend to be flirtatious and seductive but are too wrapped up in themselves to develop intimate relationships or have deep feelings toward others. As a result, their associations tend to be stormy and ultimately ungratifying. They tend to use their physical appearance as a means of drawing attention to themselves. Glitter supercedes substance.

People with histrionic personalities may be attracted to professions like modeling or acting, where they can hog the spotlight. Despite outward successes, they may lack self-esteem and strive to impress others to boost their self-worth. If they suffer setbacks or lose their place in the limelight, depressing inner doubts may emerge.

The case of Marcella shows some of these features:

Marcella was a 36-year-old, attractive, but overly made up woman who was dressed in tight pants and high heels. Her hair was in a bird's nest of the type that had been popular when she was a teenager. Her social life seemed to bounce from relationship to relationship, from crisis to crisis. Marcella sought help from the psychologist at this time because her 17-year-old daughter, Nancy, had just been hospitalized for cutting her wrists. Nancy lived with Marcella and Marcella's current boyfriend, Morris, and there were constant arguments in the apartment. Marcella recounted the disputes that took place with high drama, waving her hands, clanging the bangles that hung from her bracelets, and then clutching her breast. It was difficult having Nancy live at home, because Nancy had expensive tastes, was "always looking for attention," and flirted with Morris as a way of "flaunting her youth." Marcella saw herself as a doting mother and denied any possibility that she was in competition with her daughter.

Marcella came for a handful of sessions during which she basically ventilated her feelings and was encouraged to make decisions that might lead to a reduction of some of the pressures on her and her daughter. At the end of each session she said, "I feel so much better" and thanked the psychologist profusely. At termination of "therapy," she took the psychologist's hand and squeezed it endearingly. "Thank you so much, doctor," she said and made her exit.

■ *The Authors' Files*

Marcella also showed a number of features of narcissism, which we discuss next.

Narcissistic Personality Disorder

Narkissos was a handsome youth who, according to Greek myth, fell in love with his reflection in a spring. Because of his excessive self-love, in one version of the myth, he was transformed by the gods into the flower we know as the narcissus.

Persons with **narcissistic personality disorder** have an inflated or grandiose sense of themselves. They brag about their accomplishments and expect others to shower them with praise. They expect others to notice their special qualities, even when their accomplishments are ordinary, and they enjoy basking in the light of adulation. They are self-absorbed and lack empathy for others. Although they share certain features with histrionic personalities, such as demanding to be the center of attention, they have a much more inflated view of themselves and are less melodramatic than histrionic personalities. Sometimes they are confused with borderline personalities, but narcissists are generally better able to organize their thoughts and actions. They tend to be more successful in their careers, better able to rise to positions of status and power. Their relationships also tend to be more stable than those of borderline personalities.

A certain degree of narcissism or self-aggrandizement may represent a healthful adjustment to insecurity, a shield from criticism and failure, or a motive for achievement (Goleman, 1988). Excessive narcissistic qualities can become unhealthful, especially when cravings for reassurance and adulation are insatiable.

Table 8.2 compares "normal" self-interest with self-defeating extremes of narcissism. Up to a point, self-interest fosters success and happiness. In more extreme cases, as with narcissism, it can compromise relationships and careers.

Narcissistic personalities tend to be preoccupied with fantasies of success and power, ideal love, or recognition for brilliance or beauty. Narcissists, like histrionic personalities, may gravitate toward careers in which they can receive adulation, such as modeling, acting, or politics. Although they tend to exaggerate their accomplishments and abilities, many narcissists are successful in their occupations. But they envy those who achieve greater success. Insatiable ambition may prompt them to devote themselves tirelessly to work. They are driven to succeed, not so

Narkissos. According to one version of the Greek myth, Narkissos fell in love with his reflection in a spring. Because of his excessive self-love, the gods transformed him into a flower—the narcissus.

A person with a narcissistic personality. People with narcissistic personalities are often preoccupied with fantasies of success and power, ideal love, or recognition for their brilliance or beauty. They may pursue careers that provide opportunities for public recognition and adulation, such as acting, modeling, or politics.

Table 8.2 Features of Normal Self-Interest as Compared to Self-Defeating Narcissism

Normal Self-Interest	Self-Defeating Narcissism
Appreciating acclaim, but not requiring it in order to maintain self-esteem.	Craving adoration insatiably; requiring acclaim in order to feel momentarily good about oneself.
Being temporarily wounded by criticism.	Being inflamed or crushed by criticism and brooding about it extensively.
Feeling unhappy but not worthless following failure.	Having enduring feelings of mortification and worthlessness triggered by failure.
Feeling "special" or uncommonly talented in some way.	Feeling incomparably better than other people, and insisting upon acknowledgment of that preeminence.
Feeling good about oneself, even when other people are being critical.	Needing constant support from other people in order to maintain one's feelings of well-being.
Being reasonably accepting of life's setbacks, even though they can be painful and temporarily destabilizing.	Responding to life's wounds with depression or fury.
Maintaining self-esteem in the face of disapproval or denigration.	Responding to disapproval or denigration with loss of self-esteem.
Maintaining emotional equilibrium despite lack of special treatment.	Feeling entitled to special treatment and becoming terribly upset when one is treated in an ordinary manner.
Being empathic and caring about the feelings of others.	Being insensitive to other people's needs and feelings; exploiting others until they become fed up.

Source: Based on Goleman (1988), p. C1.

much for money as for the adulation that attends success.

Interpersonal relationships are invariably strained by narcissists' interpersonal demands and by their lack of empathy with, and concern for, other people. Narcissists seek the company of flatterers. Narcissistic personalities are often superficially charming and friendly; they draw people to them. But their interest in people is one-sided: They seek people who will serve their interests and nourish their sense of self-importance (Goleman, 1988). Narcissists have feelings of entitlement that lead them to exploit others. They treat sex partners as devices for their own pleasure or to brace their self-esteem.

The case of Bill illustrates several features of the narcissistic personality:

Most people agreed that Bill, a 35-year-old investment banker, had a certain charm. He was bright, articulate, and attractive. He possessed a keen sense of humor that drew people to him at social gatherings. He would always position himself in the middle of the room, where he could be the center of attention. The topics of conversation invariably focused on his "deals," the "rich and famous" people he had met, and his outmaneuvering of opponents. His next project was always bigger and more daring than the last. Bill loved an audience. His face *would light up when others responded to him with praise or admiration for his business successes, which were always inflated beyond their true measure. But when the conversation shifted to other people, he would lose interest and excuse himself to make a drink or to call his answering machine. When hosting a party, he would urge guests to stay late and feel hurt if they had to leave early; he showed no sensitivity to, or awareness of, the needs of his friends.*

The few friends he had maintained over the years had come to accept Bill on his own terms. They recognized that he needed to have his ego fed or that he would become cool and detached.

Bill had also had a series of romantic relationships with women who were willing to play the adoring admirer and make the sacrifices that he demanded—for a time. But they inevitably tired of the one-sided relationship or grew frustrated by Bill's inability to make a commitment or feel deeply toward them. Lacking empathy, Bill was unable to recognize other people's feelings and needs. His demands for constant attention from willing admirers did not derive from selfishness, but from a need to ward off underlying feelings of inadequacy and diminished self-esteem. It was sad, his friends thought, that Bill needed so much attention and adulation from others and that his many achievements were never enough to calm his inner doubts.

■ *The Authors' Files*

PERSONALITY DISORDERS CHARACTERIZED BY ANXIOUS OR FEARFUL BEHAVIOR

This cluster of personality disorders includes the avoidant, dependent, and obsessive-compulsive types. Although the features of these disorders differ, they share a component of fear or anxiety.

Avoidant Personality Disorder

Persons with **avoidant personality disorder** are so terrified of rejection and criticism that they are generally unwilling to enter relationships without ardent reassurances of acceptance. As a result, they may have few close relationships outside their immediate families. They also tend to avoid group occupational or recreational activities for fear of rejection. They prefer to lunch alone at their desks. They shun company picnics and parties, unless they are perfectly sure of acceptance.

A person with an avoidant personality? Avoidant personalities often keep to themselves because of fear of rejection.

Unlike schizoid personalities, with whom they share the feature of social withdrawal, avoidant personalities have interest in, and feelings of warmth toward, other people. However, fear of rejection prevents them from striving to meet their needs for affection and acceptance. In social situations, they tend to hug the walls and avoid conversing with others. They fear public embarrassment—the thought that others might see them blush, cry, or act nervously. They tend to stick to their routines and exaggerate the risks or effort involved in trying new things. They may refuse to attend a party that is an hour away on the pretext that the late drive home would be too taxing.

The case of Harold illustrates several of the features of the avoidant personality:

*H*arold, a 24-year-old accounting clerk, had dated but a few women, and he had met them through family introductions. He never felt confident enough to approach a woman on his own. Perhaps it was his shyness that first attracted Stacy. Stacy, a 22-year-old secretary, worked alongside Harold and asked him if he would like to get together sometime after work. At first Harold declined, claiming some excuse, but when Stacy asked again a week later, Harold agreed, thinking that she must really like him if she were willing to pursue him. The relationship developed quickly, and soon they were dating virtually every night. The relationship was strained, however. Harold interpreted any slight hesitation in her voice as a lack of interest. He repeatedly requested reassurance that she cared about him and evaluated every word and gesture for evidence of her feelings. If Stacy said that she could not see him because of fatigue or illness, he assumed she was rejecting him and sought reassurance. After several months, Stacy decided she could no longer accept Harold's nagging, and the relationship ended. Harold assumed that Stacy had never truly cared for him.

■ *The Authors' Files*

There is a good deal of overlap between avoidant personality disorder and social phobia, particularly between avoidant personality and a severe subtype of social phobia that involves a generalized pattern of social phobia (excessive, irrational fear of most social situations) (Herbert et al., 1992; Turner et al., 1992; Widiger, 1992). Although research evidence shows that many cases of generalized social phobia occur in the absence of avoidant personality disorder (Holt et al., 1992; Widiger, 1992), relatively fewer cases of avoidant personality occur in the absence of generalized social phobia (Widiger, 1992). All in all, it is unclear whether avoidant personality disorder represents a severe form of generalized social phobia or a distinct diagnostic category.

Dependent Personality Disorder

Dependent personality disorder describes people who are overly dependent on others. They find it difficult to do things on their own. Persons with dependent personalities may seek advice in making the smallest decision. Children or adolescents with the problem may look to their parents to select their clothes, diets, schools or colleges, even their friends. Adults with the disorder allow others to make important decisions for them. Sometimes they even permit others to make marital decisions, as in the case of Matthew:

M atthew, a 34-year-old single accountant who lives with his mother, sought treatment when his relationship with his girlfriend came to an end. His mother had objected to marriage because his girlfriend was of a different religion, and—because "blood is thicker than water"—Matthew acceded to his mother's wishes and ended the relationship. Yet he is angry with himself and at his mother because he feels that she is too possessive to ever grant him permission to get married. He describes his mother as a domineering woman who "wears the pants" in the family and is accustomed to having things her way. Matthew alternates between resenting his mother and thinking that perhaps she knows what's best for him.

Matthew's position at work is several levels below what would be expected of someone of his talent and educational level. Several times he has declined promotions in order to avoid increased responsibilities that would require him to supervise others and make independent decisions. He has maintained close relationships with two friends since early childhood and has lunch with one of them on every working day. On days his friend calls in sick, Matthew feels lost. Matthew has lived his whole life at home, except for one year away at college. He returned home because of homesickness.

■ *Adapted from Spitzer et al., 1989, pp. 123–125*

After marriage, people with dependent personality disorder may rely on spouses for decisions such as where they should live, which neighbors they should cultivate, how they should discipline the chil-

dren, what jobs they should take, how they should budget money, and where they should vacation. Like Matthew, individuals with dependent personality disorder avoid positions of responsibility. They turn down challenges and promotions, and they work beneath their potentials. They tend to be overly sensitive to criticism and are preoccupied with fears of rejection and abandonment. They may be devastated by the end of a close relationship or by the prospect of living on their own. Because of fear of rejection, they often subordinate their wants and needs to those of others. They may concur with outlandish statements and do degrading things to ingratiate themselves with others.

Dependent personality disorder is diagnosed more frequently in women. The diagnosis is often applied to women who, for fear of abandonment, tolerate husbands who openly cheat on them, abuse them, or gamble away the family's resources. Underlying feelings of inadequacy and helplessness discourage them from taking effective action. In a vicious cycle, their passivity encourages further abuse, leading them to feel yet more inadequate and helpless. The diagnosis of women with this pattern is controversial and strikes some as unfairly "blaming the victim" because women in our society are often socialized into more dependent roles. A panel convened by the American Psychological Association noted that women also encounter greater stress than men in contemporary life (Goleman, 1990c). Women are more likely than men to be subjected to second-class citizenship, which may set the stage for dependency.

Dependent personality disorder has been linked to physical problems such as hypertension, cancer, and gastrointestinal disorders like ulcers and colitis (Greenberg & Bornstein, 1988a). There also appears to be a link between dependent personality and what psychodynamic theorists refer to as "oral" behavior problems, such as smoking, eating disorders, and alcoholism (Greenberg & Bornstein, 1988b). Psychodynamic writers trace dependent behaviors to the utter dependence of the newborn baby and the baby's seeking of nourishment through oral means (suckling). From infancy, they suggest, people associate provision of food with love. Food may come to symbolize love, and persons with dependent personalities may overeat to ingest love symbolically (Greenberg & Bornstein, 1988b).

Research shows that dependent personalities are more reliant than independent personalities on other people for support and guidance (Greenberg & Bornstein, 1988a). Dependent personalities often attribute their problems to physical rather than emotional causes and seek support and advice from medical experts rather than psychologists or other counselors (Greenberg & Bornstein, 1988b).

Obsessive-Compulsive Personality Disorder

The defining features of **obsessive-compulsive personality disorder** include such traits as orderliness, perfectionism, rigidity, difficulty coping with ambiguity, difficulties expressing feelings, and meticulousness in work habits. Unlike the obsessive-compulsive anxiety disorder, people with obsessive-compulsive personality disorder do not necessarily experience outright obsessions or compulsions. If they do, both diagnoses may be appropriate.

Persons with obsessive-compulsive personality disorder are so preoccupied with perfection that they cannot complete things in a timely fashion. Their efforts inevitably fall short of their expectations and they force themselves to redo their work. Or they may ruminate about how to prioritize their assignments rather than get started. They focus on details that others perceive as trivial. As the saying goes, they often fail to see the forest for the trees. Their

"A place for everything, and everything in its place?"
People with obsessive-compulsive personalities may have invented this maxim. Many such people have excessive needs for orderliness in their environment, as suggested by this Laurie Simmons's photograph, *Red Library #2*. The "woman" in this compulsively ordered room appears to be transfixed by a missing photograph. (How perfect is *Red Library #1*?)

rigidity impairs their social relationships; they insist on doing things their way rather than compromising. Their zeal for work keeps them from participating in, or enjoying, social and leisure activities. They tend to be stingy with money. They find it difficult to make decisions; they postpone or avoid them for fear of making the wrong choice. They tend to be rigid in issues of morality and ethics because of inflexibility in personality rather than deep-seated convictions. They tend to be overly formal in relationships and find it difficult to express feelings. It is hard for them to relax and enjoy pleasant activities; they worry about the costs of such diversions.

Consider the case of Jerry:

*J*erry, *a 34-year-old systems analyst, was perfectionistic, overly concerned with details, and rigid in his behavior. Jerry was married to Marcia, a graphics artist. He insisted on scheduling their free time hour by hour and became unnerved when they deviated from his agenda. He would circle a parking lot repeatedly in search of just the right parking spot to ensure that his car would not be scraped by another. He refused to have the apartment painted for over a year because he couldn't decide on the color. He had arranged all the books in their bookshelf alphabetically and insisted that every book be placed in its proper position.*

Jerry never seemed to be able to relax. Even on vacation, he was bothered by thoughts of work that he had left behind and by fears that he might lose his job. He couldn't understand how people could lie on the beach and let all their worries evaporate in the summer air. Something can always go wrong, he figured, so how can people let themselves go?

■ *The Authors' Files*

PROBLEMS WITH THE CLASSIFICATION OF PERSONALITY DISORDERS

Problems classifying personality disorders have raised concern among researchers and clinicians. Questions remain about the reliability and validity of the diagnoses of personality disorders. There may be too much overlap among the categories to justify so many discrete categories of personality disorders. The classification system also seems to blur the distinctions between normal and abnormal variations in personality. Some categories of personality disorder, moreover, may be based on sexist presumptions. Finally, there is concern that the diagnoses may confuse labels with explanations.

Undetermined Reliability and Validity

The present DSM system sought to clarify the ambiguities in the diagnostic criteria of earlier editions by providing descriptive criteria that more tightly define particular disorders. The reliability and validity of the new definitions remain to be fully tested, however. Early indications were that reliability of Axis II personality disorder diagnoses (in DSM-III) were not as strong as desired (Drake & Vaillant, 1985). It remains to be seen whether the DSM-IV increases the reliability of these diagnoses.

Overlap Among Disorders

There is also a high degree of overlap among the personality disorders (Oldham et al., 1992). Overlap undermines the DSM's conceptual clarity or purity by increasing the number of cases that seem to fit two or more diagnostic categories (Livesley, 1985; Morey, 1988; Livesley et al., 1986). Although some personality disorders have distinct features, many disorders appear to share numerous traits. For example, Oldham and his colleagues (1992) point out that the feature "has no close friends or confidants' is a criterion for both schizotypal and avoidant personality disorders" (p. 218). The same person may have traits suggestive of dependent personality disorder (inability to make decisions or initiate activities independently) and of avoidant personality disorder (extreme social anxiety and heightened sensitivity to criticism).

This degree of overlap suggests the possibility that the DSM class of personality disorders contains too many categories (Livesley et al., 1985). One study found that as many as 25% of people with schizoid personality disorders could also be diagnosed as having avoidant personality disorders, for example (Reich & Noyes, 1986). Overall, about 2 in 3 people with personality disorders meet diagnostic criteria for more than one type of personality disorder (Widiger, 1991). Some "disorders" may thus represent different aspects of the same disorder, not separate diagnostic categories. It has been argued, for example, that the schizoid, avoidant, and schizotypal personality disorders should be regarded as different aspects of a schizoid personality (Livesley et al., 1985).

Difficulty in Distinguishing Between Variations in Normal Behavior and Abnormal Behavior

Another problem with the diagnosis of personality disorders is that they involve traits which, in lesser degrees, describe the behavior of most normal individuals. Feeling suspicious now and then does not mean that you have a paranoid personality disorder. The tendency to exaggerate your own importance does not mean that you are narcissistic. We may avoid social interactions for fear of embarrassment or rejection without having an avoidant personality disorder, and we may be especially conscientious in our work without having an obsessive-compulsive personality disorder. Because the defining attributes of these disorders are commonly occurring personality traits, clinicians should only apply these diagnostic labels when the patterns are so pervasive that they interfere with the individual's functioning or cause significant personal distress.

 It can be difficult indeed to draw the line between normal variations in behavior and personality disorders.

Sexist Biases

The positing of certain personality disorders may be sexist. The diagnostic criteria for personality disorders tend to label stereotypical feminine behaviors as pathological with greater frequency than is the case with stereotypical masculine behaviors (Kaplan, 1983). The concept of the histrionic or hysterical personality, for example, seems to be a caricature of the traditional stereotype of the feminine personality: flighty, emotional, shallow, attention-seeking. After all, if the feminine stereotype corresponds to a mental disorder, what of the masculine stereotype of the "macho male"? It may be possible to show that overly masculinized traits are associated with significant distress or impairment in social or occupational functioning in certain males: Highly masculinized males often get into many fights and experience difficulties working for female bosses. There is no personality disorder for "macho males," however. The diagnosis of dependent personality disorder may also unfairly stigmatize women who have been socialized into dependent roles as showing a "mental disorder." Women may be at greater risk of receiving diagnoses of histrionic or dependent personality disorders because clinicians perceive these patterns as existing more commonly among women or because women

Are there sexist biases in the conception of personality disorders?   The concept of the *histrionic personality disorder* seems to be a caricature of the highly stereotyped feminine personality. Why, then, is there not also something akin to a *macho male personality disorder*, which caricatures the highly stereotyped masculine personality?

are more likely than men to be socialized into these behavior patterns.

 The concepts of histrionic and dependent personality disorders may be sexist. It could be argued that the descriptions of these disorders are parodies of the traditional feminine gender-role stereotype.

Confusing Labels with Explanations

It may seem obvious that we should not confuse diagnostic labels with explanations, but in practice the distinction is sometimes clouded. If we confuse labeling with explanation, we may fall into the trap of circular reasoning. For example, what is wrong with the logic of the following statements?

1. John's behavior is antisocial.
2. Therefore, John has an antisocial personality disorder.
3. John's behavior is antisocial because he has an antisocial personality disorder.

The statements are circular in reasoning because they (1) use behavior to make a diagnosis and then (2) use the diagnosis as an explanation for the behavior. We may be guilty of circular reasoning in our everyday

speech. Consider: "John never gets his work in on time; therefore, he is lazy. John doesn't get his work in because he's lazy." The label allows for general conversation, but lacks scientific rigor. In order for a construct such as laziness to have scientific rigor, we need to understand the causes of laziness and the factors that help to maintain it. We should not confuse the label we attach to behavior with the cause of the behavior.

Moreover, the tendency to label people with disturbing behavior as personality disordered tends to overlook the social and environmental contexts in which the behavior occurs. We need to attend to the impact of specific traumatic life events, which may occur with a greater range or intensity among members of one gender or cultural group, as important factors underlying patterns of maladaptive behavior (Brown, 1986; Rosewater; 1986; Walker, 1985). The conceptual underpinnings of the personality disorders lack such a perspective. Moreover, conceptualizations of personality disorders fail to account for the social inequalities in society and the differences in power between the genders or between dominant and minority cultures that may give rise to the types of problems identified as personality disorders. For example, Brown (1988) and Walker (1986) document the significant prevalence of a history of child physical and sexual abuse among women diagnosed with personality disorders. The ways in which people cope with abuse may come to be viewed as flaws in their character, rather than viewed in terms of dysfunctional societal factors that underlie abusive relationships.

Brown (1992) argues in favor of a new category, labeled *abuse and oppression artifact disorders,* which would describe a group of disorders that are more situationally determined than the traditional personality disorders and perhaps more amenable to change. Such disorders would be characterized by a history or current experience of trauma of a repetitive nature. The stressors which accompany sexism, racism, and other forms of societal oppression are examples of such trauma. Feminist theorists, like Brown (1992), strongly urge that greater attention be focused on the societal contexts underlying maladaptive behavior, which would include attending to the power differentials in the dominant culture with respect to race, gender, ethnicity, sexual orientation, and so on, and the ways that cultural biases may creep into diagnostic conceptualizations and treatment interventions.

All in all, personality disorders are convenient labels for identifying common patterns of ineffective and ultimately self-defeating behavior, but labels do not explain their causes. Still, the development of an accurate descriptive system is an important step toward scientific explanation. The establishment of reliable diagnostic categories sets the stage for valid research into causation and treatment.

THEORETICAL PERSPECTIVES

In this section we consider theoretical perspectives on the personality disorders. Many of the theoretical accounts of disturbed personality derive from the psychodynamic model. We thus begin with a review of traditional and modern psychodynamic models.

Psychodynamic Perspectives

Traditional Freudian theory focused on Oedipal problems as the foundation for many abnormal behaviors, including personality disorders. Freud's theory of psychosexual development recounts processes by which children come to control their primitive impulses and develop concern for others. A particularly salient event in the process is the Oedipus complex. Freud believed that the moral conscience, or superego, arose from the proper resolution of the Oedipus complex. Children normally resolve the Oedipus complex by foresaking incestuous wishes for the parent of the same gender and identifying with the parent of the opposite gender. As a result, they incorporate the parent's moral principles in the form of a personality structure called the superego. Many factors may interfere with appropriate identification, however, such as a weak or absent father or an antisocial parent. Such interferences can sidetrack the normal developmental process and prevent children from developing moral constraints that prevent antisocial behavior and feelings of guilt or remorse that normally follow injurious behavior. Freud's account of moral development focused mainly on the development of males. He has been criticized for failing to account for the moral development of females.

More recent psychodynamic theories have generally focused on the earlier, pre-Oedipal period of about 18 months to 3 years, during which infants are theorized to begin to develop their identities as separate from those of their parents. These recent advances in psychodynamic theory focus on the development of the sense of self in explaining such disorders as narcissistic and borderline personality disorders.

■ **HANS KOHUT** One of the principal shapers of modern psychodynamic concepts is Hans Kohut, whose views are labeled **self psychology**. Kohut focused much of his attention on the development of the narcissistic personality.

Kohut (1966) believed that a self-image riddled with insecurity lay beneath the inflated veneers of people with narcissistic personality disorders. The narcissist's self-esteem is like a reservoir that needs to be constantly replenished lest it run dry. A steady stream of praise and attention prevents the narcissist from withering with insecurity. A sense of grandiosity helps narcissists mask their underlying feelings of worthlessness. Failures or disappointments threaten to expose these feelings and drive the narcissist into depression. Narcissists may defend themselves from despair by diminishing the importance of disappointments or failures. They may become enraged by people who fail to protect them from disappointment or decline to bathe them in reassurance, praise, and admiration. They may become infuriated by slight criticism, no matter how well intentioned. They may mask feelings of rage and humiliation by adopting a facade of cool indifference. Narcissistic personalities can make difficult psychotherapy clients because they may become enraged when therapists puncture their inflated self-images to help them develop more realistic self-concepts.

Kohut believed that early childhood is characterized by a normal stage of "healthful narcissism." Infants feel powerful, as though the world revolves around them. Infants also normally perceive older people, especially parents, as idealized towers of strength and wish to be one with them to share their power. Empathic parents reflect their children's inflated perceptions, making children feel that anything is possible and nourishing their self-esteem. Even empathic parents are critical from time to time, however, and puncture their children's grandiose sense of self. Or they fail to measure up to their children's idealized views of them. Gradually, unrealistic expectations dissolve and are replaced by more realistic appraisals. Normal childhood narcissism sets the stage for subsequent ego development. Earlier grandiose self-images form the basis for assertiveness later in childhood and set the stage for ambitious striving in adulthood. In adolescence, childhood idealization is transformed into realistic admiration for parents, teachers, and friends. In adulthood, these ideas develop into a set of internal ideals, values, and goals.

Lack of parental empathy and support, however, sets the stage for pathological narcissism in adulthood. Children who are not prized by parents may fail to develop sturdy self-esteem and be unable to tolerate even slight blows to their self-worth. Such children develop damaged self-concepts. They feel incapable of being loved and admired because of personal inadequacies or flaws. Pathological narcissism involves the mounting of grandiose facades to cloak one's perceived inadequacies. Narcissistic personalities fail to shape realistic imperfect images of themselves and others. Facades of self-perfection threaten to crumble, however. Narcissistic personalities require constant reassurance to maintain their veneers and are vulnerable to painful self-depreciation if they fail to achieve social or occupational goals.

Kohut's approach to therapy provides narcissistic clients an initial opportunity to express their grandiose self-images and to idealize the therapist. Over time, however, the therapist helps clients explore the childhood roots of their narcissism and gently points out imperfections in both client and therapist to encourage clients to form more realistic images of the self and others.

■ **OTTO KERNBERG** Modern psychodynamic views of the borderline personality also trace the disorder to difficulties in self-development in early childhood. Kernberg (1967), a leading psychodynamic theorist, views borderline personality in terms of a pre-Oedipal failure to develop a sense of constancy and unity in one's image of the self and others. Kernberg proposes that childhood failure to synthesize these contradictory images of good and bad results in **identity diffusion** and tendencies toward **splitting**—shifting back and forth between viewing oneself and other people as "all good" or "all bad."

In Kernberg's view, parents, even excellent parents, invariably fail to meet all their children's needs.

Infants therefore face the early developmental challenge of reconciling images of the nurturing, comforting "good mother" with those of the withholding, frustrating "bad mother." Failure to reconcile these opposing images into a realistic unified and stable parental image may fixate children in the pre-Oedipal period. As adults, then, they may retain the rapidly shifting attitudes that borderline personalities experience toward their therapists and others.

■ **MARGARET MAHLER** Mahler, another influential modern psychodynamic theorist, explained borderline personality disorder in terms of childhood separation from the mother figure. Mahler and her colleagues (Mahler & Kaplan, 1977; Mahler et al., 1975) believe that during the first year the infant develops a **symbiotic** attachment to its mother. *Symbiosis* is a biological term derived from Greek roots meaning "to live together" and describes life patterns in which two species lead interdependent lives. In psychology, symbiosis is likened to a state of oneness in which the child's identity is fused with the mother's. Normally, children gradually differentiate their own identities or senses of self from their mothers. The process is called **separation-individuation**. Separation is development of a separate psychological and biological identity from the mother. Individuation is recognition of the personal characteristics that define one's self-identity. Separation-individuation may be a stormy process. Children may vacillate between seeking greater independence and moving closer to, or "shadowing," the mother, which is seen as a wish for reunion. The mother may disrupt normal separation-individuation by refusing to let go of the child or by too quickly pushing the child toward independence. The tendencies of the borderline personality to react to others with ambivalence, to alternate between love and hate, is suggestive to Mahler of earlier ambivalences during the separation-individuation process. This borderline personality disorder may arise from failure to master this developmental challenge.

Psychodynamic theories of the personality disorders remain controversial. All in all, psychodynamic theory provides a rich theoretical mine for the understanding of the development of several personality disorders. But some critics contend that theories of such disorders as borderline personality disorder and narcissistic personality disorder are based largely on inferences drawn from behavior and retrospective accounts of adults, and not on observations of children (Sass, 1982). Mahler's theory has been challenged by evidence that even infants show a certain degree of psychological differentiation from others (Klein, 1981). We may also question whether direct comparisons should be made between normal childhood experiences and abnormal behaviors in adulthood. For example, the ambivalences that characterize the adult borderline personality may bear only a superficial relationship, if any at all, to children's vacillations between closeness and separation with maternal figures during separation-individuation.

Learning Perspectives

Learning theorists tend to focus more on the acquisition of behaviors than on the notion of enduring personality traits. Similarly, they think more in terms of maladaptive behaviors than of disorders of "personality." Personality traits are theorized to steer behavior—to provide consistent behavior in diverse situations. Many critics (e.g., Mischel, 1979), however, argue that behavior is actually not as consistent across situations as traits theorists would suggest. Behavior may depend more on situational demands than on inherent traits. For example, we may describe a person as lazy and unmotivated. But is this person always lazy and unmotivated? Are there not some situations in which the person may be energetic and ambitious? What differences in these situations may explain differences in behavior? Learning theorists are generally interested in defining the learning histories and circumstances that give rise to maladaptive behaviors and the reinforcers that maintain them.

Learning theorists suggest that many salient experiences that contribute to maladaptive habits of relating to others (personality disorders) occur in childhood. Repeated punishment of, or lack of reward for, childhood assertiveness and exploratory behavior may result in a dependent personality behavior pattern, for example. Obsessive-compulsive personality disorder may be connected with excessive parental discipline or overcontrol in childhood. Social-learning theorist Theodore Millon (1981) suggests that children whose behavior is rigidly controlled and punished by parents, even for slight transgressions, may develop inflexible, perfectionistic standards. As such children mature, they may strive to develop an area in which they excel, such as schoolwork or athletics, as a way of avoiding parental criticism or punishment. Overattention to a single area of development may prevent them from becoming well rounded. They may thus squelch spontaneity, avoid new challenges or risks, and develop other behaviors associated with the obsessive-compulsive personality pattern.

Millon suggests that histrionic personality disorder may be rooted in childhood experiences that connect reinforcers, such as parental attention, with physical appearance and performances for others, especially when reinforcers are dispensed inconsistently. Inconsistent attention teaches children not to take approval for granted and to strive for it continually. People with histrionic personalities may also have identified with parents who are dramatic, emotional, and attention-seeking. Extreme sibling rivalry would further heighten motivation to perform.

Social-learning theories emphasize the role of reinforcement in explaining the origins of antisocial behaviors. Ullmann and Krasner (1975) propose, for example, that antisocial personalities fail to respond to other people as potential reinforcers. Most children learn to treat others as reinforcing agents because others reinforce them with praise when they behave appropriately and punish them for misbehavior. Reinforcement and punishment provide feedback (information about social expectations) that helps children modify their behavior to maximize the chances of future rewards and minimize the risks of future punishment. As a consequence, children become socialized. They become sensitive to the demands of powerful others, usually parents and teachers, and learn to regulate their behavior accordingly. They thus adapt to social expectations. They learn what to do and what to say, how to dress and how to act to attain reinforcers.

Antisocial personalities, by contrast, may not become socialized because early learning experiences lack the consistency and predictability that help other children connect their behavior with rewards and punishments. Perhaps they were sometimes rewarded for doing the "right thing," but just as often not. They may have borne the brunt of harsh physical punishments that depended more on parental whims than on their own conduct. As adults they may not place much value on what other people expect because there was no clear connection between their own behavior and reinforcement in childhood. Snyder (1977) found that children with conduct disorders also tend to have punitive parents. Moreover, parental reinforcements are generally arbitrary—not contingent on prosocial behavior. Children may thus learn that they can do little to prevent punishment and lack the motivation to try. Although Ullmann and Krasner's views may account for some features of antisocial personality disorder, they may not adequately address the development of the "charming" type of antisocial personality, which describes people who are skillful at reading social cues produced by other people and using them for personal advantage (Smith, R.J., 1978).

Social cognitive theorist Albert Bandura has studied the role of observational learning in aggres-

What are the origins of antisocial personality disorder?
Are youth who develop antisocial personalities largely unso-
cialized because early learning experiences lack the consistency and predictability that help other children connect their
behavior with rewards and punishments? Or are they very
"socialized"—but socialized to imitate the behavior of other
antisocial youth? Are we confusing antisocial behavior with
antisocial personality disorder? To what extent does criminal
behavior or membership in gangs overlap with antisocial
personality disorder? Can environmental factors explain
how people with antisocial personality disorder maintain
their composure (their relatively low levels of arousal) under
circumstances that would induce anxiety in most of us?

sive behavior, which is one of the common components of antisocial behavior. He and his colleagues
(e.g., Bandura et al., 1963) have shown that children
acquire skills, including aggressive skills, by observing
the behavior of others. Bandura (1973, 1986) does
not believe that children and adults display aggressive
behaviors in a mechanical way. People, in fact, usually do not imitate aggressive behaviors unless they
are provoked and believe that they are more likely to
be rewarded than punished for it. Media violence and
real people may all provide children with aggressive
models (Bandura, 1973). When models get away
with misconduct, or are rewarded for misbehavior,
children may imitate them. Children may also
acquire antisocial behaviors like cheating, bullying, or
lying by direct reinforcement if they find that such
behaviors help them avoid blame or manipulate
others.

All in all, learning approaches to personality disorders, like psychodynamic approaches, have their
limitations. They are grounded in theory rather than
in prospective studies of family interactions that
presage the development of personality disorders.

Research remains to be conducted to determine
whether childhood experiences proposed by psychodynamic and learning theorists actually lead to the
hypothesized disorders.

Family Perspectives

Many theorists have argued that disturbances in family relationships may help account for the development of personality disorders. Consistent with psychodynamic formulations, researchers find that
people with borderline personality disorder *remember*
their parents as having been significantly more controlling and less caring than do reference subjects
with other psychological disorders (Zweig-Frank &
Paris, 1991). When borderline personalities recall
their earliest memories, they are more likely than
other people to paint significant others as malevolent
or evil. Their parents and others close to them were
more likely to injure them deliberately or to fail to
help them escape injuries by others (Nigg et al.,
1992). Borderline personalities report *recalling* a
higher incidence of sexual abuse and other forms of
childhood trauma than comparison groups (Herman
et al., 1989; Ogata et al., 1990; Zanarini et al., 1989).
The accuracy of such memories and reports of childhood trauma remains an open question. Again consistent with psychodynamic theory, family factors
such as parental overprotection and authoritarianism
have been implicated in the development of dependent personality traits (Bornstein, 1992).

Antisocial personalities also more frequently
experience parental loss than do normal people or
people with anxiety disorders (Greer, 1964), a finding
with implications for psychodynamic and learning
theories. Others argue that parental rejection or
neglect is an important contributor to antisocial
behavior (McCord & McCord, 1964).

In a view that straddles the psychodynamic and
learning theories, the McCords suggest that children
normally learn to associate parental approval with
conformity to parental practices and values, and disapproval with disobedience. When tempted to trans-
gress, children then feel anxious for fear of loss of
parental love. Anxiety serves as a signal that encourages the child to inhibit antisocial behavior. Eventually, the child identifies with parents and internalizes
these social controls in the form of a conscience.
When parents do not show love for their children,
identification does not occur. Children do not fear
loss of love because they have not had love. The anxiety that might have served to restrain antisocial and
criminal behavior is absent.

Parental rejection and neglect may also leave children unable to empathize with others. Children who are rebuffed by their parents may not develop warm feelings of attachment to others. Future antisocial personalities may thus develop indifference toward others or perhaps wish to develop loving relationships but lack the ability to experience genuine feelings.

The McCords cite their own research, which shows a strong connection between early childhood emotional deprivation and subsequent delinquency. They write that frequent harsh, physical punishments may temporarily coerce children into obedience. When the threat of punishment is removed, however, children lack inner restraints or "residues of conscience" to inhibit antisocial behavior. Although lack of love does not invariably cause sociopathy, the more severe the parental rejection, the more likely the child will become aggressive and lack the capacity for guilt or remorse. In the McCords' view, less severe forms of parental rejection may also interact with other factors to give rise to antisocial behavior, such as modeling effects provided by an antisocial parent.

The McCords' views may apply to some children, but certainly not to all. Although family factors may be implicated in some cases of antisocial personality disorder, many neglected children do not later show antisocial or other abnormal behaviors. We are left to develop other explanations to predict which deprived children will develop antisocial personalities or other abnormal behaviors, and which will not.

Cognitive Perspectives

Cognitively oriented psychologists have shown that the ways in which people with personality disorders interpret their social experiences influence their behavior. Antisocial adolescents, for example, tend to erroneously interpret other people's behavior as threatening (Dodge, 1985; Lochman, 1987). Perhaps because of their family and community experiences, they tend to presume that others intend them ill when they do not (Dodge & Frame, 1982). In a promising cognitive therapy method based on such findings, **problem-solving therapy**, antisocial adolescents have been encouraged to reconceptualize their social interactions as problems to be solved rather than as threats to their "manhood" (Lochman, 1992; Lochman et al., 1984). They then generate nonviolent solutions to social confrontations and, like scientists, test out the most promising ones. In the section on biological perspectives we also see that the antisocial personality's failure to profit from punish-

ment is connected with a cognitive factor: the *meaning* of the aversive stimulus.

Biological Perspectives

Little is known about biological factors in most personality disorders. Although many theorists see personality disorders as the expression of maladaptive personality traits, the potential biological facets of such traits remain for the most part unknown.

In this section we explore genetic and other factors that provide information about the biological aspects of personality disorders.

■ **GENETIC FACTORS** One approach to discovering whether or not there are biological aspects of personality disorders focuses on genetic influences. There is much evidence for familial patterns in psychological *traits* that may underlie some of the personality disorders, such as extraversion, anxiety, social shyness, and social dominance or aggressiveness (Goldsmith, 1983; McCartney et al., 1990; Pedersen et al., 1988; Plomin, 1989). Concerning the disorders themselves, there is little information concerning familial patterns for paranoid, schizoid, borderline, narcissistic, avoidant, and dependent personality disorders. Schizotypal, antisocial, and obsessive-compulsive personality disorders, however, do show suggestive familial patterns. Schizotypal personality disorder is more common among the close biological relatives of schizophrenics than among the general population, however, which is suggestive of a possible genetic continuity with schizophrenia (Kendler & Gruenberg, 1984). Obsessive-compulsive and antisocial personality disorders are both found more commonly among the close biological relatives of people who have these disorders than among the general population. Familial studies are limited because families share environmental *and* genetic factors. More direct evidence of genetic contributions in obsessive-compulsive disorder is lacking. Evidence from adoption studies suggests a possible genetic line of transmission for antisocial personality disorder, however.

Adoption studies suggest that there may be a genetic predisposition toward criminal behavior (DiLalla & Gottesman, 1991; Mednick et al., 1987). Studies of Danish people who were adopted in infancy have shown that their biological parents place them at greater risk for criminal behavior than their adoptive parents, despite the fact that their adoptive families had the opportunity to influence them for so many years (Hutchings & Mednick, 1974; Mednick et al., 1984). The Mednick team also reported that Danish adoptees whose biological fathers were criminals were at greater risk of becoming criminals than adoptees whose adoptive fathers were criminals (Hutchings & Mednick, 1977). However, the apparent conclusion that genetic factors are better predictors of criminal behavior than a shared family environment must be tempered by several considerations. First, only about 1 in 5 adoptees whose biological fathers were known to be criminals, but whose adoptive fathers were not, later became criminals themselves (Hutchings & Mednick, 1977). Genetics alone cannot thus account for the larger portion of criminal behavior; environmental influences must also be considered (Carey, 1992). Consistent with the view that heredity and environment are both involved is the finding that the highest rate (36.2%) of criminal behavior was displayed by adopted sons whose biological *and* adoptive fathers were both criminals (Hutchings & Mednick, 1977). The investigators also caution that the results of these studies may be unique to adoptees. Also consider that criminals do not necessarily show antisocial personalities and that antisocial personalities are not necessarily criminals. We thus need to consider research that focuses more directly on the antisocial personality.

Fortunately, Danish records of biological and adoptive relatives of adopted infants who later became psychopaths (antisocial personalities) have also been analyzed. The findings mirror those of the Danish criminality studies. Schulsinger (1972) found a four to five times greater incidence of psychopathy among the biological relatives of antisocial adoptees than among the adoptive relatives. Again, the size of the genetic contribution was relatively small. Environmental influences also thus appear to contribute to antisocial behavior.

■ **CHROMOSOMAL ABNORMALITIES** A chromosomal theory which briefly captured the attention of researchers was rooted in the possibility that male aggressive criminals carry two male or Y sex chromosomes and one X sex chromosome, giving them an XYY sex-chromosomal structure rather than the normal XY pattern.

In the 1960s, several men were identified who shared some interesting features: tallness, heavier-than-average beards, mild mental retardation, a history of violent behavior, *and* the XYY sex chromosome pattern (instead of the normal XY male pattern) (Jacobs et al., 1965). XYY males came to be called **supermales** because of the apparent exaggeration of masculine characteristics caused by the extra Y sex chromosome. It was soon widely speculated that overly aggressive and violent behavior, in general, might be linked to the XYY pattern. The flurry of

interest in possible chromosomal abnormalities was further stirred by the discovery that a serial killer, Richard Speck, who had been convicted of murdering eight student nurses, also had XYY sex-chromosomal structure (Montague, 1968). Other research findings of the period also suggested that an abnormally large number of men who were convicted of violent crimes fit the XYY pattern (Nielsen, 1968).

Optimism that the XYY pattern would predict potential for violence was short-lived, however. Evidence began to accumulate that the great majority of violent male offenders did not carry the extra male chromosome (Smith, R.J., 1978) and most of the criminals who did had been convicted of nonviolent crimes (Witkin et al., 1976). Only about 2% or less of male delinquents and criminals tested show the XYY structure (Jarvik et al., 1973; Rosenthal, 1970). Moreover, most supermales do not engage in crime or violence.

■ **LACK OF EMOTIONAL RESPONSIVENESS** One of the cardinal features of antisocial personality disorder is freedom from the emotions of guilt and remorse. According to Cleckley (1976), antisocial personalities can maintain their composure in stressful situations that would induce anxiety in most people. Lack of anxiety in reponse to threatening situations may point to another feature of antisocial personality disorder: the failure of punishment to induce antisocial people to relinquish antisocial behavior. Punishment seems to have little or no deterrent effect on them. For must of us, fears of getting caught and of being punished are sufficient to inhibit antisocial impulses. Antisocial personalities may not learn to inhibit their anatgonistic behavior because they experience little or no anticipatory anxiety about being apprehended and punished.

The failure of antisocial personalities to learn to avoid cues that anticipate punishment has been studied in experiments in which subjects must learn to engage in certain responses to avoid aversive stimulation such as electric shock. In an early classic study, Lykken (1957) showed that prison inmates with antisocial personalities performed more poorly than normal controls on a shock avoidance task, although their general learning ability did not differ from that of normals. Lykken reasoned that the antisocial personalities were impaired in avoidance learning ability because of unusually low levels of anticipatory anxiety.

Schachter and Latané (1964) found that prisoners with antisocial personalities performed significantly better on the Lykken avoidance learning task following receipt of injections of epinephrine (adrenaline), a hormone that increases the heart rate and other indices of autonomic arousal. Their performance apparently improved because the epinephrine had heightened their anticipatory anxiety. Other researchers (Chesno & Kilmann, 1975) showed similar results after raising antisocial subjects' levels of autonomic arousal through bursts of aversive noise rather than injections of epinephrine.

Cognitive theorists can point to research showing that the effects of aversive stimuli on people with antisocial personality disorder may depend on the *meaning* or *value* of the stimuli. Anticipation of aversive stimulation in the form of electric shock may not foster avoidance learning in antisocial personalities, but threat of punishment in the form of loss of money may do so. Schmauk (1970), for example, had subjects perform a maze-learning task under three different forms of punishment for incorrect responses: electric shock, loss of money (losing a quarter for each error from an initial "bankroll" of 40 quarters), and social disapproval (the experimenter said "Wrong" following each incorrect response). Under the shock and social punishment conditions, antisocial personalities performed more poorly than normal controls. The antisocial personalities outperformed normal controls, however, when they were threatened with forfeiture of money. Although antisocial personalities may not be deterred from misconduct by the threat of physical punishment, they may be keenly sensitive to the loss of money. Perhaps antisocial personalities learn better from their mistakes when the cost is meaningful to them.

■ AUTONOMIC NERVOUS SYSTEM REACTIVITY

Some theorists have suggested that the autonomic nervous systems (ANSs) of people with antisocial personalities may be generally underresponsive to stressful stimuli, which could explain their "immunity" to guilt and their failure to profit from punishment or show anticipatory anxiety in the face of punishment.

Electrical conductivity of the skin is a measure of ANS reactivity. When most people anticipate pain, they show sweaty palms due to overactivity of the palmar sweat glands—the so-called **galvanic skin response** (GSR). In an early study, Hare (1965) found that antisocial personalities showed lower GSR levels in anticipation of painful stimuli than normal controls. In a later study, Hare and his colleagues (1978) warned two groups of prisoners, sociopaths and nonsociopaths, to expect a blast of noise following a 12-second countdown. Nonsociopathic prisoners showed high levels of skin conductance 3 seconds into the countdown, suggestive of fear, but sociopathic prisoners failed to react until just before the blast. Even then, they showed a relatively weak GSR response.

■ THE CRAVING-FOR-STIMULATION MODEL

Other investigators have attempted to explain the antisocial personality's lack of emotional response in terms of the levels of stimulation necessary to maintain an **optimum level of arousal**. Our optimum levels of arousal are the degrees of arousal at which we feel best and function most efficiently.

Quay (1965), for one, proposed that people with antisocial personalities require a higher-than-normal threshold of stimulation to maintain an optimum state of arousal. Antisocial personalities, that is, need more stimulation to operate at peak efficiency. They are also more quickly satiated by changes in stimulation than normal people are. As a result, people with antisocial personalities require higher levels of stimulation to maintain their interest. They are quickly bored by common activities that most people find stimulating, such as reading, watching TV, or relaxing with friends. Antisocial personalities crave stimulating activities or sensation in the form of intoxicants like drugs or alcohol, motorcycling, skydiving, high-stakes gambling, or sexual adventures. A higher-than-normal threshold for stimulation would not directly cause antisocial or criminal behavior; after all, part of the "right stuff" of the nation's respected astronauts includes sensation-seeking. However, threat of boredom and inability to tolerate monotony may influence some sensation seekers to drift into crime (Smith, R.J., 1978) or reckless behavior.

In support of Quay's theory, antisocial personalities score more highly than normal people on measures of sensation-seeking (Emmons & Webb, 1974). Delinquents with antisocial personalities have been found to register lower levels of physiological reactivity, as measured by GSR, than other delinquents in response to auditory signals (Borkovec, 1970). When antisocial personalities were shown more arousing stimuli, however—in the form of nude female figures—their GSRs increased to normal levels. Antisocial personalities may thus not react as strongly as normal people do to low levels of stimulation, but highly arousing stimuli may evoke similar responses.

■ DIFFERENCES IN BRAIN WAVE PATTERNS

The electroencephalograph (EEG) has been used in the attempt to define biological differences between antisocial personalities and normal people. Early studies of brain waves suggested that brain abnormalities existed in between 31 and 58% of antisocial personalities studied. The differences usually involved a high frequency of slow brain waves that tend to occur principally among younger children (Ellingson, 1954). These findings, which were generally confirmed in reviews of more recent research (Hare, 1970; Syndulko, 1978), have led to the suggestion

QUESTIONNAIRE

The Sensation-Seeking Scale

Do you crave stimulation or seek sensation? Are you satisfied by reading or watching TV, or must you ride the big wave or bounce your motorbike over desert dunes? Zuckerman and his colleagues (1978) have found that four factors are related to sensation-seeking: (1) pursuit of thrill and adventure, (2) disinhibition (that is, proclivity to express impulses), (3) pursuit of experience, and (4) susceptibility to boredom. Sensation seekers are more likely than other people to abuse drugs, show public drunkenness, seek sexual encounters, and volunteer to participate in experiments and high-risk activities (Kohn et al., 1979; Malatesta et al., 1981; Zuckerman, 1974). *However, many sensation seekers never find themselves in conflict with the law, so sensation-seeking should not be interpreted as criminal or antisocial in itself.*

Psychologist Marvin Zuckerman (1980) has developed several sensation-seeking scales that assess the levels of stimulation people seek to feel at their best and function efficiently. A brief form of one of them follows. To assess your own sensation-seeking tendencies, pick the choice, A or B, that best depicts you. Then compare your responses to those in the key at the end of the chapter.

1. A. I would like a job that requires a lot of traveling.
   B. I would prefer a job in one location.
2. A. I am invigorated by a brisk, cold day.
   B. I can't wait to get indoors on a cold day.
3. A. I get bored seeing the same old faces.
   B. I like the comfortable familiarity of everyday friends.
4. A. I would prefer living in an ideal society in which everyone is safe, secure, and happy.

B. I would have preferred living in the unsettled days of our history.

5. A. I sometimes like to do things that are a little frightening.
   B. A sensible person avoids activities that are dangerous.
6. A. I would not like to be hypnotized.
   B. I would like to have the experience of being hypnotized.
7. A. The most important goal in life is to live it to the fullest and experience as much as possible.
   B. The most important goal in life is to find peace and happiness.
8. A. I would like to try parachute-jumping.
   B. I would never want to try jumping out of a plane, with or without a parachute.
9. A. I enter cold water gradually, giving myself time to get used to it.
   B. I like to dive or jump right into the ocean or a cold pool.
10. A. When I go on a vacation, I prefer the change of camping out.
    B. When I go on a vacation, I prefer the comfort of a good room and bed.
11. A. I prefer people who are emotionally expressive even if they are a bit unstable.
    B. I prefer people who are calm and even-tempered.
12. A. A good painting should shock or jolt the senses.
    B. A good painting should give one a feeling of peace and security.
13. A. People who ride motorcycles must have some kind of unconscious need to hurt themselves.
    B. I would like to drive or ride a motorcycle.

Sensation! What is the connection between sensation seeking and antisocial personality disorder? Do people with antisocial personalities crave stimulation because they have high optimum levels of arousal?

that the **cerebral cortex**, the outer layer of the brain that is most directly involved in thought and learning, may mature relatively more slowly in people with antisocial personalities (Reid, 1986). As a result, such people might not be as prone as other people to inhibit primitive sexual and aggressive impulses. Moreover, brain wave studies show that people with antisocial personalities require stronger stimulation to evoke a cortical response, lending support to the view that they require higher-than-normal levels of stimulation to maintain their interest (Volavka, 1990).

Hare (1970) speculated that abnormal brain wave patterns in antisocial personalities may originate from defects in the **limbic system**, which is believed to be involved in the regulation of basic emotions like fear and anxiety. Defects in the parts of the brain that normally produce anticipatory anxiety could explain why antisocial personalities fail to profit from punishment and inhibit their maladaptive behaviors (Hare, 1970). It should be recognized, however, that not all antisocial personalities reveal abnormal patterns of brain waves. Many researchers believe that even if evidence of underlying brain damage in antisocial personality disorder is found, it is unlikely to account for the wide range of personality traits and behaviors associated with the disorder (Hart et al., 1990).

Sociocultural Views

The sociocultural perspective focuses on the social conditions that contribute to personality disorders. For example, because antisocial personality disorder is believed to be more common among the lower socioeconomic classes, we might examine the particular stresses encountered by disadvantaged families. Many inner-city neighborhoods are beset by social problems such as alcohol and drug abuse, teenage pregnancy, and disorganized and disintegrating families. It is no wonder that some of the children in these families fail to receive consistent and nurturant rearing. If such children often receive little love and copious harsh punishments, their self-esteem may be reduced and lead to feelings of anger and resentment. Neglect and abuse become translated into lack of empathy and callous disregard for the welfare of others.

Children reared in poverty are also more likely to be exposed to deviant role models, such as drug dealers. Maladjustment in school may lead to alienation and frustration with the larger society (Siegel, 1992). Antisocial adolescents may lash out against the larger society, committing violent crimes or wanton vandalism. From the sociocultural perspective,

"treatment" of antisocial personality disorder focuses on redress of social injustice and amelioration of deprivation.

TREATMENT

We began the chapter with a quote from the eminent psychologist William James, who suggested that people's personalities seem to be "set in plaster" by a certain age. His view may seem to be especially applicable to many people with personality disorders, who are typically highly resistant to change.

People with personality disorders usually see their behaviors, even maladaptive, self-defeating behaviors, as natural parts of themselves. Although they may be unhappy and distressed, they are unlikely to perceive their own behavior as causative. Like Marcella, whom we described as showing features of a histrionic personality disorder, they may condemn others for their problems and believe that others, not they, need to change. Thus they usually do not seek help on their own. Or they begrudgingly acquiesce to treatment at the urging of others but drop out or fail to cooperate with the therapist. Or they may go for help when they feel overwhelmed by anxiety or depression and terminate treatment as soon as they find some relief rather than probe the personal causes of their problems.

Psychodynamic Approaches

Psychodynamic approaches are used to help people with personality disorders become more aware of the roots of their self-defeating behavior patterns and learn more adaptive ways of relating to others. Progress in therapy may be hampered by difficulties in working therapeutically with people with personality disorders, especially clients with borderline and narcissistic personality disorders. Psychodynamic therapists often report that people with borderline personalities tend to have turbulent relationships with them, sometimes idealizing them, sometimes denouncing them as uncaring. Case studies suggest that therapists feel manipulated and exploited by borderline clients' needs to test their approval, such as calling them at all hours or threatening suicide. Such clients can be exhausting and frustrating, although some successes have been reported among therapists who can handle clients' demands.

Some workers have expressed the belief that people with antisocial personality disorder are beyond the reach of psychotherapy (e.g., Cleckley,

1976). Although this view might be too broad to be accurate, it seems that antisocial personalities have not responded well to psychodynamic treatment, apparently for several reasons (Smith, R.J., 1978). One is that people with antisocial personalities, like other clients with personality disorders, rarely seek treatment voluntarily and are not usually motivated to change their behavior. Another is that antisocial personalities usually mistrust others, including therapists, making it difficult to establish effective therapeutic relationships. Despite such problems, some promising results in treating people with personality disorders within a brief, structured form of psychodynamic therapy have been recently reported (Winston et al., 1991).

Resistance to therapy also hampers therapists of other persuasions, such as behavior therapists.

Behavioral Approaches

Behavior therapists see their task as changing clients' behaviors rather than their personality structures. Many behavioral theorists do not think in terms of clients' "personalities" at all, but rather in terms of acquired maladaptive behaviors that are maintained by reinforcement contingencies. Behavior therapists therefore focus on attempting to replace maladaptive behaviors with adaptive behaviors through techniques such as extinction, modeling, and reinforcement. If clients are taught behaviors that are likely to be reinforced by other people, the new behaviors are likely to be maintained.

Behavioral marital therapists, for example, may encourage clients not to reinforce their spouses' histrionic behaviors. Treatment of avoidant personality disorder may include social skills training to help clients function more effectively in social situations, such as dating and meeting new people. Cognitive methods may be incorporated, to help socially avoidant individuals offset catastrophizing beliefs, such as exaggerated fear of being shot down or rejected by dates.

Some antisocial adolescents have been placed, often by court order, in residential and foster care programs that contain numerous behavioral elements (Reid & Balis, 1987). These programs or settings have concrete rules and clear rewards for obeying them (Barkley et al., 1976; Henggeler et al., 1986; Phillips et al., 1976; Stumphauzer, 1981). Achievement Place, founded in Kansas in the 1960s and reproduced elsewhere, reinforced prosocial behaviors, such as completing homework, and extinguished antisocial behaviors, such as using profanity (Phillips et al., 1976). Some residential programs rely on **token economies**, in which prosocial behaviors are rewarded with tokens such as plastic chips that can be exchanged for privileges.

Consider a model training program developed by Harold Cohen (Cohen & Filipczak, 1971) and his associates for delinquents in Washington, D.C. The adolescents enrolled in courses such as remedial math, history, and electronics and earned money for their achievements. Extra cash flowed for earning A's. The adolescents acquired study skills that they subsequently put to use in the public schools. They also got into fewer scrapes with the law than did controls during a 2-year follow-up period. Yet it remains unclear whether such programs reduce the risk that adolescent antisocial behavior will continue into adulthood.

Biological Approaches

Chemotherapy does not directly treat personality disorders. Agents such as antidepressants or antianxiety drugs are sometimes used to treat the distress that individuals with personality disorders may encounter, however. Such drugs cannot treat the long-standing patterns of maladaptive behavior that may give rise to distress.

Much remains to be learned about working with people who have personality disorders. The major challenges involve recruiting people who do not see themselves as being disordered into treatment and prompting them to develop insight into their self-defeating or injurious behaviors. Current efforts to help such people are too often reminiscent of the old couplet:

He that complies against his will,
Is of his own opinion still.

Samuel Butler, *Hudibras*

IMPULSE DISORDERS

Be candid. Have you ever blown your budget on a sale item? Have you ever made a bet that you could not afford? Have you ever lost it and screamed at someone, even though you knew you should be keeping cool?

Most of us keep most of our impulses under control most of the time. We usually restrain ourselves from blurting out obscenities when riled and prevent ourselves from exploding in anger. Although we may sometimes surrender to temptation and inhale a dessert that we have lusted after in our hearts, or occasionally yell at obnoxious people, we generally hold most impulses in check. Some of us, however, suffer from what the DSM diagnoses as **impulse control disorders**. These disorders are characterized by failure to resist harmful impulses, temptations, or drives (see Table 8.3). People with impulse disorders experience a rising level of tension or arousal just prior to the act, followed by a sense of relief or release after the act is completed.

Impulse control disorders have been relatively poorly studied. Little is known of their prevalence, demographics, course, or response to treatment (McElroy et al., 1992). Some investigators question the validity of the concept of the irresistible impulse. Are some impulses indeed irresistible, or are the people who characterize them as irresistible simply unwilling to forgo them (McElroy et al., 1992)? People with impulse disorders also show high rates of mood disorders, which has led some researchers to wonder whether they may actually fall within the spectrum of mood disorders (McElroy et al., 1992). We focus on two types of impulse disorders: pathological gambling and kleptomania.

Pathological Gambling

Gambling may never have been more popular in the United States. Legalized gambling is spreading in the form of state lotteries, offtrack betting (OTB) parlors, casino nights sponsored by religious and fraternal organizations, and legalized gambling meccas, like

Gambling, American style?   Gambling is big business in the United States. Although most gamblers can stop gambling whenever they want to do so, pathological or compulsive gamblers are unable to resist the urge to gamble. Many compulsive gamblers seek help only when their losses throw them into financial or emotional crisis, such as bankruptcy or divorce.

Atlantic City and Las Vegas. Perhaps 23% of Americans buy lottery tickets every week. Today, with legalized gambling available at OTB parlors and in the form of state lotteries, women and teenagers constitute more of the gambling population than ever before (Barron, 1989). Illegal betting on sporting events is also growing. Technological advances are making gambling ever more convenient—and seductive: Video slot machines and poker machines are now commonly found in diners and convenience stores, where they captivate younger players and some people who would never frequent casinos. Credit cards are used in lieu of cash in many casinos.

Most people who gamble maintain their self-control and can stop whenever they wish. Others, like the man in the following case, fall into a pattern of **pathological gambling**.

Table 8.3   Diagnostic Features of Impulse Control Disorders

1. Failure to resist the impulse, drive, or temptation to engage in an act that is harmful to the self or to others, as shown, for example, by acts of aggression (in intermittent explosive disorder), fire setting (in pyromania), or persistent and recurrent maladaptive gambling (as in pathological gambling).

2. A sense of mounting arousal or tension is experienced before the act is committed.

3. The individual experiences a sense of pleasure, release, or gratification when committing the act.

Source: Adapted from DSM-IV Draft Criteria (American Psychiatric Association, 1993), pp. R:1-R:3.

---

*T*wenty-eight years after his first two-bit bet at the race track, the double life of lies and deception caught up with an insurance executive whose gambling debts had climbed into the hundreds of thousands of dollars. The business he had built went bankrupt. His marriage ended in bitter divorce. Often, he considered killing himself.

The former executive does not look like an addict, a liar, a manipulator or someone who would ignore his two young daughters, but he admits to having been all of these.

"Gambling," he said, dragging hard on a cigarette, "took me from a good man, which I basically am, to a *person I didn't know. I was only happy when I was in action and I felt most at home when I was in action. The more I won, the more I gambled. The more I lost, the more I gambled. It was a no-win situation.*

■ *Source: "Hospital Leads Patients to Where All Bets Are Off," by G. Gately. Copyright © 1989 by The New York Times Company. Reprinted by permission.*

By the time he sought treatment, he had lost more than $1 million. Many pathological (also called compulsive) gamblers only seek treatment during a financial or emotional crisis, such as bankruptcy or divorce. Pathological gambling may take many forms, from excessive wagering on horse races or in card games and in casinos, to extravagant betting on sporting events or stock market fluctuations. Compulsive or pathological gamblers often report that they had experienced a big win, or a series of winnings, early in their gambling careers. Eventually their losses begin to mount, and they felt driven to bet with increasing desperation to reverse their luck and recoup them (Peck, 1986). Sometimes losses begin with the first bet, and pathological gamblers become trapped in a negative spiral of betting more frequently to recover losses even as their losses—and their debts—multiply.

Compulsive or pathological gambling was labeled a mental disorder with the 1980 publication of the DSM-III and is believed to be more common among men than women. Pathological gambling involves repeated failure to resist the urge to gamble, resulting in a disruptive pattern of gambling that impairs the ability to function in personal, family, or occupational roles (see Table 8.4). Pathological gambling is a progressive problem that, uncorrected, leads to rising debts, problems at work and home, and, sometimes, suicide. Pathological gamblers tend to hit rock bottom, also called **bottoming out**, a state of despair characterized by loss of control over gambling, financial ruin, suicide attempts, and shattered family relationships anywhere from 1 to 20 years after the onset of the problem (Peck, 1986).

Pathological gamblers are preoccupied with gambling. Their lives may revolve around pursuing money for stakes. Unlike casual bettors or lottery players, pathological gamblers may risk all their resources (Gately, 1989). Pathological gambling has been linked to separation and divorce, accumulation of massive debts, time lost at work or school, depression and suicide, legal and medical problems, even suicide attempts by gamblers' spouses (Lesieur & Blume, 1987). Family relationships are strained by

Table 8.4	Diagnostic Features of Pathological Gambling

Pathological gambling is characterized by a persistent and recurrent pattern of maladaptive gambling, as characterized by features such as the following:

1. Preoccupation with gambling or with obtaining money to gamble.

2. Need to increase the size or frequency of bets to achieve the desired excitement.

3. Repeated failure to cut back on or quit gambling.

4. Restlessness or irritability when unable to gamble.

5. Gambling as a means of trying to escape from problems or of trying to relieve feelings of guilt, anxiety, helplessness, or depression.

6. Repeated loss of money by gambling and returning another day ("chasing") to win back losses.

7. Lying to conceal the extent of gambling.

8. Commission of illegal acts such as fraud or forgery to finance gambling.

9. Loss or threatened loss of a key social relationship, educational opportunity, or job because of gambling.

10. Reliance on other people for financial support to ease the dire financial situation caused by gambling.

Note: Not all of these features need be present for a diagnosis to be made.

Source: Adapted from DSM-IV Draft Criteria (American Psychiatric Association, 1993), p. R:2.

the time and resources that are channeled into gambling. There is often little left for family vacations, school tuition, or monthly bills (Gately, 1989). Pathological gamblers often borrow from friends and family. When these sources dry up, they may turn to finance companies or illegal and potentially dangerous sources such as loan sharks and bookies. Pathological gamblers may attempt to reduce the stress of mounting debts by gambling yet more frequently, hoping for the "big score" that will put them "into the black." Pathological gamblers are sometimes bouncing with energy and overconfidence. At other times they are anxious or depressed.

It is not the pursuit of money alone that motivates the compulsive gambler, but also the excitement or thrill of gambling itself (Gately, 1989), as suggested by Steve B., a 46-year-old compulsive gambler from New York City who bets $150 a day on horses:

I don't dream of winning a million dollars. . . . I want to have a bet on every thoroughbred race run. My idea of gambling heaven is to sit in a horse parlor in Las Vegas and bet on every horse from 8 A.M. until 2 A.M.

[Steve had held 75 to 80 jobs in 25 years due to problems with gambling.]

Because I've gambled all my adult life, . . . I've never been able to hold a job. I'd louse up on the job because my mind was on the gambling, or I couldn't go to the racetrack. I used to devise incredibly ingenious ways to get there.

■ *Source: "States Sell Chances for Gold as a Rush Turns to Stampede," by J. J. Barron. Copyright © 1989 by The New York Times Company. Reprinted by permission.*

Many compulsive gamblers suffer from low self-esteem and were rejected or abused as children by their parents. Gambling may become a means of boosting self-esteem, of proving that they are winners. Unfortunately, they usually prove the opposite. Losing at gambling only strengthens their negative self-image, which can lead to depression and suicide.

■ **PREVALENCE OF PATHOLOGICAL GAMBLING** There may be more than 4 million pathological gamblers in the United States (Gately, 1989; Nadler, 1985). The numbers may be increasing as more states turn to legalized forms of gambling, such as lotteries and casinos, to close budget gaps (Marriott, 1992). Pathological gambling also affects family members and others whose well-being hinges on the performance of the gamblers, such as friends and employers.

The results of a New York State survey, based on a telephone sampling method, estimated the prevalence of pathological gambling at about 230,000 of New York's 13 million adults, or about 2% of the adult population (Volberg & Steadman, 1988). An additional half to three-quarters of a million reported lesser gambling problems. The typical pathological gambler was a nonwhite male, under the age of 30, who had not graduated from high school and earned $25,000 or less a year. He was more likely than nongamblers to be out of work. Earlier research on pathological gambling, by contrast, had depicted the typical pathological gambler as a middle- or upper-class white male in his 40s or 50s. Earlier findings, however, were generally based on samples that were obtained from sources like Gamblers Anonymous, college populations, or psychiatric populations and may not have represented the general population. Earlier research also frequently portrayed the pathological gambler as having a stable family and occupational life until gambling got out of hand. The New York survey, however, connected pathological gambling with nonfamily men with marginal educational and occupational backgrounds. Thus treatment efforts may need to be expanded in minority communities and to target young, poorly educated, unemployed problem gamblers. A large percentage of women was also found in the 1988 survey (36%), which suggests a need for treatment programs that target women gamblers.

■ **CHARACTERISTICS OF PATHOLOGICAL GAMBLERS** Pathological or compulsive gambling has been linked to depressive disorders (McCormick et al., 1987), early childhood trauma, and other factors. Ramirez and his colleagues (1983) consider pathological gambling to be a form of addictive behavior in that the personality characteristics of the compulsive gambler have much in common with other addictive groups, such as alcoholics and substance abusers (McCormick & Russo, 1987). Studies show that compulsive gamblers and substance abusers both tend to be self-centered, anxious, frustrated, impulsive, and manipulative (McCormick et al., 1987). Compulsive gambling is also associated with a kind of physical high and with withdrawal problems following abrupt cessation of gambling (Marriott, 1992). The Gamblers Anonymous treatment approach is also modeled after programs like Alcoholics Anonymous in which the addictive aspects of the problem are highlighted. But there may be personality differences between compulsive gamblers and substance abusers. One study compared the personality profiles of 70 compulsive gamblers and 70 alcoholics, based on the California Psychological Inventory. The gamblers showed relatively more anti-social behavior, impulsivity, and inability to delay gratification (McCormick et al., 1987)—problems that heighten the difficulties of therapists who work with them.

■ **STAGES IN THE GAMBLING "CAREER"** Lesieur and Custer (1984) describe a three-phase developmental course commonly found among pathological gamblers: winning, losing, and desperation. In the adventurous, or **winning phase**, budding gamblers see wagering as a pleasurable pastime. They thrive on the thrill of the "action." Early winnings boost self-esteem. Big wins make gamblers feel like "big shots." Nearly half of pathological gamblers report a big win in this stage, sometimes one that equals their annual salaries. In this stage, gamblers take credit for having a winning system for betting or handicapping. Losses are dismissed and attributed to external forces like "bad luck," cheating (by others), or untimely accidents (such as the football hitting a goal post on a field-goal attempt). Even during this early stage, however, gamblers often begin to borrow from friends to recoup losses.

In the middle, or **losing phase**, gamblers begin to lose, steadily. They borrow larger amounts of money to try to break even. They take out loans with finance companies, borrow from credit card accounts or credit unions, and hide transactions from their families. Married gamblers run into domestic blowups when financial pressures mount and their losses and loans are discovered. In the attempt to break even, gamblers spend progressively more time gambling and forsake work and other responsibilities. They are introduced by gambling "buddies" to other types of gambling that may bring better luck. Gamblers may lose their jobs due to repeated absences or switch to lines of work that allow more time for gambling. Gamblers may borrow from bookies and stall them for time in repaying their debts as they seek the big score.

During the **desperation phase**, gamblers become yet more obsessed with winning to break even and pay off debts. Periodic rescues may occur in the form of bailouts from relatives, but gamblers soon return to the pattern of gambling, losing, and borrowing again. Lies and deceptions are used to conceal gambling and loans. Spouses become disgusted and feel that their efforts to help are in vain. Problems on the job mount as gamblers focus on personal problems and gambling. They seek whatever means are available, legal or otherwise, to obtain money. Eventually, they panic, which leads to irrational gambling and greater risk taking. Optimism that the big win is only a bet away begins to fade, and gamblers grow restless, irritable, and fatigued. They sleep poorly and eat erratically. Periods of despair and suicidal thoughts and attempts often follow. At this stage, gamblers usually see but four ways out of their problems: running away (typically to Las Vegas or another gambling center), suicide, imprisonment, or seeking help.

■ TREATMENT OF PATHOLOGICAL GAMBLERS Various programs offer treatment to pathological gamblers. Many gamblers attend nonprofessional support groups, like Gamblers Anonymous, or seek professional counseling. Some do both (Lesieur & Custer, 1984). Gamblers Anonymous is similar in approach to Alcoholics Anonymous. The organization stresses assuming responsibility for one's behavior. It ensures the anonymity of group members to spur participation and sharing of experiences, and it helps members gain insight into their self-destructive behavior. Members make public commitments to stop

gambling and help one another resist the urge to gamble.

In addition, hospital-based or residential programs help pathological gamblers break their habits by sequestering them from their regular routines for 6 weeks or so. While they are in residence, gamblers may be introduced to Gamblers Anonymous or other support groups to help them make the transition to the community.

Few reports attest to the success of these strategies. To ensure the anonymity of participants, lay organizations like Gamblers Anonymous do not keep detailed records. Even if records were kept at Gamblers Anonymous, the dropout rate would probably be too high to be encouraging (Lesieur & Custer, 1984).

 Gamblers Anonymous groups have indeed been set up to help pathological gamblers. However, questions remain concerning the effectiveness of these groups.

Some promising results have been shown for a comprehensive treatment program in a veterans' hospital setting (Taber et al., 1987), with success, as defined by abstinence, reported for 56% (32 of 57 gamblers). The program consisted of a highly structured 28-day hospitalization for gamblers—all male veterans—who had not responded to nonresidential approaches. Upon discharge, participants who attended Gamblers Anonymous meetings fared better than those who dropped out. However, the lack of a control group and of long-term follow-up evaluations limit the validity of the results.

With pathological gambling, as with personality disorders, helping professionals are essentially dealing with individuals who make maladaptive choices and show little insight into the causes of their problems. Such clients commonly resist efforts to help them.

Kleptomania

Kleptomania derives from the Greek *kleptes*, meaning "thief," and refers to a compulsive pattern of stealing. The stolen objects are typically of little value or use to kleptomaniacs. Kleptomaniacs often give them away, return them secretly, discard them, or keep them hidden at home. In most cases, kleptomaniacs can easily afford the items. Wealthy people have been known to be compulsive shoplifters.

It is not true that kleptomania is motivated by poverty. Kleptomania is somewhat puzzling because many kleptomaniacs are well to-do.

The thefts are apparently unmotivated by anger or vengeance. The thefts are usually crimes of the moment, poorly planned, and sometimes result in arrest. Kleptomaniacs are usually inhibited by the obvious presence of guards or police officers.

Although the experience of an irresistible, repetitive pattern in kleptomania suggests common features with obsessive-compulsive disorder, kleptomania, unlike the obsessions and compulsions in obsessive-compulsive disorder, may engender intense gratification. This is an important reason for its classification as an impulse control disorder (Goldman, 1991). By contrast, the behavior of people with obsessive-compulsive disorder is considered to be disturbing or ego dystonic. Another apparent difference is that kleptomania is an end in itself, whereas obsessions and compulsions in obsessive-compulsive disorder are apparently intended to avert a future unfortunate event or situation. Nevertheless, the similarities between kleptomania and the compulsive rituals observed in obsessive-compulsive disorder may merit further study (Murray, 1992).

Kleptomania is regarded as quite rare. Shoplifting, including kleptomania-related shoplifting, is more common among women than men, although overall gender differences in the prevalence of kleptomania are uncertain.

Little research has been conducted on kleptomania (Murray, 1992). Most published reports are limited to the case studies of a few individuals and lack appropriate comparison groups. Causal factors remain unknown (Murray, 1992), although childhood abuse may play a role in the development of at least some cases (Goldman, 1991). One research group observed a high incidence of major mood disorders among a sample of 20 kleptomaniacs, suggesting a possible linkage between mood disorders and kleptomania (McElroy et al., 1991). Moreover a high prevalence of major mood disorders was found among the first-degree relatives of kleptomaniacs. Perhaps the thrill of theft is a way in which some people attempt to fend off feelings of depression.

Early psychodynamic formulations viewed kleptomania as a defense against feelings of penis envy in women and castration anxiety in men. In effect, kleptomaniacs were motivated to steal phallic objects (symbols of the penis) as a way of protecting themselves against their own apparent loss (in females) or threatened loss (in males) (Fenichel, 1945). It has not proved possible to decisively test these formulations about unconscious processes, however.

The following case illustrates the behavioral treatment of kleptomania:

The client was a 56-year-old woman, who had shoplifted every day of the preceding 14 years. Her compulsive urges to steal fit the clinical criteria which may distinguish kleptomania from other types of shoplifting, although her booty had no apparent meaning to her. Typical loot consisted of a pair of baby shoes, although there was no baby in her family to whom she could give the shoes. The compulsion to steal was so strong that she felt powerless to resist it. She told her therapist that she wished she could be "chained to a wall" (p. 213) in order to prevent her from acting out. She expressed anger that it was so easy to steal from a supermarket, in effect blaming the store for her own misconduct.

Her treatment, **covert sensitization,** *involved the imaginal pairing of aversive stimuli with the undesired behavior. In her case, the therapist directed her to imagine feeling nauseous and vomiting while stealing. For example, she pictures herself in the supermarket, approaching an object she intended to steal, and becoming nauseated and vomiting as she removed it, thereby drawing the attention of other shoppers. She was then directed to imagine herself replacing the object and consequently feeling relief from the nausea.*

In a subsequent session, she imagines the nausea starting as she approached the object, but the nausea disappeared when she turned away from it rather than removing it. She was also asked to practice the imaginal scenes on her own throughout the week, as homework assignments. She reported a decline in her urges to steal, and a reduction in stealing behavior during the treatment program. She reported only one instance of shoplifting between the completion of treatment and a 19-month follow-up evaluation.

■ *Adapted from Glover, 1985*

Although Glover's findings are promising, the report has the limitations of uncontrolled case studies. For example, we cannot know whether the treatment itself or other factors, such as the client's motivation to change her life, were responsible for her changes in behavior.

In this chapter we have considered a number of problems in which people act out on maladaptive impulses yet fail to see how their behaviors are disrupting their lives. In the following chapter we explore other maladaptive impulsive behaviors that are frequently connected with lack of self-insight: behaviors involving substance abuse.

Summary

Personality Disorders

Maladaptive or rigid behavior patterns or personality traits that are associated with states of personal distress or impair the person's ability to function in social or occupational roles are called personality disorders. People with personality disorders do not generally recognize a need to change themselves. Personality disorders may be organized into three clusters, as follow.

Personality Disorders Characterized by Odd or Eccentric Behavior

People with paranoid personality disorder are unduly suspicious and mistrustful of others, to the point that their relationships suffer. But they do not hold the more flagrant paranoid delusions typical of schizophrenia. Schizoid personality disorder describes people who have little if any interest in social relationships, show a restricted range of emotional expression, and appear distant and aloof. Schizotypal personalities appear odd or eccentric in their thoughts, mannerisms, and behavior, but not to the degree found in schizophrenia.

Personality Disorders Characterized by Dramatic, Emotional, or Erratic Behavior

Antisocial personality disorder describes people who persistently engage in behavior that violates social norms and the rights of others and who tend to show no remorse for their misdeeds. Borderline personality disorder is defined in terms of instability in self-image, relationships, and mood. Borderline personalities often engage in impulsive acts, which are frequently self-destructive. Histrionic personalities tend to be highly dramatic and emotional in their behavior. Narcissistic personalities have inflated or grandiose senses of themselves and, like histrionic personalities, demand to be the center of attention.

Personality Disorders Characterized by Anxious or Fearful Behavior

Avoidant personality disorder describes people who are so terrified of rejection and criticism that they are generally unwilling to enter relationships without unusually strong reassurances of acceptance. People with dependent personality disorder are overly dependent on others and have extreme difficulty acting independently or making even the smallest decisions on their own. People with obsessive-compulsive personality disorder have various traits such as orderliness, perfectionism, rigidity and overattention to detail, but are without the true obsessions and compulsions associated with obsessive-compulsive (anxiety) disorder.

Problems with the Classification of Personality Disorders

Various controversies and problems attend the classification of personality disorders, including lack of demonstrated reliability and validity, too much overlap among the categories, difficulty in distinguishing between variations in normal behavior and abnormal behavior, underlying sexist biases in certain categories, and confusion of labels with explanations.

Theoretical Perspectives

Traditional Freudian theory focused on unresolved Oedipal conflicts in explaining normal and abnormal personality development. More recent psychodynamic theorists have focused on the pre-Oedipal period in explaining the development of such personality disorders as narcissistic and borderline personality.

Learning theorists view personality disorders in terms of maladaptive patterns of behavior, rather than personality traits. Learning theorists seek to identify the early learning experiences and present reinforcers that may explain the development and maintenance of personality disorders.

Many theorists have argued that disturbed family relationships play roles in the development of many personality disorders. Antisocial personality disorder is connected with parental loss, rejection or neglect, and parental modeling of antisocial behavior. Cognitive theorists have focused on the role of encoding strategies in explaining tendencies of antisocial adolescents to presume that others mean them ill.

Research on biological perspectives has shown familial links in various personality disorders that are consistent with, but do not prove, genetic means of transmission. There is some research evidence that shows antisocial personalities not only lack emotional responsiveness to physically threatening stimuli but also show reduced levels of autonomic reactivity. Antisocial personalities may also require higher levels of stimulation to maintain optimal levels of arousal.

Sociocultural theorists focus on the adverse social conditions that may contribute to the development of personality disorders, especially antisocial personality. The effects of poverty, urban blight, and drug abuse can lead to family disorganization and disintegration, making it less likely that children will receive the nurturance and support to help them develop more socially adaptive behavior patterns.

Treatment

Therapists from different schools of therapy try to assist people with personality disorders to gain better awareness of their self-defeating behavior patterns and learn more adaptive ways of relating to others. Evidence of effectiveness has been lacking, largely as a result of the difficulties encountered in working therapeutically with people who are resistant to change.

Impulse Disorders

Impulse disorders involve failures to resist impulses, temptations, or drives that lead to harmful consequences to oneself or others. The person with an impulse disorder experiences a rising level of tension or arousal just preceding the act, and then a sense of relief or release when the act is committed.

Pathological gambling involves a pattern of repeated failure to resist the urge to gamble that results in impaired functioning in personal, family, or occupational roles. Some researchers view pathological gambling as a type of non-chemical addiction and have noted similarities (and some differences) in personality profiles between pathological gamblers and substance abusers. Kleptomania involves a compulsion to steal, usually involving items of little value to the person.

KEY FOR SENSATION-SEEKING SCALE

Because this is an abbreviated version of a questionnaire, no norms are applicable. However, answers that agree with the following key are suggestive of sensation-seeking:

1. A	8. A
2. A	9. B
3. A	10. A
4. B	11. A
5. A	12. A
6. B	13. B
7. A	

Robert Birmelin. *Extreme Needs.* 1989–90. Acrylic on Canvas: 90x136 inches.
Courtesy Claude Bernard Gallery. New York.

CHAPTER OUTLINE

9

Substance-Related Disorders

TRUTH  FICTION?

___ Legal substances cause more deaths through sickness and accidents than all illicit drugs combined.

___ Casual drug use among college students has mushroomed in recent years.

___ Cocaine is the most widely abused substance in the United States today.

___ Alcohol goes to women's heads more rapidly than to men's.

___ Heroin was developed during a search for a drug that would relieve pain as effectively as morphine, but without causing physical addiction.

___ Cigarettes are habit forming but not physically addictive.

___ Marijuana saps motivation.

___ A recovering alcoholic must abstain from alcohol because just one drink will lead to a binge.

*T*he planet is a supermarket of **psychoactive** chemicals, or drugs. The United States is inundated with substances that alter the mood and twist perceptions—substances that lift you up, cool you down, and turn you upside down. Many people use these substances because their friends do. Adolescents often use them because their parents and authority figures tell them not to. Some users are seeking pleasure. Others are searching for inner truth.

About half of college students have used marijuana at least once, and about 29% smoked it within the past year (Johnston et al., 1992). Many Americans rely on depressants to get to sleep at night and on stimulants to get started in the morning. In one of history's better known slanders, Karl Marx asserted that "religion . . . is the opium of the people." Heroin, however, is the actual opium of the people. The old standby alcohol is the most popular drug on campus—whether the campus is a high school or college campus (Johnston et al., 1992). In 1990, in fact, 89% of college students reported using alcohol within the past year, whereas only 1 student in 3 reported using any illicit drug (Johnston et al., 1992). Under certain conditions, the use of substances that affect mood and behavior is normal enough, at least as gauged by statistical frequency and social standards. It is normal to start the day with caffeine in the form of coffee or tea, to take wine or coffee with meals, to meet friends for a drink after work, and to end the day with a nightcap. Many of us take prescription drugs that calm us down or ease our pain. Flooding the bloodstream with nicotine by smoking is normal in the sense that about 28% of young adults in the United States have smoked within the past 30 days, and about 1 in 5 (21%) smokes daily (Johnston et al., 1992). Some psychoactive substances are illegal and are used illicitly, like cocaine, marijuana, and heroin. Others are available by prescription, like minor tranquilizers and amphetamines. Still others are available without prescription or over the counter—like cigarettes and alcohol. Ironically, the most readily available substances—cigarettes and alcohol—have caused more deaths through sickness and accidents than all illicit drugs combined.

 It is true that legal substances—alcohol and cigarettes—have caused more deaths through sickness and accidents in the United States than all illicit drugs combined.

Table 9.1 shows some results from a continuing government survey of young people in the United States, including high school seniors, college students, and young adults aged 18 to 30 (Johnston et al., 1992). Respondents are asked whether they have ever used a substance or used it during the past year, the

Table 9.1	Percentage of College Students Who Report Drug Use "During the Last 30 Days," 1981–1991										
Drug	**1981**	**1982**	**1983**	**1984**	**1985**	**1986**	**1987**	**1988**	**1989**	**1990**	**1991**
Alcohol	81.9	82.8	80.3	79.1	80.3	79.7	78.4	77.0	76.2	74.5	74.7
Cigarettes	25.9	24.4	24.7	21.5	22.4	22.4	24.0	22.6	21.1	21.5	23.2
Marijuana	33.2	26.8	26.2	23.0	23.6	22.3	20.3	16.8	16.3	14.0	14.1
Cocaine	7.3	7.9	6.5	7.6	6.9	7.0	4.6	4.2	2.8	1.2	1.0
(Crack)	NA*	NA	NA	NA	NA	NA	0.4	0.5	0.2	0.1	0.3
Other stimulants	12.3	9.9	7.0	5.5	4.2	3.7	2.3	1.8	1.3	1.4	1.0
Sedatives Barbiturates, Methaqualone	3.4	2.5	1.1	1.0	0.7	0.6	0.6	0.6	0.2	0.2	0.3
Hallucinogens	2.3	2.6	1.8	1.8	1.3	2.2	2.0	1.7	2.3	1.4	1.2
Heroin	0.0	0.0	0.0	0.0	0.0	0.0	0.1	0.1	0.1	0.0	0.1

*NA = Not available.

*Source: Johnston, L. D., Bachman, J. G., & O'Malley, P. M. (1992, January 25). Monitoring the future: A
continuing study of the lifestyles and values of youth. The University of Michigan News and Information Services:
Ann Arbor, MI.*

past 30 days, or on a daily basis. Table 9.1 reveals trends in the 30-day prevalence of the use of various substances for college students from 1981 through 1991. Note there has been a modest falloff in the 30-day prevalence of usage of alcohol and cigarettes. There have been dramatic decreases in the 30-day prevalence of usages of marijuana, cocaine, other stimulants, and sedatives. Hallucinogens other than marijuana have been used in the past 30 days by about 1 or 2% of the college population, with an apparent decline. Heroin and crack are each used by less than 1% of the college population. Although these results point to continuing declines in casual drug use among young people, hard-core drug use shows few signs of abating.

SUBSTANCE RELATED DISORDERS

The DSM-IV includes several kinds of substance-related disorders. Four kinds of major substance disorders are identified: *substance abuse, substance dependence, substance intoxication,* and *substance withdrawal.* Because psychoactive substances can also have a wide range of physical and psychological effects, use of these substances can also induce other kinds of mental disorders, including *delirium, dementia, amnestic disorder, psychotic disorder, mood disorder, anxiety disorder, sexual dysfunction,* and *sleep disorder.* Different substances have different effects, so some of these cate-

gories may apply to one, to a few, or to nearly all substances. For example, *substance intoxication* may arise following ingestion of all the psychoactive substances identified in the DSM-IV except nicotine. *Delirium* and *psychotic disorder* may arise during states of intoxication produced from ingestion of a wide range of substances including alcohol, amphetamines, cannabis (marijuana), cocaine, hallucinogens (like LSD), inhalants, opioids (such as heroin), PCP, and sedatives, but is not linked to ingestion of caffeine or nicotine.

 With some exceptions, casual drug use has actually declined among college students in recent years.

Substance Abuse, Dependence, Withdrawal, and Intoxication

Where does substance use end and abuse begin? From a legal standpoint, the answer is simple. For example, it is illegal in all states for people under the age of 21 to drink alcohol. It is also illegal to dispense prescribed drugs without prescriptions. When, however, does legal *use* of, say, alcohol cross the line and wax into *abuse*? According to the DSM, the use of a substance is considered abusive when it persists for at least a month despite the fact that it is causing or contributing to social, occupational, psychological, or physical problems. When people repeatedly miss school or work because they are drunk, or "sleeping it off," their behavior may fit the definition of **sub-**

(B)

Two of the many faces of alcohol use—and abuse.   Alcohol is our most widely used—and abused—drug. We use alcohol to celebrate our achievements and facilitate social interactions, as in photo A. Unfortunately, we sometimes use alcohol to drown our sorrows, as in photo B. Where does substance use end and substance abuse begin? According to the DSM, use becomes abuse when it persists despite the individual's knowledge that it is causing or contributing to social, occupational, psychological, or physical problems.

(A)

stance abuse. A single incident of excessive drinking at a friend's wedding would not qualify. Nor would regular consumption of low to moderate amounts of alcohol be considered abusive so long as it is not connected with any impairment in functioning. Neither the amount nor the type of drug ingested, nor whether or not the drug is illicit, is the key to defining substance abuse according to the DSM. Rather, it is whether one continues to use the drug despite the knowledge that repeated use hinders functioning in other areas of life. Substance abuse may also be defined in terms of repeated use in situations in which it is dangerous, such as driving while intoxicated. The following case illustrates how a pattern of alcohol abuse can hinder social functioning:

A 38-year-old woman and mother of four consulted a clinician upon recommendation of her priest, to whom she had confided experiencing "fits of rage" in which she struck her children and threw objects at her husband. Her children would run in terror and lock themselves in their rooms when they heard her ranting "Did you do your homework?" or "Just look at this messy house!" After these incidents, she felt guilty and ashamed. Upon interview, she admitted that these incidents were preceded by sneaking a couple of swallows of bourbon from a bottle hidden in the car. Since extreme reactions like this are not typical of a swallow or two of bourbon, the woman might be drinking more than she admits. The rage and

violent behavior which is associated with her drinking would indicate a maladaptive pattern of use of alcohol consistent with a diagnosis of alcohol abuse.

■ *Adapted from Spitzer et al., 1989*

Substance dependence involves behavior patterns that suggest impaired control over use of the substance and continued or increased use despite awareness that the substance is disrupting one's life. Substance dependence is also identified by persistent desire or previous unsuccessful attempts to cut down or control use of the substance, and by orienting one's life toward procuring and using the substance (see Table 9.2). Some features of substance dependence suggest a strong physiological component, such as tolerance and characteristic withdrawal patterns (see Table 9.2). **Tolerance** is physical habituation to a drug so that with frequent usage, higher doses are needed to attain similar effects. People who are dependent on substances frequently show characteristic withdrawal symptoms—referred to as a **withdrawal syndrome** or **abstinence syndrome**—when the degree of usage suddenly drops off. Psychoactive substances that are associated with withdrawal syndromes include alcohol, opiates, barbiturates, and antianxiety agents (minor tranquilizers), and yes, caffeine. Caffeine, the psychoactive substance found in coffee, tea, and many kinds of chocolate and soda, is apparently connected with a characteristic withdrawal syndrome, as shown in a

Table 9.2 Diagnostic Features of Substance Dependence

Substance dependence is defined as a maladaptive pattern of use that results in "significant impairment or distress," as typified by the following features occurring within the same year:

(1) Tolerance for the substance, as shown by either
   (a) the need for increased amounts of the substance to achieve the desired effect or intoxication, or
   (b) marked reduction in the effects of continuing to ingest the same amounts.

(2) Withdrawal symptoms, as shown by either
   (a) the withdrawal syndrome that is considered characteristic for the substance, or
   (b) the taking of the same substance (or a closely related substance, as when methadone is substituted for heroin) to relieve or to prevent withdrawal symptoms.

(3) Taking larger amounts of the substance, or for longer periods of time than the individual intended (e.g., person had desired to take only one drink, but after taking the first, continues drinking until severely intoxicated).

(4) Persistent desire to cut down or control intake of substance, or lack of success in trying to exercise self-control.

(5) Spending a good deal of time in activities directed toward obtaining the substance (for example, visiting several physicians to obtain prescriptions or engaging in theft), in actually ingesting the substance, or in recovering from its use. In severe cases, the individual's daily life revolves around substance use.

(6) The individual has reduced or given up important social, occupational, or recreational activities due to substance use (e.g., person withdraws from family events in order to indulge in drug use).

(7) Substance abuse is continued despite evidence of persistent or recurrent psychological, social, or physical problems either caused or exacerbated by its use (e.g., repeated arrests for driving while intoxicated).

NOTE: Not all of these features need be present for a diagnosis to be made.

Source: DSM-IV Draft Criteria (American Psychiatric Association, 1993), p. H: 1.

The withdrawal syndrome for alcohol may include such features as dryness in the mouth, nausea or vomiting, weakness, **tachycardia**, anxiety and depression, headaches, insomnia, elevated blood pressure, and fleeting **hallucinations**. In some cases of chronic alcoholism, withdrawal produces a state of **delirium tremens**, or DTs. The DTs are usually limited to chronic alcoholics who dramatically lower their intake of alcohol after many years of heavy drinking. The DTs involve intense autonomic hyperactivity (profuse sweating and tachycardia) and **delirium**—a state of mental confusion characterized by incoherent speech, **disorientation**, and extreme restlessness. Terrifying hallucinations—frequently of creepy crawling animals—may also be present.

People who experience a withdrawal syndrome often return to using the substance to relieve it. Drugs associated with substance abuse and/or dependence disorders include alcohol, opioids, stimulants such as amphetamines or cocaine, sedatives or barbiturates, prescription tranquilizers, and various psychedelic or hallucinogenic drugs such as LSD, PCP, and marijuana. Nicotine ingestion through smoking or chewing tobacco may lead to substance dependence. It is not associated with substance abuse alone because it is virtually unknown for someone to abuse nicotine without having been dependent on it. Despite the fact that the DSM considers substance abuse and dependence to be distinct diagnostic categories, the borderline between the two is not always clear (Helzer & Schuckit, 1990).

Another physiological effect of psychoactive substances is **intoxication**—also referred to as drunkenness or being high. Intoxication largely reflects the chemical actions of the psychoactive substances. The pattern of change depends on which drug is ingested, the dose, the user's biological reactivity (Erwin et al., 1984), and—to some degree—the user's expectations (Brown et al., 1980, 1985; Christiansen et al., 1982). Signs of intoxication often include confusion, belligerence, impaired judgment, inattention, and impaired motor and spatial skills. Extreme intoxication by substances such as alcohol, cocaine, opioids, and phencyclidine (PCP) can result in death, either because of the substance's biochemical effects or because of behavior patterns—such as suicide—that are connected with psychological pain or impaired judgment brought on by use of the drug. Psychoactive substances that can cause intoxication include alcohol, opioids, barbiturates, antianxiety agents (minor tranquilizers), cocaine, caffeine, and hallucinogens (such as marijuana, LSD, and phencyclidine [PCP]).

Many people abuse more than one psychoactive substance and are considered polydrug abusers.

double-blind study of 62 adults who drank about 2.5 cups of coffee per day. The subjects were switched to pills that contained either caffeine or a placebo. Coffee drinkers who took the placebo rather than caffeine were more likely to report such withdrawal symptoms as depression, anxiety, fatigue, and headache (Silverman et al., 1992).

Heroin abusers, for example, may also abuse alcohol, cocaine, stimulants, or other drugs—simultaneously or successively. Polydrug abusers encounter special problems. Ingestion of multiple drugs increases the potential for harmful overdoses, and "successful" treatment of one form of abuse may not affect, or may even exacerbate, abuse of other drugs. Some persons dependent on heroin, for example, are maintained on methadone, a synthetic narcotic that blocks the craving for heroin but does not produce a "high." In order to get high, some of them turn to cocaine.

Psychological Versus Physiological Dependence

The DSM uses the terms *substance abuse* and *substance dependence* to classify people whose usage of these substances impairs their functioning. The DSM does not label people with such disorders as being addicted to the substances. Yet the concept of addiction is widespread among professionals and laypeople alike. But what is meant by addiction?

Going without. . . Physiological dependence on a substance means that one's body has changed as a result of regular usage, as shown by the development of tolerance for the substance, by the development of a characteristic cluster of withdrawal symptoms (an abstinence syndrome), or both. This substance abuser is undergoing severe withdrawal symptoms.

People define addiction in different ways. We may define **addiction** as the habitual use of a drug that is accompanied by evidence of physiological dependence. **Physiological dependence** means that one's body has changed as a result of regular usage of a substance, as shown by the development of tolerance for the substance, by a withdrawal syndrome, or both. By contrast, **psychological dependence** involves impaired control over the use of a drug without the physiological signs of dependence.

Psychological dependence may occur in the absence of physiological dependence. People can find it difficult to control use of marijuana even though they do not develop tolerance or show a withdrawal syndrome when they stop using it. Some drugs are associated with psychological dependence but have not been conclusively shown to produce physiological dependence. These include PCP and cannabis (marijuana).

A person can also become physiologically dependent on a substance yet not become psychologically dependent. For example, people recuperating from surgery are often given narcotics derived from opium as painkillers. These patients may develop tolerance for the drugs and show withdrawal symptoms when they stop using them, yet not show evidence of habitual use or lack of control over them.

In recent years, the concept of addiction has also extended beyond the abuse of chemical substances to apply to many habitual forms of maladaptive behavior, such as pathological gambling. In the vernacular, we hear of people being addicted to love and freedom, but these do not involve physiological dependence. We limit the term *addiction* to habitual use of substances that produce physiological dependence.

Pathways to Drug Dependence

Although the progression to substance dependence varies, Weiss and Mirin (1987) suggest that there are common pathways, as outlined in a number of stages.

1. *Experimentation.* During the stage of experimentation, or occasional use, the drug temporarily makes users feel good, even euphoric. Users feel in control and believe that they can stop at any time.

2. *Routine use.* During the next stage, a period of routine use, people begin to structure their lives around the pursuit and use of drugs. Denial plays a major role at this stage, as users mask the negative consequences of their behavior to themselves and others. Values change. What had formerly been important, such as family and work, come to matter less than the drugs.

The following clinical interview illustrates how denial can mask reality. The drug user, a 48-year-old executive, was brought for a consultation by his wife. She complained that his once successful business was jeopardized by his erratic behavior, that he was grouchy and moody, and that he had spent $7,000 in the previous month on cocaine.

CLINICIAN: Have you missed many days at work recently?

EXECUTIVE: Yes, but I can afford to, since I own the business. Nobody checks up on me.

CLINICIAN: It sounds like that's precisely the problem. When you don't go to work, the company stays open, but it doesn't do very well.

EXECUTIVE: My employees are well trained. They can run the company without me.

CLINICIAN: But that's not happening.

EXECUTIVE: Then there's something wrong with them. I'll have to look into it.

CLINICIAN: It sounds as if there's something wrong with you, but you don't want to look into it.

EXECUTIVE: Now you're on my case. I don't know why you listen to everything my wife says.

CLINICIAN: How many days of work did you miss in the last two months?

EXECUTIVE: A couple.

CLINICIAN: Are you saying that you missed only two days of work?

EXECUTIVE: Maybe a few.

CLINICIAN: Only three or four days?

EXECUTIVE: Maybe a little more.

CLINICIAN: Ten? Fifteen?

EXECUTIVE: Fifteen.

CLINICIAN: All because of cocaine?

EXECUTIVE: No.

CLINICIAN: How many were because of cocaine?

EXECUTIVE: Less than fifteen.

CLINICIAN: Fourteen? Thirteen?

EXECUTIVE: Maybe thirteen.

CLINICIAN: So you missed thirteen days of work in the last two months because of cocaine. That's almost two days a week.

EXECUTIVE: That sounds like a lot but it's no big deal. Like I say, the company can run itself.

CLINICIAN: How long have you been using cocaine?

EXECUTIVE: About three years.

CLINICIAN: Did you ever use drugs or alcohol before that in any kind of quantity?

EXECUTIVE: No.

CLINICIAN: Then let's think back five years. Five years ago, if you had imagined yourself missing over a third of your workdays because of a drug, and if you had imagined yourself spending the equivalent of $84,000 a year on that same drug, and if you saw your once-successful business collapsing all around you, wouldn't you have thought that that was indicative of a pretty serious problem?

EXECUTIVE: Yes, I would have.

CLINICIAN: So what's different now?

EXECUTIVE: I guess I just don't want to think about it.

Source: Weiss, R. D., & Mirin, S. M. (1987). Cocaine. American Psychiatric Press, Inc.

As routine drug use continues, problems mount. Users devote more of their resources to their drugs. Family bank accounts are ravaged, "temporary" loans are sought from friends and family for trumped-up reasons, family heirlooms and jewelry are sold to pawnbrokers for a fraction of their value. Lying and manipulation become a way of life to cover up the drug use. The husband sells the TV set to a pawnbroker and forces the front door open to make it look like a burglary. The wife claims to have been robbed at knifepoint to explain the disappearance of a gold chain or engagement ring. Family relationships become strained as the mask of denial shatters and the consequences of drug abuse become apparent: days lost from work, unexplained absences from home, rapid mood shifts, depletion of family finances, failure to pay bills, stealing from family members, and missing family gatherings or children's birthday parties.

3. *Addiction or dependency.* Routine use becomes addiction or dependency when users feel powerless to resist drugs, either because they want to experience their effects or to avoid the consequences of withdrawal. Little or nothing else matters at this stage, as seen in the case of Eugene, a 41-year-old architect, who related the following conversation with his wife:

She had just caught me with cocaine again after I had managed to convince her that I hadn't used in over a month. Of course I had been tooting (snorting) almost every day, but I had managed to cover my tracks a little better than usual. So she said to me that I was going to have to make a choice—either cocaine or her. Before she finished the sentence, I knew what was coming, so I told her to think carefully about what she was going to say. It was clear to me that there wasn't a choice. I love my wife, but I'm not going to choose *anything* over cocaine. It's sick, but that's what things have come to. Nothing and nobody comes before my coke. (Weiss & Mirin, 1987, p. 55)

MULTICULTURAL PERSPECTIVES

Alcohol Abuse and Ethnic Minorities

Native Americans and Irish Americans have the highest U.S. incidences of alcoholism (Lex, 1987; Moncher et al., 1990). Jewish Americans have relatively low incidences of alcoholism, perhaps because Jews tend to expose children to the ritual use of wine in childhood within a religious context and impose strong cultural restraints on excessive and underage drinking.

Asian-Americans tend to drink less heavily than most other Americans, and possibly for biological reasons. Asians are more likely than African, Hispanic, and non-Hispanic white Americans to show a flushing response to alcohol. Approximately 30 to 50% of Asians show this response, which involves perceptible redness and feelings of warmth on the face, and, at higher doses, nausea, rapid heart rate, dizziness, and headaches (Ellickson et al., 1992; Newlin, 1989). Flushing may help curb excessive alcohol intake and reduce the risk of alcoholism among Asian Americans.

Researchers find, for instance, that Asians (Koreans, Taiwanese, and Hawaiian Asians) who show a more marked flushing response tend to consume less alcohol than those who show less flushing (Park et al., 1984).

Alcohol abuse appears to be taking the heaviest toll on African Americans and Native Americans (Rogan, 1986). The prevalence of **cirrhosis of the liver** (a liver disease linked to chronic alcohol abuse) among African Americans is nearly twice that among white Americans. Alcohol is implicated in almost half of homicides that involve African Americans (Williams, M., 1985). Yet Native Americans are the American ethnic group at greatest risk of incurring alcohol-related diabetes, fetal abnormalities, cirrhosis of the liver, and accident fatalities (Moncher et al., 1990). Native Americans suffer more than four times the overall U.S. death rate due to cirrhosis of the liver (Beauvais & LaBoueff, 1985). One death in four among Native American women is caused by alcohol-related cirrhosis of the liver. This figure is 37 times higher than the rate among

Alcohol and ethnic diversity. Alcohol abuse appears to be taking its heaviest toll on African Americans and Native Americans. For example, the prevalence of cirrhosis of the liver is nearly twice as high among African Americans as among white Americans. Jewish Americans have relatively low incidences of alcoholism, perhaps because they tend to expose children to the ritual use of wine in childhood and impose strong cultural restraints on excessive drinking. Asian Americans tend to drink less heavily than most other Americans, possibly because they have less biological tolerance of alcohol, as shown by a flushing response to alcohol.

white women (Moss et al., 1985). The prevalence of fetal alcohol syndrome (FAS) has been reported as more than 10 per 1,000 live births among some Native American tribes. This incidence is more than three times the overall U.S. incidence of FAS.

Many writers (e.g., Berlin, 1987) see the prevalence of alcoholism among Native Americans as a consequence of the forced attempt by Euro-American society to eradicate tribal language and culture, leading to a loss of cultural identity that sets the stage for alcoholism, drug abuse, and depression. Kahn (1982) explains the greater incidence of psychopathology among Native Americans in terms of the disruption in traditional culture caused by the appropriation of their lands by European powers and the attempts to sever them from their cultural traditions while denying them full access to the dominant Western culture. Native peoples have since lived in severe cultural and social disorganization that has resulted in high rates of psychopathology and substance abuse. Beset by such problems, Native American adults are prone to child abuse and neglect. Abuse and neglect contribute to feelings of hopelessness and depression among adolescents, who then seek to escape their feelings through alcohol and other drugs (Berlin, 1987).

Research into the acculturation hypothesis suggests that alcohol and drug abuse is greatest among Native American youths who identify least closely with traditional Native American values (that is, those who are more acculturated to the larger U.S. society). Next in level of use, however, came youth who were most closely identified with traditional Native American values. Bicultural youth, consisting of those who felt comfortable within Native American culture and the larger culture, showed the lowest abuse of alcohol and other drugs. These findings would suggest that the best adjustment (meaning the lowest levels of culture-related stress) is found among youth who have adapted to both cultures. Other factors, such as the poverty faced by many Native Americans who live on reservations, may also contribute to stress and alcohol and drug abuse.

In recent years, some Native American tribes have attempted to deal with these problems by emphasizing a return to traditional values and the development of industry to serve as sources of employment for Native American youth. Several communities have also developed specialized programs to teach young people parenting skills. They also emphasize technical and scientific training to enable young people to bring new technology to the reservation and provide a new brand of tribal leadership. As Berlin notes, being a scientist does not mean "losing respect for tradition, for ceremony and ritual, and for the traditional healers and tribal leaders" (p. 304).

■ **GATEWAY DRUGS** Alcohol and cigarettes appear to serve as *gateway drugs* to the initiation of hard drug use among adolescents (Ellickson et al., 1992). Yet use of alcohol among adolescents is so pervasive that it alone reveals little about the potential for hard drug use. Virtually all 10th graders in a sample of 4,145 West Coast adolescents had used alcohol at least once. But regular (weekly) use of alcohol indicates an increased risk of progression to hard drug use for African-American, non-Hispanic white American, and Hispanic-American adolescents. Asian-American adolescents tend to follow a somewhat different sequence: Use of hard drugs, for them, precedes increased use of alcohol. Asians tend to be more sensitive to the effects of alcohol than other ethnic groups (they "flush" more readily in response to alcohol), so it may be that for Asian Americans, heavy drinking is connected with a prior commitment to serious drug use.

Regular (weekly) cigarette smoking was also a predictor of future hard drug use for non-Hispanic white youths and for current hard drug use for Hispanic-American, African-American, and Asian-American youths. Why is cigarette smoking a marker of future hard drug use, at least among white youths? One reason may be that knowledge about the harmfulness of cigarettes is now widespread (Johnston et al., 1991), so that youthful cigarette smokers are risk takers, and risk takers may be more prone to abuse illicit drugs. Another may be that the majority of smokers' peers now disapprove of smoking—even among high school seniors (Johnston et al., 1991)—so that smoking among young people is becoming a progressively more "deviant" activity.

DEPRESSANTS

Depressants generally act by curbing activity of the central nervous system. All depressants reduce feelings of tension and anxiety and retard motor reactivity and cognitive processes. In high doses, depressants arrest vital functions and can cause death. Alcohol in large quantities usually kills by depressing respiration (breathing). There are other effects specific to each kind of depressant, however, such as providing a "rush" of pleasure. Barbiturates, methaqualone, other kinds of tranquilizers, and opioids are also depressants.

Alcohol

Perhaps no psychoactive substance has been so many things to so many people as alcohol, a drug that is classified as a **depressant**. Alcohol, which is found in such beverages as beer, wine, and so-called hard liquors or spirits such as scotch and rye, is used in many ways. It is our mealtime relaxant, our party social facilitator, our bedtime sedative. We observe holy days, laud our achievements, and express joyful wishes with alcohol. Adolescents assert their maturity with alcohol. The elderly use it to quicken circulation in peripheral parts of the body. Pediatricians have swabbed the painful gums of teething babies with alcohol. Alcohol even deals the deathblow to germs on surface wounds.

Alcohol is the most widely abused substance in the United States. Perhaps 18 million Americans have serious drinking problems (Desmond, 1987). By contrast, between 2 and 5 million people use cocaine regularly (Altman, 1988; Kolata, 1989a). Half a million use heroin regularly, and one-third to one-half million abuse sedatives.

 Alcohol, not cocaine, is the most widely abused substance in the United States.

It has been estimated that the personal and social costs of alcoholism exceed those of all illicit drugs combined. The economic costs of alcoholism—based on days lost from work, health problems associated with alcoholism, and motor vehicle accidents—are staggering (National Council on Alcoholism, 1986). Alcohol abuse is connected with lower productivity, loss of jobs, and downward movement in socioeconomic status (Baum-Baicker, 1984; Mider, 1984; Vaillant & Milofsky, 1982). Perhaps half the homeless population in the country consists of alcoholics (Desmond, 1987). Alcohol is also implicated in some 30% of reported suicides.

Alcohol, not cocaine or other drugs, is the drug of choice among young people today (Johnston et al., 1992). Although the recreational use of drugs has declined among young people since the early 1980s, alcohol abuse has declined more slowly and remains the most persistent drug problem among young peo-

ple. Drinking alcohol by people under the age of 21 is prohibited by law in all states, yet 8 million of the nation's 21 million 7th through 12th graders drink weekly, and nearly half a million report having five or more drinks at a sitting within the past 2 weeks (Johnston et al., 1992). Although use of cocaine and marijuana is becoming less socially acceptable, alcohol use by teens remains socially acceptable among peers (Johnston et al., 1991).

Table 9.3 describes alcohol use by college students in a recent year. More than 90% of students have tried alcohol, and nearly 9 out of 10 (88.3%) have used it in the past year. About 3 students in 4 (74.7%) report taking at least one drink in the last 30 days. Not many (about 4%) have had a drink every day for the past month, but more than 2 out of 5 (42.8%) report guzzling five or more drinks in a row on at least one occasion during the past 2 weeks. Such episodes of heavy drinking are connected with dangerous behavior, such as driving while intoxicated and unwise sexual activity. Consider a survey of 1,100 undergraduates taken at the University of Virginia (Grossman, 1991). Of those who drank at least five alcoholic beverages in a row on various occasions, *more than half* reported that under the influence of alcohol, they had engaged in sexual activity with someone they would not ordinarily have become involved with.

There is no universally accepted definition of **alcoholism**. The DSM does not explicitly use the term *alcoholism* for classification. Rather, the DSM classifies behavioral problems relating to alcohol and other drugs in terms of patterns of abuse and dependence. These are three of the principal patterns of alcohol abuse or dependence:

1. Regular daily drinking of large amounts of alcohol
2. Regular heavy drinking on weekends only
3. Long periods of abstention alternating with periods of binge drinking that persist for weeks or months

Table 9.3 Alcohol Use Among College Students	
Percentage who have used alcohol in their lifetime	93.6%
Percentage who have used alcohol within the past year	88.3
Percentage who have used alcohol within the past 30 days	74.7
Percentage who have used alcohol daily within the past 30 days	4.1
Percentage who had five or more drinks in a row during the last 2 weeks	42.8

Source: Johnston, L. D., Bachman, J. G., & O'Malley, P. M. (1992, January 25).

Monitoring the future: A continuing study of the lifestyles and values of youth. The University of Michigan News and Information Services: Ann Arbor, MI.

QUESTIONNAIRE

How Do You Know If You Are Hooked?

Are you dependent on alcohol? If you shake and shiver and undergo the tortures of the darned (Our editor insisted on changing this word to maintain the decorum of a textbook) when you go without a drink for a while, the answer is clear enough. Sometimes the clues are more subtle, however.

The following items, adapted from the National Council on Alcoholism's self-test, can shed some light on the question. Simply place a check mark in the yes or no column for each item. Then check the key at the end of the chapter.

		YES	NO
1.	Do you sometimes go on drinking binges?	—	—
2.	Do you tend to keep away from your family or friends when you are drinking?	—	—
3.	Do you become irritated when your family or friends talk about your drinking?	—	—
4.	Do you feel guilty now and then about your drinking?	—	—
5.	Do you often regret the things you have said or done when you have been drinking?	—	—
6.	Do you find that you fail to keep the promises you make about controlling or cutting down on your drinking?	—	—
7.	Do you eat irregularly or not at all when you are drinking?	—	—
8.	Do you feel low after drinking?	—	—
9.	Do you sometimes miss work or appointments because of drinking?	—	—
10.	Do you use more and more to get drunk or high?	—	—

Source: Adapted from Newsweek, *February 20, 1989, p. 52.*

No one of these patterns is exclusively connected with alcoholism. Yet researchers have noted some gender differences in drinking patterns among alcoholics. Male alcoholics tend to alternate between periods of heavy drinking and periods of abstinence (Hill, 1980). Women alcoholics—apparently more stable than their male counterparts—are more likely to drink steadily and are less likely to binge (Hill, 1980).

Estimates of the past-year and lifetime prevalences of alcohol and drug abuse or dependence across the five communities surveyed by the Epidemiologic Catchment Area (ECA) Study are presented in Table 9.4. Overall, about 1 in 4 men (23.8%), as compared to about 1 woman in 20 (4.6%), could be classified as suffering from alcoholism (defined in terms of alcohol abuse and/or dependence) during their lifetimes. About half as many of each gender could be classified as showing evidence of alcoholism during the past year. Lifetime prevalences of drug abuse or dependence are less common than alcoholism among men and among minority women, but curiously not among non-Hispanic white women. The ECA survey found that 7.7% of the men and 4.8% of the women met criteria for drug abuse or dependence during their lifetimes, with 4.1% of the men and 1.4% of women

showing active drug abuse or dependence disorders during the past year (see Table 9.4).

In any event, alcohol consumption in the United States apparently peaked in 1981. Perhaps because of increased public attention to alcoholism, there was a decline of about 5% in consumption rates during the early to mid-1980s (Desmond, 1987).

■ **RISK FACTORS FOR ALCOHOLISM** Investigators have identified a number of factors that place people at increased risk for developing alcoholism and alcohol-related problems. These include the following:

1. *Gender.* Men are about five times more likely than women to be diagnosed as abusive of alcohol or dependent on alcohol (see Table 9.4) (Goleman, 1992). One possible reason for this gender difference is sociocultural; perhaps tighter social constraints are placed on women. Yet it may also be that alcohol hits women harder, and not only because women usually weigh less than men. Alcohol, for example, seems to "go to women's heads" more rapidly than men's. Women are apparently more affected than men by alcohol because they have less of an enzyme that metabolizes alcohol in the stomach than men do (Lieber, 1990). Alcohol then reaches women's circu-

Table 9.4 Past Year and Lifetime Prevalence of Alcohol and Drug Abuse or Dependence (in Percentages)

	Alcohol Abuse and/or Dependence		Drug Abuse/Dependence	
	During Past Year	Lifetime	During Past Year	Lifetime
Total	6.8%	13.8%	2.7%	6.2%
Ethnicity				
Non-Hispanic white	6.7	13.6	2.7	6.3
African American	6.6	13.8	2.7	5.5
Hispanic American	9.1	16.7	2.0	4.4
Men	11.9	23.8	4.1	7.7
Non-Hispanic white	11.7	23.4	4.1	7.8
African American	11.5	23.7	3.1	7.2
Hispanic American	16.0	30.0	3.3	6.3
Women	2.2	4.6	1.4	4.8
Non-Hispanic white	2.1	4.5	1.3	5.0
African American	2.5	5.5	2.3	4.0
Hispanic American	2.5	3.8	0.7	2.5

Sources: Adapted from Helzer et al., 1991; Anthony and Helzer, 1991.

latory systems and brains relatively intact. It is almost as if women were injecting alcohol intravenously (Lieber, 1990). Not a substance to be trifled with.

 It does seem that alcohol goes to women's heads more rapidly than to men's. This is apparently because women metabolize less alcohol in the stomach than men do.

Researchers speculate that alcoholism may become more prevalent among women in the future (Helzer, 1987; Helzer et al., 1991; Kendler, 1992)—in part because social drinking has become more acceptable for women and because the gap between men and women in the prevalences of alcoholism is the narrowest in the youngest age group.

2. *Age.* The age of onset of alcoholism among men is generally in the late teens or the 20s. More than half of the cases among men develop before age 30 (Helzer et al., 1991). The problem rarely develops in men after age 45. Alcoholism in women also tends to begin early, although typically at a somewhat later age than men.

3. *Social class.* Alcoholism is found at all socioeconomic levels. Persons of low socioeconomic status are most likely to suffer the social and health correlates of excessive drinking, such as family instability, incarceration, and disease.

4. *Ethnic factors.* Ethnic factors are connected with

alcohol abuse, as noted in the feature "Alcohol Abuse and Ethnic Minorities." Native Americans and Irish Americans have the highest U.S. incidences of alcoholism, whereas Jewish Americans have relatively low incidences of alcoholism. The ECA study of five U.S. communities found the rates of alcoholism among adults to be about equal across African-American, non-Hispanic-white-American, and Hispanic-American groups (see Table 9.4) (Helzer et al., 1991). Nor did these ethnic groups vary greatly in the prevalence of drug abuse and dependence disorders among adults (Anthony & Helzer, 1991). However, Asian Americans (a group not studied in the ECA survey) tend to drink less heavily than most other Americans, possibly because they are more likely than African, Hispanic, and non-Hispanic white Americans to show a flushing response to alcohol. Alcohol, moreover, appears to be taking the heaviest toll on the health of African and Native Americans.

5. *Antisocial personality disorder.* Antisocial behavior in adolescence or adulthood poses a risk for alcoholism among adults (Helzer, 1987). The features of adolescent antisocial behavior that predict adult alcoholism include independence, rebelliousness, rejection of social rules and legal codes, poor impulse control, low tolerance for frustration, and lax moral standards (Graham & Strenger, 1988; Nathan, 1988; Vaillant, 1983). On the other hand, many alcoholics showed no antisocial tendencies in adolescence, and many antisocial adolescents do not become alcohol or drug abusers as adults (Nathan, 1988).

6. *Alcoholism in the family.* The best predictor of

problem drinking in adulthood appears to be a family history of alcohol abuse (Goodwin, 1985; Tarter & Edwards, 1986). Family members who drink may act as models ("set a poor example"). Moreover, the biological relatives of alcoholics may inherit predispositions that favor drinking, as we see in the section on theoretical perspectives.

■ ALCOHOLISM: DISEASE, MORAL DEFECT, OR BEHAVIOR PATTERN?

According to the medical perspective, substance abuse and dependence are disease processes. E. M. Jellinek (1960) set forth the axioms of this model. To Jellinek, alcoholism was a permanent, irreversible condition. Once alcoholics drink, he contended, alcohol's biochemical effects on the brain create an irresistible physical craving for more. Jellinek's ideas have contributed to the dissemination of the view that can be expressed "Once an alcoholic, always an alcoholic." Alcoholics Anonymous (AA), which has adopted Jellinek's concepts, views alcoholics as either drinking or "recovering." In other words, there is no such thing as a cured alcoholic—only an alcoholic who, through abstention, is in the process of recovering. Jellinek's concepts have also supported the idea that "just one drink" will cause an alcoholic to "fall off the wagon." In this view, the sole path to recovery for the alcoholic is abstinence.

Although the disease model has achieved prominence and wide public acceptance, the nature of alcoholism continues to be debated. For most of history, immoderate drinking was seen as a moral defect. Alcoholism was only first labeled a disease by the American Medical Association in 1966 (Desmond, 1987). Since that time, the campaign to instill this view has been so pervasive that most Americans now endorse this view (Desmond, 1987).

Yet some investigators regard alcoholism not as a disease in the medical sense of the term, but as a label to describe a harmful pattern of alcohol ingestion and related behaviors (Rohan, 1982). To them, for example, the "just-one-drink" hypothesis is not a biochemical inevitability. It is, instead, a common self-fulfilling prophecy, as we see later in the chapter.

■ PSYCHOLOGICAL EFFECTS OF ALCOHOL

The effects of drugs vary from person to person (Erwin et al., 1984). By and large they reflect the interaction of (1) the physiological effects of the substances and (2) our interpretations of those effects. What do most people expect from alcohol? Adolescent and adult samples generally report beliefs that alcohol reduces tension, diverts people from worrying, and enhances pleasurable experiences and social ability (Brown et al., 1980, 1985; Christiansen et al.,

1982; Rohsenow, 1983). These are stereotypical expectations. What *does* alcohol actually do?

For one thing, people may do many things when drinking that they would not do when sober (Lang et al., 1980; Lansky & Wilson, 1981), such as lingering longer over pornographic pictures as researchers monitor their behavior. One potential reason for the "liberating" effects of alcohol is that it impairs the information processing that usually inhibits impulses (Hull et al., 1983; Steele & Southwick, 1985). That is, when drunk, people may be less capable of envisioning the repercussions of misbehavior and less likely to dwell on social and personal standards of conduct. Perhaps the elation and euphoria brought on by alcohol help wash away misgivings. Remember, too, that alcohol is associated with a liberated social role in our culture. That is, it provides an external excuse for questionable behavior. People, after all, can claim, "It was the alcohol, not me."

Alcohol, similarly, has been connected with aggressive behavior. Department of Justice surveys have estimated that as many as one-third of prison inmates across the country had been drinking heavily immediately preceding the commission of their crimes (Desmond, 1987). Carefully controlled experiments suggest, however, that alcohol does not directly cause aggression or other crimes any more than it increases sexual response (Lang et al., 1975; Marlatt, 1981). Yet people may behave aggressively or sexually when drinking because of their expectations about the effects of alcohol, not because of its biochemical properties.

Biochemically speaking, the primary effect of alcohol is akin to that of the benzodiazepines, a class of minor tranquilizers that includes diazepam (trade name Valium) and chlordiazepoxide (Librium). Alcohol is our chief over-the-counter tranquilizer. Like the benzodiazepines, alcohol apparently heightens the sensitivity of **GABA** receptor sites (Suzdak et al., 1986). Because GABA is an inhibitory neurotransmitter, increasing the action of GABA serves to diminish overall nervous system activity.

As people drink, their senses become clouded, and balance and coordination suffer. Still higher doses act on the medulla and spinal cord, which regulate involuntary vital functions such as heart rate, respiration rate, and body temperature (Niaura et al., 1988). The slowing of these functions largely accounts for alcohol's classification as a depressant.

One of the lures of alcohol is that it induces short-term feelings of euphoria and elation that can drown self-doubts and self-criticism. Frequent use over a year or more may deepen feelings of depression, however (Aneshensel & Huba, 1983). Alcohol calms people and dulls minor aches and pains. As an intoxicant, alcohol also impairs intellectual functioning, interferes with judgment, hampers coordination, and slurs the speech. Alcohol is implicated in nearly 50% of the nation's fatal auto accidents, about 25% of fatal falls, and 30 to 50% of fatal fires and drownings (see Figure 9.1; *Alcohol and Health*, 1987; Desmond, 1987).

■ **PHYSICAL HEALTH AND ALCOHOL** Alcohol is fattening, yet habitual drinkers may be malnourished. Although it is high in calories, alcohol lacks vital nutrients like vitamins and proteins. Alcohol also impedes the body's absorption of various vitamins, including thiamine, or vitamin B_1. Chronic drinking can thus result in disorders that have been related to protein and vitamin deficiencies, including cirrhosis of the liver (linked to protein deficiency) and **alcohol amnestic disorder** (connected with vitamin B_1 deficiency) (Eckhardt et al., 1981). In cirrhosis of the liver, which causes about 14,000 annual deaths (Desmond, 1987), connective fibers supplant active liver cells, obstructing circulation of the blood. Alcohol amnestic disorder (also known as Korsakoff's syndrome) is an organic mental disorder that is characterized by glaring confusion and disorientation, memory loss for recent events, and abnormalities in eye movements.

When alcohol is metabolized, there are increases in levels of lactic and uric acids. Uric acid can give rise to gout. Chronic drinking is also connected with coronary heart disease and elevated blood pressure (Eckhardt et al., 1981). Heavy alcohol abuse is also connected with cancers of the pancreas (Heuch et al., 1983) and stomach (Popham et al., 1984), although light to moderate drinking is not known to increase the risk of stomach cancer.

Mothers who drink during pregnancy place their fetuses at risk for infant mortality, birth defects, central nervous system dysfunctions (Streissguth et al., 1983), and academic problems later on (Shaywitz et al., 1980). Many children whose mothers drink during pregnancy show **fetal alcohol syndrome** (FAS), a syndrome characterized by facial features such as a flattened nose, widely spaced eyes, and underdeveloped upper jaw, and mental retardation. FAS has been found among children of mothers who drink as little as 2 ounces of alcohol a day during the first trimester (Astley et al., 1992). The safest course for women who know or suspect they are pregnant is not to drink. Period.

Alcohol also has effects on brain cells, can trigger bleeding, can cause deterioration of the heart muscle, depresses the functioning of the immune system, and causes hormonal changes that can put a damper on the sex drive in men and disrupt the menstrual cycles of women. Despite this list of adverse effects, there is some evidence that light drinking may be healthful. Longitudinal epidemiological stud-

Figure 9.1 Estimated percentages of deaths from various causes connected with use of alcohol.
Alcohol use is apparently involved in half of the U.S. deaths due to motor vehicle accidents and homicide.
Source: Adapted from Ravenholt (1984).

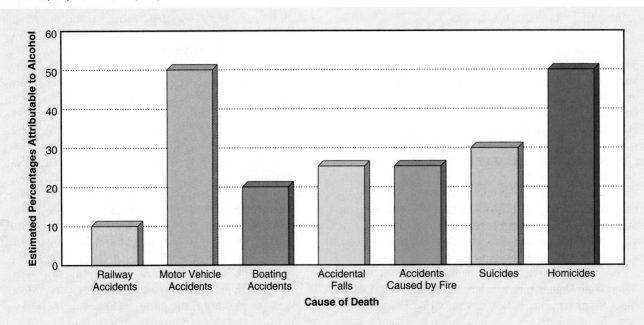

ies have observed residents of Hayward, California (Klatsky et al., 1981); Alameda County, California (Berkman et al., 1983); Framingham, Massachusetts (Friedman & Kimball, 1986); and Albany County, New York (Gordon & Doyle, 1987). They have generally shown that men who drink lightly to moderately incur fewer heart attacks and strokes and lower mortality rates than heavy drinkers *and* teetotalers. A nationwide study of 87,526 nurses found that women who imbibed 3 to 15 drinks a week had fewer strokes *caused by obstructed blood vessels in the brain* and fewer heart attacks than heavier drinkers and, again, teetotalers (Stampfer & Hennekens, 1988). However, the women were more prone toward the kind of stroke that is precipitated by excessive bleeding in the brain—a less common type of stroke.

Why may light drinking have health benefits? Some investigators (e.g., Stampfer & Hennekens, 1988) propose that light drinking elevates the amount of HDL (high-density lipoproteins, or "good cholesterol") in the blood. HDL, in turn, helps free blood vessels of blockage by LDL (low-density lipoproteins, or "bad cholesterol"). Yet the researchers who participated in the epidemiological studies do not recommend that teetotalers take up light drinking to reap its potential benefits. William Castelli, an investigator in the Framingham study, notes that people "can get the benefit [of light to moderate drinking] in other ways, such as by stopping smoking, lowering [their] cholesterol or . . . blood pressure, and [not] run the risk of becoming an alcoholic" (1988).

Sedatives and Anti-Anxiety Drugs

Barbiturates such as amobarbital, pentobarbital, phenobarbital, and secobarbital are depressants or **sedatives** with several medical uses, including alleviation of anxiety and tension, anesthetizing of pain, treatment of epilepsy and high blood pressure, and short-term treatment of insomnia. Barbiturates rapidly create physiological and psychological dependence. The multisite ECA study found that about 1% of the adult population met the criteria for a substance abuse or dependence disorder involving sedatives at some point in their lives (Anthony & Helzer, 1991).

In contrast to the profiles of young narcotics abusers, most barbiturate addicts are middle-aged people who used barbiturates initially to combat insomnia. As use persisted, however, tolerance built up so that increased doses became necessary and dependence ensued. In the process, many users

became physiologically dependent. Most physicians have grown concerned about barbiturate abuse and prefer, when prescribing drugs for relief of anxiety and tension, to prescribe anti-anxiety drugs (minor tranquilizers) such as Valium and Librium. However, it is now recognized that minor tranquilizers can also create physiological dependence. Moreover, their prolonged prescription still fails to help people alter the sources of stress in their lives.

Barbiturates are also popular street drugs because they are relaxing and produce a mild state of euphoria. High doses of barbiturates, like alcohol, produce drowsiness, slurred speech, motor impairment, irritability, and poor judgment. The effects of barbiturates last from 3 to 6 hours.

Physiologically dependent people need to be withdrawn carefully from barbiturates, under medical supervision. If they are withdrawn abruptly, they may have convulsions and die. Because of synergistic effects, a mixture of barbiturates and alcohol is about four times as powerful as either drug used by itself (Combs et al., 1980). A combination of barbiturates and alcohol is implicated in the deaths of the entertainers Marilyn Monroe and Judy Garland.

Opioids

Opioids are a group of **narcotics** derived from the opium poppy or synthetic compounds that are chemically similar. The ancient Sumerians gave this poppy its name. It means "plant of joy." The opioids include morphine, heroin, codeine, Demerol (a synthetic narcotic), and similar drugs whose major medical application is the relief of pain, or **analgesia**. According to the ECA study, 0.7% of the adult population (7 people in 1,000) currently has or has had a substance abuse or dependence disorder involving opiates (Anthony & Helzer, 1991).

Opioids appear to stimulate brain centers that regulate sensations of pleasure and pain (Goeders & Smith, 1984; Ling et al., 1984). Two revealing discoveries were made in the 1970s. One was that neurons in the brain had receptor sites into which opioids fit—like a key in a lock. The second was that people produce substances which are similar to opioids in chemical structure and dock at the same receptor sites (Goldstein, 1976). Some of these natural substances are labeled **endorphins**, which is short for "endogenous morphine"—that is, morphine coming from within. Endorphins apparently mediate the experience of pleasure and the control of pain.

■ **MORPHINE** Morphine—which receives its name from Morpheus, the Greek god of dreams—was introduced at about the time of the U.S. Civil War.

Morphine, one of the most powerful opium derivatives, was used liberally to deaden pain from wounds. Physiological dependence on morphine became known as the "soldier's disease." There was little stigma attached to dependence until morphine became a restricted substance.

■ HEROIN

Joletha Simmons is a 34-year-old heroin abuser. Flashbulbs pop as she blends heroin with water on a soda can, cooks the concoction with a flame, and sucks it into her syringe. Then, staring into a mirror, she balloons her cheek to make a vein rise in her neck and plunges the syringe in. She pauses to brush the tears from her eyes, then lowers her head, as if to pray, as the drug takes effect.

Adapted from *New York Times*, April 4, 1989, p. A26.

Photographs of Joletha appeared in the *Washington Post*. Normally fearing arrest, a person would not want evidence of his or her habit to appear in the papers. Joletha, however, took the risk because she wanted to kick her habit and hoped the publicity would gain her admission to a drug treatment program.

Shooting up. Many heroin abusers inject the substance directly into their veins. Heroin is a powerful depressant that provides a euphoric rush. Users often claim that heroin is so pleasurable that it obliterates any thought of food or sex. At the turn of the century, heroin was used to treat so many problems it was often referred to as G.O.M. ("God's own medicine").

Ironically, **heroin** was so named because, when it was derived, it was purported to make people feel "heroic." It was also hailed as the "hero" that would cure physiological dependence on morphine. Heroin was developed in 1875 during a search for a drug that would relieve pain as effectively as morphine, but without causing addiction. Chemist Heinrich Dreser transformed morphine into a new and stronger miracle drug, heroin, by means of a minor chemical change. He believed, erroneously, that heroin did not create physiological dependence.

 Heroin was in fact developed during a search for a drug that would relieve pain as effectively as morphine, but without causing physical addiction.

Heroin, like the other opioids, is a powerful depressant that can provide a euphoric rush. Users of heroin claim that it is so pleasurable it can eradicate any thought of food or sex. Soon after its initial appearance, heroin was used to treat so many problems that it became known as GOM ("God's own medicine").

Heroin is usually injected either directly beneath the skin (*skin popping*) or into a vein (*mainlining*). The positive effects are immediate. There is a powerful rush that lasts from 5 to 15 minutes and a state of satisfaction, euphoria, and well-being that lasts from 3 to 5 hours. In this state, all positive drives seem satisfied. All negative feelings of guilt, tension, and anxiety disappear. With prolonged usage, addiction can develop.

HIV—the virus that causes AIDS—can be transmitted by sharing contaminated hypodermic needles. Some heroin users have therefore turned from injecting heroin to inhaling the crystalline powder in much the same way that cocaine is inhaled (Treaster, 1991c). In some heroin treatment clinics in the New York metropolitan area, at least one-third of the addicts report they have been sniffing or snorting heroin to avoid becoming infected with HIV. Some heroin users have begun smoking heroin like crack.

The withdrawal syndrome associated with dependence on opioids can be severe. It begins within 4 to 6 hours of the last dose. Flulike symptoms progress in 3 to 5 days to rapid pulse, high blood pressure, cramps, tremors, hot and cold flashes, vomiting, insomnia, diarrhea, and—of course—craving for the drug. However, the withdrawal syndrome is variable. Although these symptoms can be uncomfortable, they are usually not devastating, especially when other drugs are prescribed to relieve them. Moreover, unlike withdrawal from barbiturates, the withdrawal syndrome rarely results in death. Many American soldiers who used heroin regularly in Vietnam are reported to have suspended usage with relatively little trouble when they returned to the United States (Bourne, 1974). Also, people given opioids in a hospital for analgesic purposes rarely become addicted.

Heroin is illegal. Because the penalties for possession or sale are high, it is also expensive. For this reason many physiologically dependent people support their habits through dealing (selling heroin), prostitution, or selling stolen goods. Heroin is a depressant, however, and its chemical effects do not directly stimulate criminal or aggressive behavior.

The numbers of new heroin users increased through 1975 but appear to have remained level since that time. However, authorities have noted increased hardcore use of heroin in recent years, apparently because of declining prices and increased potency (*More hardcore*, 1992).

STIMULANTS

Stimulants such as amphetamines and cocaine are psychoactive substances that increase the activity of the nervous system. Stimulants' other effects vary somewhat from drug to drug, and some seem to contribute to feelings of euphoria and self-confidence. Slightly less than 2% of the adult population surveyed in the ECA study had substance abuse or dependence disorders involving stimulants other than cocaine during their lifetimes (Anthony & Helzer, 1991). The prevalence of cocaine abuse was found to be 0.2% (2 people in 1,000).

Amphetamines and cocaine expedite the release of the neurotransmitters norepinephrine and dopamine and also inhibit their reuptake (their reabsorption by vesicles on presynaptic neurons). High levels of these neurotransmitters therefore remain available to the nervous system, causing continuous states of high arousal. Caffeine—the stimulant found in coffee, tea, many soft drinks, and chocolate—inhibits the reabsorption of these neurotransmitters by blocking the action of the enzymes that degrade them.

Amphetamines

The **amphetamines** are a class of stimulants that are derived from *alpha-methyl-beta-phenyl-ethyl-amine*, a colorless liquid consisting of carbon, hydrogen, and nitrogen. Amphetamines were initially used by sol-

diers during World War II to help them stay vigilant through the night. Truck drivers have used amphetamines to remain awake at the wheel. Many students have used amphetamines to help them "pull all-nighters." Amphetamines suppress the appetite and have been used widely by dieters to accelerate their metabolic rates and reduce pangs of hunger. They also enhance motor coordination and confidence, so athletes sometimes use them before meets and games.

Street names for stimulants include speed, uppers, bennies (for Benzedrine), and dexies (for Dexedrine). Amphetamines are used in high doses for their euphoric rush. Amphetamines are often taken in pill form, although some users inject liquid methamphetamine (Methedrine), the most potent form, directly into their veins. Some users inject methamphetamine for days on end to maintain an extended high. Eventually such highs come to an end. People who have been on extended highs sometimes "crash" and fall into a deep sleep or depression. Some people commit suicide on the way down.

Psychological dependence on amphetamines can develop quickly, especially among people who take them as a way of coping with depression. Tolerance also develops quickly, but it is unclear whether or not amphetamines cause physiological dependence in the form of a characteristic withdrawal syndrome. High doses can cause restlessness, irritability, hallucinations, paranoid delusions, loss of appetite, and insomnia. The hallucinations and delusions of the **amphetamine psychosis** mimic the features of paranoid schizophrenia, which has encouraged researchers to study the chemical changes induced by amphetamines as possible causes of schizophrenia.

Cocaine

Do you remember the Coca-Cola commercials proclaiming that "Coke adds life"? Because of its sugar and caffeine content, Coca-Cola should grant quite a boost. But "Coke"—Coca-Cola, that is—has not been "the real thing" since 1906. In that year the company withdrew **cocaine** from its secret formula. Coca-Cola was first brewed by a pharmacist, John Styth Pemberton, in 1886. Pemberton described his product as a "brain tonic and intellectual beverage," in part because of its cocaine content. Cocaine is a natural stimulant that is extracted from the leaves of the coca plant—the plant from which the soft drink obtained its name. Coca-Cola is still flavored with an extract from the coca plant, one that is not known to be psychoactive.

Ingestion of coca leaves has a long history among the peoples of the coca-growing regions of South America. The Inca Indians used coca to help them endure physical labor with little sleep or food (Weiss & Mirin, 1987). Europeans began to experiment with cocaine following the extraction of the drug from coca leaves in the mid-19th century. One of the prominent early advocates of cocaine, at least initially, was Sigmund Freud. Freud reported his personal experiences and those of others. As did the Incas, he found that cocaine enabled people to work longer without sleep or food. Freud also found that cocaine helped relieve pain and had positive psychoactive effects:

> The psychic effect of cocaine consists of exhilaration and lasting euphoria, which does not differ in any way from the normal euphoria of a healthy person. . . . One senses an increase of self-control and feels more vigorous and more capable of work. . . . Long lasting intensive mental or physical work can be performed without fatigue; it is as though the need for food and sleep, which otherwise makes itself felt peremptorily at certain times of the day, were completely banished. (Freud, "On Coca," 1884)

In addition to enhancing performance, cocaine heightens vigilance and bolsters confidence—properties that have made it popular among professional athletes.

Freud's recognition of cocaine's analgesic qualities blazed the path to its use as the first local anesthetic. Freud changed his views on cocaine when he learned that it was powerfully habit forming. Other notables of the late 19th and early 20th centuries who also endorsed cocaine included H. G. Wells, Thomas Edison, and Jules Verne, as well as kings, queens, and even two popes (Weiss & Mirin, 1987). Societal attitudes, like Freud's views, shifted in the early 20th century against cocaine use, based on increasing awareness of its habit-forming properties.

Cocaine's psychoactive effects may be due to its stimulation of the release of norepinephrine and dopamine and its blocking their reuptake or metabolic breakdown. These actions apparently increase neural activity in certain areas of the brain, especially in areas involved in regulating states of wakefulness, alertness, and arousal (Weiss & Mirin, 1987). Cocaine also induces pleasure, perhaps by stimulating brain systems that mediate pleasure. Dopamine may be involved in mediating this pleasure or reward mechanism. We know that laboratory rats will work for injections of cocaine by repetitively pressing a lever. They will continue to work for cocaine injections even if the neural pathways that use norepinephrine are destroyed. Their work effort plummets when the neural pathways for dopamine are destroyed. Perhaps cocaine and other drugs, particularly opioids, produce states of pleasure by activating the neurons that rely on dopamine for transmission of nerve signals (Weiss & Mirin, 1987). While it has long been believed that cocaine was not physically addicting, increasing evidence points to the addictive properties of the drug in

(A)

(B)

(C)

Some 19th-century users of cocaine. During the 19th century, many public figures experimented with cocaine as a means of bolstering their self-confidence and levels of energy. Among those who endorsed the use of a cocaine-laced tonic were authors H. G. Wells (*The Shape of Things to Come*) and Jules Verne (*20,000 Leagues Beneath the Sea*), and the inventor of the light bulb, the record player, and the motion picture—Thomas Edison. What famous psychological theorist used cocaine at about the same time? (Although Freud was initially a booster of cocaine, he changed his view of the drug when he discovered that it was habit forming.)

terms of producing a tolerance effect and an identifiable withdrawal syndrome, consisting of such symptoms as depression, reduced ability to experience pleasure, and intense cravings for the drug (Gawin et al., 1980; Gawin & Ellinwood, 1988).

Cocaine is brewed from coca leaves as a "tea," breathed in ("snorted") in powder form, and injected ("shot up") in liquid form. The rise in the use of **crack**, a hardened form of cocaine suitable for smoking that may contain more than 75% pure cocaine, has made cocaine—once the toy of the well-to-do—available to adolescents. Crack "rocks"—so called because they look like small white pebbles—are available in small ready-to-smoke amounts and considered to be the most habit-forming street drug available (Weiss & Mirin, 1987). Crack produces a prompt and potent rush that wears off in a few minutes. The rush from snorting is milder and takes a while to develop, but it tends to linger longer than the rush of crack.

Freebasing also intensifies the effects of cocaine. Cocaine in powder form is heated with ether, freeing the psychoactive chemical base of the drug, and then smoked. Ether, however, is highly flammable. Comedian Richard Pryor received extensive burns while reportedly freebasing cocaine.

The cocaine epidemic may have peaked in some respects (see Table 9.1). By 1990, as suggested by Fig-

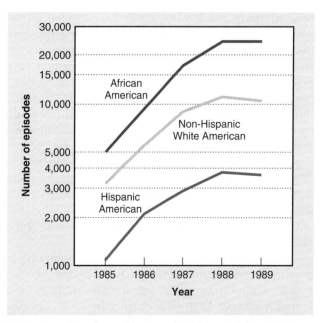

Figure 9.2 Cocaine-related emergency room episodes, according to race/ethnicity: selected emergency rooms in U.S. metropolitan areas, 1985–1989.
The numbers of cocaine-related hospital emergency room visits appeared to be topping out in the later 1980s.
Source: USDHHS Pub. No. (PHS) 91-1232, March 1991, partial reprint June 1992. Health United States 1990.

ure 9.2, a topping action in the number of cocaine-related emergency room visits was noted (USDHHS, 1991). Although the numbers of casual users of cocaine appears to be declining, there has been no corresponding reduction in the numbers of hard-core users. In fact, the number of cocaine-related deaths increased from 1988 to 1989, which was attributed to continued high use among heavy users of the drug. Still, researchers who track drug usage believe that after a decade of increasing use, the drug began to lose its appeal for millions of Americans by the end of the 1980s (Shenon, 1990).

The use of cocaine and crack among high school seniors has been dropping since the early 1980s, according to the results of nationwide surveys representing a cross-section of high school seniors in the continental United States (Johnston et al., 1991, 1992). The percentage of students reporting use of cocaine during the preceding year dropped from 6.5% in 1989 to 5.3% in 1990, and then again to 3.5% in 1991. By 1991, cocaine use among high school seniors was at the lowest level since 1975 (Johnston et al., 1992).

All told, less than a third of the high school seniors surveyed in 1990 reported using illicit drugs, as compared to 54% in 1979. For the first time since the mid-1970s, fewer than half of the students surveyed reported that they had ever tried illicit drugs (as opposed to 66% in 1982). However, rates of ciga-

A crack vial. Crack "rocks" resemble small white pebbles. Crack produces a powerful, prompt rush when smoked. Small ready-to-smoke doses are available at prices that have made them affordable to adolescents.

rette smoking and alcohol use remain at high levels, with nearly one in three seniors reporting drinking five or more alcoholic drinks in a row during the 2-week period preceding the survey and nearly 1 in 5 (19%) reporting smoking at least one cigarette a day.

The change in casual cocaine use is so dramatic that some officials have even suggested the crack and cocaine epidemics are over, at least for middle-class youth. The survey did not include high school dropouts, among whom illicit drug use, including cocaine, is more entrenched. Drug abuse among young people is apparently moving downward along the social scale and becoming increasingly focused within poorer inner city neighborhoods with high rates of school dropouts.

Officials credit anti-drug education programs as having modified the perceived harmfulness of, and social milieu for, cocaine use among students and young adults. In 1980 only about 1 in 3 18-year-olds (31%) believed that trying cocaine once or twice was harmful, as compared to 59% who felt so in 1990 (Johnston et al., 1991). In 1990, more than 9 of 10 (91.5%) 18-year-olds said they disapproved of trying cocaine even once or twice, as compared to about 3 of 4 (76%) in 1981.

■ **EFFECTS OF COCAINE** Physically, cocaine stimulates abrupt rises in blood pressure, constriction of blood vessels (with associated reduction of the oxygen supply to the heart), and acceleration of the heart rate (Altman, 1988). There are sporadic reports of respiratory and cardiovascular collapse, as with the publicized deaths of athletes Len Bias, Dave Croudip, and Don Rogers. Overdoses can give rise to restlessness, insomnia, headaches, nausea, convulsions, tremors, hallucinations, and delusions. Although intravenous use of cocaine carries the greatest risk of a lethal overdose, other forms of use can also cause fatal overdoses. Table 9.5 summarizes a number of the health risks of cocaine use.

Repeated and high-dose use of cocaine can also give rise to depression and anxiety (Weiss & Mirin, 1987). Depression may be severe enough to prompt suicidal behavior. Both initial and routine users report experiences of "crashing," or depression following cessation of cocaine use, although crashing is more common among long-term high-dose users. Psychotic behaviors have been induced by cocaine as by amphetamines, and tend to become more severe with continued use (Satel et al., 1990). Cocaine psychosis is usually preceded by a period of heightened suspiciousness, depressed mood, compulsive behavior, fault finding, irritability, and increasing paranoia (Weiss & Mirin, 1987). The psychosis may include visual and auditory hallucinations and delusions of persecution, as described in the following case:

After a while, I was convinced that there were people trying to break into my house. I didn't know who they were, but I was sure that people were after me. There was probably some reality to it too, since I really was scared that the police would come in and bust me. The only way that I felt that I could protect myself was by getting a knife. So I started sleeping with a butcher knife next to me. That didn't work for long, though, because I still felt insecure. So I felt that I had to get a gun. Every night, I went to bed with a gun on one side of me and a butcher knife on the other side. I was just waiting for someone to come in the house so that I could blow his brains out. God knows what I was going to do with the knife. I swear, I was a maniac. It wouldn't have mattered who had come to the door. If someone had come to my door at the wrong time to borrow a cup of sugar, I can tell you with 100 percent certainty, he would have been dead.

■ *Weiss and Mirin, 1987, p. 39*

Violence may occur as self-defense against delusional persecutors. Tactile hallucinations, for example of bugs crawling under the skin, may cause the user to pick at the skin until scabs form. The risk of cocaine-induced psychosis increases with chronicity and dosage levels. Cocaine abuse tends to be characterized by periodic binges that may last 12 to 36 hours, which are then followed by 2 to 5 days of abstinence, during which time the abuser may experience cravings that prompt another binge (Gawin et al., 1989).

Although cocaine has been unavailable to the general public since the Harrison Narcotic Act of 1914, it is still commonly the anesthetic of choice for surgery on the nose and throat. Cocaine, by the way, remains a stimulant, not a narcotic. Its classification as a narcotic was a legality that brought the drug under the prohibitions of the narcotics act.

Nicotine

It is no secret that cigarette smoking is dangerous. Cigarette packs sold in the United States have for years displayed notices such as "Warning: The Surgeon General Has Determined That Cigarette Smoking Is Dangerous to Your Health." Cigarette advertising is banned on radio and television. Some 400,000 lives are lost each year in the United States from smoking, mostly from lung cancer, cardiovascular disease, and chronic obstructive lung disease (USDHHS, 1991). This is nearly eight times the number who die from motor vehicle accidents. Cigarette smoking can also cause cancer of the larynx, oral cavity, and

Table 9.5 Health Risks of Cocaine Use

Physical Effects and Risks

Effects	Risks
1. Increased heart rate	Accelerated heart rate may give rise to heart irregularities that can be fatal, such as ventricular tachycardia (extremely rapid contractions) or ventricular fibrillation (irregular, weakened contractions).
2. Increased blood pressure	Rapid or large changes in blood pressure may place too much stress on a weak-walled blood vessel in the brain, which can cause it to burst, producing cerebral hemorrhage or stroke.
3. Increased body temperature	Can be dangerous to some individuals.
4. Possible grand mal seizures (epileptic convulsions)	Some grand mal seizures are fatal, particularly when they occur in rapid succession or while driving a car.
5. Respiratory effects	Overdoses can produce gasping or shallow irregular breathing that can lead to respiratory arrest.
6. Dangerous effects in special populations	Various special populations are at greater risk from cocaine use or overdose. People with coronary heart disease have died because their heart muscles were taxed beyond the capacity of their arteries to supply oxygen.

Medical Complications of Cocaine Use

Nasal Problems	When cocaine is administered intranasally (snorted), it constricts the blood vessels serving the nose, decreasing the supply of oxygen to these tissues, leading to irritation and inflammation of the mucous membranes, ulcers in the nostrils, frequent nosebleeds, and chronic sneezing and nasal congestion. Chronic use may lead to tissue death of the nasal septum, the part of the nose that separates the nostrils, requiring plastic surgery.
Lung Problems	Freebase smoking may lead to serious lung problems within 3 months of initial use.
Malnutrition	Cocaine suppresses the appetite so that weight loss, malnutrition, and vitamin deficiencies may accompany regular use.
Seizures	Grand mal seizures, typical of epileptics, may occur due to irregularities in the electrical activity of the brain. Repeated use may lower the seizure threshold, described as a type of "kindling" effect.
Sexual Problems	Despite the popular belief that cocaine is an aphrodisiac, frequent use can lead to sexual dysfunctions, such as impotence and failure to ejaculate among males, and decreased sexual interest in both sexes. Although some people report initial increased sexual pleasure with cocaine use, they may become dependent on cocaine for sexual arousal or lose the ability to enjoy sex for extended periods following long-term use.
Other Effects	Cocaine use may increase the risk of miscarriage among pregnant women. Sharing of infected needles is associated with transmission of hepatitis, endocarditis (infection of the heart valve), and HIV. Repeated injections often lead to skin infections as bacteria are introduced into the deeper levels of the skin.

Source: Adapted from Weiss and Mirin, 1987.

esophagus and may contribute to cancer of the bladder, pancreas, and kidneys. Pregnant women who smoke risk miscarriage, premature birth, and birth defects. Once it was thought that smokers' ills tended to focus on men, but today women smokers have a 30% greater risk of dying from cancer than women nonsmokers.

Largely because of health concerns, the percentage of American women and men combined who smoke declined from 42.2 in 1966 to 25.5 in 1990

Changing times. Only a couple of generations ago, cigarette advertisements featured medical doctors recommending the beneficial effects of certain brands. Today, of course, the powerful links between smoking, cancer, and other physical disorders have become widely publicized, as suggested by the American Cancer Society poster. Camels used to advertise, "I'd walk a mile for a Camel." Many heavy smokers, sad to say, wish they felt well enough to walk a mile.

("Smoking declines," 1992). (At the same time, tobacco companies are raking in money from increased overseas sales [Barry, 1991].) According to the Department of Health and Human Services, among Americans age 18 and over, the prevalence of smoking is highest for African-American men—about 39% (see Figure 9.3). The prevalence then drops off for Native-American men (37%), Puerto-Rican men (37%), non-Hispanic white men, and Mexican-American men (about 30% each), Asian-American men (25%), and Cuban-American men (24%). Women in each ethnic group are less likely to smoke than their male counterparts (Figure 9.3).

Passive smoking is associated with respiratory illnesses and other diseases in nonsmokers (Altman, 1992; Glantz & Parmley, 1991; USDHHS, 1991). Prolonged childhood exposure to second-hand smoke is a risk factor for lung cancer (Janerich et al., 1990) and various respiratory diseases of childhood, such as asthma. Because of the harmful effects of secondhand smoke, smoking has been banished from many public places such as elevators, schools, and airplanes. Many restaurants keep sections for nonsmokers. Forty-four states and Washington, D.C. have limited smoking in public places ("Smoking declines," 1992).

Today peer pressure favors *not* smoking. More than 70% of young adults aged 18 to 30 perceive smoking a pack of cigarettes a day as highly risky and disapprove of smoking (Johnston et al., 1991). Many people now see smoking as "deviant" behavior and are openly hostile toward people who assail them with secondhand smoke.

A profile of smokers is found in Figure 9.4. Table 9.6 provides government statistics on the smoking behavior of college students. All these figures showed declines from 1981 through 1991.

■ **COMPONENTS OF TOBACCO SMOKE** Tobacco smoke contains many constituents, including *carbon monoxide*, *hydrocarbons* (or *"tars"*), and *nicotine*.

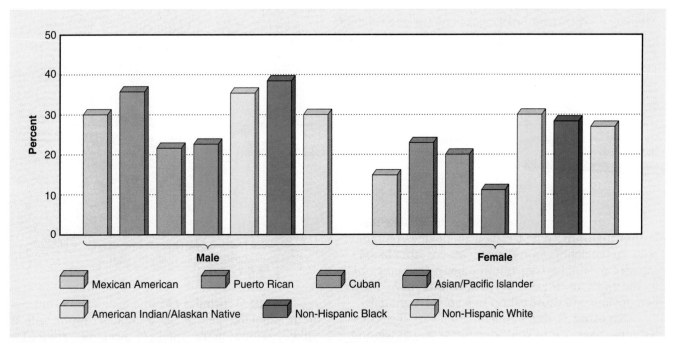

Figure 9.3 Current U.S. cigarette smokers among people 18 years of age and above, according to gender and race/ethnicity.
The prevalences of smoking are highest for African-American men and Native American men. Women in each ethnic group are less likely to smoke than their male counterparts.

Source: USDHHS Pub. No. (PHS) 91-1232, March 1991, partial reprint June 1992. Health United States 1990.

Figure 9.4 Cigarette smokers in the United States, according to gender, race/ethnicity, and level of education.
People with higher levels of education are less likely to smoke.

Source: Based on data in the Surgeon General's Report (1987), Centers for Disease Control.

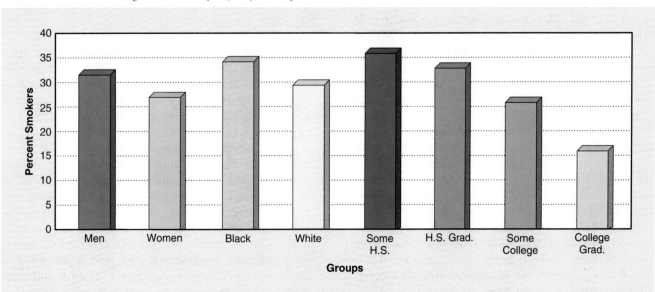

Table 9.6 Cigarette Smoking Among College Students	
Percentage who have smoked within the past year	35.6
Percentage who have smoked within the past 30 days	23.2
Percentage who have smoked daily within past 30 days	13.8
Percentage who have smoked half a pack or more within the past 30 days	8.0

Source: Johnston, L. D., Bachman, J. G., & O'Malley, P. M. (1992, January 25).
Monitoring the future: A continuing study of the lifestyles and values of youth. The University of Michigan News and Information Services: Ann Arbor, MI.

Oxygen is transported through the bloodstream by **hemoglobin**. When carbon monoxide combines with hemoglobin, however, it lessens the blood's capacity to supply oxygen to the body. One outcome is shortness of breath. **Hydrocarbons** have been demonstrated to cause cancer in laboratory animals.

Nicotine is the stimulant found in cigarettes. Nicotine gives rise to cold, clammy skin, nausea and vomiting, dizziness and faintness, and diarrhea—all of which account for the discomforts of novice smokers. Nicotine also induces a discharge of adrenaline, which generates a rush of autonomic activity including rapid heartbeat and release of stores of sugar into the blood. Nicotine quells the appetite and grants a sort of psychological "kick" (Grunberg, 1991).

■ **NICOTINE DEPENDENCE** Nicotine is the substance that creates physiological dependence on cigarette smoking (Lichtenstein & Glasgow, 1992). Nicotine dependence, in the form of cigarette smoking, is characterized by some degree of tolerance and a characteristic withdrawal syndrome, which is typical of addictive drugs (Pomerleau et al., 1986). As tolerance for nicotine increases, the smoking rate increases, until it levels off at about one or two packs a day. The withdrawal syndrome for nicotine includes lack of energy, nervousness, lightheadedness and dizziness, drowsiness, headaches, fatigue, irregular bowels, insomnia, cramps, palpitations, sweating, tremors, and craving for cigarettes (Pomerleau et al., 1986).

Research evidence documents the addictive aspects of cigarette smoking. Smokers regulate their smoking patterns to maintain fairly even blood levels of nicotine. Smokers raise their cigarette consumption, take more puffs, or inhale harder as compensatory measures when high-nicotine cigarettes are replaced with low-nicotine brands (Schneider, 1987; Taylor & Killen, 1991). Regular smokers also increase their nicotine intake if given certain drugs that speed the rate of elimination of nicotine from the body in the excretion of urine (Benowitz & Jacob, 1985).

 Cigarettes are *not* just habit forming. Nicotine, the stimulant found in cigarette smoke, gives rise to physiological dependence (physical addiction).

The DSM includes nicotine dependence, not cigarette smoking per se, as a mental disorder. It is unknown how many smokers meet the criteria for this diagnosis (Hughes et al., 1987). It may be important to know whether or not a smoker is physiologically dependent on nicotine because various treatment techniques can be employed to help would-be quitters manage dependency aspects of smoking. For example, nicotine-replacement therapy in the form of nicotine chewing gum or nicotine skin patches is available to help dependent smokers quit.

Unlike many other drugs, nicotine does not generally hinder performance of mental and physical tasks. Smokers are thus not usually impaired in their social or occupational functioning.

PSYCHEDELICS

Psychedelics, also known as **hallucinogenics**, are a class of drugs that produce sensory distortions or hallucinations. There are major alterations in color perception and hearing. Various hallucinogenics may also have additional effects, such as relaxation and euphoria or, in some cases, panic.

The hallucinogenics include such drugs as lysergic acid diethylamide (LSD), psilocybin, and mescaline. Psychoactive substances that are similar in effect to psychedelic drugs are marijuana (cannabis) and phencyclidine (PCP). Mescaline is derived from the peyote cactus and has been used for centuries by Indians in the Southwest, Mexico, and Central America in religious ceremonies, as has psilocybin, which is derived from certain mushrooms. LSD, PCP, and marijuana are more commonly used in North America.

There is little or no evidence that these drugs give rise to physiological dependence, although there is no question that people can become psychologically dependent on them—as they can on practically anything. The lifetime prevalence of substance abuse disorders involving psychedelic drugs was found to be 0.4% (4 people in 1,000) in the adult population, according to the ECA multisite survey (Anthony & Helzer, 1991).

LSD

LSD is the acronym for lysergic acid diethylamide, a synthetic hallucinogenic drug that was discovered by the Swiss chemist Albert Hoffman in 1938. Hoffman penned his initial experience with LSD as follows:

> I was forced to stop my work in the laboratory . . . and to go home, as I was seized by a particular restlessness associated with the sensation of mild dizziness. On arriving home, I lay down and sank into a kind of drunkenness which was not unpleasant and which was characterized by extreme activity of imagination. As I lay in a dazed condition with my eyes closed (I experienced daylight as disagreeably bright) there surged upon me an uninterrupted stream of fantastic images of extraordinary plasticity and vividness and accompanied by an intense, kaleidoscopelike play of colours. This condition gradually passed off after about two hours. (Hoffman, 1971, p. 23)

In addition to the vivid parade of colors and visual distortions produced by LSD, users have claimed that it "expands consciousness" and opens new worlds—as if they were looking into some reality beyond the usual reality. Sometimes they believe they have achieved great insights during the LSD "trip," but when it wears off they usually cannot implement or even summon up these discoveries.

LSD apparently decreases the action of serotonin, a neurotransmitter that inhibits neural firing. LSD may also increase utilization of dopamine. Because LSD curbs the action of an inhibiting neurotransmitter and increases dopamine activity, brain activity escalates, in this case giving rise to a flurry of colorful sensations or hallucinations.

LSD trips are somewhat unpredictable. Many frequent users have nothing but good trips. Others have had one bad trip and sworn off. Barber's review of the literature (1970) suggests that the rare psychotic reactions which occur are usually confined to users with a history of abnormal behaviors.

Some users have **flashbacks**—distorted perceptions or hallucinations that occur days, weeks, or longer after usage but mirror the LSD trip. Such flashbacks may stem from chemical changes in the

An LSD trip. LSD is an hallucinogenic drug that gives rise to a vivid parade of colors and visual distortions. Some users have claimed to have achieved great insights while "tripping," but when the drug wears off, they usually cannot summon up or implement these "insights."

brain produced by LSD, but Heaton and Victor (1976) and Matefy (1980) submit a psychological explanation.

Heaton and Victor (1976) found that LSD users who undergo flashbacks are more oriented toward fantasy, more willing to let their thoughts wander, and more prone toward focusing on internal sensations. If they should encounter sensations similar to a trip, they may construe them as flashbacks and let themselves focus on them indefinitely, encouraging a replay of the experience in which people may fill in the gaps psychologically.

Matefy (1980) found that "trippers" who report flashbacks also show greater capacity to become engrossed in role playing and hypothesized that flashbacks may amount to nothing more than enacting a trip. This does not mean that people who claim to have flashbacks are lying. They may be more willing to surrender control over internal sensations to try to alter their states of consciousness and seek peak experiences. Users who do not report flashbacks prefer to be more in charge of their thoughts and are more concerned about meeting the demands of daily life.

Phencyclidine (PCP)

PCP—referred to as "angel dust" on the streets—was developed as an anesthetic in the 1950s but was discontinued as such when the hallucinatory side effects of the drug were discovered. It became popular as a street drug in the 1970s because it is readily manufactured and relatively inexpensive.

The effects of PCP, like most drugs, are dose related. In addition to causing hallucinations, PCP accelerates the heart rate and blood pressure and causes sweating, flushing, and numbness. It also has dissociating effects—causing users to feel as if there is some sort of invisible barrier or wall between themselves and their environments. Dissociation can be experienced as pleasant, engrossing, or frightening, depending on the user's expectations, mood, setting, and so on. Overdoses can give rise to drowsiness and a blank stare, convulsions, and, now and then, coma; paranoia and aggressive behavior; and accidents that result from perceptual distortion.

Marijuana

Marijuana is produced from the *Cannabis sativa* plant. Marijuana helps some people to relax; others to elevate their moods. Marijuana sometimes produces mild hallucinations, so it is regarded as a minor hallucinogenic. The major psychoactive substance in marijuana is **delta-9-tetrahydrocannabinol**, or THC. THC is found in branches and leaves of the plant but is highly concentrated in the resin of the female plant. **Hashish**, or "hash," is also derived from the resin. Although it is more potent than marijuana, hashish has similar effects.

Marijuana usage burgeoned throughout the so-called Swinging Sixties and the 1970s but the drug then lost some of its cachet. As one high school senior in Manhattan put it, "It's not cool anymore" (Treaster, 1991b, p. A1). She added that her classmates were "really scared about getting into college and getting good jobs, and doing drugs doesn't help" (Treaster, 1991b, p. B4). Many young people in her parent's generation viewed marijuana as part of a social movement associated with exploring alternative lifestyles or dropping out of mainstream society. Today, however, most young people are seeking to "drop in" and find a place for themselves in society. U.S. marijuana use apparently peaked in 1979, when 31.5 million Americans were believed to have used the drug. By 1990, the numbers of marijuana users had dropped by more than a third, to 20.5 million (Treaster, 1991b). In terms of percentages, nearly 18% of Americans over the age of 12 smoked marijuana in 1979, as contrasted with 10% in 1990. Although conclusive evidence of damaging long-term consequences has been lacking, about 75% of Americans aged 19 to 22 now believe that regular use of marijuana entails great risk—up from 44% in 1980 (Johnston et al., 1991). More than half of this age group now disapprove of experimentation with marijuana; more than two-thirds disapprove of occasional use; and about 90% disapprove of regular use (Johnston et al., 1991). Still, marijuana remains the nation's most popular illicit drug, although its prevalence does not compare with alcohol's.

■ PSYCHOACTIVE EFFECTS OF MARIJUANA

Marijuana smokers report different sensations at various levels of intoxication. The early stages of intoxication are usually characterized by restlessness, which is supplanted by serenity. Moderate to strong intoxication leads to increased perceptions of self-insight, creative thinking, and empathy for others. Some users report that marijuana helps them socialize, but the friendliness that typifies early intoxication may give way to self-absorption and social withdrawal as the smoker becomes higher (Fabian & Fishkin, 1981). Strongly intoxicated people perceive time as passing more slowly. A song of a few minutes may seem to last an hour. There is increased awareness of bodily sensations, such as heartbeat. Smokers also report that strong intoxication heightens sexual sensations. Visual hallucinations may occur.

Strong intoxication can cause smokers to become disoriented. If their moods are euphoric, disorientation may be construed as harmony with the universe. Yet some smokers find strong intoxication disturbing. An accelerated heart rate and sharpened awareness of bodily sensations cause some smokers to fear that their hearts will "run away" with them. Some smokers are frightened by disorientation and fear that they will not "come back." High levels of intoxication now and then induce nausea and vomiting.

Regular use of marijuana does not appear to cause physiological dependence. Tolerance is a mark of dependence, but with marijuana, **reverse tolerance** has been reported. Regular users of marijuana frequently need progressively *less* of it to achieve similar effects. Perhaps some of the substances in marijuana smoke require a long time to be metabolized. The effects of smoking would then be added to those of the chemicals tarrying in the body. But regular users also have expectations that may interact with even mild bodily cues to produce results formerly achieved through higher doses.

Although it may not be physically addictive, regular marijuana use can lead to psychological dependence. Concern has also been raised that marijuana may give rise to **amotivational syndrome**, which saps achievement motivation, melts ambition, and impairs concentration. This fear has been fueled by correlational evidence that heavy collegiate smokers do not struggle to succeed with the intensity shown by nonsmokers or occasional smokers. We cannot ignore the selection factor in such studies. That is, people who choose to smoke heavily may differ in basic ways from people who do not (Maugh, 1982). For example, heavy smokers may be more committed to fantasy and emotional experience than to self-regulation and academic excellence. Their general approach to life could underlie their relative lack of ambition and their ingestion of marijuana. Still other investigations find no cognitive effects from heavy use of marijuana over a 7-year period (Schaeffer et al., 1981).

 It is unclear whether or not marijuana saps motivation (leads to amotivational syndrome). The research problem involves a selection factor: People who choose to rely heavily on marijuana may already be less ambitious and achievement oriented than those who do not.

Whatever the final outcome of research into its psychological effects, there are other reasons to be concerned about marijuana use. The Institute of Medicine of the National Academy of Sciences notes that marijuana impairs perception and motor coordination and thus makes driving and the operation of other machines dangerous. It impairs short-term memory and slows learning. Although it induces positive mood changes in many users, some people report anxiety and confusion; there are also occasional reports of psychotic reactions. Marijuana elevates the heart rate to about 140 to 150 beats per minute and, in some people, raises blood pressure. These changes are particularly taxing to people with hypertension and heart disease. Finally, marijuana smoke contains even higher amounts of carcinogenic hydrocarbons than tobacco smoke.

THEORETICAL PERSPECTIVES

People use psychoactive substances for various reasons. Some begin to use drugs in adolescence because of peer pressure, or because they believe that drugs make them seem more sophisticated or grown up. Some adolescents use drugs as a way of rebelling against their parents or society at large. Regardless of why they get started, people are more likely to stick with drugs if drugs make them feel good. For example, most adolescents imbibe alcohol to "get high," not to establish that they are adults (Carman et al., 1983). Many people smoke cigarettes for the pleasure they provide. Others smoke to help them relax when they are tense and, paradoxically, to give them a kick or a lift when they are tired.

People who are anxious about their jobs or social lives may be drawn to the calming effects of alcohol, marijuana (in certain doses), tranquilizers, and sedatives. People with low self-confidence and self-esteem may be drawn to the ego-bolstering effects of amphetamines and cocaine. Many poor young people attempt to escape the poverty, anguish, and tedium of inner city life through heroin and similar drugs (Hollister, 1983). More well-to-do adolescents may rely on drugs to manage the transition from dependence to independence and major life changes concerning jobs, college, and lifestyles.

Let us consider various theoretical perspectives on substance abuse and dependence.

Biological Perspectives

There are a number of biological perspectives on substance abuse and dependence. One involves the biological mechanisms by which substances create physiological dependence. Another involves the search for genetic factors in abuse and dependence.

■ **WITHDRAWAL SYNDROMES** Researchers are discovering biological pathways by which substances may give rise to physiological dependence. One potential pathway involves endorphins. Endorphins and opioids dock at the same receptor sites in the brain, for example. Normally, the brain produces a certain level of endorphins, giving rise to a sort of psychological steady state of comfort and potential to experience pleasure. However, when the body becomes habituated to opioids, it may stop producing endorphins, in which case the user may come to depend on opioids for feelings of comfort, relief from pain, and feelings of pleasure. When habitual use of opioids is then discontinued, feelings of discomfort and little aches and pains may be magnified until the body resumes adequate production of endorphins. The interim discomfort might underlie part of the withdrawal syndrome for opioids. More research is needed, however, to document the role of endorphins in mediating withdrawal syndromes.

■ **GENETIC FACTORS** Evidence for a biological predisposition to alcoholism (Tarter & Edwards, 1986) and other kinds of substance dependence has been accumulating. Alcoholism does run in families (Goodwin, 1985). The sons of alcoholics are at greater risk than the sons of nonalcoholics of abusing alcohol themselves (Pihl et al., 1990). However, a familial pattern in alcoholism does not in itself implicate genetic factors because the home environment is likely to be affected by an alcoholic parent. Researchers have thus turned to twin and adoption studies to tease out the relative contributions of genetic and other factors.

Monozygotic (MZ) twins have identical genetic heritages, whereas fraternal or dizygotic (DZ) twins share only half of their genes. If genetic factors make a significant contribution to alcoholism, it would thus be expected that MZ twins would show about twice the concordance rate for alcoholism as DZ twins. The evidence is mixed. One recent twin study showed a greater concordance rate for MZ twins than DZ twins for alcohol abuse for males, but not for females (Pickens et al., 1991). However, a recent twin study of 1,080 adult pairs of women twins found that MZ twins were significantly more likely than DZ twins to share alcoholic drinking patterns (Kendler et al., 1992). Another study of MZ and DZ twins suggested that there is a substantial genetic role for early-onset alcoholism in males but only a modest role in alcoholism in females and in late-onset alcoholism in males (McGue et al., 1992).

Further evidence for the role of biological factors in alcoholism is found in adoption studies in which children are reared apart from their biological parents. Most studies report that the biological *sons* of alcoholic parents have about four times the risk of becoming alcoholic than the biological sons of nonalcoholic parents, whether they are reared by their biological fathers or by nonalcoholic adoptive parents (see Figure 9.5) (Cadoret et al., 1980; Goodwin, 1985; Helzer, 1987; Schuckit, 1987).

Still another source of genetic evidence is found in cross-species research. Scientists can conduct kinds of research with lower animals that would be unethical—and impractical—with humans. Research with rodents has shown most laboratory rats and mice favor plain water and will not imbibe water laced with alcohol. Nevertheless, by inbreeding rodents who show even slight tendencies to ingest alcohol, strains of animals have been bred that prefer alcohol to water. With rodents it is also possible to control for environmental influences, so that the liquid preferences are shown to be genetic in origin (Newlin & Thomson, 1990). Rodents, of course, are not people. Still, evidence that predispositions toward preferences for alcoholic beverages can be genetically transmitted in other mammalian species cannot be taken lightly.

In 1990, researchers identified a gene that may play a key role in the development of some forms of alcoholism (Altman, 1990a; Goleman, 1990c). The gene is linked to dopamine receptors in the brain. The gene was present in 77% of the brains of 35 peo-

Figure 9.5 Alcohol-related problems in adoptees of alcoholic biological parents (probands) and nonalcoholic biological parents (controls).
There is a higher percentage of drinking problems among the children of parents of drinking problems, although the children were reared by nonalcoholic adoptive parents. Such evidence supports a role for genetic factors in alcoholism.
Source: Adapted from Goodwin et al. (1973).

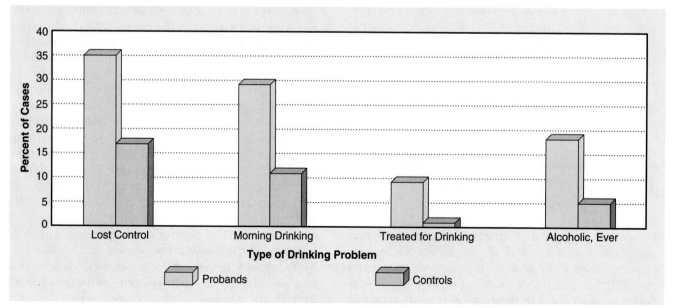

ple who had died from alcohol-related causes, but in only 28% of the brains of deceased nonalcoholics (Noble & Blum, 1990). The detection of the gene raises hopes for two developments: (1) a blood test to identify people who are genetically vulnerable to alcoholism, and (2) drugs that may modify or block the gene's actions to prevent alcoholism. The mechanism by which the gene may influence the development of alcoholism remains unknown, but it may lead to disruption of the activity of dopamine receptors which might, in turn, enhance the pleasure derived from alcohol and hence increase cravings for alcohol (Altman, 1990a).

Recent research sheds further light on biological differences between sons of alcoholics and sons of nonalcoholics that are likely to have a genetic component. A genetic vulnerability to alcoholism may involve a combination of reaping greater pleasure from alcohol and a capacity for greater biological tolerance (Newlin & Thomson, 1990; Pihl et al., 1990). Men with alcoholic biological parents or siblings metabolize alcohol more rapidly than men without alcoholics in the immediate biological family (Schuckit & Rayses, 1979). People who metabolize alcohol relatively quickly can tolerate larger doses and are less likely to develop upset stomachs, dizziness, and headaches when they drink. Better tolerance of alcohol does not compel people to drink. When they do drink, however, they can imbibe large enough quantities to generate euphoric feelings, and they are also spared negative reactions—at least in the short run. These factors may increase their risk of developing problems in moderating their drinking.

The sons of alcoholic fathers have also been shown to be more tense and to have lower levels of the neurotransmitter GABA (Moss, 1990). GABA is an inhibitory neurotransmitter found throughout the gray matter of the central nervous system. GABA regulates nervous activity by preventing neurons from overly exciting their neighbors. Inadequate action of GABA apparently contributes to feelings of anxiety and tension. When the sons of alcoholic fathers consumed an alcoholic drink, they became less tense and their GABA levels rose to the level of the group composed of sons of nonalcoholic fathers. Perhaps the sons of alcoholics have inherited an irregularity in GABA action, which leads them to feel anxious and to use alcohol to quell their nervousness (Goleman, 1990a). Researchers suspect that some alcoholics have deficiencies in other neurotransmitters, such as serotonin, which make them impulsive and likely to abuse any available drug, including alcohol (Goleman, 1990a).

The brain wave patterns of the biological sons of alcoholics may also differ from those of the sons of nonalcoholics. Results are consistent with those concerning the action of GABA: The sons of alcoholics appear to produce fewer alpha waves, which are linked to states of relaxation (Schuckit, 1987). When the sons of alcoholics drink, they show a relatively greater increase in the production of alpha waves. It may thus be that the sons of alcoholics are more likely to use alcohol to promote feelings of relaxation (Schuckit, 1987).

In sum, the present research suggests that genetics account for perhaps 50 to 60% of the factors that contribute to alcoholism (Goleman, 1992c). Although genetics appears to play an important role, there is thus ample "room" for other factors (Cadoret et al., 1986), which is highlighted by the finding that at least one-third of alcoholics show no family history of alcoholism (Schuckit, 1983). The development of alcoholism most probably reflects the interaction of biological, psychological, social, cultural, and environmental factors. Genetic factors may create an inborn tolerance for alcohol and a tendency to find alcohol more relaxing. Other salient factors may include instability in the early home environment, a father in a low-status job (Cloninger et al., 1983, 1984), the ready availability of alcohol, permissive social attitudes about drunkenness, and peer pressure (Schuckit, 1987).

Some theorists suggest that the tendency to become physiologically dependent on nicotine may also be influenced by genetics (Carmelli et al., 1992; Hughes & Hatsukami, 1987). A study reported in the *New England Journal of Medicine* was based on the smoking patterns of 4,775 pairs of twins who served in the U.S. armed forces during World War II. The twins were surveyed in the late 1960s and again in the early 1980s. There were higher concordance rates for MZ than DZ twins on factors such as current smoking of cigarettes, cigars, or pipes, and on quitting. The researchers (Carmelli et al., 1992) conclude that there were "moderate" genetic influences on patterns of lifetime smoking.

Learning Perspectives

Learning theorists propose that substance-related behaviors are largely learned and can, in principle, be unlearned. They focus on the roles of conditioning and observational learning in substance abuse and dependence. We also consider the social-learning variables of outcome and self-efficacy expectancies.

■ **OPERANT CONDITIONING** Behaviors related to substance abuse and dependence may be acquired through reinforcement. Drug use may become habitual because of the pleasure or positive reinforcement provided by drugs. Drugs like cocaine can apparently directly stimulate pleasure mechanisms in the brain, providing direct positive reinforcement (Wise, 1988). In animal studies, for example, the injection of psychoactive drugs like cocaine has been made contingent on the performance of various tasks, such as pressing a lever (Weiss & Mirin, 1987). Laboratory animals will learn to repeatedly press the lever for cocaine. When cocaine reinforcement is then made intermittent, they will "work longer and harder" to attain it.

Researchers can estimate the reinforcing power of drugs by comparing the rates at which animals perform operant responses, such as pressing a lever, to receive them. Animals will perform to receive a wide range of drugs, including amphetamines, nicotine, barbiturates, opioids, alcohol, and PCP. Performance rates are most dramatic for cocaine, however. *Rhesus monkeys will work continuously for cocaine until they die* (Weiss & Mirin, 1987).

People may initially use a substance because of social influence, trial and error, or social observation. In the case of alcohol, they learn that the substance can produce euphoria, reduce anxiety and tension, and release behavioral inhibitions. Alcohol can thus be reinforcing when it is used to combat depression (by producing euphoric feelings, even if short-lived), to combat tension (by functioning as a tranquilizer), or to help people sidestep moral conflicts (for example, by dulling awareness of moral prohibitions against sexual behavior or aggression). Social reinforcers are also made available by substance abuse, such as the approval of drug-abusing companions and, in the cases of depressants and stimulants, the (temporary) surmounting of social shyness.

■ ALCOHOL AND TENSION REDUCTION

Theorists have long maintained that people drink to reduce tension. The tension-reduction theory of alcohol predicts that people drink more as the level of stress in their lives mounts. Research suggests that the relationship between stress and alcohol may be moderated by psychological factors such as styles of coping and alcohol expectancies and by gender. A study of a random sample of 1,316 African-American and white adult drinkers revealed that drinking increased in relation to the level of stress among one group of men: men who tend to use avoidant forms of emotional coping with stress and who have positive expectations about the effects of alcohol. That is, they tend to deny negative emotions or to try not to think about them (Cooper et al., 1992). Positive alcohol expectancies involve beliefs that alcohol produces pleasure, reduces anxiety and tension, and makes one more powerful, aggressive, and self-expressive.

Men who had less positive expectations of alcohol and who were willing to face and deal with negative feelings were actually *less* likely to drink under stress. Drinking in women was unrelated to stress, regardless of their style of coping or expectancies about alcohol.

■ REINFORCEMENT VALUE OF SMOKING CIGARETTES

Cigarette smoking is apparently positively reinforced by the stimulating effects of nicotine. The pleasures of nicotine are produced rapidly by drawing cigarette smoke into the lungs. The nicotine in cigarette smoke readily passes the blood–brain barrier and reaches the brain in 7 to 10 seconds following each puff, which is less time than it takes heroin to reach the brain following injection into the bloodstream (Schneider, 1987). Blood levels of nicotine are elevated within minutes. Cigarette smoking can quickly become a strong habit because of the frequency of reinforcement (number of puffs) and the physical dependence on nicotine that develops with repeated use.

■ SUBSTANCE ABUSE AS SELF-MEDICATION FOR DEPRESSION AND ANXIETY

Alcohol and other drugs are often used as self-medication for depression and anxiety (Schmeck, 1988). Stimulants temporarily elevate the mood, whereas depressants like alcohol quell anxiety. Although alcohol and other drugs may alleviate emotional distress, they do not treat underlying anxiety or mood disorders. Rather than learning to solve personal problems, people who medicate themselves with drugs may face additional substance-related problems.

Sad to say, vicious cycles may be initiated. Because long-term drinking has depressing effects, people who drink to manage feelings of depression may actually deepen them. They are then more likely to crave the short-term euphoric effects of alcohol. Because alcohol can relax inhibitions, people under the influence are more likely to do things that produce guilt and social difficulties, compounding their problems. They may then crave fast liquid relief for these problems.

■ NEGATIVE REINFORCEMENT

Once people become physiologically dependent on substances, **negative reinforcement** comes into play. For example, in chronic alcoholics, resumption of drinking becomes negatively reinforced by relief from withdrawal symptoms such as tachycardia, profuse sweating, and "shakes." Withdrawal symptoms are perceived by smokers and ex-smokers as significant obstacles to quitting smoking and as prompting relapses (Katz & Singh, 1986). Smokers who are able to quit are occasionally bothered by urges to smoke but have learned to manage them.

■ THE CONDITIONING MODEL OF CRAVING

Principles of classical conditioning may also help to explain the cravings for drugs experienced by people who are or were dependent (Weiss & Mirin, 1987). Cravings may thus be seen as conditioned responses rather than reflections of chemical deficiencies. Cravings are triggered by cues (conditioned stimuli) that were associated with use of the substance. Socializing with certain companions ("drinking buddies") or passing a liquor store may elicit conditioned cravings for alcohol. Sensations of anxiety or depression that were paired with use of alcohol or drugs may also elicit cravings. The following case illustrates conditioned cravings to environmental cues:

A 29-year-old man was hospitalized for the treatment of heroin addiction. After four weeks of treatment, he returned to his former job, which required him to ride the subway past the stop at which he had previously bought his drugs. Each day, when the subway doors opened at this location, [he] experienced enormous craving for heroin, accompanied by tearing, a runny nose, abdominal cramps, and gooseflesh. After the doors closed, his symptoms disappeared, and he went on to work.

■ *Weiss and Mirin, 1987, p. 71*

Similarly, some people are primarily "stimulus smokers." They reach for a cigarette in the presence of smoking-related stimuli such as seeing someone smoke or smelling smoke. Smoking becomes a strongly conditioned habit because it is paired repeatedly with many situational cues—watching TV, finishing dinner, driving in the car, studying, drinking or socializing with friends, sex, and, for some, using the bathroom.

The conditioning model of craving is strengthened by research which shows that alcoholics tend to salivate more than nonalcoholics to the sight and smell of alcohol (Monti et al., 1987). In Pavlov's classic experiment, a salivation response was conditioned in dogs by repeatedly pairing the sound of a bell (a neutral or conditioned stimulus) with the presentation of food powder (an unconditioned stimulus). Salivation among alcoholics can also be viewed as a conditioned response to alcohol-related cues. Whereas salivating to a bell may be harmless, salivating at a bottle of Scotch, or at a picture of a bottle in a magazine ad, can throw the alcoholic who is trying to remain abstinent into a tailspin. Problem drinkers

who show the greatest salivary response to alcohol cues may be at greatest risk of relapse and profit from treatment designed to extinguish their responses to alcohol-related cues (Monti et al., 1987). A treatment combining exposure and response prevention is helpful to many individuals with obsessive-compulsive disorder. Perhaps a treatment that combines exposure to alcohol-related cues but prevents drinking would help extinguish cravings for alcohol.

■ OBSERVATIONAL LEARNING

Social-learning theory has inspired research on the modeling of substance abuse. In a typical experiment, subjects are asked to participate in groups of two in "taste tests" of alcoholic beverages (Caudill & Marlatt, 1975). However, each group consists of a genuine subject and a confederate of the experimenter. During the tests, the accomplice is asked to drink first and models heavy or light drinking. The amount that the real subject then drinks is used as a measure of effects of modeling.

Research along these lines has demonstrated modeling effects on drinking rates among men and women who drink heavily in social situations, but not necessarily among light drinkers (e.g., Caudill & Marlatt, 1975; Lied & Marlatt, 1979). Light drinkers seem better able to resist modeling effects and to rely more on self-imposed limits.

The modeling effect may in part explain the increased risk of alcoholism among children of alcoholics. Young men from families in which there is at least one alcoholic—perhaps a parent or a sibling—are more strongly affected by drinking models than men without family histories of alcoholism (Chipperfield & Vogel-Sprott, 1988). Children who are reared with alcoholics may be less likely to learn from family members to regulate their drinking. They may thus become more reliant on the observed behavior of other drinkers (Chipperfield & Vogel-Sprott, 1988). When drinking companions drink to excess, they are more likely to follow their lead.

■ OUTCOME EXPECTANCIES AND SUBSTANCE ABUSE

People's beliefs or expectancies about the outcomes of using substances influence their decisions concerning usage (Schafer & Brown, 1991; Stacy et al., 1991). People who hold positive expectancies of drugs' effects are more likely to use them (Schafer & Brown, 1991). Most people believe that alcohol reduces tension, diverts attention from their problems, heightens their pleasure and social abilities, and alters experiences for the better. Even 12- to 14-year-olds with little or no history of drinking hold positive expectancies, which suggests that positive outcome expectancies may be based more on cultural stereotypes than experience (Christiansen & Goldman, 1983).

People of various ages who hold more positive expectancies about alcohol may be more likely to become problem drinkers. Among adolescents, positive expectancies are more strongly related than family drinking patterns to the likelihood of drinking (Christiansen & Goldman, 1983). Adolescent alcohol abusers are more likely than nonabusers to expect alcohol to enhance their social skills (for example, make them more relaxed, outgoing, assertive, and carefree in social interactions), improve cognitive functioning (reduce their worries and increase their sense of personal power), hone motor skills, enhance sexual pleasure and performance, induce feelings of relaxation, and stimulate them (Brown et al., 1987). In another study, expectancies that alcohol reduces tension were the best predictor of problem drinking among college students (Brown, 1985a). Such expectancies were also a stronger predictor of relapse among treated alcoholics than variables like marital or employment status, stress, and social support, or participation in an aftercare program (Brown, 1985b).

■ **SELF-EFFICACY EXPECTANCIES** Part of the appeal of substances such as alcohol lies in their ability to enhance self-efficacy expectancies directly (by enhancing feelings of energy, power, and well-being) and indirectly (by reducing stressful states of arousal, such as anxiety) (Wilson, 1987). Cocaine similarly enhances self-efficacy expectancies, an outcome sought in particular by performance-conscious athletes. People may therefore come to rely on substances in challenging situations where they doubt their abilities. Alcohol can also help protect one's sense of self-efficacy by shunting criticism for socially unacceptable behavior from the self to the alcohol. People who "screw up" while drinking can maintain their self-esteem by attributing their shortcomings to the alcohol.

Cognitive Perspectives

Much evidence has supported the role of cognitive factors in substance abuse and dependence. The influence of cognitive factors touches on abusers' attitudes, beliefs, and expectancies.

■ **DOES ONE SLIP CAUSE SUBSTANCE ABUSERS TO GO ON BINGES? PERHAPS WHAT YOU BELIEVE IS WHAT YOU GET** According to the disease model of alcoholism, abstainers who binge after just one drink do so largely for biochemical reasons. Experimental research, however, suggests that cognitive factors may be more important. In fact, the one-drink hypothesis may be explained by the drinker's expectancies rather than the biochemical properties of alcohol.

Studies of the one-drink hypothesis, like many other studies on alcohol, are made possible by the fact that the taste of vodka can be cloaked by tonic water. In a classic study by Marlatt and his colleagues (1973), subjects were led to believe that they were participating in a taste test. Alcoholics and social drinkers who were informed that they were sampling an alcoholic beverage (vodka) drank significantly more than counterparts who were informed that they were sampling a nonalcoholic beverage. The expectations of alcoholics and social drinkers alike turned out to be the crucial factors that predicted the amount

Outcome expectancies and alcohol abuse. People who hold more positive expectancies about alcohol may be more likely to drink excessively. Adolescent alcohol abusers often expect that alcohol will enhance their social skills, reduce their worries, enhance their sexual pleasure and performance, induce feelings of relaxation, and stimulate them. Who are the people in this picture and what do they expect from alcohol?

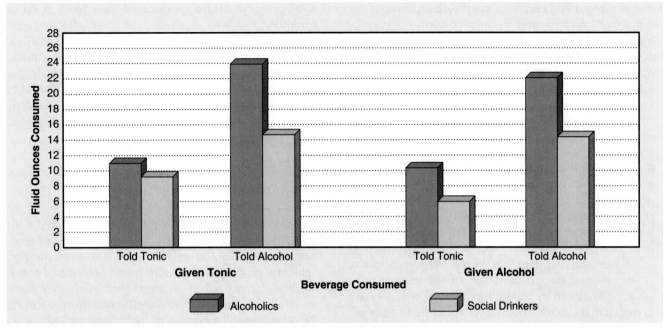

Figure 9.6 Must alcoholics fall off the wagon if they have one drink?
It is widely believed that alcoholics will lose control if they have just one drink. Will they? If so, why? Laboratory research by Marlatt and his colleagues suggests that the tendency of alcoholics to drink to excess following a first drink may be the result of a self-fulfilling prophecy rather than a craving. Like the dieter who eats a piece of chocolate, alcoholics may assume that they have lost control because they have fallen off the wagon and then go on a binge. This figure shows that alcoholics in the Marlatt study drank more when they were led to believe that the beverage contained alcohol, regardless of its actual content. It remains unclear, however, whether binge drinking by alcoholics in real-life settings can be explained as a self-fulfilling prophecy.

Source: Adapted from Marlatt et al. (1973).

consumed (see Figure 9.6). *The actual content of the beverages was immaterial.*

Marlatt (1978) explains the one-drink effect as a self-fulfilling prophecy. If alcoholics believe that just one drink will cause loss of control, they perceive the outcome as predetermined when they drink. Their drinking—even taking one drink—may thus escalate into a binge. When individuals who were formerly physiologically dependent on alcohol share this belief—which is propounded by many groups, including AA—they may interpret "just one drink" as "falling off the wagon." Marlatt's point is that the "mechanism" of falling off the wagon due to one drink is cognitive, reflecting one's expectations about the effects of the drink, and not physiological. This expectation is an example of what Aaron Beck refers to as *absolutist thinking*. When we insist on seeing the world in black and white rather than shades of gray, we may interpret one bite of dessert as proof that we are off our diets, or one cigarette as proof that we are hooked again. Rather than telling ourselves, "Okay, I goofed, but that's it. I don't have to have more," we encode our lapses as catastrophes and transform them into relapses.

Despite the widespread acceptance of the disease model of alcoholism, the belief that just one drink will lead to a binge may be a self-fulfilling prophecy. "Just one drink" is more likely to lead to a binge when the drinker *believes* it will.

Still, alcohol-dependent people who believe that they may go on a drinking binge if they have just one drink are well advised to abstain rather than place themselves in a situation that they feel they may not be able to manage.

■ **SUBSTANCE ABUSE AND DECISION-MAKING PROCESSES** From a decision-making perspective, people choose whether or not to use substances according to their weighing of the expected positive and negative consequences. Cox and Klinger (1988) propose that such decisions can be made on the basis of weighing the anticipated short-term and long-term consequences of drinking alcohol. Consider problem drinkers who face the choice to drink or not to drink every day. They may be aware of the eventual negative consequences of drinking (e.g., getting fired or divorced), but expectations of immediate relief from anxiety and feelings of pleasure may be more prominent at a given moment. They thus decide to drink. The problem drinker may or may not be aware of such decisions, or of decisions to engage in the chain of behaviors that lead to problem drinking—such as whether or not to take a route from work that runs past a favorite watering hole.

■ **THE SELF-AWARENESS MODEL**   Have you ever known anyone to use drugs after flunking a test or receiving a poor job appraisal? According to Hull's (1987) self-awareness model, depressants can create a psychological shield that protects users from negative social feedback. Alcohol, for example, reduces self-awareness by clouding perception of negative environmental cues (knowledge of the test grade or job appraisal) and by rendering the drinker less aware of negative feedback from others about past behavior.

Laboratory studies have exposed highly self-aware subjects and others to various kinds of feedback on laboratory tasks, then given them the opportunity to "sample" wines. In a study by Hull (1987), one group of highly self-aware subjects was told that they had carried out laboratory tasks poorly. Another self-aware group was told that they had succeeded. The evaluations were actually made at random. The group who received failure feedback drank significantly more alcohol during the subsequent "taste tests" than the group who received success feedback. Alcohol may have been used by the highly self-aware group who "failed" as a means of not having to deal with negative information about themselves. Subjects who are less self-aware usually do not drink more when they are exposed to failure feedback (Hull & Young, 1983). They may not need the shield of alcohol to screen out the negative information. In a field test of the model, Hull and his colleagues (Hull et al., 1986) studied relapse (return to drinking) among people who had been detoxified from alcohol. Relapse was connected with negative events that reflected poorly on highly self-aware subjects' abilities. There was no connection between such events and relapse among subjects who were less self-aware. Similarly, adolescents who received high scores on a measure of self-awareness drank more frequently after they got poor grades than adolescents who scored low on self-awareness (Hull et al., 1986).

However, other researchers (e.g., Chassin et al., 1988) have not found that highly self-aware adolescents use alcohol as a way of dealing with getting into trouble with the law, getting poor grades in school, or getting fired from a job. It should also be noted that research does not generally show that alcohol reliably reduces self-awareness (Frankenstein & Wilson, 1984), so the central premise of the theory remains in doubt.

Additional research is necessary to examine the conditions under which the self-awareness model may explain substance use and abuse. Use of alcohol probably has multiple causes, so failure of a model to explain all patterns of abuse does not necessarily impugn its value in explaining some patterns of abuse.

Sociocultural Perspectives

Cultural and religious factors are also connected with the consumption of alcohol and drugs. Rates of alcohol abuse, as noted earlier, vary across ethnic and religious groups. Let us note here some other sociocultural factors. Church attendance, for example, is generally connected with abstinence from alcohol. Perhaps people who are more willing to engage in culturally sanctioned activities, such as churchgoing, are also more likely to adopt culturally sanctioned prohibitions against excessive drinking. Yet women have begun to drink and smoke more as they have entered the male-dominated work force (Nathan & Skinstad, 1987).

Use of alcohol and drugs often occurs within a group or social setting. We go drinking with friends, or entertain over drinks at home. A good wine list is a sign of class in a restaurant. Drinking is determined, in part, by where we live, whom we worship with, and by the social or cultural norms that regulate our behavior. Cultural attitudes can encourage or discourage problem drinking.

Adolescents (and preadolescents) are exposed to peers who use drugs. In a survey of 563 11th and 12th graders from two southwestern communities, association with peers who used drugs was the single greatest predictor of drug usage (Swaim et al., 1989).

Psychodynamic Perspectives

According to traditional psychodynamic theory, alcoholism reflects certain features of the oral-dependent personality. Alcoholism is, by definition, an oral behavior pattern. Psychodynamic theory connects immoderate drinking with other oral traits, such as dependence and depression, and traces the origins of these traits to fixation in the oral stage of psychosexual development. Excessive drinking in adulthood symbolizes efforts to attain oral gratification.

Psychodynamic theorists also view smoking as an oral fixation, although they have not been able to predict who will or will not smoke. Sigmund Freud smoked upward of 20 cigars a day despite several vain attempts to desist. Although he contracted cancer and had to have his jaw replaced, he would still not surrender his "oral fixation." He eventually succumbed to cancer of the mouth in 1939 at the age of 83, after years of agony.

Research support for these psychodynamic concepts is mixed. Some research suggests, for example, that alcoholics are more likely to be dependent than the general population (McCord et al., 1960). It is unclear, however, whether dependence contributes to or stems from problem drinking (Vaillant & Milofsky, 1982). Chronic drinking, for example, is connected with loss of employment and downward movement in social status, both of which would render drinkers more reliant on others for support. Moreover, an empirical connection between dependence and alcoholism does not establish that alcoholism represents an oral fixation due to unconscious childhood conflict.

Too, many—but certainly not all—alcoholics have antisocial personalities which are characterized by independence-seeking as expressed through rebelliousness and rejection of social and legal codes (Graham & Strenger, 1988; Vaillant, 1983). It appears that there may be different personality subtypes among substance abusers and it would be unfair to characterize them all as dependent.

In sum, there are many perspectives on substance abuse and dependence. It appears that in some cases genetic factors and the early home environment give rise to predispositions to abuse and dependence. In adolescence and adulthood, expectations—which may reflect cultural stereotypes, personal experiences, and cognitive factors—seem to affect decisions whether or not to use a substance. When physiological dependence occurs, people may use a substance to avert withdrawal symptoms. It appears that no single model or perspective can fully explain substance abuse and dependence. These behavior patterns apparently represent complex interactions among biological, psychological, social, cultural, and environmental factors.

TREATMENT

There have been and remain a vast variety of nonprofessional, biological, and psychological approaches to substance abuse and dependence. However, treatment has been a frustrating endeavor. In many, perhaps most cases, dependent people really do not want to discontinue the substances they are abusing. Most cocaine abusers, for example, like most abusers of alcohol and other drugs, do not seek treatment on their own (Carroll & Rounsaville, 1992). Those who do not seek treatment tend to be heavy abusers who deny the negative impact of cocaine on their lives and dwell within a social milieu that fails to encourage them to get help (Carroll & Rounsaville, 1992). When people do come for treatment, helping them through a withdrawal syndrome is usually straightforward enough, as we shall see. However, helping them to pursue a life devoid of their preferred substances is more problematic. Moreover, treatment takes place in a setting—such as the therapist's office, a support group, a residential center, or a hospital—in which abstinence is valued and encouraged. Then the individual returns to the work, family, or street settings in which abuse and dependence were instigated and maintained. The problem of returning to abuse and dependence following treatment—that is, of *relapse*—can thus be more troublesome than the problems involved in initial treatment. For this reason, recent treatment efforts have focused on relapse prevention.

Another complication is that many substance abusers also have psychological disorders and vice versa. Most clinics and treatment programs focus on only one of these problems rather than treating them simultaneously, however. This narrow focus results in poorer treatment outcomes, including more common rehospitalizations, among those with dual diagnoses. (Polcin, 1992). It has been estimated that 20 to 70% of all those who have other mental disorders—and 50 to 70% of the young adults with other mental disorders—merit a dual diagnosis that includes substance abuse (Polcin, 1992).

Biological Approaches

Various biological approaches have been introduced to treat substance abuse and dependence. For people who are physiologically dependent, biological treatment oftens begins with **detoxification**—that is, helping physiologically dependent people safely through the withdrawal syndrome. Continued treatment is then provided through psychological counseling or peer support. Researchers are also searching for chemical compounds that will block cravings for various substances without incurring risks of abuse or dependence themselves.

■ **DETOXIFICATION** Detoxification is often carried out in a hospital setting to provide the dependent person with as much support as possible. In the case of alcohol and barbiturates, hospitalization allows medical personnel to monitor the development of potentially dangerous withdrawal symptoms, such as convulsions. Dependent people are sometimes given tranquilizers, such as Librium and Valium, to help mute withdrawal symptoms. Detoxification to alcohol takes about a week. When tranquilizers are used to cope with subsequent urges to drink, however, people can be caught up in a sort of game of "musical drugs."

■ **DISULFIRAM** A chemotherapeutic approach to the treatment of alcohol abuse is found in the drug disulfiram (brand name Antabuse). When alcohol is ingested within 12 hours of taking disulfiram, a strong aversive reaction including nausea, sweating, flushing, rapid heart rate, reduced blood pressure, and vomiting is induced (Murray, 1989a). Disulfiram is intended to discourage use of alcohol by engendering an anticipatory fear reaction, but well-designed studies have not documented its effectiveness (Murray, 1989a). For one thing, people who want to drink can simply not take disulfiram.

■ **ANTIDEPRESSANTS** Antidepressants have shown some promise in stemming cravings for cocaine in some abusers shortly after they discontinue the drug, according to some preliminary research findings, but they are no panacea (Kolata, 1989a). In a recent double-blind controlled study (Gawin et al., 1989), cocaine abusers given the antidepressant desipramine were two to three times as likely to remain abstinent for several weeks during a 6-week treatment program as abusers given a placebo drug or another medication, lithium carbonate. Fifty-nine percent of those given the antidepressant maintained abstinence for at least 3 to 4 consecutive weeks, as compared to an average of 21% in the other conditions. Desipramine may facilitate neural processes that underlie feelings of pleasure in everyday experiences. If substance abusers are more capable of deriving pleasure from nondrug-related activities, they may be less likely to return to cocaine to induce pleasurable feelings. This study only followed subjects for 6 weeks following abstinence, however. Long-term effects of desipramine need to be studied further.

■ **NICOTINE REPLACEMENT THERAPY** One promising development in the pharmacological treatment of cigarette smoking is nicotine replacement therapy in the form of a prescription gum (brand name Nicorette) and nicotine transdermal (skin) patches. Many regular smokers, perhaps the great majority, are nicotine dependent. The use of nicotine replacements helps to avert withdrawal symptoms

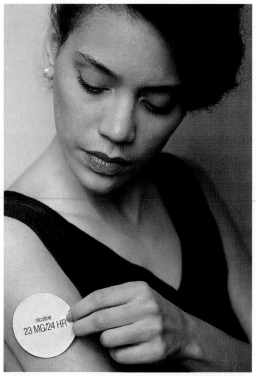

Is the path to abstinence from smoking skin deep? Forms of nicotine replacement therapy—such as nicotine transdermal (skin) patches and chewing gum that contains nicotine—allow people to continue to receive nicotine when they quit smoking. Nicotine replacement therapy has been shown to be significantly more effective than placebos in helping people quit smoking, but it does not address the behavioral components of addiction to nicotine, such as the habit of smoking while drinking alcohol. Nicotine replacement therapy is apparently more effective when it is combined with behavior therapy that focuses on changing smoking habits.

when dependent smokers discontinue cigarettes. Once the smoking habit is suspended, ex-smokers can wean themselves from the sources of nicotine replacement.

A review of placebo-controlled studies of nicotine-chewing-gum treatment supports its usefulness in quitting smoking (Baille et al., 1990). Early double-blind studies also show that nicotine transdermal patches lead to higher initial smoking cessation rates than placebo patches do (Tonnesen et al., 1991; Transdermal Nicotine Study Group, 1991). But what about long-term results?

Nicotine patches, like nicotine gum, may help quell the physiological components of withdrawal, but they have no effect on the behavioral components of the addiction, such as the habit of smoking while drinking alcohol (Weiss, 1992). As a result, nicotine replacement is relatively ineffective in promoting long-term changes unless it is combined with behavior therapy that focuses on changing smoking habits. In one recent study, nicotine gum failed to improve long-term abstinence from cigarette smoking when given in the absence of behavioral therapy (Killen et al., 1990). However, a combination of nicotine replacement therapy and behavioral counseling is apparently more effective than either approach alone (Killen et al., 1990; Lichtenstein & Glasgow, 1992). Early evidence on the effectiveness of nicotine patches shows that smokers who quit with them stand about the same chances of relapse as people who quit without them (Weiss, 1992). By 6 months after quitting smoking, fewer than half of the smokers who quit using patches or not using patches remain abstinent. For reasons such as these, psychologists have devised a number of methods referred to as relapse-prevention training (discussed later in the chapter).

■ **METHADONE MAINTENANCE PROGRAMS**
Methadone is an **opioid**—similar to an opium derivative in chemical structure, but synthesized in the laboratory. Methadone is used to treat physiological dependence on heroin in the same way that heroin was once used to treat physiological dependence on morphine. Methadone is slower acting than heroin and does not provide the thrilling rush, however. Methadone programs are usually publicly financed and hence relieve heroin-dependent people of the need to engage in illicit activity to support their habits. It can be taken indefinitely. On the other hand, people treated with methadone can be conceptualized as swapping dependence on one drug for dependence on another.

Methadone is taken orally in single doses in the clinic setting. Ironically, methadone has also become

MULTICULTURAL PERSPECTIVES

Treatment of Alcoholism Among Ethnic Minority Groups

Treatment approaches to alcoholism involve common themes such as recognizing the problem, increasing awareness of the reasons for drinking, and developing the motivation to refrain from drinking (Moss et al., 1985). Moreover, they attend to factors that cut across ethnic groups, such as financial problems. Yet many members of ethnic minority groups resist traditional treatment approaches because they feel excluded from full participation in society (Westermeyer, 1984). Native American alcoholic women, for example, tend to respond less favorably to traditional alcoholism counseling than white women (Rogan, 1986). Hurlburt and Gade (1984) attribute this difference to the resistance of Native American women to "white man's" authority. They suggest that the early stages of intervention might be more successful in overcoming this resistance if treatment were provided by Native American counselors.

The use of counselors from the client's own ethnic group is an example of a culturally sensitive treatment approach. Culturally sensitive approaches pay special attention to ethnic factors in alcoholism (Rogan, 1986). Culturally sensitive programs that address all facets of the human being, including racial and cultural identity, can nurture pride that helps people resist the temptation to cope with stress through chemicals (Rogan, 1986).

Treatment providers may also be more successful if they recognize and incorporate indigenous forms of healing into the treatment process (Rogan, 1986). For example, spirituality is an important aspect of traditional Native American culture, and spiritualists have played important roles as natural healers. Seeking the assistance of a spiritu-

alist may help improve the counseling relationship (Knox, 1985). Likewise, given the importance of the church in African-American and Hispanic-American culture, counselors working with alcoholics from these groups may be more successful when they draw on clergy and church members as resources in the treatment process.

Culturally sensitive treatment for alcoholism. Culturally sensitive treatment of drinking problems address all aspects of the person, including ethnic factors and the nurturance of pride in one's cultural identity. Ethnic pride may help people resist the temptation to cope with stress through alcohol and other substances.

desirable as a street drug because users have found that if they inject it rather than take it orally, it can provide sensations similar to those of heroin. One study compared a combination of paraprofessional (lay) drug counseling, professional psychotherapy, and methadone maintenance to paraprofessional drug counseling and methadone maintenance alone among 93 male veterans. The addition of professional psychotherapy produced significantly better results on a battery of tests of abnormal behaviors (Woody et al., 1987). Perhaps skillful therapy better helps people manage stress and develop adaptive behaviors than chemicals alone or chemicals and lay counseling.

■ **NALOXONE** Another drug, **naloxone**, prevents users from becoming high if they subsequently take heroin. Some people are placed on naloxone after being withdrawn from heroin. However, the basic limitation of naloxone is identical to that of disulfiram: People can choose not to use it. Drugs like naloxone also do not provide the positive reinforcement yielded by heroin. It thus fails to motivate heroin users to undertake a heroin-free lifestyle.

Drugs like disulfiram and methadone are apparently more useful when they are combined with counseling, job training, and stress management—processes that provide substance abusers the skills they need to embark on a life in the mainstream culture.

Nonprofessional Support Groups

Despite the complexity of the factors contributing to substance abuse and dependence, these problems are frequently handled by laypeople or nonprofessionals. Such people often have or had the problems themselves. For example, self-help group meetings are sponsored by organizations like Alcoholics Anonymous (AA), Narcotics Anonymous, and Cocaine Anonymous. These groups promote abstinence and provide members an opportunity to discuss their feelings and experiences in a supportive group setting. More experienced group members (sponsors) support newer members during periods of crisis or potential relapse. The meetings are without charge.

■ **ALCOHOLICS ANONYMOUS**

> "It's the first drink that gets you drunk."
> "One day at a time."
>
> AA Slogans

Many laypeople and professionals consider **Alcoholics Anonymous** to provide the most effective treatment for problem drinkers. AA was begun in the 1930s. Although it is run by laypeople, it is based on the disease model of alcoholism. AA assumes that alcoholics are never cured, regardless of how long they abstain from alcohol or how well they control their drinking. Instead of being "cured," alcoholics are seen as "recovering." It is also assumed that people need help in order to stop drinking. AA is so deeply embedded in the consciousness of helping professionals that many of them automatically refer newly detoxified people to AA as the follow-up agency.

The AA experience is in part spiritual, in part group supportive, in part cognitive. Participants in AA meetings are encouraged to recognize their powerlessness over alcohol and seek the help of a "higher power," which discourages some potential members, including agnostics and atheists who prefer not to seek divine support. Prayer and meditation are urged upon members to help them get in touch with their higher power. The meetings themselves provide group support. So does the buddy, or sponsoring system, which encourages members to call each other for support when they feel tempted to drink.

AA claims to have a high success rate, one in the neighborhood of 75% (Wallace, 1985). Critics note that percentages this high are based on personal testimony—a series of anecdotes—rather than on careful surveys or experiments. Moreover, such estimates include only persons who attend meetings for extended periods. As many as 90% of those who try AA drop out after a handful of meetings (Miller, 1982). AA fails to keep records of members in order to protect their anonymity (Brownell et al., 1986). AA also fails to use control groups in assessing the effectiveness of treatment (O'Connor & Daly, 1985). Therefore, we cannot rule out a selection factor as possibly being at least partly responsible for any benefits attributed to AA. Perhaps some people who apparently benefit from AA actually improve because they have decided to change their lives.

Al-Anon, begun in 1951, is a spinoff of AA that supports the spouses, partners, and parents of alcoholics. There are some 26,000 Al-Anon groups nationwide (Desmond, 1987). Another spinoff of AA, Alateen, provides support to children of alcoholics, helping them to see that they are not to blame for their parents' drinking and are thus undeserving of the guilt they may feel. A nonreligious alternative to AA, Rational Recovery, is acquiring some followers (Hall, 1990).

■ **NARCOTICS ANONYMOUS AND COCAINE ANONYMOUS** Narcotics Anonymous and Cocaine Anonymous also urge members to admit their powerlessness, to place their faith in a higher power, and to make use of a buddy system. The problems of evaluating the effectiveness of these programs parallel the problems of evaluating AA.

In the following case of a cocaine abuser, individual therapy was combined with support group meetings sponsored by Narcotics Anonymous:

Paul A., a 31-year-old accountant, entered psychotherapy after his wife told him to either seek treatment for his cocaine abuse or leave the house. He had been treating his wife and son cruelly, was neglecting responsibilities at work, and had experienced numerous bouts of depression. The major focus of his first two months of psychotherapy was stopping his cocaine use. His therapist encouraged Paul to attend Narcotics Anonymous meetings, and they discussed the feelings, events, and places that stimulated his desire for cocaine. Paul's therapist also taught him techniques that could help him avoid drug use even when his craving for cocaine was high.

As Paul's preoccupation with cocaine diminished with a lengthening period of abstinence, the focus of his psychotherapy began to shift toward the initial precipitants for his drug use: anxiety about becoming a father (he began heavy cocaine use during his wife's pregnancy), and his own unresolved relationships with his abusive alcoholic father. As he began to learn more about these issues, he gained a greater sense of mastery over his emotions, and his desire to escape from uncomfortable feelings decreased.

■ *Weiss and Mirin, 1987, p. 126*

Residential Approaches

In residential approaches, substance abusers live at their treatment centers, such as hospitals and therapeutic communities. Hospitalization may be recommended when substance abusers cannot exercise self-control in their usual environments, when dependent users cannot tolerate withdrawal symptoms, and when abusers' behavior is self-destructive or dangerous to others (Weiss & Mirin, 1987). Outpatient treatment is less costly and is often indicated when withdrawal symptoms are less severe, clients are committed to changing their behavior, and environmental support systems, such as families, strive to help clients make the transition to a drug-free lifestyle.

When alcoholism was given disease status by the American Medical Association in 1966, only a few medically based treatment programs existed, such as the renowned Hazelden program in Minnesota (Desmond, 1987). Since then, many thousands have come into being (Desmond, 1987). Some of these programs, like the Betty Ford Clinic, have received a great deal of media attention.

Most inpatient programs use an extended 28-day detoxification, or drying-out, period, an approach initiated at Hazelden in 1949. Clients are helped through withdrawal symptoms in a few days. Then the emphasis shifts to counseling about the destructive effects of alcohol and combating distorted ideas or rationalizations. Within the disease model, the goal of abstinence is urged (Desmond, 1987).

Getting started. This woman is being admitted to a drug rehabilitation center, in which the first step will be helping her safely withdraw from chemical dependence. She will then be faced with the ongoing challenge of developing a lifestyle that is devoid of drugs.

It has not been demonstrated that most alcoholics require hospitalization (some certainly do). A review of studies comparing outpatient and inpatient programs revealed no overall difference in relapse rates (Miller & Hester, 1986). However, medical insurance may not cover outpatient treatment, which may encourage many problem drinkers to admit themselves for inpatient care.

A number of residential therapeutic communities are also in use. Some of them have part- or full-time professional staffs. Others are run completely by laypeople. One of the earliest communities was Synanon, which followed the disease-model belief that substance abusers differ from other people in basic ways and must abstain completely from their habits. Participants were required to assume progressive responsibilities. They began by maintaining their personal hygiene, beds, and rooms, and, eventually, they worked to contribute to community life. Lapses were confronted harshly in regular and spontaneous group sessions. Members were also confronted about their excuses for failing to take responsibility for themselves and about their denial of the damage being done by their abuse. Members shared their life experiences to help each other develop productive ways of handling stress. Synanon has long since closed its doors, but its communal approach has served as a model for other communities such as Daytop Village and Phoenix House.

Assessment of the results of these therapeutic communities, like AA, suffers from an absence of controlled studies. Like AA, therapeutic communities have high numbers of early dropouts. In addition, many former members who managed to remain substance-free while they dwelled in these communities and helped treat others relapsed when they returned to the world outside.

Psychodynamic Approaches

Psychoanalysts view substance abuse and dependence as symptomatic of conflicts that are rooted in childhood experiences. Focusing on substance abuse or dependence per se is seen to offer, at most, a superficial type of therapy. It is assumed that if the underlying conflicts are resolved, abusive behavior will also subside as more mature forms of gratification are sought. Traditional psychoanalysts also assume that programs directed solely at abusive behavior will be of limited benefit because they fail to address the underlying psychological causes of abuse.

There are many reports of successful psychodynamic case studies with substance abusers, particularly with problem drinkers. However, there is a dearth of controlled and replicable research studies.

The effectiveness of psychodynamic methods for treating substance abuse and dependence thus remains unclear.

Behavioral Approaches

Behavioral approaches to substance abuse and dependence focus on modifying abusive and dependent behavior patterns. The issue to many behaviorally oriented therapists is not whether substance abuse and dependence are diseases but whether or not abusers can learn to change their behavior when they are faced with temptation.

■ **SELF-CONTROL STRATEGIES** Self-control training focuses on helping abusers develop skills they can use to change their abusive behavior. Behavior therapists focus on three components of substance abuse:

1. The *antecedent* cues or stimuli (A's) that prompt or trigger abuse,
2. The abusive *behaviors* (B's) themselves, and
3. The reinforcing or punishing *consequences* (C's) that maintain or discourage abuse.

Table 9.7 shows the kinds of strategies that are used to modify the "ABCs" of substance abuse.

■ **AVERSIVE CONDITIONING** In **aversive conditioning**, painful or aversive stimuli are paired with substance abuse or abuse-related stimuli to make abuse less appealing. In the case of problem drinking, tastes of different alcoholic beverages are usually paired with chemically induced nausea and vomiting or with electric shock (Wilson, 1991). As a consequence, alcohol may come to elicit an aversive conditioned response, such as fear or nausea, that inhibits drinking. Avoidance of alcohol is then negatively reinforced by relief from aversive responses.

In one large-scale study of aversive conditioning in the treatment of alcoholism, 63% of the 685 people treated remained abstinent for 1 year afterward, and about a third remained abstinent for at least 3 years (Wiens & Menustik, 1983). A review article concluded there was consistent evidence that chemical aversion treatment (pairing alcohol ingestion with emetically induced nausea) produced 1-year abstinence rates of approximately 60% (Elkins, 1991). A 60% abstinence rate is considered reasonably successful, given the recalcitrance of alcoholism to treatment. Wilson (1991) counters, however, that emetic therapy is costly and intrusive, and has not been shown to be superior to less costly treatment methods. Moreover, it seems that aversive conditioned

Table 9.7   Self-Control Strategies for Modifying the "ABC's" of Substance Abuse

1. Controlling the A's (Antecedents) of Substance Abuse:

Substance abusers become conditioned to a wide range of external (environmental) and internal stimuli (body states). Substance abusers may begin to break these stimulus–response connections by:

- Removing drinking and smoking paraphrenalia from the home—all alcoholic beverages, beer mugs, carafes, ashtrays, matches, cigarette packs, lighters, etc.
- Restricting the stimulus environment in which drinking or smoking is permitted. Use the substance only in a stimulus-deprived area of their homes, such as the garage, bathroom, or basement. All other stimuli that might be connected to using the substance are removed—there is no TV, reading materials, radio or telephone. In this way, substance abuse becomes detached from many controlling stimuli.
- Not socializing with substance abusers, by avoiding situations linked to abuse—bars, the street, bowling alleys, etc.
- Frequenting substance-free environments—lectures or concerts, a gym, museums, evening classes. By socializing with nonabusers, sitting in nonsmoking cars of trains, eating in restaurants without liquor licenses.
- Managing the internal triggers for abuse. By practicing self-relaxation or meditation and not taking the substance when tense. By expressing angry feelings by writing them down or self-assertion, not by taking the substance. By seeking counseling for prolonged feelings of depression, not alcohol, pills, or cigarettes.

2. Controlling the B's (Behaviors) of Substance Abuse:

People can prevent and interrupt substance abuse by:

- Using response prevention—breaking abusive habits by physically preventing them from occurring or making them more difficult. By not bringing alcohol home or cigarettes to the office.
- Using competing responses when tempted. By being prepared to handle substance-related situations with appropriate ammunition—mints, sugarless chewing gum, etc. By taking a bath or shower, walking the dog, walking around the block, taking a drive, calling a friend, spending time in a substance-free environment, practicing meditation or relaxation, or exercising when tempted, rather than using the substance.
- Making abuse more laborious—buying one can of beer at a time; storing matches, ashtrays, and cigarettes far apart; wrapping cigarettes in foil to make smoking more cumbersome; pausing for 10 minutes when struck by the urge to drink, smoke, or use another substance and asking oneself, "Do I really need *this* one?"

3. Controlling the C's (Consequences) of Substance Abuse:

Substance abuse has immediate positive consequences such as pleasure, relief from anxiety and withdrawal symptoms, and stimulation. People can counter these intrinsic rewards and alter the balance of power in favor of nonabuse by:

- Rewarding themselves for nonabuse and punishing themselves for abuse.
- Switching to brands of beer and cigarettes they don't like.
- Setting gradual substance-reduction schedules and rewarding themselves for sticking to them.
- Punishing themselves for failing to meet substance-reduction goals. Substance abusers can assess themselves, say, 10 cents for each slip and donate the cash to an unpalatable cause, such as a brother-in-law's birthday present.
- Rehearsing motivating thoughts or self-statements—like writing reasons for quitting smoking on index cards. For example:

Each day I don't smoke adds another day to my life.
Quitting smoking will help me breathe deeply again.
Foods will smell and taste better when I quit smoking.
Think how much money I'll save by not smoking.
Think how much cleaner my teeth and fingers will be by not smoking.
I'll be proud to tell others that I kicked the habit.
My lungs will become clearer each and every day I don't smoke.

Smokers can carry a list of 20 to 25 such statements and read several of them at various times throughout the day. They can become parts of one's daily routine, a constant reminder of one's goals.

responses are readily extinguished because exposure to alcohol in real-life settings is not paired with chemical or electrical aversion.

Aversive conditioning for smoking aims at making once pleasurable cigarette smoke aversive through some form of overexposure. In **rapid smoking**, for example, smokers puff at a faster than usual rate, about once every 6 seconds until they begin to feel nauseated. The nausea acts as an unconditioned stimulus that becomes paired with smoking-related conditioned stimuli such as the taste and aroma of cigarette smoke, the feel of the cigarette in the hand, and so on. After repeated pairings, cigarette smoke becomes aversive and smokers are motivated to avert it by quitting. Generally speaking, the long-term results of rapid smoking and other forms of aversive conditioning in maintaining abstinence from smoking have ranged from poor to modestly successful (Brandon et al., 1987; Glasgow & Lichtenstein, 1987; Sateia, 1987; Schwartz, 1987). Taylor and Killen (1991) report an average quit rate across studies of

rapid smoking at 1-year follow-up of 25%. Interest in rapid smoking appears to have waned (Taylor & Killen, 1991), in part because questions persist about the safety of drawing so much nicotine and carbon monoxide into the body so quickly.

Behavior therapists have also used **covert sensitization**—a form of aversive conditioning that employs imaginal rather than actual aversive stimuli. For example, clients are instructed to imagine becoming nauseous and vomiting when taking a drink or puffing a cigarette. The scenes typically end with rejection of the substance and feelings of relief. Evidence from controlled studies of the efficacy of covert sensitization in treating substance abuse is lacking, however.

■ **SOCIAL SKILLS TRAINING**   Social skills training helps people develop effective interpersonal responses in social situations that prompt substance abuse. Assertiveness training, for example, may be used to teach alcoholic clients how to fend off social

---

The Controlled Social Drinking Controversy

The disease model of alcoholism contends that alcoholics who have just one drink will lose control and go on a binge. Some professionals, however, like Linda and Mark Sobell, have argued that behavior modification self-control techniques can teach many alcoholics to engage in **controlled social drinking**—to have a drink or two without necessarily falling off the wagon.

The contention that alcoholics can learn to drink moderately remains controversial. The proponents of the disease model of alcoholism, who have wielded considerable political strength, stand strongly opposed to attempts to teach controlled social drinking.

To support their contention, the Sobells published the results of an experiment with 20 alcoholics who were taught to control their drinking. The Sobells (1973, 1976, 1984) reported that 85% of their subjects remained in control of their drinking at a 2-year follow-up. However, a research group critical of the Sobells (Pendery et al., 1982) published its own follow-up of the Sobells' subjects. The group claimed that only one person had remained successful at controlled social drinking. Most had returned to uncontrolled drinking on many occasions, and four of the group had died from alcohol-related causes.

Yet other investigators have found that controlled social drinking is a reasonable treatment goal for younger, less alcohol-dependent problem drinkers who are headed on the road toward chronic alcoholism (Miller & Muñoz, 1983; Pomerleau et al., 1977; Sanchez-Craig et al., 1984; Sanchez-Craig & Wilkinson, 1986/1987; Strickler et al., 1976; Wallace et al., 1988; Vogler et al., 1975). Evidence supporting controlled social drinking programs for chronic alcoholics, however, remains lacking. Interest in controlled social drinking programs has also waned, largely because of strong opposition from professionals and lay organizations committed to the abstinence model.

Controlled drinking programs may be best suited for alcohol abusers who reject the goal of total abstinence, who have failed in programs requiring abstinence, who have a relatively short history of problem drinking, and who do not show severe withdrawal symptoms (Lawson, 1983; Sobell et al., 1990). On the other hand, controlled social drinking may not be appropriate for individuals who believe in the goal of abstinence, who are taking medications that may negatively interact with alcohol, who incur health risks from drinking even small amounts of alcohol, who have histories of severe intoxication ("alcohol binges") or withdrawal symptoms, or who have failed in previous controlled drinking programs (Lawson, 1983).

pressures to drink (Lawson, 1983). Behavioral marital therapy seeks to improve marital communication and a couple's problem-solving skills to relieve marital stresses that can trigger abuse. Couples may learn how to use written behavioral contracts. One such contract might stipulate that the substance abuser agrees to abstain from drinking or to take Antabuse, while his or her spouse agrees to refrain from comments about past drinking and the probability of future lapses.

Relapse-Prevention Training

The word **relapse** derives from Latin roots meaning "to slide back." From 50 to 90% of those who quit alcohol and other habit-forming substances will eventually return to them, or relapse (Brownell et al., 1986a, 1986b). It is estimated that about 3 out of 4 relapses to alcohol abuse occur in response to negative emotional states such as depression or anxiety, to interpersonal conflict, or to social pressures to resume drinking (Lawson, 1983). Problem drinkers who relapse are more likely than those who do not to have encountered stress (Grant, 1990), such as loss of a loved one or economic problems. They are also more likely than alcoholics who maintain sobriety to rely on avoidance methods of coping, such as denial. Successful abstainers tend to have more social and family resources and support to draw on in handling stress (Havassy et al., 1991).

Research suggests that virtually any behavioral treatment enables as many as 50 to 80% of smokers to quit—at least temporarily (Sateia, 1987). Another picture emerges when we consider relapse rates, however. Six-month to 1-year follow-up abstinence rates deteriorate to 20 to 25% for behavioral interventions overall (Sateia, 1987).

Because of the prevalence of relapse, behaviorally oriented therapists have devised a number of methods referred to as **relapse-prevention training**. Such training helps substance abusers cope with temptations and high-risk situations to prevent *lapses*—that is, slips—from becoming full-blown relapses (Marlatt & Gordon, 1980). High-risk situations include negative mood states, such as depression, anger, or anxiety; interpersonal conflict (e.g., marital problems or conflicts with employers); and socially conducive situations such as "the guys getting together." Participants learn to cope with these situations, for example, by learning self-relaxation skills to counter anxiety and learning to resist social pressures to resume use of the substance. Trainees are also taught to avoid practices that might prompt a relapse, such as keeping alcohol on hand for friends.

Although it contains many behavioral strategies, relapse-prevention training is a cognitive-behavioral technique in that it also focuses on substance abusers' *interpretations* of any lapses or slips that may occur, such as smoking a first cigarette or taking a first drink following quitting. Clients are taught how to avoid the so-called **abstinence violation effect** (AVE)—the tendency to overreact to a lapse—by learning to reorient their thinking about lapses and slips. People who have a slip may be more likely to relapse if they attribute their slip to self-perceived weaknesses and experience guilt and shame (Curry, 1987). For example, consider a skater who slips on the ice (Marlatt & Gordon, 1985). Whether or not the skater gets back up and continues to perform depends largely on whether the skater sees the slip as an isolated and correctable event or as a sign of complete failure.

In contrast to the disease model, which contends that alcoholics automatically lose control if they take a single drink, the relapse-prevention model assumes that whether or not a lapse becomes a relapse depends on the person's interpretation of the lapse (Marlatt & Gordon, 1985). Self-defeating attributions such as "What's the use? I'm just doomed to fail" trigger depression, resignation, and resumption of problem drinking. Participants in relapse-prevention training programs are encouraged to view lapses as temporary setbacks that provide opportunities to learn what kinds of situations lead to temptation and how they can avoid or cope with such situations. If they can learn to think, "Okay, I had a slip, but that doesn't mean that all is lost unless I believe that it is," they are less likely to catastrophize lapses and subsequently relapse. Another relapse-prevention approach enhances social support by training smokers' spouses or partners to be more helpful in maintaining abstinence (for example, McIntyre-Kingsolver et al., 1986). Social support appears to play a key role in determining relapse in abstinence-based programs for alcoholism, drug abuse, and cigarette smoking (Havassy et al., 1991). The aspect of support that most strongly reduced the risk of relapse was the presence of a spouse or close friend who was available to provide help, comfort, and understanding.

All in all, efforts to help people discontinue substance abuse and dependence have been mixed at best. Many abusers really do not want to discontinue use of these substances. They would prefer, if possible, to avert their negative consequences. Unfortunately, negative outcomes frequently take some time to develop—perhaps decades in the cases of alcohol and cigarettes—whereas the pleasures of the next drink, puff, or fix are immediate.

In many cases, particularly with lay support groups and residential programs, treatment outcomes have not been adequately evaluated, so that most claims of success are unsubstantiated. Moreover, because of lack of funds, many thousands of substance abusers who would like treatment find it unavailable. Even the apparently well-controlled experiments run by some investigators frequently employ a "shotgun" approach of behavioral and cognitive techniques so that it is unclear which ones—if any—are helpful. In addition, it is one thing to help abusers and dependent people initially discontinue usage of the substances that entice them. It is another to help them prevent relapse.

In the case of inner-city youth who have become trapped within a milieu of street drugs and hopelessness, the availability of culturally sensitive counseling and job training opportunities would be of considerable benefit in helping them assume more productive social roles. The challenge is clear: to develop cost-effective ways of helping people recognize the negative effects of substances and forgo the powerful and immediate reinforcements they provide.

Summary

Patterns of Substance Abuse and Dependence

According to the DSM, substance abuse disorders involve continued or repeated use of a substance despite awareness that it causes or aggravates one's problems, or repeated use in dangerous situations, such as driving while intoxicated. Substance dependence disorders, which often include signs of physiological dependence, involve loss of control over substances and continued use despite knowledge of adverse effects.

Substance abuse, at least casual patterns of abuse, has apparently declined among most young adults in recent years, perhaps because of publicity about drugs' harmful effects. Many so-called hard-core substance abusers are not accessible to standard survey techniques, however.

Depressants

Depressants discussed in the chapter include alcohol, sedatives and minor tranquilizers, and opioids.

Alcohol is the most widely abused drug in the United States. Effects of alcohol include intoxication, impaired coordination, slurred speech, and impaired intellectual functioning. Chronic alcohol abuse has been connected with disorders such as alcohol amnestic disorder (Korsakoff's syndrome), cirrhosis of the liver and other physical disorders, and with fetal alcohol syndrome.

Barbiturates are depressants or sedatives that have been used medically for relief of anxiety and short-term insomnia, among other uses.

Opioids such as morphine and heroin are derived from the opium poppy. Others are synthesized. Used medically for relief of pain, they are strongly addictive.

Stimulants

Stimulants increase the activity of the nervous system. Although the effects differ somewhat from drug to drug, they may produce feelings of euphoria and self-confidence.

Amphetamines and cocaine increase the availability of neurotransmitters in the brain, heightening states of arousal. High doses can produce an amphetamine psychosis, which mimics features of paranoid schizophrenia.

Cocaine tends to enhance alertness and performance, bolster confidence, and induce states of pleasure. Crack, a hardened smokable form of cocaine, is quickly habit forming. Use of cocaine is associated with various health risks that can lead to sudden death, as in the case of some athletes, or the development of chronic health problems.

Repeated use of nicotine, usually in the form of cigarette smoking, can lead to a physiological dependence.

Psychedelics

The hallucinogenics include LSD, psilocybin, and mescaline. Other drugs with similar effects are cannabis (marijuana) and phencyclidine (PCP). There is little evidence that these drugs induce physiological dependence, although psychological dependence may occur.

LSD is a synthetic drug that can induce hallucinations, which can recur at later times in the form of flashbacks. PCP—"angel dust"—can induce feelings of dissociation and hallucinations. It remains unclear whether marijuana produces an amotivational syndrome or other long-term cognitive effects. But its short-term negative effects on motor performance and on memory and learning, its ability to elevate the heart rate and perhaps blood pressure, and its carcinogenic potential all raise serious concerns about its use.

Theoretical Perspectives

Biological perspectives focus on uncovering the biological pathways that may explain mechanisms of physiological dependence. The disease model treats problems of substance abuse and dependence as disease processes. Learning theorists view substance abuse disorders as maladaptive behavior patterns that are largely acquired by means of conditioning and observational learning. Cognitive perspectives have focused on roles of attitudes, beliefs, and expectancies in substance abuse and dependence. Research suggests that the one-drink effect may be a self-fulfilling prophecy. Sociocultural perspectives have focused on the adoption of culturally sanctioned prohibitions against excessive drinking in explaining differences among various ethnic and religious groups in rates of alcoholism. Social factors, such as peer pressure, also influence the development of substance abuse. Psychodynamic theorists view problems of substance abuse, such as excessive drinking and habitual smoking, as signs of oral fixation.

Treatment

Biological approaches to substance abuse disorders include detoxification; the use of disulfiram, methadone, naloxone, and other chemical preparations; and nicotine replacement strategies. Biological approaches are apparently more effective when they are combined with psychotherapy or behavior therapy. Residential treatment approaches include hospitals and therapeutic communities. Nonprofessional support groups, like Alcoholics Anonymous and Narcotics Anonymous, promote abstinence within a supportive group setting.

Psychodynamic therapists focus on uncovering the inner conflicts, originating in childhood, that are believed to be at the root of substance abuse problems. Behavior therapists focus on helping substance abusers change problem behaviors in the present through such techniques as self-control training, aversive conditioning, and skills training approaches. Regardless of the initial success of a treatment technique, relapse remains a pressing problem in treating substance abusers. Relapse-prevention training employs cognitive-behavioral techniques to help ex-abusers cope with high-risk situations and to prevent lapses from becoming relapses by helping participants to interpret lapses in less damaging ways.

KEY FOR "HOW DO YOU KNOW IF YOU ARE HOOKED?" QUESTIONNAIRE

Any "yes" answer suggests that you may be dependent on alcohol. If you have answered any of these questions in the affirmative, we suggest that you seriously examine what your drinking means to you.

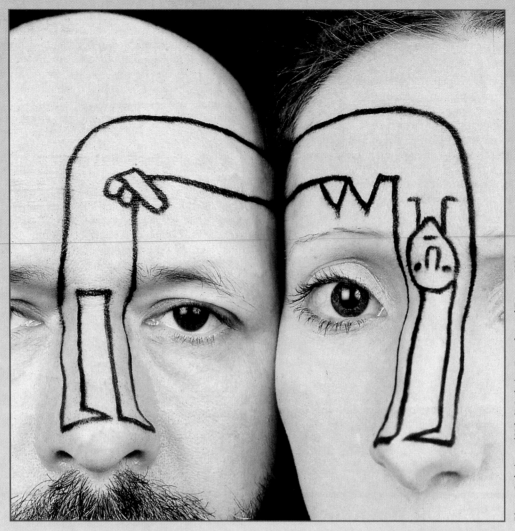

Rimma Gerlovina and Valeriy Gerlovina, Romulus and Remus, 1989. Ektacolor print: 37½ × 37½. Steinbaum Krauss Gallery, New York.

CHAPTER OUTLINE

10

Sexual and Gender Identity Disorders and Variations in Sexual Behavior

TRUTH  FICTION?

___ In some cultures in the world, victims of rape are often blamed for the crime.

___ A gay male or lesbian sexual orientation is caused by hormone imbalances.

___ People have been transformed into members of the other gender through surgery.

___ Some people are sexually aroused by violence.

___ Rapists are mentally ill.

___ People who wear revealing bathing suits are exhibitionists.

___ People who like to watch their spouses disrobe are voyeurs.

___ Some people cannot become sexually aroused unless they are subjected to pain or humiliation by others.

___ Orgasm is a reflex.

___ Sexual dysfunctions are rare.

___ Men are always eager for sex.

___ People who love one another have satisfying sexual relations.

LEARNING OBJECTIVES

When you have completed your study of Chapter 10, you should be able to:

1. Describe sociocultural factors in conceptions of what sexual behaviors are normal and abnormal.

2. Discuss the changes in the DSM concerning the classification of homosexuality as a mental disorder.

3. Discuss the psychological adjustment of gay men and lesbians.

4. Discuss theoretical perspectives on sexual orientation.

5. Discuss issues concerning "therapy" of gay men and lesbians.

6. Describe gender identity disorder.

7. Describe the process of gender reassignment and discuss its success.

8. Discuss the incidence of rape.

9. Discuss theoretical perspectives on the causes of rape.

10. Discuss the effects of rape on victims.

11. Discuss the treatment of rape victims and of rapists.

12. Define and describe the features of various paraphilias.

13. Describe the effects of childhood sexual abuse on victims.

14. Discuss theoretical perspectives on the paraphilias.

15. Discuss treatment of persons with paraphilias.

16. Describe the phases of the sexual response cycle.

17. Define and describe the features of various sexual dysfunctions.

18. Discuss theoretical perspectives on sexual dysfunctions.

19. Discuss treatment of the sexual dysfunctions.

*O*ff the fog-bound shore of Ireland lies the isle of Inis Beag.[1] From the air it is a verdant jewel, warm and enticing. From the ground, the perspective is different.

For example, the inhabitants of Inis Beag believe that normal women do not have orgasms and that those who do must be deviant (Messenger, 1971). Premarital sex is virtually unknown. Women participate in sexual relations in order to conceive children and pacify their husbands' lustful urges. They need not be concerned about being called on for frequent performances, because the men of Inis Beag believe, groundlessly, that sex saps their strength. Relations on Inis Beag take place in the dark—literally and figuratively, and with the nightclothes on. Consistent with local standards of masculinity, the man ejaculates as quickly as he can. Then he rolls over and goes to sleep, without concern for his partner's satisfaction. Women do not complain, however, as they are reared to believe that it is abnormal for them to experience sexual pleasure.

If Inis Beag is not your cup of tea, perhaps the ambience of Mangaia will strike you as more congenial. Mangaia is a Polynesian pearl. Languidly Mangaia lifts out of the azure waters of the Pacific. Inis Beag and Mangaia are on opposite sides of the world—literally and figuratively.

From childhood, Mangaian children are expected to explore their sexuality through masturbation (Marshall, 1971). Mangaian teenagers are encouraged by their elders to engage in sexual relations. They will be found on hidden beaches or beneath the sheltering fronds of palms, industriously practicing skills acquired from their elders. Mangaian women usually reach orgasm numerous times before their partners do. Young men vie to see who is more skillful in helping their partners attain multiple orgasms.

The inhabitants of Mangaia and Inis Beag have like anatomic features and the same hormones pulse through their bodies. Their attitudes and cultural values about what is normal and abnormal differ vastly, however. Their attitudes affect their sexual behavior and the enjoyment they attain—or do not attain—from sex. In sex, as in other areas of behavior, the lines between the normal and the abnormal are not always drawn precisely. Sex, like eating, is a natural function. Yet this natural function has been profoundly affected by cultural, religious, and moral beliefs, custom, folklore, and superstition.

Even in the United States today, we find attitudes as diverse as those on Inis Beag and Mangaia. Some people feel guilty about any form of sexual activity and thus reap little if any pleasure

---
[1]Inis Beag is actually a pseudonym for an Irish folk community.

from sex. Others, who see themselves as the children of the sexual revolution, may worry about whether they have become free enough or skillful enough in their sexual activity.

NORMAL AND ABNORMAL IN SEXUAL BEHAVIOR

In the realm of sexual behavior, our conceptions of what is normal and what is not are clearly influenced by sociocultural factors. Various patterns of sexual behavior that might be considered abnormal in Inis Beag, such as masturbation, premarital intercourse, and oral-genital sex, are normal in American society, statistically speaking, because more people report these behaviors than deny them (Blumstein & Schwartz, 1983; Hunt, 1974). Behavior is sometimes labeled as abnormal because it deviates from the norms of one's society. Yet consider a handful of the variations in sexual behavior and attitudes that we find around the world:

- Because women's breasts are eroticized in Western culture, Western laws and social codes require that they usually be shielded from public view. Yet the kinds of stimuli that are considered sexually arousing vary enormously from culture to culture. In some societies, breasts are considered of interest to nursing children only, and that is because the children connect them with food. Women in such societies often go bare-breasted when the weather permits. Among the Abkhasian people in the southern part of the former Soviet Union, men are sexually aroused by women's armpits (Benet, 1974). Women's armpits may thus be seen by their husbands only (Kammeyer, 1990).

- The incest taboo is one of the few sexual beliefs that is found universally across the world. Even so, some societies believe that men and women who eat together are engaging in a mild form of sexual activity. Societies with such beliefs thus forbid brothers and sisters from eating together (Kammeyer et al., 1990).

- Kissing is a highly popular form of mild petting in Western culture but is unknown among such cultures as the Siriono of Bolivia and the Thonga of Africa. The Thonga were shocked when they first observed European visitors kissing, and one man exclaimed, "Look at them—they eat each others' saliva and dirt."

- Sexual fidelity is highly valued nearly everywhere in the United States. Nevertheless, it is considered polite among the Native American Aleut people of Alaska for a husband to offer his wife to a visitor.

- In the patriarchal society of Pakistan, the Hudood Ordinance has resulted in prison sentences for some women who have accused men of raping them. The ordinance accords more believability to men's testimony than to women's testimony. Women are sometimes even prevented from offering testimony. As a result, some women who charge men with rape have thus been prosecuted for adultery, whereas their assailants, claiming that any sexual contact was consensual, have been acquitted (Schork, 1990). If this Pakistani ordinance

A.

B.

What is normal and what is abnormal in the realm of sexual and sexually related behavior patterns? The cultural context must be considered in defining what is normal and what is abnormal. The people in these photographs—and the ways in which they cloak or expose their bodies—would be quite out of place in one another's societies.

sounds "foreign" to you, however, you may wish to reflect on some of the reasons that the great majority of women who are raped in the United States fail to report the crimes to authorities. As we see later in the chapter, the victim is often blamed for the crime in the United States as well.

 In some cultures in the world, victims of rape are indeed often blamed for the crime. The United States is one such culture.

Sexual behavior may also be considered abnormal if it is self-defeating, harms others, or causes personal distress, among other criteria. This chapter considers sexual and gender identity disorders and variations in sexual behavior. We address the topics of sexual orientation, gender identity disorder, rape, paraphilias, and sexual dysfunctions. In doing so, we explore several questions that probe the boundaries between abnormality and normality. For example, is a gay male or lesbian sexual orientation a mental disorder? Where does sexual encouragement end and rape begin? Are people who commit rape or who coerce children into sexual behavior mentally disordered, criminal, or both? Are some instances of voyeurism or exhibitionism normal and others abnormal? When is it considered abnormal to have difficulty becoming sexually aroused or reaching orgasm?

SEXUAL ORIENTATION

Western society has historically been unkind to gay men and lesbians. Within the Judeo-Christian tradition, sexual activity with members of one's own gender has been condemned as sinful or immoral. The Book of Genesis, which tells of the destruction of Sodom by the hand of God, is actually ambiguous about exactly what behavior brought down the God's wrath, but Pope Gregory III attributed the city's annihilation to sex between men—in his view, "a vice . . . abominable in the sight of God."

Gay male and lesbian sexual orientations also met with the disapproval of many scholars in the scientific community. Sigmund Freud, though compassionate toward gay men and lesbians, nevertheless maintained that their sexual orientation represented arrested psychosexual development.

The first edition of the DSM, the DSM-I (1952), designated homosexuality as a mental disorder. In 1973, the members of the American Psychiatric Association voted to drop homosexuality from the DSM listing of mental disorders. However, the category of **ego-dystonic homosexuality** was created for gay men and lesbians who were distressed about their sexual orientation and wanted to become heterosexual. (Of course, no disorder called "ego-dystonic heterosexuality" was instituted for people who might be distressed by their heterosexual orientation.) The

L'Abandon (Les Deux Amies). Lesbian lovers are the subject of this painting by Henri de Toulouse-Lautrec.

DSM-III-R reclassified ego-dystonic homosexuality under a catchall diagnostic category "Sexual Disorder Not Otherwise Specified." This diagnosis could be made on the basis of persistent and marked distress or confusion about one's sexual orientation. The DSM-IV continues to consider "persistent and marked distress about one's sexual orientation" to be a "Sexual Disorder Not Otherwise Specified." As written, the diagnostic criteria could apply equally to heterosexuals, bisexuals, gay males, and lesbians.

Defining Sexual Orientation

Sexual orientation refers to the direction of one's sexual attraction toward, and desire for romantic relationships with, one's own or the opposite gender. Men whose erotic feelings are directed toward other men and who desire to form romantic relationships with men are called **gay males**. Women who are sexually attracted to, and desire to form romantic relationships with, other women are referred to as **lesbians** (after *Lesbos,* a Greek island on which, according to legend, sexual behavior between women was idealized). People who are sexually attracted to, and desire to form romantic relationships with, people of the opposite gender are called **heterosexuals**. Some people have erotic attractions to and romantic interests in people of both genders; they are called **bisexuals**. Sexual orientation is *not* to be considered a sexual preference (Money, 1987). The term *preference* denotes a voluntary choice; research does not show that people choose to have a gay male or lesbian sexual orientation anymore than they choose to have a heterosexual sexual orientation (American Psychological Association, 1991).

In keeping with the suggestions of the American Psychological Association's (1991) Committee on Lesbian and Gay Concerns, we are using the terms *gay male* and *lesbian* instead of *homosexual* in our discussion of sexual orientation. As noted by the Committee, there are several problems with the word *homosexual:* One, because it has been historically associated with concepts of deviance and mental illness, it may perpetuate negative stereotypes of gay men and lesbians. Two, the term is often used to refer to men only, thus rendering lesbians invisible. Third, it is often ambiguous in meaning—that is, does it refer to sexual behavior or sexual orientation?

Sexual activity with members of one's own gender does not in itself signify a gay male or lesbian sexual orientation. It may reflect a lack of heterosexual opportunities or ritualistic cultural practices, as in the case of the New Guinean Sambian people. American adolescent males may experiment with mutual masturbation. Men in prisons may similarly turn to each other as sexual outlets. Sambian male youths engage exclusively in sexual practices with older males, because it is believed that they must drink "men's milk" to achieve the fierce manhood of the head hunter (Money, 1987). They become exclusively heterosexual when they reach a marriageable age, however.

Kinsey and his colleagues (1948, 1953) devised a "heterosexual–homosexual" continuum that places people according to their frequency of sexual contacts with, and the intensity of their sexual attraction to, members of their own gender. Persons in category 0 were classified as "exclusively heterosexual." People at scale points 1 or 2 were considered "predominantly heterosexual," and at scale points 4 or 5, "predominantly homosexual." Those in category 6 were classified as "exclusively homosexual." Most subjects fell into the first (0) category. As many as 37% of the men and 13% of the women in Kinsey's samples had had at least one sexual experience with a person of the same gender following puberty, but only about 4% of his male subjects and 1 to 3% of his female subjects could be classified as "exclusively homosexual." About 2% of the men and 1% of the women in a 1970s survey commissioned by the Playboy Foundation (Hunt, 1974) reported a gay male or lesbian orientation. Most people with sexual experience with people of the same gender, however, limited their contacts to adolescent experimentation. Most researchers continue to use the Kinsey scale or a modification of it to classify sexual orientation (Sanders et al., 1990). The proportions of gay males and lesbians in the population, as well as the prevalences of sexual experiences with people of one's own gender, do not appear to have changed much since Kinsey's time (Fay et al., 1989; Gordon & Snyder, 1989). June Reinisch (1990), the present director of the Kinsey Institute, estimates that over 25% of U.S. men today have had at least one adolescent or adult sexual experience with another man.

Kinsey considered people rated 3 as bisexual. Among his 20- to 35-year-old respondents, 9 to 32% of the males and 4 to 11% of the females were rated 3. Some people believe that one cannot be equally attracted to men and women. Some think of bisexuals as fence-sitters who, perhaps for fear of leaving their spouses or general social rejection, are reluctant to recognize their gay male or lesbian sexual orientation. It may be that bisexuality is a genuine sexual orientation, however, rather than a cover for a gay male or lesbian sexual orientation (Gordon & Snyder, 1989).

Adjustment of Gay Males and Lesbians

Despite the social ostracism, prejudice, and discrimination faced by gay men and lesbians in our society, research has not shown that they are more emotionally unstable or subject to more mental disorders, such as depression or anxiety, than heterosexuals (Reiss, 1980). Research evidence also suggests that bisexuals are about as well adjusted as gay men, lesbians, and heterosexuals (Coleman, 1987).

There is no one gay lifestyle. Gay men and lesbians are found at all socioeconomic and occupational levels and live a variety of lifestyles. Bell and Weinberg (1978) found that the adjustment of gay men and lesbians in San Francisco was linked to their lifestyles. "Close couples" who lived as though they were married appeared as well-adjusted as married heterosexuals. Gay men and women who led other lifestyles showed various levels of adjustment. Gay men who lived by themselves and had few if any sexual contacts tended to be more poorly adjusted. So, too, are many heterosexuals who lead similar lifestyles. Heterosexual, gay male, and lesbian couples tend to report similar levels of satisfaction in their relationships (Kurdek & Schmitt, 1986; Peplau & Cochran, 1990).

Gay males as a group have been more likely than lesbians to engage in casual sex with numerous partners (Bell & Weinberg, 1978). However, because of the threat of AIDS today, many gay males have adopted safer sex practices, such as using condoms, limiting their number of sex partners, reducing the frequency of anal intercourse, and relying more on masturbation as a sexual release (Centers for Disease Control, 1990; Lourea et al., 1986; Schechter et al., 1984; Siegel et al., 1988). Lesbians have been generally more likely to seek sexual activity within the bounds of a committed relationship. A recent survey reported that about 3 lesbians in 4, but only about 1 gay male in 2, were currently involved in steady relationships (Peplau & Cochran, 1990).

Theoretical Perspectives

Theoretical understandings of sexual orientation have been mainly approached from the psychodynamic, learning, and biological perspectives.

■ **PSYCHODYNAMIC PERSPECTIVES** Traditional psychodynamic theory suggests that children enter the world open to all forms of sexual stimulation. Prior to internalizing social inhibitions, children are **polymorphously perverse.** Through normal resolution of the Oedipus complex, boys identify with their fathers and seek the (presumably) heterosexual stimulation that sexually arouses their fathers. Girls, through normal resolution of the Electra complex, identify with their mothers and also seek heteroerotic stimulation. A boy who does not resolve the Oedipus complex properly may sexually identify with his mother and even "transform himself into her" (Freud, 1922/1959, p. 40). Castration anxiety, the residue of an unresolved Oedipus complex, persists in later life. When sexually mature, the man cannot tolerate sex with women, whose lack of a penis arouses latent fears of castration within himself. The vaginal cavity itself looms as a threat of possible injury or loss of his penis. He consequently turns to other men for sexual satisfaction, for they too possess a penis and do not unconsciously arouse the fear of the potential loss of his own. A girl who does not successfully resolve the Electra complex may become a lesbian, "exhibit markedly masculine traits in the conduct of her later life, choose a masculine vocation, and so on" (p. 50). The residue of her unresolved Electra complex is continued penis envy, the striving to become a man by acting like a man and seeking sexual satisfaction with women. In Freud's view, both

A gay male close couple. Research shows that gay male close couples are as well adjusted as heterosexual married couples. Although there is much individual variation among people of every sexual orientation, gay males and lesbians are as well adjusted overall as heterosexuals.

gay males and lesbians are fixated in the phallic stage of psychosexual development.

Thus, according to Freud:

1. There are no biological predispositions toward sexual orientation.
2. A gay male or lesbian sexual orientation is linked to the assumption of the gender-role stereotypes of the opposite gender. That is, gay males will show feminine personality traits and behavioral tendencies; lesbians, masculine traits and tendencies.
3. Sexual orientation is not established until the phallic stage of development.

Over the years psychoanalyst Irving Bieber (1962, 1976) has investigated the origins of a gay male sexual orientation by means of the case study. In 1962, he reported the results of questionnaires filled out by 77 psychiatrists on 106 gay male clients. In 1976, he reported the results of similar surveys with gay male clients themselves. Bieber claimed to find a "classic pattern" among gay males of a dominant, "smothering" mother and a passive father. The mothers were overprotective, seductive, and jealous concerning their sons. The fathers were generally aloof, unaffectionate, and hostile toward them. The parents were often unhappy, and the mother substituted a "close-binding" relationship with her son for the failed relationship with her husband.

Bieber's view is that the "classic pattern" causes boys to fear contacts with females. A female partner unconsciously represents the male's mother. Desire for her stirs unconscious fear of retaliation by the father—that is, castration anxiety. As a result, the

vagina seems an unsafe place. The gay male lover's penis provides reassurance against castration anxiety.

There are major problems with Bieber's research. The subjects, first of all, were all in analysis, and many wanted to become heterosexual. We thus cannot generalize to well-adjusted gay men. Second, the analysts may have chosen cases that confirmed their psychodynamic perspectives. Third, many gay men have engaged in sexual intercourse with women without arousing any apparent fear of their genitals. Fourth, although Pillard (1990) found research evidence that gay males describe themselves as more distant from their fathers and closer to their mothers during childhood than do heterosexual controls, many males whose families fit the "classic pattern" are heterosexual. Pillard's research is also correlational and allows multiple interpretations. Were the sons pushed away by their fathers? Or did the fathers become more distant because their sons pushed them away or failed to respond to their attempts to involve them in stereotypical father-son activities? Fifth, many gay males report being closer to their fathers than their mothers in childhood (Bell et al., 1981). All in all, there is much variation among the families of gay men as well as among those of lesbians, and no single pattern applies to all cases (Isay, 1990).

■ **LEARNING PERSPECTIVES** Many learning theorists agree with psychoanalysts that children come into the world capable of learning to respond to any form of pleasurable sexual stimulation. Then the approaches diverge. Psychoanalysts focus on theoretical unconscious processes. Learning theorists focus largely on processes of conditioning.

Are there connections between a gay male sexual orientation and the father–son relationship? Bieber's research suggested there was a classic pattern in the developmental relationships between gay males and their parents. Other researchers find a great deal of variation in the relationships between gay males (and heterosexual males) and their parents.

According to principles of classical conditioning, children may become sexually aroused by stimuli that are associated with past sexual pleasures. Enjoyable early sexual encounters with people of the same gender may condition children to repeat such experiences. Similarly, pain, fear, or the threat of social disapproval attached to sexual attractions to, or activities with, people of the same gender may lead children to respond to such attractions or activities with anxiety.

According to principles of operant conditioning, as set forth by Kinsey and his colleagues, reinforcement of early sexual experiences (like orgasm achieved through interaction with members of one's own gender) can influence the development of one's sexual orientation. If sexual motivation is high and the only available partners are of the same gender, as is the case for many adolescents, youngsters may experiment with sexual behavior with members of their own gender. If the experiments are repeatedly reinforced by pleasure, they may become habitual (Van Wyk, 1984). Or perhaps males who had early punitive experiences with females, including their mothers, learned to avoid contacts with females. If they had more rewarding contacts with males and had opportunities for sexual experimentation with males that proved gratifying, they may have gone on to develop a gay male sexual orientation.

Learning theorists point to developmental experiences akin to those noted by Bieber. Many gay males recall their mothers as cold and demanding of attention. Their mothers preferred them (the sons) to their fathers, interfered in their relations with girls, and encouraged feminine gender-role behavior patterns (Evans, 1969). The sons also spent little time with their fathers and reported negative attitudes toward and fear of their fathers.

There are problems with learning perspectives. Many gay males and lesbians are aware of their orientations *before* they have overt sexual contacts (Bell et al., 1981). Thus, we cannot attribute their orientations to early reinforcement of sexual behavior by persons of the same gender. And remember the Sambian males: Repeated homosexual experiences do not sway Sambian youth from their eventual exclusive heterosexuality.

Also, in a society that denigrates gay male and lesbian sexual orientations, children are unlikely to develop the expectancy that sexual behavior with members of their own gender will be reinforcing for them. In other words, they are unlikely to strive to imitate gay male or lesbian models. Nor is there any evidence that being reared by gay male or lesbian parents leads to the development of a gay or lesbian sexual orientation. Richard Green (1978) studied 37 children reared in sexually atypical households. Most

of them had lesbian mothers. All but one child developed gender-stereotyped preferences for toys, games, and ways of relating to other people. Researchers also find that the children of lesbian mothers cannot be distinguished from children of heterosexual mothers in their sexual orientations and general adjustment (Green et al., 1986).

■ **BIOLOGICAL PERSPECTIVES** Biological theories focus primarily on genetic and hormonal factors. There is considerable evidence of familial patterns in sexual orientation (Pillard, 1990; Pillard & Weinrich, 1986). In one study, 22% of the brothers of 51 primarily gay men were either gay or bisexual themselves. This is about four times the percentage that is found in the general population (Pillard & Weinrich, 1986). Although this evidence is consistent with a genetic explanation, families share environments as well as genes.

Twin studies shed further light on possible genetic factors. Carefully conducted twin studies generally find higher concordance rates for sexual orientation in gay males and their twins among monozygotic (MZ) twins than among dizygotic (DZ) twins (Bailey & Pillard, 1991; Eckert et al., 1986; McConaghy & Blaszczynski, 1980). Bailey and Pillard (1991) found, for example, that 52% of the MZ twin brothers of gay men in their sample were also gay as opposed to a 22% concordance rate for DZ twins. These twins were not reared apart, however, and MZ twins are more likely than DZ twins to be reared alike. Their greater concordance rates may thus also reflect social environmental factors, or the likelihood that MZ twins react more similarly than DZ twins to similar social environmental influences (Bancroft, 1990). Although the evidence points to a role for genetic factors in determining sexual orientation, genetics alone does not appear to determine one's sexual orientation in a "robot-like" fashion (Money, 1987). Other influences, such as early life experiences, may also play a part.

What of a role for sex hormones? Because hormones strongly influence the sexual behavior of lower animals (Crews & Moore, 1986), researchers have investigated possible hormonal differences between heterosexuals and gay men and women. However, research evidence has not reliably linked sexual orientation to current (adult) levels of male or female sex hormones (Feder, 1984). Another possibility concerns the prenatal effects of sex hormones. Prenatal sex hormones can masculinize or feminize the brain structures of laboratory animals along gender-specific lines with respect to mating behavior. One contemporary theorist, Lee Ellis (1990; Ellis & Ames, 1990), believes that sexual orientation in humans is prenatally determined and dependent on a complex interaction of genetic, neurological, hormonal, and environmental factors (such as the level of stress the mother encounters during pregnancy) affecting the development of the fetal brain. Why maternal stress? Stress causes the release of hormones such as adrenaline and cortisol, which can interact with testosterone *in utero* and perhaps affect the prenatal development of the brain. Perhaps the brains of some gay males have been prenatally feminized, and the brains of some lesbians have been masculinized (Money, 1987).

F Sexual orientation is not determined by *current* hormonal imbalances. However, prenatal hormonal factors may well play a role in sexual orientation.

Intriguing findings have been reported concerning possible structural differences in the brains of gay and heterosexual men. Based on autopsies of the brains of 19 gay and 16 (presumably) heterosexual men, a neurobiologist, Simon LeVay, reported that a forward (anterior) region of the hypothalamus was relatively smaller in size in the brains of the gay men (LeVay, 1991). Moreover, this brain region was of similar size in the brains of the gay men and those of a comparison group of six presumably heterosexual women, but was larger in the brains of the heterosexual men than of those of the women. The significance of these findings in explaining sexual orientation remains uncertain. For one thing, LeVay's subjects had died of complications from AIDS. The structural differences he reported could have been related to the effects of the disease rather than to sexual orientation. This alternative explanation appeared unlikely, however, because LeVay discovered that the brains of several heterosexual men who died of AIDS did not show this size difference. Still, LeVay's findings were based on a small sample of cases and need to be confirmed on larger samples. Nor can we say whether the structural differences LeVay reported were prenatally determined. We should also be careful not to conclude from this evidence that biology is destiny. Commenting on LeVay's findings, a government scientist, Richard Nakamura, noted that LeVay's findings "shouldn't be taken to mean that you're automatically homosexual if you have a structure of one size versus a structure of another size" (Angier, 1991a).

All in all, the determinants of gay male and lesbian sexual orientations remain mysterious and complex—as mysterious and complex as the determinants of heterosexual sexual orientations.

Changing Sexual Orientation

Most gay men and lesbians—indeed, the great majority—do not seek to change their sexual orientations. By the same token, most heterosexuals do not seek to change their sexual orientation. Most people consider their sexual orientations to be integral parts of their self-identities.

Sigmund Freud recognized that psychoanalysis had limited success in changing people's sexual orientations. In a letter to a mother of a gay son, Freud wrote,

> What analysis can do for your son runs in a different line [from changing sexual orientation]. If he is unhappy, neurotic, torn by conflicts, inhibited in his social life, analysis may bring him harmony, peace of mind, full efficiency, whether he remains [gay] or gets changed. (Cited in Jones, 1953, p. 534)

Numerous learning-based behavioral treatments have been devised to induce heteroerotic responses among gay men. (Research on lesbians has been scant.) In one approach, *aversive conditioning*, gay males receive electric shock while they view slides of sexual activity between men. The slide is then removed, or replaced with a picture of heterosexual activity, and the shock is simultaneously suspended. The viewer thus comes to associate relief from anxiety with heterosexual activity. In the technique of *orgasmic reconditioning*, gay men masturbate while they view slides of sexual activity between men. Prior to reaching orgasm, pictures of heterosexual activity are introduced, so that orgasm becomes associated with heteroerotic stimuli. *Social skills training* (which relies on coaching, modeling, and role playing) has been used to enhance the abilities of gay men to develop relationships with women. Reliable evidence that such learning-based methods change clients' sexual *orientations*—rather than simply influence their behavior—remains lacking.

William Masters and Virginia Johnson (1979) used methods employed in treating sexual dysfunctions in heterosexual couples to "reverse" the sexual orientations of gay men and lesbians. (We elaborate on the applications of these methods to heterosexual couples later in the chapter.) As an example, they had gay males engage in pleasurable activities with women, such as mutual massage and genital stimulation, under relaxed conditions. Masters and Johnson reported failure rates of less than 25% for subjects they treated. More than 7 of 10 treated subjects continued to show heterosexual activity by the time of a 5-year follow-up (Schwartz & Masters, 1984). Critics note that Masters and Johnson's clients included many bisexuals. Some clients were married. Some of the "gay men" sought treatment because they were romantically involved with women. All of these gay men, for one reason or another, *wanted* to change their sexual orientation. They thus fail to represent the gay community at large. Nor are changes in sexual behavior (for example, increased heterosexual activity) the same thing as a change in sexual orientation.

Many therapists refuse to try to reverse a person's sexual orientation. If a gay male or lesbian sexual orientation is not an illness, why try to cure it? Isay (1990), a psychoanalyst, contends that gay men and lesbians usually seek therapy only because of problems that stem from social pressure and prejudice, not because they would prefer to have intimate relationships with people of the opposite gender. In such cases, he argues that the therapist should try to help unburden clients of the conflicts caused by these external pressures and help them improve their lives as gay men and lesbians rather than try to change their sexual orientations.

GENDER IDENTITY DISORDER

Our **gender identity** is our sense of being male or being female. Gender identity is normally based on anatomic gender. In the normal run of things, our gender identity is consistent with our anatomic gender. In **gender identity disorder**, however, there is a conflict between one's anatomic gender and one's gender identity.

Gender identity disorder may begin in childhood. Children with the disorder find their anatomic genders to be sources of persistent and intense distress. The diagnosis is not used simply to label "tomboyish" girls and "sissyish" boys. It is applied to children who persistently repudiate their anatomic traits (girls might insist on urinating standing up or assert that they do not want to grow breasts; boys may find their penis and testes revolting) or who are preoccupied with clothing or activities that are stereotypic of the other gender (see Table 10.1).

About five times as many boys as girls have gender identity disorder (Zucker & Green, 1992). The disorder takes many paths. It can come to an end or abate markedly by adolescence, with the child becoming more accepting of her or his gender identity. It may persist into adolescence or adulthood. The child may develop a gay male or lesbian sexual orientation at about the time of adolescence (Zucker & Green, 1992).

A number of cases of gender identity disorder among adults have been widely publicized. In 1953, for example, headlines were made by an ex-GI who

Table 10.1   Clinical Features of Gender Identity Disorder

(a) A strong, persistent identfication with the other gender

   At least four of the following features are required to make the diagnosis in children:

   (1) Repeated expression of the desire to be a member of the other gender (or expression of the belief that the child does belong to the other gender)

   (2) Preference for wearing clothing stereotypical of members of the other gender

   (3) Presence of persistent fantasies about being a member of the other gender, or assumption of parts played by members of the other gender in make-believe play

   (4) Desire to participate in leisure activities and games considered stereotypical of the other gender

   (5) Strong preference for playmates who belong to the other gender (at ages when children typically prefer playmates of their own gender)

   Adolescents and adults typically express the wish to be of the other gender, frequently "pass" as a member of the other gender, wish to live as a member of the other gender, or believe that their emotions and behavior typify the other gender

(b) A strong, persistent sense of discomfort with one's anatomic gender or with the behaviors that typify the gender role of that gender

   In children, these features are commonly present: Boys state that their external genitals are repugnant or that it would be better not to have them, show aversion to "masculine" toys, games, and rough-and-tumble play. Girls prefer not to urinate while sitting, express the wishes not to grow breasts or to menstruate, or show aversion to "feminine" clothing

   Adolescents and adults typically state that they were born the wrong gender and express the wish for medical intervention (e.g., hormone treatments or surgery) to rid them of their own sex characteristics and simulate the characteristics of the other gender

(c) There is no "intersex condition," such as ambiguous sexual anatomy, that might give rise to such feelings

(d) The features cause serious distress or impair key areas of occupational, social, or other functioning

Source: DSM-IV Draft Criteria (American Psychiatric Association, 1993), p. 0:9.

journeyed to Denmark for a "sex-change operation." She then became known as Christine Jorgensen. More than 2,500 gender-reassignment surgeries have been reported since in the United States. One of the better known cases is that of the tennis player Dr. Renée Richards, who was formerly Dr. Richard Raskin. Gender-reassignment surgery does not trans-

(A)

(B)

Before and after.
Transsexual Dr. Renée Richards is shown before gender-reassignment surgery as Dr. Richard Raskin (A) and afterward (B) Richards competed professionally on the women's tennis circuit and once served as a coach of Martina Navratlova.

form one into a person of the opposite gender, if what is meant by gender reassignment is the implantation of the internal reproductive organs of the opposite gender. Rather, the surgery attempts to construct a likeness of the external genitalia of the opposite gender. The surgery is more precise in fashioning the external genitals in male-to-female than in female-to-male transsexuals. People who have such operations can engage in sexual activity, even achieve orgasm, yet they are incapable of conceiving or bearing children.

Earlier editions of the DSM used the diagnosis of **transsexualism** for people who have reached puberty, harbor persistent discomfort because of the belief that their anatomic gender is wrong for them, and are preoccupied with transforming their sex characteristics to those of the other gender. The DSM-III-R had separate diagnostic categories for *gender identity disorder of childhood, transsexualism,* and *gender identity disorder of adolescence or adulthood, nontranssexual type.* The DSM-IV uses the single diagnostic category, *gender identity disorder,* for people of all ages and for people who show various levels of desire for medical intervention to change their gender. As noted in Table 10.1, however, the clinical features vary somewhat according to the age of the individual. To be consistent with the changes in diagnostic practices, we refer in the text to gender identity disorder rather than to transsexualism.

Unlike a gay male or lesbian sexual orientation, gender identity disorder is very rare. (People with gender identity disorder should not be confused with

gay males or lesbians. The latter groups have erotic interests in members of their own gender but their gender identities are consistent with their anatomic gender.) Sexual attractions in themselves do not appear to be central in importance. Some people with gender identity disorder, for example, are specified as "sexually attracted to neither" males or females in the DSM-IV. That is, they deny ever experiencing strong sexual feelings. Others are specified as sexually attracted to males, to females, or to both. People with gender identity disorder who are sexually attracted to members of their own anatomic gender are unlikely to consider themselves to be gay males or lesbians. Nature's gender assignment is a mistake in their eyes. From their perspective, they are trapped in the body of the wrong gender.

■ **GENDER REASSIGNMENT** Surgery is only one part of a complex process of gender reassignment. The first step is a thorough evaluation to determine that the person seeking reassignment appears competent to make such a decision. If the person were seeking change because of paranoid delusions, for example, surgeons would refuse the request. Next, a lifetime of hormone treatments are begun. In the case of people who undergo gender reassignment from male to female, estrogen is taken to stoke the development of female secondary sex characteristics, leading to the rounding of the hips, breast development, softening of the skin, and suppression of beard growth. In the case of people who undergo gender reassignment from female to male, male sex hormones (androgens) are taken to foster the development of male secondary sex characteristics, leading to the deepening of the voice, muscular development, a masculine pattern of hair growth, and a loss of fatty deposits in the breasts and hips. Surgeons cannot construct or implant the internal sexual organs or **gonads** of the other gender, however. Before surgery, the person is also usually required to live for a year or so as a member of the other gender. Cross-living allows the individual and the treatment team to make some prediction of postoperative adjustment.

For people who undergo gender reassignment from male to female, the penis and testicles are removed. Then tissue from the penis is used to construct an artificial vagina, so that sensitive nerve endings are preserved that can provide sexual sensations. For people who undergo gender reassignment from female to male, the surgeon removes the internal sex organs (ovaries, fallopian tubes, uterus) and flattens the breasts by removing the remaining fatty tissue. Through a series of operations, an artificial penis and scrotum are constructed. The urethra, the tube that carries urine from the bladder, is rerouted, permitting the person to urinate while standing, which appears to be a source of psychological gratification. Various methods may be used to permit the artificial penis to approximate erection, including the implantation of prosthetic rods.

It is not true that people have become members of the other gender through surgery. Instead, their external genitals are fashioned to the appearance of those of the opposite gender. Although they can experience sexual sensations and achieve orgasm, they cannot reproduce. Whether people think of themselves as being male or female is another matter.

■ **POSTOPERATIVE ADJUSTMENT** In the 1960s, shortly after gender reassignment became available in the United States, reports of postoperative adjustment were generally favorable. However, an influential study by Meyer and Reter (1979) at the prestigious gender identity clinic at John Hopkins University reported very negative findings. The researchers found more positive results among a control group of patients with gender identity disorder who did not receive gender reassignment than among those who did. The Meyer and Reter study led to the abandonment of gender-reassignment surgery at Johns Hopkins, to the closing of its gender identity clinic, and cast a pall over gender-reassignment surgery nationwide. Looking back, however, it appears that the termination of the Johns Hopkins program may have reflected political pressures from the community as well as these negative findings (Lothstein, cited in Abramowitz, 1986). Other

researchers have also claimed that Meyer and Reter used unscientific measures of psychological adjustment (Abramowitz, 1986; Fleming et al., 1981). Moreover, the positive adjustment of some people with gender identity disorder who are not reassigned does not mean that reassignment is not useful for others (Pauly, 1981).

Recent reviewers find more positive outcomes for those undergoing gender-reassignment surgery (Kockott & Fahrner, 1987; Lundstrom et al., 1984; Pauly, 1981; Pauly & Edgerton, 1986), especially when safeguards are taken to restrict surgical treatment to the most appropriate cases (Lothstein, 1982). In one study, all but 1 of 42 postoperative male-to-females indicated that they would make the same decision if they were again faced with the choice. The great majority reported experiencing greater sexual pleasure as a "woman" (Bentler, 1976). Abramowitz (1986) reported at least some improvement in psychological functioning following surgery in about 2 of 3 cases. By and large, this meant that the patients were less unhappy with their lives following the surgery, not that they suddenly became ecstatic. Generally speaking, patients with gender identity disorder are poorly adjusted before surgery. Many continue to show signs of maladjustment, such as social isolation and loneliness, afterward. Medical complications also occur in about 1 in 2 cases following surgery (Lindermalm et al., 1986).

Men seeking gender reassignment outnumber women applicants by perhaps 3 or 4 to 1, but outcomes are generally more favorable for female-to-male cases. One reason may be society's greater acceptance of women who desire to live as men (Abramowitz, 1986). Another reason appears to be that females with gender identity disorder are generally better adjusted than their male counterparts before surgery (Pauly, 1974; Kockott & Fahrner, 1988). Male-to-female patients whose surgery left no telltale signs (such as scarring of the breasts or leftover erectile tissue) were found to be better adjusted than those whose surgery was less successful in allowing them to "pass" as women (Ross & Need, 1989). In this study, the support received from friends and family following gender reassignment also played a role in adjustment. Nearly 10% of males who undergo gender ressignment, as compared to 4 to 5% of females who do so, experience negative outcomes, such as need for hospitalization, psychosis, requests for reversal surgery, even suicide (Abramowitz, 1986).

A review of international studies reported positive results from gender-reassignment surgery in about 90% of cases overall (Lundstrom et al., 1984). A large-scale study at the gender identity clinic of the Clarke Institute of Psychiatry in Toronto reported that

116 postoperative patients were found to be generally well adjusted and were generally satisfied with the results of their surgery a year later (Blanchard et al., 1985). Males and females both reported lower levels of anxiety, depression, and other psychological complaints a year following, than prior to, surgery, and more than 9 of 10 reported they would make the same decision to undergo surgery had they to do it all over again. Another study of 141 Dutch patients with gender identity disorder also reported positive results (Kuiper & Cohen-Kettenis, 1988). However promising the results of these studies may be, they are limited by the absence of nonsurgical control groups.

■ **THEORETICAL PERSPECTIVES** Theoretical views of the development of gender identity disorder parallel to some degree those seeking to explain the development of a gay male or lesbian sexual orientation. Psychodynamic theorists point to extremely close mother–son relationships, parents with empty relationships, fathers who are absent or detached (Stoller, 1969). These family circumstances may foster strong identification with the mother in young males, leading to a reversal of expected gender roles and identity. Girls with weak ineffectual mothers and strong masculine fathers may overly identify with their fathers and develop a psychological sense of themselves as "little men."

Learning theorists similarly point to father absence in the case of boys—to the unavailability of a strong male role model. Socialization patterns might have affected children who were reared by parents who had wanted children of the other gender and who strongly encouraged cross-gender dressing and patterns of play.

People with gender identity disorder often show cross-gender preferences in toys, games, and clothing very early in childhood. If there are critical early learning experiences in gender identity disorder, they may occur at preschool ages. Prenatal hormonal imbalances may also be involved. Perhaps the brain is "masculinized" or "feminized" by sex hormones during certain stages of prenatal development. The brain could become differentiated as to gender in one direction while the genitals develop in the other direction (Money, 1987). All told, we presently lack a clear understanding of the development or causes of gender identity disorder.

RAPE

The commission of rape is not classified as a mental disorder within the DSM system. Rape is nonetheless abnormal in that it is socially unacceptable, violates social norms, and is grievously harmful to its victims. Rape is also often connected with such diagnosable mental disorders as antisocial personality and sexual sadism.

Forcible rape refers to the use of force, violence, or threats of violence to coerce victims into sexual activity. **Statutory rape** is defined as sexual activity with a person who is unable to give consent, either because of being under the age of consent or because of mental disability, even though the person may cooperate with the rapist.

FBI records show that in the United States, 102,555 forcible rapes were reported in 1990 (41 reported rapes per 100,000 persons) (Uniform Crime Reports, 1990). The prevalence of rapes that are reported to authorities in the United States is 20 times greater than the rate in Japan and 13 times greater than the rate in Great Britain ("Women under assault," 1990). Even so, the great majority of rapes—perhaps 90% or more—may go unreported (Gibbs, 1991). Young women are most at risk of being raped, with about 6 of 10 rape victims being less than 18 years of age at the time of the rape (*Unsettling Report on an Epidemic of Rape*, 1992). Yet women of all ages, as well as races and socioeconomic levels, have been victims.

Victimization surveys ask random samples of people whether they have ever been raped and thus provide information about unreported rapes as well as reported rapes (Harney & Muehlenhard, 1991). Based on a compilation of official records and victimization surveys, researchers estimate that between 15 and 25% of U.S. women have been raped or will be raped at some point during their lifetimes (Calhoun & Atkeson, 1991). In about 4 of 5 cases overall, the assailant is known to the victim ("acquaintance rape") (Gibbs, 1991; *Unsettling Report on an Epidemic of Rape*, 1992), but they are not usually intimate acquaintances or lovers (Koss, 1988).

A large-scale survey of 3,187 women and 2,972 men attending 32 colleges across the nation revealed that a disturbingly high percentage of the women reported they had been victims of rape (15.4%) or attempted rape (12.1%) (Koss et al., 1987). In nearly 90% of the reported rapes among these college women, the victim was acquainted with the rapist (Koss, 1988; see Figure 10.1). Acquaintance rapes are especially likely to be underreported to police because the victims may not perceive them as crimes. About 1 in 13 men surveyed (7.7%) admitted to committing or attempting rape (Koss et al., 1987). Further analysis of the data showed that nearly 4% of the women reported being victims of rape or attempted rape within 6 months of the survey. Most of these rapes had taken place on campus.

Date rape is a kind of acquaintance rape. Men who commit date rape may assume that willingness

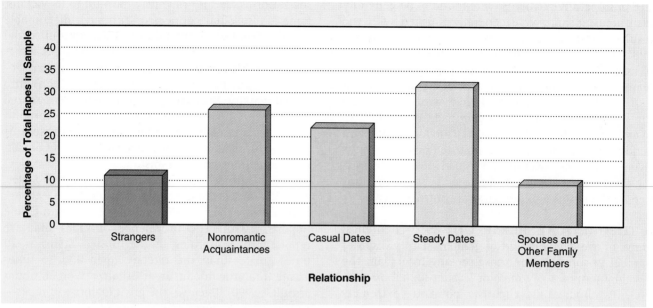

Figure 10.1 Relationships between rapists and their victims.
According to a large-scale survey of more than 3,000 college women at 32 colleges, the great majority of rapes of college women were committed by acquaintances of the victims, including dates, nonromantic acquaintances, and family members.
Source: Adapted from Koss (1988).

Kristine, Amy, and Karen. These college women are among the many thousands who have been allegedly raped by dates. Although women are counseled not to walk on deserted, dark streets or through alleyways, most rapes are committed by their acquaintances, not by strangers.

to accompany them home, or even acceptance of a date, signifies assent to sexual activity, or that women are somehow obligated to reciprocate with sex if their dates take them to dinner and treat them to a good time. Other date rapists presume that women who go to singles bars and similar places are in effect expressing tacit agreement to sexual activity with men who show interest in them. Date rapists may also assume

that women who resist their advances are merely trying to avoid looking "easy." Unlike stranger rape, in which wholesale force or threats are used from the beginning, date rape usually follows a chain of steps from gentle urging to more intense advances to outright physical coercion (Gibbs, 1991).

The question of consent is basic to determining whether a sexual act constitutes rape. Unlike stranger rape, date rape occurs under conditions in which sexual relations could occur consensually, so the issue of consent can become ambiguous. In court cases, such as those involving William Kennedy Smith and Mike Tyson, the defendant may claim that sexual activity was consensual. Charges of date rape may come down to his word against hers. Her word may be less persuasive to a jury if she had freely consented to consensual acts such as sharing dinner, going to the movies together, going to the man's room or home, sharing a drink, and kissing or petting beforehand.

Theoretical Perspectives

There is no single kind of rape or rapist (Siegel, 1992). Some rapists who have feelings of shyness and inadequacy report that they cannot find willing partners. They lack social skills for interacting with the opposite gender (Overholser & Beck, 1986). Others are basically antisocial and tend to act out on their impulses regardless of the cost to the victim. Many antisocial rapists have long records as violent offenders (Prentky & Knight, 1991; Siegel, 1992). For still other rapists, violence appears to enhance sexual arousal, so they are motivated to combine sex with aggression (Barbaree & Marshall, 1991).

 It is true that some people are sexually aroused by violence. For example, violence appears to enhance sexual arousal in some rapists.

Other rapists, who were abused as children, may humiliate women as a way of expressing anger and power over women, and of taking revenge (Groth & Birnbaum, 1979).

■ **PSYCHOLOGICAL FACTORS** Groth and Hobson (1983) argue that the seeking of sexual gratification has little to do with rape. On the basis of clinical experience with more than 1,000 rapists, Groth and Hobson hypothesize the existence of three basic kinds of rape: anger rape, power rape, and sadistic rape. The anger rape is a savage, unpremeditated attack triggered by feelings of hatred and resentment. Anger rapists often use more force than necessary to gain compliance to take revenge for humiliations they have suffered—or believe they have suffered—at the hands of women. The power rapist is basically motivated by the desire to control another person. Groth and Hobson (1983) suggest that power rapists use rape to try "to resolve disturbing doubts about [their] masculine identity and worth, [or] to combat deepseated feelings of insecurity and vulnerability" (p. 165). Sadistic rapes frequently employ torture and **bondage**, merging sex and aggression. Sadistic rapists are most likely to mutilate their victims.

Cognitive theorists recognize that our thoughts and beliefs influence our actions. Some rapists, particularly date rapists, tend to misread women's expressed wishes (Lipton et al., 1987). They assume that dates who say "No" really mean yes and are merely playing male-female games. Consider the comments of a college student who raped his date:

I first met her at a party. She looked really hot, wearing a sexy dress that showed off her great body. We started talking right away. I knew that she liked me by the way she kept smiling and touching my arm while she was speaking. She seemed pretty relaxed so I asked her back to my place for a drink. . . . When she said yes, I knew that I was going to be lucky!

When we got to my place, we sat on the bed kissing. At first, everything was great. Then, when I started to lay her down on the bed, she started twisting and saying she didn't want to. Most women don't like to appear too easy, so I knew that she was just going through the motions. When she stopped struggling, I knew that she would have to throw in some tears before we did it.

She was still very upset afterwards, and I just don't understand it! If she didn't want to have sex, why did she come back to the room with me? You could tell by the way she dressed and acted that she was no virgin, so why she had to put up such a big struggle I don't know. (Trenton State College, 1991)

■ **SOCIOCULTURAL FACTORS** Many rapists cannot be distinguished by means of interviews and psychological tests from nonrapists. Many show no impairment in general functioning or in reality testing (Dean & de Bruyn-Kops, 1982). The "normality" of rapists suggests that socialization factors may play an important role.

 Actually, the great majority of rapists have not been shown to be mentally disordered. Rape is a violent crime, not a symptom of a mental disorder. This is not to imply that rapists or acts of rape are normal; it is to point out that rape is a form of social deviance, not a mental disorder, and that rapists should be held accountable under the law.

Many social critics assert that our culture may actually breed rapists by socializing men into sexually dominant and aggressive roles that are associated with stereotypical concepts of masculinity (Burt, 1980; Lisak, 1991; Malamuth et al., 1991; Prentky & Knight, 1991; Stermac et al., 1990). Research with college students supports the links between stereotypical masculinity and tendencies to commit or condone rape. Studies show that college men who adhere more strictly to the stereotypes of the tough competitive male report a greater likelihood of committing rape, are more accepting of pressure and violence against women, more prone to blame rape victims than rapists, and more sexually aroused by portrayals of rape than are men holding less rigid stereotypes (Check & Malamuth, 1983; Muehlenhard & Falcon, 1990). Sociocultural influences also reinforce themes that often underlie rape, such as the cultural belief that a masculine man is expected to be sexually assertive and overcome a woman's resistance until she "melts" in his arms (Stock, 1991).

Cultural Myths That Create a Climate That Supports Rape

Many of us, including many professionals, harbor myths about rape. These myths tend to deny the impact of the assault and also to place blame on the victim rather than her assailant. They contribute to a social climate that is too often lenient toward rapists and unsympathetic toward victims. Complete the following questionnaire to learn whether you harbor some of the more common myths.

Martha Burt (1980) has compiled the following statements concerning rape. Read each of them and indicate whether you believe it to be true or false. Then turn to the key at the end of the chapter to learn the implications of your answers.

T F 1. A woman who goes to the home or apartment of a man on their first date implies that she is willing to have sex.

T F 2. Any female can get raped.

T F 3. One reason that women falsely report a rape is that they frequently have a need to call attention to themselves.

T F 4. Any healthy woman can successfully resist a rapist if she really wants to.

T F 5. When women go around braless or wearing short skirts and tight tops, they are just asking for trouble.

T F 6. In the majority of rapes, the victim is promiscuous or has a bad reputation.

T F 7. If a girl engages in necking or petting and she lets things get out of hand, it is her own fault if her partner forces sex on her.

T F 8. Women who get raped while hitchhiking get what they deserve.

T F 9. A woman who is stuck-up and thinks she is too good to talk to guys on the street deserves to be taught a lesson.

T F 10. Many women have an unconscious wish to be raped, and may then unconsciously set up a situation in which they are likely to be attacked.

T F 11. If a woman gets drunk at a party and has intercourse with a man she's just met there, she should be considered "fair game" to other males at the party who want to have sex with her too, whether she wants to or not.

T F 12. Many women who report a rape are lying because they are angry and want to get back at the man they accuse.

T F 13. Many, if not most, rapes are merely invented by women who discovered they were pregnant and wanted to protect their reputation.

Source: Items adopted from Burt, M. R. (1980). Cultural myths and support for rape. Journal of Personality and Social Psychology, 38, 217–230. Copyright © 1990 by the American Psychological Association. Reprinted by permission.

Victims of Rape

Rape victims suffer more than the rape itself. Many victims are distraught following rape (Calhoun & Atkeson, 1991). They cry often and suffer insomnia. They report loss of appetite, headaches, irritability, anxiety and depression, and menstrual irregularity (Norris & Feldman-Summers, 1981). Some become sullen, withdrawn, and mistrustful (McArthur, 1990). Because of society's tendency to blame the victim for the assault, some victims also have misplaced feelings of guilt and shame (McArthur, 1990). Some women also fear notifying their husbands and boyfriends about the assault, for fear that they will be blamed or considered unfaithful (Moss et al., 1990). Victims often develop sexual dysfunctions such as lack of sexual desire and difficulty becoming sexually aroused (Becker et al., 1983, 1986). Of a sample of 222 rape victims, 88% reported lack of sexual desire and some fear of sex (Becker et al., 1984). At the very least, many women do not reap the level of sexual enjoyment they had experienced before the assault (Calhoun & Atkeson, 1991). Many victims express fear of contracting AIDS from the assault (Baker et al., 1990). Many rape victims show signs of post-traumatic stress disorder (PTSD), including intrusive memories of the rape, nightmares, emotional numbing, and heightened autonomic arousal (Moscarello, 1990; Winfield et al., 1990).

Based on interviews with rape victims at Boston City Hospital and follow-up conversations, Burgess and Holmstrom (1974) concluded that many rape victims suffer from a two-phase **rape trauma syndrome**. The first, or acute, phase usually lasts for several weeks following the rape. Many victims are disorganized during the acute phase. Victims may cry uncontrollably or show an unrealistic composure, which often gives way to venting of feelings later on. Feelings of anger, fear, nervousness, guilt, shame, powerlessness, and self-blame are common (Roehl & Gray, 1984). Physical symptoms reflect specific injuries that require medical attention and stress-related symptoms such as headaches, nausea, and insomnia. The second phase, called the long-term reorganization phase, may last for years (Sales et al., 1984). (Women raped 2 to 46 years prior to survey interviews were found to be more anxious, fearful, and depressed than nonvictims [Santiago et al., 1985].) During this phase, many women change their lives—like moving to safer surroundings—to decrease the likelihood of recurrent assaults and help them manage the emotional aftermath of the attack.

A population survey of households in the Los Angeles area (Burnam et al., 1988) compared the frequencies of diagnosable mental disorders in victims and nonvictims of sexual assault (see Figure 10.2). Sexual assault was defined as pressured or forced sex-

ual contact in childhood or adulthood, including acts of rape, molestation, and childhood sexual abuse. Assault victims were two to four times as likely to show major depression, anxiety disorders, and substance abuse disorders in adulthood than individuals without a history of assault (Burnam et al., 1988). Men with a history of assault were as likely as women to develop these disorders, except that men developed alcohol or drug problems at a later age. Childhood assault was more closely linked to adult psychopathology than assault in adulthood.

Treatment of Rape Victims

Treatment of rape victims is often a two-phase process that assists victims to cope with the immediate aftermath of rape and then to promote long-term adjustment. Crisis intervention provides victims with emotional support and information to help them see to their immediate needs as well as to help them develop strategies for coping with the trauma (Resick

Figure 10.2 Frequencies of diagnosable mental disorders in victims and nonvictims of sexual assault
Assault victims were two to four times as likely as nonvictims to show disorders such as depression, anxiety disorders, and substance abuse.
Source: Burnam et al (1988).

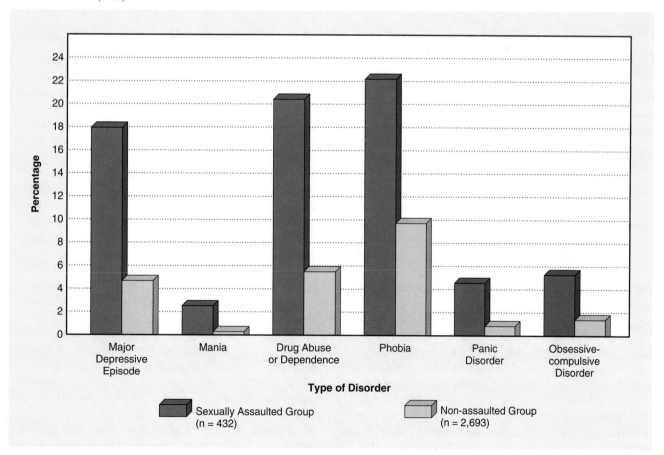

Rape crisis counseling.   Rape crisis centers help rape victims cope with the trauma of rape. They provide victims with emotional support and help them obtain medical and legal services. But for many victims of rape, anxiety, fears, depression, and other psychological problems endure for years.

& Schnicke, 1990). Longer term treatment may be designed to help victims cope with undeserved feelings of guilt and shame, lingering feelings of anxiety and depression, and the interpersonal and sexual problems they may have developed with the men in their lives (Becker & Skinner, 1984).

Treatment of Rapists

Treatment of the rape victim means supporting her (the vast majority of victims are women) through the crisis period and helping foster long-term adjustment. "Treatment" of the rapist can refer to measures that help him "adjust" to feelings of inadequacy and other deficiencies that may be implicated in his crime—*and* to treatments which are intended to protect society from him.

Most convicted rapists are incarcerated to punish them and protect society from them, not for treatment. In prison, they may receive psychotherapy or rehabilitation to prepare them for reentry into society, but the results of prison-based treatment programs are not encouraging. Consider a study of 54 rapists who received aversive conditioning and other forms of treatment at a Canadian facility. Within an average of 46 months following release from prison, 28% had been convicted of another sexual crime and 43% had been convicted of either a sexual crime or another crime of violence (Rice et al., 1990). All in all, the effectiveness of psychological and other rehabilitative efforts with rapists has not been demonstrated (Furby et al., 1989).

Biological approaches to treating rapists have aimed at reducing their sex drives. In some European countries, rapists who claimed that they could not control their sex drives have been castrated (their testes have been surgically removed) to reduce the secretion of testosterone which activates the sex drive (Wille & Beier, 1989). (The rapists voluntarily underwent castration as an alternative to incarceration.) Although many castrated rapists do report lowered sex drives, they can retain their sexual interest and remain capable of erection. Some have repeated their crimes (Heim, 1981).

The use of castration with rapists has declined because of mixed effectiveness and ethical concerns about its invasive character and irreversibility. Antiandrogen drugs, such as Depo-Provera, temporarily lower the production of the male sex hormone testosterone and thereby reduce sexual drives and perhaps the propensity to act on deviant sexual urges (Hucker et al., 1988; Ingersoll & Patton, 1991). Yet sex offenders may not reliably take the drug (Hucker et al., 1988), and chemicals do not change antisocial personalities or assist rapists to resolve their underlying hostilities toward women or needs for social dominance that prompt sexual aggression. Nor is there adequate evidence to show that antiandrogen drugs actually curb recidivism in the long run among rapists (Cooper, 1986).

PARAPHILIAS

The word *paraphilia* was coined from the Greek roots *para*, meaning "to the side of," and *philos*, meaning "loving." In the **paraphilias**, people show sexual arousal ("loving") in response to stimuli that are unusual or bizarre ("to the side of" normally arousing stimuli). According to the DSM-IV, paraphilias involve recurrent, powerful sexual urges and fantasies that center on either (1) nonhuman objects such as underwear, shoes, leather, or silk, (2) humiliation or experience of pain in oneself or one's partner, or (3) children and other persons who do not grant consent.

The diagnosis requires that the paraphilic urges are recurrent, powerful, and persistent over a period of at least six months. The person receiving the diagnosis must have acted out on the urges or must be distinctly distressed by them. The diagnosis can be made purely on the basis of the person's reported paraphilic fantasies, if they cause personal distress. Overt paraphilic behavior is not required.

Some persons who receive the diagnosis can function sexually in the absence of paraphilic stimuli

Rape Prevention

Given the incidence of rape, it is useful to be aware of strategies that may prevent it. Rape prevention follows two paths. The first concerns suggestions from *The New Our Bodies, Ourselves* (Boston Women's Health Book Collective, 1993) for averting stranger rape. The second involves suggestions for averting date rape (Rathus & Fichner-Rathus, 1994). By listing strategies for rape prevention, we do not mean to imply that rape victims are responsible for falling prey to an attack. The responsibility for any act of sexual violence lies with the perpetrator, not with the victim, and perhaps with society for fostering attitudes that underlie sexual violence.

Preventing Stranger Rape

- Establish signals and plans with other women in the building or neighborhood.
- List first initials only in the phone directory and on the mailbox.
- Use dead-bolt locks.
- Lock windows and install iron grids on first-floor windows.
- Keep doorways and entries well lit.
- Have keys handy for the car or the front door.
- Do not walk by yourself after dark.
- Avoid deserted areas.
- Do not allow strange men into the apartment or the house without checking their credentials.
- Keep the car door locked and the windows up.
- Check out the backseat of the car before getting in.
- Don't live in a risky building.
- Don't give rides to hitchhikers (that includes women hitchhikers).
- Don't converse with strange men on the street.
- Shout "Fire!" not "Rape!" People flock to fires but circumvent scenes of violence.

Preventing Date Rape

- Avoid getting into secluded situations until you know your date very well. (As noted in the questionnaire "Cultural Myths," some men interpret a date's willingness to accompany them to their room as an agreement to engage in sexual activity.)
- Be wary when a date attempts to control you in any way, such as frightening you by driving rapidly or taking you some place you would rather not go.
- Stay sober. We often do things we would not otherwise do—including sexual activity with people we might otherwise reject—when we have had too many drinks. Be aware of your limits.
- Be very assertive and clear concerning your sexual intentions. Some rapists, particularly date rapists, tend to misinterpret women's wishes. If their dates begin to implore them to stop during kissing or petting, they construe pleading as "female gameplaying." So if kissing or petting is leading where you don't want it to go, speak up.
- When dating a person for the first time, try to date in a group.
- Encourage your college or university to offer educational programs about date rape. The University of Washington, for example, offers students lectures and seminars on date rape and provides women with escorts to get home. Brown University requires all first-year students to attend orientation sessions on rape.
- Talk to your date about his attitudes toward women. If you get the feeling that he believes that men are in a war with women, or that women try to "play games" with men, you may be better off dating someone else.
- You can find out about attitudes by discussing items from the questionnaire with a man you are considering dating. You can say something like, "You know, my friend's date said that . . . What do you think about it?" It's a good way to find out if he has attitudes that can lead to trouble.

or fantasies. Others resort to paraphilic stimuli under stress. Still others cannot become sexually aroused unless these stimuli are used, in actuality or in fantasy. For some individuals, the paraphilia is their exclusive means of attaining sexual gratification.

Some paraphilias are relatively harmless and victimless. Among these are fetishism and transvestic fetishism. Others—exhibitionism, pedophilia, and some cases of sadism—have unwilling victims. A most harmful paraphilia is sexual sadism when acted out with a nonconsenting partner. Voyeurism falls somewhere in between because the "victim" does not typically know that he or she is being watched.

People with paraphilias usually do not consider themselves to be mentally disordered. They are generally seen by the mental health system when they get into conflict with their partners or with society. With the exceptions of sexual masochism and some isolated cases of other disorders, paraphilias are almost never diagnosed in women.

Now let us consider a number of the paraphilias.

Exhibitionism

Exhibitionism is the recurrent, powerful urge to expose one's genitals to an unsuspecting stranger in order to surprise, shock, or sexually arouse the victim. The exhibitionist may masturbate while fantasizing about or actually exposing himself. The disorder appears to be almost exclusively limited to males (Freund & Blanchard, 1986). The victims are almost always females.

Exhibitionists are typically not interested in actual sexual contact with the victim and are therefore not usually considered dangerous. Nevertheless, victims may believe themselves in great danger and may be traumatized by the act. Victims are probably best advised to show no reaction to exhibitionists, to just continue on their way, if possible. It would be unwise to insult an exhibitionist, lest it provoke a violent reaction. Although most of them are not violent, 1 in 10 has considered or attempted rape (Gebhard et al., 1965). Nor do we recommend an exaggerated show of shock or fear; it tends to reinforce the exhibitionist.

Some researchers view exhibitionism as a means of indirectly expressing hostility toward women, perhaps because of perceptions of having been wronged by women in the past or of not being noticed or taken seriously by them (Geer et al.,

1984). Exhibitionists tend to be shy, dependent, lacking in social and sexual skills, even socially inhibited (Dwyer, 1988). Some doubt their masculinity and hold feelings of inferiority (Blair & Lanyon, 1981). Their victims' revulsion or fear boosts their sense of mastery of the situation and heightens their sexual arousal.

Consider the case of Michael:

Michael was a 26-year-old, handsome, boyish-looking married male with a 3-year-old daughter. He had spent about one-quarter of his life in reform schools and in prison. As an adolescent he had been a fire-setter. As a young adult, he had begun to expose himself. He came to the clinic without his wife's knowledge because he was exposing himself more and more often—up to three times a day—and he was afraid that he would eventually be arrested and thrown into prison again.

Michael said he liked sex with his wife, but it wasn't as exciting as exposing himself. He couldn't prevent his exhibitionism, especially now, when he was between jobs and worried about where the family's next month's rent was coming from. He loved his daughter more than anything and couldn't stand the thought of being separated from her.

Michael's method of operation was as follows: He would look for slender adolescent females, usually near the junior high school and the senior high school. He would take his penis out of his pants and play with it while he drove up to a girl or a small group of girls. He would lower the car window, continuing to play with himself, and ask them for directions. Sometimes the girls didn't see his penis. That was okay. Sometimes they saw it and didn't react. That was okay, too. When they saw it and became flustered and afraid, that was best of all. He would start to masturbate harder, and now and then he managed to ejaculate before the girls had departed.

Michael's history was unsettled. His father had left home before he was born, and his mother had drunk heavily. He was in and out of foster homes throughout his childhood, "all over" the capital district area of New York State. Before he was 10 years old he was involved in sexual activities with neighborhood boys. Now and then the boys also forced neighborhood girls into petting, and Michael had mixed feelings when the girls got upset. He felt bad for them, but he also enjoyed it. A couple of times girls seemed horrified at the sight of his penis, and it made him "really feel like a man. To see that look, you know, with a girl, not a woman, but a girl—a slender girl, that's what I'm after."

■ *The Authors' Files*

Exhibitionism. Exhibitionism is a paraphilia in which people seek sexual arousal or gratification through exposing themselves to unsuspecting victims. Exhibitionists are usually not interested in actual sexual contact with the victim.

Professional stripteasers and swimmers in revealing swimsuits are not usually exhibitionists. Both groups may seek to sexually arouse, but generally not to shock, observers.

It is not true that people who wear revealing bathing suits are exhibitionists. Exhibitionists are almost always men and are motivated by the wish to shock and dismay the people they expose themselves to, not to show off the attractiveness of their bodies.

The chief motive of the stripteaser, of course, may simply be to earn a living.

Fetishism

The French *fétiche* is thought to derive from the Portuguese *feitico*, referring to a "magic charm." In this case, the "magic" lies in the object's ability to sexually arouse. The chief feature of **fetishism** is recurrent, powerful sexual urges and arousing fantasies involving inanimate objects, such as an article of clothing (bras, panties, hosiery, boots, shoes, leather, silk, and the like). It is normal for men to like the sight, feel, and smell of their lovers' undergarments. The fetishist, however, may prefer the object to the person and may not be able to become sexually aroused without it. Fetishists often experience sexual gratification by masturbating while fondling the object, rubbing it, or smelling it, or by having their partners wear it during sexual activity.

The origins of fetishes may be traced to early childhood in many cases. Most of the rubber fetishists in one research sample were able to recall first experiencing a fetishistic attraction to rubber sometime between the age of 4 and 10 (Gosselin & Wilson, 1980).

Transvestic Fetishism

The chief feature of **transvestic fetishism** is recurrent, powerful urges and related fantasies involving cross-dressing for purposes of sexual arousal. Other fetishists can be satisfied by handling objects such as women's clothing while they masturbate; transvestites want to wear them. Transvestites typically don women's clothes in private and masturbate while imagining that other men are attracted to them in their finery. Some frequent transvestite clubs. Gay men may cross-dress to attract other men or because it is fashionable to masquerade as women in their social circles. Males with gender identity disorder

cross-dress because of gender discomfort associated with wearing men's clothing. Cross-dressing among gay men and males with gender identity disorder is seldom performed for the sake of sexual gratification, and is thus not considered to be a form of transvestic fetishism. Nor are female impersonators who cross-dress for theatrical purposes considered to be transvestites. For reasons such as these, the diagnosis is limited to heterosexuals.

Most transvestites are married and engage in sexual activity with their wives, but they seek additional sexual gratification through dressing as women, as in the case of Archie:

*A*rchie was a 55-year-old plumber who had been cross-dressing for many years. There was a time when he would go out in public as a woman, but as his prominence in the community grew, he became more afraid of being discovered in public. His wife Myrna knew of his "peccadillo," especially since he borrowed many of her clothes, and she also encouraged him to stay at home, offering to help him with his "weirdness." For many years his paraphilia had been restricted to the home.

The couple came to the clinic at the urging of the wife. Myrna described how Archie had imposed his will on her for 20 years. Archie would wear her undergarments and masturbate while she told him how disgusting he was. (The couple also regularly engaged in "normal" sexual intercourse, which Myrna enjoyed.) The cross-dressing situation had come to a head because a teenaged daughter had almost walked into the couple's bedroom while they were acting out Archie's fantasies.

With Myrna out of the consulting room, Archie explained how he grew up in a family with several older sisters. He described how underwear had been perpetually hanging all around the one bathroom to dry. As an adolescent Archie experimented with rubbing against articles of underwear, then with trying them on. On one occasion a sister walked in while he was modeling panties before the mirror. She told him he was a "dredge to society" and he straightaway experienced unparalleled sexual excitement. He masturbated when she left the room, and his orgasm was the strongest of his young life.

Archie did not think that there was anything wrong with wearing women's undergarments and masturbating. He was not about to give it up, regardless of whether his marriage was destroyed as a result. Myrna's main concern was finally separating herself from Archie's "sickness." She didn't care what he did anymore, so long as he did it by himself. "Enough is enough," she said.

That was the compromise the couple worked out in marital therapy. Archie would engage in his fantasies by *himself. He would choose times when Myrna was not at home, and she would not be informed of his activities. He would also be very, very careful to choose times when the children would not be around.*

Six months later the couple were together and content. Archie had replaced Myrna's input into his fantasies with transvestic-sadomasochistic magazines. Myrna said, "I see no evil, hear no evil, smell no evil." They continued to have sexual intercourse. After a while, Myrna even forgot to check to see which underwear had been used.

■ *The Authors' Files*

Voyeurism

The chief feature of **voyeurism** is either acting upon or being strongly distressed by recurrent, powerful sexual urges and related fantasies involving watching unsuspecting people, generally strangers, who are undressed, disrobing, or engaging in sexual activity. The purpose of watching, or "peeping," is to attain sexual excitement. The voyeur does not usually seek sexual activity with the person being observed.

Are individuals who enjoy watching their mates disrobe in their presence or attending pornographic films voyeurs? The answer is no. The people who are observed know that they are being observed by their mates or will be observed by film audiences. We should also note that feelings of sexual arousal while watching our mates undress or observing sex scenes in R- and X-rated films fall within the normal spectrum of human sexuality.

 People who like to watch their spouses disrobe are *not* necessarily voyeurs. Enjoying seeing others undress is completely normal. Voyeurs choose unsuspecting victims, and they generally prefer watching to doing.

The voyeur usually masturbates while watching, or while fantasizing about watching. For some voyeurs, peeping is the exclusive sexual outlet. Voyeurs are known to place themselves in risky situations. The prospects of being found out or injured apparently heighten the excitement.

Frotteurism

The French *frottage* refers to the artistic technique of making a drawing by rubbing against a raised object. The chief feature of the paraphilia of **frotteurism** is

recurrent, powerful sexual urges and related fantasies involving rubbing against or touching a nonconsenting person. Frotteurism generally occurs in crowded places, such as subway cars, buses, or elevators. It is the rubbing or touching, not the coercive aspect of the act, that is sexually arousing to the man. He may imagine himself enjoying an exclusive, affectionate sexual relationship with the victim. Because the physical contact is brief and furtive, frotteurs stand only a small chance of being caught by authorities. Even the victims may not realize at the time what has happened or register much protest (Spitzer et al., 1989). In the following case example, a frotteur victimized about a thousand women over a period of years but was arrested only twice:

Charles, 45, was seen by a psychiatrist following his second arrest for rubbing against a woman in the subway. He would select as his target a woman in her 20s as she entered the subway station. He would then position himself behind her on the platform and wait for the train to arrive. He would then follow her into the subway car and when the doors closed would begin bumping against her buttocks, while fantasizing that they were enjoying having intercourse in a loving and consensual manner. About half of the time he would reach orgasm. He would then continue on his way to work. Sometimes when he hadn't reached orgasm, he would change trains and seek another victim. While he felt guilty for a time after each episode, he would soon become preoccupied with thoughts about his next encounter. He never gave any thought to the feelings his victims might have about what he had done to them. While he was married to the same woman for 25 years, he appears to be rather socially inept and unassertive, especially with women.

■ *Adapted from Spitzer et al., 1989, pp. 106–107. Reprinted from Rathus, Nevid, and Fichner-Rathus, 1993, p. 552*

Pedophilia

Pedophilia derives from the Greek *paidos*, meaning "child." The chief feature of pedophilia is recurrent, powerful sexual urges and related fantasies that involve sexual activity with prepubescent children. The pedophile must be an individual of at least 16 years of age who is at least 5 years older than the victim. Pedophiles are almost always males, although there are some cases of female pedophiles reported (Cooper et al., 1990; Mathews et al., 1990). Some pedophiles are attracted only to children. Others are attracted to adults as well.

Pedophilic behavior may include exhibitionism, kissing, fondling, oral sex, anal intercourse and, in the case of girls, vaginal intercourse (Knudsen, 1991). Genital fondling is most common (Knudsen, 1991). Some pedophiles look at or undress children only. Children are not worldly wise, and pedophiles frequently inform the children that they are "educating" them, "showing them something," or doing something that they will "like." Some pedophiles are incestuous and limit their activity to family members; others to children outside the family.

A national telephone victimization survey of more than 2,600 U.S. adults revealed that nearly 27% of the women and 16% of the men reported having been sexually abused as children (Finkelhor et al., 1990). The sexual abuse of children cuts across all racial, ethnic, and economic boundaries (Alter-Reid et al., 1986). Child sexual abuse, like rape, is underreported to authorities, with perhaps only 1 in 3 or 1 in 4 cases reported (Alter-Reid et al., 1986). Not all child molesters are true pedophiles, however. The clinical definition is brought to bear only when sexual attraction to children is recurrent and persistent. Some molesters engage in pedophilic acts or experience such urges only occasionally or during times of opportunity.

Sometimes the pedophile threatens the child or the child's family with physical harm to prevent disclosure. Children rarely report sexual abuse for fear that they will be blamed for it. Often the symptoms of abuse are "masked" and become expressed as school problems, fears, or eating or sleeping problems (Finkelhor, 1990; Miller-Perrin & Wurtele, 1988). Yet no single behavioral pattern is reliably associated with child sexual abuse (Miller-Perrin & Wurtele, 1988). Sometimes a pediatrician discovers physical evidence of sexual abuse.

Despite the stereotype, most pedophiles are not "dirty old men" who hang around schoolyards in raincoats. They are usually (otherwise) law-abiding, respected citizens in their 30s or 40s. Most are married or divorced and have children of their own. Pedophiles are usually well acquainted with their victims, either relatives or friends of the family. Many cases of pedophilia are not isolated incidents. They may be a series of acts that begin when children are very young and continue for many years until they are discovered or the relationship is broken off (Finkelhor, 1990). When abuse occurs, it is more likely to be repeated than to occur on only one occasion (Kolko, 1988).

The origins of pedophilia are complex and varied. Some pedophiles fit the stereotype of being weak, shy, socially inept, and isolated men who are threatened by mature relationships and turn to children for sexual gratification because children are less critical and demanding (Ames & Houston, 1990; Overholser & Beck, 1986). In other cases, it may be that childhood sexual experiences with other children were so enjoyable that the pedophile, as an adult, is attempting to recapture the excitement of earlier years. De Young (1982), among others, hypothesizes that some pedophiles who were sexually abused by adults as children may now be reversing the situation in an effort to establish feelings of mastery.

■ **INCEST** The term *incest* derives from the Latin roots *in-*, meaning "not," and *castus*, meaning chaste. Sagarin defines incest as "marriage and/or sexual intercourse between persons [consanguineously] of so close a relationship that the act is proscribed and punished by virtue of the closeness of that kinship tie" (1977, p. 128). True incest refers only to people who are related by blood, but the law may also proscribe relationships between, say, stepfathers and stepdaughters.

The DSM does not have a diagnostic category for incest. Instead, diagnosticians making the diagnosis of pedophilia specify whether or not the offense is limited to incest.

Fourteen percent of the men and 8% of the women in Hunt's (1974) national survey reported some kind of sexual contact with relatives. Brother-sister incest is the most common type of incest and is probably greatly underreported (Waterman & Lusk, 1986). A survey of 800 undergraduates at a New England college found that 21% of the men and 39% of the women reported a sexual experience with a sibling of the opposite gender, whereas 4% reported incestuous relationships with their fathers (Finkelhor, 1980). Genital fondling and display were the most common incestuous activities (Finkelhor, 1980).

Incest often occurs within the context of broad family disruption, as when parents have dysfunctional marriages or are alcoholic or abusive (Alter-Reid et al., 1986; Sirles & Franke, 1989; Waterman, 1986). Sociocultural factors, such as poverty, overcrowding, and social or geographical isolation may also contribute to incest (Waterman, 1986).

Gebhard and his colleagues (1965) found that many fathers who committed incest with their daughters were religiously devout, fundamentalistic, and moralistic. Such men, when sexually frustrated, may be less likely to find extramarital and extrafamilial sexual outlets. In many cases, the father is under stress but does not find adequate emotional and sexual support from his wife (Gagnon, 1977). He turns to a daughter as a wife surrogate. The girl is often mature enough to have assumed household chores.

Perhaps, in the father's fantasies, she has become the "woman of the house." These men's wives often seem surprised by revelations of incest, despite obvious clues and even their daughters' repeated complaints. Sometimes the wife seems involved in a tacit conspiracy to allow the abuse to continue to preserve the family or because of fear of the abuser.

■ **EFFECTS OF SEXUAL ABUSE** Victims of child sexual abuse are at increased risk of a wide range of psychological problems and complaints including anxiety, anger and aggressive behavior, eating disorders, sexual promiscuity, drug abuse, self-destructive behavior including suicide attempts, sexual dysfunctions, lack of trust, low self-esteem, social withdrawal, and psychosomatic problems such as stom-

achaches and headaches (Finkelhor, 1990; Goodwin et al., 1990; McLaren & Brown, 1989; Wolfe, 1990). Many victims of childhood sexual abuse—like many victims of rape—also show signs of post-traumatic stress disorder (PTSD), such as flashbacks, nightmares, emotional numbing, and feelings of detachment from others (Finkelhor, 1990).

■ **TREATMENT** Because most cases of child sexual abuse go unreported, survivors of abuse may not receive psychotherapy for overcoming trauma-related feelings of anger and (misplaced) guilt until adulthood (Alter-Reid et al., 1986). Sex therapy may help adult survivors surmount sexual dysfunctions and fears (Douglas et al., 1989). Group therapy may help them face their feelings in a supportive setting with

MULTICULTURAL PERSPECTIVES

Effects of Childhood Sexual Abuse on African-American and White Women

Gail Wyatt (1990) investigated childhood sexual abuse in a sample of 126 African-American women and 122 white women in Los Angeles County. The subjects were matched on such variables as marital status, number of children, and education. The operational definition of childhood sexual abuse was broad, including acts such as exhibitionism, fondling, oral sex, and sexual intercourse.

The prevalence of abuse was similar in both groups. Nearly 1 woman in 2 had suffered at least one incident of abuse, and nearly 40% of these incidences had gone unreported to authorities. The African-American women were somewhat less likely to report abuse to their immediate family members or to the police. However, they were nearly twice as likely to have informed extended family members as were the white women, a finding that underscores the importance of the extended family to African Americans. African-American women were more likely than white women (35% versus 22%) to avoid reporting abuse for fear of repercussions. The African-American women may have felt more vulnerable to the financial adversity that their families would have had to endure if the abuser—often their mothers' boyfriends or their stepfathers on whom the family was financially dependent—had been forced to leave the home. White women more often expressed fear of being blamed for the abuse as a reason for nonreporting (36%) than did African-American women (23%).

The psychological impact of abuse was similar on both groups. African-American and white women were

Out in the open. Many victims of childhood sexual abuse are reluctant to report their experiences to family members or authorities because of fear of repercussions, such as being blamed for the abuse or—when the abuser is the father or the mother's boyfriend—for breaking up the home.

both likely to feel violated and to harbor feelings of fear, disgust, and anger. Both groups were prone to face sexual problems as adults. The African-American women were more prone to recount that the experience had affected their feelings toward men. They were particularly likely to avoid men who reminded them of the abuser. Yet broadly speaking, the similarities in the responses of the two groups of women eclipsed the differences.

people who have undergone similar trauma (Alexander et al., 1989).

When sexual abuse is uncovered in childhood, a multicomponent treatment approach may be recommended. It may include individual therapy for the victim and her or his parents; group therapy for an adolescent victim; play or art therapy for a younger child; marital counseling; and family therapy for the parents and all the children (Waterman, 1986). Family therapy may help the family restructure relationships and avoid blaming the victim (Fish & Faynik, 1989). The effectiveness of treatment programs for sexually abused children remains to be demonstrated, however (Waterman et al., 1986; Wolfe, 1990).

Sexual Masochism

Sexual masochism derives its name from the Austrian novelist Ritter Leopold von Sacher-Masoch (1835–1895), who wrote stories and novels about men who sought sexual gratification from women inflicting pain on them, often in the form of flagellation (being beaten or whipped). Some writers have attributed the desire to be flagellated to the practice of disciplining children with the rod, which was commonplace in the 19th century. But if such an origin was sufficient explanation, Reay Tannahill, author of *Sex in History* (1980), notes that the wish to be flagellated would have become "an international pandemic" (p. 382). It did not.

Sexual masochists either act on or are distressed about recurrent, powerful sexual urges and related fantasies that involve being humiliated, bound, flogged, or made to suffer in other ways. In some cases, the sexual masochists cannot attain sexual gratification in the absence of pain or humiliation.

 It is true that some people cannot become sexually aroused unless they are subjected to pain or humiliation by others. This pattern of abnormal behavior is referred to as sexual masochism.

Some masochists bind or mutilate themselves. Some engage partners, who may be prostitutes, to restrain them (bondage), blindfold them (sensory bondage), paddle, or whip them. Some want to be urinated or defecated upon or subjected to verbal abuse.

A most dangerous expression of masochism is **hypoxyphilia**, in which participants are sexually aroused by being deprived of oxygen—for example by using a noose, plastic bag, chemical, or pressure on the chest during a sexual act, such as masturbation.

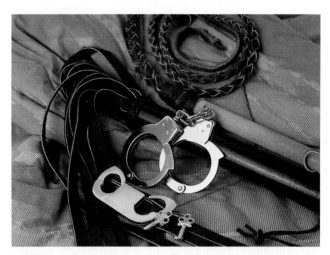

S & M paraphernalia. Some of the devices used by sadists and masochists.

The oxygen deprivation is usually accompanied by fantasies of asphyxiating or being asphyxiated by a lover. Hypoxyphiliacs generally discontinue their activity before they lose consciousness, but occasional deaths result from miscalculation.

Sexual Sadism

Sexual sadism is named after the infamous Marquis de Sade, the 18th-century Frenchman who wrote stories about the pleasures of achieving sexual gratification by inflicting pain or humiliation on others. The marquis's first novel, *Justine,* is also his best known. The virtuous Justine is bound and spread-eagled so that bloodhounds can savage her. She seeks refuge with a surgeon who tries to vivisect her. Then she falls into the clutches of a saber-wielding mass murderer. After tiring of Justine's purity, Nature releases her by hurling a timely thunderbolt. The marquis justified his tales by arguing that the men in them are only carrying out Nature's bloody, barbarous laws. To the marquis, the universe was basically evil. Evil acts, then, were consistent with natural law. In virtue lay misery and ruin. Vice was the path to prosperity and fulfillment.

Sexual sadists have recurrent, powerful urges and related fantasies of acts in which they are sexually aroused by the physical suffering or humiliation of a victim. Sadists either act out their fantasies or are disturbed by them. **Sadomasochism** describes a mutually gratifying interaction between a sadist and a masochist. Some sadists recruit consenting partners into their routines, who may be lovers or wives with a masochistic streak, or prostitutes. Still others stalk and assault nonconsenting victims. Sadistic rapists fall into this last group. Most rapists, however, do not seek to become sexually aroused by inflicting pain on their victims; they may even lose sexual interest when they see their victims in pain.

Many people have occasional sadistic or masochistic fantasies or engage in sex play involving simulated forms of sadomasochism with their partners. The clinical diagnosis is not usually brought to bear unless sexual masochists or sadists are distressed by their behavior or fantasies, or they act them out in ways that are harmful to themselves or others.

Other Paraphilias

There are many other paraphilias. These include making obscene phone calls ("telephone scatologia"), necrophilia (sexual urges or fantasies involving sexual contact with corpses), partialism (sole focus on part of the body), zoophilia (sexual urges or fantasies involving sexual contact with animals), and sexual arousal associated with feces (coprophilia), enemas (klismaphilia), and urine (urophilia).

Theoretical Perspectives

Psychodynamic theorists see many paraphilias as defenses against castration anxiety. They generally link sexual deviations to Oedipal fixations. The thought of the penis disappearing within the vagina is unconsciously equated with castration. The paraphile therefore averts castration anxiety by displacing sexual arousal into safer activities—for example, undergarments, children, or watching others. Transvestic fetishism symbolizes denial that women do not have penises, which eases castration anxiety. The transvestite sequesters his sex organ beneath women's clothing, unconsciously providing evidence of women's (and his own) safety. The shock and dismay shown by the exhibitionist's victim provides unconscious reassurance that he does, after all, have a penis. The sadist unconsciously identifies with his father—the "aggressor" of his Oedipal fantasies—and relieves anxiety by enacting the role of the castrater. Some psychoanalytic theorists see masochism as a way of coping with conflicting feelings about sex. Masochists are basically guilty about sex, that is, but they can enjoy it as long as they believe they are being punished for it. Others view masochism as the redirection inward of aggressive impulses originally aimed at the powerful, threatening father. Like the child who is relieved when his inevitable punishment is over, the masochist gladly accepts bondage and flagellation in the place of castration.

Learning theorists explain paraphilias in terms of conditioning and observational learning. Some

object or activity becomes inadvertently associated with sexual arousal. The object or activity then gains the capacity to elicit sexual arousal. For example, a boy who glimpses his mother's stockings on the towel rack while he is masturbating may go on to develop a fetish for stockings (Breslow, 1989). Orgasm in the presence of the object reinforces the erotic connection, especially when it occurs repeatedly. Yet if fetishes were acquired by mechanical association, we would expect fetishists to be attracted to stimuli that are inadvertently and repeatedly connected with sexual activity, such as bedsheets, pillows, even ceilings (Breslow, 1989). Yet such is not the case. The *meaning* of the stimulus also apparently plays a role. Perhaps the development of fetishes depends on the person's ability to eroticize certain types of stimuli (like women's undergarments) and incorporate them within their erotic and masturbatory fantasies.

Fetishes can often be traced to early childhood. Consider the development of rubber fetishes. Reinisch (1990) speculates that the earliest awareness of sexual arousal or response (such as erection) may have been connected with rubber pants or diapers such that an association was made between the two, setting the stage for the development of the fetish.

Like other patterns of abnormal behavior, paraphilias may involve multiple biological, psychological, and sociocultural factors. Money and Lamacz (1990) hypothesize a multifactorial model that traces the development of paraphilias to childhood. They suggest that childhood experiences etch a pattern, or "lovemap," in the brain that determines the kinds of stimuli and behaviors that come to sexually arouse people. In the case of paraphilias, such lovemaps become "vandalized" by early traumatic experiences, such as incest, physical abuse or neglect, and excessively harsh antisexual child rearing. Yet not all children who undergo such experiences develop paraphilias. Perhaps some children are more vulnerable to developing distorted lovemaps than others. The precise nature of such a vulnerability remains to be defined.

Treatment of Paraphilias

Therapists of various theoretical persuasions have attempted to treat clients with paraphilias. Psychoanalysts, for example, attempt to help paraphiles by bringing childhood sexual conflicts into awareness so they can be resolved in the light of the individual's adult personality. Favorable results from individual case studies appear in the literature from time to time, but there is a dearth of controlled investigations to support the efficacy of psychodynamic treatment of paraphilias.

I see many possible areas for problems in a set-up such is this one! (See note below)

Sexual and Gender Identity Disorders and Variations in Sexual Behavior 391

Various treatments have been spawned by the behavioral and cognitive perspectives. Consider systematic desensitization. The premise is that deep muscle relaxation is incompatible with the tensions of sexual arousal, so responding to a series of progressively more arousing stimuli, while remaining relaxed, should disconnect arousal from deviant stimuli. In one case study, a transvestic fetishist who had become attracted to his mother's lingerie at the age of 13 was taught to relax and presented with audiotaped transvestic and fetishistic themes (Fensterheim & Kanter, 1980). He played the tapes daily while remaining relaxed and reported no fetishistic activity at follow-ups. An uncontrolled case study, however, limits interpretations about cause and effect.

In aversive conditioning, the stimulus that elicits sexual arousal (for example, panties) is paired repeatedly with an aversive stimulus (for example, electric shock) in the belief that the stimulus will acquire aversive properties. Electric shock was used with a socially inhibited fetishist who masturbated while wearing or fantasizing about women's panties (Kushner, 1977). He was shocked while imagining, viewing photos of, or holding panties. After 41 sessions distributed over 14 weeks, he reported absence of fetishistic fantasies. He was then desensitized to fear of contacts with the opposite gender and went on to enjoy heterosexual relationships.

Covert sensitization, the most common form of aversion therapy used to treat sex offenders in the United States (McConaghy, 1990), is a variation of aversive conditioning in which a stimulus that elicits sexual arousal is paired in the imagination with an aversive stimulus. In an unusual broad-scale application, 38 pedophiles and 62 exhibitionists, more than half of whom were court-referred, were treated by pairing imaginary aversive odors with fantasies of the problem behavior (Maletzky, 1980). Clients were instructed to fantasize pedophilic or exhibitionist scenes. Then:

> At a point . . . when sexual pleasure is aroused, aversive images are presented. . . . Examples might include a pedophiliac fellating a child, but discovering a festering sore on the boy's penis; an exhibitionist exposing to a woman but then suddenly being discovered by his wife or the police; or a pedophiliac laying a young boy down in a field, only to lie next to him in a pile of dog feces.
>
> Maletzky, 1980, p. 308

Maletzky used this treatment weekly for 6 months, then followed it with "booster sessions" every 3 months over a 3-year period. The procedure resulted in at least a 75% reduction of the deviant activities and fantasies for over 80% of the subjects at follow-up periods of up to 36 months. Treatment was equally effective for self- and court-referred clients.

In orgasmic reconditioning, the person becomes sexually aroused in any way he can, but then focuses attention on appropriate images or fantasies during orgasm. Davison (1977) reports reducing sadistic fantasies in an otherwise inhibited 21-year-old college man by reinforcing nonsadistic fantasies. The client was instructed to attain erection in any way that he could, but then to masturbate while looking at photos of *Playboy* models. Orgasm was thus paired with "normal" imagery, which eventually attained the capacity to elicit sexual arousal. The client also received social skills training to help him develop heterosexual relationships.

Although there are many reports of successful behavioral treatment of various paraphilias, controlled studies are lacking. Less successful results have also appeared. Rice and her colleagues (1991) investigated the effects of behavioral treatment (mainly electric aversion therapy) among 136 child molesters who were incarcerated in a maximum security psychiatric institution. A 6-year follow-up study revealed that the behavioral treatment had no effect on recidivism (return to incarceration) for sexual offenses. More broadly, investigators note many problems that attend the treatment of the paraphilias:

1. Paraphiliacs usually do not want or seek treatment, at least not voluntarily. They are generally seen by health professionals when forced to do so by a judge, their families, or their sex partners, or because of fear of exposure, prosecution, or humiliation (Spitzer et al., 1989).

2. Helping professionals may consider it unethical to serve at the behest of the judicial process to attempt to alter the behavior of remanded or incarcerated sex offenders who may not be in a position to render full, voluntary consent.

3. Therapy is usually unsuccessful when clients are resistant or recalcitrant.

4. Sex offenders usually insist that they cannot control their impulses. Therapists usually find that accepting personal responsibility for one's actions is essential to change.

SEXUAL DYSFUNCTIONS

We now consider a very different class of sexual disorders: **sexual dysfunctions**. The sexual dysfunctions are characterized by lessened or inhibited sexual interest, pleasure, or response. Sexual dysfunctions do not involve problems in gender identity or socially deviant behavior patterns. Because they are quite

Are big "hooters" and sprawling vaginas NORMAL ?!? Also, why was it assumed that the man's "normal" orientation should be heterosexual?!?

When a source of pleasure becomes a source of anxiety. Many couples encounter sexual difficulties. Sexual dysfunctions are a source of personal distress to oneself or one's partner and can often lead to friction between the partners. Problems in communication can give rise to or exacerbate sexual dysfunctions.

commonplace, they may not be considered abnormal from the statistical perspective. Psychologists focus on sexual dysfunctions because they are a source of distress to oneself and/or one's sex partner.

To provide perspective on the sexual dysfunctions, we first describe normal patterns of sexual response. Then we explore the types of sexual dysfunctions and the methods of treatment that help people overcome them.

The Sexual Response Cycle

Sexual dysfunctions interfere with the initiation or completion of the sexual response cycle. Much of our understanding of the sexual response cycle is based on the pioneering work of sex researchers William Masters and Virginia Johnson. The DSM describes the sexual response cycle as consisting of four phases:

1. *Appetitive Phase.* This phase involves sexual fantasies and the desire to engage in sexual activity. The occurrence of sexual fantasies and desires are quite normal; the question is, "How much (or how little) sexual interest is normal?"

2. *Excitement Phase.* This phase involves the physical changes and feelings of pleasure that occur during the process of sexual arousal. In response to sexual stimulation the heart rate, respiration rate, and blood pressure increase. Sexual excitement involves two essential sexual reflexes—erection in the man and

vaginal lubrication ("wetness") in the woman. In men, erection occurs as blood vessels in chambers of loose tissue within the penis dilate to permit an increased blood flow to expand the tissues. In women, the breasts swell and the nipples become erect. Blood engorges the genitals, causing the clitoris to expand. The vagina lengthens and dilates, and lubrication appears.

3. *Orgasm Phase.* In both genders, sexual tension peaks and is released through involuntary rhythmic contractions of the pelvic muscles. Orgasm, like erection and lubrication, is a reflex. In men, muscles at the bottom of the penis contract, causing semen to be expelled. In women, muscles surrounding the outer third of the vagina contract reflexively. In men and women, the first contractions are strongest and spaced at 0.8-second intervals (five contractions in 4 seconds). Ensuing contractions are weaker and farther apart.

 It is true that orgasm is a reflex. People cannot will or force an orgasm. Nor can they will or force other sexual reflexes, such as erection and vaginal lubrication. People can only set the stage for these sexual responses and let them happen.

People can set the stage for orgasm by receiving adequate sexual stimulation and having an accepting attitude toward sexual pleasure. People cannot force or will an orgasm, however. Attempts to compel an orgasm are often counterproductive.

4. *Resolution Phase.* Relaxation and a sense of well-being occur. During this phase, men are physiologically incapable of reachieving erection and orgasm for a period of time. Women, however, may be able to maintain a high level of sexual excitement with continued stimulation and experience multiple orgasms in swift succession. During the sexual revolution of the 1960s and 1970s, awareness of this capacity caused some women to think that they ought not be satisfied with just one orgasm. This is the flip side of the old saw that sexual enjoyment is appropriate for men only. In sex, as in other areas of life, oughts and shoulds are often arbitrary demands that elicit feelings of anxiety and inadequacy.

Types of Sexual Dysfunctions

The DSM-IV groups most dysfunctions within these categories:

1. Sexual desire disorders
2. Sexual arousal disorders
3. Orgasm disorders
4. Sexual pain disorders

Accurate estimates of the prevalence of sexual dysfunctions are hard to come by. Nonetheless, a review of community surveys suggests that more than one-third of the men currently experience premature (too rapid) ejaculation (Spector & Carey, 1990; see Table 10.2). Fewer report problems in achieving or maintaining erections (male erectile disorder) or reaching orgasm (male or female orgasm disorder). Given the hesitance of many people to admit to such problems, the actual prevalences may be higher. Single people may be at greater risk of incurring sexual dysfunctions than married people, in part because singles may feel less secure in their sexual relationships and because they may lack familiarity with the sexual preferences of their partners.

 Sexual dysfunctions are actually quite common.

In some cases, the sexual dysfunction has existed throughout the individual's lifetime, and is labeled a *lifelong dysfunction*. In the case of *acquired dysfunctions*, the problem begins following a period (or at least one occurrence) of normal functioning. In the case of a *situational dysfunction*, the problem occurs in some situations, (for example, with one's spouse), but not in others (for example, with a lover or when masturbating). In the case of a *generalized dysfunction*, the problem occurs in all situations with all partners.

■ **SEXUAL DESIRE DISORDERS** Disorders of sexual desire or appetite include hypoactive sexual desire disorder and sexual aversion disorder.

People with **hypoactive sexual desire disorder** show little or no sexual interest or desire. Typically there is an absence or virtual absence of sexual fantasies. Clinicians weigh various factors in reaching a diagnostic impression, such as the client's lifestyle,

sociocultural factors (for example, cultural attitudes toward sexuality), the quality of the relationship between the client and her or his partner, and the client's age and gender. There is no universally agreed-upon normal level of sexual desire. College students may experience 300 or more sexual thoughts, fantasies, and feelings over the course of a day. Other people may rarely, if ever, experience sexual desires (Goleman, 1988a). Couples usually seek help when one or both partners recognize that the level of sexual activity in the relationship is deficient or has waned to the point that little desire or interest remains. Sometimes the lack of desire is limited to one partner. In other cases, both partners may feel sexual urges, but anger and conflict concerning other issues inhibit sexual interaction. Although problems in sexual desire were only first included in the DSM in 1980, they have become the most common presenting complaint seen by sex therapists today (LoPiccolo & Friedman, 1988). As reported in a survey of sex therapists, nearly a third (31%) of couples treated for sexual problems complain of differences in sexual desire between the partners (Goleman, 1988a). Some problems that are categorized as problems in arousal or orgasm may reflect underlying lack of desire. Sex therapists usually advocate that couples who want different frequencies of sexual activity arrive at a compromise. They do not invariably encourage the less interested partner to meet all the needs of the other (Goleman, 1988a).

A gender shift has apparently occurred among clients who seek help for lack of sexual desire. In the 1970s, women accounted for most (70%) of the cases (LoPiccolo & Friedman, 1988), but by the 1980s, men were accounting for most (60%) of the cases (Spector & Carey, 1990). The reasons for the shift are not fully understood, but it is clear that the cultural assumption that men are always eager for sex is a myth.

Men are not always eager for sex. Men are actually likely to outnumber women among those seeking help for lack of sexual desire.

People with **sexual aversion disorder** have a strong aversion to genital sexual contact and avoid all or nearly all genital contact with a partner. They may, however, desire and enjoy affectionate contact or nongenital sexual contact. Their aversion to genital contact may stem from childhood sexual abuse, rape, or other traumatic experiences. In other cases, deep-seated feelings of sexual guilt or shame may impair sexual response. In men, the diagnosis is often connected with a history of erectile failure (Spark, 1991).

Table 10.2 Estimated Current Prevalence of Sexual Dysfunctions in Percentages of Respondents Reporting the Problem

Premature ejaculation	36–38
Male erectile disorder	4–9
Male orgasmic disorder	4–10
Female orgasmic disorder	5–10

Source: Adapted from Spector and Carey, 1990.
Reprinted with permission from Rathus, Nevid, & Fichner-Rathus, 1993, p. 445.

Such men may associate sexual opportunities with feelings of failure and shame. Their partners may similarly develop aversions to sexual contact because of this history of anxiety and frustration.

■ **SEXUAL AROUSAL DISORDERS** Disorders of sexual arousal involve either a lack of sexual pleasure or excitement during sex, or difficulty achieving or sustaining the physiological changes—lubrication and erection—that allow completion of sexual activity.

In women, sexual arousal is characterized by lubrication of the vaginal walls that makes entry by the penis possible. In men, sexual arousal is characterized by erection. Almost all women now and then have difficulty becoming or remaining lubricated. Almost all men have occasional difficulty attaining or maintaining an erection through intercourse. The diagnoses of **female sexual arousal disorder** and **male erectile disorder** (also called *sexual impotence* or *erectile dysfunction*) are reserved for persistent or recurrent problems in becoming aroused.

■ **ORGASM DISORDERS** There are three orgasm disorders: **female orgasmic disorder**, **male orgasmic disorder**, and **premature ejaculation**.

Orgasmic disorder refers to persistent or recurrent delay in reaching orgasm following what the clinician judges to be an "adequate" amount of sexual stimulation. Some women require manual (hand) clitoral stimulation to reach orgasm during coitus. Years ago, psychodynamically oriented theorists distinguished "clitoral orgasms" from "vaginal orgasms." Clitoral orgasms were achieved through masturbation and were considered emblematic of fixation in the phallic stage. Vaginal orgasms were achieved through sexual intercourse (coitus) and considered emblematic of mature genital sexuality. Masters and Johnson (1966), however, found only one kind of orgasm, physiologically speaking, regardless of the main source of sexual stimulation. Many authorities (for example, LoPiccolo, 1985) argue that women who achieve orgasm during intercourse through a combination of penile thrusting and direct stimulation to the clitoris by her own hand or her partner's should not consider themselves sexually dysfunctional. Women who reliably achieve orgasm through manual or oral stimulation by their partners, and who enjoy intercourse even though they do not achieve climax during coitus, should also be reassured of their normality.

In men, recurrent or persistent difficulty in achieving orgasm following a normal pattern of sexual interest and excitement is termed male orgasmic disorder. This disorder is relatively rare and has received very little attention in the clinical literature (LoPiccolo, 1990). Men with this problem can usually reach orgasm through masturbation but not through intercourse. Because of its infrequency, there are only a few isolated case studies on the problem (Dow, 1981; Rathus, 1978; Schull & Spenkle, 1980). In the DSM-III-R, the female and male orgasmic disorders were referred to as *inhibited (male or female) orgasm*. The DSM-IV diagnostic labels are more descriptive and objective. That is, the DSM-IV labels do not presume that some process (psychological, biological, or an interaction of the two) has obstructed or suppressed orgasm. The new labels properly serve to identify and classify the problems, thus separating description from (presumed) explanation.

Premature ejaculation is defined as recurrent or persistent ejaculation with minimal sexual stimulation. It can occur prior to, upon, or shortly after penetration, but before the man desires it. Note the subjective elements. In making the diagnosis, the clinician weighs the man's age, the novelty of the partner, and the frequency of sexual activity. Occasional experiences of rapid ejaculation, such as when the man is with a new partner or is very highly aroused, fall within the normal spectrum. More persistent patterns of premature ejaculation would occasion a diagnosis of the disorder.

■ **SEXUAL PAIN DISORDERS** In **dyspareunia**, sexual intercourse is associated with recurrent pain in the genital region. **Vaginismus** is involuntary spasm of the muscles surrounding the vagina, making sexual intercourse painful or impossible.

Theoretical Perspectives

Sexual dysfunctions reflect biological, psychological, and other factors.

■ **BIOLOGICAL PERSPECTIVES** Many cases of sexual dysfunction stem from biological factors. Diabetes, coronary heart disease, lung disorders, multiple sclerosis, kidney disease, sexually transmitted diseases, and side effects of various drugs are some of the biological factors that can interfere with sexual desire, arousal, and orgasm (Conte, 1986; LoPiccolo, 1985; Segraves, 1988; Spark, 1991). When the clinician finds evidence that a general medical condition is causally related to the sexual dysfunction, the diagnosis includes the specification "due to general medical condition." Similarly, when there is evidence that the sexual dysfunction could be accounted for by the use of, or withdrawal from, a psychoactive substance, the classification of a "substance-induced sexual dysfunction" is used.

Researchers are finding that the male sex hormone testosterone plays a pivotal role in sexual interest and functioning in both men and women (both genders produce testosterone in varying amounts) (Carani et al., 1990; Sherwin et al., 1985). Men with deficient production of testosterone may lose sexual interest and the capacity for erections (Spark, 1991). Women whose adrenal glands and ovaries have been removed (so that they no longer produce testosterone) may gradually lose sexual interest and the capacity for sexual response. Although hormonal deficiencies may play a role in some cases of sexual dysfunction, researchers find that most men and women with sexual dysfunction have normal hormonal levels (Schreiner-Engle et al., 1989; Spark, 1991; Stuart et al., 1987).

Many temporary physical conditions give rise to problems in desire, arousal, and orgasm—even to sexual pain. Fatigue impairs sexual response, frequently leading to genital pain if the couple persist in attempting intercourse. Depressants such as tranquilizers, alcohol, and narcotics also lessen sexual response (Schiavi, 1990; Segraves, 1988; Spark, 1991). These effects are normally isolated unless people do not recognize their causes and attach too much meaning to them. That is, if you are intoxicated and you do not know that alcohol suppresses sexual response, you may wonder whether there is something wrong with you. Biological factors may thus interact with psychological factors to lead to a persistent problem. Because of your concern, you may try to bear down during your next sexual opportunity, causing anxiety that may further interfere with normal sexual response. A second failure may strengthen self-doubts, which creates more anxiety, which stems performance, which leads to repeated failure experiences, and so on in a vicious cycle.

■ **PSYCHODYNAMIC PERSPECTIVES** Psychodynamic hypotheses generally revolve around presumed conflicts of the phallic stage (Fenichel, 1945). Mature genital sexuality is believed to require successful resolution of the Oedipus and Electra complexes. Dysfunctional men are presumed to suffer from unconscious castration anxiety. Sexual intercourse elicits fear of retaliation by the father, rendering the vagina unsafe. Erectile dysfunction "saves" the man from having to enter the vagina. Premature ejaculation allows him to "escape" rapidly and may also represent unconscious hatred of women (Kaplan, 1974). Orgasmic disorder prevents him from completing the act and unconsciously minimizes his guilt and fear. Rapid ejaculation serves the unconscious purpose of expressing hatred through soiling the woman and denying her sexual pleasure.

What are the effects of alcohol on sexual performance? Alcohol often serves as a social facilitator and may boost self-confidence, but it can also dampen sexual responsiveness and sexual performance. Failure to recognize how alcohol may have contributed to problems in sexual performance may lead people to approach future sexual opportunities with nagging self-doubts. Such doubts can set into motion a vicious circle by producting anxiety that hampers performance and intensifies self-doubts.

In women, enduring penis envy engenders hostility. The woman fixated in the phallic stage punishes her partner for bearing a penis and does not permit the organ to bring her pleasure, as in female sexual arousal disorder. Vaginismus may express an unconscious wish to castrate her partner (Kaplan, 1974). In orgasmic disorder, she has failed to overcome penis envy and transfer erotic feelings from the clitoris to the vagina. She thus prevents orgasm from occurring through intercourse. It is difficult to test the validity of the psychoanalytic concepts because they involve unconscious conflicts, like castration anxiety and penis envy, that cannot be scientifically observed. Evidence for these views relies on case studies that involve interpretation of patients' histories. Case-study accounts are open to rival interpretations, however.

■ **LEARNING PERSPECTIVES** Behaviorists largely focus on the role of conditioned anxiety in the sexual dysfunctions. The occurrence of physically or psychologically painful experiences associated with sexual activity may cause a person to respond to sexual encounters with anxiety that is strong enough to counteract sexual pleasure and performance. People with aversions to sex, orgasmic disorder, and vaginismus may harbor feelings of revulsion that are connected with histories of sexual abuse or rape.

Sexual fulfillment is also based on the learning of sexual competencies. Sexual competencies, like other competencies, are built on knowledge and skill. Knowledge and skills are acquired through learning experiences. We learn what makes us and others feel good through trial and error, by reading and talking about sex, and perhaps, by viewing sex films or videotapes. Some dysfunctional individuals were reared in environments in which discussions of sex were shunned and early sexual experimentation was harshly punished. Such early learning may inhibit later sexual exploration, which can limit the acquisition of sexual knowledge and skills.

■ **COGNITIVE PERSPECTIVES** Albert Ellis (1977b) points out that irrational beliefs and attitudes may contribute to sexual dysfunctions. Consider the irrational beliefs that we must have the approval at all times of everyone who is important to us and that we must be thoroughly competent at everything we do. If we cannot abide the occasional disappointment of others, we may catastrophize the significance of one frustrating sexual episode. If we insist that every sexual rendezvous be perfect, we set the stage for inevitable failure.

Helen Singer Kaplan (1974) notes problems that can occur with our ability to regulate our levels of sexual arousal. Premature ejaculators, for example, may be poor at cognitively gauging their degrees of sexual arousal. As a consequence, they would not call on self-control strategies, such as temporarily suspending stimulation, in time to delay ejaculation.

■ **PROBLEMS IN RELATIONSHIPS** "It takes two to tango," to coin a phrase. Sexual relations are usually no better than other facets of relationships or marriages (Perlman & Abramson, 1982). Couples who harbor resentments toward one another may choose the sexual arena for combat. Communication problems, moreover, are linked to general marital dissatisfaction. Couples who find it difficult to communicate their sexual desires may lack the means to help their partners become more effective lovers.

The following case illustrates how sexual arousal disorder may be connected with problems in the relationship:

After living together for six months, Paul and Petula are contemplating marriage. But a problem has brought them to a sex therapy clinic. As Petula puts it, "For the last two months he hasn't been able to keep his erection after he enters me." Paul is 26 years old, a lawyer; Petula, 24, is a buyer for a large department store. They both grew up in middle-class, suburban families, were introduced through mutual friends and began having intercourse, without difficulty, a few months into their relationship. At Petula's urging, Paul moved into her apartment, although he wasn't sure he was ready for such a step. A week later he began to have difficulty maintaining his erection during intercourse, although he felt strong desire for his partner. When his erection waned, he would try again, but would lose his desire and be unable to achieve another erection. After a few times like this, Petula would become so angry that she began striking Paul in the chest and screaming at him. Paul, who at 200 pounds weighed more than twice as much as Petula, would just walk away, which angered Petula even more. It became clear that sex was not the only trouble spot in their relationship. Petula complained that Paul preferred to spend time with his friends and go to baseball games than to spend time with her. When together at home, he would become absorbed in watching sports events on television, and showed no interest in activities she enjoyed—attending the theater, visiting museums, etc. Since there was no evidence that the sexual difficulty was due to either organic problems or depression, a diagnosis of male erectile disorder was given. Neither Paul or Petula was willing to discuss their nonsexual problems with a therapist. While the sexual problem was treated successfully with a form of sex therapy modeled after techniques developed by Masters and Johnson, and the couple later married, Paul's ambivalences continued, even well into their marriage, and there were future recurrences of sexual problems as well.

■ Adapted from Spitzer et al., 1989, pp. 149–150

■ **SOCIOCULTURAL PERSPECTIVES** At the turn of the century, an Englishwoman said that she would "close her eyes and think of England" when her husband approached her for sexual relations. This old-fashioned stereotype suggests how sexual pleasure was once considered exclusively a male preserve—that sex, for women, was primarily a duty. Mothers usually informed their daughters of the conjugal duties before the wedding, and girls encoded sex as just one of the ways in which women serviced the needs of others. Women who harbor such stereotypical attitudes toward female sexuality may be unlikely to become aware of their sexual potentials. In addition, sexual anxieties may transform negative expectations into self-fulfilling prophecies. Sexual dysfunctions in men, too, may be linked to severely restricted sociocultural beliefs and sexual taboos.

A CLOSER LOOK

Assessment of Problems in Sexual Arousal

Masters and Johnson (1970) believed that the overwhelming majority of erectile problems are psychological in origin. Today, researchers recognize that physiological factors play a more prominent role in sexual dysfunctions than was previously believed (Rajfer et al., 1992). Physiological factors may actually account for the majority of cases of erectile disorders (Reinisch, 1990). Many cases involve a combination of physiological and psychological factors (Meisler & Carey, 1990; Mohr & Beutler, 1990). But how is the clinician to know whether a man's erectile problems are basically biological or psychological in origin?

Clinicians rely on laboratory tests (to measure testosterone levels), physical examination, history taking, and a technique called nocturnal penile **tumescence**, or NPT (Conte, 1986; Mohr & Beutler, 1990). For many years it has been known that men normally attain a number of erections while they are asleep. Lack of erections during sleep would strongly suggest organic causes for erectile problems.

NPT provides a direct measure of erection during sleep. Erection normally occurs during so-called rapid-eye-movement (REM) sleep—the period of sleep that is associated with dreaming and indicated by the rapid darting of the eyeballs beneath the closed lids. NPT is usually carried out over three nights while changes in tumescence are monitored continuously by devices such as the **penile strain gauge** (Karacan, 1982; Kaya et al., 1979). However, NPT has been criticized for producing too many false negatives (men with organic pathologies who produce normal NPT results) and false positives (men without organic problems who show abnormal NPT results) (LoPiccolo, 1986). Overall, the test is believed to lead to misleading findings in perhaps 1 in 5 cases (Meisler & Carey, 1990). In sum, the NPT test is considered suggestive of organic causes, but not conclusive (Mohr & Beutler, 1990).

More informal means have also been used to monitor nighttime erections, such as fastening the penis with a plastic snap gauge or a ring of perforated gummed stamps and looking for signs of breakage in the morning. However, the reliability of these techniques has also been questioned (LoPiccolo, 1986).

No single test or marker for organically based erectile dysfunction has been universally accepted (Sakheim, 1987). It has been suggested that the assessment of the causes of impotence should be multifaceted and include examinations by a urologist and a mental health professional (Saypol et al., 1983).

Physiological devices have also been created to measure sexual arousal in women, but these efforts have lagged those undertaken for men (Conte, 1986). Most methods employ a **plethysmograph**, which is a tampon-shaped probe that is placed in the vagina and measures vaginal blood engorgement according to the amount of light reflected from the vaginal wall (Geer et al., 1974; Hoon et al., 1976). Engorgement of the genitals is one of the chief components of sexual arousal. The plethysmograph shows whether women show normal patterns of sexual arousal in response to sexual stimulation. But plethysmographs are expensive and require trained personnel and laboratory settings. In addition, sexual response in the laboratory may not be an accurate analogue of sexual response in more natural interpersonal settings (Conte, 1986).

Note, too, that objectively (physiologically) measured sexual arousal does not necessarily correspond to subjective self-reports of sexual arousal (Heiman, 1978; Kockott et al., 1980; Morokoff & Heiman, 1980). Perhaps objective and subjective measures of sexual arousal do not assess the same thing. Scientists may be tempted to assume that objective devices assess "the real thing," but without evidence we cannot conclude that one measure is more valid than another (Conte, 1986). Assessing sexual arousal from multiple vantage points, including self-reports, physiological measures, and behavioral ratings, may increase the accuracy of diagnosis of sexual dysfunctions and lead to more fruitful treatment plans (Conte, 1986).

Modern psychodynamic theorists, like Helen Singer Kaplan (1974), suggest that women may hold anger and other negative feelings toward men that lead to sexual dysfunctions and stem from sociocultural factors rather than from penis envy. Women in our society are often socialized to sacrifice for and submit to their husbands, which may engender rebellion that finds expression through sexual dysfunctions.

Javier (1993) notes, for example, the idealization within many Hispanic cultures of the *marianismo* stereotype, which derives its name from the Virgin Mary. From this sociocultural perspective, the ideal virtuous woman "suffers in silence" as she submerges her needs and desires to those of her husband and children. She is the provider of joy, even in the face of her own pain or frustration. It is not difficult to imagine that some women who adopt these stereo-

Is ALL the research being currently done on sexual dysfunctionality heterosexually biased, or is it being assumed that the findings on straight men can accordingly be applied to gay men?

A CLOSER LOOK

Does Anxiety Really Interfere with Sexual Performance?

 Anxiety plays a key role in sexual dysfunction in several theoretical models. Masters and Johnson (1970) emphasized that performance anxiety involving fears of inadequacy deter effective sexual functioning. Nearly all sex therapy programs aim directly or indirectly to reduce anxiety to restore sexual response.

Ironically, under certain conditions anxiety may increase sexual arousal. Prior exposure to an anxiety-inducing film, as compared to prior exposure to a neutral film, can facilitate self-reported sexual response to a sexually explicit film in both women (Hoon et al., 1977) and men (Wolchik et al., 1980).

In a study by David Barlow and his colleagues (1983) that was intended to simulate conditions of performance anxiety, sexually functional male volunteers were shown an explicit sexual film under one of three conditions:

1. A contingent threat condition, in which the subjects were informed there was a 60% chance they would receive a mild electric shock if they did not achieve an adequate level of sexual arousal;

2. A noncontingent threat condition in which subjects were informed that the likelihood of shock was unrelated to their level of sexual arousal or any other response;

3. A no-shock control condition, in which a light signaled them that no shock would be delivered.

Sexual arousal was measured by a penile strain gauge. Although no shocks were administered in any condition, the expectation of contingent shock was intended as an analogue of performance anxiety, because the likelihood of shock depended on achieving a certain level of arousal. It turned out that both threat conditions *increased* sexual arousal. Expectation of contingent threat actually produced the highest level of arousal.

A subsequent study by the Barlow group (Beck et al., 1984) used the same method with sexually functional and sexually dysfunctional men. In contrast to sexually func-

tional men, sexually dysfunctional men showed reduced levels of sexual arousal to both conditions of threat. "Performance anxiety," as defined in these experiments, apparently plays a different role in sexually functional and dysfunctional men. It apparently facilitates sexual arousal in functional men and impedes arousal in dysfunctional men.

In other studies, the response of the woman in erotic films and audiotapes is manipulated. When she acts as though she is highly aroused, and her male partner is not, sexually functional male viewers show higher levels of sexual arousal. Sexually dysfunctional men show lower levels of sexual arousal, presumably because the aroused woman is perceived as being very demanding of her partner (Abrahamson et al., 1985). Watching a highly aroused partner may evoke performance-related fears among sexually dysfunctional men. By contrast, the sexually functional men may have encoded the aroused woman as a sexual stimulus that heightened their own arousal.

Sexually dysfunctional men tend to report more negative emotions, principally depression, while viewing erotic films, whereas normal men report more pleasurable experiences (Abrahamson et al., 1985; Beck, 1984; Heiman & Rowland, 1983). The sexual context may evoke more unpleasant associations for men with sexual problems because it reminds them of their failure experiences. Men with psychologically based dysfunctions are more likely to underestimate their level of sexual arousal while watching erotic films, as measured by comparing self-report estimates to penile measurements, as compared to nondysfunctional men and men with organically based sexual dysfunction (Barlow, 1986; Sackheim, 1984). Sexually dysfunctional men may also see themselves as less able to control their sexual response compared to sexually functional men (Barlow, 1986).

In another study, sexually dysfunctional males, as compared to functional males, paid more attention to their own thoughts, sensations, and feelings when erotic stimuli were presented (Beck & Barlow, 1986). The sexually functional men focused more attention on the erotic stimuli and less on their performance.

---

typical expectations may find it difficult to assert their own needs for sexual gratification or may express resistance to this cultural ideal by becoming sexually unresponsive.

■ **PERFORMANCE ANXIETY Performance anxiety**, or fear of whether we shall be able to perform successfully, is a prominent factor in many cases of

sexual dysfunction. People with performance anxiety may focus on recollections of past failures and expectations of repeated failure rather than absorb themselves in their erotic sensations and fantasies (Barlow, 1986). Performance anxiety can make it difficult for a man to achieve or maintain erection, as well as cause him to ejaculate prematurely. Performance anxiety can also prevent a woman from becoming

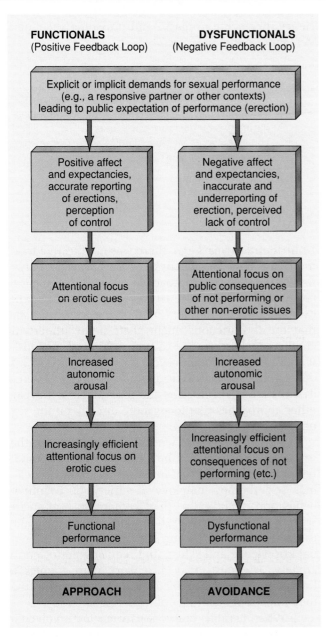

FUNCTIONALS
(Positive Feedback Loop)

DYSFUNCTIONALS
(Negative Feedback Loop)

Explicit or implicit demands for sexual performance
(e.g., a responsive partner or other contexts)
leading to public expectation of performance (erection)

Positive affect
and expectancies,
accurate reporting
of erections,
perception
of control

Negative affect
and expectancies,
inaccurate and
underreporting of
erection, perceived
lack of control

Attentional focus
on erotic cues

Attentional focus on
public consequences
of not performing or
other non-erotic issues

Increased
autonomic
arousal

Increased
autonomic
arousal

Increasingly efficient
attentional focus on
erotic cues

Increasingly efficient
attentional focus on
consequences of not
performing (etc.)

Functional
performance

Dysfunctional
performance

APPROACH

AVOIDANCE

Barlow (1986) proposes a model of erectile dysfunction that considers these cognitive factors (see Figure 10.3). In dysfunctional men, pressures to perform sexually lead to

Figure 10.3   Barlow's model of erectile dysfunction.
Anxiety may have different effects on sexually functional and dysfunctional men. Perhaps because dysfunctional men expect to fail, they focus on the anticipated feelings of shame and embarrassment rather than on erotic stimuli. Their concerns then heighten their anxiety, impairing their performance and distracting them from erotic cues. Functional men, by contrast, may expect to succeed and focus more attention on erotic stimuli, heightening their sexual response.

Source: Barlow, D. H. (1986). Cause of sexual dysfunction: The role of anxiety and cognitive interference. Journal of Consulting and Clinical Psychology, 54, 140–148. Copyright © 1986 by the American Psychological Association. Reprinted by permission.

negative affect (depression); expectancies of failure; inaccurate underestimates of erectile response; and perceived lack of control over sexual response. Because they expect to fail, dysfunctional men center on the anticipated consequences of failure—such as shame or embarrassment, apologies, and the need to explain themselves—rather than on erotic cues. Their preoccupations heighten anxiety, impairing their performance and distracting them from erotic stimuli. Sexual encounters are avoided because they are encoded as opportunities for repeated failure, frustration, and self-defeat.

When sexually functional men are stimulated by a responsive partner or an erotic film, they experience pleasurable affect and positive expectancies, perceive themselves to be in control, and accurately gauge their sexual response. They focus on erotic cues that may increase anxiety or autonomic arousal, but not to the point of interfering with sexual response. Mild anxiety may actually enhance sexual arousal. By centering on erotic cues, functional men become more aroused, successfully engage in sexual activity, and heighten their outcome and self-efficacy expectancies—all leading to increased approach tendencies.

The Barlow model highlights the role of interfering cognitions in sexual dysfunctions among men and women. Interfering cognitions include expectancies of failure that are evoked by performance demands. They heighten anxiety to the point of impairing sexual performance. In a vicious cycle, the more people focus on interfering cognitions, the more difficult it will be for them to perform sexually—and the more likely they will be to focus on interfering cognitions in the future. Although the model was derived from research on men, Barlow believes that it may also help explain sexual dysfunctions in women.

adequately lubricated or contribute to orgasmic dysfunction.

In Western cultures, the connection between a man's sexual performance and his sense of manhood is deeply ingrained. The man who repeatedly fails to perform sexually may begin to see himself as a total failure, despite other accomplishments in life. With so much of his self-esteem riding on the line whenever he makes love, it is little wonder that anxiety

about the quality of his performance—performance anxiety—may mount to a point that it inhibits erection. Sexual opportunities are no longer connected with expectations of relaxation, pleasure, and sexual fulfillment. They are transformed into tests of manhood and he may respond to them by bearing down and trying to will (force) an erection. Willing an erection may backfire because erection is a reflex that cannot be forced. The man may become preoccupied with erectile failure—setting the stage for more anxiety and subsequent failure. His partner may try to be comforting and supportive. She may say, "It's no big deal. It can happen to anyone. Don't worry about it. It will get better in time." But words may be insufficient to relieve his feelings of inadequacy.

One client who suffered erectile dysfunction described his feelings of sexual inadequacy this way:

I always felt inferior, like I was on probation, having to prove myself. I felt like I was up against the wall. You can't imagine how embarrassing this was. It's like you walk out in front of an audience that you think is a nudist convention and it turns out to be a tuxedo convention.

■ *The Authors' Files*

Another man described how performance anxiety led him to prepare for sexual relations as though he were psyching himself up for a big game:

At work I have control over what I do. With sex, you don't have control over your sex organ. I know that my mind can control what my hands do. But the same is not true of my penis. I had begun to view sex as a basketball game. I used to play in college. When I would prepare for a game, I'd always be thinking, "Who was I guarding that night?" I'd try to psych myself up, sketching out in my mind how to play this guy, thinking through all possible moves and plays. I began to do the same thing with sex. If I was dating someone, I'd be thinking the whole evening about what might happen in bed. I'd always be preparing for the outcome. I'd sketch out in my mind how I was going to touch her, what I'd ask her to do. But all the time, right through dinner or the movies, I'd be worrying that I wouldn't get it up. I kept picturing her face and how disappointed she'd be. By the time we did go to bed, I was paralyzed with anxiety.

■ *The Authors' Files*

Women, too, may equate their self-esteem with their ability to reach frequent and intense orgasms. Yet when men and women try to bear down to will arousal or lubrication, or to force an orgasm, they may find that the harder they try, the more these responses elude them. Thirty years ago the pressures concerning sex often revolved around the issue

"Should I or shouldn't I?" Today, however, the pressures for both men and women are often based more on achieving performance goals relating to proficiency at reaching orgasm and providing their partners with sexual pleasure.

 People do not necessarily have satisfying sexual relations when they love one another. Many factors—ranging from early traumatic experiences to lack of sexual competencies to biological problems to performance anxiety—can interfere with sexual satisfaction.

Sex Therapy

Until about 25 years ago, there was no effective treatment for most sexual dysfunctions. Psychoanalytic forms of therapy approached sexual dysfunctions indirectly, for example. It was assumed that sexual dysfunctions represented underlying conflicts, and that the dysfunctions might abate if the underlying conflicts—the presumed causes of the dysfunctions—were resolved through psychoanalysis. A lack of evidence that psychoanalytic approaches reversed sexual dysfunctions led clinicians and researchers to develop other approaches that focus more directly on the sexual problems themselves.

Most contemporary sex therapists assume that sexual dysfunctions can be treated by directly modifying the couple's sexual interactions. Broadly speaking, sex therapy employs a variety of cognitive-behavioral techniques that center on enhancing self-efficacy expectancies, improving a couple's ability to communicate, fostering sexual competencies (sexual knowledge and skills), and reducing performance anxiety. Therapists may also work with couples to help them iron out problems in the relationship that may impede sexual functioning.

When feasible, both sex partners are involved in therapy. In some cases, however, individual therapy may be preferable, as we shall see.

■ THE MASTERS AND JOHNSON APPROACH

In the approach pioneered by Masters and Johnson (1970), the therapists are a female and male team that educates the couple and directs them through a sequence of homework assignments. Masters and Johnson employed an intensive 2-week therapy format in which couples would travel to their clinic, lodge in a local hotel, and focus entirely on their relationship during the treatment period. Anxieties and resentments usually surfaced in meetings between the couple and the therapists, and they were discussed. The focus was on behavioral change, however.

Most sex therapists do not demand that clients suspend all other responsibilities for a 2-week period. The necessity of the female and male team has also been questioned. Also, in some instances, *bibliotherapy*—or self-treatment of dysfunctioning by following a written guide—has also been of help (see Dodge et al., 1982).

■ THE HELEN SINGER KAPLAN APPROACH

Kaplan's (1974) approach is notable because it combines behavioral and psychodynamic methods. She attributes sexual dysfunctions to the interaction of immediate causes (poor technique, performance anxiety, marital conflict, and lack of communication) and remote causes (unresolved internal conflicts that predispose people to encounter anxiety in the expression of their sexual needs). Kaplan begins therapy with the direct behavioral approach to sex therapy. She uses brief insight-oriented (psychodynamic) therapy when remote causes apparently impede client response to the behavioral approach. In this way, she brings to the surface the inner conflicts that may have impeded sexual interest or responsiveness.

Let us survey some of the more common sex therapy techniques that are used to treat sexual dysfunctions.

■ DISORDERS OF AROUSAL

Women who have difficulty becoming sexually aroused and men with erectile problems are first educated to the fact that they need not "do" anything to become aroused. As long as their problems are psychological, not organic, they need only experience sexual stimulation under relaxed, nonpressured conditions, so that disruptive cognitions and anxiety do not inhibit reflexive responses.

Masters and Johnson have the couple counter performance anxiety by engaging in **sensate focus exercises**. These are nondemand sexual contacts—sensuous exercises that do not demand sexual arousal in the form of vaginal lubrication or erection. Partners begin by massaging one another without touching the genitals. The partners learn to "pleasure" each other and to "be pleasured" by following and giving verbal instructions and by guiding each other's hands. The method fosters both communication skills and sexual skills and also countermands anxiety. After several sessions, the genitals are included. When sexual excitement is achieved, the couple do not straightaway engage in intercourse because intercourse would create demands. After excitement is attained reliably, however, the couple engage in a relaxed sequence of other sexual activities, culminating in intercourse.

A number of similar sex therapy methods were employed in the case of Victor P.

Victor P., a 44-year-old concert violinist, was eager to show the therapist reviews of his concert tour. A solo violinist with a distinguished orchestra, Victor's life revolved around practice, performances, and reviews. He dazzled audiences with his technique and the energy of his performance. As a concert musician, Victor had exquisite control over his body, especially his hands. Yet he could not control his erectile response in the same way. Since his divorce seven years earlier, Victor had been troubled by recurrent episodes of erectile failure. Time and time again he had become involved in a new relationship, only to find himself unable to perform sexually. Fearing repetition, he would sever the relationship. He was unable to face an audience of only one. For a while he dated casually, but then he met Michelle.

Michelle was a writer who loved music. They were a perfect match because Victor, the musician, loved literature. Michelle, a 35-year-old divorcée, was exciting, earthy, sensual, and accepting. The couple soon grew inseparable. He would practice while she would write—poetry mostly, but also short pieces for women's magazines. Unlike some women Victor met who did not know Bach from Bartok, Michelle held her own in conversations with Victor's friends and fellow musicians over late night dinner at Sardi's. They kept their own apartments; Victor needed his own space and solitude for practice.

*In the nine months of their relationship, Victor was unable to perform on the stage that mattered most to him—his canopied bed. It was just so frustrating, he said. "I would become erect and then just as I approach her to penetrate, pow! It collapses on me." Victor's history of nocturnal erections and erections during light petting suggested that he was basically suffering from performance anxiety. He was bearing down to force an erection, much as he might try to learn the fingering of a difficult violin piece. Each night became a command performance in which Victor served as his own severest critic. Victor became a spectator to his own performance, a role that Masters and Johnson refer to as **self-spectatoring**. Rather than focus on his partner, his attention was riveted on the size of his penis. As noted by the late great pianist Vladimir Horowitz, the worst thing a pianist can do is watch his fingers. Perhaps the worst thing a man with erectile problems can do is watch his penis.*

To break the vicious cycle of anxiety, erectile failure, and more anxiety, Victor and Michelle followed a sex therapy program (Rathus & Nevid, 1977) modeled after the Masters-and-Johnson-type treatment. The aim was to restore the pleasure of sexual activity, unfettered by anxiety. The couple was initially instructed to abstain from attempts at intercourse to free Victor from any pressure to perform. The couple progressed through a series of steps:

1. *Relaxing together in the nude without any touching, such as when reading or watching TV together.*

2. *Sensate focus exercises.*

3. *Genital stimulation of each other manually or orally to orgasm.*

4. *Nondemand intercourse (intercourse performed without any pressure on the man to satisfy his partner). The man may afterward help his partner achieve orgasm by using manual or oral stimulation.*

5. *Resumption of vigorous intercourse (intercourse involving more vigorous thrusting and use of alternative positions and techniques that focus on mutual satisfaction). The couple is instructed not to catastrophize occasional problems that may arise.*

The therapy program helped Victor overcome his erectile disorder. Victor was freed of the need to prove himself by achieving erection on command. He surrendered his post as critic. Once the spotlight was off the bed, he became a participant and not a spectator.

■ *The Authors' Files*

■ **DISORDERS OF ORGASM** Women with orgasmic disorder often harbor underlying beliefs that sex is dirty or sinful. They may have been taught not to touch themselves. They are often anxious about sex and have not learned, through trial and error, what kinds of sexual stimulation will arouse them and help them reach orgasm. Treatment in these cases includes modification of negative attitudes toward sex. When orgasmic disorder reflects the woman's feelings about or relationship with her partner, treatment requires working through these feelings or enhancing the relationship.

In either case, Masters and Johnson work with the couple and first use sensate focus exercises to lessen performance anxiety, open channels of communication, and help the couple acquire pleasuring skills. Then during genital massage and, later, during intercourse, the woman directs her partner in the caresses and techniques that stimulate her. By taking charge the woman is also psychologically freed from the stereotype of the passive, submissive female role.

Many researchers find that a program of directed masturbation is most effective for helping preorgasmic women—women who have never achieved orgasm through any means (Andersen, 1981; Heiman & LoPiccolo, 1987; LoPiccolo & Stock, 1986; McMullen & Rosen, 1979). Even Masters and Johnson, who prefer a couples approach, reported in 1966 that masturbation is the most efficient way for women and men to reach orgasm. Masturbation provides people with a chance to learn about their own bodies and to give themselves pleasure without reliance on a partner. Masturbation programs educate women about their sexual anatomy and encourage them to experiment with self-caresses at their own pace and to incorporate sexual fantasies and imagery during self-stimulation. They are not distracted by external pressures to please a partner. Pleasure helps counter sexual anxiety, and women learn gradually to bring themselves to orgasm, sometimes with the help of an electric vibrator. Once women can masturbate to orgasm, additional couples treatment can facilitate but does not guarantee transference to orgasm with a partner (Heiman & LoPiccolo, 1987; LoPiccolo & Stock, 1986).

Although scant attention in the scientific literature has been focused on male orgasmic disorder, the standard treatment, barring any underlying organic problem, focuses on increasing sexual stimulation and reducing performance anxiety (LoPiccolo, 1990; LoPiccolo & Strock, 1986).

Masters and Johnson also use sensate focus exercises in treating premature ejaculation so that couples learn to give and take pleasure under nondemanding conditions. When the couple is ready to undertake sexual activity, they use the so-called *squeeze technique*, in which the tip of the penis is squeezed by the man's partner when the man is about to ejaculate and then released. The squeeze technique, which should be learned only through personal instruction, temporarily prevents ejaculation. Through repeating the procedure, the man gradually learns to extend intercourse without ejaculating.

In 1956, urologist James Semans suggested the so-called *stop-start* or *stop-and-go* technique for premature ejaculation. The man and his partner just suspend sexual activity when he is about to ejaculate and then resume stimulation when his sensations abate. Repeated practice enables him to regulate ejaculation by sensitizing him to the cues that precede ejaculation.

■ **VAGINISMUS AND DYSPAREUNIA** Vaginismus is a conditioned reflex involving the involuntary constriction of the vaginal opening. It represents a psychologically based fear of penetration, rather than a physical defect or disorder (LoPiccolo & Stock,

A CLOSER LOOK

Biological Treatments of Male Erectile Disorder

Biological approaches in treating male erectile disorder dysfunction include surgical implants, hormonal treatment, use of muscle relaxants, and vascular surgery (LoPiccolo & Stock, 1986). There are several types of penile implants (Spark, 1991). One is a prosthetic device made of two rods of silicone. They are implanted in the penis and remain in a semirigid position that permits intercourse. Another implant requires more extensive surgery. Cylinders are implanted in the penis. They are attached to a small reservoir of fluid inserted in the abdomen and to a tiny pump placed in the scrotum (the sac holding the testes) or elsewhere. When the man wants an erection, he squeezes the pump. Fluid enters the cylinders, creating an erection. Men with implants and their partners are generally satisfied with the results (Anderson & Wold, 1986; Beutler et al., 1984). However, long-term follow-ups have identified a number of poorer outcomes, perhaps as many as 40% (LoPiccolo & Stock, 1986; Spark, 1991).

Hormone treatments are often helpful for men with abnormally low levels of male sex hormones but not for men whose hormone levels are within normal limits (Carani et al., 1990; Spark, 1991). Because hormone treatments can have side effects, such as liver damage, they should not be undertaken lightly (LoPiccolo & Stock, 1986).

The muscle relaxant *papaverine* has been used to help relax the muscles that surround the spongy tissues in the penis, allowing blood to flow more freely into the penis, causing it to become erect within a few minutes (Althof et

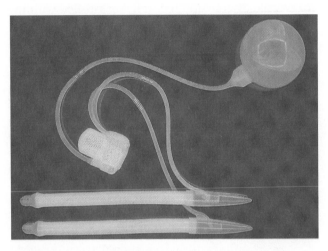

Implants. One kind of penile implant consists of the two cylinders shown here that make the penis rigid when fliud from the reservoir (top right) is pumped into them by squeezing the pump (lower middle) that is usually inserted in the scrotum.

al., 1989; Mohr & Beutler, 1990). The man is instructed by a physician how to inject the drug directly into the penis prior to sexual intercourse. Due to side effects, such as pain or bruises from the injections, self-injection programs have high dropout rates (Althof et al., 1989).

Vascular surgery may be effective in rare cases in which blockage in the blood vessels prevents blood from swelling the penis, or in which the penis is structurally defective (LoPiccolo & Stock, 1986; Mohr & Beutler, 1990).

1986). Treatment for vaginismus involves a combination of relaxation techniques and the use of vaginal dilators. The woman herself regulates the insertion of the dilators (rods of varying diameter) and proceeds at her own pace to avoid discomfort (LoPiccolo & Stock, 1986). The method is generally successful as long as it is unhurried. Because women with vaginismus often have histories of sexual molestation or rape, psychotherapy for the psychological effects of experiences may be part of the treatment program (LoPiccolo & Stock, 1986). Treatment of dyspareunia is usually focused on treating the underlying condition, often a medical problem, causing pain during coitus. Sometimes dyspareunia is secondary to vaginismus and abates when vaginismus is successfully treated.

■ **EVALUATION OF SEX THERAPY** The influence of Masters and Johnson in the development of treatment approaches for sexual dysfunction has been extraordinary (Barlow, 1986). Since the publication of *Human Sexual Inadequacy* in 1970, innovations have largely centered on variations of the Masters-and-Johnson approach (Barlow, 1986).

Masters and Johnson (1970) claimed an overall success rate of 80% in treating sexual dysfunctions. Although Masters and Johnson's techniques were innovative, their evaluation of their own success has been criticized on numerous grounds. For example, they did not operationally define degrees of improvement, nor did they adequately follow up clients to see whether "reversals" (of sexual problems) remain reversed (Adams, 1980; Zilbergeld & Evans, 1980).

Other researchers report more modest levels of success in treating sexual dysfunctions, especially erectile dysfunction. Whereas Masters and Johnson reported success rates of treating erectile dysfunction ranging from 50 to 74%, more recent estimates of success have ranged as low as 30% (Barlow, 1986; Crown & D'Ardenne, 1982). Still, most men treated for erectile dysfunction report being satisfied with the effects of sex therapy (Mohr & Beutler, 1990) and the addition of biological treatments has meant that virtually all men with erectile disorders can be helped in one way or another (Reinisch, 1990). Reported success rates in treating vaginismus have ranged as high as 80% (Hawton & Catalan, 1990) to 100% (Masters & Johnson, 1970). Success rates above 90% have been reported in treating premature ejaculation through either the squeeze or stop-start techniques (Kilmann & Auerbach, 1979). Using masturbation as the primary technique, LoPiccolo (1990) reports an overall success rate of 95% in helping approximately 150 preorgasmic women achieve orgasm. Most of the women (about 85%) were also able to achieve orgasm through direct genital stimulation provided by their partners. By contrast, only about 40% were able to achieve orgasm during intercourse. Many couples who believed it was important for the woman to reach orgasm during intercourse were able to accomplish this end by combining manual clitoral stimulation with sexual intercourse (LoPiccolo & Strock, 1986).

All in all, the success rates reported for sex therapy techniques are encouraging (see LoPiccolo, 1990), especially when we remember that only one generation ago there were no effective treatments for the sexual dysfunctions.

SUMMARY

Normal and Abnormal in Sexual Behavior

Sexual behavior is largely influenced by sociocultural factors. What is considered normal in one culture may be considered abnormal in another.

Sexual Orientation

A gay male or lesbian sexual orientation is not considered a mental disorder, but people who are persistently confused or distressed about their sexual orientation may be considered disordered. Gay males and lesbians have not been shown to be more psychologically disturbed than heterosexuals. The origins of sexual orientation are complex and may involve multiple factors, including prenatal hormonal factors and early social learning experiences.

Gender Identity Disorder

Gender identity disorder pertains to people who find their anatomic gender to be a source of persistent and intense distress. People with the disorder may seek to change their sex organs to resemble those of the opposite gender, and many undergo gender-reassignment surgery to accomplish this purpose.

Rape

Rape is a violent crime, not a sexual disorder. The desires to dominate women or express hatred toward them may be more prominent motives for rape than sexual desire. A sociocultural perspective suggests that cultural attitudes, such as stereotypes of male aggressiveness and social dominance, underlie propensities to rape. Rape victims often suffer acute and long-term effects, described as a rape trauma syndrome.

Paraphilias

Paraphilias are sexual deviations involving patterns of arousal to stimuli such as nonhuman objects (for example, shoes or clothes), humiliation or the experience of pain in oneself or one's partner, or children. Paraphilias include exhibitionism, fetishism, transvestic fetishism, voyeurism, frotteurism, pedophilia, sexual masochism, and sexual sadism. Although some paraphilias are essentially harmless (such as fetishism), others, such as pedophilia and sexual sadism, often harm nonconsenting victims. Paraphilias may be caused by the interaction of biological, psychological, and social factors. Efforts to treat paraphilias are compromised by the fact that most paraphiles do not wish to change.

Sexual Dysfunctions

Sexual dysfunctions include sexual desire disorders (hypoactive sexual desire disorder and sexual aversion disorder), sexual arousal disorders (female sexual arousal disorder and male erectile disorder), orgasm disorders (female and male orgasmic disorders and premature ejaculation), and sexual pain disorders (dyspareunia and vaginismus). Sexual dysfunctions can stem from biological factors (such as disease or the effects of alcohol and other drugs), psychological factors (such as performance anxiety, unresolved conflicts, or lack of sexual competencies), and sociocultural factors (such as sexually restrictive cultural learning). Sex therapy focuses on directly modifying problematic sexual behavior by enhancing self-efficacy expectancies, teaching sexual competencies, improving sexual communication, and reducing performance anxiety.

SCORING KEY FOR RAPE MYTHS SCALE

All of the items are false, with the exception of item 2, which is true. The key issue is whether you endorse cultural beliefs which contribute to a social climate that legitimizes rape. As an example, if you believe that women unconsciously desire to be raped, you may also believe that rape victims are responsible for their victimization. Such attitudes tend to excuse the perpetrator and blame the victim.

Rainer Fetting, Red Square Face, 1984. Oil on canvas and wood: 94 × 85¾ inches. Virginia Museum of Fine Arts. Gift of the Sydney and Francis Lewis Foundation.

CHAPTER OUTLINE

11

Schizophrenia and Other Psychotic Disorders

TRUTH or FICTION?

____ Many schizophrenic people show no emotional response to tragic events.

____ Schizophrenics occupy 1 hospital bed in 4 in the United States.

____ Some people show schizophrenic-type behaviors, including flagrant delusions and hallucinations, but they cannot be diagnosed as schizophrenic until half a year later.

____ Hallucinations are rare and a sign of mental disorder.

____ Some schizophrenics sustain unusual, uncomfortable positions for hours and will not respond to questions or comments during these periods.

____ A 54-year-old female hospitalized schizophrenic was conditioned to cling to a broom by being given cigarettes as reinforcers.

____ A child with two schizophrenic parents will develop schizophrenia about 90% of the time.

____ Schizophrenics are more likely to have been born during the winter than at other times of the year.

____ Schizophrenics have cold, overprotective mothers.

____ Antipsychotic medications cure many cases of schizophrenia.

____ Teaching families how to relate to schizophrenic members and solve family problems reduces the incidence of recurrent acute episodes.

____ Some people are deluded that they are loved by a famous person.

LEARNING OBJECTIVES

When you have completed your study of Chapter 11, you should be able to:

1. Discuss the contributions of Emil Kraepelin, Eugen Bleuler, and Kurt Schneider to the concept of schizophrenia.

2. Discuss the changes in the definition of schizophrenia that have occurred from the time of Kraepelin to the present day.

3. Discuss the prevalence of schizophrenia in the general population.

4. Describe various patterns of the course of schizophrenia, referring to the concepts of *acute episode*, *prodromal phase*, and *residual phase*.

5. Distinguish among schizophrenia, brief psychotic disorder, and schizophreniform disorder.

6. Discuss the concept of schizophrenia-spectrum disorders and distinguish among schizophrenia, schizotypal personality disorder, and schizoaffective disorder.

7. Discuss the disturbances in thought and speech that characterize schizophrenia.

8. Discuss deficits in attention, referring to recent psychophysiological research.

9. Discuss perceptual disturbances in schizophrenia.

10. Discuss emotional disturbances in schizophrenia.

11. Discuss the disturbances in self-identity, volition, interpersonal behavior, and psychomotor behavior in schizophrenia.

12. Discuss the historical changes in the classification of types of schizophrenia.

13. Distinguish between the disorganized, catatonic, paranoid, undifferentiated, and residual types of schizophrenia.

14. Discuss the process–reactive dimension of schizophrenia, the positive and negative "symptoms" of schizophrenia, and Type I and Type II schizophrenia.

15. Discuss psychodynamic, learning, biological, family, and sociocultural perspectives on schizophrenia.

16. Describe and evaluate research on genetic factors, biochemical factors, viral infections, and brain damage.

17. Discuss evidence for the diathesis–stress model of schizophrenia.

18. Discuss biological, psychoanalytic, learning-based, psychosocial-rehabilitation, and family intervention treatments of schizophrenia.

19. Discuss research concerning the effects and side effects of antipsychotic medication.

20. Discuss the features of delusional disorder and differentiate the disorder from paranoid schizophrenia and paranoid personality disorder.

Schizophrenia is perhaps the most puzzling and disabling of the mental disorders. It is the clinical syndrome that best corresponds to popular conceptions of madness or lunacy. Schizophrenia often elicits fear, misunderstanding, and condemnation rather than sympathy and concern (Carpenter, 1987). Schizophrenia strikes at the heart of the person. It strips the mind of the intimate connections between thoughts and emotions and fills it with distorted perceptions, false ideas, and illogical conceptions, as in the case of Angela:

Angela was 19 years old. Her boyfriend Jaime insisted that she come to the emergency room because she had cut her wrists. When she was questioned, her attention wandered. She seemed transfixed by creatures in the air, or by something she might be hearing. It seemed as though she had an invisible earphone.

Angela explained that she had slit her wrists at the command of the "hellsmen." Then she became terrified. Later she related that the hellsmen had cautioned her not to disclose their existence. Angela had been fearful that the hellsmen would punish her for her indiscretion.

Jaime related that Angela and he had been living together for nearly a year. They had initially shared a modest apartment in town. But Angela did not like being around other people and persuaded Jaime to rent a cottage in the country. There Angela spent much of her days making fantastic sketches of goblins and monsters. She occasionally became agitated and behaved as though invisible beings were issuing directions. Her words would begin to become jumbled.

Jaime would try to persuade her to go for help, but she would resist. Then the wrist cutting began. Jaime believed that he had made the bungalow secure by removing all knives and blades. But Angela always found a sharp object.

Then he would bring Angela to the hospital against her protests. Stitches would be put in, she would be held under observation for a while, and she would be medicated. She would recount that she cut her wrists because the hellsmen had informed her that she was bad and had to die. After a few days in the hospital, she would disavow hearing the hellsmen and insist on discharge.

Jaime would take her home. The pattern would repeat itself.

■ *The Authors' Files*

When the emergency room team examined Angela's wrists and learned that she thought that she had been following the dictates of "hellsmen," they began to surmise that she was afflicted by schizophrenia. Schizophrenia touches every facet of victims' lives. During acute episodes, schizophrenia is characterized by

delusions, hallucinations, illogical thinking, incoherent speech, and bizarre behavior. Between acute episodes, schizophrenics may still be unable to think clearly and may lack an appropriate emotional response to the people and events in their lives. They may speak in a flat tone and show little if any facial expressiveness.

Although researchers are immersed in probing the psychological and biological foundations of schizophrenia, the disorder remains in many ways a mystery. In this chapter, we examine how research has illuminated our understanding of schizophrenia. We also consider a number of other psychotic disorders, including brief psychotic disorder, schizophreniform disorder, schizoaffective disorder, and delusional disorder.

HISTORY OF THE CONCEPT OF SCHIZOPHRENIA

Although various forms of "madness" have afflicted people throughout the course of history, no one knows how long the behavior pattern we now label schizophrenia existed before it was first described as a medical syndrome by Emil Kraepelin in 1893 (Boffey, 1986). Modern conceptualizations of schizophrenia have been largely shaped by the contributions of Kraepelin, Eugen Bleuler, and Kurt Schneider.

Emil Kraepelin

Kraepelin (1856–1926), one of the fathers of modern psychiatry, called the disorder **dementia praecox**. The term derived from the Latin *dementis,* meaning "out" (*de-*) of one's "mind" (*mens*), and the roots that form the word *precocious,* meaning "before" one's

level of "maturity." *Dementia praecox* thus refers to premature impairment of mental abilities. Kraepelin believed that dementia praecox was a disease process that was caused by specific, although unknown, bodily pathology (Hoenig, 1983).

Kraepelin wrote that dementia praecox involves the "loss of the inner unity of thought, feeling, and acting." The syndrome begins early in life, and the course of deterioration eventually results in complete "disintegration of the personality" (Kraepelin, 1909–1913, Vol. 2, p. 943). Kraepelin's description of dementia praecox includes behavior patterns such as delusions, hallucinations, and odd motor behaviors—the behavior patterns that typically characterize the disorder today.

Eugen Bleuler

In 1911, the Swiss psychiatrist Eugen Bleuler (1857–1939) renamed dementia praecox *schizophrenia,* from the Greek *schistos,* meaning "cut" or "split," and *phren,* meaning "brain." In doing so, Bleuler was focusing on the major characteristic of the syndrome, the splitting of the brain functions that give rise to cognition, feelings or affective responses, and behavior. A schizophrenic, for example, might giggle inappropriately when discussing an upsetting event, or might show no emotional expressiveness in the face of tragedy.

Eugen Bleuler

Emil Kraepelin

It is true that many schizophrenic people show no emotional response to tragic events. Their affect is said to be flat or blunted.

Although the Greek roots of *schizophrenia* mean "split brain," schizophrenia should not be confused with the dissociative disorder of multiple personality, which is frequently referred to as "split personality" by laypeople. In multiple personality, the personality apparently divides into two or more personalities, but each personality usually shows better integrated cognitive, affective, and behavioral functioning than is the case in schizophrenia. In schizophrenia, the splitting cleaves cognition, affect, and behavior. There may thus be little agreement between the thoughts and the emotions, or between the individual's perceptions of reality and what is truly happening.

Although Bleuler accepted Kraepelin's description of the symptoms of schizophrenia, he did not accept Kraepelin's views that schizophrenia necessarily begins early in life and inevitably follows a deteriorating course. Bleuler proposed that schizophrenia follows a more variable course. In some cases, acute episodes occur intermittently. In others, there might be limited improvement rather than inevitable deterioration.

Bleuler believed that schizophrenia could be recognized on the basis of four primary features or symptoms. Today, we refer to them as the **four A's**:

1. **Associations**. Associations or relationships among thoughts become disturbed. We now call this type of disturbance "thought disorder" or "looseness of associations." *Looseness of associations* means that ideas are strung together with little or no relationship among them; nor does the speaker appear to be aware of the lack of connectedness. Overtly, the person's speech becomes rambling and confused.

2. **Affect**. Affect or emotional response becomes flattened or inappropriate. The individual may show a lack of response to upsetting events, or burst into laughter at hearing that a family member or friend has died.

3. **Ambivalence**. Schizophrenics hold ambivalent or conflicting feelings toward others, loving and hating them at the same time.

4. **Autism**. Autism is withdrawal into a private fantasy world that is not bound by principles of logic.

In Bleuler's view, hallucinations and delusions represent "secondary symptoms"—symptoms that accompany the primary symptoms but do not define the disorder. In more recent years, however, other theorists (Schneider, 1957) have proposed that hallucinations and delusions are key, or primary, features of schizophrenia. Bleuler was also strongly influenced by psychodynamic theory. He came to believe that the content of hallucinations and delusions could be explained by the schizophrenic's attempt to replace the external world with a world of fantasy.

Bleuler's contributions led to the adoption of a broader definition of schizophrenia and brought the diagnostic category into more common use. Bleuler's ideas were especially influential in the United States. U.S.-trained professionals began to use the diagnosis more freely than their European counterparts, who were more influenced by Kraepelin's narrower definition of the disorder. The diagnosis of schizophrenia was broadened in the United States even beyond Bleuler's criteria to include people who showed combined features of schizophrenia and mood disorders. These cases are now generally classified separately from schizophrenia under the category of **schizoaffective disorder**.

Kurt Schneider

Another influential developer of modern concepts of schizophrenia was the German psychiatrist Kurt Schneider (1887–1967). Schneider believed that Bleuler's criteria (his "four A's") were too vague for diagnostic purposes and that they failed to adequately distinguish schizophrenia from other disorders, such as bipolar disorder.

Schneider's (1957) most notable contribution was to discriminate between the features of schizophrenia that he believed are central to diagnosis, which he termed **first-rank symptoms**, and so-called **second-rank symptoms**, which he believed are found not only in schizophrenia, but also in other psychoses and in some nonpsychotic disorders such as personality disorders. In Schneider's view, if first-rank symptoms are present and cannot be accounted for by organic factors, a diagnosis of schizophrenia is justified. Hallucinations and delusions are prominent first-rank symptoms. Disturbances in mood and confused thinking are considered second-rank symptoms. Although Schneider's ranking of behaviors helped distinguish schizophrenia from other disorders, we now know that first-rank symptoms are sometimes found among people with other disorders, especially manic disorders (Mellor, 1982). One study, for example, found that 13% of diagnosed manics showed evidence of first-rank symptoms of schizophrenia (Wing & Nixon, 1975), such as hallucinations and delusions. Although first-rank symptoms are clearly associated with schizophrenia, they are not unique to it (Mellor, 1982).

Hallucinations? According to Kurt Schneider, hallucinations and delusions are numbered among the first-rank symptoms of schizophrenia—that is, the symptoms of schizophrenia that are central to the diagnosis. So-called second-rank symptoms are found in other disorders as well. Schneider considered confusion and disturbances in mood to be second-rank symptoms.

Contemporary Diagnostic Practices

Although most mental health professionals accept the view that schizophrenia is an identifiable behavior pattern, there has been widespread disagreement over the best way to define it. During the 1950s and 1960s, Bleuler's broad view of schizophrenia was widely accepted in the United States (Andreasen, 1987). By the 1960s, British psychiatrists had adopted the more stringent criteria for defining schizophrenia, based on the first-rank symptoms identified by Kurt Schneider. The U.S. broadening of the definition of schizophrenia led to relatively more cases of schizophrenia being diagnosed in the United States than in Europe. In one study, nearly twice as many patients in a Brooklyn, New York, mental hospital were diagnosed as schizophrenic as were those in a mental hospital outside London, England. Yet a re-evaluation of the diagnoses in both hospitals according to stricter criteria revealed no significant differences in the incidence of the disorder (Leff, 1977).

The DSM-III diagnostic system, introduced in 1980, narrowed the criteria for defining schizophrenia, which led to a tightening of diagnostic practices, especially in the United States. All in all, the same person might or might not have been diagnosed as schizophrenic depending on the country in which she or he was seen and when the diagnostic evaluation was made.

The progressive tightening of diagnostic criteria with the DSM-III and the DSM-IV helped improve the overall consistency or reliability of the diagnosis of schizophrenia (Strachan, 1986). The down side of tightening the diagnostic criteria is that the description of the diagnostic category of schizophrenia may have become so narrow that many people with the disorder may be excluded from the diagnosis (Andreasen, 1990).

The contributions of Kraepelin, Bleuler, and Schneider are expressed in modified form in the present DSM diagnostic system. Although the diagnostic code incorporates many of the features of schizophrenia identified by these early contributors, it is not limited, as Kraepelin had proposed, to cases in which there is a course of progressive deterioration. The narrower DSM-III and DSM-IV criteria have placed into other diagnostic categories persons with mood disorders complicated by psychotic behavior (for example, schizoaffective disorders) and people with schizophrenic-like thinking but without overt psychotic behavior (schizotypal personality disorder). The DSM-IV criteria for schizophrenia also require that psychotic behaviors be present at some point during the course of the disorder and that signs of the disorder be present for at least 6 months. People with briefer forms of psychosis are placed in diagnostic categories that may be connected with more favorable outcomes. Table 11.1 describes the major clinical criteria for schizophrenia.

Table 11.1 Major Clinical Features of Schizophrenia

A. Two or more of the following must be present for a significant portion of time over the course of a 1-month period:

   (1) delusions   *auditory of 2 or more*
   (2) hallucinations → *voices, significant to diagnose*
   (3) speech which is either incoherent or characterized by marked loosening of associations
   (4) disorganized or catatonic behavior
   (5) negative features (e.g., flattened affect)

B. Functioning in such areas as social relations, work, or self-care during the course of the disorder is markedly below the level achieved prior to the onset of the disorder. If the onset develops during childhood or adolescence, there is a failure to achieve the expected level of social development.

C. Signs of the disorder have occurred continuously for a period of at least 6 months. This 6-month period must include an active phase lasting at least a month in which psychotic symptoms (listed in A) which are characteristic of schizophrenia occur.

D. Schizoaffective and mood disorders have been ruled out.

E. The disorder cannot be attributed to the effects of a substance (e.g., substance abuse or prescribed medication) or to a general medical condition.

Source: Adapted from the DSM-IV Draft Criteria (American Psychiatric Association, 1993), p. I:1.

 It is true that schizophrenics occupy 1 hospital bed in 4 in the United States.

The ECA study failed to find significant gender differences in the rates of schizophrenia (Keith et al., 1991). Although the diagnosis of schizophrenia was more prevalent among African Americans than white Americans, the difference disappeared when factors such as socioeconomic level, age, gender, and marital status were taken into account (Keith et al., 1991). However, the prevalence of schizophrenia among Hispanic Americans, especially men, was lower than that among either white Americans or African Americans (Keith et al., 1991). There is a tendency, however, for African Americans and Hispanic Americans who suffer from mood disorders to be misdiagnosed as schizophrenic (Loring & Powell, 1988). Schizophrenia may thus be overdiagnosed in members of these minority groups. Such misdiagnosis may result from the stereotyping of minority group members as "out of control" by many non-Hispanic white mental health professionals.

Yet patterns of symptoms also appear to vary among population groups. African-American schizophrenics may be more likely than white-American schizophrenics to exhibit hallucinations, disorientation, and displays of anger, whereas white-American schizophrenics may be more likely to display incoherent delusions (Chu et al., 1985). African-American schizophrenics, as a group, also appear to be less severely impaired than white-American schizophrenics (Fabrega et al., 1988).

PREVALENCE OF SCHIZOPHRENIA

Schizophrenia is a problem of enormous proportions. The multisite Epidemiologic Catchment Area (ECA) study of five U.S. communities reported an overall prevalence of schizophrenia in the general adult population of 1.3%. This percentage means that more than 2 million people in the United States would warrant a diagnosis of schizophrenia at some point in their lives (Keith et al., 1991). Other epidemiological studies estimate a slightly lower percentage, 1% (Keith et al., 1991). Nearly 1 million people in the United States are treated for schizophrenia each year. This number amounts to about 15% of the total number of people receiving treatment for any type of behavioral problem (Rosenstein et al., 1989). Schizophrenics also occupy more than half of the hospital beds in this country in facilities for the mentally disordered and retarded, and one-quarter of all hospital beds (Boffey, 1986).

PHASES OF SCHIZOPHRENIA

Schizophrenia typically develops in late adolescence or early adulthood, at the very time that people are making their way from the family into the world outside. People who develop schizophrenia become increasingly disengaged from society. They fail to function in the expected roles of student, worker, or spouse, and their families and communities grow intolerant of their deviant behavior.

In some cases, the onset of the disorder is acute. It occurs suddenly, within a few weeks or months. The individual may have been well adjusted and shown few if any signs of behavioral disturbance. Then a rapid transformation in personality and behavior leads to an acute psychotic episode.

In other cases, there is a slower, more gradual decline in functioning. It may take years before psy-

MULTICULTURAL PERSPECTIVES

Schizophrenia or *Nervios*?
What's in a Name?—Quite a Lot, Apparently

The term *schizophrenia* is connected with a certain stigma in our society and with the expectation that the disorder is enduring (Jenkins & Karno, 1992). Yet to many Mexican Americans, a person with schizophrenia is perceived as suffering from *nervios* ("nerves"), a cultural label that is attached to a wide range of troubled behaviors, including anxiety, schizophrenia, and depression, and carries less stigmata and more positive expectations than the label of schizophrenia (Jenkins, 1988; Jenkins & Karno, 1992). Researchers believe that the label *nervios* may have the effect of destigmatizing the schizophrenic:

> Since severe cases of *nervios* are not considered blameworthy or under an individual's control, the person who suffers its effects is deserving of sympathy, support, and special treatment. Moreover, severe cases of *nervios* are potentially curable. It is interesting to note that Mexican-descent relatives do not adopt another possible cultural label for craziness, *loco*. As a *loco*, the individual would be much more severely stigmatized and considered to be out of control with little chance for recovery. . . .
>
> Defining the problem as *nervios*, a common condition that in its milder forms afflicts nearly everyone, provides them a way of identifying with and minimizing the problem by claiming that the ill relative is "just like me, only more so."
>
> Jenkins and Karno, 1992, pp. 17–18

Family members may respond differently to schizophrenic relatives if they ascribe aspects of their behavior to

Schizophrenia or an attack of *nervios*? Many Mexican Americans perceive people with schizophrenia to be suffering from *nervios* ("nerves"), a cultural label that is connected with problems such as anxiety, schizophrenia, and depression. The label *nervios* carries less stigma and more positive expectations than that of schizophrenia, and may be connected with more positive outcomes.

a temporary or curable condition, which they believe can be altered by willpower, than if they believe that the behavior is caused by a permanent brain abnormality. It remains to be seen whether different ways of conceptualizing the problems of schizophrenics across cultures are connected with differences in behavior patterns or rates of recurrent episodes among persons with the disorder.

---

chotic behaviors emerge, although early signs of deterioration may be observed. This period of deterioration is called the **prodromal phase**. It is characterized by waning interest in social activities and increasing difficulty in meeting the responsibilities of daily living. At first, such people seem to take less care of their appearance. They fail to bathe regularly or they wear the same clothes repeatedly. Over time, their behavior may become increasingly odd or eccentric. There are lapses in job performance or schoolwork. Their speech may become increasingly vague and rambling. At first these changes in personality may be so gradual that they raise little concern among friends and families. They may be attributed to "a phase" that the person is passing through. But as behavior becomes more bizarre—like hoarding

food, collecting garbage, or talking to oneself on the street—the acute phase of the disorder begins. Frankly psychotic symptoms develop, such as wild hallucinations, delusions, and increasingly bizarre behavior.

Following acute episodes, schizophrenics may enter the **residual phase**, in which their behavior returns to the level that was characteristic of the prodromal phase. Although schizophrenics may be free of active psychotic behaviors during the residual phase, they may continue to be impaired by a deep sense of apathy, by difficulties in thinking or speaking clearly, and by the harboring of unusual ideas, such as beliefs in telepathy or clairvoyance. Such patterns of behavior make it difficult for them to assume social roles as wage earners, marital partners, or students.

Full return to normal behavior is uncommon but may occur. For many, a chronic pattern characterized by occasional relapses and continued impairment between acute episodes develops.

BRIEFER FORMS OF PSYCHOSIS

Although we tend to link psychotic behavior with schizophrenia, some brief psychotic episodes do not progress to schizophrenia. The DSM-IV category of **brief psychotic disorder** applies to a psychotic disorder that lasts from a day to a month and is characterized by at least one of the following features: delusions, hallucinations, disorganized speech, or disorganized or catatonic behavior. If the disorder occurs in response to a major source of stress, such as the loss of a loved one or exposure to brutal traumas in wartime, the clinician notes that the disorder occurred following exposure to a marked stressor or stressors. In the DSM-III-R, a brief psychotic disorder with one or more marked stressors was termed a *brief reactive psychosis*. A person may be diagnosed as having a brief psychotic disorder without marked stressor(s) when no precipitating event(s) can be identified. If the episode occurs within 4 weeks of childbirth, the clinician may use the diagnostic classification, *brief psychotic disorder with postpartum onset*.

Schizophreniform disorder consists of abnormal behaviors identical to those in schizophrenia that have persisted for at least 1 month but less than 6 months. They thus do not yet justify the diagnosis of schizophrenia. Although some cases have good outcomes, in others the disorder persists beyond 6 months and is reclassified as schizophrenia. Researchers find substantial deficits in cognitive functioning (problems with thought, memory, and concentration) among schizophreniform patients which are similar to those shown by chronic schizophrenics (Hoff et al., 1992). There may thus be a continuity between the two conditions.

It is true that people who show bizarre schizophrenic-type behaviors cannot be diagnosed as schizophrenic until half a year later. This is because schizophrenia is conceptualized as a persistent disorder. Briefer disorders that resemble schizophrenia are labeled brief psychotic disorder and schizophreniform disorder.

SCHIZOPHRENIA-SPECTRUM DISORDERS

Some people have persistent patterns of unusual thinking or emotional responses that seem to lie within the broader spectrum of schizophrenic problems, but may not fit the stringent definition of schizophrenia. The schizophrenia spectrum includes related disorders that vary in severity from milder personality disorders (schizoid, paranoid, and schizotypal types) to schizophrenia (Andreasen, 1987).

The schizophrenia spectrum may also include schizoaffective disorder, which is characterized by prominent psychotic behaviors and disturbances in mood, such as mania or depression. Schizoaffective disorder has been described as something of a "mixed bag." It refers to a mixed group of psychotic and mood-disordered behaviors that are seen by some as a form of severe mood disorder and by others as a syndrome that lies between mood disorders and schizophrenia (Andreasen, 1987). Researchers in one recent study found that schizoaffective disorder is associated with somewhat better prognosis (outcome) than schizophrenia (Grossman et al., 1991). When evaluated at 2-, 4-, and 5-year intervals following hospitalization, people with schizoaffective disorder fared better in social functioning and displayed less symptomatology than schizophrenics. Nevertheless, they showed poorer functioning than people with unipolar (major depression) or bipolar disorder.

Some investigators believe that schizophrenia-spectrum disorders share a common genetic link. There appears to be a greater than average incidence of schizoaffective disorders among the relatives of schizophrenics and a greater than average incidence of schizophrenia among the relatives of people with schizoaffective disorder (Kendler et al., 1985; Maj et al., 1991). Researchers also suspect a possible genetic link between schizotypal personality disorder and schizophrenia (Siever et al., 1990b).

The distinction between schizophrenia and schizophrenia-spectrum disorders may be more a matter of degree than of kind. Differences in genetic vulnerability or environmental stress may prompt development of milder or more severe forms of a common schizophrenic-type disorder (Andreasen, 1987). For now, though, the generally accepted diagnostic practice is to adopt the narrower definition of schizophrenia, which sorts out disorders such as schizotypal and schizoid personality disorders, and schizoaffective disorder, from schizophrenia per se.

FEATURES OF SCHIZOPHRENIA

Schizophrenia is a pervasive disorder that affects a wide range of psychological processes involving cognition, affect, and behavior. Many people diagnosed as schizophrenic show only a few of the behavior patterns listed in Table 11.1. Schizophrenics at some time or another may show delusions, problems with associative thinking, and hallucinations, but not necessarily all at once. There are also different kinds or types of schizophrenia, characterized by different behavior patterns. No one behavior pattern is unique to schizophrenia, nor is any one behavior pattern invariably present among schizophrenics.

Male schizophrenics appear to differ from female schizophrenics in several ways. They tend to show an earlier age of onset, a poorer history of adjustment prior to exhibiting the disorder, more cognitive impairment, more behavioral deficits, and a poorer response to chemotherapy (Goldstein & Tsuang, 1990). These differences have led researchers to speculate that females and males may differ in their relative risks of developing different forms of schizophrenia (Goldstein & Tsuang, 1990). Perhaps schizophrenia involves different areas of the brain in men and women, which may explain differences in the features of the disorder between the genders.

Impaired Level of Functioning

In schizophrenia, there is a marked decline in occupational and social functioning. Schizophrenics may have difficulty holding a conversation, forming friendships, holding a job, or taking care of their personal hygiene.

Disturbances in Thought and Speech

Schizophrenia is characterized by disturbances in thinking and in the conveyence of thoughts through coherent, meaningful speech. Disturbances in thinking may be expressed in terms of the content and the form of thought.

■ **DISTURBANCES IN THE CONTENT OF THOUGHT** The most prominent disturbance in the content of thought involves delusions, or false beliefs that remain fixed in the person's mind despite their illogical bases and lack of evidence to support them. They tend to remain unshakeable even in the face of disconfirming evidence. Delusions may take many forms, including *delusions of persecution* (e.g., "The CIA is out to get me"), *delusions of reference* ("People on the bus are talking about me," or "People on television are making fun of me"), *delusions of being controlled* (believing that one's thoughts, feelings, impulses, or actions are controlled by external forces, such as agents of the devil), and *delusions of grandeur* (believing oneself to be Jesus or believing that one is on a

special mission, or having grand but illogical plans for saving the world). People with delusions of persecution may think that they are being pursued by the Mafia, FBI, CIA, or some other group. A woman with delusions of reference believed that television news correspondents were broadcasting coded information about her. A man with delusions of this type expressed the belief that the walls of his house had been bugged by his neighbors. Other delusions include beliefs that one has committed unpardonable sins, is rotting away from a horrible disease, or that the world or oneself do not really exist. Other commonly occurring delusions include *thought broadcasting* (believing that one's thoughts are somehow transmitted to the external world so that others can overhear them), *thought insertion* (believing that one's thoughts have been planted in one's mind by an external source), and *thought withdrawal* (believing that thoughts have been removed from one's mind). Mellor (1970) offers the following examples of thought broadcasting, thought insertion, and thought withdrawal:

> *Thought Broadcasting:* A 21-year-old student reported, "As I think, my thoughts leave my head on a type of mental ticker-tape. Everyone around has only to pass the tape through their mind and they know my thoughts" (p. 17).
> *Thought Insertion:* A 29-year-old housewife reported that when she looks out of the window, she thinks, "The garden looks nice and the grass looks cool, but the thoughts of [a man's name] come into my mind. There are no other thoughts there, only his. . . . He treats my mind like a screen and flashes his thoughts on it like you flash a picture" (p. 17).
> *Thought Withdrawal:* A 22-year-old woman experienced the following: "I am thinking about my mother, and suddenly my thoughts are sucked out of my mind by a phrenological vacuum extractor, and there is nothing in my mind, it is empty" (pp. 16–17).

Schizophrenia is not the only diagnostic category characterized by delusional thinking. People in a manic episode may experience delusions of grandeur. They may believe that they hold a unique relationship to God or that they have some special mission to fulfill. People with a "pure" delusional disorder may hold delusions of jealousy or persecution that appear so convincing that others may accept them at face value. Psychotic behavior may also occur in major depression, usually in the form of delusions of guilt (beliefs that one is being persecuted because of some transgression) or somatic delusions (false, persistent beliefs that cancer is eating away at one's body). Delusions in schizophrenia tend to be more bizarre and more often involve features of thought insertion and thought broadcasting than do delusions associated with mood or other mental disorders (Junginger et al., 1992). In contrast, grandiose delusions (exaggerated perceptions of self-importance) tend to occur more commonly among people with bipolar or schizoaffective disorder.

■ **DISTURBANCES IN THE FORM OF THOUGHT** Unless we are engaged in daydreaming or purposefully letting our thoughts wander, our thoughts tend to be tightly knit together. The connections (or associations) between our thoughts tend to be logical and coherent. Schizophrenics tend to think in a disorganized, illogical fashion, however. In schizophrenia, the form or structure of thought processes as well as their content is often disturbed. Clinicians label this type of disturbance a **thought disorder**.

A thought disorder is recognized by the breakdown in the organization, processing, and control of thoughts (Holzman, 1986). Looseness of associations, which we now regard as a cardinal sign of thought disorder, is one of Bleuler's four A's. Schizophrenics' speech is often jumbled, with parts of words combined incoherently or words strung together to make meaningless rhymes. Their speech may jump from one topic to another, but convey little useful information. Schizophrenics are usually unaware that their thoughts and behavior appear abnormal. In severe cases of loosened associations, their speech may become completely incoherent or incomprehensible. Another common sign of thought disorder is poverty of content of speech (that is, speech that is coherent but lacks informational value because it is too vague, abstract, concrete, stereotypic, or repetitive). Less commonly occurring signs of thought disorder include **neologisms** (a word made up by the speaker that has little or no meaning to others), **perseveration** (inappropriate but persistent repetition of the same words or train of thought), **clanging** (stringing together of words or sounds on the basis of rhyming, such as, "I know who I am but I don't know Sam"), and **blocking** (involuntary abrupt interruption of speech or thought).

Many but not all schizophrenics manifest a thought disorder (Harrow & Marengo, 1986; Marengo & Harrow, 1985). Some schizophrenics appear to think and speak coherently, but have disordered content of thought as evidenced by the presence of delusions (Andreasen, 1986). Nor is disordered thought unique to schizophrenia; it has been found in milder form among normal people (Andreasen, 1986; Andreasen & Grove, 1986), especially when they are tired or under stress. Disordered thought is also found among other diagnostic groups, such as persons with mania (Andreasen & Grove, 1986; Oltmanns et al., 1985). Thought disorders among manics tend to be short lived and reversible, however. Schizophrenics tend to show more

persistent or recurrent abnormalities in thinking (Andreasen & Grove, 1986; Harrow & Marengo, 1986).

Thought disorder in schizophrenia occurs most often during acute episodes, but it may linger into residual phases. Thought disorders that persist beyond acute episodes are connected with poorer prognoses (Harrow & Marengo, 1986; Marengo & Harrow, 1987), perhaps because lingering thought disorders are reflective of more severe disorders (Harrow & Marengo, 1986).

Deficits in Attention

To read this book you must screen out background noises and other environmental stimuli. The ability to focus on relevant stimuli is basic to learning and thinking. Kraepelin and Bleuler suggested that schizophrenia involves a breakdown in the processes of attention. Schizophrenics appear to have difficulty filtering out irrelevant distracting stimuli, a deficit that impairs their ability to focus their attention and organize their thoughts (Asarnow et al., 1991; Elkins et al., 1992; Grillon et al., 1990). Researchers suspect that schizophrenics are easily distractible at least in part because of a neurological dysfunction that interferes with the allocation of attention and the filtering out of unessential information (Grillon et al., 1990). The mother of a schizophrenic son described her son's difficulties in filtering out extraneous sounds:

> . . . his hearing is different when he's ill. One of the first things we notice when he's deteriorating is his heightened sense of hearing. He cannot filter out anything. He hears each and every sound around him with equal intensity. He hears the sounds from the street, in the yard, and in the house, and they are all much louder than normal. (Anonymous, 1985, p. 1; cited in Freedman et al., 1987, p. 670)

Schizophrenics appear to be *hypervigilant* or acutely sensitive to extraneous sounds, especially during the early stages of the disorder. During acute episodes, they may become flooded by these stimuli, overwhelming their ability to make sense of their environments. Through measuring the brain's involuntary brain wave responses to auditory stimuli, researchers have found that brains of schizophrenics are less able than those of normal people to inhibit or screen out responses to extraneous auditory signals (Freedman et al., 1987).

The neurobiology of these sensory disturbances is not fully clear. Researchers are investigating a possible "gating" mechanism in the brain that may be responsible for filtering extraneous stimuli, much like closing a gate in a road can stem the flow of traffic

Are schizophrenic people overwhelmed by irrelevant stiumlation that distracts them from useful information? Schizophrenics appear to have difficulty filtering out extraneous information. This deficit impairs their ability to focus their attention and organize their thoughts. The deficit may reflect a neurological dysfunction that interferes with the allocation of attention and the filtering out of superfluous information.

(Freedman et al., 1987). Such sensory deficits appear to run in the families of schizophrenics, which could point to an underlying genetic mechanism (Freedman et al., 1987).

Cognitively oriented researchers have focused on the role of information processing in explaining deficits in attention. Information processing refers to the mechanisms by which the individual receives, stores, and processes information from the outside world. Experimental studies have shown that schizophrenics may have deficits in the early stages of information processing—that is, in transferring the immediate sensory impression that is formed in the brain by external stimuli, such as light or sound, into short-term memory (Braff & Saccuzzo, 1985; Miller et al., 1979). People who have difficulty processing sensory information are handicapped indeed in their attempts to understand the outer world. Their environments may be perceived as confused and fragmentary.

The belief that schizophrenics suffer from attentional deficiencies is supported by various studies which focus on psychophysiological aspects of attention. Evidence is accumulating that schizophrenics have deficits in the automatic brain processes that regulate attention to external stimuli.

■ **DEFICIENCIES IN ORIENTING RESPONSE**
When you are exposed to a stimulus, such as an auditory tone or a flash of light, you experience a pattern of automatic or involuntary psychophysiological responses, called the **orienting response** (OR), that alerts your brain to the presence of the stimulus. Orienting responses include pupil dilation, brain wave patterns connected with states of attention, and

changes in the electrical conductivity of the skin—that is, galvanic skin response (GSR).

Studies conducted in the United States, Britain, and Germany (Bernstein, 1987; Bernstein et al., 1988) have shown that 40 to 50% of schizophrenics fail to demonstrate a normal OR, as measured by GSR, to auditory tones. This subgroup of schizophrenics also appears to be distinguished by deficits including emotional withdrawal and cognitive impairment (Bernstein, 1987; Bernstein et al., 1981). In medical terminology, these deficits are called the **negative symptoms** of schizophrenia—those involving behavioral deficits. Schizophrenics with normal ORs tend to show behavioral excesses or so-called **positive symptoms** of schizophrenia, such as the more dramatic, excited, overt schizophrenic behaviors like delusions, hallucinations, and bizarre behavior (Bernstein et al., 1981; Straube, 1979). Perhaps the attentional difficulties in at least some schizophrenics are related to failure of the brain mechanisms that normally allocate attention to incoming stimuli.

■ **EYE MOVEMENT DYSFUNCTIONS** Eye movement dysfunction refers to an impairment in the ability to visually track a stimulus as it moves across one's field of vision. Researchers suspect that eye movement dysfunctions may be a genetic marker for schizophrenia. Eye movement dysfunctions appear to be specific to schizophrenia and occur relatively infrequently among other psychotic groups and among normals (Iacono et al., 1992). They do not appear to be under voluntary control—subjects, that is, are not simply refusing to cooperate with the experimental task. Thus, these attentional difficulties appear to involve a defect in the automatic or involuntary processes related to visual attention. Eye movement dysfunctions have consistently been found among schizophrenics (Clementz & Sweeney, 1990). Eye movement dysfunction also tends to run in families of schizophrenics (Clementz et al., 1992; Holzman et al., 1988; Iacono et al., 1992). The import of eye movement for our understanding of schizophrenia remains unclear, however (Clementz & Sweeney, 1990). For example, not all schizophrenics or their family members show eye movement abnormalities. There may thus be different genetic pathways associated with different subtypes of schizophrenia.

Eye movement dysfunctions have also been found to be more common in persons with schizotypal personality disorder (but not in persons with other personality disorders) in relation to normal controls. This finding lends support to the belief that schizotypal disorder may be biologically linked to schizophrenia within a spectrum of schizophrenia-related disorders (Siever et al., 1990b).

■ **EVENT-RELATED POTENTIALS** Researchers are also studying the brain wave patterns, called event-related potentials, or ERPs, that occur in response to external stimuli. ERPs have been broken down into components that emerge at various intervals following the presentation of a stimulus such as a flash of light or an auditory tone. Early components (brain wave patterns occurring within the first 250 milliseconds [ms], or one-quarter of a second, of exposure to a stimulus) may be involved in registering the stimulus in the brain. Later components such as the P300 component (a brain wave pattern that typically occurs about 300 ms, or three-tenths of a second, after a stimulus) are thought to be involved with processes involving attention to the stimulus.

Schizophrenics show early (less than 250 ms) ERP components of greater than expected magnitude in response to tactile stimuli. Perhaps these brain wave patterns result in abnormally high levels of sensory information reaching higher brain centers, producing *sensory overload*. This finding supports the view that schizophrenics may be deficient in their ability to filter out distracting stimuli. Research has also shown lower than expected levels of P300 brain wave patterns in schizophrenics in response to auditory tones (Baribeau-Brown et al., 1983), which suggests the possibility that schizophrenics have difficulties extracting meaningful information from stimuli such as lights, sounds, and touches (Holzman, 1987). Evidence with ERPs is thus consistent with the view that schizophrenics may be flooded with high levels of sensory information and have greater difficulty

extracting useful information from it. As a result, they may be confused and find it difficult to filter out irrelevant stimuli such as extraneous noises.

In sum, biological and cognitive research suggests that schizophrenics find it difficult to interpret sensory input and to ignore distracting stimuli. Research also suggests that schizophrenics may benefit from cognitive retraining that helps them to attend to relevant stimuli (Brenner et al., 1992).

Perceptual Disturbances

*E*very so often during the interview, Sally would look over her right shoulder in the direction of the office door, and smile gently. When asked why she kept looking at the door, she said that the voices were talking about the two of us just outside the door and she wanted to hear what they were saying. "Why the smile?" Sally was asked. "They were saying funny things," she replied, "like maybe you thought I was cute or something." ■

*E*ugene was flailing his arms wildly in the hall of the psychiatric unit. Sweat seemed to pour from his brow, and his eyes darted about with agitation. He was subdued and injected with haloperidol (brand name Haldol) to reduce his agitation. When he was about to be injected he started shouting, "Father, forgive them for they know not . . . forgive them . . . father . . ." His words became jumbled. Later, after he had calmed down, he reported that the ward attendants had looked to him like devils or evil angels. They were red and burning, and steam issued from their mouths.

■ *The Authors' Files*

Hallucinations, the most common form of perceptual disturbance among schizophrenics, are images that are perceived in the absence of external stimulation. They are difficult to distinguish from reality. For Sally, the voices coming from outside the consulting room were real enough, even though no one was there. Hallucinations may involve any of the senses. Auditory hallucinations ("hearing voices") are most common. Tactile hallucinations (such as tingling, electrical, or burning sensations) and somatic hallucinations (feeling like snakes are crawling inside one's belly) are also common. Visual hallucinations (seeing things that are not there), gustatory hallucinations (tasting things), and olfactory hallucinations (smelling things) are rarer.

Auditory hallucinations occur in about 70% of cases of schizophrenia (Cleghorn et al., 1992). In

A painting by a schizophrenic man. This picture was painted by a young man who reported monsters—apparent hallucinations—like the one pictured here crawling on the floor. He also reported that the chairs next to his bed had turned into devils.

auditory hallucinations, the voices may be experienced as female or male and as originating inside or outside one's head (Asaad & Shapiro, 1986). Schizophrenics may hear voices conversing about them in the third person, debating their virtues or faults.

Some schizophrenics experience *command hallucinations*—voices that instruct them to perform certain acts, such as harming themselves or others. Researchers find that command hallucinators report greater aggression and self-punishment themes in their hallucinations than do noncommand hallucinators (Rogers et al., 1990). Angela, for example, was instructed by the "hellsmen" to commit suicide. Schizophrenics who experience command hallucinations are often hospitalized for fear that they may harm themselves or others. Yet command hallucinations often go undetected by professionals because command hallucinators deny or are unwilling to discuss them (Rogers et al., 1990).

The research is mixed on how frequently schizophrenics comply with command hallucinations. One study found no greater incidence of violent or dangerous behavior between hallucinators with and without command hallucinations (Hellerstein et al., 1987). In this study, the majority of people who had hallucinations commanding them to commit acts of violence apprently ignored them. The study took place in a secured hospital setting, however. Another study of command hallucinators revealed that more than half (56%) reportedly complied with a command on at least one occasion. Nearly half (44%) complied frequently or very frequently (Rogers et al., 1990).

Visual hallucinations among schizophrenics appear to be more common in non-Western cultures (Ndetei & Singh, 1983; Ndetei & Vadher, 1984). In one study conducted in an English hospital in Kenya, researchers found that schizophrenics of African, Asian, or Jamaican background were about twice as likely to experience visual hallucinations as schizophrenics of European background (Ndetei & Vadher, 1984).

Hallucinations are not unique to schizophrenics. People with major depression and mania have been reported to experience hallucinations (Bentall, 1990). Nor are hallucinations invariably a sign of psychopathology. Cross-cultural evidence shows that they are common and valued in some developing countries (Bentall, 1990). Even in developed countries, studies show that about 10% of the people sampled report having experienced occasional hallucinations (Bentall, 1990). Normal people sometimes experience hallucinations during the course of a religious experience or ritual (Asaad & Shapiro, 1986). Participants in such experiences may report fleeting trancelike states with visions or other perceptual aberrations. We may all hallucinate in the form of dreams or in response to hallucinogenic drugs. Hallucinations may also occur during grief reactions, when images of the deceased may appear, and in other stressful conditions. In most cases, grief-induced hallucinations can be differentiated from psychotic hallucinations in that the individual can distinguish them from reality.

 It may actually be that all people may hallucinate in one way or another. Yet the great majority of people are not schizophrenic.

Bentall (1990) views the hallucinations of psychiatric patients as involving lack of skill or ability to distinguish between real and imaginary events. They tend to confuse real and imaginary (hallucinations) events, that is.

Drug-induced hallucinations tend to be visual and often involve abstract shapes such as circles or stars, or flashes of light. Schizophrenic hallucinations, in contrast, tend to be more fully formed and complex. Hallucinations (for example, of bugs crawling on one's skin) may also occur during delirium tremens (the DTs), which often occur as part of the withdrawal syndrome for chronic alcoholism. Hallucinations may also occur as side effects of medications or in neurological disorders, such as Parkinson's disease.

■ **CAUSES OF HALLUCINATIONS** The causes of psychotic hallucinations remain unknown, but speculations abound (Asaad & Shapiro, 1986). Disturbances in brain chemistry are suspected as playing a causal role. The neurotransmitter dopamine has been implicated because antipsychotic drugs that block dopamine activity also tend to reduce hallucinations. Conversely, drugs that lead to increased production of dopamine tend to induce hallucinations. Because hallucinations resemble dreamlike states, it is also possible that hallucinations are types of daytime dreams connected with a failure of brain mechanisms that normally prevent dream images from intruding on waking experiences.

Hallucinations may also represent a type of subvocal inner speech (Cleghorn et al., 1992). Many of us talk to ourselves from time to time, although we usually keep our mutterings beneath our breaths (subvocal) and recognize the voice as our own. Do auditory hallucinations among schizophrenics represent projections of their own internal voices, or self-speech, onto external sources? In one recent experiment, 14 of 18 hallucinating schizophrenics reported that the voices disappeared when they engaged in a procedure that prevented them from talking to themselves beneath their breaths (Bick & Kinsbourne, 1987). Similar results were obtained for 18 of 21 normal subjects who reportedly experienced hallucinations in response to hypnotic suggestions.

Researchers who study brain metabolism report finding similarities (and some differences) in the metabolic patterns observed in the language regions of the cerebral cortex during auditory hallucinations and those observed in normal subjects who are listening to their own voices (Cleghorn et al., 1992). Researchers also find evidence of similar electrical activity in the auditory cortex of the brain during

auditory hallucinations and in response to real sounds (Tiihonen et al., 1992).

Even if theories linking subvocal speech to auditory hallucinations stand up to further scientific inquiry, they cannot account for hallucinations in other sensory modalities, such as visual, tactile, or olfactory hallucinations (Bentall, 1990).

Emotional Disturbances

Disturbances of affect or emotional response in schizophrenia are typified by blunted affect—also called *flat* affect—and by inappropriate affect. Flat affect is inferred from the absence of emotional expression in the face and voice. Schizophrenics may speak in a monotone and maintain an expressionless face, or "mask." They may not experience a normal range of emotional response to people and events. Or their emotional responses may be inappropriate, like giggling at bad news.

It is not fully clear, however, whether the emotional blunting of schizophrenics is a disturbance in the ability to express emotions, to report the presence of emotions, or to actually experience emotions (Berenbaum & Oltmanns, 1990). Schizophrenics, in other words, may experience emotions even if their experiences are not communicated to the world outside.

Other Disturbances or Impairments

Schizophrenics may become confused about their personal identities—the cluster of attributes and characteristics that define themselves as individual people and give meaning and direction to their lives. They may fail to recognize themselves as unique individuals and be unclear as to how much of what they experience are parts of themselves. In psychodynamic terms, this phenomenon is sometimes referred to as loss of *ego boundaries*. They may also have difficulty adopting a third-party perspective and fail to perceive their own behavior and verbalizations as socially inappropriate in a given situation (Carini & Nevid, 1992; Harrow & Quinlan, 1985).

Disturbances of volition are most often seen in the residual or chronic state and are characterized by loss of initiative to pursue goal-directed activities. Schizophrenics may be unable to carry out plans and may lack interest or drive. Apparent ambivalence toward choosing courses of action may block goal-directed activities.

Schizophrenics may show highly excited or wild behavior, or slow to a state of **stupor**. They may exhibit odd gestures and bizarre facial expressions, or become unresponsive and curtail spontaneous movement. In extreme cases, as in catatonic schizophrenia, schizophrenics may seem unaware of the environment or maintain a rigid posture. Or they may move about in an excited but seemingly purposeless manner.

Schizophrenics manifest significant impairment in their interpersonal relationships. They tend to withdraw from social interactions and become absorbed in private thoughts and fantasies. Or they cling so desperately to others that they make them uncomfortable. Schizophrenics may become so dominated by their own fantasies that they become autistic—that is, lose touch with the outside world.

TYPES OF SCHIZOPHRENIA

There are various forms or types of schizophrenia. Kraepelin listed three types of schizophrenia: paranoid, catatonic, and hebephrenic (now called disorganized type). Bleuler included a fourth type, called **simple schizophrenia**, to describe a milder form of schizophrenia that is characterized by disorganized thinking, odd behavior, and excessively vague speech, but without active psychotic features like hallucinations or delusions. Simple schizophrenia is no longer a diagnostic category in the DSM system. People who may have formerly received this diagnosis may fit the present criteria for *schizotypal personality disorder*, however—a form of personality disturbance that resembles a less severe form of schizophrenia. As noted earlier, some researchers believe that schizotypal personality disorder and schizophrenia share a common genetic linkage.

The DSM-IV lists three specific types of schizophrenia: *disorganized, catatonic,* and *paranoid.* Schizophrenics who display active psychotic features, such as hallucinations, delusions, incoherent speech, or confused or disorganized behavior, but who do not meet the specifications of the other types are considered to be of an *undifferentiated type.* Others who have no prominent psychotic features at the time of evaluation but have some residual features (for example, social withdrawal, peculiar behavior, blunted or inappropriate affect, strange beliefs or thoughts) would be classified *residual type.*

Disorganized Type

The **disorganized type** describes schizophrenics who display such features as confused behavior, incoherence, loose associations, vivid, frequent hallucinations, flattened affect, and disorganized delusions that often involve sexual or religious themes. Social impairment is frequent among disorganized schizophrenics. They also display silliness and giddiness of mood, giggling and talking nonsensically. They often neglect their appearance and hygiene and lose control of their bladders and bowels.

Consider the case of Emilio:

A person diagnosed with disorganized schizophrenia. One of the features of disorganized schizophrenia is grossly inappropriate affect, as shown by this young man who continuously giggles and laughs for no apparent reason.

A 40-year-old man who looks more like 30 is brought to the hospital by his mother, who reports that she is afraid of him. It is his twelfth hospitalization. He is dressed in a tattered overcoat, baseball cap, and bedroom slippers, and sports several medals around his neck. His affect ranges from anger (hurling obscenities at his mother) to giggling. He speaks with a childlike quality and walks with exaggerated hip movements and seems to measure each step very carefully. Since stopping his medication about a month ago, his mother reports, he had been hearing voices and looking and acting more bizarrely. He tells the interviewer he has been "eating wires" and lighting fires. His speech is generally incoherent and frequently falls into rhyme and clanging associations. His history reveals a series of hospitalizations since the age of 16. Between hospitalizations, he lives with his mother, who is now elderly, and often disappears for months at a time, but is eventually picked up by the police for wandering in the streets.

■ *Adapted from Spitzer et al., 1989, pp. 137–138*

Catatonic Type

The **catatonic type** describes schizophrenics who have markedly impaired motor behavior, characterized by a slowing of activity that progresses to a stupor but may switch abruptly into an agitated phase. Catatonic schizophrenics may show unusual mannerisms or grimacing, or hold bizarre, apparently strenuous postures for hours, even as their limbs become stiff or swollen. A striking feature is **waxy flexi-**

A person diagnosed with catatonic schizophrenia. Catatonic schizophrenics may remain in unusual, difficult positions for hours, even though their limbs become stiff or swollen. They may seem oblivious to their environment, even to people who are talking about them. Yet they may later say that they heard what was being said. Periods of stupor may alternate with periods of agitation.

bility, which involves the adoption of a fixed posture into which they have been positioned by others.

 Some schizophrenics do sustain unusual, uncomfortable positions for hours and will not respond to questions or comments during these periods. This behavior pattern is referred to as *waxy flexibility* and is a feature of catatonic schizophrenia.

Catatonics are often mute and show no evidence of attending to those around them. Later they may report that they heard what others were saying at the time, however.

A 24-year-old man had been brooding about his life. He professed that he did not feel well, but could not explain his bad feelings. While hospitalized he initially sought contact with people, but a few days later was found in a statuesque position, his legs contorted in an awkward-looking position. He refused to talk to anyone and acted as if he couldn't see or hear anything. His face was an expressionless mask. A few days later, he began to talk, but in an echolalic or mimicking way. For example, he would respond to the question, "What is your name?" by saying, "What is your name?" He could not care for his needs and required to be fed by spoon.

■ *Adapted from Arieti, 1974, p. 40*

Paranoid Type

The **paranoid type** describes schizophrenics who are preoccupied with one or more delusions or have frequent auditory hallucinations (American Psychiatric Association, 1993). Their behavior and speech does not show the marked disorganization typical of the disorganized type, nor is there a prominent display of flattened or inappropriate affect or catatonic behavior. Their delusions often involve themes of grandeur or persecution. They may also have delusions of jealousy. They may believe, for example, that their spouse or lover is unfaithful despite a lack of evidence. They may also become highly agitated, confused, and fearful.

There was a certain sadness about Cara. Perhaps it was because her delusions seemed to represent her desire to be loved and treated as someone important. Cara, 20, was diagnosed as a paranoid schizophrenic. She told the psychologist that she couldn't wait until her twenty-first

On the run? Paranoid schizophrenics hold systematized delusions that commonly involve themes of persecution and grandeur. They usually do not show the degree of confusion, disorganization, or disturbed motor behavior evinced by disorganized or catatonic schizophrenics. Unless they are discussing the areas in which they are delusional, their thought processes may appear to be relatively intact.

birthday, when "Mr. (Nelson) Rockefeller," then the vice president, would whisk her away to Washington and present her with her inheritance—38 million dollars. She explained that Mr. Rockefeller was actually her real father and that her mother was lying when she denied it. In fact, her real father had abandoned the family when Cara was 7. On other occasions, Cara claimed to be an heiress of the Kennedy family, "Kim Kennedy." She believed that newscasters on television were sending her secret messages from Mr. Rockefeller and that one of them, newsman Dan Rather, was sending her love messages. She reported that she received telepathic messages from Mr. Rockefeller, telling her when she could expect his arrival. The thoughts just popped into her mind, she claimed, but she knew they were his. She believed that there were enemies of Mr. Rockefeller who worked for the FBI who wanted to kill her and who hid in the bushes around her house, waiting for her to come out. For weeks before her hospitalization, she refused to leave home, barricading herself in the attic. When hospitalized, she reported that she had heard men on her roof, laughing about her and threatening to kill her.

■ *The Authors' Files*

DIMENSIONS OF SCHIZOPHRENIA

In addition to the various types of schizophrenia, researchers generally agree that there are various patterns of disorder that are useful to categorize as dimensions. Such dimensions include the process–reactive dimension, dimensions defined by positive and negative features or symptoms, and Type I–Type II schizophrenia.

The Process–Reactive Dimension

In some cases, schizophrenia appears to develop slowly or insidiously. No clearly identified stressor appears to evoke the changes in functioning. This pattern, called **process schizophrenia**, has traditionally been associated with more persistent impairment and less favorable outcomes than **reactive schizophrenia**. Reactive schizophrenia has a more sudden onset. It typically follows precipitating stressors such as moving away from home or the death of a parent.

Reactive schizophrenics generally achieve a higher level of social, school, and vocational functioning before the acute phase of the disorder (called *premorbid adjustment*) than did process schizophrenics. The higher the level of premorbid adjustment, the better the eventual outcome or, in medical terminology, the **prognosis** (Huber et al., 1980; Strauss et al., 1977). Premorbid adjustment has been found to be a better predictor of outcome than the severity of the disorder during the acute phase (Moller et al., 1982).

Many reactive schizophrenics appeared normal before the abrupt onset of the disorder. Many had friends, held jobs, and did well at school. Process schizophrenics, by contrast, tended to show poorer social development. They typically failed to achieve an adequate social, educational, or occupational adjustment before the acute features of schizophrenia emerged.

Changes in diagnostic practices may have limited the prognostic value of the process–reactive distinction. Studies from the 1960s and 1970s generally showed that reactive schizophrenics had better prognoses than process schizophrenics but were based on the broader conception of schizophrenia contained in the DSM-II. In 1980, the DSM-III adopted a narrower definition of schizophrenia, and many people with schizophrenic-type behavior were assigned to other categories, such as schizotypal personality disorder, schizoaffective disorder, brief reactive psychoses, and schizophreniform disorders. Studies conducted with subjects who meet the tighter DSM-III criteria for schizophrenia have generally failed to demonstrate the prognostic value of the process–reactive dimension. Schizophrenics defined by DSM-III and DSM-IV criteria tend to be limited to the more chronic process type (Harrow et al., 1986; Harrow & Westermeyer, 1987; Herron, 1987). Yet the process–reactive dimension may still predict outcomes among the broader schizophrenia-spectrum of disorders that includes schizotypal personality disorders and schizoaffective disorders, among others (Herron, 1987).

Positive and Negative Symptoms

Another system of classification in schizophrenia is based on the features or symptoms of the disorder. Some behavior patterns associated with schizophrenia, labeled *negative symptoms*, represent behavioral deficits or the absence of normal behaviors. Other features, called *positive symptoms*, represent excessive or distorted behaviors. Negative symptoms include flattened affect, poverty of speech or of thought processes, a slowing-down of movement and psychological functioning (psychomotor retardation), loss of pleasure or interest in activities, and social withdrawal (Andreasen, 1987). Positive symptoms include the more florid or active signs of the disorder, such as bizarre behavior, hallucinations and delusions, and thought disorder (Andreasen, 1987). African-American schizophrenics seem to exhibit fewer negative symptoms of schizophrenia than their white counterparts (Fabrega et al., 1988).

Positive symptoms may involve a defect in the inhibitory mechanisms that would normally control excessive or distorted behaviors. Negative symptoms appear to represent the more enduring or persistent characteristics of schizophrenia. The presence of the negative symptoms of schizophrenia is associated with poorer premorbid functioning, lower educational level, more gradual onset, few if any remissions during the early years of the disorder, and a progressive decline in functioning that leads to enduring disability (Andreasen et al., 1990; Fenton & McGlashan, 1991; McGlashan & Fenton, 1992). Positive symptoms tend to occur during acute episodes and then disappear (Carpenter et al., 1988). Even when the schizophrenic is free of the more dramatic positive features of the disorder, like hallucinations and delusions, she or he may continue to be impaired by the persistence of the more enduring negative characteristics of blunted emotions and poverty of speech (Marengo & Harrow, 1987).

Research suggests that positive symptoms may also persist into the residual phase among some schiz-

ophrenics. In one study (Marengo & Harrow, 1987), a group of young schizophrenics was examined for 2 years following hospitalization for evidence of thought disorder, a positive symptom of schizophrenia. A high number of them continued to have problems with thought processes. Forty percent (16 of 41) showed persistent thought disorder, and an additional 37% (15 of 41) showed intermittent thought disorder (Marengo & Harrow, 1987). Not surprisingly, the more persistent the thought disorder, the poorer the person's adjustment to community living, as measured by rates of employment and rehospitalization. Thought disorder persisted in many cases even among schizophrenics who continued to take antipsychotic medication.

Type I–Type II Schizophrenia

The intriguing possibility has been posed that positive and negative symptom pictures may represent distinct processes in schizophrenia (McGlashan & Fenton, 1992) or even correspond to two different subtypes of schizophrenia: Type I and Type II schizophrenia (Crow, 1980a, 1980b). Type I schizophrenia is characterized by abrupt onset, positive symptoms (for example, hallucinations, delusions, and looseness of associations), preserved intellectual ability, and more favorable response to antipsychotic medication. Type II schizophrenia corresponds to a pattern consisting of negative symptoms (flattened or blunted affect, social withdrawal, poverty of speech), greater chronicity and intellectual impairment, and poorer response to antipsychotic drugs.

Because Type I schizophrenia is believed to respond more favorably to antipsychotic drugs and such drugs affect the levels of the neurotransmitter dopamine in the brain, Type I schizophrenia may involve a breakdown in the regulation or supply of dopamine (Crow, 1981). The behavior pattern, course of disorder, and lack of responsiveness to medication associated with Type II schizophrenia, however, suggests a different developmental process, perhaps one that involves a structural deficit or cell loss in the brain.

The Type I–Type II hypothesis has stimulated a great deal of research. The evidence does not fully support the view that schizophrenia consists of two distinct behavior patterns, however, (Meltzer, 1985, 1987). Some investigators (for example, Berquier & Ashton, 1991; Kay, 1990; Meltzer, 1985, 1987; Mortimer et al., 1990; Rosen et al., 1984) find that only a minority of schizophrenics can be classified as exhibiting either predominantly positive or negative symptoms. They argue that positive and negative symptoms do not define distinct subtypes of schizophrenia but rather separate dimensions that can coexist in the same individual. There is also evidence that dopamine activity is greater, not lesser, among schizophrenics with evidence of structural damage in the brain, another point that is inconsistent with the Type I–Type II model (van Kammen et al., 1986). Still, some researchers argue that the Type I–Type II model remains a useful way of categorizing some subtypes of schizophrenia (Andreasen et al., 1990).

THEORETICAL PERSPECTIVES

The understanding of schizophrenia has been approached from the major theoretical perspectives. The causes of schizophrenia remain unknown, but are generally believed to involve the interaction of genetic, psychological, social, and environmental influences. In the next sections we examine the contributions of psychodynamic, learning, biological, family, and sociocultural perspectives to our understanding of the factors that may contribute to schizophrenia.

Psychodynamic Perspectives

According to the psychodynamic perspective, schizophrenia represents the overwhelming of the ego by primitive sexual or aggressive impulses from the id. These impulses threaten the ego and give rise to intense intrapsychic conflict. Under such threat, the person regresses to an early period in the oral stage, referred to as *primary narcissism.* In this period, the infant has not yet learned that the world and it are distinct entities. ("Secondary" narcissism describes self-involvement at a later age, like during adolescence.) Because the ego mediates the relationship between the self and the outer world, this breakdown in ego functioning accounts for the schizophrenic's detachment from reality. Input from the id causes fantasies to become mistaken for reality, giving rise to hallucinations and delusions. Primitive impulses may also carry more weight than social norms and be expressed in bizarre, socially inappropriate behavior.

Freud's followers, such as Erik Erikson and Harry Stack Sullivan, placed more emphasis on interpersonal than intrapsychic factors. Sullivan (1962), for example, who devoted much of his life's work to schizophrenia, emphasized the importance of impaired mother–child relationships, arguing that they can set the stage for gradual withdrawal from other people. In early childhood, anxious and hostile interactions between the child and parent lead the

Withdrawing into oneself? Henry Stack Sullivan and some other psychodynamic theorists see schizophrenics as withdrawing into private fantasy worlds, largely because of severely disturbed relationships with their mothers.

child to take refuge in a private fantasy world. A vicious cycle ensues: The more the child withdraws, the less opportunity there is to develop a sense of trust in others and the social skills necessary to establish intimacy. Then the weak bonds between the child and others prompt social anxiety and further withdrawal. This cycle continues until young adulthood. Then, faced with an increasing set of demands at school or work and in intimate relationships, the person becomes overwhelmed with anxiety and withdraws completely into a world of fantasy.

Critics of Freud's views point out that schizophrenic behavior and infantile behavior are not much alike, so that schizophrenia cannot be explained by regression. Critics of Freud and modern psychodynamic theorists note that psychodynamic explanations are *post hoc,* or retrospective. Early child–adult relationships are recalled from the vantage point of adulthood rather than observed longitudinally. Psychoanalysts have not been able to demonstrate that certain early childhood experiences or family patterns predict schizophrenia.

Learning Perspectives

Learning theorists attempt to explain schizophrenic behavior through principles of conditioning and observational learning. From this perspective, for example, people may learn to "emit" schizophrenic behaviors when they are more likely than normal behavior to be reinforced, as suggested by Ullmann and Krasner (1975).

Ullmann and Krasner focused on the reinforcement value of social stimulation. Schizophrenics may grow up in unreinforcing environments because of disturbed family patterns or other environmental influences. Thus, they never learn to respond appropriately to social stimuli. Instead, as Sullivan too had argued, they attend increasingly to private or idiosyncratic stimuli. Other people perceive them as strange, and they suffer social rejection. In a vicious cycle, rejection spurs feelings of alienation; alienation, in turn, engenders more bizarre behavior. Patterns of bizarre behavior may be maintained by the unintentional reinforcement they receive from some people in the form of attention and expressions of sympathy.

Support for this view is found in operant conditioning studies in which bizarre behavior is shaped by reinforcement. Experiments with schizophrenics show, for example, that reinforcement affects the frequency of bizarre versus normal verbalizations and that hospital patients can be shaped into performing odd behaviors. In a classic case example, Haughton and Ayllon (1965) conditioned a 54-year-old female chronic schizophrenic to cling to a broom. A staff member gave her the broom to hold and, when she did so, another staff member gave her a cigarette. This pattern was repeated several times. Soon the woman could not be parted from the broom. But the fact that reinforcement can influence people to engage in peculiar behavior does not demonstrate that the bizarre behaviors characterizing schizophrenia can be accounted for by learning.

A 54-year-old female hospitalized schizophrenic was in fact conditioned to cling to a broom by being given cigarettes as reinforcers. The issue is the extent to which principles of learning can account for the bizarre behavior patterns shown by schizophrenics.

There are other shortcomings to these behavioral explanations. For example, many of us grow up in harsh or punishing circumstances, but do not retreat into private worlds of fantasy or display bizarre behavior. Many schizophrenics also grow up in homes that are supportive and socially reinforcing.

Moreover, schizophrenic behaviors fall into patterns that are unlikely to occur by chance and then be reinforced to the point that they become learned habits.

■ **A SOCIAL-LEARNING PERSPECTIVE** Social-learning theorists suggest that modeling of schizophrenic behavior can occur within the mental hospital. In that setting, patients may begin to model themselves after their fellow patients who act strangely. Hospital staff may inadvertently reinforce schizophrenic behavior by paying more attention to those patients who exhibit more bizarre behavior. This understanding is consistent with the observation that schoolchildren who disrupt the class garner more attention from their teachers than well-behaved children do.

Perhaps some forms of schizophrenic behavior can be explained by the principles of modeling and reinforcement. However, many people come to display schizophrenic behavior patterns without prior exposure to other schizophrenics. In fact, the onset of schizophrenic behavior patterns is more likely to lead to hospitalization than to result from hospitalization.

Biological Perspectives

Biological perspectives focus on the role of genetics and other biological factors in schizophrenia. There is considerable evidence to support biological bases for schizophrenia.

■ **GENETIC FACTORS** Evidence for a genetic contribution to the development of schizophrenia is strong (Gottesman, 1991). Schizophrenia, like many other disorders, tends to run in families. The familial incidence of schizophrenia is usually studied by identifying schizophrenics in mental hospitals and then consulting health registers and community informants to determine the incidence of schizophrenia and other disorders among their relatives. Despite some differences in methodology, studies in Sweden, Iceland, and the United States have found that the risk of psychotic disorders (including schizophrenia and other psychotic disorders) is about four times greater among the first-degree relatives (full siblings, parents, and children) of schizophrenics than among the general population (Karlsson, 1982).

Figure 11.1 shows the pooled results of European studies on family incidence of schizophrenia conducted from 1920 to 1978. The closer the genetic relationship between identified schizophrenics and their family members, the greater the likelihood (or concordance rate) of schizophrenia or probable schizophrenia in their relatives. Figure 11.1 also shows

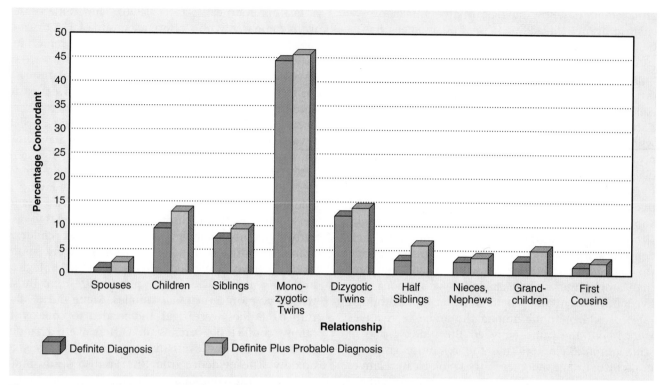

Figure 11.1 The familial risk of schizophrenia.
Generally speaking, the more closely one is related to people who have developed schizophrenia, the greater the risk of developing schizophrenia oneself. Monozygotic (MZ) twins, whose genetic heritages overlap fully, are much more likely than dizygotic (DZ) twins, whose genes overlap by 50%, to be concordant for schizophrenia.
Source: Adapted from Gottesman et al (1987).

that the rate of schizophrenia among the spouses of schizophrenics is akin to that in the general population: 1%. Because spouses generally share the environment but not a genetic relationship with their mates, sharing an environment with a schizophrenic does not appear to increase the risk of becoming schizophrenic—at least in adulthood. Note also that the concordance rate among identical (MZ) twins is between 40 and 50%. Since MZ twins share 100% of their genes, schizophrenia appears to be determined, at least in part, by other-than-genetic factors.

The evidence of increased rates of concordance among close genetic relatives of schizophrenics is consistent with a genetic explanation, but the European data did not control for other factors that may explain this concordance, such as the relatives' sharing of home environments. Other sources of data, specifically twin and adoption studies, shed further light on genetic factors in schizophrenia.

Adoption studies provide the strongest evidence for a genetic contribution to schizophrenia (Gottesman et al., 1987). Because children in such studies are reared apart from their biological parents, the studies help sort out genetic and environmental factors.

In an early study, Heston (1966) located 47 children of schizophrenic mothers (so-called *high-risk,* or HR children) who were adopted or sent to live with relatives soon after birth. The percentage of these adoptees who went on to develop schizophrenia was 16.6, as compared to 0% among a group of 50 reference cases consisting of adoptees who were also reared by foster mothers but whose biological mothers were not schizophrenic.

In a Danish study, U.S. and Danish researchers examined official registers and found 39 high-risk (HR) adoptees who had been reared apart from schizophrenic biological mothers (Rosenthal et al., 1968, 1975). Denmark is popular for such studies for several reasons (Mednick et al., 1987): (1) a national population register makes it possible for researchers to locate adopted children; (2) the Danish population is relatively stable and homogeneous in ethnic background; and (3) the registers also maintain health records and social statistics that provide researchers with information such as causes of death, criminal records, and records of psychiatric hospitalization.

In the studies by Rosenthal and his colleagues, 3 of the 39 HR adoptees (8%) were diagnosed as schizophrenic, as compared to 0% of a reference group of 47 adoptees whose biological parents had no psychiatric history. In addition, the HR adoptees had a higher incidence of schizophrenia-spectrum disorders.

Other investigators have approached the question of heredity in schizophrenia from the opposite direction. U.S. researcher Seymour Kety and Danish colleagues (Kety et al., 1968, 1975, 1978) used official records to find 33 index cases of Danish children who had been adopted early in life and later diagnosed as schizophrenic. They compared the rates of diagnosed schizophrenia in the biological and adoptive relatives of the index cases with those of the relatives of a matched reference group that consisted of adoptees with no psychiatric history. The results strongly supported the genetic explanation. The incidence of diagnosed schizophrenia was greater among the biological relatives of the schizophrenic adoptees than among the adoptive relatives with whom they lived but shared no genetic relationship. Although rates of schizophrenia among the adoptive relatives were about the same between the index group of schizophrenic adoptees and the reference group of nonschizophrenic adoptees, the biological relatives of the schizophrenic adoptees were significantly more likely to have been diagnosed as schizophrenic. It thus appears that the incidence of schizophrenia follows that of shared genes, not shared environments.

Still another approach, the **cross-fostering study**, has yielded additional evidence of genetic factors in schizophrenia. In this approach, investigators compare the incidence of schizophrenia among children of schizophrenic and nonschizophrenic biological parents who were reared by either schizophrenic or nonschizophrenic adoptive parents. Another Danish study by Wender and his colleagues (Wender et al., 1974) found the incidence of schizophrenia related to the presence of schizophrenia in the children's biological parents, but not in their adoptive parents. High-risk children (children of schizophrenic biological parents) were almost twice as likely to develop schizophrenia as those of nonschizophrenic biological parents, regardless of whether or not they were reared by a schizophrenic parent. It is also notable that adoptees whose biological parents were nonschizophrenics were placed at no greater risk of developing schizophrenia by being reared by a schizophrenic adoptive parent than by a nonschizophrenic parent. In sum, a genetic relationship with a schizophrenic seems to be the most prominent risk factor for developing the disorder (Watt, 1982).

Research from Finland suggests that heredity interacts with environmental influences in determining vulnerability to schizophrenia. The Finnish study examined 112 (HR) offspring of schizophrenic mothers born between 1972 and 1979 who were adopted at birth (Tienari et al., 1987, 1990). These index cases were compared with a reference group of 135 cases—matched adopted children of nonschizophrenic biological parents. Although the children in the study have not yet reached or passed the age of greatest risk for the emergence of schizophrenia, the evidence to date shows that the HR children are about twice as likely as the reference children to have developed a severe psychological disorder. HR children have also shown a greater percentage of psychotic disorders (7%) than the reference children (1.5%).

Environmental factors appear to be playing a role in the Finnish study. All of the index cases who developed psychotic disorders were reared by disturbed adoptive families. Moreover, index children reared by disturbed adoptive families were more likely to have developed other serious psychological problems, such as borderline personality, than those reared by more functional families. Some of the disturbed families were rigid and tended to cope with family conflict by denying it. Others were chaotic; they showed low levels of trust and high levels of anxiety. The evidence from the Finnish study indicates that the combination of genetic factors and a disruptive family environment increase the risk of severe psychological disorders, including psychotic disorders. A serious drawback to the Finnish study, however, is that it is retrospective, not prospective. The disturbed family relationships could thus represent the reaction of the families to the emergence of behavioral problems in their troubled offspring instead of a contribution factor (Goldstein, 1987b).

■ **MODELS OF GENETIC TRANSMISSION**
Although the role of genetics in schizophrenia appears convincing (Weintraub, 1987), the mode of transmission remains unknown (Watt, 1982). Researchers have proposed three general models that may account for the genetic transmission of schizophrenia:

1. *The Distinct Heterogeneity Model.* The **distinct heterogeneity model** proposes that schizophrenia comprises a number of disorders; some are caused by genetic defects that may be traced to particular genes and some by environmental factors. Catatonic schizophrenia, for example, may be a distinct disorder caused by a genetic abnormality on a particular chromosome. Other genes on the same or other chromosomes may be responsible for other schizophrenic behavior patterns.

2. *The Monogenic Model.* The **monogenic model** proposes that all forms of schizophrenia can be traced to a single defective gene. This model of causation is believed to account for genetic dis-

eases such as Huntington's disease (discussed in Chapter 12). The model proposes that a single defective gene would cause schizophrenia in all individuals who receive the gene from both parents (**homozygotes**) but only in a small number of those who receive it from only one parent (**heterozygotes**) (Murray & Reveley, 1986). However, the single-gene theory does not seem to fit the evidence of patterns of transmission in twin and family studies, although it may account for some cases (Murray & Reveley, 1986; McGue & Gottesman, 1989).

3. *The Multifactorial-Polygenic Model.* The **multifactorial-polygenic model** (MFP) proposes a threshold effect. Schizophrenia, from this perspective, is caused by the interactive or combined effects of genes and environmental factors, such as prenatal and postnatal biological trauma, and psychosocial stress. These factors produce schizophrenic behavior when they interact to raise the person's susceptibility above a critical point referred to as a threshold. This model fosters research into the relative contributions of genetic and environmental factors.

Other genetic models combine features of these three. Schizophrenic behavior, for example, could result from the interaction of a single gene and environmental stressors. The evidence favoring the single-gene model appears slim (Faraone & Tsuang, 1985), however, and most contemporary researchers seem to favor the multifactorial-polygenic model (Gottesman et al., 1987).

Although genetic studies strongly suggest a role for heredity in the development of schizophrenic behavior, many relatives of schizophrenics—including MZ twins—do not share the disorder. Hence factors other than heredity contribute to schizophrenic behavior.

■ **THE DIATHESIS–STRESS MODEL: INTEGRATING BIOLOGICAL AND PSYCHOSOCIAL FACTORS** In 1962, psychologist Paul Meehl proposed an integrative model that led to the development of the diathesis–stress model. In a manner consistent with the multifactorial-genetic approach, Meehl suggested that certain people possess a genetic predisposition to schizophrenia which is expressed behaviorally only if they are reared in stressful environments (Meehl, 1962, 1972).

More recently, Zubin and Spring (1977) formulated the diathesis–stress model, which views schizophrenia in terms of the interaction of a diathesis, or predisposition to develop the disorder, with environmental stressors. Schizophrenics inherit a diathesis that makes them more vulnerable than other people to the effects of stress. A psychotic episode may occur in people with a diathesis for schizophrenia when the level of stress exceeds the person's threshold. Sources of stress may include early biological trauma, rearing by a schizophrenic parent, or emotional or physical deprivation that may result from family conflict. On the other hand, if environmental stress remains below the person's stress threshold, schizophrenia may never develop.

■ **LONGITUDINAL STUDIES** Longitudinal studies provide additional support for the tenet of the diathesis–stress model that environmental factors interact with genetic factors to increase or decrease the likelihood of schizophrenic behavior. Longitudinal studies ideally begin before the emergence of the behavior pattern in question and follow its course. In this way, investigators consider which early characteristics predict whether a person will develop a targeted behavior pattern such as schizophrenia.

Longitudinal studies require a commitment of many years and substantial cost. Because schizophrenia only occurs in 1 to 2% of the general population, researchers have focused on high-risk children (children of one or more schizophrenic biological parents), since they are more likely to develop the disorder. Research has shown that 10 to 25% of children with one schizophrenic parent and 35 to 46% of children with two schizophrenic parents develop schizophrenia or a schizophrenia-spectrum disorder during adulthood (Erlenmeyer-Kimling & Cornblatt, 1987; Gottesman, 1991).

 Fewer than 50% of the children of two schizophrenic parents develop schizophrenia themselves, not 90%. Even the MZ twins of schizophrenics develop the disorder somewhat less than 50% of the time.

Researchers look for differences between HR children and other children to search for factors, or **markers**, that may predispose HR children to schizophrenia (e.g., Szymanski et al., 1991). If we understand these early indicators, we may be able to identify children at greatest risk and devise intervention programs that may prevent the development of schizophrenia (Goldstein & Tuma, 1987).

Perhaps the best known longitudinal study was undertaken by Sarnoff Mednick and his colleagues in Denmark (Mednick & Schulsinger, 1965). In 1962, the Mednick group identified 207 HR children and 104 reference subjects who were matched for factors like gender, social class, age, and education (Mednick et al., 1987). The children from both groups ranged in age from 10 to 20 years, with a mean of 15 years. None showed signs of disturbance when first interviewed.

Five years later, at an average age of 20, the children were reexamined. By then 20 of the HR children were found to have demonstrated abnormal behavior, but not necessarily a schizophrenic episode (Mednick & Schulsinger, 1968). The children who showed abnormal behavior, referred to as the HR "sick" group, were then compared with a matched group of 20 HR children from the original sample who remained well functioning (an HR "well" group) and a matched group of 20 low-risk (LR) subjects. It turned out that the mothers of the HR "well" offspring had experienced easier pregancies and deliveries than those of the HR "sick" group or the LR group. Seventy percent of the mothers of the HR "sick" children had had serious complications during pregnancy or delivery. Thus it may be that complications in pregnancy or childbirth interact with genetic influences to produce serious forms of abnormal behavior later in life. Babies of schizophrenic mothers are at greater than expected risk of these types of complications, such as low birth weights (Goodman & Emory, 1992).

Perhaps complications during pregnancy or childbirth produce brain damage that eventually leads to schizophrenia among genetically vulnerable (HR) people (Berquier & Ashton, 1991; Mednick, 1970; Parnas et al., 1982b). The low rate of complications during pregnancy and birth in the HR "well" group suggests that normal pregnancies and births may help protect HR children from developing schizophrenia (Mednick et al., 1987).

A later evaluation in 1972 showed that 8.6% (15 in total) of the HR offspring, but only 1% of the LR group, met the diagnostic criteria for schizophrenia used at the time. Seventeen percent of the HR cases but only 1% of the LR cases were diagnosed as borderline schizophrenic (now called schizotypal personality disorder) (Mednick et al., 1987; Schulsinger, 1976).

Although these results support genetic and other biological influences in schizophrenia, the quality of parenting may also play a role. HR children who developed schizophrenia in the Danish study had poorer relationships with their parents than HR children who eventually became schizotypal or showed no pattern of abnormal behavior (Mednick et al., 1987).

Mednick and his colleagues (1987) believe that HR children who become schizophrenic or schizotypal share a genetic vulnerability that explains common developmental deficiencies. Both groups were similarly passive and had shorter attention spans in

infancy than HR children who developed normally (Parnas et al., 1982a; Silverton et al., 1985). In adolescence, both groups showed more signs of thought disorder and less empathy for other people. Mednick and his colleagues (1987) speculate that the genetically transmitted component in schizophrenia is actually schizotypal personality disorder. Perhaps this personality disturbance progresses to schizophrenia only when the child is exposed to stressful events such as complications during pregnancy or delivery and/or poor parenting.

An Israeli study examined a sample of 50 children who had one schizophrenic parent (Marcus et al., 1987). Some of these HR children were reared by their parents in the community. Others were reared communally on a kibbutz and had limited exposure to their parents. The sample was compared to 50 children of normal parents who were reared in similar environments. Assessments were conducted in 1985, when the subjects were aged 26 to 32. Nearly half (48%) of the HR children who were available for testing showed evidence of diagnosable patterns of abnormal behavior, as compared to 9% of the reference group. Twenty percent (9 of 46) of the HR children, but none from the reference groups, were diagnosed as schizophrenic or as showing a schizophrenia-spectrum disorder, such as schizotypal personality disorder.

The HR children reared by their schizophrenic parents were no more likely at the time of the assessment to have developed schizophrenia than were those HR children raised on the kibbutz. This finding suggests that the lessened exposure of children to their schizophrenic parents (by removing them to the kibbutz) did not affect their risk of developing schizophrenia. It could be, however, that the unique environment of being reared on a kibbutz may present an environmental stressor that offsets the lessened contact with the schizophrenic parent.

The Israeli study also identified a subgroup of HR children who showed neuropsychological deficits during childhood and who later developed schizophrenia (Marcus et al., 1987). The deficits of these children were similar to those of children diagnosed as having attention-deficit disorder, which is characterized by hyperactivity and problems in attention and concentration. This subgroup also showed poor social adjustment: Males displayed antisocial and withdrawn behavior. Females harbored feelings of rejection and of not fitting in, but did not show the overt behavioral problems of the males. Some HR children thus show childhood evidence of neuropsychological and social deficits that may be markers for the development of schizophrenia in early adulthood.

Investigators in the United States are also looking for early indicators of schizophrenia by following

HR children in longitudinal studies. Researchers in one study find striking evidence of deficiencies in attention and in social competence during childhood in HR children (Weintraub, 1987). The HR children were rated by their teachers as more deviant and by their parents as more prone to emotional upsets and distractibility. Their classmates tended to see them as being different and described them as withdrawn, abrasive, and socially inept (Weintraub, 1987; Weintraub & Neale, 1984). Other researchers have found evidence of a greater than expected frequency of problems in social, intellectual, and emotional development in HR children through the age of 4 (Sameroff et al., 1987). However, it is too early to tell whether the early developmental problems identified by these researchers in HR children predict the development of schizophrenia.

At Emory University in Atlanta, researchers have followed the children of schizophrenic, depressed, and normal mothers from birth through 5 years (Goodman, 1987). The children were predominantly African Americans from poor single-parent families. Testing at various age intervals revealed that children of schizophrenic mothers had more problems than the other groups. The schizophrenic offspring were less socially competent than the other children and more often had multiple deficits. Schizophrenic mothers were also rated as providing a poorer child-rearing environment. They were less emotionally responsive and provided fewer learning experiences, toys, and games. HR children may not only carry increased genetic risk; poor rearing by schizophrenic parents may also contribute to early developmental problems.

■ **PROTECTIVE AND VULNERABILITY FACTORS IN HR CHILDREN** Although the reasons are unclear, some HR children are apparently invulnerable to developing schizophrenia, even when they are reared in stressful environments (Weintraub, 1987). Perhaps invulnerable children have some yet unidentified physiological factor that protects them from developing schizophrenia (Marcus et al., 1987). Perhaps environmental factors such as availability of a supportive family environment protects them.

There is some evidence that healthful styles of parental communication, including parental ability to express positive feelings, contributes to the school adjustment of HR children (Wynne et al., 1987). Children whose schizophrenic parents have intermittent acute episodes also show fewer developmental deficits than children of schizophrenic parents with more chronic disorders (Wynne et al., 1987). The Emory University study found that the most socially competent HR children had the most positive child-rearing environments—even within poor single-

Protective factors in high-risk children. A supportive and nurturing environment may reduce the likelihood of developing schizophrenia among high-risk children (that is, children who have one or more schizophrenic biological parents).

parent families. These environments often included a secondary caregiver who helped meet their needs, such as a boyfriend of the mother or a relative (Goodman, 1987).

Although these longitudinal studies have not yet run their course, a number of factors have emerged that may place HR children at greater or lesser risk for developing schizophrenia (see Table 11.2). A limitation of studying HR children as a model of the development of schizophrenia is that it is not clear whether the "markers" which seem to increase vulnerability among children of schizophrenic parents will generalize to the majority of schizophrenics who do not have schizophrenic parents (Goldstein, 1987a).

■ **BIOCHEMICAL FACTORS** Contemporary biological investigations of schizophrenia have focused on the role of the neurotransmitter dopamine (Meltzer, 1987). The **dopamine theory** posits that schizophrenia involves an overreactivity of dopamine receptors in the brain—the receptor sites on postsynaptic neurons into which molecules of dopamine lock (Davis et al., 1991).

Yet schizophrenics do not appear to produce more dopamine than other people. Instead, they appear to *utilize* more of it. But why? Research suggests that schizophrenics may have a greater-than-normal number of dopamine receptors in their brains or that their receptors may be overly sensitive to dopamine (Black et al., 1988; Davis et al., 1991; Mackay et al., 1982; Snyder, 1984).

The dopamine theory evolved from observing the effects of the group of stimulants called **amphet-**

Table 11.2 Possible Risk Factors Associated with Vulnerability to Schizophrenia in Children of Schizophrenics ("HR" children)

High-Risk (Vulnerability) Factors	Low-Risk (Protective) Factors
Maternal anxiety during pregnancy[a]	Lesser severity of maternal illness[b]
Psychotic status of mother in the period of 6 months to 2 years following the birth[a]	Older age of mothers[b]
	Higher education and IQ of mother[b]
Severity of maternal mental illness[c]	Prior work experience of mother[b]
Negative attitudes of mother toward pregnancy[a]	Presence of secondary caregiver (e.g., spouse, boyfriend, or other relative)[b]
Low social class[c]	
Family conflict, marital discord, and lack of parenting skills[d]	Mother's healthy communication with the child, father's expression of positive emotions in a free play situation, and balance between child-initiated and parent-initiated activities in free play situation[e]
Chronic mental illness in the mentally disturbed parent[e]	
Deviant (confused) communication style and expression of hostile feelings toward the child[e]	Absence of severe environmental trauma in the form of pregnancy and birth complications[f]
Attentional deficits and social problems relating to withdrawal and antisocial behavior in males and feelings of social rejection in females[f]	Supportive and nurturing rearing environment[g]
Complications during pregnancy and delivery[g]	

[a]Swedish high-risk study (McNeil & Kaiij, 1978)
[b]Emory University Project on Children of Disturbed Parents (Goodman, 1987)
[c]Rochester Longitudinal Study (Sameroff et al., 1987)
[d]Stony-Brook High-Risk Project (Weintraub, 1987)
[e]University of Rochester Child and Family Study (Wynne et al., 1987)
[f]Israeli high-risk study (Marcus et al., 1987)
[g]Danish high-risk study (Mednick et al., 1987)

amines. It appears that amphetamines increase the concentration of dopamine in the synaptic cleft by blocking its reuptake by presynaptic vesicles. High doses of amphetamines prompt behavior in normal people that mimics paranoid schizophrenia. Among schizophrenics, even low doses of amphetamines exacerbate schizophrenic behavior (Meltzer, 1979; Meltzer & Stahl, 1976; Snyder, 1980; van Kammen, 1977).

Another source of evidence for the dopamine model is found in the effects of the **phenothiazines**, a class of drugs that is often effective in the treatment of schizophrenia. Phenothiazines such as Thorazine and Mellaril apparently block the action of dopamine at the receptor sites on postsynaptic neurons (Creese et al., 1978; Turkington, 1983). As a consequence, phenothiazines inhibit excessive transmission of neural impulses that may give rise to schizophrenic behavior.

Another source of evidence is based on autopsies of deceased schizophrenics. Postmortem exami-

nation of the brains of schizophrenics does show evidence of increased *numbers* of dopamine receptor sites in certain parts of the brain (see Mackay, 1980)—findings consistent with the dopamine hypothesis. However, findings of autopsies may be contaminated by the fact that many subjects had regularly used antipsychotic drugs to treat their disorders, possibly altering their brain chemistry.

Still, the evidence supporting the dopamine theory remains inconclusive. Researchers have not yet determined that overreactivity of dopamine receptors causes schizophrenic behavior. Although most investigators believe that dopamine plays some role in schizophrenia, research suggests that the dopamine hypothesis may not apply to all schizophrenics and that dopamine activity may play a larger role in explaining flagrant behavior patterns (positive symptoms) than the negative symptoms or deficits of schizophrenia (Mackay, 1980; Meltzer, 1987; Meltzer & Stahl, 1976). It also appears that decreased, not increased, dopamine reactivity may be connected with some of the negative symptoms of schizophrenia (Davis et al., 1991; Meltzer, 1987). We also need to learn more about how various neurotransmitters interact to increase our understanding of the biochemistry of schizophrenia.

■ **VIRAL INFECTIONS** Could schizophrenia be caused by a slow-acting virus that attacks the developing brain of a fetus or newborn child? Prenatal rubella (German measles), a viral infection, is a cause of later mental retardation. Could another virus give rise to schizophrenia?

Viral infections are more prevalent in the winter months. The viral theory could therefore account for an excess number of schizophrenics being born in the winter (Hare, 1979). Other factors could also explain seasonal differences in the schizophrenic births, however, such as seasonal variations in nutrition during pregnancy (Hare, 1979). The apparent greater incidence of winter births among schizophrenics may also be a statistical artifact of failure to account for the fact that the incidence of schizophrenia increases with age. That is, individuals born in the early (winter) months of the year might be more likely to be diagnosed as schizophrenic than those born later in the same year because they are slightly older (Lewis, 1989).

What is the connection between schizophrenia and being born in the winter? Evidence that schizophrenics are more likely than other people to be born during winter months has suggested the possibility that viral attacks—which are more common during the winter—may heighten the probability that a fetus or newborn child will develop schizophrenia. Yet direct evidence of a link between schizophrenia and viral infection is lacking.

A Danish study, however, revealed findings that are too powerful to be simply explained by the fact that winter-born children are slightly older than others born in the same year. The Danish study examined the (HR) children of schizophrenic mothers and found that they were most likely to develop schizophrenia when they were born in urban settings during the winter months (Machón et al., 1983). The winter-urban HR children showed a 23.3% incidence of schizophrenia, as compared to 1% in the general population and 8.9% among HR children in general. This evidence seems to support the viral theory because viral infections are also more contagious in congested urban settings, especially during the cold winter months. However, it is not known whether or not the children who developed schizophrenia had actually suffered a viral attack as fetuses or neonates.

Schizophrenics are in fact more likely to have been born during the winter than at other times of the year. However, the reasons for this seasonal variation are unclear.

Note also that in October and early November of 1957, the Finnish capital Helsinki was swept by a serious virus epidemic (Mednick et al., 1987). Sarnoff Mednick and his colleagues studied the incidence of schizophrenia among people who were fetuses during the epidemic. The results are intriguing. People who were exposed to the epidemic during the second trimester of prenatal development had greater-than-average frequencies of admission to a mental hospital with a diagnosis of schizophrenia than people born during the same period of the year during the previous 6 years. They also had more admissions for schizophrenia than people who were exposed to the epidemic during the first or third trimesters of prenatal development (Mednick et al., 1990). Although most of the organ systems are formed during the first trimester, the brain is still undergoing crucial developments during the second trimester. Perhaps it is not merely exposure to a viral infection, but the timing of the exposure during pregnancy, that predicts schizophrenia.

Berquier and Ashton (1991) suggest that birth complications and viral influences may be involved in the development of schizophrenia in genetically vulnerable people. In the absence of an identified viral agent, however, the evidence for the viral theory of schizophrenia remains indirect. Even if viral agents were discovered, they would probably account for but a small fraction of cases of schizophrenia (Meltzer, 1987).

■ **BRAIN ABNORMALITIES**   Brain-imaging methods have revealed evidence of structural abnormalities in the brains of schizophrenics, strengthening the view that brain abnormalities may play a role in schizophrenia.

Positron emission tomography (the PET scan) provides information about the metabolic processes of the brain—that is, the brain's use of oxygen. The faster the metabolic rate, the higher the level of brain activity. PET scans of the brains of schizophrenics find lower-than-normal metabolic rates in the frontal lobes and basal ganglia (Buchsbaum & Haier, 1987; Buchsbaum et al., 1982a) (see Figure 11.2). The frontal lobes and the basal ganglia are involved in the regulation of attention, so these findings coincide with psychological evidence of deficits in attention among schizophrenics. However, the brain metabolism of the scanned schizophrenics may have been affected by their histories of use of antipsychotic medication, even though they were drug free at the time of the study.

Researchers have also examined differences in blood flow to the brain in schizophrenics and normals as an index of differences in rates of brain activity. The bloodstream carries oxygen to the brain, so blood flow is another indicator of metabolic processes. Studies that examined the rate of blood flow to the whole brain have failed to show overall differences between schizophrenics and normals (Buchsbaum & Haier, 1987; Gur et al., 1985), but differences in regional patterns of blood flow have been discovered. Normal people have relatively greater blood flow in the frontal areas of the cerebral cortex as compared to

the posterior regions, whereas schizophrenics show less marked regional differences. These findings are consistent with the brain metabolism studies that show lower-than-normal metabolic rates in schizophrenics in the frontal lobes.

Brain functions in schizophrenics are also studied by means of computer-assisted EEG (electroencephalography) techniques, such as brain-electrical activity mapping (BEAM) and computer electroencephalographic topography (CET). In CET, a computer analyzes the input from electrodes placed at 16 or more points on the scalp. The computer then generates a simulated map of electrical activity of the brain. The various regions of the brain are colored in by the computer with areas of relatively greater activity indicated by "warm" colors (yellows and oranges) and areas of relative inactivity indicated by "cool colors" (blues and purples). CET technology has begun to map out differences such as the following in brain activity between schizophrenics and normals:

1. Schizophrenics produce lower rates of alpha waves than normals (Bernstein et al., 1981; Itil, 1977) (see Figure 11.3). Alpha waves are an idling brain rhythm that usually occurs during times of relaxation or rest, generally with the eyes closed. Alpha activity can be interrupted upon opening the eyes or when the individual is engaged in a cognitive task (Buchsbaum & Haier, 1987).

2. Delta waves may indicate states of drowsiness or lower levels of arousal in the higher (cortical) brain regions (Buchsbaum & Haier, 1987). Schizophrenics have been found to produce higher-than-normal levels of delta waves (Spohn & Patterson, 1979), especially in the

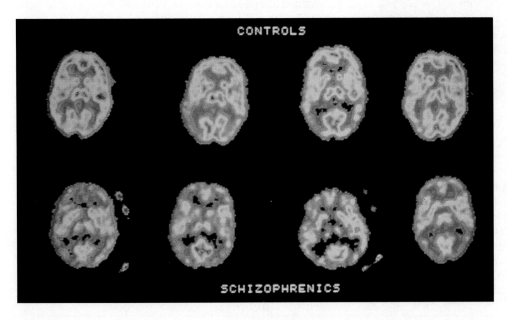

CONTROLS

SCHIZOPHRENICS

Figure 11.2 PET scans of normal people and schizophrenics.
Positron emission tomography (PET scan) evidence of the metabolic processes of the brain show relatively less metabolic activity in the frontal lobes of the brains of schizophrenics. PET scans of the brains of four normal people are shown in the top row, and PET scans of the brains of four schizophrenics are shown below.

Schizophrenia and Other Psychotic Disorders

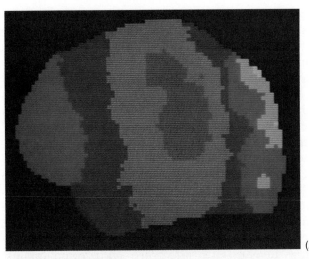
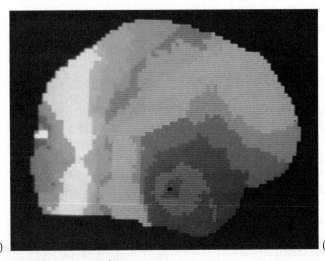

(A)　　　　　　　　　　　　　　　　　　(B)

Figure 11.3 CET maps of the brains of a schizophrenic person as compared to normal individuals.
In computer electroencephalographic topography (CET), a computer generates a map of the electrical activity of the brain from input from electrodes placed at multiple sites on the scalp. The regions of the brain are color coded so that areas of relatively greater activity are indicated by warm colors (yellows and oranges) and areas of relative inactivity are indicated by cool colors (blues and purples). Here we see evidence of lower levels of alpha wave activity in the occipital lobe of the brain of a schizophrenic subject (A) as compared to a composite of 16 normal subjects (B). Alpha waves usually occur during times of relaxation or rest.

frontal lobes (Buchsbaum et al., 1982b; Morihisa et al., 1983). This production is consistent with PET scan findings of lower metabolic rates in the frontal lobes in schizophrenics. Thus, schizophrenics have abnormally low levels of activity, metabolic and electrical, in their frontal lobes.

The significance of these findings in explaining schizophrenia remains undetermined.

Computerized axial tomography (the CAT scan) and magnetic resonance imaging (MRI) have also revealed brain abnormalities among schizophrenics, such as the enlargement of the brain ventricles (the

Figure 11.4 Structural changes in the brain of a schizophrenic patient (top) as compared with that of a normal subject.
The magnetic resonance imaging (MRI) of the brain of the schizophrenic subject (A) shows a relatively shrunken hippocampus (yellow) and relatively enlarged fluid-filled ventricles (gray) when compared to the structures of the normal subject (B). The MRI was conducted by schizophrenia researcher Nancy C. Andreasen.

Source: Gershon, E.S., & Rieder, R.O. (1992). Major disorders of mind and brain. Scientific American, 267, p. 128.

(A)　　　　　　　　　　　　　　　　　　(B)

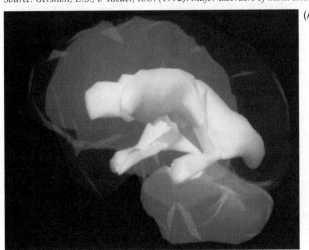
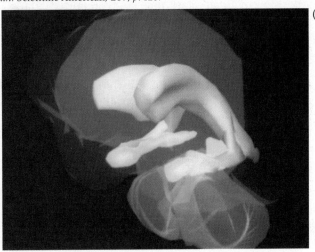

hollow spaces in the brain) and other measures of brain atrophy (Meltzer, 1987; Pandurangi et al., 1988; Raz & Raz, 1990; Shelton & Weinberger, 1986; Weinberger et al., 1983; Weinberger & Wyatt, 1982) (see Figure 11.4). Ventricular enlargement is found to be more prominent among male schizophrenics (Flaum et al., 1990; Raz & Raz, 1990), which is consistent with the view that male schizophrenics are at greater risk of neurological damage than female schizophrenics. Although the causes of ventricular enlargement in schizophrenia remain unknown, increased ventricular size is seen by some as an index of brain damage occurring during pregnancy or early life, which together with a genetic vulnerability may predispose some individuals to schizophrenia (Raz & Raz, 1990). However, evidence of brain deterioration in the brains of mature schizophrenics does not tell us whether or not these signs of brain damage preceded the development of the disorder, or are themselves a consequence of the disorder or its treatment.

Some research suggests that ventricular enlargements are more common among schizophrenics with poorer premorbid histories, poorer response to antipsychotic drugs, greater evidence of negative symptoms, and more chronic cognitive impairment (Andreasen, 1987; Weinberger et al., 1980). Perhaps these structural abnormalities play a greater part in the development of cases whose clinical profiles correspond to Type II schizophrenia, as described by Crow (1980a). Researchers have speculated that this type of schizophrenia may be caused by structural brain damage (loss of vital brain tissue), rather than by disturbances in the reactivity of dopamine receptors. However, some researchers (e.g., Luchins et al., 1983; Pandurangi et al., 1988) have been unable to replicate research that relates negative symptomatology to brain abnormalities such as enlarged ventricles. Evidence that schizophrenics with more negative symptoms have a greater degree of ventricular enlargement thus remains mixed (Andreasen et al., 1990). Moreover, at least one study reported that most schizophrenic subjects were within the normal range for ventricular size (Gur et al., 1991).

Note also that ventricular enlargement may not be unique to schizophrenia. People with bipolar disorder have also been found to show enlarged ventricles, although the enlargement appears to be modest in size and less prominent than that seen in schizophrenia (Swayze et al., 1990).

Magnetic resonance imaging (MRI) also reveals anatomical structures within the brain. One MRI study (Andreasen et al., 1986a) found evidence of smaller-than-normal frontal lobes, craniums, and cerebrums in schizophrenics. Others using MRI have found structural differences between the brains of identical twins in which one twin member was schizophrenic and the other was not (Suddath et al., 1990). Researchers find that in almost all cases the brains of the schizophrenic twin members had larger ventricles and showed more evidence of other structural defects than did the brains of their (nonschizophrenic) co-twins. Studying identical twins offers researchers the advantage of controlling for genetic factors because identical twins have identical genes. Hence, any observed differences between them reflect factors other than genetics. Although genetic factors may account for a predisposition to schizophrenia, the Suddath study shows that other factors must be involved in the brain damage associated with schizophrenia. The nature of these factors—whether they involve viral infections, birth complications, brain traumas suffered early in life or during prenatal development, or environmental influences in childhood—remains an open question. Still, these structural defects may not be related to schizophrenia per se. They may be related to other factors that are connected with schizophrenia, such as histories of stress, hospitalization, and drug therapy.

Researchers have also failed to reveal any particular brain abnormality that is unique to schizophrenia. A number of the abnormalities found in the brains of schizophrenics are also found in the brains of individuals with other diagnoses, such as mood disorders (Meltzer, 1987). The specific role that such abnormalities play in schizophrenia is thus clouded. And so it goes as researchers attempt to disentangle the complex web of factors that account for the mysteries of schizophrenia.

In sum, biological factors are clearly implicated in schizophrenia. Estimates based on family and twin data suggest a heritability factor in schizophrenia of about .76, meaning that 76% of the risk of developing schizophrenia is accounted for by genetic factors and 24% is not (Gottesman et al., 1987). Other estimates of the genetic contribution range from 71 to 91% (Kendler & Robinette, 1983). Yet the specific mode of inheritance in schizophrenia remains unknown (Hallmayer et al., 1992).

Brain imaging reveals evidence of decreased metabolic, circulatory, and electrical activity in areas of the brain that are involved in processes of attention, specifically the frontal lobes. However, the significance of these findings of brain abnormalities remains questionable because they may represent the effects of the disorder and may not be specific to schizophrenia. These brain abnormalities may also be found in some other mental disorders, and their relationship to the symptoms and course of schizophrenia remains unclear (Szymanski et al., 1991). Nor has a definitive biological marker for schizophrenia yet been identified (Szymanski et al., 1991). Some potential markers, like eye movement disorders (see p. 417) may suggest an increased potential for schizophrenia in persons at genetic risk, but even deficiencies in visual tracking are not definite indications that schizophrenia will develop.

All in all, the development of schizophrenia appears to involve a complex interaction of biological, psychological, social, and environmental factors (McGue & Gottesman, 1989; Weiss et al., 1991).

Family Theories

Family theories of schizophrenia examine the contributions of disturbed family relationships to the development and course of schizophrenia.

■ **THE SCHIZOPHRENOGENIC MOTHER** Early family theories of schizophrenia focused on the role of a "pathogenic" family member, such as the **schizophrenogenic mother** (Fromm-Reichmann, 1948, 1950). In what some feminists view as historic psychiatric sexism, the schizophrenogenic mother was described as cold, aloof, overprotective, and domineering. She was characterized as stripping her children of self-esteem, stifling their independence, and forcing them into dependency on her. Children reared by such mothers were believed to be at special risk for developing schizophrenia if their fathers were passive and failed to counteract the pathogenic influences of the mother. Despite extensive research, however, it has not been shown that the mothers of schizophrenics fit the stereotypical picture of the schizophrenogenic mother (Hirsch & Leff, 1975).

 Despite theoretical assumptions, extensive research has *not* shown that schizophrenics have cold, overprotective, "schizophrenogenic" mothers.

■ **THE DOUBLE-BIND HYPOTHESIS** In the 1950s, family theorists began to focus on the role of disturbed communications in the family. One of the more prominent theories, put forth by Gregory Bateson and his colleagues (1956), was that **double-bind communications** contributed to the development of schizophrenia. A double-bind communication transmits two mutually incompatible messages. In a double-bind communication with a child, a mother might freeze up when the child approaches her and then scold the child for keeping a distance. Whatever the child does, she or he is wrong. With repeated exposure to such double binds, the child's thinking may

become disorganized and chaotic. The double-binding mother prevents discussion of her inconsistencies because she cannot admit to herself that she is unable to tolerate closeness. Note this vignette:

> A young man who had fairly well recovered from an acute schizophrenic episode was visited in the hospital by his mother. He was glad to see her and impulsively put his arm around her shoulders whereupon she stiffened. He withdrew his arm and she asked, "Don't you love me anymore?" He then blushed and she said, "Dear, you must not be so easily embarrassed and afraid of your feelings." The patient was able to stay with her only a few minutes more and following her departure he assaulted an aide.
>
> Bateson et al., 1956, p. 251

Perhaps double-bind communications serve as a source of family stress that increase the risk of schizophrenia in genetically vulnerable individuals. In more recent years, investigators have broadened the investigation of family factors in schizophrenia by viewing the family in terms of a system of relationships among the members, rather than singling out mother–child or father–child interactions. Research has begun to identify stressful factors in the family that may interact with a genetic vulnerability in leading to the development of schizophrenia. Two principal sources of family stress that have been studied are patterns of deviant communications and negative emotional expression in the family.

■ **COMMUNICATION DEVIANCE** Communication deviance describes a pattern of parental communication marked by excessive vagueness or blurring of meaning in parental speech and by parental inability to focus in on what the child is saying (Goleman, 1984). Parents who are high in communication deviance tend to attack their children personally rather than offer constructive criticism and may subject them to double-bind communications. They also tend to interrupt the child with intrusive, negative comments. They are prone toward telling the child what she or he "really" thinks rather than allowing the child to formulate her or his own thoughts and feelings (Goleman, 1984).

Parents of schizophrenics show higher levels of communication deviance than parents of nonpsychotic people (Miklowitz et al., 1991). A longitudinal study at UCLA found that parental communication deviance predicted the development of schizophrenia among a sample of behaviorally troubled adolescents who were not schizophrenic at the time of their initial assessment (Goldstein, 1987a, 1987b). Ten of twenty (50%) of the adolescents whose parents were high in communication deviance were diagnosed 15 years later as suffering from a schizophrenia-spectrum disorder (that is, schizophrenia or a related diagnosis like schizotypal personality disorder or schizoaffective disorder). Only 1 in 12 adolescents from low communication deviance families and 5 of 19 from moderate communication deviance families were similarly diagnosed.

Considering the emotional climate in the adolescent's family sharpened the prediction of development of schizophrenia in the UCLA study (Goldstein, 1987b). Adolescents most likely to develop schizophrenia-spectrum disorders were reared by families who interacted in a more negative emotional manner and in which the parents were high in communication deviance. Communication deviance and hostile family interactions may represent two sources of family stress that act, within the diathesis–stress model, to heighten the risk of schizophrenia among genetically vulnerable individuals.

Yet we cannot conclude that communication deviance is causally related to the development of schizophrenia. The causal pathway may work in the opposite direction. Perhaps communication deviance is a parental reaction to the behavior of disturbed children. Parents may learn to use odd language as a way of coping with children who continually interrupt and confront them (Miklowitz et al., 1991). Or perhaps parents and children share genetic traits that become expressed as disturbed communications and increased vulnerability toward schizophrenia, without there being a causal link between the two.

The UCLA study was limited to adolescents who were showing evidence of behavioral disturbance. It remains to be seen whether these factors predict the risk of schizophrenic-type disorders among children who are free of overt behavioral problems. It would also be desirable to study all of the offspring in the family, not just the one at greatest risk, in an effort to determine why some children in disturbed families develop schizophrenic-type disorders and others do not.

■ **EXPRESSED EMOTION**   Another measure of disturbed family communications is labeled expressed emotion (EE). EE focuses on the amount of expressed negative emotion that family members direct toward the schizophrenic family member (Leff & Vaughn, 1985; Vaughn & Leff, 1976, 1981). In research studies, EE is usually measured according to three criteria: the number of critical comments expressed by the relative about the patient; hostility expressed toward the patient (almost always associated with high levels of criticism); and emotional overinvolvement, as shown by excessive protectiveness and intrusive expressions of concern.

Acute episodes among schizophrenics in low EE families have been found to recur less frequently in

the first 2 years following hospitalization than they do in high EE families (Leff & Vaughn, 1981) (see Figure 11.5). Low EE families may actually serve to protect, or buffer, the schizophrenic individual from the adverse impact of outside stressors and help prevent recurrent episodes (Strachan, 1986). EE has also been shown to predict recurrence even when the initial level of disturbance of the schizophrenic's behavior is statistically controlled (Brown et al., 1972). EE in the family also appears unrelated to the degree of abnormality in the schizophrenic's behavior at discharge (Vaughn & Leff, 1976). Taken together, these data suggest that high EE may play a causal role in determining the course of schizophrenia (Strachan, 1986) and is not simply a reaction of the family to greater deviance on the schizophrenic's part. However, questions of cause and effect remain unresolved; other behavioral differences between the schizophrenics in high and low EE families may account for differences in outcomes, rather than the differences in their families per se. Moreover, most of the research showing relationships between EE status and recurrence have been conducted on male schizophrenics (Hogarty, 1985), so the relevance of the findings to female schizophrenics remains unknown. We should also note that many schizophrenics are detached from their families and have little if any

Figure 11.5   Relapse rates of schizophrenics in high and low EE families.
Schizophrenics whose families are high in expressed emotion (EE) are at greater risk of relapse than those whose families are low in EE. Whereas low-EE families may help protect the schizophrenic family member from environmental stressors, high-EE families may impose additional stress.
Source: Adapted from Leff & Vaughn (1981).

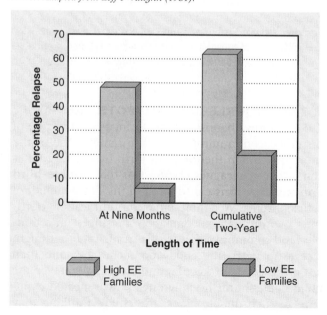

Families of Schizophrenics: Roles for Cultural Factors

Relationships between expressed emotion and rates of recurrence of schizophrenia have been drawn largely from research with non-Hispanic white samples in England and the United States (Karno et al., 1987). Because family patterns are often influenced by cultural factors, researchers have begun to explore whether the EE construct has value in predicting recurrence of schizophrenia in other cultures. Some cross-cultural support for the prognostic value of the construct comes from a study of low-income, relatively unacculturated Mexican-American family members of schizophrenic patients (Karno et al., 1987). Paralleling findings with the non-Hispanic white British and American families, high levels of EE (that is, critical, hostile, and emotionally overinvolved attitudes and behaviors) among key family members in the Mexican-American sample were associated with an increased risk of relapse among schizophrenic family members who lived with their families after hospitalization.

Some cross-cultural differences in EE have also begun to emerge. Much lower prevalences of high EE behaviors, as compared with the non-Hispanic white British and American families, were found among the Mexican-American families and among another sample of family members of schizophrenics from northern India (Wig et al., 1987). The non-Hispanic white families thus tended to be more openly critical of their schizophrenic family members than were family members from these other cultural backgrounds.

Other researchers find that the extended family structure often found in traditional cultures may offer an emotional and financial buffer against the hardships imposed by the schizophrenic's behavioral excesses and deficiencies. In Western settings, these burdens are more likely to be borne by the nuclear family (Lefley, 1990). Such differences remind us of the need to take cultural factors into account when examining relationships between family factors and schizophrenia.

contact with them (Goldstein, 1987b). Family factors thus cannot account for recurrent episodes among them.

The EE construct has been criticized by relatives who feel that they are being blamed by mental health professionals for the disturbed family member's problems (Strachan, 1986). However, research on EE and other family stress factors helps focus attention on the need to help family members change their style of relating to each other, which may reduce the stress imposed on the schizophrenic member (Leff et al., 1982) and improve family harmony.

■ **FAMILY FACTORS IN SCHIZOPHRENIA: CAUSES OR SOURCES OF STRESS**   There is little if any evidence that families are responsible for directly causing schizophrenia in their offspring. If rearing factors cause schizophrenia, we would expect that the foster (nonbiologically related) siblings of adoptees who become schizophrenic, and who were reared by the same adoptive parents, would be at greater risk of schizophrenia than the biological siblings of these schizophrenic adoptees who were reared in different families (Kety, 1980). However, evidence from a study in Iceland shows just the opposite results. The biological siblings of 8 schizophrenic adoptees showed a greater prevalence of schizophrenia than did their foster siblings (Karlsson, 1966). Similar findings were obtained based on a sample of 12 schizophrenic adoptees in Denmark (Kety, 1980). The small numbers of schizophrenic adoptees in these studies limits the significance of their findings, however.

Moreover, the (HR) offspring of schizophrenic parents who are reared in some other environment are about as likely to develop schizophrenia as HR children who are reared by their own (schizophrenic) parents (Heston, 1966; Karlsson, 1966; Kety et al., 1968, 1975; Marcus et al., 1987; Rosenthal et al., 1968). Too, children who are born to normal parents but reared by schizophrenic adoptive parents are not at greater-than-normal risk of developing schizophrenic disorders (Wender et al., 1974). Nor is there empirical support for the view that family factors can account for schizophrenia in children who do not have a genetic vulnerability.

What then is the role of family factors in schizophrenia? Disturbed patterns of emotional interaction and communication in the family may represent a source of stress that may increase the likelihood of the development or recurrence of schizophrenia among individuals with a genetic disposition for the disorder. Some researchers suggest that the less contact schizophrenics have with high-stress relatives, the better they are able to function in the community (Vaughn & Leff, 1976). Removing schizophrenics from stressful family environments for at least some part of the day through sheltered workshops, employment, and day treatment programs may lessen the impact of high-stress families and improve the chances of successful community adjustment. Outcomes may also be improved if schizophrenics and their families are taught ways of coping with stress, and if families are taught to be less critical and more supportive of their schizophrenic members. Counseling programs that help family members of chronic schizophrenics learn to express their feelings without attacking or criticizing the schizophrenic may help prevent family conflicts that damage the schizophrenic's adjustment (Spiegel & Wissler, 1986).

Sociocultural Perspectives

The sociocultural model views schizophrenic behavior in terms of the relationship between the individual and society. Researchers suspect that such factors as overcrowding, poor diet and sanitation, and inadequate health care contribute to increased risk of schizophrenia, at least among people with a genetic vulnerability (Kety, 1980). Some adherents to the sociocultural model believe that it is necessary to eradicate social ills or stressors that may give rise to schizophrenic behavior, such as poverty, discrimination, and overcrowding, rather than focus on changing the behavior of schizophrenic people.

Research findings show that schizophrenia is most common among the lower socioeconomic classes (Kety, 1980). A classic study conducted by Hollingshead and Redlich (1958) in New Haven, Connecticut, showed that the rate of schizophrenia was twice as high among the lowest socioeconomic class than among the second lowest. More recent evidence from the ECA study showed that schizophrenia was five times more prevalent at the lowest rung of the socioeconomic ladder than it was at the highest (Keith et al., 1991). Low socioeconomic status may be a *consequence* and not an *antecedent* of schizophrenia, however. Schizophrenics may drift downward in social status because they lack the social skills and cognitive abilities to function at higher levels. Disproportionate numbers of schizophrenics may thus wind up in impoverished areas.

Evidence for the hypothesis that schizophrenics drift downward in socioeconomic status is mixed. Some evidence is supportive (Turner & Wagonfield, 1967); other evidence is not (Dunham, 1965; Hollingshead & Redlich, 1958). Perhaps both views are partly correct. Although many schizophrenics drift downward occupationally in comparison to their fathers' occupations, many schizophrenics are also reared in families from the lower socioeconomic classes. The stresses of poverty may thus also play a role in the development of schizophrenia.

Other sociocultural theorists have attempted to explain schizophrenic behavior in terms of the social role of the mental patient in society. Thomas Scheff (1966), for example, claims that once mental patients are assigned a diagnostic label, like schizophrenia, they are selectively reinforced for behavior that is consistent with the label. Mental patients act crazy, in other words, because they are expected to do so. Scheff's theory may help to explain the **institutionalization syndrome**, a pattern of behavior of institutional residents associated with passivity and dependency. Patients in institutions are frequently rewarded for following orders, not complaining, and not making personal decisions. Although role theory may explain some aspects of schizophrenic behavior, especially in institutional settings, it does not account for disturbances in thinking and perception, such as thought disorder and hallucinations.

The Scottish psychiatrist R. D. Laing straddles the sociocultural and humanistic-existential perspectives. He views the schizophrenic's flight into fantasy as a means of coping with intolerably stressful life conditions. Laing regards schizophrenia as a search for a more authentic identity in a world that squelches individuality and requires people to adopt socially acceptable public selves, or "masks." The stresses of conforming can shatter the facade of socially acceptable behavior and cause the individual to retreat into a private fantasy world. In this private world, the schizophrenic undertakes a personal journey of discovery to find her or his true inner self. Laing regards schizophrenia as a valiant act of defiance, not as an illness. To Laing, schizophrenia "is a special sort of strategy that a person invents in order to live in an unlivable situation" (1964, p. 186).

In Laing's view, schizophrenic speech is not meaningless chatter. Laing argues that we should try to understand the meaning that these behaviors hold for the individual in light of the way the individual experiences herself or himself in the world. Schizophrenics need guidance and support to help them resolve the split between their true and false selves and to give their lives new meaning.

Laing and his followers established therapeutic residences built on his theoretical model. In such residences, deviant behavior is tolerated more so than in traditional treatment centers, and schizophrenics are encouraged to reach a more authentic identity. However, there is little if any evidence to support the therapeutic value of Laing's approach. On the other hand, Laing's assertion that schizophrenia reflects family pressures and stress has received some support from research on family factors in schizophrenia.

TREATMENT

There is no cure for schizophrenia. Treatment of the disorder is often multifaceted, incorporating chemotherapeutic, psychological, and rehabilitative approaches.

Most schizophrenics in organized mental health settings are treated with some form of antipsychotic medication, which is intended to control the more flagrant behavior patterns—such as hallucinations and delusions—and to decrease the risk of recurrent episodes among schizophrenics without active (positive) symptoms.

Biological Approaches

Various biological approaches have been used in the treatment of schizophrenia, including electroconvulsive therapy (ECT), psychosurgery, and chemotherapy. Today psychosurgery has been all but discontinued, and ECT is used only rarely with schizophrenics. Chemotherapy is the principal method of treatment.

The advent of antipsychotic drugs—also referred to as major tranquilizers or *neuroleptics*—in the 1950s revolutionized the treatment of schizophrenia and provided the impetus for large-scale releases of mental patients to the community (deinstitutionalization). Medication has helped control the more flagrant behavior patterns of schizophrenia and reduced the need for long-term hospitalization (Bellack, 1986; Mackay, 1980; Spohn et al., 1986). Yet for many mental patients today, entering a hospital is like going through a revolving door. That is, they are repeatedly admitted and discharged within relatively brief time frames (Bellack & Mueser, 1990). Many are simply discharged to the streets once they are stabilized on medication and receive little if any follow-up care, which often leads to a pattern of chronic homelessness punctuated by brief stays in the hospital. Only a small proportion of schizophrenics who are discharged from long-term care facilities are successfully reintegrated into the community (Bellack & Mueser, 1990).

Some of the more common classes of antipsychotic drugs include the phenothiazines chlorpromazine (Thorazine), thioridazine (Mellaril), trifluoperazine (Stelazine), and fluphenazine (Prolixin). Haloperidol (Haldol) is chemically distinct from the phenothiazines but produces similar effects (Crammer et al., 1982). The ways in which these drugs lessen psychotic behaviors are not fully known. Evidence is accumulating, however, that their therapeutic action involves the blocking of dopamine receptors in the brain (Marder & May, 1986). Another type of drug, clozapine (trade name Clozaril) was approved for use in 1990. Researchers suspect that clozapine has a broader spectrum of action than other neuroleptics. It appears to affect both dopamine and norepinephrine receptors in the brain and to help alleviate negative as well as positive symptoms of schizophrenia (Honigfeld & Patin, 1991; Pickar et al.,

1992). Other neuroleptics have been generally less effective in reducing negative symptoms.

The effectiveness of antipsychotic drugs has been repeatedly demonstrated in double-blind, placebo-controlled studies. Yet a substantial minority of schizophrenics receive little benefit from traditional neuroleptics, and there are no clear-cut factors that determine who will best respond (Bellack, 1986; Kane, 1987; May & Goldberg, 1978). Empirical studies and reviews of the literature reveal that clozapine helps one-third to two-thirds of seriously disturbed schizophrenic patients who do not respond to other neuroleptics such as Thorazine and Prolixin (Green & Salzman, 1990; Perry et al., 1991; Pickar et al., 1992). A German study was even more optimistic. It found that 85% of treatment-resistant schizophrenics who were treated with clozapine showed some improvement (Naber & Hippius, 1990). Schizophrenics who do not respond to other drugs but who are given clozapine also show reduced rates of rehospitalization and hospitalization costs (Honigfeld & Patin, 1991).

Yet medication alone is insufficient to meet the multifaceted needs of schizophrenics. Green and Salzman (1990) note that even clozapine needs to be supplemented with psychosocial and psychoeducational programs to help patients develop better social skills and adjust to demands of community living. Researchers recognize that a comprehensive model of care is needed, which might include such elements as medication, medical care, family therapy, social skills training, crisis intervention, rehabilitation services, housing and other social services, and provisions to ensure a continuity of care between the hospital and the community (Bellack & Mueser, 1990).

Schizophrenics typically receive maintenance doses of antipsychotic drugs once their flagrant symptoms abate. Continued medication reduces the risk of recurrent episodes and rehospitalization (Carpenter, 1986; Kane, 1987) (see Figure 11.6). One study compared a continuous medication regimen to a targeted medication approach in which medication was withdrawn and readministered only if symptoms worsened. Continuous medication resulted in less frequent rehospitalizations and more days employed during a 2-year period (Carpenter et al., 1990). But continued medication is no panacea. Half (50%) of the schizophrenics who were maintained reliably on long-acting injectible medication had recurrent episodes (Hogarty, 1979). Problems with recurrent episodes cannot simply be attributed to failure to take the drugs as prescribed (Kane, 1987; Strachan, 1986).

The literature shows that the long-term use of traditional neuroleptic drugs (other than clozapine) may cause a potentially irreversible form of brain damage called **tardive dyskinesia** (TD). TD is a movement disorder that affects the face, mouth,

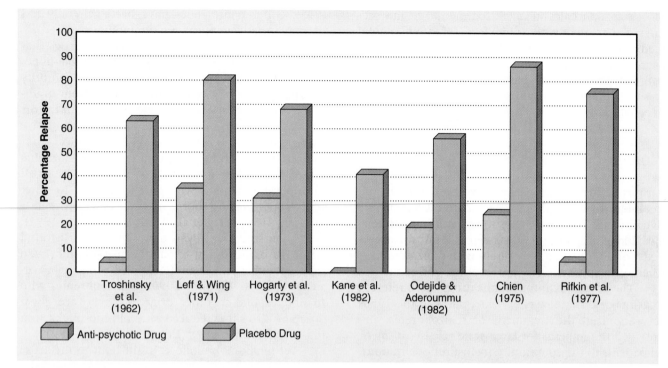

Figure 11.6 Relapse rates at 12-month follow-ups: Maintenance drug versus placebo.
Many studies show that schizophrenic patients who are switched to placebo drugs once they are discharged from the hospital are significantly more likely to relapse than schizophrenics who receive antipsychotic drugs.

neck, trunk, or extremities. TD generally occurs among persons who are treated with antipsychotics for 6 months or longer (Marder & May, 1986). It can take different forms, the most common of which is frequent eye blinking (Gardos et al., 1987). Other signs of TD consist of mouth and eye movements, lip smacking and puckering, facial grimacing, and involuntary movements of the limbs and trunk (Marder & May, 1986). The risk of TD seems to increase with age, and TD is especially common among older female patients (Smith & Baldessarini, 1980). Although most TD-related problems in movement are mild, some affected individuals become seriously disabled and have difficulties breathing, talking, or eating (Marder & May, 1986). No treatment for TD has been shown to be both safe and effective (Kane, 1987). Although some schizophrenics with TD show improvement when antipsychotic drugs are discontinued, many remain permanently and severely disabled.

TD occurs with alarming frequency among patients treated for extended periods with antipsychotic drugs (Carpenter, 1986). The rate among those treated for a year or longer has been estimated to be at least 10 to 20% (Task Force Report, American Psychiatric Association, 1980). Others estimate that about 4% of antipsychotic drug users will develop the

disorder each year for at least the first 5 or 6 years of treatment (Kane et al., 1986a). The risk of these potentially disabling side effects requires physicians to carefully weigh the risks and benefits of long-term treatment with these drugs (Kane, 1987).

Various treatment strategies are being explored to lower the risk of TD, such as lower dosages and intermittent (noncontinuous) regimens (Carpenter, 1986). Patients who receive lower doses of these drugs also exhibit a significantly lower incidence of early signs of TD (Kane et al., 1985; Kane et al., 1986b), but the long-term safety and efficacy of this approach need to be established. Preliminary findings suggest that dosages as low as 10 to 20% of customary levels may be nearly as effective in reducing the incidence of recurrent episodes (Carpenter, 1986). Low-dosage patients who experience recurrent psychotic behaviors can often be restabilized in the community by means of a stepped-up dosage of medication (Kane, 1987). Then dosages may be lowered again.

Clozapine apparently does not lead to TD (Fischbach, 1992), but it has other side effects. The primary concern is agranulocytosis, a potentially lethal disorder in which the body produces inadequate supplies of white blood cells. The disorder affects 1 to 2% of patients who use the drug (Green &

Salzman, 1990; Honigfeld & Patin, 1991). Because the onset of agranulocytosis is suggested by lowered white blood cell counts, users of clozapine receive regular blood tests (Freudenheim, 1991; Honigfeld & Patin, 1990; Miller, 1993). Another concern is the risk of seizures, which is apparently dose related. About 1 patient in 10 who takes clozapine for 1 year will experience seizures (Green & Salzman, 1990).

Perhaps as many as 20% of schizophrenics do not require continuous antipsychotic medication to maintain themselves in the community (Fenton & McGlashan, 1987). Schizophrenics who have acquired social and occupational skills, and those who are recovering from an initial acute episode, may be less likely to need maintenance medication. The social or family environment faced upon discharge from the hospital may also help determine the schizophrenic's ability to adapt to the community with or without medication. Yet clinicians are presently unable to determine with reasonable accuracy which schizophrenics can manage effectively without continued medication.

 Antipsychotic medications do *not* cure schizophrenia. In most cases they do help control the bizarre, flagrant behavior patterns that characterize acute episodes.

Psychoanalytic Approaches

Freud did not believe that traditional psychoanalysis was well suited to the treatment of schizophrenia. Schizophrenics' withdrawal into a fantasy world would prevent them from forming a meaningful relationship with the psychoanalyst. The techniques of classical psychoanalysis, Freud wrote, must "be replaced by others; and we do not know yet whether we shall succeed in finding a substitute" (cited in Arieti, 1974, p. 532).

Other psychoanalysts such as Harry Stack Sullivan and Frieda Fromm-Reichmann adapted psychoanalytic techniques specifically for schizophrenics. However, research has failed to demonstrate the effectiveness of psychoanalytic or psychodynamic therapy with schizophrenics (Carpenter, 1986; Gunderson et al., 1984; May & Tuma, 1976; Mosher & Keith, 1980; Stanton et al., 1984). In one carefully controlled study (May & Tuma, 1976), for example, psychoanalytic treatment proved to be less effective than antipsychotic drugs. Nor did psychoanalytic treatment increase the effectiveness of drug therapy when the two were combined. In light of such results, some critics have argued that further research on the use of psychodynamic therapies with schizophrenics is not warranted (Klerman, 1984). Perhaps

MULTICULTURAL PERSPECTIVES

Treatment of Schizophrenia Among Asian Americans

 Ethnic differences may come into play in determining medication dosages for effective treatment of schizophrenia and sensitivity to side effects. Asians, for example, tend to require smaller doses of neuroleptics than Caucasians to achieve an optimal response. Asians also tend to experience more side effects from the same dosage.

Ethnicity may also play a role in the family's involvement in the treatment process. Researchers report that in a study of 26 Asian-American and 26 white American schizophrenics, family members of the Asian subjects were more frequently involved in the treatment program (Lin et al., 1991). For example, the Asian-American patients were more likely to be accompanied to their medication evaluation sessions by family members. The authors believe that the greater family involvement among Asian Americans represents the relatively stronger sense of family responsibility in Asian cultures. Non-Hispanic white Americans are more likely to emphasize individualism and self-responsibility.

This finding highlights the value of working with the family in treating Asian-American schizophrenics. The failure of clinicians to include the family often compromises the value of therapy among Asian Americans and causes many of them to drop out of therapy prematurely (Lin et al., 1978). Yet these findings also underscore the need to enlist greater participation from family members of white-American schizophrenics. The neglect or rejection of the schizophrenic within the family may play an important role in premature treatment termination and poorer outcomes.

supportive psychoeducational approaches that help prepare schizophrenics for societal roles, in combination with drug treatment, would be more helpful than psychodynamic approaches (Kane, 1987).

Learning-Based Approaches

Behavioral or learning-based approaches to schizophrenia generally involve the direct modification of schizophrenic behaviors and the development of more adaptive behaviors. Learning-based approaches are problem oriented and help prepare schizophrenics for community roles. Therapy methods include techniques such as (1) selective reinforcement of behavior (like providing staff attention for appropriate behavior and extinguishing bizarre verbalizations through withdrawal of staff attention); (2) the token economy, in which individuals are rewarded for appropriate behavior with tokens, such as plastic chips, that can be exchanged for tangible reinforcers such as desirable goods or privileges; and (3) social skills training, in which clients are taught conversation skills and other appropriate social behaviors through coaching, modeling, behavior rehearsal, and feedback.

■ **SOCIAL-LEARNING PROGRAMS** Promising results have emerged from studies applying intensive learning-based approaches in hospital settings. A classic study by Paul and Lentz (1977) compared traditional hospital treatment of chronic schizophrenics with two intensive psychosocial programs that were intended to enhance independent functioning. One applied social-learning principles to help schizophrenics acquire more appropriate behaviors. The other, milieu therapy, was based on the model of the **therapeutic community** and involved schizophrenics in group decision making. The subjects in the study were considered hard-core schizophrenics who had been generally unresponsive to antipsychotic medication (Paul et al., 1972).

The psychosocial treatments were run on adjoining wards and shared some common features. Subjects in both could progress through a series of steps toward less restrictive treatment settings, earn greater privileges, and assume more responsibilities along the way. Both programs were run around the clock.

The social-learning program employed a token economy. Behaviors reinforced by tokens included attendance at meetings, maintenance of proper grooming, and appropriate verbal communications. Tokens could be exchanged for rewards like food, privacy time, passes, and other privileges. Signs were posted that listed the numbers of tokens available for performing specific behaviors and the numbers of tokens needed to earn particular rewards.

In the milieu program, subjects were divided into small living groups that were responsible for delegating responsibilities, such as preparing meals. Groups were encouraged to spend free time together and to use peer pressure to promote adaptive behavioral changes. Subjects and staff held group meetings to discuss and vote on issues that affected living conditions on the ward. This exercise in democracy may not seem so radical an idea, but the typical mental hospital at the time of the study tended to treat patients like dependent children, telling them how to behave and offering them little responsibility. The therapeutic community attempts to involve schizophrenics in the governing process as a way of preparing them for responsible community roles upon discharge.

Both psychosocial treatments yielded significantly better results than the standard hospital regimen, as measured by increased adaptive behavior in the hospital, decreased need for medication, and improved community functioning. The social-learning program also produced markedly better results than the milieu treatment (see Figure 11.7). Schizophrenics in the social-learning program reduced the frequency of bizarre behavior to a small fraction of baseline levels—at far less cost than the comparison treatments. The average social-learning program participant improved by more than 1,200% in overall measures of interpersonal and communicative skills. Perhaps the most telling statistics involved discharge and community tenure because the ultimate goal of treating hospitalized patients is to restore them to successful functioning in the community. Nearly all of the social-learning program subjects (97.5%) were able to be discharged and to remain in the community for a minimum of 90 days, as compared to 71% of the milieu-therapy participants and 45% of the control (standard treatment) participants. Social-learning program participants also remained in the community longer than participants in the other conditions.

From the standpoint of clinical effectiveness and cost of treatment, it is clear that the intensive social-learning program was the treatment of choice (Glynn & Mueser, 1986). However, there are prerequisites that may limit the applicability of this approach. Such programs require strong administrative support, skilled treatment leaders, extensive staff training, and continuous quality control (Glynn & Mueser, 1986).

■ **SOCIAL SKILLS TRAINING** Social skills training programs apply principles of social-learning theory to teach participants specific social and vocational skills. Social skills training has been used extensively (Morrison & Bellack, 1984) to help schizophrenics acquire specific social skills such as assertiveness skills and general conversational skills. Such skills facilitate adjustment in the community.

Although different approaches to skills training have been developed, the basic model uses role-playing exercises within a group format. Participants practice skills such as starting or maintaining conversations with new acquaintances and receive feedback and reinforcement from the therapist and other group members (Liberman et al., 1986). The first step might be a dry run in which the participant role-plays the targeted behavior, such as asking strangers for bus directions. The therapist and other group members then praise the effort and provide constructive

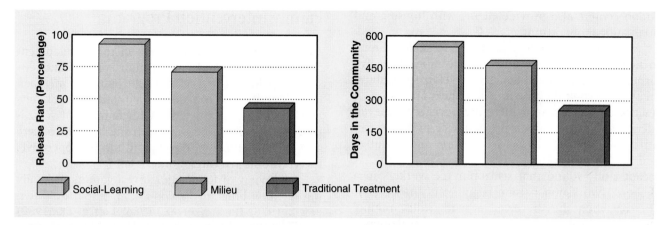

Figure 11.7 Some measures of outcome from the Paul and Lentz study.
This figure shows the release rates and community tenure (days in the community) of schizophrenics in the three conditions studied by Paul and Lentz: (1) social-learning-based treatment, (2) milieu treatment, and (3) traditional hospital treatment. Nearly all of the subjects in the social-learning program (97.5%) were able to be discharged and to remain in the community for a minimum of 90 days, as compared to 71% of the milieu therapy participants and 45% of the control (standard treatment) participants. Subjects in the social-learning program also remained in the community longer than subjects who received the other conditions.

Source: Glynn & Mueser (1986).

feedback. Role playing is augmented by techniques such as modeling (observation of the therapist or other group members enacting the desired behavior), direct instruction (specific directions for enacting the desired behavior), shaping (reinforcement for successive approximations to the target behavior), and coaching (therapist use of verbal or nonverbal prompts to elicit a particular desired behavior in the role play). Participants are given homework assignments to practice the behaviors in the settings in which they live, such as on the hospital ward or in the community. The aim is to enhance generalization or transfer of training to other settings. Training sessions may also be run in stores, restaurants, schools, and other **in vivo** settings.

Several controlled studies report success for social skills training as a means of improving interpersonal behavior (Bellack et al., 1984; Eisler et al., 1978; Hogarty, 1986; Wallace & Liberman, 1985). Reviews of outcome studies reveal that social skills training for schizophrenics has led to marked improvements in various social skills, including assertiveness skills, conversational skills, and job interview skills (Bellack & Mueser, 1990; Benton & Schroeder, 1990). Social skills training can also be credited with improved discharge rates and reductions in relapse rates. Yet social skills training has had only modest effects on overall measures of functioning, which suggests that it is not the solution to all of the problems faced by schizophrenics. Social skills

training is perhaps most appropriately seen as one component of a multifaceted treatment approach.

Psychosocial Rehabilitation

Schizophrenics typically have difficulties functioning in social and occupational roles. These problems limit their ability to adjust to community life even in the absence of overt psychotic behavior. Many older long-hospitalized schizophrenics who have been resettled in the community are particularly ill prepared to handle the tasks of daily living, such as cooking, shopping, or traveling around town. Many younger schizophrenics have markedly deficient social skills, even though they have spent only short periods of time in mental hospitals (Anthony & Liberman, 1986).

A number of self-help clubs and more structured psychosocial rehabilitation centers have sprung up to help schizophrenics find places in society. Many centers were launched by nonprofessionals or by schizophrenics themselves because mental health agencies often failed to provide comparable services (Anthony & Liberman, 1986). Early examples of self-help clubs were Fountain House and Horizon House, both of which were founded by formerly hospitalized schizophrenics. Each provided clients with social support and assistance. Multiservice psychosocial rehabilitation centers also provide clients with housing and occupational opportunities.

These centers often make use of skills training to help clients learn how to handle money, resolve disputes with family members, develop friendships, take buses, cook their own meals, shop, and so on. A review of the research literature reveals that even clients with severe abnormal behavior problems can learn useful skills relating to self-care, and cognitive and social functioning (Anthony et al., 1984). A recent study found that schizophrenic workers in a sheltered workshop became significantly more productive when they received a work skills training program which contained the following elements: direct instruction in specific job tasks, step-by-step modeling of task performance, and rehearsal of tasks with corrective and positive feedback from the trainer and co-workers (Sauter & Nevid, 1991).

The rehabilitation model teaches that disabled individuals can achieve their potentials if they are given the support and structure they need and if the expectations and demands placed on them are consistent with their capacities. Both the client and the family should be helped to adjust their expectations to attainable levels (Anthony & Liberman, 1986).

Development of community support programs and tax incentives for employers who hire mental patients are additional examples of how society can help provide mental patients with the support they need to lead more productive lives. Consider the following case:

> *A 30-year-old male with a 15-year history of being in and out of private and state psychiatric hospitals decided he would like to get a job in the community after being in a psychosocial work adjustment program for 1 year. He did not have a good work history; for example, 6 months was the longest he had ever been able to hold a job. Using the targeted job tax credit legislation as an incentive to the employer, the psychiatric rehabilitation team was able to find the disabled person a job working in a video repair shop, a job consistent with the client's interests and talents. To keep his job at the repair shop, the client needed to learn the skills of taking orders from authority figures (showing understanding of what others say and expressing his own thoughts and feelings to others). The team also made the environment more supportive of the client by educating the employer to the client's needs. The team obtained employer agreement on reducing the initial work load until the disabled person became comfortable with the new environment.*

> ■ *Adapted from Anthony and Liberman, 1986, p. 553*

Family Intervention Programs

Family conflict may play a role in the development and course of schizophrenia. Family conflicts and tensions can heap stress on the schizophrenic member, increasing the risk of recurrent episodes. Researchers and clinicians have worked with families of schizophrenics to help them cope with the burdens of care and to assist them in developing more cooperative, less confrontative ways of interrelating.

A review of four major investigations of family intervention programs (Faloon et al., 1982; Goldstein et al., 1978; Hogarty et al., 1986; Leff et al., 1982) revealed that, as compared to control groups, each program produced significant reductions in rates of recurrent schizophrenic episodes at 6- to 9-month follow-ups (Strachan, 1986). All of the schizophrenic subjects in these studies, those treated within a family treatment approach and controls, received continuous medication. Thus, the effects of family intervention added to the effects accounted for by medication. Although there were differences in the programs, they all shared features such as a focus on the practical aspects of everyday living, educating family members about schizophrenia and teaching them how to relate to the schizophrenic family member, improving communication in the family, and fostering effective coping skills for handling family problems and disputes.

Controlled investigations of family intervention programs have consistently demonstrated reductions in the risk of recurrent episodes as compared to pure drug treatment or drug treatment plus individual therapy (Goldstein, 1987b). One question that remains unanswered is whether these approaches prevent recurrent episodes or merely delay them (Goldstein, 1987b). Nor do all schizophrenics live with their families. Perhaps similar psychoeducational programs can be applied to nonfamily environments for schizophrenics, such as foster care homes or board-and-care homes (Strachan, 1986).

 Teaching families how to relate to schizophrenic members and solve family problems has been shown to reduce the incidence of recurrent acute episodes.

In sum, no single treatment approach meets all the needs of schizophrenics. An integrated, comprehensive model of treatment may be most effective in helping schizophrenics achieve maximal social adjustment (Anthony & Liberman, 1986). This model may consist of drug therapy, hospitalization as needed, hospital-based social-learning programs, family intervention programs, skills training programs, social self-help clubs, and rehabilitation programs.

DELUSIONAL DISORDER

It may surprise you to learn that some forms of paranoid thinking affect normal people from time to time. Most of us feel suspicious of other people's motives at times or feel that others may have it in for us or are talking about us behind our backs. Among normals, however, paranoid thinking is usually short lived and does not disrupt daily functioning (Haynes, 1986).

People who hold persistent, clearly delusional paranoid beliefs may be classified as suffering from a **delusional disorder**. The diagnosis applies to people with persistent delusions that often but not always involve paranoid themes. In delusional disorders, the delusional beliefs concern events that may possibly occur, such as the infidelity of a spouse, persecution by others, or attracting the love of a famous person. The apparent plausibility of these beliefs may lead others to take them seriously and check them out before concluding that they are unfounded. Apart from the delusion, the individual's behavior does not show evidence of obviously bizarre or odd behavior, as we see in the following case:

*M*r. *Polsen, a married 42-year-old postal worker, was brought to the hospital by his wife because he had been insisting that there was a contract out on his life. Mr. Polsen told the doctors that the problem had started some four months ago when he was accused by his supervisor of tampering with a package, an offense that could have cost him his job. When he was exonerated at a formal hearing, his supervisor was "furious" and felt publically humiliated, according to Mr. Polsen. Shortly afterwards, Mr. Polsen reported, his co-workers began avoiding him, turning away from him when he walked by, as if they didn't want to see him. He then began to think that they were talking about him behind his back, although he could never clearly make out what they were saying. He gradually became convinced that his co-workers were avoiding him because his boss had put a contract on his life. Things remained about the same for two months, when Mr. Polsen began to notice several large white cars cruising up and down the street where he lived. This frightened him and he became convinced there were hit men in these cars. He then refused to leave his home without an escort and would run home in panic when he saw one of these cars approaching. Other than the reports*

of his belief that his life was in danger, his thinking and behavior appeared entirely normal on interview. He denied experiencing hallucinations and showed no other signs of psychotic behavior, except for the queer beliefs about his life being in danger. The diagnosis of Delusional Disorder, Persecutory type seemed the most appropriate, since there was no evidence that a contract had been taken on his life (hence, a persecutory delusion) and there was an absence of other clear signs of psychosis that might support a diagnosis of a schizophrenic type disorder.

■ *Adapted from Spitzer et al., 1989, pp. 122–123*

Mr. Polsen's delusional belief that "hit teams" were pursuing him was treated with antipsychotic medication in the hospital setting and faded in about 3 weeks. His belief that he had been the subject of an attempted "hit" stuck in his mind, however. A month following admission, he stated, "I guess my boss has called off the contract. He couldn't get away with it now without publicity" (Spitzer et al., 1989, p. 123).

Although delusions frequently occur in schizophrenia, delusional disorders are believed to be distinct from schizophrenia. Persons with delusional disorders do not exhibit the confused or jumbled thinking that is characteristic of schizophrenia. Hallucinations, when they occur, are not as prominent. Delusions in schizophrenia are embedded within a larger array of disturbed thoughts, perceptions, and behavior. In delusional disorders, the delusion itself may be the only clear sign of abnormality. Also, the paranoid content in paranoid schizophrenia is generally less coherent and more bizarre than that of delusional disorders. Whereas schizophrenics may believe that their minds are controlled by "psychics" or other external forces, paranoid thinking in delusional disorders often seems plausible. Unlike schizophrenics, persons with delusional disorders are generally able to function effectively in their work, although their interpersonal relationships may suffer because of their delusional concerns. Such people appear quite normal when their delusions are not being discussed.

Delusional disorders should also be distinguished from another disorder in which paranoid thinking is present—paranoid personality disorder. People with paranoid personality disorders may hold exaggerated or unwarranted suspicions of others, but not outright delusions as are found among people with delusional disorders or paranoid schizophrenia. A person with paranoid personality disorder may believe that he was passed over for a promotion because his boss had it in for him, but he would not maintain the unfounded belief that his boss had put a contract on his life.

A CLOSER LOOK

The Love Delusion

Erotomania, or the love delusion, is a delusional disorder in which the individual believes that he or she is loved by someone of high social status, even though the individual may have only a passing or even a nonexistent relationship with the alleged lover (Goldstein, 1986). Although the love delusion was once thought to be predominantly a female disorder, recent reports suggest that it may not be a rarity among men. It has been suggested, for example, that John Hinckley, Jr., who attempted to assassinate President Ronald Reagan reportedly to impress actress Jodie Foster, could be considered a case of erotomania (Stone, 1984). Although women with erotomania may have a potential for violence when their attentions are rebuffed, men with this condition appear more likely to threaten or commit acts of violence in the pursuit of the objects of their unrequited desires (Goldstein, 1986). Antipsychotic medications may reduce the intensity of the delusion but do not appear to eliminate the delusion (Segal, 1989). Nor is there evidence that psychotherapy helps people with erotomania. The prognosis is thus bleak, and people with erotomania may harass their love objects for many years. Mental health professionals also need to be aware of the potential for violence in the management of people who possess these delusions of love (Goldstein, 1986; Segal, 1989).

The following cases provide some examples of the love delusion:

Mr. A., a 35-year-old man, was described as a "love-struck" suitor of a daughter of a former President of the United States. He was arrested for repeatedly harrassing the woman in an attempt to win her love, although they were actually perfect strangers. Refusing to adhere to the judge's warnings to stop pestering the woman, he placed numerous phone calls to her from prison and was later transferred to a psychiatric facility, still declaring that they were very much in love.

Mr. B. was arrested for breaching a court order to stop pestering a famous pop singer. A 44-year-old farmer, Mr. B. had followed his love interest across the country, constantly bombarding her with romantic overtures. He was committed to a psychiatric hospital, but maintained the belief that she'd always wait for him.

Then there was Mr. C., a 32-year-old businessman, who believed that a well-known woman lawyer had fallen in love with him following a casual meeting. He constantly called and sent flowers and letters, declaring his love. While she repeatedly rejected his advances and eventually filed criminal charges for harrassment, he felt that she was only testing his love by placing obstacles in his path. He abandoned his wife and business and his functioning declined. When the woman continued to reject him, he began sending her threatening letters and was committed to a psychiatric facility.

■ *Adapted from Goldstein, 1986, p. 802*

 Some people do suffer from the delusion that they are loved by a famous person. They are said to have a delusional disorder, erotomanic type.

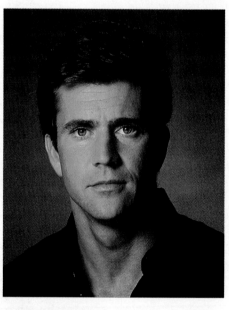

Is one of these people in love with you? People with *erotomania*—that is, the love delusion—may believe they are loved by a "star" or someone of high social status, even though they have never met.

Table 11.3 Types of Delusional Disorders

Type	Description
Erotomanic type	Beliefs that someone of higher social status, such as movie star or political figure, is in love with you.
Grandiose Type	Inflated beliefs about your worth, importance, power, knowledge, or identity, or beliefs that you hold a special relationship to a deity or a famous person. Cult leaders who believe they have special mystical powers of enlightenment may have delusional disorders of this type.
Jealous Type	Delusions of jealousy in which the person may become convinced, without due cause, that his or her lover is unfaithful. The delusional person may misinterpret certain clues as signs of unfaithfulness, such as spots on the bedsheets.
Persecutory Type	The most common type of delusional disorder, persecutory delusions involve themes of being conspired against, followed, cheated, spied upon, poisoned or drugged, or otherwise maligned or mistreated. Persons with such delusions may repeatedly institute court actions, or even commit acts of violence, against those who they perceive are responsible for their mistreatment.
Somatic Type	Delusions involving physical defects, disease, or disorder. Persons with these delusions may believe that foul odors are emanating from their bodies, or that internal parasites are eating away at them, or that certain parts of their body are unusually disfigured or ugly, or not functioning properly despite evidence to the contrary.
Mixed Type	Delusions typify more than one of the other types; no single theme predominates.

Source: Adapted from DSM-IV Draft Criteria (American Psychiatric Association), p. I:5.

Various kinds of delusional disorders are described in Table 11.3. Delusional disorders are relatively uncommon. Once a delusion is established, it may persevere, although the individual's concern about it may wax and wane over the years. In other cases, the delusion may disappear entirely for periods of time and then recur. Sometimes the disorder permanently disappears.

In this chapter we focused on schizophrenia, perhaps the most severe form of mental disturbance. Research into the origins of schizophrenia highlights roles for biological and other factors. In the next chapter we turn to mental disorders that are directly caused by known biological abnormalities, such as strokes and brain tumors, or in which biological causes are presumed but have not yet been fully explicated, such as Alzheimer's disease.

Summary

History of the Concept of Schizophrenia

Emil Kraepelin was the first to describe schizophrenia. He labeled the disorder *dementia praecox* and believed that it was a disease that develops early in life and follows a progressively deteriorating course. Eugen Bleuler renamed the disorder *schizophrenia* and believed that its course is more variable. He also distinguished between primary symptoms (the four A's) and secondary symptoms. Kurt Schneider distinguished between first-rank symptoms that define the disorder and second-rank symptoms that occur in schizophrenia and other disorders.

Prevalence of Schizophrenia

Schizophrenia is believed to affect 1 to 2% of the population.

Phases of Schizophrenia

Schizophrenia usually develops in late adolescence or early adulthood. Its onset may be abrupt or gradual. The period of deterioration preceding the onset of acute symptoms is called the prodromal phase. An acute episode involves the emergence of clear psychotic features. The residual phase is characterized by a level of functioning that was typical of the prodromal phase.

Schizophrenia-Spectrum Disorders

Schizophrenia-spectrum disorders refer to schizophrenic-type disorders that range in severity from milder personality disorders, such as schizotypal and schizoid types, to schizophrenia itself and schizoaffective disorder.

Features of Schizophrenia

Among the more prominent features of schizophrenia are disorders in the content of thought (delusions) and form of thought (thought disorder), as well as the presence of perceptual distortions (hallucinations) and emotional disturbances (flattened or inappropriate affect). There are also dysfunctions in the brain processes that regulate attention to the external world.

Types of Schizophrenia

The disorganized type describes schizophrenics with grossly disorganized behavior and thought processes. The catatonic type describes schizophrenics with grossly impaired motor behaviors, such as those who maintain fixed postures or remain mute for long periods of time. Paranoid type describes those who hold paranoid delusions that tend to be complex and systematized. The undifferentiated type is a catch-all category that applies to schizophrenics with active psychotic behaviors who do not fit other types. The residual type applies to those in a residual phase who do not have prominent psychotic behaviors at the time of evaluation.

Dimensions of Schizophrenia

Researchers have identified various dimensions of schizophrenia. Process schizophrenia is associated with a gradual decline in functioning, whereas reactive schizophrenia is characterized by an acute onset. Process schizophrenia has historically been associated with more unfavorable prognoses (outcomes) than reactive schizophrenia.

Researchers have also distinguished between the positive symptoms, or behavioral excesses, of schizophrenia and the negative symptoms, or behavioral deficits, of the disorder. Some researchers believe that these symptom clusters correspond to two basic types of schizophrenia: Type I schizophrenia (positive symptoms, abrupt onset, preserved intelligence, more favorable response to antipsychotic drugs) and Type II schizophrenia (negative symp-

toms, gradual onset, greater chronicity and intellectual impairment, and poorer response to antipsychotic drugs).

Theoretical Perspectives

In the traditional psychodynamic model, schizophrenia represents a regression to a psychological state corresponding to early infancy in which the proddings of the id produce bizarre, socially deviant behavior and give rise to hallucinations and delusions. Learning theorists propose that schizophrenic behavior may result from lack of social reinforcement, which leads to gradual detachment from the social environment and increased attention to an inner world of fantasy. Modeling and selective reinforcement of bizarre behavior may explain some schizophrenic behaviors in the hospital setting.

Research has demonstrated strong linkages between biological factors and schizophrenia. Evidence for genetic factors comes from studies of family patterns of schizophrenia, twin studies, and adoption studies. The mode of genetic transmission remains unknown. Environmental factors also play a role in schizophrenia, and many researchers have adopted the diathesis–stress model to account for the interaction between a genetic predisposition (diathesis) and environmental factors. The diathesis–stress model has been supported by studies of children of schizophrenic biological parents among whom environmental stress apparently increases the risk of the disorder.

Most researchers believe that the neurotransmitter dopamine plays a role in schizophrenia, especially in the more flagrant features of the disorder. Some researchers also believe that complications during pregnancy and birth, such as a viral infection, heighten the risk of schizophrenia in genetically vulnerable people. Evidence of brain dysfunctions and structural damage in schizophrenia is accumulating, but researchers are uncertain about causal pathways.

Family factors such as communication deviance and expressed emotion may act as sources of stress that increase the risk of development or recurrence of schizophrenia among people with a genetic predisposition.

The sociocultural perspective focuses on the roles of social ills such as poverty and overcrowding in the development of schizophrenia.

Treatment

Treatment of schizophrenia tends to be multifaceted, incorporating pharmacological and psychosocial approaches. Antipsychotic medication is not a cure but tends to stem the more flagrant aspects of the disorder and to reduce the need for hospitalization and the risk of recurrent episodes. Antipsychotic drugs are connected with potentially severe side effects and patient response to them needs to be monitored closely.

Psychoanalytic approaches have not been shown to be effective in treating schizophrenia. Learning-based approaches, such as token economy systems and social skills training, have achieved some success in increasing adaptive behavior among schizophrenics. Psychosocial-rehabilitation approaches help schizophrenics adapt more successfully to occupational and social roles in the community. Family intervention programs help families cope with the burdens of care, communicate more clearly, and learn more helpful ways of relating to the patient.

Delusional Disorder

People with delusional disorder hold delusional beliefs that are apparently plausible and less bizarre than schizophrenic delusions. The delusion itself is often the only clear sign of abnormality, whereas schizophrenic delusions are embedded within a more general pattern of disturbed thoughts, perceptions, and behaviors.

Andres Serrano. Locked Brains, 1990. Cibachrome, silicone, plexiglas, wood frame: 40 × 60 inches. Courtesy of Paula Cooper Gallery, New York.

CHAPTER OUTLINE

12

Delirium, Dementia, Amnestic and Other Cognitive Disorders

TRUTH  FICTION?

___ A man with a brain tumor patted the heads of fire hydrants and parking meters in the belief they were children.

___ The most frequently identified cause of delirium is abrupt withdrawal from alcohol or other drugs.

___ Dementia is a normal function of the aging process.

___ Alzheimer's disease is found only among the elderly.

___ Alzheimer's disease is caused by aluminum ingestion.

___ After a motorcycle accident, a medical student failed to recognize the woman he had married a few weeks earlier.

___ Football players and prize-fighters can recover completely—display no lingering cognitive deficits—from being knocked out.

___ When the symptoms of syphilis disappear by themselves, there is nothing to be concerned about.

___ Julius Caesar and Vincent van Gogh suffered from epilepsy.

*I*n *The Man Who Mistook His Wife for a Hat*, neurologist Oliver Sacks (1985) tells of Dr. P., a distinguished musician and teacher who had lost the ability to recognize objects visually. For example, Dr. P. failed to recognize the faces of his students at the music school. When a student spoke, however, Dr. P. immediately recognized his or her voice. Not only did the professor fail to discriminate faces visually, but sometimes he perceived faces where none existed. He patted the heads of fire hydrants and parking meters, which he took to be children. He warmly addressed the rounded knobs on furniture. These peculiarities were generally dismissed as jokes and laughed off by Dr. P. and his colleagues. After all, Dr. P. was well known for his oddball humor and jests. But Dr. P.'s music remained as accomplished as ever, his general health seemed fine, and so these misperceptions seemed little to be concerned about.

Not until three years later did Dr. P. seek a neurological evaluation. His ophthalmologist had found that although Dr. P.'s eyes were healthy, he had problems interpreting visual stimulation. So he made the referral to Dr. Sacks, a neurologist. When Sacks engaged Dr. P. in conversation, Dr. P.'s eyes fixated oddly on miscellaneous features of Dr. Sack's face—his nose, then his right ear, then his chin, sensing parts of his face but apparently not connecting them in a meaningful pattern. When Dr. P. sought to put on his shoe after a physical examination, he confused his foot with the shoe. When preparing to leave, Dr. P. looked around for his hat, and then . . .

> [Dr. P.] reached out his hand, and took hold of his wife's head, tried to lift it off, to put it on. He had apparently mistaken his wife for a hat! His wife looked as if she was used to such things.
>
> Sacks, 1985, p. 10

Dr. P.'s peculiar behavior may seem amusing to some, but his loss of visual perception was tragic. Although Dr. P. could identify abstract forms and shapes—a cube, for example—he no longer recognized the faces of his family, or his own. Some features of particular faces would strike a chord of recognition. For example, he could recognize a picture of Einstein from the distinctive hair and mustache, and a picture of his own brother from the square jaw and big teeth. But he was responding to isolated features, not grasping the facial patterns as wholes.

Sacks recounts a final test:

> It was still a cold day, in early spring, and I had thrown my coat and gloves on the sofa.
>
> "What is this?" I asked, holding up a glove.
>
> "May I examine it?" he asked, and, taking it from me, he proceeded to examine it as he had examined the geometrical shapes.

"A continuous surface," he announced at last, "infolded on itself. It appears to have"—he hesitated—"five outpouchings, if this is the word."

"Yes," I said cautiously. "You have given me a description. Now tell me what it is."

"A container of some sort?"

"Yes," I said, "and what would it contain?"

"It would contain its contents!" said Dr. P., with a laugh. "There are many possibilities. It could be a change-purse, for example, for coins of five sizes. It could . . ."

I interrupted the blarney flow. "Does it not look familiar? Do you think it might contain, might fit, a part of your body?"

No light of recognition dawned on his face.

No child would have the power to see and speak of "a continuous surface . . . infolded on itself," but any child, any infant, would immediately know a glove as a glove, see it as familiar, as going with a hand. Dr. P. didn't. He saw nothing as familiar. Visually, he was lost in a world of lifeless abstractions.

Sacks, 1985, p. 13

Later, we might add, Dr. P. accidentally put the glove on his hand, exclaiming, "My God, it's a glove!" (Sacks, 1985, p. 13). His brain immediately seized the pattern of **tactile** information, although his visual brain centers were powerless to provide a confirmatory interpretation. Dr. P., that is, showed lack of visual knowledge—a symptom referred to as visual **agnosia**, derived from Greek roots meaning "without

knowledge." Still, Dr. P.'s musical abilities and verbal skills remained intact. He was able to function, to dress himself, take a shower, and eat his meals by singing various songs to himself—for example, eating songs and dressing songs—that helped him coordinate his actions. However, if his dressing song was interrupted while he was dressing himself, he would lose his train of thought and be unable to recognize not only the clothes that his wife had laid out but also his own body. When the music stopped, so did his ability to make sense of the world. Sacks later learned that Dr. P. had a massive tumor in the area of the brain that processes visual information. Dr. P. was apparently unaware of his deficits, having filled his visually empty world with music in order to function and imbue his life with meaning and purpose.

It is true that a man with a brain tumor patted the heads of fire hydrants and parking meters in the belief that they were children. The tumor caused dysfunctions in the parts of his brain that processed visual information.

Dr. P.'s case is unusual in the peculiarity of his symptoms, but it illustrates the universal dependence of psychological functioning on an intact brain. The case also shows how some people adjust—sometimes so gradually that the changes are all but imperceptible—to developing physical or organic problems. Mr. P.'s visual problems might have been relatively more debilitating in a person who was less talented or who had less social support to draw on.

COGNITIVE DISORDERS WITH ORGANIC ORIGINS

In this chapter we consider cognitive disorders that have organic origins. In many disorders discussed in earlier chapters, there is *possible* involvement of organic factors, ranging from genetic influences to imbalances in neurotransmitters. Consider the apparent roles of dopamine in schizophrenia and norepinephrine in the mood disorders, for example. In the disorders covered in this chapter, however, there is clear or assumed organic causation, such as trauma to the brain, disease, or nutritional imbalances. In disorders with *possible* organic involvement, such as schizophrenia and the mood disorders, the causal connections between specific organic factors (in these cases, neurotransmitters) and mental disorders have not been fully revealed. Put it another way: Disorders like schizophrenia and bipolar disorder are known to have biological *correlates*, but the significance of these

Does his singing help him coordinate his actions? In a celebrated case study of a pattern of abnormal behavior with organic origins, "Dr. P.," who was discovered to be suffering from a brain tumor, could no longer gather visual information. Yet he could continue to eat meals and wash and dress himself so long as he could sing to himself.

correlates in accounting for the disorders has not been clearly established. The disorders discussed in this chapter, however, either have known biological causes or are presumed to be caused by biological factors that have not yet been uncovered.

When the brain is damaged by injury, stroke, or progressive deterioration, there may be a rapid or gradual decline in intellectual, social, and occupational functioning. Affected people may become completely dependent on others to meet basic needs in feeding, toileting, and grooming. In some cases, these problems result from intoxication by, or withdrawal from, alcohol or other drugs, or from the ingestion of toxins. Although the disorders discussed in this chapter all involve known or presumed biological causes, it appears that psychological and environmental factors also play a role in determining symptoms and victims' personal abilities to cope with cognitive and physical deficits.

DSM-IV Classification

Most of the disorders discussed in this chapter are a subclass of mental disorders that the DSM-IV refers to as **cognitive disorders**. The essential feature of cognitive disorders is that they are associated with temporary or permanent dysfunctions of the brain. Like other mental disorders, cognitive disorders affect cognitive abilities and daily functioning, such as thought and memory, feeling states, personal hygiene, and grooming. The cognitive disorders differ from other mental disorders in that there is either known biological causality in each case, or else the disorder is presumed to be caused by biological factors that have not yet been uncovered. The biological causes in many cases give rise to a wide range of significant, even life-threatening physical impairments. Yet the cognitive or mental features of each disorder are also striking, which is why they are referred to as cognitive disorders. In this chapter, we discuss the cognitive disorders shown in Table 12.1.

The major cognitive disorders include *delirium*, *dementia*, and *amnestic disorders*. Cognitive disorders are sometimes caused by intoxication or withdrawal from psychoactive substances, such as alcohol. The draft criteria for DSM-IV listed three kinds of substance-induced cognitive disorders: *substance-induced delirium*, *substance-induced persisting dementia*, and *substance-induced persisting amnestic disorder*. Substance-induced persisting dementia and substance-induced persisting amnestic disorders are by definition enduring or persistent problems. Substance-induced delirium develops during drug intoxication or withdrawal and can be short-lived.

Table 12.1	Deliria, Dementias, and Amnestic Disorders
Deliria	Delirium due to a General Medical Condition
	Substance-Induced Delirium
Dementias	Dementia of the Alzheimer's Type
	Vascular Dementia
	Dementia due to Other General Medical Conditions
	Dementia due to HIV Disease
	Dementia due to Head Trauma
	Dementia due to Parkinson's Disease
	Dementia due to Huntington's Disease
	Dementia due to Pick's Disease
	Dementia due to Other General Medical Condition (e.g., hypothyroidism, brain tumor, vitamin B12 deficiency)
	Substance-Induced Persisting Dementia
Amnestic Disorders	Amnestic Disorder due to a General Medical Condition (transient or chronic)
	Substance-Induced Persisting Amnestic Disorder

Source: DSM-IV Draft Criteria (American Psychiatric Association, 1993), pp. F:1–F:9.

Cognitive disorders are classified on Axis I of the DSM-IV, whereas the medical condition responsible for the problem is listed on Axis III. If, for example, a person is diagnosed as having Dementia of the Alzheimer's Type on Axis I, Alzheimer's Disease itself is noted on Axis III. Again, if Dementia Due to HIV Disease is the diagnosis listed on Axis I, HIV Disease is also coded on Axis III.

A number of changes in the classification of delirium, dementia, and amnestic disorders have occurred from the DSM-III-R to the DSM-IV. The DSM-III-R used the category of *organic mental disorders* to classify brain dysfunctions that resulted in cognitive impairments such as delirium, dementia, and amnesia. One of the most notable changes was the elimination of the term *organic* from the diagnostic classification. A problem with the earlier use of the term *organic* for these disorders was the implication that other mental disorders, such as schizophrenia and bipolar disorder, are by definition *non*organic. As argued by Spitzer and his colleagues (1992c), however, evidence for biological factors in these so-called nonorganic disorders is mounting.

Although it is not classified as a cognitive disorder, we also discuss epilepsy in this chapter. Epilepsy involves a brain dysfunction characterized by disturbances in the electrical rhythms of the brain, which induce seizures and produce changes in states of consciousness. Epilepsy can be caused by biological problems as wide ranging as brain tumors, high fever during infancy, or head injuries. Epilepsy, moreover, is among the more common disorders of the brain, affecting 1 to 2% of the population.

Diagnostic Problems

The diagnosis of cognitive disorders with organic origins can be a difficult task. Brain damage may result in a variety of symptoms, depending on such factors as the location and extent of the damage, the person's coping ability, and, as in the case of Dr. P., the availability of social support. Damage to a given area of the brain may not produce the same symptoms in different people because of minor structural or functional differences, because of subtle differences in the site of the damage, or because of psychological factors—like histories of learning—that interact with organic factors. Moreover, organic factors sometimes cause abnormal behavior patterns such as depression, disorientation, and suspiciousness. These patterns resemble those occurring in other mental disorders, such as depressive disorders and schizophrenia.

Neurological examinations and neuropsychological testing are used to detect brain damage. Imaging techniques such as CAT and PET scans probe for organic defects that are not revealed by neurological examination. CAT scans generally help clinicians identify structural defects like tumors, whereas PET scans provide insight into apparently structurally intact regions that are made dysfunctional by strokes or other causes. Many organic conditions are treatable or reversible, particularly when they are diagnosed early. A timely and thorough evaluation can thus spell the difference between recovery and impairment—in some cases, between life and death. The appropriate treatment for a cognitive disorder may differ appreciably from that for a similar condition without clear organic causes. For example, cognitive disorders caused by brain tumors may be treated successfully with surgery, not with psychotherapy.

The extent and location of brain damage largely determine the range and severity of impairment. By and large, the more widespread the damage, the greater and more extensive the impairment in functioning. The location of the damage is also critical because many brain structures or regions perform specialized functions. Damage to the temporal lobe, for example, is associated with defects in memory and attention, whereas damage to the occipital lobe may result in visual-spatial deficits, such as Dr. P.'s loss of ability to recognize familiar faces.

DELIRIUM

Delirium derives from the Latin roots *de-*, meaning "from," and *lira*, meaning "line" or "furrow." It means straying from the line, or the norm, in perception, cognition, and behavior. Delirium is characterized by severe difficulty in concentration and by psychological disorganization that is disclosed by rambling, incoherent speech (see Table 12.2). Delirious people find it difficult to tune out irrelevant stimuli or to shift their attention to new tasks. They may speak excitedly, but their speech lacks meaning and coherence (Freemon, 1981). Disorientation as to time and place is common. Disorientation to person (the identities of oneself and others) is not. Delirious people may report hallucinations, especially visual hallucinations. Perceptual disturbances may include misinterpreta-

Table 12.2   Features of Delirium

	Level of Severity		
	Mild	**Moderate**	**Severe**
Emotion	Apprehension	Fear	Panic
Cognition and perception	Confusion, racing thoughts	Disorientation, delusions	Meaningless mumbling, vivid hallucinations
Behavior	Tremors	Muscle spasms	Seizures
Autonomic activity	Abnormally fast heartbeat (tachycardia)	Perspiration	Fever

Source: Adapted from Freemon, 1981, p. 82.

tions of sensory stimuli (for example, confusing an alarm clock for a fire bell), or illusions (feeling as if the bed has an electrical charge passing through it). There can be marked slowing of movement into a state resembling catatonia. There can be rapid fluctuations between restlessness and stupor. Restlessness is typified by insomnia; agitated, aimless movements; even bolting out of bed or striking out at nonexistent objects. This may alternate with periods in which victims have to struggle to stay awake.

Unlike dementia, which involves a progressive deterioration of mental functioning, delirium may clear up spontaneously or be completely reversed through resolution of the underlying organic condition. The course of delirium is relatively brief, usually about a week, rarely longer than a month. If the organic condition persists or deteriorates, however, delirium may progress to coma or death. During the course of delirium, people's mental states will often fluctuate between periods of clarity ("lucid intervals"), which are most common in the morning, and periods of confusion and disorientation. Delirium is generally worse in the dark and following sleepless nights.

Delirium is believed to result from a combination of generalized disturbance of the brain's metabolic processes and imbalances in the levels of neurotransmitters. As a result, the ability to process information is impaired and confusion reigns. The abilities to think and speak clearly, interpret sensory stimuli, and attend to the environment decline. Delirium may occur abruptly, as with seizures or head injuries, or it may develop gradually over hours or days, generally because of infection, fever, or metabolic disorders. The most common causes of delirium are infection, head trauma, seizures, metabolic disturbances caused by diseases of the liver or kidneys, hypoglycemia (low blood sugar), thiamine deficiencies, and intoxication or withdrawal from psychoactive substances. Often the cause cannot be identified.

The DTs

States of delirium may also result from ingestion of toxic substances. Potentially lethal mushrooms, for example, can produce delirium that is accompanied by vivid hallucinations. The most common cause of delirium is abrupt withdrawal from drugs, most commonly alcohol (Freemon, 1981).

It is true that the most frequently identified cause of delirium is abrupt withdrawal from alcohol or other drugs.

The DSM-IV diagnosis of Alcohol-Induced Delirium, with onset during withdrawal, has historically been termed **delirium tremens**, or *the DTs*. The DTs sometimes follow abrupt withdrawal from alcohol, especially when use has been chronic. Tremors become evident within the first hours of withdrawal. Convulsive seizures may occur after 24 hours, then subside, and the person may appear normal for the next day or two (Freemon, 1981). Then an acute period of delirium begins in which the patient may be terrorized by wild and frightening hallucinations, like "bugs crawling down walls" or on the skin. The DTs can last for a week or more and are best treated in a hospital setting, where the patient can be carefully monitored and the symptoms treated with tranquilizers and environmental support. The following case illustrates the psychological problems that characterize the DTs:

A divorced carpenter, 43 years of age, is brought to a hospital emergency department by his sister. She reports that he has at least a 5-year history of consuming large amounts of alcohol (a fifth of cheap wine) on a daily basis. He has had many blackouts from drinking, and he has lost several jobs due to drinking. He ran out of money three days earlier, at which time he stopped drinking abruptly, and he has been begging for money to buy his meals. On examination, he seems keyed up, talking almost non-stop in an unfocused and rambling manner. He appears confused and believes that the doctor is his brother, calling him by his brother's name. There is evidence of a hand tremor, and he picks at "bugs" that he believes he sees on the hospital bedsheets. He is disoriented as to place and time; he apparently thinks that he is in a parking lot of a supermarket rather than a hospital. He is apprehensive and fears that an impending holocaust is about to end the world. He has difficulty concentrating. His perceptions apparently drift into hallucinations of fiery car crashes that seem to be prompted by sounds of hospital carts crashing against each other in the hallways.

■ *Adapted from Spitzer et al., 1989, pp. 224–226.*

DEMENTIAS

Most of us experience mild declines in memory by about the age of 50. We display minor decrements in visual-spatial skills by age 60, and some slight decrements in language skills and abstract thinking ability by about age 70 (National Institute of Mental Health,

A CLOSER LOOK

Organic and Psychological Changes in the Elderly

How old would you be if you didn't know how old you was?

Satchel Paige

Old age isn't so bad when you consider the alternative.

Maurice Chevalier

Many physical changes occur with aging. Changes in calcium metabolism cause the bones to grow brittle and heighten the risk of breaks from falls. The skin grows less elastic, creating wrinkles and folds. The senses become less keen, so that older people see and hear less acutely. The elderly need more time (called *reaction time*) to respond to stimuli, whether they are driving or taking intelligence tests. For example, elderly drivers require more time to react to traffic signals and other cars. Our immune system functions less effectively with increasing age, so that we become more vulnerable to illness.

Cognitive changes occur as well. The elderly exhibit some drop-off in general cognitive ability as gauged by intelligence tests. The decline is sharpest on timed items, like the performance scales of the Wechsler Adult Intelligence Scale. We understand little about the causes of these declines in cognitive functioning (Storandt, 1983). Loss of motivation and of sensory acuity play a part. B. F. Skinner (1983) contended that much of the decline reflects an "aging environment"—not an aging person. That is, much of the behavior of older people goes unreinforced, especially after retirement. Consider that nursing home residents who are reinforced for retaining recent events display improved scores on memory tests (Langer et al., 1979; Wolinsky, 1982). Some cognitive changes may reflect psychological problems, like depression, rather than the physical aspects of aging (Albert, 1981). In such cases, the dementia is not considered a feature of an organic mental disorder. If the underlying depression is treated, cognitive performance may also improve. Depression often goes unrecognized among the elderly, however.

Depression in the Elderly Depression is epidemic among the elderly—the most common emotional problem they face (Butler & Lewis, 1982). According to the National Institute on Aging, at least 15% of people over the age of 65 suffer from some degree of depression, with perhaps 1 in 5 of these experiencing major depression ("Fifteen percent of aged are depressed," 1992). Rates of depression are even higher among elderly residents of nursing homes, with estimates for depression ranging as high as 25%. One-quarter to one-third of 150 elderly medical inpatients in one Veteran's Administration Hospital had diagnosable mental conditions, with the majority of these meeting the criteria for a depressive disorder (Rapp et al., 1988). Suicide is also most frequent among the elderly (McIntosh, 1985).

What changes take place as we age? How do they affect our moods?   Although some declines in cognitive and physical functioning are connected with aging, elderly people who remain active and engage in rewarding activities can be highly satisfied with their lives.

Depressive disorders occur commonly in people suffering from various brain disorders, several of which, like Alzheimer's disease and stroke, disproportionately affect the elderly (Teri, 1992). Researchers estimate that depressive disorders occur among 10 to 30% of Alzheimer's disease patients (Sweet et al., 1992; Teri, 1992); 40 to 50% of Parkinson's disease patients (Cummings, 1992; Rao et al., 1992; Sweet et al., 1992); and about 50% of stroke victims (Sweet et al., 1992). In the case of Parkinson's disease, depression may not only be a reaction to coping with the disease; it may also result from neurobiological changes in the brain that are caused by the disease (Rao et al., 1992).

A longitudinal study of 2,032 people 65 years of age and older from rural Iowa tracked depressive features across a 6-year period (Wallace & O'Hara, 1992). Researchers found that depressive features increased across the 6-year period, which indicates that depression may increase with age among older people. Women were generally more likely than men to report feelings of depression, but the gender gap narrowed with increasing age as the level of depression among men caught up.

Infirm older people may be at yet greater risk of depression. Depressed elderly people who encounter worsening health tend to encounter more persistent depression. Improvement in health is associated with remission of depression (Kennedy et al., 1991). Elderly people who are in poor health and who lack social support are at greatest risk of depression (Phifer & Murrell, 1986). Concerning the importance of social support, one study showed that elderly men encountered more depression following the loss of a close family member (other than their spouses) than did elderly women (Siegel & Kuykendall, 1990). Elderly men who are widowed and who did not belong to a church or synagogue, and who consequently had less available social supports, were most at risk of depression. The researchers suspect that widowers have more limited social support networks than widows and are less likely to have confidants outside marriage who might provide support.

The elderly may be especially vulnerable to depression because of the stresses of coping with the life events of the so-called golden years—retirement; physical illness or incapacitation; placement in a residential facility or nursing home; the deaths of a spouse, siblings, lifetime friends, and acquaintances; or the need to care for a spouse whose condition is declining. Retirement, whether voluntary or forced, may sap the sense of meaningfulness in life. Deaths of relatives and friends not only induce grief but remind the elderly of their own advanced years and reduce the availability of social supports. Elderly adults may feel incapable of forming new friendships or finding new goals in life. Evidence suggests that the chronic strain of coping with a demented person can lead to depression in the caregiver, even in the absence of evidence of prior vulnerability to depression. In one study, 30% of elderly spousal caregivers experienced a depressive disorder, versus only 1% of age-matched controls during the same time period (Dura et al., 1990).

Despite the prevalence of depression in the elderly, hospital physicians often fail to recognize it. In one study of elderly hospitalized medical patients, physicians detected depression in only 8.7% of those who were diagnosed as depressed by researchers (Rapp et al., 1988). Depression sometimes goes undetected because it is masked by physical complaints and sleeping problems (Kazniak & Allender, 1985). Physicians may also be less likely to recognize depression in the elderly than in middle-aged or young people because they tend to focus more on elderly patients' physical complaints (Rapp et al., 1988).

Memory Functioning and Depression The effects of depression on memory functioning in the elderly appear to be variable. Some studies find memory deficits among elderly depressed people; others do not (Niederehe, 1986). Unlike irreversible dementias such as those attributed to Alzheimer's disease, the memory loss and cognitive impairment that characterize depression among the elderly can lift when the depression lifts (Salzman & Gutfreund, 1986). However, when depression occurs among patients already afflicted with dementia, as in Alzheimer's disease, a rapid and dramatic worsening of cognitive functioning may occur.

Depression and memory loss in the elderly may accompany bereavement. Such problems may be resolved as grief resolves and survivors learn to cope on their own, however (Salzman & Gutfreund, 1986):

Mrs. A. was a 71-year-old retired schoolteacher. Her husband died after a 3-year bout with intestinal cancer. Although his death was expected and prepared for, she was nevertheless overcome by emotion. She had been a highly functioning, scholarly woman who read widely, yet Mrs. A. was suddenly unable to think clearly. She noticed her striking forgetfulness. So did her children, who had come to support her during the period of

1987). Despite earlier beliefs that people naturally grow senile as they age, the processes of normal aging involve modest declines in intellectual abilities. Significant declines in intellectual functioning, or **dementia**, are not considered a normal function of the aging process, but rather a sign of a degenerative brain disorder.

 It is *not* true that dementia is considered a normal function of the aging process. Rather it is considered a sign of a degenerative brain disorder.

Dementia is defined by deterioration in mental abilities such as memory, problem-solving skills, and abstract thinking that is sufficient to impair social and occupational functioning (Davies, 1988). Screening and testing on neurological and neuropsychological tests can help distinguish dementias from normal aging processes (NIMH, 1987). Generally speaking, the decline in intellectual functioning in dementia is more rapid and severe.

The causes of dementia include brain diseases such as Alzheimer's disease and Pick's disease, and the lasting effects of chronic intoxication, infections, strokes, and tumors. In some cases dementia can be halted or reversed, especially when it is caused by certain tumors and treatable infections, or when it results from depression or substance abuse (NIMH, 1987). Most dementias are irreversible, however. Alzheimer's disease represents the most common form of irreversible dementia.

mourning. Mrs. A. had difficulty recalling where she had placed things. Now and then she forgot the day of the week and the date. She felt incapable of shopping for groceries because it was too arduous to make change. Although she would make lists as a way of reminding herself of her chores, she would misplace the lists and forget about them. She could not concentrate to read or watch television. If she did watch for a while, she did not remember what she had seen. She recurrently called her children by the wrong name, and was particularly prone to calling her son by her deceased husband's name. As the weeks elapsed, however, the forgetfulness, disorientation, and diminished capacity for concentration gradually dissipated. After about half a year, Mrs. A. returned to her normal level of intellectual functioning and has continued to function adequately.

■ *Adapted from Salzman and Gutfreund, 1986, p. 258*

Some depressed older people complain of memory problems even though their memory functioning is average or above average (Williams et al., 1987). Perceptions of memory impairment among some depressed elderly people may be a kind of cognitive distortion, one that is characteristic of the tendency of depressed people in general to devalue their abilities. There are also more dysfunctional attitudes, feelings of hopelessness, and negative automatic thoughts among elderly depressed people than among their nondepressed age-mates (Lam et al., 1987).

Treating Depression in Older People Antidepressants like imipramine and mild tranquilizers like alprazolam have been used with mixed results to treat depressed older people (Feighner, 1982; Teri, 1992). Psychological approaches appear to provide hopeful alternatives to drug therapy. In one study, cognitive therapy was effective in reducing depression and improving sleeping patterns among elderly subjects (Beutler et al., 1987). Treatment with alprazolam, by contrast, led to no improvement in subjective feelings of depression or physical complaints.

Zeiss and Lewinsohn (1986) proposed a cognitive-behavioral treatment model that is tailored to the life problems of the elderly. They suggest ways in which therapists can help depressed elderly people cope more effectively with events such as the loss of loved ones or with physical illness. Therapists also help elderly clients challenge self-defeating attitudes, such as the belief that they are too old to change or to learn new behaviors.

Teri (1992) describes a behavioral treatment of depression for patients with dementia that she developed at the University of Washington. Her approach assumes that depressive behaviors are maintained through reinforcement contingencies and thus alters the patterns of reinforcement made available to elderly patients. For example, Teri uses a Pleasant Events Schedule to identify activities that elderly patients might still enjoy and increases patients' involvement in them. She creates conditions under which patients retain as much independence as possible. Under these conditions, patients' remaining cognitive and functional abilities are maximized. Preliminary data show that this method has a significant impact on lifting depression among the demented elderly, as assessed by standardized measures of depression. Although behavioral treatment for depression among the demented elderly is promising, Teri suggests that clinicians consider the use of drug therapy with this patient group when behavior therapy fails.

Dementia of the Alzheimer's Type

Alzheimer's disease (AD) is a progressive form of mental deterioration that is believed to account for more than half of the cases of dementia in the general population (Selkoe, 1992). Two to 4 million Americans are estimated to be afflicted with the disease (Growdon, 1992; Kolata, 1991a, 1991b; Teri & Wagner, 1992). Epidemiological studies of East Boston and Framingham, Massachusetts (see Figure 12.1) show that AD afflicts about 10% of people over the age of 65, with the risk increasing dramatically with advanced age (Evans et al., 1989; Selkoe, 1992). Although AD is strongly connected with aging, it is a disease and not a consequence of normal aging of the brain (Kolata, 1991a).

 Alzheimer's disease is *not* found only among the elderly. However, its incidence rises with age, and it is most likely to afflict people aged 75 and above.

AD is characterized by progressive deterioration in mental functions including memory, language, and problem-solving ability (Crystal, 1988; Wilson & Kazniak, 1986). Isolated memory losses are not indicative of AD (e.g., forgetting where one put one's glasses) and may occur normally as part of the aging process, but suspicion of AD is raised when cognitive impairment affects the individual's ability to function in daily work and social roles (Davies, 1988).

A study of 107 AD patients revealed that psychotic symptoms (delusions and/or hallucinations) appeared in about 1 in 3 patients (Jeste et al., 1992).

The appearance of psychotic symptoms was apparently connected with greater cognitive impairment and more rapid deterioration. Alzheimer's patients are frequently depressed or suicidal, but their doctors may overlook the danger signs or disregard them (Shuchman, 1990; Teri & Wagner, 1992). Depression among Alzheimer's patients strains caregivers and is also associated with greater impairment in the patient's ability to perform the tasks of daily life (Teri & Wagner, 1992).

Alzheimer's disease was first described in 1907 by the German physician Alois Alzheimer (1864–1915). During an autopsy of a 56-year-old woman who had suffered from severe dementia, he found

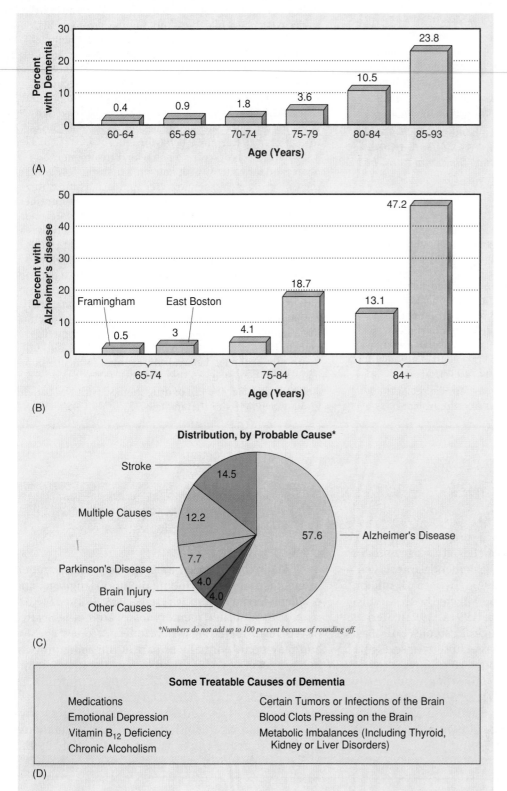

(A)

(B)

(C)

(D)

Figure 12.1 Prevalence of Alzheimer's disease among the elderly in two community studies in Massachusetts.
Epidemiological studies of East Boston and Framingham, Massachusetts, found that the prevalence of Alzheimer's disease (AD) increased sharply with age among the elderly. Overall, AD affects about 10% of the population over the age of 65. The lower prevalences reported in the Framingham study were likely due to the narrower criteria used by the Framingham group to diagnose the disease.

Source: From "Aging Brain, Aging Mind," By Dennis J. Selkoe. Copyright © 1992 by Scientific American, Inc. All rights reserved.

two brain abnormalities that are now regarded as signs of the disease (Tomlinson et al., 1970): neuritic plaques (portions of degenerative brain tissue) and neurofibrillary tangles (twisted bundles of nerve cells). The darkly shaded areas in the photo to the right in Figure 12.2 suggest how these neurological changes affect brain activity.

Positron emission tomography (the PET scan) provides measures of glucose and oxygen consumption in areas of the brain that might be affected in AD and other dementias. Comparative PET scans of AD patients and normal elderly reference groups show evidence of generally reduced metabolic rates in AD patients of about 33 to 37% (Ferris et al., 1980). Researchers have also found a negative correlation between metabolic rate and cognitive performance: The greater the cognitive impairment, the lower the metabolic rate (de Leon et al., 1983; Frackowiak et al., 1981). The fact that metabolic changes in the brains of AD patients appear to be widespread suggests that AD may affect multiple areas of the brain (de Leon et al., 1986).

Patients who are suspected of having AD also show evidence of reduced blood flow in the brain (Yamaguchi et al., 1980), but the significance of these findings remains unclear (de Leon et al., 1986). One possibility supported by research showing reduced brain metabolic activity in AD patients is that in AD, brain tissue degenerates to the point where it requires less nutrients, such as glucose, that are transported by blood to fuel brain cell activity. Thus, the supply of blood to the brain as well as the metabolic rate in affected areas of the brain is reduced (de Leon et al., 1986).

Alzheimer's disease. Alzheimer's disease can devastate patients' families. Spouses usually provide the bulk of daily care. This man has been caring for his wife for several years, and he believes that his hugs and kisses sometimes prompt his wife to murmur his name

■ **DIAGNOSIS** There is no clear-cut test for AD (Cohen, 1986). The diagnosis of AD is based on a process of exclusion, and is given only when detectable causes of dementia are eliminated (Eisdorfer & Cohen, 1980). Diagnosticians try to rule out other medical conditions that mimic AD (Crystal, 1988), as well as other abnormal behavior patterns, such as severe depression, that might account for memory loss and impaired cognitive functioning.

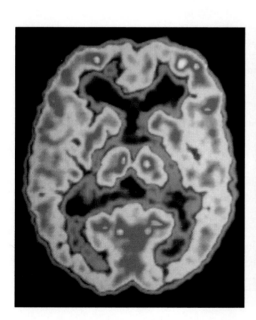

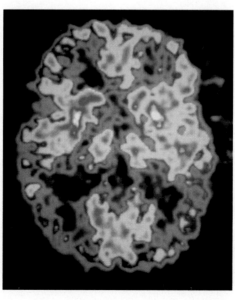

Figure 12.2 PET scans of brains from a healthy aged adult (left) and a patient with Alzheimer's disease (right).
The darkly shaded areas in the photo to the right suggest how the neurological changes associated with Alzheimer's disease (as marked by the excess of dark shading) impair brain activity.

Source: Robert P. Friedland, Case Western Reserve University, courtesy of Clinical Neuroimaging, © 1988 *by John Wiley and Sons, Inc.*

Estimates of misdiagnoses range from under 10% to more than 50%, however, even at the hands of specialists such as neurologists (Gurland & Cross, 1986).

A confirmatory diagnosis of AD is only made upon inspection of brain tissue by biopsy or autopsy (Davies, 1988). However, biopsy is rarely performed because of the risk of hemorrhaging or infection (Crystal, 1988), and autopsy, of course, occurs too late to help the patient.

■ **FEATURES OF ALZHEIMER'S DISEASE**   The disease is progressive; cognitive functioning generally declines with the duration of the illness (Teng et al., 1987). We usually find only limited memory problems and subtle personality changes during the early stages (see Table 12.3). Alzheimer's patients may first have trouble managing their finances; remembering recent events or basic information such as telephone numbers, area codes, zip codes, and the names of their grandchildren; and performing numerical computations (Reisberg et al., 1986). A business manager who once handled millions of dollars may become unable to add two numbers (Davies, 1988). There may be subtle personality changes, such as signs of

Table 12.3   The Global Deterioration Scale (GDS) for Assessment of Alzheimer's Disease

GDS Stage	Clinical Phase	Clinical Characteristics	Diagnosis
1 = No cognitive decline	Normal	No subjective complaints of memory deficit. No memory deficit evident on clinical interview.	Normal
2 = Very mild cognitive decline	Forgetfulness	Subjective complaints of memory deficits. No objective deficits in employment or social situations. Appropriate concern with respect to symptomatology.	Normal aged
3 = Mild cognitive decline	Early confusional	Earliest clear-cut deficits. Decreased performance in demanding employment and social settings. Objective evidence of memory deficit obtained only with an intensive interview. Mild to moderate anxiety accompanies symptoms.	Compatible with incipient Alzheimer's disease
4 = Moderate cognitive decline	Late confusional	Clear-cut deficit on careful clinical interview. Inability to perform complex tasks. Denial is dominant defense mechanism. Flattening of affect and withdrawal from challenging situations occur.	Mild Alzheimer's disease
5 = Moderately severe cognitive decline	Early dementia	Patients can no longer survive without some assistance. Patients are unable during interview to recall a major relevant aspect of their current lives. Persons at this stage retain knowledge of many major facts regarding themselves and others. They invariably know their own names and generally know their spouses and children's names. They require no assistance with using the toilet and eating, but may have some difficulty choosing the proper clothing to wear.	Moderate Alzheimer's disease
6 = Severe cognitive decline	Middle dementia	May occasionally forget the name of the spouse upon whom they are entirely dependent for survival. Will be largely unaware of all recent events and experiences in their lives. Will require some assistance with activities of daily living. Personality and emotional changes occur.	Moderately severe Alzheimer's disease
7 = Very severe cognitive decline	Late dementia	All verbal abilities are lost. Frequently there is no speech at all—only grunting. Incontinent of urine; requires assistance toileting and feeding. Loses basic psychomotor skills (for example, ability to walk).	Severe Alzheimer's disease

Source: Reprinted with permission from Reisberg et al., 1982. Copyright © 1982 by American Psychiatric Association.

withdrawal in people who had been outgoing or irritability in people who had been gentle (Davies, 1988). In these early stages, people with AD generally appear neat and well groomed and are generally cooperative and socially appropriate.

As AD progresses to a level of moderate severity, people find it harder to manage everyday tasks and require some assistance (Reisberg et al., 1986). They may be unable to select clothes for the season or the occasion. They may be unable to recall their addresses or the names of family members. When they drive, they begin making mistakes, such as failing to stop at stop signs or accelerating when they should be braking.

Some AD patients are not aware of their deficits. Others deny them (Dieckmann et al., 1988). At first they may attribute their problems to other causes (Davies, 1988), such as stress or fatigue. Denial may protect AD patients in the early or mild stages of the disease from recognition that their intellectual abilities are in decline (Reisberg et al., 1986). Denial is suspected when there is a clear discrepancy between the realities of patients' conditions and their reported perceptions of their conditions. On the other hand, those who recognize their problems may become depressed by them.

As AD progresses, people become more severely impaired. At the moderately severe level, they encounter difficulties in various aspects of personal functioning, such as toileting and bathing themselves (Reisberg et al., 1986). There are large gaps in their memories for recent events. Patients cannot recall their complete addresses but may remember parts of them. Or they may forget the name of the president but be able to recall his or her last name if given the first name. They may fail to recognize familiar people or forget their names (Mendez et al., 1992; Reisberg et al., 1986). They often make mistakes in recognizing themselves in mirrors (Mendez et al., 1992). Memory for remote events is also affected. They are generally unable to recall the names of their schools, parents, or birthplaces. They may no longer be able to speak in full sentences. Verbal responses may be limited to a few words.

Psychomotor coordination becomes impaired. Patients may begin walking in shorter, slower steps. They may no longer be able to sign their names, even when assisted by others. They may have difficulty handling a knife and fork. Agitation becomes a prominent feature at this stage, and victims may act out in response to the threat of having to contend with an environment that no longer seems controllable. Patients may pace or fidget, or display aggressive behavior such as yelling, throwing, or hitting. Patients may wander off because of restlessness and be unable to find their way back.

Victims at this stage may start talking to themselves or experience visual hallucinations or paranoid delusions. They may believe that someone is attempting to harm them or is stealing their possessions, or that their spouses are unfaithful to them. They may believe that their spouses are actually other people.

At the most severe stage, cognitive functions decline to the point where sufferers are essentially helpless. They become incontinent, are unable to communicate or walk, and require assistance in toileting and feeding. They may be entirely mute and inattentive to the environment.

Several of the principal features of Alzheimer's disease, including disorientation, memory loss, and behavior problems, are illustrated by the following case:

A 65-year-old draftsman began to have problems remembering important details at work; at home he began to have difficulty keeping his financial records up-to-date and remembering to pay bills on time. His intellectual abilities progressively declined, forcing him eventually to retire from his job. Behavioral problems began to appear at home, as he grew increasingly stubborn and even verbally and physically abusive toward others when he felt thwarted.

On neurological examination, he displayed disorientation as to place and time, believing that the consultation room was his place of employment and that the year was "1960 or something," when it was actually 1982. He had difficulty with even simple memory tests, failing to remember any of six objects shown to him ten minutes earlier, not recalling the names of his parents or siblings, or the name of the President of the United States. His speech was vague and filled with meaningless phrases. He couldn't perform simple arithmetical computations, but he could interpret proverbs correctly.

Shortly following the neurological consultation, the man was placed in a hospital since his family was no longer able to control his increasingly disruptive behavior. In the hospital, his mental abilities continued to decline, while his aggressive behavior was largely controlled by major tranquilizers (antipsychotic drugs). He was diagnosed as suffering from a Primary Degenerative Dementia of the Alzheimer type. He died at age 74, some 8 years following the onset of his symptoms.

■ *Adapted from Spitzer et al., 1989, pp. 131–132*

Victims' difficulties in recalling recent events may stem from breakdown of the biological processes involved in consolidating memories (Hart, 1987).

Although intellectual functioning declines progressively in AD, certain cognitive functions appear to remain relatively intact. A study of 141 Alzheimer's patients showed that they performed fairly well at repeating words or phrases that were just spoken to them (Teng et al., 1987). They also were generally able to follow written commands, which suggests that written notes may help them partially to compensate for memory deficits and to better organize their behavior. AD patients find it difficult to complete more complicated tasks, however, such as spelling words backward or copying complex designs. Earlier age of onset of AD was associated with poorer cognitive functioning, when the duration of illness was kept constant. Perhaps the form of AD that strikes patients earlier in life is more severe.

The Global Deterioration Scale, or GDS (Reisberg et al., 1982), shows the magnitude or "stage" of cognitive decline associated with normal aging and with various degrees of severity of Alzheimer's disease (see Table 12.3). Keep in mind, however, that forgetfulness among the aged may fall within the spectrum of normal aging. It is not necessarily an early sign of Alzheimer's disease. A study of 40 people who averaged 69 years of age and complained of forgetfulness (GDS Stage 2) were found 3½ years later to be alive and functioning well in the community (Reisberg et al., 1986). Only 5% of them showed notable cognitive deterioration during the 3½ years. Elderly people (and some of us not quite that advanced in years) complain of not remembering names as well as they used to, or of forgetting names that were once well known to them. Although mild forgetfulness may concern people, it need not impair their social or occupational functioning (Reisberg et al., 1986).

■ IMPACT ON THE FAMILY: A FUNERAL THAT NEVER ENDS?

Alzheimer's disease touches on people's deepest fears, namely fears of losing control of one's mind, one's thoughts, one's actions, one's environment. Families who helplessly watch their loved ones slowly deteriorate have been described as attending a "funeral that never ends" (Aronson, 1988). Living with a person with advanced AD may seem like living with a stranger, so profound are the changes in the person's personality and behavior.

At least 2 of 3 persons with AD and related disorders live at home (Gurland & Cross, 1986). Eventually, they require round-the-clock attention from family members (Gelman et al., 1989), placing incredible strains on the members of the family who shoulder the burden of care. Spouses usually provide the bulk of care, often with the assistance of their children, principally their daughters or daughters-in-law (Aronson, 1988). The children, usually middle-aged, are caught (some describe it as being "sandwiched") between the demands of caring for a demented parent and tending to their own children, marriages, and careers. The stress caused by the symptoms of advanced AD, such as wandering away, aggressiveness, destructiveness, incontinence, screaming, and remaining awake at night all contribute to the level of stress imposed on the caregivers (Gurland & Cross, 1986).

Families who no longer can shoulder the burden of care may seek to place the AD patient in a nursing home or long-term care facility. Generally speaking, it is the ability of the family to support the AD patient financially and emotionally, and not the degree of dementia or impairment of functioning, that determines whether or not afflicted people become institutionalized (Aronson, 1988). About 60% of nursing home residents suffer from dementias of one type or another (Davies, 1988). Because Medicare, the system of health care for the elderly, does not cover long-term custodial care in nursing homes for victims of dementia, families must either foot the bill themselves or seek subsidized care (Medicaid) for indigent patients (Aronson, 1988).

Self-help groups have been established to provide families of AD patients with emotional support and opportunities to share information about the disease. More than a thousand support groups—composed of individuals who are living through or have lived through caring for family members with AD—have been started by the Alzheimer's Disease and Related Disorders Association (ADRDA) (Marks, 1988).

■ THEORETICAL PERSPECTIVES

The plaques that characterize Alzheimer's disease are believed by many scientists to destroy the adjacent brain tissue, which leads to loss of memory function, confusion, and other symptoms of the disease (Angier, 1990). These plaques appear to be composed of fibrous protein fragments, known as beta amyloid. For some reason, possibly genetic mutation, the plaques break off from a larger protein during metabolic processes and cluster together in strings that attract remnants of other nerve cells, forming stiff ropelike patches, or plaques.

There is evidence of genetic transmission of AD. The risk of contracting AD is estimated to be about four times greater among first-degree relatives of AD patients—parents, siblings, or offspring—than among the general population (Crystal, 1988; Mohs et al., 1987). Perhaps 10 to 30% of AD cases are transmitted genetically (Cowley, 1989). Evidence for a genetic basis to Alzheimer's disease is strengthened by research in which a particular gene that researchers have linked to Alzheimer's disease was implanted into mouse embryos. Gene implantation led to the development in adulthood of the characteristic plaques and neurofibrillary tangles associated with the disease in people (Gordon et al., 1991). Like human Alzheimer's patients, the mice also showed evidence of massive brain cell death. Scientists have also been able to trace the genetic transmission of Alzheimer's across several generations in humans (Benson et al., 1991). Scientists studying stored tissue samples from three generations of one family affected by Alzheimer's showed that every family member who developed the disease had inherited the defective gene.

On a biochemical level, researchers suspect that dying nerve cells in the brain may release enzymes which lead protein fragments (that then form plaques) to break off. Other factors, such as an environmental toxin or an underlying infection, may also play causal roles (Kolata, 1991). An understanding of the biochemical stages through which plaques are formed may enable researchers to develop drugs that block their formation (Kolata, 1991).

Other biochemical research focuses on possible roles for imbalances in brain neurotransmitters, especially acetylcholine (ACh). AD patients show reduced levels of ACh in their brains (Davies, 1988), perhaps because of loss of brain cells in an area of the brain, the nucleus basalis of Meynert, that manufactures ACh (Coyle et al., 1983; Whitehouse et al., 1982).

Electroencephalographic evidence reveals a relative slowing in brain wave activity among AD patients (Albert et al., 1986) that may reflect reductions in the activity of neurotransmitters like ACh. There is also some evidence that ACh deficiencies give rise to AD symptoms. For example, normal young people who take a drug inhibiting the activity of the brain cells that normally respond to ACh undergo memory losses similar to those observed among older people with similar losses (Drachman & Leavitt, 1974).

Various other casual agents may be involved in AD. Some researchers suggest that AD may be triggered by a slow-acting virus that destroys the brain cells which produce ACh, but the evidence is sketchy (Davies, 1988). Others have postulated that AD may be linked to brain traumas. Aluminum toxicity has also been suggested, based largely on findings of abnormal concentrations of aluminum in the brains of AD victims (Crowley, 1989). The theory suggests that susceptible persons who are exposed to large amounts of the metal in food, water, or deodorants may eventually develop the disease (Kolata, 1992). However, the evidence for aluminum toxicity as a causal factor in AD is inconclusive.

 Metal poisoning may play some role in Alzheimer's disease, but most authorities consider the evidence inconclusive.

■ **TREATMENT** Because AD is connected with lessened ACh in the brain, chemotherapy has aimed at heightening ACh levels. One drug under study is tacrine, which inhibits the breakdown of ACh by decreasing the action of an enzyme that metabolizes ACh. In a 6-week double-blind, placebo-controlled study of tacrine with 632 patients with "probable" Alzheimer's disease, use of tacrine was connected with statistically significant *decreases in the rate of loss* of cognitive performance, as judged by cognitive tests that measure such abilities as word recognition (Davis et al., 1992). There were no significant differences between treated and control subjects in physicians' ratings of the subjects' overall functioning, however. Because there were no signs that tacrine led to meaningful changes in subjects' ability to function in everyday tasks, the effects of the medication can be considered modest at best (Growdon, 1992). Moreover, tacrine was connected with side effects such as headaches, gastrointestinal symptoms, and elevated enzyme levels that could lead to liver damage (Davis et al., 1992). Because of the risk of side effects, tacrine has been made available only on a limited basis under strict study conditions. We still lack an effective and safe treatment for AD.

The treatment for irreversible dementias like AD largely consists of therapeutic support and tranquilizing medication to help control the emotional agitation and inappropriate behavior that accompanies severe dementias. Early diagnosis of AD may not stem cognitive deterioration, but it allows the families of AD victims a chance to set aside money, make retirement plans, or make a change in residence to ensure access to adequate care (Crystal, 1988). People who are suspected of having AD should also be evaluated quickly because other conditions that produce AD-like symptoms, such as stroke or depression, may be treatable or reversible (Dieckmann et al., 1988). The depression that is frequently connected with AD may also be treatable by psychotherapy or antidepressant medication (Dieckmann et al., 1988). Behavioral problems associated with AD may also be treated by behavioral and chemotherapeutic approaches. Clearly, much remains to be learned about the causes and treatment of AD.

Vascular Dementia

The brain, like other living tissues, depends on the bloodstream to supply it with oxygen and glucose and to carry away its metabolic wastes. Mental functioning can be impaired when normal circulation to and within the brain is disrupted, for example by strokes and cerebral hemorrhages. Repeated strokes can also cause a form of dementia called multi-infarct dementia or *vascular dementia*.

■ **STROKES** When the blood supply to the brain is cut off by a clot in a blood vessel, the parts of the brain that are normally supplied by that vessel may be damaged or destroyed, causing a cerebrovascular accident, or CVA. A CVA is more commonly called a stroke. In one type of stroke, a *cerebral thrombosis*, a blood clot forms within a blood vessel and blocks or *occludes* circulation. In another type of stroke, a *cerebral embolism*, a blood clot or another substance, such as an air bubble or fatty globule, travels from elsewhere in the body and becomes lodged within the blood vessel, occluding circulation. *Atherosclerosis* (the buildup of fatty nodules along the interior walls of blood vessels) constricts the vessels, thereby increasing the likelihood of either type of stroke.

The effects of a stroke depend on the extent of the brain damage and can be severe—fatal, in fact. Some trivial ("silent") strokes do not affect key brain regions and produce only minor effects. Most stroke victims need to adjust to some degree of permanent impairment, however. Survivors may experience paralysis or loss of sensation on one side of the body, loss of speech (aphasia), and impaired memory. Some cannot walk on their own. Many victims find it difficult to adjust to their loss of functioning. As a consequence, they may have unstable moods that fluctuate between depression and rage.

Aphasia, which refers to the partial or complete loss of ability to comprehend and produce language, is a common effect of stroke. There are sensory or receptive aphasias and motor or expressive aphasias. In sensory aphasias, people have difficulty comprehending language but retain the ability to express themselves. In motor aphasias, ability to express one's thoughts is impaired, but the person can understand language. Motor aphasics may not be able to summon up the names of familiar objects when they try to speak, or they may scramble the normal order of words.

One of the more famous self-descriptions of aphasia is by a 19th-century medical scientist, Jacques Lordat:

> When I wanted to speak I could not find the right expression. . . . My thoughts were ready, but the sounds that should convey them to my informant were no longer at my disposal . . . I was no longer able to grasp the ideas of others, for the [aphasia] that prevented me from speaking made me incapable of understanding the sounds I heard quickly enough to grasp their meaning.
>
> Quoted in Freemon, 1981, p. 156

■ **CEREBRAL HEMORRHAGE** In a *cerebral hemorrhage*, a blood vessel in the brain ruptures, causing blood to leak into brain tissue, damaging or destroying it. The weakness in the vessel wall that permits it to rupture may be a congenital defect or a result of hypertension, which may gradually weaken the walls of blood vessels. Sometimes the causes remain unknown.

The effects of a cerebral hemorrhage depend on the size of the ruptured vessel and the area of the brain affected. A victim of a cerebral hemorrhage typically experiences sudden loss of consciousness and lapses into a coma, which may be accompanied by convulsions. Extensive hemorrhage can be lethal. Survivors may experience symptoms like those suffered by stroke victims, including aphasias, disturbances in memory and judgment, and motor problems such as paralysis.

■ **MULTI-INFARCT DEMENTIA** Multi-infarct dementias (MIDs) are caused by repeated strokes or other forms of brain damage. A stroke occurs when a blood clot cuts off the supply of blood to part of the brain. The areas of the brain that are affected may cease to function, and the victim may suffer disabilities in motor, speech, and cognitive functions. Death may also occur. Single strokes may produce gross impairments in specific functions, such as an aphasia (the loss of the ability to speak or to comprehend speech), but single strokes do not typically cause the more generalized cognitive declines that define dementia. Multi-infarct dementia generally results from multiple strokes that occur at different times and that have cumulative effects on a wide range of mental abilities.

Multi-infarct dementias are symptomatically similar to Alzheimer's disease (AD), including loss of memory and language ability, agitation and emotional instability, and loss of ability to care for one's own basic needs. AD is characterized by insidious onset and gradual decline of mental functioning. MID, however, tends to occur abruptly and to follow a stepwise deterioration of rapid changes in cognitive functioning, with the declines believed to reflect the effects of additional strokes (Brinkman et al., 1986). In MID, certain cognitive functions may remain relatively intact in the early course of the disorder, leading to a pattern of patchy deterioration in which islands of mental competence remain while other abilities suffer gross impairment, depending on the particular areas of the brain that have been damaged.

Dementia due to HIV Disease

Human immunodeficiency virus (HIV), the virus that causes AIDS, can invade the central nervous system (Levy et al., 1985), causing a cognitive disorder, dementia due to HIV disease. This cognitive disorder leads to progressive impairment in cognitive functioning and motor behavior (Tross & Hirsch, 1988). Persons with AIDS who develop dementia tend to decline faster and succumb sooner than do those with AIDS who remain free of dementia (Levy et al., 1984). Dementia is rare in persons with HIV who have not yet developed full-blown AIDS, however (Altman, 1989a).

The first signs of dementia may mimic depression: impaired concentration, apathy, social withdrawal, difficulty recalling recent events, and lack of emotional responsiveness (blunted or flat affect) (Faulstich, 1987). Early neurological signs include problems in walking, muscle coordination (ataxia), and reflexes. Cognitive functioning declines rapidly within 2 months of the appearance of symptoms (Tross & Hirsch, 1988). AIDS patients are often aware of their deteriorating cognitive abilities, and may respond with depression and anger (Tross & Hirsch, 1988). As the disease progresses, dementia grows more severe, taking the form of delusions, disorientation, and marked impairments in memory and thought. In its later stages, the dementia may resemble the profound deficiencies found among Alzheimer's victims. Eventually patients may experience seizures, mutism, and coma, leading to death (Faulstich, 1987).

Dementia due to Head Trauma

Head trauma can injure the brain. Such injury is caused by jarring, banging, or cutting brain tissue, usually because of accident or assault. There are several types of brain traumas, including concussions, contusions, and lacerations. Specific changes in personality following traumatic injury to the brain vary with the site and extent of the injury, among other factors (Prigatano, 1992). Damage to the frontal lobe, for example, is associated with a range of emotional changes involving alterations of mood and personality (Stuss et al., 1992).

■ **CONCUSSION** One type of brain trauma is the **concussion**—epidemic among football players and boxers—which involves the momentary loss of consciousness resulting from a violent blow to, or jarring of, the head. The loss of consciousness may last from a second or two to a few minutes. Recovery is usually complete, without lingering effects.

 Football players and prize-fighters can often recover completely from being knocked out, without lingering cognitive effects.

In severe cases, however, concussions can produce delirium and agitation, and victims have amnesia for the events directly preceding the injury. In some cases, a post-traumatic syndrome may persist for weeks or months following the injury. Such syndromes are characterized by headaches, anxiety, insomnia, depression, and memory deficits. Notable permanent brain damage is rare.

■ **CONTUSION** A more serious type of brain trauma, the **contusion**, is produced by jarring the brain so hard that the soft brain tissue is pounded against the hard bone of the skull and bruised. A coma typically results and may last for hours or days. Hemorrhaging may require surgery to repair the damage or stop the bleeding. Upon awakening, victims may have problems with cognitive functions and speech, but functioning is usually regained in about a week. Repeated concussions and contusions, however, such as those incurred by professional boxers,

Heading toward a concussion? Concussions are epidemic among boxers and some other athletes, such as football players. Concussions involve transient loss of consciousness from a blow to the head. Severe cases can produce delirium and agitation.

can cause lasting brain damage and give rise to dementia and emotional instability. Boxers who suffer from this condition, called the "punch-drunk syndrome" or *traumatic encephalopathy* (*encephalopathy* derives from Greek roots meaning "something wrong in the head"), experience cognitive and physical symptoms like slurring of speech, shaky or unsteady gait, emotional problems, memory deficits, dizziness, and tremors.

■ **LACERATION** The most serious type of brain trauma, a **laceration**, is an injury caused by a foreign object that pierces the skull and damages brain tissue. The extent of the damage is related to the location and extent of the injury. Although a severe laceration can cause immediate death, survivors often suffer permanent brain damage that results in major mental and physical impairments. Sometimes, however, the victim "luckily" experiences only minor damage or no permanent effects.

Dementia due to Parkinson's Disease

Parkinson's disease was identified by the physician James Parkinson in 1817. Parkinson treated several patients who suffered from a degenerative process that was characterized by shaking or tremors, rigidity, disturbances in posture (leaning forward), and lack of control over body movements. Parkinson's disease afflicts between 400,000 and 1 million people in the

Parkinson's disease. Parkinson's disease is characterized by tremors, rigidity, disturbances in posture, and lack of control over body movements. There is also evidence of cognitive and perceptual impairment, especially during the later stages of the disease. Here a physician examines a Parkinson's patient for signs of motor impairment.

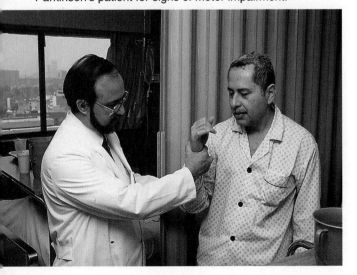

United States (Cowley, 1992). It affects men and women about equally and most often strikes between the ages of 50 and 69 (Knight et al., 1988).

Parkinson's patients may be able to exercise control over the shaking or tremors, but only briefly. Some victims cannot walk at all. Others walk laboriously, in a crouch. Parkinson's patients execute voluntary body movements with difficulty, have poor control over fine motor movements, such as finger control, and have sluggish reflexes. Parkinson's patients look expressionless, as if they are wearing masks, a symptom that apparently reflects the degeneration of brain tissue that controls facial muscles. It is particularly difficult for patients to engage in sequences of complex movements, such as those required to sign their names. Patients with the disease may be unable to coordinate two movements at the same time, as seen in this description of a patient who had difficulty walking and reaching for his wallet at the same time:

A 58-year-old man was walking across the hotel lobby in order to pay his bill. He reached into his inside jacket pocket for his wallet. He stopped walking instantly as he did so and stood immobile in the lobby in front of strangers. He became aware of his suspended locomotion and resumed his stroll to the cashier; however, his hand remained rooted in his inside pocket, as though he were carrying a weapon he might display once he arrived at the cashier.

■ *Adapted from Knight et al., 1988*

Parkinson's disease involves the destruction of neurons in the basal ganglia of the brain, specifically in a region called the *substantia nigra* ("black substance"), which lies below the cerebral cortex and is involved in controlling body movements (Kolata, 1991b). In some cases, the damage or destruction is considered to be drug-induced (Rajput et al., 1984; Widner et al., 1992). Major tranquilizers like Thorazine or Stelazine are known to induce Parkinsonian side effects, for example. Other possible causes, such as viruses, environmental toxins, and arteriosclerosis, have also been noted (Knight et al., 1988; Rajput et al., 1984). In most cases, however, the cause remains unknown.

Some Parkinson's victims suffer cognitive impairments, but they tend to be more subtle than those exhibited by Alzheimer's patients (Knight et al., 1988). Despite marked motor disability, intellectual functions appear to remain intact in most Parkinson's patients in the early stages of the disease. Patients in the later stages seem to experience greater deficits in memory, language, and perceptual skills. Parkinson's patients often become socially withdrawn and are at greater-than-average risk for depression (Cummings, 1992). Depression may be due to difficulty in coping with the disease or to the biochemical changes that are part and parcel of the disease (Rao et al., 1992).

The cells that are affected in Parkinson's disease are involved in the manufacture and storage of the neurotransmitter dopamine (Freed et al., 1992; Spencer et al., 1992; Widner et al., 1992). Thus, the disease may be related to deficiencies in the amount of dopamine available to the brain. The drug L-dopa, first used in the 1970s, is converted to dopamine in the brain. It brought hope to Parkinson's patients by increasing the levels of dopamine in the brain (Rajput et al., 1984). About 80% of Parkinson's patients showed significant improvements in their tremors and motor symptoms following treatment with L-dopa (Helme, 1982). L-dopa helps control the symptoms and slows the progress of the disease, but it does not cure it. Moreover, L-dopa loses its effectiveness as the disease progresses, so that most patients continue to deteriorate (Kolata, 1991b). The drug is often rendered useless within 10 years of treatment (Cowley, 1992).

Little progress has been made in treating Parkinson's disease since the introduction of L-dopa. Recent research findings raise hopes that new approaches may be in the offing, however. For example, two research groups independently reported finding a brain chemical that protects and stimulates the nerve cells that die or are disabled in sufferers of Parkinson's disease (Hefti et al., 1991; Hyman et al., 1991). The significance of this finding in developing specific interventions to protect these nerve cells from damage or to rejuvenate disabled cells remains to be determined.

Other research groups (e.g., Freed et al., 1992; Spencer et al., 1992; Widner et al., 1992) have transplanted dopamine-producing neurons from the brains of aborted fetuses into the brains of Parkinson's patients. The hope is that fetal cells will take root in the recipient's brain and produce dopamine, replenishing the loss of this vital brain chemical in Parkinson sufferers (Cowley, 1992). Many of the patients receiving the brain-tissue implants gained more control over motor and speech functions and showed less need of L-dopa. However, they were not restored to normal (Cowley, 1992). Fetal tissue is used because it is more plastic than tissue from deceased children or adults (that is, more adaptable to surviving and functioning in the host brain), and it is also less likely to stimulate an immune response in the host and thus be rejected (Garry et al., 1992).

Many questions are raised by this treatment approach, however. Some are moral and ethical. A debate is underway, for example, about whether it is proper to use tissues from electively aborted fetuses in research or treatment (Garry et al., 1992; Kassirer & Angell, 1992). Some people worry that successful therapy of this sort could lead to the purposeful conception and abortion of fetuses for medical purposes. Other questions about this approach reflect the early stage of the research (Fahn, 1992). For example: Exactly how much fetal tissue is effective? How long do benefits last? Will the brain of the host regulate dopamine secretion by transplanted cells? Will this treatment reverse Parkinson's disease or merely delay its progress?

Dementia due to Huntington's Disease

Huntington's disease, also known as Huntington's chorea, was first recognized by the neurologist George Huntington in 1872. Huntington's disease involves a progressive deterioration of the **basal ganglia**, especially of the *caudate nucleus* and the *putamen*, which primarily affects neurons that produce ACh and **GABA**.

The symptoms may appear in childhood but usually begin in the prime of adulthood, between the ages of 30 and 50. The most prominent physical symptoms of the disease are involuntary, jerky movements of the face (grimaces), neck, limbs, and trunk—in contrast to the poverty of movement that typifies Parkinson's disease. These twitches are termed *choreiform*, which derives from the Greek *choreia*, meaning "dance." The psychological effects of the disease involve progressive dementia with severe memory loss (Caine et al., 1977). Unstable moods, alternating with states of apathy and depression, are common. As the disorder progresses, paranoia may develop and patients may become suicidally depressed. Eventually, there is loss of control of bodily functions, leading to death, which generally occurs within 15 years after the onset.

One of the victims of Huntington's disease was the folksinger Woody Guthrie, who gave us the song "This Land Is Your Land," among others. He died of Huntington's disease in 1967, after 22 years of battling the malady. Like many other victims of Huntington's disease, Guthrie was misdiagnosed as an alcoholic. He spent several years in a number of mental hospitals before the correct diagnosis was made. When the symptoms first appeared, he said it felt as though he were drunk. He would become clumsy and fly into fits of despair and rage. Slowly, the disease progressed. He could no longer play the guitar.

Eventually, he could not speak. Doctors could do nothing to prevent his decline and death.

Research into genetic testing of families suggests that the disease can be attributed to a defective gene that lies near the tip of chromosome 4 (Blakeslee, 1992). The gene is apparently connected with *mitochondria,* which are factors in cells that manufacture energy and fuel basic life processes. In addition to producing cognitive and motor impairments, problems in energy metabolism cause people with Huntington's disease to lose weight rapidly (Young, 1992). As a by-product of energy metabolism gone awry, lactic acid builds up and kills cells in the brain. Researchers are therefore investigating the potential benefits of drugs and vitamins that lower levels of lactic acid (Young, 1992).

Huntington's disease is transmitted genetically from either parent to children of either gender. People who have a parent with Huntington's disease stand a 50% chance of inheriting the gene (Blakeslee, 1992). People who inherit the gene eventually contract the disease.

Until recently, children of Huntington's disease victims had to wait until the symptoms developed—usually in midlife—to learn whether they had inherited the disease. A genetic test has been developed that can detect carriers of the defective gene—those who will eventually develop the disease should they live long enough. Eventually, perhaps, genetic engineering may provide a means of modifying the defective gene or its effects. Researchers are also closely scrutinizing the effects of transplants of fetal brain tissue into Parkinson's patients because variations of this procedure might have benefits for people with Huntington's disease (Fahn, 1992). Because researchers have not yet developed ways to cure or control Huntington's disease, some potential carriers, like folksinger Arlo Guthrie, whose father was Woody Guthrie, prefer not to know whether they have inherited the gene.

Dementia due to Pick's Disease

Pick's disease gives rise to a progressive dementia that is symptomatically similar to AD (Davies, 1988). Symptoms include memory loss and social inappropriateness, such as a loss of modesty or the display of flagrant sexual behavior (Davies, 1988). Diagnosis is confirmed only upon autopsy by the *absence* of the neurofibrillary tangles and plaques that are found in AD and by the presence of other abnormal structures—Pick's bodies—in nerve cells (Heston et al., 1987). Pick's disease is believed to account for perhaps 5% of dementias. It occurs most frequently between the ages of 60 and 70, and the risk declines

Arlo Guthrie. Arlo Guthrie's father, folksinger Woody Guthrie, died from Huntington's disease. Huntington's chorea involves a progressive deterioration of the basal ganglia, resulting in motor impairment, deterioration in cognitive functioning, and eventual death. The disease is transmitted genetically, and the onset generally occurs between the ages of 30 and 50. Arlo stands a 50% chance of inheriting the disease from his father.

with advancing age after 70 (Heston & Mastry, 1982). Men are more likely than women to suffer from Pick's disease (Heston et al., 1987).

Pick's disease appears to run in families, and a genetic component is suspected in its etiology (Heston et al., 1987). It has been estimated that members of the immediate family of victims of Pick's disease have an overall risk of 17% of contracting the disease by age 75 (Heston et al., 1987).

Dementia and Other Psychological Problems due to General Medical Conditions

Conditions in this category include brain tumors, nutritional deficiencies, endocrine disorders, and infections of the brain.

■ **BRAIN TUMORS** Benign and malignant (cancerous) brain tumors can cause serious cognitive disorders in addition to the threats they pose to our physical health (see Figure 12.3). The skull prevents the brain from expanding, so even a benign tumor can press against and damage the surrounding tissue. Malignant brain tumors can be primary (that is, originate in the brain), or secondary (spread or *metastasize* to the brain from other cancerous sites in the body). In either case, they are made up of cells that proliferate rapidly and destroy adjacent healthy cells.

The symptoms produced by a brain tumor depend on the tumor's size and location. Memory problems sometimes represent the first signs of a tumor. Recurrent headaches are another sign. Because such early signs also occur in many other disorders, the possibility of a brain tumor is often overlooked. As the tumor grows, symptoms worsen, giving rise to persistent, severe headaches, seizures, disorientation, memory impairment, vomiting, changes in vision, motor impairment, and, in some cases, dementia. The personality may also be affected. Depression, flat or blunted affect, and confusion are some of the personality changes observed in patients with brain tumors. Some patients become slovenly in their dress or careless in their work. Some tumors are operable and can be removed by surgery, so early detection and treatment is critical. Inoperable malignancies sometimes respond to radiation.

■ **NUTRITIONAL DEFICIENCIES** Nutritional imbalances or deficiencies may also affect cognitive functioning. Chronic alcoholics, as noted in the section on amnestic disorders, may neglect their diets and develop such disorders as *alcohol persisting amnestic disorder* (more widely known as *Korsakoff's syndrome*) as a result.

Figure 12.3 A CAT scan showing a tumor.
This CAT scan of a 67-year-old man shows a tumor on the left side of the brain (the right side of the photograph). The tumor is the dark, roughly circular region.

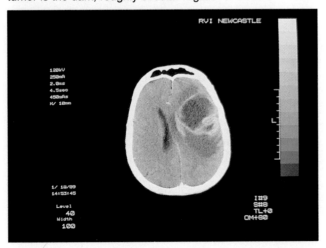

A deficiency of niacin, a B vitamin, causes **pellagra**, which derives its name from the Latin *pellis*, meaning "skin," and the Greek *agra*, meaning "seizure." Pellagra gives rise to physical symptoms like diarrhea and skin eruptions (hence the name), and to psychological symptoms such as anxiety, depression, loss of memory for recent events, and problems in concentration. If left untreated, hallucinations and delirium may result, and eventually death. Because of greater attention to diet and an improved standard of living, pellagra is now uncommon in the United States. It is more common in developing countries where diets are nutritionally unbalanced and consist mainly of cornmeal. Except in the most advanced cases, treatment with a diet rich in niacin and other key vitamins is an effective treatment.

Beriberi (a reduplication of the Sinhalese word meaning "weakness") is another disease caused by thiamine deficiency. It is thus found commonly among alcoholics and others whose diet is lacking in thiamine, sometimes occurring together with pellagra. Beriberi is characterized by nerve disorders that produce difficulties in memory and concentration, irritability, fatigue and lethargy, lack of appetite, insomnia, irritability, and loss of appetite.

■ **ENDOCRINE DISORDERS** Because hormones are released directly into the bloodstream and travel throughout the body, including the brain, overactivity or underactivity of endocrine glands can affect psychological as well as physical functions.

The thyroid gland secretes **thyroxin**, which is involved in the regulation of the metabolic rate. Hyperthyroidism (also called *Grave's disease*) is caused by oversecretion of thyroxin, which accelerates the metabolism and produces weight loss, "bug eyes," and psychological effects such as excitability, insomnia, anxiety, restlessness, even transient delusions or hallucinations. Former President George Bush and first lady Barbara Bush were treated for Grave's disease.

Hypothyroidism, which results from abnormally low levels of thyroxin, may cause **cretinism** in childhood, a condition characterized by stunted growth and mental retardation. In adulthood, hypothyroidism, also called *myxedema*, slows the metabolism and is associated with physical changes such as dry skin and weight gain, and psychological changes such as sluggishness and fatigue, difficulties in concentration and memory, depression, and dementia in some cases. The widespread use of iodized salt, which prevents thyroid deficiencies, has greatly reduced the occurrence of hypothyroidism in the United States.

Victims of Grave's disease. Former President George Bush and first lady Barbara Bush both suffer from Grave's disease, which is caused by oversecretion of thyroxin.

The adrenal glands, which are located above the kidneys, consist of an outer layer, or cortex, and an internal core, or medulla. The adrenal cortex secretes steroids, which enhance resistance to stress and regulate metabolism of carbohydrates. Cortical underactivity may result in **Addison's disease** (after the English physician, Thomas Addison), which is characterized by weight loss, low blood pressure, fatigue, irritability, lack of motivation, social withdrawal, and depression. Cortical overactivity, or **Cushing's syndrome** (after the American physician, Harvey Cushing), is a relatively rare disease generally affecting young women. Cushing's syndrome is characterized by physical symptoms such as weight gain, fatigue, and muscle weakness, and psychological features such as negative mood states that may fluctuate between depression and anxiety.

■ **INFECTIONS OF THE BRAIN** Infections of the brain may damage or destroy neural tissue and have profound mental and physical effects. We consider several major types of brain infection, including encephalitis, meningitis, and neurosyphilis.

Encephalitis **Encephalitis** is derived from Greek roots meaning "inflammation" (*-itis*) in "the head" (*kephale*). It refers to any kind of infection of the brain. Most infections are caused by viruses carried by mosquitoes, ticks, and other insects. Inanimate objects that penetrate the brain, such as shrapnel or bullets, cause structural damage, may carry infectious organisms, and also leave orifices that allow other infectious organisms to enter. In other cases, infections from other parts of the body spread to the brain.

An epidemic of encephalitis, suspected of being caused by an influenza virus carried by mosquitoes, spread throughout Europe and the United States around the time of World War I. It was called sleeping sickness because it induced prolonged periods of lethargy and sleepiness, which were followed by periods of irritability and excitability. Epidemics of encephalitis are practically unknown today in developed nations, but outbreaks of encephalitis—along with infestations of insects—continue to plague developing nations.

Delirium can occur during the acute phase of encephalitis, and some patients suffer convulsions or coma. Changes in personality also occur, especially in young children, and survivors may be left with psychological symptoms like irritability, restlessness, depression, and dementia. There is usually an apparently complete physical recovery, but some effects may linger: tremors, paralysis in the arms or legs, speech and hearing problems, and, in the case of afflicted infants, mental retardation.

Meningitis Another type of infection that afflicts the central nervous system, **meningitis**, involves acute inflammation of the membranes, or meninges (from the Greek *meningos*, meaning "membrane") that cover the spinal cord and brain. Various microbes, such as viruses, bacteria, and protozoa, may cause meningitis. The most common cause is the meningococcus (from the Greek *kokkos*, meaning "kernel" or "berry") bacterium, which is also responsible for most epidemics. If treated early with antibiotics, this form of meningitis can generally be cured. If left untreated, however, it may lead to coma and death. Victims typically experience a high fever, convulsions, severe headache, muscle stiffness and pain, vomiting, drowsiness, impaired concentration, irritability, and memory impairment. When contracted in infancy, meningitis, like encephalitis, may cause mental retardation because of its effects on developing brain tissue.

Neurosyphilis **General paresis** (from the Greek *parienai*, meaning "to relax") is a form of mental deterioration—or "relaxation," in its most negative connotation—that results from neurosyphilis, a form of syphilis in which the disease organism directly attacks the brain and central nervous system. General paresis is of historical significance to abnormal psychology. The 19th-century discovery of the connection between this form of dementia and a concrete physical illness, syphilis, strengthened the medical model and held out the promise that organic causes would eventually be found for other abnormal behavior patterns.

Syphilis is a sexually transmitted disease caused by the bacterium *Treponema pallidum.* Syphilis is almost always transmitted through genital, oral-genital, or anal contact with an infected person, but it may also be transmitted from mother to fetus through the placenta. If left untreated, syphilis undergoes several stages of development, beginning with the appearance of a painless chancre (a round hard sore with raised edges) at the site of the infection about 2 to 4 weeks following contact. Although the chancre disappears spontaneously within a few weeks, the infection continues to fester. During the secondary stage, beginning a few weeks to a few months later, a skin rash appears, which consists of reddish raised bumps. This rash also eventually disappears, and the infection enters a latency stage, which may last from 1 to 40 years, in which the infection appears dormant. The bacteria are multiplying and invading sites throughout the body, however. They sometimes destroy nerve cells in the spinal cord that control motor responses. Sometimes they attack brain tissue. In the late stage of the infection, the damage caused by the bacteria produces a wide range of symptoms, including—when the brain is attacked directly—general paresis.

It is *not* true that there is nothing to be concerned about if the symptoms of syphilis disappear by themselves. Syphilis may apparently lie dormant for many years, yet then strike the central nervous system, producing the symptoms of general paresis.

General paresis is associated with physical symptoms like tremors, slurred speech, impaired motor coordination, and, eventually, paralysis—all of which are suggestive of *relaxed* control over the body. Psychological signs include shifts in mood states, blunted emotional responsiveness, and irritability; delusions; changes in personal habits, such as suspension of personal grooming and hygiene; and progressive intellectual deterioration, including impairments of memory, judgment, and comprehension. Some paretic patients grow euphoric and entertain delusions of grandiosity. Others become lethargic and depressed. Eventually, paretic patients lapse into a state of apathy and confusion, characterized by the inability to care for themselves or to speak intelligibly. Death eventually ensues, either because of renewed infection or because of the damage caused by the existing infection.

Late-stage syphilis once accounted for 10 to 30% of admissions to psychiatric hospitals. However, advances in detection and the development of antibiotics that cure the infection has sharply reduced the incidences of late-stage syphilis and the development of general paresis. The effectiveness of treatment depends on when antibiotics are introduced and the extent of central nervous system damage. In cases where extensive tissue damage has been done, antibiotics can stem the infection and prevent further damage, thereby producing some improvement in intellectual performance. They cannot restore patients to their premorbid levels of functioning, however.

AMNESTIC DISORDERS

Amnestic disorders (amnesia) are characterized by a dramatic decline in memory functioning that is not connected with states of delirium or dementia. Amnesia is typified by the inability to learn new information (short-term memory) and to recall previously accessible information from the past (long-term memory). Problems with short-term memory may be revealed by inability to remember the names of, or to recognize, people the person met 5 or 10 minutes earlier. Immediate memory, as measured by ability to repeat back a series of numbers, seems to be unimpaired. The number series is unlikely to be recalled later, however, no matter how often it is rehearsed.

Amnestic disorders frequently follow a traumatic event, such as a blow to the head, an electric shock, or an operation. A head injury may prevent people from remembering events that occurred shortly before the accident. The victim of an automobile accident or a football player who is knocked unconscious may be unable to remember events that occurred within several minutes of the injury. The accident victim may not remember leaving the house. The football player may not remember leaving the locker room. Consider the following case:

A medical student was rushed to the hospital after he was thrown from a motorcycle. His parents were with him in his hospital room when he awakened. As his parents were explaining what had happened to him, the door suddenly flew open and his flustered wife, whom he had married a few weeks earlier, rushed into the room, leaped onto his bed, and began to caress him and expressed her great relief that he was not seriously

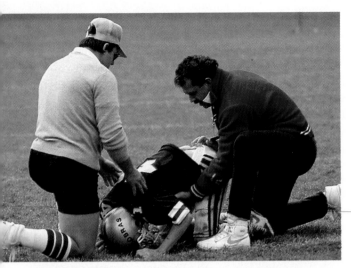

Amnestic disorder.   An amnestic disorder can follow a traumatic injury such as a blow to the head. This football player may not be able to recall the events that happened just prior to his being tackled, nor the collision itself.

injured. After several minutes of expressing her love and reassurance, his wife departed and the flustered student looked at his mother and asked: "Who is she?"

■ *Adapted from Freemon, 1981, p. 96*

 It is true that after a motorcycle accident, a medical student failed to recognize the woman he had married a few weeks earlier.

The medical student's long-term memory loss not only included memories dating to the accident but also farther back to before he was married or had met his wife. Like most victims of post-traumatic amnesia, the medical student recovered his memory fully.

In amnestic disorders, recall of recently acquired information often suffers greater decrements than memory of distant events. Amnestic people are more likely to remember events from their childhood than last evening's dinner, for example. Amnestic syndrome produces some disorientation, and amnestic people may attempt to fill the gaps in their memories with imaginary events. They tend to lack insight into their loss, however, and they may deny their memory problems. Or they may admit that they have a memory problem but appear apathetic about it, showing a kind of emotional blandness.

Although amnestic people may suffer profound memory losses, their general intelligence tends to remain within a normal range (Butters et al., 1978). Memory loss in pure amnesia may thus be distinguished from that occurring in progressive dementias like Alzheimer's disease, in which memory and intellectual functioning both deteriorate (Butters et al., 1986). Early detection and diagnosis of the causes of memory problems are vital to many sufferers, because 20 to 30% of them are correctable (Cohen, 1986).

Other causes of amnesia include brain surgery, sudden loss of oxygen to the brain **(hypoxia)**, infection, and **infarction** (blockage) of the blood vessels supplying the brain.

Korsakoff's syndrome. Chronic alcoholics are prone to developing this disorder, which is characterized by profound deficits in memory and acquisition of new information. Korsakoff's is connected with thiamine deficiency, which is a common condition among chronic alcoholics.

Alcohol Persisting Amnestic Disorder

A common cause of amnestic disorder is thiamine deficiency due to chronic abuse of alcohol. Alcoholics tend to take poor care of their nutritional needs and may not follow a diet that is rich enough in vitamin B_1, or thiamine. Thiamine deficiencies may produce an irreversible form of brain damage called **alcohol persisting amnestic disorder**, or **Korsakoff's syndrome**. Korsakoff's syndrome is not limited to alcoholics, however. It has been reported in other groups who experience thiamine deficiencies, such as prisoners of war.

Korsakoff's syndrome produces substantial losses in short- and long-term memories and inability to form new memories. These memory deficits are believed to result from the loss of brain tissue due to bleeding (Victor et al., 1971). Despite these memory losses, patients with Korsakoff's syndrome may retain their general level of intelligence (Huppert & Piercy, 1979). They are often described as being superficially friendly but lacking in insight, unable to discriminate between actual events and wild stories they invent to fill the gaps in their memories. Korsakoff sufferers sometimes become grossly disoriented and confused and require custodial care.

Korsakoff's syndrome often follows an acute attack of **Wernicke's disease**, another brain disorder caused by thiamine deficiency. Wernicke's disease is characterized by confusion and disorientation, difficulty maintaining balance while walking **(ataxia)**, and paralysis of the muscles that control eye movements. These symptoms may pass, but the person is often left with Korsakoff's syndrome and enduring memory impairment. If, however, Wernicke's disease is treated promptly with major doses of vitamin B_1, Korsakoff's syndrome may not ensue. Once Korsakoff's syndrome has set in, it is usually permanent, although slight improvement is possible with treatment.

EPILEPSY

CASSIUS: *What, did Caesar swound?[1]*
    CASCA: *He fell down in the market place and foamed at the mouth and was speechless.*
 BRUTUS: *'Tis very like—he hath the falling sickness.*

Shakespeare, *Julius Caesar*, I, ii.

Epilepsy—which Shakespeare referred to as "the falling sickness"—has struck not only Julius Caesar, but other notables such as Alexander the Great, Peter the Great, Lord Byron, Feodor Dostoevsky, Thomas Edison, and Vincent van Gogh.

 Julius Caesar and Vincent van Gogh did in fact suffer from epilepsy.

Consider the stigma the epileptic has had to endure. Traditionally, victims of epilepsy have been feared and shunned. Their wild gyrations during seizures have been taken as signs of possession or insanity. They have been made to feel that they are different, that they should keep their distance and not expect to lead a full life, marry, or rear children. They have been humiliated in ways that were never imposed on victims of most other diseases, causing them to develop feelings of inadequacy, shame, and embarrassment. In many cases, the emotional toll of epilepsy places a greater burden on sufferers than the physical effects. Because of these attitudes, many epileptics hide their disorders. Many physicians avoid using the term, largely because of the social stigma, preferring to label epilepsy a seizure disorder (Lechtenberg, 1984).

Epilepsy is not a disease in itself, but rather a manifestation of as many as 500 underlying disorders, such as a brain tumor, high fever during infancy, or a head injury (Blakeslee, 1988b). Epilepsy tends to be a chronic condition that typically lasts for many years (Seidenberg & Berent, 1992). It is characterized by disturbances in the electrical rhythms of the brain, which take the form of seizures and produce changes in states of consciousness (see Table 12.4). The seizures may begin several years after the initial trauma. Sometimes the seizures disappear during adolescence; in other cases, they continue for a lifetime. Some forms of epilepsy may be inherited, but most are not.

Epilepsy is among the most common neurological disorders, affecting 1 to 2% of the population (Hauser & Hesdorffer, 1990a; Herman & Whitman,

Table 12.4   Early Signs of Epilepsy
Wandering
Staring spells
Memory gaps
Bedwetting
Violent muscle spasms in sleep
Nocturnal tongue-biting

Source: Lechtenberg, 1984.

---

[1]Swoon, or faint.

1992). New cases of epilepsy occur most frequently among children under the age of 2 and among adults over the age of 65 (McLin, 1992). In fact, more than half of all cases of epilepsy begin before the age of 2 (Seidenberg & Berent, 1992). Approximately 5 to 10 children in 1,000 become epileptic (Seidenberg & Berent, 1992).

Children with epilepsy commonly fail to perform to the level of their ability in school, in large part because their seizures tend to interfere with attention and learning (Seidenberg & Berent, 1992). Psychosocial factors such as lowered teacher and parent expectations of children with epilepsy and the development of a negative self-concept may also play a role. Behavioral problems are also a frequent accompaniment of epilepsy in childhood, although it is difficult to pinpoint the causes.

Evidence is beginning to accumulate that some people with epilepsy are at increased risk of various types of psychological problems, including mood disorders, anxiety, personality changes, psychosis, and suicide (McLin, 1992). Researchers have highlighted the problem of depression in particular (Hauser & Hesdorffer, 1990a; Robertson, 1989). The unpredictability of seizure activity in many people with epilepsy can lead to feelings of learned helplessness, possibly setting the stage for depression (Hermann & Whitman, 1992). Fears that continuing seizures may harm one's physical and psychological health can compound feelings of depression and anxiety. The stigma (both real and perceived) that is attached to epilepsy in the general community can also impair self-esteem (Seidenberg & Berent, 1992) and lead to feelings of shame, as well as to tendencies to conceal the condition (Hermann & Whitman, 1992).

Epilepsy that can be attributed to definite causes such as tumors or brain trauma is called *acquired* or *symptomatic epilepsy*. Cases of unknown origin are called *idiopathic epilepsy*. People with idiopathic epilepsy are believed to have subtle brain abnormalities that are not identifiable by current techniques for studying the functioning of the brain (Lechtenberg, 1984).

Various factors may precipitate an epileptic attack. Even in patients whose seizures are generally well controlled by medication, sleeplessness, infection, trauma, abuse of alcohol or drugs, even flashing lights can trigger attacks (Lechtenberg, 1984). In some epileptics, one night of sleeplessness may evoke an attack. Others who apparently suffer from the same type of epilepsy may be able to go sleepless for days before incurring an attack. The most common cause of recurrent seizures is haphazard use of prescribed anticonvulsive medication. Hormonal changes may induce seizures at about the time of menstruation in female epileptics.

Epileptics often experience warning signs of the impending attack, called an **aura**. The aura embodies peculiar sensations or involuntary movements that are part of the seizure but experienced as separate (Lechtenberg, 1984). Auras can vary from person to person. Some people experience automatic behaviors like lip-smacking, grimacing, or spitting; or they feel compelled to turn their heads to the side. Others have sensations like unpleasant odors or tastes, feelings of depersonalization, fright, nausea, or a sense of *déja vu*—that they have previously experienced the events that are occurring. Some auras are experienced as generalized feelings of strangeness or peculiarity ("funny feelings"). Auras can usually be

Victims of epilepsy. A number of noted historic figures have suffered from epilepsy, including Julius Caesar who, in the Shakespearian play given his name, was said to suffer from "the falling sickness." Other epilepsy sufferers include the Russian ruler Peter the Great, shown in the painting to the right by Louis Caravaque, and the French postimpressionist Vincent van Gogh, shown in the self-portrait to the left.

described vividly as they occur and afterward, but people typically do not remember the convulsions themselves. Auras may help sufferers reduce the risk of injury by helping them prepare for seizures.

Types of Epilepsy

Because there are many kinds of epilepsy, it might be more appropriate to speak of epilep*sies.* *Tonic-clonic epilepsy* is the most severe type of seizure. It entails a generalized convulsive or *grand mal seizure* in which abnormal activity in both hemispheres of the brain causes a sudden loss of consciousness and convulsive, jerking movements of the body. The seizure often occurs without warning, although it may be preceded by an aura that typically consists of a few seconds of sickness or light-headedness. The attack itself may last from a few seconds to a few minutes. There are two phases of muscle activity: a *tonic phase* and a *clonic phase.* In the tonic phase, the muscles in the torso and limbs are rigidified. The legs are extended, the fists clenched, and the arms may be outstretched and forced tight against the body. This is followed by the *clonic stage,* involving strong muscle contractions of a rhythmic or clonic pattern that produce violent spasms alternating with moments of relaxation. During grand mal seizures, victims may lose bladder or bowel control and bite their tongues. They do not, however, swallow their tongues (Brody, 1992e). Grand mal seizures can frighten witnesses. Seeing someone fall to the ground and thrash about wildly can cause bystanders to turn away or flee. Informed bystanders, however, can help prevent tongue biting or breaking of teeth by placing—not forcing—an object like a folded handkerchief between the back teeth of the victim on one side of the mouth (Miller, 1978). The object should be too large to swallow. Care should be taken during insertion so that the good samaritan's fingers are not bitten. If you want to help, do not try to force the mouth open; wait until it momentarily relaxes. You may also help the person by putting something soft under the head, by removing eyeglasses, loosening tight clothing, removing sharp or hard objects from the area, and, following the seizure, turning the person to one side to permit drainage from the mouth (Brody, 1992e). You should remain with the person until the person is fully conscious, alert, and oriented, but do not offer them anything to eat or drink (Brody, 1992e). When consciousness is regained, victims may experience confusion and fatigue, or fall into a deep sleep. Upon awakening, victims may have no memory of the seizure, although they may learn of it from evidence of urination or soreness of the tongue.

Sufferers of grand mal seizures do not generally "outgrow" the disorder with age, but they may go for years or decades without a seizure. Anticonvulsive medications generally suppress recurrence of seizures (Lechtenberg, 1984).

In *petit mal epilepsy* (absence-type epilepsy) the individual experiences *absence attacks* or *petit mal seizures.* These are momentary lapses in consciousness that occur suddenly without a warning aura and usually last for a few seconds. Petit mal seizures are not accompanied by the violent spasms or falling that characterize grand mal seizures. The disorder is most common in children between the ages of 6 and 12. Petit mal seizures typically disappear during adolescence, but they may change to another type in adulthood, such as grand mal or psychomotor seizures (Lechtenberg, 1984). Petit mal seizures are characterized by transient loss of consciousness and lack of responsiveness to the environment. The victim may seem to be "staring into space." Attacks may occur repeatedly throughout the day. During such seizures, victims may seem as though they are frozen in place, as if someone had pushed the pause button on a VCR and frozen the action for a few seconds. Afterward, they pick up where they had left off, often unaware of the intervening lapse and without the confusion and fatigue that usually attend a grand mal seizure. Petit mal seizures can go unrecognized because victims may appear to be momentarily lost in thought or daydreaming.

Victims of *psychomotor* or *temporal lobe* epilepsy retain motor control but experience a loss of contact with reality that may last up to a few minutes. Sufferers of psychomotor seizures may look lost in a trance but can continue to carry out mechanical or routine tasks such as walking down the street or repetitive household chores. Psychomotor epilepsy usually begins after puberty and is thought to account for 20 to 30% of cases (Lechtenberg, 1984). Psychomotor seizures generally begin in the temporal lobe of the brain, although some do not. (Other types of epilepsy may also involve temporal lobe disturbance.) Some psychomotor seizures are characterized by abrupt, unusual, and apparently aimless behaviors such as running away, wandering off, crying or laughing, or urinating in public. There may also be hallucinations or delusional thinking. After an attack, victims may be confused and disoriented for 10 to 20 minutes. Some occasionally exhibit anger or violence while thus confused. When normal consciousness returns, the anger or violence is usually forgotten or partially recalled with embarrassment and remorse.

In *Jacksonian* or *focal* epilepsy, the seizures originate from specific brain sites and affect circumscribed parts of the body. Depending on the affected area of the brain, such seizures may consist of nothing more than finger twitching, a leg spasm, or numbness or

Table 12.5   Myths and Facts About Epilepsy

Myth	Fact
All seizures involve convulsions.	Seizures involve disturbances in the brain's electrical activity and may or may not include convulsions.
During a seizure, an epileptic blanks out.	Some seizures involve complete loss of awareness; others involve minimal changes in the state of consciousness.
Epileptics typically experience different types of seizures.	Most epileptics experience only one type of seizure.
Having a seizure means that one is epileptic.	An isolated seizure may be a passing phenomenon—such as a response to a head trauma or brain infection. Following recovery, the individual may have no greater risk of recurrent seizures than the average person.
If I have an epileptic parent, then I'm bound to get it too.	Although some neurological disorders that cause seizures may be inherited, children of an epileptic parent have less than a 3% chance of developing recurrent epilepsy. Epilepsy attributable to a head trauma is not at all inherited.
Epileptics are intellectually impaired because their brains have been damaged by their seizures.	Most people with idiopathic epilepsy (epilepsy with no known cause) show no sign of mental impairment.
Epileptics have disturbed personalities.	Epileptics can have perfectly normal personalities. Some have psychological problems that stem from coping with stigma. Learning to take precautions to avoid precipitants of seizures (for example, alcohol, exhaustion) and to take medication reliably are also stressful demands that can affect adjustment.
Men with epilepsy may commit rape during their seizures.	Some seizures may include unusual sexual behaviors that appear purposeless and not characteristic of the individual's usual behavior, such as public undressing or masturbation; however, men do not commit rapes, or make purposeful sexual advances, during seizures.
Family members should come to accept the epileptic as totally dependent on them.	Adequately controlled epilepsy is more of a manageable problem than a calamity. Even when control of seizures requires restrictions, epileptics can look forward to social and financial independence.

Source: Adapted from Lechtenberg (1984).

tingling of the skin. Victims usually remain alert, although seizures occasionally spread to other parts of the brain and progress to grand mal attacks. Some focal seizures produce visual or auditory phenomena, such as flashing lights or visual or auditory hallucinations. Table 12.5 dispels a number of myths about epilepsy.

Treatment of Epilepsy

Anticonvulsant medications, such as Dilantin and phenobarbital, can control seizures in 50% or more of the patient population (Hauser & Hesdorffer,

1990a; Lechtenberg, 1984). Patients may have to use the medication—even if they are free of seizures—for many years (Lechtenberg, 1984). When seizures cannot be controlled by medication, surgery is sometimes used either to correct neurological defects that trigger seizures or to make changes that decrease their likelihood or intensity (Blakeslee, 1988b).

The organic disorders connected with abnormal behavior are thus quite a mixed bag. Their causes, symptoms, courses, and treatments—where available—vary greatly. For these reasons, the way in which they are classified as mental disorders remains a subject of discussion among professionals.

SUMMARY

Cognitive Disorders with Organic Origins

In cognitive disorders with organic origins, there is frank or assumed organic causation, such as progressive degeneration, trauma to the brain, disease, or nutritional imbalances. The essential feature of cognitive disorders is that

they are associated with temporary or permanent dysfunctions of the brain.

Delirium

Delirium is a state of mental confusion characterized by symptoms such as impaired attention, disorientation, disorganized thinking and rambling speech, reduced level of consciousness, and perceptual disturbances. Delirium is most commonly caused by alcohol withdrawal, as in the form of delirium tremens.

Dementias

Dementia involves cognitive deterioration or impairment, as seen by memory deficits, impaired judgment, personality changes, and disorders of higher cognitive functions such as problem-solving ability and abstract thinking. Dementia is not a normal consequence of aging but a sign of a degenerative brain disorder. There are various causes of dementias, such as Alzheimer's disease, Pick's disease, chronic intoxication, brain infections, tumors, and strokes. Depression is common among the elderly and may be associated with memory deficits that can lift as the depression clears, which is not the case in the more progressive dementias, such as those caused by Alzheimer's disease.

Alzheimer's disease (AD) involves progressive deterioration in cognitive and personality functioning and self-care skills. There is no cure or effective treatment for AD. Research into its causes has focused on genetic factors, imbalances in neurotransmitters—especially in acetylcholine—and aluminum toxicity.

Human immunodeficiency virus (HIV) can attack the central nervous system, causing a progressive decline in mental and motor functioning.

Vascular dementias result from strokes (blood clots that block the supply of blood to parts of the brain, damaging or destroying brain tissue) and cerebral hemorrhages. Survivors of strokes often experience paralysis and loss of sensation in some parts of the body, as well as loss of speech (aphasia) and impaired memory. A cerebral hemorrhage involves the rupture of a blood vessel in the brain, which leaks blood into brain cavities that can damage or destroy sensitive brain tissue. Survivors, like stroke victims, are often faced with disturbances in motor, speech, and cognitive abilities. Multi-infarct dementia (MID) refers to dementias that are caused by repeated strokes or other forms of brain damage.

Head traumas may injure the brain by jarring, banging, or cutting brain tissue. Delirium, agitation, and amnesia may result in severe concussions. Contusions can lead to coma, cognitive impairment, and emotional problems. Lacerations can be lethal or lead to permanent major cognitive impairment.

Parkinson's disease is characterized by involuntary shaking or tremors, motor disabilities, and possible cognitive impairment. Parkinson's disease involves destruction of brain tissue in the substantia nigra of the brain, which is involved in controlling body movements. The disease involves reductions in the level of dopamine in the brain.

Huntington's disease is a genetically transmitted disease that involves progressive deterioration in the basal ganglia, which primarily affects neurons that produce ACh and GABA. The symptoms usually first appear between the ages of 30 and 50 and involve involuntary, jerky movements of the face (grimaces), neck, limbs, and trunk, or so-called choreiform movements, which are accompanied by

dementia. The disease is progressive and death usually occurs within 15 years.

Pick's disease is denoted by the presence of Pick's bodies in the nerve cells and the absence of the neurofibrillary tangles and plaques found in AD.

Brain tumors, whether benign or malignant, can cause psychological difficulties such as memory impairment, changes in personality, disorientation, and dementia. Pellagra, which is caused by deficiencies of niacin, can give rise to psychological symptoms such as anxiety, depression, loss of memory for recent events, problems in concentration, and hallucinations and delirium. Beriberi is caused by thiamine deficiency and often produces impairment in memory and concentration, lethargy, lack of appetite, and irritability. Hyperthyroidism produces such physical effects as accelerated metabolism and such psychological effects as excitability, insomnia, anxiety, and restlessness. In childhood, hypothyroidism can result in cretinism, which is characterized by stunted growth and mental retardation. In adulthood, hypothyroidism slows the metabolism and is associated with such psychological changes as sluggishness and fatigue, difficulties in concentration and memory, depression, and possibly dementia. Underactivity of the adrenal cortex may cause Addison's disease, which is associated with weight loss, low blood pressure, fatigue, irritability, lack of motivation, social withdrawal, and depression. Overactivity of the adrenal cortex can produce Cushing's syndrome, which is characterized by various physical and emotional problems. Brain tissue may be damaged or destroyed by infections, and thus give rise to mental and physical impairments. Encephalitis is an inflammation of the brain that may be caused by injuries or infections. Encephalitis is often associated with states of delirium, and convulsions or coma during acute stages. Meningitis is an infection of the central nervous systems that involves acute inflammation of the membranes that cover the spinal cord and brain. Both encephalitis and meningitis can lead to mental retardation if contracted during infancy. Neurosyphilis is a sexually transmitted disease in which the brain is attacked by the bacterium that causes syphilis, which can result in a state of dementia called general paresis.

Amnestic Disorders

Amnestic disorders involve deficits in short-term or long-term memory. The most common cause of amnestic syndrome is alcohol amnestic disorder, or Korsakoff's syndrome, which involves a thiamine deficiency typically associated with patterns of chronic alcohol abuse.

Epilepsy

Epilepsy, which may result from hundreds of underlying disorders, involves disturbances in the brain's electrical rhythms that take the form of seizures and produce changes in states of consciousness. Epilepsy is generally treated with anticonvulsive medication or surgery.

Karel Appel, Close Together, 1976. Painted wood: height 31 inches. Courtesy of Jane Kahan Gallery, New York.

CHAPTER OUTLINE

13

Abnormal Behavior in Childhood and Adolescence

TRUTH  FICTION?

___ Many behavior patterns that are normal for children would be considered abnormal among adults.

___ Boys are more likely than girls to develop disorders in childhood and adolescence.

___ People with severe mental retardation outnumber those with mild retardation by about 2 to 1.

___ Some people can recall verbatim every story they read in a newspaper.

___ Sugar causes hyperactivity.

___ Stimulants calm many hyperactive children.

___ Some children refuse to go to school because they believe that terrible things may happen to their parents while they are away.

___ Therapists have used Puerto Rican folktales to help Puerto Rican children adjust to the demands of living in mainstream U.S. society.

___ You cannot be too rich or too thin.

___ Some college women keep their weight down by making themselves vomit after they go on eating binges.

___ It is normal for children who have acquired daytime control over their bladders to have accidents during the night for a year or more.

LEARNING OBJECTIVES

When you have completed your study of Chapter 13, you should be able to:

1. Discuss ways of determining what is normal and abnormal in childhood and adolescence.

2. Discuss risk factors for disorders in childhood and adolescence.

3. Discuss theoretical perspectives on autism.

4. Differentiate between autism and childhood schizophrenia.

5. Discuss treatment of autism.

6. Describe the assessment of mental retardation.

7. Describe levels of severity of mental retardation.

8. Discuss the causes of mental retardation.

9. Discuss methods of testing for genetic defects.

10. Discuss intervention in cases of mental retardation.

11. Discuss the savant syndrome.

12. Describe types of learning disorders.

13. Discuss theoretical perspectives on learning disorders.

14. Discuss approaches to remediating learning disorders.

15. Describe types of communication disorders.

16. Describe types of disruptive behavior and attention-deficit disorders.

17. Discuss theoretical perspectives on disruptive behavior and attention-deficit disorders.

18. Discuss treatment of disruptive behavior and attention-deficit disorders.

19. Discuss the features and treatment of anxiety disorders affecting children and adolescents.

20. Describe the features and treatment of depression in childhood and adolescence.

21. Discuss the problem of adolescent suicide.

22. Describe the eating disorders of anorexia nervosa and bulimia nervosa.

23. Discuss theoretical perspectives on these eating disorders.

24. Discuss the treatment of these eating disorders.

25. Discuss theoretical perspectives on enuresis and encopresis.

26. Discuss treatment of these disorders.

Insanity is hereditary. You can get it from your children.

Sam Levenson

*A*t the age of 5½ your second author's daughter Jordan would do the following in the course of a day:

- Repeat verbatim several scenes from the Mel Brooks films *Spaceballs* and *Young Frankenstein*
- Change her clothing five or six times
- Drink orange juice from a baby bottle
- Play "Heart and Soul" on the piano a dozen times
- Punch her 7-year-old sister and her father
- Awaken several times during the night screaming
- Curse like a marine (or like a Mel Brooks film character)
- Curl up on a couch and play with her toes
- Demand that one of her parents help wipe her after she made "poo"
- Lisp
- Attain (prekindergarten) achievement test scores in the 99th percentile

After the monster goes wild, Igor, Dr. Frankenstein's assistant in *Young Frankenstein*, confesses to the good doctor that he had found the brain of "Abby Someone" for the experiment in rejuvenation. "Abby who?" asks Dr. Frankenstein. "Abby Normal," admits Igor.

Many times Jordan's parents asked themselves whether her behavior was normal or, well, "abby-normal." To determine what is normal and abnormal among children and adolescents, not only do we consider the criteria outlined in Chapter 1. We also weigh what is to be expected given the child's age, gender, family and cultural background, and the sundry developmental transformations that are taking place (Garber, 1984; Sroufe & Rutter, 1984). Many problems are first identified when the child enters school. They may have existed earlier but been tolerated, or unrecognized as problematic, in the home. Sometimes the stress of starting school contributes to their onset.

NORMAL AND ABNORMAL IN CHILDHOOD AND ADOLESCENCE

There are diverse criteria for defining abnormal behavior in children, just as there are in adults. Some children and adolescents exhibit bizarre behavior patterns. Others engage in self-defeating behavior, such as refusing to eat or going on a binge and then

"*Pop, am I experiencing a normal childhood?*"

making themselves vomit. Others display deficiencies in intellectual growth, as in mental retardation. Some act in ways that are socially inappropriate, as in conduct disorders. Other behavior disorders, such as those that involve anxiety and depression, are mainly characterized by distress in the child. Keep in mind, however, that what is socially acceptable at one age, such as intense fear of strangers at about 9 months, may be socially unacceptable at more advanced ages.

 Many behavior patterns that would be considered abnormal among adults—such as intense fear of strangers and lack of bladder control—are perfectly normal for children at certain ages.

Problems in childhood and adolescence often have a special poignancy. Many of them occur at ages when children have little capacity to cope. Many of them prevent children from fulfilling their developmental potentials.

Psychotherapy with children has been approached from various perspectives and differs in important respects from therapy with adults. Children may not have the verbal skills to express their feelings through speech or the ability to sit in a chair through a therapy session. Therapy methods must be tailored to the level of the child's cognitive, physical, social, and emotional development. For example, psychodynamic therapists have developed techniques of **play therapy** in which children enact family conflicts symbolically through their play activities, such as by "play-acting" with dolls or puppets. Or they might be given drawing materials and asked to draw

pictures, in the belief that their drawings will reflect their underlying feelings.

RISK FACTORS FOR DISORDERS IN CHILDHOOD AND ADOLESCENCE

The problems encountered in childhood and adolescence are varied, yet a number of risk factors apply to many if not most of them. Some factors are biological. Others are cognitive or social, such as undesirable life changes, family conflict, and parental neglect and abuse. One primary risk factor, however, is gender. Boys are at greater risk for developing childhood problems ranging from autism to hyperactivity to elimination disorders. Problems of anxiety and depression also affect boys more often than girls, by a ratio of about 3 to 1 (Achenbach, 1982). In adolescence, however, anxiety and mood disorders become more common among girls and remain so throughout adulthood. The eating disorders of anorexia and bulimia, which usually begin in adolescence, predominantly affect girls. Let us examine other risk factors for developmental disorders.

 Boys are generally more likely than girls to encounter disorders of anxiety and depression in early childhood. By adolescence, girls are more likely to experience such problems and also eating disorders.

Biological Risk Factors

Prenatal factors, birth complications, premature birth, and low birth weight all heighten the risk of maladaptive behavior in childhood (Lewis et al., 1988). Serious illnesses also place the child at greater risk of behavioral and emotional problems (Anthony, 1972). Run-of-the-mill bacterial and viral infections apparently do not increase the risk of these problems, however.

Genetic factors appear to play a role in childhood and adolescent disorders. Autism, learning disorders, hyperactivity, antisocial behavior, anxiety disorders, even eating disorders all seem to occur more commonly among the close biological relatives of people who are affected by these problems. One review of the literature noted that the biological relatives of adolescents who are hospitalized for schizophrenic, mood, or antisocial personality disorders present diagnostic evidence of similar problems at greater than expected rates (Strober, 1986).

MULTICULTURAL PERSPECTIVES

Multicultural Influences on Judgments of Children's Behavior as Normal or Abnormal

Cultural beliefs help determine whether people view behavior as normal or abnormal. People who base judgments of normality only on standards derived from their own cultures risk being ethnocentric when they view the behavior of people in other cultures as abnormal (Kennedy et al., 1984). The problem is of special concern regarding child psychopathology. Because children rarely label their own behavior as abnormal, definitions of normality depend largely on how a child's behavior is filtered through the lenses by which parents in a particular culture view that behavior (Lambert et al., 1992; Weisz et al., 1988). Cultures may vary with respect to the types of behaviors they classify as unacceptable or abnormal as well as the threshold for labeling child behaviors as deviant or socially unacceptable (Weisz et al., 1992). Researchers find that parents in different cultures do judge the unusualness of behavior from different perspectives (Lambert et al., 1992).

For example, researchers sought to investigate the question, "When a child has psychological problems, what determines whether adults will consider the problem serious or whether they will seek professional help?" (Weisz et al., 1988, p. 601). To do so, Weisz and associates (1988) presented vignettes to Thai and American parents, teachers, and clinical psychologists. The vignettes depicted two children, one with problems characterized by "overcontrol" (for example, shyness and fears) and one with problems characterized by undercontrol (for example, disobedience and fighting). The Thai parents rated *both* sets of problems as less serious (see Figure 13.1) and worrisome than Ameri-

How serious is this problem? Thai parents might judge the behavior shown by these children to be less serious than American parents would. Thai-Buddhist values tolerate broad variations in children's behavior and assume that it will change for the better.

can parents, and as more likely to improve without treatment as time passed. Such an interpretation is embedded within traditional Thai-Buddhist beliefs and values. Thai-Buddhist values tolerate broad variations in children's behavior. They assume that change is inevitable and that children's behavior will eventually change for the better. Differences between cultural groups were greater for parents and teachers than for psychologists, which suggests that professional training in a common scientific tradition might offset cultural differences.

Psychosocial Risk Factors

Stress apparently heightens the risk of psychological and behavioral as well as physical problems among children. In one study of children aged 6 to 9, undesirable life events and daily hassles predicted maladaptive behavior (Wertlieb et al., 1987). Family conflicts and instabilities appear to contribute to anxieties, depression, and conduct disorders in children, and to eating disorders in adolescents.

Cognitive factors such as expectancies are also intertwined with maladaptive behavior patterns in childhood. For example, when presented with social opportunities, such as happening upon another child who has a ball, outgoing, popular children are likely

to report thinking something like, "I was thinking that he/she would be nice and let me play." Socially withdrawn children are more likely to have expectancies such as "I was afraid that she/he didn't want me to play" (Stefanek et al., 1987). Aggressive children also report self-defeating expectancies, particularly the assumption that others intend them ill. Children's expectancies, like those of adults, influence their actions and can become self-fulfilling prophecies—for better or worse.

Rejection by peers (Parker & Asher, 1987) and parents appears to place children at increased risk. A 40-year longitudinal study of 253 males first contacted between the ages of 5 and 9 found that social rejection placed them at significant risk for premature

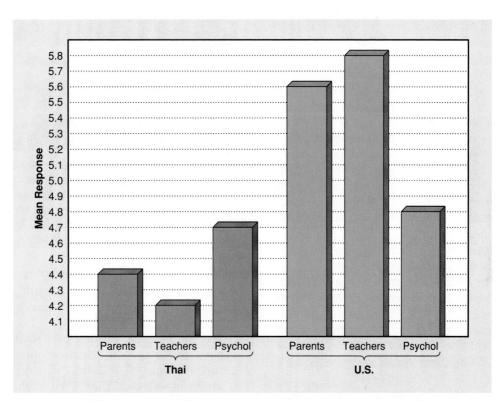

Figure 13.1 **Ratings by Thai and U.S. parents, teachers, and psychologists of the seriousness of children's behavioral problems.**
Researchers presented vignettes of children with problems characterized by overcontrol (for example, shyness and fears) and undercontrol (for example, disobedience and fighting) to Thai and American parents, teachers and psychologists. The Thai parents rated both sets of problems as less serious and worrisome than American parents, and as more likely to improve without treatment. The Thai parents apparently assume that people change and that their children's behavior will eventually change for the better.

Source: Weisz et al. Journal of Consulting and Clinical Psychology, 56, 601–609. Copyright ©1988 by the *American Psychological Association. Reprinted by permission.*

death, conviction for felonies, and various disorders, including alcoholism (McCord, 1983). Cause and effect are somewhat clouded, however. Although social rejection is painful for most children (and adults), children sometimes display maladaptive behaviors that prompt rejection and portend later difficulties.

Parental abuse and neglect also place children at risk. Researchers have found that children who suffer parental abuse or severe neglect are at greater risk in adolescence of lowered intelligence, depression and suicide, and substance abuse. They are also more likely than other children to be arrested for a crime as adolescents ("Study finds severe effects from childhood abuse," 1991 February 18) and as adults (Widom, 1989). Physical abuse can lead to neuropsy-

chological deficits that impair verbal, perceptual, and motor skills (Tarter et al., 1984); diminish performance on intelligence tests; and interfere with academic achievement (Amerman et al., 1986). Abuse can also disturb patterns of attachment and exploratory behavior. Abused children are less apt than nonabused peers to venture out to explore their surroundings (Aber & Allen, 1987). Abused children, even preschoolers, are more apt to be depressed and aggressive than nonabused children (Hoffman-Plotkin & Twentyman, 1984; Kazdin et al., 1985).

Various biological and psychosocial factors thus appear to place children and adolescents at risk for maladaptive behavior patterns. Now let us consider some of these problems, beginning with autism.

AUTISM

Peter nursed eagerly, sat and walked at the expected ages. Yet some of his behavior made us vaguely uneasy. He never put anything in his mouth. Not his fingers nor his toys—nothing. . . .

More troubling was the fact that Peter didn't look at us, or smile, and wouldn't play the games that seemed as much a part of babyhood as diapers. He rarely laughed, and when he did, it was at things that didn't seem funny to us. He didn't cuddle, but sat upright in my lap, even when I rocked him. But children differ and we were content to let Peter be himself. We thought it hilarious when my brother, visiting us when Peter was 8 months old, observed that "That kid has no social instincts, whatsoever." Although Peter was a first child, he was not isolated. I frequently put him in his playpen in front of the house, where the schoolchildren stopped to play with him as they passed. He ignored them, too.

It was Kitty, a personality kid, born two years later, whose responsiveness emphasized the degree of Peter's difference. When I went into her room for the late feeding, her little head bobbed up and she greeted me with a smile that reached from her head to her toes. And the realization of that difference chilled me more than the wintry bedroom.

Peter's babbling had not turned into speech by the time he was 3. His play was solitary and repetitive. He tore paper into long thin strips, bushel baskets of it every day. He spun the lids from my canning jars and became upset if we tried to divert him. Only rarely could I catch his eye, and then saw his focus change from me to the reflection in my glasses. . . .

[Peter's] adventures into our suburban neighborhood had been unhappy. He had disregarded the universal rule that sand is to be kept in sandboxes, and the children themselves had punished him. He walked around a sad and solitary figure, always carrying a toy airplane, a toy he never played with. At that time, I had not heard the word that was to dominate our lives, to hover over every conversation, to sit through every meal beside us. That word was autism.

■ *Eberhardy, 1967*

Autism, or *autistic disorder*, is one of the severest disorders of childhood. Autistic children, like Peter, seem utterly alone in the world, despite parental efforts to bridge the gulf that divides them.

Autism derives from the Greek *autos*, meaning "self." The term *autism* was first used in 1906 by the Swiss psychiatrist Eugen Bleuler to refer to a peculiar

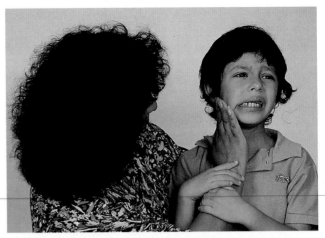

Autism. Autism, one of the most severe childhood disorders, is characterized by pervasive deficits in the ability to relate to and communicate with others, and by a restricted range of activities and interests. Autistic children, like the one shown here, lack the ability to relate to others and seem to live in their own private worlds.

style of thinking among schizophrenics. (Autism is one of Bleuler's "four A's.") Autistic thinking is the tendency to view oneself as the center of the universe—to believe that external events somehow refer to oneself. In 1943, another psychiatrist, Leo Kanner, applied the diagnosis "early infantile autism" to a group of disturbed children who seemed unable to relate to others, as if they lived in their own private world. Unlike children suffering from mental retardation, autistic children seemed to shut out any input from the outside world, creating a kind of "autistic aloneness" (Kanner, 1943).

A large community-based study in the state of Utah showed a prevalence of autism of 4 cases among 10,000 people (Ritvo et al., 1989a). Autism usually, but not always, developed by about 30 months of age. The Utah researchers found that rates of autism did not vary with race, religion, or parent's occupation or educational level (Ritvo et al., 1989a).

Autism seems always to have been with Peter. In the case of Eric, however, the disorder apparently developed between the ages of 12 and 24 months:

"People used to say to me they hoped they [would have] a baby just like mine," Sarah said of Eric, 3 years old at the time. As an infant, Eric smiled endearingly, laughed, and hugged. He uttered a dozen words by his first birthday. By 16 months he had memorized the alphabet and could read some signs. "People were very impressed," Sarah said.

Gradually, things changed, but it took months for Sarah to realize that Eric had a problem. At the age of 2, other members of Eric's play group bubbled with conversation. Eric had abandoned words completely. Instead, Eric combined letters and numbers in idiosyncratic ways, such as "B-T-2-4-6-Z-3."

Eric grew increasingly withdrawn. His diet was essentially self-limited to peanut butter and jelly sandwiches. He spent hour after hour arranging letters and numbers on a magnetic board. But the "symptom" that distressed Sarah most was impossible to measure: when she gazed into Eric's eyes, she no longer saw a "sparkle."

■ *Adapted from Martin, 1989*

Autism is three to four times more common among boys. Perhaps the most poignant feature of autism is the child's utter aloneness (see Table 13.1). Other features include communication problems and ritualistic or stereotyped behavior. Autistic children may be mute. If some language skills are present, they may be characterized by peculiar usage, as in echolalia (parroting back what the child has heard in a high-pitched monotone); pronoun reversals (using "you" or "he" instead of "I"); use of words that have meaning only to those who have intimate knowledge of the child; and tendencies to raise the voice at the end of sentences, as if asking a question. Nonverbal

communication may also be impaired or absent. For example, autistic children may not engage in eye contact or display facial expressions. Most autistic children repeat purposeless stereotyped movements interminably—twirling, flapping their hands, or rocking back and forth with their arms around their knees. Sometimes they mutilate themselves, even as they cry out in pain. They may bang their heads, slap their faces, bite their hands and shoulders, or pull out their hair. Autistic children may also throw sudden tantrums or panics. Another feature of autism is aversion to environmental changes—a feature termed "preservation of sameness." When familiar objects are moved even slightly from their usual places, autistic children may throw tantrums or cry continually until their placement is restored. Like Eric, autistic children may insist on eating the same food every day.

Autism as a Pervasive Developmental Disorder

Autistic disorder is classified as a **pervasive developmental disorder** in the DSM-III-R and the DSM-IV. Pervasive developmental disorders affect widespread aspects of development: cognitive, social, and emotional (Prior, 1984; Waterhouse & Fein, 1984).

Table 13.1	Diagnostic Features of Autistic Disorder	
A.	Diagnosis requires a combination of features from the following groups. Not all of the features from each group need be present for a diagnosis to be made.	
(1)	Impaired social interactions	1. Impairment in the nonverbal behaviors such as facial expressiveness, posture, gestures and eye contact that normally regulate social interaction
		2. Does not develop age-appropriate peer relationships
		3. Failure to express pleasure in the happiness of other people
		4. Does not show social or emotional reciprocity (give and take)
(2)	Impaired communication	1. Delay in development of spoken language (nor is there an effort to compensate for this lack through gestures)
		2. When speech development is adequate, there is nevertheless lack of ability to initiate or sustain conversation
		3. Shows abnormalities in form or content of speech (e.g., stereotyped or repetitive speech as in echolalia; idiosyncratic use of words; speaking about the self in the second or third person—using "you" or "he" to mean "I")
		4. Does not show spontaneous social or imaginative (make-believe) play
(3)	Restricted, repetitive and sterotyped behavior patterns	1. Shows restricted range of interests
		2. Insists on routines (e.g., always uses same route to go from one place to another)
		3. Shows stereotyped movements (e.g., hand flicking, head banging, rocking, spinning)
		4. Shows preoccupation with parts of objects (e.g., repetitive spinning of wheels of toy car) or unusual attachments to objects (e.g., carrying a piece of string)
B.	Onset occurs prior to the age of 3 through display of abnormal functioning in one or more of the following: social behavior, communication, or imaginative play.	

Source: Adapted from DSM-IV Draft Criteria (American Psychiatric Association, 1993), pp. E:3-E:4.

Pervasive developmental disorders were generally classified as forms of *psychoses* in earlier editions of the DSM. They were thought to reflect childhood forms of adult psychoses like schizophrenia because they shared features such as social and emotional impairment, oddities of communication, and stereotyped motor behaviors. Research has shown that they are distinct from adult psychoses, however. Their symptoms do not overlap entirely, and their presence does not predict psychosis in adulthood very well. Only very rarely in these children is there evidence of the prominent hallucinations or delusions that would justify a diagnosis of schizophrenia. Pervasive developmental disorders, of which autistic disorder is the major subtype, are now classified separately from the psychoses.

Autistic children are often described by their parents as having been "good babies" early in infancy. This generally means that they were not demanding. As they develop, however, autistic children begin to reject physical affection, such as cuddling, hugging, and kissing (Schopler & Mesibov, 1984). Their speech development begins to fall behind the norm. Although Eric did quite well through his first 16 months, there is often a dearth of babbling during the first year.

Autistic children are bound by ritual. The teacher of a 5-year-old autistic girl learned to greet her every morning by saying, "Good morning, Lily, I am very, very glad to see you" (Diamond et al., 1963). Although Lily would not respond to the greeting, she would shriek if the teacher omitted even one of the *verys*.

Autistic children apparently fail to develop a differentiated self-concept (Ferrari & Matthews, 1983). Nearly all normal 2-year-olds recognize their reflections in a mirror, but about 30% of autistic children between the ages 3 and 12 fail to recognize themselves (Spiker & Ricks, 1984). Despite their unusual behavior, autistic children are often quite attractive.

Autistic children often have an "intelligent look" about them. However, as measured by scores on standardized tests, their intellectual development tends to lag below the norm. A large community-based survey in Utah revealed that 6 out of 10 autistics scored below 70 on standardized IQ tests (Ritvo et al., 1989a). Low IQ scores may be in part attributable to failure to pay attention to the examiner or the tasks at hand, however. Perhaps 5 to 30% of autistic children score in the average range on intelligence tests (Yirmiya & Sigman, 1991). Still, even those who function at an average level of intelligence show deficits in activities requiring the ability to symbolize, such as recognizing emotions, engaging in symbolic play, and conceptual problem solving. They also display difficulty in attending to tasks that involve interacting with other people.

Theoretical Perspectives

The causes of autism remain unknown. Early views of autism focused on pathological family relationships. Kanner and his colleagues (e.g., Kanner & Eisenberg, 1955) suggested that autistic children were reared by cold, detached parents who were dubbed "emotional refrigerators." Psychoanalyst Bruno Bettelheim (1967) also focused on the family by suggesting that extreme self-absorption is the child's defense against parental rejection. The parents rear the child in an emotionally and socially desolate atmosphere in which the child's efforts to develop language and social skills wither. The child surrenders efforts to develop mastery over the external world and withdraws into a world of fantasy. The pathological insistence on preservation of sameness represents the child's rigid, defensive efforts to impose order and predictability.

Interestingly, the rocking of the autistic child looks very much like the rocking shown by rhesus monkey infants who are reared in social isolation. The appearance of a cross-species parallel may strengthen the belief that autism stems from emotional isolation, even if the parents occupy the same home.

Research, however, has not supported the assumption—so devastating to many parents—that they are in fact frosty and remote (Hoffmann & Prior, 1982). Of course there is truth to the notion that parents and autistic children do not relate to one another very well, but causal connections are clouded. Rather than rejecting their children and thus fostering autism, parents of autistic children may grow somewhat aloof because their efforts to relate to their children repeatedly meet with failure. Aloofness then becomes a result of autism, not a cause.

Today most practitioners are careful not to blame the parents for their children's autism. In earlier years it was more common to find cases like the following in which parents felt doubly damned by their children's misfortunes and by some members of the mental health community:

> "*I* knew we were in for it when I started reading the literature," remarked Nancy, the 36-year-old parent of an autistic son, John. "When [my husband] and I sought help for John, we were struck by a certain lack of empathy. One psychiatrist sort of looked beyond us or through us, as if we weren't sincere in our desire to help John.

"There was this one time I'll never forget. Someone working on her master's degree was trying to give John an intelligence test . . . [The psychiatrist] and I were watching through this one-way mirror. She kept on grabbing John's face and aiming it toward her to try to get his attention. After this went on for a while, John let out one of his shrieks, and he just went on and on. I could see that the [tester] and the psychiatrist were going to just wait it out, even if it lasted for hours. I went in and took John out of there."

"'Isn't it a little late for that?' [the psychiatrist] asked when I was walking out with John. I didn't even stop to ask him what he meant. I just got John out of there as fast as I could."

■ *The Authors' Files*

Psychologist O. Ivar Lovaas and his colleagues (1979) offer a cognitive-learning perspective on autism. They suggest that autistic children have perceptual deficits which limit them to processing only one stimulus at a time. As a result, autistic children are slow to learn by means of classical conditioning (association of stimuli). From the learning-theory perspective, children become attached to their primary caregivers because they are associated with primary reinforcers like food and hugging. Autistic children, however, attend either to the food or the cuddling and do not connect it with the parent.

Cognitive theorists have focused on the kinds of cognitive deficits shown by autistic children and the possible relationships among them. Rutter (1983), for example, suggests that cognitive and language deficits are primary and give rise to social problems. Autistic children appear to have difficulty integrating information from various senses (Ornitz, 1974; Ritvo, 1976). At times they seem hypersensitive to stimulation. At other times they are so insensitive that an observer might wonder whether or not they are deaf. Perceptual-cognitive deficits seem to diminish their capacity to make use of information—to comprehend and apply social rules (Wing, 1972).

Biological views of autism have achieved increased prominence in recent years. Biological perspectives focus on presumed malfunctions in the organization of the central nervous system that governs the processing of information and may underlie cognitive-perceptual deficits (Greenspan & Porges, 1984). Evidence is found in the rather specific pattern of cognitive dysfunctioning that characterizes autistic children (Hoffmann & Prior, 1982). It is unlikely that any particular pattern of child rearing could account for the highly similar patterns of bizarre behavior shown by autistic children around the world. The

features of autism also resemble patterns that sometimes follow brain diseases such as encephalitis and congenital syphilis.

Many theorists also suspect neurological damage because of the sundry impairments in mental functioning, including mental retardation, language deficits, bizarre motor behavior, even seizures (Ritvo & Ritvo, 1992; Zilbovicius et al., 1992). Certain neurological signs like drooling and lack of coordination are found in most autistic children (Hoffmann & Prior, 1983). Damage in the cerebral cortex might account for seizures, failure to integrate perceptual information, and language problems. Some believe that the site of cerebral dysfunction may lie in the left, or dominant, hemisphere, which tends to govern language and analytic functions—two areas of major deficiency in autistic children. So-called right-brain functions, like visual-motor skills, are relatively more normal among autistic children (Prior, 1979).

Many autistic children do show abnormalities in brain waves, as measured by the electroencephalograph (EEG), especially a pattern of brain wave activity that is associated with persistent states of heightened arousal. It has been hypothesized that dysfunction of brain structures involved in regulating levels of arousal, such as the reticular formation, may lead to a failure to maintain states of arousal at a proper level (Rimland, 1984). But hard evidence of the specific sites of brain pathology that might account for autism has remained elusive. MRI studies of the brain have not to date produced evidence of any structural abnormalities associated with autism (for example, Garber & Ritvo, 1992; Garber et al., 1989). In sum, despite the widespread belief that brain abnormalities underlie autism, researchers have not yet found any one pattern of brain dysfunction, or any particular site in the brain, that is specifically associated with the disorder (Zilbovicius et al., 1992). Perhaps autism is a syndrome stemming from multiple causes involving more than one type of brain abnormality (Ritvo & Ritvo, 1992).

Most autistic children have higher-than-normal levels of serotonin and dopamine. Moreover, stimulants like amphetamines, which heighten levels of dopamine, exacerbate the symptoms of autistic children—as they exacerbate the symptoms of adult schizophrenics. Yet the role of neurotransmitters in the development of autism remains unclear and requires further study.

If there is brain dysfunction in autistic children, where does it originate? Evidence of genetic factors is accumulating. For example, in one twin study, 4 of 11 monozygotic (identical) twins of autistic children showed the disorder, as compared with none of 10 dizygotic (fraternal) twins of autistic children (Folstein & Rutter, 1978). Moreover, another 4 of the identical twins shared one or more signs of autism, such as lagging language development or pronoun reversal. According to the epidemiological study of autism in the state of Utah, the risk that a later-born sibling of an autistic child would develop autism was about 1 in 10 (8.6%), which is 215 times greater than the risk of autism in the general population (Ritvo et al., 1989b). This evidence lends further support to a genetic means of transmission in autism. Genetic factors appear to play a relatively stronger role among autistic individuals who are also severely mentally retarded (Baird & August, 1985).

Brain dysfunction in autistics may also be linked to congenital disorders and birth complications. For example, whereas autism strikes about 0.2% of the general population, it is found among 8 to 10% of children with congenital rubella (German measles)—a notable discrepancy (Chess et al., 1971). Yet another hypothesis grows out of the finding that mothers of autistic children are more likely to suffer spontaneous abortions and threatened miscarriages. Perhaps these complications, and autism, are caused by prenatal damage at the hands of the mother's immune systems (Stubbs et al., 1985). The mother's immune system may attack the fetus as it would an invading organism.

Treatment

Psychodynamically oriented treatments for autism have included psychotherapy, play therapy, and placement of children in residential facilities largely governed by Bruno Bettelheim's ideas. The residences aim to provide children with the warmth presumed to be lacking in the home. Unconditional support is intended to help autistic children form secure attachments to other people who then become introjected as positive self-images (Sanders, 1974). Children are also given the chance to influence their environments. Their demands are met so long as they are not self-injurious.

Bettelheim claimed that some 42% of the children in residence at his Orthogenetic School in Chicago have benefited from treatment (1967). However, the criteria for improvement have been inconsistent and Bettelheim's observations may have been colored by his expectations. Other reports suggest that residential treatment and psychodynamically oriented psychotherapy are less effective than behavioral approaches (Rimland, 1977).

Although most behaviorists do not contend that autism is caused by faulty learning, they suggest that principles of learning may be helpful in treating autistic behavior. There are reports that operant conditioning methods (that is, systematic use of rewards and punishments) have encouraged autistic children to pay attention to therapists (Lovaas, 1977), to play with other children (Romanczyk et al., 1975), and to stop self-mutilative behavior. Techniques like extinction (withholding reinforcement following a response) are sometimes effective for behaviors like head banging, but a great many unreinforced trials (trials that are ignored) may be required to eliminate the response. In one case, 1,800 head bangs over 8 days were required before the response was eliminated (Simmons & Lovaas, 1969). The problem seems

Contact. One of the principal therapeutic tasks in working with autistic children is the establishment of interpersonal contact. Psychodynamic therapists emphasize the importance of continual support to help the autistic child form secure attachments. Behavior therapists use reinforcers to increase adaptive social behaviors, such as paying attention to the therapist and playing with other children. Behavior therapists may also use punishments to suppress self-mutilative behavior.

to be that many repetitive behavior patterns—like rocking and self-injurious behaviors—are maintained by internal reinforcements such as increased stimulation. Therefore, withdrawal of social reinforcers may have little if any effect.

Use of aversive stimulation such as spanking and, in extreme cases, electric shock, is more effective than extinction. Lovaas reported that painful but apparently non-injurious electric shock can eliminate self-mutilation within a minute of application (Lovaas, 1970). Using electric shock with children raises moral, ethical, and legal concerns, of course. Lovaas has countered that failure to eliminate self-injurious behavior places the child at greater risk of physical harm and denies children the opportunity to participate in other kinds of therapy. Lovaas also suggests that the use of aversive stimulation should be combined with positive reinforcement for acceptable alternate behaviors (Simmons & Lovaas, 1969).

Because autistic children show behavioral deficits, a central focus of behavior modification is the development of new behavior. New behaviors are maintained by reinforcements, so it is important to teach autistic children, who often respond to people as they would to a piece of furniture, to accept people as reinforcers. People can be established as reinforcers by pairing praise with primary reinforcers like food. Then social reinforcement (praise) and primary reinforcers (food) can be used to shape and model toileting behaviors, speech, and social play (Lovaas et al., 1966). The involvement of families and residential treatment personnel in these behavioral programs prompts the maintenance and generalization of behavioral changes (Anderson et al., 1986; Romanczyk, 1986).

The results of a long-term study showed significant benefits for intensive behavioral treatment (Lovaas, 1987). Autistic children received 40 hours of one-to-one behavior modification each week for at least 2 years. Significant intellectual and educational gains were reported for 9 of the 19 children (47%) in the program. The children who improved achieved normal IQ scores and were able to succeed in the first grade. Only 2% of a control group that did not receive the intensive treatment achieved similar gains. Although these are among the most promising results to date in the treatment of autistic children, longer term follow-ups remain to be reported.

Biological approaches have had some limited impact in the treatment of autism. It is understood that amphetamines exacerbate autistic and schizophrenic behavior patterns, apparently by heightening the action of dopamine in each case. In contrast, major tranquilizers, which lessen dopamine activity, have been found to diminish many aspects of autistic behavior, including rocking and self-mutilation (Campbell et al., 1982; Clark & Witherspoon, 1984). However, there is little evidence that drugs foster the cognitive and language development of autistic children.

■ **THE LONG-TERM VIEW** Over the years only a small minority of autistic children—perhaps 5%—have developed into self-sufficient and independent adults (DeMyer et al., 1981; Kernberg, 1979; Rutter, 1983). For example, a follow-up study at a Canadian regional research center showed that more than half of the treated children remained institutionalized, and 90% remained intellectually deficient. Only a few held jobs or lived independently (Wolf & Goldberg, 1986).

The long-term prospects may differ for autistic children who are retarded and those who are not (Prior, 1984). Language skills, which correlate with overall intellectual development, are also predictive of future adjustment. It remains to be seen whether efforts to promote language development will lead to long-term improvements.

Autism Versus Childhood Schizophrenia

The DSM no longer includes a separate category for childhood schizophrenia. Use of the label schizophrenia is preferred for the relatively rare instances in which a schizophrenic disorder develops in childhood. **Childhood schizophrenia**, like adult schizophrenia, is marked by confusion and disorientation, social withdrawal, speech problems, odd motor behaviors, loose associations, delusions, and hallucinations. Children who have received the diagnosis often report bizarre imaginary events, which suggests that their ways of perceiving the world are severely distorted. The onset of childhood schizophrenia is usually after 30 months of age (autism usually begins earlier), and it affects boys and girls equally (autism disproportionately affects boys). Autistic children generally show indifference to other people, although they may become attached to inanimate objects. Schizophrenic children, by contrast, appear to become excessively attached to their parents. They may cling to them and shriek at minor separations. Children labeled as childhood schizophrenics do not show the intellectual and language deficiencies displayed by autistic children. Kernberg (1979) claims that major tranquilizers are reasonably effective in treating childhood schizophrenia, as they are in the adult version of the disorder. It nevertheless remains unclear that schizophrenia in childhood is the equivalent of schizophrenia in adulthood.

MENTAL RETARDATION

The great majority of mentally retarded people fall in the mild range of severity. They are generally capable of independent functioning, although they may require some guidance and support.

Mental retardation involves a broad delay in the development of cognitive and social functioning. The course of development of mentally retarded children is variable. Many improve over time, especially if they receive support, guidance, and enriched educational opportunities. Mentally retarded children reared in impoverished environments may fail to improve or may deteriorate further in relation to other children.

Mental retardation is generally assessed by a combination of formal intelligence tests and observation of adaptive functioning. The DSM-IV uses three criteria in diagnosing mental retardation: (1) an IQ score of approximately 70 or below on a test like the Wechsler Intelligence Scale for Children (WISC) or the Stanford-Binet; (2) evidence of impaired functioning in adaptive behavior; and (3) onset of the disorder before age 18. People whose behavior is impaired fail to meet the standards of behavior that are expected of someone of the same age within a given cultural setting. They do not develop comparable social and communication skills or become adequately independent and self-sufficient. For infants, task-related judgments of subaverage intellectual functioning may be used in place of IQ scores because tests of infant intelligence either do not yield reliable IQ scores, or IQ scores at all.

Mental retardation varies in severity, as shown in Table 13.2. Most mentally retarded children (about 85%) fall into the mildly retarded range. These children are generally capable of meeting basic academic demands such as learning to read simple passages. They can eventually function independently in adulthood, although they may require some guidance and support. Table 13.3 provides a description of the deficits and abilities associated with various degrees of mental retardation.

Causes of Retardation

In many cases, mental retardation can be traced to biological causes, including chromosomal and genetic disorders, infectious diseases, and brain damage. In cases where there is no evidence of biological defects, an impoverished home environment is suspected as a cause of, or contributor to, retardation.

■ **DOWN SYNDROME AND OTHER CHROMOSOMAL ABNORMALITIES** The most common chromosomal abnormality linked to mental retardation is **Down syndrome** (formerly called Down's syndrome), which is characterized by an extra or third chromosome on the 21st pair of chromosomes, resulting in 47 chromosomes rather than the normal complement of 46 (see Figure 13.2). Down syndrome occurs in about 1 in 800 births. It usually occurs when the 21st pair of chromosomes in either the egg or the sperm fails to divide normally, resulting in an extra chromosome. Chromosomal abnormalities become more likely as parents age (Hamamy et al., 1990), so expectant couples in their 30s or older often undergo prenatal genetic tests (see feature "Genetic Counseling and Prenatal Testing") to detect Down syndrome and other genetic abnormalities. Down syndrome can be traced to a defect in the mother's chromosomes in about 95% of cases (Antonarakas et al., 1991), with the remainder attributable to defects in the father's sperm.

People with Down syndrome are recognizable by certain physical features, such as a round face, broad, flat nose, and small, downward-sloping folds

Table 13.2 Levels of Mental Retardation		
Degree of Severity	**Approximate IQ Range**	**Percentage of Mentally Retarded Within Range**
Mild mental retardation	50–70	Approximately 85%
Moderate mental retardation	35–49	10
Severe mental retardation	20–34	3–4
Profound mental retardation	Below 20	1–2

Source: Adapted from DSM-IV Draft Criteria (American Psychiatric Association, 1993), p. E:1.

Table 13.3	Levels of Retardation, Typical Ranges of IQ Scores, and Types of Adaptive Behaviors Shown		
Approximate IQ Score Range	Preschool Age 0–5 Maturation and Development	School Age 6–21 Training and Education	Adult 21 and Over Social and Vocational Adequacy
Mild 50–70	Often not noticed as retarded by casual observer, but is slower to walk, feed self, and talk than most children.	Can acquire practical skills and useful reading and arithmetic to a 3rd to 6th grade level with special education. Can be guided toward social conformity.	Can usually achieve social and vocational skills adequate to self-maintenance; may need occasional guidance and support when under unusual social or economic stress.
Moderate 35–49	Noticeable delays in motor development, especially in speech; responds to training in various self-help activities.	Can learn simple communication, elementary health and safety habits, and simple manual skills; does not progress in functional reading or arithmetic.	Can perform simple tasks under sheltered conditions; participates in simple recreation; travels alone in familiar places; usually incapable of self-maintenance.
Severe 20–34	Marked delay in motor development; little or no communication skill; may respond to training in elementary self-help—e.g., self-feeding.	Usually walks, barring specific disability; has some understanding of speech and some response; can profit from systematic habit training.	Can conform to daily routines and repetitive activities; needs continuing direction and supervision in protective environment.
Profound Below 20	Gross retardation; minimal capacity for functioning in sensorimotor areas; needs nursing care.	Obvious delays in all areas of development; shows basic emotional responses; may respond to skillful training in use of legs, hands, and jaws; needs close supervision.	May walk, may need nursing care, may have primitive speech; will usually benefit from regular physical activity; incapable of self-maintenance.

Reprinted from S. A. Rathus. Psychology, *5th ed. (Fort Worth: Harcourt Brace Jovanovich, 1993), p. 331.*

Learning to function.
Although persons with Down syndrome suffer from deficits in learning and development, most can learn to function productively with encouragement and training.

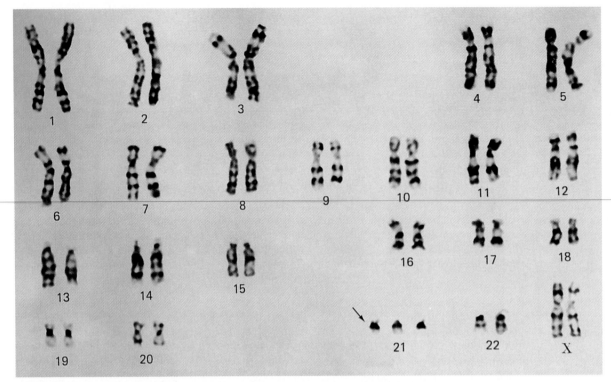

Figure 13.2 Trisomy 21—the chromosomal condition that gives rise to Down syndrome.
Down syndrome is connected with an extra chromosome on the 21st pair of chromosomes, so the person has 47 chromosomes rather than the normal complement of 46. Here the extra chromosome on the 21st pair is indicated by an arrow.

of skin at the inside corners of the eyes that gives the impression of slanted eyes. Children with Down syndrome are also characterized by a protruding tongue, small, squarish hands and short fingers, a curved fifth finger, and disproportionately small arms and legs in relation to their bodies. Nearly all of these children are mentally retarded and many suffer from physical problems, such as malformations of the heart and respiratory difficulties. Sadly, most die by middle age. In their later years, they tend to suffer memory losses and experience childish emotions that represent a form of senility (Kolata, 1985).

Children with Down syndrome suffer various deficits in learning and development. They tend to be uncoordinated and to lack proper muscle tone, which makes it difficult for them to carry out physical tasks and engage in play activities like other children. Down syndrome children suffer memory deficits, especially for information presented verbally, which makes it difficult for them to learn in school. They also have difficulty following instructions from teachers and expressing their thoughts or needs clearly in speech. Despite their disabilities, most can learn to read, write, and perform simple arithmetic, if they receive appropriate schooling and the right encouragement.

Although less common than Down syndrome, chromosomal abnormalities on the sex chromosome may also result in mental retardation, such as in Klinefelter's syndrome and Turner's syndrome. Klinefelter's syndrome, which only occurs among males, is characterized by the presence of an extra X sex chromosome, resulting in an XXY sex chromosomal pattern rather than the XY pattern that men normally have. Men with this XXY pattern fail to develop appropriate secondary sex characteristics, resulting in enlarged breasts, poor muscular development, and infertility. Mild retardation occurs frequently among these men.

Found only among females is Turner's syndrome, which is characterized by the presence of a single X sex chromosome instead of the normal two. Although such girls develop normal external genitals, their ovaries remain poorly developed, producing reduced amounts of estrogen. As women, they tend to be shorter than average and infertile. They also tend to show evidence of mild retardation, especially in skills relating to math and science.

■ **FRAGILE X SYNDROME AND OTHER GE-NETIC ABNORMALITIES** Fragile X syndrome is the most common type of inherited mental retardation. The disorder is believed to be caused by a mutated gene on the X sex chromosome (Angier, 1991b). The defective gene is located in an area of the chromosome that appears fragile, hence the name *fragile X syndrome*. Fragile X syndrome causes mental retardation in every 1,000 to 1,500 males and (generally less severe) mental handicaps in every 2,000 to 2,500 females (Angier, 1991b; Rousseau et al., 1991).

As a cause of mental retardation, fragile X syndrome is second only to Down syndrome (Angier, 1991b). The effects of fragile X syndrome range from mild learning disabilities to retardation so profound that those affected can hardly speak or function.

Females normally have two X sex chromosomes, whereas males have only one. For females, having two X sex chromosomes seems to provide some protection against the disorder if the defective gene turns up on one of the two chromosomes (Angier, 1991b). This may explain why the disorder usually has more profound effects on males than on females. Yet the mutation does not always manifest itself. Many males and females carry the fragile X mutation but show no clinical evidence of it. Yet they can pass along the syndrome to their offspring.

A genetic test can detect the presence of the mutation by direct DNA analysis (Rousseau et al., 1991) and may be of help to prospective parents in genetic counseling. Prenatal testing of the fetus is also possible (Sutherland et al., 1991). Although there is no treatment for fragile X syndrome, identifying the defective gene is the first step toward understanding how the protein produced by the gene functions to produce the disability, which may lead to the development of treatments for the disorder (Angier, 1991b).

Phenylketonuria (PKU) is a genetic disorder transmitted by a recessive gene that is found in 1 person in 60 (Brody, 1990b). The gene prevents the child from metabolizing the amino acid *phenylalanine,* which is found in many foods. Consequently, phenylalanine and its derivative, phenylpyruvic acid, accumulate in the body, causing damage to the central nervous system that results in mental retardation and emotional disturbance. The presence of PKU can be detected among newborns by analyzing blood or urine samples. Although there is no cure for PKU, children with the disorder may suffer less damage or develop normally if they are placed on a diet low in phenylalanine soon after birth (Brody, 1990b). Such children receive protein supplements that compensate for their nutritional loss.

Tay-Sachs disease is also caused by recessive genes. Tay-Sachs disease, which mostly afflicts Jews of Eastern European ancestry, is a fatal degenerative disease of the central nervous system. About 1 in 25 American Jews is a carrier of the recessive gene responsible for the disorder. The chance that both members of a Jewish couple carry the gene is thus about 1 in 625. Children who are afflicted by Tay-Sachs suffer gradual loss of muscle control, deafness and blindness, retardation and paralysis, and eventually die before the age of 5.

■ **PRENATAL FACTORS** Some cases of mental retardation are caused by maternal infections or substance abuse during pregnancy. Rubella (German measles) in the mother, for example, can be passed along to the unborn child, causing brain damage that results in retardation and plays a role in autism. Although the mother may experience mild symptoms or none at all, the effects on the fetus can be tragic. Other maternal diseases that may cause retardation in the child include syphilis, **cytomegalovirus**, and genital herpes.

Widespread programs that immunize women against rubella before pregnancy and tests for syphilis during pregnancy have reduced the risk of transmission of these infections to children. Most children who contract genital herpes from their mothers do so during delivery by coming into contact with the herpes simplex virus that causes the disease in the birth canal. Caesarean sections (C sections) reduce the risk of the baby's coming into contact with the virus during outbreaks.

Drugs that the mother ingests during pregnancy may pass through the placenta to the child. Some can cause severe birth deformities and mental retardation. The tranquilizer thalidomide, for example, was prescribed in the 1960s to control morning sickness in pregnant women until it became known that children whose mothers had used the drug were often born with undeveloped limbs and mental retardation. Children whose mothers drink alcohol during pregnancy are often born with a condition called **fetal alcohol syndrome**, which is characterized by mental retardation and various physical abnormalities, such as a flattened nose, widely separated eyes, reduced head size, and lower than average height and weight.

Birth complications, such as oxygen deprivation or head injuries, place children at risk for neurological disorders, including mental retardation. Prematurity also places children at risk of retardation and other developmental problems. Brain infections, such as encephalitis and meningitis, or traumas during infancy and early childhood can cause mental retardation and other health problems. Children who

A CLOSER LOOK

Genetic Counseling and Prenatal Testing

Genetic counseling has become widely used as a method to help parents avert genetic tragedies. The genetic counselor takes information about couple's ages and genetic background characteristics in order to determine the probabilities of genetic or chromosomal defects in their offspring. Some couples whose offspring are at high risk for these defects decide to adopt rather than bear children of their own.

Various genetic tests for pregnant women have been developed to help detect the presence of genetic and chromosomal abnormalities in their fetuses, such as Down syndrome, fragile X syndrome, and Tay-Sachs disease. In *amniocentesis,* which is usually conducted about 14 to 15 weeks following conception, a sample of amniotic fluid is drawn with a syringe from the amniotic sac that contains the fetus. Cells from the fetus can then be separated from the fluid, allowed to grow in a culture, and examined for the presence of biochemical and chromosomal abnormalities. In *chorionic villus sampling,* or CVS, small pieces of the hairlike material (villi) on the amniotic sac are snipped for analysis. CVS can be performed at 9 to 12 weeks after conception.

Because these tests carry some risk of miscarriage and infection, they are usually performed only on women at greater genetic risk, such as those above the age of 35 or with other children who are genetically damaged. CVS provides earlier results than amniocentesis, but it is somewhat riskier, so most physicians prefer to use amniocentesis (Rosenthal, 1991). The use of ultrasound to guide the placement of the needle in amniocentesis has made it possible for physicians to perform amniocentesis as early as 10 to 12 weeks (Rosenthal, 1991). Down syndrome may also be detected on the basis of a blood test, the alpha-fetoprotein test. The results of this test are not considered conclusive, however. A positive finding may thus be followed up

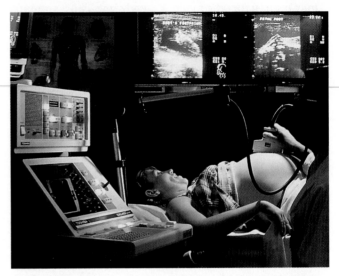

Amniocentesis.   In amniocentesis, a physician extracts a sample of amniotic fluid to test for biochemical and chromosomal abnormalities. Here the physician uses ultrasound to determine the location of the fetus to help prevent accidental injury to it while placing the syringe in the mother's abdomen.

by amniocentesis. Blood tests are also used to detect carriers of Tay-Sachs disease and other disorders (Cunningham & Gilstrap, 1991; Hobbins, 1991).

In the future, it may be possible to control the effects of defective genes during prenatal development. Today, however, expectant couples who are informed that their unborn children are genetically defective grapple with the often agonizing decision about whether or not to have an abortion. The question of abortion in such cases raises painful moral and personal dilemmas, not only for the affected families but for society at large.

---

ingest toxins, such as paint chips containing lead, may also suffer brain damage that produces mental retardation.

■ **CULTURAL-FAMILIAL CAUSES** Most cases of mental retardation fall in the mild range of severity. No apparent biological cause or distinguishing physical feature sets many mildly retarded children apart from other children. It is widely believed that psychosocial factors, such as an impoverished social environment, either cause or contribute to the devel-

opment of mental retardation in such children. In these cases, retardation is considered to be **cultural-familial**. Children in impoverished families may lack toys, books, or opportunities to interact with adults in intellectually stimulating ways. Consequently, they may fail to develop appropriate language skills or become unmotivated to learn the skills that are valued in contemporary society. Economic burdens, such as the need to hold multiple jobs, may prevent their parents from spending time reading to them, talking to them at length, and exposing them to creative play or trips to museums and parks. They may spend most of their days glued to the TV set. The parents, most of whom were also reared in poverty, may lack the reading or communication skills to help shape the development of these skills in their children. A vicious cycle of poverty and impoverished intellectual development may be repeated from generation to generation.

Children with this form of retardation may respond dramatically when provided with enriched learning experiences, especially at the earlier ages. Social programs like Head Start, for example, have helped children at risk of cultural-familial retardation to function within the normal range of ability (Barnett & Escobar, 1990; Hauser-Cram et al., 1991; Zigler et al., 1992).

■ **INTERVENTION** The services that mentally retarded children require to meet the developmental challenges they face depend in part on the level of severity of retardation. With appropriate training, children with mild retardation may approach a sixth grade level of competence. They can acquire vocational skills that allow them to minimally support themselves through meaningful work. Many such children can be mainstreamed in regular classes. At the other extreme, the profoundly mentally retarded may need institutional care or placement in a residential care facility in the community, like a group home. Placement in an institution is often based on the need to control destructive or aggressive behavior, not because of severity of the individual's intellectual impairment. Consider the case of a child with moderate retardation:

*T*he mother pleaded with the emergency room physician to admit her 15-year-old son, claiming that she couldn't take it anymore. Her son, a Down syndrome patient with an IQ of 45, had alternated since the age of 8 between living in institutions and at home. Each visiting day he pleaded with his mother to take him home, and after about a year at each placement, she would bring him home but find herself unable to control his behavior. During temper tantrums, he would break dishes and destroy furniture and had recently become physically assaultive toward his mother, hitting her on the arm and shoulder during a recent scuffle when she attempted to stop him from repeatedly banging a broom on the floor.

■ *Adapted from Spitzer et al., 1989, pp. 338–340*

In 1975, Congress passed the Education for All Handicapped Children Act, Public Law 94-142, which required public schools to provide handicapped children with free public education that is appropriate to their needs. PL 94-142 was an impetus for a massive increase in special education programs for children with mental retardation and other handicapping conditions like physical disability. To ensure the appropriateness of the educational experience for each handicapped child, school officials must adapt the educational program to the needs of the particular student. This often involves a multidisciplinary approach, in which professionals from different disciplines evaluate the child and recommend services and training experiences that are suited to the child's special needs. Some communities, however, have been slow to conform with the law because Congress has not appropriated the funds that are needed to ensure compliance. Local governments may be unwilling to raise taxes to pay for special education services.

Controversy remains concerning whether mentally retarded children should be mainstreamed in regular classes or placed in special education classes. Some mildly retarded children may achieve better when they are mainstreamed (Robinson & Robinson, 1976). Others may not do so well in regular classes. They may find them to be overwhelming and withdraw from their schoolmates (Linton & Juul, 1980).

Imparting skills. In 1975, Congress enacted legislation requiring public schools to provide handicapped children with education that meets their individual needs. Here a teacher demonstrates wood-sanding techniques to a severely retarded adolescent.

A CLOSER LOOK

The Savant Syndrome

Got a minute? Try the following:

1. Without referring to a calendar, calculate the day of the week that March 15, 2079, will fall on.

2. List the prime numbers between 1 and 1 billion. (Hint: the list starts 1, 2, 3, 5, 7, 11, 13, 17 . . .)

3. Repeat verbatim the newspaper stories you read over coffee this morning.

4. Sing accurately every note played by the first violin in Beethoven's Ninth Symphony.

These tasks are impossible for all but a very few. Ironically, those of us who are most likely to be able to accomplish these feats—*idiots savants*—are autistic, retarded, or both.

The idiot savant (derived from the French *savoir*, meaning "to know") has been described as possessing "islands of mental ability in a sea of mental handicap and disability" (Treffert, 1988, p. 563). Idiots (pronounced *id-ee-oh*) savants have severe mental deficiencies but possess some remarkable mental abilities. The prevalence of the savant syndrome within the retarded population is estimated at about .06%, or 1 case in 2,000 (Hill, 1977). Prevalence rates are reported to be higher among autistic populations. Most idiots savants, like most autistic people, are male (Treffert, 1988). Among a sample of 5,400 autistic people, 531 cases (9.8%) were reported by parents to have the savant syndrome (Rimland, 1978). Because they want to think of their children as special, however, parents might overreport the incidence of the savant syndrome.

Several hundred savants have been described in this century. They are reported to have shown remarkable but circumscribed mental skills, such as calendar calculating and rare musical talent, both of which stand in contrast to their limited general intellectual abilities. Idiots savants also have outstanding memories. Just as we learn about health

Savant syndrome. Dustin Hoffman (right) won the Oscar for best actor for his portrayal of an autistic savant with a remarkable capacity for numerical calculation in the film *Rainman*. Tom Cruise (left) played his brother. Hoffman was able to capture the sense of emotional detachment and isolation of his autistic character.

by studying illness, we may be able to learn more about normal mechanisms of memory by studying people in whom memory stands apart from other aspects of mental functioning (Treffert, 1988).

The label *savant syndrome* is preferable to the more common, but pejorative term *idiot savant*. The phenomenon occurs more frequently in males by a ratio of about 6 to 1. The special skills of the savant tend to appear out of the blue and may disappear as suddenly. Some savants engage in lightning calculations. A 19th-century enslaved person in Virginia, Thomas Fuller, "was able to calculate the number of seconds in 70 years, 17 days, and 12 hours in a minute and one half, taking into account the 17 leap years that would have occurred in the period" (Smith, 1983).

There has also been a trend toward deinstitutionalization of the more severely mentally retarded. The Developmentally Disabled Assistance and Bill of Rights Act, which Congress passed in 1975, provided that persons with mental retardation have the right to receive appropriate treatment in the least restrictive treatment setting. In New York State, the number of mentally retarded people in institutions shrank from 26,000 in 1971 to 7,000 in 1991 (Winerip, 1991). New York has closed 5 of its institutions for the mentally retarded and expects to eventually close the remaining 15. Michigan is the closest among the larger states to closing all its institutions, and has dropped its inpatient census from 12,000 to 700 dur-

ing the past 20 years. Mentally retarded people who are capable of functioning in the community have the right to receive less restrictive care than is provided in large institutions. Many moderately or severely retarded adolescents and adults are capable of living outside the institution and have been placed in supervised group homes. Residents typically share household responsibilities and are encouraged to participate in meaningful daily activities, such as training programs or sheltered workshops. Others live with their families and attend structured day programs. Mildly retarded adults often work in outside jobs and live in their own apartments or share apartments with other mildly retarded persons. Although the

There are also cases of blind savants who could play back any musical piece, no matter how complex, or repeat long passages of foreign languages without losing a syllable. Some savants make exact estimates of elapsed time. One could reportedly repeat verbatim the contents of a newspaper he had just heard; another could repeat backward what he had just read (Tradgold, 1914, cited in Treffert, 1988).

 Ability to recall news stories verbatim is shown by some individuals with the savant syndrome.

Sacks (1985) describes the case of savant twins, who were apparently incapable of simple computations and seemed to lack any knowledge of division and multiplication. Yet they immediately "perceived" relationships among numbers. Upon seeing a bunch of matches that had fallen to the floor, they called out "111," the correct number, too quickly to have counted. Then one twin exclaimed "37," having factored 111 into three equal parts, apparently automatically. It was as if the number had sundered itself into three. The twins were also capable of recognizing prime numbers—integers that can be divided by no other whole numbers but themselves and the number one—although they could not derive prime numbers logically. Linguists like Noam Chomsky theorize that people are neurologically "prewired" to grasp the deep structure that underlies all human languages. Perhaps, Sacks speculates, the brain circuits of savants like the twins are wired with a "deep arithmetic"—an innate structure for perceiving mathematical relationships that is analogous to the prewiring that allows people to perceive and produce language.

Various theories have been presented to explain the savant syndrome (Treffert, 1988). Some believe that savants have unusually well developed memories that allow them to record and scan vast amounts of information. It has been suggested that savants may inherit two sets of hereditary factors, one for retardation and the other for special abilities. Perhaps it is coincidental that their special abilities and their mental handicaps were inherited in common. Other theorists suggest that the left and right hemispheres of savants' cerebral cortexes are organized in an unusual way. This latter belief is supported by research suggesting that the special abilities of savants often involve skills associated with right hemisphere functioning. Still other theorists suggest that savants learn special skills to compensate for their lack of more general skills, perhaps as a means of coping with their environment, or perhaps as a means of earning social reinforcements. Perhaps the savant's skills in concrete functions, like calculation, compensate for their lack of abstract thinking ability. Some, finally, attribute savant syndrome to prolonged periods of sensory deprivation. A barren social environment could have prompted the savant to concentrate on "trivial" pursuits like memorizing obscure facts or learning calendar calculating. In blind or deaf savants, sensory deprivation takes a literal meaning. Among autistics, attending to minute details may derive from inability to focus on stimuli beyond an extremely narrow range. Yet many savants are not blind, deaf, or socially deprived; they have been reared in stimulus-rich environments.

Recent research has pointed to possible gender-linked left hemisphere damage occurring prenatally or congenitally. Compensatory right hemisphere development might then take place, establishing specialized brain circuitry that processes concrete and narrowly defined kinds of information (Treffert, 1988). An environment that reinforces savant abilities and provides opportunities for practice and concentration would give further impetus to the development of these unusual abilities. Still, the savant syndrome remains a mystery.

large-scale dumping of mental patients in the community from psychiatric institutions resulted in massive social problems and swelled the ranks of America's homeless population (see Chapters 14 and 15), deinstitutionalization of the mentally retarded has largely been a success story that has been achieved with rare dignity (Winerip, 1991).

Mentally retarded children and adults may need psychological counseling to help them adjust to life in the community. Many have difficulty making friends and may become socially isolated. Problems with self-esteem are also common, especially because mentally retarded people are often demeaned and ridiculed. Supportive counseling may be supplemented with behavioral techniques that help retarded people acquire skills in areas such as hygiene, work, and social relationships.

Behavioral approaches teach basic hygienic behaviors such as toothbrushing, self-dressing, and hair-combing. In the example of toothbrushing, the therapist might first define the component parts of the targeted behavior (for example, picking up the toothbrush, wetting the toothbrush, taking the cap off the tube, putting the paste on the brush, etc.) (Kissel et al., 1983). The therapist might then shape the desired behavior by using such techniques as *verbal instruction* (for example, "Jim, pick up the toothbrush"); *physical guidance* (physically guiding the client's hand in performing the desired response); and *reward* (use of positive verbal reinforcement) for successful completion of the desired response ("That's really good, Jim"). Such behavioral techniques have been shown to be effective in teaching a simple but remunerative vocational skill (that is, stamping return addresses on envelopes) to a group of severely retarded adult women who were so handicapped that they were essentially nonverbal (Schepis et al., 1987). Such techniques may help people who are more severely retarded develop adaptive capacities that can enable them to perform more productive roles. Social skills training focuses on the development of conversational skills and job interviewing skills, among others (Kelly et al., 1980).

LEARNING DISORDERS

Nelson Rockefeller served as governor of New York State and as vice president of the United States. He was brilliant and well educated. However, despite the best of tutors, he always had trouble reading. Rockefeller suffered from **dyslexia**, which derives from the Greek roots *dys-*, meaning "bad," and *lexikon*, meaning "of words." Dyslexia is a kind of **learning disorder** (also called a *learning disability*). Mental retardation involves a general delay in intellectual development. People with learning disorders, by contrast, may be generally intelligent, even gifted, but show inadequate development in reading, math, or writing skills that impair school performance or daily activities.

The exact numbers of people with learning disorders are unknown, but it has been estimated that as many as 10% of the general population are dyslexic to some degree (Meir, 1971). Boys are more than two to four times as likely as girls to develop problems in reading and writing. Learning disorders tend to run a chronic course. The more severe the problem is in childhood, the more likely it is to affect adult development (Spreen, 1988). Children with learning disorders tend to perform poorly in school. They are often viewed as failures by their teachers and their families. It is not surprising that most of them develop low expectations and problems in self-esteem by the age of 9. Moreover, their academic and personal problems tend to worsen as time passes (Wenar, 1983).

Authorities do not all agree on the definition of learning disorders. One approach considers children to be learning disordered if they perform at two grade levels or more below their age levels or grade levels

(Morris, 1988). However, children advance more rapidly at younger ages, so a second grader performing at a kindergarten level is relatively more deficient than an eighth grader performing at a sixth grade level. A specific cutoff point, like the 2-year discrepancy, seems arbitrary. A second approach considers children learning disordered when they underperform on standardized tests of specific academic skills in relation to what children of comparable intelligence achieve. The intelligence–achievement gap is the criterion suggested in the DSM.

Some authorities limit the diagnosis of learning disorders to children who are "at least average" in intelligence, so as to more clearly distinguish learning disorders from mental retardation. However, there is no universally accepted standard for determining what is meant by "at least average" (Morris, 1988). Sometimes an IQ score of 90 is used as the lower boundary of average intelligence. In other cases, IQ scores as low as 70 are considered low average as opposed to mentally retarded. Other authorities suggest that even children whose IQ scores fall within the retarded range may be considered learning disordered if their achievement on tests of academic skills does not keep pace with that of children of comparable potential.

An act of Congress, the Congressional Education for All Handicapped Children Act of 1975, drew a distinction among learning disorders and learning problems that stem from causes such as mental retardation; emotional disorders; perceptual or motor handicaps; and cultural, economic, or environmental disadvantage. The exclusion of learning problems that might be attributable to such environmental causes as cultural or economic disadvantage from the purview of learning disorders has drawn fire on political and scientific grounds. It has been argued, for example, that attributing the disproportionately high incidence of academic failures among poor children to impoverished environments, as opposed to potentially treatable learning disorders, is tantamount to expecting them to fail (Morris, 1988). The underlying message to the child—and the child's school system—seems to be: Why bother to make special efforts to help them succeed in school? Refusal to accept failure from poor children, on the other hand, might encourage them—and their teachers—to do everything they can to remediate specific deficits in learning.

Types of Learning Disorders

There are several types of learning disorders, including *mathematics disorder*, *disorder of written expression*, and *reading disorder*. These disorders were classified as *academic skills disorders* in the DSM-III-R.

■ **MATHEMATICS DISORDER** Mathematics disorder describes children with deficiencies in arithmetic skills. They may have problems understanding basic mathematical terms or operations, such as addition or subtraction; decoding mathematical symbols (+, =, etc.); or learning multiplication tables. The problem may become apparent as early as the first grade (age 6) but is not generally recognized until about the third grade (age 8).

■ **DISORDER OF WRITTEN EXPRESSION** Disorder of written expression refers to children with grossly deficient writing skills. The impairment may be characterized by errors in spelling, grammar, or punctuation, or by difficulty in composing sentences and paragraphs. Severe writing difficulties generally become apparent by age 7 (second grade), although milder cases may not be recognized until the age of 10 (fifth grade) or later.

■ **READING DISORDER** Reading disorder—dyslexia—characterizes children who have poorly developed skills in recognizing words and comprehending written text. Dyslexia is believed to affect 4 to 5% of the U.S. population—about 12 million people (Blakeslee, 1991). Dyslexic children may read laboriously and distort, omit, or substitute words when reading aloud. Dyslexic children have trouble decoding letters. Dyslexic children may perceive letters upside down (*w* for *m*) or in reversed images (*b* for *d*). Dyslexia is usually apparent by the age of 7, coinciding with the second grade, although it is sometimes recognized in 6-year-olds.

Dyslexia. Dyslexic children have difficulty decoding words. Note the reversal of the letters *w* and *l* in the *owl* in this picture of a dyslexic girl completing a writing exercise.

Theoretical Perspectives

Hypotheses of learning disorders tend to focus on cognitive-perceptual problems and possible underlying neurological factors. Many learning disabled children show problems in visual or auditory perception. They may lack the capacity to copy words or to discriminate geometric shapes. Other children have short attention spans or are hyperactive.

Research findings suggest that dyslexia may stem from a brain abnormality that involves the senses of vision, hearing, and touch (Blakeslee, 1991). There is evidence of impaired visual processing in dyslexics that would be consistent with a defect in a major visual relay station in the brain involved in sequencing the flow of visual information from the retina to the visual cortex of the brain (Livingstone et al., 1991). Inspection of the autopsied brains of dyslexic people showed that this relay station was smaller and less well organized than that in normal people. As a result, the brains of dyslexic people may not be able to decipher a rapid succession of visual stimuli, such as those involved in decoding letters and words. Words may thus become blurry, fuse together, or seem to jump off the page—problems reported by dyslexic people (Blakeslee, 1991). Dysfunctions in other sensory pathways involving the senses of hearing and touch may also be involved in learning disorders. Research also shows that children with reading impairments have difficulty with tasks requiring rapid auditory discrimination of sounds (for example, distinguishing "ba" from "da" in speech). Similarly, reading-impaired children have difficulty distinguishing a rapid succession of tactile stimuli (Blakeslee, 1991). For example, if dyslexics are asked to put their hands under a table and one of their fingers is touched, they can identify which one. Yet if two fingers are touched in rapid succession, they discern only a single touch (Blakeslee, 1991).

Researchers caution that the findings of brain abnormalities in visual pathways in the brain were based on a small number of subjects. If such findings are confirmed with larger samples, it may lead the way to early detection of dyslexia through visual tests. Hopes are raised that specialized treatment programs might be developed and introduced in early childhood to enable affected children to become capable of learning to read by the time they begin formal schooling (Blakeslee, 1991).

Learning disorders also appear to run in families (see Figure 13.3). Sons of dyslexic fathers and mothers have been found to run 39 and 35% risks, respectively, of developing dyslexia. This is 5 to 7 times the risk among sons of nondyslexic parents (Vogler et al., 1985). Daughters of dyslexic parents of either gender

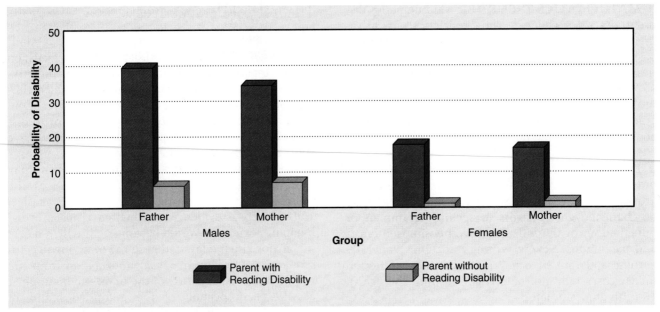

Figure 13.3   Familial risk of developmental reading disorder (dyslexia).
Boys are at greater risk than girls of developing dyslexia, and children of both genders whose parents are dyslexic are at relatively greater risk. Although these data are consistent with a genetic explanation of the etiology of dyslexia, it is also possible that dyslexic parents do not provide their children with the types of stimulation such as books and reading bedtime stories that foster reading skills.

Source: Adapted from Vogler et al. (1985).

run a 17 to 18% chance of developing dyslexia. These figures are 10 to 12 times greater than the risk among girls whose parents are not dyslexic. These figures do not control for environmental influences, however, and may thus reflect sociocultural factors as well as genetic factors.

Twin studies provide more direct support for a genetic component in dyslexia (Pennington & Smith, 1988). One twin study found 64 identical (MZ) twins pairs and 55 fraternal (DZ) twin pairs in which at least one twin was dyslexic (DeFries et al., 1987). The concordance rate for dyslexia was significantly higher among the MZ twin pairs who fully share their genetic pools, as compared to the DZ twins who share only half of their genetic inheritance.

Intervention

Approaches to intervention for learning disorders include the following (Lyon & Moats, 1988):

1. *The psychoeducational model.* Psychoeducational approaches emphasize children's strengths and preferences, rather than attempt to correct assumed underlying deficiencies. For example, a child who

retains auditory information better than visual information might be taught verbally, for example by using tape recordings, rather than by using written materials.

2. *The behavioral model.* The behavioral model assumes that academic learning is built on a hierarchy of basic skills, or "enabling behaviors." In order to read effectively, one must first learn to recognize letters, then attach sounds to letters, then combine letters and sounds into words, and so on. The child's learning competencies are assessed to determine where deficiencies lie in the hierarchies of skills. An individualized program of instruction and reinforcement helps the child acquire the skills to perform academic tasks.

3. *The medical model.* This model assumes that learning disorders are symptoms of biologically based deficiencies in cognitive processing. Proponents suggest that remediation should be directed at the underlying pathology rather than the learning disorder. If the child has a visual defect that makes it difficult to follow a line of text, treatment should aim to remediate the visual deficit, perhaps through visual-tracking exercises. Improvement in reading ability would be expected to follow.

4. *The neuropsychological model.* This approach borrows from the psychoeducational and medical models. It assumes that learning disorders reflect underlying biologically based deficits in processing information (medical model). It also assumes that remediation should be academic in focus (psychoeducational). Subject matter should be adapted to bypass inefficient brain regions and appeal to more efficient or intact neural systems.

5. *The linguistic model.* The linguistic approach focuses on children's basic language deficiencies, like recognizing how sounds and words are strung together to create meaning, which can give rise to problems in reading, spelling, and finding the words to express themselves. Adherents to this model teach language skills sequentially, helping the student grasp the structure and use of words (Wagner & Torgesen, 1987).

6. *The cognitive model.* This model focuses on how children organize their thoughts when they learn academic material. Within this perspective, children are helped to learn by (1) recognizing the nature of the learning task, (2) applying effective problem-solving strategies to complete tasks, and (3) monitoring the success of their strategies. Children with arithmetic problems might be guided to break down a math problem into its component tasks, think through the steps necessary to complete each task, and evaluate their performance at each step to judge how to proceed. Children are shown a systematic approach to problem solving that can be applied to diverse academic tasks.

■ **EVALUATION** The medical model is currently limited by lack of evidence that underlying deficiencies are correctable or that such improvements foster academic skills (Lyon & Moats, 1988; Wong, 1986). There is also a lack of evidence for the psychoeducational approach. (Brady, 1986; Lyon & Moats, 1988). The neuropsychological approach has not yet been fully tested. In contrast, the behavioral model has produced impressive results in improving the skills of children with problems in reading and arithmetic (Koorland, 1986). It remains to be seen whether or not these gains will generalize beyond the training environment. The linguistic approach has received some support, but not enough to advocate widespread use in treating children with reading and spelling deficiencies (Lyon & Moats, 1988). The cognitive model, too, has received some support, but many learning disordered children have not developed enough basic knowledge in their problem areas to use it to think through problems (Lyon & Moats, 1988).

COMMUNICATION DISORDERS

Communication disorders, formerly called *language and speech disorders* in the DSM-III-R, involve difficulties in understanding or using language. The category of communication disorders includes *expressive language disorder, mixed receptive/expressive language disorder, phonological disorder,* and *stuttering.* Each of these disorders interferes with academic or occupational functioning or ability to communicate socially. Table 13.4 contains a listing of the DSM-IV classification scheme for learning disorders and communication disorders.

Expressive language disorder involves impairment in the use of spoken language, such as slow vocabulary development, errors in tense, difficulties recalling words, and problems producing sentences of appropriate length and complexity for the individual's age. Affected children may also have a phonological or articulation disorder, compounding their speech problems.

Mixed receptive/expressive language disorder refers to children who have difficulties both understanding and producing speech. Problems with understanding speech (receptive language skills) occur with accompanying problems in expressing speech; hence the mixed type diagnosis. There may

Table 13.4	DSM-IV Classification of Learning Disorders and Communication Disorders
Learning Disorders	Reading Disorder Mathematics Disorder Disorder of Written Expression
Communication Disorders	Expressive Language Disorder Mixed Receptive/Expressive Language Disorder Phonological Disorder Stuttering

Source: DSM-IV Draft Criteria (American Psychiatric Association, 1993), pp. C:1, C:2.

be difficulty understanding words or sentences. In some cases, children have difficulty understanding certain word types (such as words expressing differences in quantity—*large, big,* or *huge*), spatial terms (such as *near* or *far*), or sentence types (such as sentences that begin with the work *unlike*). Other cases are marked by difficulties understanding simple words or sentences.

Phonological disorder or *articulation disorder* involves difficulties in articulating the sounds of speech in the absence of defects in the oral speech mechanism or neurological impairment. Children with the disorder may omit, substitute, or mispronounce certain sounds—especially *ch, f, l, r, sh* and *th* sounds, which are usually articulated properly by the early school years. It may sound as if they are uttering "baby talk." In more severe cases, there are problems articulating sounds usually mastered during the preschool years: *b, m, t, d, n,* and *h.* Speech therapy is often helpful, and milder cases often resolve themselves by the age of 8.

Stuttering refers to disturbances in the ability to speak fluently with appropriate timing of speech sounds. The lack of normal fluency must be inappropriate for the person's age in order to justify the diagnosis. Stuttering is characterized by one or more of the following characteristics: (1) repetitions of sounds and syllables; (2) prolongations of certain sounds; (3) interjections of inappropriate sounds; (4) broken words, such as pauses occurring within a spoken word; (5) blocking of speech; (6) circumlocutions (substitutions of alternative words to avoid problematic words); (7) displaying an excess of physical tension when emitting words; and (8) repetitions of monosyllabic whole words (for example "I-I-I-I am

glad to meet you.") (American Psychiatric Association, 1993).

DISRUPTIVE BEHAVIOR AND ATTENTION-DEFICIT DISORDERS

The category of *disruptive behavior and attention-deficit disorders* refers to a diverse range of problem behaviors and includes *attention-deficit/hyperactivity disorder, conduct disorder,* and *oppositional defiant disorder.* These disorders are socially disruptive and usually more upsetting to other people than to those who receive these diagnoses.

Attention-Deficit/Hyperactivity Disorder

Many parents believe that their children are not attentive toward them—that they run around on whim and do things in their own way. Some inattention, especially in early childhood, is normal enough. In **attention-deficit/hyperactivity disorder** (ADHD), however, children display impulsivity, inattention, and **hyperactivity** that are considered inappropriate to their developmental levels. Although some children with deficits in attention do not display hyperactivity, those who do show a relatively greater range of problems behaviors, including poorer self-control, greater impulsivity, greater lethargy and daydreaming, and more serious aggressive, oppositional, and

Attention-deficit/hyperactivity disorder (ADHD). ADHD is 6 to 9 times more common in boys than girls. It is characterized by attentional difficulties, restlessness, impulsivity, excessive motor behavior (continuous running around or climbing), and temper tantrums.

antisocial behavior (Barkley et al., 1990). ADHD often occurs together with other psychiatric disorders, such as conduct disorder, oppositional defiant disorder, mood disorders, anxiety disorder, learning disorders, mental retardation, and borderline personality disorder (Biederman et al., 1991).

ADHD is far from rare. ADHD is recognized in about 3 to 5% of schoolchildren (Angier, 1991a) and is the most common cause of childhood referrals to mental health agencies (Trites & Caprade, 1983). Boys are 3 to 9 times more likely than girls to be identified as having ADHD (Angier, 1991). Although inattention appears to be the basic problem (McGee et al., 1985), there are associated problems such as inability to sit still for more than a few moments (Angier, 1991), bullying, temper tantrums, stubbornness, and failure to respond to punishment (Hechtman & Weiss, 1983) (see Table 13.5).

Activity and restlessness impair the ability of ADHD children to function in school. They seem incapable of sitting still. They fidget and squirm in their seats, butt into other children's games, have outbursts of temper, and may engage in dangerous behavior, such as running into the street without looking (Campbell, 1985; Douglas, 1983; Whalen & Henker, 1985). All in all, they can drive parents and teachers to despair.

ADHD is associated with impaired academic performance. Affected children may fail to follow or remember instructions or complete assignments. They disrupt classes and other children, so that they get into fights and are frequently unpopular. Excessive motor activity declines by adolescence, but problems in attention may persist into adulthood. ADHD-related problems, such as underachievement, poor self-image, and impaired social relationships, can persist for a lifetime.

Where does "normal" age-appropriate overactivity end and hyperactivity begin? Assessment of the degree of hyperactive behavior is crucial because many normal children are called "hyper" from time to time. Some critics of the ADHD diagnosis argue that it merely labels children who are difficult to control as mentally disordered or sick. Most normal children, especially boys, are highly active during the early school years. Proponents of the diagnosis counter that there is a difference in quality between normal overactivity and ADHD. Normally overactive children are usually goal directed and can exert voluntary control over their own behavior. ADHD children appear hyperactive without reason and do not seem to be able to conform their own behavior to the demands of teachers and parents. Put it another way: Normal children can sit still and concentrate for a while when they want to do so; hyperactive children seemingly cannot.

Table 13.5 Diagnostic Features of Attention-Deficit Hyperactivity Disorder (ADHD)

Kind of Problem	Specific Behavior Pattern
Lack of Attention	Fails to attend to details or makes careless errors in schoolwork, etc. Has difficulty sustaining attention in schoolwork or play Doesn't appear to pay attention to what is being said Fails to follow through on instructions or to finish work Has trouble organizing work and other activities Avoids work or activities that require sustained attention Loses work tools (e.g., pencils, books, assignments, toys) Becomes readily distracted Forgetful in daily activities
Hyperactivity	Fidgets with hands or feet or squirms in his or her seat Leaves seat in situations such as the classroom in which remaining seated is required Is constantly running around or climbing on things Has difficulty playing quietly
Impulsivity	Frequently "calls out" in class Fails to wait his/her turn in line, games, etc.

In order to receive a diagnosis of ADHD, the disorder must begin by the age of 7, must have significantly impaired academic, social, or occupational functioning, and must be characterized by a designated number of clinical features shown in this table occurring over a 6-month period in at least two settings such as school, at home, or at work.

Adapted from DSM-IV Draft Criteria (American Psychiatric Association, 1993), pp. E:8–E:9.

A CLOSER LOOK

Hold That Twinkie! Does Sugar Cause Hyperactivity?

It is a popular belief that children's intake of sugar is related to various problem behaviors, such as poor attention span, hyperactivity, and irritability. Approximately half (45%) of the pediatricians and family physicians polled in a survey recommend low sugar diets for hyperactive children (Rosen et al., 1988). Parents and teachers may assume that sugar heightens children's activity levels because sugar provides a quick source of energy.

Despite these commonly held assumptions, a review of the literature does not support a consistent relationship between sugar and hyperactivity. As many studies report that sugar enhances goal-directed behavior as worsens it (Milich et al., 1986). Nor does the sugar substitute aspartame (Nutra-Sweet) appear to have disruptive effects on behavior (Kruesi et al., 1987).

 Actually, it has not been demonstrated that sugar contributes to hyperactivity.

Despite lack of experimental evidence that sugar contributes to hyperactivity, some questions remain. It may be that some children are more adversely affected by sugar than others (Milich et al., 1986). Perhaps children who habitually consume sugar respond differently to sugar than those who avoid it or use it sparingly. Individual differences among children thus need to be considered in future research. Future studies should also address the question of whether there are long-term effects of continuous exposure to high doses of sugar. In the meantime, there is no evidence that sugar causes or exacerbates hyperactivity or other forms of disruptive behavior. Still, the clear relationships of sugar to tooth decay, poor nutrition, and obesity argue against excessive consumption (Milich et al., 1986).

■ **THEORETICAL PERSPECTIVES** Although the causes of ADHD are not known, both environmental and biological influences may play causal roles. For example, environmental factors are suggested by evidence that ADHD children are more likely than other children to be reared in unstable families, as characterized by marital breakups and frequent moves. Biological linkages are suspected on the basis of several lines of evidence. Relatives of both boys and girls with attention-deficit disorder show an increased prevalence of the disorder themselves, which is suggestive of a familial mode of transmission (Faraone et al., 1991). The mothers of hyperactive children often had difficult pregnancies. ADHD children are also more likely than other children to have mothers who abused alcohol or other drugs during pregnancy. As infants, hyperactive children were more prone to neurological disorders, such as encephalitis and seizures.

Yet most ADHD children do not show clear signs of neurological damage. Whether or not there is frank evidence of brain damage in ADHD children, it is possible that their nervous systems are less mature than those of unaffected children. This hypothesis receives some support from the observed gender ratio of affected children because the nervous systems of boys mature more slowly than those of girls. We shall see that the effects of stimulants on ADHD children also offer some support to the hypothesis of organic causes. The feature "Hold That Twinkie!" notes that researchers have also explored whether hyperactivity may be connected with dietary factors.

■ **TREATMENT** Treatments for ADHD are primarily biological and cognitive-behavioral. The most common treatment is pharmacological—the use of stimulants such as Ritalin (methylphenidate) and amphetamines. Nearly 9 of 10 ADHD children in a recent survey had been treated with Ritalin (Wolraich et al., 1990). It may seem ironic that stimulants are used to treat children who are overactive. The rationale is that hyperactivity reflects inability of the (possibly immature) cerebral cortex to inhibit more primitive parts of the brain. The drugs, in theory, facilitate cortical control over more primitive, lower brain centers. As in the case of Eddie, although stimulant medication can help reduce restlessness and increase attention, it is hardly a panacea:

Nine-year-old Eddie is a problem in class. His teacher complains that he is so restless and fidgety that the rest of the class cannot concentrate on their work. He hardly ever sits still. He is in constant motion, roaming the classroom, talking to other children while they are working. He has been suspended repeatedly for outrageous behavior, most recently swinging from a fluorescent light fixture and unable to get himself down. His mother reports that Eddie has been a problem since he was a toddler. By the age of 3 he had become unbearably restless and demanding. He has never needed much sleep and always awakened before anyone else in the family, making his way downstairs and wrecking things in the living room and kitchen. Once, at the age of 4, he unlocked the front door and wandered into traffic, but was rescued by a passer-by.

Psychological testing shows Eddie to be average in academic ability, but to have a "virtually nonexistent" attention span. He shows no interest in television or in games or toys that require some concentration. He is unpopular with peers and prefers to ride his bike alone or to play with his dog. He has become disobedient at home and at school and has stolen small amounts of money from his parents and classmates.

Eddie has been treated with methylphenidate (Ritalin), but it was discontinued because it had no effect on his disobedience and stealing. However, it did seem to reduce his restlessness and increase his attention span at school.

■ *Adapted from Spitzer et al., 1989, pp. 315–317*

 Stimulants do calm many hyperactive children, apparently by fostering cortical control over more primitive structures of the brain.

Although the use of stimulants in the treatment of ADHD is not without its critics, researchers find stimulant therapy to be safe and effective when carefully monitored (Dulcan, 1986; Wolraich et al., 1990). The most commonly prescribed and researched stimulant, methylphenidate, causes the release of dopamine from presynaptic neurons and decreases the reuptake of dopamine (Dulcan, 1986). Stimulants have the paradoxical effect of decreasing motor activity in ADHD children, as measured, for example, by time spent out of one's seat and foot movements in the classroom (Dulcan, 1986). The normal (voluntary) high activity levels shown in physical education classes and on weekends are not disrupted, however. Stimulant medication also reduces annoying, disruptive, and aggressive behaviors among hyperactive children (e.g., Abikoff & Gittelman, 1985; Hinshaw, 1991; Klorman et al., 1988; Whalen et al., 1987). The stimulant Ritalin allows many ADHD children to concentrate on tasks, perhaps for the first times in their lives (Angier, 1991a).

Yet stimulant therapy has not been shown to foster academic achievement, although it is associated with improved cognitive abilities on laboratory tasks that measure distractability, impulsivity, and attention (Dulcan, 1986). This lack of consistency is puzzling to many researchers. It suggests that medication alone cannot compensate for educational deficiencies.

Use of stimulants with ADHD children has been controversial. Although short-term side effects are generally resolved in 2 to 3 weeks or following dosage reduction or use of "drug holidays" (Dulcan, 1986; Whalen & Henker, 1991), the long-term effects of stimulant medication use are not well known (Dulcan, 1986). Initial weight loss may occur, which is due to the appetite-suppressing effects of stimulants. But what of the effects of stimulant medication on the growth process? Researchers to date have found no apparent effect of stimulant therapy on eventual height (Gittelman-Klein & Mannuzza, 1990). In one study, 61 boys who were treated with Ritalin for childhood hyperactivity attained normal stature in adulthood and did not differ in height from nonhyperactive controls. Although stimulant use slowed the children's growth during their early years, the lag was offset by an accelerated or compensatory growth rate (called a growth rebound) after termination of the drug (Gittelman-Klein & Mannuzza, 1990).

Cognitive-behavioral programs are also used in the treatment of ADHD. For example, teachers have been trained to systematically dispense social reinforcers, such as praise, for appropriate behavior in the classroom. Such operant conditioning methods have shown some success in decreasing hyperactivity and increasing the time spent on academic work (O'Leary et al., 1976). Cognitive techniques have been developed to teach children strategies for exercising self-control and solving problems (Douglas et al., 1976; Kendall & Braswell, 1985).

Many studies have been undertaken to compare the effectiveness of stimulants with psychological approaches and with approaches that combine pharmacological and psychological methods. The outcomes of such studies are in conflict. Some suggest that behavioral and cognitive techniques do not augment the effectiveness of stimulants (Abikoff & Gittleman, 1985; Brown et al., 1985). Others suggest that stimulants do not augment the effectiveness of behavioral interventions (Gadow, 1985). Some researchers believe that a combination of cognitive behavioral approaches and stimulant medication will ultimately prove to be the most effective treatment for ADHD (Hinshaw et al., 1984; Pelham et al., 1980; Whalen & Henker, 1991). We need carefully controlled studies to tease out the effective elements of multiple treatment programs.

We note in passing a nutritional approach to treating hyperactivity described by pediatrician Ben Feingold in the book *Why Your Child Is Hyperactive.* The so-called Feingold diet eliminates junk foods, artificial food coloring, preservatives, salicylates, and other chemicals. However, only 5 to 10% of the children given the Feingold diet who have been studied show behavioral improvements (Barkley, 1981; Dulcan, 1986; Henker & Whalen, 1980). Moreover, the changes observed in those who improve are not as dramatic as those induced by methylphenidate. Nor have other nutrition-related factors, such as food allergies, vitamin deficiencies, or sugar, been empirically related to hyperactivity (Barkley, 1981; Dulcan, 1986).

■ **ADHD CHILDREN AND THE FUTURE**
ADHD usually declines by adolescence, further supporting the hypothesis that hyperactivity reflects immaturity of the nervous system. Some hyperactive children show no evidence of continued impairment as adolescents or young adults (Cantwell, 1988; Lambert, 1987; Mannuzza et al., 1988). Others, however, continue to show persistent problems, such as difficulties getting along with others, poor academic performance, negative self-concept, antisocial behavior, substance abuse, and poor work histories (Cantwell, 1988; Mannuzza et al., 1991; Weiss, 1985). Hyperactive children are also more likely than others to become delinquents, be suspended from school, and to require continued interventions in adolescence (see Figure 13.4) (Lambert et al., 1987). Still, most formerly hyperactive children have attained jobs and are satisfied with their lives by young adulthood (Weiss et al., 1979).

Conduct Disorder

Although they both involve disruptive behavior, **conduct disorder** differs a great deal from ADHD (Hinshaw, 1987). Whereas ADHD children seem literally incapable of controlling their behavior, children with conduct disorders purposefully engage in patterns of antisocial behavior that violate social norms and the rights of others (Hinshaw, 1987). Whereas ADHD children throw temper tantrums, children diagnosed as conduct disordered are intentionally aggressive and cruel. They may steal or destroy property. In adolescence they may commit rape, armed robbery, even homicide. They may cheat in school—when they bother to attend—and lie to cover their tracks. They frequently engage in substance abuse and sexual activity. Like antisocial adults, many conduct-disordered children are callous and apparently do not experience guilt or remorse for their misdeeds. Conduct-disordered children frequently have academic problems, such as poor reading, math, and expressive language skills, but their disorders do not prevent them from paying attention in class. Although there are differences between ADHD and conduct disorder, some children with conduct disorder also display a

Figure 13.4 Interventions received by adolescents who were earlier diagnosed as hyperactive.
Adolescents who were diagnosed as hyperactive during earlier childhood were more likely than those who were not diagnosed as hyperactive to receive the kinds of interventions shown in this figure.
Source: Adapted from Lambert et al. (1987).

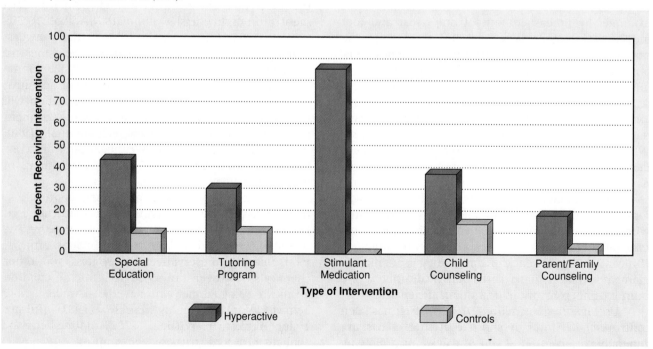

pattern of short attention span and hyperactivity that may justify a double diagnosis.

Conduct disorder involves such behaviors as breaking and entering, stealing, running away from home, lying, fire-setting, truancy, destruction of property, physical cruelty to people or animals, sexual coercion, use of a weapon, and starting fights. Conduct disorders are much more common among boys than girls. They usually begin just before or during puberty and tend to become stable. Longitudinal studies show that elementary school children with conduct disorders are more likely than other children to engage in delinquent acts as early adolescents (Spivack et al., 1986; Tremblay et al., 1992). Antisocial behavior in the form of delinquent acts (stealing, truancy, vandalism, fighting or threatening others, and so on) during early adolescence (ages 14 to 15) has also been found to predict alcohol and substance abuse in late adolescence, especially among males (Boyle et al., 1992; Windle, 1990).

Conduct disorder and **oppositional defiant disorder** appear to be related but separate disruptive behavior disorders (Loeber et al., 1991). Children who are diagnosed with oppositional defiant disorder show negativistic and defiant behavior, but without the serious violations of the rights of others and level of aggression that characterize conduct disorders. Research with boys shows that oppositional boys may lie and be mildly aggressive, but those with conduct disorders are even more aggressive and more likely to violate the rights of others (Loeber et al., 1991). Oppositional defiant disorder usually develops earlier and may lead to a conduct disorder (Loeber et al., 1991).

■ **THEORETICAL PERSPECTIVES** Genetic factors may play a role in conduct and oppositional defiant disorders. Researchers find that parents of children with oppositional defiant disorders and severe conduct disorders display high rates of antisocial personality disorder and substance abuse (Frick et al., 1992). Whether the link between these parental characteristics and disruptive behaviors in the child is genetic or stems from some psychosocial mechanisms, such as parental modeling of antisocial behaviors, remains an open question (Frick et al., 1992). However, there is increasing evidence from adoption studies that genetic factors are involved in the development of antisocial behavior. Antisocial behavior, that is, is more likely to be found among the biological parents than the adoptive parents of adopted children with conduct disorders (Mednick, 1985).

The families of children with conduct disorders tend to be characterized by negative and coercive interactions (Dadds et al., 1992). Children with conduct disorders are often highly demanding, noncompliant, and oppositional in relating to other family members. Family members often reciprocate by displaying negative behaviors in turn. Conduct disorders in children sometimes develop in families torn by marital conflict (Christensen et al., 1983; Emery, 1982; Forehand et al., 1986). Disruptive behavior may also be connected with parental distress. For example, mothers who suffer from depression tend to perceive their children as more disruptive than others view them. Such mothers also display poor parenting behaviors—such as vague and interrupted commands—that tend to foster disruptive behavior in their children (Forehand et al., 1988). Mothers of children with conduct disorders are also more likely than other mothers to be inconsistent in their use of discipline and less able to supervise their children's behavior (Frisch, 1992).

Some investigations focus on the ways in which disruptive children process information. For example, aggressive children tend to be biased in their processing of social information: They may assume that others intend them ill when they do not (Akhtar & Bradley, 1991; Dodge et al., 1990; Lochman, 1992). They usually blame others for the scrapes they get into. They believe that they are misperceived and treated unfairly.

■ **TREATMENT** The treatment of conduct disorders remains a challenge. Psychotherapy has not generally been shown to help disruptive children change their behavior. Placing children with conduct disorders in programs or treatment settings with explicit rules and clear rewards for obeying them may offer greater promise (Barkley et al., 1976; Cohen & Filipczak, 1971; Henggeler et al., 1986). Such programs usually rely on operant conditioning procedures that involve systematic use of rewards and punishments.

Many conduct disordered children, especially boys, display aggressive behavior. Researchers find that aggressive children are less able than nonaggressive peers to generate alternate (nonviolent) responses to social provocations (Akhtar & Bradley, 1991). Cognitive-behavioral problem-solving therapy has been used to teach antisocial and aggressive boys to reconceptualize social provocations as problems to be solved rather than as challenges to their manhood that must be answered with violence. In empirical studies, aggressive boys have been trained to use calming thoughts to inhibit impulsive behavior and to generate and try out nonviolent solutions to social conflicts (Kazdin et al., 1992; Lochman, 1992; Lochman et al., 1984). These approaches have helped reduce aggressive, antisocial, and disruptive behavior, and increase appropriate behavior.

Researchers have shown that problem-solving therapy with 7- to 13-year-olds who had been hospitalized for aggressive behavior was more effective than alternative treatments in reducing aggression at home and school (Kazdin et al., 1987). Despite their relative improvement, however, a majority of the children receiving problem-solving skills training in this study remained generally poorly adjusted, highlighting the intractability of antisocial behavior.

Sometimes the disruptive child's parents are brought into the treatment process (Kazdin et al., 1992). Henggeler and his colleagues (Brunk et al., 1987; Henggeler, 1982; Henggeler et al., 1986) have developed a "family-ecological" approach based on Urie Bronfenbrenner's (1979) ecological theory. Like Bronfenbrenner, Henggeler sees children as embedded within various social systems—family, school, criminal justice, community, and so on. He focuses on how juvenile offenders affect and are affected by the systems with which they interact. The techniques themselves are not unique. Rather, the family-ecological approach tries to change children's relationships with multiple systems to end disruptive interactions.

The following example illustrates the involvement of the parents in the behavioral treatment of a case of oppositional defiant disorder:

B illy was a 7-year-old second grader referred by his parents. The family was relocated frequently because the father was in the navy. Billy usually behaved when his father was taking care of him, but he was noncompliant with his mother and yelled at her when she gave him instructions. His mother was incurring great stress in the effort to control Billy, especially when her husband was at sea.

Billy had become a problem at home and in school during the first grade. He ignored and violated rules in both settings. Billy failed to carry out his chores and frequently yelled at and hit his younger brother. When he acted up, his parents would restrict him to his room or the yard, take away privileges and toys, and spank him. But all of these measures were used inconsistently. He also played on the railroad tracks near his home and twice the police had brought him home after he had thrown rocks at cars.

A home observation showed that Billy's mother often gave him inappropriate commands. She interacted with him as little as possible and showed no verbal praise, physical closeness, smiles, or positive facial expressions or gestures. She paid attention to him only when he misbehaved. When Billy was noncompliant, she would *yell back at him and then try to catch him to force him to comply. Billy would then laugh and run from her.*

Billy's parents were informed that the child's behavior was a product of inappropriate cueing techniques (poor directions), a lack of reinforcement for appropriate behavior, and lack of consistent sanctions for misbehavior. They were taught the appropriate use of reinforcement, punishment, and **time out***. The parents then charted Billy's problem behaviors to gain a clearer idea of what triggered and maintained them. They were shown how to reinforce acceptable behavior and use time out as a contingent punishment for misbehavior. Billy's mother was also taught relaxation training to help desensitize her to Billy's disruptions. Biofeedback was used to enhance the relaxation response.*

During a 15-day baseline period, Billy behaved in a noncompliant manner about four times per day. When treatment was begun, Billy showed an immediate drop to about one instance of noncompliance every two days. Follow-up data showed that instances of noncompliance were maintained at a bearable level of about one per day. Fewer behavioral problems in school were also reported, even though they had not been addressed directly.

■ *Adapted from Kaplan, 1986, pp. 227–230*

ANXIETY IN CHILDHOOD AND ADOLESCENCE

Anxieties and fears are a normal feature of childhood, just as they are a normal feature of adult life. Children face many fears and anxieties that are deemed normal because they are commonplace and seem to reflect natural cognitive-developmental processes. For example, during the second half of the first year, it is normal for children to develop separation anxiety from caregivers and fear of strangers. Other common childhood anxieties concern supernatural and imaginary creatures, being left alone or in the dark, attack by animals, noise, pain, and injury. Certain fears tend to decline during the first 6 years, such as fears of noises, strange people and objects, and pain. Other fears tend to increase, such as fears of animals, ridicule, the dark, and true sources of danger. These trends are quite normal.

Anxiety is considered abnormal, however, when it is excessive and interferes with normal academic or social functioning. Children, like adults, may suffer from various phobias, such as specific phobia and

Avoidance. Children with social phobias often avoid contact with strangers. Avoidant children tend to be excessively shy and socially withdrawn. They have difficulty interacting with other children.

social phobia, and from the more pervasive form of anxiety that is characteristic of generalized anxiety disorder (GAD). *Separation anxiety disorder,* however, is a diagnostic category that applies only to children.

Children who have social phobias typically have normal needs for affection and acceptance, and they develop warm relationships with family members. Their avoidance of people outside the family interferes with their development of peer relationships, however. They tend to be shy and withdrawn. They usually avoid playgrounds and other children in the neighborhood. Their distress at being around other children at school can also impede their academic progress. Such problems tend to develop after normal fear of strangers fades, at age 2½ or later. Problems with anxiety may be complicated by depression and isolation because anxious children typically fail to establish social relationships outside the immediate family. In some cases, children avoid other children because of lack of experience in relating to them, although they can relate relatively well to adults.

Children with generalized anxiety disorder are generally apprehensive and fretful. Although specific

phobias and social phobias may also be found in these children, their worries are not limited to one or two specific objects or events. Their fears extend to future events like visits to the doctor and tests, and to past events, such as whether or not they said the right thing to a peer or responded to a test item correctly. They are also greatly concerned about their competence in social relationships, school, and sports. Overanxious children often report anxiety-related physical symptoms such as headaches and stomachaches.

Separation Anxiety Disorder

It is normal for children to show anxiety when they are separated from their caregivers (Ainsworth & Bowlby, 1991). Mary Ainsworth (1989), who has chronicled the development of attachment behaviors, notes that separation anxiety is a normal feature of the child–caregiver relationship and begins during the first year. The sense of security normally provided by bonds of attachment apparently encourages children to explore their environments and become progressively independent of their caregivers (Bowlby, 1988).

Separation anxiety disorder is diagnosed when separation anxiety is persistent and excessive or inappropriate for the child's developmental level. That is, 3-year-olds ought to be able to attend

Separation anxiety. In separation anxiety disorder, children show persistent anxiety when separated from their parents that is inconsistent with their developmental level. Such children tend to cling to their parents and resist even brief separations.

preschool without nausea and vomiting brought on by anxiety. Six-year-olds ought to be able to attend first grade without persistent dread that they or their parents will come to harm. Children with this disorder tend to cling to their parents and follow them around the house. They may voice concerns about death and dying and insist that someone stay with them while they are falling asleep. Other features of the disorder include nightmares, stomachaches, nausea, and vomiting when separation is anticipated (as on school days), pleading with parents not to leave, or throwing tantrums when parents are about to depart. They may refuse to attend school for fear that something will happen to their parents while they are away. The disorder appears to affect boys and girls in equal numbers.

TF Some children with separation anxiety disorder do refuse to go to school because they believe that terrible things may happen to their parents while they are away.

In previous years, separation anxiety disorder was usually referred to as *school phobia*. Separation anxiety disorder may occur at preschool ages, however. Today most cases in which younger children refuse to attend school are viewed as stemming from separation anxiety. In adolescence, however, refusal to attend school is also frequently connected with academic and social concerns, in which cases the label of separation anxiety disorder would not apply.

The development of separation anxiety disorder frequently follows a stressful life event, such as illness, the death of a relative or pet, or a change of schools or homes. Alison's problems followed the death of her grandmother:

*A*lison's grandmother died when Alison was 7 years old. Her parents decided to permit her request to view her grandmother in the open coffin. Alison took a tentative glance from her father's arms across the room, then asked to be taken out of the room. Her 5-year-old sister took a leisurely close-up look, with no apparent distress.

Alison had been concerned about death for two or three years by this time, but her grandmother's passing brought on a new flurry of questions: "Will I die?," "Does everybody die?," and so on. Her parents tried to reassure her by saying, "Grandma was very, very old, and she also had a heart condition. You are very young and in perfect health. You have many, many years before you have to start thinking about death."

Alison also could not be alone in any room in her house. She pulled one of her parents or her sister along with her everywhere she went. She also reported nightmares about her grandmother and, within a couple of days, insisted on sleeping in the same room with her parents. Fortunately, Alison's fears did not extend to school. Her teacher reported that Alison spent some time talking about her grandmother, but her academic performance was apparently unimpaired.

Alison's parents decided to allow Alison time to "get over" the loss. Alison gradually talked less and less about death, and by the time 3 months had passed, she was able to go into any room in her house by herself. She wanted to continue to sleep in her parents' bedroom, however. So her parents "made a deal" with her. They would put off the return to her own bedroom until the school year had ended (a month away), if Alison would agree to return to her own bed at that time. As a further incentive, a parent would remain with her until she fell asleep for the first month. Alison overcame the anxiety problem in this fashion with no additional delays.

■ *The Authors' Files*

Theoretical understandings of excessive anxiety in children to some degree parallel explanations of anxiety disorders in adults. Psychoanalytic theorists argue that childhood anxieties and fears, like their adult counterparts, symbolize unconscious conflicts. Cognitive theorists suggest that anxious children, like anxious adults, can make perfectionistic self-demands that set themselves up for failure. Expecting the worst, combined with low self-confidence, encourages avoidance of feared activities—with friends, in school, and elsewhere. Negative expectations may also heighten feelings of anxiety to the point where they impede performance. Learning theorists suggest that the occurrence of generalized anxiety may touch upon broad themes, such as fears of rejection or failure, that carry across situations. Perhaps underlying fears of rejection or self-perceptions of inadequacy generalize to most areas of social interaction and achievement.

Whatever the causes, overanxious children may profit from the anxiety-control techniques discussed in Chapter 5, such as gradual exposure and relaxation training. In one example, relaxation training combined with instructing children to recognize and challenge irrational expectations was shown to help some fearful or overanxious children (Kendall & Williams, 1981).

DEPRESSION IN CHILDHOOD AND ADOLESCENCE

The stereotype is that childhood is the happiest time of life. Most children enjoy protection from their parents and are unencumbered by adult responsibilities. From the perspective of aging adults, their bodies seem made of rubber and free of aches. They have apparently boundless energy.

Despite the stereotype, depression is common among children and adolescents. About 10% of the 10-year-olds in one survey described themselves as being tearful, unhappy, or distressed (Rutter et al., 1981). Perhaps one-quarter to one-half of children with diagnosable mental disorders meet criteria for depressive disorders (Asarnow & Carlson, 1985). Though rare, major depression has even been found among preschoolers (Kashany et al., 1986). The features of major depression among children are similar to those that characterize the disorder in adults (Ryan et al., 1987). A study of 30 children who were hospitalized for depression found cognitive patterns also associated with adult depressive disorders: a sense of hopelessness, low self-esteem, and low self-efficacy expectancies concerning their ability to solve their problems (McCauley et al., 1988). Depressed children

also report feelings of sadness and of being alone, crying, and apathy (Carey et al., 1987). They also complain of insomnia, fatigue, and poor appetite. However, children of various ages show relatively poor appetites, so we need to be aware of developmental norms before we draw conclusions about children's behavior. Some depressed children may refuse to attend school, express fears of their parents' dying, and cling to their parents or retreat to their rooms. Many depressed children and adolescents have suicidal thoughts. Some attempt suicide (Asarnow & Carlson, 1985).

Adolescents who develop depression are at much greater risk of having other psychological disorders as well. Among depressed male adolescents, conduct or oppositional disorders are common; depressed female adolescents are likely to have eating disorders (Rohde et al., 1991). Depressed children also tend to be deficient in academic and social skills as compared to nondepressed peers (Cole, 1990). Perhaps they are less likely to receive social reinforcements because they fail to perform as well as their peers in school and play activities.

Many depressed children neither report nor are aware of feelings of depression, however. Depressed children may not report feeling sad even though they appear tearful and sad (Carlson & Garber, 1986). Part of the problem is cognitive-developmental. Children are not usually capable of recognizing internal feeling states until about the age of 7. The capacity for **con-**

Is this child too young to be depressed? Although we tend to think of childhood as the happiest and most carefree time of life, depression is actually quite common among children and adolescents. Depressed children may report feelings of sadness and lack of interest in previously enjoyable activites. Many, however, do not report or are not aware of feelings of depression, even though they may look depressed to observers. Depression may also be masked by other problems, such as conduct or school-related problems, physical complaints, and overactivity.

MULTICULTURAL PERSPECTIVES

Culturally Sensitive Therapies for Puerto Rican Children

Psychoanalysis, cognitive-behavior therapy, play therapy, drug therapy, family therapy—these are a sample of the kinds of therapies commonly used to help children in the United States cope with adjustment problems and patterns of abnormal behavior. Yet research suggests that culturally sensitive therapies, ones that are specifically tailored to the cultural backgrounds and needs of children from diverse cultural groups, are also of value.

Costantino and his colleagues (1986), for example, adapted traditional Puerto Rican folktales, or *cuentos*, as modeling examples in treating Puerto Rican children with behavior problems. The *cuentos* featured child protagonists who served as models for adaptive behavior. The stories were read aloud by the therapists and the children's mothers, and were followed by group discussion of the behavior and feelings of the main character and the moral of the story. The final element in such sessions was role playing, in which children were given the opportunity to imitate the adaptive behavior exemplified by the main character in dramatizations of the story.

***Cuento* therapy.** *Cuento* therapy is a culturally sensitive form of psychotherapy in which stories *(cuentos)* are used to model examples of adaptive behavior for Puerto Rican children who are experiencing behavior problems.

It is true that therapists have used adapted Puerto Rican folktales (*cuento* therapy) to help Puerto Rican children adjust to the demands of living in mainstream U.S. society.

Another culturally sensitive type of therapy that has been found to be useful with Puerto Rican youth is hero/heroine therapy. In one study of this approach, Malgady and his colleagues (1990a) used biographical stories of Puerto Rican heroes and heroines to foster ethnic pride and identity in Puerto Rican adolescents and to expose them to successful adult models. The models enacted ways of achieving and of coping with life stressors commonly encountered within the Puerto Rican community, many of which involve cultural conflict and discrimination.

Culturally sensitive therapies such as *cuento* therapy and hero/heroine therapy rest on the assumption that cultural conflicts underlie many of the problems encountered by immigrant and ethnic minority children and adolescents in the United States (Malgady et al., 1990b). It is too early to tell whether such culturally sensitive approaches are more effective than traditional approaches, but present evidence indicates that such approaches are superior to no treatment (Malgady et al., 1990b).

crete operations by about that age apparently contributes to the development of self-perception of internal feeling states (Glasberg & Aboud, 1982). But children may not be able to identify negative feeling states like depression in themselves until adolescence (Larson et al., 1990).

Although children, especially younger children, may not report depressed feelings, depression may be inferred from their behavior. Like adult depressives, depressed children show less social activity and less emotional expression (less often smiling, for example) than do nondepressed peers (Kazdin et al., 1985). In some cases, however, depression in childhood is "masked" by behaviors that do not appear directly related to depression. Conduct disorders, academic problems, physical complaints, and even hyperactivity may stem, now and then, from unrecognized depression. Among adolescents, aggressive and sexual *acting out* may be signs of underlying depression (Carlson, 1980).

Correlates and Treatment of Depression in Childhood and Adolescence

Some of the correlates of childhood depression are situational. Exposure to negative life events, such as parental conflict or unemployment, places children, especially younger children, at increased risk for depression (Nolen-Hoeksema et al., 1992). Depression and suicidal behavior in childhood are frequently related to family problems and conflicts (Kaslow & Rehm, 1985).

As children mature and their cognitive abilities increase, however, cognitive factors, such as attributional styles, appear to play a relatively stronger role in the development of depression. Older children (sixth and seventh graders) who adopt a pessimistic explanatory style (who attribute negative events to internal, stable, and global causes, and who attribute positive events to external, unstable, and specific causes) are more likely than children with an optimistic explanatory style to report features of depression (Nolen-Hoeksema et al., 1992). All in all, the distorted cognitions of children include the following (Leitenberg et al., 1986; McCauley et al., 1988; Nolen-Hoeksema et al., 1992):

1. Expecting the worst (pessimism)
2. Catastrophizing the consequences of negative events
3. Assuming personal responsibility for negative outcomes, even when it is unwarranted
4. Selectively attending to the negative aspects of events

Depressed children and adolescents, like depressed adults, tend to adopt a cognitive style that is characterized by negative attitudes toward themselves and the future. Self-perceptions of incompetence have been linked to low self-esteem, helplessness, and depression in children and adolescents (McCranie & Bass, 1984; Nolen-Hoeksema et al., 1992; Weisz et al., 1987). Self-perception of incompetence is not always a cognitive distortion, of course. Children who are perceived by peers as having multiple incompetencies—difficulties performing in academic, social, and athletic domains, for example—are at greater risk of developing depression than children who are perceived by their peers as having fewer incompetencies (Cole, 1991). For some children as for some adults, treatment of depression may involve fostering social and other skills.

Although there are links between cognitive factors and depression, it remains to be determined whether children become depressed because they think depressing thoughts, whether depression causes changes in cognitive style, or whether depression and cognitive styles interact in more complex ways.

Although childhood depression has been traditionally treated with psychodynamic therapy, cognitive-behavioral approaches have been gaining prominence. As with adults, cognitive-behavioral therapy for childhood depression may focus on helping the child acquire more effective social skills to increase the likelihood of obtaining social reinforcement. Children are also trained to practice thinking and talking to themselves in more rational ways. Family therapy is often used to resolve family conflicts and reorganize family relationships in ways that members can be more supportive of each other.

Some evidence supports a role for genetics in childhood depression. Children of depressed parents are more likely to become depressed than children of nondepressed parents (Beardslee et al., 1983). This does not prove the case for genetic transmission, however, because parents may influence their children through their interactions with them as well as by passing along their genes. Low utilization of the neurotransmitters serotonin and norepinephrine may be implicated in childhood depression as well as adult depression. However, evidence from most controlled trials has failed to show that antidepressants which increase utilization of these transmitters are more effective than placebos in the treatment of childhood depression (Pliszka, 1991).

Suicide Among Children and Adolescents

Suicide is relatively uncommon among younger children. In the most recent year for which statistics were available as this book went to press, only 240 suicides were reported nationwide among children aged 5 to 14 (Brody, 1992b). Even so, suicide is the third leading cause of death among children and the second leading cause among older teenagers (Brody, 1992b). Some apparent accidental deaths, such as those due to falling from a window, may actually be suicides as well. The suicide rate for adolescents aged 15 to 19 is about 8 per 100,000 (USDHHS, 1991) and has tripled since the 1950s (Neiger, 1988).

Despite the commonly held view that children and adolescents who talk about suicide are only venting their feelings, young people who do intend to kill themselves may very well talk about it (Brody, 1992b). In fact, those who discuss their plans are the ones most likely to carry them out. Moreover, children and adolescents who have survived suicide attempts are most likely to try it again (Brody, 1992b). Unfortunately, parents tend not to take their children's suicidal talk seriously. They often refuse treatment for their children, or terminate treatment prematurely.

Several risk factors have been identified for suicide among children and adolescents (Brody, 1992b; Neiger, 1988; Shafi, 1986):

1. *Gender.* Girls, like women, are three times more likely than boys to attempt suicide. Boys, like men, are more likely to succeed, however, perhaps because boys, like men, are more apt to use lethal means, such as guns. The presence of a loaded handgun in the house turns out to be the greatest risk factor for completed suicide among children, even those as young as 5 (Brody, 1992b).

2. *Age.* Young people in late adolescence or early adulthood (ages 15 to 24) are at greater risk than younger adolescents.

3. *Geography.* Adolescents in less populated areas are more likely to commit suicide. Adolescents in the more rural western regions of the United States have the highest suicide rate.

4. *Race.* In the 15 to 24 age group, Native Americans commit suicide nearly twice as often as white Americans (USDHHS, 1991). The suicide rates for African-, Asian-, and Hispanic-American youth are about 30 to 60% lower than that of non-Hispanic white youth (USDHHS, 1991).

5. *Depression.* Depression, especially when combined with low self-esteem, is a major risk factor for suicide among adolescents.

6. *Previous suicidal behavior.* One-quarter of adolescents who attempt suicide are repeaters. More than 80% of adolescents who take their lives have talked about it before doing so. Suicidal teenagers may carry lethal weapons, talk about death, make suicide plans, or engage in risky or dangerous behavior.

7. *Strained family relationships.* Family problems are present among about 75% of adolescent suicide attempters. The problems include family instability and conflict (Asarnow et al., 1987), parental abuse, neglect, rejection, or disciplinary inconsistency.

8. *Stress.* Many suicides among young people are directly preceded by a traumatic event that produces extreme stress or anxiety, such as the breakup of a relationship with a girlfriend or boyfriend, unwanted pregnancy, getting arrested or getting into trouble in school, moving to a new school, or having to take an important test (Brody, 1992b). In one study of 120 adolescents who committed suicide in the New York metropolitan area, most took their lives within hours of expecting trouble or getting into trouble (Brody,

1992b). Most young people seem to be able to cope with stressful events, but suicidal youngsters often become so filled with anxiety and dread that they see no alternative to suicide (Brody, 1992b).

9. *Substance abuse* in the adolescent's family, or by the adolescent.

10. *Social contagion.* Adolescent suicides sometimes occur in clusters, especially when a suicide or a group of suicides receives widespread publicity (Kessler et al., 1990; Phillips & Carstensen, 1986). Adolescents may romanticize suicide as a heroic act of defiance. There are often suicides or attempts among the siblings, friends, parents, or adult relatives of suicidal adolescents. Adolescent suicides may occur in bunches in a community, especially when adolescents are subjected to mounting academic pressures, such as competing for admission to college. Perhaps the suicide of a family member or schoolmate renders suicide a more "real" option for managing stress or punishing others. Perhaps the other person's suicide gives the adolescent the impression that he or she is "doomed" to commit suicide. Note the case of Pam:

*P*am was an exceptionally attractive 17-year-old who was hospitalized after cutting her wrists. "Before we moved to [an upper-middle-class town in Westchester County]," she told the psychologist, "I was the brightest girl in the class. Teachers loved me. If we had had a yearbook, I'd have been the most likely to succeed. Then we moved, and suddenly I was hit with it. Everybody was bright, or tried to be. Suddenly I was just another ordinary student planning to go to college.

"Teachers were good to me, but I was no longer special, and that hurt. Then we all applied to college. Do you know that 90 percent of the kids in the high school go on to college? I mean four-year colleges? And we all knew—or suspected—that the good schools had quotas on kids from here. I mean you can't have 30 kids from our senior class going to Yale or Princeton or Wellesley, can you? You're better off applying from Utah.

"Then Kim got her early-acceptance rejection from Brown. Kim was number one in the class. Nobody could believe it. Her father'd gone to Brown and Kim had almost 1500 SATs. Kim was out of commission for a few days—I mean she didn't come to school or anything— and then, boom, she was gone. She offed herself, kaput, no more, the end. Then Brian was rejected from Cornell. A few days later, he was gone, too. And I'm like, 'These kids were better than me.' I mean their grades and their SATs were higher than mine, and I was going to apply to Brown and Cornell. I'm like, 'What chance do I have? Why bother?'"

■ *The Authors' Files*

The reader can identify how catastrophizing cognitions can play a role in such tragic cases. Consistent with the literature on suicide among adults, suicidal children make less use of active problem-solving strategies in handling stressful situations. They may see no other way out of their perceived failures or stresses. As with adults, one approach to working with suicidal children involves helping them challenge distorted thinking and generate alternate strategies for handling the problems and stressors they face.

EATING DISORDERS

It is normal enough for young children to be fussy eaters. Even the (partial) hunger strikes of 2-year-olds occur quite often. The eating habits of some children and adolescents, however, are extreme enough to impair their health and social adjustment. Children, like adults, can become obese, and much of the time, obese children develop into obese adults. Children and adolescents can also develop eating disorders such as **anorexia nervosa** and **bulimia nervosa**. While these eating disorders can also affect adults, they usually begin in adolescence, which is why they are discussed in this chapter. Anorexia nervosa and bulimia nervosa are also related because they affect many more girls than boys and involve preoccupations with weight control and maladaptive ways of keeping weight down.

Anorexia Nervosa

*K*aren was the 22-year-old daughter of a renowned English professor. She had begun her college career full of promise at the age of 17, but two years ago, after "social problems" occurred, she had returned to live at home and taken progressively lighter course loads at a local college. Karen had never been overweight, but about a year ago her mother noticed that she seemed to be gradually "turning into a skeleton."

Karen spent literally hours every day shopping at the supermarket, butcher, and bakeries; and in conjuring up gourmet treats for her parents and younger siblings. Arguments over her lifestyle and eating habits had divided the family into two camps. The camp led by her father called for patience; that headed by her mother demanded confrontation. Her mother feared that Karen's father would "protect her right into her grave" and wanted Karen placed in residential treatment "for her

own good." The parents finally compromised on an outpatient evaluation.

At an even 5 feet, Karen looked like a prepubescent 11-year-old. Her nose and cheekbones protruded crisply. Her lips were full, but the redness of the lipstick was unnatural, as if too much paint had been dabbed on a corpse for the funeral. Karen weighed only 78 pounds, but she had dressed in a stylish silk blouse, scarf, and baggy pants so that not one inch of her body was revealed.

Karen vehemently denied that she had a problem. Her figure was "just about where I want it to be" and she engaged in aerobic exercise daily. A deal was struck in which outpatient treatment would be tried as long as Karen lost no more weight and showed steady gains back to at least 90 pounds. Treatment included a day hospital with group therapy and two meals a day. But word came back that Karen was artfully toying with her food—cutting it up, sort of licking it, and moving it about her plate—rather than eating it. After 3 weeks Karen had lost another pound. At that point, her parents were able to persuade her to enter a residential treatment program, where her eating behavior could be more carefully monitored.

■ *The Authors' Files*

Anorexia nervosa. Karen Carpenter was a popular recording star who died from a heart attack in her early 30s. It is believed that her long struggle with anorexia nervosa contributed to her death. She weighed but 80 pounds at one point toward the end of her life. Is anorexia encouraged by the contemporary cultural ideal of the slender female?

Anorexia derives from the Greek roots *an-*, meaning "without," and *orexis*, meaning "a desire for." *Anorexia* thus means "without desire for [food]," which can be something of a misnomer because some anorexic people report hunger. However, food may impress them as repugnant, and they may refuse to eat more than is absolutely necessary to maintain a minimal weight for their ages and heights. Often, they starve themselves to the point where they become dangerously emaciated.

 Perhaps you cannot be too rich, but you can be dangerously thin, as in the case of anorexia nervosa.

By and large, anorexia develops in early to late adolescence, between the ages of 12 and 18, although earlier and later onsets are sometimes found. It is found in females by a ratio of 20 to 1 (American Psychiatric Association, 1987). Anorexia nervosa and bulimia nervosa were once considered very rare, but they are becoming increasingly common in the United States and other developed countries (Kagan & Squires, 1984; Killen et al., 1986; Mitchell & Eckert, 1987; Popue et al., 1984; Pyle et al., 1986). Perhaps as many as 1 in every 100 female adolescents could be considered anorexic, according to the clinical features shown in Table 13.6.

The typical pattern of anorexia begins after menarche when the girl notices added weight and insists that it must come off. Extreme dieting and, often, excessive exercise, continue unabated after the initial weight-loss goal is achieved, however—even after their families and others express concern. Anorexic girls almost always deny that they are losing too much weight or wasting away. They may proffer their stressful exercise regimens as evidence. Women with eating disorders are more likely than normal women to view themselves as heavier than

they are (Horne et al., 1991). In a study of the distortion of body images among anorexic women, Penner and his colleagues (1991) studied women who averaged 31% below their ideal body weights, according to Metropolitan Life Insurance Company charts. Ironically, the women overestimated the sizes of parts of their bodies to be 31% larger than their actual sizes! Whereas others may perceive anorexic women like Karen to be skin and bones, anorexic girls and women often sit before the mirror and see themselves not as they are but as they were.

Although the thought of eating is repugnant to anorexic girls, some experience strong hunger. Loss of appetite is rare. They may be constantly around food. Also, like Karen, they may absorb themselves in cookbooks, assume family shopping chores, and prepare fancy dinners for others.

Although the typical anorexic or bulimic person is a young white female from a family of higher socioeconomic status, anorexia is becoming more prevalent among other social groups and older age groups (Mitchell & Eckert, 1987). Anorexia and bulimia are relatively less common among African and Asian Americans (Nevo, 1985; Jones et al., 1980).

■ MEDICAL COMPLICATIONS OF ANOREXIA

Anorexics can incur serious medical complications (Kaplan & Woodside, 1987). They may lose as much as 35% of their body weight and develop anemia. Anorexic females are also likely to encounter dermatological problems like dry, cracking skin; fine, downy hair; even a yellowish discoloration that may persist for years after weight is regained. Cardiovascular complications include heart irregularities, hypotension (low blood pressure), and associated dizziness upon standing, sometimes causing blackouts. Decreased food ingestion can cause gastrointestinal problems like constipation, abdominal pain, and obstruction or paralysis of the bowels or intestines. Menstrual irregularities are common, and amenor-

---

Table 13.6 Diagnostic Features of Anorexia Nervosa

A. Refusal to maintain weight beyond the minimal normal weight for one's age and height; for example, a weight at least 15% below normal

B. Strong fear of putting on weight or becoming fat, despite being thin

C. A distorted body image in which one's body—or part of one's body—is perceived as fat, though others perceive the person as thin.

D. In case of females who have had menarche, absence of three or more consecutive mentrual periods.

Adapted from the DSM-IV Draft Criteria (American Psychiatric Association, 1993), p. P:1.

rhea (absence or suppression of menstruation) is part and parcel of the clinical definition of anorexia in females. Muscular weakness and abnormal growth of bones may occur, causing loss of height and **osteoporosis**.

A review of 33 studies on anorexic females found reported mortality rates ranging from 0 to 22%. The consensus, however, seems to place the overall mortality rate at about 4% or a little less (Herzog et al., 1988). About half of these fatalities are due to direct complications of anorexia, such as inanition (a state of weakness from eating or drinking too little) and severe imbalances in **electrolytes**. About 1 in 4 result from suicide (Herzog et al., 1988; Hsu, 1980, 1987). The remaining deaths are attributed to various causes, including accidents, lung disease, and unspecified factors.

Bulimia Nervosa

Nicole has only opened her eyes, but already she wishes it was time for bed. She dreads going through the day, which threatens to turn out like so many other days of her recent past. Each morning she wonders, is this the day that she will be able to get by without being obsessed by thoughts of food? Or will she "blow it again" and spend the day gorging herself? Today is the day she will get off to a new start, she promises herself. Today she will begin to live like a normal person. Yet she is not convinced that it is really up to her.

Nicole starts the day with eggs and toast. Then she goes to work on cookies; doughnuts; bagels smothered with butter, cream cheese, and jelly; granola; candy bars; and bowls of cereal and milk—all within 45 minutes. Then she cannot take in any more food and turns her attention to purging what she has eaten. She goes to the bathroom, ties back her hair, turns on the shower to mask any noise she will make, drinks a glass of water, and makes herself vomit. Afterward she vows, "Starting tomorrow, I'm going to change." But she suspects that tomorrow may be just another chapter of the same story.

■ *Adapted from Boskind-White & White, 1983, p. 29*

Nicole suffers from bulimia nervosa. *Bulimia* derives from the Greek roots *bous*, meaning "ox" or "cow," and *limos*, meaning "hunger." The unpretty picture inspired by the origin of the term is one of continuous eating, like a cow chewing its cud. Bulimia nervosa is an eating disorder characterized by recurrent episodes of gorging on large quantities of food fol-

lowed by purging, such as by self-induced vomiting, in order to maintain a normal weight (see Table 13.7). Bulimics often use two or more strategies for purging, such as vomiting and use of laxatives (Tobin et al., 1992). Whereas anorexics are extremely thin, bulimic individuals are usually of normal weight. However, they share excessive concern about their shapes and weight.

Most bulimics gag themselves to induce vomiting following bingeing episodes, although some vomit after every meal. Most bulimics attempt to conceal their behavior. Although less common, some bulimics use laxatives or compulsive exercise to control their weight. Bulimics live in fear of gaining weight. In one study, 15 female bulimics aged 18 to 25 were matched with 15 nondisordered women according to age, gender, and body shape. Subjects were asked to imagine a weight gain of 5 pounds (Cutts & Barrios, 1986). Bulimics were more highly aroused by the weight-gain imagery, as assessed by subjective report and physiological measures. Although bulimics share with anorexics an overconcern with body shape and weight, bulimics do not pursue extreme thinness. Their ideal weights are similar to those of normal women (Fairburn et al., 1986).

The average age for onset of bulimia is the late teens, when concerns about dieting and expression of body dissatisfaction are at their greatest (Agras & Kirkley, 1986). Bulimic women spend significantly more time than nonbulimic women thinking about food and their weight (Zotter & Crowther, 1991). Bulimics tend to be slightly overweight preceding the

---

Table 13.7   Diagnostic Features of Bulimia Nervosa

A. Recurrent episodes of binge eating (gorging) as shown by both:
   (1) Eating an unusually high quantity of food during a 2-hour period, and
   (2) Sense of loss of control over food intake during the episode

B. Regular inappropriate behavior to prevent weight gain such as self-induced vomiting, abuse of laxatives or diuretics, fasting, or vigorous exercise

C. A minimum average of two episodes a week of binge eating and inappropriate accompanying behavior to prevent weight gain over a period of at least 3 months

D. Persistent overconcern with the shape and weight of one's body

Adapted from DSM-IV Draft Criteria (American Psychiatric Association, 1993), pp. P:1-P:2.

development of bulimia, and the binge-purge cycle usually follows a period of highly restrictive dieting. Binge eating tends to alternate with dietary restraint and is often precipitated by emotional distress or unpleasant events (Fairburn et al., 1986). The binge itself usually occurs in secret and involves consumption of usually forbidden fattening foods with little regard for taste or texture. Binge eaters typically feel that they lack control over their eating (Wilson & Walsh, 1991) and may consume 5,000 to 10,000 calories at a sitting. The episode continues until the bulimic is spent or exhausted, suffers painful stomach distention, induces vomiting, or runs out of food. Drowsiness, guilt, and depression usually ensue, but bingeing is initially pleasant because of release from dietary constraints. In between binges, bulimics may maintain rigid controls over eating (Fairburn et al., 1986).

According to community-based studies, 85 to 90% of bulimic people are female (Carlat & Camargo, 1991). Most are in their 20s and come from the middle or upper socioeconomic classes. About one-quarter are married (Fairburn et al., 1986). The incidence of bulimia is much higher than that of anorexia, and concern about the disorder has generated much publicity and controversy. Although some researchers see bulimia as reaching alarming proportions on college campuses (Halmi, 1981; Pyle et al., 1986), others consider such notions of alarm to be overstated (Kolata, 1988b).

One problem in estimating the incidence of bulimia lies in how the problem is defined. Bingeing itself is quite common, with 1 to 3 women in 4 and 2 to 3 men in 5 reporting occasional binge eating episodes (Mitchell & Eckert, 1987). However, bingeing alone does not constitute bulimia (see Table 13.7). A study at the University of Pennsylvania found that about 1.3 to 5% of college women and 0.1% of the college men at the University of Pennsylvania met DSM criteria for bulimic disorder, but the incidences of occasional bulimic behaviors were higher (Schott & Stunkard, 1987). A national survey of collegians reported that 1% of college women and 0.2% of college men met the DSM criteria for bulimia nervosa (Kolata, 1988b). Overall, survey results show that bulimia affects between 1 and 10% of U.S. women and spans all socioeconomic groups (Fluoxetine Bulimia Nervosa Collaborative Study Group, 1992).

 Some college women do keep their weight down by making themselves vomit after they go on eating binges. A recurrent pattern of binge eating and purging defines the disorder of bulimia nervosa.

■ MEDICAL COMPLICATIONS OF BULIMIA

Bulimia is also associated with many medical complications (Kaplan & Woodside, 1987). Many of these stem from repeated vomiting. There may be irritations of the skin around the mouth due to frequent contact with stomach acid, blockage of salivary ducts, decay of tooth enamel, and dental cavities. The acid from the vomit may damage taste receptors on the palate, which might make the bulimic less sensitive to the taste of vomit with repeated purgings (Rodin et al., 1990). Decreased sensitivity to the aversive taste of vomit may play a role in maintaining the purging behavior (Rodin et al., 1990). Cycles of bingeing and vomiting may cause abdominal pain, hiatus hernia, and other abdominal complaints. Stress on the pancreas may produce pancreatitis (inflammation), which is a medical emergency (Kaplan & Woodside, 1987). Excessive use of laxatives may cause bloody diarrhea and laxative dependency, so that the person cannot have normal bowel movements without laxatives. In the extreme, the bowel can lose its reflexive eliminatory response to pressure from waste material. Bingeing on large quantities of salty food may cause convulsions and swelling. Repeated vomiting or abuse of laxatives can lead to potassium deficiency, producing muscular weakness, cardiac irregularities, even sudden death—especially among bulimics who use diuretics. As with anorexics, menstruation may come to a halt.

Theoretical Perspectives on Eating Disorders

The link between anorexia and menarche has led psychodynamic theorists to suggest that anorexia may represent the girl's unconscious effort to remain a prepubescent child. By maintaining the veneer of childhood, pubescent girls may avoid dealing with such adult issues as increased independence and separation from their families, sexual maturation, and assumption of personal responsibilities. Because of the loss of fatty deposits, their breasts and hips flatten. Menstrual periods cease. In their fantasies, perhaps, they remain children, sexually undifferentiated.

Conflicts relating to autonomy have been implicated in the development of anorexia nervosa and bulimia (Strauss & Ryan, 1987). Psychodynamically oriented writers note that anorexic girls have difficulties separating from their families and consolidating separate, individuated identities (Bruch, 1973; Minuchin et al., 1978). The results of a recent study showed that anorexic women were less well defined than normal women in how they saw themselves as

QUESTIONNAIRE

The Fear of Fat Scale

Fear of body fat motivates eating disorders like anorexia and bulimia. The Goldfarb Fear of Fat scale (Goldfarb et al., 1985) measures the degree to which people fear becoming fat. The scale may help identify individuals at risk of developing eating disorders. It differentiates between anorexics and normal women, and between bulimics and nonbulimics. Dieters, however, also score higher on the scale than nondieters.

To complete the Fear of Fat scale, read each of the following statements and write in the number that best represents your own feelings and beliefs. Then check the key at the end of the chapter.

    1 = very untrue
    2 = somewhat untrue
    3 = somewhat true
    4 = very true

____ 1. My biggest fear is of becoming fat.

____ 2. I am afraid to gain even a little weight.

____ 3. I believe there is a real risk that I will become overweight someday.

____ 4. I don't understand how overweight people can live with themselves.

____ 5. Becoming fat would be the worst thing that could happen to me.

____ 6. If I stopped concentrating on controlling my weight, chances are I would become very fat.

____ 7. There is nothing that I can do to make the thought of gaining weight less painful and frightening.

____ 8. I feel like all my energy goes into controlling my weight.

____ 9. If I eat even a little, I may lose control and not stop eating.

____ 10. Staying hungry is the only way I can guard against losing control and becoming fat.

Source: Goldfarb L. A., Dynens, E. M., & Gerrard, M. (1985). The Goldfarb fear of fat scale. Journal of Personality Assessment, 49, 329–332.

being separate from their parents and families (Strauss & Ryan, 1987).

Some learning theorists view anorexia as a type of weight phobia. Excessive, irrational fears of putting on weight may reflect the tendencies in our culture to idealize the slender female form. Learning theorists also see purging among bulimics as a means of reducing the anxiety and fear that binge eating engenders in individuals who fear gaining weight (Rosen & Leitenberg, 1982). Purging reduces fear of weight gain following bingeing, so that fear reduction negatively reinforces the preceding binge-purge pattern. Purging may be seen as a compulsive ritual that is reinforced by anxiety reduction, just as compulsive hand washing and checking in obsessive-compulsives may be reinforced by relief from the anxiety induced by obsessive thoughts (Leitenberg et al., 1988).

Bulimia nervosa may be connected with relatively poor social relationships. One study of 21 bulimic college women and a matched control group of 21 normal women found that the bulimic women had more social problems. The bulimic women believed that less social support was available to them. They reported a higher occurrence of social conflict, particularly with family members (Grissett & Norvell, 1992). The bulimic women also rated themselves, and were judged by others, as less socially skillful than the control group. Although causal links between social skills and eating disorders remain to be elaborated, researchers wonder if enhancing bulimic women's social skills may increase the quality of their relationships and reduce their tendencies to use food in maladaptive ways.

There is also a strong connection between dieting and bulimia. Bulimic women, that is, invariably have histories of dieting (Ruderman & Besbeas, 1992). Dieting itself does not give rise to bulimia, however; bulimics tend to have more psychological problems and lower self-esteem than other dieters, which may make them more vulnerable to progress from dieting to bulimia (Ruderman & Besbeas, 1992).

Regardless of the factors that initiate eating disorders, social reinforcers may maintain them. Children with eating disorders may quickly become the focus of attention of their families, and receive attention from their parents that might otherwise be lacking.

■ **FAMILY FACTORS AND SYSTEMS** Some theorists focus on the brutal effect that self-starvation has on parents. They suggest that some adolescents use refusal to eat to punish their parents for feelings of loneliness and alienation they experience in the home. One related study compared the mothers of adolescents with eating disorders to the mothers of normal adolescents. Mothers of the adolescents with the eating disorders were more likely to be unhappy about their families' functioning, to have their own problems with eating and dieting, to believe that their daughters ought to lose weight, and to regard their daughters as unattractive (Pike & Rodin, 1991). Is binge eating, as suggested by Humphrey (1986), a metaphoric effort to gain the nurturance and comfort that the mother is denying her daughter? Does purging represent the symbolic upheaval of negative feelings toward the family?

Bulimics, in contrast with normal women, perceive their families as less expressive and cohesive, but as more often in conflict (Johnson & Flach, 1985; Ordman & Kirschenbaum, 1986). Families of bulimics perceive their family relationships as more conflicted and detached, less mutually supportive, and less structured than families of normal subjects (Humphrey, 1986a). Similar findings characterize the family patterns of bulimic anorexics—females who binge and purge but, in contrast to bulimics, do not maintain normal weight levels (Humphrey, 1987). Parents of bulimic anorexics tend to place their daughters in double binds by communicating mixed messages: They pay lip service to encouraging autonomy but at the same time wrest control from their daughters. Bulimic daughters, in turn, show ambivalence toward their parents. They alternate between being submissive though resentful and being self-assertive.

All in all, the families of females with eating disorders are more often conflicted and disengaged but less cohesive and nurturant than those of reference groups. They seem less capable of promoting independence in their children (Strober & Humphreys, 1987). Note, however, that the preponderance of this research is retrospective—relying on accounts of family patterns in individuals already identified as eating disordered. Therefore, it is unclear whether the identified family patterns contribute to the initiation of eating disorders, or whether eating disorders disrupt family life. The truth probably lies in an interaction between the two.

From the **systems perspective**, families are systems that regulate themselves in ways that minimize the open expression of conflict and reduce the immediate need for overt change. Within this perspective, anorexic girls may be seen as helping to maintain the shaky balances and harmonies that are found in dysfunctional families by displacing attention from family conflicts and marital tensions onto themselves (Minuchin et al., 1978). The anorexic girl

may become the *identified patient*, although the family unit is actually dysfunctional.

■ **BIOLOGICAL FACTORS**   Over the years, most theorists have attributed anorexia nervosa and bulimia nervosa to psychological origins. Recent research has also implicated biological factors, however. For example, some cases may reflect problems in the hypothalamus. The neurotransmitters norepinephrine and dopamine stimulate animals to eat when they act on parts of the hypothalamus, and these animals, like bulimic bingers, show preference for carbohydrates (Kaplan & Woodside, 1987; Leibowitz, 1986; Mitchell & Eckert, 1987; Wurtman & Wurtman, 1984). The neurotransmitter serotonin, by contrast, seems to induce satiation, thereby suppressing appetite and especially the desire for carbohydrates (Halmi et al., 1986; Kaplan & Woodside, 1987). Biological conditions that increase the action of serotonin could thus inhibit the desire to eat, as in some cases of anorexia. Perhaps conditions that suppress the action of serotonin, which normally inhibits appetite for carbohydrates, cause episodic carbohydrate bingeing, as found in many cases of bulimia.

These hypotheses receive some support from observed relationships between mood and eating disorders. Norepinephrine and serotonin imbalances are implicated in both kinds of disorders. Many bulimic females are also depressed or present some depressive features (Fairburn & Cooper, 1984; Fairburn et al., 1986; Hudson et al., 1984; Piran et al., 1985). Bulimic females often respond favorably to antidepressant drugs (Pope et al., 1983; Pope & Hudson, 1982; Rosebush, 1986; Walsh et al., 1982). Another source of evidence is that immediate (first-degree) relatives of bulimics are more likely than the immediate relatives of normal people to display mood disorders (Kassett et al., 1989). Immediate relatives of bulimics have been found, in fact, to have mood disorders in about the same proportion as the relatives of people with bipolar disorders (Hudson et al., 1983). Bulimia often occurs together with many kinds of mental disorders, including alcoholism, major depression, and such anxiety disorders as panic disorder, phobia, and generalized anxiety disorder (Kendler et al., 1991). Perhaps some bulimics binge as a form of attempted self-medication for such problems (Johnson & Larson, 1982).

Although eating disorders tend to run in families, it is unlikely that genetic factors fully explain them. Perhaps biological factors involving genetics and neurotransmitters provide a diathesis or predisposition for eating disorders, but their development depends on the interaction of genetic factors with family, social, cultural, and environmental pressures (Strober & Humphrey, 1987).

A CLOSER LOOK

Body Image and the Idealization of Thinness

Perhaps many men have claimed that they were leafing through *Playboy* magazine to study cultural standards for beauty. Garner and his colleagues (1980) actually did so, however. Their aim was to document the increasing pressures on women to be slender. To carry out their aim, they compared pictures of *Playboy* centerfolds, Miss America contestants, and models from women's magazines over the past few decades. Sure enough, they found that the idealized models of the feminine form have become progressively thinner and more boyish over the years. In contrast to the large-breasted ideals of the 1950s, the models' busts and hips have become smaller in proportion to their waistlines.

As the cultural ideal slims down, women with average or heavier-than-average figures come under more pressure to control their weight. Agras and Kirkley (1986) documented cultural interest in losing weight by tabulating the diet articles printed in three women's magazines since the year 1900: *Ladies' Home Journal, Good Housekeeping*, and *Harper's Bazaar*. Diet articles were absent until the 1930s. During the 1930s and 1940s, only about one article appeared in every 10 issues. During the 1950s and 1960s, the number of diet articles jumped to about one in every other issue. During the 1980s, however, the number mushroomed to about 1.3 articles per issue. In recent years, that is, there has been an average of *more than one* diet article per issue!

It is no secret that among today's college-age and adult women there is a widespread belief that one's figure is heavier than the ideal (Fallon & Rozin, 1985; Rozin & Fallon, 1987). Today, however, even children express dissatisfaction with their body images. One study surveyed the body-figure preferences of 670 children between the ages of 10½ and 15 (Cohn et al., 1987). *Both* genders were generally dissatisfied with their bodies. Boys wanted to be heavier than they were and girls, thinner. As in the Fallon and Rozin studies, when girls were asked to describe the ideal female figure, they chose a figure that was thinner than they and also thinner than the figure preferred by boys. Boys, on the other hand, had an ideal body shape that was heavier than they were themselves and heavier than the figure they believed that girls would prefer.

Boys will naturally grow heavier as they mature and gain muscle mass. Their bodies will thus conform more closely to their perceived ideal. Girls, unfortunately, are likely to experience a greater discrepancy between their own body shapes and their ideals as their busts fill out and their hips grow rounder. The discrepancy between the girls' perceived and ideal figures was in fact greater among the older girls in the study (Cohn et al., 1987). Even as they

The cultural ideal?   The idealization of the slender feminine form in our society can place young women under pressure to conform to an unrealistic, idealized concept of thinness. These cultural pressures can place them at risk of developing an eating disorder.

enter adolescence, contemporary girls have already developed an unrealistic desire for thinness that can lead to unhappiness and perceptions of "failure," setting the stage for the development of eating disorders.

As suggested by Boskind-White and White (1986),

. . . if the toxic chain reaction of the terror of fat, fad diets, and eating disorders is to be broken, it is essential for the public to be properly informed regarding the dangers inherent in severe caloric deprivations. The media and fashion industry must take responsibility and introduce models who are womanly and fit rather than emaciated and unhealthy. Only then will women, young and old, begin to value themselves enough to reject inappropriate roles and implement more effective coping strategies with respect to food (pp. 363–364).

Treatment of Anorexia Nervosa and Bulimia Nervosa

Eating disorders are difficult to treat. Anorexic patients are frequently hospitalized. They may then be given drugs to heighten hunger and inhibit vomiting. Behavioral treatment is also commonly used, with reinforcements made contingent on appropriate eating and weight gain. Commonly used reinforcers include ward privileges and social opportunities (Hsu, 1980). Behavior therapy is often combined with psychodynamic therapy to probe for deeper psychological conflicts (Bruch, 1973), or with family therapy to resolve underlying family conflicts (Minuchin et al., 1980). In one encouraging study (Rosman et al., 1976), more than 4 out of 5 anorexic young women whose families had received family therapy retained weight gains in follow-up evaluations. The results of another treatment study, however, revealed that most anorexic women continued to perceive themselves as overweight, even though their weights averaged 8% below their professed ideal weights (Nussbaum et al., 1985). Although the women in the study had maintained or increased their weight gains 2 years following the treatment program, such persistent distortions in body image suggest that the longer term outlook for anorexics who are "successfully" treated may be in doubt.

Research has begun to accumulate that supports the effectiveness of cognitive-behavioral therapy for bulimia (Fairburn et al., 1991; Wilson et al., 1991). Bulimics are often treated successfully in outpatient programs that focus on developing appropriate eating habits, preventing binge eating and vomiting, and replacing distorted beliefs about food and dieting with more adaptive beliefs. Hospitalization is reserved for those who require more intensive medical interventions or who appear suicidal (Mitchell & Eckert, 1987).

To eliminate self-induced vomiting, many cognitive-behavior therapists use the behavioral technique of exposure coupled with response prevention that is helpful with many obsessive-compulsive people (Leitenberg et al., 1984). In this technique, the bulimic is exposed to eating forbidden foods while the therapist stands by to prevent vomiting until the urge to purge passes. Bulimics thus learn to tolerate violations of their dietary rules without resorting to purging. In one study, 20 of 34 (nearly 60%) of bulimic women who received 11 exposure-and-response-prevention sessions reduced their binge-purge episodes by 80% or more. Fourteen resumed normal eating patterns and demonstrated complete cessation of vomiting (Gioles et al., 1985).

Many cognitive-behavior therapists are also using cognitive restructuring to modify some of the irrational beliefs that maintain bulimia. Bulimics display rigid, distorted beliefs about which foods are good or bad, for example. They hold themselves to unrealistic, perfectionistic eating restrictions and engage in dichotomous (all or nothing) thinking that predisposes them to purge when they slip even a little from their rigid diets. They also tend to overemphasize their appearance in their evaluations of their self-worth.

A combination of the exposure-with-response-prevention technique and cognitive restructuring appears to be more effective than cognitive restructuring alone (Ordman & Kirschenbaum, 1985; Wilson et al., 1986). Relapse-prevention techniques are also of help. Bulimics may be asked to visualize situations that prompt bingeing and to imagine ways of managing them.

Drug therapy has also helped many persons with eating disorders (McCann & Agras, 1990; Mitchell & Eckert, 1987; Pope et al., 1983; Rodin & Slochower, 1976; Rosebush, 1986). Serotonin suppresses the appetite by inducing feelings of satiation. The drug cyproheptadine, which checks the action of serotonin, has been used to facilitate weight gains in a number of anorexics (Halmi et al., 1986). Researchers suspect that antidepressants may act to reduce binge eating by suppressing appetite and thereby increasing dietary control, rather than by elevating mood (McCann & Agras, 1990). In one double-blind, placebo-controlled study with bulimic subjects, antidepressant medication resulted in a 91% decrease in bingeing, compared to a 19% *increase* among subjects who were given an inert placebo (Hughes et al., 1986). When the placebo-control group later crossed over and received the active drug, 10 of 12 improved significantly. A more recent double-blind study pitted the antidepressant fluoxetine (Prozac) against a placebo in a study of 387 bulimic women. Overall, treatment with Prozac (60 mg a day) was associated with reduced carbohydrate craving, binge eating, and vomiting episodes; and also with reduced depression (Fluoxetine Bulimia Nervosa Collaborative Study Group, 1992).

The efficacy of antidepressant medication in treating bulimia may suggest that bulimia is a type of mood disorder. As the medication resolves the underlying mood disorder, the eating problems abate. Not necessarily. Antidepressant drugs may have effects other than treating depression, such as affecting the brain mechanisms that regulate appetite. If the drugs had been labeled "antibulimics" and not antidepressants, would we wonder whether depression is a type of eating disorder?

ELIMINATION DISORDERS

Fetuses and newborn children eliminate waste products reflexively. As children develop, they are trained to *inhibit* the natural reflexes that govern urination and bowel movements. In the classic *Patterns of Child Rearing*, Robert Sears and his colleagues (1957) reported that American children were toilet trained, on the average, at 18 months. However, nighttime bladder accidents occurred frequently until about 24 months. Today most children in the United States achieve bladder control between the ages of 2 and 3. They continue to have nighttime accidents for another year or so, however.

In toilet training, as in many other areas of development, maturation plays a crucial role. During the first year, only the exceptional child can be toilet trained. By the third year, toilet training is usually rapid and smooth. According to the DSM-IV, children who do not become toilet trained by a reasonable age and who do not have organic conditions that might impair control of elimination are said to have *enuresis*, *encopresis*, or both.

Enuresis

Enuresis derives from the Greek roots *en-*, meaning "in," and *ouron*, meaning "urine." **Enuresis** is failure to control urination after one has reached the "normal" age for attaining such control. Conceptions of what age is normal for achieving control can vary among clinicians. DSM-IV standards are shown in Table 13.8. Enuresis, like so many other developmental disorders, is more common among boys.

Nighttime accidents are referred to as *bed wetting*. Achieving bladder control at night is more difficult than achieving daytime control. When asleep at night, children must learn to wake up when they feel

---

Table 13.8 Diagnostic Features of Enuresis
The child repeatedly wets bedding or clothes (whether intentional or involuntary)
The child's chronological age is at least 5 (or child is at an equivalent developmental level)
The behavior occurs at least twice a week for 3 months or causes significant impairment in functioning or distress
The disorder does not have an organic basis

Adapted from DSM-IV Draft Criteria (American Psychiatric Association, 1993), pp. E:16–E:17.

---

the pressure of a full bladder and then go to the bathroom to relieve themselves. The younger the "trained" child is, the more likely she or he is to wet the bed at night. Nighttime accidents often occur for a year or so after the child no longer wets during the day.

 It is perfectly normal for children who have acquired daytime control over their bladders to have nighttime accidents for a year or more.

■ **THEORETICAL PERSPECTIVES** Numerous psychological explanations of enuresis have been advanced. Psychodynamic explanations suggest that enuresis may represent the expression of hostility toward children's parents because of harsh toilet training. It may represent regression in response to the birth of a sibling or some other stressor or life change, such as starting school or suffering the death of a parent or relative. Learning theorists point out that enuresis occurs most commonly in children whose parents attempted to train them early. Early failures may have connected anxiety with efforts to control the bladder. Conditioned anxiety, then, induces rather than curbs urination.

Genetics may also be involved; the DSM reports that the concordance rate for enuresis is higher among MZ twins than among DZ twins. Genetic factors may regulate the rate of development of cortical control over eliminatory reflexes.

Bed wetting, the most common type of enuresis, usually occurs during the deepest stage of sleep and may reflect immaturity of the nervous system. In most cases bed wetting resolves itself by adolescence, and usually by the age of 8.

■ **TREATMENT** Enuresis usually resolves itself as children mature. Behavioral methods have been shown to be helpful when enuresis endures or causes parents or children great distress, however. Such methods condition children to wake up when their bladders are full. One reasonably dependable example is Mowrer's bell-and-pad method (Doleys, 1977).

The problem in bed wetting is that children continue to sleep despite bladder tension that awakens most other children. As a consequence, they reflexively urinate in bed. Psychologist O. Hobart Mowrer pioneered the bell-and-pad method in which a special pad is placed beneath the sleeping child. When the pad is wet, an electrical circuit closes, causing a bell to ring and the sleeping child to waken. After several repetitions, most children learn to wake up in response to bladder tension—*before* they wet the pad. The technique is usually explained through principles of classical conditioning. In the bell-and-pad method, *tension in children's bladder* is paired repeatedly with a stimulus (a bell) that wakes them up. The bladder tension (conditioned stimulus, or CS) comes to elicit the same response (waking up—the conditioned response, or CR) which is elicited by the bell (the unconditioned stimulus, or US). Variations of the bell-and-pad method have also been used successfully with adult enuretics (van Son et al., 1990).

Encopresis

Encopresis derives from the Greek roots *en-* and *kopros*, meaning "feces." **Encopresis** is lack of control over bowel movements that is not caused by an organic problem. It occurs in a child with a mental and chronological age of 4 or above. Soiling, like enuresis, is more common among boys. The overall incidence of soiling is lower than that of enuresis, however. Between 1 and 2% of children at the ages of 7 and 8 have problems with soiling. Encopresis rarely occurs among adolescents by the middle teens (Schaefer, 1979), except among the profoundly or severely retarded.

Soiling, unlike enuresis, is more likely to happen during the day. It can thus be keenly embarrassing to the child. Classmates often avoid or ridicule soilers. Because feces have a strong odor, teachers may find it hard to act as though nothing of consequence has happened. Parents, too, are eventually galled by recurrent soiling and may increase their demands for self-control and employ powerful punishments for failure. Because of all this, the child may start to hide soiled underwear (Ross, 1981). Such children may distance themselves from classmates, or feign sickness to stay at home. Their levels of anxiety concerning soiling increase. Because anxiety (arousal of the sympathetic branch of the autonomic nervous system) promotes bowel movements, control may become yet more elusive.

When soiling is involuntary, it is often associated with constipation, impaction, or retention that results in subsequent overflow. Constipation may be related to psychological factors, such as fears associated with defecating in a particular place or with a more general pattern of negativistic or oppositional behavior. Or constipation may be related to physiological factors, such as complications from an illness or from medication. Much less frequently, encopresis is deliberate or intentional.

Soiling often appears to follow harsh punishment of an accident or two, particularly in children who are already highly stressed or anxious. Harsh punishment may rivet children's attention on soiling. They may then ruminate about soiling, raising their level of anxiety so that self-control is impaired.

Operant conditioning methods may be helpful in dealing with soiling. They employ rewards (by praise and other means) for successful attempts at self-control and mild punishments for continued accidents (for example, gentle reminders to attend more closely to bowel tension and having the child clean her or his own underwear). When encopresis persists, thorough medical and psychological evaluation is recommended to determine possible causes and appropriate treatments.

SUMMARY

Normal and Abnormal in Childhood and Adolescence

In differentiating between normal and abnormal behavior in childhood and adolescence, we consider children's ages, genders, family and cultural backgrounds, and developmental levels.

Risk Factors for Disorders in Childhood and Adolescence

Researchers have identified various risk factors for disorders of childhood and adolescence: gender; biological risk factors, such as genetics, prenatal factors, birth complications, premature birth, low birth weights, and childhood illnesses; and psychosocial factors, such as stress, family conflict, cognitive factors, lack of acceptance, and parental neglect and abuse.

Autism

Autism is a pervasive developmental disorder. Autistic children shun affectionate behavior, engage in stereotyped behavior, attempt to preserve sameness, and engage in peculiar speech habits such as echolalia, pronoun reversals, and idiosyncratic speech. The causes of autism remain unknown.

Mental Retardation

Mental retardation is a general delay in the development of intellectual and adaptive abilities. Most cases fall in the mildly retarded range. In many cases, as with Down syndrome and fragile X syndrome, there are clear biological causes.

Learning Disorders

Learning disorders are specific deficits in the development of arithmetic, writing, or reading skills. Intervention mainly attempts to remediate specific skill deficits.

Communication Disorders

Communication disorders involve impaired understanding or use of language. They include expressive language disorder, mixed receptive/expressive language disorder, phonological disorder, and stuttering.

Disruptive Behavior and Attention-Deficit Disorders

Disruptive behavior disorders include attention-deficit/hyperactivity disorder (ADHD), conduct disorder, and oppositional defiant disorder. ADHD is characterized by impulsivity, inattention, and hyperactivity. Stimulant medication is generally effective in reducing hyperactivity, but it has not led to general academic gains. Children with conduct disorders intentionally engage in antisocial behavior.

Anxiety in Childhood and Adolescence

Children with separation anxiety disorder show excessive anxiety when separated from their parents. Some children show persistent and excessive avoidance of contact with strangers. Some children have excessive or unrealistic anxieties and worries.

Depression in Childhood and Adolescence

Depressed children, especially younger children, may not report or be aware of feeling depressed. Depression may also be masked by seemingly unrelated behaviors, such as conduct disorders. Although rare, suicide in children does occur and threats should be taken seriously. Risk factors for adolescent suicide include gender, age, geography, race, depression, past suicidal behavior, strained family relationships, stress, substance abuse, and social contagion.

Eating Disorders

Two major types of eating disorders, anorexia nervosa and bulimia nervosa, tend to begin in adolescence. They affect many more girls than boys and involve preoccupations with weight control and maladaptive ways of trying to keep weight down. Anorexia nervosa involves maintenance of weight at least 15% below normal levels, intense fears of becoming overweight, distorted body image, and in females, amenorrhea. Bulimia nervosa involves preoccupation with weight control and body shape, repeated binges, and regular purging to keep weight down.

Elimination Disorders

Enuresis and encopresis are not due to organic causes and are more common among boys. The bell-and-pad method conditions enuretic children to respond to bladder tension.

NORMS FOR THE FEAR OF FAT SCALE

Comparative scores are available for women only. You may compare your own score on the Fear of Fat Scale to those obtained by the following groups:

Group	N	Mean
Nondieting college women (women satisfied with their weight)	49	17.30
General female college population	73	18.33
College women who are dissatisfied with their weight and have been on three or more diets during the past year	40	23.90
Bulimic college women (actively bingeing and purging)	32	30.00
Anorexic women in treatment	7	35.00

Keep the following in mind as you interpret your score:

1. The Goldfarb samples are quite small.
2. A score at a certain level does not place you in that group; it merely means that you report an equivalent fear of fat. In other words, a score of 33.00 does *not* indicate that you are bulimic or anorexic. It means that your self-reported fear of fat approximates those reported by bulimic and anorexic women in the Goldfarb study.

Source of data: Goldfarb, L. A., Dykens, E. M., & Gerrard, M. (1985). The Goldfarb Fear of Fat Scale. Journal of Personality Assessment, 49, 329–332.

Alfredo Castaneda, Quien te lo dijo?, 1973. Oil on masonite, 15¾ × 57⅞ inches. Mary-Anne Martin/Fine Art, New York

CHAPTER OUTLINE

14

Methods of Therapy and Treatment

TRUTH **or** FICTION?

___ In some states, anyone can set up shop as a psychotherapist.

___ Some psychotherapists ask clients to lie down on a couch and express whatever thoughts come to mind.

___ Some psychotherapists believe that the goal of psychotherapy is to teach clients to be themselves.

___ Some therapists actively dispute their clients' most cherished beliefs.

___ People cannot overcome their problems unless they gain insight into the origins of their problems in long-term psychotherapy.

___ Group therapy is less expensive than individual therapy, but individual therapy is preferable for clients who can afford it.

___ There are so many problems in evaluating the effectiveness of psychotherapies that it is premature to claim that psychotherapy has been shown to be of value.

___ A psychotic Haitian man responded positively to a form of therapy that included the lifting of a curse by a *vodou* priest.

___ Electroconvulsive therapy is helpful in many cases of depression that do not respond to other forms of therapy.

___ Drugs have not been found helpful in treating abnormal behavior problems.

*C*arla, a 19-year-old college sophomore, had been crying more or less continuously for several days. She felt that her life was falling apart—that her college aspirations were in a shambles and that she was a disappointment to her parents. The thought of suicide had crossed her mind. She could not seem to drag herself out of bed in the morning and had withdrawn from her friends. Her misery had seemed to descend on her from nowhere, although she could pinpoint some pressures in her life: a couple of poor grades at school, a recent breakup with a boyfriend, some adjustment problems with roommates.

Carla was clearly depressed and met the diagnostic criteria associated with major depression. Had she broken her leg, her treatment from a qualified professional would have followed a fairly standard course. Yet treatment of emotional disorders like depression may be approached from different therapeutic perspectives. The treatment that Carla would receive would likely depend on the type of helping professional she consulted as well as the particular therapist's orientation. A psychiatrist might recommend a course of antidepressant medication, perhaps in combination with some form of psychotherapy. A cognitively oriented psychologist might suggest a program of cognitive therapy to help Carla identify dysfunctional thoughts that might be underlying her depressed mood, whereas a psychodynamic therapist might recommend that she begin psychoanalytically oriented therapy to uncover inner conflicts believed to lie at the root of her depression.

In earlier chapters we examined how helping professionals treat specific disorders, such as depression. In this chapter we focus on the therapies themselves. We first consider therapeutic elements that are shared by psychodynamic, humanistic-existential, behavioral, and cognitive approaches. We then examine the goals and techniques of each school of therapy and review the evidence supporting the effectiveness of psychotherapy approaches. Although most approaches to psychotherapy have focused on the individual, we will see that some approaches extend the therapeutic focus to the group, as in group, family, and marital therapy. We also review biological approaches to treatment—**psychotropic** or psychotherapeutic drugs, electroconvulsive therapy (ECT), and psychosurgery. We then explore the roles of the hospital and the community mental health center in the contemporary mental health system and the changes brought about by deinstitutionalization.

PSYCHOTHERAPY

Psychotherapy is a systematic interaction between a client and a therapist that incorporates psychological principles to help bring about changes in the client's behaviors, thoughts, and feelings in order to help the client overcome abnormal behavior, solve problems in living, or develop as an individual. Let us consider these features of psychotherapy more closely:

1. *Systematic interaction.* The process of psychotherapy involves systematic interactions between clients and therapists. "Systematic" means that therapists structure such interactions with plans and purposes that reflect their theoretical points of view.

2. *Psychological principles.* Psychotherapists draw on psychological principles, research, and theory in their practice.

3. *Behavior, thoughts, and feelings.* Psychotherapy may be directed at behavioral, cognitive, and emotional domains to help clients overcome psychological problems and lead more satisfying lives.

4. *Abnormal behavior, problem solving, and personal growth.* At least three groups of clients are assisted by psychotherapy. First are people with abnormal behavior problems such as mood disorders, anxiety disorders, or schizophrenia. Second are people who seek help for personal problems that are not regarded as abnormal, such as social shyness or confusion about career choices. Third are people who seek personal growth. For them, psychotherapy is a means of self-discovery that may help them reach their potentials as, for example, parents, creative artists, performers, or athletes.

Psychotherapies share other features as well. For one, psychotherapies involve verbal interactions. Psychotherapies are "talking therapies"—forms of interchange between clients and therapists that involve talking or conversation. In some cases, there is much verbal discussion between clients and therapists. In others, such as traditional psychoanalysis, clients do most of the talking. In each case, skillful therapists are attentive listeners. Attentive listening is an active, not a passive, activity. Therapists listen carefully to what clients are saying in order to understand as clearly as possible what they are experiencing and attempting to convey. Skillful therapists are also sensitive to clients' nonverbal cues, such as ges-

tures that may indicate underlying feelings or conflicts. Therapists also seek to convey empathy through words as well as nonverbal gestures, such as establishing eye contact and leaning forward to indicate interest in what the client is saying. Therapist empathy is a consistent predictor of therapy outcome. Clients of therapists who are perceived as warmer and more empathic show greater improvement than clients of other therapists, whether in psychodynamic therapy (Luborsky et al., 1988) or cognitive-behavior therapy (Burns & Nolen-Hoeksema, 1992).

Another common feature of psychotherapies is the instilling in clients of a sense of hope of improvement (Bandura, 1986; Wolpe, 1985). Clients generally enter therapy with expectations of receiving help to overcome their problems. Responsible therapists do not promise results or guarantee cures. They do instill hope, however, that they can help clients deal with their problems. Positive expectancies can become a type of self-fulfilling prophecy by leading clients to mobilize their efforts toward overcoming their problems. Responses to positive expectancies are termed *placebo effects* or *expectancy effects.*

The common features of psychotherapy that are not specific to any one form of therapy, such as the encouragement of hope, and the display of empathy and attentiveness on the part of the therapist (Marziali & Alexander, 1991) are often referred to as **nonspecific factors**. Nonspecific factors may have therapeutic benefits in addition to the specific benefits of particular forms of therapy.

Types of Psychotherapists

Therapies reflect the theoretical orientations of the therapists. Some therapists adopt psychodynamic approaches; others, behavioral, cognitive, family systems, humanistic-existential, or eclectic approaches, to name a few. Therapists also differ in their professional backgrounds and training. The three major professional groups whose members receive training and experience in psychotherapy are clinical psychologists, psychiatrists, and psychiatric social workers. Unfortunately, many states do not limit the use of the title *therapist* to trained professionals. In such states, anyone can identify her or himself as a therapist and perform "therapy" without a license. Thus, people seeking help are advised to inquire about the training and licensure of helping professionals.

 It is true that in some states, anyone can set up shop as a psychotherapist.

■ **CLINICAL PSYCHOLOGISTS** A clinical psychologist is a psychologist trained in the assessment, diagnosis, and treatment of psychological problems. All psychologists, including clinical psychologists, must have at least a master's degree. In most states, they must have a doctoral degree (PhD, EdD, or PsyD) to be licensed to practice psychology. Psychologists use various techniques to diagnose psychological problems, including clinical interviews, psychological tests, and behavioral observations. Psychologists use psychotherapy as a means of treating these problems. Psychologists often receive extensive training in research, which helps them conduct studies in clinical settings and critically evaluate the clinical literature.

■ **PSYCHIATRISTS** Psychiatrists are licensed physicians who have earned medical degrees such as the MD (Doctor of Medicine) or DO (Doctor of Osteopathy). They have also completed a postdoctoral residency program in psychiatry that provides specialized training in diagnosing and treating psychological problems. Like psychologists, psychiatrists conduct psychotherapy and conduct diagnostic interviews. Unlike psychologists,[1] they can prescribe drugs and administer other biological treatments, such as ECT. Psychiatrists may rely on psychologists for psychological testing to help determine a diagnosis or course of treatment.

---

[1]However, some psychologists are being trained in specialized postdoctoral programs to prescribe psychotropic medications. The issue of prescription privileges for psychologists continues to be hotly debated among psychologists and between psychologists and psychiatrists.

■ **PSYCHIATRIC SOCIAL WORKERS** Psychiatric social workers earn a graduate degree in social work at the master's level (Master of Social Work; MSW) or doctoral level (Doctor of Social Work; DSW). They receive supervised training in helping people adjust and utilize social support services and community agencies. Many psychiatric social workers conduct psychotherapy or specialize in marital or family therapy.

We now consider major approaches to psychotherapy.

PSYCHODYNAMIC THERAPIES

Psychoanalysis is the form of psychodynamic therapy originated by Sigmund Freud. Practitioners of psychoanalysis, or *psychoanalysts,* view psychological problems as rooted in early childhood experiences and unconscious conflicts. Although they have much in common with traditional psychoanalysis, more recent *psychoanalytic* or *psychodynamic* therapies tend to be briefer, to focus more on issues concerning present relationships, and to follow a somewhat different format (Strupp, 1992).

Traditional Psychoanalysis

Freud used psychoanalysis to help clients gain insight into, and resolve, unconscious conflicts. Working through these conflicts, the ego would be freed of the

Freud's consulting room at 19 Berggasse in Vienna. The room, in which Freud conducted traditional psychoanalysis, is peopled with a lively array of statuettes and figures.

need to maintain defensive behaviors—such as phobias, obsessive-compulsive behaviors, hysterical complaints, and the like—that shield it from recognition of inner turmoil.

Freud summed up the goal of psychoanalysis by saying, "Where id was, there shall ego be." This meant, in part, that psychoanalysis could help shed the light of awareness, represented by the conscious ego, on the inner workings of the id. But Freud did not expect, or intend, that clients should seek to become conscious of all repressed material—of all their impulses, wishes, fears, and memories. The aim, rather, was to replace defensive behavior with more adaptive behavior. By so doing, clients could find gratification without incurring social or self-condemnation.

Through this process a man with a phobia of knives might become aware that he had been repressing impulses to vent a murderous rage against his father. The phobic avoidance of contact with knives serves a hidden purpose of keeping these homocidal impulses in check. Another man might come to realize that unresolved anger toward his dominating or rejecting mother has sabotaged his intimate relationships with women during his adulthood. A woman with a loss of sensation in her hand which could not be explained medically might come to see that she harbored guilt over urges to masturbate. The loss of sensation may have prevented her from acting on these urges. Through confronting hidden impulses and the conflicts they produced, clients learn to sort out their feelings and find more constructive and socially acceptable ways of satisfying the urgings of the id. The ego is then freed to focus on more constructive interests.

The major methods that Freud used to accomplish these goals were free association, dream analysis, and analysis of the transference relationship.

■ **FREE ASSOCIATION** You are asked to lie down on a couch and to say anything that enters your mind. The psychoanalyst (or *analyst* for short) sits in a chair behind you, out of direct view. For the next 45 or 50 minutes, you let your mind wander, saying whatever pops in, or saying nothing at all. The analyst remains silent most of the time, prompting you occasionally to utter whatever crosses your mind, no matter how seemingly trivial, no matter how personal. This process continues, typically for three or four sessions a week, for a period of several years. At certain points in the process, the analyst offers an **interpretation**, drawing your attention to connections between your disclosures and unconscious conflicts.

Free association is the process of uttering uncensored thoughts as they come to mind. Free association is believed to gradually break down the defenses that block awareness of unconscious processes. Clients are told not to censor or screen out thoughts, but to let their minds wander "freely" from thought to thought. Psychoanalysts do not believe that the process of free association is truly free. Repressed impulses press for expression or release, leading to a **compulsion to utter**. Although free association may begin with small talk, the compulsion to utter eventually leads the client to disclose more meaningful material.

The ego continues to try to avert the disclosure of threatening impulses and conflicts. Consequently, clients may show **resistance**—an unwillingness or inability to recall or discuss disturbing or threatening material. Clients might report that their minds suddenly go blank when they venture into sensitive areas. They might switch topics abruptly, or accuse the analyst of trying to pry into material that is too personal or embarrassing to talk about. Or they might conveniently "forget" the next appointment after a session in which sensitive material is touched upon. The analyst monitors the dynamic conflict between the "compulsion to utter" and resistance. Signs of resistance are often suggestive of meaningful material. Now and then, the analyst brings interpretations of this material to the attention of the client to help the client gain better **insight** into deep-seated feelings and conflicts.

■ **DREAM ANALYSIS** To Freud, dreams represented the "royal road to the unconscious." During sleep, the ego's defenses are lowered and unacceptable impulses find some form of expression in dreams. Because the defenses are not completely eliminated, the impulses take a disguised or symbolized form in dreams. In psychoanalytic theory, dreams have two levels of content:

1. **Manifest content**: the material of the dream that the dreamer experiences and reports, and

2. **Latent content**: the unconscious material that the dream symbolizes or represents. A man might dream of flying in an airplane. Flying is the apparent or manifest content of the dream. Freud believed that flying may symbolize erection, so perhaps the latent content of the dream

reflects unconscious issues related to fears of impotence. Such symbols may vary from person to person. Analysts therefore ask clients to free-associate to the manifest content of the dream to provide clues to the latent content.

■ **TRANSFERENCE** Freud found that clients not only responded to him as an individual, but also in ways that reflected their feelings and attitudes toward other important people in their lives. A young female client might respond to him as a father figure, **displacing**, or transferring, onto Freud her feelings toward her own father. A man might also view him as a father figure, responding to him as a rival in a manner that Freud believed might reflect the man's unresolved Oedipal complex.

The process of analyzing and working through the **transference relationship** is considered an essential component of psychoanalysis. Freud believed that the transference relationship provides a vehicle for the reenactment of childhood conflicts with parents. Clients may react to the analyst with the same feelings of anger, love, or jealousy they felt toward their own parents. Freud termed the enactment of these childhood conflicts the *transference neurosis*. This "neurosis" had to be successfully analyzed and worked through for clients to succeed in psychoanalysis.

Childhood conflicts usually involve unresolved feelings of anger or rejection, or needs for love. For example, a client may interpret any slight criticism by the therapist as a devastating blow, transferring feelings of self-loathing that the client had repressed from childhood experiences of parental rejection. Transferences may also distort or color the client's relationships with others, such as a spouse or employer. Clients might relate to their spouses as they had to their parents, perhaps demanding too much from them or unjustly accusing them of being insensitive or uncaring. Or they might not give new friends or lovers the benefit of a fair chance, if they had been mistreated by others who played similar roles in their past. The analyst helps the client recognize transference relationships, especially the therapy transference, and to work through the residues of childhood feelings and conflicts that lead to self-defeating behavior in the present.

According to Freud, transference is a two-way street. Freud felt that he transferred his feelings onto his clients—perhaps viewing a young man as a competitor or a woman as a rejecting love interest. Freud referred to the feelings that he projected onto clients as **countertransference**. Psychoanalysts in training are expected to undergo psychoanalysis themselves to help them uncover motives that might lead to countertransferences in their therapeutic relationships. In their therapeutic training, psychoanalysts learn to monitor their own reactions in therapy, so as to become better aware of when and how countertransferences intrude upon the therapy process.

Although the analysis of the therapy transference is a crucial element of psychoanalytic therapy, it generally takes months or years for a transference relationship to develop and be resolved. This is one reason why psychoanalysis is typically a lengthy process.

Modern Psychodynamic Approaches

Although some psychoanalysts continue to practice traditional psychoanalysis in much the same manner as Freud, briefer and less intensive forms of psychodynamic treatment have emerged (Koss et al., 1986; Zaiden, 1982). These newer approaches are often referred to as "psychoanalytic psychotherapy," "psychoanalytically oriented" therapy, or "psychodynamic therapy." They are able to reach clients who are seeking briefer and less costly forms of treatment, perhaps once or twice a week. Economic pressures are leading many psychodynamic therapists to emphasize briefer forms of treatment (Strupp, 1992). With the advent of managed care systems such as health maintenance organizations (HMOs), traditional long-term psychodynamic psychotherapy is likely to become a luxury that is available to only a very few (Strupp, 1992).

Like Freudian psychoanalysis, newer psychody-

Modern psychodynamic psychotherapy. Modern psychodynamic therapists engage in more direct face-to-face interactions with clients than traditional psychoanalysts. Modern psychodynamic approaches are also generally briefer and focus more on the direct exploration of clients' defenses and transference relationships.

namic approaches aim to reveal unconscious motives and break down resistances and psychological defenses. New approaches may also focus more than traditional approaches on clients' current relationships and on helping clients make productive behavior changes. Because of the briefer format, therapy may entail a more open and direct exploration of the client's defenses and transference relationships than was traditionally the case. Unlike the traditional approach, the client and therapist generally sit facing each other. Rather than offer an occasional interpretation, the therapist engages in more frequent verbal give-and-take with the client.

In the following vignette of an interaction between a modern psychodynamic therapist and a client, we see that the therapist (analyst) engages the client in more direct verbal exchanges than would be expected in traditional psychoanalysis. Also note how the analyst focuses on the issue of the client's competitiveness toward him. In the psychodynamic framework, this competitiveness may be seen as a type of transference of the client's unresolved Oedipal rivalry with his own father.

---

*P*ATIENT: *. . . I continue to have success, but I have been feeling weak and tired. I saw my doctor yesterday and he said there's nothing organically wrong.*

ANALYST: *Does anything come to mind in relation to weak and tired feelings?*

P: *I'm thinking of the way you looked last year after you came out of the hospital [The patient was referring to a hospitalization that, in fact, I had the previous year during which time our treatment sessions were suspended].*

A: *Do you recall how you felt when you saw me looking that way?*

P: *It made me upset, even guilty.*

A: *But why guilty?*

P: *I'm not sure why I said that. There was nothing to feel guilty about.*

A: *Perhaps you had some other feelings.*

P: *Well it's true that at one point I felt faintly pleased that I was young and vigorous and you seemed to be going downhill. As a matter of fact I had that thought again last night when I thought of how well I have been doing.*

A: *Perhaps then . . . you imagined I felt badly because you were going uphill while I was going down.*

P: *That feels correct and I think that I may even want that to happen. [The patient looks distressed and then goes off on another topic.]*

A: *It's interesting how you felt what you were talking about after you said that you could sense wanting me to go downhill and you going up. Clearly you're not very comfortable when you contrast your state with mine—to your advantage.*

P: *Well you know I've never felt comfortable when thinking of myself outdoing you in any way. And when it comes to our states of health, the idea is particularly distressing.*

A: *I wonder now if the weak and tired feelings that you spoke about earlier in the session aren't related to what we're discussing now. Perhaps your weak and tired feelings represent an identification with me brought on by your feeling guilty about your successes, since that implies that you are outdoing me. Perhaps you felt that you were making me ill again with your wishes and thus you had to punish yourself by making yourself ill. Your discomfort with feeling that in certain respects you're surpassing me is posing a problem for you.*

■ Silverman, 1984, pp. 226–227

Some modern psychodynamic therapies focus more on the role of the ego and less on the role of the id. Therapists adopting this view believe that Freud placed too much emphasis on the sexual and aggressive impulses and underplayed the importance of the ego. These therapists, such as Heinz Hartmann, are generally described as **ego analysts**. Other modern psychoanalysts, such as Melanie Klein and Margaret Mahler, are identified with object-relations approaches to psychodynamic therapy. **Object-relations** therapists focus on helping people separate their own ideas and feelings from the elements of others that they have incorporated or introjected within themselves. They can then develop more as individuals—as their own persons.

HUMANISTIC-EXISTENTIAL THERAPIES

Psychodynamic therapies tend to focus on unconscious processes, such as internal conflicts. By contrast, humanistic-existential therapies focus on clients' subjective, conscious experiences. Humanistic-existential therapies also focus more on what clients are experiencing in the present—the here and now—rather than on the past. But there are also similarities between the psychodynamic and the humanistic-existential therapies. Both assume that the past affects present behavior and feelings and both seek to expand clients' self-insight.

Person-Centered Therapy

Carl Rogers (1951), the founder of **person-centered therapy**, or **client-centered therapy,** believed that people have natural motivational tendencies toward growth, fulfillment, and health. In Rogers's view, psychological disorders develop largely from the roadblocks that others place in the journey toward self-actualization. When others are selective in their approval of our childhood feelings and behavior, we may come to disown the criticized parts of ourselves. To earn social approval, we may don social masks or facades. We learn "to be seen and not heard" and may become deaf even to our own inner voices. Over time, we may develop distorted self-concepts that are consistent with others' views of us but are not of our own making and design. As a result, we may become poorly adjusted, unhappy, and confused as to who and what we are.

 Some psychotherapists, such as person-centered therapists, do believe that the goal of psychotherapy is to teach clients to be themselves.

Well-adjusted people make choices and take actions that are consistent with their personal values and needs. Rogers's approach to therapy, *person-centered therapy*, creates conditions of warmth and acceptance in the therapeutic relationship that help clients become more aware and accepting of their true selves. Rogers was a major shaper of contemporary psychotherapy, and was rated the single most influential psychotherapist in a survey of therapists (Smith, 1982). Rogers did not believe that therapists should impose their own goals or values on their clients. His focus of therapy, as the name implies, is centered on the person.

Person-centered therapy is *nondirective*. The client, not the therapist, takes the lead and directs the course of therapy. The therapist mirrors or reflects the client's expressed feelings to help him or her get in touch with deeper feelings and parts of the self that had become disowned because of social condemnation. The therapist reflects back or paraphrases the client's disclosures without interpreting them or passing judgment on them. Here we see how a therapist reflects back the client's disclosures to help her clarify and explore her feelings:

CLIENT: *Now—one of the things that . . . had worried me was . . . living at the dorm, it's hard—not to just sort of fall in with a group of people . . . that aren't interesting, but just around. Well, I . . . found that I had been spending a lot more time with a group of people that I didn't find interesting—All of them are pleasant people . . . but well, there were a lot of things that I didn't have in common. . . . So, now I find that I'm . . . getting away from that group a little bit. And . . . being with people who are a little bit more stimulating, and people that I really find I have more interests in common with.*

COUNSELOR: *That is, you've really chosen to draw away from the group you're just thrown in with by chance, and you pick people whom you want more to associate with. Is that it?*

CLIENT: *That's the idea. . . . I haven't taken any great steps by leaps and bounds. But, well, one of the girls lives on my floor and she would come and knock on the door and say . . . that she wanted to eat lunch . . . or all of us are going down to eat at twelve. Well, it used to be hard for me to say, "Well, no. I would like to eat at 12:30 . . . so I can eat lunch and go to my one-thirty class." And so I'd stop whatever I was doing and drag down at twelve with the group. Well, now I say, occasionally, "Well, that isn't convenient for me . . . I'd rather eat earlier . . . And then another thing is that . . . with the group of kids that I was eating with, I felt that I had just sort of been dragged into the group, almost. They . . . had sort of pulled me in with a group of their friends that I wouldn't have picked, myself, especially. And . . . so that I found that all my time was being taken up with these people, and now I'm beginning to seek out people that I prefer myself . . . rather than being drawn in with the bunch.*

COUNSELOR: *You find it a little more possible, I gather, to express your real attitudes in a social situation, like wanting to go to lunch or not wanting to go to lunch, and also to . . . make your own choice of friends, and people that you want to mix with. . . .*

CLIENT: *I mean at first . . . I tried to see if I was just withdrawing from this bunch of kids I'd been spending my time with, and I'm sincere in thinking that . . . it's not a withdrawal, but it's more of an assertion of my real interests.*

COUNSELOR: *M-hm. In other words, you've tried to be self-critical in order to see if you're just running away from the situation, but you feel really, it's an expression of your positive attitudes.*

CLIENT: *I—I think it is.*

■ *Rogers, 1951, pp. 154–155*

Rogers stressed the importance of creating a warm therapeutic relationship that would encourage the client to engage in self-exploration and self-expression. The effective person-centered therapist should possess four basic qualities or attributes: *unconditional positive regard, empathic understanding, genuineness,* and *congruence.* First, the therapist must be able to express **unconditional positive regard** for clients. In contrast to the conditional approval that the client may have received from parents and others in the past, the therapist must be unconditionally accepting of the client as a person, even if the therapist sometimes objects to the client's choices or behaviors. Unconditional positive regard provides clients with a sense of security that encourages them to explore their feelings without fear of disapproval. As clients feel accepted or prized for themselves, they are encouraged to accept themselves in turn. To Rogers, every human being has intrinsic worth and value. Traditional psychodynamic theory holds that people are basically motivated by primitive forces, such as sexual and aggressive impulses. Rogers believed, however, that people are basically good and are motivated to pursue *pro* social goals.

Therapists with **empathic understanding** are able to reflect or mirror accurately their clients' experiences and feelings. Therapists try to see the world through their clients' eyes or frames of reference. They listen actively to clients and set aside their own judgments and interpretations of events. Empathic understanding encourages clients to get in touch with feelings of which they may be only dimly aware.

Genuineness is the ability to be open about one's feelings. Rogers admitted that he had negative feelings at times during therapy sessions, typically boredom, but that he attempted to express these feelings openly rather than hide them (Bennett, 1985).

Congruence refers to the fit between one's thoughts, feelings, and behavior. The congruent person is one whose behavior, thoughts, and feelings are integrated and consistent. Congruent therapists serve as models of psychological integrity to their clients.

Gestalt Therapy

Another type of humanistic therapy, **Gestalt therapy**, was developed by Fritz Perls (1893–1970). Perls was trained as a traditional psychoanalyst but developed an approach to therapy that reflected the humanistic-existential emphasis on the client's subjective experiences in the here and now. Perls adopted the German term *Gestalt,* meaning "shape" or "form," to reflect his interest in helping clients blend conflicting parts of their personalities into an integrated whole. Perls retained the Freudian belief that psychological disorders reflect internal conflicts, but he also believed that clients must focus on how conflicts affect their experience of themselves and their relationships today rather than dwell on their origins. Gestalt therapists use structured exercises to help expand clients' awareness of their feelings and self-defeating ways of relating to others. Whereas person-centered therapists are nondirective and warm and accepting of their clients, Gestalt therapists are directive and confrontational, even hostile sometimes, because they attempt to break through clients' defenses and help them recognize their underlying conflicts.

One Gestalt exercise intended to increase awareness of internal conflicts is the **dialogue**. In this technique, clients verbally enact or confront the

Fritz Perls

opposing elements in their personalities. One example is the conflict between two parts of the personality that Perls labeled the "top dog" and the "underdog." Your top dog might conservatively command you, "Don't stick your neck out. Play it safe. You might lose everything if you take chances." Your underdog, the opposing personality element, might become frustrated and rise to assert, "You'll never get out of this rut if you don't take on new challenges." Becoming aware of these disparate elements in the personality can lead to an integration that may involve a compromise between both opposing parts.

In other exercises, clients might be encouraged to recognize feelings they may have been denying by arguing in support of ideas which are opposite to their expressed beliefs. Or they might role-play with their therapists encounters with people in their lives toward whom they have conflicted relationships, in order to bring out the strong feelings that these conflicts evoke.

Like traditional psychoanalysts, Perls focused on clients' dreams. Perls believed that the elements of dreams represented the disowned parts of the personality. To help clients get in touch with these parts, Perls would ask them to role-play the elements in their dreams. In one case, for example, a client (Jim) reported a recurring dream in which he sees a wheel coming toward him, growing to immense size as it bears down on him. Perls asks the client, "If you were this wheel, . . . what would you do with Jim?" Jim replies, "I am just about to roll over Jim" (Perls, 1971, p. 127). Perls encouraged Jim to take the part of the wheel to help him recognize that "the wheel" represented his fears about taking decisive action. Through exercises such as this, Jim is helped to become more aware of the energy he has been wasting worrying and can begin to take greater control of his life.

Existential Therapies

Existential therapists and humanistic therapists share an emphasis on helping clients become more aware of their conscious experiences and make personal choices that give their lives meaning and a sense of fulfillment. They also emphasize the uniqueness of the individual. Some of the more prominent existential therapists include the Swiss psychiatrists Ludwig Binswanger and Medard Boss, and the American psychologist Rollo May. Another existential therapist was the Viennese psychiatrist Victor Frankl, who developed **logotherapy**, a form of therapy designed to help clients find meaning in their lives. Existential therapists owe much of their intellectual heritage to the European existential philosophers, in particular

Rollo May

the Danish philosopher Sören Kierkegaard and the German philosophers Martin Heidegger and Edmund Husserl, and the French philosopher Jean-Paul Sartre.

Many existential therapists, especially those who trained or practiced in Europe, also incorporate psychodynamic concepts in their approach to therapy, such as the analysis of defenses that people use to distort their feelings and experiences. Whereas Rogerian therapists emphasize acceptance and empathetic understanding of the client, existential therapists stress the importance of coming to terms with the fundamental questions of existence, of recognizing the finality of life and of one's personal responsibility for making choices that give life meaning and purpose.

COGNITIVE THERAPIES

There is nothing either good or bad, but thinking makes it so.

Shakespeare, *Hamlet*

In these words, Shakespeare did not mean to imply that misfortunes or ailments are painless or easy to manage. His point, rather, is that the ways in which we evaluate upsetting events can heighten our discomfort and impair our ability to cope. Several hundred years later, cognitive therapists adopted this simple but elegant expression as a kind of motto for their approach to therapy.

Like humanistic-existential therapists, cognitive therapists believe that people can make genuine choices that help them develop their potentials. Cognitive therapists share with Carl Rogers and Fritz Perls the belief that therapy should address the here and now. Whereas Rogers and Perls help clients probe deep-seated feelings, however, cognitive therapists focus on the clients' beliefs, automatic types of thinking, and self-defeating attitudes that create or compound their emotional problems. Like psychodynamic therapists, cognitive therapists also focus on fostering client self-insight, but they aim to increase their clients' awareness of current cognitions, not of distant sources of unconscious conflict. Cognitive therapists aim to help clients *change* the maladaptive cognitions that are believed to underlie psychological problems and gain a more accurate picture of themselves and others.

Let us focus on two major cognitive therapies, Albert Ellis's rational-emotive therapy (RET), and Aaron Beck's cognitive therapy.

Rational-Emotive Therapy

Albert Ellis (1977a, 1985, 1987) believes that the adoption of irrational, self-defeating beliefs gives rise to psychological problems and negative feelings. A salient irrational belief is that one must almost always have the love and approval of the important people in one's life. Ellis finds it understandable to want other people's approval and love, but he argues that it is irrational for us to believe that we cannot survive without it. Another irrational belief is that we must be thoroughly competent and achieving in everything we seek to accomplish. We are usually doomed to fall short of these irrational expectations. When we do fall short, such expectations engender negative emotional consequences, such as depression and lowered self-esteem. Psychological disorders, like anxiety or depressive disorders, are not directly caused by negative events, but rather by viewing them through the dark-colored glasses of irrational beliefs. Thinking irrationally transforms challenging events, like forthcoming examinations, into looming disasters. Ellis's rational-emotive therapy seeks to free people from such irrational beliefs and their consequences. Rational-emotive therapists actively *dispute* irrational beliefs and their premises and assist clients to develop more rational, adaptive beliefs.

 Some therapists do actively dispute their clients' most cherished beliefs. Rational-emotive therapists are one example.

Ellis and Dryden (1987) describe the case of a 27-year-old woman, Jane, who was socially inhibited and particularly shy with attractive men. Through RET, Jane identified some of her underlying irrational beliefs, such as "I must speak well to people I find attractive" and "When I don't speak well and impress people as I should, I'm a stupid, inadequate person!" (p. 68). Ellis helped Jane discriminate between these irrational beliefs and rational alternatives, such as "If people do reject me for showing them how anxious I am, that will be most unfortunate, but I can stand it" (p. 68). RET encouraged Jane to debate or dispute irrational beliefs by posing challenging questions to herself, (1) "*Why* must I speak well to people I find attractive?" and, (2) "When I don't speak well and impress people, how does that make me a *stupid and inadequate person*?" (p. 69). Jane learned to form rational responses to her self-questioning, for example, (1) "There is no reason I must speak well to people I find attractive, but it would be desirable if I do so, so I shall make an effort—but not kill myself—to do so," and, (2) "When I speak poorly and fail to impress people, that only makes me a *person who spoke unimpressively this time*—not a *totally stupid or inadequate person.*" (p. 69).

Jane also rehearsed more rational ideas several times a day. Examples included, "I would like to speak well, but I never *have to,*" and, "When people I favor reject me, it often reveals more about them and their tastes than about me" (pp. 69–70). After 9 months of RET, Jane was able to talk comfortably to men she found attractive and was preparing to take a job as a teacher, a position she had previously avoided due to fear of facing a class.

Ellis recognizes that irrational beliefs may be formed on the basis of early childhood experiences. Changing them requires finding rational alternatives in the here and now, however. Rational-emotive therapists also help clients substitute more effective interpersonal behavior for self-defeating or maladaptive behavior. Ellis often gives clients specific tasks or homework assignments, like disagreeing with an overbearing relative or asking someone for a date. He assists them in practicing or rehearsing adaptive behaviors.

Beck's Cognitive Therapy

As formulated by psychiatrist Aaron Beck and his colleagues (for example, Beck, 1991; Beck & Freeman, 1990; Beck & Haaga, 1992), cognitive therapy, like RET, focuses on clients' maladaptive cognitions. Cognitive therapists encourage clients to recognize how errors in thinking ("cognitive distortions") affect their moods and impair their behavior. Cognitive therapists help clients recognize and change these disruptive patterns of thinking.

To help clients see the relationship between their thoughts and feelings, cognitive therapists utilize homework assignments which require them to record the thoughts that are prompted by upsetting events and to connect them with their emotional responses (Burns & Beck, 1978). Beck and his colleagues also make use of behavioral homework assignments, such as encouraging depressed clients to fill their free time with structured activities, like shopping or completing work around the house. Carrying out such tasks serves to counteract the apathy and loss of motivation that tend to characterize depression and may also provide concrete evidence of competence, which helps combat self-perceptions of helplessness and inadequacy (Beck et al., 1979).

Another type of homework assignment involves reality testing. Clients are asked to test out their negative beliefs in the light of reality. For example, a depressed client who feels unwanted by everyone might be asked to call two or three friends on the phone to gather data about the friends' reactions to the calls. The therapist might then ask the client to report on the assignment: "Did they immediately hang up the phone? Did they seem pleased that you called? Did they express any interest at all in talking to you again or getting together sometime? Does the evidence support the conclusion that *no one* has any interest in you?" Such exercises help clients replace distorted cognitions with rational alternatives.

Consider this case in which a depressed man was encouraged to test his belief that he was about to be fired from his job. The case also illustrates several cognitive distortions or errors in thinking, such as selectively perceiving only one's flaws (in this case, self-perceptions of laziness) and expecting the worst (expectations of being fired):

A 35-year-old man, a frozen foods distributor, had suffered from chronic depression since his divorce six years earlier. During the past year the depression had worsened and he found it increasingly difficult to call upon customers or go to the office. Each day that he avoided working made it more difficult for him to go to the office and face his boss. He was convinced that he was in imminent danger of being fired since he had not made any sales calls for more than a month. Since he had not earned any commissions in a while, he felt he was not adequately supporting his two daughters and was concerned that he wouldn't have the money to send them to college. He was convinced that his basic problem was laziness, not depression. His therapist pointed out the

illogic in his thinking. First of all, there was no real evidence that his boss was about to fire him. His boss had actually encouraged him to get help and was paying for part of the treatment. His therapist also pointed out that judging himself as lazy was unfair because it overlooked the fact that he had been an industrious, successful salesman before he became depressed. While not fully persuaded, the client agreed to a homework assignment in which he was to call his boss and also make a sales call to one of his former customers. His boss expressed support and reassured him that his job was secure. The customer ribbed him about "being on vacation" during the preceding six weeks but placed a small order. The client discovered that the small unpleasantness he experienced in facing the customer and being teased paled in comparison to the intense depression he felt at home while he was avoiding work. Within the next several weeks he gradually worked himself back to a normal routine, calling upon customers and making future plans. This process of viewing himself and the world from a fresh perspective led to a general improvement in his mood and behavior.

■ *Adapted from Burns and Beck, 1978, pp. 124–126*

RET and cognitive therapy have much in common, especially the focus on helping clients replace self-defeating thoughts and beliefs with more rational ones. Perhaps the major difference between the two approaches is one of therapeutic style. RET therapists tend to be more confrontational and forceful in their approach to disputing clients' irrational beliefs (Dryden, 1984; Ellis et al., 1989; Marzillier, 1980). Cognitive therapists tend to adopt a more gentle, collaborative approach in helping clients discover the distortions in their thinking.

BEHAVIOR THERAPY

Behavior therapy, which is also referred to as *behavior modification*, employs techniques derived from learning theories to assist clients to make adaptive behavioral changes. Behavior therapists focus on helping clients make overt behavioral changes. They also frequently use cognitive techniques to modify clients' cognitive distortions and self-defeating beliefs (Wilson, 1982). Many common behavioral techniques, in fact, such as systematic desensitization and covert sensitization, make use of cognitive processes like visual imagery. Behavior therapists insist that therapeutic outcomes be assessed in terms of behavioral changes that can be observed and measured, however, such as the ability to approach a phobic stimulus which a client had previously avoided.

Like the humanistic-existential and cognitive schools of therapy, behavior therapists focus on the here and now. They also seek to foster client self-insight in the sense of helping clients gain a better awareness of the circumstances in which their problem behaviors occur and the early learning experiences that may have led to their development. Because the focus is on changing behavior—not on personality change or deep probing into the past—behavior therapy is relatively brief. Behavior-change programs typically last from a day to a few months. Behavior therapists, like other therapists, seek to develop warm therapeutic relationships with clients, but they believe that the special efficacy of behavior therapy derives from the learning-based techniques (Wolpe, 1985), rather than from the quality of the therapeutic relationship.

Throughout the textbook we have described behavior therapy techniques for treating such problems as phobias, obsessive-compulsive disorder, depression, conduct disorders in childhood, and sexual dysfunctions. Let us review several behavior therapy techniques.

Methods of Fear Reduction

Behavior therapy first gained acclaim for the innovation of a number of methods for reducing fears and phobias—problems that had proved resistant to insight-oriented therapies. Among these methods are systematic desensitization, gradual exposure, and modeling.

■ **SYSTEMATIC DESENSITIZATION Systematic desensitization** reduces fears and phobias by presenting, usually through imagination, a hierarchy of phobic stimuli to a client who remains relaxed, usually by means of progressive relaxation (see Chapter 4). While maintaining muscle relaxation, the client is asked to imagine (or perhaps view, as through a series of slides) progressively more anxiety-arousing scenes. If fear is evoked, the client focuses on restoring muscle relaxation. The process is repeated until the scene can be tolerated without anxiety. The client then progresses to the next scene in the *fear-stimulus hierarchy*. The procedure is continued until the person can remain relaxed while imagining the most distressing scene in the hierarchy.

■ **GRADUAL EXPOSURE** In **gradual exposure** (also called *in vivo,* meaning "in life," exposure), phobic clients expose themselves to a hierarchy of actual anxiety-evoking stimuli while they try to remain relaxed. As in systematic desensitization, the client progresses up the hierarchy at her or his own pace. In Chapter 5 we reported the case of Kevin, an elevator phobic who overcame his fears through gradual exposure. Gradual exposure is often combined with cognitive techniques, such as replacing anxiety-arousing irrational thoughts with calming rational thoughts.

■ **MODELING Modeling** is a form of observational learning in which clients first observe and then imitate others who approach or interact with fear-evoking situations or objects. After observing the model, the client may be assisted or guided by the therapist or the model in performing the target behavior. The client receives ample reinforcement from the therapist for each attempt. Modeling approaches have been pioneered by Albert Bandura and his colleagues, who have shown remarkable success in using modeling techniques to treat various phobias, especially fears of animals, such as snakes and dogs (Bandura et al., 1967, 1969, 1974).

Modeling. Modeling techniques are often used to help people overcome phobic behaviors. Here a woman models approaching and petting a dog to a phobic child. As the phobic child observes the woman harmlessly engage in the desired behavior, he is more likely to imitate the behavior.

■ **THE SYMPTOM-SUBSTITUTION CONTRO-VERSY** Psychoanalysts consider phobias to be symptomatic of unconscious conflicts. They have argued that treating the symptom (that is, the phobia) without dealing with the underlying conflict may only prompt the emergence of alternate symptoms—that is, **symptom substitution**. Behavior therapists contend, however, that maladaptive behavior is itself the problem, and not necessarily a symptom of a deeper problem. Research has favored the behaviorist position. Systematic desensitization, for example, has been found effective in treating phobias (Marks, 1982; Paul, 1969; Smith & Glass, 1977) without any apparent evidence of the emergence of symptom substitution as a problem (Deffenbacher & Suinn, 1988). Moreover, people who overcome problem behaviors such as phobias are more likely to experience other benefits, such as greater self-confidence and ability to participate in a wider range of activities, rather than secondary problems.

People may be able to overcome many kinds of problems whether or not they have insight into their origins. It has not been shown, for example, that brief behavioral methods lead to symptom substitution.

Aversive Conditioning

Whereas fear-reduction methods attempt to *disconnect* fears from target stimuli, **aversive conditioning** aims to *connect* fear with problem behaviors. Whereas fear-reduction methods instill *approach* behaviors, aversive conditioning inspires *avoidance* behaviors.

Aversive conditioning involves the pairing of painful or aversive stimuli with unwanted behaviors, such as cigarette smoking, problem drinking, or deviant sexual responses. For example, to help problem drinkers control their intake of alcohol, the tastes of alcoholic beverages can be paired with electric shock or with drugs that induce nausea or vomiting (Elkins, 1991; Wiens & Menustik, 1983; Wilson, 1991). Smokers have been treated with some success with a form of aversive conditioning called *rapid smoking*, in which the rate of puffing is increased to the point that smoking becomes a noxious event (Lichtenstein, 1982; Taylor et al., 1991). Some success has also been reported with the use of aversive conditioning for treating self-injurious behaviors in autistic children (Bucher & Lovaas, 1968). It may seem paradoxical that aversive stimulation in the form of electric shock can sometimes stop such self-punishing behaviors as repeated head banging in autistic children. Perhaps the head banging is rein-

forced by the stimulation it provides, or by attention from others, and not because of the physical pain it induces. The long-term results of aversive conditioning are frequently disappointing, however, especially with sexual deviations and problems of smoking or alcohol abuse. Unless alternative behaviors are learned that become reinforcing in themselves, the problem behavior often returns when the individual is no longer faced with the immediate aversive consequences.

Covert sensitization is a technique for pairing the unwanted behavior (e.g., smoking, problem drinking, sexual interest in children) with aversive stimulation in imagination. The problem drinker, for example, may imagine becoming nauseated shortly after taking a drink at an office party, even to the point of imagining vomiting on the carpet in full view of all of his or her employer and co-workers. Covert sensitization for smoking may be more effective when combined with other techniques than when used alone (Taylor et al., 1991). Covert sensitization has become the most common form of aversion therapy used to treat sex offenders in the United States (McConaghy, 1990), although it is usually used in the context of a broader treatment program.

Operant Conditioning

Operant conditioning is based on the assumption that what happens after responses is more important than what precedes them (Delprato & Midgley, 1992; Glenn et al., 1992; Hineline, 1992) and thus focuses on the use of reinforcement to foster acquisition of adaptive responses and to extinguish maladaptive responses. Operant conditioning techniques have a wide range of applications. For example, parents and teachers may be trained to reinforce their children systematically for appropriate behavior by expressing appreciation and to extinguish inappropriate behavior by ignoring it (Gewirtz & Peláez-Nogueras, 1992; Schlinger, 1992). In institutional settings, **token economy** systems allow patients to earn tokens for performing adaptive behaviors, such as self-grooming or making their beds. The tokens can eventually be exchanged for desired rewards. Token economy systems have been used to help hospitalized schizophrenics develop more cooperative, prosocial behaviors, for example (Paul & Lentz, 1977). Token systems have also been used successfully in treating children with conduct disorder problems. In one application, conduct-disordered children received tokens for engaging in helpful behaviors, like volunteering, and gave up tokens when they engaged in such inappropriate behaviors as inattention and arguing (Schneider & Byrne, 1987). In the following case example, a token reinforcement program was used to improve a child's academic functioning in a classroom setting:

The child was a third-grade student who was inattentive to her teacher's instructions and refused to complete school assignments or participate with her classmates in school projects. Most of her time at school was spent dawdling or daydreaming. Her parents reported that she had few friends and lacked social skills. A token reinforcement program was designed that rewarded her for "on-task" behavior at school—following her teacher's instructions, completing assignments, and cooperating in class projects. The measure of outcome was the number of reading units the child completed. During a baseline period, the child completed zero reading units. Beans were then used as tokens that the child could earn for on-task behavior and exchange for special privileges. For example, the behavior of "reading first in a reading group" earned three beans. Staying after school to work on special projects with the teacher earned nine beans. The number of reading units climbed to 12 during the first three months of treatment and then to 36 during the last three treatment months. The child also showed increased social participation with friends and greater acceptance by her peers.

■ *Adapted from Walker, C.E., et al., 1981, pp. 147–148*

Social Skills Training

Social skills training is used to help clients develop effective social skills and counter social anxieties. Social skills training has, for example, helped aggressive people express themselves in a nonthreatening manner and helped chronic schizophrenics cope more effectively with the demands of community living. A type of social skills training called **assertiveness training** helps unassertive people speak up for their rights and communicate their feelings, needs, and interests.

Social skills training usually includes such techniques as self-monitoring, coaching, modeling, practice or behavior rehearsal, and feedback. In *self-monitoring,* clients are instructed to keep a running diary of upsetting social interactions in order to identify examples of social avoidance and awkward behavior. The therapist may then *coach* (provide instruction in) more effective social behavior or *model* (demonstrate) more effective behavior. The client then practices (engages in *behavior rehearsal* of) the behavior in role-playing exercises as the therapist provides constructive *feedback.* The therapist is attentive not only to what the client says and does in the practice opportunities, but also to the client's posture, tone of voice, and facial expressions.

Social skills training is often conducted in a group treatment setting. In the role-play enactments, group members can take the parts of important people in each other's lives, such as parents, spouses, employers, or potential dates. Homework assignments are used to provide clients with opportunities to practice newly acquired behaviors in real-life settings.

Self-Control Techniques

Whereas insight-oriented therapists have traditionally encouraged clients to uncover the "meanings" of problem habits such as smoking or excessive drinking, behavior therapists directly train people in self-control or self-management skills. Self-control training can be used for a wide range of problem behaviors such as nail-biting, inadequate study habits, overeating, and substance abuse.

Self-control strategies involve changing the A's, or stimulus antecedents, which trigger the problem behavior; the B's, or problem behaviors themselves; and the C's, or reinforcement consequences that follow. Smokers, for example, may be instructed to reduce their contact with smoking-related cues (the A's), stretch the chain of behaviors that leads to smoking a cigarette (the B's), and reward or punish themselves (the C's) for meeting or exceeding their smoking reduction goals. Examples of the ABC's of weight control are provided in Chapter 4 (see p. 161). The ABC's of substance abuse are provided in Chapter 9 (see p. 359).

Self-control training often begins with a **functional analysis** of the problem behavior—that is, a systematic study of the antecedent stimuli or cues that trigger it and the reinforcers that maintain it. For example, smokers may be asked to track each cigarette smoked, jotting down the time of day it was smoked, the presence of any cues that may have triggered the urge, including internal cues (for example, negative emotions, sensations of hunger) and external cues (seeing someone else smoking), and the reinforcement consequences (feelings of pleasure, relief from anxiety, relaxation, and so forth). A functional analysis can reveal stimulus and reinforcement patterns that can be modified to foster self-control. For example, a smoker may find that smoking occurs most often in response to feelings of boredom or loneliness and is maintained by the stimulation that it provides. By filling in unstructured time with stimulating activities, preferably in nonsmoking environments, the smoker may be able to cut down substantially the number of cigarettes smoked.

Other Methods

There are many other forms of behavior therapy that were considered in our discussions of specific disorders. **Biofeedback training**, for example, is often used as a relaxation technique or for treatment of stress-related physical problems, such as headaches or hypertension (Chapter 4). Relaxation techniques, such as progressive relaxation, are used not only in the context of systematic desensitization, but also for treatment of generalized anxiety (Chapter 5) and stress-related physical problems like headaches and hypertension (Chapter 4).

Cognitive-Behavior Therapy

The parallel interest in the development of cognitive psychology and information processing in the 1970s and 1980s focused attention on the role of cognitions

Biofeedback training (BFT).   BFT is often used in the treatment of such stress-related problems as headaches and hypertension. Here clients use a biofeedback device to learn to relax by focusing on their galvanic skin response (GSR), a sign of bodily arousal that is associated with states of anxiety or tension.

in psychopathology and the treatment of psychological disorders. Cognitive-behavior therapy developed from the attempt to integrate therapeutic techniques that focus not only on overt behavior but also on dysfunctional thoughts and cognitions (Wilson, 1978). Cognitive-behavior therapy draws on the assumptions that cognitions and information processing play important roles in the genesis and maintenance of maladaptive behavior and that the impact of external events is mediated by cognitive processes (Beidel & Turner, 1986). Despite its recent development, cognitive-behavior therapy has become the most widely emphasized therapeutic orientation in doctoral training programs in clinical psychology in the United States (see Figure 14.1) (Nevid et al., 1986, 1987).

There is no unified approach among cognitive-behavior therapists but rather an assortment of approaches that combine behavioral and cognitive techniques. For example, a cognitive-behavior therapist might treat a person with a depressive disorder with a combination of Beck's cognitive-therapy techniques and behavioral techniques that focus on increasing the availability of reinforcement. The following case illustration of cognitive-behavior therapy shows how behavioral (exposure) and cognitive (cognitive restructuring) techniques were used in the treatment of agoraphobia:

Mrs. X was a 41-year-old woman with a 12-year history of agoraphobia. She feared venturing into public places alone and required her husband or children to accompany her from place to place. In-vivo (actual) exposure sessions were arranged in a series of progressively more fearful encounters—a fear-stimulus hierarchy. The first step in the hierarchy, for example, involved taking a shopping trip while accompanied by the therapist. After accomplishing this task, she gradually moved upwards in the hierarchy. By the third week of treatment, she was able to complete the last step in her hierarchy—shopping by herself in a crowded supermarket. Cognitive restructuring was conducted along with the exposure training. Mrs. X was asked to imagine herself in various fearful situations and to report the self-statements she experienced. The therapist helped her identify disruptive self-statements, such as "I am going to make a fool of myself." This particular self-statement was challenged by questioning whether it was realistic to believe that she would actually lose control, and, secondly, by disputing the belief that the consequences of losing control, were it to happen, would truly be disastrous. She progressed rapidly with treatment and became capable of functioning more independently. But she still harbored concerns about relapsing in the future. The therapist focused at this point on deeper cognitive structures involving her fears of abandonment by the people she loved if she were to relapse and be unable to attend to their needs. In challenging these beliefs, the therapist helped her realize that she was not as helpless as she perceived herself to be and that she was loved for other reasons than her ability to serve others. She also explored the question, "Who am I improving for?" She realized that she needed to find reasons to overcome her phobia that were related to meeting her own personal needs, not simply the needs of her loved ones. At a follow-up interview nine months after treatment, she was functioning independently, which allowed her to pursue her own interests, such as taking night courses and seeking a job.

■ *Adapted from Biran, 1988, pp. 173–176*

It could be argued that any behavioral method involving mental imagery, such as systematic desensitization or covert sensitization, bridges behavioral and cognitive domains. Cognitive therapies such as Ellis's rational-emotive therapy and Beck's cognitive therapy might also be regarded as forms of cognitive-behavior therapy because they incorporate cognitive and behavioral treatment methods. The dividing lines between the psychotherapies may not be as clearly drawn as authors of textbooks—who are given the task of classifying them—might desire. Not only are traditional boundaries between the cognitive and behavioral therapies blurring, but many therapists adopt an eclectic approach in which they incorporate principles and techniques from various therapeutic perspectives.

ECLECTICISM IN PSYCHOTHERAPY

Eclectic therapists incorporate principles and techniques from different therapeutic orientations to enhance their overall therapeutic effectiveness (Wolfe & Goldfried, 1988). An eclectic therapist might use behavior therapy techniques to help a client change specific maladaptive behaviors, for example, along with psychodynamic techniques to help the client gain insight into the childhood roots of the problem.

Contemporary therapists are thus increasingly looking beyond the theoretical barriers that divide one school of psychotherapy from another in an effort to define what is common among the schools of therapy and what is useful in each of them (Beitman et al., 1989). During the 1940s and 1950s, psychotherapy was virtually synonymous with

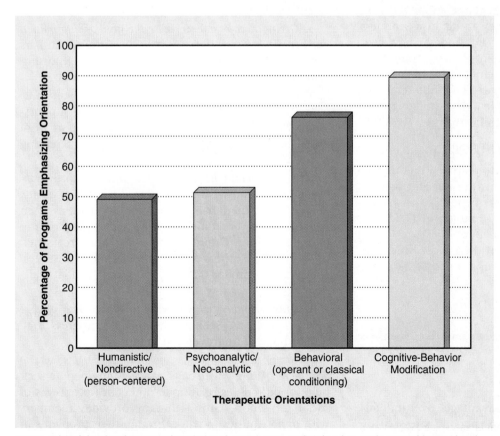

Figure 14.1 Therapeutic orientations receiving at least moderate emphasis in U.S. doctoral programs in clinical psychology.
Based on the results of a survey of 96 directors of clinical psychology doctoral training programs, this graph shows the percentages of training programs that were judged by their directors to place at least moderate emphasis on various therapeutic orientations. More than 9 out of 10 programs stressed training in cognitive-behavior modification (also called cognitive-behavior therapy). This suggests that cognitive-behavioral techniques will probably continue to grow in influence. Each of the approaches was emphasized by at least half of the programs, indicating that each of these major therapeutic models continues to be widely represented.

Source: Original data based on survey by Coletti et al. (1983). Data analysis based on results reported by Nevid et al. (1986, 1987).

psychodynamic therapy. Few other psychotherapy approaches had much impact on psychotherapists or on public awareness (Garfield, 1981, 1982). In more recent surveys, however, the largest single group of psychologists and psychotherapists have identified themselves as eclectic in orientation (DeMaria, 1988; Norcross & Prochaska, 1982a, 1982b; Smith, 1982). The percentages of respondents in these surveys who identified themselves as psychodynamic or psychoanalytic ranged from 12 to 30%. The percentages describing themselves as eclectic ranged from 31 to 58%. Researchers find that therapists who adopt an eclectic approach tend to be older and more experienced (Beitman et al., 1989). Perhaps they have learned through experience of the value of drawing on diverse contributions to the practice of therapy.

An Integrative Approach: Toward a Seamless Psychotherapy?

Eclecticism has different meanings for different therapists. Some therapists are *technical eclectics*. They draw on techniques from different schools of therapy without necessarily adopting the theoretical positions that spawned the techniques (Lazarus et al., 1992). Other therapists are *integrative eclectics*. They attempt to synthesize and integrate diverse theoretical approaches—to sew together different therapeutic elements from diverse approaches so that they result in a seamless psychotherapy (Wachtel, 1991). Today, however, integrative psychotherapy remains largely more of an aspiration than a reality (Wachtel, 1991). Research has yet to be undertaken to assess how different psychotherapies may be integrated to best advantage toward increasing therapeutic effectiveness (Wolfe & Goldfried, 1988).

Research is also needed to identify the basic principles of change shared by various therapeutic orientations and to investigate the specific factors, processes, and therapeutic ingredients that each particular approach has to offer (Beitman et al., 1989; Lazarus et al., 1992; Prochaska et al., 1991).

We now consider forms of therapy in which the focus of therapy extends to groups of people, families, and married couples.

GROUP THERAPY

Group therapy has several advantages over individual treatment. For one, group therapy is less costly because several clients are treated at the same time.

Many clinicians also believe that group therapy may be more effective in treating groups of clients who have similar problems, such as complaints relating to anxiety, depression, lack of social skills, or adjustment to divorce or other life stresses. The group format provides clients with the opportunity to learn how people with similar problems cope with them and provides the social support of the group as well as the therapist. The particular approach to treatment reflects the theoretical orientation of the therapist or group leader. In psychoanalytic groups, for example, an emphasis may be placed on interpretations and working through transferences that emerge between group members or between group members and the therapist. Person-centered groups seek to create an accepting atmosphere for clients to explore their deeper feelings without fears of social criticism. In behavior therapy groups, people with similar problems may undergo a group administration of techniques such as systematic desensitization and social skills training.

All in all, group therapy has certain advantages over individual treatment, including the following:

1. *Group therapy is less costly.*

2. *Group therapy allows greater access to limited therapist resources.* Therapists may not have the time to see all the people who request assistance in a one-to-one treatment format.

3. *Group therapy may increase the fund of information and experience that clients can draw on.* Group members can share their life experiences, providing information on ways of solving one another's problems.

4. *Group therapy provides group support for appropriate behavior.* Clients may expect therapists to be supportive toward them, but an outpouring of support from one's peers may have greater impact on increasing self-esteem and self-confidence.

5. *Group therapy helps clients recognize that their problems are not unique (and therefore they are not alone).* People who experience psychological difficulties often feel that they are different than other people, and perhaps inferior. Group members are often reassured to learn that others have made similar mistakes, experienced similar failures, and had similar self-doubts.

6. *Group members who improve provide a source of hope for other members.* Seeing other people progress may bolster hope of improvement in others.

7. *Group therapy provides opportunities for learning to deal more effectively with other people.* Many people seek help for difficulties relating to others or for reasons of social inhibition. Group therapy provides members with opportunities to work through their problems in relating to others. For example, the therapist or other

Group therapy. What are some of the advantages of group therapy over individual therapy? What are some of its disadvantages?

members may point out to a particular member when he or she acts in a bossy manner or tends to withdraw when criticized—patterns of behavior that may mirror the behavior they show in their relationships with others outside the group. Group members may also rehearse social skills with one another in a supportive atmosphere. Members may role-play important people in each other's lives to hone interpersonal skills.

Not only is group therapy usually less expensive than individual therapy, it is also sometimes preferable because of the availability of group reinforcement and the fund of knowledge that can be tapped in the group setting. A central issue for therapists is to identify clients who are more likely to profit from one type of therapy or another.

Despite these advantages, clients may prefer individual therapy for various reasons. For one, clients might not wish to disclose their problems to others in a group. Some clients prefer the individual attention of the therapist. Others are too socially inhibited to feel comfortable in a group setting—even though they might be the ones who could most profit from a group experience. Because of such concerns, group therapists require that group disclosures be kept confidential, that group members relate to each other supportively and nondestructively, and that group members receive the attention that they need.

There are several specialized forms of group therapy. In **psychodrama**, a technique developed by Jacob Moreno in the 1920s, group members role-play or reenact emotionally laden scenes from each other's lives in the form of stage plays. For example, a man might reenact a conflict with his father by having other group members play the roles of the father and other important people who played some part in the conflict. To Moreno, psychodrama was a vehicle for expression of painful or hostile feelings in a supportive setting that helped members achieve insight into their own behavior and gain a more realistic understanding of the behavior of others. By coming to terms with these conflicts, members could be freed of the social inhibitions that limited their spontaneity and ability to form meaningful relationships with others.

Encounter groups are specialized forms of group therapy that emerged from the humanistic movement in the 1960s. Encounter groups aim to foster increased self-awareness by focusing on how members relate to each other in a setting in which open expression of feelings is encouraged. Encounter groups are not appropriate for people with serious psychological problems. Rather, they are intended for people who are fairly well adjusted but seek personal growth and heightened awareness of their own needs and feelings and the ways they relate to others. Encounter groups seek to meet these needs through a process of intense encounters or direct confrontations between strangers. Some groups are held as marathon encounters that may run continuously for 12 or more hours at a time. Reflecting the humanistic approach, encounter groups stress the interactions taking place in the here and now. They focus on expression of genuine feelings, not on interpretation or on discussions of the past. When a group member is perceived by the others as hiding behind a social mask or facade, the others might descend on the person en masse and try to rip the mask off to encourage the person to express his or her true feelings.

Such confrontational tactics can be damaging if they force overly rapid disclosure of intimate feelings that the person is not yet able to handle, or if the person feels attacked or scapegoated by the others in the group. Responsible leaders try to maintain control of the group to prevent such abuses and to keep it moving in a direction that facilitates personal growth and self-awareness.

Evidence from controlled studies examining the effectiveness of group therapy is mixed. One review of the group therapy literature showed results that favored group therapy over placebo or no-treatment conditions, for example, but the studies comprising the analysis tended to be plagued by poor methodologies (Kaul & Bednar, 1986). Moreover, there is a lack of evidence that directly compares each form of group therapy with a comparable form of individual therapy.

Family and Marital Therapy

In **family therapy**, it is the family, not the individual, that is the unit of treatment. Family therapy aims to help troubled families resolve their conflicts and problems so that the family functions better as a unit and individual family members are subjected to less stress from family conflicts.

Faulty patterns of communications within the family often contribute to family problems. In family therapy, family members are helped to communicate more effectively and to air their disagreements constructively. Family conflicts often emerge at transitional points in the life cycle when family patterns are altered by changes in one or more members. Conflicts between parents and children, for example, often emerge when adolescent children seek greater independence or autonomy. Family members with low self-esteem may be unable to tolerate different attitudes or behaviors from other members of the family, and may resist their efforts to change or grow more independent. Family therapists work with families to resolve these conflicts and help them adjust to life changes among family members.

Family therapists are sensitive to families' tendencies to scapegoat one family member as the source of the problem, or the "identified client." Disturbed families seem to adopt a sort of myth: Change the identified client, the "bad apple," and the "barrel," or family, will once again become functional. Family therapists encourage familes to work together to resolve their disputes and conflicts, instead.

One widely adopted approach to family therapy, called *conjoint family therapy,* was developed by Virginia Satir (1967). Satir conceptualized the family in terms of a pattern or *system* of communications and interactions that need to be studied and changed to enhance the family unit as well as the growth of individual family members.

Family therapy. In family therapy, the family, not the individual, is the unit of treatment. Family therapists help family members communicate more effectively with one another, for example, to air their disagreements in ways that are not hurtful to individual members. Family therapists also try to prevent one member of the family from becoming the scapegoat for the family's problems.

Another prominent approach to family therapy is **structural family therapy** (Minuchin, 1974). This approach also adopts a family systems model of abnormal behavior. It conceptualizes problem behaviors of individual members of the family as characteristics of the family system, that is, rather than as individual problems. Individual members may develop psychological or physical problems in response to stressful problems in family role relationships. Family systems usually resist the efforts of individual members to change them. Structural family therapists analyze the family roles played by individual members and help families restructure themselves so that members can relate to each other in more supportive ways. For example, a child may feel in competition with other siblings for a parent's attention and develop enuresis, or bed wetting, as a means of securing attention. The structural family therapist would help the family understand the hidden messages in the child's behavior and assist the family to make changes in their relationships to meet the child's needs more adequately. In so doing, the therapist shows the family how the member with the identified problem (enuresis) is responding to wider problems in the family.

Marital therapy may be considered a subtype of family therapy, in which the family unit is the marital couple. Like other forms of family therapy, marital therapy focuses on improving communication and analyzing role relationships in order to improve the marital relationship. For example, one partner may play a dominant role and resist any request to share power with the other. The marital therapist would help bring these role relationships into the open, so

MULTICULTURAL PERSPECTIVES

Ethnic Matching of Clients and Therapists

The great majority of psychotherapists in the United States are non-Hispanic white Americans whose primary language is English. Are such therapists as effective in treating minority clients as therapists from the clients' own ethnic group?

Must the ethnic backgrounds of therapists and clients match? According to the cultural responsiveness hypothesis, therapy is more effective when the therapist and the client share the same ethnic background. Evidence is mixed on the issue, although it is clear that clients who are not fluent in English profit from meeting with therapists who can converse with them in their own languages.

The so-called *cultural responsivenessness hypothesis* suggests that clients will respond better to therapy when the therapist is similar to them in ethnic and language background (Sue et al., 1991). The evidence is mixed on whether or not ethnic matching increases therapeutic benefits (Sue, 1988). A recent large-scale study of the mental health system in Los Angeles County found at least partial support for the cultural responsiveness hypothesis (Sue et al., 1991). On the one hand, therapist-client matching was associated with lower rates of premature termination (dropping out after only one session) and greater length of treatment for all groups (African, Mexican, non-Hispanic white, and Asian Americans). Ethnic matching, however, was unrelated to treatment outcome, except for Mexican Americans. It thus appears from this study that ethnic matching had a greater effect in general on retaining clients in therapy than it did on eventual outcome. For Mexican Americans and Asian Americans who did not speak English as their primary language, however, ethnic and language matching was associated with both retention in therapy and outcome. Language matching as well as ethnic matching may be of greater value to clients who are not native English speakers.

Whatever the benefits of matching therapists to clients on the basis of ethnicity might be, it is important to recognize that ethnicity alone is not a sole determinant of therapeutic effectiveness. Therapist sensitivity and ability to establish rapport are likely to be critical factors in determining therapeutic effectiveness, whether one is treating clients of the same or different ethnicity (Sue, 1988).

that alternative ways of relating to one another could be explored that would lead to a more satisfying relationship.

EVALUATING THE EFFECTIVENESS OF PSYCHOTHERAPY

There are thus many kinds of psychotherapy. Therapies have been spawned by different theoretical perspectives to meet the needs of individuals and groups. But does psychotherapy work? Is it effective? Are some forms of therapy more effective than others? Are some forms of therapy more effective for some types of clients or for some types of problems than for others?

In order to address these questions, researchers must carefully specify the conditions of treatment, such as characteristics of the clients, the therapists, and the type of therapy itself, and measure the results broadly enough to evaluate multiple dimensions of change. Let us first consider issues concerning the design of psychotherapy research studies. Then we review evidence concerning the effectiveness of psychotherapy.

Specifying the Conditions of Treatment

In a well-designed study, the investigator clearly specifies the type of therapy investigated, as well as the characteristics of the therapists and clients who participated. By specifying these characteristics, some of which are listed in Table 14.1, researchers can better determine the factors that might influence the results of psychotherapy. A particular form of therapy, for example, may be more effective when practiced by a therapist of the same gender as the client than when practiced by a therapist of the opposite gender. Or certain types of therapy may be more effective for certain types of clinical problems than for others.

Measuring Therapy Outcomes

Psychotherapy researchers measure the effects of therapy from several vantage points to help ensure that their measures encompass various dimensions of change. Perhaps the most straightforward method of assessing the effectiveness of psychotherapy is to

Table 14.1 Factors Connected with the Effectiveness of Psychotherapy

Client Factors	Age, gender, educational level, ethnicity, marital status, prior treatment history, type of problem or diagnostic category, length or duration of problem, severity of problem, age of onset of problem
Therapist Factors	Training and level of experience, therapeutic orientation, age, gender, ethnicity
Treatment Factors	Type of treatment or therapeutic approach (for example, behavioral, cognitive, psychoanalytic, etc.), format of treatment (individual, group, couple), setting of treatment (inpatient, outpatient, day hospital, etc.), length of treatment, frequency of treatment sessions, length of treatment sessions

measure the status of clients' presenting complaints before therapy (at *pretreatment*) and then again immediately following therapy (at *posttreatment*). For example, clients might rate the frequency or severity of various complaints such as anxiety and depression on a complaint or symptom inventory. The difference between pretreatment and posttreatment scores on the complaint inventory would be used as a measure of treatment outcome. There might also be a follow-up assessment taken at perhaps a 6-month or 1-year interval to evaluate whether treatment gains were lasting.

Most researchers consider self-reports to be an important dimension of change because only clients can directly appraise their own subjective complaints. Clients may also be the only ones who can measure the frequency of occurrence of certain behaviors, such as level of consumption of alcohol or cigarette smoking, or of certain abnormal behavior patterns, such as the occurrence of panic attacks or hallucinations. Self-reports are prone to response biases or distortions, however (see Chapter 3). In a therapy program for smoking cessation, for example, subjects may report that they have quit smoking when they have not done so, in order to please the experimenter or to avoid losing face. To control for such response biases, the experimenter might seek to verify self-reports of abstinence by biochemical means, such as testing a sample of their breath for carbon monoxide or analyzing a sample of their saliva for telltale signs of nicotine in the body.

Researchers also need to attend to important domains of change. A phobia, for example, may be measured by means of the client's self-reported anxiety when exposed to the phobic situation, and also according to the client's overt behavior (ability to approach the phobic stimulus) and physiological responses (heightened autonomic nervous system activity). Subjects frequently show greater change in one response domain than in another (Lang, 1968; Rachman & Hodgson, 1974). For example, an elevator phobic might succeed in the behavioral goal of taking an elevator ride to the top floor but still report feeling jumpy and register a physiological response (heightened heart rate) during the ride. The relative independence of these response domains emphasizes the value of measuring effects in several response domains, especially in the case of fear or anxiety.

Different therapies are connected with different outcome goals. Some forms of therapy, like behavior therapy, focus on goals that can be defined and measured in behavioral terms—as again in the case of the former elevator phobic who can now ride unassisted. But cognitive therapists seek to alter the ways in which individuals interpret the world and to help them replace distorted beliefs with rational alternatives. Evaluations of cognitive therapy outcomes often include paper-and-pencil measures of irrational beliefs and attitudes, along with measures of behavioral change and self-reports of relief from symptom complaints. Although private events like thoughts and beliefs are not directly observed or measured, they can be inferred on the basis of clients' verbal or self-reports. Investigations of person-centered therapy often include paper-and-pencil measures of changes in self-concept or self-acceptance as a marker of therapeutic change. But strict behaviorists might challenge the validity of measures that are not based on direct observation. Psychoanalysts, too, might object to measures based on the individual's self-reports, arguing that conscious experience does not reflect unconscious motives and conflicts. And what of the forms of therapy, like psychoanalysis or person-centered therapy, that seek to foster such goals as insight, personality change, and self-actualization? Is it fair to measure their outcomes by the same yardsticks that might apply to behavior therapies or cognitive therapies? Because each person's self-insights, or growth potentials, are unique, moreover, it may be impossible to measure how much insight or growth an individual has experienced compared to others. Might it be most useful to base judgments of such outcomes on the therapist's clinical judgment? Unfortunately, because they have a vested interest in believing that their clients benefit from therapy, therapists may not be unbiased judges. So the researcher needs to consider, when choosing measures, the goals that the particular form of therapy attempts to achieve and the possible sources of response bias that might distort the results.

Table 14.2 contains examples of outcome measures in psychotherapy research that represent various response domains.

Table 14.2   Types of Outcome Measures in Psychotherapy Research

Response Domain	Types of Measures
Self-Report	Symptom complaints Disturbing emotions Frequencies of specific behaviors (for example, smoking rate, use of alcohol or drugs) Holding irrational or dysfunctional beliefs Frequency of specific disruptive thoughts
Reports from Others	Spousal reports of smoking abstinence or employment Parent reports of childhood behavior problems Therapist reports or ratings of symptoms or problem behaviors Supervisor reports of work performance
Behavioral	Direct observation or monitoring of specific problem behaviors (for example, hyperactivity, conduct problems) Behavioral tasks or homework assignments, such as approaching a phobic object or situation
Physiological	Heart rate Brain wave patterns (EEG) Skin conductivity (GSR) Analysis of blood, saliva, or urine specimens
Personality or Personal Growth	Personality tests (for example, the MMPI or Rorschach) Measures relating to values or purposes in life Measures relating to self-esteem, self-acceptance, and self-actualization

Analyses of Psychotherapy Effectiveness

In 1952, the psychologist Hans Eysenck published a review of psychotherapy research that sent shock waves through the psychotherapy community (Eysenck, 1952). Eysenck concluded on the basis of the evidence he compiled that the rate of improvement in psychotherapy among neurotic clients was no greater than the rate of **spontaneous remission**. Whether or not neurotic clients received therapy, that is, two-thirds reported substantial improvement within a period of 2 years.

■ **META-ANALYTIC STUDIES** Reviews of more recent research paint a more positive picture of the effectiveness of psychotherapy, however. Such reviews are often based on the method of **meta-analysis**, which is a statistical technique for averaging the results of large numbers of studies in order to determine levels of overall effectiveness (Landman & Dawes, 1982).

In the most frequently cited meta-analysis of psychotherapy research, Smith and Glass (1977) analyzed the results of some 375 controlled studies comparing various types of therapies (psychodynamic, behavioral, humanistic, etc.) against control groups. The results of their analyses showed that the average psychotherapy client in these studies was better off than 75% of the clients who remained untreated. In 1980, Smith and Glass and their colleague Miller reported the results of a larger analysis based on 475 controlled outcome studies, which showed that the average person who received therapy was better off at the end of treatment than 80% of those who did not (Glass & Kliegl, 1983; Smith et al., 1980). The fact that the average client benefited from psychotherapy does not mean that every client benefited. Negative outcomes do occur. Some clients deteriorate. Others experience little if any improvement. People who receive other types of intervention, such as drug therapy or electroconvulsive therapy (ECT), may also fail to respond positively or experience adverse effects.

More recent meta-analyses also show positive outcomes for psychotherapy. For example, a meta-analysis based on 60 studies appearing in the scientific literature from 1977 to 1986 showed that behavior therapy produced stronger effects than placebo or nonspecific treatments (Bowers & Clum, 1988). Brody (1990) challenged Bowers and Clum's meta-analysis on methodological grounds, however, claiming, for example, that they failed to include the most relevant outcome measures. Another meta-analysis by Crits-Christoph (1992) included well-controlled studies of the efficacy of various forms of specific brief forms of psychodynamic psychotherapy. This study found substantial benefits in relation to waiting-list control conditions and effects about equal in magnitude among psychodynamic, behavior, cognitive, and drug therapies (Crits-Christoph, 1992). Translated into percentages, the average person receiving brief psychodynamic therapy showed greater improvement than 85% of those clients placed on waiting lists, with improvement measured in terms of relief from complaints such as anxiety and depression. Much smaller differences were obtained when the analysts compared the brief psychodynamic therapies to alternate therapies, such as self-help conditions.

Although meta-analyses have presented evidence for the effectiveness of psychotherapy, the use of this statistical technique has met with some criticisms:

1. *Inclusion of poorly designed studies.* Computer specialists have a saying, "Garbage in, garbage out." Despite the use of highly sophisticated statistical techniques, the end result of a set of calculations is only as good as the input on which the calculations are based. The results of meta-analyses may thus be flawed if the studies that were included in the analyses were faulty in design, as is true of many of the studies by Smith, Glass, Bowers, Clum, and others. On the other hand, meta-analysis of studies of high methodological quality actually reveals psychotherapy to be more effective than meta-analysis that is based on more poorly designed studies (Landman & Dawes, 1982).

2. *The "apples and oranges" problem.* The question of whether or not psychotherapy *in general* is effective tends to overlook the roles that client, therapist, and treatment factors may play in determining treatment effectiveness. Computing an overall averaged result for different forms of therapy that are tackling different types of problems is akin to mixing apples and oranges in a blender and then tasting the mixture to evaluate the taste of one fruit or the other. The resultant mix reveals little about the value of particular forms of therapy for particular problems or clients. The "apples and oranges" problem can be overcome by breaking down the meta-analysis into smaller components that examine the effects of various combinations of treatments, clients, and therapists.

3. *Publication bias.* Meta-analyses generally include studies that are available for analysis because they appear in scientific journals. Such journals are more likely to publish studies that produce significant findings than studies that do not, however (Greenwald, 1975). As a result, meta-analyses may be biased toward findings that support the effectiveness of psychotherapy. On the other hand, it is unlikely that

publication bias fully accounts for the apparent effectiveness of psychotherapy (Brown, 1987).

4. *Nonrepresentativeness of studies.* Many of the studies included in the Smith and Glass meta-analysis (and similar meta-analyses, such as that conducted by Shapiro and Shapiro in 1982) are not based on actual clients receiving therapy in clinics or private practice. Many of these studies take place in university settings and recruit college volunteers who are suffering from relatively minor problems (like snake phobia or nonassertiveness). It is not clear that the results of such studies generalize to clinical practice. On the other hand, the effectiveness of psychotherapy is also supported by meta-analyses which include only studies that use actual clients rather than student volunteers (Andrews & Harvey, 1981).

Despite the problems in conducting psychotherapy research, evidence of the effectiveness of psychotherapy has been encouraging. It also appears that the greatest gains in psychotherapy are achieved in the first several months of treatment (Howard et al., 1986), and that these gains tend to be lasting (Nicholson & Berman, 1983).

Comparing the Effectiveness of Different Forms of Psychotherapy

There are but a few well-designed treatment studies that directly compare different forms of therapy with each other. One difficulty in mounting such studies is to secure permission from subjects, and clinic administrators, that assignments to the alternate types of treatment are to be randomized (so as to balance groups on subject characteristics). Another problem is ensuring that the therapists representing the competing therapies are equally well trained and experienced and willing to accept clients at random. Bias is introduced when clinicians select clients they feel most capable of working with effectively. Also, the measures of results must be compatible with the goals of each kind of treatment, and the durations of treatment must be comparable.

One of the few examples of a comparative treatment study was reported by Sloane and his colleagues (Sloane et al., 1975). Subjects in this study were college students who sought treatment at the Temple University Outpatient Clinic. The subjects were randomly assigned to either psychoanalytic therapy, behavior therapy, or a waiting-list control condition. Both treatment groups received 4 months of therapy. The psychoanalytic treatment consisted of

a short-term insight-oriented approach, whereas the behavior therapy approach included such techniques as assertiveness training and systematic desensitization. All of the participating therapists were experienced clinicians. The measures of outcome included ratings of client improvement by clinicians who were not part of the treatment program, client self-ratings, and structured interviews to determine work and social adjustment. The results immediately following treatment showed that both behavior therapy and psychoanalytic therapy produced significantly greater improvement than the waiting-list control condition, but the treatments did not significantly differ from each other. The independent clinicians rated 80% of the behavior therapy and psychoanalytic therapy clients to be improved, as compared to 48% of the waiting-list controls. These gains were maintained at a follow-up evaluation 8 months later, at which time there were still no significant differences between the treatment approaches.

Researchers also use meta-analysis to determine whether different therapies produce different degrees of benefit. Meta-analysis can be used to reveal the average benefit or size of effect associated with therapy in general, or, when broken down further, with particular types of therapy as measured against control groups. Smith and colleagues (1980) reported that effect sizes for several of the major schools of therapy, including psychodynamic, humanistic (Gestalt and person-centered), and behavior modification, were quite similar. Generally speaking, the average client treated by these methods was better off than 70 to 80% of untreated controls. Does this mean that these therapeutic approaches were about equally effective? Perhaps, but not necessarily. There may be differences among these therapies such as the types of clinical problems they treat, their therapeutic goals, and the types of outcome measures that are used to evaluate each. For example, if a particular therapy was used to treat more difficult cases, we would be more impressed by a given effect size than we might if more responsive subjects were treated.

It is thus insufficient to ask which therapy works best. We must ask, Which therapy works best for which type of problem? Which clients are best suited for which type of therapy? What are the advantages and limitations of particular therapies? Behavior therapy, for example, has shown impressive results in treating phobias, obsessive-compulsive disorders, and sexual dysfunctions, and in improving the adaptive functioning of schizophrenics and other institutionalized populations. Psychodynamic and humanistic-existential approaches may be more effective in fostering self-insight and personality growth. Cognitive therapy has demonstrated impressive results in treating depression and anxiety disor-

Is the Effectiveness of Psychotherapy Attributable to Nonspecific Factors?

Do various psychotherapies work because of their specific treatment techniques or because of the features—called **nonspecific treatment factors**—that they share? Meta-analytic studies reveal only negligible differences in outcomes among the various therapies when such therapies are compared to control groups (Crits-Christoph, 1992; Smith et al., 1980). Such minor differences suggest that the effectiveness of psychotherapy may have more to do with the features they share than with the techniques that set them apart (Stiles et al., 1986). It is also possible that research studies have not been sufficiently sensitive to differences in effectiveness among therapies in the treatment of specific clinical problems (Kazdin et al., 1986; Stiles et al., 1986).

The nonspecific factors in psychotherapy stem largely from the therapist-client relationship. Such factors include the engendering of positive expectancies to combat feelings of helplessness and hopelessness (Klein & Rabkin, 1984; Rounsaville et al., 1987), the strength of the therapeutic relationship (Marziali & Alexander, 1991), the empathy shown by the therapist (Burns & Nolen-Hoeksema, 1992; Luborsky et al., 1988), along with the general support, warmth, and attention that clients receive from their therapists. If it is true that the effects of therapy stem more from the therapist-client relationship than from specific therapeutic techniques, perhaps psychotherapists should be encouraged to focus more on developing these nonspecific factors than specific interventions.

On the other hand, research findings are accumulating that reveal that the effectiveness of psychotherapy is due to more than just nonspecific factors. Meta-analysis has been used to provide evidence that specific forms of therapy, such as behavior therapy and psychodynamic therapy, produce larger treatment effects than those produced by nonspecific treatment approaches that provide support and instill hope (Barker et al., 1988; Landman & Dawes, 1982; Shapiro & Shapiro, 1982). Psychotherapy (mostly behavioral in emphasis) has also been found to be about twice as effective as well-designed nonspecific therapies that instill equal expectancies of improvement (Barker et al., 1988). Findings from a study of brief (12-session) psychodynamic therapy for clients suffering a stress-related reaction showed that positive outcomes reflected specific therapeutic techniques and not simply nonspecific factors (Jones et al., 1988). All in all, psychotherapies appear to be complex processes that incorporate common features such as support, attention, and concern, along with specific techniques that foster adaptive change.

---

ders. Researchers remain challenged to determine what treatment, practiced by whom, and under what conditions, is most effective for each kind of client. We also need more evidence of the effectiveness of various forms of psychotherapy with ethnic minorities. For example, although much evidence has been gathered to demonstrate the effectiveness of behavioral approaches in treating anxiety disorders among non-Hispanic white Americans, we know little about the effectiveness of behavior therapy in treating anxiety disorders among African Americans (Turner, 1992).

 Although there are many problems in evaluating the effectiveness of psychotherapies, the weight of the evidence suggests that psychotherapy is indeed helpful and that its effectiveness is due to a combination of both nonspecific and specific factors.

MULTICULTURAL ISSUES IN PSYCHOTHERAPY

In our evaluation of the effectiveness of psychotherapy, we noted that we must not only consider whether clients who receive therapy, generally speaking, are better off than those who do not. We must also consider what kind of therapy is most effective for what kind of client and for what kind of problem. Part of that appraisal involves considering how cultural and ethnic factors relate to therapeutic process.

In this section, we consider some of the issues involved in treating African Americans, Asian Americans, Hispanic Americans, and Native Americans. It is clear that clinicians must avoid stereotypes and be sensitive to the values, languages, and cultural beliefs of members of minority groups they treat in psychotherapy (Comas-Diaz & Griffith, 1988; Lee & Richardson, 1991).

African Americans

The cultural history of African Americans must be understood in the context of a history of extreme racial discrimination (Boyd-Franklin, 1989; Butts, 1980; Greene, 1990). African Americans have needed to develop coping mechanisms for managing the racism they encounter in such areas as employment, housing, education, and access to health care (Greene, 1993a, 1993b). For example, the sensitivity of many African Americans to the potential for maltreatment and exploitation has been a survival tool that may take the form of a heightened level of suspiciousness or reserve (Greene, 1986). Therapists need to be aware of the tendency of African-American clients to minimize their vulnerability by being less self-disclosing, especially in earlier stages of therapy (Ridley, 1984). Therapists should not confuse such suspiciousness with paranoia, however (Boyd-Franklin, 1989; Greene, 1986; Grier & Cobbs, 1968).

In addition to whatever psychological problems an African-American client may present, the therapist often needs to assist the client to develop coping mechanisms to deal with societal racial barriers. Therapists also need to be attuned to tendencies of some African Americans to internalize within their self-concepts the negative stereotypes about blacks that are perpetuated in the dominant culture (Greene, 1985a; 1992b; 1992c; Pinderhughes, 1989).

Therapists must also be culturally literate and aware of their own feelings and attitudes about African Americans (Greene, 1985a; 1992b; 1992c; Pinderhughes, 1989). Therapists are exposed to the same negative stereotypes about African Americans as other people in society and must recognize how the incorporation of these stereotypes, if left unexamined, can become destructive to the therapeutic relationships they form with African-American clients. In effect, therapists must be willing to confront their own racism and prejudices and work to replace these attitudes with more realistic appraisals of African Americans (Mays, 1985).

Therapists must also be aware of the cultural characteristics associated with African-American families, such as strong kinship bonds between family members, often including people who are not biologically related (for example, a close friend of a parent may have some parenting role and may be addressed as an "Aunt"), strong religious and spiritual orientation, multigenerational households, adaptibility and flexibility of gender roles (African-American women have a long history of working outside the home), and distribution of child-care responsibilities among different family members (Boyd-Franklin, 1989; Collins, 1987; Ferguson-Peters, 1985; Greene, 1990; McAdoo, 1983). For example, grandmothers often assume significant parenting responsibilities and may be referred to by the children as "mother." A therapist who is unfamiliar with this cultural tradition may find it confusing that the child experiences the grandmother as the psychological parent.

Among African Americans, there is often the assumption that one is supposed to be able at all

How can non-Hispanic white therapists be sensitive to the experiences and needs of African-American clients? In order to help African-American clients, therapists from other ethnic groups need to be familiar with various aspects of African-American culture and in touch with their own tendencies to stereotype African Americans.

times to manage one's problems and be strong in the face of stress. Any sign of emotional weakness carries such a strong negative stigma that people who encounter anxieties, feelings of depression, or even normal reactions to stress may perceive themselves as having a "nervous breakdown" (Boyd-Franklin, 1989; Childs, 1990; Greene, 1993b). Yet the cultural expectation that they should just "get over it" on their own often delays their seeking help until the problem becomes serious.

Asian Americans

Sue (1991) explains various ways in which cultural influences affect the utilization and effectiveness of mental health services for Asian Americans. Mental health problems carry a severe social stigma among Asian Americans, which may avert them from recognizing problems and seeking help to deal with them. Asian Americans, especially recent immigrants, may also have little understanding of, or faith in, Western models of psychotherapy. The emphasis in Western psychotherapy on the open expression of feelings may conflict with traditional Asian tendencies to refrain from public displays of emotion. Asians may also prefer structured, unambiguous approaches to solving problems, which may conflict with the open-ended, unstructured, and often ambiguous style of Western insight-oriented psychotherapies. Asians, that is, may regard the therapist as an authority figure who should give them direct advice to help them solve their problems, whereas the traditional Western therapist may prefer to help clients clarify their feelings and reach their own decisions, rather than tell them what to do. Moreover, Asian Americans may have a different conception of mental health. They may believe that mental health arises from turning one's thoughts away from painful experiences or "morbid" thoughts, whereas traditional Western psychotherapy focuses on getting in touch with painful thoughts and feelings. For these and other reasons, many Asian Americans may find Western psychotherapy to be incompatible with their values and beliefs.

Clinicians also note that Asians often express psychological complaints in terms of physical symptoms. The tendency to somaticize emotional problems may be attributed to differences in communication styles (Zane & Sue, 1991). That is, Asians may use somatic terms to convey emotional distress.

Culturally sensitive therapists not only understand the beliefs and values of other cultures, but also integrate this knowledge within the therapy process.

Such therapists need to assess the client's willingness and ability to express personal feelings, and to tailor therapy to match the client's cultural expectations. Consider the therapeutic relationship between therapists and Japanese clients. Traditional Japanese culture values restraint in talking about oneself and one's feelings. Therapists thus need to be patient and not expect instant self-disclosures from Japanese-American clients (Henkin, 1985).

In some cases, there may also be inherent role conflicts between the goals of therapy and the values of a particular culture. For example, therapeutic approaches that emphasize the importance of individuality and self-determination may be inappropriate in treating Japanese or others who strongly adhere to cultural values which emphasize the importance of the group over the individual (Henkin, 1985).

Hispanic Americans

Although Hispanic-American subcultures differ in various respects, many of them share certain cultural values and beliefs, such as adherence to a strong patriarchal (male-dominated) family structure and strong kinship ties. De La Cancela and Guzman (1991) identify some other values shared by many Hispanic Americans:

> One's identity is in part determined by one's role in the family. The male, or *macho*, is the head of the family, the provider, the protector of the family honor, and the final decision maker. The woman's role (*marianismo*) is to care for the family and the children. Obviously, these roles are changing, with women entering the work force and achieving greater educational opportunities. Cultural values of *respeto* (respect), *confianza* (trust), *dignidad* (dignity), and *personalismo* (personalism) are highly esteemed and are important factors in working with many [Hispanic Americans]. (p. 60)

Therapists need to be sensitive to these cultural factors, if they are to be successful in developing effective interventions with Hispanic-American clients. They need to recognize, for example, value conflicts that may occur between the traditional Hispanic-American value of interdependency on the family with the value of independence and self-reliance which is stressed in white non-Hispanic American culture (De la Cancela & Guzman, 1991). Psychotherapeutic interventions should respect differences in values rather than attempt to impose values of majority cultures on people from ethnic minority groups. Therapists should also be trained to reach beyond the confines of their offices to work within the Hispanic-American community itself, in settings which impact on the daily lives of Hispanic Americans, such as social clubs, *bodegas* (neighborhood groceries), beauty and barber shops, as well as with building superintendents ("el super"), many of whom in our large urban areas are Hispanic American.

Although many therapists recognize the importance of cultural factors in psychotherapy, some therapists have gone further by developing culturally sensitive approaches to therapy. For example, Malgady and his colleagues (Malgady et al., 1990b) describe several forms of culturally specific psychotherapy in providing mental health services to Hispanic Americans. Malgady and his colleagues cite the cultural distance between the typically lower socioeconomic class Hispanic-American client and the typically middle-class, white non-Hispanic-American therapist as the root of the difficulty in treating Hispanic-American clients. Malgady and his colleagues outline some therapeutic approaches that they believe might close the gap between mental health service providers and Hispanic-American clients:

1. Recruiting bicultural/bilingual staff and creating a therapeutic atmosphere that is accepting of Hispanic-American cultural values.

2. Using treatment methods that are in keeping with Hispanic-American clients' cultural values. One might, for example, adopt Ruiz's (1981) recommendation to tailor the type of treatment to the client's level of acculturation.

3. Incorporating clients' cultural values in therapy. An example of integrating cultural values directly into psychotherapy is found in the use of *cuento therapy* with Puerto Rican children by Malgady and his colleagues (see Chapter 13). *Cuento therapy* is a storytelling technique that adapts Hispanic folktales, or cuentos, to model therapeutic themes or morals. The child characters in the folktales embody socially desirable beliefs, values, and behaviors.

Nevid and Javier (1992) adapted a form of *cuento therapy* within a smoking cessation program for Hispanic-American smokers. As part of a multicomponent behavioral program, they developed a series of videotape vignettes featuring Hispanic-American characters in culturally laden scenes depicting smoking cessation themes. One vignette, for example, focused on debunking the belief that smoking represents macho behavior; another underscored the importance of familial values in Hispanic-American culture by having characters commit themselves to a smoking-cessation program for the "love of their children and themselves." The portrayals of the characters in the vignettes modeled adaptive smoking-cessation behaviors and served as focal points for group discussions among participants and group leaders.

Native Americans

Kahn (1982) argues that if mental health professionals are to be successful in helping Native Americans, they must do so within a context that is relevant and sensitive to Native Americans' customs, culture, and values. Prevention efforts should focus on strengthening cultural cohesion, identity and pride, and helping Native American peoples regain a sense of mastery over the world in which they live. In some cases, language and cultural differences create so great a gap between Native American peoples and the dominant culture that only trained Native American mental health counselors may be effective as service providers. Among the Papago Indians in Arizona (Kahn et al., 1981), utilization of mental health services was virtually nil until culturally sensitive programs with indigenous counselors were developed (Kahn, 1982).

Therapists can use indigenous ceremonies that are part of the client's cultural or religious traditions. To do so, mental health professionals need to be knowledgeable about methods of therapy and about traditional Native and mainstream Western cultures, and attempt to integrate the two (Timpson et al., 1988). Lefley (1990) notes that purification and cleansing rites are therapeutic for many Native American peoples in the United States and elsewhere, like among the African-Cuban *santeria*, the Brazilian *umbanda*, and the Haitian *vodou*. Cleansing rites are often sought by people who believe that their problems are caused by failure to placate malevolent spirits or to perform mandatory rituals (Lefley, 1990).

■ **LIFTING THE CURSE FROM TECHNICAL ECLECTICISM?** Lefley (1984) recounts the case of a hospitalized psychotic Haitian man who remained acutely psychotic after 10 days of hospital treatment. According to his own belief system, the patient's problems were due to a curse that had to be lifted. In a cross-cultural example of technical eclecticism, a *vodou* priest (called a *boungan*) was invited to perform curative rituals. The patient calmed down at once, was stabilized on medications, and soon sent home.

 It is true that a psychotic Haitian man responded positively to a form of therapy that included the lifting of a curse by a *vodou* priest.

A CLOSER LOOK

Feminist Psychotherapy

Feminist psychotherapy has its theoretical origins in feminist political theory, philosophy, and ethics. Feminist ideology challenges the validity of gender-role stereotypes and expectations that have traditionally maintained patterns of male dominance and female subordination in our society (Lerman & Porter, 1990; Greene, 1993c).

Feminist therapy emerged as a response to male dominance of mental health professions and institutions. It challenges the apparent role played by the mental health establishment in maintaining social inequities between men and women, and between members of the dominant culture and those of ethnic minority groups. Although feminist therapists use a variety of therapeutic techniques, they are guided by the common goal of raising awareness of the harmful effects of discrimination, such as the effects of job discrimination on the basis of gender, race, or sexual orientation, and of the treatment of women as sexual objects.

Feminist therapists also challenge the tendency of traditional psychotherapies to label as normal those attributes identified with the male-dominated mainstream culture, and to label as abnormal those attributes associated with femininity and with minority cultures.

How does feminist therapy challenge traditional psychotherapies?   Feminist therapy challenges the validity of gender-role stereotypes and traditional inequalities of power between men and women, and between people who represent the dominant culture and ethnic minority groups. Feminist therapists argue that the traditional mental health establishment has a tendency to label forms of behavior which run counter to the interests of the male-dominated culture as pathological. For example, do women who act assertively suffer from unresolved penis envy?

Feminist therapists object to the use of gender-role stereotypes to support cultural beliefs in male superiority and female inferiority. Similarly, they object to using cultural differences, such as differences in child-rearing practices, as a basis for characterizing minority cultural groups as inferior to majority cultural groups. They advocate a more respectful appreciation of cultural and gender differences and contend that the existence of differences between groups does not imply that one group is inferior or superior to another.

Feminist therapists note that women's and minority group members' expressions of anger and suspiciousness toward dominant group members may be appropriate responses to prejudice and discrimination. For example, the anger or suspiciousness that African Americans direct toward white Americans is perceived as a normal adaptation to living in a prejudiced society. Moreover, feminist therapists assert that traditional psychotherapies have failed to recognize the harmful effects of sexist, racist, and heterosexist biases. Traditional therapies have consequently mislabeled the appropriate negative reactions of women, minority group members, and gay males and lesbians to their mistreatment as dysfunctional or maladaptive. Feminists argue that traditional therapies label any behaviors that do not serve the interests of the dominant group as problematic.

Feminist therapy further assails traditional approaches for their failure to challenge and label as pathological the discriminatory and destructive behaviors of dominant group members. For example, feminist therapists view racist, sexist, and heterosexist behaviors as pathological, not the negative reactions of the victims of these behaviors.

Feminist therapy also demands that therapists explore and understand their own social biases and the role of those biases in their work as therapists. Like sociocultural theorists, feminist theorists assume that social inequality, rather than individual psychopathology, often plays a prominent role in creating and maintaining many of the problems presented by clients in psychotherapy, particularly when those clients are members of oppressed groups (Brown, 1992). Feminist therapy challenges therapists to pay greater attention to the social contexts in which people are socialized, and to the origins of social rules or customs that sanction destructive behaviors in members of the dominant culture and punish similar behaviors in nondominant group members. Therapists of all persuasions are also asked to attend to inequalities in power between men and women in a male dominated society, and between members of the dominant culture and those of ethnic minority groups, economically disadvantaged persons, and gay men and lesbians.

BIOLOGICAL THERAPIES

There is a growing emphasis in American psychiatry on biological bases of abnormal behavior, or **biological psychiatry** (Pardes, 1986; van Praag, 1988). Biological psychiatry seeks biological defects that might explain abnormal behavior and on the use of biological approaches, such as drugs and ECT, to treat it. The trend toward biological psychiatry has been spurred by recent scientific advancements (Pardes, 1986), such as the development of brain-imaging techniques like MRI. Knowledge is also expanding concerning the role of neurotransmitters in abnormal behaviors. Such knowledge may lead to the development of new drugs to correct neurotransmitter imbalances. In experimental work that a few years ago would have seemed science fiction, researchers are attempting to repair defective brain tissues by implanting new brain structures. For example, there is hope that implanting brain cells that produce acetylcholine will help Alzheimer's patients.

Molecular geneticists are also mapping out the chromosomal segments (genes) that are connected with various mental disorders. One day it may become common practice to repair or replace problematic genes (Pardes, 1986).

Current biological approaches to the treatment of abnormal behaviors include drug therapy (**chemotherapy**), electroconvulsive shock therapy (ECT), and psychosurgery. Biological approaches are administered by medical doctors, many of whom have specialized training in psychiatry or **psychopharmacology**. Many family physicians or general practitioners also prescribe psychoactive or **psychotropic drugs** for their patients, however.

Although the biological or medical approaches have had dramatic success in treating some forms of abnormal behavior, they also have their limitations. For one, biological therapies may have unwelcome or dangerous side effects. The phenothiazines can lead to tardive dyskinesia, for example, and ECT may be associated with memory losses. There is also the potential for abuse. One of the most commonly prescribed minor tranquilizers, Valium, has become a major drug of abuse among people who become psychologically and physiologically dependent on it. Psychosurgery has been all but eliminated as a form of treatment because of serious harmful effects of earlier procedures.

Drug Therapy

■ **MINOR TRANQUILIZERS** For many years, the minor tranquilizer Valium was the most widely prescribed drug in the world. Valium is a member of the *benzodiazepine* family (anxiolytic drugs) and is often prescribed for treatment of anxiety, insomnia, and tension. Other benzodiazepines include chlordiazepoxide (Librium), oxazepam (Serax), and fluraxepam (Dalmane). Valium and these other tranquilizers are believed to depress the level of activity in certain parts of the central nervous system (CNS). In turn, the CNS decreases the level of sympathetic nervous system activity, reducing the respiration rate and heart rate, and lessening feelings of anxiety and tension (Caplan et al., 1983). Minor tranquilizers grew in popularity when physicians became concerned about the use of more potent sedatives, such as barbiturates, which are highly addictive and extremely dangerous when taken in overdoses or mixed with alcohol. The minor tranquilizers also can, and often do, lead to dependence, however. People who are dependent on Valium may go into convulsions when they abruptly stop taking it. Deaths have been reported among people who mix Valium with alcohol, or who are unusually sensitive to it. There are other less severe side effects, such as fatigue, drowsiness, and impaired motor coordination that might nonetheless impair the ability to function, or to operate an automobile. Regular usage of the drugs can produce tolerance, requiring higher dosages for continued effectiveness (Gillin, 1991). Quite commonly, patients become involved in tugs-of-war with their physicians as they demand increased dosages despite their physicians' concerns about the potential for abuse and dependence.

Drug therapy. Drug therapy is the most common biological treatment of abnormal behavior problems. Among the many different types of psychotropic drugs are minor tranquilizers, major tranquilizers (neuroleptics), antidepressants, and lithium. Stimulants, such as Ritalin, are also used in the treatment of attention-deficit hyperactivity disorder (ADHD).

When used on a short-term basis, minor tranquilizers can be safe and effective in the treatment of anxiety. Drugs do not teach people more adaptive ways of solving their problems, however, and may encourage them to rely on a chemical agent to cope with stress rather than develop active means of coping. Drug therapy is thus often combined with psychotherapy to help people with anxiety complaints deal with the psychological and situational bases of their problems. However, combining drug therapy and psychotherapy may present special problems and challenges. For one, drug-induced relief from anxiety may reduce clients' motivation to try to solve their problems. For another, medicated clients who develop skills for coping with stress in psychotherapy may fail to retain what they have learned once the tranquilizers are discontinued, or find themselves too tense to employ their newly acquired skills.

Rebound anxiety is another problem associated with regular use of minor tranquilizers. Many people who regularly use minor tranquilizers report that anxiety or insomnia returns in more severe form once they discontinue them. For some, this may represent a fear of not having the drugs to depend on. For others, rebound anxiety might reflect changes in biochemical processes that are not well understood at present (Chouinard et al., 1983).

■ **MAJOR TRANQUILIZERS** Major tranquilizers, or **neuroleptics**, are called antipsychotic drugs because they are commonly used to treat the more flagrant features of psychosis, such as hallucinations, delusions, and states of confusion. Many of these drugs, including Thorazine, Mellaril, Prolixin, and Stelazine, belong to the **phenothiazine** class of chemicals. Phenothiazines are generally believed to block the action of dopamine at receptor sites in the brain. Research along these lines, which supported the dopamine theory of schizophrenia, was reviewed in Chapter 11. Clozapine (brand name Clozaril), a neuroleptic of a different chemical class than the phenothiazines, is helpful in treating many seriously disturbed schizophrenics, perhaps one-third to two-thirds, who were previously unresponsive to other neuroleptics (Green & Salzman, 1990; Naber & Hippius, 1990; Perry et al., 1991; Pickar et al., 1992). The use of clozapine must be carefully monitored, however, because of potentially dangerous side effects (Freudenheim, 1991).

Neuroleptics are generally effective in reducing agitation, hallucinations, and delusions (Gilman et al., 1990; May, 1975; Watson et al., 1978) without the sedation associated with barbiturates. Although they can control psychotic behaviors, they do not effect a cure because the psychotic features often return following withdrawal from the medication. In larger doses, they can produce apathy and fatigue and have been misused by hospital personnel as a form of punishment for unruly behavior. Most antipsychotic drugs are less effective in treating the so-called negative features of schizophrenia, such as apathy, withdrawal, and social deficits, although clozapine appears to be more effective in treating such symptoms (Honigfeld & Patin, 1990; Pickar et al., 1992). Major tranquilizers have reduced the need for more restrictive forms of treatment for severely disturbed patients, such as physical restraints and confinement in padded cells, and have lessened the need for long-term hospitalization. The introduction of major tranquilizers in the mid-1950s was one of the major factors that led to the massive exodus of chronic mental patients from state institutions that has occurred in the intervening years. Many ex-hospital patients have been able to resume family life and hold jobs while continuing to take their medications.

Because most neuroleptics block the action of dopamine, they often lead to symptoms resembling those of Parkinson's disease, including muscular rigidity and tremors (Calne, 1977; Kimble, 1988). Parkinsonian side effects can often be controlled by drugs that are also used in the treatment of Parkinsonism. However, the long-term use of antipsychotic drugs (possibly excepting Clozapine) is also associated with some serious side effects that may be irreversible, the most severe of which is the disabling motor condition called tardive dyskinesia (see Chapter 11). Psychiatrists have been urged to exercise prudence in prescribing long-term use of neuroleptics because of the danger of tardive dyskinesia and other serious potential side effects (Baldessarini & Cohen, 1987). Researchers are also experimenting with lowered dosages, intermittent drug regimens, and alternate medications to reduce the risk of such side effects.

■ **ANTIDEPRESSANTS** People with major depression are often helped with drugs called **antidepressants**. Between 60 and 70% of people with depressive disorders respond positively to some degree to tricyclic antidepressants (Georgotas & McCue, 1988). Yet the overall effectiveness of tricyclic medications, in terms of the degree to which they alleviate depression, appears to be modest (Greenberg et al., 1992).

Imbalances in the neurotransmitters norepinephrine and serotonin have been linked to depression (see Chapter 7). Although it is generally believed that antidepressants increase the amount of these neurotransmitters at crucial sites in the brain, the precise mechanism of action of these drugs in treating depression is not yet clear. Nor is it understood why antidepressants often have beneficial effects on other disorders, such as panic disorder (see Chapter 5), obsessive-compulsive disorder (see Chapter 5), and eating disorders (see Chapter 13). As research continues we may find that these disorders also involve dysregulation of neurotransmitters, such as norepinephrine and serotonin.

There are several types of antidepressant drugs, including *tricyclics*, **monoamine oxidase (MAO) inhibitors**, and *serotonin reuptake inhibitors*. The first two kinds of antidepressants increase the supplies of norepinephrine and serotonin in the brain, but in different ways (see Chapter 7). The third increases the action of serotonin. The MAO inhibitors include such drugs as phenelzine (Nardil) and isocarboxazid (Marplan). Some of the more common tricyclics are imipramine (Tofranil), amitriptyline (Elavil), and doxepin (Sinequan). Tricyclics are more commonly prescribed because they are generally considered more effective. Moreover, people who use MAO inhibitors must follow strict dietary restrictions. Serotonin reuptake inhibitors include fluoxetine (Prozac) and sertraline (Zoloft), whose chemical properties differ from those of other antidepressants.

A number of head-to-head comparisons between cognitive therapy and antidepressant medication have been reported. In a major multisite/government-sponsored study of the treatment of depression, the effectiveness of an antidepressant medication (imipramine) was compared to that of cognitive therapy, interpersonal psychotherapy, and a placebo control condition (Elkin et al., 1989). The short-term results following the 16-week treatment period showed that both psychological treatment approaches, cognitive therapy and interpersonal therapy, were about equally effective to each other and to antidepressant medication in alleviating depression. The results were complicated by the finding that cognitive therapy did not outperform the placebo control condition, in which subjects received a placebo drug combined with supportive counseling from an experienced psychiatrist. Some limited evidence favored interpersonal psychotherapy and the active drug treatment (imipramine) in comparison to the placebo control condition, however.

In most other comparisons of cognitive therapy and drug therapy for depression, cognitive therapy has shown itself to be at least comparable in effectiveness to the tricyclic antidepressants (Hollon et al., 1991; Imber et al., 1990; Robinson et al., 1990; Wexler & Cicchetti, 1992). Cognitive therapy may also provide greater protection against a recurrence of depression following termination of treatment (Hollon & Beck, 1986; Hollon et al., 1991). Critics, however, have challenged these results, contending, for example, that the medication conditions in these studies adopted standard dosage protocols and thus failed to adjust dosages to optimal levels as would be the case in routine treatment (Meterissian & Bradwejn, 1989).

Antidepressants tend to relieve the physical or vegetative features of depression. For example, they tend to reduce sleep difficulties and disturbances of appetite, and to increase energy levels (Lyons et al., 1985; Weissman et al., 1981). As a result, people with depressive disorders may be able to make better use of psychotherapy to deal with the social and cognitive deficits that are associated with these disorders. There is some research showing the combination of drug therapy and psychotherapy to be more effective in treating depression than drug therapy alone (Conte et al., 1986). Yet most research has in fact *failed* to show that the combination of antidepressant medication and psychotherapy increases the effectiveness of either form of treatment alone (Burns & Nolen-Hoeksema, 1992; Robinson et al., 1990; Wexler & Cicchetti, 1992). Moreover, cognitive-behavior therapy has been shown to be of benefit even in cases of endogenous depression in which there is evidence of biological dysfunction such as disturbed sleep patterns (Thase et al., 1991). Still, antidepressant medication may be most appropriate for depressives who fail to respond to psychotherapy alone (Steward et al., 1990). Recognize, too, that some depressives who fail to respond to drug therapy may respond favorably to psychotherapy. All in all, more research is needed to specify which clients will profit best from drug therapy, from psychotherapy, or from a combination of the two.

■ **LITHIUM** Lithium carbonate, a salt of the metal lithium in tablet form, has demonstrated remarkable effectiveness in treating manic and depressive episodes in bipolar disorder and reducing their recurrences (see Chapter 7). Because of its potential toxicity, the blood levels of patients maintained on lithium must be carefully monitored. Like diabetics who must take insulin through their lifetimes to control their diabetes, people with bipolar disorder may have to continue using lithium indefinitely to control the disorder. Figure 14.2 summarizes the actions of some kinds of psychotropic drugs. Table 14.3 lists psychotropic drugs according to their drug class and category.

Electroconvulsive Therapy

In 1939, the Italian psychiatrist Ugo Cerletti introduced the technique of **electroconvulsive therapy** (ECT) in psychiatric treatment. Cerletti had observed the practice in some slaughterhouses of using electric

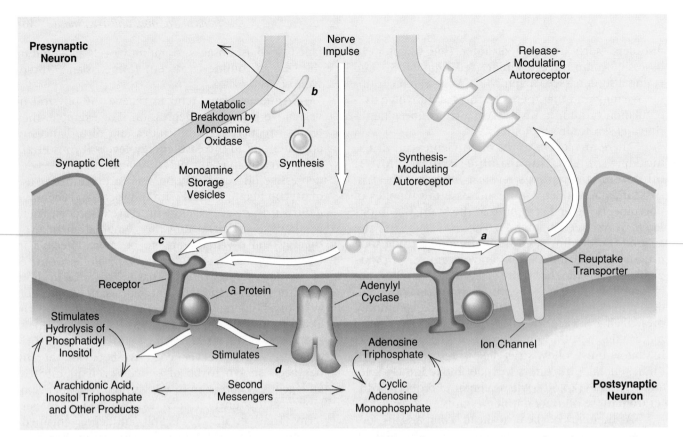

Figure 14.2 **Actions of psychotropic drugs.** Psychotropic drugs act in various ways on presynaptic and postsynaptic neurons. Some antidepressants, such as fluoxetine (Prozac), and tricyclics like imipramine (Tofranil), block the reuptake (the return to storage vesicles in the presynaptic reuron) (a) of monoamines such as norepinephrine and serotonin. Other antidepressants, called monoamine oxidase (MAO) inhibitors (b), block the actions of an enzyme, monoamine oxidase, that normally breaks down monoamines. In either case, the drugs increase the availability of monoamines in the synapse. Some drugs affect the postsynaptic neuron by either blocking monoamine receptors or enhancing their ability to respond. Haloperidol (Haldol), for example, is an antipsychotic drug that blocks dopamine receptors on the postsynaptic cell (c). Other drugs affect how the receiving or postsynaptic neuron responds by interfering with the cascading chemical changes (d) that occur after a receptor is activated. For example, some drugs, such as lithium carbonate used to treat bipolar disorder, inhibit the synthesis of second-messenger chemicals (d) that normally takes place following activation of a receptor.

Source: From "Major Disorders of Mind and Brain," by Elliot S. Gerhon and Ronald O. Rieder. Copyright © 1992 by Scientific American, Inc. All rights reserved.

Electroconvulsive therapy (ECT). ECT is helpful in many cases of severe or prolonged depression that do not respond to other forms of treatment. Still, its use remains controversial because of potential side effects.

shock to render animals unconscious. He observed that the shocks also produced convulsions. Cerletti incorrectly believed, as did other researchers in Europe at the time, that convulsions of the type found in epilepsy were incompatible with schizophrenia and that a method of inducing convulsions might be used to cure schizophrenia.

After the introduction of the phenothiazines in the 1950s, the use of ECT became generally limited to the treatment of severe depression. The introduction of antidepressants has limited the use of ECT even further today. The American Psychiatric Association (1990) now recommends that ECT be used to treat major depression only in people who do not respond to antidepressant medication. Evidence suggests that about 50% of depressives who fail to respond to anti-

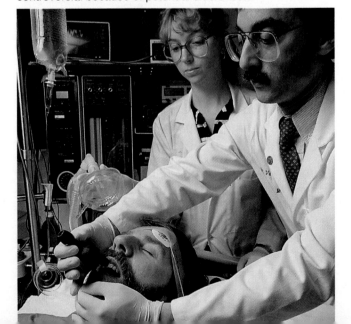

Table 14.3 Psychotropic Drugs

Category	Drug Class	Generic Name	Trade Name
Antianxiety agents (also called minor tranquilizers or anxiolytics)	Benzodiazepines	Diazepam	Valium
		Chlordiazepoxide	Librium
		Clorazepate	Tranxene
		Oxazepam	Serax
		Lorazepam	Ativan
	Triazolobenzodiazepine	Alprazolam	Xanax
	Propanediols	Meprobamate	Miltown
			Equanil
	Hypnotics	Flurazepam	Dalmane
Antipsychotic drugs (also called neuroleptics or major tranquilizers)	Phenothiazines	Chlorpromazine	Thorazine
		Thioridazine	Mellaril
		Mesoridazine	Serentil
		Perphenazine	Trilafon
		Trifluoperazine	Stelazine
		Fluphenazine	Prolixin
	Thioxanthenes	Chlorprothixene	Taractan
		Thiothixene	Navane
	Butyrophenones	Haloperidol	Haldol
	Dibenzoxazepines	Loxapine	Loxitane
	Dibenzodiazepine	Clozapine	Clozaril
Antidepressants	Tricyclic antidepressants (TCAs)	Imipramine	Tofranil
		Desipramine	Norpramin
		Amitriptyline	Elavil
		Doxepin	Sinequan
		Nortriptyline	Aventyl
		Protriptyline	Vivactil
	MAO inhibitors (MAOIs)	Phenelzine	Nardil
		Isocarboxazid	Marplan
		Tranylcypromine	Parnate
	Serotonin reuptake inhibitors	Fluoxetine	Prozac
		Sertraline	Zoloft
Antimanic Agents		Lithium carbonate	Lithane
		Carbamazapine	Tegretol
Stimulants		Methylphenidate	Ritalin

depressants show significant improvement following ECT (Sackheim et al., 1990).

ECT remains a source of controversy for several reasons. First, many people, including many professionals, are uncomfortable about the idea of passing an electric shock through a person's head, even if the level of shock is closely regulated and the convulsions are controlled by drugs. Second are the potential side effects. ECT often produces dramatic relief from severe depression (Coffey & Weiner, 1990), but concerns remain about its potential for inducing lasting memory losses (Breggin, 1990; Roueche, 1980). Researchers are investigating alternative regimens for delivering shock that minimize the risk of memory impairment but maintain therapeutic effectiveness. Third are the questions of relative efficacy. The relative effectiveness of ECT as compared to antidepressant drugs, to sham (simulated) ECT, and to cognitive behavior therapy remains unclear. Fourth, no one yet knows why ECT works, although it is suspected that it might help correct neurotransmitter imbalances in the brain (Coffey & Weiner, 1990).

 ECT is actually helpful in many cases of depression that do not respond to other forms of therapy. However, ECT is usually considered a treatment of last resort because of its possible side effects and because its therapeutic mechanisms remain unknown.

Psychosurgery

Psychosurgery is yet more controversial than ECT. The most widely practiced form of psychosurgery is the **prefrontal lobotomy**, which has been used with severely disturbed patients. In a prefrontal lobotomy, the nerve pathways linking the thalamus to the prefrontal lobes of the brain are surgically severed. The operation was based on the theory that extremely disturbed patients suffer from overexcitation of emotional impulses that emanate from the lower brain centers, such as the thalamus and hypothalamus. It was believed that by severing the connections between the thalamus and the higher brain centers in the frontal lobe of the cerebral cortex, the patient's violent or aggressive tendencies could be controlled. The prefrontal lobotomy was developed by the Portuguese neurologist Antonio Egas Moniz and was introduced to the United States in the 1930s. More than a thousand mental patients received the operation by 1950. Although the operation did reduce violent and agitated behavior in many cases, it was not always successful. In a cruel ironic twist, one of Moniz's treatment failures later shot him, leaving him paralyzed from a bullet that lodged in his spine.

Many distressing side effects are associated with the prefrontal lobotomy, including hyperactivity, impaired learning ability and reduced creativity, distractibility, apathy, overeating, withdrawal, epileptic-type seizures, and even death. The occurrence of these side effects, combined with the introduction of the phenothiazines, has led to the virtual elimination of the operation.

Several more sophisticated psychosurgery techniques have been introduced in more recent years for various purposes. Generally speaking, they are limited to smaller parts of the brain and produce less damage than the prefrontal lobotomy. These operations have been performed to treat such problems as intractable aggression, depression, and psychotic behavior; chronic pain; some forms of epilepsy (Valenstein, 1980); and persistent obsessive-compulsive disorder (Hay et al., 1991; Sachdev et al., 1992). Follow-up studies of such procedures have shown marked improvement in about one-third to one-half of the cases (Corkin, 1980; Hay et al., 1991; Mirsky & Orzack, 1980; Sachdev et al., 1992). Yet concerns about possible adverse effects of psychosurgery continue to limit the applicability of this approach.

Evaluation of Biological Approaches

There is little doubt that the use of psychotropic drugs has helped many people with severe psychological problems. Many thousands of formerly hospitalized schizophrenics, for example, are able to function more effectively in the community because of antipsychotic drugs. Antidepressant drugs have been demonstrated to help in the treatment of depression and appear to have therapeutic benefits in treating

other disorders, such as panic disorder, obsessive-compulsive disorder, and eating disorders.

 Actually, drugs have been found helpful in many cases, particularly in cases involving more severe patterns of abnormal behavior.

On the other hand, in the case of depression, it may be that some forms of psychotherapy are as effective as drug therapy. Moreover, problems persist with respect to the side effects of various psychotropic drugs. In addition, minor tranquilizers have often become drugs of abuse among people who become dependent on them for relieving the effects of stress rather than seeking more adaptive ways of solving their problems. Medical practitioners have often been too quick to use their prescription pads to help people with anxiety complaints, rather than to help them examine their lives or refer them for psychological treatment. Physicians often feel pressured, of course, by patients who seek a chemical solution to their life problems.

Cultural or ethnic differences may play a role in responsiveness to psychotropic medications (Lefley, 1990; Lesser, 1992). African Americans, for example, tend to show a better response to antidepressants and phenothiazines than other groups. Hispanic Americans tend to show lower effective dosage levels (Lawson, 1986). Some clinical evidence indicates that African Americans, as compared to white Americans, show a quicker response to tricyclic antidepressants but may encounter more side effects (Lesser, 1992). Cultural differences may also play a role in determining acceptability of medication or even the preferred method of drug administration (Lefley, 1990). For example, evidence from several samples shows greater resistance to taking pills among African-American patients (Page et al., 1983; Weidman, 1978). Sharing of medications within the family is a common practice among Hispanic Americans in New York (Rivera, 1988).

Although controversies concerning the use of ECT persist, there is increasing evidence of its effectiveness in helping people overcome severe depression that might not be responsive to psychotherapy or antidepressant medication (Coffey & Weiner, 1990; Janicak et al., 1985; National Institute of Mental Health, 1985; Scovern & Kilmann, 1980). Moreover, ECT may help reduce the risk of suicide among severely depressed people (Martin et al., 1985).

While we continue to learn more about the biological foundations of abnormal behavior patterns, the interface between biology and behavior can be considered a two-way street (Pardes, 1986). Researchers have uncovered links between psychological factors and many physical disorders and conditions. Researchers are also investigating whether the combination of psychological and drug treatments for such problems as depression, anxiety disorders, and substance abuse disorders, among others, may increase the therapeutic benefits of either of the two approaches alone. Although American psychiatry has become increasingly "medicalized" in recent years, some within the psychiatric community have warned their colleagues not to overlook the role of psychological factors in explaining and treating mental disorders (van Praag, 1988).

HOSPITALIZATION AND COMMUNITY-BASED CARE

People receive mental health services within various settings, including hospitals, outpatient clinics, community mental health centers, and private practices. In this section we explore the purposes of hospitalization and the movement toward community-based care. Due to *deinstitutionalization*—the policy of shifting the burden of care from the state hospitals to the community—an exodus has taken place from state mental hospitals. We will see that deinstitutionalization has had a profound impact on the delivery of mental health services as well as on the larger community. First, let us consider some of the factors that may inhibit the use of mental health services by ethnic minorities in our society.

Ethnic Differences in Use of Mental Health Services

Consider the case of Kenyata:

Kenyata, an African-American woman in her early twenties, was brought to the emergency room of a general hospital by the police. She physically resisted the police and the emergency-room attendants. Moreover, her speech seemed muddled and difficult to decipher. The attending psychiatrist had Kenyata restrained and gave her large doses of a major tranquilizer. The police explained that Kenyata had tried to knife her boyfriend, Jimmy. They had brought her to the hospital rather than arrest her because she had a history of "mental problems."

Kenyata had been admitted to another hospital across the river on previous occasions. The psychiatrist telephoned that hospital and was told that Kenyata's diagnosis was schizophrenia. Since Kenyata was uncooperative during an attempted interview, he admitted her involuntarily to the hospital psychiatric unit and entered the reported diagnosis in her chart. An admission note explained her violence and resistance as "schizophrenic negativism."

Kenyata was not schizophrenic. Her speech had been unintelligible in the emergency room, but she had been drinking and had used many Black-English expressions. Kenyata had grown up in the ghetto and dropped out of school early. She had engaged in prostitution and child abuse. She was hostile, mistrustful, and largely untrusting of, and noncommunicative with, white mental-health professionals. Yet she was "treated" for schizophrenia—that is, hospitalized and drugged.

■ *Adapted from Rathus, 1993, pp. 606–607*

Kenyata's case is not unique. African Americans are more likely than non-Hispanic white Americans to be admitted to mental hospitals (Rosenstein et al., 1987) and to be committed to such institutions involuntarily (Lindsey & Paul, 1989). The question is, why? Relationships between ethnicity and prevalence of mental disorders are complex, to say the least. African Americans are overrepresented among the lower socioeconomic groups in our society and the lower strata on the socioeconomic ladder do tend to have higher prevalences of severe mental disorders that often lead to hospitalization, such as schizophrenia. So perhaps socioeconomic differences come into play. But, as noted by Rathus (1993), Kenyata's case highlights the stereotyping and lack of sensitivity to cultural and language differences that ethnic minorities, especially the poor, may encounter within the mental health system.

The other side of the coin is underutilization of outpatient-based mental health services by ethnic minorities. For example, African Americans tend to receive fewer aftercare services in the community upon discharge from mental hospitals than white Americans (Solomon, 1988). Nor are mental health clinics the first places where African Americans typically go for help for emotional problems. African Americans seeking mental health interventions turn most often to the church and second to the emergency room of the local general hospital (Lewis-Hall, 1992). The National Survey of African Americans found that slightly more than half (54%) of those who reported experiencing feelings of a "nervous breakdown" failed to consult any type of professional for help with their problems (Neighbors, 1992).

Hispanic Americans, particularly Mexican Americans, also tend to underutilize outpatient services (Hough et al., 1987). Past discrimination may play a role in determining underutilization of mental health services by Mexican Americans (Sanchez & Mohl, 1992). If minority clients perceive non-Hispanic white therapists as cold and insensitive, they are less likely to place their trust in them. Others have found that Hispanic Americans who encounter emotional problems are more likely to seek assistance from friends and relatives, or from spiritualists, than to reach out to mental health facilities, which they perceive as cold and impersonal institutions (De La Cancela & Guzman, 1991). Hispanic people are also more likely to seek assistance for emotional problems from primary care physicians than from psychologists or psychiatrists.

Cheung (1991) notes several barriers that may help to explain the underutilization of mental health services by ethnic minorities, including the following:

1. *Institutional or structural barriers.* People from minority groups often fail to use mental health services because they believe that such services will be unresponsive to their needs. Facilities may be inaccessible to minority group members because they are located at a considerable distance from their homes or because of lack of public transportation. Most facilities only operate during daytime work hours, which means they are inaccessible to minority group members who are unable to take time off. Moreover, minorities feel that staff members often make them feel stupid for not being familiar with clinic procedures and that their requests for assistance often become tangled in red tape.

2. *Cultural barriers.* Many recent immigrants, especially those from Southeast Asian countries, have had little if any previous contact with mental health professionals. They may hold different conceptions of mental health problems or view mental health problems as less severe than physical problems. In some ethnic minority subcultures, the family is expected to take care of members who have mental breakdowns and may resist seeking outside assistance because of guilt engendered by the belief that seeking outside help would represent rejection of the family member and would embarrass the family. Other barriers include cultural differences between minority group members who are typically of lower socio-economic status and mostly white, middle-class staff members, and incongruence between the cultural practices of minority group members and the techniques used by mental health professionals. For example, Asian immigrants may find little value in talking about their problems or may be uncomfortable expressing their feelings to strangers. In many ethnic minority groups, personal and interpersonal problems are brought to trusted elders in the family or religious leaders, not to outside professionals.

3. *Language barriers.* Differences in language make it difficult for minority group members to describe their problems or obtain the services that are needed. Many mental health services do not have staff members who can communicate in the languages used by ethnic minority residents in their communities.

4. *Economic barriers.* Minority group members often live in economically distressed areas that have limited resources. Studies show that communities with more limited resources are unable to provide the range and accessibility of services to the public of wealthier communities, which have more resources available.

Cheung (1991) concludes that greater utilization of mental health services will depend to a great extent on the ability of the mental health system to develop programs which consider these cultural fac-

A language barrier? People from various ethnic minority groups do not make use of mental health services because of language barriers.

tors and build staffs that consist of culturally sensitive providers, including minority mental health professionals and paraprofessionals. Changes in traditional patterns of underutilization may be in the offing. For example, investigators in a recent study in Texas failed to find differences in dropout rates in psychotherapy or in length of treatment between Mexican-American and non-Hispanic white American clients (Sanchez & Mohl, 1992).

Roles for Hospitalization

Different types of hospitals provide different types of care. Municipal and community-based hospitals tend to focus on short-term care for people with serious psychological problems who need a structured hospital environment to help them through an acute crisis. In such cases, psychotropic drugs and other biological treatments, such as ECT for severe cases of depression, are often used in combination with short-term psychotherapy. Hospitalization may be followed by outpatient treatment. Many private care hospitals provide longer term care or are specialized to help people withdraw safely from alcohol or drugs.

The state mental hospital system has traditionally served as the bastion of long-term residential care. Unfortunately, state hospitals have historically failed to provide decent living conditions and the structured treatment needed to restore chronic mental patients to community life. This failure sparked the shift toward community-based care earlier in this century. Prior to deinstitutionalization, patients on back wards were essentially *warehoused*. That is, they were left to live out their lives with little hope or expectation of recovery or return to the community. Many received little professional care and were abused by poorly trained and supervised staffs.

Most state hospitals today are better managed and provide more humane care than those of the 19th and early 20th centuries, but here and there deplorable conditions persist. Today's state hospital is generally more treatment oriented and focuses on preparing residents to return to community living. Many state hospitals have developed structured treatment environments that incorporate token economy systems and milieu approaches (see Chapter 11). State hospitals today often function, under deinstitutionalization, as part of an integrated, comprehensive approach to treatment. They provide the structured environment that is needed for people who are unable to function in a less restrictive community setting. When hospitalization restores patients to a higher level of functioning, the patients are reintegrated in the community and provided with follow-up care and transitional residences, if needed, to help them adjust to community living. Patients may be rehospitalized as needed in a state hospital if a community-based hospital is not available, or if they require more extensive care than a community hospital can provide. For younger and less intensely disturbed people, the state hospital stay is typically briefer than it was in the past, lasting only until their condition allows them to reenter society. Elderly chronic patients may be unprepared to handle the most rudimentary tasks (shopping, cooking, cleaning, and so on) of independent life, however—in part because the state hospital may be the only home such patients have known as adults.

The Community Mental Health Center

Community mental health centers (CMHCs) perform many functions in the effort to reduce the need for hospitalization of new patients and rehospitalization of formerly hospitalized patients. A primary function of the CMHC is to help discharged mental patients adjust to the community by providing continuing care and closely monitoring their progress. Unfortunately, not enough CMHCs have been established to serve the needs of the hundreds of thousands of ex-hospital patients and to try to prevent the need for hospitalization of new patients by providing intervention services and alternatives to full hospitalization, such as day hospital programs. Patients in day hospitals attend structured therapy and vocational rehabilitation programs in a hospital setting during the day but are returned to their families or homes at night. Many CMHCs also administer transitional treatment facilities in the community, such as halfway houses, which provide a sheltered living environment to help discharged mental patients gradually adjust to the community as well as to provide people in crisis with an alternative to hospitalization. CMHCs also serve in consultative roles to other professionals in the community, such as training police officers to handle disturbed people. Many of the features of the CMHC focus on prevention, such as crisis intervention, consultation, and halfway houses. In Chapter 15 we take a closer look at the ways in which mental health professionals seek to meet the challenge of prevention. We also take a further look at one of our most vexing social problems: homelessness among ex-hospitalized mental patients.

Let us now take a closer look at the movement toward deinstitutionalization of mental patients. Has deinstitutionalization achieved the goal of reintegrating mental patients into society, or does it remain a promise that is largely unfulfilled?

A halfway house. Halfway houses are transitional (community) facilities that provide sheltered opportunities for mental patients to reenter society. Here, former institutionalized patients who live together in a community residence operate a small home renovation business.

The Movement Toward Deinstitutionalization

By the mid-20th century, the deplorable conditions that existed in many public mental hospitals led to calls for reforms of the mental health system. Understaffed and underfunded, many institutions at the time provided only minimal attention to the needs of the patients.

In 1961, a congressional commission issued a report that was sharply critical of existing psychiatric hospitals and called for sweeping reforms (Joint Commission on Mental Illness and Health, 1961). This report spearheaded the movement that would eventually be called *deinstitutionalization*. The thrust of the commission's report was to promote reintegration of mental patients in the community:

> The objective of modern treatment of persons with major mental illness is to enable the patient to maintain himself in the community in a normal manner. To do so, it is necessary (1) to save the patient from the debilitating effects of institutionalization as much as possible, (2) if the patient requires hospitalization, to return him to home and community life as soon as possible, and (3) thereafter to maintain him in the community as long as possible (p. 270).

The call for reform of the mental health system led to the creation of a nationwide system of community mental health centers (CMHCs) by an act of Congress in 1963. By 1980, over 700 CMHCs had been established (Keisler & Sibulkin, 1987), providing alternatives to hospitalization to many people in need of care. The advent of phenothiazines in the 1950s provided a second impetus toward deinstitutionalization. The phenothiazines helped control many of the flagrant features of schizophrenia, allowing thousands of hospitalized patients to be returned to families, jobs, or sheltered living environments in the community.

Deinstitutionalization has cut the state mental hospital population by about 80% since 1955 (Kiesler & Sibulkin, 1987). This change is more striking when it is expressed in terms of the proportion of the population that is housed in state mental hospitals. In 1955, 339 of every 100,000 people resided in such hospitals (Bachrach, 1987). Today, only 50 of 100,000 people do.

Other factors also played roles in the exodus of mental patients to the community. Civil libertarians and patients' rights advocates brought the dehumanizing conditions in many psychiatric hospitals into closer public scrutiny (Grob, 1983). Community-based care was promoted as a more humane alternative to long-term hospitalization. Increased attention to patients' rights led to landmark court cases which established minimal standards of care that state institutions must provide (see Chapter 15). Given these standards, which would have raised hospital care costs significantly, state legislators who were eager to reduce costs to taxpayers may have found it more expedient to release large numbers of patients to the community (Grob, 1983).

Other economic factors also contributed to deinstitutionalization. Many CMHCs were seeded by federal funding, for example, whereas the large state institutions largely depended on state funding (Grob, 1983). Moreover, the introduction of federal disability subsidies in the 1960s, such as the Supplemental Security Income (SSI) disability program, provided a source of revenue that could be passed along to nursing home and group care ("board-and-care") home operators in the community. Community providers could thus offer alternative residential treatment to formerly hospitalized patients and others who might have been hospitalized in earlier times (Shadish et al., 1989).

Evaluation of Deinstitutionalization

Deinstitutionalization has often been criticized for failing to live up to its expectations (Elpers, 1987). Critics have charged that many hospital patients were merely dumped into the community. These patients were ill prepared to handle the demands of community living and unable to obtain required services in the community.

New, promising technologies exist to improve community-based care for people with chronic mental disorders—for example, psychosocial rehabilitation centers, family psychoeducational groups, supported housing and work programs, and social skills training (Anthony et al., 1990). Unfortunately, too few of the people who might benefit from such services actually receive them.

A 1991 government report found that 249 of the 600 community mental health centers across the United States that had received federal funds had failed to provide even the basic services, such as emergency care and outpatient clinics, which they were required to offer (Hilts, 1991). Failure to provide such services is seen by experts in the mental health field as one of the "reasons for the growing number of homeless mentally ill people now wandering the streets of American cities untreated" (Hilts, 1991). Although the agency responsible for oversee-

ing the community mental health system, the National Institute of Mental Health, felt that the problems were not as widespread as the government report alleged, it is clear that many centers fail to provide adequate services to severely disturbed or formerly institutionalized clients.

With supportive services lacking, additional burdens are placed on already strained public support systems, such as public housing and social services. Lacking adequate support, mental patients may face more dehumanizing conditions on the street, under deinstitutionalization, than they did in mental hospitals (Warner, 1989; Wines, 1988). Many factors may account for the unfulfilled promises of deinstitutionalization.

1. *Lack of community support services.* Insufficient funds were shifted from state hospitals to community services. State governments were unable or unwilling to commit additional funds to develop community care facilities. Patients were thus frequently left unsupervised.

2. *Community resistance.* The "not-in-my-backyard" (NIMBY) syndrome prevented the establishment of community care facilities and group homes in many communities. Many people are willing to support the establishment of community services for the mentally ill—in *someone else's* community, that is.

3. *Lack of public housing.* Many of the homeless in our urban centers are ex-hospital patients or people with psychiatric disturbances who might have been hospitalized in earlier times, but who now wander from place to place for lack of decent affordable housing and community support services.

4. *Limits of psychotropic drugs.* Psychotropic drugs did not help restore the deficits in social and occupational functioning of many long-hospitalized schizophrenics (Shadish et al., 1989).

A study of ex-hospital patients in Chicago (Lurigio & Lewis, 1989) places the problems of deinstitutionalization in perspective. The study found that the overwhelming majority of discharged mental patients were poor, unemployed, and on welfare. They lacked job skills and close family ties. A substantial number were homeless. Aftercare services were generally inadequate. The researchers saw little hope that these people could escape from poverty and despair to lead more productive lives. Most eventually returned to the state hospitals, which had provided the only stable environment and source of support they had known.

All in all, deinstitutionalization has failed to

restore a reasonable quality of life to vast numbers of discharged patients. Nor has it decreased their dependency on mental health services or helped them to meet their basic needs (Shadish et al., 1989). Many remain in custodial-type nursing homes that resemble the back wards of the institutions from which they were released. Many others are homeless.

Although the net results of deinstitutionalization may not have yet lived up to expectations, a number of successful community-oriented programs have been developed (Lamb, 1982; Stein & Tess, 1978; Talbott, 1981). Deinstitutionalization has worked best for those who experience acute episodes of disturbed behavior, for those who are hospitalized briefly and then returned to their homes, families, and jobs (Shadish et al., 1989). If deinstitutionaliza-

tion is to eventually succeed for all patients, patients must be provided with continuing care and afforded opportunities for decent housing, gainful employment, and training in social and vocational skills (Goering et al., 1984; Lurigio & Lewis, 1989).

The ability of community facilities to help maintain new patients in the community appears to have been more successful. A review of 10 controlled experiments in which severely disturbed people were randomly assigned to receive either hospitalization or outpatient treatment failed to find even one experiment that showed better results for hospitalization (Kiesler, 1982). Outpatient treatment generally outperformed hospitalization in terms of the ability of the person to maintain independent living arrangements, stay in school, and find a job.

SUMMARY

Psychotherapy

Psychotherapies involve systematic interactions between therapists and clients that incorporate psychological principles to help clients overcome abnormal behavior, solve problems in living, or develop as individuals. Psychotherapies employ theory-based specific treatment factors and nonspecific factors such as the quality of the therapeutic relationship and the instillation of hope.

Psychodynamic Therapies

Psychodynamic therapies originated with psychoanalysis, the approach to treatment developed by Freud. Psychoanalysts use techniques such as free association and dream analysis to help people gain insight into their unconscious conflicts and work them through in the light of their adult personalities. More recent psychoanalytic therapies are generally briefer and less intensive.

Humanistic-Existential Therapies

Humanistic-existential approaches focus on the client's subjective, conscious experience in the here and now. Rogers's person-centered therapy helps people increase their awareness and acceptance of inner feelings that had met with social condemnation and been disowned. The effective person-centered therapist possesses the qualities of unconditional positive regard, empathetic understanding, genuine-

ness, and congruence. Perls's Gestalt therapy helps people integrate disparate elements in their personalities through structured exercises. Existential therapies focus on helping clients get in touch with their subjective experiences and make personal choices that will imbue life with meaning and a sense of purpose.

Cognitive Therapies

Cognitive therapies focus on modifying the maladaptive cognitions that are believed to underlie emotional problems and self-defeating behavior. Ellis's rational-emotive therapy focuses on disputing the irrational beliefs that occasion emotional distress and substituting adaptive behavior for maladaptive behavior. Beck's cognitive therapy focuses on helping clients identify, challenge, and replace distorted cognitions, such as tendencies to magnify negative events and minimize personal accomplishments.

Behavior Therapy

Behavior therapy applies principles of learning to help people make adaptive behavioral changes. Behavior therapy techniques include systematic desensitization, gradual exposure, modeling, aversive conditioning, operant conditioning approaches, social skills training, self-control techniques, biofeedback training, and relaxation techniques. Cognitive-behavior therapy integrates the behavioral and cognitive approaches.

Eclecticism in Psychotherapy

Therapists who adopt an eclectic approach incorporate principles and techniques from different therapeutic orientations and may or may not attempt to integrate these techniques within a unified theory.

Group Therapy

Group therapy has several advantages over individual treatment, such as reduced costs, opportunities for shared learning experiences and mutual support, and increased utilization of scarce therapist resources. The particular approach to group therapy depends on the orientation of the therapist.

Family and Marital Therapy

Family therapists work with conflicted families to help them resolve their differences. Family therapists focus on clarifying family communications, resolving role conflicts, guarding against scapegoating individual members, and helping members develop greater autonomy. Marital therapists focus on helping couples improve their communications and resolve their differences.

Evaluating the Effectiveness of Psychotherapy

Psychotherapy researchers have generated encouraging evidence of the effectiveness of psychotherapy. Although there are few well-designed head-to-head comparative treatment studies, the results of meta-analyses of research studies that compare psychotherapy with control groups supports the efficacy of various approaches to psychotherapy.

Multicultural Issues in Psychotherapy

Therapists need to take cultural factors into account in determining the appropriateness of Western forms of psychotherapy for different cultural groups. Some groups may, for example, have different views of the importance of the autonomy of the individual, or may place more value on spiritual than psychotherapeutic interventions.

Biological Therapies

Biological approaches include drug therapy, electroconvulsive shock therapy (ECT), and psychosurgery. Minor tranquilizers such as Valium may relieve short-term anxiety but do not directly help people solve their problems. Neuroleptics help relieve flagrant psychotic features, but regular use of most antipsychotic drugs has been associated with a risk of disabling side effects. Antidepressants have been shown to be effective in treating depressive disorders, but it has not been shown that antidepressant medication is superior overall to psychotherapy. Lithium has been shown to be effective in treating bipolar disorder. ECT is often associated with dramatic relief from severe depression, but questions remain about side effects. Psychosurgery is conducted only rarely because of adverse consequences.

Hospitalization and Community-Based Care

The mental hospital provides a structured treatment environment for people in acute crisis and for those who are unable to adapt to community living. The mental hospital today aims to restore patients to community functioning and incorporates treatment approaches such as biological therapies, psychotherapies, structured living environments, and drug and alcohol rehabilitation. Deinstitutionalization has greatly reduced the population of state mental hospitals, but has not yet fulfilled its promise to restore mental patients to a reasonable quality of life in the community. Community mental health centers provide continuing care to ex-hospitalized patients, crisis intervention, partial hospitalization and halfway house programs, and community consultation.

Marisol, Poor Family I, 1986. Mixed Media: 6'6" × 13' × 7'.
Courtesy Sidney Janis Gallery, New York. © Marisol/VAGA, New York

CHAPTER OUTLINE

15

Contemporary and Legal Issues

TRUTH  FICTION?

___ People with mental disorders are more likely than the general population to exhibit dangerous behavior.

___ An attempt to assassinate the president of the United States was seen by millions of television viewers, but the would-be assassin was found not guilty by a court of law.

___ People who are found not guilty of a crime by reason of insanity may remain confined to a mental hospital indefinitely—for many years longer than they would have been sentenced to prison, if they had been found guilty.

___ It is possible for a defendant to be held competent to stand trial but still be judged not guilty of a crime by reason of insanity.

___ Therapists may not disclose confidential information about clients to third parties, even when their clients threaten violence to the third parties.

___ Many of the nation's homeless are discharged into the streets from mental hospitals without adequate arrangements for community care.

*L*arry Hogue—the "wild man" of West 96th Street. Hogue, a homeless veteran of the Vietnam War who dwells in the alleyways and doorways of New York's Upper West Side. Hogue, a middle-aged man who goes barefoot in winter, eats from garbage cans, and mutters to himself (Dugger, 1992). Hogue, who reportedly stalked a teacher and threatened to cook and eat her fawn-colored Akita. Hogue, who reportedly becomes violent when he smokes crack and was once arrested for pushing a schoolgirl in front of a school bus (Shapiro, 1992). (Miraculously, she escaped injury.) Hogue, who has a history of some 40 arrests and hospitalizations (Wickenhaver, 1992). Hogue, for whom the criminal justice systems and mental health systems are nothing but revolving doors. Hogue, whom many regard as the living embodiment of the cracks in our mental health, criminal justice, and social services systems.

What does society do about Larry Hogue? What does society do about Joyce Brown?

Joyce Brown? Joyce Brown is a middle-aged woman who also lives on the streets of New York. At one time she slept above a hot air vent on the sidewalk on the Upper East Side of Manhattan, in the midst of some of the most expensive real estate in the world. Sometimes she was observed defecating in her clothes or on the sidewalk. She hurled insults at strangers and refused to go to a shelter, preferring to live in the streets, despite the obvious dangers of potential attack and the risks of exposure to the elements.

In New York, a program had begun in the early 1980s to provide outreach services to the homeless people in need of psychological treatment. Teams of specialists, each consisting of a nurse, a social worker, and a psychiatrist, were charged with the task of identifying and monitoring behaviorally disordered homeless people, helping them obtain services, bringing them soup and sandwiches, and taking them to the hospital if they were deemed to represent an immediate threat to themselves or others under the authority provided by the state laws governing psychiatric commitment, even if it was against the individual's will. In 1987, however, the standing orders for the team were broadened, requiring them to pick up disturbed homeless individuals who they felt posed a foreseeable, if not necessarily an immediate threat to themselves or others, and to bring them to a psychiatric facility for treatment, either with or without their consent. Joyce Brown was the first individual that the teams had involuntarily committed under the expanded guidelines for commitment.

"The Wild Man of West 96th Street." Larry Hogue, the so-called Wild Man of West 96th St. in New York City, has become a symbol of the cracks in the mental health, criminal justice, and social services systems.

At Bellevue Psychiatric Hospital where she was brought for evaluation, Brown was diagnosed by three psychiatrists as a paranoid schizophrenic who held delusional beliefs, and she was judged to be in need of treatment. Joyce Brown decided to fight back. She claimed that she was sane and had a basic right to live her life as she saw fit, even if it offended other people. As long as she committed no crime, what right did society have to deprive her of her liberty? Yes, she admitted, she had defecated in the streets. But there were no public rest rooms available, and establishments such as restaurants had refused her access.

Brown enlisted the aid of the local chapter of the American Civil Liberties Union (ACLU). ACLU psychiatrists also examined Brown and found her behavior not to be abnormal. A hearing was held before a judge to decide whether Brown was to remain in the hospital. The judge ruled in favor of Joyce Brown, but the city had the ruling overturned on appeal. Brown's lawyers then appealed that ruling. While the case meandered its way through the courts, Joyce Brown remained in the hospital, although the doctors were prevented from treating her with antipsychotic drugs against her will. Because she refused medication, the doctors released her, claiming there was little they could do for her.

Brown believed that the issue was not the normality of her behavior but the failure of society to provide decent housing for the underprivileged. Lacking the means to afford housing, she claimed to have the right to live her life as she saw fit, even if it meant living on the street. The mayor at the time, Ed Koch, defended his program to an interviewer. The

city had held her against her will, he said, not because she offended passersby, but because it was compassionate to help those who cannot fend for themselves.

Joyce Brown? Where is she now? Having won her fight not to be treated for mental illness, Brown was recently seen and heard ranting and raving on West 42nd Street, near a Travelers Inn where she has stayed from time to time (Wickenhaver, 1992). And what of the outreach program that forcibly removed Joyce Brown from the street? A follow-up study of the first year of implementation of the program to involuntarily remove psychiatrically disturbed homeless people from the streets and provide them psychiatric care in a hospital setting found that half of those initially treated in a city hospital were transferred for long-term care to a state psychiatric center (Marcos et al., 1990). The investigators believe that many of those transferred to the state psychiatric facility were severely impaired and would most probably have deteriorated further, both physically and psychologically, had they not been removed from the streets and involuntarily placed in a hospital.

The cases of Larry Hogue and Joyce Brown touch on the more general issue of how to balance the rights of the individual with the rights of society. Do people, for example, have the right to live on the streets under unsanitary conditions? There are those who argue that a just and humane society has the right and responsibility to care for people who are perceived to be incapable of protecting their own best interests, even if "care" means involuntarily committing them to a psychiatric institution. Do people who are obviously mentally disturbed have the right to refuse treatment? Do psychiatric institutions have the right to inject them with antipsychotic and other drugs against their will? When severely disturbed people break the law, should society respond to them with the criminal justice system or with the mental health system?

In this chapter we consider psychiatric commitment and other issues that arise from society's response to abnormal behavior, such as the rights of patients in institutions, the use of the insanity defense in criminal cases, and the responsibility of professionals to warn individuals who may be placed at risk by the dangerous behavior of their clients. We see that the standard for psychiatric commitment rests, in part, on a determination of dangerousness. We thus consider whether health professionals can predict dangerousness. The chapter concludes with a discussion of two major challenges faced by professionals today: meeting the needs of homeless people with mental disorders and seeking ways of preventing or lessening the impact of abnormal behaviors in society.

PSYCHIATRIC COMMITMENT

Legal placement of people in psychiatric institutions against their will is called **civil**, or psychiatric, **commitment**. Through civil commitment, individuals who are deemed to be mentally disordered and to be a threat to themselves or others may be involuntarily confined to psychiatric institutions to provide them with treatment and help ensure their own safety and that of others. Civil commitment should be distinguished from legal or criminal commitment, in which an individual who has been acquitted of a crime by reason of insanity is placed in a psychiatric institution for treatment. In **legal commitment**, a criminal's unlawful act is judged by a court of law to be the result of a mental disorder or defect that should be dealt with by having the individual committed to a psychiatric hospital where treatment can be provided, rather than having the individual incarcerated in a prison.

Civil commitment should also be distinguished from voluntary hospitalization, in which an individual voluntarily seeks treatment in a psychiatric institution, and can, with adequate notice, leave the institution when she or he so desires. Even in such cases, however, when hospital staff perceive a voluntary patient who is requesting discharge to present a threat to her or his own welfare or to others, the staff

may petition the court to change the patient's legal status from voluntary to involuntary.

Involuntary placement of an individual in a psychiatric hospital usually requires that a petition be filed by a relative or a professional. Psychiatric examiners may be empowered by the court to evaluate the person in a timely fashion, after which a judge hears psychiatric testimony and decides whether or not to commit the individual. In the event of commitment, the law usually requires periodic legal review and recertification of the patient's involuntary status. The legal process is intended to ensure that people are not indefinitely "warehoused" in psychiatric hospitals. Hospital staff must demonstrate the need for continued inpatient treatment.

Legal safeguards are usually in place to protect people's civil rights in commitment proceedings. Defendants have the right to due process and to be assisted by an attorney, for example. On the other hand, when defendants are deemed to present a clear and imminent threat to themselves or others, the court may order immediate hospitalization until a more formal commitment hearing can be held. Such emergency powers are usually limited to a specific period, like 72 hours. During this time a formal commitment petition must be filed with the court or the individual has a right to be discharged.

Standards for psychiatric commitment have been tightened over the past generation, and the rights of individuals who are subject to commitment proceedings more strictly protected. In the past, psychiatric abuses were more commonplace. People were often committed without clear evidence that they posed a threat. Not until 1979, in fact, did the

Should she be committed to a psychiatric institution? People must be judged as dangerous in order to be psychiatrically hospitalized against their wills. This photograph of emergency workers pulling a woman away from a ledge after she threatened to jump leaves little doubt about the dangerousness of her behavior. But professionals have not demonstrated they can reliably predict future dangerousness.

U.S. Supreme Court rule, in *Addington v. Texas,* that in order for individuals to be hospitalized involuntarily, they must be judged to be both "mentally ill" and to present clear and present danger to themselves or others.

Few would argue that contemporary tightening of civil commitment laws better protects the rights of the individual. Some call for the complete abolition of psychiatric commitment, however, on the grounds that commitment deprives the individual of liberty in the name of therapy, and that such loss of liberty cannot be justified in a free society. One vocal and persistent critic of the civil commitment statutes is psychiatrist Thomas Szasz (Szasz, 1970a). Szasz argues that the label of *mental illness* is a societal invention which transforms social deviance into medical illness. In Szasz's view, people should not be deprived of their liberty because their behavior is perceived to be different or socially disruptive. According to Szasz, people who violate the law should be prosecuted for criminal behavior, not confined to a psychiatric hospital. Although psychiatric commitment may prevent some people from acting violently, it *does* violence to many more by depriving them of liberty:

> The mental patient, we say, *may be* dangerous: he may harm himself or someone else. But we, society, *are* dangerous: we rob him of his good name and of his liberty, and subject him to tortures called "treatments" (Szasz, 1970b, p. 279).

Szasz's strident opposition to institutional psychiatry and his condemnation of psychiatric commitment have focused attention on abuses in the mental health system. Szasz has also convinced many professionals to question the legal, ethical, and moral questions raised by coercive psychiatric treatment in the forms of involuntary hospitalization and forced medication. Many caring and concerned professionals draw the line at abolishing psychiatric commitment, however. They argue that people may not be acting in their considered best interests when they threaten suicide or harm to others, or when their behavior becomes so disorganized that they cannot meet their basic needs.

PREDICTING DANGEROUSNESS

In order to be psychiatrically committed, people must be judged to be dangerous to themselves or others. Professionals are thus responsible for making accurate predictions of dangerousness to determine whether people should be involuntarily hospitalized or maintained involuntarily in the hospital. But how accurate are professionals in predicting dangerousness? Do

Who is the most dangerous?   Is it the apparently drunk driver (A)? Is it the institutionalized psychiatric patient (B)? Or is it the scheming corporate executives (C)? Critics of the mental health system, such as psychiatrist Thomas Szasz, point out that drunk drivers account for more injuries and deaths than paranoid schizophrenics, although paranoid schizophrenics are more likely to be committed. Others have suggested that those corporate executives who knowingly make decisions jeopardizing the health of employees and consumers to maximize profits are guilty of corporate violence that accounts for more deaths and injuries than other types of crime.

(A)   (B)   (C)

professionals have special skills or clinical wisdom that renders their predictions accurate, or are their predictions no more accurate than those of laypeople?

Psychiatric raters in one study were able to agree among themselves fairly well in their assessments of dangerousness to self and others and of the need for psychiatric commitment of patients seen for psychiatric evaluation in an emergency room setting (Lidz et al., 1989). These results do not mean that the psychiatrists were correct in their judgments, but rather that their judgments were reliable in that the raters tended to agree with each other.

Although predictions of dangerousness by mental health professionals may be fairly reliable, there is little research evidence to support their validity—that is, their accuracy. In one study, for example, two psychiatrists examined each of 257 people who were accused of felony crimes but remanded to a psychiatric hospital because they were judged incompetent to stand trial (Coccoza & Steadman, 1979). The psychiatrists judged 60% of the defendants as dangerous and 40% as not dangerous. The subjects were then followed through their hospitalizations and for a period of 3 years after discharge. The results showed that the people judged to be dangerous by the psychiatrists were actually slightly *less* likely (14% versus 16%) than those judged nondangerous to be rearrested for violent crimes.

There is apparently a general tendency for professionals to *overpredict* dangerousness—that is, to label many individuals as dangerous when they are not (Monahan, 1981). The American Psychological Association (1978) and the American Psychiatric Association (1974) have both gone on record as stating that neither psychologists nor psychiatrists, respectively, can predict violence among the people they treat. The prediction problem has been cited by some as grounds for the abandonment of dangerousness as a criterion for civil commitment (Siegel, 1973; Rabkin & Zitrin, 1982).

Nor is it clear that people with mental disorders are especially prone to violence toward others. People with mental disorders who have no history of violent behavior are no more likely than the general population to exhibit dangerous behavior in the future (Monahan, 1981).

People with mental disorders who have no prior history of violent behavior are actually no more likely than the general population to exhibit dangerous behavior in the future.

Nor does the research evidence support the public perception that schizophrenics, as a group, are more violent or dangerous than nonschizophrenics (Monahan & Steadman, 1983). (However, some schizophrenics, like some nonschizophrenics, are indeed violent.)

Despite the evidence, therapists may err on the side of caution and overpredict the potential for dangerous behavior because they believe that failure to predict violence may have more serious consequences than overprediction. On the other hand, overprediction of dangerousness deprives many people of liberty on the basis of fears that turn out to be groundless. According to Szasz and other critics of the practice of psychiatric commitment, the commitment of the many to prevent the violence of the few is a form of preventive detention that violates the basic principles on which the United States was founded.

Problems in Predicting Dangerousness

Various factors are believed to account for inaccurate predictions of dangerousness, including the following.

■ **THE POST-HOC PROBLEM**   Recognizing violent tendencies after a violent incident occurs (post hoc) is easier than predicting it (ad hoc). It is often said that hindsight is 20/20. Like Monday morning quarterbacking, it is easier to piece together fragments of people's prior behaviors as evidence of their violent tendencies *after* they have committed acts of violence. Predicting a violent act before the fact is a more difficult task, however.

The problem of major depression provides another example. Clinicians often have little difficulty (post hoc) finding social, financial, and other factors in patients' circumstances that could be said to have contributed to a major depressive episode. Yet many people are in similar difficult social and financial situations, and it remains difficult (ad hoc) to predict which ones will develop a major depressive episode.

■ **THE PROBLEM IN LEAPING FROM THE GENERAL TO THE SPECIFIC**   Generalized perceptions of violent tendencies may not predict specific acts of violence. Most people who have "general tendencies" toward violence may never act out on them. Nor is classification within a diagnostic category that is associated with aggressive or dangerous behavior, such as antisocial personality disorder, a sufficient basis for predicting specific violent acts in individuals (Bloom & Rogers, 1987).

■ **PROBLEMS IN DEFINING DANGEROUS-NESS** One difficulty in assessing the predictability of dangerousness is the lack of agreement in defining the criteria for labeling behavior as violent or dangerous. There is no universal agreement on the definition of violence or dangerousness. Most people would agree that crimes such as murder, rape, and assault are acts of violence. There is less agreement, even among authorities, for labeling other acts—for example, driving recklessly, harshly criticizing one's spouse or children, destroying property, selling drugs, shoving into people at a tavern, or stealing cars—as violent or dangerous.

Szasz argues that decisions on which dangerous acts are considered grounds for commitment are value judgments:

> Drunken drivers are dangerous both to themselves and to others. They injure and kill many more people than, for example, persons with paranoid delusions of persecution. Yet, people labeled "paranoid" are readily committable, while drunken drivers are not.
> Some types of dangerous behavior are even rewarded. Race-car drivers, trapeze artists, and astronauts receive admiration and applause. . . . Thus, it is not dangerousness in general that is at issue, but rather the manner in which one is dangerous (Szasz, 1963, p. 46).

Professional boxers, football players, and hockey players reap huge financial rewards and public acclaim for engaging in violent and dangerous behaviors that are *socially acceptable*. Some suggest that corporate executives who expose consumers or employees to risks to their health or personal safety are guilty of committing corporate violence (or *suite* crime as opposed to *street* crime), which accounts for more deaths and injuries than all other types of crimes (Monahan et al., 1979). Consider, for example, the dangerousness of business owners and corporate executives who produce and market cigarettes despite widespread knowledge of the harm caused by these substances. Clearly, the determination of which behaviors are regarded as dangerous involves moral and political judgments within a given social context (Monahan, 1981).

■ **BASE-RATE PROBLEMS** The prediction of dangerousness is complicated by the fact that violent acts like murder, assault, or suicide are infrequent or rare events at the individual level within the general population, even if newspaper headlines sensationalize them regularly. Other rare events—like earthquakes—are also difficult to predict with any degree of certainty concerning when or where they will strike.

The relative difficulty of making predictions of infrequent or rare events is known as the base-rate problem. Consider the example the problem of suicide prediction. If the suicide rate in a given year has a low base rate of about 1% of a clinical population, the likelihood of accurately predicting that any given person in this population will commit suicide is not very favorable. You would be correct 99% of the time if you predicted that any given individual in this population would *not* commit suicide in a given year. But to predict the nonoccurrence of suicide in every case would mean that you would fail to predict the relatively few cases in which suicide does occur, even though virtually all of your predictions would likely be correct. Yet predicting the one likely case of suicide among each hundred people in the population is likely to be tricky. You would be wrong most of the time if you predicted that three or more people would commit suicide in a given year (even if 1 of the 3 did commit suicide).

When clinicians make predictions, they weigh the relative risks of incorrectly failing to predict the occurrence of a behavior (a false negative) against the consequences of incorrectly predicting it (a false positive). Clinicians often err on the side of caution by overpredicting dangerousness. Say that a person makes a veiled threat to harm herself or himself ("I don't know how I can go on. I often feel that I'd like to take all the pills at once and end it all."). The clinician might decide that the person is a serious suicide risk and needs to be hospitalized, voluntarily or involuntarily. If the person is hospitalized and suicide does not occur, the clinician is in a position to claim that the hospitalization may have prevented suicide. On the other hand, had the clinician not sought commitment and had the person committed suicide, the clinician could be accused of exercising poor professional judgment. From the clinician's perspective, erring on the side of caution might seem like a no-lose situation. Yet many people who are committed to an institution under such circumstances are denied their liberty when they would not actually have taken their lives.

■ **THE UNLIKELIHOOD OF DISCLOSURE OF DIRECT THREATS OF VIOLENCE** How likely is it that truly dangerous people will disclose their intentions to a health professional who is evaluating them or to their own therapist? The client in therapy is not likely to inform a therapist of a clear threat such as "I'm going to kill _____ next Wednesday morning." Threats are more likely to be vague and nonspecific, as in "I'm so sick of _____; I could kill her," or "I swear he's driving me to murder." In such cases, therapists must infer dangerousness from hostile gestures and veiled threats. Vague, indirect threats of violence are less reliable indicators of dangerousness than specific, direct threats.

■ THE DIFFICULTY OF PREDICTING BEHAVIOR IN THE COMMUNITY FROM BEHAVIOR IN THE HOSPITAL

Much of the research on the accuracy of clinical predictions of dangerousness is based on the predictions of the long-term dangerousness of hospitalized patients when they are discharged. Clinicians largely base such predictions on patients' behavior in the hospital. Violent or dangerous behavior may be situation specific, however. A model patient who is able to adapt to a structured environment like that of a psychiatric hospital may be unable to cope with pressures of independent communal life. Accuracy is improved when predictions of potential violence are based on the person's past community behavior, such as a history of violent incidents, rather than on the person's behavior in the hospital setting (Klassen & O'Connor, 1988).

In sum, it may be expecting too much of clinicians to ask them to make long-term predictions of dangerousness. It is one thing to predict dangerousness of people in emergency situations in which they appear to be "out of control" and may be threatening others verbally or brandishing a weapon. It is another to predict potential violence in the indeterminate future. The results of one study support the view that predictions of imminent dangerousness are reasonably accurate. This study (McNeil & Binder, 1987) examined predictions of imminent dangerousness that were made at the time of admission following an emergency civil commitment. People who were judged by hospital staff to be dangerous when admitted to the hospital engaged in more acts of violence during the first 72 hours of hospitalization than did involuntarily committed patients who were not considered dangerous at the point of admission. As many as 2 out of 3 people who were judged to be violent to others engaged in a violent behavior within the first 3 days of hospitalization.

Note that the McNeil and Binder (1987) study did not address the question of whether the people who were judged to be imminently dangerous at admission would have committed dangerous acts *in the community* if they had *not* been hospitalized. To learn whether such people would be violent if they were left in the community, researchers would have to conduct a controlled study in which people who are judged to be imminently dangerous are assigned at random to be either hospitalized or permitted to remain in the community (Monahan, 1981). Such a study is unlikely to be conducted because it would require that people who are believed to be significant threats to themselves or others be left to their own devices.

PATIENTS' RIGHTS

We have considered society's right to hospitalize involuntarily people who are judged to be mentally ill and to pose a threat to themselves or others. What happens following commitment, however? Do involuntarily committed patients have the right to receive or demand treatment? Or can society just warehouse them in psychiatric facilities indefinitely without treating them? Consider the opposite side of the coin as well: May people who are involuntarily committed refuse treatment? Such issues—which have been brought into public light by landmark court cases—fall under the umbrella of *patients' rights*. Generally speaking, the history of abuses in the mental health system, as highlighted in such popular books and movies as *One Flew Over the Cuckoo's Nest*, have led to a tightening of standards of care and adoption of legal guarantees to protect patients' rights. The legal status of some issues, such as the right to treatment, remains unsettled, however.

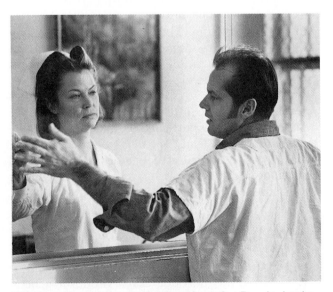

What are the rights of mental patients? Popular books and films such as *One Flew Over the Cuckoo's Nest* with Jack Nicholson and Louise Fletcher have highlighted many of the abuses of mental hospitals. In recent years, a tightening of standards of care and the adoption of legal safeguards have protected the rights of mental patients.

Right to Treatment

One might assume that mental health institutions which accept people for treatment will provide them with treatment. Not until the landmark federal court case of *Wyatt v. Stickney* (1972), however, did a federal court establish a minimum standard of care to be provided by hospitals. The case was a class action suit against Stickney, the Commissioner of Mental Health for the State of Alabama, brought on behalf of Ricky Wyatt, a mentally retarded young man, and other patients at a state hospital and school in Tuscaloosa.

The federal district court in Alabama held both that the hospital had failed to provide treatment to Wyatt and others and that living conditions at the hospital were inadequate and dehumanizing. The court described the hospital dormitories as "barnlike structures" that afforded no privacy to the residents. The bathrooms had no partitions between stalls, the patients were outfitted with shoddy clothes, the wards were filthy and crowded, the kitchens were unsanitary, and the food was substandard. In addition, the staff was inadequate in numbers and poorly trained. The court held that mental hospitals must, at a minimum, provide the following:

1. A humane psychological and physical environment,
2. Qualified staff in numbers sufficient to administer adequate treatment, and
3. Individualized treatment plans (*Wyatt v. Stickney*, 334 Supp., p. 1343, 1975).

The court established that the state was obliged to provide adequate treatment for people who were involuntarily confined to psychiatric hospitals. The court further ruled that to commit people to hospitals for treatment involuntarily, and then not to provide treatment, violated their rights to due process under the law.

The court specifically required at least 2 psychiatrists, 12 nurses, 1 doctoral-level psychologist, and 2 master's-level social workers for every 250 patients. Physical, recreational, and social conditions had to be improved, as shown in Table 15.1. Although the ruling of the court was limited to Alabama, many other states have followed suit and revised their mental hospital standards to ensure that involuntarily committed patients are not denied basic rights.

Other court cases have further clarified patients' rights.

■ **O'CONNOR V. DONALDSON** The 1975 case of Kenneth Donaldson is another landmark in patients' rights. Donaldson, a former patient at a state hospital

Table 15.1 Partial Listing of The Patient's Bill of Rights Under *Wyatt v. Stickney*

1. Patients have rights to privacy and to be treated with dignity.
2. Patients shall be treated under the least restrictive conditions that can be provided to meet the purposes that commitment was intended to serve.
3. Patients shall have rights to visitation and telephone privileges unless special restrictions apply.
4. Patients have the right to refuse excessive or unnecessary medication. In addition, medication may not be used as a form of punishment.
5. Patients shall not be kept in restraints or isolation except in emergency conditions in which their behavior is likely to pose a threat to themselves or others and less restrictive restraints are not feasible.
6. Patients shall not be subject to experimental research unless their rights to informed consent are protected.
7. Patients have the right to refuse potentially hazardous or unusual treatments, such as lobotomy, electroconvulsive shock, or aversive behavioral treatments.
8. Unless it is dangerous or inappropriate to the treatment program, patients shall have the right to wear their own clothing and keep possessions.
9. Patients have rights to regular exercise and to opportunities to spend time outdoors.
10. Patients have rights to suitable opportunities to interact with the opposite gender.
11. Patients have rights to humane and decent living conditions.
12. No more than six patients shall be housed in a room and screen or curtains must be provided to afford a sense of privacy.
13. No more than eight patients shall share one toilet facility, with separate stalls provided for privacy.
14. Patients have a right to nutritionally balanced diets.
15. Patients shall not be required to perform work that is performed for the sake of maintenance of the facility.

in Florida, sued two hospital doctors on the grounds that he had been involuntarily confined without receiving treatment for 14 years, despite the fact that he posed no serious threat to himself or others. Donaldson had been originally committed on the basis of a petition filed by his father who had perceived him

Kenneth Donaldson. Donaldson points to the U.S. Supreme Court decision which ruled that people who are considered mentally ill but not dangerous cannot be confined against their will if they can be maintained safely in the community.

as delusional. Despite the facts that Donaldson received no treatment during his confinement and was denied grounds privileges and occupational training, his repeated requests for discharge were denied by the hospital staff. He was finally released when he threatened to sue the hospital. Once discharged, Donaldson did sue his doctors and was awarded damages of $38,500 from O'Connor, the superintendent of the hospital. The case was eventually argued before the U.S. Supreme Court.

Court testimony established that although the hospital staff had not perceived Donaldson to be dangerous during his hospitalization, they had refused to release him. The hospital doctors argued that continued hospitalization had been necessary because they had believed that Donaldson was unlikely to adapt successfully to community living. The doctors had prescribed antipsychotic medications as a course of treatment, but Donaldson had refused to take them because of his Christian Science beliefs. As a result, he received only custodial care.

The U.S. Supreme Court held that "mental illness [alone] cannot justify a State's locking a person up against his will and keeping him indefinitely in simple custodial confinement. . . . There is still no constitutional basis for confining such persons involuntarily if they are dangerous to no one and can live safely in freedom" (p. 2493). The ruling addressed patients who are not considered dangerous. It is not yet clear whether the same constitutional rights would be applied to committed patients who are judged to be dangerous.

In its ruling on *O'Connor v. Donaldson*, the Supreme Court did not deal with the larger issue of

the rights of patients to receive treatment. The ruling does not directly obligate state institutions to treat involuntarily committed, nondangerous people, because the institutions may elect to release them instead.

The Supreme Court did touch on the larger issue of society's rights to protect itself from individuals who are perceived as offensive. In delivering the opinion of the court, Justice Potter Stewart wrote,

> May the State fence in the harmless mentally ill solely to save its citizens from exposure to those whose ways are different? One might as well ask if the State, to avoid public uneasiness, could incarcerate all who are physically unattractive or socially eccentric. Mere public intolerance or animosity cannot constitutionally justify the deprivation of a person's physical liberty (*O'Connor v. Donaldson*, 95 S. Ct. 2486, 1975).

■ ***YOUNGBERG V. ROMEO*** In a 1982 case, *Youngberg v. Romeo*, the U.S. Supreme Court more directly addressed the issue of the patient's right to treatment. Even so, it seemed to retreat somewhat from the patients' rights standards established in *Wyatt v. Stickney*. Nicholas Romeo, a 33-year-old profoundly retarded man who was unable to talk or care for himself, had been institutionalized in a state hospital and school in Pennsylvania. While in the state facility he had a history of injuring himself through his violent behavior and was often kept in restraints. The case was brought by the patient's mother who alleged that the hospital was negligent in not preventing his injuries and for routinely using physical restraints for prolonged periods while not providing adequate treatment.

The Supreme Court ruled that involuntarily committed patients, like Nicholas, have a right to be confined in less restrictive conditions, such as being freed from physical restraints whenever it is reasonable to do so. The Supreme Court ruling also included a limited recognition of the committed patient's right to treatment. The Court held that institutionalized patients have a right to minimally adequate training to help them function free of physical restraints, but only to the extent that such training can be provided in *reasonable* safety. The determination of reasonableness, the Court held, should be made on the basis of the judgment of the qualified professionals in the facility. The federal courts should not interfere with the internal operations of the facility, the Court held, because "there's no reason to think judges or juries are better qualified than appropriate professionals in making such decisions" (p. 2462). The courts should only second-guess the judgments of qualified professionals, the Supreme Court held, when such judgments are determined to depart from professional standards of practice. But the Supreme Court did not address the broader issues of the rights of committed patients to receive training that might eventually enable them to function independently outside the hospital.

Right to Refuse Treatment

Consider the following scenario. A person, John Citizen, is involuntarily committed to a mental hospital for treatment. The hospital staff determines that John suffers from a psychotic disorder, paranoid schizophrenia, and should be treated with antipsychotic medications, such as major tranquilizers. John, however, decides not to comply with treatment. He claims that the hospital has no right to treat him against his will. The hospital staff seeks a court order to mandate treatment, arguing that it makes little sense to involuntarily commit people unless the hospital is empowered to treat them as the staff deems fit.

Does an involuntary patient, like John, have the right to refuse treatment? If so, does this right conflict with states' rights to commit people to mental institutions to receive treatment for mental disorders? One might also wonder whether people who are judged in need of involuntary hospitalization are competent enough to make decisions about which treatments are in their best interests.

The rights of committed patients to refuse psychotropic medications was tested in the 1979 case of *Rogers v. Okin,* in which a Massachusetts federal district court imposed an injunction on a Boston state hospital that prohibited the forced medication of patients except in emergency situations. The court ruled that committed patients could not be forcibly medicated, except in the case of emergency—for example, when patients' behavior posed a significant threat to themselves or others. The court recognized that a patient may be unwise to refuse medication, but that a patient with or without a mental disorder has the right to exercise bad judgment so long as the effects of the "error" do not impose "a danger of physical harm to himself, fellow patients, or hospital staff" (p. 1367).

Many professionals were outraged by this court ruling. As one psychiatrist put it, patients who refused medications would literally find themselves "rotting with their rights on" (Gutheil, 1980). Others, however, viewed the court decision in more favorable terms, seeing it as a means of ensuring that hospitalized patients would be treated with greater dignity and would be more likely to receive proper treatment (Cole, 1982).

Although statutes and regulations vary from state to state, cases in which hospitalized patients refuse medications are often first brought before an independent review panel. If the panel rules against the patient, the case may then be brought before a judge who makes the final decision about whether or not the patient is to be forcibly medicated.

In actual practice, the number of refusals of medication is generally low, about 10% overall (Appelbaum & Hoges, 1986). Furthermore, between 70 and 90% of refusals that reach the review process are eventually overridden (Appelbaum & Hoges, 1986).

Let us note that voluntarily admitted patients have always had the right to refuse treatment. They may also sign themselves out of the hospital, even if their doctors believe that they should remain. Hospitals may petition the court to change patients' commitment status from voluntary to involuntary if the staff believes that patients are dangerous and in need of treatment, however.

Most professionals, including many of those who initially challenged the rights of involuntarily hospitalized mental patients to refuse treatment, now recognize that some type of independent review board is useful to ensure that the type of treatment that patients receive is appropriate. The adoption of carefully conducted review procedures may help reduce the potential for inappropriate prescription of medications (Appelbaum, 1988). Some psychiatrists, like Paul Appelbaum, go further and suggest that the medication of all involuntary patients should be subject to an independent review process, whether the patients refuse them or not, so that compliant patients do not receive treatment that is inferior to that of resistant patients.

The incorporation of independent review panels into hospital practices is a laudable goal. But it raises the question of who is to be charged with handling this review process. In Appelbaum's view, review panels should be controlled by psychiatrists because psychiatrists are best prepared by virtue of their training and experience to evaluate the need for medications and other biological treatments, such as ECT. It might be argued, however, that allowing psychiatrists to monitor the use of medications is tantamount to allowing the fox to guard the chicken coop. Psychiatrists may be unwilling to second-guess their colleagues. Appelbaum recognizes that psychiatrists who review a patient's refusal to accept medication generally overrule the patient in favor of the prescribing physician. As he puts it, "When physicians act like judges, they still tend to think like physicians" (p. 417). An independent review panel that incorporates the opinions of psychiatrists and other mental health professionals might provide more of a forum for discussion on divergent opinions.

Our discussion of legal issues and abnormal behavior now turns to the controversy concerning the **insanity defense**.

THE INSANITY DEFENSE

As President Ronald Reagan stepped out of the Washington Hilton on March 31, 1981, gunshots rang out. Secret Service agents pulled out their weapons and formed a human shield around the president as another agent shoved him into a waiting limousine, which then sped away to a hospital. At first, the president did not know that he had been wounded. He said later that it sounded like firecrackers. Agents seized the gunman, John Hinckley, a 25-year-old drifter. Not only had the president been wounded. James Brady, his press secretary, was hit by a stray bullet that shattered his spine, leaving him partially paralyzed. A Secret Service agent was also shot.

Hinckley had left a letter in his hotel room revealing his hope that his assassination of the president would impress a young actress, Jodie Foster. Hinckley had never met Foster but had a crush on her.

There was never any question at the trial that Hinckley had fired the wounding bullets, but the prosecutor was burdened to demonstrate beyond a reasonable doubt that Hinckley had had the capacity, at the time of the assassination attempt, to control his

Jodie Foster. John Hinckley reportedly attempted to assassinate President Reagan in order to impress Ms. Foster, whom he had seen in the film *Taxi Driver* but never met. In the film, Robert DeNiro, who portrayed a paranoid schizophrenic, rescued Foster's character from a life of prostitution. Hinckley's attorneys claimed that their client experienced similar rescue fantasies.

behavior and appreciate its wrongfulness. The defense presented testimony that portrayed Hinckley as an incompetent schizophrenic who suffered under the delusion that he would achieve a "magic union" with Foster as a result of killing the president. The prosecutor portrayed Hinckley as making a conscious and willful choice to kill the president. The prosecution further argued that whatever mental disorder Hinckley might have had did not prevent him from controlling his behavior.

The jury sided with the defense, finding Hinckley not guilty by reason of insanity.

 It is true that a man who was seen by millions of television viewers attempting to assassinate the president of the United States was found not guilty by a court of law. He was found "not guilty by reason of insanity."

The verdict led to a public outcry across the country, with many calling for the abolition of the insanity defense. Public opinion polls taken several days after the Hinckley verdict was returned showed that the

Was he insane when he committed his crime? John W. Hinckley, Jr., attempted to assassinate President Ronald Reagan in 1981 but was found not guilty by reason of insanity. The public outrage over the Hinckley verdict led to a reexamination of the insanity plea in many states.

public had little confidence in the psychiatric testimony that had been offered at the trial (Slater & Hans, 1984). One objection focused on the fact that once the defense presented evidence to support a plea of insanity, the federal prosecutor had the responsibility of proving *beyond a reasonable doubt* that the defendant was sane. It can be difficult enough to demonstrate that someone is sane or insane in the present, so imagine the problems that attend proving that someone *was* sane at the time a criminal act was committed.

In the aftermath of the Hinckley verdict, the federal government and some states have changed their statutes to shift the burden of proof to the defense to prove *insanity.* This shift relieves the prosecution of the burden of proving sanity beyond a reasonable doubt. In some states, such as Idaho and Montana, the insanity defense had been abolished long before the Hinckley case. Even the American Psychiatric Association went on record as stating that psychiatric expert witnesses should not be called on to render opinions about whether defendants can control their behavior. In the opinion of the psychiatric association, these are not medical judgments that psychiatrists are trained to provide.

Despite the few celebrated cases, like the Hinckley case, in which the insanity defense was put in the public spotlight, successful insanity defenses typically occur in fewer than 1% of cases in which they are pleaded (Pasewark, 1981; Phillips et al., 1988; Rogers et al., 1983; Weiner, 1985). Nor do psychiatric experts offer conflicting testimony to the degree that the public generally believes. In a study in Alaska, psychiatrists who were called as expert witnesses agreed with each other's testimony 79% of the time (Phillips & Wolf, 1988). Conflicting psychiatric testimony was presented in only 1.5% of all criminal cases in the Alaskan study in which psychiatric testimony was presented, and in 7 of 10 of these cases the defendant was found guilty. However uncommon, when battles between opposing witnesses did occur, the result was unlikely to lead to acquittal.

Perceptions of the use of the insanity defense tend to stray from the facts. A study in Wyoming asked state legislators to estimate the percentage of cases that had resulted in an insanity verdict among 21,012 felony cases that were tried in the state. The legislators, presumably knowledgeable about the law in their own state, estimated, on the average, that the insanity plea had been offered in 21% of these cases and that successful defenses occurred in about 8.5% of felony cases overall (Pasewark & Pantle, 1979). Laypeople who were interviewed provided estimates that were about twice as large as those given by the state legislators (Pasewark & Seidenzahl, 1979). In fact, the actual frequency of insanity pleas was 102

(less than 0.5% of the total cases) and only one defendant in these cases was acquitted. The net result of these findings is that changes in the insanity defense, or its abolition, may prevent some few flagrant cases of abuse, but they are not likely to afford the public much broader protection.

Although the public outrage over the Hinckley and other celebrated insanity verdicts has led to a reexamination of the insanity defense (see feature "The GBMI Verdict"), society has long held to the doctrine of free will as a basis for determining respon-

A CLOSER LOOK

The GBMI Verdict—Guilty But Mentally Ill

In 1975, well before the Hinckley verdict, Michigan became the first state to adopt a new legal standard—the GBMI, or "guilty-but-mentally-ill," verdict (Robey, 1978). The GBMI verdict offers juries the option of finding a defendant both guilty and mentally ill, if they determine that the defendant is mentally ill but that the mental illness did not cause the defendant to commit the crime. The GBMI verdict provides that people so convicted may be imprisoned but also receive treatment while in prison. Their mental condition may also be taken into account in future parole hearings (Maeder, 1985). In the wake of the Hinckley acquittal, six additional states adopted the GBMI verdict, with four of these states adopting the verdict in the very month following the Hinckley verdict (Maeder, 1985).

Although it is clear that the GBMI was intended to reduce the number of NGRI (not guilty by reason of insanity) verdicts, this outcome has apparently not occurred. In Michigan, for example, approximately the same number of insanity acquittals were returned in the years directly preceding and following the adoption of the GBMI alternative, approximately 50 to 60 per year (Smith & Hall, 1982). About 34 defendants per year, on the average, received the GBMI verdict in Michigan in the years following its passage, and these defendants would probably have been found guilty anyway had the GBMI verdict not been available (Smith & Hall, 1982). It is also clear that the availability of mental health treatment in prison settings, and the consideration of mental health criteria in parole hearings, is not limited to GBMI defendants. It appears that the GBMI verdict is a social experiment that has not yet proved its usefulness and is seen by some as merely a means of stigmatizing defendants who are found guilty as also being mentally ill (Maeder, 1985).

sibility for wrongdoing. The doctrine of free will, as applied to criminal responsibility, requires that people can be held guilty of a crime only if they are judged to have been in control of their actions at the time of commission of the crime. Not only must it be determined by a court of law that a defendant had committed a crime beyond a reasonable doubt, but the issue of the individual's state of mind must be considered as well in determining guilt. The court must thus rule not only on whether a crime was committed, but on whether or not an individual is held *morally responsible* and *deserving* of punishment. The insanity defense is based on the belief that when a criminal act derives from a distorted state of mind, and not from the exercise of free will, the individual should not be punished but rather treated for the underlying mental disorder. The insanity defense has a long legal history.

Legal Bases of the Insanity Defense

We can find in modern law three major court rulings that bear on the insanity defense. The first involved a case in Ohio in 1834 in which it was ruled that people cannot be held responsible if they are compelled to commit criminal actions because of impulses that they are unable to resist.

The second major legal test of the insanity defense is referred to as the M'Naghten rule, based on a case in England in 1843 of a Scotsman, Daniel M'Naghten, who had intended to assassinate the prime minister of England, Sir Robert Peel. Instead, he killed Peel's secretary whom he had mistaken for the prime minister. M'Naghten claimed that the voice of God had commanded him to kill Lord Peel. The English court acquitted M'Naghten on the basis of insanity, finding that the defendant had been ". . . labouring under such a defect of reason, from disease of the mind, as not to know the nature and quality of the act he was doing; or, if he did know it, that he did not know he was doing what was wrong." The M'Naghten rule, as it has come to be called, holds that people do not bear criminal responsibility if, by reason of a mental disease or defect, they either have no knowledge of their actions or are unable to tell right from wrong.

To find the third major case that helped lay the foundation for the modern insanity defense we must jump more than 100 years to 1954 and the case of *Durham v. United States*. In this case, the presiding judge, David Bazelon, held that the "accused [person] is not criminally responsible if his unlawful act was the product of mental disease or mental defect" (pp. 874–875). Under the Durham rule, juries were expected to decide not only whether the accused suffered from a mental disease or defect, but also whether this mental condition was causally connected to the criminal act. The court recognized that criminal intent is a precondition of criminal responsibility:

> The legal and moral traditions of the western world require that those who, of their own free will and with evil intent . . . commit acts which violate the law, shall be criminally responsible for those acts. Our traditions also require that where such acts stem from and are the product of a mental disease or defect . . . moral blame shall not attach, and hence there will not be criminal responsibility (*Durham v. United States*, 214 F2d 862, D.C. circ. 1954).

The intent of the Durham rule was to reject as outmoded the two earlier standards of legal insanity, the irresistible impulse rule and the "right–wrong" principle under the M'Naghton rule. Judge Bazelon argued that the "right–wrong test" was outmoded because the concept of "mental disease" is broader than the ability to recognize right from wrong. The legal basis of insanity should thus not be judged on but one feature of a mental disorder, such as deficient reasoning ability. The irresistible impulse test was denied because the court recognized that in certain cases, criminal acts arising from "mental disease or defect" may occur in a cool and calculating manner rather than in the manner of a sudden, irresistible impulse.

The Durham rule, however, has proved to be unworkable for several reasons, such as a lack of precise definitions of such terms as *mental disease* or *mental defect* (Fingarette, 1972; Maeder, 1985). Courts were confused, for example, about issues such as whether a personality disorder, like antisocial personality disorder, constituted a "disease." It also proved difficult for juries to draw conclusions about whether an individual's "mental disease" was causally connected to the criminal act. Without clear or precise definitions of terms, juries came to rely increasingly on expert psychiatric testimony, often serving as little more than rubber stamps as their verdicts endorsed the testimony of expert witnesses (Maeder, 1985).

By 1972, the Durham rule had failed and was replaced in many jurisdictions by a set of legal guidelines formulated by the American Law Institute (ALI) to define the legal basis of insanity (Maeder, 1985). These guidelines, which essentially combined the M'Naghten principle with the irresistible impulse principle, included the following provisions:

1. A person is not responsible for criminal conduct if at the time of such conduct as a result of mental disease or defect he lacks substantial capacity either to appreciate the criminality (wrongful-

ness) of his conduct or to conform his conduct to the requirements of law.

2. . . . the terms "mental disease or defect" do not include an abnormality manifested only by repeated criminal or otherwise antisocial conduct (American Law Institute, 1962, p. 66).

The first guideline incorporates aspects of the M'Naghten test (being unable to appreciate right from wrong) and the irresistible impulse test (being unable to conform one's behavior to the requirements of law) of insanity. The second guideline asserts that repeated criminal behavior (like a pattern of drug dealing) is not sufficient in itself to establish a mental disease or defect that might relieve the individual of criminal responsibility. Although many legal authorities believe that the ALI guidelines are an improvement over earlier tests, questions remain as to whether a jury composed of ordinary citizens can be expected to make complex judgments about the defendant's state of mind, even on the basis of expert testimony. Under the ALI guidelines, juries must determine whether defendants lack substantial capacity to be aware of, or capable of, conforming their behavior to the law. By adding the term *substantial capacity* to the legal test, the ALI guidelines may also broaden the legal basis of the insanity defense because this may imply that defendants need not be completely incapable of controlling their criminal actions in order to meet the legal test of not guilty by reason of insanity.

Under our system of justice, juries must struggle with the complex question of determining criminal responsibility, not merely criminal actions. But what of those individuals who successfully plead not guilty by reason of insanity? Should they be committed to a mental institution for a fixed sentence, as they might have been had they been incarcerated in a penal institution? Or should their commitments be of an indeterminate term and their release depend on their mental status? The legal basis for answering such questions was decided in the following case of Michael Jones, whose acquittal by reason of insanity resulted in involuntary commitment to a mental hospital for a period that turned out to be seven times longer than the maximum prison sentence for the crime.

■ **DETERMINING THE TERM OF CRIMINAL COMMITMENT** The issue of determinate versus indeterminate commitment was addressed in the case of Michael Jones (*Jones v. United States*), who was arrested in 1975 and charged with petty larceny for attempting to steal a jacket from a Washington, D.C., department store. Jones was first committed to a public mental hospital, St. Elizabeth's Hospital (which,

incidentally, is the hospital where John Hinckley remains committed as of this writing). Jones was diagnosed by a hospital psychologist as suffering from paranoid schizophrenia and was kept hospitalized until he was judged competent to stand trial, about 6 months later. Jones offered a plea of not guilty by reason of insanity, which the court accepted without challenge, remanding him to St. Elizabeth's. Despite the fact that Jones's crime carried a maximum sentence of 1 year in prison, Jones's repeated attempts to obtain release were denied in subsequent court hearings.

His appeal was eventually heard by the U.S. Supreme Court *7 years* after he was hospitalized. The Supreme Court reached its decision in 1983. It ruled against Jones's appeal and affirmed the decision of the lower courts that he was to remain in the hospital. The Supreme Court thereby established a principle that individuals who are acquitted by reason of insanity "constitute a special class that should be treated differently" than civilly committed individuals. They may be committed for an indefinite period to a mental institution under criteria that require a less stringent level of proof of dangerousness than would ordinarily be applied in cases of civil commitment.

 It is true that people who are found not guilty of a crime by reason of insanity may remain confined to a mental hospital indefinitely—for many years longer than they would have been sentenced to prison, if they had been found guilty.

Among other things, the Supreme Court ruling in *Jones v. the United States* provides that the usual and customary sentences that the law provides for particular crimes have no bearing on criminal commitment. In the words of the Court,

> different considerations underlie commitment of an insanity acquittee. As he was not convicted, he may not be punished. His confinement rests on his continuing illness and dangerousness. . . . There simply is no necessary correlation between severity of the offense and length of time necessary for recovery (*Jones v. United States*, 103 S.Ct. 3043, 1983).

The ruling held that a person who is criminally committed may be confined "to a mental institution until such time as he has regained his sanity or is no longer a danger to society" (p. 3053). As in the case of Michael Jones, insanity acquittees may remain confined in a mental institution for longer than they would have been sentenced to prison. It is also possible, however, that such persons could be released earlier than they might have been released from prison, if their "mental condition" is found to have improved. A person acquitted of a serious crime by virtue of the insanity defense may even be released within a few weeks or months, although, practically speaking, it is doubtful that improvement would be established so quickly. Public outrage over a speedy release, especially for a major crime, might also prevent rapid release.

The indeterminateness of legal or criminal commitment raises various questions. Is it reasonable to deny people like Michael Jones their liberty for an indefinite and possibly life-long term for a relatively minor crime, such as petty larceny? On the other hand, is justice served by acquitting perpetrators of heinous crimes by reason of insanity and then allowing them the opportunity for an early release if they are deemed by professionals to be able to rejoin society?

The Supreme Court's ruling in *Jones v. United States* seems to imply that one must separate the notion of legal sentencing from that of legal or criminal commitment. The former, in which sentences are scaled according to the seriousness of the crime, rests on the principle that the punishment should fit the crime. In legal or criminal commitment, however, persons acquitted of their crimes by reason of insanity are guiltless in the eyes of the law. They must be treated, not punished, until such time that their mental status has improved to the point which permits them to safely reenter society.

Perspectives on the Insanity Defense

The insanity defense places special burdens on juries. In assessing criminal responsibility, the jury is expected to determine not only that a crime was committed by the accused, but also the defendant's state of mind at the time of commission of the crime. In rejecting the Durham decision, courts have relieved psychiatrists and other expert witnesses from bearing the burden of responsibility for determining whether or not the defendant's behavior is a product of a "mental disease or defect." But is it reasonable to assume that juries of people from all walks of life are better able to assess defendants' states of mind than mental health professionals? In particular, how can a jury evaluate the testimony of expert conflicting witnesses? The task imposed on the jury is made even more difficult by the mandate to decide whether or not the defendant was mentally incapacitated *at the time* of the crime. The defendant's courtroom behavior may bear little resemblance to his or her behavior during the crime.

Another challenge to the insanity defense has been raised by Thomas Szasz and others who deny the existence of mental illness itself. If mental illness does not exist, then the insanity defense becomes groundless. Szasz argues that the insanity defense is ultimately degrading because it strips people of personal responsibility for their behavior. People who break laws are criminals, Szasz argues, and should be prosecuted and sentenced accordingly. Acquittal of defendants by reason of insanity treats them as nonpersons, as unfortunates who are not deemed to possess the basic human qualities of free choice, self-determination, and personal responsibility. We are each responsible for our behavior, Szasz contends, and we should each be held accountable for our misdeeds.

Szasz argues that the insanity defense has historically been invoked in crimes which were particularly heinous or perpetrated against persons of high social rank. When persons of low social rank commit crimes against persons of higher status, Szasz argues, the effect of the insanity defense is to direct attention away from the social ills that may have motivated the crime. Despite Szasz's contention, however, the insanity defense is invoked in many cases of less shocking crimes or in cases involving persons from similar social classes.

How, then, are we to evaluate the insanity defense? To abolish the insanity defense in all forms would be to reverse hundreds of years of a legal tradition that has recognized that people are not to be held responsible for their criminal behavior when their ability to control themselves is impaired by a mental disorder or defect.

Consider a hypothetical example. John Citizen commits a crime, say a heinous crime like murder, while acting on a delusional belief that the victim was intent on assassinating him. The accused claims that voices from his TV set informed him of the identity of the assailant and commanded him to kill the assailant to save himself and other potential victims. Cases like this are thankfully rare. Few mentally disturbed persons, even few psychotics, commit violent crimes, and even fewer commit murder.

In reaching a judgment on the insanity plea, we need to consider whether we believe that the law should allow special standards to apply in cases such as our hypothetical case, or whether one standard of criminal responsibility should apply to all. If we assert the legitimacy of the insanity defense in some cases, we still need a standard of insanity that can be interpreted and applied by juries of ordinary citizens. The furor over the Hinckley verdict suggests that issues concerning the insanity plea remain unsettled.

COMPETENCY TO STAND TRIAL

There is a basic rule of law that those who stand accused of crimes must be able to understand the charges and proceedings brought against them and be able to participate in their own defense. The concept of competency to stand trial should not be confused with the legal defense of insanity. A defendant can be held competent to stand trial but judged not guilty by reason of insanity. A clearly delusional person, for example, may understand the court proceedings and be able to confer with defense counsel, but still be acquitted by reason of insanity. On the other hand, a person may be incapable of standing trial at a particular time, but be tried and acquitted or convicted later on when competency is restored.

> **T**
> **oR**
> **F**
> It is true that a defendant can be held competent to stand trial but still be judged not guilty of a crime by reason of insanity.

Far more people are confined to mental institutions on the basis of a determination that they lack competency to stand trial than on the basis of an insanity verdict. There may be 45 people committed under the competency to stand trial criteria for every 1 committed following a verdict of not guilty by reason of insanity (Steadman, 1979).

People who are declared incompetent to stand trial are generally confined to a mental institution until they are deemed competent or a determination is made that they are unlikely to ever regain competency. Abuses may occur, however, if the accused are kept incarcerated for indefinite periods awaiting trial. In earlier years, it was not uncommon for people who were declared incompetent to have their trials delayed for months or years until they were judged ready to stand trial, if indeed they were ever judged to be competent. In 1972, however, the U.S. Supreme Court ruled in the case of *Jackson v. Indiana* that a person could not be kept in a mental hospital awaiting trial longer than it would take to determine whether treatment was likely to restore competency. If it did not seem that the person would ever become competent, even with treatment, the individual would have to be either released or committed under the procedures for civil commitment.

A 1992 ruling by the U.S. Supreme Court, in the case of *Medina v. California*, held that the burden of proof for determining incompetence to stand trial lies with the defendant, not the state (Greenhouse, 1992). This decision may speed the trials of many people who commit crimes and whose competency is in question.

THE DUTY TO WARN

Consider the following mock dialogue between a therapist and an 18-year-old client:

CLIENT: I just can't take my father anymore. I swear, I'm going to pick something up and bust his head the next time I see him.

THERAPIST: Are you saying that you might really act on these feelings and hurt your father?

CLIENT: (after a pause): I tell you, I might just do it. I just don't know what I might do if I got that mad.

THERAPIST: You know what you're telling me is pretty scary. I think your father has a right to know that you have these feelings.

CLIENT: Are you going to tell him?

THERAPIST: I'd prefer if we told him together. But if not, I'll have to tell him. It's my duty to warn him. You remember that I explained to you that I have a responsibility to reveal certain information you tell me if it poses a threat to yourself or others. I think this is one of those times. Sometimes when we say things like wanting to hurt someone else, we are really looking for someone to help us with those feelings. I want you to know that I'm here to help you with those feelings, but I also have a responsibility to others to warn them if there is a threat made against them.

One of the most difficult dilemmas that a therapist may face, like the one in the hypothetical vignette, is whether or not to disclose confidential information that may protect third parties from harm. Information that a client discloses in psychotherapy is generally protected as privileged communication, which carries a right to confidentiality. But this right is not absolute. Courts have determined that a therapist is obliged to breach confidentiality under certain conditions, such as when there is clear and compelling evidence that an individual poses a serious threat to others.

A California case, *Tarasoff v. the Regents of the University of California*, established the legal basis for the therapist's **duty to warn**.

The Tarasoff Case

In 1969, a graduate student at the University of California at Berkeley, Prosenja Poddar, a native of India, became depressed when his romantic overtures toward a young woman, Tatiana Tarasoff, were rebuffed. Poddar entered psychotherapy with a psychologist at a student health facility, during the course of which he informed the psychologist that he intended to kill Tatiana when she returned from her summer vacation. The psychologist, concerned about Poddar's potential for violence, first consulted with his colleagues and then notified the campus police. He informed them that Poddar was dangerous and

recommended that he be taken to a facility for psychiatric treatment.

Poddar was subsequently interviewed by the campus police. They believed that he was rational and released him after he promised to keep his distance from Tatiana. Poddar then terminated treatment with the psychologist, and shortly afterward killed Tatiana. He shot her with a pellet gun when she refused to allow him entry to her home and then repeatedly stabbed her as she fled into the street. Poddar was found guilty of the lesser sentence of voluntary manslaughter, rather than murder, based on testimony of three psychiatrists that Poddar suffered from diminished mental capacity and paranoid schizophrenia. Under California law, his diminished capacity prevented the finding of malice that was necessary for conviction on a charge of first- or second-degree murder. Following a prison term, Poddar returned to

---

A CLOSER LOOK

The Dilemma of AIDS and the Duty to Warn

Imagine that you are a clinical psychologist and are treating a carrier of the AIDS virus (the *human immunodeficiency virus* or H.I.V.) for a psychological problem. The client—let's call him Jim—is a heterosexual married male who contracted H.I.V. from intravenous drug use. He discloses that he fears telling his wife about his history of drug use or that he carries H.I.V. for fear she might leave him. Despite your repeated suggestions that he inform his wife of the potential risk of engaging in unprotected sex, Jim refuses.

As Jim's therapist, you face an ethical dilemma. Do you owe Jim the duty of protecting the confidentiality of his disclosures, or does your duty to warn a third party of a serious threat take precedence? Is the potential of spreading the AIDS virus to a sex partner of sufficient risk to constitute a clear and convincing threat that would place a *Tarasoff* burden on you as the therapist?

As of this writing, the courts have failed to provide clear direction to therapists with respect to their obligation to protect others from dangerous sexual or drug-injecting behavior of H.I.V.-infected clients (Knapp & VanderCreek, 1990). In July 1988, the American Medical Association (AMA), which represents the nation's physicians, broke with its long-standing tradition of protecting patient confidentiality by voting to encourage physicians to warn the sex partners of H.I.V.-infected patients if they can find no other way of alerting them to the danger. The AMA encouraged government officials to develop legislation to

Must the psychologist warn this man's wife that his patient is infected with H.I.V.? Should all communications from clients to psychologists be kept confidential? If health professionals are obligated to warn third parties of dangers to them disclosed by their clients, should they warn sex partners of people who are infected with H.I.V.—the virus that leads to AIDS—that they may contract the infection from their clients?

require tracing of sexual contacts in order to "solicit, identify, and notify" sex partners of patients with H.I.V. or AIDS patients. The AMA resolution called on physicians to first attempt to persuade H.I.V./AIDS patients to cease activities

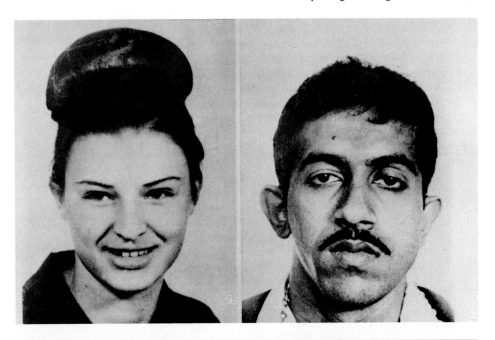

Tatiana Tarasoff and Prosenjit Poddar. Poddar, Tatiana's killer, was a rejected suitor who had made threats against her to his therapist at a university health center. Poddar was subsequently convicted of voluntary manslaughter in her death. A suit brought by Tatiana's parents against the university led to a landmark court ruling that established an obligation on therapists to warn third parties of threats made against them by their clients.

that would put their partners at risk. If persuasion fails, then the physician is encouraged to notify the authorities. If the authorities fail to act, the physician is called on to directly notify and provide counseling to the sex partner at risk. However, the AMA recognizes that the legal right for physicians to breach confidentiality in H.I.V./AIDS cases is prohibited by law in certain states and that new legislation will be necessary to provide legal immunity if physicians are to carry through these resolutions.

Physicians are trained to weigh medical evidence and make informed judgments of the relative risks of contracting physical diseases. However, are psychologists and other nonmedical professionals required to evaluate the medical risks that a client's behavior poses to third parties, like the sex partners of people infected with H.I.V.? Does requiring psychologists to render judgments about the risk of physical contagion compel them to go beyond their areas of expertise?

One argument holds that the obligations imposed on therapists by the *Tarasoff* decision require them to make judgments about the risks posed by their clients' behaviors and to warn individuals who may be placed in danger by these behaviors. To extend *Tarasoff* to disclosures about H.I.V. status, the argument continues, is to place an unfair burden on psychologists to render an opinion concerning the dangerousness of their clients' medical conditions. Several perplexing questions arise from placing this duty on psychologists (Defendant's Argument; Girardi et al., 1988):

1. What if the psychologist is faced with a client who is clearly a high-risk candidate for H.I.V.-infection (that is, a person who shares dirty needles to inject drugs) but refuses to be tested?

2. What if a client whose behavior places him or herself in a high-risk category becomes ill with symptoms associated with H.I.V. infection but refuses to be tested?

Should we require psychologists to evaluate their clients' medical conditions and judge whether their clients have AIDS or are likely to carry H.I.V.? Should we then require them to disclose this suspicion to their clients' sex partners? If we say yes, should we not also require therapists to disclose these suspicions to the sex partners of *all* clients who are members of groups who have been hit hard by the AIDS epidemic, such as gay males, people who inject drugs, and prostitutes, if they refuse to have themselves tested?

Some have argued that professionals without medical training should not be expected to render such judgments (Defendant's argument; Girardi et al., 1988). Others (for example, Plaintiff's argument; Girardi et al., 1988) argue that *Tarasoff* places a burden on therapists to make judgments about the dangers that a client's behavior poses to a third party. Therapists would not be expected to render medical opinions. Rather, they would be required to consider whether Jim's behavior—his stated refusal to inform his sex partner of the fact that he carries H.I.V.—is a form of dangerous behavior that would place her at risk of infection. This argument holds that the risk of contracting H.I.V. through unprotected sex, or by sharing contaminated needles, is so widely understood that any mental health professional, whether medically trained or not, should recognize the dangers posed to a third party.

This debate is certain to continue as society grapples with the legal, medical, and psychological consequences of the AIDS epidemic. Psychologists and other professionals will be faced with difficult ethical choices as they weigh their responsibilities to protect client confidentiality against their legal and ethical obligations to warn individuals who may be infected with H.I.V. by their clients.

India, where he reportedly made a new life for himself (Schwitzgebel & Schwitzgebel, 1980).

Tatiana's parents, however, sued the university. They claimed that the university health center had failed in its responsibility to warn Tatiana of the threat that was made against her by Poddar. The Supreme Court of the State of California agreed with the parents. They ruled that a therapist who has reason to believe that a client poses a serious threat to another person is obligated to warn the potential victim. This obligation is not met by notifying police. This ruling imposed on therapists a duty-to-warn obligation when their clients show the potential for violence by making threats against others.

The ruling recognized that the rights of the intended victim outweigh the rights of confidentiality. Under *Tarasoff,* the therapist does not merely have a *right* to breach confidentiality and warn potential victims of danger, but is *obligated* by law to divulge such confidences to the victim.

 It is actually the case that psychologists are required in many states to reveal confidential information to third parties who have been threatened by their clients.

The duty-to-warn provision poses ethical and practical dilemmas for psychologists and other psychotherapists. Psychotherapists, in states that apply the *Tarasoff* obligation, have a duty to assess the potential violence of their clients, *even though professionals are not generally able to predict dangerousness with a high degree of accuracy.* Under *Tarasoff,* then, therapists may actually feel obliged to protect their personal interests and those of others by breaching confidentiality on the mere suspicion that their clients harbor violent intentions toward third parties. Because there are very few cases in which clients' threats are carried out, the *Tarasoff* ruling may serve to deny many clients their rights to confidentiality in order to prevent such rare instances. Although some clinicians may "overreact" to *Tarasoff* and breach confidentiality without sufficient cause (Roth & Meisel, 1978), it can be argued that the interests of the few potential victims outweigh the interests of the many who may suffer a loss of confidentiality.

Although therapists apparently possess no special ability to predict dangerousness, the *Tarasoff* ruling obliges them to judge whether or not their clients' disclosures indicate a clear intent to harm others. In the *Tarasoff* case, the threat was obvious enough to prompt the therapist to breach confidentiality by requesting the help of campus police. In most cases, however, threats are not so clear cut. There remains a lack of clear criteria for determining whether or not a therapist "should have known" that a client was dangerous before a violent act occurs (Fulero, 1988). In the absence of guidelines that specify the criteria that therapists should use to fulfill their duty to warn, they, like the therapist in the hypothetical example, must rely on their best subjective judgments.

Although the intent of the *Tarasoff* decision was to protect potential victims, it may inadvertently increase the risks of violence when applied to clinical practice (Stone, 1976). For example,

1. *Clients may be less willing to confide in their therapists.* Under the obligations imposed on therapists by *Tarasoff,* clients may be less willing to confide violent urges to their therapists, making it more difficult for therapists to help them diffuse these feelings before they are acted upon.

2. *Potentially violent people may be less likely to enter therapy.* People with violent tendencies may be less willing to enter therapy for fear that disclosures made to a therapist may be revealed.

3. *Therapists may be less likely to probe violent tendencies for fear of legal complications.* To protect themselves and their careers, therapists may avoid asking clients questions concerning potential violence in the belief that they are legally protected if they remain ignorant of them (Wise, 1978). Therapists might also avoid accepting patients for treatment who are believed to have violent tendencies.

It is unclear whether *Tarasoff* has protected lives or endangered lives. It is clear, however, that *Tarasoff* has raised concerns for clinicians who are trying to meet their legal responsibilities under *Tarasoff* and their clinical responsibilities to their clients.

In the wake of the *Tarasoff* decision, we might also ask, "How far might the duty to warn be extended?" Might a therapist be responsible for protecting society at large when more generalized threats are made that do not identify a specific victim? To date, the *Tarasoff* ruling has not been extended to cases in which generalized threats are made (Knapp & VanderCreek, 1982). In Vermont, however, the *Tarasoff* decision has been extended to include a duty to warn in situations when threats against property are made (*Peck v. Counseling Service of Addison County,* 1985).

The *Tarasoff* decision carries the force of law only in California. Other states vary in terms of their statutes that apply in duty-to-warn cases. Therapists must be aware of the statutes and legal precedents that exist in the particular states in which they practice. Therapists must also not lose sight of the primary therapeutic responsibility to their clients when legal issues arise. They must balance the obligation to meet their responsibilities under duty-to-warn provisions with the need to help their clients resolve the feelings of rage and anger that give rise to violent threats.

FACING THE CHALLENGE OF HOMELESSNESS AND ABNORMAL BEHAVIOR

Do the Joyce Browns and Larry Hogues of our society, like other homeless people, represent a personal failure or a failure by society to provide services and housing that would enable disadvantaged citizens to lead secure and productive lives? In this section, we address the problem of the psychiatric homeless—people whose problems include homelessness *and* mental disturbance.

The homeless are a diverse population with diverse needs. Some are homeless because of such adverse life circumstances as prolonged unemployment, family dissolution, or the lack of affordable housing, not because of mental disorders. Yet many

How to Help? Outreach services are needed to provide assistance to psychiatric homeless people who avoid seeking help from the mental health system.

are ex-hospitalized mental patients. Many homeless people also have alcohol- and drug-related problems (Levine & Huebner, 1991; Toro & Wall, 1991). Rates of alcohol abuse range from 30 to 40% and drug abuse from 10 to 15% of homeless adults (McCarty et al., 1991). According to recent studies, about one-half to three-fourths of homeless adults have at least one identifiable mental disorder or alcohol or drug disorder (Fischer & Breakey, 1991). About one-third suffer from severe mental disorders such as schizophrenia, mood disorders, and schizoaffective disorders (Dennis et al., 1991; Levine & Rog, 1990; Rossi, 1990) and perhaps one-quarter to two-fifths have been hospitalized in the past for psychiatric disorders (Tessler & Dennis, 1989). About 10 to 20% of the homeless could be given dual diagnoses of substance abuse along with a severe mental disorder (Drake et al., 1991). Generally speaking, drug abuse and living in an urban area are associated with increased risk of homelessness among psychiatric patients (Susser et al., 1991).

A survey of two beach communities in Los Angeles County illustrates the prevalence of psychiatric problems among the homeless. Of 529 homeless adults surveyed in these communities, 44% had prior hospitalizations for psychiatric or alcohol- or drug-related problems (Gelberg et al., 1988). Homeless people with past psychiatric hospitalizations were more likely to have psychiatric problems, including alcohol and drug abuse, and to engage in criminal activities than were those without such hospitalizations. Figure 15.1 shows the frequencies of various types of disturbed behavior among the homeless people in this study.

Most alcoholic homeless adults do not fit the stereotype of the older, heavily dependent, male skid-row bum (Fischer & Breakey, 1992). Alcoholism is now found among homeless men and women of all ages. A study of 223 men in municipal shelters in New York City found evidence of a history of drug or alcohol abuse in nearly 3 of 5 (58%) (Susser et al., 1989). A study of 76 homeless adults in Buffalo found that 2 of 3 could have been diagnosed as having a substance abuse or dependence disorder at some time in their lives (Toro & Wall, 1991). In the New York City study, nearly 3 in 4 (71%) of the homeless men showed evidence of mental disorders or excessive substance use.

Homelessness among people with psychiatric problems is not limited to urban areas. In rural areas, too, schizophrenics and others with severe mental disorders may lack available or consistent housing, although unstable living arrangements rather than outright homelessness is a more common occurrence (Drake et al., 1991).

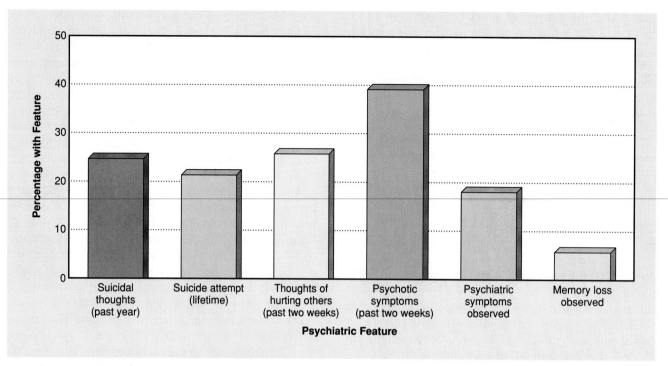

Figure 15.1 Psychiatric features of homeless adults.
Many, but not all, homeless people have psychiatric problems. The results of a survey of psychiatric features among a homeless population in two beach communities in Los Angeles County are represented in this graph. About 1 in 4 reported experiencing suicidal thoughts or making a suicide attempt and nearly 1 in 5 showed psychiatric symptoms when interviewed.

Source: Adapted from Gelberg et al. (1988).

Homelessness and Deinstitutionalization

The elevated numbers of the homeless in our urban centers can be traced, at least in part, to the policy of deinstitutionalization (Lamb, 1984). Many of the homeless are former hospital patients who were essentially dumped into local communities following discharge and left with little if any support. Also, some of the younger psychiatric homeless population might have been hospitalized in earlier times, but are now, in the wake of deinstitutionalization, directed toward community support programs, when they are available (Dennis et al., 1991). The lack of available housing and transitional care facilities and effective case management play important roles in accounting for homelessness among the psychiatrically disturbed (Golden, 1990b; Lamb & Lamb, 1990). The functional deficits associated with mental disorders are also seen as contributing factors, such as disorganized thinking and actions, poor problem-solving skills, and severe paranoia that prevents the individual from accepting help from others (Lamb & Lamb, 1990). Many are also immobilized by depression. As a vicious cycle, the stresses of homelessness may worsen the individual's mental condition, which in turn makes it more difficult for individuals to extricate themselves from prolonged homelessness. Then, too, substance abuse often plays an important role in the mounting problems the psychiatric homeless face.

Some of the psychiatric homeless are repeatedly hospitalized for brief stays in community-based hospitals during acute episodes. Like Larry Hogue, they move back and forth between the hospital and the community as though caught in a revolving door. Frequently, they are released from the hospital with inadequate arrangements for housing and community care. Some are left essentially to fend for themselves. In the Los Angeles study, the majority of homeless adults with past psychiatric treatment had not attended an outpatient facility for more than 5 years, and only 8% had sought help from community mental health centers (Gelberg et al., 1988). These findings underscore the lack of continuity of care for the psychiatric homeless.

It is true that many of the nation's homeless are discharged into the streets from mental hospitals without adequate arrangements for community care.

Community Programs for the Psychiatric Homeless

The many problems of the homeless tax the efforts of society to help them (Gelberg et al., 1988). The mental health system alone does not have the resources to resolve the multifaceted problems faced by the psychiatric homeless population (Chavetz & Goldfinger, 1984). Helping the psychiatric homeless escape from homelessness will at the least require a combination of efforts, representing an integration of mental health and alcohol and drug abuse programs, access to decent, affordable housing, and the provision of other social services (Arce et al., 1983; Dennis et al., 1991).

Mental health systems also require better means for tracking ex-hospital patients and providing them with follow-up care. Community-based clinics often have difficulty locating their follow-up-care clients because many of them wander city streets and have no fixed addresses. New York State's mental health system was reportedly unable to track many of the psychiatric patients that it had released from state institutions (Cummings, 1988). Six months following the release of 60 patients in one study, 38% had failed to maintain contact with state agencies and their whereabouts were unknown. The study also revealed that there were few support services available to help them adjust to community life. In New York State, the report noted, between 80,000 and 100,000 patients are discharged from psychiatric hospitals and mental health centers each year. With a lack of follow-up care, many wind up among the homeless on city streets.

Other pressing obligations compromise the abilities of the federal and state governments to provide comprehensive community care. Federal funding support never reached the levels that were promised when the deinstitutionalization movement was ushered in during the early 1960s. The community mental health movement requires community support and adequate financial resources if it is to succeed (James, 1987).

The psychiatric homeless population lacks secure, affordable housing in addition to continuity of care. Mental health agencies may be able to overcome community resistance to accepting discharged mental patients by demonstrating that mental patients are not simply dumped in the community but are closely monitored in supervised residences. The psychiatric homeless also need social services, medical services, and drug and alcohol counseling. These services are likely to be more effective if they are integrated within a single treatment facility near where homeless people congregate (Frances & Goldfinger, 1986). Drug- and alcohol-free homes and residences can also play important roles in the process of drug and alcohol rehabilitation (McCarty et al., 1991).

Yet psychiatrically disturbed homeless people typically do not seek out mental health services (Arana, 1990). Some health professionals therefore advocate the development of aggressive outreach services to reach them (Frances & Goldfinger, 1986). In an effort to reach the psychiatrically homeless population, New York State has assigned each of 500 case managers to 10 discharged patients to help them obtain community services (Cummings, 1988). It is too early to tell what impact such outreach programs will have in serving the needs of discharged patients.

Programs involving mobile outreach, more intensive case management, drop-in centers, and shelter-based programs, among other approaches, have been developed (Dennis et al., 1991). Outreach workers may first need to build trust, by offering coffee or sandwiches and listening to the concerns expressed by homeless people during unstructured visits. Other researchers (Barrow et al., 1989) have found that provision of basic services (for example, food, showers, medical services, mailboxes) by drop-in centers offer strong incentives for the psychiatric homeless to enter treatment. Still, despite such attempts, the numbers of homeless adults who become involved in treatment remains small, which reflects the lack of connectedness between homeless people and the mental health system (Barrow et al., 1989). Mental health and rehabilitation programs that are placed directly on site in settings which typically serve large numbers of homeless people, such as the shelter care system, may be more successful in maximizing involvement in these programs than those based in clinic or hospital settings (Caton et al., 1990).

Although the number of specialized programs for the psychiatric homeless population have greatly increased in recent years, they still only reach a small fraction of those in need (Dennis et al., 1991). The federal government, through the National Institute of Mental Health, has begun funding demonstration projects that focus on providing psychiatric homeless adults with comprehensive mental health services (Dennis et al., 1991).

Some professionals call for reinstitutionalization

as needed (see Lamb, 1990). However, many professionals and laypeople express concerns about a return to the warehousing that typified the earlier period of institutionalization. One factor discouraging rehospitalization is the cost. In New York State, for example, psychiatric hospitalization is estimated to cost $70,000 per year per patient, as compared to perhaps $13,000 a year for alternate community-based treatment that would involve residence in state-run group homes or rehabilitated apartments in city-owned buildings, along with supervision by case workers (*"Hide the Homeless?"* 1991).

Other professionals are concerned that aggressive outreach programs will infringe on the freedom of homeless people, further stigmatize them, and possibly fail to help them (Mossman & Perlin, 1992). An alternate proposal is to focus on the social problems faced by the homeless, like championing efforts to meet their basic needs for housing, food, and clothing, and broadening access to outpatient treatment (Mossman & Perlin, 1992).

All in all, the problems of the psychiatric homeless population remain a complex problem for the mental health system and the general public.

FACING THE CHALLENGE OF PREVENTION

"An ounce of prevention is worth a pound of cure"—so goes the saying. How can society gather knowledge and mobilize its resources to help prevent mental health problems from occurring or to intervene early in their development?

Perhaps the earliest reference to prevention is found in the Bible. In the Book of Genesis, Joseph interprets a dream of pharaoh as foretelling that 7 years of famine would follow 7 years of plenty. Joseph urged pharaoh to store grain when crops were plentiful to prevent starvation in the lean years.

Today we stockpile vital supplies like grain and oil to ameliorate the effects of shortages. In medical science, the development of vaccines has helped protect people from contracting such diseases as smallpox and polio. In the mental health system, however, resources are generally directed toward treating mental health problems rather than attempting to prevent them from developing. In recent years, however, a movement toward prevention has received impetus from research programs that demonstrate the cost effectiveness of preventing problems from arising and reducing their severity when they do arise.

There are three levels of **prevention**: primary prevention, secondary prevention, and tertiary prevention. **Primary prevention** aims to prevent the development of mental disorders. **Secondary prevention** is the marshalling of efforts to intervene early in the development of these problems in order to prevent them from becoming more severe. **Tertiary prevention** attempts to reduce the impact of these problems, for example, by providing rehabilitation services to discharged patients to prevent rehospitalization. In the following sections we take a closer look at these types of prevention.

Primary Prevention

Primary prevention aims to prevent problems by uncovering and eliminating their underlying causes. Efforts at primary prevention may be stymied by lack of knowledge about their causes. For instance, until researchers discovered that AIDS is caused by a virus and how that virus is transmitted, AIDS prevention efforts were superficial and tentative.

Some relationships between cause and effect are well established. Improved prenatal and perinatal care have helped prevent the development of various childhood illnesses, for example. Counseling pregnant women to avoid using alcohol or helping them to quit smoking also prevents the development of a variety of problems in their children. Advances in genetic engineering may soon permit treatment of the fetus to prevent the expression of many genetic defects.

Food stamp programs and school lunch programs have been developed to provide children with adequate nutrition in their formative years to fend off the development of some physical and mental disorders. The field of **health psychology** addresses primary prevention of physical illness through encouraging healthful lifestyle changes, such as quitting smoking, controlling weight, or managing stress.

Even though we lack concrete evidence of the causes of many psychological problems, various primary prevention programs are based on the belief that early childhood stresses, or states of emotional or physical deprivation, set the stage for developmental problems. Structured learning experiences such as the Head Start program have been established to help children believed to be at academic risk develop their potential. Recognition that parents who abuse their children were often themselves abused as children has spurred the development of greater child protection efforts and programs to help troubled families. Prevention programs have been developed to reduce pregnancies, drug abuse, and smoking among adolescents.

(A)

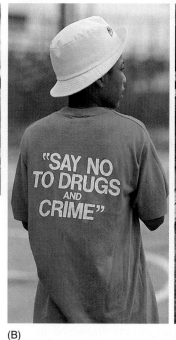

Primary prevention. Primary prevention takes many forms, including programs focused on enhancing skills in early childhood, such as (A) this Head Start nursery school program for 3- to 4-year-olds; (B) drug prevention programs such as this "Just Say No" program that targets preteens in Oakland, California; and (C) community-based programs that seek to improve the quality of housing, such as this housing rehabilitation program in San Antonio, Texas.

(B)　　　　　　　　　　　　　　(C)

Some proponents of primary prevention believe that society must address social problems such as poverty, discrimination, lack of economic opportunity, inadequate housing, and chronic joblessness that may contribute to mental disorders and violence within families. This approach—a *systems-level strategy*—focuses on changing society rather than changing individuals (Cowen, 1985). However, implementation of major societal changes can represent momentous undertakings. Obstacles include differences in opinions concerning what changes are needed, the costs of such changes, and the time that would be required to implement such changes (Cowen, 1985). The *person-centered approach* alternatively focuses on helping individuals cope more effectively with their life stressors (Cowen, 1985).

Person-centered approaches may be distinguished along two dimensions (Cowen, 1985): *situation-focused approaches* and *competence-enhancement approaches*. Situation-focused approaches provide services to people who are facing specific life stressors such as divorce, loss of a loved one, or loss of a job. Competence-enhancement approaches train people in skills or competencies that they can use as needed to cope with potential stressors.

Support services to families undergoing a divorce provide an example of a situation-based approach to primary prevention. Research evidence has linked divorce to the development of physical and psychological problems in family members (Cowen, 1985). Support services such as divorce

counseling may thus help families cope with the financial and emotional consequences of divorce.

A competence-enhancement approach to primary prevention is illustrated in the work of Spivack and his associates (1976). The Spivak group has shown that childhood behavior problems are often related to deficiencies in problem-solving skills, such as the inability to conceive alternative solutions to problems or to anticipate the effects of one's actions. Because deficiencies in problem-solving skills seem to set the stage for adjustment problems, Spivak and his group developed a primary prevention approach in which children from an inner-city Head Start program were taught problem-solving skills. Children who received training in problem solving showed better adjustment a year later than children who did not receive the intervention program.

Secondary Prevention

Secondary prevention employs early detection and intervention to nip the development of serious or long-term mental health problems in the bud. Secondary prevention in mental health programs takes various forms, such as crisis intervention, self-help groups, telephone hot lines, community consultation, and early intervention.

When people are in acute crises or extremely stressful situations that overwhelm their ability to cope, they may not be able to wait for scheduled

MULTICULTURAL PERSPECTIVES

"Soulbeat": A Culture-Specific Program for Preventing Substance Abuse Among African Americans

 Maypole and Anderson (1987) describe a culturally specific substance abuse prevention program for African Americans. Called "Soulbeat," this east Arkansas program reached out to families and youth through the schools and African-American churches in the community. The African-American church represents a major support system in the African-American community and can serve an important role in efforts to prevent substance abuse and other problems.

The prevention program focused on the staging of culturally sensitive plays and skits in the churches and schools. Young people enacted the pertinent roles in the plays. The plays served as learning experiences for both the actors and the audience. They helped expand these groups' knowledge about the effects of substance abuse on individuals and families in the African-American community. They also highlighted themes such as the role played by group peer pressure in the development of substance abuse problems.

By working with the institutions that are inherent parts of the lives of diverse ethnic groups, psychologists reach individuals who might otherwise fail to receive the benefits of their knowledge and skills.

---

appointments or to follow a long-term course of treatment. *Crisis intervention* involves the coordination of emergency services to provide immediate help. This may take the form of a *telephone hot line*, staffed by professionals or nonprofessionals who are especially trained to provide crisis services such as support, information, and referral. Crisis intervention may also involve face-to-face short-term crisis therapy, in which the therapist helps the individual or family cope with immediate stressors such as the loss of a loved one or a devastating illness or accident. The therapist provides reassurance, support, guidance, information, and counseling. In cases of acute psychological distress, a crisis intervention team may be called on to coordinate treatment services to prevent the need for hospitalization.

Self-help groups support people in acute crises, such as following the loss of loved ones. People in such groups show understanding of each other's con-

cerns and impart information that can help other members cope. Some self-help programs provide support to parents coping with the emotional consequences of miscarriage, stillbirth, or infant death. These self-help groups, which have become a rapidly growing movement in the United States (Blakeslee, 1988), counter the tendencies of well-meaning but misguided observers—for example, family members, doctors, and friends—to deny or minimize the emotional anguish that parents experience following the death of a baby. One mother who lost several babies shortly after birth said, "I was told not to think about it, that I was young and could have another one, that my loss was less significant because it was an infant. . . . It was not treated as an important loss" (Blakeslee, 1988, p. B13). Failing to recognize and confront the emotional pain of bereavement may lead to enduring emotional scars.

The *telephone hot line* is another example of secondary prevention. Hot lines for suicidal people, adolescent runaways, and rape victims have been established throughout the United States and Canada. These services are usually staffed by nonprofessionals, although psychologists or psychiatrists may supervise or consult. The suicide hot line aims to dissuade people at the brink of suicide not to take their lives and arranges referrals for treatment to help suicidal people cope with the stressors they face. Telephone hot lines protect the anonymity of callers, so as to reach people who may be reluctant to identify themselves.

Community consultation also represents a form of secondary prevention. **Community psychology** is the branch of psychology that specifically focuses on the role of social systems within the community in preventing and remedying maladaptive behavior and emotional disturbance. Community psychologists often consult with other professionals in the community such as police officers, teachers, and employers who have frequent contact with high-risk populations. Community psychologists and other mental health professionals can thus reach more people in need than would be possible through individual contacts. For example, mental health professionals may help train teachers to identify early signs of emotional disturbance in their students so that early intervention can be arranged. Or they may help train police officers become more skillful in handling family conflicts, which may prevent their escalation.

Early intervention, another type of secondary prevention, treats people as early as possible once problems arise to prevent further declines in functioning and help restore functioning. An example of early intervention is seen in an experimental program that provided treatment to problem drinkers who were in the early stages of alcohol abuse (Alden, 1988). In

MULTICULTURAL PERSPECTIVES

Community-Wide Crisis Intervention: An Israeli Example

An example of a community-wide crisis intervention occurred in Israel in the aftermath of a devastating school bus accident (Toubiana et al., 1988). In the early morning hours of a day in June 1985, a bus carrying Israeli children to a celebration marking the end of the school year was struck at a railroad crossing by a speeding train. Nineteen children and three adults were killed and a number of other children injured. Children in other buses witnessed the accident. Within hours of the tragedy, a psychologist was summoned to the school to support and counsel the surviving children and their families and teachers. During the next several days, the psychologist consulted with teachers to help them handle disturbed children, sometimes providing direct support to the children in helping them "ventilate," or express, their feelings through various activities, such as group discussion, drawings, and poetry. Children who were unable to attend class were seen individually by the psychologist. Mental health workers found many traumatic reactions among schoolmates. Frightening nightmares involving scenes of the accident were reported by 70% of the children. Many of the surviving children experienced acute bereavement or grief reactions. No attempt was made to distance the children from their memories of the traumatic experience. Rather, the children were encouraged to honor the memories of the deceased children in memorials, by visiting the injured children in the hospital, by visits to bereaved parents, and by expressing their feelings about the deceased children in writing or pictures.

A short-term approach to treatment was adopted that was similar in many respects to the treatment employed in helping Israeli soldiers cope with combat stress reactions. In both cases, there is an emphasis on early intervention and opportunities for people in distress to share feelings with people undergoing similar reactions. Counselors mobilize positive expectations by informing distressed individuals that their reactions are normal and that they will recover in time. Ventilation or expression of feelings in a supportive environment is encouraged to allow the release of emotions that are associated with the stressful event. Therapists also encourage people to resume their regular routines as early as possible.

---

traditional programs directed toward alcoholics, abstinence is considered the only acceptable goal of treatment. This experimental program established moderate drinking as its goal because the program developers recognized that problem drinkers in the early stages of alcohol abuse may be less willing to commit themselves to abstinence. Intervention consisted of a 12-week program that focused on self-management skills such as (1) self-monitoring of drinking patterns and blood alcohol levels; (2) setting weekly goals for drinking rate and blood alcohol levels; (3) slowing the rate of consumption by diluting drinks and slowing the pace of drinking; (4) avoiding contact with stimulus cues associated with drinking, such as avoiding bars or social events associated with drinking; and (5) developing alternative behaviors that might substitute for drinking. Initial results on the effectiveness of the early intervention program were encouraging (Alden, 1988).

Secondary prevention efforts that trained college students at risk for alcohol problems to curb alcohol intake have also shown promising results (Kivlahan et al., 1990). Investigators in this program trained participants over an 8-week period to gauge their blood alcohol levels accurately, to set limits on drinking, and to prevent relapses. A 1-year follow-up evaluation showed that program participants reported drinking less alcohol than control subjects.

Tertiary Prevention

Much of tertiary prevention focuses on reducing the impact of severe mental disorders by providing aftercare services to people who were formerly institutionalized. Aftercare aims to foster community adjustment and prevent rehospitalization. Examples of aftercare services include rehabilitation and structured workshop services, outpatient treatment, day hospitals (day-only hospitalized-based programs for people residing at home or in the community), halfway houses, and community support services. People who receive aftercare services have been found to be less likely to return to the hospital (Glasscote, 1978).

Halfway houses, a major component of aftercare services, serve both secondary and tertiary prevention purposes. A **halfway house** provides a structured living environment in the community for patients who do not require the more restrictive environment of an institution. By providing services for people in the early stages of distress, the halfway house may serve a secondary prevention function by helping to stave off a further decline in functioning. The halfway house may also serve the tertiary prevention function of providing ex-hospital patients with a—well—halfway measure that serves as a transition to independent community living.

Halfway houses are usually private homes that have been converted to accommodate groups of patients. The residents usually share meals and participate in group meetings. Some halfway houses provide structured work experiences. Others are more informally structured and allow residents to pursue their own occupational training or educational opportunities. Typically, most staff members are non-professionals. Psychologists and other professionals are available for consultation or supervision. A live-in counselor may be available to offer support and ensure that house regulations are followed. Residents tend to adjust more successfully when they perceive the house environment to be closer to their conception of their ideal living environment, along such dimensions as degree of structure, order and organization, and level of staff support, than when there is a poorer fit (Nevid et al., 1980). Halfway houses that place higher expectations on their residents with respect to work responsibilities and self-governance are generally more successful in helping residents achieve higher levels of independent functioning (Fairweather, 1980; Fairweather et al., 1969; Lamb & Goertzel, 1971).

Yet there is a nationwide shortage of well-run halfway houses. A major problem in establishing additional halfway houses is community resistance. Community residents often object to the presence of mental patients in their midst and may wrongly perceive the residents as dangerous or object to the sight of people whose behavior seems bizarre or strange.

A Final Word on Prevention

Psychologists, like other helping professionals, tend to focus on providing care to those who have identifiable problems or are clearly in need. They tend to react to needs for treatment as they arise, rather than spearhead social reforms, such as programs to improve housing conditions and improve nutrition and health care for populations in high-risk categories, that might eventually reduce the prevalence of mental disorders. Proactively promoting social and environmental changes that might enhance psychological functioning might reduce human suffering as well as the costs of caring for people with mental health problems.

We opened this book by noting that despite the public impression that abnormal behavior affects only the few, it actually affects nearly every one of us in one way or another. If we all work together to foster research into the causes, treatment, and prevention of abnormal behavior, perhaps we can meet the multifaceted challenges that abnormal behavior poses to so many of us and to our society at large.

SUMMARY

Psychiatric Commitment

The legal process by which people are placed in psychiatric institutions against their will is called psychiatric or civil commitment. Psychiatric commitment is intended to provide treatment to people who are deemed to suffer from mental disorders and to pose a threat to themselves or others. Legal or criminal commitment, by comparison, involves the placement of a person in a psychiatric institution for treatment who has been acquitted of a crime by reason of insanity. In voluntary hospitalization, people voluntarily seek treatment in a psychiatric facility, and can leave of their own accord, unless a court rules otherwise.

Predicting Dangerousness

Although people must be judged dangerous to be placed involuntarily in a psychiatric facility, mental health professionals have not demonstrated any special ability to predict dangerousness. Factors that may account for the failure to predict dangerousness include (1) recognizing violent tendencies post hoc is easier than predicting it; (2) generalized perceptions of violent tendencies may not predict specific acts of violence; (3) lack of agreement in defining violence or dangerousness; (4) base-rate problems; (5) unlikelihood of direct threats of violence; and (6) predictions based on hospital behavior may not generalize to community settings.

Patients' Rights

Landmark court cases have clarified patients' rights in psychiatric facilities. In *Wyatt v. Stickney*, a court in Alabama imposed a minimum standard of care. In *O'Connor v. Donaldson*, the U.S. Supreme Court ruled that nondangerous mentally ill people could not be held in psychiatric facilities against their will if such people could be maintained safely in the community. In *Youngberg v. Romeo*, the U.S. Supreme Court ruled that involuntarily confined patients have a right to less restrictive types of treatment and to receive training to help them function. Court rulings, such as that of *Rogers v. Okin* in Massachusetts, have established that patients have a right to refuse medication, except in case of emergency.

The Insanity Defense

Three court cases established legal precedents for the insanity defense. In 1834, a court in Ohio applied a principle of irresistible impulse as the basis of an insanity defense. The M'Naghten rule, based on a case in England in 1843, treated the failure to appreciate the wrongfulness of one's action as the basis of legal insanity. The *Durham* rule was based on a case in the United States in 1954 in which it was held that persons did not bear criminal responsibility if their criminal behavior was the product of "mental disease or mental defect." People who are criminally committed may be hospitalized for an indefinite period of time, with their eventual release dependent on a determination of their mental status.

Competency to Stand Trial

People who are accused of crimes but are incapable of understanding the charges against them or assisting in their own defense can be found incompetent to stand trial and remanded to a psychiatric facility. In the case of *Jackson v. Indiana*, the U.S. Supreme Court placed restrictions on the length of time a person judged incompetent to stand trial could be held in a psychiatric facility.

The Duty to Warn

Although information disclosed by a client to a therapist generally carries a right to confidentiality, the California *Tarasoff* ruling held that therapists have a duty or obligation to warn third parties of threats made against them by their clients.

Facing the Challenge of Homelessness and Abnormal Behavior

Many homeless people are ex-hospitalized mental patients or people who might have been hospitalized involuntarily under laxer standards for commitment in earlier times.

Facing the Challenge of Prevention

Primary prevention involves efforts to prevent the development of illness and abnormal behaviors. Secondary prevention involves efforts at early intervention to forestall the development of more severe problems. Tertiary prevention involves efforts that focus on reducing the impact of existing problems or need for rehospitalization.

Glossary

Abnormal psychology. The branch of psychology that deals with the description, causes, and treatment of abnormal behavior.

Abstinence syndrome. See *withdrawal syndrome*.

Abstinence violation effect. The tendency in people trying to maintain abstinence from a substance, such as alcohol or cigarettes, to overreact to a lapse with feelings of guilt and a sense of resignation that may then trigger a full-blown relapse.

Acculturation. The process of adapting to a new or different culture.

Acetylcholine. A type of neurotransmitter that is involved in the control of muscle contractions. Abbreviated *ACh*.

Acrophobia. Excessive, irrational fear of heights.

Acute stress disorder. A traumatic stress reaction occurring in the days and weeks following exposure to a traumatic event.

Addison's disease. A disease caused by underactivity of the adrenal cortex.

Adjustment disorder. A maladaptive reaction to an identified stressor or stressors that occurs shortly following exposure to the stressor(s) and results in impaired functioning or signs of emotional distress that exceed what would normally be expected in the situation. The reaction may be resolved if the stressor is removed or the individual learns to adapt to it successfully.

Adrenaline. A hormone produced by the adrenal medulla that is involved in stimulating the sympathetic division of the autonomic nervous system. Also called *epinephrine*.

Aerobic exercise. Exercises such as running or swimming that condition the lungs and hearts by requiring sustained increases in the consumption of oxygen by the body.

Affect. (AF-fect). Emotion or feeling state that is attached to objects, ideas, or life experiences.

Agnosia. A disturbance of sensory perception.

Agoraphobia. Excessive, irrational fear of open places.

AIDS dementia complex. A form of dementia that is believed to result from an infection of the brain caused by the AIDS virus.

Al-Anon. An organization sponsoring support groups for family members of alcoholics.

Alarm reaction. The first stage of the general adaptation syndrome following response to a stressor, it is characterized by heightened sympathetic activity.

Alcohol persisting amnestic disorder. See *Korsakoff's syndrome*.

Alcoholism. Physiological dependence on alcohol that results in impaired personal, social, or physical functioning.

Alzheimer's disease. A progressive brain disease characterized by gradual loss of memory and intellectual functioning, personality changes, and eventual loss of ability to care for oneself.

Ambivalent. Holding conflicting feelings toward another person or goal, such as both loving and hating the same person.

Ambulatory. Able to walk about on one's own.

Amenorrhea. Absence of menstruation—a symptom of anorexia nervosa.

Amnestic disorders. Disturbances of memory associated with inability to learn new material and recall past events.

Amotivational syndrome. A loss of ambition or motivation to achieve, which has been connected with use of marijuana.

Amphetamine psychosis. A psychotic state induced by ingestion of amphetamines.

Amphetamines. Types of stimulants, such as Dexedrine and Benzedrine. Abuse can trigger an amphetamine psychosis that mimics acute episodes of schizophrenia.

Anaerobic exercise. Exercise such as weight lifting that does not demand sustained increase in consumption of oxygen.

Anal-expulsive. In psychodynamic theory, a personality type characterized by excessive self-expression, such as extreme sloppiness or messiness.

Anal fixation. In psychodynamic theory, attachment to objects and behavior that characterized the anal stage.

Anal-retentive. In psychodynamic theory, a personality type characterized by excessive needs for self-control, such as extreme neatness and punctuality.

Anal stage. The second stage of psychosexual development in Freud's theory, in which gratification is achieved through anal activities, such as by the elimination of bodily wastes.

Analgesia. A state of relief from pain without loss of consciousness.

Analogue. Something that resembles something else in many respects.

Analogue study. A method of research that involves the simulation of naturally occurring conditions in a controlled setting.

Analytical psychology. Jung's psychodynamic theory, which emphasizes such concepts as the collective unconscious, the existence of archetypes, and the notion of the self as a unifying force of personality.

Anhedonia. A state characterized by inability to experience pleasure.

Anorexia nervosa. An eating disorder, primarily affecting young women, which is characterized by maintenance of an abnormally low body weight, distortions of body image, intense fears of gaining weight, and, in females, amenorrhea.

Antecedents. Factors of events that precede other events. Antecedents may or may not be causally connected to the events that follow.

Antibodies. Substances produced by white blood cells that identify and destroy antigens.

Antidepressants. Types of drugs that act to relieve depression. Tricyclics, MAO inhibitors, and serotonin reuptake inhibitors are the major classes of antidepressants.

Antigens. A substance that triggers an immune system response to it (the contraction for *anti*body *gen*erator).

Antisocial personality disorder. A type of personality disorder that is characterized by a chronic pattern of antisocial and irresponsible behavior and lack of remorse. Also referred to as *psychopathy* and *sociopathy*.

Anxiety. An emotional state characterized by physiological arousal, unpleasant feelings of tension, and a sense of apprehension, foreboding, and dread about the future.

Anxiety disorder. A type of mental disorder in which anxiety is the prominent feature. Formerly labeled *neurosis*.

Aphasia. Impaired ability to understand or express oneself through speech.

Archetypes. Jung's concept of primitive images or concepts that reside in the collective unconscious.

Arteriosclerosis. A disease involving thickening and hardening of the arteries.

Assertiveness training. A set of techniques in behavior therapy, generally consisting of modeling, feedback, and behavior rehearsal, that is intended to train clients to become more self-expressive and capable of standing up for their rights.

Asylum. Historic: an institution that cared for the mentally ill. Also, a safe place or refuge.

Ataxia. Loss of muscle coordination.

Atherosclerosis. A disease process consisting of arteriosclerosis with the deposition of fatty substances along the walls of the arteries.

Attention-deficit/hyperactivity disorder. A behavior disorder of childhood that is characterized by excessive motor activity and inability to focus one's attention.

Attributional style. A personal style for explaining cause-and-effect relationships between events.

Aura. A warning sign or cluster of symptoms preceding the occurrence of a migraine headache or epileptic seizure.

Authentic. In the humanistic-existential model, a term that describes choices and actions which reflect on our true feelings and needs.

Autism. (1) The absorption in daydreaming and fantasy. (2) A disorder in childhood characterized by failure to relate to others, lack of speech, disturbed motor behaviors, intellectual impairment, and demands for sameness in the environment. Also one of Bleuler's "Four A's," describing one of the primary symptoms of schizophrenia.

Automatic thoughts. Thoughts that seem to pop into one's mind. In Aaron Beck's theory, automatic thoughts that reflect cognitive distortions induce negative feelings like anxiety or depression.

Autonomic nervous system. The division of the peripheral nervous system that regulates the activities of glands and involuntary functions, such as respiration, heartbeat, and digestion. Abbreviated *ANS*. Also see *sympathetic* and *parasympathetic* branches of the ANS.

Aversive conditioning. A behavior therapy technique in which a maladaptive response is paired with exposure to an aversive stimulus, such as electric shock or nausea, so that a conditioned aversion develops toward the stimuli associated with the maladaptive response. Also termed *aversion therapy.*

Avoidant disorder of childhood or adolescence. A childhood behavior disorder characterized by excessive fear and avoidance of strangers.

Avoidant personality disorder. A type of personality disorder characterized by avoidance of social relationships due to fears of rejection.

Axon. The long thin part of the neuron along which nervous impulses travel.

Barbiturates. Types of depressants that are sometimes used to relieve anxiety or induce sleep, but which are highly addictive.

Basal ganglia. Ganglia located between the thalamus and the cerebrum in the brain that are involved in the coordination of motor activity.

Baseline. A period of time preceding the implementation of a treatment. Used to gather data regarding the rate of occurrence of the target behavior before treatment is introduced.

Behavior genetics. The field of study that addresses the role of genetics in the explanation of behavior.

Behavior modification. The application of principles of learning to the bringing about of desired behavioral changes.

Behavior therapy. See *behavior modification.*

Behavioral assessment. The approach to clinical assessment that focuses on the objective recording or description of the problem behavior, rather than inferences about personality traits.

Behavioral interview. An approach to clinical interviewing which focuses on relating the problem behavior to antecedent stimuli and reinforcement consequences.

Behavioral rating scale. A method of behavioral assessment that involves the use of a scale to record the frequency of occurrence of target behaviors.

Behaviorism. The school of psychology that defines psychology as the study of observable or overt behavior and focuses on investigating the relationships between stimuli and responses.

Behaviorist. One who adheres to the school of behaviorism.

Benzodiazepines. The class of minor tranquilizers that includes Valium and Librium.

Bereavement. The normal experience of suffering following the loss of a loved one.

Beriberi. A nutritional disorder caused by thiamine deficiency.

Biofeedback training. A method of feeding back to the individual information about bodily functions so that the person is able to gain better control over these functions. Abbreviated *BFT.*

Biological markers. Biological characteristics that identify people with greater vulnerability to particular disorders.

Biological psychiatry. The movement within modern psychiatry that focuses on biological explanations and treatments of mental disorders.

Bipolar. Characterized by opposites, as in *bipolar disorder.*

Bipolar disorder. A disorder characterized by mood swings between states of extreme elation and severe depression. Formerly called *manic depression.*

Bisexuals. People who are attracted to and interested in forming romantic relationships with members of both genders.

Blind. In the context of research design, a state of being unaware of whether or not one has received a treatment.

Blocking. (1) A disruption of self-expression of threatening or emotionally laden material. (2) In schizophrenics, a condition of suddenly becoming silent with loss of memory for what they had just discussed.

Bondage. A form of sadomasochism involving the binding of the arms or legs of oneself or one's partner during sexual activity.

Borderline personality disorder. A type of personality disorder that is characterized by abrupt shifts in mood, lack of a coherent sense of self, and unpredictable, impulsive behavior.

Bottoming out. A state of despair characterized by financial ruin, suicide attempts, and shattered family relationships that is experienced by many pathological gamblers.

Brain electrical activity mapping. A method of brain imaging that involves the computer analysis of data from multiple electrodes that are placed on the scalp in order to reveal areas of the brain with relatively higher or lower levels of electrical activity. Abbreviated *BEAM.*

Brief psychotic disorder. A psychotic disorder lasting from a day to a month that often follows exposure to a major stressor.

Bulimia nervosa. An eating disorder characterized by a recurrent pattern of binge eating followed by self-induced purging and accompanied by persistent overconcern with body weight and shape.

Cardiovascular disorders. Diseases of the cardiovascular system, such as coronary heart disease, hypertension, and arteriosclerosis.

Case. In the context of abnormal psychology, an individual who is identified as having a particular disorder or as receiving a treatment.

Case study. A carefully drawn biography that is typically constructed on the basis of clinical interviews, observations, psychological tests, and, in some cases, historical records.

Castration anxiety. In psychodynamic theory, the boy's unconscious fear that he will be castrated as a form of punishment for having incestuous wishes for his mother.

Catastrophize. To exaggerate or magnify the negative consequences of events; to blow things out of proportion.

Catatonic type. The subtype of schizophrenia characterized by gross disturbances in motor activity, such as catatonic stupor.

Catecholamine hypothesis. The belief that decreased availability of norepinephrine produces depression and increased levels produce mania.

Catecholamines. A group of chemically related substances that function as neurotransmitters in the brain (dopamine and norepinephrine) and as hormones (epinephrine and norepinephrine).

Catharsis. (1) The discharge of states of tension associated with repression of threatening impulses or material. (2) The free expression or purging of feelings. Also called *abreaction*.

Causal relationship. A relationship between two factors or events in which one is necessary and sufficient to bring about the other. Also called a *cause-and-effect relationship*.

Central nervous system. The brain and spinal cord.

Cerebellum. A part of the hindbrain involved in coordination and balance.

Cerebral cortex. The wrinkled surface area of the cerebrum, often referred to as gray matter because of the appearance produced by the high density of cell bodies. Associative thinking is generally assumed to occur in the cerebral cortex.

Cerebrum. The large mass of the forebrain, consisting of two hemispheres.

Chemotherapy. In the context of abnormal psychology, the use of psychoactive drugs to treat abnormal behavior patterns. Also referred to as *drug therapy*.

Childhood schizophrenia. The development of a schizophrenic disorder in childhood; considered a relatively rare occurrence.

Choleric. Having or showing bad temper.

Chromosomes. The structures found in the nuclei of cells that carry the units of heredity, or *genes*.

Cirrhosis of the liver. A liver disease often associated with prolonged alcohol abuse.

Civil commitment. The legal process involved in placing an individual in a mental institution, even against his or her will. Also called psychiatric commitment.

Clanging. In schizophrenics, the tendency to string words together because they rhyme or sound alike.

Classical conditioning. A simple form of learning in which a previously neutral stimulus (the conditioned stimulus) comes to elicit the response (the conditioned response) that is usually elicited by a second stimulus as a result of being paired repeatedly with the second stimulus. Also called *Pavlovian conditioning*.

Claustrophobia. Excessive, irrational fear of small tight places.

Client-centered therapy. Another name for Carl Rogers's *person-centered therapy*.

Closed-ended questions. Questionnaire or test items that have a limited range of response options.

Cocaine. A stimulant derived from coca leaves. The hardened, smokable form of cocaine is called *crack*.

Coefficient alpha. A measure of internal consistency or reliability: the average intercorrelation among the items composing a particular scale or test.

Cognition. Mental processes such as sensation and perception, memory, intelligence, language, thought, and problem solving.

Cognitive disorders. A category of mental disorders characterized by impaired cognitive abilities and daily functioning in which biological causation is either known or presumed.

Cognitive restructuring. A cognitive therapy method that involves replacing irrational or self-defeating thoughts and attitudes with rational alternatives.

Cognitive social theory. See *social-learning theory*.

Cognitive-specificity hypothesis. In Aaron Beck's theory, the belief that links different feeling states like depression and anxiety to particular kinds of automatic thoughts.

Cognitive therapy. (1) The name of Aaron Beck's kind of psychotherapy, which challenges the distorted thought patterns that give rise to or exacerbate clients' problems. (2) More generally, a form of psychotherapy that addresses clients' cognitive processes, usually their self-defeating attitudes.

Cognitive triad of depression. In Aaron Beck's theory, the view that depression derives from the adoption of negative views of oneself, the environment, and the future.

Collective unconscious. In Carl Jung's theory, the hypothesized storehouse of archetypes and racial memories.

Comatose. In a coma, a state of deep prolonged unconsciousness.

Community psychology. The branch of psychology that focuses on changing social systems in the community in the interest of preventing and remedying maladaptive behavior.

Competencies. In social-learning theory, a type of person variable characterized by knowledge and skills.

Compulsion. A persistent and apparently irresistible urge to repeat a certain act or ritualistic behavior, such as compulsive hand washing.

Compulsion to utter. In psychodynamic theory, the urge to verbally express repressed material.

Computerized axial tomography. The generation of a computer-enhanced image of the internal structures of the brain by means of passing a narrow X-ray beam through the head at different angles. Abbreviated *CAT scan*.

Concordance. Agreement.

Concrete operations. The stage of cognitive development in Jean Piaget's theory that corresponds to the development of logical thought processes involving the relationships among objects with respect to such properties as conservation and reversibility.

Concurrent validity. A type of test validity that is determined on the basis of the statistical relationship or correlation between the test and a criterion measure taken at the same point in time.

Concussion. A blow to, or jarring of, the head that results in momentary loss of consciousness or disruption of brain functioning.

Conditional positive regard. In Carl Rogers's theory, valuing other people on the basis of whether their behavior meets with one's approval.

Conditioned response. (1) In classical conditioning, a learned or acquired response to a previously neutral stimulus. (2) A response to a conditioned stimulus. Abbreviated *CR*.

Conditioned stimulus. A previously neutral stimulus that comes to evoke a conditioned response following repeated pairings with a stimulus (unconditioned stimulus) that had already evoked that response. Abbreviated *CS*.

Conditions of worth.   Standards by which one judges the worth or value of oneself or others.

Conduct disorder.   A pattern of abnormal behavior in childhood characterized by disruptive, antisocial behavior.

Congruence.   In Carl Rogers's theory, the fit between one's self-concept and one's thoughts, behaviors, and feelings. One of the principal characteristics of effective person-centered therapists.

Conscious.   Aware.

Construct.   (CON-struct). A hypothetical concept such as *id* or *hunger* that is proposed to exist within people and help explain behavior.

Construct validity.   (1) The degree to which a test or instrument measures the hypothetical construct that it purports to measure. (2) In experiments, the degree to which treatment effects can be accounted for by the theoretical mechanisms or constructs that are represented by the independent variables.

Content validity.   (1) The degree to which the content of a test or measure represents the content domain of the construct it purports to measure. (2) The degree to which the content of a test or measure covers a representative sample of the behaviors associated with the construct dimension or trait in question.

Continuous amnesia.   A form of dissociative amnesia in which the person loses the memory of all events occurring since the problem began.

Contrasted groups approach.   A method of concurrent validity in which group membership is used as the criterion by which the validity of a test is measured. The ability of the test to differentiate between two or more comparison groups (for example, schizophrenics vs. normals) is taken as evidence of concurrent validity.

Control subjects.   Subjects who do not receive the experimental treatment or manipulation but for whom all other conditions are held constant.

Controlled social drinking.   A controversial approach to treating problem drinkers in which the goal of treatment is the maintenance of controlled social drinking in moderate amounts, rather than total abstinence.

Contusion.   Brain trauma caused by jarring the brain with sufficient force that the brain is shifted and pressed against the skull, causing structural damage to the soft brain tissue.

Conversion disorder.   A type of somatoform disorder characterized by loss or impairment of physical function in the absence of any organic causes that might account for the changes. Formerly called *hysteria* or *hysterical neurosis.*

Corpus callosum.   A thick bundle of fibers that connects the two hemispheres of the brain.

Correlation.   A relationship or association between two or more variables. A correlation between variables may suggest, but does not prove, that a causal relationship exists between them.

Correlation coefficient.   A statistic that expresses the strength and direction (positive or negative) of the relationship between two variables.

Corticosteroids.   Steroids manufactured by the adrenal cortex that are involved in regulating the metabolism of carbohydrates and which increase resistance to stress by stemming inflammation and allergic reactions. Also called *cortical steroids.*

Countertransference.   In psychoanalysis, the transfer of feelings that the analyst holds toward other persons in her or his life onto the client.

Covert sensitization.   A technique of aversive conditioning that aims to help a client discontinue undesired behavior by associating the behavior with imagined aversive stimuli.

Crack.   The hardened, smokable form of cocaine.

Creative self.   In Alfred Adler's theory, the self-aware part of the personality that strives to achieve its potential.

Cretinism.   A disorder caused by thyroid deficiency in childhood that is characterized by stunted growth and mental retardation.

Criterion validity.   The degree to which a test or instrument correlates with an independent, external criterion (standard) representing the construct or trait that the test or instrument is intended to measure. There are two general types of criterion validity: concurrent validity and predictive validity.

Cross-fostering study.   A method of determining heritability of a trait or disorder by examining differences in prevalence among adoptees reared by either adoptive parents or biological parents who possessed the trait or disorder in question. Evidence that the disorder followed biological, rather than adoptive parentage favors the heritability of the trait or disorder.

Cultural-familial retardation.   A milder form of mental retardation that is believed to result, or at least be influenced by, impoverishment in the child's home environment.

Culture-bound.   Referring to patterns of behavior that are found only within a specific cultural context.

Culture-related.   Referring to patterns of behavior that are strongly related to the factors that define a specific cultural context, but which are also found in other cultures.

Cushing's syndrome.   A relatively rare disease that is caused by overactivity of the adrenal cortex and involves both physical and psychological changes.

Cyclothymic disorder.   A mood disorder characterized by a chronic pattern of mild mood swings between depression and mania that are not of sufficient severity to be classified as bipolar disorder.

Cytomegalovirus.   A maternal disease that carries a risk of mental retardation to the unborn child.

Defense mechanisms.   In psychodynamic theory, the reality-distorting strategies used by the ego to shield itself from conscious awareness of anxiety-evoking or troubling material.

Deinstitutionalization.   The practice of discharging large numbers of hospitalized mental patients to the community and of reducing the need for new admissions through the development of alternative treatment approaches such as halfway houses and crisis intervention services.

Delirium. A state of mental confusion, disorientation, and extreme difficulties focusing attention.

Delirium tremens. A withdrawal syndrome that often occurs following a sudden decrease or cessation of drinking in chronic alcoholics that is characterized by extreme restlessness, sweating, disorientation, and hallucinations. Abbreviated *DTs.*

Delta-9-tetrahydrocannabinol. The major active ingredient in marijuana. Abbreviated *THC.*

Delusion. A firmly held but inaccurate belief that persists despite evidence that it has no basis in reality.

Delusional disorder. A type of psychosis characterized by the presence of persistent delusions, often of a paranoid nature, that do not have the bizarre quality of the type often found in paranoid schizophrenia. Other than the delusion itself, the person's behavior may appear entirely normal.

Dementia. A state of deterioration of mental functioning, involving impairment of memory, thinking, judgment, use of language, and ability to carry through purposeful movements, and eventually resulting in personality changes.

Dementia praecox. The term given by Kraepelin to the disorder we now call schizophrenia.

Demonological model. The model that explains abnormal behavior in terms of supernatural forces, such as possession or a pact with the devil.

Dendrites. The rootlike structures at the end of the neuron that receive nerve impulses from other neurons.

Dependent personality disorder. A type of personality disorder characterized by difficulties making independent decisions and overly dependent behaviors.

Dependent variable. A measure of outcome in a scientific study that is assumed to be dependent on the effects of the independent variable.

Depersonalization. Feelings of unreality or detachment from one's self or one's body, as if one were a robot or functioning on automatic pilot, or observing oneself from outside.

Depersonalization disorder. A disorder characterized by persistent or recurrent episodes of depersonalization.

Depressant. A drug that lowers the level of activity of the central nervous system.

Derealization. Loss of the sense of reality of one's surroundings, experienced in terms of strange changes in one's environment (for example, people or objects changing size or shape), or in the sense of the passage of time.

Description. In science, the representation of observations without interpretation or inferences as to their nature or meaning. Description can be contrasted with inference, which is the process of drawing conclusions based on observations.

Desperation phase. The latter stage of pathological gambling in which the gambler hits rock bottom.

Determinant. (1) A factor that establishes (gives rise to) and sets limits, as on behavior. (2) A factor that is believed to govern responses to the Rorschach inkblot test—properties such as form, shading, texture, or color, and sense of movement implied by the features of the blot or the percept that the respondent imposes on the blot.

Detoxification. The process of ridding the system of alcohol or drugs under supervised conditions in which withdrawal symptoms can be monitored and controlled.

Deviation IQ. An intelligence quotient that is derived by determining the deviation between the individual's score and the norm (mean).

Dialogue. In Gestalt therapy, a technique in which one enacts a confrontation between two opposing parts of one's personality, such as between one's top dog and underdog.

Diathesis-stress. A model of abnormal behavior that posits that abnormal behavior patterns, such as schizophrenia, involve the interaction of genetic and environmental influences. In this model, a genetic predisposition, or diathesis, increases the individual's vulnerability to develop the disorder in response to stressful life circumstances. If, however, the level of stress is kept under the person's particular threshold, the disorder may never develop, even among people with the genetic predisposition.

Disorganized type. The subtype of schizophrenia that is characterized by disorganized behavior, bizarre delusions, and vivid hallucinations. Formerly *hebephrenic schizophrenia.*

Disorientation. A state of mental confusion or lack of awareness with respect to time, place, or the identity of oneself or others.

Displacement. In psychodynamic theory, a type of defense mechanism that involves the transferring of impulses toward threatening or unacceptable objects onto more acceptable or safer objects.

Disruptive behavior disorders. A category of behavior disorders in childhood involving socially disruptive behavior patterns, including attention-deficit hyperactivity disorder, conduct disorder, and oppositional defiant disorder.

Dissociative amnesia. A type of dissociative disorder in which a person experiences memory losses in the absence of any identifiable organic cause. But general knowledge and skills are usually retained.

Dissociative disorder. A category of disorders involving sudden changes in consciousness or self-identity, including dissociative amnesia, dissociative fugue, and dissociative identity disorder and depersonalization disorder.

Dissociative fugue. A type of dissociative disorder in which one suddenly flies from one's life situation, travels to a new location, assumes a new identity, and has amnesia for autobiographical information. The person usually retains skills and other abilities and may appear to others in the new environment to be leading a normal life.

Dissociative identity disorder. A dissociative disorder in which a person has two or more distinct, or alter, personalities.

Distinct heterogenity model. A model of genetic transmission of schizophrenia which proposes that schizophrenia represents a number of different disorders, each having its own distinct causes that may involve genetic defects that can be traced to particular genes or environmental factors.

Dizygotic twins. Twins who develop from separate fertilized eggs. Also called fraternal twins. Abbreviated *DZ twins*. Often contrasted with *monozygotic (MZ) twins* in studies of heritability of particular traits or disorders.

Dopamine. A neurotransmitter of the catecholamine class that is involved in Parkinson's disease and is believed to play a role in schizophrenia. See *dopamine theory.*

Dopamine theory. The biochemical theory of schizophrenia which proposes that schizophrenia involves the action of dopamine.

Double-bind communications. A pattern of communication involving the transmission of contradictory or mixed messages without acknowledgment of the inherent conflict; posited by some theorists to play a role in the development of schizophrenia.

Double depression. Persons diagnosed with both major depression and dysthymia.

Down syndrome. A condition caused by a chromosomal abnormality involving an extra chromosome on the 21st pair ("trisomy 21"), it is characterized by mental retardation and various physical abnormalities. Formerly called *mongolism* and *Down's syndrome.*

Drive for superiority. In Adler's theory, a term describing the desire to compensate for feelings of inferiority.

Duty to warn. An obligation imposed on therapists to warn third parties of threats made against them by the therapists' clients. The *Tarasoff* case established the legal basis for duty to warn provisions.

Dyslexia. A type of learning disorder characterized by impaired reading ability.

Dyspareunia. Persistent or recurrent pain experienced during or following sexual intercourse.

Dysthymic disorder. A mild but chronic type of depressive disorder.

Eclectic. The adoption of principles or techniques from various systems or theories.

Ego. In psychodynamic theory, the psychic structure corresponding to the concept of the self. The ego is governed by the reality principle and is responsible for finding socially acceptable outlets for the urgings of the id. The ego is characterized by the capacity to tolerate frustration and delay gratification.

Ego analyst. Psychodynamically oriented therapists who are influenced by ego psychology.

Ego dystonic. Behavior or feelings that are perceived to be foreign or alien to one's self-identity.

Ego-dystonic homosexuality. A termed used in the DSM to refer to a sense of discomfort with their sexual orientation that may be experienced by gay males or lesbians who would prefer to have a heterosexual orientation.

Ego ideal. In Freud's view, the configuration of higher social values and moral ideals embodied in the superego.

Ego identity. In Erik Erikson's view, the sense of personal identity: the achievement of a firm sense of who one is and what one stands for.

Ego psychology. The approach of modern psychodynamic theorists which posits that the ego has energy and strivings of its own apart from the id. Ego psychologists focus more on the conscious strivings of the ego than on the hypothesized unconscious functioning of the id.

Ego syntonic. Behavior or feelings that are perceived as natural or compatible parts of the self.

Electra complex. In psychodynamic theory, the term used to describe the conflict in the young girl during the phallic stage of development involving her longing for her father and her resentment of her mother.

Electroconvulsive therapy. The induction of a convulsive seizure by means of passing an electric current through the head; used primarily in the treatment of severe depression. Abbreviated *ECT.*

Electrodermal response. Changes in the electrical conductivity of the skin following exposure to a stimulus.

Electroencephalograph. An instrument for measuring the electrical activity of the brain (brain waves). Abbreviated *EEG.*

Electrolytes. Nonmetallic substances that serve as electrical conductors. In the body, electrolytes, such as dissolved salt, play vital roles in cell functioning, such as the maintenance of appropriate fluid balance in cells.

Electromyograph. An instrument for measuring muscle tension that is often used in biofeedback training. Abbreviated *EMG.*

Emotion-focused coping. A style of coping with stress that attempts to minimize emotional responsiveness rather than deal with the source of stress directly (for example, the use of denial to avoid thinking about the stress, or the use of tranquilizers to quell feelings of anxiety).

Empathic understanding. In Carl Rogers's theory, the ability to understand a client's experiences and feelings from the client's frame of reference. It is considered one of the principal characteristics of effective person-centered therapists.

Encephalitis. An inflammation of the brain.

Encoding. The stage of information processing that involves the modification of information for placement in memory.

Encopresis. Loss or lack of bowel control beyond the age of expected control that cannot be accounted for by physical causes.

Encounter group. A specialized form of group therapy or group process that focuses on increased self-awareness in a setting that encourages open expression of feelings.

Endocrine system. The system of ductless glands in the body that directly secretes hormones into the bloodstream.

Endogenous. Referring to abnormal behavior patterns that appear to arise from one's nature (genetic factors) rather than one's nurture (environmental influences).

Endorphins. Natural substances that function as neurotransmitters in the brain and are similar in their effects to morphine.

Enuresis. Loss or lack of bladder control beyond the age of expected control that cannot be accounted for by physical causes.

Epidemiological method. A method of research involved in tracking the rates of occurrence of particular disorders among different groups.

Epilepsy. A group of disorders caused by temporary sudden changes in the electrical activity of the brain that result in convulsive seizures or changes in the level of consciousness or motor activity.

Erogenous zone. A part of the body that is sensitive to sexual stimulation.

Eros. Freud's concept of the basic life instinct, which seeks to preserve and perpetuate life.

Erotomania. A form of delusional disorder characterized by delusional beliefs that one is loved by someone of high social status, even though one may have only a passing or even a non-existent relationship with the alleged lover. Also called the *love delusion*.

Estrogen. A female sex hormone involved in promoting growth of female sexual characteristics and regulating the menstrual cycle.

Etiology. Cause or origin; the study of causality.

Exhaustion stage. The third stage of the general adaptation syndrome (GAS), which is characterized by a lowering of resistance, increased parasympathetic activity, and possible physical deterioration.

Exhibitionism. A type of paraphilia occurring almost exclusively in males, in which the man experiences persistent and recurrent sexual urges and sexually arousing fantasies involving the exposure of his genitals to a stranger and either has acted on these urges or feels strongly distressed by them.

Exorcism. A ritual intended to expel demons or evil spirits from a person believed to be possessed.

Expectancies. In social-learning theory, a person variable describing people's predictions. Expectancies may refer to signs that suggest the occurrence of other events and to the outcomes of particular behaviors, as in "if-then" statements.

Experimental method. A scientific method that aims to discover cause-and-effect relationships by means of manipulating the independent variable(s) and observing their effects on the dependent variable(s).

Experimental subject. (1) In an experiment, a subject receiving a treatment or intervention, in contrast to a *control subject*. (2) More generally, one who participates in an experiment.

External attribution. In the reformulated helplessness theory, a type of attribution involving the belief that the cause of an event involves factors outside the self. Contrast with *internal attribution*.

External validity. A type of experimental validity involving the degree to which the experimental results can be generalized to other settings and populations.

Extinguish. In classical conditioning, to weaken a conditioned response by presenting the conditioned stimulus in the absence of the unconditioned stimulus. In operant conditioning, to weaken a previously reinforced response by withholding or withdrawing reinforcement.

Extraversion. A personality trait describing someone whose interests and attention are directed to people and things outside the self. Extraverted people tend to be sociable, outgoing, and self-expressive. Opposite of *introversion*.

Face validity. An aspect of content validity: the degree to which the content of a test or measure bears an apparent or obvious relationship to the constructs or traits it is purported to measure.

Factitious disorder. A type of mental disorder characterized by the intentional fabrication of psychological or physical symptoms for no apparent gain.

Factor analysis. A statistical technique for determining relationships that exist among items, such as items on psychological tests or personality scales.

False negative. An incorrect appraisal that people are free of a particular disorder when in fact they are not.

Family therapy. A form of therapy in which the family unit is treated as the client.

Fat cells. Cells that store fat. Also called *adipose tissue*.

Fear. An unpleasant negative emotion characterized by the perception of a specific threat, sympathetic nervous system activity, and tendencies to avoid the feared object.

Fear-stimulus hierarchy. An ordered series of increasingly more fearful stimuli. Used in the behavioral techniques of *systematic desensitization* and *gradual exposure*.

Feedback. Information about one's behavior.

Female sexual arousal disorder. A type of sexual dysfunction in women involving difficulties becoming sexually aroused, as defined by a lack of vaginal lubrication or failure to maintain sufficient lubrication to complete the sexual act, or lack of sexual excitement or pleasure during sexual activity.

Fetal alcohol syndrome. A cluster of symptoms appearing in children whose mothers drank alcohol during certain stages of pregnancy, characterized by distinct facial features and developmental delays. Abbreviated *FAS*.

Fetishism. A type of paraphilia in which a person uses an inanimate object or a body part (*partialism*) as a focus of sexual interest and as a source of arousal.

Fight-or-flight reaction. The hypothesized inborn tendency to respond to a threat by means of fighting the threat or fleeing.

First-rank symptoms. In Kurt Schneider's view, the primary features of schizophrenia, such as hallucinations and delusions, that distinctly characterize the disorder.

Fixation. In psychodynamic theory, arrested development in the form of attachment to objects of an earlier stage that occurs as the result of excessive or inadequate gratification at that stage.

Flashback. (1) The vivid reexperiencing of a past event, which may be difficult to distinguish from current reality. (2) The experience of sensory distortions or hallucinations occurring days or weeks after usage of LSD or other hallucinogenic drug that mimics the drug's effects.

Forced-choice format. A method of structuring test questions that requires respondents to select among a set number of possible answers.

Forcible rape. The legal term for rape or forced sexual intercourse with a nonconsenting person.

Form level. The appropriateness of fit between a person's response to a

Rorschach inkblot and the features of the blot itself.

Four A's. In Bleuler's view, the primary characteristics of schizophrenia: *(loose) associations, (blunted or inappropriate) affect, ambivalence,* and *autism.*

Frame of reference. In Carl Rogers's view, the person's unique patterning of attitudes, perceptions, and beliefs about the world, according to which the person evaluates events.

Free association. In psychoanalysis, the method of verbalizing thoughts as they occur without any conscious attempt to edit or censure them.

Freebasing. A method of ingesting cocaine by means of heating the drug with ether to separate its most potent component (its "free base") and then smoking the extract.

Frotteurism. A type of paraphilia characterized by recurrent sexual urges or sexually arousing fantasies involving bumping and rubbing against nonconsenting persons for sexual gratification. The person has either acted on these urges or is strongly distressed by them.

Frustration. (1) The thwarting of a motive or pursuit of a goal. (2) The emotion produced by the thwarting of a motive or pursuit of a goal.

Functional analysis. Analysis of behavior in terms of antecedent stimuli and consequent stimuli (potential reinforcers).

GABA. Gamma-aminobutyric acid (GABA), an inhibitory neurotransmitter, believed to play a role in anxiety.

Galvanic skin response. A measure of the change in electrical activity of the skin that is caused by increased activity of the sweat glands that accompanies states of sympathetic nervous system arousal, such as when the person is anxious. Abbreviated *GSR.*

Gamma-aminobutyric acid (GABA). See *GABA.*

Gastrointestinal disorders. Disorders of the stomach and intestines, such as ulcers or colitis.

Gender identity. One's psychological sense of being female or being male.

Gender-identity disorder. A disorder in which the individual believes that her or his anatomic gender is inconsistent with her or his psychological sense of being female or male.

General adaptation syndrome. In Selye's view, the body's three-stage response to states of prolonged or intense stress. Abbreviated *GAS.*

General paresis. A degenerative brain disorder that occurs during the final stage of syphilis.

Generalized amnesia. A form of dissociative amnesia in which people lose memories of their entire lives, although they retain their basic habits, tastes, and skills.

Generalized anxiety disorder. A type of anxiety disorder characterized by general feelings of dread and foreboding and heightened states of sympathetic arousal. Formerly referred to as *free-floating anxiety.*

Genes. The units found on chromosomes that carry heredity.

Genetic predisposition. A tendency to develop a behavior pattern that is determined by one's heredity.

Genetics. The science of heredity.

Genital stage. In psychodynamic theory, the fifth stage of psychosexual development that corresponds to mature sexuality and is characterized by the expression of libido through sexual intercourse with an adult member of the opposite gender.

Genotype. (1) The genetic constitution of an individual or a group. (2) The sum total of traits that one inherits from one's parents.

Genuineness. In Carl Rogers's view, the ability to recognize and express one's true feelings. Genuineness is considered to be a characteristic of the effective person-centered therapist.

Gestalt therapy. The approach to psychotherapy originated by Fritz Perls that seeks to help people integrate the conflicting parts of their personalities through directive exercises designed to help people perceive their whole selves.

Global attribution. In the reformulated helplessness theory, a type of attribution involving the belief that the cause of an event involved generalized, rather than specific factors. Contrast with *specific attribution.*

Gonads. The sex glands of an organism that have reproductive functions: the testes in men, the ovaries in women.

Gradual exposure. In behavior therapy, a method of overcoming fears through a stepwise process of direct exposure to increasingly fearful stimuli.

Group therapy. A form of psychotherapy in which several individuals receive treatment at the same time in a group format.

Halfway house. A protected or supervised environment in the community, which provides a bridge or compromise between living in the psychiatric hospital and independent community living.

Hallucination. A perception that occurs in the absence of an external stimulus that is confused with reality.

Hallucinogenic. A substance that gives rise to hallucinations.

Hashish. A drug derived from the resin of the marijuana plant— *Cannabis sativa.* Often called *hash.*

Health psychology. The branch of psychology involved in the study of the relationships between psychological factors (e.g., coping styles, belief patterns, overt behaviors) and physical illness. Health psychology seeks to apply knowledge of these relationships to help people lower their risk of developing disease or improving their ability to cope with disease through making adaptive behavioral and cognitive changes.

Hemoglobin. The red compound found in red blood cells that carries oxygen from the lungs to the tissues and carries away carbon dioxide from the tissues to the lungs.

Heroin. A type of opiate or narcotic drug derived from morphine that has strong addictive properties.

Heterozygote. A plant or animal that is a hybrid, inheriting genes for two unlike characteristics.

Hierarchy of needs. In Abraham Maslow's theory, the ordered series of needs that motivate behavior.

High strain. Referring to jobs that impose great stress on workers.

Histrionic personality disorder. A type of personality disorder characterized by excessive needs to be the center of attention and to receive reassurance, praise, and approval from others. Such persons often appear overly dramatic and emotional in their behavior.

Homosexuality. The sexual orientation characterized by erotic interest in, and development of romantic relationships with members of one's own gender.

Homozygotes. A plant or organism having genes with like characteristics.

Hormones. Substances secreted by endocrine glands that regulate bodily functions and promote the development or growth of body structures.

Hot reactors. Persons whose response to stress is characterized by accelerated heart rate and constriction of the blood vessels in the peripheral areas of the body.

Humors. Historic: the vital bodily fluids considered responsible for one's disposition and health, as in Hippocrates's belief that the health of the body and mind depended on the balance of four humors in the body: phlegm, black bile, blood, and yellow bile.

Huntington's disease. A degenerative disease that is transmitted genetically and is characterized by jerking and twisting movements, psychotic behavior, and mental deterioration.

Hydrocarbons. Chemical compounds consisting of hydrogen and carbon, which are a constituent of cigarette smoke.

Hyperactivity. An abnormal behavior pattern found most often in young boys that is characterized by difficulties maintaining attention and extreme restlessness.

Hypertension. High blood pressure.

Hyperthyroidism. A physical condition caused by excesses of the hormone thyroxin, it is characterized by excitability, insomnia, and weight loss. Also called *Grave's disease.*

Hyperventilation. A pattern of overly rapid breathing associated with anxiety in which one breathes off too much carbon dioxide, leading to feelings of light-headedness and further distress.

Hypnosis. A trancelike state induced by suggestions in which one is generally passive and responsive to the commands of the hypnotist.

Hypoactive sexual desire disorder. Persistent or recurrent lack of sexual interest or sexual fantasies.

Hypochondriasis. A somatoform disorder that is characterized by persistent beliefs that one has a serious medical condition despite the lack of medical evidence to support such beliefs.

Hypoglycemia. A metabolic disorder involving low levels of blood sugar that is characterized by lack of energy, dizziness, and shakiness.

Hypomanic episodes. Mild manic episodes.

Hypothalamus. A structure in the lower middle part of the brain that is involved in regulating body temperature, emotion, and motivation.

Hypothesis. An assumption that is tested through experimentation.

Hypothyroidism. A physical condition caused by deficiencies of the hormone thyroxin that is characterized by sluggishness and lowered metabolism.

Hypoxia. Deficiencies in the supply of oxygen to the brain or other organs.

Hypoxyphilia. A paraphilia in which a person seeks sexual gratification by being deprived of oxygen by means of using a noose, plastic bag, chemical, or pressure on the chest.

Hysteria. Former term for *conversion disorder.*

Id. In psychodynamic theory, the unconscious psychic structure that is present at birth. The id contains instinctive drives and is governed by the pleasure principle.

Ideas of persecution. A form of delusional thinking characterized by false beliefs that one is being persecuted or victimized by others.

Ideas of reference. A form of delusional thinking in which a person reads personal meaning into the behavior of others or external events that are completely independent of the person.

Identification. (1) In psychodynamic theory, the process of incorporating the personality or behavior of others. (2) In social-learning theory, a process of imitation by which children acquire behaviors similar to those of role models.

Identity diffusion. See *role diffusion.*

Immune surveillance theory. The belief that cancer results from a breakdown in the body's immune system in which the immune system fails to mark and destroy mutant cells, allowing them to spread.

Immune system. The body's system for recognizing and destroying antigens (foreign bodies) that invade the body, mutated cells, and worn-out cells.

Impotence. See *male erectile disorder.*

Impulse control disorders. Disorders involving the failure to control impulses that result in harm to oneself or others, such as pathological gambling or kleptomania.

In vivo. In real life.

Independent variable. A factor in an experiment that is manipulated so that its effects can be measured or observed.

Individual psychology. The psychodynamic theory developed by Alfred Adler.

Individual response specificity. The belief that people respond to the same stressor in idiosyncratic ways.

Infarction. The development of an infarct, or area of dead or dying tissue, resulting from the blocking or obstruction of blood vessels normally serving that tissue.

Inference. A conclusion that is drawn from data.

Inferiority complex. In Adler's view, the feelings of inferiority that are believed to be a central source of motivation.

Inflammation. The response to an injured part in which increased blood flow brings an increased number of white blood cells and results in reddening, warming, and swelling of the area.

Inhibited orgasm. Persistent or recurrent delay in achieving orgasm following an adequate period of sexually stimulating activity.

Inquiry. In Rorschach terminology, the phase of the testing process in which the examiner poses probing questions to uncover the factors that determined the subject's responses.

Insanity defense. A form of legal defense in which a defendant in a criminal case pleads innocence on the basis of insanity.

Insight. In psychotherapy, the attainment of awareness and understanding of one's true motives and feelings.

Institutionalization syndrome. A behavioral pattern characteristic of patients in institutional settings that is marked by dependency, obedience to authority, and passivity.

Intake interview. The process of gathering information from new clients through the use of a structured series of questions.

Intelligence. (1) The global capacity to understand the world and cope with its challenges. (2) The trait or traits associated with successful performance on intelligence tests.

Intelligence quotient. A measure of intelligence derived on the basis of scores on an intelligence test. It is called a quotient because it was originally derived by dividing a respondent's *mental age* by her or his actual age. Abbreviated *IQ.*

Interjudge reliability. A measure of reliability of a test based on the agreement between raters.

Internal attribution. In the reformulated helplessness theory, a type of attribution involving the belief that the cause of an event involved factors within oneself. Contrasted with *external attribution.*

Internal consistency. Reliability as measured by the cohesiveness or interrelationships of the items on a test or scale.

Internal validity. A type of experimental validity involving the degree to which manipulation of the independent variable(s) can be causally related to changes in the dependent variable(s).

Interpretation. In psychoanalysis, an explanation of a client's behavior or verbalizations offered by the analyst.

Intoxication. A state of drunkenness.

Introjection. In psychodynamic theory, the process of unconsciously incorporating features of the personality of another person within one's own ego structure.

Involuntary. Automatic or without conscious direction, as in the cases of bodily processes like heartbeat and respiration.

Kleptomania. An impulse control disorder characterized by compulsive stealing.

Knob. The swollen ending of an axon terminal.

Koro syndrome. A culture-related somatoform disorder, found primarily in China, in which people fear that their genitals are shrinking and retracting into the body.

Korsakoff's syndrome. A form of brain damage that is associated with chronic thiamine deficiency. The syndrome may occur among chronic alcoholics and is characterized by memory loss, disorientation, and the tendency to invent memories to replace lost memories (confabulation). Also called *alcohol persisting amnestic disorder.*

La belle indifférence. A French term describing the lack of concern over one's symptoms displayed by some people with conversion disorder.

Laceration. The most serious type of brain trauma, this involves an injury to the brain that is caused by a foreign object that pierces the skull, such as a bullet or a piece of shrapnel.

Latency stage. According to psychoanalytic theory, the fourth stage of psychosexual development, which is characterized by repression of sexual impulses.

Latent content. In psychodynamic theory, the underlying or symbolic content of dreams.

Learned helplessness. In Seligman's model, a behavior pattern characterized by passivity and perceptions of lack of control that develops because of a history of failure to be able to exercise control over one's environment.

Learning disorder. Noted deficiency in a specific learning ability, which is remarkable because of the individual's general intelligence and exposure to learning opportunities.

Legal commitment. The legal process involved in confining a person found "not guilty by reason of insanity" in a mental institution; also called *criminal commitment.*

Leukocytes. White blood cells. Leukocytes comprise part of the body's immune system.

Libido. In psychodynamic theory, the energy of eros, the life instinct. Generally, sexual drive or energy.

Limbic system. A group of brain structures in the lower part of the cerebrum that are involved in memory and motivation.

Localized amnesia. A form of dissociative amnesia in which memory is lost for all events occurring during a particular period of time.

Locus of control. One's perception of the site (internal or external) of the capacity to generate reinforcement. People who believe that they have the capacity to generate or attain reinforcements are said to have an internal locus of control. People who rely on others or luck for reinforcement are said to have an external locus of control.

Logotherapy. A type of existential therapy developed by Viktor Frankl that focuses on helping people find meaning in their lives.

Longitudinal studies. Research studies in which subjects are followed over time. Longitudinal studies have helped researchers identify factors in early life that may predict the later development of disorders such as schizophrenia.

Losing phase. A middle phase of a "gambling career" in which losses begin to mount and gambling may increase in the attempt to break even.

LSD. See *lysergic acid diethylamide.*

Lysergic acid diethylamide. A type of hallucinogenic drug.

Magnetic resonance imaging. Formation of a computer-generated image of the anatomical details of the brain by measuring the signals that these structures emit when the head is placed in a strong magnetic field. Abbreviated *MRI.*

Major depression. A severe mood disorder characterized by the occurrence of major depressive episodes in the absence of a history of manic episodes. Major depression is characterized by a range of features such as depressed mood, lack of interest or pleasure in usual activities, lack of energy or motivation, and changes in appetite or sleep patterns.

Major tranquilizer. A type of tranquilizer used primarily in the treatment of psychotic behavior, such as Thorazine. Also called an *antipsychotic* drug.

Male erectile disorder. A sexual dysfunction in males, characterized by difficulty in achieving or maintaining erection during sexual activity.

Malingering. Faking illness so as to avoid or escape work or other duties, or to obtain benefits.

Manic. Relating to mania, as in the manic phase of a bipolar disorder.

Manic episode. A period of unrealistically heightened euphoria, extreme restlessness, and excessive activity characterized by disorganized behavior and impaired judgment. Alternates with major depressive episodes in bipolar disorder.

Manifest content. In psychodynamic theory, the reported content or apparent meaning of dreams.

Mantra. In meditation, a resonant sounding word or sound that is repeated to induce a state of relaxation and a narrowing of consciousness.

Marijuana. An hallucinogenic-type drug derived from the *Cannabis sativa* plant.

Markers. (1) Characteristics that identify individuals who are most vulnerable to a particular disorder or who are already afflicted with the disorder. Studies of HR (high-risk) children aim to identify potential markers for schizophrenia. The DST (dexamethasone suppression test) may represent a possible biological marker for depression.

Medical model. A biological perspective in which abnormal behavior is viewed as symptomatic of underlying illness.

Medulla. An area of the hindbrain involved in the regulation of heartbeat and respiration.

Melancholia. A state of severe depression.

Meningitis. An inflammation of the meninges, or membranes covering the brain and spinal cord, often caused by a bacterial infection.

Mental age. The age equivalent that corresponds to a person's level of intelligence, as measured by performance on the Stanford Binet Intelligence Scale.

Mental retardation. (1) A generalized delay or impairment in the development of intellectual and adaptive abilities. (2) Substantially lower intellectual functioning, as determined by an IQ of 70 or below.

Mental status examination. A structured clinical evaluation to determine various aspects of the client's mental functioning.

Meta-analysis. A statistical technique for combining the results of different studies into an overall average. In psychotherapy research, meta-analysis is used to compute the average benefit or size of effect associated with psychotherapy overall, or with different forms of therapy, in relation to control groups.

Metabolic rate. The rate at which energy is consumed in the body.

Methadone. An artificial narcotic that lacks the rush associated with heroin, which is used to help heroin addicts abstain from heroin without incurring an abstinence syndrome.

Model. In social-learning theory, a person whose behavior patterns are imitated by others.

Modeling. In behavior therapy, a technique for helping a client acquire new behavior by means of having the therapist or members of a therapy group demonstrate a target behavior that is then imitated by a client.

Monoamine oxidase (MAO) inhibitors. Antidepressants that act to increase the availability of neurotransmitters in the brain by inhibiting the actions of an enzyme, monoamine oxidase, that normally breaks down or degrades neurotransmitters (norepinephrine and serotonin) in the synaptic cleft.

Monogenic model. A single-gene model of genetic transmission in schizophrenia.

Monozygotic twins. Twins who develop from the same fertilized egg and therefore share identical genes. Also called identical twins. Abbreviated *MZ twins*. Contrast with fraternal, or *dizygotic (DZ) twins*.

Mood. The pervasive quality of an individual's emotional experience, as in depressed mood, anxious mood, or elated mood.

Mood disorder. A type of disorder characterized by disturbances of mood, as in depressive disorders (major depression or dysthymia) or bipolar disorders (bipolar disorder and cyclothymia).

Moral principle. In psychodynamic theory, the principle that governs the superego to set moral standards and enforce adherence to them.

Moral therapy. A 19th-century treatment philosophy that emphasized that hospitalized mental patients should be treated with care and understanding in a pleasant environment, not shackled in chains.

Morphine. A strongly addicting narcotic drug derived from the opium poppy that relieves pain and induces feelings of well-being.

Motor cortex. The part of the cerebral cortex, located in the frontal lobe, that is involved in controlling muscular responses.

Mourning. Normal feelings or expressions of grief following a loss. See *bereavement*.

Movement. In Rorschach terminology, responses to the Rorschach test that involve perceptions of the figures as animated (for example, running, dancing or flying), which may be suggestive of intelligence and creativity on the part of the respondent.

Multifactorial-polygenic model. A model of genetic transmission of schizophrenia which maintains that schizophrenia is caused by the interactive or combined effects of multiple genes and environmental influences.

Multi-infarct dementia. A form of mental deterioration that is caused by multiple strokes or other forms of brain damage.

Multiphasic. Referring to several aspects of the personality, as in the Minnesota Multiphasic Personality Inventory.

Münchausen syndrome. A type of factitious disorder characterized by the feigning of medical symptoms for no apparent purpose other than getting admitted or remaining in hospitals.

"Musterbation." Albert Ellis's term for a type of rigid thought pattern characterized by the tendency to impose absolutist expectations on oneself: One thinks that one "must" achieve a certain goal, as in "I *must* get an A in this course or else!"

Myocardial infarction. A breakdown of the tissue of the heart due to an obstruction of the blood vessels that supply blood to the affected area—a heart attack.

Myocarditis. An inflammation of the muscle tissue of the heart (myocardium).

Naloxone. A drug that prevents users from becoming high if they subsequently take heroin. Some people are placed on naloxone after being withdrawn from heroin to prevent return to heroin.

Narcissistic personality disorder. A type of personality disorder characterized by the adoption of an inflated self-image, demands for constant attention and admiration, among other features.

Narcotics. Drugs, such as opiates, that are used for pain relief and treatment of insomnia, but which have addictive potential.

Naturalistic-observation method. A method of scientific research in which the behavior of subjects is carefully and unobtrusively observed and measured in their natural environments.

Negative correlation. A statistical relationship between two variables such that increases in one variable are associated with decreases in the other.

Negative reinforcer. A reinforcer whose removal increases the frequency of an operant behavior. Anxiety, pain, and social disapproval often function as negative reinforcers; their removal tends to increase the rate of the immediately preceding behavior. Contrast with *positive reinforcer.*

Negative symptoms. The deficits or behavioral deficiencies associated with schizophrenia, such as social skills deficits, social withdrawal, flattened affect, poverty of speech and thought, psychomotor retardation, failure to experience pleasure in pleasant activities.

Neo-Freudians. A term used to describe the "second generation" of theorists who followed in the Freudian tradition. On the whole, neo-Freudians (such as Jung, Adler, Horney, Sullivan) placed greater emphasis on the importance of cultural and social influences on behavior and lesser importance on sexual impulses and the functioning of the id.

Neologisms. A type of disturbed thinking associated with schizophrenia involving the coining of new words.

Neuroleptics. A group of antipsychotic drugs used in the treatment of schizophrenia, such as the phenothiazines (Thorazine, Mellaril, etc.).

Neurons. Nerve cells.

Neuropsychology. The field of psychology that focuses on the study of relationships between the brain and behavior.

Neurosis. The type or types, respectively, of nonpsychotic behavioral disturbances characterized chiefly by the use of defensive behaviors to control anxiety, in which the person is generally able to function but is impaired in some aspect(s) of functioning. Plural: *neuroses.*

Neurotic anxiety. In psychodynamic theory, the feelings of anxiety that stem from the unconscious perception of threat that unacceptable impulses may rise to the level of consciousness or become expressed in overt behavior.

Neuroticism. A trait describing a general neurotic quality involving such characteristics as anxious, worrisome behavior, apprehension about the future, and avoidance behavior.

Neurotransmitter. A chemical substance that serves as a type of messenger by transmitting neural impulses from one neuron to another.

Nicotine. A stimulant found in tobacco smoke.

Nonspecific treatment factors. The characteristics that are not specific to any one form of psychotherapy, but tend to be shared by psychotherapies, such as the attention a client receives from a therapist and the therapist's encouragement of the client's sense of hope and positive expectancies.

Norepinephrine. A type of neurotransmitter of the catecholamine class.

Nuclear magnetic resonance. See *magnetic resonance imaging.*

Obesity. Excessive body weight or plumpness, often defined as weighing at least 20% above one's ideal body weight.

Objective tests. Tests that allow a limited, specified range of response options or answers so that they can be scored objectively.

Object-relations. The person's relationships to the internalized representations or "objects" of others' personalities that have been introjected within the person's ego structure. See *object-relations theory.*

Object-relations theory. In psychodynamic theory, the viewpoint that focuses on the influences of the internalized representations (called "objects") within the person's ego structure of the personalities of parents and other figures of strong attachment.

Obsession. A recurring or nagging thought or image that seems beyond the individual's ability to control.

Obsessive-compulsive disorder. A type of anxiety disorder characterized by the occurrence of obsessional thoughts and/or compulsions to perform certain actions.

Obsessive-compulsive personality disorder. A type of personality disorder characterized by rigid ways of relating to others, perfectionistic tendencies, lack of spontaneity, and excessive attention to details.

Oedipus complex. In psychodynamic theory, the conflict that occurs during the phallic stage of development in which the boy incestuously desires his mother and perceives his father as a rival for his mother's love and attention. The counterpart in girls involves incestuous desires to possess the father, combined with jealous rivalry with the mother for father's love and resentment of the mother, whom she blames for lacking a penis.

Open-ended questions. A type of question that provides an unlimited range of response options.

Operant conditioning. A form of learning in which the organism acquires new behaviors on the basis of reinforcement.

Opiate. A type of depressant drug with strong addictive properties that is derived from the opium poppy and provides relief from pain and feelings of euphoria.

Opioid. A natural or synthetic (artificial) drug with opiatelike properties and effects.

Oppositional defiant disorder. A disorder in childhood or adolescence characterized by excessive oppositionality or tendencies to refuse requests from parents and others.

Optimum level of arousal. The level of arousal associated with peak performance and maximum feelings of well-being.

Oral stage. In psychodynamic theory, the first of Freud's stages of psychosexual development, during which pleasure is primarily sought through such oral activities as sucking and biting.

Orienting response. An unlearned pattern of responses to an incoming stimulus, including pupil dilation, particular brain wave patterns associated with states of attention, and changes in the electrical conductivity of the skin (GSR).

Osteoporosis. A physical disorder caused by calcium deficiency that is characterized by extreme brittleness of the bones.

Overanxious disorder. A disorder in childhood or adolescence characterized by excessive anxiety or worrisome behavior.

Panic disorder. A type of anxiety disorder characterized by the repeated occurrence of episodes of intense anxiety or panic.

Paranoid. Referring to irrational suspicions.

Paranoid personality disorder. A type of personality disorder characterized by persistent suspiciousness of the motives of others, but not to the point of holding clear-cut delusions.

Paranoid type. A subtype of schizophrenia characterized by hallucinations and systematized delusions, commonly involving themes of persecution.

Paraphilias. Sexual deviations or types of sexual disorders in which the person experiences recurrent sexual urges and sexually arousing fantasies involving nonhuman objects (such as articles of clothing), inappropriate or nonconsenting partners (for example, children), or situations producing humiliation or pain to oneself or one's partner. The paraphiliac has either acted on such urges or is strongly distressed by them.

Parasympathetic. Relating to the activity of the parasympathetic branch of the autonomic nervous system. See *sympathetic division*.

Parkinson's disease. A progressive disease of the basal ganglia, it is characterized by muscle tremor and shakiness, rigidity, difficulty walking, poor control over fine body movements, lack of facial muscle tonus, and cognitive impairment in some cases, especially in later stages of the disorder.

Pathogen. An organism such as a bacterium or virus that can cause disease.

Pathological gambler. A person who gambles habitually despite consistent losses. A compulsive gambler.

Peak experience. In humanistic theory, a brief moment of rapture that stems from the realization that one is on the path toward self-actualization.

Pellagra. A disease caused by deficiency of niacin characterized by skin eruptions and various behavioral features.

Penile strain gauge. A device for measuring the size of penile erection.

Performance anxiety. Fear relating to the threat of failing to perform adequately.

Peripheral nervous system. The part of the nervous system that consists of the somatic nervous system and the autonomic nervous system.

Perseveration. The persistent repetition of the same thought or response.

Person-centered therapy. Carl Rogers's method of psychotherapy, emphasizing the establishment of a warm, accepting therapeutic relationship that frees clients to engage in process of self-exploration and self-acceptance.

Person variables. In social-learning theory, the influences on behavior of characteristics relating to the person, including encoding strategies, competencies, expectancies, subjective values, and self-regulatory systems and plans.

Personal constructs. In George Kelly's theory, the personal dimensions of judgment by which individuals evaluate events, such as strong-weak, good-bad, and so on.

Personality disorders. Types of abnormal behavior patterns involving excessively rigid patterns of behaviors, or ways of relating to others, that ultimately become self-defeating because their rigidity prevents adjustment to external demands.

Pervasive developmental disorder. A disorder characterized by gross impairment in the development of a broad array of skills relating to social, cognitive, and language functioning.

Phallic stage. In psychodynamic theory, Freud's third stage of psychosexual development, characterized by sexual interest focused on the phallic region and the development of incestuous desires for the parent of the opposite gender and rivalry with the parent of the same gender (the Oedipus complex).

Phenothiazines. A group of antipsychotic drugs or "major tranquilizers" used in the treatment of schizophrenia.

Phenotype. The representation of the total array of traits of an organism, as influenced by the interaction of nature (genetic factors) and nurture (environmental factors).

Phenylketonuria. A genetic disorder that prevents the metabolization of phenylpyruvic acid, leading to mental retardation. Abbreviated *PKU*.

Phlegmatic. Slow and stolid.

Phobia. An excessive irrational fear that is out of proportion to the degree of danger in a stimulus or a situation.

Phrenologist. Practitioner of the study of bumps on a person's head as indications of the individual's underlying traits or characteristics.

Pick's disease. A form of dementia, similar in its features to Alzheimer's disease, but characterized by the presence of specific abnormalities (Pick's bodies) in nerve cells and the absence of the neurofibrillary tangles and plaques found in Alzheimer's disease.

Placebo. (pluh-SEE-bo). An inert medication or form of bogus treatment that is intended to control for the effects of expectancies. Sometimes referred to as a "sugar pill."

Play therapy. A form of psychodynamic therapy with children in which play activities and objects are used as a means of helping children symbolically enact family conflicts or express underlying feelings or personal problems.

Pleasure principle. In psychodynamic theory, the governing principle of the id, involving the demands for immediate gratification of instinctive needs.

Polygenic. Traits or characteristics that are determined by more than one gene.

Polymorphously perverse. In psychodynamic theory, the belief that humans are born with the capacity of achieving sexual gratification through various ways, such as heterosexual, homosexual, and autoerotic (pleasure from one's body organs) activities.

Pons. A brain structure, located in the hindbrain, which is involved in respiration.

Population. A total group of people, other organisms, or events.

Pornography. Portrayals of explicit sexual activity that are intended to sexually arouse the observer.

Positive correlation. A statistical relationship between two variables such that increases in one variable are associated with increases in the other.

Positive reinforcers. Types of reinforcers that increase the frequency of behavior when they are presented. Food and social approval are generally, but not always, positive reinforcers. Contrast with *negative reinforcer*.

Positive symptoms. The more flagrant features of schizophrenia associated with behavioral excesses, such as hallucinations, delusions, bizarre behavior, and thought disorder.

Positron-emission tomography. A brain-imaging technique in which a computer-generated image of the neural activity of regions of the brain is formed by tracing the amounts of glucose used in the various regions. Abbreviated *PET scan*.

Possession. In demonology, a type of superstitious belief in which abnormal behavior is taken as a sign that the individual has become possessed by demons or the devil, usually as a form of retribution or the result of making a pact with the devil.

Postpartum depression. Persistent and severe mood changes that occur following childbirth.

Post-traumatic stress disorder. A type of disorder involving impaired functioning following exposure to a traumatic experience, such as combat, physical assault or rape, or natural or technological disasters. The person experiences such problems as reliving or reexperiencing the trauma, intense fear, avoidance of event-related stimuli, generalized numbing of emotional responsiveness, and heightened autonomic arousal.

Preconscious. In psychodynamic theory, descriptive of material that lies outside of present awareness but which can be brought into awareness by focusing attention. See also *unconscious*.

Predictive validity. The degree to which a test response or score is predictive of some criterion behavior (such as school performance) in the future.

Prefrontal lobotomy. A form of psychosurgery in which certain neural pathways in the brain were severed in the attempt to control disturbed behavior.

Pregenital. In psychodynamic theory, referring to characteristics that are typical of stages of psychosexual development that precede the genital stage.

Premature ejaculation. A type of sexual dysfunction involving a persistent or recurrent pattern of ejaculation occurring during sexual activity at a point before the man desires it.

Prepared conditioning. The belief that people are genetically prepared to acquire fear responses to certain classes of stimuli, such as fears of large animals, snakes, heights, or even strangers. Although the development of such phobias may have had survival value to our prehistoric ancestors, such behavior patterns may be less functional today.

Presenting problem. The complaint that prompts initial contact with a helping professional.

Pressured speech. An outpouring of speech in which words seem to surge urgently for expression, as in a manic state.

Primary gains. In psychodynamic theory, the relief from anxiety obtained through the development of a neurotic symptom.

Primary prevention. Efforts placed on preventing the development of psychological or medical problems before they start.

Primary process thinking. In psychodynamic theory, the mental process in infancy by which the id seeks gratification of primitive impulses by means of imagining that it possesses what it desires. Thinking which is illogical, magical, and fails to discriminate between reality and fantasy.

Primary reinforcers. Natural reinforcers or stimuli that have reinforcement value without learning. Water, food, warmth, and relief from pain are examples of primary reinforcers. Contrast with *secondary reinforcers*.

Primary sex characteristics. The characteristics that distinguish the genders and are directly involved in reproduction, such as the sex organs.

Problem-focused coping. A form of coping with stress characterized by directly confronting the source of the stress.

Problem-solving therapy. A form of therapy that focuses on helping people develop more effective problem-solving skills.

Process schizophrenia. A type of schizophrenia characterized by gradual onset, poor premorbid functioning, and poor outcomes. Contrast with *reactive schizophrenia*.

Prodromal phase. (1) A stage in which the early features or signs of a disorder become apparent. (2) In schizophrenia, the period of decline in functioning that precedes the development of the first acute psychotic episode.

Progesterone. A female sex hormone involved in promoting the growth and development of the sex organs and helping to maintain pregnancy.

Prognosis. A prediction of the probable course or outcome of a disorder.

Projection. In psychodynamic theory, a defense mechanism in which one's own impulses are attributed to another person.

Projective test. A psychological test that presents ambiguous or vague stimuli into which the examinee is believed to project her or his own personality and unconscious motives in making a response. The Rorschach and TAT are examples of projective tests.

Prophylactic. Relating to a device, drug, or remedy designed to preserve health or prevent disease.

Psychiatric commitment. See *civil commitment.*

Psychiatrist. A physician who specializes in the diagnosis and treatment of emotional disorders.

Psychic. (1) Relating to mental phenomena. (2) A person who claims to be sensitive to supernatural forces.

Psychic determinism. The belief that emotions and behavior are caused by the interplay of internal mental processes.

Psychoactive. Describing chemical substances or drugs that have psychological effects.

Psychoanalysis. (1) The theoretical model of personality developed by Sigmund Freud. (2) The method of psychotherapy developed by Sigmund Freud.

Psychoanalytic theory. The theoretical model of personality developed by Freud. Also called *psychoanalysis.*

Psychodrama. The method of group therapy developed by Moreno in which people express emotional responses and enact conflicts with significant others in their lives through dramatized role enactments.

Psychodynamic model. The theoretical model of Freud and his followers in which behavior is viewed as the product of clashing forces within the personality.

Psychological dependence. Reliance, as on a substance, although one may not be physiologically dependent on the substance.

Psychological hardiness. A cluster of stress-buffering traits characterized by commitment, challenge, and control.

Psychologist. A person with advanced graduate training in psychology. A clinical psychologist is a type of psychologist who specializes in abnormal behavior.

Psychometric approach. A method of psychological assessment which seeks to use psychological tests to identify and measure the reasonably stable traits in an individual's personality that are believed to largely determine the person's behavior.

Psychomotor retardation. A general slowing down of motor behavior and psychological functioning.

Psychoneuroimmunology. The field of scientific investigation that studies relationships between psychological factors, such as coping styles, attitudes, and behavior patterns, and immunological functioning.

Psychopharmacology. The field of study that examines the effects of drugs on behavior and psychological functioning and that explores the use of psychoactive drugs in the treatment of emotional disorders.

Psychophysiological. Referring to physiological correlates or underpinnings of psychological events.

Psychosexual. Descriptive of the stages of human development in Freud's theory in which sexual energy (libido) becomes expressed through different erogenous zones of the body during different developmental stages.

Psychosis. A type of major psychological disorder in which people show impaired ability to interpret reality and difficulties in meeting the demands of daily life. Schizophrenia is a prominent example of a psychotic disorder. Plural: *psychoses.*

Psychosocial. Relating to interpersonal relationships and social interactions that influence behavior and development.

Psychosocial development. Erikson's theory of personality development that extends through multiple stages of development from infancy through old age.

Psychotherapy. A method of helping involving a systematic interaction between a therapist and a client that uses psychological principles to influence the client's thoughts, feelings, or behaviors in order to help that client overcome abnormal behavior or adjust to problems in living.

Psychotropic drugs. Drugs that are used in the treatment of emotional disorders whose main effects are psychological or behavioral.

Punishments. Unpleasant stimuli that suppress the frequency of the behaviors they follow.

Quasi-experiment. A method of research that is "similar to" the experimental method, except that experimental and control subjects are not assigned to their respective groups by random assignment. Hence, a selection factor may operate to distort results. See *selection factor.*

Random sample. A sample that is drawn in such a way that every member of a population has an equal probability of being selected.

Rape trauma syndrome. A cluster of symptoms that victims often experience in the aftermath of rape.

Rapid flight of ideas. A characteristic of manic behavior involving rapid speech and changes of topics.

Rapid smoking. A method of aversive conditioning in which cigarettes are inhaled more rapidly than usual, making smoking an aversive experience.

Rapport. In psychotherapy, the interpersonal relationship between a therapist and a client that is characterized by harmony, trust, and cooperation.

Rational-emotive therapy. Albert Ellis's method of cognitive therapy, which focuses on helping clients challenge and correct irrational beliefs that produce emotional and behavioral difficulties.

Rationalization. In psychodynamic theory, a type of defense mechanism involving a process of self-deception in the form of finding justifications for unacceptable impulses, ideas, or behavior.

Reactive schizophrenia. A type of schizophrenia characterized by relatively abrupt onset that is believed to be precipitated by stressful or traumatic events. Contrast with *process schizophrenia.*

Reality anxiety. The concept in psychodynamic theory relating to reality-based fear.

Reality principle. In psychodynamic theory, the governing principle of the ego that involves consideration of what is socially acceptable and practical in gratifying needs.

Reality testing. The ability to perceive the world accurately and to distinguish reality from fantasy.

Rebound anxiety. The occurrence of strong anxiety following withdrawal from a tranquilizer.

Receptor site. A part of a dendrite on the receiving neuron that is structured to receive a neurotransmitter.

Rehearsal. In behavior therapy, a practice opportunity in which a person enacts a desired response and receives feedback from others.

Reinforcement. A stimulus that increases the frequency of the response that it follows. See *positive* and *negative,* and *primary* and *secondary reinforcers.*

Relapse. A recurrence of a problem behavior or disorder.

Relapse-prevention training. A cognitive-behavioral technique used in the treatment of addictive behaviors that employs behavioral and cognitive strategies to resist temptations and prevent lapses from becoming relapses.

Relaxation training. A technique for acquiring skills of self-relaxation, such as progressive muscle relaxation.

Reliability. In psychological assessment, the consistency of a measuring instrument, such as a psychological test or rating scale. There are various ways of measuring reliability, such as test–retest reliability, internal consistency, and interrater reliability. Also see *validity.*

Repression. In psychodynamic theory, a type of defense mechanism involving the ejection from awareness of anxiety-provoking ideas, images, or impulses, without the conscious awareness that one has done so.

Residual phase. In schizophrenia, the phase of the disorder that follows an acute phase, characterized by a return to a level of functioning that was typical of the prodromal phase.

Resistance. During psychoanalysis, the blocking of thoughts or feelings that would evoke anxiety if they were consciously experienced. Resistance may also take the form of missed sessions by the client or the client's verbal confrontation with the analyst as threatening material is about to be uncovered.

Resistance stage. In Selye's view, the second stage of the general adaptation syndrome, involving the attempt to withstand prolonged stress and preserve bodily resources. Also called the *adaptation stage.*

Response. A reaction to a stimulus.

Reticular activating system. A part of the brain involved in processes of attention, sleep, and arousal. Abbreviated *RAS.*

Reverse tolerance. The acquisition of decreased tolerance for a psychoactive drug such that lesser amounts of the substance become capable, over time, of producing the same effects as greater amounts.

Reward. A pleasant stimulus or event that increases the frequency of the behavior it follows.

Role diffusion. In Erikson's theory, a state of confusion, aimlessness, insecurity, and heightened susceptibility to the suggestions of others that is associated with the failure to acquire a firm sense of ego identity during adolescence.

Sadomasochism. Sexual activities between partners involving the attainment of gratification by means of inflicting and receiving pain and humiliation.

Sample. Part of a population.

Sanguine. A cheerful disposition.

Schizoaffective disorder. A type of psychotic disorder in which individuals experience both severe mood disturbance and features associated with schizophrenia.

Schizoid personality disorder. A type of personality disorder characterized by a persistent lack of interest in social relationships, flattened affect, and social withdrawal.

Schizophrenia. An enduring psychosis that involves failure to maintain integrated personality functioning, impaired reality testing, and disturbances in thinking. Common features of schizophrenia include delusions, hallucinations, flattened or inappropriate affect, and bizarre behavior. Also see *schizophreniform disorder, schizotypal personality disorder,* and *brief reactive psychosis.*

Schizophreniform disorder. A psychotic disorder lasting less than 6 months in duration with features that resemble schizophrenia.

Schizophrenogenic mother. The type of mother, described as cold but also overprotective, that was believed to be capable of causing schizophrenia in her children. Research has failed to support the validity of this concept.

Schizotypal personality disorder. A type of personality disorder characterized by eccentricities or oddities of thought and behavior but without clearly psychotic features. Many persons formerly called *simple schizophrenics* would be given this diagnosis today.

Second-rank symptoms. In Goldstein's view, symptoms associated with schizophrenia that also occur in other mental disorders.

Secondary gains. Benefits associated with neuroses or other disorders, such as expressions of sympathy and increased attention from others, and release from ordinary responsibilities.

Secondary prevention. An approach to prevention that focuses on the early detection and treatment of physical or psychological problems.

Secondary process thinking. In psychodynamic theory, the reality-based thinking processes and problem-solving activities of the ego.

Secondary reinforcers. Stimuli that gain reinforcement value through their association with established reinforcers. Money and social approval are typically secondary reinforcers. Contrast with *primary reinforcers.*

Secondary sex characteristics. The physical traits that differentiate men from women but which are not directly involved in reproduction, such as the depth of the voice and the distribution of bodily hair.

Sedatives. Types of depressant drugs that reduce states of tension and restlessness and induce sleep.

Selection factor. A kind of confound or bias in experimental or quasi-experimental studies in which differences between experimental and control groups are due to differences in the types of subjects comprising the groups, rather than to the independent variable. It is called a selection factor because it involves a bias in the process by which subjects were selected for the treatment and control groups.

Selective abstraction. In Beck's theory, a type of cognitive distortion involving the tendency to selectively focus only on the parts of one's experiences that reflect on one's flaws and to ignore those aspects that reveal one's strengths or competencies.

Selective amnesia. A type of dissociative amnesia involving the loss of memory for disturbing events that occurred during a certain time period.

Self. The center of one's consciousness that organizes one's sensory impressions and governs one's perceptions of the world. The sum total of one's thoughts, sensory impressions, and feelings.

Self-actualization. In humanistic psychology, the tendency to strive to become all that one is capable of being. The motive that drives one to reach one's full potential and express one's unique capabilities.

Self-efficacy expectations. Our beliefs that we can accomplish certain tasks or bring about desired results through our own efforts.

Self-esteem. One's sense of worth or value as a human being.

Self-ideals. The mental image or representation of what we expect ourselves to be.

Self-insight. Awareness of the relationships between one's behavior and one's motivations, needs, and wants.

Self-monitoring. In behavioral assessment, the process of recording or observing one's own behavior, thoughts, or emotions.

Self-psychology. Hans Kohut's theory which describes processes that normally lead to the achievement of a cohesive sense of self, or in narcissistic personality disorder, to a grandiose, but fragile sense of self.

Self-spectatoring. The tendency to observe one's behavior as if one were a spectator of oneself. People with sexual dysfunctions often become self-spectators in the sense of focusing their attention during sexual activity on the response of their sex organs rather than on their partners or the sexual stimulation itself.

Sensate focus exercises. In sex therapy, the mutual pleasuring activities between the partners that is focused on the partners taking turns giving and receiving physical pleasure.

Sensorium. The person's entire sensory apparatus. The term is used by clinicians to refer to the client's focusing of attention, capacity for concentration, and level of awareness of the world.

Sensory cortex. The part of the cerebral cortex, located in the parietal lobe, that receives sensory stimulation.

Separation anxiety disorder. A childhood disorder characterized by extreme fears of separation from parents or others on whom the child is dependent.

Separation-individuation. In Margaret Mahler's theory, the process by which young children come to separate psychologically from their mothers and come to perceive themselves as separate and distinct persons.

Serotonin. A type of neurotransmitter, imbalances of which have been linked to mood disorders and anxiety.

Serotonin-reuptake inhibitor. A type of antidepressant medication that prevents serotonin from being taken back up by the transmitting neuron, thus increasing its action.

Serum cholesterol. A fatty substance (cholesterol) in the blood serum that has been implicated in cardiovascular disease.

Set point. A value that regulatory mechanisms in the body attempt to maintain. For example, these regulatory mechanisms may try to maintain a certain body weight by adjusting the rate of metabolism.

Sexual aversion disorder. A type of sexual dysfunction characterized by aversion to, and avoidance, of genital sexual contact.

Sexual masochism. A type of paraphilia characterized by sexual urges and sexually arousing fantasies involving receiving humiliation or pain in which the person has either acted on these urges or is strongly distressed by them.

Sexual sadism. A type of paraphilia or sexual deviation characterized by recurrent sexual urges and sexually arousing fantasies involving inflicting humiliation or physical pain on sex partners in which the person has either acted on these urges or is strongly distressed by them.

Significant. In statistics, a magnitude of difference that is taken as indicating meaningful differences between groups because of the low probability that it occurred by chance.

Simple schizophrenia. See *schizotypal personality disorder*.

Single-case experimental designs. A type of case study in which the subject (case) is used as his or her own control by varying the conditions to which the subject is exposed (by use of a *reversal* phase) or by means of a *multiple-baseline* design.

Situation variables. In social-learning theory, the external influences on behavior, such as rewards and punishments.

Social phobia. An excessive fear of engaging in behaviors that involve public scrutiny.

Social-learning theory. A learning-based theory that emphasizes observational learning and incorporates roles for both situation and person variables in determining behavior. Also termed *cognitive social theory*.

Social skills training. In behavior therapy, a technique for helping people acquire or improve their social skills. Assertiveness training can be considered a form of social skills training.

Sociocultural perspective. A model of abnormal behavior which places emphases on the social and cultural influences that lead to deviant behavior, rather than on pathological influences within the person. More broadly, the model which interprets behavior within a larger social and cultural context.

Sodium lactate. A chemical substance that has been found to induce panic in some people, especially among panic-prone people.

Soma. A cell body.

Somatic nervous system. The division of the peripheral nervous system that relays information from the sense organs to the brain and transmits messages from the brain to the skeletal muscles, resulting in body movements.

Somatization disorder. A type of somatoform disorder involving recurrent multiple complaints that cannot be explained by any clear physical causes. Also called *Briquet's syndrome.*

Somatoform disorders. Disorders in which people complain of physical (somatic) problems, although no physical abnormality can be found. See *conversion disorder, hypochondriasis,* and *somatization disorder.*

Somatosensory cortex. That part of the cerebral cortex that is involved in the perception of tactile stimulation and in the regulation of voluntary motor activity.

Specific attribution. In the reformulated helplessness theory, a type of attribution involving the belief that the cause of an event involved specific, rather than generalized, factors. Contrast with *global attribution.*

Specific phobias. A persistent but excessive fear of a specific object or situation, such as a fear of heights or of small animals.

Splitting. A term describing the inability of some persons (especially borderline personalities) to reconcile the positive and negative aspects of themselves and others into a cohesive integration, resulting in sudden and radical shifts between strongly positive and strongly negative feelings.

Spontaneous recovery. The recurrence of an extinguished response as a function of the passage of time.

Spontaneous remission. The sudden resolution of a psychological or physical problem or disorder. Resolution of such a problem without treatment.

Stable attribution. In the reformulated helplessness theory, a type of attribution involving the belief that the cause of an event involved stable, rather than changeable, factors. Contrast with *unstable attribution.*

Standard scores. Scores that indicate the relative standing of raw scores in relation to the distribution of normative scores. For example, raw scores on the MMPI scales are converted into standard scores that indicate the degree to which each of the individual raw scores deviates from the mean.

Standardized interview. A highly structured form of clinical interviewing that makes use of a series of specific questions to help the clinician reach a diagnosis.

Statutory rape. A legal term referring to sexual intercourse with a minor, even with the minor's consent.

Steroids. A group of hormones including testosterone, estrogen, progesterone, and corticosteroids.

Stimulus. (1) An aspect of the environment that produces a change in an organism's behavior (a response). (2) A form of physical energy, such as sound or light, that impinges on the senses.

Stratified random sample. A random sample that was drawn in such a way that certain identified subgroups within the population were represented in the sample in relation to their numbers in the population.

Stress. The demand made on an organism to adapt or adjust.

Structural family therapy. A form of family therapy which analyzes the structure of the family unit in terms of the role relationships and communications that exist within the family.

Structural hypothesis. In Freud's theory, the belief that the clashing forces within the personality could be divided into three psychic structures: the id, the ego, and the superego.

Structured interview. A means by which an interviewer obtains clinical information from a client by asking a fairly standard series of questions concerning such issues as the client's presenting complaints or problems, mental state, life circumstances, and psychosocial or developmental history.

Stupor. A state of relative or complete unconsciousness in which the person is not generally aware of, or responsive to, the environment, as in a *catatonic stupor.*

Subjective values. The values that individuals place on objects or events.

Substance abuse. The continued use of a psychoactive drug despite the knowledge that it is causing or contributing to a persistent or recurrent social, occupational, psychological, or physical problem.

Substance dependence. Impaired control over the use of a psychoactive drug and continued or even increased use despite awareness that the substance is disrupting one's life. Substance dependence is often characterized by physiological dependence.

Superego. In psychodynamic theory, the psychic structure that represents the incorporation of the moral values of the parents and important others and that floods the ego with guilt and shame when it falls short of meeting those standards. The superego is governed by the moral principle and consists of two parts, the conscience and the ego ideal.

Supermales. Males who possess the XYY chromosomal structure, which has been associated with exaggerated male characteristics such as heavier beards, and which was linked in some earlier research to violent tendencies in some cases.

Survey method. A method of scientific research in which large samples of people are questioned by use of a survey instrument.

Survivor guilt. The feelings of guilt often experienced by survivors of calamities.

Symbiotic. (1) In biology, the living together of two different but interdependent organisms. (2) In Mahler's object-relations theory, the term used to describe the state of oneness that normally exists between mother and infant in which the infant's identity is fused with the mother's.

Sympathetic. Pertaining to the division of the autonomic nervous system that becomes active to meet the demands of stress, as in adjusting to cold temperatures, or in expending bodily reserves of energy through physical exertion or through emotional reactions, such as anxiety or fear. See *parasympathetic.*

Symptom substitution. The appearance of a new symptom as a substitute for one which has been removed or suppressed. In psychodynamic terms, a symptom, such as phobia, represents an indirect expression of an unconscious conflict. In this view, the removal of a symptom without the resolution of the underlying conflict would be expected to lead to the emergence of another symptom that would represent the continuing conflict.

Synapse. A junction between the terminal knob of one neuron and the dendrite or soma of another through which the nerve impulses pass.

Syndrome. A cluster of symptoms that is characteristic of a particular disorder.

Syphilis. A type of sexually transmitted disease, implicated in its final stages of causing a mental disorder called *general paresis*.

Systematic desensitization. A behavior therapy technique for overcoming phobias by means of exposure (in imagination or by means of slides) to progressively more fearful stimuli while one remains deeply relaxed.

Systems perspective. The view that problems reflect the systems (family, social, school, ecological, etc.) in which they are embedded.

Tachycardia. Abnormally rapid heartbeat.

Tactile. Pertaining to the sense of touch.

Taijin-kyofu-sho. A psychiatric syndrome found in Japan that involves excessive fear of offending or causing embarrassment to others. Abbreviated *TKS*.

Tardive dyskinesia. A movement disorder characterized by involuntary movements of the face, mouth, neck, trunk, or extremities that is caused by long-term use of antipsychotic medications.

Tay-Sachs disease. A disease of lipid metabolism that is genetically transmitted and generally results in death in early childhood.

Temporal stability. The consistency of test responses across time, as measured by test–retest reliability.

Terminals. In neuropsychology, the small branching structures found at the tips of axons.

Tertiary prevention. An approach to prevention that focuses on reducing the level of impairment of distressed individuals. See *primary* and *secondary prevention.*

Test–retest reliability. A method for measuring the reliability of a test by means of comparing (correlating) the scores of the same examinees on separate occasions.

Testosterone. A male sex hormone (steroid), produced by the testes, that is involved with promoting growth of male sexual characteristics and sperm.

Thalamus. A structure in the brain that is involved in relaying sensory information to the cortex and in processes relating to sleep and attention.

Theory. (1) A plausible or scientifically defensible explanation of events. (2) A formulation of the relationships underlying observed events. Theories are helpful to scientists because they provide a means of organizing observations and lead to predictions about future events.

Therapeutic community. A treatment setting, such as in a special ward in a hospital or in a community residence, in which the interactions among the residents and staff are structured to serve a therapeutic purpose.

Thermistor. A small device that is strapped to the skin for registering body temperature, as used in biofeedback training.

Thought disorder. Disturbances in thinking characterized by various features, especially the breakdown in logical associations between thoughts.

Thought insertion. A type of delusion in which people believe that their thoughts have been planted in their minds from external sources.

Thyroxin. A hormone produced by the thyroid gland that increases the metabolic rate.

Time out. A behavioral technique in which an individual who emits an undesired behavior is removed from an environment in which reinforcers are available and placed in an unreinforcing environment for a period of time as a form of punishment. Time out is frequently used in behavioral programs for modifying behavior problems in children, in combination with positive reinforcement for desirable behavior.

Token economies. Behavioral treatment programs in institutional settings in which a controlled environment is constructed such that people are reinforced for desired behaviors by receiving tokens (such as poker chips) that may be exchanged for desired rewards or privileges.

Tolerance. Physical habituation to a drug so that with frequent usage, higher doses are needed to attain similar effects.

Transcendental meditation. A popular form of meditation introduced to the United States by the Maharishi Mahesh Yogi which focuses on the repeating of a mantra to induce a meditative state. Abbreviated *TM.*

Transference relationship. In psychoanalysis, the client's transfer or generalization to the analyst of feelings and attitudes the client holds toward important figures in his or her life.

Transsexualism. A type of gender identity disorder characterized by feelings of being trapped inside a body of the wrong gender.

Transvestic fetishism. A type of paraphilia in heterosexual males characterized by recurrent sexual urges and sexually arousing fantasies involving dressing in female clothing in which the person has either acted on these urges or is strongly distressed by them. Also termed *transvestism.*

Trephining. A harsh prehistoric practice of cutting a hole in a person's skull, possibly as an ancient form of surgery for brain trauma, or possibly as a means of releasing the demons that prehistoric people may have believed caused abnormal behavior in the afflicted persons.

Trichotilliomania. A type of impulse control disorder involving persistent failure to resist urges to pull one's own hair out, producing noticeable hair loss.

Tricyclics. A group of antidepressant drugs that increase the activity of norepinephrine and serotonin in the brain by interfering with the reuptake of these neurotransmitters by transmitting neurons. Also called TCAs (tricyclic antidepressants).

Tumescence. A swelling or a swollen part, as in penile tumescence (erection).

Two-factor model. O. Hobart Mowrer's belief that both operant and classical conditioning are involved in the acquisition of phobic responses. Basically, the fear component of phobia is acquired by means of classical conditioning (pairing of a previously neutral stimulus with an aversive stimulus); the avoidance component is acquired by means of operant conditioning (relief from anxiety negatively reinforces avoidance behavior).

Type A behavior pattern. A pattern of behavior characterized by a sense of time urgency, competitiveness, and hostility. Abbreviated *TABP*.

Ulcers. Open sores, as in the stomach lining.

Unconditional positive regard. In Carl Rogers's view, the expression of unconditional acceptance of another person's basic worth as a person, regardless of whether one approves of all of the behavior of the other person. The ability to express unconditional positive regard is considered a quality of an effective person-centered therapist.

Unconditioned response. An unlearned response or a response to an unconditioned stimulus. Abbreviated *UR* or *UCR*.

Unconditioned stimulus. A stimulus that elicits an instinctive or unlearned response from an organism. Abbreviated *US* or *UCS*.

Unconscious. (1) In psychodynamic theory, pertaining to impulses or ideas that are not readily available to awareness, in many instances because they are kept from awareness by means of *repression*. (2) Also in psychodynamic theory, the part of the mind that contains repressed material and primitive urges of the id. (3) More generally, a state of unawareness or loss of consciousness.

Unipolar. Pertaining to a single pole or direction, as in unipolar (depressive) disorders. Contrast with *bipolar disorder.*

Unobtrusive. Not interfering.

Unstable attribution. In the reformulated helplessness theory, a type of attribution involving the belief that the cause of an event involved changeable, rather than stable, factors. Contrast with *stable attribution.*

Vacillate. To move back and forth.

Vaginal plethysmograph. A device for measuring sexual arousal in females as a function of the amount of blood congestion in the vaginal cavity.

Vaginismus. A type of sexual dysfunction characterized by the recurrent or persistent contraction of the muscles surrounding the vaginal entrance, making penile entry while attempting intercourse difficult or impossible.

Validity. (1) With respect to tests, the degree to which a test measures the traits or constructs that it purports to measure. (2) With respect to experiments, the degree to which an experiment yields scientifically accurate and defensible results.

Validity scales. Groups of test items that serve to detect whether the results of a particular test are valid or whether a person responded in a random manner or in a way that was intended to create a favorable or unfavorable impression.

Variables. Conditions that are measured (dependent variables) or manipulated (independent variables) in scientific studies.

Voyeurism. A type of paraphilia characterized by recurrent sexual urges and sexually arousing fantasies involving the act of watching unsuspecting others who are naked, in the act of undressing, or engaging in sexual activity, in which the person has either acted on these urges or is strongly distressed by them.

Waxy flexibility. A feature of catatonic schizophrenia in which a person's limbs are moved into a certain posture or position, which the person then rigidly maintains for a lengthy period of time.

Weaning. The process of accustoming a child to eat solid food, rather than seek nourishment through breast feeding or sucking a baby bottle.

Wernicke's disease. A brain disorder associated with chronic alcoholism that is characterized by confusion, disorientation, and difficulties maintaining balance while walking (ataxia). If left untreated, it may lead to *Korsakoff's syndrome.*

Winning phase. The first stage in a "gambling career," marked by perceptions of gambling as a pleasant pastime, in which early winnings boost self-esteem. But pathological gamblers eventually progress to stages of *losing* and *desperation.*

Withdrawal syndrome. The characteristic cluster of withdrawal symptoms following the sudden reduction or abrupt cessation of use of a psychoactive substance after physiological dependence has developed.

World view. The prevailing view of the times (English translation of the German *Weltanschauung*).

References

Abelson, H., Cohen, R., Heaton, E., & Slider, C. (1970). Public attitudes toward and experience with erotic materials. In *Technical reports of the Commission on Obscenity and Pornography* Vol. 6. Washington, DC: U.S. Government Printing Office.

Abend, S. M., Porder, M. S., & Willick, M. S. (1983). *Borderline patients: Psychoanalytic perspectives*. New York: International Universities Press.

Aber, J. L., & Allen, J. (1987). Effects of maltreatment on young children's socioemotional development: An attachment theory perspective. *Developmental Psychology, 23*, 406–414.

Abikoff, H., & Gittleman, R. (1985). Hyperactive children treated with stimulants: Is cognitive training a useful adjunct? *Archives of General Psychiatry, 72*, 953–961.

Abraham, K. (1948). The first pregenital stage of the libido. In D. Bryan & A. Strachey (Eds.), *Selected papers of Karl Abraham, M.D.* London: Hogarth Press. (Original work published 1916)

Abrahamson, D. J., Barlow, D. H., Beck, J. G., Sackheim, D. K., & Kelly, J. D. (1985). The effects of attentional focus and partner responsiveness on sexual responding: Replication and extension. *Archives of Sexual Behavior, 14*, 361–371.

Abramowitz, S. (1986). Psychosocial outcomes of sex reassignment surgery. *Journal of Consulting and Clinical Psychology, 54*, 183–189.

Abrams, D. B., et al. (1987). Psychosocial stress and coping in smokers who relapse or quit. *Health Psychology, 6*, 289–303.

Abrams, R., & Fink, M. (1984). The present status of unilateral ECT: Some recommendations. *Journal of Affective Disorders, 7*, 245–247.

Abrams, R., et al. (1983). Bilateral versus unilateral electroconvulsive therapy-efficacy in melancholia. *American Journal of Psychiatry, 140*, 463–465.

Abramson, L. T., Seligman, M. E. P., & Teasdale, J. D. (1978). Learned helplessness in humans: Critique and reformulation. *Journal of Abnormal Psychology, 87*, 49–74.

Achenbach, T. M. (1978). The Child Behavior Profile: I. Boys aged 6 through 11. *Journal of Consulting and Clinical Psychology, 46*, 478–488.

Achenbach, T. M. (1982). *Developmental psychopathology* (2nd ed.). New York: Wiley.

Achenbach, T. M., & Edelbrock, C. S. (1979). The Child Behavior Profile: I. Boys aged 12–16 and girls aged 6–11 and 12–16. *Journal of Consulting and Clinical Psychology, 47*, 223–233.

Ackerman, S. H., Manaker, S., & Cohen, M. I. (1981). Recent separation and the onset of peptic ulcer disease in older children and adolescents. *Psychosomatic Medicine, 43*, 305–310.

Adams, K. M. (1984). Luria left in the lurch: Unfulfilled promises are not valid tests. *Journal of Clinical Neuropsychology, 6*, 455–458.

Adams, V. (1980, August). Sex therapists in perspective. *Psychology Today*, 35–36.

Affleck, G., Tennen, H., Croog, S., & Levine, S. (1987). Causal attribution, perceived benefits, and morbidity after a heart attack: An 8-year study. *Journal of Consulting and Clinical Psychology, 55*, 29–35.

Agras, W. S., & Kirkley, B. G. (1986). Bulimia: Theories of etiology. In K. D. Brownell & J. P. Foreyt (Eds.), *Handbook of eating disorders* (pp. 367–378). New York: Basic.

AIDS policy: Confidentiality and disclosure. (1988). Official Actions. *American Journal of Psychiatry, 145*, 541.

Ainsworth, M. D. S. (1989). Attachments beyond infancy. *American Psychologist, 44*, 709–716.

Ainsworth, M. D. S., & Bowlby, J. (1991). An ethological approach to personality development. *American Psychologist, 46*, 333–341.

Akhtar, A. (1987). Schizoid personality disorder: A synthesis of developmental, dynamic, and descriptive features. *American Journal of Psychotherapy, 41*, 499–517.

Akhtar, N., & Bradley, E. J. (1991). Social information processing deficits of aggressive children: Present findings and implications for social skills training. *Clinical Psychology Review, 11*, 621–644.

Akhtar, S. (1988). Four culture-bound psychiatric syndromes in India. *International Journal of Social Psychiatry, 34*, 70–74.

Akiskal, H. S. (1983). Dysthymic disorder: Psychopathology of proposed chronic depressive subtypes. *American Journal of Psychiatry, 140*, 11–20.

Albert, M. S. (1981). Geriatric neuropsychology. *Journal of Consulting and Clinical Psychology, 49*, 835–850.

Albert, M. S., Naeser, M. A., Duffy, F. H., & McAnulty, G. (1986). CT and EEG validators for Alzheimer's disease. In L. W. Poon (Ed.), *Handbook for clinical memory assessment of older adults* (pp. 383–392). Washington, DC: American Psychological Association.

Alcohol and Health. (1987). Rockville, MD: National Institute of Alcohol Abuse and Alcoholism.

Alden, L. E. (1988). Behavioral self-management controlled-drinking strategies in a context of secondary prevention. *Journal of Consulting and Clinical Psychology, 56*, 280–286.

Alexander, A. B. (1981). Asthma. In S. N. Haynes & L. Gannon (Eds.), *Psychosomatic disorders: A psychophysiological approach to etiology and treatment*. New York: Praeger.

Alexander, F. (1939). Emotional factors in essential hypertension. *Psychosomatic Medicine, 1,* 153–216.

Alexander, F. (1950). *Psychosomatic Medicine.* New York: Norton.

Alexander, P. C., et al. (1989). A comparison of group treatments of women sexually abused as children. *Journal of Consulting and Clinical Psychology, 57,* 479–483.

Allderidge, P. (1979). Hospitals, madhouses and asylums: Cycles in the care of the insane. *British Journal of Psychiatry, 134,* 1476–1478.

Allen, M. G. (1976). Twin studies of affective illness. *Archives of General Psychiatry, 33,* 1476–1478.

Alloy, L. B., & Abramson, L. Y. (1988). Depressive realism: Four theoretical perspectives. In L. B. Alloy (Ed.), *Cognitive processes in depression* (pp.223–265). New York: Guilford Press.

Alloy, L. B., & Clements, C. M. (1992). Illusion of control: Invulnerability to negative affect and depressive symptoms after laboratory and natural stressors. *Journal of Abnormal Psychology, 101,* 234–245.

Alter-Reid, K., Gibbs, M. S., Lachenmeyer, J. R., Sigal, J., & Mossoth, N. A. (1986). Sexual abuse of children: A review of the empirical findings. *Clinical Psychology Review, 6,* 249–266.

Althof, S. E., et al. (1989). Why do so many people drop out from auto-injection therapy for impotence? *Journal of Sex and Marital Therapy, 15,* 121–129.

Altman, L. K. (1988, January 26). Cocaine's many dangers: The evidence mounts. *New York Times,* p. C3.

Altman, L. K. (1989a, April 24). Experts on AIDS, citing new data, push for testing. *New York Times,* pp. 1, B8.

Altman, L. K. (1990a, April 18). Scientists see a link between alcoholism and a specific gene. *New York Times,* pp. A1, A18.

Altman, L. K. (1990b, May 29). The evidence mounts on passive smoking. *New York Times,* pp. C1, C8.

Altman, L. K. (1991, June 18). W.H.O. says 40 million will be infected with AIDS virus by 2000. *New York Times,* p. C3.

Altman, L. K. (1992, October 7). Passive smoking tied to risk of cancer in autopsy study. *New York Times,* p. C13.

American Psychiatric Association. (1974). *Clinical aspects of the violent individual.* Washington, DC: American Psychiatric Association.

American Psychiatric Association (1987). Diagnostic and statistical manual of mental disorders (3rd eds., rev.). Washington, DC: Author.

American Psychiatric Association. (1987a). *Electroconvulsive Therapy, Task Force Report 14.* Washington, DC: Author.

American Psychiatric Association. (1987b). *Dexamethasone suppression test: An overview of its current status in psychiatry.* Washington, DC: Author.

American Psychiatric Association. (1988). AIDS Policy: Confidentiality and disclosure. *American Journal of Psychiatry, 145,* 541.

American Psychiatric Association (1990). *The practice of electroconvulsive therapy.* Washington, DC: American Psychiatric Press.

American Psychiatric Association (1991). The APA task force report on benzodiazepine dependence, toxicity, and abuse. [Editorial]. *American Journal of Psychiatry, 148,* 151–152.

American Psychiatric Association (1993). *DSM-IV Draft Criteria (3/1/93).* Task Force on DSM-IV. Washington, D.C.: American Psychiatric Press, Inc.

American Psychological Association. (1978). Report of the Task Force on the Role of Psychology in the Criminal Justice System. *American Psychologist, 33,* 1099–1113.

American Psychological Association, Committee on Lesbian and Gay Concerns. (1991). Avoiding heterosexual bias in language. *American Psychologist, 46,* 973–974.

Ames, M. A., & Houston, D. A. (1990). Legal, social, and biological definitions of pedophilia. *Archives of Sexual Behavior, 19,* 333–342.

Ammerman, R. T., Cassisi, J. E., Herson, M., & Van Hasselt, V. B. (1986). Consequences of physical abuse and neglect in children. *Clinical Psychology Review, 6,* 291–310.

Anastasi, A. (1983). Evolving trait concepts. *American Psychologist, 38,* 175–184.

Andersen, B. L. (1981). A comparison of systemic desensitization and directed masturbation in the treatment of primary orgasmic dysfunction in females. *Journal of Consulting and Clinical Psychology, 49,* 568–570.

Andersen, B. L. (1992). Psychological interventions for cancer patients to enhance the quality of life. *Journal of Consulting and Clinical Psychology, 60,* 552–568.

Andersen, B. J., & Wold, F. M. (1986). Chronic physical illness and sexual behavior. *Journal of Consulting and Clinical Psychology, 54,* 168–175.

Anderson, L. P. (1991). Acculturative stress: A theory of relevance to black Americans. *Clinical Psychology Review, 11,* 685–702.

Andreasen, N. C. (1986). Scale for the Assessment of Thought, Language, and Communication (TLC). *Schizophrenia Bulletin, 12,* 473–482.

Andreasen, N. C. (1987a). The diagnosis of schizophrenia. *Schizophrenia Bulletin, 13,* 1–8.

Andreasen, N. C. (1987b). Creativity and mental illness: Prevalence rates in writers and their first-degree relatives. *American Journal of Psychiatry, 144,* 1288–1292.

Andreasen, N. C. (1990, August/September). Schizophrenia. In American Psychiatric Association, *DSM-IV Update.* Washington, DC: American Psychiatric Association.

Andreasen, N. C., & Flaum, M. (1991). Schizophrenia: The characteristic symptoms. *Schizophrenia Bulletin, 17* 27–49.

Andreasen, N. C., & Grove, W. M. (1986). Thought, language, and communication in schizophrenia: Diagnosis and prognosis. *Schizophrenia Bulletin, 12,* 348–359.

Andreasen, N., et al. (1986). Structural abnormalities in the frontal system in schizophrenia. *Archives of General Psychiatry, 43,* 136–144.

Andreasen, N. C., et al. (1990). Positive and negative symptoms in schizophrenia. *Archives of General Psychiatry, 47,* 615–621.

Andrews, G., & Harvey, R. (1981). Does psychotherapy benefit neurotic patients? *Archives of General Psychiatry, 38,* 1203–1208.

Aneshensel, C. S., & Huba, G. J. (1983). Depression, alcohol use, and smoking over one year: A four-wave longitudinal causal model. *Journal of Abnormal Psychology, 92,* 134–150.

Angier, N. (1990a, May 29). Scientists link protein fragments to Alzheimer's. *New York Times,* p. C3.

Angier, N. (1990b, December 13). If anger ruins your day, it can shrink your life. *New York Times,* B23.

Angier, N. (1991a,). Kids who can't sit still. *New York Times,* Section 4A, pp. 30–33.

Angier, N. (1991b, May 30). Gene causing common type of retardation is discovered. *New York Times,* pp. A1, B11.

Angle, H. V., Johnson, T., Grebenkemper, N. S., & Ellinwood, E. H. (1979). Computer interview support for clinicians. *Professional Psychology, 10,* 49–57.

Anonymous. (1985, June 13). Schizophrenia—a mother's agony over her son's pain. *Chicago Tribune,* Section 5, pp. 1–3.

Anthony, J. C., & Helzer, J. E. (1991). Syndromes of drug abuse and dependence. In L. N. Robins & D. A. Regier (Eds.), *Psychiatric disorders in America: The Epidemiologic Catchment Area Study* (pp. 116–154). New York: The Free Press.

Anthony, W. A., Cohen, M. R., & Cohen, B. (1984). Psychiatric rehabilitation. In J. Talbott (Eds.), *The chronic mental patient: Five years later* (pp. 213–252). New York: Grune & Stratton.

Anthony, W. A., Cohen, M., & Kennard, W. (1990). Understanding the current facts and principles of mental health systems planning. *American Psychologist, 45,* 1249–1256.

Anthony, W. A., & Liberman, R. P. (1986). The practice of psychiatric rehabilitation: Historical, conceptual, and research base. *Schizophrenia Bulletin, 12,* 542–559.

Antonarakas, S. E., et al. (1991). Prenatal origin of the extra chromosome in trisomy 21 as indicated by analysis of DNA polymorphisms. *New England Journal of Medicine, 324,* 872–876.

Antoni, M. H. (1987). Neuroendocrine influences in psychoimmunology and neoplasia: A review. *Psychology and Health, 1,* 3–24.

Antoni, M. H., Levine, J., Tischer, P., Green, C., & Millon, T. (1986). Refining personality assessments by combining MCMI high-point profiles and MMPI codes: IV. MMPI 89/98. *Journal of Personality Assessment, 50,* 65–72.

Antoni, M. H., Tischer, P., Levine, J., Green, C., & Millon, T. (1985). Refining personality assessments by combining MCMI high-point profiles and MMPI codes, Part I: MMPI code 28/82. *Journal of Personality Assessment, 49,* 392–398.

Antoni, M. H., et al. (1990). Psychoneuroimmunology and HIV-1. *Journal of Consulting and Clinical Psychology, 58,* 38–49.

Antoni, M. H., et al. (1991). Cognitive-behavioral stress management intervention buffers distress responses and immunologic changes following notification of HIV-1 seropositivity. *Journal of Consulting and Clinical Psychology, 59,* 906–915.

APA Task Force on Laboratory Tests in Psychiatry. (1987). *American Journal of Psychiatry, 144,* 1253–1262.

Appelbaum, P. S. (1988). The right to refuse treatment with antipsychotic medications: Retrospect and prospect. *American Journal of Psychiatry, 145,* 413–419.

Appelbaum, P. S., & Hoges, K. (1986). The right to refuse treatment: What the research reveals. *Behavioral Sciences and the Law, 4,* 279–292.

Arana, G. W., Baldessarini, R. J., & Ornstein, M. (1985). The dexamethasone suppression test for diagnosis and prognosis in psychiatry: Commentary and review. *Archives of General Psychiatry, 42,* 1193–1204.

Arana, J. D. (1990). Characteristics of homeless mentally ill inpatients. *Hospital and Community Psychiatry, 41,* 674–676.

Arce, A. A., Tadlock, M., Vergare, M. J., & Shapiro, S. H. (1983). A psychiatric profile of street people admitted to an emergency shelter. *Hospital and Community Psychiatry, 34,* 812–817.

Arieti, S. (1974). *Interpretation of schizophrenia* (2nd ed.). New York: Basic.

Arkin, R. M., Detchon, C. S., & Maruyama, G. M. (1982). Roles of attribution, affect, and cognitive interference in test anxiety. *Journal of Personality and Social Psychology, 43,* 1111–1124.

Aronson, M. K. (1988). Patients and families: Impact and long-term-management implications. In M. K. Aronson (Ed.), *Understanding Alzheimer's disease* (pp. 74–78). New York: Scribner's.

Aronson, T. A. (1987). A naturalistic study of imipramine in panic disorder and agoraphobia. *American Journal of Psychiatry, 144,* 1014–1019.

Aronson, T. A. (1989). A critical review of psychotherapeutic treatments of the borderline personality: Historical trends and future directions. *Journal of Nervous and Mental Disease, 177,* 511–528.

Asaad, G., & Shapiro, B. (1986). Hallucinations: Theoretical and clinical overview. *American Journal of Psychiatry, 143,* 1088–1097.

Asarnow, J. R., & Carlson, G. A. (1985). Depression self-rating scale: Utility with child psychiatric inpatients. *Journal of Consulting and Clinical Psychology, 53,* 491–499.

Asarnow, J. R., Carlson, G. A., & Guthrie, D. (1987). Coping strategies, self-perceptions, hopelessness, and perceived family environments in depressed and suicidal children. *Journal of Consulting and Clinical Psychology, 55,* 361–366.

Asarnow, R. F., et al. (1991). Span of apprehension in schizophrenia. In J. Zubin, S. Steinhauer, & J. Gruzelier (Eds.), *Handbook of schizophrenia: Vol. 5. Neuropsychology, psychophysiology, and information-processing* (pp. 353–370). Amsterdam: Elsevier Science.

Ayllon, T., & Haughton, E. (1962). Control of the behavior of schizophrenic patients by food. *Journal of the Experimental Analysis of Behavior, 5,* 343–352.

Azrin, N. H., & Peterson, A. L. (1989). Reduction of an eye tick by controlled blinking. *Behavior Therapy, 20,* 467–473.

Bachrach, L. L. (1989). Deinstitutionalization: A semantic analysis. *Journal of Social Issues, 45,* 161–171.

Bailey, J. M., & Pillard, R. C. (1991). A genetic study of male sexual orientation. *Archives of General Psychiatry, 48,* 1089–1096.

Baille, A., Mattick, R. P., & Webster, P. (1990). *Review of published treatment outcome literature on smoking cessation: Preparatory readings for the Quality Assurance Project Smoking Cessation Expert Committee* (National Campaign Against Drug Abuse, National Drug and Alcohol Research Center, Working Paper No. 1). Sydney, Australia: University of New South Wales.

Baker, T. C., et al. (1990). Rape victims' concerns about possible exposure to HIV infection. *Journal of Interpersonal Violence, 5,* 49–60.

Bal, D. G. (1992). Cancer in African Americans. *Ca—A Cancer Journal for Clinicians, 42,* 5–6.

Baldessarini, R. J., & Cohen, B. M. (1987). Drs. Baldessarini and Cohen reply. *American Journal of Psychiatry, 144,* 262.

Baldwin, L. C. (1990). Child abuse as an antecedent of multiple personality disorder. *American Journal of Occupational Therapy, 44,* 978–983.

Balleza, M. (1992, October 9). A new mental disorder appears in abuse cases. *New York Times,* p. D16.

Bancroft, J. (1990). Commentary: Biological contributions to sexual orientation. In D. P. McWhirter, S. A. Sanders, & J. M. Reinisch (Eds.), *Homosexuality/heterosexuality: Concepts of sexual orientation* (pp. 101–111). New York: Oxford University Press.

Bandura, A. (1973). *Aggression: A social learning analysis.* Englewood Cliffs, NJ: Prentice-Hall.

Bandura, A. (1982). Self-efficacy mechanism in human agency. *American Psychologist, 37,* 122–147.

Bandura, A. (1986). *Social foundations of thought and action: A social-cognitive theory.* Englewood Cliffs, NJ: Prentice-Hall.

Bandura, A., Barr-Taylor, C., Williams, S. L., Mefford, I. N., & Barchas, J. D. (1985). Catecholamine secretion as a function of perceived coping self-efficacy. *Journal of Consulting and Clinical Psychology, 53,* 406–414.

Bandura, A., Blanchard, E. B., & Ritter, B. (1969). The relative efficacy of desensitization and modeling approaches for inducing behavioral,

affective, and cognitive changes. *Journal of Personality and Social Psychology, 13,* 173–199.

Bandura, A. J., Grusen, J. E., & Menlove, F. L. (1967). Relative efficacy of desensitization and modeling approaches for inducing behavioral, affective, and attitudinal changes. *Journal of Personality and Social Psychology, 5,* 16–23.

Bandura, A., Jeffery, R. W., & Wright, C. L. (1974). Efficacy of participant modeling as a function of response induction aids. *Journal of Abnormal Psychology, 83,* 56–64.

Bandura, A., & Rosenthal, T. L. (1966). Vicarious classical conditioning as a function of fear arousal. *Journal of Personality and Social Psychology, 3,* 54–62.

Bandura, A., Ross, S. A., & Ross, D. (1963). Imitation of film-mediated aggressive models. *Journal of Abnormal and Social Psychology, 66,* 3–11.

Bandura, A., Taylor, C. B., Williams, S. L., Medford, I. N., & Barchas, J. D. (1985). Catecholamine secretion as a function of perceived coping self-efficacy. *Journal of Consulting and Clinical Psychology, 53,* 406–414.

Barbaree, H. E., & Marshall, W. L. (1991). The role of male sexual arousal in rape: Six models. *Journal of Consulting and Clinical Psychology, 59,* 621–631.

Barber, T. X. (1970). *LSD, marihuana, yoga, and hypnosis.* Chicago: Aldine.

Baribeau-Brown, J., Picton, T. W., & Gosselin, J. Y. (1983). Schizophrenia: A neurophysiological evaluation of abnormal information processing. *Science, 219,* 874–876.

Barker, S. L., Funk, S. C., & Houston, B. K. (1988). Psychological treatment versus nonspecific factors: A meta-analysis of conditions that engender comparable expectations for improvement. *Clinical Psychology Review, 8,* 579–594.

Barkin, R., Braun, B. G., & Kluft, R. P. (1986). The dilemma of drug therapy for multiple personality disorder. In B. G. Braun (Ed.), *Treatment of multiple personality disorder.* Washington, DC: American Psychiatric Press.

Barkley, R. A. (1981). *Hyperactive children: A handbook for diagnosis and treatment.* New York: Guilford Press.

Barkley, R. A., DuPaul, G. J., & McMurray, M. B. (1990). Comprehensive evaluation of attention deficit disorder with and without hyperactivity as defined by research criteria. *Journal of Consulting and Clinical Psychology, 58,* 775–789.

Barkley, R. A., Hasting, J. E., & Tousel, S. E. (1976). Evaluation of a token system for juvenile delinquents in a residential setting. *Journal of Behavior Therapy and Experimental Psychiatry, 7,* 227–230.

Barlow, D. H. (1986). Causes of sexual dysfunction: The role of anxiety and cognitive interference. *Journal of Consulting and Clinical Psychology, 54,* 140–148.

Barlow, D. H. (1988). *Anxiety and its disorders: The nature and treatment of anxiety and panic.* New York: Guilford Press.

Barlow, D. H. (1991). Introduction to the special issue on diagnoses, definitions, and *DSM–IV:* The science of classification. *Journal of Abnormal Psychology, 100,* 243–244.

Barlow, D. H., Blanchard, E. B., Vermilyea, J. A., Vermilyea, B. B., & DiNardo, P. A. (1986). Generalized anxiety and generalized anxiety disorder: Description and reconceptualization. *American Journal of Psychiatry, 143,* 40–44.

Barlow, D. H., Sackheim, D. K., & Beck, J. G. (1983). Anxiety increases sexual arousal. *Journal of Abnormal Psychology, 92,* 49–54.

Barlow, D. H., et al. (1985). The phenomenon of panic. *Journal of Abnormal Psychology, 94,* 320–328.

Barnett, P. A., & Gotlib, I. (1988). Psychosocial functioning and depression: Distinguishing

among antecedents, concomitants, and consequences. *Psychological Bulletin, 104,* 97–126.

Barnett, W. S., & Escobar, C. M. (1990). Economic costs and benefits of early intervention. In S. J. Meisels & J. P. Shonkoff (Eds.), *Handbook of early childhood intervention.* New York: Cambridge University Press.

Baron, M., Gruen, R., Asnis, L., & Lord, S. (1985). Familial transmission of schizotypal and borderline personality disorder. *Journal of Clinical Psychology, 142,* 927–934.

Barron, J. (1989, May 28). States sell chances for gold as rush turns to stampede. *New York Times,* p. 24.

Barrow, S. M., et al. (1989). *Effectiveness of programs for the mentally ill homeless.* New York: New York State Psychiatric Institute.

Barry, M. (1991). The influence of the U.S. tobacco industry on the health, economy, and environment of developing countries. *New England Journal of Medicine, 324,* 917–920.

Barsky, A. J., Wyshak, G., & Klerman, G. L. (1992). Psychiatric comorbidity in DSM-III-R hypochondriasis. *Archives of General Psychiatry, 49,* 101–108.

Baskin, D. (1984). Cross-cultural conceptions of mental illness. *Psychiatric Quarterly, 56,* 45–53.

Baskin, D., Bluestone, H., & Nelson, M. (1981). Ethnicity and psychiatric diagnosis. *Journal of Clinical Psychology, 37,* 529–537.

Basow, S. (1992). *Gender: Stereotypes and roles* (3rd ed.). Pacific Grove, CA: Brooks/Cole.

Bateson, G. D., Jackson, D., Haley, J., & Weakland, J. (1956). Toward a theory of schizophrenia. *Behavioral Science, 1,* 251–264.

Baum-Baicker C. (1984). Treating and preventing alcohol abuse in the workplace. *American Psychologist, 39,* 454.

Beal, D. M., et al. (1991). Safety and efficacy of fluoxetine. *American Journal of Psychiatry, 148,* 1751.

Beardslee, W. R., et al. (1983). Children of parents with major affective disorder: a review. *American Journal of Psychiatry, 140,* 825–832.

Beauvais, F., & LaBoueff, S. (1985). Drug and alcohol abuse intervention in American Indian communities. Special Issue: Intervening with special populations. *International Journal of the Addictions, 20,* 139–171.

Beck, A. T. (1976). *Cognitive therapy and the emotional disorders.* New York: International Universities Press.

Beck, A. T. (1985). Theoretical perspectives on clinical anxiety. In A. H. Tuma & J. D. Maser (Eds.), *Anxiety and the anxiety disorders.* Hillsdale, NJ: Erlbaum.

Beck, A. T. (1991). Cognitive therapy: A 30-year retrospective. *American Psychologist, 46,* 368–375.

Beck, A. T., Brown, G., Berchick, R. J., Stewart, B. L., & Steer, R. A. (1990). Relationship between hopelessness and ultimate suicide. *American Journal of Psychiatry, 147,* 190–195.

Beck, A. T., Brown, G., Steer, R. A., Eidelson, J. I., & Riskind, J. H. (1987). Differentiating anxiety and depression: A test of the cognitive content-specificity hypothesis. *Journal of Abnormal Psychology, 96,* 179–183.

Beck, A. T., Emery, G., & Greenberg, R. L. (1985). *Anxiety disorders and phobias: A cognitive perspective.* New York: Basic.

Beck, A. T., & Freeman, A. (1990). *Cognitive therapy of personality disorders.* New York: Guilford Press.

Beck, A. T., & Haaga, D. A. F. (1992). The future of cognitive therapy. *Psychotherapy, 29,* 34–38.

Beck, A. T., Laude, R., & Bohnert, M. (1974). Ideational components of anxiety neurosis. *Archives of General Psychiatry, 31,* 319–325.

Beck, A. T., Rush, A. J., Shaw, B. F., & Emery, G. (1979). *Cognitive therapy of depression.* New York: Guilford Press.

Beck, A. T., Ward, C. H., Mendelson, M., Mock, J., & Erbaugh, J. (1961). An inventory for measuring depression. *Archives of General Psychiatry, 4,* 561–571.

Beck, A. T., & Young, J. E. (1986). Depression. In D. H. Barlow (Ed.), *Clinical handbook of psychological disorders* (pp.206–244). New York: Guilford Press.

Beck, A. T., et al. (1990). Relationship between hopelessness and ultimate suicide: A replication with psychiatric outpatients. *American Journal of Psychiatry, 147,* 190–195.

Beck, A. T., et al. (1992). A crossover study of focused cognitive therapy for panic disorder. *American Journal of Psychiatry, 149,* 778–783.

Beck, J. G. (1984). *The effect of performance demand and attentional focus on sexual responding in functional and dysfunctional men.* Unpublished doctoral dissertation, State University of New York at Albany.

Beck, J. G., & Barlow, D. H. (1986). The effects of anxiety and attentional focus on sexual responding: II. Cognitive and affective patterns in erectile dysfunction. *Behaviour Research and Therapy, 24,* 19–26.

Becker, J. V., Skinner, L. J., & Abel, G. G. (1983). Sequelae of sexual assault: The survivor's perspective. In J. G. Greer & I. R. Stuart (Eds.), *The sexual aggressor* (pp. 240–266). New York: Van Nostrand Reinhold.

Becker, J. V., Skinner, L. J., Abel, G. G., & Cichon, J. (1984). Time-limited therapy with sexually dysfunctional sexually assaulted women. *Journal of Social Work and Human Sexuality, 3,* 97–115.

Becker, J. V., et al. (1986). Level of postassault sexual functioning in rape and incest victims. *Archives of Sexual Behavior, 15,* 37–49.

Begleiter, H., Parjesz, B., Bihari, B., & Kissin, B. (1984). Event-related brain potentials in boys at risk for alcoholism. *Science, 225,* 1493–1496.

Beidel, D. C., & Turner, S. M. (1986). A critique of the theoretical bases of cognitive-behavioral theories and therapy. *Clinical Psychology Review, 6,* 177–199.

Beitman, B. D. (1987). Panic attacks and their treatment: An introduction. *Journal of Integrative and Eclectic Psychotherapy, 6,* 412–420.

Bell, A. P., & Weinberg, M. S. (1978). *Homosexualities: A study of diversity among men and women.* New York: Simon & Schuster.

Bell, A. P., Weinberg, M. S., & Hammersmith, S. K. (1981). *Sexual preference: Its development in men and women.* Bloomington: University of Indiana Press.

Bellack, A. S. (1986). Schizophrenia: Behavior therapy's forgotten child. *Behavior Therapy, 17,* 199–214.

Bellack, A. S., & Mueser, K. T. (1990). Schizophrenia. In A. S. Bellack, M. Hersen, & A. E. Kazdin (1990). *International handbook of behavior modification and therapy.* (2nd ed.) (pp. 353–370). New York: Plenum Press.

Bellack, A. S., Turner, S. M., Hersen, M., & Luber, R. F. (1984). An examination of social skills training for chronic schizophrenic patients. *Hospital and Community Psychiatry, 35,* 1023–1028.

Belsher, G., & Costello, C. G. (1988). Relapse after recovery from unipolar depression: A critical review. *Psychological Bulletin, 104,* 84–96.

Bender, L. (1938). A visual motor gestalt test and its clinical use. *Research Monograph of the American Orthopsychiatric Association, 3* (XI), 176.

Benet, S. (1974). *Abkhasians: The long living people of the Caucasus.* New York: Holt, Rinehart & Winston.

Bennett, D. (1985). Rogers: More intuition in therapy. *APA Monitor, 16,* 3.

Bennett, G. (1986). Behavior therapy for obesity: A quantitative review of the effects of selected treatment characteristics on outcome. *Behavior Therapy, 17,* 554–562.

Benowitz, N. L., & Jacob, P., III. (1985). Nicotine renal excretion rate influences nicotine intake during cigarette smoking. *Journal of Pharmacological and Experimental Therapeutics, 234,* 153–155.

Ben-Porath, Y. S., Butcher, J. N., & Graham, J. R. (1991). Contribution of the MMPI-2 content scales to the differential diagnosis of schizophrenia and major depression. *Psychological Assessment, 3,* 634–640.

Benson, H. (1975). *The relaxation response.* New York: Morrow.

Benson, H., Manzetta, B. R., & Rosner, B. (1973). Decreased systolic blood pressure in hypertensive subjects who practiced meditation. *Journal of Clinical Investigation, 52,* 8.

Bentall, R. P. (1990). The illusion of reality: A review and integration of psychological research on hallucinations. *Psychological Bulletin, 107,* 82–95.

Bentler, P. M. (1976). A typology of transsexualism: Gender identity theory and data. *Archives of Sexual Behavior, 5,* 567–584.

Benton, M. K., & Schroeder, H. E. (1990). Social skills training with schizophrenics: A meta-analytic evaluation. *Journal of Consulting and Clinical Psychology, 58,* 741–747.

Berger, P. A. (1978). Medical treatment of mental illness. *Science, 200,* 974–981.

Bergler, E. (1957). *Homosexuality: Disease or way of life.* New York: Hill & Wang.

Berkman, L. F., & Breslow, L. (1983). *Health and ways of living: The Alameda County study.* New York: Oxford University Press.

Berkman, L. F., & Syme, S. L. (1979). Social networks, host resistance, and mortality: A nine-year follow-up study of Alameda County residents. *American Journal of Epidemiology, 109,* 186–204.

Berlin, I. N. (1987). Effects of changing Native American cultures on child development. *Journal of Community Psychology, 15,* 299–306.

Bernstein, A. S. (1987). Orienting response research in schizophrenia: Where we have come from and where we might go. *Schizophrenia Bulletin, 13,* 623–641.

Bernstein, A. S., et al. (1981). Bilateral skin conductance, finger pulse volume, and EEG orienting response to tone of differing intensities in chronic schizophrenics and controls. *Journal of Nervous and Mental Disease, 169,* 513–528.

Bernstein, A. S., et al. (1988). Schizophrenia is associated with altered orienting activity; depression with electrodermal (cholinergic?) deficit and normal orienting response. *Journal of Abnormal Psychology, 97,* 3–12.

Bernstein, E. M., & Putnam, F. W. (1986). Development, reliability, and validity of a dissociation scale. *Journal of Nervous and Mental Disease, 174,* 727–735.

Bernstein, I. L. (1985). Learned food aversions in the progression of cancer and its treatment. In N. S. Braverman & P. Bernstein (Eds.), *Experimental assessments and clinical application of conditioned food aversions. Annals of the New York Academy of Sciences, 443.*

Bernstein, R. L., & Gaw, A. C. (1990). Koro: Proposed classification for DSM-IV. *American Journal of Psychiatry, 147,* 1670–1674.

Berquier, A., & Ashton, R. (1991). A selective review of possible neurological etiologies of schizophrenia. *Clinical Psychology Review, 11,* 645–661.

Bertelsen, A., Harvald, B., & Hauge, M. (1977). A Danish twin study of manic depressive disorders. *British Journal of Psychiatry, 130,* 330–351.

Bettelheim, B. (1967). *The Empty Fortress.* New York: Free Press.

Beutler, L. E., et al. (1984). Women's satisfaction with partners' penile implants. *Urology, 24,* 552–558.

Beutler, L. E., et al. (1985). *Comparative follow-up evaluations: Patients with inflatable and noninflat-*

able penile protheses. Manuscript submitted for publication.

Beutler, L. E., et al. (1987). Group cognitive therapy and alprazolam in the treatment of depression in older adults. *Journal of Consulting and Clinical Psychology, 55,* 550–556.

Bick, P. A., & Kinsbourne, M. (1987). Auditory hallucinations and subvocal speech in schizophrenic patients. *American Journal of Psychiatry, 144,* 222–225.

Bieber, I. (1976). A discussion of "Homosexuality: The ethical challenge." *Journal of Consulting and Clinical Psychology, 44,* 163–166.

Biederman, J., et al. (1991). Comorbidity of attention deficit hyperactivity disorder with conduct, depressive, anxiety, and other disorders. *American Journal of Psychiatry, 148,* 564–577.

Bigler, E. D., & Ehrenfurth, J. W. (1981). The continued inappropriate singular use of the Bender Visual Motor Gestalt Test. *Professional Psychology, 12,* 562–569.

Billings, A. G., Cronkite, R. C., & Moos, R. H. (1983). Social-environmental factors in unipolar depression: Comparisons of depressed patients and nondepressed controls. *Journal of Abnormal Psychology, 92,* 119–133.

Biran, M. (1988). Cognitive and exposure treatment for agoraphobia: Re-examination of the outcome research. *Journal of Cognitive Psychotherapy: An International Quarterly, 2,* 165–178.

Black, D. W., Yates, W. R., & Andreasen, N. C. (1988). Schizophrenia, schizophreniform disorder, and delusional paranoid disorders. In J. A. Talbott, R. E. Hales, & S. C. Yudofsky (Eds.), *Textbook of psychiatry.* Washington, DC: American Psychiatric Press.

Blair, C. D., & Lanyon, R. I. (1981). Exhibitionism: A critical review of the etiology and treatment. *Psychological Bulletin, 89,* 439–463.

Blakeley, M. K. (1985). Is one woman's sexuality another woman's pornography? The question behind a major legal battle. *Ms.,* pp. 37–47, 120–123.

Blakeslee, S. (1988, September 8). New groups aim to help parents face grief when a newborn dies. *The New York Times,* p. B13.

Blakeslee, S. (1990, September 20). Study links emotions to second heart attacks. *New York Times,* p. B8.

Blakeslee, S. (1991). Study ties dyslexia to brain flaw affecting vision and other senses. *New York Times,* pp. A1, A30.

Blakeslee, S. (1992, October 27). Unusual clues help in long fight to solve Huntington's disease. *New York Times,* p. C3.

Blanchard, E. B. (1987). Long-term effects of behavioral treatment of chronic headache. *Behavior Therapy, 18,* 375–385.

Blanchard, E. B. (1992a). Introduction to the special issue on behavioral medicine: An update for the 1990s. *Journal of Consulting and Clinical Psychology, 60,* 491–492.

Blanchard, E. B. (1992b). Psychological treatment of benign headache disorders. *Journal of Consulting and Clinical Psychology, 60,* 537–551.

Blanchard, E. B., Andrasik, F., Guarnieri, P., Neff, D. F., & Rodichok, L. D. (1987). Two-, three-, and four-year follow-up on the self-regulatory treatment of chronic headache. *Journal of Consulting and Clinical Psychology, 55,* 257–259.

Blanchard, E. B., Kalb, L. C., Pallmeyer, T. P., & Gerardi, R. (1982). The development of a psychophysiological assessment procedure for posttraumatic stress disorder in Vietnam veterans. *Psychiatric Quarterly, 4,* 220–229.

Blanchard, E. B., et al. (1985). Behavioral treatment of 250 chronic headache patients: A clinical replication series. *Behavior Therapy, 16,* 308–327.

Blanchard, E. B., et al. (1990a). Placebo-controlled evaluation of abbreviated progressive muscle relaxation and of relaxation combined with cognitive therapy in the treatment of tension headache. *Journal of Consulting and Clinical Psychology, 58,* 210–215.

Blanchard, E. B., et al. (1990b). A controlled evaluation of thermal biofeedback and thermal feedback combined with cognitive therapy in the treatment of vascular headache. *Journal of Consulting and Clinical Psychology, 58,* 216–224.

Blanchard, E. B., et al. (1991). The role of regular home practice in the relaxation treatment of tension headache. *Journal of Consulting and Clinical Psychology, 59,* 467–470.

Blanchard, R., Steiner, B. W., & Clemmensen, L. H. (1985). Gender dysphoria, gender reorientation, and the clinical management of transsexualism. *Journal of Consulting and Clinical Psychology, 53,* 295–304.

Blashfield, R. K., & Draguns, J. G. (1976). Evaluative criteria for psychiatric classification. *Journal of Abnormal Psychology, 85,* 140–150.

Blatt, S. (1986). Where have we been and where are we going? *Journal of Personality Assessment, 50,* 343–346.

Blehar, M. C., Weissman, M. M., Gershon, E. S., & Hirschfeld, R. M. A. (1988). Family and genetic studies of affective disorders. *Archives of General Psychiatry, 45,* 289–292.

Bliss, E. L. (1984). A symptom profile of patients with multiple personalities, including MMPI results. *Journal of Nervous and Mental Disease, 172,* 197–202.

Bliss, E. L., & Jeppsen, E. A. (1985). Prevalence of multiple personality among inpatients and outpatients. *American Journal of Psychiatry, 142,* 250–251.

Bloom, B. L. (1992). Computer assisted psychological intervention: A review and commentary. *Clinical Psychology Review, 12,* 169–197.

Bloom, J. D., & Rogers, J. L. (1987). The legal basis of forensic psychiatry: Statutorily mandated psychiatric diagnosis. *American Journal of Psychiatry, 144,* 847–853.

Blumenthal, D. (1988, October 9). Dieting reassessed. *New York Times Magazine: Part 2. The Good Health Magazine,* pp. 24–25, 53–54.

Blumenthal, J. A., & Emery, C. S. (1988). Rehabilitation of patients following myocardial infarctions. *Journal of Consulting and Clinical Psychology, 56,* 374–381.

Blumenthal, J. A., et al. (1987). Effects of exercise on the Type A behavior pattern. *Psychosomatic Medicine, 49,* 204.

Blumenthal, S. J. (1985). *Suicide and suicide prevention.* (Comm. Pub. No. 98-497). Washington DC: U.S. Government Printing Office.

Blumstein, P., & Schwartz, P. (1983). *American couples.* New York: Morrow.

Boffey, P. M. (1986, March 16). Schizophrenia: Insights fail to halt rising toll. *New York Times,* pp. 1, 32–33.

Bonn, J. A., Readhead, C. P. A., & Timmons, B. H. (1984). Enhanced adaptive behavioral response in agoraphobic patients pretreated with breathing retraining. *Lancet,* pp. 665–669.

Boor, M. (1982). The multiple personality epidemic. *Journal of Nervous and Mental Disease, 170,* 302–304.

Boorstin, D. J. (1983). *The discoverers: A history of man's search to know his world and himself.* New York: Random House.

Booth-Kewley, S., & Friedman, H. S. (1987). Psychological predictors of heart disease: A quantitative review. *Psychological Bulletin, 101,* 343–362.

Borkovec, T. D. (1970). Autonomic reactivity to sensory stimulation in psychopathic, neurotic, and normal juvenile delinquents. *Journal of Consulting and Clinical Psychology, 35,* 217–222.

Borkovec, T. D., & Mathews, A. M. (1988). Treatment of nonphobic anxiety disorders: A comparison of nondirective, cognitive, and coping desensitization therapy. *Journal of Consulting and Clinical Psychology, 56,* 877–884.

Borkovec, T. D., Mathews, A. M., Chambers, A., Ebrahimi, S., Lytle, R., & Nelson, R. (1987). The effects of relaxation training with cognitive therapy or nondirective therapy and the role of relaxation-induced anxiety in the treatment of generalized anxiety. *Journal of Consulting and Clinical Psychology, 55,* 883–888.

Bornstein, M. R., Bellack, A. S., & Hersen, M. (1977). Social-skills training for unassertive children: A multiple-baseline analysis. *Journal of Applied Behavior Analysis, 10,* 183–195.

Bornstein, R. F. (1992). The dependent personality: Developmental, social, and clinical perspectives. *Psychological Bulletin, 112,* 3–23.

Boskind-White, M., & White, W. C., Jr. (1983). *Bulimarexia: The binge-purge cycle.* New York: Norton.

Boskind-White, M., & White, W. C., Jr. (1986). Bulimarexia: A historical-sociocultural perspective. In K. D. Brownell & J. P. Foreyt, *Handbook of eating disorders: Physiology, psychology, and treatment of obesity, anorexia, and bulimia* (pp. 353–378). New York: Basic.

Boston Women's Health Book Collective. (1984). *The New Our Bodies, Ourselves.* New York: Simon & Schuster.

Bourne, P. G. (1972). The Viet Nam veteran: Psychosocial casualties. *Psychiatry in Medicine, 3,* 23–27.

Bowers, T. G., & Clum, G. A. (1988). Relative contribution of specific and nonspecific treatment effects: Meta-analysis of placebo-controlled behavior therapy research. *Psychological Bulletin, 103,* 315–323.

Bowlby, J. (1988). *A secure base.* New York: Basic.

Boyd, J. H., & Weissman, M. M. (1981). Epidemiology of affective disorders: A reexamination and future directions. *Archives of General Psychiatry, 38,* 1039–1046.

Boyd-Franklin, N. (1989). *Black families in therapy: A multisystems approach.* New York: Guilford Press.

Boyle, M. H., et al. (1992). Predicting substance use in late adolescence: Results from the Ontario Child Health Study Follow-up. *American Journal of Psychiatry, 149,* 761–767.

Braddock, L. (1986). The dexamethasone suppression test: Fact and artifact. *British Journal of Psychiatry, 148,* 363–374.

Brady, S. (1986). Short-term memory, phonological processing, and reading ability. *Annals of Dyslexia, 36,* 138–153.

Braff, D. L., & Saccuzzo, D. P. (1985). The time course of information-processing deficits in schizophrenia. *American Journal of Psychiatry, 142,* 170–174.

Brandon, T. H., Zelman, D. C., & Baker, T. B. (1987). Effects of maintenance sessions on smoking relapse: Delaying the inevitable? *Journal of Consulting and Clinical Psychology, 55,* 780–782.

Braun, B. G. (1988). *Treatment of multiple personality disorder.* Washington, DC: American Psychiatric Press.

Breggin, P. R. (1990, August 30). Electroshock's damage. *New York Times,* p. A22.

Breggin, P. R. (1992, September 18). U.S. hasn't given up linking genes to crime. *New York Times,* p. A34.

Breier, A., Charney, D. S., & Heninger, G. R. (1986). Agoraphobia with panic attacks: Development, diagnostic stability, and course of illness. *Archives of General Psychiatry, 43,* 1029–1036.

Brenner, H. D., et al. (1992). Treatment of cognitive dysfunctions and behavioral deficits in schizophrenia. *Schizophrenia Bulletin, 18,* 21–26.

Breslow, N. (1989). Sources of confusion in the study and treatment of sadomasochism. *Journal of Social Behavior and Personality, 4,* 263–274.

Brill, A. A. (1938). Introduction. In A. A. Brill (Ed.), *The basic writings of Sigmund Freud* (pp. 3–34). New York: Random House.

Brinkman, S. D., Largen, J. W., Jr., Cushman, L., Braun, P. R., & Block, R. (1986). Clinical validators: Alzheimer's disease and multi-infarct dementia. In L. W. Poon (Ed.), *Handbook for clinical memory assessment of older adults* (pp. 307–313). Washington, DC: American Psychological Association.

Brody, J. E. (1988a, May 5). Sifting fact from myth in the face of asthma's growing threat to American children. *New York Times,* p. B19.

Brody, J. E. (1988c, October 11). Studies unmasks origins of brutal migraines. *New York Times,* pp. C1, C10.

Brody, J. E. (1990b, June 7). A search to bar retardation in a new generation. *New York Times,* p. B9.

Brody, J. E. (1992b,). Suicide myths cloud efforts to save children. *New York Times,* pp. C1, C3.

Brody, J. E. (1992d, May 15). Study finds a liquid diet works (but not for the 50% who quit). *New York Times,* p. B7.

Brody, J. E. (1992e, November 11). Epilepsy need not interfere with living a normal life. *New York Times,* p. C14.

Brody, N. (1990). Behavior therapy versus placebo: Comment on Bowers and Clum's meta-analysis. *Psychological Bulletin, 107,* 106–109.

Bronfrenbrenner, U. (1979). *The Ecology of Human Development: Experiments by Nature and Design.* Cambridge, MA: Harvard University Press.

Brown, G. W., Birley, J. L. T., & Wing, J. K. (1972). Influence of family life on the course of schizophrenic disorders: A replication. *British Journal of Psychiatry, 121,* 241–258.

Brown, J. (1987). A review of meta-analyses conducted on psychotherapy outcome research. *Clinical Psychology Review, 7,* 1–24.

Brown, L. S. (1992). A feminist critique of the personality disorders. In L. Brown & M. Balou (Eds.), *Personality and psychopathology: Feminist reappraisals.* (pp. 206–228). New York: Guilford Press.

Brown, R. T., Wynne, M. E., & Medenis, R. (1985). Methylphenidate and cognitive therapy: A comparison of treatment approaches with hyperactive boys. *Journal of Abnormal Child Psychology, 13,* 69–87.

Brown, S. A. (1985a). Expectancies versus background in the prediction of college drinking patterns. *Journal of Consulting and Clinical Psychology, 53,* 123–130.

Brown, S. A. (1985b). Reinforcement expectancies and alcohol treatment outcome after one year. *Journal of Studies on Alcohol, 46,* 304–308.

Brown, S. A., Creamer, V. A., & Stetson, B. A. (1987). Adolescent alcohol expectancies in relation to personal and parental drinking patterns. *Journal of Abnormal Psychology, 96,* 117–121.

Brown, S. A., Goldman, M. S., & Christiansen, B. A. (1985). Do alcohol expectancies mediate drinking patterns of adults? *Journal of Consulting and Clinical Psychology, 53,* 512–519.

Brown, S. A., Goldman, M. S., Inn, A., & Anderson, L. R. (1980). Expectations of reinforcement from alcohol. Their domain and relation to drinking patterns. *Journal of Consulting and Clinical Psychology, 48,* 419–426.

Brownell, K. D. (1988,). Yo-yo dieting. *Psychology Today,* pp. 20–23.

Brownell, K. D. (1991). Dieting and the search for the perfect body: Where physiology and culture collide. *Behavior Therapy, 22,* 1–12.

Brownell, K. D., Marlatt, G. A., Lichtenstein, E., & Wilson, G. T. (1986). Understanding and preventing relapse. *American Psychologist, 41,* 765–782.

Brownell, K. D., & Wadden, T. A. (1992). Etiology and treatment of obesity: Understanding a serious, prevalent, and refractory disorder. *Journal of Consulting and Clinical Psychology, 60,* 505–517.

Bruch, H. (1973). *Eating disorders: Obesity, anorexia and the person within.* New York: Basic.

Brunk, M., Hengeggeler, S. W. & Whelan, J. P. (1987). Comparison of multisystematic therapy and parent training in the brief treatment of child abuse and neglect. *Journal of Consulting and Clinical Psychology, 55,* 171–178.

Buchsbaum, M. S., et al. (1982a). Cerebral glucography with positron tomography: Use in normal subjects and in patients with schizophrenia. *Archives of General Psychiatry, 39,* 251–259.

Buchsbaum, M. S., et al. (1982b). New methods to determine the CNS effects of antigeriatric compounds: EEG topography and glucose use. *Drug Development Research, 2,* 489–496.

Buchsbaum, M. S., & Haier, R. J. (1987). Functional and anatomical brain imaging: Impact on schizophrenia research. *Schizophrenia Bulletin, 13,* 115–132.

Buchsbaum, M. S., et al. (1984). The Genain quadruplets: Electrophysiological, positron emission and X-ray tomographic studies. *Psychiatry Research, 13,* 95–108.

Bumberry, W., Oliver, H. M., & McClure, J. N. (1978). Validation of the Beck Depression Inventory in a university population using psychiatric estimate as the criterion. *Journal of Consulting and Clinical Psychology, 46,* 150–155.

Burgess, A., & Holmstrom, L. (1974). Rape trauma syndrome. *American Journal of Psychiatry, 131,* 981–986.

Buriel, R., Calzada, S., & Vazquez, R. (1982). The relationship of traditional Mexican American culture to adjustment and delinquency among three generations of Mexican American male adolescents. *Hispanic Journal of Behavioral Sciences, 4,* 41–55.

Burish, T. G., Carey, M. P., Krozely, M. G., & Greco, F. A. (1987). Conditioned side effects induced by cancer chemotherapy: Prevention through behavioral treatment. *Journal of Consulting and Clinical Psychology, 55,* 42–48.

Burish, T. G., Snyder, S. L., & Jenkins, R. A. (1991). Preparing patients for cancer chemotherapy: Effect of coping preparation and relaxation interventions. *Journal of Consulting and Clinical Psychology, 59,* 518–525.

Burke, K. C., et al. (1990). Age at onset of selected mental disorders in five community populations. *Archives of General Psychiatry, 47,* 511–518.

Burman, B., Mednick, S. A., Machon, R. A., Parnas, J., & Schulsinger, F. (1987). Children at high-risk for schizophrenia: Parent and offspring perceptions of family relations. *Journal of Abnormal Psychology, 96,* 364–366.

Burnam, M. A., et al. (1988). Sexual assault and mental disorders in a community population. *Journal of Consulting and Clinical Psychology, 56,* 843–850.

Burnam, M. A., Hough, R. L., Karno, M., Escobar, J. I., & Telles, C. A. (1987). Acculturation and lifetime prevalence of psychiatric disorders among Mexican Americans in Los Angeles. *Journal of Health and Social Behavior, 28,* 89–102.

Burns, D. D. (1980). *Feeling good: The new mood therapy.* New York: Morris.

Burns, D. D., & Beck, A. T. (1978). Modification of mood disorders. In J. P. Foreyt and D. P. Rathjen (Eds.), *Cognitive behavior therapy: Research and application* (pp. 109–134). New York: Plenum.

Burns, D. D., & Nolen-Hoeksema, S. (1992). Therapeutic empathy and recovery from depression in cognitive-behavioral therapy: A structural equation model. *Journal of Consulting and Clinical Psychology, 60,* 441–449.

Burt, M. R. (1980). Cultural myths and supports for rape. *Journal of Personality and Social Psychology, 38,* 217–230.

Butler, G. (1989). Issues in the application of cognitive and behavioral strategies to the treatment of social phobia. *Clinical Psychology Review, 9,* 91–106.

Butler, G., Fennell, M., Robson, P., & Gelder, M. (1991). Comparison of behavior therapy and cognitive behavior therapy in the treatment of generalized anxiety disorder. *Journal of Consulting and Clinical Psychology, 59,* 167–175.

Butler, G., Gelder, M., Hibbert, G., Cullington, A., et al. (1987). Anxiety management: Developing effective strategies. *Behaviour Research and Therapy, 25,* 517–522.

Butler, R. N., & Lewis, M. I. (1982). *Aging and mental health* (3rd ed.). St. Louis: Mosby.

Butters, N., Martone, M., White, B., Granholm, E., & Wolfe, J. (1986). Clinical validators: Comparisons of demented and amnesic patients. In L. W. Poon (Ed.), *Handbook for clinical memory assessment of older adults* (pp. 337–352). Washington, DC: American Psychological Association.

Butters, N., Sax, D., Montgomery, K., & Tarlow, S. (1978). Comparison of the neuropsychological deficits associated with early and advanced Huntington's disease. *Archives of Neurology, 35,* 585–589.

Byrne, D. (1977). The imagery of sex. In Money, J., & Musaph, H. (Eds.), *Handbook of sexology* (pp. 327–350). New York: Elsevier/North Holland.

Byrne, D. G., Whyte, H. M., & Butler, K. L. (1981). Illness behaviour and outcome following survived myocardial infarction: A prospective study. *Journal of Psychosomatic Research, 25,* 97–107.

Cadoret, R. J., Cain, C. A., & Grove, W. M. (1980). Development of alcoholism in adoptees raised apart from alcoholic biologic relatives. *Archives of General Psychiatry, 37,* 561–563.

Cadoret, R. J., Troughton, E., O'Gorman, T. W., & Heywood, E. (1986). An adoption study of genetic and environmental factors in drug abuse. *Archives of General Psychiatry, 43,* 1131–1136.

Caetano, R. (1987). Acculturation and drinking patterns among U.S. Hispanics. *British Journal of Addiction, 82,* 789–799.

Caine, E. D., Ebert, M. H., & Weingartner, H. (1977). An outline for the analysis of dementia: The memory disorder of Huntington's disease. *Neurology, 27,* 1087–1092.

Calhoun, K. S., & Atkeson, B. M. (1991). *Treatment of rape victims: Facilitating social adjustment.* New York: Pergamon Press.

Calne, D. B. (1977). Developments in the pharmacology and therapeutics of Parkinsonism. *Annals of Neurology, 1,* 111–119.

Cameron, N. (1963). *Personality development and psychopathology: A dynamic approach.* Boston: Houghton Mifflin.

Campbell, D. T., & Stanley, J. C. (1963). Experimental and quasi-experimental designs for research on teaching. In N. L. Gage (Ed.), *Handbook of research on teaching.* Chicago: Rand McNally.

Campbell, S. B. (1985). Hyperactivity in preschoolers: Correlates and prognostic implications. *Clinical Psychology Review, 5,* 405–428.

Campbell, S. B., & Cohn, J. F. (1991). Prevalence and correlates of postpartum depression in first-time mothers. *Journal of Abnormal Psychology, 101,* 594–599.

Cantor, P. C. (1976). Personality characteristics found among youthful female suicide attempters. *Journal of Abnormal Psychology, 85,* 324–329.

Carani, C., et al. (1990). Effects of androgen treatment in impotent men with normal and low levels of free testosterone. *Archives of Sexual Behavior, 19,* 223–234.

Card, J. J. (1987). Epidemiology of posttraumatic stress disorder in a national cohort of Vietnam veterans. *Journal of Clinical Psychology, 43,* 6–17.

Cardin, V. A., McGill, C. W., & Falloon, I. R. H. (1986). An economic analysis: Costs, benefits, and effectiveness. In I. R. H. Falloon (Ed.), *Family management of schizophrenia* (pp. 115–123). Baltimore: Johns Hopkins University Press.

Carey, G. (1992). Twin imitation for antisocial behavior: Implications for genetic and family environment research. *Journal of Abnormal Psychology, 101,* 18–25.

Carey, M. P., & Burish, T. G. (1987). Providing relaxation training to cancer chemotherapy patients: A comparison of three delivery techniques. *Journal of Consulting and Clinical Psychology, 55,* 732–737.

Carey, M. P., & Burish, T. G. (1988). Etiology and treatment of the psychological side effects associated with cancer chemotherapy: A critical review and discussion. *Psychological Bulletin, 104,* 307–325.

Carey, M. P., Faulstich, M. E., Gresham, F. M., Ruggiero, L., & Enyart, P. (1987). Children's Depression Inventory: Construct and discriminant validity across clinical and nonreferred (control) populations. *Journal of Consulting and Clinical Psychology, 55,* 755–761.

Carini, M. A., & Nevid, J. S. (1992). Social appropriateness and impaired perspective in schizophrenia. *Journal of Clinical Psychology, 48,* 170–177.

Carlat, D. J., & Camargo, C. A. (1991). Review of bulimia nervosa in males. *American Journal of Psychiatry, 148,* 831–843.

Carlson, G. A. (1980). Unmasking masked depression in children and adolescents. *American Journal of Psychiatry, 137,* 445–449.

Carlson, G. A., & Garber, J. (1986). Developmental issues in the classification of depression in children. In M. Rutter, C. Izard, & P. Read (Eds.), *Depression in young people: Developmental and clinical prospectives* (pp. 399–434). New York: Guilford.

Carlson, G. A., & Miller, D. C. (1981). Suicide affective disorder and women physicians. *American Journal of Psychiatry, 138,* 1330–1335.

Carmelli, D., Swan, G. E., Robinette, D., & Fabstiz, R. (1992). Genetic influences on smoking—a study of male twins. *New England Journal of Medicine, 327,* 829–833.

Carpenter, W. T., Jr. (1986). Thoughts on the treatment of schizophrenia. *Schizophrenia Bulletin, 12,* 527–539.

Carpenter, W. T., Jr., Heinrichs, W., & Wagmen, E. N. (1988). Deficit and nondeficit forms of schizophrenia: The concept. *American Journal of Psychiatry, 145,* 578–584.

Carpenter, W. T., Jr., et al. (1990). Continuous versus targeted medication in schizophrenic outpatients: Outcome results. *American Journal of Psychiatry, 147,* 1139–1148.

Carroll, E. M., Rueger, D. B., Foy, D. W., & Donahoe, C. P. (1985). Vietnam combat veterans with posttraumatic stress disorder: An analysis of marital and cohabiting adjustment. *Journal of Abnormal Psychology, 94,* 329–337.

Carroll, K. M., & Rounsaville, B. J. (1992). Contrast of treatment-seeking and untreated cocaine abusers. *Archives of General Psychiatry, 49,* 464–471.

Carver, C. S., & Gaines, J. G. (1987). Optimism, pessimism, and postpartum depression. *Cognitive Therapy & Research, 11,* 449–462.

Caton, C. L. M., et al. (1990). An evaluation of a mental health program for homeless men. *American Journal of Psychiatry, 147,* 286–289.

Caudill, B. D., & Marlatt, G. A. (1975). Modeling influences in social drinking: An experimental analogue. *Journal of Consulting and Clinical Psychology, 43,* 405–415.

Centers for Disease Control. (1985). *Suicide surveillance, 1970–1980.* Washington, DC: Department of Health and Human Services.

Centers for Disease Control. (1990). Estimates of HIV prevalence and projected AIDS cases; Summary of a workshop, October 31–November 1, 1989. *Morbidity and Mortality Weekly Report,* February 23, 110–119.

Cerny, J., Barlow, D. H., Craske, M. G., & Himadi, W. G. (1987). Couples treatment of agoraphobia: A two-year follow-up. *Behavior Therapy, 18,* 401–415.

Chadda, R. K., & Ahuja, N. (1990). Dhat syndrome: A sex neurosis of the Indian subcontinent. *British Journal of Psychiatry, 156,* 577–579.

Chan, D. W. (1991). The Beck Depression Inventory: What difference does the Chinese version make? *Psychological Assessment, 3,* 616–622.

Chang, S. C. (1984). Review of I. Yamashita "Taijin-kyofu." *Transcultural Psychiatric Research Review, 21,* 283–288.

Chassin, L., Mann, L. M., & Sher, K. J. (1988). Self-awareness theory, family history of alcoholism, and adolescent alcohol involvement. *Journal of Abnormal Psychology, 97,* 206–217.

Chavetz, L., & Goldfinger, S. M. (1984). Residential instability in a psychiatric emergency setting. *Psychiatric Quarterly, 56,* 20–34.

Check, J. V. P., & Malamuth, N. M. (1983). Sex-role stereotyping and reactions to depictions of stranger versus acquaintance rape. *Journal of Personality and Social Psychology, 45,* 344–356.

Chesno, F. A., & Kilmann, P. R. (1975). Effects of stimulation intensity on sociopathic avoidance learning. *Journal of Abnormal Psychology, 84,* 144–151.

Chess, S., Korn, S. J., & Fernandez, P. B. (1971). *Psychiatric Disorders of Children with Congenital Rubella.* New York: Brunner/Mazel.

Cheung, F. (1991). The use of mental health services by ethnic minorities. In H. F. Myers et al. (Eds.), *Ethnic minority perspectives on clinical training and services in psychology* (pp. 23–31). Washington, DC: American Psychological Association.

Cheung, F., Song, W., & Butcher, J. N. (1991). An infrequency scale for the Chinese MMPI. *Psychological Assessment, 3,* 648–653.

Childs, E. K. (1990). Therapy, feminist ethics, and the community of color with particular emphasis on the treatment of black women. In H. Lerman & N. Porter (Eds.), *Feminist ethics in psychotherapy* (pp. 195–203). New York: Springer.

Chipperfield, B., & Vogel-Sprott, M. (1988). Family history of problem drinking among young male social drinkers: Modeling effects on alcohol consumption. *Journal of Abnormal Psychology, 97,* 423–428.

Chouinard, G., et al. (1983). New concepts on benzodiazepine therapy: Rebound anxiety and new indications for the more potent benzodiazepines. *Progress in Neuro-Psychopharmacology and Biological Psychiatry, 7,* 669–673.

Christensen, A., et al. (1983). Parental characteristics and interactional dysfunction in families with child behavioral problems: a preliminary investigation. *Journal of Abnormal Child Psychology, 11,* 153–166.

Christiansen, B. A., & Goldman, M. S. (1983). Alcohol related expectancies versus demographic/background variables in the prediction of adolescent drinking. *Journal of Consulting and Clinical Psychology, 52,* 249–257.

Christiansen, B. A., Goldman, M. S., & Inn, A. (1982). Development of alcohol-related expectancies in adolescence. *Journal of Consulting and Clinical Psychology, 50,* 336–344.

Chronicle of Higher Education (1992, March 18). Pp. A35–A44.

Clark, D. M. (1986). A cognitive approach to panic. *Behaviour Research and Therapy, 24,* 461–470.

Clark, D. M., Salkovskis, P. M., & Chalkley, A. J. (1985). Respiratory control as a treatment for panic attacks. *Journal of Behavior Therapy and Experimental Psychiatry, 16,* 23–30.

Clark, M., & Witherspoon, O. (1984, May 28). Using drugs to fight autism. *Newsweek,* pp. 90–91.

Cleckley, H. (1976). *The mask of sanity* (5th ed.). St. Louis: Mosby. (Originally published in 1941.)

Cleghorn, J. M., et al. (1992). Toward a brain map of auditory hallucinations. *American Journal of Psychiatry, 149,* 1062–1069.

Clementz, B. A., & Sweeney, J. A. (1990). Is eye movement dysfunction a biological marker for schizophrenia? A methodological review. *Psychological Bulletin, 108,* 77–92.

Cloninger, C. R., Bohman, M., Sigvardsson, S., & von Knorring, A. L. (1984). Psychopathology in adopted-out children of alcoholics. In M. Galanter (Ed.), *Recent developments in alcoholism* (pp. 37–51). New York: Plenum Press.

Cloninger, C. R., Reich, T., & Yokoyama, S. (1983). Genetic diversity, genome organization, and investigation of the etiology of psychiatric diseases. *Psychiatric Developments, 3,* 225–246.

Coffey, C. E., & Weiner, R. D. (1990). Electroconvulsive therapy: An update. *Hospital and Community Psychiatry, 41,* 515–521.

Cohen, D. (1986). Psychopathological perspectives: Differential diagnosis of Alzheimer's disease and related disorders. In L. W. Poon (Ed.), *Handbook for clinical memory assessment of older adults* (pp. 81–88). Washington, DC: American Psychological Association.

Cohen, H. L., & Filipczak, J. (1971). *A new learning environment.* San Francisco: Jossey-Bass.

Cohen, L. A. (1987, November). Diet and cancer. *Scientific American,* pp. 42–48, 533–534.

Cohen, S., Evans, G. W., Stokols, D., & Krantz, D. S. (1986). *Behavior, health, and environmental stress.* New York: Plenum.

Cohen, S., Tyrrell, D. A. J., & Smith, A. P. (1991). Psychological stress and susceptibility to the common cold. *New England Journal of Medicine, 325,* 606–612.

Cohen, S., & Wills, T. A. (1985). Stress, social supports and the buffering hypothesis. *Psychological Bulletin, 98,* 310–357.

Cohn, L. D., et al. (1987). Body-figure preferences in male and female adolescents. *Journal of Abnormal Psychology, 96,* 276–279.

Cole, D. A. (1990). Relation of social and academic competence to depressive symptoms in childhood. *Journal of Abnormal Psychology, 99,* 422–429.

Cole, D. A. (1991). Preliminary support for a competency-based model of depression in children. *Journal of Abnormal Psychology, 100,* 181–190.

Cole, R. (1982). Patient's rights vs. doctor's rights: Which should take precedence? In A. E. Doudera & J. P. Swazy (Eds.), *Refusing treatments in mental health institutions: Values and conflict.* Ann Arbor, AUPHA Press.

Coleman, E. (1987). Bisexuality: Challenging our understanding of sexual orientation. *Sexuality and Medicine, 1,* 225–242.

Collins, P. H. (1990). *Black feminist thought: Knowledge, consciousness, and the politics of empowerment.* Boston: Unwin Hyman.

Comas-Diaz, L., & Griffith, E. (1988). Introduction: On culture and psychotherapeutic care. In L. Comas-Diaz & E. Griffith (Eds.), *Clinical guidelines in cross-cultural mental health.* New York: Wiley.

Combs, B. J., Hales, D. R., & Williams, B. K. (1980). *An invitation to health.* Menlo Park, CA: Benjamin/Cummings.

Commission on the Review of the National Policy Toward Gambling, (1978). *Gambling in America: The Final Report.* Washington, DC: U.S. Government Printing Office.

Costantino, G., Malgady, R. G., & Rogler, L. H. (1986). Cuento therapy: A culturally sensitive modality for Puerto Rican children. *Journal of Consulting and Clinical Psychology, 54,* 639–645.

Conte, H. R. (1986). Multivariate assessment of sexual dysfunction. *Journal of Consulting and Clinical Psychology, 54,* 149–157.

Conte, H. R., Plutchik, R., Wild, K., & Karasu, T. B. (1986). Combined psychotherapy and pharmacotherapy for depression: A systematic analysis of the evidence. *Archives of General Psychiatry, 43,* 471–479.

Cook, E. W., III, Melamed, B. G., Cuthbert, B. N., McNeil, D. W., & Lang, P. J. (1988). Emotional imagery and the differential diagnosis of anxiety. *Journal of Consulting and Clinical Psychology, 56,* 734–740.

Cook, T. D., & Campbell, D. T. (1979). *Quasi-experimentation: Design and analysis issues for field settings.* Chicago: Rand McNally.

Coons, P. M. (1986). Treatment progress in 20 patients with multiple personality disorder. *Journal of Nervous and Mental Disease, 174,* 715–721.

Coons, P. M., Bowman, E. S., & Pellow, T. A. (1989). Post-traumatic aspects of the treatment of victims of sexual abuse and incest. *Psychiatric Clinics of North America, 12,* 325–327.

Cooper, A. J. (1986). Progestogens in the treatment of male sex offenders; A review. *Canadian Journal of Psychiatry, 31,* 73–79.

Cooper, A. J., et al. (1990). A female sex offender with multiple paraphilias: A psychologic, physiologic (laboratory sexual arousal) and endocrine case study. *Canadian Journal of Psychiatry, 35,* 334–337.

Cooper, M. L., et al. (1992). Stress and alcohol use: Moderating effects of gender, coping, and alcohol expectancies. *Journal of Abnormal Psychology, 101,* 139–152.

Cooper, S. J., et al. (1986). Post-mortem neurochemical findings in suicide and depression: A study of the serotonergic system and imipramine binding in suicide victims. In J. W. W. Deakin (Ed.), *The biology of depression* (pp. 53–70). Proceedings of a meeting of the Biological Group of the Royal College of Psychiatrists held at Manchester University, 1985. Washington, DC: American Psychiatric Press.

Cordes, C. (1985). Common threads found in suicide. *APA Monitor, 16* (10), 11.

Corkin, S. (1980). A prospective study of cingulotomy. In E. S. Valenstein (Ed.), *The psychosurgery debate.* San Francisco: Freeman.

Cormier, W. H., & Cormier, L. S. (1985). *Interviewing strategies for helpers.* Monterey, CA: Brooks/Cole.

Coryell, W., Endicott, J., & Keller, M. (1992a). Major depression in a nonclinical sample: Demographic and clinical risk factors for first onset. *Archives of General Psychiatry, 49,* 117–125.

Coryell, W., Endicott, J., & Keller, M. (1992b). Rapidly cycling affective disorder: Demographics, diagnosis, family history, and course. *Archives of General Psychiatry, 49,* 126–131.

Costa, P. T., Jr., & McCrae, R. R. (1985). Hypochondriasis, neuroticism, and aging: When are somatic complaints unfounded? *American Psychologist, 40,* 19–28.

Costa, P. T., Jr., Zonderman, A. B., McCrae, R. R., & Williams, R. B., Jr. (1985). Content and comprehensiveness in the MMPI: An item factor analysis in a normal adult sample. *Journal of Personality and Social Psychology, 48,* 925–933.

Cowen, E. L. (1985). Person-centered approaches to primary prevention in mental health: Situation-focused and competence-enhancement.

American Journal of Community Psychology, 13, 31–48.

Cowley, G. (1989, December 18). Medical mystery tour: What causes Alzheimer's disease, and how does it ruin the brain? *Newsweek,* pp. 59–63.

Cowley, G. (1992, December 7). Progress on Parkinson's: Tissue from aborted fetuses can bring relief. *Newsweek,* p. 68.

Cox, B. J., et al. (1992). Situations and specific coping strategies associated with clinical and nonclinical panic attacks. *Behaviour Research & Therapy, 30,* 67–69.

Cox, W. M., & Klinger, E. (1988). A motivational model of alcohol use. *Journal of Abnormal Psychology, 97,* 168–180.

Coyle, J. T., Price, D. L., & DeLong, M. R. (1983). Alzheimer's disease: A disorder of cortical cholinergic innervation. *Science, 219,* 1184–1190.

Coyne, J. C. (1976). Toward an interactional description of depression. *Psychiatry, 39,* 14–27.

Coyne, J. C., Kessler, R. C., Tal, M., Turnbull, J., Wortman, C. B., & Greden, J. F. (1987). Living with a depressed person. *Journal of Consulting and Clinical Psychology, 55,* 347–352.

Craighead, L. W. (1984). Sequencing of behavior therapy and pharmacotherapy for obesity. *Journal of Consulting and Clinical Psychology, 52,* 190–199.

Craighead, L. W., & Agras, W. S. (1991). Mechanisms of action in cognitive-behavioral and pharmacological interventions for obesity and bulimia nervosa. *Journal of Consulting and Clinical Psychology, 59,* 115–125.

Craighead, L. W., Stunkard, A. J., & O'Brien, R. M. (1981). Behavior therapy and pharmacotherapy for obesity. *Archives of General Psychiatry, 38,* 763–768.

Crammer, J., Barraclough, B., & Heine, B. (1982). *The use of drugs in psychiatry* (2nd ed.). London: Invicta Press (The Royal College of Physicians).

Craske, M. G., Brown, T. A., & Barlow, D. H. (1991). Behavioral teratment of panic disorder: A two-year follow-up. *Behavior Therapy, 22,* 289–304.

Creamer, M., Burgess, P., & Pattison, P. (1992). Reaction to trauma: A cognitive processing model. *Journal of Abnormal Psychology, 101,* 452–459.

Creese, I., Burt, D. R., & Snyder, S. H. (1978). Biochemical actions of neuroleptic drugs. In L. L. Iverson, S. D. Iverson, & S. H. Snyder (Eds.), *Handbook of psychopharmacology* (Vol. 10, New York: Plenum.

Crews, D., & Moore, M. C. (1986). Evolution of mechanisms controlling mating behavior. *Science, 231,* 121–125.

Crits-Christoph, P. (1992). The efficacy of brief dynamic psychotherapy: A meta-analysis. *American Journal of Psychiatry, 149,* 151–158.

Crow, T. J. (1980a). Molecular pathology of schizophrenia: More than one disease process? *British Medical Journal, 280,* 66–68.

Crow, T. J. (1980b). Positive and negative schizophrenic symptoms and the role of dopamine. *British Journal of Psychiatry, 137,* 383–386.

Crow, T. J. (1980c). Positive and negative schizophrenic symptoms and the role of dopamine: A debate. *British Journal of Psychiatry, 137,* 379–383.

Crown, S., & D'Ardenne, D. (1982). Symposium on sexual dysfunction: Controversies, methods, results. *British Journal of Psychiatry, 140,* 70–77.

Crystal, A. J. (1988). The diagnosis of Alzheimer's disease and other dementing disorders. In M. K. Aronson (Ed.) *Understanding Alzheimer's disease.* New York: Macmillan.

Cummings, C. (1988, August 15). Panel says care is still lacking for mentally ill. *New York Times,* p. B2.

Cummings, J. L. (1992). Depression and Parkinson's disease: A review. *American Journal of Psychiatry, 149,* 443–454.

Cunningham, F. G., & Gilstrap, L. C. (1991). Maternal serum alpha-fetoprotein screening. *New England Journal of Medicine, 325,* 55–57.

Curb, J. D., & Marcus, E. B. (1991). Body fat and obesity in Japanese-Americans. *American Journal of Clinical Nutrition, 53,* 1552S–1555S.

Cutts, T. F., & Barrios, B. A. (1986). Fear of weight gain among bulimic and nondisturbed females. *Behavior Therapy, 17,* 626–636.

Dadds, M. R., et al. (1992). Childhood depression and conduct disorder: II. An analysis of family interaction patterns in the home. *Journal of Abnormal Psychology, 101,* 505–513.

Davidson, J. M., et al. (1982). Hormonal replacement and sexuality in men. *Clinics in Endocrinology and Metabolism, 11,* 599–623.

Davies, P. (1988). Alzheimer's disease and related disorders: An overview. In M. K. Aronson (Ed.), *Understanding Alzheimer's disease* (pp. 3–14). New York: Scribner's.

Davis, K. L., et al. (1991). Dopamine in schizophrenia: A review and reconceptualization. *American Journal of Psychiatry, 148,* 1474–1486.

Davis, K. L., et al (1992). A double-blind, placebo-controlled multicenter study of tacrine for Alzheimer's disease. *New England Journal of Medicine, 327,* 1253–1259.

Davison, G. C. (1977). Elimination of a sadistic fantasy by a client-controlled counterconditioning technique. In J. Fischer & H. Gochios (Eds.), *Handbook of behavior therapy with sexual problems.* New York: Pergamon Press.

Dawber, T. B. (1980). *The Framingham study: The epidemiology of atherosclerotic disease.* Cambridge, MA: Harvard University Press.

Deakin, J. F. W., & Crow, T. J. (1986). Monoamines, rewards and punishments—the anatomy and physiology of the affective disorders. In J. W. W. Deakin (Ed.), *The biology of depression.* Proceedings of a meeting of the Biological Group of the Royal College of Psychiatrists held at Manchester University, 1985. Washington, DC: American Psychiatric Press.

Dean, C. W., & deBruyn-Kops, E. (1982). *The crime and consequences of rape.* Springfield, IL: Charles C Thomas.

Deffenbacher, J. L., & Suinn, R. M. (1988). Systematic desensitization and the reduction of anxiety. *The Counseling Psychologist, 16,* 9–30.

DeFries, J. C., Fulker, D. W., & LaBuda, M. C. (1987). Reading disability in twins: Evidence for a genetic etiology. *Nature, 329,* 537–539.

De La Cancela, V., & Guzman, L. P. (1991). Latino mental health service needs: Implications for training psychologists. In H. F. Myers et al. (Eds.), *Ethnic minority perspectives on clinical training and services in psychology* (pp. 59–64). Washington, DC: American Psychological Association.

de Leon, M. J., George, A. E., & Ferris, S. H. (1986). Computed tomography and positron emission tomography correlates of cognitive decline in aging and senile dementia. In L. W. Poon (Ed.), *Handbook for clinical memory assessment of older adults* (pp. 367–382). Washington, DC: American Psychological Association.

de Leon, M. J., et al. (1983). Computed tomography and positron emission transaxial tomography evaluations of normal aging and Alzheimer's disease. *Journal of Cerebral Blood Flow and Metabolism, 3,* 391–394.

de Young, M. (1982). *The sexual victimization of children.* Jefferson, NC: McFarland & Company.

D'Elia, G., & Raotma, H. (1975). Is unilateral ECT less effective than bilateral ECT? *British Journal of Psychiatry, 126,* 83–89.

Delprato, D. J., & Midgley, B. D. (1992). Some fundamentals of B. F. Skinner's behaviorism. *American Psychologist, 47,* 1507–1520.

Dennis, D. L., et al. (1991). A decade of research and services for homeless mentally ill persons. *American Psychologist, 46,* 1129–1138.

Dent, D. N. T., & Teasdale, J. D. (1988). Negative cognitions and the persistence of depression. *Journal of Abnormal Psychology, 97,* 29–34.

Depue, R. A., Slater, J. F., Wolfstetter-Kausch, H., Klein, D., Goplerud, E., & Farr, D. (1981). A behavioral paradigm for identifying persons at risk for bipolar depressive disorders: A conceptual framework and five validational studies [Monograph]. *Journal of Abnormal Psychology, 90,* 381–437.

DeRubeis, R. J., et al. (1990). How does cognitive therapy work? Cognitive change and symptom change in cognitive therapy and pharmacotherapy for depression. *Journal of Consulting and Clinical Psychology, 58,* 862–869.

Desmond, E. W. (1987, November). Out in the open: Changing attitudes and new research give fresh hope to alcoholics. *Time Magazine,* pp. 80–90.

Devan, G. S. (1987). Koro and schizohrenia in Singapore. *British Journal of Psychiatry, 150,* 106–107.

Devannand, D. P., et al. (1991). Absence of cognitive impairment after more than 100 lifetime ECT treatments. *American Journal of Psychiatry, 148,* 929–932.

Devins, G. M., Binik, Y. M., Hollomby, D. J., Barre, P. E., & Guttmann, R. D. (1981). Helplessness and depression in end-stage renal disease. *Journal of Abnormal Psychology, 90,* 531–545.

Diamond, E. L. (1982). The role of anger and hostility in essential hypertension and coronary heart disease. *Psychological Bulletin, 92,* 410–433.

Dieckmann, L., Zarit, S. H., Zarit, J. M., & Gatz, M. (1988). The Alzheimer's Disease Knowledge Test. *The Gerontologist, 28,* 402–407.

DiLalla, L. F., & Gottesman, I. I. (1991). Biological and genetic contributors to violence—widom's untold tale. *Psychological Bulletin, 109,* 125–129.

Doane, J. A., Faloon, I. R. H., Goldstein, M. J., & Mintz, J. (1985). Parental affective style and the treatment of schizophrenia. *Archives of General Psychiatry, 42,* 34–42.

Dodge, K. A. (1985). Attributional bias in aggressive children. *Advances in Cognitive Behavioral Research and Therapy, 4,* 73–110.

Dodge, K. A., & Frame, C. L. (1982). Social cognitive biases and deficits in aggressive boys. *Child Development, 53,* 620–635.

Dodge, K. A., Price, J. M., Bachorowski, J., & Newman, J. P. (1990). Hostile attributional biases in severely aggressive adolescents. *Journal of Abnormal Psychology, 99,* 385–392.

Dodge, L. J. T., Glasgow, R. E., & O'Neill, H. K. (1982). Bibliotherapy in the treatment of female orgasmic dysfunction. *Journal of Consulting and Clinical Psychology, 50,* 442–443.

Dohrenwend, B. P., & Shrout, P. E. (1985). "Hassles" in the conceptualization and measurement of life stress variables. *American Psychologist, 40,* 780–785.

Dohrenwend, B. S., Dohrenwend, B. P., Dodson, M., & Shrout, P. E. (1984). Symptoms, hassles, social supports and life events: The problem of confounded measures. *Journal of Abnormal Psychology, 93,* 222–230.

Doleys, D. M. (1977). Behavioral Treatments for nocturnal enuresis in children: a review of the literature. *Psychological Bulletin, 8,* 30–54.

Dollard, J., & Miller, N. E. (1950). *Personality and psychotherapy.* New York: McGraw-Hill.

Donnerstein, E. I. (1980). Aggressive erotica and violence against women. *Journal of Personality and Social Psychology, 39,* 269–277.

Donnerstein, E. I., & Linz, D. G. (1984,). Sexual violence in the media: A warning. *Psychology Today,* pp. 14–15.

Donnerstein, E. I., & Linz, D. G. (1987). *The question of pornography.* New York: Free Press.

Douglas, A. R., Matson, I. C., & Hunter, S. (1989). Sex therapy for women incestuously abused as children. *Sexual and Marital Therapy, 4,* 143–159.

Douglas, V. I. (1983). Attentional and cognitive problems. In M. Rutter (Ed.), *Developmental neuropsychiatry* (pp. 280–329). New York: Guilford Press.

Douglas, V. I., Parry, P., Marton, P., & Garson, C. (1976). Assessment of a cognitive training program for hyperactive children. *Journal of Abnormal Child Psychology, 4,* 389–410.

Dow, S. (1981). Retarded ejaculation. *Journal of Sex and Marital Therapy, 7,* 49–53.

Doyne, E. J., et al. (1987). Running versus weight lifting in the treatment of depression. *Journal of Consulting and Clinical Psychology, 55,* 748–754.

Drachman, D. A., & Leavitt, J. (1974). Human memory and the cholinergic system. *Archives of Neurology, 30,* 113–121.

Drake, R. E., Osher, F. C., & Wallach, M. A. (1991). Homelessness and dual diagnosis. *American Psychologist, 46,* 1149–1158.

Drake, R. E., & Vaillant, G. E. (1985). A validity study of axis II of DSM III. *American Journal of Psychiatry, 142,* 553–558.

Drake, R. E., et al. (1991). Housing instability and homelessness among rural schizophrenic patients. *American Journal of Psychiatry, 148,* 211–215.

Dryden, W. (1984). *Rational-emotive therapy: Fundamentals and innovations.* London: Croom Helm.

Dubbert, P. M. (1992). Exercise in behavioral medicine. *Journal of Consulting and Clinical Psychology, 60,* 613–618.

Duffy, F. H. (1982). Topographic display of evoked potentials: Clinical applications of Brain Electrical Activity Mapping (BEAM). *Annals of the New York Academy of Science, 388,* 183–196.

Duffy, F. H., et al. (1980). Dyslexia: Regional differences in brain electrical activity by topographic mapping. *Annals of Neurology, 7,* 412–420.

Dugger, C. W. (1992, September 3). Threat only when on crack, homeless man foils system. *New York Times,* pp. A1, B4.

Dulcan, M. K. (1986). Comprehensive treatment of children and adolescents with attention deficit disorders: The state of the art. *Clinical Psychology Review, 6,* 539–570.

Dunham, H. W. (1965). *Community and schizophrenia: An epidemiological analysis.* Detroit: Wayne State University Press.

Dura, J. R., Stukenberg, K. W., & Kiecolt-Glaser, J. K. (1990). Chronic stress and depressive disorders in older adults. *Journal of Abnormal Psychology, 99,* 284–290.

Durham v. United States, 214 F. 2d 862, D.C. circ. (1954).

Durkheim, E. (1958). *Suicide.* (J. A. Spaulding & G. Simpson, Trans.). New York: Free Press. (Original work published 1897)

Dwyer, M. (1988). Exhibitionism/voyeurism. *Journal of Social Work and Human Sexuality, 7,* 101–112.

Eaton, W. W., Dryman, A., & Weissman, M. M. (1991). Panic and phobia. In L. N. Robins & D. A. Regier (Eds.), *Psychiatric disorders in America: The Epidemiologic Catchment Area Study* (pp. 155–179). New York: The Free Press.

Eaves, G., & Rush, A. J. (1984). Cognitive patterns in symptomatic and remitted unipolar major depression. *Journal of Abnormal Psychology, 93,* 31–40.

Eberhardy, F. (1967). The view from "the couch." *Journal of Child Psychological Psychiatry, 8,* 257–263.

Eckenrode, J. (1984). Impact of chronic and acute stressors on daily reports of mood. *Journal of Personality and Social Psychology, 46,* 907–918.

Eckert, E. D., Bouchard, T. J., Bohlen, J., & Heston, L. L. (1986). Homosexuality in monozy-

gotic twins reared apart. *British Journal of Psychiatry, 148,* 421–425.

Eckhardt, M. J., et al. (1981). Health hazards associated with alcohol consumption. *Journal of the American Medical Association, 246,* 648–666.

Egeland, J. A., et al. (1983). Amish study, II: The impact of cultural factors on diagnosis of bipolar illness. *American Journal of Psychiatry, 140,* 67–71.

Ehlers, A., & Breuer, P. (1992). Increased cardiac awareness in panic disorder. *Journal of Abnormal Psychology, 101,* 371–382.

Ehlers, A., Margraf, J., Roth, W. T., Barr-Taylor, C., & Birbaumer, N. (1988). Anxiety induced by false heart rate feedback in patients with panic disorder. *Behaviour Research and Therapy, 26,* 1–11.

Eisdorfer, C., & Cohen, D. (1980). Diagnostic criteria for primary neuronal degeneration of the Alzheimer type. *Journal of Family Practice, 11,* 553–557.

Eisenbruch, M. (1992). Toward a culturally sensitive DSM: Cultural bereavement in Cambodian refugees and the traditional healer as taxonomist. *Journal of Nervous and Mental Disease, 180,* 8–10.

Eisler, R. M., Blanchard, E. B., Fitts, H., & Williams, J. G. (1978). Social skill training with and without modeling for schizophrenic and non-psychotic hospitalized psychiatric patients. *Behavioral Modification, 2,* 147–172.

Eliot, R. S., & Buell, J. C. (1983). The role of the central nervous system in sudden cardiac death. In T. M. Dembroski, T. Schmidt, & G. Blunchen (Eds.), *Biobehavioral bases of coronary-prone behavior.* New York: Karger.

Elkin, I., et al. (1989). National Institute of Mental Health treatment of depression collaborative research program: General effectiveness of treatments. *Archives of General Psychiatry, 46,* 971–982.

Elkins, I. J., et al. (1992). Span of apprehension in schizophrenic patients as a function of distractor masking and laterality. *Journal of Abnormal Psychology, 101,* 53–60.

Elkins, R. A. (1991). An appraisal of chemical aversion (emetic therapy) approaches to alcoholism treatment. *Behaviour Research and Therapy, 29,* 387–413.

Ellickson, P. L., Hays, R. D., & Bell, R. M. (1992). Stepping through the drug use sequence: Longitudinal scalogram analysis of initiation and regular use. *Journal of Abnormal Psychology, 101,* 441–451.

Ellicott, A., et al. (1990). Life events and the course of bipolar disorder. *American Journal of Psychiatry, 147,* 1194–1198.

Ellingson, R. J. (1954). Incidence of EEG abnormality among patients with mental disorders of apparently non-organic origin: A critical review. *American Journal of Psychiatry, 111,* 263–275.

Ellis, A. (1977a). *Anger: How to live with and without it.* Secaucus, NJ: Citadel Press.

Ellis, A. (1977b). The basic clinical theory of rational-emotive therapy. In A. Ellis & R. Grieger (Eds.), *Handbook of rational-emotive therapy.* New York: Springer.

Ellis, A. (1985). Cognition and affect in emotional disturbance. *American Psychologist, 40,* 471–472.

Ellis, A. (1987). The impossibility of achieving consistently good mental health. *American Psychologist, 42,* 364–375.

Ellis, A., & Dryden, W. (1987). *The practice of rational emotional therapy.* New York: Springer.

Ellis, A., Young, J., & Lockwood, G. (1989). Cognitive therapy and rational-emotive therapy: A dialogue. *Journal of Cognitive Psychotherapy, 1,* 205–256.

Ellis, L. (1990). Prenatal stress may affect sex-typical behaviors of a child. *Brown University Child Behavior and Development Letter, 6,* (1) 1–3.

Elpers, J. R. (1987). Are we legislating reinstitutionalization? *American Journal of Orthopsychiatry, 57,* 441–446.

Emery, R. E., & O'Leary, K. D. (1982). Children's perceptions of marital discord and behavior problems of boys and girls. *Journal of Abnormal Child Psychology, 10,* 11–24.

Emmelkamp, P. M. G., & Kuipers, A. C. M. (1979). Agoraphobia: A follow-up study four years after treatment. *British Journal of Psychiatry, 134,* 352–355.

Emmons, T. D., & Webb, W. W. (1974). Subjective correlates of emotional responsivity and stimulation seeking in psychopaths, normals, and acting-out neurotics. *Journal of Consulting and Clinical Psychology, 42,* 620.

Epstein, L. H., & Perkin, K. A. (1988). Smoking, stress, and coronary heart disease. *Journal of Consulting and Clinical Psychology, 56,* 342–349.

Erdman, H. P., et al. (1987). A comparison of the Diagnostic Interview Schedule and clinical diagnosis. *American Journal of Psychiatry, 144,* 1477–1480.

Erikson, E. H. (1963). *Childhood and society.* New York: Norton.

Erikson, E. H. (1975). *Life history and the historical moment.* New York: Norton.

Erlenmeyer-Kimling, L., & Cornblatt, B. (1987). The New York High-Risk Project: A follow-up report. *Schizophrenia Bulletin, 13,* 451–461.

Ernsberger, P. (1987). Complications of the surgical treatment of obesity. *American Journal of Psychiatry, 144,* 833–834.

Ernst, N. D., & Harlan, W. R. (1991). Obesity and cardiovascular disease in minority populations: Executive summary. *American Journal of Clinical Nutrition, 53,* 1507S–1511S.

Ernster, V. L., Sacks, S. T., Selvin, S., & Petrakis, N. L. (1979). Cancer incidence by marital status: U. S. Third National Cancer Survey. *Journal of the National Cancer Institute, 63,* 585–587.

Evans, D. A., et al. (1989). Prevalence of Alzheimer's disease in a community population of older persons. *Journal of the American Medical Association, 262,* 2551–2556.

Evans, R. B. (1969). Childhood parental relationships of homosexual men. *Journal of Consulting and Clinical Psychology, 33,* 129–135.

Exner, J. E. (1978). *The Rorschach: A comprehensive system, Vol. 2.* New York: Wiley.

Exner, J. E., & Weiner, I. B. (1982). *The Rorschach: A comprehensive system, Vol. 3.* New York: Wiley.

Eysenck, H. J. (1952). The effects of psychotherapy: An evaluation. *Journal of Consulting Psychology, 16,* 319–324.

Eysenck, H. J. (1991). *Smoking, personality, and stress: Psychosocial factors in the prevention of cancer and coronary heart disease.* New York: Springer-Verlag.

Fabian, J. L. (1991). "Koro: Proposed classification for DSM-IV": Comment. *American Journal of Psychiatry, 148,* 1766.

Fabian, W. D., Jr., & Fishkin, S. M. (1981). A replicated study of self-reported changes in psychological absorption with marijuana intoxication. *Journal of Abnormal Psychology, 90,* 546–553.

Fabrega, H., Jr. (1990). Hispanic mental health research: A case for cultural psychiatry. *Hispanic Journal of Behavioral Sciences, 12,* 339–365.

Fabrega, H., Jr. (1992). Diagnosis interminable: Toward a culturally sensitive DSM-IV. *Journal of Nervous and Mental Disease, 180,* 5–7.

Fabrega, H., Jr., Mezzich, J., & Ulrich, R. F. (1988). Black-white differences in psychopathology in an urban psychiatric population. *Comprehensive Psychiatry, 29,* 285–297.

Fahn, S. (1992). Fetal-tissue transplants in Parkinson's disease. *New England Journal of Medicine, 327,* 1589–1590.

Fairbank, J. A., & Nicholson, R. A. (1987). Theoretical and empirical issues in the treatment of posttraumatic stress disorder in Vietnam veterans. *Journal of Clinical Psychology, 43,* 44–55.

Fairburn, C. G., & Cooper, P. J. (1984). The clinical features of bulimia nervosa. *British Journal of Psychiatry, 144,* 238–246.

Fairburn, C. G., Cooper, Z., & Cooper, P. J. (1986). The clinical features and maintenance of bulimia nervosa. In K. D. Brownell & J. P. Foreyt (Eds.), *Handbook of eating disorders* (pp. 389–404). New York: Basic.

Fairburn, C. G., Kirk, J., O'Connor, M., & Cooper, P. J. (1986). A comparison of two psychological treatments for bulimia nervosa. *Behavior Research and Therapy, 24*(6), 629–643.

Fairburn, C. G., et al. (1991). Three psychological treatments for bulimia nervosa: A comparative trial. *Archives of General Psychiatry, 48,* 463–469.

Fairweather, G. W., Sanders, D. H., Maynard, H., Cressler, D. L., & Bleck, D. S. (1969). *Community life for the mentally ill: An alternative to institutional care.* Chicago: Aldine.

Fallon, A. E., & Rozin, P. (1985). Sex differences in perceptions of desirable body shape. *Journal of Abnormal Psychology, 94,* 102–105.

Falloon, I. R. H., et al. (1982). Family management in the prevention of exacerbations of schizophrenia. *New England Journal of Medicine, 306,* 1437–1440.

Falloon, I. R. H., et al. (1985). Family management in the prevention of morbidity of schizophrenia: Clinical outcome of a two-year longitudinal study. *Archives of General Psychiatry, 42,* 887–896.

Falste, R. (1988, October 9). The myth about teen-agers. *New York Times Magazine: Part 2. (The Good Health Report Magazine),* pp. 19, 76.

Fann, W. E., Karacan, I., Pokerny, A. D., & Williams, R. L. (1982). *Phenomenology and the treatment of psychophysiological disorders.* New York: Spectrum Publications.

Faraone, S. V., Kremen, W. S., & Tsuang, M. T. (1990). Genetic transmission of major affective disorders: Quantitative models and linkage analyses. *Psychological Bulletin, 108,* 109–127.

Faraone, S. V., & Tsuang, M. T. (1985). Quantitative models of the genetic transmission of schizophrenia. *Psychological Bulletin, 98,* 41–66.

Faraone, S. V., et al. (1991). A family-genetic study of girls with DSM-III attention deficit disorder. *American Journal of Psychiatry, 148,* 112–117.

Farrell, A. D., Camplair, P. S., & McCullough, L. (1987). Identification of target complaints by computer interview: Evaluation of the Computerized Assessment System for Psychotherapy Evaluation and Research. *Journal of Consulting and Clinical Psychology, 55,* 691–700.

Faulstich, M. E. (1987). Psychiatric aspects of AIDS. *American Journal of Psychiatry, 144,* 551–556.

Fava, M. (1991). Does fluoxetine increase the risk of suicide? *Harvard Mental Health Letter, 7*(7), 8.

Fawcett, J., et al. (1987). Clinical predictors of suicide in patients with major defective disorders: A controlled prospective study. *American Journal of Psychiatry, 144,* 35–40.

Fawcett, J., et al. (1990). Time-related predictors of suicide in major affective disorder. *American Journal of Psychiatry, 147,* 1189–1194.

Fawzy, F. I., et al. (1990). A structured psychiatric intervention for cancer patients. *Archives of General Psychiatry, 47,* 729–735.

Fay, R. E., et al. (1989). Prevalence and patterns of same-gender sexual contact among men. *Science, 243* 338–348.

Feder, H. H. (1984). Hormones and sexual behavior. *Annual Review of Psychology, 35,* 165–200.

Feighner, J. P. (1982). Benzodiazepines as antidepressants. *Modern Problems in Pharmopsychiatry, 18,* 197–213.

Felton, B. J., & Revenson, T. A. (1984). Coping with chronic illness: A study of illness controllability and the influence of coping strategies on psychological adjustment. *Journal of Consulting and Clinical Psychology, 52,* 343–353.

Fenichel, O. (1945). *The psychoanalytic theory of neurosis.* New York: Norton.

Fensterheim, H., & Kanter, J. S. (1980). Behavioral approach to sexual disorders. In B. Welman & J. Money (Eds.), *Handbook of human sexuality.* Englewood Cliffs, NJ: Prentice Hall.

Fenton, W. S., & McGlashan, T. H. (1987). Sustained remission in drug-free schizophrenic patients. *American Journal of Psychiatry, 144,* 1306–1309.

Fenton, W. S., & McGlashan, T. H. (1991). Natural history of schizophrenia subtypes: II. Positive and negative symptoms and long-term course. *Archives of General Psychiatry, 48,* 978–986.

Ferguson-Peters, M. (1985). Racial socialization of young black children. In H. & J. L. McAdoo, *Black children* (pp. 159–173). Beverly Hills, CA: Sage.

Ferris, S. H., et al. (1980). Positron emission tomography in the study of aging and senile dementia. *Neurobiology of Aging, 1,* 127–131.

Fibel, B., & Hale, W. D. (1978). The generalized expectancy for success scale—new measure. *Journal of Consulting and Clinical Psychology, 46,* 924–931.

Fieve, R. R. (1975). *Moodswings: The third revolution in psychiatry.* New York: Morrow.

Fifteen percent of elderly are depressed. (1992, July 9). *New York Times,* p. C10.

Fingarette, H. (1972). *The meaning of criminal insanity.* Berkeley: University of California Press.

Finkelhor, D. (1980). Sex among siblings: A survey on prevalence, variety, and effects. *Archives of Sexual Behavior, 9,* 171–194.

Finkelhor, D. (1990). Early and long-term effects of child sexual abuse: An update. *Professional Psychology: Research and Practice, 21,* 325–330.

Fischer, P. J., & Breakey, W. R. (1992). The epidemiology of alcohol, drug, and mental disorders among homeless persons. *American Psychologist, 46,* 1115–1128.

Fish, V., & Faynik, C. (1989). Treatment of incest families with the father temporarily removed: A structural approach [Special Issue: Childhood sexual abuse]. *Journal of Strategic and Systemic Therapies, 8,* 53–63.

Fishbain, D. A. (1991). "Koro: Proposed classification for DSM-IV": Comment. *American Journal of Psychiatry, 148,* 1765–1766.

Fisher, J. D., & Fisher, W. A. (1992). Changing AIDS-risk behavior. *Psychological Bulletin, 111,* 455–474.

Fisher, S., & Greenberg, R. (Eds.). (1978). *The scientific evaluation of Freud's theories and therapy: A book of readings.* New York: Basic.

Flaskerud, J. H., & Hu, L. (1992). Relationship of ethnicity to psychiatric diagnosis. *Journal of Nervous and Mental Disease, 180,* 296–303.

Flaum, M., Arndt, S., & Andreasen, N. C. (1990). The role of gender in studies of ventricle enlargement in schizophrenia: A predominantly male effect. *American Journal of Psychiatry, 145,* 1327–1332.

Fleming, M. Z., Cohen, D., Salt, P., Jones, D., & Jenkins, S. (1981). A study of pre- and post-surgical transsexuals: MMPI characteristics. *Archives of Sexual Behavior, 10,* 161–170.

Fleming, M. Z., MacGowan, B. R., Robinson, L., Spitz, J., & Salt, P. (1982). The body image of the postoperative female-to-male transsexual. *Journal of Consulting and Clinical Psychology, 50,* 461–462.

Fluoxetine Bulimia Nervosa Collaborative Study Group. (1992). Fluoxetine in the treatment of bulimia nervosa: A multicenter, placebo-controlled, double-blind trial. *Archives of General Psychiatry, 49,* 139–147.

Foa, E. B. (1990, August/September). Obsessive-compulsive disorder. In American Psychiatric Association, *DSM-IV Update.* Washington, DC: American Psychiatric Association.

Foa, E. B., Steketee, G., & Grayson, J. B. (1985). Imaginal and in vivo exposure: A comparison with obsessive-compulsive checkers. *Behavior Therapy, 16,* 292–302.

Folkman, S., & Lazarus, R. S. (1986). Stress processes and depressive symptomatology. *Journal of Abnormal Psychology, 95,* 107–113.

Folstein, S. & Rutter, M. (1978). A twin study of individuals with infantile autism. In M. Rutter & E. Schopler (Eds.) *Autism: A Reappraisal of Concepts and Treatment.* New York: Plenum Press.

Forehand, R., Brody, G., Slotkin, J., Fauber, R., McCombs, A., & Long, N. (1988). Young adolescent and maternal depression: Assessment, interrelations, and family predictors. *Journal of Consulting and Clinical Psychology, 56,* 422–426.

Forehand, R., Brody, G., & Smith, K. (1986). Contributions of child behavior and marital dissatisfaction to maternal perceptions of child maladjustment. *Behaviour Research & Therapy, 24,* 43–48.

Forehand, R., Lautenschlager, G. J., Faust, J., & Graziano, W. G. (1986). Parent perceptions and parent-child interactions in clinic-referred children: A preliminary investigation of the effect of maternal depressive moods. *Behaviour Research and Therapy, 24,* 73–75.

Foreyt, J. P., & Goodrick, G. G. (1991). Factors common to successful therapy for the obese patient. *Medicine and Science in Sports and Exercise, 23,* 292–297.

Foster, S. L., & Cone, J. D. (1986). Design and use of direct observation procedures. In A. R. Ciminiero, K. S. Calhoun, & H. E. Adams (Eds.), *Handbook of behavioral assessment* (2nd ed.) (pp. 253–324). New York: Wiley.

Fowler, R. D. (1985). Landmarks in computer-assisted psychological assessment. *Journal of Consulting and Clinical Psychology, 53,* 748–759.

Foy, D. W., Resnick, H. S., Sipprele, R. C., & Carroll, E. M. (1987). Premilitary, military, and postmilitary factors in the development of combat-related posttraumatic stress disorder. *The Behavior Therapist, 10,* 3–9.

Frackowiak, R. S. J., Pozzilli, C., Legg, N. J., DuBoulay, G. H., Marshall, J., Lenzi, G. L., & Jones, T. (1981). Regional cerebral oxygen supply and utilization in dementia: A clinical and physiological study with oxygen-15 and positron tomography. *Brain, 104,* 753–778.

Frances, A., & Goldfinger, S. M. (1986). "Treating" a homeless mentally ill patient who cannot be managed in a shelter system. *Hospital and Community Psychiatry, 37,* 577–579.

Frankenstein, W., & Wilson, G. T. (1984). Alcohol's effects on self-awareness. *Addictive Behaviors, 9,* 323–328.

Frankl, V. E. (1959). *Man's search for meaning.* Boston: Beacon Press.

Franklin, J. A. (1987). The changing nature of agoraphobic fears. *British Journal of Clinical Psychology, 26,* 127–133.

Freed, C. R., et al. (1992). Survival of implanted fetal dopamine cells and neurologic improvement 12 to 46 months after transplantation for Parkinson's disease. *New England Journal of Medicine, 327,* 1549–1555.

Freedman, R., et al. (1987). Neurobiological studies of sensory gating in schizophrenia. *Schizophrenia Bulletin, 13,* 669–678.

Freemon, F. R. (1981). *Organic mental disease.* Jamaica, NY: Spectrum.

Freud, S. (1959). *Group psychology and the analysis of the ego.* (James Strachey, ed. and trans.). London: Hogarth Press. (Original work published 1922).

Freud, S. (1959). Analysis of a phobia in a 5-year-old boy. In A. & J. Strachey (Ed. & Trans.), *Collected papers* (Vol. 3, New York: Basic. (Original work published 1909).

Freud, S. (1957). Mourning and melancholia. In J. Rickman (Ed.), *A general selection from the works of Sigmund Freud*. Garden City, NY: Doubleday. (Original work published 1917).

Freudenheim, M. (1991, May 25). Medicaid payment ordered for drug for schizophrenia. *New York Times*, pp. A1, A10.

Freund, K., & Blanchard, R. (1986). The concept of courtship disorder. *Journal of Sex and Marital Therapy, 12,* 79–92.

Frick, P. J., et al. (1992). Familial risk factors to oppositional defiant disorder and conduct disorder: Parental psychopathology and maternal parenting. *Journal of Consulting and Clinical Psychology, 60,* 49–55.

Fried, R., & Golden, W. L. (1989). The role of psychophysiological hyperventilation assessment in cognitive behavior therapy. *Journal of Cognitive Psychotherapy: An International Quarterly, 3* 5–14.

Friedman, M., et al. (1984). Alteration of Type A behavior and reduction in cardiac recurrences in postmyocardial infarction patients. *American Heart Journal, 108,* 237–248.

Friedman, M., et al. (1986). Alteration of Type A behavior and its effect on cardiac recurrences in postmyocardial infarction patients: Summary results of the recurrent coronary prevention project. *American Heart Journal, 112,* 653–665.

Fromm-Reichmann, F. (1948). Notes on the development of treatment of schizophrenics by psychoanalytic psychotherapy. *Psychiatry, 11,* 263–273.

Fromm-Reichmann, F. (1950). *Principles of intensive psychotherapy*. Chicago: University of Chicago Press.

Frye, J. S., & Stockton, R. A. (1982). Discriminant analysis of posttraumatic stress disorder among a group of Vietnam veterans. *American Journal of Psychiatry, 139,* 52–56.

Fulero, S. M. (1988). Tarasoff: 10 Years Later. *Professional Psychology: Research and Practice, 19,* 184–190.

Fullerton, D. I., Cayner, J. J., & McLaughlin-Reidel, T. (1978). Results of a token economy. *Archives of General Psychiatry, 35,* 1451–1453.

Furby, L., Weinrott, M. R., & Blackshaw, L. (1989). Sex offender recidivism: A review. *Psychological Bulletin, 105,* 3–30.

Gadow, K. D. (1985). Relative efficacy of pharmacological, behavioral, and combination treatment for enhancing academic performance. *Clinical Psychology Review, 5,* 513–533.

Gagnon, J. H. (1977). *Human sexualities.* Glenview, IL: Scott Foresman.

Galassi, J. P. (1988). Four cognitive-behavioral approaches: Additional considerations. *The Counseling Psychologist, 16* (1), 102–105.

Garber, H. J., & Ritvo, E. R. (1992). Magnetic resonance imaging of the posterior fossa in autistic adults. *American Journal of Psychiatry, 149,* 245–247.

Garber, H. R., et al. (1989). A magnetic resonance imaging study of autism: normal fourth ventricle size and absence of pathology. *American Journal of Psychiatry, 146,* 532–534.

Garcia, M., & Marks, G. (1989). Depressive symptomatology among Mexican-American adults: An examination with the CES-D scale. *Psychiatry Research, 27,* 137–148.

Gardos, G., Cole, J. O., Salomon, M., & Schniebolk, S. (1987). Clinical forms of severe tardive dyskinesia. *American Journal of Psychiatry, 144,* 895–902.

Garfield, S. L. (1981). Psychotherapy: A 40-year appraisal. *American Psychologist, 36,* 174–183.

Garfield, S. L. (1982). Eclecticism and integration in psychotherapy. *Behavior Therapy, 13,* 610–623.

Garner, D. M., Garfinkel, P. E., Schwartz, D. M., & Thompson, M. G. (1980). Cultural expectations of thinness in women. *Psychological Reports, 47,* 483–491.

Garner, D. M., & Wooley, S. C. (1991). Confronting the failure of behavioral and dietary treatments for obesity. *Clinical Psychology Review, 11,* 729–780.

Garry, D. J., et al. (1992). Are there really alternatives to the use of fetal tissue from elective abortions in transplantation research? *New England Journal of Medicine, 327,* 1592–1595.

Garssen, B., de Ruiter, C., & Van Dyck, R. (1992). Breathing retraining: A rational placebo? *Clinical Psychology Review, 12,* 141–153.

Gately, G. (1989, January 22). Hospital leads patients to where all bets are off. *New York Times*, p. 31.

Gawin, F. H., et al. (1989). Desipramine facilitation of initial cocaine abstinence. *Archives of General Psychiatry, 46,* 117–121.

Gebhard, P. H., Gagnon, J. H., Pomeroy, W. B., & Christenson, C. V. (1965). *Sex offenders: An analysis of types.* New York: Harper & Row.

Geer, J., Heiman, J., & Leitenberg, H. (1984). *Human sexuality.* Englewood Cliffs, NJ: Prentice-Hall.

Geer, J., Morokoff, P., & Greenwood, P. (1974). Sexual arousal in women: The development of a measurement device for vaginal blood volume. *Archives of Sexual Behavior, 3,* 559–564.

Gelberg, L., Linn, L. S., & Leake, B. D. (1988). Mental health, alcohol and drug use, and criminal history among homeless adults. *American Journal of Psychiatry, 144,* 191–196.

Gelernter, C. S., et al. (1991). Cognitive-behavioral and pharmacological treatments of social phobia: A controlled study. *Archives of General Psychiatry, 48,* 938–945.

Gelman, D. (1988, August 29). Treating war's psychic wounds: Stress disorder among Vietnam vets may be rising. *Newsweek*, pp. 62–64.

Gelman, D., Hager, M., & Quade, V. (1989, December 18). The brain killer. *Newsweek*, pp. 54–56.

Georgotas, A., & McCue, R. E. (1986). Benefits and limitations of major pharmacological treatment for depression. *American Journal of Psychotherapy, 40,* 370–376.

Gershon, E. S., & Rieder, R. O. (1992). Major disorders of mind and brain. *Scientific American, 267,* (3), 126–133.

Gewirtz, J. L., & Peláez-Nogueras, M. (1992). B. F. Skinner's legacy to human infant behavior and development. *American Psychologist, 47,* 1411–1422.

Gibbs, N. (1991, June 3). When is it rape? *Time Magazine*, pp.48–54.

Gil, K. M., et al. (1990). The relationship of negative thoughts to pain and psychological distress. *Behavior Therapy, 21,* 349–362.

Gillin, J. C. (1991). The long and the short of sleeping pills. *New England Journal of Medicine, 324,* 1735–1736.

Gilman, A. G., et al. (1990). *Goodman and Gilman's the pharmacological basis of therapeutics* (8th ed.). New York: Pergamon.

Girardi, J. A., Keese, R. M., Traver, L. B., & Cooksey, D. R. (1988). Psychotherapist responsibility in notifying individuals at risk for exposure to HIV. *Journal of Sex Research, 25,* 1–27.

Gitlin, M. J., & Pasnau, R. O. (1989). Psychiatric syndromes linked to reproductive function in women: A review of current knowledge. *American Journal of Psychiatry, 146,* 1413–1422.

Gittleman-Klein, R., & Klein, D. F. (1969). Premorbid asocial adjustment and prognosis in schizophrenia. *Journal of Psychiatric Research, 7,* 35–53.

Gittleman-Klein, R., & Mannuzza, S. (1990). Hyperactive boys almost grown up. *Archives of General Psychiatry, 45,* 1131–1134.

Glantz, S. A., & Parmley, W. W. (1991). Passive smoking and heart disease: Epidemiology, physiology, and biochemistry. *Circulation, 83,* 1–12.

Glasberg, R., & Aboud, F. (1982). Keeping one's

distance from sadness: children's self-reports of emotional experience. *Developmental Psychology, 18,* 287–293.

Glaser, R., Kiecolt-Glaser, J. K., Speicher, C. E., & Holliday, J. E. (1985). Stress, loneliness, and changes in herpes virus latency. *Journal of Behavioral Medicine, 8,* 249–260.

Glaser, R., Rice, J., Speicher, C. E., Stout, J. C., & Kiecolt-Glaser, J. K. (1986). Stress depresses interferon production by leukocytes concomitant with a decrease in natural killer cell activity. *Behavioral Neuroscience, 100,* 675–678.

Glaser, R., et al. (1987). Stress-related immune suppression: Health implications. *Brain, Behavior, and Immunity, 1,* 7–20.

Glaser, R., et al. (1991). Stress-related activation of Epstein-Barr virus. *Brain, Behavior, and Immunity, 5,* 219–232.

Glasgow, R. E., & Lichtenstein, E. (1987). Long-term effects of behavioral smoking cessation interventions. *Behavior Therapy, 18,* 297–324.

Glass, G. V., & Kliegl, R. M. (1983). An apology for research intergration in the study of psychotherapy. *Journal of Consulting and Clinical Psychology, 51,* 28–41.

Glasscote, R. (1978). What programs work and what programs do not work for chronic mental patients? In J. A. Talbott (Ed.), *The chronic mental patient: Problems, solutions and recommendations for a public policy.* Washington, DC: American Psychiatric Association.

Glenn, S. S., Ellis, J., & Greenspoon, J. (1992). On the revolutionary nature of the operant as a unit of behavioral selection. *American Psychologist, 47,* 132b–132a.

Gleser, G., Green, B., & Winget, C. (1981). *Prolonged psychosocial effects of disaster: A study of Buffalo Creek.* New York: Academic Press.

Glover, J. H. (1985). A case of kleptomania treated by covert sensitization. *British Journal of Clinical Psychology, 24,* 213–214.

Glynn, S., & Mueser, K. T. (1986). Social learning for chronic mental inpatients. *Schizophrenia Bulletin, 12,* 648–668.

Golden, C. J., Hammeke, T. A., & Purisch, A. D. (1980). *The Luria-Nebraska Neuropsychological Battery: Manual.* Los Angeles: Western Psychological Services.

Golden, T. (1990a, March 12). Was illness at bridges in the minds of workers. *New York Times*, pp. B1, B4.

Golden, T. (1990b, April 2). Ill, possibly violent, and no place to go. *New York Times*, pp. A1, B4.

Goldfarb, L. A., Dykens, E. M., & Gerrard, M. (1985). The Goldfarb Fear of Fat Scale. *Journal of Personality Assessment, 49,* 329–332.

Goldfried, M., & Zax, M. (1965). The stimulus value of the TAT. *Journal of Projective Techniques, 29,* 46–57.

Goldman, H. H., Taub, C. A., & Regier, D. A. (1983). The multiple functions of the state mental hospital. *American Journal of Psychiatry, 140,* 296–300.

Goldman, M. J. (1991). Kleptomania: Making sense of the nonsensical. *American Journal of Psychiatry, 148,* 986–996.

Goldsmith, H. H. (1983). Genetic influences on personality from infancy to adulthood. *Child Development, 54,* 331–355.

Goldstein, A. (1976). Opioid peptides (endorphins) in pituitary and brain. *Science, 193,* 1081–1086.

Goldstein, J. M., & Tsuang, M. T. (1990). Gender and schizophrenia: An introduction and synthesis of findings. *Schizophrenia Bulletin, 16,* 179–183.

Goldstein, M. J. (1987a). The UCLA high-risk project. *Schizophrenia Bulletin, 13,* 505–514.

Goldstein, M. J. (1987b). Psychosocial issues. *Schizophrenia Bulletin, 13,* 157–171.

Goldstein, M. J., Rodnick, E. H., Evans, J. R., May, P. R. A., & Steinberg, M. R. (1978). Drug and family therapy in the aftercare of acute schizophrenics. *Archives of General Psychiatry, 35,* 1169–1177.

Goldstein, M. J., & Tuma, A. H. (1987). High-risk research: Editors' introduction. *Schizophrenia Bulletin, 13,* 369–371.

Goldstein, R. B., et al. (1991). The prediction of suicide: Sensitivity, specificity, and predictive value of a multivariate model applied to suicide among 1906 patients with affective disorders. *Archives of General Psychiatry, 48,* 418–422.

Goldstein, R. L. (1986). Erotomania. *American Journal of Psychiatry, 143,* 802.

Goleman, D. (1984, December 11). Schizophrenia: Early signs found. *New York Times,* pp. C1, C16.

Goleman, D. (1988a, October 18). Chemistry of sexual desire yields its elusive secrets. *New York Times,* pp. C1, C15.

Goleman, D. (1988b, November 1). Narcissism looming larger as root of personality woes. *New York Times: Science Times,* pp. C1, C16.

Goleman, D. (1988c, December 13). Obsessive disorder: Secret toll is found. *New York Times,* pp. C1, C11.

Goleman, D. (1990a,). The quiet comeback of electroshock therapy. *New York Times,* p. B5.

Goleman, D. (1990b,). Scientists pinpoint brain irregularities in drug addicts. *New York Times,* pp. C1, C7.

Goleman, D. (1990,c,). Women's depression is higher. *New York Times.*

Goleman, D. (1992c, October 14). Study ties genes to drinking in women as much as in men. *New York Times,* p. C14.

Gonzalez, D. (1992, November 15). What's the problem with "Hispanic"? Just ask a "Latino." *New York Times,* Section 4, p. 6.

Good, B., & Good, M. D. (1985). The cultural context of diagnosis and therapy: A view from medical anthropology. In M. Miranda & H. H. L. Kitano (Eds.), *Mental health research in minority communities: Development of culturally sensitive training programs* (pp. 1–27). Rockville, MD: National Institute of Mental Health.

Goodman, S. H. (1987). Emory University project on children of disturbed parents. *Schizophrenia Bulletin, 13,* 411–423.

Goodman, S. H., & Emory, E. K. (1992). Perinatal complications in births to low socioeconomic status schizophrenic and depressed women. *Journal of Abnormal Psychology, 101,* 225–229.

Goodman, W. K., et al. (1989). Efficacy of fluvoxamine in obsessive-compulsive disorder. *Archives of General Psychiatry, 46,* 36–44.

Goodman, W. K., et al. (1990). Specificity of serotonin reuptake inhibitors in the treatment of obsessive-compulsive disorder. *Archives of General Psychiatry, 47,* 577–585.

Goodwin, D. W. (1985). Alcoholism and genetics. *Archives of General Psychiatry, 42,* 171–174.

Goodwin, F. K., & Jamision, K. R. (1987). Bipolar disorders. In R. E. Hales and A. J. Frances (Eds.), *American Psychiatric Association Annual Review (Vol. 6).* Washington, DC: American Psychiatric Press.

Goodwin, J. M., Cheeves, K., & Connell, V. (1990). Borderline and other severe symptoms in adult survivors of incestuous abuse. *Psychiatric Annals, 20,* 22–32.

Gordon, S., & Snyder, C. W. (1989). *Personal issues in human sexuality: A guidebook for better sexual health* (2nd ed.). Boston: Allyn & Bacon.

Gordon, T., & Doyle, J. T. (1987). Drinking and mortality: The Albany Study. *American Journal of Epidemiology, 125,* 263–270.

Gormally, J., Sipps, G., Raphael, R., Edwin, D., & Varvil-Weld, D. (1981). The relationship between maladaptive cognitions and social anxiety. *Journal of Consulting and Clinical Psychology, 49,* 300–301.

Gorman, J. M., et al. (1985). Lactate infusions in obsessive-compulsive disorder. *American Journal of Psychiatry, 142,* 864–866.

Gosselin, C., & Wilson, G. (1980). *Sexual variations.* New York: Simon & Schuster.

Gotlib, I. H. (1984). Depression and general psychopathology in university students. *Journal of Abnormal Psychology, 93,* 19–30.

Gotlib, I. H., et al. (1991). Prospective investigation of postpartum depression: Factors involved in onset and recovery. *Journal of Abnormal Psychology, 100,* 122–132.

Gottesman, I. I. (1991). *Schizophrenia genesis: The origins of madness.* New York: Freeman.

Gottesman, I. I., McGuffin, P., & Farmer, A. E. (1987). Clinical genetics as clues to the "real" genetics of schizophrenia. *Schizophrenia Bulletin, 13,* 23–47.

Gould, R., Miller, B. L., Goldberg, M. A., & Benson, D. F. (1986). The validity of hysterical signs and symptoms. *Journal of Nervous and Mental Disease, 174,* 593–597.

Graham, J. R. (1990). *MMPI-2: Assessing personality and psychopathology.* New York: Oxford University Press.

Graham, J. R., & Strenger, V. E. (1988). MMPI characteristics of alcoholics: A review. *Journal of Consulting and Clinical Psychology, 56,* 197–205.

Graham, N. M. H. et al. (1992). The effects on survival of early treatment of human immunodeficiency virus infection. *New England Journal of Medicine, 326,* 1037–1042.

Green, A. I., & Salzman, C. (1990). Clozapine: Benefits and risks. *Hospital and Community Psychiatry, 41,* 379–380.

Green, A. R., & Goodwin, G. M. (1986). Antidepressants and monoamines: Actions and interactions. In J. W. W. Deakin (Ed.), *The biology of depression* (pp. 174–189). Proceedings of a meeting of the Biological Group of the Royal College of Psychiatrists held at Manchester University, 1985. Washington, DC: American Psychiatric Press.

Green, B. L., Grace, M. C., Lindy, J. D., Titchener, J. L., & Lindy, J. G. (1983). Levels of functional impairment following a civilian disaster: The Beverly Hills Supper Club fire. *Journal of Consulting and Clinical Psychology, 51,* 573–580.

Green, B. L., et al. (1990b). Risk factors for PTSD and other diagnoses in a general sample of Vietnam veterans. *American Journal of Psychiatry, 147,* 729–733.

Green, R., Mandel, J., Hotvedt, M., Gray, J., & Smith, L. (1986). Lesbian mothers and their children: A comparison with solo parent heterosexual mothers and their children. *Archives of Sexual Behavior, 15,* 167–184.

Greenberg, P. D. (1987). Tumor immunology. In D. P. Stites et al. (Eds.), *Basic and clinical immunology* (6th ed.) Norwalk, CT: Appleton & Lange.

Greenberg, R. P., & Bornstein, R. F. (1988a). The dependent personality: I. Risk for physical disorders. *Journal of Personality Disorders, 2,* 126–135.

Greenberg, R. P., & Bornstein, R. F. (1988b). The dependent personality: II. Risk for psychological disorders. *Journal of Personality Disorders, 2,* 136–143.

Greenberg, R. P., Bornstein, R. F., Greenberg, M. D., & Fisher, S. (1992). A meta-analysis of antidepressant outcome under "blinder" conditions. *Journal of Consulting and Clinical Psychology, 60,* 664–669.

Greene, B. A. (1985). Considerations in the treatment of black patients by white therapists. *Psychotherapy, 22,* 389–393.

Greene, B. A. (1986). When the therapist is white and the patient is black: Considerations for psychotherapy in the feminist heterosexual and lesbian communities. *Women and Therapy, 5,* 41–65.

Greene, B. A. (1990). Sturdy bridges: The role of African American mothers in the socialization of African American children. *Women and Therapy, 10,* 205–225.

Greene, B. A. (1992a). Racial socialization: A tool in psychotherapy with African American children. In L. Vargas & J. Koss (Eds.), *Working with culture: Psychotherapeutic interventions with ethnic minority children and adolescents* (pp. 63–81). San Francisco: Jossey-Bass.

Greene, B. A. (1992b). Black feminist psychotherapy. In E. Wright (Ed.), *Psychoanalysis and feminism: A critical dictionary* (pp. 34–35). Oxford: Basil Blackwell.

Greene, B. A. (1992c). Still here: A perspective on psychotherapy with African American women. In J. Chrisler & D. Howard (Eds.), *New directions in feminist psychology.* New York: Springer.

Greene, B. A. (1993a, Spring). Psychotherapy with African American women: The integration of feminist and psychodynamic approaches. *Journal of Training and Practice in Professional Psychology.*

Greene, B. A. (1993b). African American women. In L. Comas-Diaz & B. Greene (Eds.), *Women of color and mental health.* New York: Guilford Press.

Greene, B. A. (1993a, in press). Psychotherapy with African American women: The integration of feminist and psychodynamic approaches. *Journal of Training and Practice in Professional Psychology.*

Greenhouse, L. (1992, June 23). Defendants must prove incompetency. *New York Times,* p. A17.

Greenwald, A. G. (1975). Consequences of prejudice against the null hypothesis. *Psychological Bulletin, 82,* 1–20.

Greenspan, S. I., & Porges, S. W. (1984). Psychopathology in infancy and early childhood: Clinical perspectives on the organization of sensory and affective-thematic experience. *Child Development, 55,* 49–70.

Greer, S. (1964). Study of parental loss in neurotics and sociopaths. *Archives of General Psychiatry, 11,* 177–180.

Grier, W., & Cobbs, P. (1968). *Black rage.* New York: Basic.

Griffith, J. (1983). Relationship between acculturation and psychological impairment in adult Mexican-Americans. *Hispanic Journal of Behavioral Sciences, 5,* 431–459.

Griffith, J. (1985). A community survey of psychological impairment among Anglo-and Mexican Americans and its relationship to service utilization. *Community Mental Health Journal, 21,* 28–41.

Grillon, C., et al. (1990). Increased distractibility in schizophrenic patients. *Archives of General Psychiatry, 47,* 171–179.

Grissett, N. I., & Norvell, N. K. (1992). Perceived social support, social skills and quality of relationships in bulimic women. *Journal of Consulting and Clinical Psychology, 60,* 293–299.

Grob, G. N. (1983). *Mental illness and American society, 1875–1940.* Princeton, NJ: Princeton University Press.

Grossman, L. S., et al. (1991). Outcome of schizoaffective disorder at two long-term follow-ups; Comparisons with outcome of schizophrenia and affective disorders. *American Journal of Psychiatry, 148,* 1359–1365.

Groth, A. N., & Birnbaum, H. J. (1979). *Men who rape.* New York: Plenum.

Groth, A., & Hobson, W. (1983). The dynamics of sexual assault. In L. Schlesinger & E. Revitch (Eds.), *Sexual dynamics of antisocial behavior.* Springfield, IL: Charles C. Thomas.

Growdon, J. H. (1992). Treatment for Alzheimer's disease. *New England Journal of Medicine, 327,* 1306–1308.

Grünbaum, A. (1985). Cited in Goleman, D. J. (1985, January 15). Pressure mounts for analyst to prove theory is scientific. *New York Times*, pp. C1, C9.

Grunberg, N. E. (1991). Smoking cessation and weight gain. *New England Journal of Medicine, 324*, 768–769.

Guarnaccia, P. J., Rubio-Stipec, M., & Canino, G. (1989). Ataques de nervios in the Puerto Rican diagnostic interview schedule: The impact of cultural categories on psychiatric epidemiology. *Culture, Medicine and Psychatrity, 13*, 275–295.

Gunderson, J. G., et al. (1984). Effects of psychotherapy in schizophrenia: II. Comparative outcome of two forms of treatment. *Schizophrenia Bulletin, 10*, 564–598.

Gunderson, J. G., & Phillips, K. A. (1991). A current view of the interface between borderline personality disorder and depression. *American Journal of Psychiatry, 148*, 967–975.

Gunderson, J. G., & Singer, M. T. (1986). Defining borderline patients: An overview. In M. H. Stone (Ed.), *Essential papers on borderline disorders* (pp. 453–474). New York: New York University Press.

Gur, R. E., et al. (1985). Brain function in psychiatric disorders. *Archives of General Psychiatry, 42*, 329–334.

Gur, R. E., et al. (1991). Magnetic resonance imaging in schizophrenia: I. Volumetric analysis of brain and cerebrospinal fluid. *Archives of General Psychiatry, 48*, 407–412.

Gurland, B. J., & Cross, P. S. (1986). Public health perspectives on clinical memory testing of Alzheimer's disease and related disorders. In L. W. Poon (Ed.), *Handbook for clinical memory assessment of older adults* (pp. 11–20). Washington, DC: American Psychological Association.

Gutheil, T. G. (1980). In search of true freedom: Drug refusal, involuntary medication, and "rotting with your rights on." *American Journal of Psychiatry, 137*, 327–328.

Gwinup, G. (1975). Effects of exercise alone on the weight of obese women. *Archives of Internal Medicine, 135*, 676–680.

Haaga, D. A. (1987). Treatment of the type A behavior pattern. *Clinical Psychology Review, 7*, 557–574.

Haaga, D. A. F., Dyck, M. J., & Ernst, D. (1991). Empirical status of cognitive theory of depression. *Psychological Bulletin, 110*, 215–236.

Haas, G. L., Clarkin, J. F., & Glick, I. D. (1985). Marital and family treatment of depression. In E. E. Beckham & W. R. Leber (Eds.), *Handbook of depression: Treatment, assessment and research* (pp. 151–183). Homewood, IL: Dorsey Press.

Hackett, T. P., Cassem, H. H., & Wishnie, H. (1968). The coronary-care unit: An appraisal of its psychologic hazards. *New England Journal of Medicine, 279*, 1365–1370.

Hallmayer, J., et al. (1992). Exclusion of linkage between the serotonin receptor and schizophrenia in a large Swedish kindred. *Archives of General Psychiatry, 49*, 216–219.

Halmi, K. A., Eckert, E., LaDu, T. J., & Cohen, J. (1986). Treatment efficacy of cyproheptadine and amitriptyline. *Archives of General Psychiatry, 43*, 177–181.

Hamamy, H., et al. (1990). Consanguinity and the genetic control of Down syndrome. *Clinical Genetics, 37*, 24–29.

Hamilton, E. W., & Abramson, L. Y. (1983). Cognitive patterns and major depressive disorders: A longitudinal study in a hospital setting. *Journal of Abnormal Psychology, 92*, 173–184.

Hammen, C., & de Mayo, R. (1982). Cognitive correlates of teacher stress and depressive symptoms: Implications for attributional models of depression. *Journal of Abnormal Psychology, 91*, 96–101.

Hammen, C., et al. (1992). Psychiatric history and stress: Predictors of severity of unipolar depression. *Journal of Abnormal Psychology, 101*, 45–52.

Hammond, O. (1988). Needs assessment and policy development: Native Hawaiians as Native Americans. *American Psychologist, 43*, 383–387.

Harding, J. J. (1989). Postpartum psychiatric disorders: A review. *Comprehensive Psychiatry, 30*, 109–112.

Hare, E. (1979). Schizophrenia as an infectious disease. *British Journal of Psychiatry, 135*, 468–470.

Hare, R. D. (1965). Temporal gradient of fear arousal in psychopaths. *Journal of Abnormal Psychology, 70*, 442–445.

Hare, R. D. (1970). *Psychopathy: Theory and research*. New York: Wiley.

Hare, R. D. (1986). Criminal psychopaths. In J. C. Yuille (Ed.), *Police selection and training: The role of psychology* (pp. 187–206). Dordrecht, Netherlands: Martinos Nijhoff.

Hare, R. D., Frazelle, J., & Cox, D. N. (1978). Psychopathy and physiological responses to threat of an aversive stimulus. *Psychophysiology, 15*, 165–172.

Hare, R. D., McPherson, L. M., & Forth, A. E. (1988). Male psychopaths and their criminal careers. *Journal of Consulting and Clinical Psychology, 56*, 710–714.

Harney, P. A., & Muehlenhard, C. L. (1991). Rape. In E. Grauerholz & M. A. Koralewski (Eds.), *Sexual coercion: A sourcebook on its nature, causes, and prevention* (pp. 3–16). Lexington, MA: Lexington.

Harrell, T. H., & Ryon, N. B. (1983). Cognitive-behavioral assessment of depression: Clinical validation of the Automatic Thoughts Questionnaire. *Journal of Consulting and Clinical Psychology, 51*, 721–725.

Harris, L. (1988). *Inside America*. New York: Vintage.

Harrow, M., & Marengo, J. T. (1986). Schizophrenic thought disorder at followup: Its persistence and prognostic significance. *Schizophrenia Bulletin, 12*, 373–393.

Harrow, M., & Quinlan, D. M. (1985). *Disordered thinking and schizophrenic psychopathology*. New York: Gardner Press.

Harrow, M., & Westermeyer, J. F. (1987). Process-reactive dimension and outcome for narrow concepts of schizophrenia. *Schizophrenia Bulletin, 13*, 361–368.

Harrow, M., Westermeyer, J. F., Silverstein, M., Strauss, B. S., & Cohler, B. J. (1986). Prediction of outcome in schizophrenia: The process-reactive dimension. *Schizophrenia Bulletin, 12*, 195–207.

Hart, B. M., Reynolds, N. J., Baer, D. M., Brawley, E. R., & Harris, F. R. (1968). Effects of contingent and non-contingent social reinforcement on the cooperative play of a pre-school child. *Journal of Applied Behavior Analysis, 1*, 73–76.

Hart, R. P. (1987). Rate of forgetting in dementia and depression. *Journal of Consulting and Clinical Psychology, 55*, 101–105.

Harwood, A. (1981). Mainland Puerto Ricans. In A. Harwood (Ed.), *Ethnicity and medical care*. Cambridge, MA: Harvard University Press.

Hatfield, E., Sprecher, S., & Traupman, J. (1978). Men's and women's reactions to sexually explicit films: A serendipitous finding. *Archives of Sexual Behavior, 6*, 583–592.

Haughton, E., & Ayllon, T. (1965). Production and elimination of symptomatic behavior. In L. P. Ullmann & L. Krasner (Eds.), *Case studies in behavior modification*. New York: Holt, Rinehart and Winston.

Hauser, W. A., & Hesdorffer, D. C. (1990a). *Epilepsy: Frequency, causes and consequences*. New York: Demos.

Hauser-Cram, P., Pierson, D. E., Walker, D. K., & Tivnan, T. (1991). *Early education in the public schools*. San Francisco: Jossey-Bass.

Havassy, B. E., Hall, S. M., & Wasserman, D. A. (1991). Social support and relapse: Commonalities among alcoholics, opiate users, and cigarette smokers. *Addictive Behaviors, 16*, 235–246.

Hawkrigg, J. J. (1975). Agoraphobia. *Nursing Times, 71*, 1280–1282.

Hawton, K., & Catalan, J. (1990). Sex therapy for vaginismus: Characteristics of couples and treatment outcomes. *Sexual and Marital Therapy, 5*, 39–48.

Hay, P. J., et al. (1991). Magnetic resonance imaging and outcome following psychosurgery in patients with obsessive-compulsive disorder. *Biological Psychiatry, 29*, (Suppl.), 701S. (Abstract).

Haynes, S. G., & Feinleib, M. (1980). Women, work, and coronary heart disease: Prospective findings from the Framingham heart study. *American Journal of Public Health, 70*, 133–141.

Haynes, S. N. (1986). A behavioral model of paranoid behaviors. *Behavior Therapy, 17*, 266–287.

Hays, R. B., Turner, H., & Coates, T. J. (1992). Social support, AIDS-related symptoms, and depression among gay men. *Journal of Consulting and Clinical Psychology, 60*, 463–469.

Heaton, R. K., & Victor, R. G. (1976). Personality characteristics associated with psychedelic flashbacks in natural and experimental settings. *Journal of Abnormal Psychology, 85*, 83–90.

Hechtman, L., & Weiss, G. (1983). Long-term outcome of hyperactive children. *American Journal of Orthopsychiatry, 53*, 522–541.

Heiby, E., & Becker, J. D. (1980). Effect of filmed modeling on the self-reported frequency of masturbation. *Archives of Sexual Behavior, 9*, 115–122.

Heiby, E. M., Campos, P. E., Remick, R. A., & Keller, F. D. (1987). Dexamethasone suppression and self-reinforcement correlates of clinical depression. *Journal of Abnormal Psychology, 96*, 70–72.

Heim, N. (1981). Sexual behavior of castrated sex offenders. *Archives of Sexual Behavior, 10*, 11–20.

Heiman, J. R. (1978). Uses of psychophysiology in the assessment and treatment of sexual dysfunction. In J. LoPiccolo & L. LoPiccolo (Eds.), *Handbook of sex therapy* (pp. 123–135). New York: Plenum Press.

Heiman, J. R., & LoPiccolo, J. (1987). *Becoming orgasmic* (2nd ed.). Englewood Cliffs, NJ: Prentice Hall.

Heiman, J. R., & Rowland, D. L. (1983). Affective and physiological sexual patterns: The effects of instructions on sexually functional and dysfunctional men. *Journal of Psychosomatic Research, 27*, 105–116.

Heimberg, R. G. (1989). Cognitive and behavioral treatments for social phobia: A critical analysis. *Clinical Psychology Review, 9*, 107–128.

Heimberg, R. G., et al. (1987). Attributional style, depression, and anxiety: An evaluation of the specificity of depressive attributions. *Cognitive Therapy and Research, 11*, 537–550.

Heimberg, R. G., et al. (1990). Cognitive behavioral group treatment for social phobia: Comparison with a credible placebo control. *Cognitive Therapy and Research, 14*, 1–23.

Hellerstein, D., Frosch, W., & Koenigsberg, H. W. (1987). The clinical significance of command hallucinations. *American Journal of Psychiatry, 144*, 219–221.

Helms, J. E. (1992). Why is there no study of cultural equivalence of standardized cognitive ability testing? *American Psychologist, 47*, 1083–1101.

Helzer, J. E. (1987). Epidemiology of alcoholism. *Journal of Consulting and Clinical Psychology, 55*, 284–292.

Helzer, J. E., et al. (1985). A comparison of clinical and diagnostic interview schedule diagnoses. *Archives of General Psychiatry, 42,* 657–666.

Helzer, J. E., Burnam, A., & McEvoy, L. T. (1991). Alcohol abuse and dependence. In L. N. Robins & D. A. Regier (Eds.), *Psychiatric disorders in America: The Epidemiologic Catchment Area Study* (pp. 81–115). New York: The Free Press.

Helzer, J. E., & Schuckit, M. A. (1990, August/September). Substance use disorders. In American Psychiatric Association, *DSM-IV Update.* Washington, DC: American Psychiatric Association.

Hendin, H., & Haas, A. P. (1991). Suicide and guilt as manifestation of PTSD in Vietnam combat veterans. *American Journal of Psychiatry, 148,* 586–591.

Henggeler, S. W., et al. (1986). Multisystemic treatment of juvenile offenders: Effects on adolescent behavior and family interaction. *Developmental Psychology, 22,* 132–141.

Henker, B., & Whalen, C. K. (1980). The changing faces of hyperactivity: Retrospect and prospect. In C. K. Whalen and B. Henker (Eds.), *Hyperactive children* (pp. 321–363). New York: Academic Press.

Henkin, W. A. (1985). Toward counseling the Japanese in America: A cross-cultural primer. *Journal of Counseling and Development, 63,* 500–503.

Herbert, J. D., Hope, D. A., & Bellack, A. S. (1992). Validity of the distinction between generalized social phobia and avoidant personality disorder. *Journal of Abnormal Psychology, 101,* 332–339.

Herman, C. P., & Polivy, J. (1980). Restrained eating. In A. J. Stunkard (Ed.), *Obesity* (pp. 208–225). Philadelphia: Saunders.

Herman, C. P., Polivy, J., Lank, C. N., & Heatherton, T. F. (1987). Anxiety, hunger, and eating behavior. *Journal of Abnormal Psychology, 96,* 264–269.

Hermann, B., & Whitman, S. (1992). Psychopathology in epilepsy: The role of psychology in altering paradigms of research, treatment, and prevention. *American Psychologist, 47,* 1134–1138.

Herrell, J. M. (1975). Sex differences in emotional response to "erotic literature." *Journal of Consulting and Clinical Psychology, 43,* 921.

Herron, W. G. (1987). Evaluating the process-reactive dimension. *Schizophrenia Bulletin, 13,* 357–359.

Hertz, M. R. (1986). Rorschach bound: A 50-year memoir. *Journal of Personality Assessment, 50,* 396–416.

Herzog, D. B., Keller, M. B., & Lavori, P. W. (1988). Outcome in anorexia and bulimia nervosa: A review of the literature. *Journal of Nervous and Mental Disease, 176,* 131–143.

Heston, L. L. (1966). Psychiatric disorders in foster home reared children of schizophrenic mothers. *British Journal of Psychiatry, 112,* 819–825.

Heston, L. L., & Mastri, A. R. (1982). Age at onset of Pick's and Alzheimer's dementia: Implications for diagnosis and research. *Journal of Gerontology, 37,* 422–424.

Heston, L. L., White, J. A., & Mastri, A. R. (1987). Pick's disease: Clinical genetics and natural history. *Archives of General Psychiatry, 44,* 409–411.

Heuch, I., et al. (1983). Use of alcohol, tobacco and coffee, and risk of pancreatic cancer. *British Journal of Cancer, 48,* 637–643.

Hibbert, G. A. (1984). Ideational components of anxiety. *British Journal of Psychiatry, 144,* 618–624.

Hide the homeless? [Editorial]. (1991, November 11). *New York Times,* p. A14.

Hill, S. Y. (1980). Introduction: The biological consequences. In *Alcoholism and alcohol abuse among women: Research issues.* Rockville, MD:

National Institute on Alcohol Abuse and Alcoholism.

Hilts, P. J. (1991, October 9). Report is critical of mental clinics. *New York Times,* p. L25.

Hineline, P. N. (1992). A self-interpretive behavior analysis. *American Psychologist, 47,* 1274–1286.

Hinshaw, S. P. (1987). On the distinction between attentional deficits/hyperactivity and conduct problems/aggression in child psychopathology. *Psychological Bulletin, 101,* 443–463.

Hinshaw, S. P. (1991). Stimulant medication and the treatment of aggression in children with attentional deficits. *Journal of Clinical Child Psychology, 20,* 301–312.

Hirsch, S. R., & Leff, J. P. (1975). *Abnormalities in parents of schizophrenics.* Oxford: Oxford University Press.

Hirschfeld, R. M. A., & Cross, C. (1982). Epidemiology of affective disorders. *Archives of General Psychiatry, 39,* 35–46.

Hobbins, J. C. (1991). Diagnosis and management of neural-tube defects today. *New England Journal of Medicine, 324,* 690–691.

Hoelscher, T. J., Lichstein, K. L., Fischer, S., & Hegarty, T. B. (1987). Relaxation treatment of hypertension: Do home relaxation tapes enhance treatment outcome? *Behavior Therapy, 18,* 33–37.

Hoenig, J. (1983). The concept of schizophrenia: Kraepelin-Bleuler-Schneider. *British Journal of Psychiatry, 142,* 547–556.

Hoff, A., et al. (1992). Neuropsychological functioning of first-episode schizophreniform patients. *American Journal of Psychiatry, 149,* 898–903.

Hoffman, A. (1971). LSD discoverer disputes "chance" factor in finding. *Psychiatric News, 6,* 23–26.

Hoffman, W., & Prior, M. (1982). Neuropsychological dimensions of autism in children: a test of the hemispheric dysfunction hypotheses. *Journal of Clinical Neuropsychology, 4,* 27–42.

Hoffman-Plotkin, D., & Twentyman, C. T. (1984). A multimodal assessment of behavioral and cognitive deficits in abused and neglected preschoolers. *Child Development, 55,* 794–802.

Hogarty, G. E., Schroeder, N. R., Ulrich, R., Mussare, N., Peregino, F., & Herron, E. (1979). Fluphenazine and social therapy in the aftercare of schizophrenic patients. *Archives of General Psychiatry, 36,* 1283–1294.

Hogarty, G. E. (1985). Expressed emotion and schizophrenic relapse: Implications from the Pittsburgh study. In M. Alpert (Ed.), *Controversies in schizophrenia* (pp. 354–365). New York: Guilford Press.

Hogarty, G. E., et al. (1986). Family psychoeducation, social skills training, and maintenance chemotherapy in the aftercare of schizophrenia. *Archives of General Psychiatry, 43,* 633–642.

Holden, A. E., Jr., & Barlow, D. H. (1986). Heart rate and heart rate variability recorded in vivo in agoraphobics and nonphobics. *Behavior Therapy, 17,* 26–42.

Hollestedt, C., et al. (1983). Outcome of pregnancy in women treated at an alcoholic clinic. *Acta Psychiatrica Scandanavia, 67,* 236–248.

Hollingshead, A. B., & Redlich, F. C. (1958). *Social class and mental illness: A community study.* New York: Wiley.

Hollon, S. D., & Beck, A. T. (1979). Cognitive therapy for depression. In P. C. Kendall and S. D. Hollon (Eds.), *Cognitive-behavioral interventions: Theory, research and procedures* (pp. 153–196). Orlando, FL: Academic Press.

Hollon, S. D., & Kendall, P. C. (1980). Cognitive self-statements in depression: Development of an automatic thoughts questionnaire. *Cognitive Therapy and Research, 4,* 383–395.

Hollon, S. D., Shelton, R. C., & Loosen, P. T. (1991). Cognitive therapy and pharmacother-

apy for depression. *Journal of Consulting and Clinical Psychology, 59,* 88–99.

Holmes, D. S. (1984). Meditation and somatic arousal reduction: A review of the experimental evidence. *American Psychologist, 39,* 1–10.

Holmes, D. S. (1985). To meditate or to simply rest, that is the question: A response to the comments of Shapiro. *American Psychologist, 40,* 722–725.

Holmes, D. S., Solomon, S., Cappo, B. M., & Greenberg, J. L. (1983). Effects of transcendental meditation versus resting on physiological and subjective arousal. *Journal of Personality and Social Psychology, 44,* 1244–1252.

Holmes, T. H., & Rahe, R. H. (1967). The social readjustment rating scale. *Journal of Psychosomatic Research, 11,* 213–218.

Holroyd, K. A., et al. (1991). A comparison of pharmacological (amitryptyline HCL) and nonpharmacological (cognitive-behavioral) therapies for chronic tension headaches. *Journal of Consulting and Clinical Psychology, 59,* 387–393.

Holt, C. S., Heimberg, R. G., & Hope, D. A. (1992). Avoidant personality disorder and the generalized subtype of social phobia. *Journal of Abnormal Psychology, 101,* 318–325.

Holzman, P. S. (1986). Thought disorder in schizophrenia: Editor's introduction. *Schizophrenia Bulletin, 12,* 342–347.

Holzman, P. S. (1987). Recent studies of psychophysiology in schizophrenia. *Schizophrenia Bulletin, 13,* 49–75.

Holzman, P. S., Shenton, M. E., & Solovay, M. R. (1986). Quality of thought disorder in differential diagnosis. *Schizophrenia Bulletin, 12,* 360–372.

Honigfeld, G., & Patin, J. (1990). A two-year clinical and economic follow-up of patients on clozapine. *Hospital and Community Psychiatry, 41,* 882–885.

Hoon, P., Wincze, J., & Hoon, E. (1977). A test of reciprocal inhibition: Are anxiety and sexual arousal in women mutually inhibitory? *Journal of Abnormal Psychology, 86,* 65–74.

Hopkins, J., Campbell, S. B., & Marcus, M. (1987). Role of infant-related stressors in postpartum depression. *Journal of Abnormal Psychology, 96,* 237–241.

Horne, L. R., Van Vactor, J. C., & Emerson, S. (1991). Disturbed body image in patients with eating disorders. *American Journal of Psychiatry, 148,* 211–215.

Hough, R. L., et al. (1987). Utilizaiton of health and mental services by Los Angeles Mexican Americans and non-Hispanic whites. *Archives of General Psychiatry, 44,* 702–709.

House, J. S., Robbins, C., & Metzner, H. L. (1982). The association of social relationships and activities with mortality: Prospective evidence from the Tecumseh Community Health Study. *American Journal of Epidemiology, 116,* 123–140.

Howard, K. I., Kopta, S. M., Krause, M. S., & Orlinksky, D. E. (1986). The dose-effect relationship in psychotherapy. *American Psychologist, 41,* 159–164.

Howard-Pitney, B., et al. (1992). Psychological and social indicators of suicide ideation and suicide attempts in Zuni adolescents. *Journal of Consulting and Clinical Psychology, 60,* 473–476.

Hrncir, E. J., Speller, G. M., & West, M. (1985). What are we testing? *Developmental Psychology, 21,* 226–232.

Hsu, L. K. G. (1980). Outcome of anorexia nervosa: A review of the literature (1954 to 1978). *Archives of General Psychiatry, 37,* 1041–1046.

Hsu, L. K. G. (1987). Treatment of anorexia nervosa: Dr. Hsu replies. *American Journal of Psychiatry, 144,* 260–261.

Huber, G., Gross, G., & Chuettler, R. (1980). Longitudinal studies of schizophrenic patients. *Schizophrenia Bulletin, 6,* 592–605.

Hucker, S., Langgevin, R., & Bain, J. (1988). A double blind trail of sex drive reducing medication in pedophiles. *Annals of Sex Research, 1,* 227–242.

Hudson, J. I., Pope, H. G., & Jonas, J. M. (1984). Treatment of bulimia with antidepressants: Theoretical considerations and clinical findings. In A. J. Stunkard & E. Stellar (Eds.), *Eating and its disorders* (pp. 259–273). New York: Raven Press.

Hudson, J. I., Pope, H. G., Jr., Jonas, J. M., & Yurgelun-Todd, D. (1983). Family history study of anorexia nervosa and bulimia. *British Journal of Psychiatry, 142,* 133–138, 428–429.

Hugdahl, K., & Ohman, A. (1977). Effects of instruction on acquisition and extinction of electrodermal response to fear-relevant stimuli. *Journal of Experimental Psychology: Human Learning and Memory, 3,* 608–618.

Hughes, J. R., Gust, S. W., & Pechacek, T. F. (1987). Prevalence of tobacco dependence and withdrawal. *American Journal of Psychiatry, 144,* 205–208.

Hughes, J. R., & Hatsukami, D. K. (1987). Criteria of a pharmacologic withdrawal syndrome: Reply. *Archives of General Psychiatry, 44,* 392.

Hughes, P. L., Wells, L. A., Cunningham, C. J., & Ilstrup, D. M. (1986). Treating bulimia with desipramine. *Archives of General Psychiatry, 43,* 182–186.

Hull, J. G. (1987). Self-awareness model. In H. T. Blane & K. E. Leonard (Eds.), *Psychological theories of drinking and alcoholism* (pp. 272–304). New York: Guilford Press.

Hull, J. G., & Young, R. D. (1983). Self-consciousness, self-esteem, and success-failure as determinants of alcohol consumption in male social drinkers. *Journal of Personality and Social Psychology, 44,* 1097–1109.

Hull, J. G., Young, R. D., & Jouriles, E. (1986). Applications of the self-awareness model of alcohol consumption: Predicting patterns of use and abuse. *Journal of Personality and Social Psychology, 51,* 790–796.

Humphrey, L. L. (1986a). Family dynamics in bulimia. In S. C. Feinstein et al. (Eds.), *Adolescent psychiatry.* Chicago: University of Chicago Press.

Humphrey, L. L. (1986b). Family relations in bulimic-anorexic and non-distressed families. *International Journal of Eating Disorders, 5,* 223–232.

Humphrey, L. L. (1987). A comparison of bulimic-anorexic and non-distressed families using structural analysis of social behavior. *Journal of the American Academy of Child Psychiatry, 26,* 248–255.

Humphrey, L. L. (in press). Family wide distress in bulimia. In D. Cannon & T. Baker (Eds.), *Addictive disorders: Psychological assessment and treatment.* New York: Praeger.

Hunt, M. (1974). *Sexual behavior in the 1970s.* Chicago: Playboy Press.

Hunt, T., & Weber, J. (Producers). (1989). *NOVA: Confronting the Killer Gene* [Telecast]. Boston: WGBH Educational Foundation.

Huppert, F. A., & Piercy, M. (1979). Normal and abnormal forgetting in organic amnesia: Effect of locus of lesion. *Cortex, 15,* 385–390.

Hurlburt, G., & Gade, E. (1984). Personality differences between Native American and Caucasian women alcoholics: Implications for alcoholism counseling. *White Cloud Journal, 3,* 35–39.

Hutchings, B., & Mednick, S. A. (1974). Registered criminality in the adoptive and biological parents of registered male adoptees. In S. A. Mednick, F. Schulsinger, J. Higgins, & B. Bell (Eds.), *Genetics, environment and psychopathology.* New York: Elsevier.

Hutchings, B., & Mednick, S. A. (1977). Criminal-ity in adoptees and their adoptive and biological parents: A pilot study. In S. A. Mednick & K. O. Christensen (Eds.), *Biosocial bases of criminal behavior.* New York: Gardner Press.

Iacono, W. G., et al. (1992). Smooth-pursuit eye tracking in first-episode psychotic patients and their relatives. *Journal of Abnormal Psychology, 101,* 104–116.

Imber, S. D., et al. (1990). Mode-specific effects among three treatments for depression. *Journal of Consulting and Clinical Psychology, 58,* 352–359.

Ingram, R. E. (1990). Self-focused attention in clinical disorders: Review and a conceptual model. *Psychological Bulletin, 107,* 156–176.

Ingram, R. E. (1991). Tilting at windmills: A response to Pyszczynski, Greenberg, Hamilton, and Nix. *Psychological Bulletin, 110,* 544–550.

Isay, R. A. (1990). Psychoanalytic theory and the therapy of gay men. In D. P. McWhirter, S. A. Sanders, & J. M. Reinisch (Eds.), *Homosexuality/heterosexuality: Concepts of sexual orientation* (pp. 283–303). New York: Oxford University Press.

Israel, E., et al. (1990). The effects of a 5-lipoxy-genase inhibitor on asthma induced by cold, dry air. *New England Journal of Medicine, 323,* 1740–1744.

Itel, T. (1977). Qualitative and quantitative EEG findings in schizophrenia. *Schizophrenia Bulletin, 3,* 61–79.

Jacobs, P. A., Brunton, M., Melville, M. M., Brittain, R. P., & McClemont, W. F. (1965). Aggressive behavior, mental subnormality, and the XYY male. *Nature, 208,* 1351–1352.

Jacobs, T. J., & Charles, E. (1980). Life events and the occurrence of cancer in children. *Psychosomatic Medicine, 42,* 11–24.

Jacobsen, F. M., Wehr, T. A., Skewer, R. A., Sack, D. A., & Rosenthal, N. E. (1987). Morning versus midday phototherapy of seasonal affective disorder. *American Journal of Psychiatry, 144,* 1301–1305.

Jacobson, N. S., Wilson, L., & Tupper, C. (1988). The clinical significance of treatment gains resulting from exposure-based interventions for agoraphobia: A reanalysis of outcome data. *Behavior Therapy, 19,* 539–554.

Jamison, K. K., & Akiskal, H. S. (1983). Medication compliance in patients with bipolar disorder. *Psychiatric Clinics of North America, 6,* 175–192.

Janerich, D. T., et al. (1990). Lung cancer and exposure to tobacco smoke in the household. *New England Journal of Medicine, 323,* 632–636.

Janet, P. (1889). *L'automatisme psychologique.* Paris: Alcan.

Janicak, P. G., et al. (1985). Efficacy of ECT: A meta-analysis. *American Journal of Psychiatry, 142,* 297–302.

Jarvik, L. F., Klodin, V., & Matsuyama, S. S. (1973). Human aggression and the extra Y chromosome: Fact or fiction. *American Psychologist, 28,* 674–676.

Javier, R. A. (1993). Cited in Rathus, S. A. (1993). *Psychology* (5th ed.). Fort Worth TX: Harcourt Brace Jovanovich.

Jeffery, R. W. (1988). Dietary risk factors and their modification in cardiovascular disease. *Journal of Consulting and Clinical Psychology, 56,* 350–357.

Jellinek, E. M. (1960). *The disease concept of alcoholism.* New Haven, CT: College and University Press.

Jemmott, J. B., et al. (1983,). Academic stress, power motivation, and decrease in secretion rate of salivary secretory immunoglobin A. *Lancet,* pp. 1400–1402.

Jenike, M. A., et al. (1990). A controlled trial of fluvoxamine in obsessive-compulsive disorder: Implications for a serotonergic. *American Journal of Psychiatry, 147,* 1209–1215.

Jenkins, C. D. (1988). Epidemiology of cardiovascular diseases. *Journal of Consulting and Clinical Psychology, 56,* 324–332.

Jenkins, J. H. (1988). Ethnopsychiatric interpretations of schizophrenic illness; The problem of *nervios* within Mexican-American families. *Culture, Medicine, and Psychiatry, 12,* 301–329.

Jenkins, J. H., & Karno, M. (1992). The meaning of expressed emotion: Theoretical issues raised by cross-cultural research. *American Journal of Psychiatry, 149,* 9–21.

Jeste, D. V., et al. (1992). Cognitive deficits of patients with Alzheimer's disease with and without delusions. *American Journal of Psychiatry, 149,* 184–188.

Johnson, C., & Flach, A. (1985). Family characteristics of 105 patients with bulimia. *American Journal of Psychiatry, 142,* 1321–1324.

Johnson, C., & Larson, R. (1982). Bulimia: An analysis of mood and behavior. *Psychosomatic Medicine, 44,* 341–351.

Johnson, F. N. (Ed.). (1975). *Lithium research and therapy.* New York: Academic Press.

Johnson, J. D. (1985). A mechanism to inhibit input activation and its dysfunction in schizophrenia. *British Journal of Psychiatry, 146,* 429–435.

Johnston, L. D., Bachman, J. G., & O'Malley, P. M. (1992, January 25). Monitoring the future: A continuing study of the lifestyles and values of youth. Ann Arbor: University of Michigan News and Information Services.

Johnston, L. D., O'Malley, P. M., & Bachman, J. G. (1991). Drug use among American high school seniors, college students and young adults. DHHS Publication No. (ADM) 91-1835. Rockville, MD: National Institute on Drug Abuse.

Joiner, T. E., Alfano, M. S., & Metalsky, G. I. (1992). When depression breeds contempt: Reassurance seeking, self-esteem, and rejection of depressed college students by their roommates. *Journal of Abnormal Psychology, 101,* 165–173.

Joint Commission on Mental Illness and Health. (1961). *Action for mental health: Final report of the Joint Commission on Mental Illness and Health.* New York: Basic.

Jones, D. J., Fox, M. M., Babigan, H. M., & Hutton, H. E. (1980). Epidemiology of anorexia nervosa in Monroe County, New York, 1960–1976. *Psychosomatic Medicine, 42,* 551–558.

Jones, E. (1953). *The life and work of Sigmund Freud.* New York: Basic.

Jones v. United States, 103 S. Ct. 3043 (1983).

Junginger, J., Barker, S., & Coe, D. (1992). Mood theme and bizarreness of delusions in schizophrenia and mood psychosis. *Journal of Abnormal Psychology, 101,* 287–292.

Jurkovic, G. J. (1980). The juvenile delinquent as a moral philosopher: A structural-developmental perspective. *Psychological Bulletin, 88,* 709–727.

Kagan, D. M., & Squires, R. L. (1984). Eating disorders among adolescents: Patterns and prevalence. *Adolescence, 19,* 15–29.

Kagan, J. (1984). *The nature of the child.* New York: Basic.

Kahn, M. W. (1982). Cultural clash and psychopathology in three aboriginal cultures. *Academic Psychology Bulletin, 4,* 553–561.

Kahn, M. W., Hannah, M., Hinkin, C., Montgomery, C., & Pitz, D. (1987). Psychopathology on the streets: Psychological assessment of the homeless. *Professional Psychology: Research and Practice, 18,* 580–586.

Kahn, M. W., Henry, J., & Lejero, L. (1981). Indigenous mental health paraprofessionals on an Indian reservation. In M. O. Wagonfeld & S. S. Rakin, *Paraprofessionals in human services.* New York: Human Sciences Press.

Kammeyer, K. C. W. (1990). *Marriage and family:*

A foundation for personal decisions. (2nd ed.). Boston: Allyn & Bacon, Inc.

Kane, J. M. (1987). Treatment of schizophrenia. *Schizophrenia Bulletin, 13,* 133–156.

Kane, J. M., Rifkin, A., Woerner, M., & Sarantakos, S. (1986a). Dose response relationships in maintenance drug treatment for schizophrenia. *Psychopharmacology Bulletin, 22,* 205–235.

Kane, J. M., Woerner, M. S., Borenstein, M., Wegner, J., & Lieberman, J. (1986b). Integrating incidence and prevalence of tardive dyskinesia. *Psychopharmacology Bulletin, 22,* 254–258.

Kane, J. M., et al. (1985). High-dose versus low-dose strategies in the treatment of schizophrenia. *Psychopharmacology Bulletin, 21,* 533–537.

Kannel, W. B., McGee, D. L., & Castelli, W. P. (1984). Latest perspectives on cigarette smoking and cardiovascular disease: The Framingham Study. *Journal of Cardiac Rehabilitation, 4,* 267–277.

Kanner, A. D., Coyne, J. C., Schaefer, C., & Lazarus, R. S. (1981). Comparison of two modes of stress measurement: Daily hassles and uplifts versus major life events. *Journal of Behavioral Medicine, 4,* 1–39.

Kanner, L. (1943). Autistic disturbances of affective content. *Nervous Child, 2,* 217–240.

Kanner, L., & Eisenberg, L. (1955). Notes on the follow-up studies of autistic children. In P. Hoch & J. Zubin (Eds.), *Psychopathology of Childhood.* New York: Grune & Stratton.

Kaplan, A. S., & Woodside, D. B. (1987). Biological aspects of anorexia nervosa and bulimia nervosa. *Journal of Consulting and Clinical Psychology, 55,* 645–653.

Kaplan, H. S. (1974). *The new sex therapy: Active treatment of sexual dysfunctions.* New York: Brunner/Mazel.

Kaplan, S. J. (1986). *The private practice of behavior therapy: A guide for behavioral practitioners.* New York: Plenum.

Karacan, I. (1982). Nocturnal penile tumescence as a biologic marker assessing erectile dysfunction. *Psychosomatics, 23,* 349, 351–353, 356–357, 359–360.

Karasek, R. A., Baker, D., Marxer, F., Ahlbom, A., & Theorell, T. (1981). Job decision latitude, job demands, and cardiovascular disease: A prospective study of Swedish men. *American Journal of Public Health, 71,* 694–705.

Karasek, R. A., Theorell, T. G., Schwartz, J., Pieper, C., & Alfredsson, L. (1982). Job, psychological factors and coronary heart disease: Swedish prospective findings and U.S. prevalence findings using a new occupational inference method. *Advances in Cardiology, 29,* 62–67.

Karlsson, J. L. (1966). *The biological basis of schizophrenia.* Springfield, IL: Thomas.

Karlsson, J. L. (1982). Family transmission of schizophrenia: A review and synthesis. *British Journal of Psychiatry, 140,* 600–606.

Karno, M., et al. (1987). Expressed emotions and schizophrenic outcome among Mexican-American families. *Journal of Nervous and Mental Disease, 175,* 143–151.

Karno, M., et al. (1988). The epidemiology of obsessive-compulsive disorder in five U.S. communities. *Archives of General Psychiatry, 45,* 1094–1099.

Kassett, J. A., et al. (1989). Psychiatric disorders in the first-degree relatives of probands with bulimia nervosa. *American Journal of Psychiatry, 146,* 1468–1471.

Kassirer, J. P., & Angell, M. (1992). The use of fetal tissue in research on Parkinson's disease. *New England Journal of Medicine, 327,* 1591–1592.

Katona, C. L. E., et al. (1986). Platelet binding and neuroendocrine responses in depression.

In J. W. W. Deakin (Ed.), *The biology of depression* (pp. 121–136). Proceedings of a meeting of the Biological Group of the Royal College of Psychiatrists held at Manchester University, 1985. Washington, DC: American Psychiatric Press.

Katz, R. C., & Singh, N. N. (1986). Reflections on the ex-smoker: Some finding on successful quitters. *Journal of Behavioral Medicine, 9,* 191–202.

Kaul, T. J., & Bednar, R. L. (1986). Experiential group research: Results, questions, and suggestions. In S. L. Garfield & A. E. Bergin (Eds.), *Handbook of psychotherapy and behavior change: An evaluative analysis* (3rd ed.). New York: Wiley.

Kay, S. R. (1990). Significance of the positive-negative distinction in schizophrenia. *Schizophrenia Bulletin, 16,* 635–652.

Kaya, N., Moore, C., & Karacan, I. (1979). Nocturnal penile tumescence and its role in impotence. *Psychiatric Annals, 9,* 426–431.

Kazdin, A. E. (1984). *Behavior modification in applied settings.* Homewood, NJ: Dorsey Press.

Kazdin, A. E., et al. (1985). Depressive symptoms among physically abused and psychiatrically disturbed children. *Journal of Abnormal Psychology, 94,* 298–307.

Kazdin, A. E., Esveldt-Dawson, K., French, N. H., & Unis, A. S. (1987). Problem-solving skills training and relationship therapy in the treatment of antisocial child behavior. *Journal of Consulting and Clinical Psychology, 55,* 76–85.

Kazdin, A. E., Siegel, T. D., & Bass, D. (1992). Cognitive problem-solving skills training and parent management training in the treatment of antisocial behavior in children. *Journal of Consulting and Clinical Psychology,* 733–747.

Kazniak, A. W., & Allender, J. R. (1985). Psychological assessment of depression in older adults. In G. M. Chaisson-Stewart (Ed.), *Depression in the elderly: An interdisciplinary approach* (pp. 107–160). New York: Wiley.

Kearins, J. M. (1981). Visual spatial memory in Australian aboriginal children in desert regions. *Cognitive Psychology, 13,* 434–460.

Keefe, F. J., Dunsmore, J., & Burnett, R. (1992). Behavioral and cognitive-behavioral approaches to chronic pain: Recent advances and future directions. *Journal of Consulting and Clinical Psychology, 60,* 528–536.

Keesey, R. E. (1986). A set-point theory of obesity. In K. D. Brownell & J. P. Foreyt (Eds.), *Handbook of eating disorders: Physiology, psychology, and treatment of obesity, anorexia, and bulimia.* New York: Basic Books.

Keith, S. J., Regier, D. A., & Rae, D. S. (1991). Schizophrenic disorders. In L. N. Robins & D. A. Regier (Eds.), *Psychiatric disorders in America: The Epidemiologic Catchment Area Study* (pp. 33–52). New York: The Free Press.

Keller, M. B. (1990). Diagnostic and course of illness variables pertinent to refractory depression. In A. Tasman, et al. (Eds.), *Review of Psychiatry,* Vol. 9. Washington, DC: American Psychiatric Press.

Keller, M. B., First, M., & Koscis, J. H. (1990, August/September). Major depression and dysthymia. In American Psychiatric Association, *DSM-IV Update.* Washington, DC: American Psychiatric Association.

Kellner, R. (1990). Somatization: Theories and research. *Journal of Nervous & Mental Disease, 178,* 150–160.

Kelly, G. A. (1955). *The psychology of personal constructs* (Vols. 1 & 2). New York: Norton.

Kelly, G. A. (1958). Man's construction of his alternatives. In G. Lindzey (Ed.), *Assessment of human motives.* New York: Holt, Rinehart and Winston.

Kelly, J. A., Brasfield, T. L., & St. Lawrence, J. S. (1991). Predictors of vulnerability to AIDS

risk behavior relapse. *Journal of Consulting and Clinical Psychology, 59,* 163–166.

Kelly, J. A., Wildman, B. G., & Berler, E. S. (1980). Small group behavioral training to improve the job interview skills repertoire of mildly retarded adolescents. *Journal of Applied Behavior Analysis, 13,* 461–471.

Kelly, J. A., et al. (1989). Behavioral intervention to reduce AIDS risk activities. *Journal of Consulting and Clinical Psychology, 57,* 60–67.

Kelly, J. A., & Murphy, D. A. (1992). Psychological interventions with AIDS and HIV: Prevention and treatment. *Journal of Consulting and Clinical Psychology, 60,* 576–585.

Kelly, J. A., et al. (1992). AIDS/HIV risk behavior among the chronic mentally ill. *American Journal of Psychiatry, 149,* 886–889.

Kendall, P. C., & Braswell, L. (1985). *Cognitive-behavioral therapy for impulsive children.* New York: Guilford Press.

Kendall, P. C., & Williams, C. L. (1981). Behavioral and cognitive-behavioral approaches to outpatient treatment with children. In W. E. Craighead, A. E. Kazdin, & M. J. Mahoney, *Behavior Modification: Principles, Issues, and Applications* (2d ed.), Boston: Houghton Mifflin.

Kendell, R. E. (1983). Hysteria. In G. F. M. Russell & L. A. Hersov (Eds.), *Handbook of psychiatry: Vol. 4. The neuroses and personality disorders* (pp. 232–246). Cambridge: Cambridge University Press.

Kendler, K. (1992). Cited in Goleman, D. (1992, October 14). Study ties genes to drinking in women as much as in men. *New York Times,* p. C14.

Kendler, K. S., & Gruenberg, A. M. (1984). An independent analysis of the Danish Adoption Study of Schizophrenia. *Archives of General Psychiatry, 41,* 555–564.

Kendler, K. S. Gruenberg, A. M., & Tsuang, M. T. (1985). Psychiatric illness in first-degree relatives of schizophrenic and surgical control patients, a family study using DSM-III criteria. *Archives of General Psychiatry, 42,* 770–779.

Kendler, K. S., & Robinette, C. D. (1983). Schizophrenia in the National Academy of Sciences National Research Council Twin Registry: A 16-year update. *American Journal of Psychiatry, 140,* 1551–1563.

Kendler, K. S., et al. (1991). The genetic epidemiology of bulimia nervosa. *American Journal of Psychiatry, 148,* 1627–1637.

Kendler, K. S., et al. (1992a). A population-based twin study of major depression in women: The impact of varying definitions of illness. *Archives of General Psychiatry, 49,* 257–266.

Kendler, K. S., et al. (1992b). Generalized anxiety disorder in women. *Archives of General Psychiatry, 49,* 267–272.

Kendler, K. S., et al. (1992c). The genetic epidemiology of phobias in women: The interrelationship of agoraphobia, social phobia, situational phobia, and simple phobia. *Archives of General Psychiatry, 49,* 273–281.

Kennedy, B., & Flick, G. R. (1991). Classification of koro. *American Journal of Psychiatry, 148,* 1278–1279.

Kennedy, G., Kelman, H. R., & Thomas, C. (1991). Persistence and remission of depressive symptoms in late life. *American Journal of Psychiatry, 148,* 174–178.

Kennedy, S., Scheirer, J., & Rogers, A. (1984). The price of success: Our monocultural science. *American Psychologist, 390,* 966–967.

Kernberg, O. F. (1975). *Borderline conditions and pathological narcissism.* New York: Jason Aronson.

Kernberg, P. F. (1979). Childhood schizophrenia and autism: a selective review. In L. Bellak (Ed.), *Disorders of the schizophrenic syndrome.* New York: Basic Books.

Kessler, R. C., et al. (1990). Clustering of teenage suicides after television news stories about suicides: A reconsideration. *American Journal of Psychiatry, 145,* 1379–1383.

Kessler, R. C., et al. (1991). Stressful life events and symptom onset in HIV infection. *American Journal of Psychiatry, 148,* 733–738.

Kety, S. S. (1980). The syndrome of schizophrenia: Unresolved questions and opportunities for research. *British Journal of Psychiatry, 136,* 421–436.

Kety, S. S., Rosenthal, D., Wender, P. H., & Schulsinger, F. (1968). The types of prevalence of mental illness in the biological and adoptive families of adopted schizophrenics. In D. Rosenthal & S. S. Kety (Eds.), *The transmission of schizophrenia.* Oxford: Pergamon Press.

Kety, S. S., Rosenthal, D., Wender, P. H., Schulsinger, F., & Jacobsen, B. (1975). Mental illness in the biological and adoptive families of adoptive individuals who have become schizophrenic: A preliminary report based on psychiatric interviews. In R. R. Fieve, D. Rosenthal, & H. Brill (Eds.), *Genetic research in psychiatry.* Baltimore: Johns Hopkins University Press.

Kety, S. S., Rosenthal, D., Wender, P. H., Schulsinger, F., & Jacobsen, B. (1978). The biological and adoptive families of adopted individuals who become schizophrenic. In C. Wynne, R. L. Cromwell, & S. Mathysse (Eds.), *The nature of schizophrenia* (pp. 25–37). New York: Wiley.

Keyes, D. (1982). *The minds of Billy Milligan.* New York: Bantam.

Kiecolt-Glaser, J. K., et al. (1987). Marital quality, marital disruption, and immune function. *Psychosomatic Medicine, 49,* 13–34.

Kiecolt-Glaser, J. K., & Glaser, R. (1992). Psychoneuroimmunology: Can psychological interventions modulate immunity? *Journal of Consulting and Clinical Psychology, 60,* 569–575.

Kiecolt-Glaser, J. K., Speicher, C. E., Holliday, J. E., & Glaser, R. (1984). Stress and the transformation of lymphocytes in Epstein-Barr virus. *Journal of Behavioral Medicine, 7,* 1–12.

Kiecolt-Glaser, J. K., et al. (1985). Psychosocial enhancement of immunocompetence in a geriatric population. *Health Psychology, 4,* 25–41.

Kiecolt-Glaser, J. K., et al. (1987). Chronic stress and immunity in family caregivers of Alzheimer's disease victims. *Psychosomatic Medicine, 49,* 523–535.

Kiecolt-Glaser, J. K., et al. (1988). Marital discord and immunity in males. *Psychosomatic Medicine, 50,* 213–229.

Kiesler, C. A. (1982). Mental hospitalization and alternative care. *American Psychologist, 37,* 349–360.

Kiesler, C. A. & Sibulkin, A. E. (1987). *Mental hospitalization: Myths and facts about a national crisis.* Newbury Park, CA: Sage.

Killen, J. D., Fortmann, S. P., Newman, B., & Varady, A. (1990). Evaluation of a treatment approach combining nicotine gum with self-guided behavioral treatments for smoking relapse prevention. *Journal of Consulting and Clinical Psychology, 58,* 85–92.

Killen, J. D., et al. (1986). Self-induced vomiting and laxative and diuretic use among teenagers. *Journal of the American Medical Association, 225,* 1417–1449.

Kilmann, P. R., & Auerbach, R. (1979). Treatments of premature ejaculation and psychogenic impotence: A critical review of the literature. *Archives of Sexual Behavior, 8,* 81–100.

Kimball, D. P. (1988). *Biological psychology.* New York: Holt, Rinehart, & Winston.

Kinsey, A. C., Pomeroy, W. B., & Martin, C. E. (1948). *Sexual behavior in the human male.* Philadelphia: Saunders.

Kinsey, A. C., Pomeroy, W. B., Martin, C. E., & Gebhard, P. H. (1953). *Sexual behavior in the human female.* Philadelphia: Saunders.

Kissel, R. C., Whitman, T. L., & Reid, D. H. (1983). An institutional staff training and self-management program for developing multiple self-care skills in severely-profoundly retarded individuals. *Journal of Applied Behavior Analysis, 16,* 395–415.

Kivlahan, D. R., Marlatt, G. A., Fromme, K., Coppel, D. B., & Williams, E. (1990). Secondary prevention with college drinkers: Evaluation of an alcohol skills training program. *Journal of Consulting and Clinical Psychology, 58,* 805–810.

Klag, M. J. (1991). Cited in Leary, W. E. (1991, February 6). Social links are seen in black stress. *New York Times,* p. A16.

Klassen, D., & O'Connor, W. A. (1988). Predicting violence in schizophrenic and non-schizophrenic patients: A prospective study. *Journal of Community Psychology, 16,* 217–227.

Klatsky, A. L., Freidman, G. D., & Siegelaub, A. B. (1981). Alcohol and mortality: A ten-year Kaiser-Permanente experience. *Annals of Internal Medicine, 95,* 139–145.

Kleiman, D. (1988, November 7). A day in a mental hospital, a dream of life outside. *New York Times,* pp. B1, B2.

Klein, D. F., & Rabkin, J. G. (1984). Specificity and strategy in psychotherapy research and practice. In R. L. Spitzer & J. R. W. Williams (Eds.), *Psychotherapy research: Where are we and where should we go?* New York: Guilford Press.

Klein, D. N., & Depue, R. A. (1985). Obsessional personality traits and risk for bipolar affective disorder: An offspring study. *Journal of Abnormal Psychology, 94,* 291–297.

Klein, D. N., Taylor, E. B., Dickstein, S., & Harding, K. (1988). Primary early-onset dysthymia: Comparison with primary nonbipolar nonchronic major depression on demographic, clinical, familial, personality, and socioenvironmental characteristics and short-term outcome. *Journal of Abnormal Psychology, 97,* 387–398.

Klein, M. (1981). On Mahler's autistic and symbiotic phases: An exposition and evaluation. *Psychoanalysis and Contemporary Thought, 4,* 69–105.

Klein, M., et al. (1952). *Developments in psychoanalysis.* London: Hogarth Press.

Klein, M. H., et al. (1985). A comparative outcome study of group psychotherapy versus exercise treatments for depression. *International Journal of Mental Health, 13,* 148–175.

Kleiner, L., & Marshall, W. L. (1985). Relationship difficulties and agoraphobia. *Clinical Psychology Review, 5,* 581–595.

Kleinman, A. (1987). Anthropology and psychiatry: The role of culture in cross-cultural research on illness. *British Journal of Psychiatry, 151,* 447–454.

Klerman, G. L. (1984). Ideology and science in the individual psychotherapy of schizophrenia. *Schizophrenia Bulletin, 10,* 608–612.

Klerman, G. L., et al. (1991). Panic attacks in the community: Social morbidity and health care utilization. *Journal of the American Medical Association, 265,* 742–746.

Klerman, G. L., & Weissman, M. M. (1989). Increasing rates of depression. *Journal of the American Medical Association, 261,* 2229–2235.

Klerman, G. L., Weissman, M. M., Rounsaville, B. J., & Chevron, E. S. (1984). *Interpersonal psychotherapy of depression.* New York: Basic.

Klorman, R., et al. (1988). Effects of methylphenidate on attention-deficit hyperactivity disorder with and without aggressive/noncompliant features. *Journal of Abnormal Psychology, 97,* 413–422.

Klosko, J. S., Barlow, D. H., Tassinari, R., & Cerny, J. A. (1990). A comparison of alprazolam and behavior therapy in treatment of panic disorder. *Journal of Consulting and Clinical Psychology, 58,* 77–84.

Kluft, R. P. (1984a). An introduction to multiple personality disorder. *Psychiatric Annals, 14,* 19–24.

Kluft, R. P. (1984b). Multiple personality in childhood. *Psychiatric Clinics of North America, 7,* 121–135.

Kluft, R. P. (1986). Three high functioning multiples. *Journal of Nervous and Mental Disease, 174,* 722–726.

Kluft, R. P. (1987). First-rank symptoms as a diagnostic clue to multiple personality disorder. *American Journal of Psychiatry, 144,* 293–298.

Kluznik, J. C., Speed, N., Van Valkenburg, C., & Magraw, R. (1986). Forty-year follow-up of United States prisoners of war. *American Journal of Psychiatry, 143,* 1443–1446.

Knapp, S., & Vandercreek, L. (1982). Tarasoff: Five years later. *Professional Psychology, 13,* 511–516.

Knapp, S., & Vandercreek, L. (1990). Application of the duty to protect to HIV-positive patients. *Professional Psychology: Research and Practice, 21,* 161–166.

Knight, R. G., Godfrey, H. P. D., & Shelton, E. J. (1988). The psychological deficits associated with Parkinson's disease. *Clinical Psychology Review, 8,* 391–410.

Knudsen, D. D. (1991). Child sexual coercion. In E. Grauerholz & M. A. Koralewski (Eds.), *Sexual coercion: A sourcebook on its nature, causes, and prevention* (pp. 17–28). Lexington, MA: Lexington.

Kobasa, S. C. (1979). Stressful life events, personality, and health: An inquiry into hardiness. *Journal of Personality and Social Psychology, 37,* 1–11.

Kobasa, S. C., Maddi, S. R., & Kahn, S. (1982). Hardiness and health: A prospective study. *Journal of Personality and Social Psychology, 42,* 168–177.

Kobasa, S. C., Maddi, S. R., & Zola, M. A. (1983). Type A and hardiness. *Journal of Behavioral Medicine, 6,* 41–51.

Kockott, G., & Fahrner, E. (1987). Transsexuals who have not undergone surgery: A follow-up study. *Archives of Sexual Behavior, 16,* 511–522.

Kockott, G., & Fahrner, E. (1988). Male-to-female and female-to-male transsexuals: A comparison. *Archives of Sexual Behavior, 17,* 539–545.

Kockott, G., Feil, W., Ferstl, R., Aldenhoff, J., & Besinger, U. (1980). Psychophysiological aspects of male sexual inadequacy: Results of an experimental study. *Archives of Sexual Behavior, 9,* 477–493.

Kohn, P. M., Barnes, G. E., & Hoffman, F. M. (1979). Drug-use history and experience seeking among adult male correctional inmates. *Journal of Consulting and Clinical Psychology, 47,* 708–715.

Kohut, H. (1966). Forms and transformations of narcissism. *Journal of the American Psychoanalytic Association, 14,* 243–272.

Kolata, G. (1988, August, 25). Epidemic of dangerous eating disorder may be false alarm. *New York Times,* p. B16.

Kolata, G. (1989a, March 7). Some addicts find medication can ease craving for cocaine. *New York Times,* pp. C4.

Kolata, G. (1990a,). Where fat is problem, heredity is the answer, studies find. *New York Times,* B9.

Kolata, G. (1990b, September 11). Gene for key brain protein isolated. *New York Times,* p. C3.

Kolata, G. (1991a, February 26). Alzheimer's

researchers close in on causes. *New York Times,* pp. C1, C7.

Kolata, G. (1991b, March 21). Chemical is found to shield cells in Parkinson's disease. *New York Times,* p. B10.

Kolata, G. (1991b, November 8). Studies cite 10.5 years from infection to illness. *New York Times,* p. B12.

Kolata, G. (1991a, November 9). For heterosexuals, diagnosis of AIDS is often unmercifully late. *New York Times,* p. 32.

Kolata, G. (1992,). New Alzheimer's study questions link to metal. *New York Times,* p. C2.

Kolko, D. J. (1988). Educational programs to promote awareness and prevention of child sexual victimization: A review and methodological critique. *Clinical Psychology Review, 8,* 195–209.

Kolko, D. J., & Rickard-Figueroa, J. L. (1985). Effects of video games on the adverse corollaries of chemotherapy in pediatric oncology patients: A single-case analysis. *Journal of Consulting and Clinical Psychology, 53,* 223–228.

Koorland, M. A. (1986). Applied behavior analysis and the correction of learning disabilities. In J. K. Torgesen & B. Y. L. Wong (Eds.), *Psychological and educational perspectives on learning disabilities* (pp. 297–328). Orlando, FL: Academic Press.

Koss, M. P. (1988). Stranger and acquaintance rape: Are there differences in the victim's experience? *Psychology of Women Quarterly, 12,* 1–24.

Koss, M. P., Butcher, J. L., & Strupp, H. H. (1986). Brief psychotherapy methods in clinical research. *Journal of Consulting and Clinical Psychology, 54,* 60–67.

Koss, M. P., Gidycz, C. A., & Wisniewski, N. (1987). The scope of rape: Incidence and prevalence of sexual aggression and victimization in a national sample of higher education students. *Journal of Consulting and Clinical Psychology, 55,* 162–170.

Kosson, D. S., Smith, S. S., & Newman, J. P. (1990). Evaluating the construct validity of psychopathy in black and white male inmates: Three preliminary studies. *Journal of Abnormal Psychology, 99,* 250–259.

Kotses, H., et al. (1991). Long-term effects of biofeedback-induced facial relaxation on measures of asthma severity in children. *Biofeedback and Self Regulation, 16,* 1–21.

Kovacs, M., & Beck, A. T. (1978). Maladaptive cognitive structure in depression. *American Journal of Psychiatry, 135,* 525–533.

Kozol, N. J., et al. (1985). *Epidemiology of heroin: 1964–1984.* Rockville, MD: National Institute on Drug Abuse.

Kraepelin, E. (1909–1913). *Psychiatrie* (8th Ed.). Leipzig: J. A. Barth.

Kramer, L. (1990, July 16). A "Manhattan Project" for AIDS. *New York Times,* A15.

Krantz, D. S. (1980). Cognitive processes and recovery from heart attack: A review and theoretical analysis. *Journal of Human Stress, 6,* 27–38.

Krantz, D. S., Contrada, R. J., Hills, D. R., & Friedler, E. (1988). Environmental stress and biobehavioral antecedents of coronary heart disease. *Journal of Consulting and Clinical Psychology, 56,* 333–341.

Krantz, D. S., Grunberg, N. E., & Baum, A. (1985). Health psychology, *Annual Review of Psychology, 36,* 349–383.

Krantz, S. E., & Moos, R. H. (1988). Risk factors at intake predict nonremission among depressed patients. *Journal of Consulting and Clinical Psychology, 56,* 863–869.

Kraus, R. F., & Buffler, P. A. (1979). Sociocultural stress and the American native in Alaska: An analysis of changing patterns of psychiatric illness and alcohol abuse among Alaska natives. *Culture, Medicine, and Psychiatry,* 11–15.

Krauss, P., & Brown, G. M. (1988). Drugs and the DST: Need for a reappraisal. *American Journal of Psychiatry, 145,* 666–674.

Kruesi, M. J. P., et al. (1987). Effects of sugar and aspartame on aggression and activity in children. *American Journal of Psychiatry, 144,* 1487–1490.

Kuczmarski, R. J. (1992). Prevalence of overweight and weight gain in the United States. *American Journal of Clinical Nutrition, 55* (Suppl.), 495S–502S.

Kuiper, B., & Cohen-Kettenis, P. (1988). Sex reassignment surgery: A study of 141 Dutch transsexuals. *Archives of Sexual Behavior, 17,* 439–457.

Kurdek, L. A., & Schmitt, J. P. (1986). Relationship quality of partners in heterosexual married, heterosexual cohabiting, gay, and lesbian relationships. *Journal of Personality and Social Psychology, 51,* 711–720.

Kushner, M. (1977). The reduction of a longstanding fetish by means of aversive conditioning. In J. Fischer & H. Gochios (Eds.), *Handbook of behavior therapy with sexual problems.* New York: Pergamon Press.

LaCroix, A. Z., & Haynes, S. G. (1987). Gender differences in the stressfulness of workplace roles: A focus on work and health. In R. Barnett, G. Baruch, & L. Biener (Eds.), *Gender and stress* (pp. 96–121). New York: Free Press.

Lacks, P. E., Bertelson, A. D., Ganz, L., & Kunkel, J. (1983). The effectiveness of three behavioral treatments for different degrees of sleep-onset insomnia. *Behavior Therapy, 14,* 593–605.

Laguerre, M. S. (1981). Haitian Americans. In A. Harwood (Ed.), *Ethnicity and medical care.* Cambridge, MA: Harvard University Press.

Laing, R. D. (1964). Is schizophrenia a disease? *International Journal of Social Psychiatry, 10,* 184–193.

Laing, R. D. (1976, July 20). Round the bend. *New Statesman.*

Lam, D. H., Brewin, C. R., Woods, R. T., & Bebbington, P. E. (1987). Cognition and social adversity in the depressed elderly. *Journal of Abnormal Psychology, 96,* 23–26.

Lamb, H. R. (1982). *Treating the long-term mentally ill: Beyond deinstitutionalization.* San Francisco: Jossey-Bass.

Lamb, H. R. (1984). Deinstitutionalization and the homeless mentally ill. In H. R. Lamb (Ed.), *The homeless mentally ill: A Task Force Report of the American Psychiatric Association* (pp. 55–74). Washington, DC: American Psychiatric Association.

Lamb, H. R., & Goertzel, V. (1971). Discharge of mental patients: Are they really in the community? *Archives of General Psychiatry, 24,* 29–34.

Lamb, H. R., & Lamb, D. M. (1990). Factors contributing to homelessness among the chronically and severely mentally ill. *Hospital and Community Psychiatry, 41,* 301–305.

Lambert, M. C., et al. (1992). Jamaican and American adult perspectives on child psychopathology: Further exploration of the threshold model. *Journal of Consulting and Clinical Psychology, 60,* 64–72.

Lambert, N. M., Hartsough, C. S., Sassone, D., & Sandoval, J. (1987). Persistence of hyperactivity symptoms from childhood to adolescence and associated outcomes. *American Journal of Orthopsychiatry, 57,* 22–32.

Landman, J. T., & Dawes, R. M. (1982). Psychotherapy outcome: Smith and Glass' conclusions stand up under scrutiny. *American Psychologist, 38,* 504–516.

Lang, A. R., Goeckner, D. J., Adesso, V. J., & Marlatt, G. A. (1975). Effects of alcohol on aggression in male social drinkers. *Journal of Abnormal Psychology, 84,* 508–518.

Lang, A. R., Searles, J., Lauerman, R., & Adesso, V. J. (1980). Expectancy, alcohol, and sex guilt as determinants of interest in and reaction to sexual stimuli. *Journal of Abnormal Psychology, 89,* 644–653.

Lang, J. G., Munoz, R. F., Bernal, G., & Sorenson, J. L. (1982). Quality of life and psychological well-being in a bicultural Latino community. *Hispanic Journal of Behavioral Sciences, 4,* 433–450.

Lang, P. J. (1968). Fear reduction and fear behavior: Problems in treating a construct. In J. M. Schlein (Ed.), *Research in Psychotherapy* (Vol. III, pp. 90–102). Washington, DC: American Psychological Association.

Lang, P. J. (1985). The cognitive psychophysiology of emotion: Fear and anxiety. In A. H. Tuma & J. D. Maser (Eds.), *Anxiety and the anxiety disorders* (pp. 131–170). Hillsdale, NJ: Erlbaum.

Lang, P. J., & Lazovik, A. D. (1963). Experimental desensitization of a phobia. *Journal of Abnormal and Social Psychology, 66,* 519–525.

Langer, E. J., Rodin, J., Beck, P., Weinan, C., & Spitzer, L. (1979). Environmental determinants of memory improvement in late adulthood. *Journal of Personality and Social Psychology, 37,* 2003–2013.

Langford, H. G., et al. (1985). Dietary therapy slows the return of hypertension after stopping prolonged medication. *Journal of the American Medical Association, 253,* 657–664.

Lansky, D., & Wilson, G. T. (1981). Alcohol, expectations, and sexual arousal. *Journal of Abnormal Psychology, 90,* 35–45.

LaPerriere, A. R., et al. (1990). Exercise intervention attenuates emotional distress and natural killer cell decrements following notification of positive serologic status for HIV-1. *Biofeedback and Self-Regulation, 15,* 229–242.

LaPerriere, A. R., et al. (1991). Aerobic exercise training in an AIDS risk group. *International Journal of Sports Medicine, 12,* S53–S57.

Larson, R. W., Raffaelli, M., Richards, M. H., Ham, M., & Jewell, L. (1990). Ecology of depression in late childhood and early adolescence: A profile of daily states and activities. *Journal of Abnormal Psychology, 99,* 92–102.

Lawson, D. M. (1983). Alcoholism. In M. Hersen (Ed.), *Outpatient behavior therapy: A clinical guide* (pp. 143–172). New York: Grune & Stratton.

Lazarus, A. A., Beutler, L. E., & Norcross, J. C. (1992). The future of technical eclecticism. *Psychotherapy, 29,* 11–20.

Lazarus, R. S., DeLongis, A., Folkman, S., & Gruen, R. (1985). Stress and adaptational outcomes: The problem of confounded measures. *American Psychologist, 40,* 770–779.

Lazarus, R. S., & Folkman, S. (1984). *Stress, appraisal, and coping.* New York: Springer.

Leary, W. E. (1991, February 6). Social links are seen in black stress. *New York Times,* p. A16.

Le Shan, L. (1966). An emotional life-history pattern associated with neoplastic disease. *Annals of New York Academy of Sciences, 125,* 780–792.

Lear, M. W. (1988, July 3). Mad malady. *New York Times Magazine,* pp. 21–22.

Lechtenberg, R. (1984). *Epilepsy and the family.* Cambridge, MA: Harvard University Press.

Ledray, L. E. (1990). Counseling rape victims: The nursing challenge. *Perspectives in Psychiatric Care, 26,* 21–27.

Lee, C. C., & Richardson, B. L. (1991). *Multicultural issues in counseling: New approaches to diversity.* Alexandria, VA: AACD.

Lefcourt, H. M., Miller, R. S., Ware, E. E., & Sherk, D. (1981). Locus of control as a modifier of the relationship between stressors and moods. *Journal of Personality and Social Psychology, 41,* 357–369.

Lefcourt, H. M., & Martin, R. A. (1986). *Humor and life stress: Antidote to adversity.* New York: Springer-Verlag.

Leff, J. (1977). International variations in the diagnosis of schizophrenia. *British Journal of Psychiatry, 131,* 329–338.

Leff, J., Kuipers, L., Berkowitz, R., Eberlein-Vries, R., & Sturgeon, D. (1982). A controlled trial of social intervention in the families of schizophrenic patients. *British Journal of Psychiatry, 141,* 121–134.

Leff, J., & Vaughn, C. (1981). The role of maintenance therapy and relatives' expressed emotion in relapse of schizophrenia: A two-year follow-up. *British Journal of Psychiatry, 139,* 102–104.

Leff, J., & Vaughn, C. (1985). *Expressed emotion in families.* New York: Guilford Press.

Lefley, H. P. (1990). Culture and chronic mental illness. *Hospital and Community Psychiatry, 41,* 277–286.

Lehrer, P. M., Sargunaraj, D., & Hochron, S. (1992). Psychological approaches to the treatment of asthma. *Journal of Consulting and Clinical Psychology, 60,* 639–643.

Leibowitz, S. F. (1986). Brain monoamines and peptides: Role in the control of eating behavior. *Federation Proceedings, 45,* 599–615.

Leishman, K. (1987, February). Heterosexuals and AIDS. *Atlantic Monthly,* pp. 39–58.

Leitenberg, H., Gross, J., Peterson, J., & Rosen, J. C. (1984). Analysis of an anxiety model and the process of change during exposure plus response prevention treatment of bulimia nervosa. *Behavior Therapy, 15,* 3–20.

Leitenberg, H., Rosen, J. C., Gross, J., Nudelman, S., & Vara, L. S. (1988). Exposure plus response-prevention treatment of bulimia nervosa. *Journal of Consulting and Clinical Psychology, 56,* 535–541.

Leitenberg, H., Yost, L. W., & Carroll-Wilson, M. (1986). Negative cognitive errors in children: Questionnaire development, normative data, and comparisons between children with and without self-reported symptoms of depression, low self-esteem, and evaluation anxiety. *Journal of Consulting and Clinical Psychology, 54,* 528–536.

Lesieur, H. R., & Blume, S. B. (1987). The South Oaks Gambling Screen (SOGS): A new instrument for the identification of pathological gamblers. *American Journal of Psychiatry, 144,* 1184–1188.

Lesieur, H. R., Blume, S. B., & Zoppa, R. M. (1986). Alcoholism, drug abuse, and gambling. *Alcoholism: Clinical and Experimental Research, 10,* 33–38.

Lesieur, H. R., & Custer, R. L. (1984, July). Pathological gambling: Roots, phases, and treatment. *ANNALS, AAPSS, 474,* 146–156.

Le Shan, L. (1966). An emotional life-history pattern associated with neoplastic disease. *Annals of the New York Academy of Sciences, 125,* 780–793.

Lesser, I. (1992, December). Ethnic differences in response to psychotropic drugs. Paper presented at a symposium *Anxiety Disorders in African Americans,* presented by the State University of New York Health Science Center at Brooklyn, NY.

LeVay, S. (1991). A difference in hypothalamic structure between heterosexual and homosexual men. *Science, 253,* 1034–1037.

Levin, A. P., Schneier, F. R., & Liebowitz, M. R. (1989). Social phobia: Biology and pharmacology. *Clinical Psychology Review, 9,* 129–140.

Levine, I. S., & Huebner, R. B. (1991). Homeless persons with alcohol, drug, and mental disorders. *American Psychologist, 46,* 1113–1114.

Levine, I. S., & Rog, D. J. (1990). Mental health services for homeless mentally ill persons. *American Psychologist, 45,* 963–968.

Levine, J., et al. (1987). The role of denial in recovery from coronary heart disease. *Psychosomatic Medicine, 49,* 109–117.

Levine, J., Warrenburg, S., Kerns, R., Schwartz, G., Delaney, R., Fontana, A., Gradman, A., Smith, S., Scott, A., & Cascione, R. (1987). The role of denial in recovery from coronary heart disease. *Psychosomatic Medicine, 49,* 109–117.

Levy, R. M., Pons, V. G., & Rosenblum, M. L. (1984). Central nervous system mass lesions in the acquired immune deficiency syndrome (AIDS). *Journal of Neurosurgery, 61,* 9–16.

Levy, S. M., Herberman, R. B., Maluish, A. M., Schlien, B., & Lippman, M. (1985). Prognostic risk assessment in the primary breast cancer by behavioral and immunological parameters. *Health Psychology, 4,* 99–113.

Lewinsohn, P. M. (1974). A behavioral approach to depression. In R. J. Friedman & M. M. Katz (Eds.), *The psychology of depression: Contemporary theory and research.* Washington, DC: Winston-Wiley.

Lewinsohn, P. M., Antonuccio, D., Steinmetz, J., & Terry, L. (1984). *The coping with depression course: A psychoeducational intervention for unipolar depression.* Eugene, OR: Castalia.

Lewinsohn, P. M., Duncan, E. M., Stanton, A. K., & Hautzinger, M. (1986). Age at first onset for nonpolar depression. *Journal of Abnormal Psychology, 95,* 378–383.

Lewinsohn, P. H., & Libet, J. M. (1972). Pleasant events, activity schedules and depression. *Journal of Abnormal Psychology, 79,* 291–295.

Lewinsohn, P., Steinmetz, J., Larson, D., & Franklin, J. (1981). Depression-related cognitions: Antecedent or consequence? *Journal of Abnormal Psychology, 90,* 213–219.

Lewinsohn, P. M., Teri, L., & Wasserman, D. (1983). Depression. In M. Hersen (Ed.), *Outpatient behavior therapy: A practical guide* (pp. 81–108). New York: Grune & Stratton.

Lewinsohn, P. M., et al. (1991). Cognitive-behavioral treatment for depressed adolescents. *Behavior Therapy, 21,* 385–401.

Lewis, M. S. (1989a). Age incidence and schizophrenia: Part I. The season of birth controversy. *Schizophrenia Bulletin, 15,* 59–73.

Lewis, R. J., Dlugokinski, E. L., Caputo, L. M., & Griffin, R. B. (1988). Children at risk for emotional disorders: Risk and resource dimensions. *Clinical Psychology Review, 8,* 417–440.

Lewis-Hall, F. (1992, December). Overview of DSM-III-R: Focus on panic disorder and obsessive-compulsive disorder. Paper presented at a symposium *Anxiety Disorders in African Americans,* presented by the State University of New York Health Science Center at Brooklyn, NY.

Lewy, A. J. (1987). The psychopharmacological effect of light in seasonal affective disorder. *Psychopharmacology Bulletin, 23,* 347–348.

Lex, B. W. (1987). Review of alcohol problems in ethnic minority groups. *Journal of Consulting and Clinical Psychology, 55,* 293–300.

Ley, R. (1985). Blood, breath, and fears: A hyperventilation theory of panic attacks and agoraphobia. *Clinical Psychology Review, 5,* 271–285.

Ley, R. (1991). The efficacy of breathing retraining and the centrality of hyperventilation in panic disorder: A reinterpretation of experimental findings. *Behaviour Research and Therapy, 29,* 301–304.

Liberman, R. P., et al. (1986). Training skills in the psychiatrically disabled: Learning, coping and competence. *Schizophrenia Bulletin, 12,* 631–647.

Lichtenstein, E. (1982). The smoking problem: A behavioral perspective. *Journal of Consulting and Clinical Psychology, 50,* 804–819.

Lichtenstein, E., & Glasgow, R. E. (1992). Smoking cessation: What have we learned over the past decade? *Journal of Consulting and Clinical Psychology, 60,* 518–527.

Lichtenstein, E., Glasgow, R. E., & Abrams, D. B. (1986). Social support in smoking cessation: In search of effective interventions. *Behavior Therapy, 17,* 607–619.

Lichtenstein, E., Harris, D., Birchler, G., Wahl, J., & Schmahl, D. (1973). Comparison of rapid smoking, warm, smoky air, and attention placebo in the modification of smoking behavior. *Journal of Consulting and Clinical Psychology, 40,* 92–98.

Lidz, C. W., et al. (1989). Commitment: The consistency of clinicians and the use of legal standards. *American Journal of Psychiatry, 146,* 176–181.

Lieber, C. S. (1990, January 14). Cited in "Barroom biology: How alcohol goes to a woman's head." *The New York Times,* p. E24.

Liebowitz, M. R., et al. (1984). Lactate provocation of panic attacks: I. Clinical and behavioral findings. *Archives of General Psychiatry, 41,* 764–770.

Liebowitz, M. R., et al. (1985a). Specificity of lactate infusions in social phobia versus panic disorders. *American Journal of Psychiatry, 142,* 947–949.

Liebowitz, M. R., et al. (1985b). Psychopharmacological treatment of social phobia. *Psychopharmacology Bulletin, 21,* 610–614.

Liebowitz, M. R., Gorman, J. M., Fyer, A. J., & Klein, D. F. (1985c). Social phobia: Review of a neglected anxiety disorder. *Archives of General Psychiatry, 42,* 729–736.

Lied, E. R., & Marlatt, G. A. (1979). Modeling as a determinant of alcohol consumption: Effect of subject sex and prior drinking history. *Addictive Behaviors, 4,* 47–54.

Lin, K., et al. (1991). Ethnicity and family involvement in the treatment of schizophrenic patients. *Journal of Nervous and Mental Disease, 179,* 631–633.

Lin, T. Y., et al. (1978). Ethnicity and patterns of help-seeking. *Culture, Medicine, and Psychiatry, 2,* 3–14.

Lindemalm, G., Korlin, D., & Uddenberg, N. (1986). Long-term follow-up of "sex change" in 134 male to female transsexuals. *Archives of Sexual Behavior, 15,* 187–210.

Lindsey, K. P., & Paul, G. L. (1989). Involuntary commitments to public mental institutions: Issues involving the overrepresentation of blacks and assessment of relevant functioning. *Psychological Bulletin, 106,* 171–183.

Linehan, M. M., Camper, P., Chiles, J. A., Strosahl, K., & Shearin, E. (1987). Interpersonal problem solving and parasuicide. *Cognitive Therapy and Research, 11,* 1–12.

Ling, G. S. F., et al. (1984). Separation of morphine analgesia from physical dependence. *Science, 226,* 462–464.

Linton, T. E., & Juul, K. D. (1980). Mainstreaming: Time for reassessment. *Educational Leadership, 37,* 433–437.

Linz, D. (1985). *Sexual violence in the media: Effects on male viewers and implications for society.* Unpublished doctoral dissertation, University of Wisconsin, Madison.

Linz, D. (1989). Exposure to sexually explicit materials and attitudes toward rape: A comparison of study results. *Journal of Sex Research, 26,* 50–84.

Linz, D., Donnerstein, E., & Penrod, S. (1988). The effects of long-term exposure to violent and sexually degrading depictions of women. *Journal of Personality and Social Psychology, 55,* 758–767.

Lipton, D. N., McDonel, E. C., & McFall, R. M. (1987). Heterosocial perception in rapists. *Journal of Consulting and Clinical Psychology, 55,* 17–21.

Lisak, D. (1991). Sexual aggression, masculinity, and fathers. *Signs, 16,* 238–262.

Litman, G., & Topman, A. (1983). Outcome studies on techniques in alcoholism treatment. In M. Galanter (Ed.), *Recent developments in alcoholism* (Vol. 1). New York: Plenum.

Litz, B. T. (1992). Emotional numbing in combat-related post-traumatic stress disorder: A critical review and reformulation. *Clinical Psychology Review, 12,* 417–432.

Livesley, W. J. (1985). The classification of personality disorder: II. The problem of criteria. *Canadian Journal of Psychiatry, 30,* 359–362.

Livesley, W. J., West, M., & Tanney, A. (1985). Historical comment on DSM-III schizoid and avoidant personality disorders. *American Journal of Psychiatry, 142,* 1344–1347.

Livesley, W. J., West, M., & Tanney, A. (1986). Doctor Livesley and associates reply. *American Journal of Psychiatry, 143,* 1062–1063.

Livingstone, M., et al. (1991). Physiological and anatomical evidence for a magnocellular defect in developmental dyslexia. *Proceedings of the National Academy of Sciences, 88,* 7943–7947.

Lloyd, C., Alexander, A. A., Rice, D. G., & Greenfield, N. S. (1980). Life events as predictors of academic performance. *Journal of Human Stress, 6,* 15–25.

Lochman, J. E. (1987). Self- and peer perceptions and attributional biases of aggressive and nonaggressive boys in dyadic interactions. *Journal of Consulting and Clinical Psychology, 55,* 404–410.

Lochman, J. E. (1992). Cognitive-behavioral intervention with aggressive boys: Three-year follow-up and preventive effects. *Journal of Consulting and Clinical Psychology, 60,* 426–432.

Lochman, J. E., Burch, P. R., Curry, J. F., & Lampron, L. B. (1984). Treatment and generalization effects of cognitive behavioral and goal setting interventions with aggressive boys. *Journal of Consulting and Clinical Psychology, 52,* 915–916.

Loeber, R., Lahey, B. B., & Thomas, C. (1991). Diagnostic conundrum of oppositional defiant disorder and conduct disorder. *Journal of Consulting and Clinical Psychology, 100,* 379–390.

Loewenstein, R. J. (1991). Psychogenic amnesia and psychogenic fugue: A comprehensive review. *Annual Review of Psychiatry, 10,* 223–247.

Lombroso, C. T., & Duffy, F. H. (1982). Brain electrical activity mapping as an adjunct to CT scanning. In R. Canger, F. Angeleri & J. K. Penry (Eds.), *Advances in epileptology: 11th Epilepsy International Symposium* (pp. 83–88). New York: Raven Press.

López, S. R., & Hernandez, P. (1986). How culture is considered in evaluations of psychopathology. *Journal of Nervous and Mental Diseases, 176,* 598–606.

López, S. R., & Núñez, J. A. (1987) Cultural factors considered in selected diagnostic criteria and interview schedules. *Journal of Abnormal Psychology, 96,* 270–272.

LoPiccolo, J. (1985, September). *Advances in diagnosis and treatment of sexual dysfunction.* Paper presented at the 28th annual meeting of the Society for the Scientific Study of Sex, San Diego.

LoPiccolo, J. (1990). Sexual dysfunction. In A. S. Bellack, M. Hersen, & A. E. Kazdin (1990). *International handbook of behavior modification and therapy.* (2nd ed.) (pp. 575–564). New York: Plenum Press.

LoPiccolo, J., & Friedman, J. (1988). Broad-spectrum treatment of low sexual desire: Integration of cognitive, behavioral, and systemic therapy. In S. Leiblum & R. Rosen (Eds.), *Sexual desire disorders.* New York: Guilford Press.

LoPiccolo, J., & Lobitz, W. C. (1972). The role of masturbation in the treatment of orgasmic dysfunction. *Archives of Sexual Behavior, 2,* 163.

LoPiccolo, J., & Stock, W. E. (1986). Treatment of sexual dysfunction. *Journal of Consulting and Clinical Psychology, 54,* 158–167.

Loring, M., & Powell, B. (1988). Gender, race, and DSM III: A study of objectivity of psychiatric diagnostic behavior. *Journal of Health and Social Behavior, 29,* 1–22.

Lothstein, L. M. (1982). Sex reassignment surgery: Historical, bioethical, and theoretical issues. *American Journal of Psychiatry, 139,* 417–426.

Lourea, O., Rila, M., & Taylor, C. (1986). Sex in the age of AIDS. Paper presented to the Western Region Conference of the Society for the Scientific Study of Sex, Scottsdale, AZ.

Lovaas, O. I. (1977). *The Autistic Child: Language Development Through Behavior Modification.* New York: Halstead Press.

Lovaas, O. I. (1987). Behavioral treatment and normal educational and intellectual functioning in young autistic children. *Journal of Consulting and Clinical Psychology, 55,* 3–9.

Lovejoy, M. (1982). Expectations and the recovery process. *Schizophrenia Bulletin, 8,* 605–609.

Lubin, B., Larsen, R. M., & Matarazzo, J. D. (1984). Patterns of psychological test usage in the United States: 1935–1982. *American Psychologist, 39,* 451–454.

Lubin, B., Larsen, R. M., Matarazzo, J. D., & Seever, M. (1985). Psychological test usage patterns in five professional settings. *American Psychologist, 40,* 857–861.

Luborsky, L., et al. (1988). *Who will benefit from psychotherapy? Predicting therapeutic outcomes.* New York: Basic.

Luchins, D. J., Levine, R. R., & Meltzer, H. Y. (1983). Lateral ventricular size, psychopathology and medication response in the psychoses. *Biological Psychiatry, 19,* 29–44.

Ludolph, P. S. (1985). How prevalent is multiple personality? *American Journal of Psychiatry, 142,* 1526–1527.

Lundstrom, B., Pauly, I., & Walinder, J. (1984). Outcome of sex reassignment surgery. *Acta Psychiatrica Scandinavica, 70,* 289–294.

Lurigio, A. J., & Lewis, D. A. (1989). Worlds that fail: A longitudinal study of urban mental patients. *Journal of Social Issues, 45,* 79–90.

Lykken, D. T. (1957). A study of anxiety in the sociopathic personality. *Journal of Abnormal and Social Psychology, 55,* 6–10.

Lynn, R. (1977). The intelligence of the Japanese. *Bulletin of the British Psychological Society, 30,* 69–72.

Lynn, R. (1982). IQ in Japan and in the United States shows a growing disparity. *Nature, 297,* 222–223.

Lyon, F. R., & Moats, L. C. (1988). Critical issues in the instruction of the learning disabled. *Journal of Consulting and Clinical Psychology, 56,* 830–835.

Lyons, J. S., Rosen, A. J., & Dysken, M. W. (1985). Behavioral effects of tricyclic drugs in depressed patients. *Journal of Consulting and Clinical Psychology, 53,* 17–24.

Machón, R. A., Mednick, S. A., & Schulsinger, F. (1983). The interaction of seasonality, place of birth, genetic risk and subsequent schizophrenia in a high risk sample. *British Journal of Psychiatry, 143,* 383–388.

Mackay, A. V. P. (1980). Positive and negative symptoms and the role of dopamine. *British Journal of Psychiatry, 137,* 379–383.

Mackay, A. V. P., et al. (1982). Increased brain dopamine and dopamine receptors in schizophrenia. *Archives of General Psychiatry, 39,* 991–997.

MacPhillamy, D. J., & Lewinsohn, P. M. (1974). Depression as a function of levels of desired and obtained pleasure. *Journal of Abnormal Psychology, 83,* 651–657.

Maddi, S. R., & Kobasa, S. C. (1984). *The hardy executive: Health under stress.* Homewood, IL: Dow Jones-Irwin.

Maeder, T. (1985). *Crime and madness: The origins and evolution of the insanity defense.* New York: Harper & Row.

Maher, W. B., & Maher, B. A. (1985). Psychopathology: I. From ancient times to the eighteenth century. In G. A. Kimble and K. Schlesinger (Eds.), *Topics in the history of psychology* (Vol. 2). Hillsdale, NJ: Erlbaum.

Mahler, M., & Kaplan, L. (1977). Developmental aspects in the assessment of narcissistic and so-called borderline personalities. In P. Hartocollis (Ed.), *Borderline personality disorders: The concept, the syndrome, the patient* (pp. 71–85). New York: International Universities Press.

Mahler, M. S., Pine, F., & Bergman, A. (1975a). The borderline syndrome: The role of the mother in the genesis and psychic structure of the borderline personality. *International Journal of Psychoanalysis, 56,* 163–177.

Maier, S. F., & Seligman, M. E. P. (1976). Learned helplessness: Theory and evidence. *Journal of Experimental Psychology (General), 105,* 3–46.

Mail, P., & McDonald, D. (1980). *Tulapai to Tokay.* New Haven: HRAF Press.

Maj, M., et al. (1991). A family study of DSM-III-R schizoaffective disorder, depressive type, compared with schizophrenia and psychotic and nonpsychotic major depression. *American Journal of Psychiatry, 148,* 612–616.

Maj, M., et al. (1992). Pattern of recurrence of illness after recovery from an episode of major depression: A prospective study. *American Journal of Psychiatry, 149,* 795–800.

Malamuth, N. M. (1984). Aggression against women: Cultural and individual causes. In N. M. Malamuth & E. Donnerstein (Eds.), *Pornography and sexual aggression* (pp. 19–52). Orlando, FL: Academic Press.

Malamuth, N. M., & Check, J. V. P. (1981). The effects of mass media exposure on acceptance of violence against women: A field experiment. *Journal of Research in Personality, 15,* 436–446.

Malamuth, N. M., et al. (1991). Characteristics of aggressors against women: Testing a model using a national sample of college students. *Journal of Consulting and Clinical Psychology, 59,* 670–681.

Malatesta, V. J., Sutker, P. B., & Treiber, F. A. (1981). Sensation seeking and chronic public drunkenness. *Journal of Consulting and Clinical Psychology, 49,* 282–294.

Maletsky, B. M. (1980). Self-referred vs. court-referred sexually deviant patients: Success with assisted covert sensitization. *Behavior Therapy, 11,* 306–314.

Malgady, R. G., Rogler, L. H., & Costantino, G. (1990b). Culturally sensitive psychotherapy for Puerto Rican children and adolescents: A program of treatment outcome research. *Journal of Consulting and Clinical Psychology, 58,* 704–712.

Malloy, P. F., Fairbank, J. A., & Keane, T. M. (1983). Validation of a multimethod assessment of posttraumatic stress disorder in Vietnam veterans. *Journal of Consulting and Clinical Psychology, 51,* 488–494.

Malmo, R. B., & Shagass, C. (1949). Physiological study of symptom mechanism in psychiatric patients under stress. *Psychosomatic Medicine, 11,* 25–29.

Maloney, M. P., & Ward, M. P. (1976). *Psychological assessment: A conceptual approach.* New York: Oxford University Press.

Mann, J., Tarantola, D., & Netter, T. W. (1992). *AIDS in the world 1992.* Cambridge, MA: Harvard University Press.

Mannuzza, S., Gittelman-Klein, R., Bonagura, N., Horowitz-Konig, P. H., & Shenker, R. (1988). Hyperactive boys almost grown up: II. Status of subjects without a mental disorder. *Archives of General Psychiatry, 45,* 13–18.

Mannuzza, S., et al. (1991). Hyperactive boys almost grown up: V. Replication of psychiatric status. *Archives of General Psychiatry, 48,* 77–83.

Marcos, L. R., et al. (1990). Psychiatry takes to

the streets: The New York City initiative for the homeless mentally ill. *American Journal of Psychiatry, 147,* 1557–1561.

Marcus, D. K., & Nardone, M. E. (1992). Depression and interpersonal rejection. *Clinical Psychology Review, 12,* 433–449.

Marcus, J., et al. (1987). Review of the NIMH Israeli Kibbutz-City study and the Jerusalem infant development study. *Schizophrenia Bulletin, 13,* 425–438.

Marder, S. R., & May, P. R. A. (1986). Benefits and limitations of neuroleptics and other forms of treatment in schizophrenia. *American Journal of Psychotherapy, 40,* 357–369.

Marengo, J., & Harrow, M. (1985). Thought disorder: A function of schizophrenia, mania, or psychosis? *Journal of Nervous and Mental Disease, 173,* 35–41.

Marengo, J., & Harrow, M. (1987). Schizophrenic thought disorder at follow-up: A persistent or episodic course? *Archives of General Psychiatry, 44,* 651–659.

Margraf, J., Ehlers, A., & Roth, W. T. (1986). Biological models of panic disorder and agoraphobia: A review. *Behavior Research and Therapy, 24,* 553–567.

Markman, H. J., Floyd, F. J., Stanley, S. M., & Staraasli, R. D. (1988). Prevention of marital distress: A longitudinal investigation. *Journal of Consulting and Clinical Psychology, 56,* 210–217.

Marks, I. M. (1982). Toward an empirical clinical science: Behavioral psychotherapy in the 1980s. *Behavior Therapy, 13,* 63–81.

Marks, I. M. (1985). Behavioral treatment of social phobia. *Psychopharmacology Bulletin, 21,* 615–618.

Marks, I. M. (1987). Behavioral aspects of panic disorder. *American Journal of Psychiatry, 144,* 1160–1165.

Marks, I. M., et al. (1989). The "efficacy" of alprazolam in panic disorder and agoraphobia: A critique of recent reports. *Archives of General Psychiatry, 46,* 668–670.

Marks, J. (1978). *The benzodiazepines: Use, overuse, misuse, abuse.* Baltimore: University Park Press.

Marks, J. (1988). Alzheimer support groups: A framework for survival. In M. K. Aronson (Ed.), *Understanding Alzheimer's disease* (pp. 188–197). New York: Scribner's.

Marks, M. P., et al. (1992). Are anxiety symptoms and catastrophic cognitions directly related? *Journal of Anxiety Disorders, 5,* 247–254.

Marlatt, G. A. (1978). Craving for alcohol, loss of control, and relapse: A cognitive-behavioral analysis. In P. E. Nathan, G. A. Marlatt, & T. Loberg (Eds.), *Alcoholism: New directions in behavioral research and treatment* (pp. 271–314). New York: Plenum.

Marlatt, G. A., Demming, B., & Reid, J. B. (1973). Loss of control drinking in alcoholics: An experimental analogue. *Journal of Abnormal Psychology, 81,* 233–241.

Marlatt, G. A., & Gordon, J. R. (1985). *Relapse prevention: Maintenance strategies in the treatment of addictive behaviors.* New York: The Guilford Press.

Marlatt, G. A., & Rohsenow, D. J. (1981). The think-drink effect. *Psychology Today,* pp. 60–69.

Marriott, M. (1992, November 21). Fervid debate on gambling: Disease or moral weakness? *New York Times,* pp. A1, A22.

Marshall, D. (1971). Sexual behavior on Mangaia. In D. Marshall & R. Suggs (Eds.), *Human sexual behavior: Variations in the ethnographic spectrum.* Englewood Cliffs, NJ: Prentice-Hall.

Marshall, W. L. (1989). Pornography and sex offenders. In D. Zillmann & J. Bryant (Eds.), *Pornography: Research advances and policy considerations* (pp. 185–214). Hillsdale, NJ: Lawrence Erlbaum Associates.

Martelli, M. F., Auerbach, S. M., Alexander, J., & Mercuri, L. G. (1987). Stress management in the health care setting: Matching interventions with patient coping styles. *Journal of Consulting and Clinical Psychology, 55,* 201–207.

Martin, D. (1989, January 25). Autism: Illness that can steal a child's sparkle. *New York Times,* p. B1.

Martin, R. A., & Lefcourt, H. M. (1983). Sense of humor as a moderator of the relation between stressors and moods. *Journal of Personality and Social Psychology, 45,* 1313–1324.

Martin, R. L., et al. (1985). Mortality in a follow-up of 500 psychiatric outpatients: I. Total mortality. *Archives of General Psychiatry, 42,* 47–54.

Martinez, F. D., Cline, M., & Burrows, B. (1992). Increased incidence of asthma in children of smoking mothers. *Pediatrics, 89,* 21–26.

Marttunen, M. J., et al. (1991). Mental disorders in adolescent suicide: DSM-III-R Axes I and II diagnoses in suicides among 13–19-year-olds in Finland. *Archives of General Psychiatry, 48,* 834–839.

Marx, E. M., Williams, J. M. G., & Claridge, G. C. (1992). Depression and social problem solving. *Journal of Abnormal Psychology, 101,* 78–86.

Marziali, E., & Alexander, L. (1991). The power of the therapeutic relationship. *American Journal of Orthopsychiatry, 61,* 383–391.

Marzillier, J. S. (1980). Cognitive therapy and behavioural practice. *Behaviour Research and Therapy, 18,* 249–258.

Masand, P., & Mantosh, D. (1991). Association of fluoxetine with suicidal ideation. *American Journal of Psychiatry, 148,* 1603–1604.

Maslow, A. H. (1963). The need to know and the fear of knowing. *Journal of General Psychology, 68,* 111–124.

Masters, W. H., & Johnson, V. E. (1966). *Human sexual response.* Boston: Little, Brown.

Masters, W. H., & Johnson, V. E. (1970). *Human sexual inadequacy.* Boston: Little, Brown.

Masters, W. H., & Johnson, V. E. (1979). *Homosexuality in perspective.* Boston: Little, Brown.

Matefy, R. (1980). Role-playing theory of psychedelic flashbacks. *Journal of Consulting and Clinical Psychology, 48,* 551–553.

Mathews, A. M. (1990). Why worry? The cognitive function of anxiety. *Behaviour Research and Therapy, 28,* 455–468.

Mattick, R. P., & Peters, L. (1988). Treatment of severe social phobia: Effects of guided exposure with and without cognitive restructuring. *Journal of Consulting and Clinical Psychology, 56,* 251–260.

Maugh, T. H. (1982). Marijuana "justifies serious concern." *Science, 215,* 1488–1489.

Mavissakalian, M. (1987). Initial depression and response to imipramine in agoraphobia. *Journal of Nervous and Mental Disease, 175,* 358–361.

Mavissakalian, M., & Michelson, L. (1986). Two-year follow-up of exposure and imipramine treatment of agoraphobia. *American Journal of Psychiatry, 143,* 1106–1112.

Mavissakalian, M., Michelson, L., Greenwald, D., Kornblith, S., & Greenwald, M. (1983). Cognitive-behavioral treatment of agoraphobia: Paradoxical intention vs. self-statement training. *Behavior Research and Therapy, 21,* 75–86.

Mavissakalian, M., & Perel, J. (1985). Imipramine in the treatment of agoraphobia: Dose-response relationships. *American Journal of Psychiatry, 142,* 1032–1036.

Mavissakalian, M. R., & Perel, J. M. (1989). Imipramine dose-response relationship in panic disorder with agoraphobia. *Archives of General Psychiatry, 46,* 127–131.

May, P. R. (1975). A follow-up study of treatment of schizophrenia. In R. L. Spitzer & D. F. Klein (Eds.), *Evaluation of psychological therapies.* Baltimore: Johns Hopkins University Press.

May, P. R. A., & Goldberg, S. C. (1978). Prediction of schizophrenic patient's response to pharmacotherapy. In M. A. Lipton, A. DiMascio, &

K. F. Killam (Eds.), *Psychopharmacology: A generation of progress* (pp. 1139–1153). New York: Raven Press.

May, P. R. A., & Tuma, A. H. (1976). The Paul H. Hoch Award Lecture: A follow-up study of the results of treatment of schizophrenia. In R. L. Spitzer & D. F. Klein (Eds.), *Evaluation of psychological therapies* (pp. 256–284). Baltimore: Johns Hopkins University Press.

Maypole, D. E., & Anderson, R. B. (1987). Culture-specific substance abuse prevention for blacks. *Community Mental Health Journal, 23,* (2), 135–139.

Mays, V. M. (1985). The Black American and psychotherapy: The dilemma. *Psychotherapy, 22,* 379–388.

McArthur, M. J. (1990). Reality therapy with rape victims. *Archives of Psychiatric Nursing, 4,* 360–365.

McCann, U. D., & Agras, W. S. (1990). Successful treatment of nonpurging bulimia nervosa with desipramine: A double-blind, placebo-controlled study. *American Journal of Psychiatry, 147,* 1509–1513.

McCartney, K., Harris, M. J., & Bernieri, F. (1990). Growing up and growing apart: A developmental meta-analysis of twin studies. *Psychological Bulletin, 107,* 226–237.

McCarty, D., et al. (1991). Alcoholism, drug abuse, and the homeless. *American Psychologist, 46,* 1139–1148.

McCauley, E., Mitchell, J. R., Burke, P., & Moss, S. (1988). Cognitive attributes of depression in children and adolescents. *Journal of Consulting and Clinical Psychology, 56,* 903–908.

McClelland, D. C. (1958). Methods of measuring human motivation. In J. W. Atkinson (Ed.), *Motives in fantasy, action, and society.* Princeton, NJ: Van Nostrand.

McClelland, D. C. (1989). Motivational factors in health and disease. *American Psychologist, 44,* 675–683.

McClelland, D. C., Alexander, C., & Marks, E. (1982). The need for power, stress, immune functions, and illness among male prisoners. *Journal of Abnormal Psychology, 91,* 61–70.

McClelland, D. C., & Kirshnit, C. (1988). The effect of motivational arousal through films on salivary immunoglobulin A. *Psychology and Health, 2,* 31–52.

McConaghy, N. (1990). Sexual deviation. In A. S. Bellack, M. Hersen, & A. E. Kazdin (1990). *International handbook of behavior modification and therapy.* (2nd ed.) (pp. 565–580). New York: Plenum Press.

McConaghy, N., & Blaszczynski, A. (1980). A pair of monozygotic twins discordant for homosexuality: Sex-dimorphic behavior and penile volume responses. *Archives of Sexual Behavior, 9,* 123–124.

McCord, J. (1983). A 40-year prospective on effects of child abuse and neglect. *Child Abuse and Neglect, 7,* 265–270.

McCord, W., & McCord, J. (1964). *The psychopath: An essay on the criminal mind.* New York: Van Nostrand.

McCord, W., McCord, J., & Gudeman, J. (1960). *Origins of alcoholism.* Stanford, CA: Stanford University Press.

McCormick, R. A., Taber, J., Kruedelbach, N., & Russo, A. (1987). Personality profiles of hospitalized pathological gamblers: The California Personality Inventory. *Journal of Clinical Psychology, 43,* 521–527.

McCranie, E. W., & Bass, J. D. (1984). Childhood family antecedents of dependency and self-criticism: Implications for depression. *Journal of Abnormal Psychology, 93,* 3–8.

McCreadie, R. G., Main, C. J., & Dunlap, R. A. (1978). Token economy, pimozide and chronic schizophrenia. *British Journal of Psychiatry, 133,* 179–181.

McCutchan, J. A. (1990). Virology, immunology,

and clinical course of HIV infection. *Journal of Consulting and Clinical Psychology, 58,* 5–12.

McElroy, S. L., et al. (1991). Kleptomania: A report of 20 cases. *American Journal of Psychiatry, 148,* 652–657.

McElroy, S. L., et al. (1992). The DSM-III-R impulse control disorders not elsewhere classified; Clinical characteristics and relationship to other psychiatric disorders. *American Journal of Psychiatry, 149,* 318–325.

McGee, R., & Feehan, M. (1991). Are girls with problems of attention underrecognized? *Journal of Psychopathology and Behavioral Assessment, 13,* 187–198.

McGlashan, T. H., & Fenton, W. S. (1992). The positive-negative distinction in schizophrenia: Review of natural history validators. *Archives of General Psychiatry, 49,* 63–72.

McGovern, F. J., & Nevid, J. S. (1986). Evaluation apprehension on psychological inventions in a prison-based setting. *Journal of Consulting and Clinical Psychology, 54,* 576–578.

McGrath, E., Keita, G. P., Strickland, B. R., & Russo, N. F. (1990). *Women and depression: Risk factors and treatment issues.* Washington DC: American Psychological Association.

McGue, M., & Gottesman, I. I. (1989). A single dominant gene still cannot account for the transmission of schizophrenia. *Archives of General Psychiatry, 46,* 478–479.

McGue, M., Pickens, R. W., & Sivkis, D. S. (1992). Sex and age effects on the inheritance of alcohol problems: A twin study. *Journal of Abnormal Psychology, 101,* 3–17.

McGuffin, P., & Katz, R. (1986). Nature, nurture and affective disorder. In J. W. W. Deakin (Ed.), *The biology of depression* (pp. 26–52). Proceedings of a meeting of the Biological Group of the Royal College of Psychiatrists held at Manchester University, 1985. Washington, DC: American Psychiatric Press.

McKinney, R. E., et al. (1991). A multicenter trial of oral zidovudine in children with advanced human immunodeficiency virus disease. *New England Journal of Medicine, 324,* 1018–1025.

McIntosh, J. L. (1985). Suicide among the elderly: Levels and trends. *American Journal of Orthopsychiatry, 55,* 288–293.

McIntyre-Kingsolver, K., Lichtenstein, E., & Mermelstein, R. J. (1986). Spouse training in a multicomponent smoking-cessation program. *Behavior Therapy, 17,* 67–74.

McKusick, L., et al. (1987, June). Prevention of HIV infection among gay and bisexual men: Two longitudinal studies. Paper presented to the Third International Conference on AIDS, Washington, DC.

McLean, P. D., & Hakstian, A. R. (1990). Relative endurance of unipolar depression treatment effects: Longitudinal follow-up. *Journal of Consulting and Clinical Psychology, 58,* 482–488.

McLeod, J. D., Kessler, R. C., & Landis, K. R. (1992). Speed of recovery from major depressive episodes in a community sample of married men and women. *Journal of Abnormal Psychology, 101,* 277–286.

McLin, W. M. (1992). Introduction to issues in psychology and epilepsy. *American Psychologist, 47,* 1124–1125.

McMullen, S., & Rosen, R. C. (1979). Self-administered masturbation training in the treatment of primary orgasmic dysfunction. *Journal of Consulting and Clinical Psychology, 47,* 912–918.

McNally, R. (1987). Preparedness and phobias: A review. *Psychological Bulletin, 101,* 283–303.

McNally, R. J. (1990). Psychological approaches to panic disorder: A review. *Psychological Bulletin, 108,* 403–419.

McNally, R. J., Cassiday, K. L., & Calamari, J. E. (1990). Taijin-kyofu-sho in a Black American woman: Behavioral treatment of a "culture-bound" anxiety disorder. *Journal of Anxiety Disorders, 4,* 83–87.

McNally, R. J., & Foa, E. B. (1987). Cognition and agoraphobia: Bias in the interpretation of threat. *Cognitive Therapy and Research, 11,* 567–581.

McNally, R. J., Riemann, B. C., & Kim, E. (1990). Selective processing of threat cues in panic disorder. *Behaviour Research and Therapy, 28,* 407–412.

McNeil, D. E., & Binder, R. L. (1987). Predictive validity of judgements of dangerousness in emergency civil commitment. *American Journal of Psychiatry, 144,* 197–200.

McNeil, T. F., & Kaiij, L. (1978). Obstetrical factors in the development of schizophrenia: Complications in the births of preschizophrenics and in reproduction by schizophrenic parents. In L. C. Wynne, R. L. Cromwell, & S. Matthysse (Eds.), *The nature of schizophrenia: New approaches to research and treatment.* New York: Wiley.

Mead, M. (1935). *Sex and temperament in three primitive societies.* New York: Morrow.

Mednick, S. A. (1970). Breakdown in individuals at high risk for schizophrenia: Possible predispositional perinatal factors. *Mental Hygiene, 54,* 50–63.

Mednick, S. A., Gabrielli, W. F., & Hutchings, B. (1984). Genetic influences in criminal convictions: Evidence from an adoption cohort. *Science, 224,* 891–894.

Mednick, S. A., Machon, R. A., & Huttunen, M. O. (1990). An update on the Helsinki influenza project. *Archives of General Psychiatry, 47,* 292.

Mednick, S. A., Moffitt, T. E., & Stack, S. (1987). *The causes of crime: New biological approaches.* New York: Cambridge University Press.

Mednick, S. A., Parnas, J., & Schulsinger, F. (1987). The Copenhagen High-Risk project, 1962–86. *Schizophrenia Bulletin, 13,* 485–495.

Mednick, S. A., & Schulsinger, F. (1965). A longitudinal study of children with a high risk for schizophrenia: A preliminary report. In S. Vandenberg (Ed.), *Methods and goals in human behavior genetics* (pp. 255–296). New York: Academic Press.

Mednick, S. A., & Schulsinger, F. (1968). Some pre-morbid characteristics related to breakdown in children with schizophrenic mothers. In D. Rosenthal & S. S. Kety (Eds.), *The transmission of schizophrenia* (pp. 267–291). New York: Pergamon Press.

Meehan, P. J., et al. (1991). Attempted suicide among young adults: Progress toward a meaningful estimate of prevalence. *American Journal of Psychiatry, 149,* 41–44.

Meehl, P. E. (1962). Schizotaxia, schizotypy, schizophrenia. *American Psychologist, 17,* 827–838.

Meehl, P. E. (1972). A critical afterword. In I. I. Gottesman & J. Shields (Eds.), *Schizophrenia and genetics: A twin study vantage point* (pp. 367–415). New York: Academic Press.

Mehrabian, A., & Weinstein, L. (1985). Temperament characteristics of suicide attempters. *Journal of Consulting and Clinical Psychology, 53,* 544–546.

Meichenbaum, D., & Deffenbacher, J. L. (1988). Stress inoculation training. *The Counseling Psychologist, 16* (1), 69–90.

Meichenbaum, D., & Turk, D. (1976). The cognitive-behavioral management of anxiety, anger, and pain. In P. O. Davidson (Ed.), *The behavioral management of anxiety, depression, and pain.* New York: Brunner/Mazel.

Meisler, A. W., & Carey, M. P. (1990). A critical reevaluation of nocturnal penile tumescence monitoring in the diagnosis of erectile dysfunction. *Journal of Nervous and Mental Disease, 178,* 78–89.

Meissner, W. W. (1980). Psychoanalysis and sexual disorders. In B. J. Wolman & J. Money (Eds.), *Handbook of human sexuality.* Englewood Cliffs, NJ: Prentice-Hall.

Mellor, C. S. (1970). First rank symptoms of schizophrenia. *British Journal of Psychiatry, 177,* 15–23.

Mellor, C. S. (1982). The present status of first rank symptoms. *British Journal of Psychiatry, 140,* 423–424.

Meltzer, H. Y. (1985). Dopamine and negative symptoms in schizophrenia; Critique of the Type I-Type II hypothesis. In M. Alpert (Ed.), *Controversies in schizophrenia: Changes and constancies* (pp. 110–136). New York: Guilford Press.

Meltzer, H. Y. (1987). Biological studies in schizophrenia. *Schizophrenia Bulletin, 13,* 77–111.

Meltzer, H. Y., & Stahl, S. M. (1976). The dopamine hypothesis of schizophrenia: A review. *Schizophrenia Bulletin, 2,* 19–76.

Menaghan, E. G., & Lieberman, M. A. (1986). Changes in depression following divorce: A panel study. *Journal of Marriage and the Family, 17,* 319–328.

Mendelson, J. H., Miller, K. D., Mello, N. K., Pratt, H., & Schmitz, R. (1982). Hospital treatment of alcoholism: A profile of middle income Americans. *Alcoholism: Clinical and Experimental Research, 6,* 377–383.

Mendez, M., et al. (1992). Disturbances of person identification in Alzheimer's disease: A retrospective study. *Journal of Nervous and Mental Disease, 180,* 94–96.

Mendlewicz, J., & Rainer, J. D. (1977). Adoption study supporting genetic transmission in manic depressive illness. *Nature, 268,* 326–329.

Merckelbach, H., Arntz, A., & de Jong, P. (1991). Conditioning experiences in spider phobics. *Behaviour Research and Therapy, 29,* 301–304.

Messenger, J. (1971). Sex and repression in an Irish folk community. In D. Marshall & R. Suggs (Eds.), *Human sexual behavior: Variations in the ethnographic spectrum.* Englewood Cliffs, NJ: Prentice-Hall.

Metcalfe, M., & Goldman, E. (1965). Validation of an inventory for measuring depression. *British Journal of Psychiatry, 111,* 240–242.

Meyer, J. K., & Reter, D. J. (1979). Sex reassignment: Follow-up. *Archives of General Psychiatry, 36,* 1010–1015.

Michael, C. C., & Funabiki, D. (1985). Depression, distortion and life stress: Extended findings. *Cognitive Therapy and Research, 9,* 659–666.

Michelson, L. K., & Marchione, K. (1991). Behavioral, cognitive, and pharmacological treatments of panic disorder with agoraphobia: Critique and synthesis. *Journal of Consulting and Clinical Psychology, 59,* 100–114.

Michelson, L., et al. (1990). Panic disorder: Cognitive-behavioral treatment. *Behaviour Research and Therapy, 28,* 141–151.

Mider, P. A. (1984). Failures in alcoholism and drug dependence prevention and learning from the past. *American Psychologist, 39,* 183.

Miklowitz, D. J., et al. (1991). Communication deviance in families of schizophrenic and manic patients. *Journal of Abnormal Psychology, 100,* 163–173.

Milich, R., Wolraich, M., & Lindgren, S. (1986). Sugar and hyperactivity: A critical review of empirical findings. *Clinical Psychology Review, 6,* 493–513.

Miller, B. J. (1978). *The complete medical guide.* (4th ed.). New York: Simon & Schuster.

Miller, E. (1987). Hysteria: Its nature and explanation. *British Journal of Clinical Psychology, 26,* 163–173.

Miller, I. W., Klee, S. H., & Norman, W. H. (1982). Depressed and nondepressed inpatients' cognitions of hypothetical events, experimental tasks, and stressful life events. *Journal of Abnormal Psychology, 91,* 78–81.

Miller, I. W., & Norman, W. H. (1986). Persistence of depressive cognitions within a sub-group of depressed patients. *Cognitive Therapy and Research, 10,* 211–224.

Miller, R. E. (1987). Method to study anhedonia

in hospitalized psychiatric patients. *Journal of Abnormal Psychology, 96,* 41–45.

Miller, S., Saccuzzo, D., & Braff, D. (1979). Information processing deficits in remitted schizophrenics. *Journal of Abnormal Psychology, 88,* 446–449.

Miller, S. D., et al. (1991). Optical differences in multiple personality disorder: A second look. *Journal of Nervous and Mental Disease, 179,* 132–135.

Miller, T. Q., et al. (1991). Reasons for the trend toward null findings in research on Type A behavior. *Psychological Bulletin, 110,* 469–485.

Miller, W. R. (1982). Treating problem drinkers: What works? *The Behavior Therapist, 5,* 15–18.

Miller, W. R., & Hester, R. K. (1986). Inpatient alcoholism treatment: Who benefits? *American Psychologist, 41,* 794–805.

Miller, W. R., & Muñoz, R. F. (1983). *How to control your drinking* (2nd ed.). Albuquerque: University of New Mexico Press.

Miller-Perrin, C. L., & Wurtele, S. K. (1988). The child sexual abuse prevention movement: A critical analysis of primary and secondary approaches. *Clinical Psychology Review, 8,* 313–329.

Millon, T. (1981). *Disorders of personality DSM-III: Axis II.* New York: Wiley.

Millon, T. (1982). *Millon Clinical Multiaxial Inventory manual* (3rd ed.). Minneapolis: National Computer Systems.

Mineka, S. (1991, August). Paper presented to the annual meeting of the American Psychological Association, San Francisco. (Cited in Turkington, C. [1991]. Evolutionary memories may have phobia role. *APA Monitor, 22* [11], 14.)

Minuchin, S. (1974). *Families and family therapy.* Cambridge, MA: Harvard University Press.

Minuchin, S., Rosman, B. L., & Baker, L. (1978). *Psychosomatic families: Anorexia nervosa in context.* Cambridge, MA: Harvard University Press.

Miranda, J., Persons, J. B., & Nix-Byers, C. (1990). Endorsement of dysfunctional beliefs depends on current mood state. *Journal of Abnormal Psychology, 99,* 237–241.

Mirsky, A. F., & Orzack, M. H. (1980). Two retrospective studies of psychosurgery. In E. S. Valenstein (Ed.), *The psychosurgery debate.* San Francisco: Freeman.

Mirsky, I. A. (1958). Physiologic, psychologic and social determinants in the etiology of duodenal ulcer. *American Journal of Digestive Diseases, 3,* 285–315.

Mischel, W. (1979). On the interface of cognition and personality: Beyond the person-situation debate. *American Psychologist, 34,* 740–754.

Mischel, W. (1986). *Introduction to personality* (4th ed.). New York: Holt, Rinehart and Winston.

Mitchell, J. E., & Eckert, E. D. (1987). Scope and significance of eating disorders. *Journal of Consulting and Clinical Psychology, 55,* 628–634.

Mittelmark, M. B., et al. (1986). Community-wide prevention of cardiovascular disease: Education strategies of the Minnesota Heart Health Program. *Preventive Medicine, 15,* 1–17.

Mittelmark, M. B., et al. (1987). Predicting experimentation with cigarettes: The Childhood Antecedents of Smoking Study. *American Journal of Public Health, 77,* 206–208.

Mizes, J. S., Landolf-Fritsche, B., & Grossman-McKee, D. (1987). Patterns of distorted cognitions in phobic disorders: An investigation of clinically severe simple phobics, social phobics, and agoraphobics. *Cognitive Therapy & Research, 11,* 583–592.

M'Naughton, 10 Cl & F, 200, 8 Eng. Rep. 718 (H & L) 1843.

Mohr, D. C., & Beutler, L. E. (1990). Erectile dysfunction: A review of diagnostic and treatment procedures. *Clinical Psychology Review, 10,* 123–150.

Mohs, R. C., Breitner, J. C., Silverman, J. M., & Davis, K. L. (1987). Alzheimer's disease: Morbid risk among first-degree relatives approximates 50% by 90 years of age. *Archives of General Psychiatry, 44,* 405–408.

Mokuau, N. (1990). The impoverishment of native Hawaiians and the social work challenge. *Health and Social Work, 15,* 235–242.

Moller, H. J., Zerssen, D., von, Werner-Eilert, K., & Wuschner-Stockheim, M. (1982). Outcome in schizophrenic and similar paranoid psychoses. *Schizophrenia Bulletin, 8,* 99–108.

Monahan, J. (1981). *A clinical prediction of violent behavior:* (DHHS Publication, ADM 81–921). Rockville, MD: National Institute of Mental Health.

Monahan, J., Novaco, R., & Geis, G. (1979). Corporate violence: Research strategies for community psychology. In T. Sarbin (Ed.), *Challenges to the criminal justice system.* New York: Human Sciences.

Monahan, J., & Steadman, H. J. (1983). Crime and mental disorder: An epidemiological approach. In A. Morris & M. Tomroy (Eds.), *Crime and justice: An annual review of research.* Chicago: University of Chicago Press.

Moncher, M. S., Holden, G. W., & Trimble, J. E. (1990). Substance abuse among Native-American youth. *Journal of Consulting and Clinical Psychology, 58,* 408–415.

Money, J. (1987). Sin, sickness, or status? Homosexual gender identity and psychoneuroendocrinology. *American Psychologist, 42,* 384–399.

Money, J., & Lamacz, M. (1990). *Vandalized lovemaps.* Buffalo, NY: Prometheus.

Monroe, S. M. (1982). Life events and disorder: Event-symptom associations and the course of disorder. *Journal of Abnormal Psychology, 91,* 14–24.

Monroe, S. M. (1983). Major and minor life events as predictors of psychological distress: Further issues and findings. *Journal of Behavioral Medicine, 6,* 189–205.

Monroe, S. M., Bromet, E. J., Connell, M. M., & Stener, S. C. (1986). Social support, life events, and depressive symptoms: A 1-year prospective study. *Journal of Consulting and Clinical Psychology, 54,* 423–431.

Monroe, S. M., Kupfer, D. J., & Frank, E. (1992). Life stress and treatment course of recurrent depression: 1. Response during index episode. *Journal of Consulting and Clinical Psychology, 60,* 718–724.

Montague, A. (1968). Chromosomes and crime. *Psychology Today,* pp. 43–49.

Monti, P. M., et al. (1987). Reactivity of alcoholics and nonalcoholics to drinking cues. *Journal of Abnormal Psychology, 96,* 122–126.

Moon, J. R., & Eisler, R. M. (1983). Anger control: An experimental comparison of three behavioral treatments. *Behavior Therapy, 14,* 493–505.

Moore, R. D., et al. (1991). Zidovudine and the natural history of the acquired immunodeficiency syndrome. *New England Journal of Medicine, 324,* 1412–1416.

More hardcore. (1992, November 19). *Newsday,* p. 73.

Morey, L. C. (1988). Personality disorders in DSM-III and DSM-III-R: Convergence, coverage, and internal consistency. *American Journal of Psychiatry, 145,* 573–577.

Morihisa, J. M., Duffy, F. H., & Wyatt, R. J. (1983). Brain electrical activity mapping (BEAM) in schizophrenic patients. *Archives of General Psychiatry, 40,* 719–728.

Morin, C. M., & Azrin, N. H. (1988). Behavioral and cognitive treatments of geriatric insomnia. *Journal of Consulting and Clinical Psychology, 56,* 748–753.

Morokoff, P. J., & Heiman, J. R. (1980). Effects of erotic stimuli on sexually functional and dysfunctional women: Multiple measures before and after sex therapy. *Behaviour Research and Therapy, 18,* 127–137.

Morris, R. D. (1988). Classification of learning disabilities: Old problems and new approaches. *Journal of Consulting and Clinical Psychology, 56,* 789–794.

Morrison, J. (1989). Childhood sexual histories of women with somatization disorder. *American Journal of Psychiatry, 146,* 239–241.

Morrison, R. L., & Bellack, A. S. (1984). Social skills training. In A. S. Bellack (Ed.), *Schizophrenia: Treatment, management and rehabilitation* (pp. 247–279). Orlando, FL: Grune & Stratton.

Morrison, R. L., & Bellack, A. S. (1987). Social functioning of schizophrenic patients: Clinical and research issues. *Schizophrenia Bulletin, 13,* 715–725.

Mortimer, A. M., et al. (1990). The positive-negative dichotomy in schizophrenia. *British Journal of Psychiatry, 157,* 41–49.

Moscarello, R. (1990). Psychological management of victims of sexual assault. *Canadian Journal of Psychiatry, 35,* 25–30.

Mosher, L. R., & Keith, S. J. (1980). Psychosocial treatment: Individual, group, family, and community support approaches. *Schizophrenia Bulletin, 6,* 10–41.

Moss, F., et al. (1985). Sobriety and American Indian problem drinkers. *Alcoholism Treatment Quarterly, 2,* 81–96.

Moss, M., Frank, E., & Anderson, B. (1990). The effects of marital status and partner support on rape trauma. *American Journal of Orthopsychiatry, 60,* 379–391.

Mossman, D., & Perlin, M. L. (1992). Psychiatry and the homeless mentally ill: A reply to Dr. Lamb. *American Journal of Psychiatry, 149,* 951–957.

Muehlenhard, C. L., & Falcon, P. L. (1990). Men's heterosocial skill and attitudes toward women as predictors of verbal sexual coercion and forceful rape. *Sex Roles, 23,* 241–259.

Mullen, B. & Suls, J. (1982). The effectiveness of attention and rejection as coping styles: A meta-analysis of temporal differences. *Journal of Psychosomatic Research, 26,* 43–49.

Murray, H. A. (1943). *Thematic Apperception Test: Pictures and manual.* Cambridge, MA: Harvard University Press.

Murray, J. B. (1989a). Alcoholism: Etiologies proposed and therapeutic approaches tried. *Genetic, Social, and General Psychology Monographs, 115,* 81–121.

Murray, J. B. (1989b). Geophysical variables and behavior: VLII. Seasonal affective disorder and phototherapy. *Psychological Reports, 64,* 787–801.

Murray, J. B. (1992). Kleptomania: A review of the research. *Journal of Psychology, 126,* 131–138.

Murray, R. M., & Reveley, A. M. (1986). Genetic aspects of schizophrenia: Overview. In A. Kerr and P. Snaith (Eds.), *Contemporary issues in schizophrenia* (pp. 261–267). Avon, England: Bath Press.

Murray, R. M., et al. (1983). Current genetic and biological approaches to alcoholism. *Psychiatric Developments, 2,* 179–192.

Naber, D., & Hippius, H. (1990). The European experience with use of clozapine. *Hospital and Community Psychiatry, 41,* 886–890.

Nadi, N. S., Nurnberger, J. I., & Gershon, E. S. (1984). Muscarinic cholinergic receptors on skin fibroblasts in familiar affective disorder. *New England Journal of Medicine, 311,* 225–230.

Nadler, L. B. (1985). The epidemiology of pathological gambling: Critique of existing research and alternative strategies. *Journal of Gambling Behavior, 1,* 35–50.

Nathan, P. E. (1988). The addictive personality is the behavior of the addict. *Journal of Consulting and Clinical Psychology, 56,* 183–188.

Nathan, P. E., & Skinstad, A. H. (1987). Outcomes

of treatment for alcohol problems: Current methods, problems, and results. *Journal of Consulting and Clinical Psychology, 55,* 332–340.

National Cancer Institute (1991, August 22). Cited in *New York Times,* Lung cancer is said to overtake heart trouble as smokers' peril, p. B10.

National Center for Health Statistics. (1967). *Suicide in the United States, 1950-1964.* Washington, DC: U. S. Department of Health, Education, and Welfare.

National Council on Alcoholism. (1986). *Facts on alcoholism.* New York: Author.

National Institute of Mental Health. (1985). *Electroconvulsive therapy: Consensus development conference statement.* Bethesda, MD: Office of Medical Applications of Research.

National Institute of Mental Health. (1987). *Differential diagnosis of dementing diseases.* NIH Consensus Development Conference Statement, Vol. 6, No. 11. Bethesda, MD: Author.

Ndetei, D. M., & Singh, A. (1983). Hallucinations in Kenyan schizophrenic patients. *Acta Psychiatrica Scandinavica, 67,* 144–147.

Ndetei, D. M., & Vadher, A. (1984). A comparative cross-cultural study of the frequencies of hallucination in schizophrenia. *Acta Psychiatrica Scandinavica, 70,* 545–549.

Neal, A. M., & Turner, S. M. (1991). Anxiety disorders research with African Americans: Current status. *Psychological Bulletin, 109,* 400–410.

Needles, D. J., & Abramson, L. Y. (1990). *Journal of Abnormal Psychology, 99,* 156–165.

Neiger, B. L. (1988). Adolescent suicide: Character traits of high-risk teenagers. *Adolescence, 23,* 469–475.

Neighbors, H. (1992, December). The help seeking behavior of black Americans: A summary of the National Survey of Black Americans. Paper presented at a symposium, *Anxiety Disorders in African Americans,* presented by the State University of New York Health Science Center at Brooklyn, NY.

Nelson, J. C., Mazure, C. M., & Jatlow, P. I. (1990). Value of the DST for predicting response of patients with major depression to hospitalization and desipramine. *American Journal of Psychiatry, 147,* 1488–1492.

Nemiah, J. C. (1978). Psychoneurotic disorders. In A. M. Nicholi (Ed.), *Harvard guide to modern psychiatry.* Cambridge, MA: Harvard University Press.

Neugebauer, R. (1979). Medieval and early modern theories of mental illness. *Archives of General Psychiatry, 36,* 477–484.

Neuringer, C. (1982). Affect configurations and changes in women who threaten suicide following a crisis. *Journal of Consulting and Clinical Psychology, 50,* 182–186.

Nevid, J. S., Capurso, R., & Morrison, J. K. (1980). Patient's adjustment to family-care as related to their perceptions of real-ideal differences in treatment environments. *American Journal of Community Psychology, 8,* 117–120.

Nevid, J. S., & Javier, R. A. (1992, June). *"SI, PUEDO" smoking cessation program for Hispanic smokers.* Paper presented at the forum on Minority Health Issues for an Emerging Majority, National Institutes of Health, Washington, D.C.

Nevid, J. S., Lavi, B., & Primavera, L. H. (1986). Cluster analysis of training orientations in clinical psychology. *Professional Psychology: Research and Practice, 17,* 367–370.

Nevid, J. S., Lavi, B., & Primavera, L. H. (1987). Principal components analysis of therapeutic orientations of doctoral programs in clinical psychology. *Journal of Clinical Psychology, 43,* 723–729.

Newlin, D. B. (1989). The skin-flushing response: Autonomic, self-report, and conditioned response to repeated administrations of alcohol in Asian men. *Journal of Abnormal Psychology, 98,* 421–425.

Newlin, D. B., & Thomson, J. B. (1990). Alcohol challenge with sons of alcoholics: A critical review and analysis. *Psychological Bulletin, 108,* 383–402.

Newman, J. P., Patterson, C. M., & Kosson, D. S. (1987). Response perseveration in psychopaths. *Journal of Abnormal Psychology, 96,* 145–148.

Newmark, C. S., Frerking, R. A., Cook, L., & Newmark, L. (1973). Endorsement of Ellis's irrational beliefs as a function of psychopathology. *Journal of Clinical Psychology, 29,* 300–302.

Nezu, A. M., & Carnevale, G. J. (1987). Interpersonal problem solving and coping reactions of Vietnam veterans with posttraumatic stress disorder. *Journal of Abnormal Psychology, 96,* 155–157.

Nezu, A. M., & Ronan, G. F. (1985). Life stress, current problems, problem solving, and depressive symptoms: An integrative model. *Journal of Consulting and Clinical Psychology, 53,* 693–697.

Niaura, R. S., et al. (1988). Relevance of cue reactivity to understanding alcohol and smoking relapse. *Journal of Abnormal Psychology, 97,* 133–152.

Nicholson, R. A., & Berman, J. S. (1983). Is follow-up necessary in evaluating psychotherapy? *Psychological Bulletin, 93,* 261–278.

Niederehe, G. (1986). Depression and memory impairment in the aged. In L. W. Poon (Ed.), *Handbook for clinical memory assessment of older adults* (pp. 226–237). Washington, DC: American Psychological Association.

Nielsen, J. (1968). The XYY syndrome in a mental hospital. *British Journal of Criminology, 8,* 186–203.

Nigg, J. T., et al. (1992). Malevolent object representations in borderline personality disorder and major depression. *Journal of Abnormal Psychology, 101,* 61–67.

Nolen-Hoeksema, S. (1991). Responses to depression and their effects on the duration of depressive episodes. *Journal of Abnormal Psychology, 100,* 569–582.

Nolen-Hoeksema, S., Girgus, J. S., & Seligman, M. E. P. (1992). Predictors and consequences of childhood depressive symptoms: A 5-year longitudinal study. *Journal of Abnormal Psychology, 101,* 405–422.

Nolen-Hoeksema, S., Morrow, J., & Fredrickson, B. L. (1992). *The effects of response styles on the duration of depressed mood: A field study.* Manuscript submitted for publication.

Norris, F. H. (1992). Epidemiology of trauma: Frequency and impact of different potentially traumatic events on different demographic groups. *Journal of Consulting and Clinical Psychology, 60,* 409–418.

Norris, J., & Feldman-Summers, S. (1981). Factors related to the psychological impacts of rape on the victim. *Journal of Abnormal Psychology, 90,* 562–567.

Norton, G. R., Harrison, B., Hauch, J., & Rhodes, L. (1985). Characteristics of people with infrequent panic attacks. *Journal of Abnormal Psychology, 94,* 216–221.

Norton, G. R., & Rhodes, L. (1983). *Characteristics of people with infrequent panic attacks: A preliminary analysis.* Unpublished manuscript, University of Winnipeg.

NOVA. (1989, March 28). *Confronting the killer gene.* Boston: WGBH Educational Foundation.

Novaco, R. (1974). *A treatment program for the management of anger through cognitive and relaxation control.* Unpublished doctoral dissertation, Indiana University.

Novaco, R. (1977b). A stress inoculation approach to anger management in the training of law enforcement officers. *American Journal of Community Psychology, 5,* 327–346.

Novello, A. C. (1991). Women and HIV infection. *Journal of the American Medical Association, 265,* 1805.

Noyes, R., et al. (1986). Relationship between panic disorder and agorphobia: A family study. *Archives of General Psychiatry, 43,* 227–232.

Noyes, R., et al. (1991). Controlled discontinuation of benzodiazepine treatment for patients with panic disorders. *American Journal of Psychiatry, 148,* 517–523.

Nussbaum, M., et al. (1985). Follow-up investigation of patients with anorexia nervosa. *Journal of Pediatrics, 106,* 835–840.

O'Connor, A., & Daly, J. (1985). Alcoholics: A twenty year follow-up study. *British Journal of Psychiatry, 146,* 645–647.

O'Connor, G. T., et al. (1989). An overview of randomized trials of rehabilitation with exercise after myocardial infarction. *Circulation, 80,* 234–244.

O'Connor, R. D. (1969). Modification of social withdrawal through symbolic modeling. *Journal of Applied Behavior Analysis, 2,* 15–22.

O'Connor v. Donaldson, 95 S. Ct. 2486 (1975).

Oetting, E. R., & Beauvais, F. (1990). Adolescent drug use: Findings of national and local surveys. *Journal of Consulting and Clinical Psychology, 58,* 385–394.

Office of Technology Assessment, U.S. Congress (1987, April). *Losing a million minds: Confronting the tragedy of Alzheimer's disease* (OTA-BA-323). Washington, DC: U.S. Government Printing Office.

O'Hara, M. W., Zekoski, E. M., Philipps, L. H., & Wright, E. J. (1990). Controlled prospective study of post partum mood disorders: comparison of child bearing & non-child bearing women. *Journal of Abnormal Psychology, 99,* 3–15.

O'Hara, M. W., et al. (1991). Prospective study of postpartum blues: Biological and psychosocial factors. *Archives of General Psychiatry, 48,* 801–806.

Ohman, A., Fredrikson, M., Hugdahl, K., & Rimmo, P. (1976). The premise of equipotentiality in human classical conditioning: Conditioned electrodermal responses to potentially phobic stimuli. *Journal of Experimental Psychology: General, 105,* 313–337.

O'Leary, A. (1990). Stress, emotion, and human immune functions. *Psychological Bulletin, 108,* 383–382.

O'Leary, K. D., Pelham, W. E., Rosenbaum, A., & Price, G. H. (1976). Behavioral treatment of hyperkinetic children: An experimental evolution of its usefulness. *Clinical Pediatrics, 15,* 510–515.

Oldham, J. M., et al. (1992). Diagnosis of DSM-III-R personality disorders by two structured interviews: Patterns of comorbidity. *American Journal of Psychiatry, 149,* 213–220.

Olinger, J. L., Kuiper, N. A., & Shaw, B. F. (1987). Dysfunctional attitudes and stressful life events: An interactive model of depression. *Cognitive Therapy and Research, 11,* 25–40.

Ollendick, T. H., et al. (1992). Sociometric status and academic, behavioral, and psychological adjustment: A five-year longitudinal study. *Journal of Consulting and Clinical Psychology, 60,* 80–87.

Olmsted, M. P., & Garner, D. M. (1986). The significance of self-induced vomiting as a weight-control method among non-clinical samples. *International Journal of Eating Disorders, 5,* 683–700.

Oltmanns, T. F., Murphy, R., Berenbaum, H., & Dunlop, S. R. (1985). Rating verbal communication impairment in schizophrenia and affective disorders. *Schizophrenia Bulletin, 11,* 292–299.

Ordman, A. M., & Kirschenbaum, D. S. (1985). Cognitive-behavioral therapy for bulimia: An initial outcome study. *Journal of Consulting and Clinical Psychology, 53,* 305–313.

Ordman, A. M., & Kirschenbaum, D. S. (1986). Bulimia: Assessment of eating, psychological adjustment, and familial characteristics. *International Journal of Eating Disorders, 5,* 865–876.

Ornitz, E. M. (1974). The modulation of sensory input and motor output in autistic children. *Journal of Autism and Childhood Schizophrenia, 4,* 197–215.

Öst, L. (1987). Age of onset in different phobias. *Journal of Abnormal Psychology, 96,* 223–229.

Öst, L. (1992). Blood and injection phobia: Background and cognitive, physiological, and behavioral variables. *Journal of Abnormal Psychology, 101,* 68–74.

Öst, L., Salkovskis, P. M., & Hellström, K. (1991). One-session therapist-directed exposure vs. self-exposure in the treatment of spider phobia. *Behavior Therapy, 22,* 289–304.

Overholser, J. C., & Beck, S. (1986). Multimethod assessment of rapists, child molesters, and three control groups on behavioral and psychological measures. *Journal of Consulting and Clinical Psychology, 54,* 682–687.

Overmier, J. B. L., & Seligman, M. E. P. (1967). Effect of inescapable shock upon subsequent escape and avoidance learning. *Journal of Comparative and Physiological Psychology, 63,* 28–33.

Padgett, V. R., Brislin-Slütz, J. A., & Neal, J. A. (1989). Pornography, erotica, and attitudes toward women: The effects of repeated exposure. *Journal of Sex Research, 26,* 479–491.

Paffenbarger, R. S., Jr., et al. (1984). A natural history of athleticism and cardiovascular health. *Journal of the American Medical Association, 252,* 491–495.

Paffenbarger, R. S., Jr., et al. (1986). Physical activity, all-cause mortality, and longevity of college alumni. *New England Journal of Medicine, 314,* 605–613.

Pagel, M., & Becker, J. (1987). Depressive thinking and depression: Relations with personality and social resources. *Journal of Personality and Social Psychology, 52,* 1043–1052.

Palinkas, L. A., et al. (1992). Ethnic differences in stress, coping, and depressive symptoms after the Exxon *Valdez* oil spill. *Journal of Nervous and Mental Disease, 180,* 287–295.

Pandurangi, A. K., Bilder, R. M., Rieder, R. O., Mukherjee, S., & Hamer, R. M. (1988). Schizophrenic symptoms and deterioration: Relation to computed tomographic findings. *Journal of Nervous and Mental Disease, 176,* 200–206.

Pardes, H. (1986). Neuroscience and psychiatry: Marriage or coexistence? *American Journal of Psychology, 143,* 1205–1212.

Park, J. Y., et al. (1984). The flushing response to alcohol use among Koreans and Taiwanese. *Journal of Studies on Alcohol, 45,* 481–485.

Parker, K. C. H., Hanson, R. K., & Hinsley, J. (1988). MMPI, Rorschach, and WAIS: A meta-analytic comparison of reliability, stability, and validity. *Psychological Bulletin, 103,* 367–373.

Parnas, D. J., Schulsinger, F., Schulsinger, H., Teasdale, T. W., & Mednick, S. A. (1982a). Behavioral precursors of the schizophrenia spectrum: A prospective study. *Archives of General Psychiatry, 39,* 658–664.

Parnas, D. J., et al. (1982b). Perinatal complications and clinical outcome within the schizophrenia spectrum. *British Journal of Psychiatry, 140,* 416–420.

Pasewark, R. A. (1981). Insanity plea: A review of the research literature. *Journal of Psychiatry and Law, 9,* 357–401.

Pasewark, R. A., & Pantle, M. L. (1979). Insanity plea: Legislators' view. *American Journal of Psychiatry, 136,* 222–223.

Pato, M. T., et al. (1991). Controlled comparison of buspirone and clomipramine in obsessive-compulsive disorder. *American Journal of Psychiatry, 148,* 127–129.

Paul, G. L. (1969). Outcome of systematic desensitization II: Controlled investigations of individual treatment, technique variations, and current status. In C. M. Franks (Ed.), *Behavior therapy: Appraisal and status.* New York: McGraw-Hill.

Paul, G. L., & Lentz, R. J. (1977). *Psychosocial treatment of chronic mental patients: Milieu versus social-learning programs.* Cambridge, MA: Harvard University Press.

Paul, G. L., Tobias, L. T., & Holly, B. L. (1972). Maintenance psychotropic drugs in the presence of active treatment programs. A triple blind withdrawal study with long-term mental patients. *Archives of General Psychiatry, 27,* 106–115.

Pauli, P., et al. (1991). Anxiety induced by cardiac perceptions in patients with panic attacks: A field study. *Behaviour Research and Therapy, 29,* 137–145.

Pauly, I. B. (1974). Female transsexualism: Part 1. *Archives of Sexual Behavior, 3,* 487–508.

Pauly, I. B. (1981). Outcome of sex reassignment surgery for transsexuals. *Australian and New Zealand Journal of Psychiatry, 15,* 45–51.

Pauly, I. B., & Edgerton, M. (1986). The gender-identity movement. *Archives of Sexual Behavior, 15,* 315–329.

Pavlov, I. (1927). *Conditioned reflexes.* London: Oxford University Press.

Paykel, E. S. (1979). Predictors of treatment response. In E. S. Paykel & A. Coppen (Eds.), *Psychopharmacology of affective disorders.* Oxford, England: Oxford University Press.

Paykel, E. S. (1982). Life events and early environments. In E. S. Paykel (Ed.), *Handbook of affective disorders.* New York: Guilford Press.

Paykel, E. S., & Hale, A. S. (1986). Recent advances in the treatment of depression. In J. W. W. Deakin (Ed.), *The biology of depression* (pp. 153–173). Proceedings of a meeting of the Biological Group of the Royal College of Psychiatrists held at Manchester University, 1985. Washington, DC: American Psychiatric Press.

Peck, C. P. (1986). A public mental health issue: Risk-taking behavior and compulsive gambling. *American Psychologist, 41,* 461–465.

Peck v. Counseling Service of Addison County, 499 A.2d 422, Vermont Supreme Court Docket 83–062 (June 14, 1985).

Pedersen, N. L., Plomin, R., McClearn, G. E., & Friberg, L. (1988). Neuroticism, extraversion, and related traits in adult twins reared apart and reared together. *Journal of Personality and Social Psychology, 55,* 950–957.

Pelham, W. E., et al. (1985). Behavioral and stimulant treatment of hyperactive children: A therapy study with methylphenidate probes in a within-subjects design. *Journal of Applied Behavior Analysis, 13,* 221–236.

Pelham, W. E., Jr., & Murphy, H. A. (1986). Attention deficit and conduct disorders. In M. Hersen (Ed.), *Pharmacological and behavioral treatment: An integrative approach.* New York: Wiley.

Pell, S., & Fayerweather, W. E. (1985). Trends in the incidence of myocardial infarction and in associated mortality and morbidity in a large employed population, 1957–1983. *New England Journal of Medicine, 312,* 1005–1011.

Pendery, M. L., Maltzman, I. M., & West, L. J. (1982). Controlled drinking by alcoholics? New findings and a re-evaluation of a major affirmative study. *Science, 217,* 169–174.

Pennebaker, J. W., Kiecolt-Glaser, J. K., & Glaser, R. (1988). Disclosure of traumas and immune function: Health implications for psychother-

apy. *Journal of Consulting and Clinical Psychology, 56,* 239–245.

Penner, L. A., Thompson, J. K., & Coovert, D. L. (1991). Size overestimation among anorexics: Much ado about very little? *Journal of Abnormal Psychology, 100,* 90–93.

Pennington, B. F., & Smith, S. D. (1988). Genetic influences on learning disabilities: An update. *Journal of Consulting and Clinical Psychology, 56,* 817–823.

Peplau, L. A., & Cochran, S. D. (1990). A relationship perspective on homosexuality. In D. P. McWhirter, S. A. Sanders, & J. M. Reinisch (Eds.), *Homosexuality/heterosexuality: Concepts of sexual orientation* (pp. 321–349). New York: Oxford University Press.

Perez, F. I., Stump, D. A., Gay, J. R. A., & Hart, V. R. (1976). Intellectual performance in multi-infarct dementia and Alzheimer's disease: A replication study. *Canadian Journal of Neurological Sciences, 3,* 181–187.

Perez, F. I., et al. (1975b). Analysis of intellectual and cognitive performance in patients with multi-infarct dementia, vertebrobasilar insufficiency with dementia, and Alzheimer's disease. *Journal of Neurology, Neurosurgery, and Psychiatry, 38,* 533–540.

Perez-Stable, E. (1991, May). *Health promotion among Latinos: What are the priorities?* Chancellor's Distinguished Lecture, University of California, Irvine.

Perkins, D. (1982). The assessment of stress using life events scales. In L. Goldberger & S. Brenitz (Eds.), *Handbook of stress: Theoretical and clinical aspects.* New York: Free Press.

Perlman, J. D., & Abramson, P. R. (1982). Sexual satisfaction among married and cohabitating individuals. *Journal of Consulting and Clinical Psychology, 50,* 458–460.

Perls, F. S. (1971). *Gestalt therapy verbatim.* New York: Bantam.

Perry, C. L., Klepp, K., & Shultz, J. M. (1988). Primary prevention of cardiovascular disease: Community-wide strategies for youth. *Journal of Consulting and Clinical Psychology, 56,* 358–364.

Perry, C. L., et al. (1987). Promoting healthy eating and physical activity patterns among adolescents: Slice of life. *Health Education Research: Theory and Practice, 2,* 93–104.

Perry, P. J., et al. (1991). Clozapine and norclozapine plasma concentrations and clinical response of treatment-refractory schizophrenic patients. *American Journal of Psychiatry, 148,* 231–235.

Persad, E. (1990). Electroconvulsive therapy in depression. *Canadian Journal of Psychiatry, 35,* 175–182.

Petersen, S. E., et al. (1988). Positron emission tomographic studies of the cortical anatomy of single-word processing. *Nature, 331,* 585–589.

Peterson, C., Schwartz, S. M., & Seligman, M. E. P. (1981). Self-blame and depressive symptoms. *Journal of Personality and Social Psychology, 41,* 253–259.

Peterson, C., Villanova, P., & Raps, C. S. (1985). Depression and attributions: Factors responsible for inconsistent results in the published literature. *Journal of Abnormal Psychology, 94,* 165–168.

Pettiti, D. B., & Friedman, G. D. (1985). Cardiovascular and other diseases in smokers of low-yield cigarettes. *Journal of Chronic Diseases, 38,* 582–588.

Pfohl, B. (1991). Histrionic personality disorder: A review of available data and recommendations for DSM-IV. *Journal of Personality Disorders, 5,* 150–166.

Phifer, J. F., & Murrell, S. A. (1986). Etiologic factors in the onset of depressive symptoms in older adults. *Journal of Abnormal Psychology, 93,* 282–291.

Phillips, D. P., & Carstensen, L. S. (1986). Clustering of teenage suicide after television news stories about suicide. *New England Journal of Medicine, 315,* 685–689.

Phillips, E. L., Phillips, E. A., Fixsen, D. L., & Wolf, M. M. (1971). Achievement place: Modifications of the behaviors of pre-delinquent boys within a token economy. *Journal of Applied Behavior Analysis, 4,* 45–59.

Philipps, L. H., & O'Hara, M. W. (1991). Prospective study of postpartum depression: 4 1/2-year follow-up of women and children. *Journal of Abnormal Psychology, 100,* 151–155.

Phillips, M. R., Wolf, A. S., & Coons, D. J. (1988). Psychiatry and the criminal justice system: Testing and myths. *American Journal of Psychiatry, 145,* 605–610.

Pickar, D., et al. (1992). Clinical and biological response to clozapine in patients with schizophrenia: Crossover comparison with fluphenazine. *Archives of General Psychiatry, 49,* 345–353.

Pickens, R. W., et al. (1991). Heterogeneity in the inheritance of alcoholism: A study of male and female twins. *Archives of General Psychiatry, 48,* 19–28.

Pigott, T. A., et al. (1990). Controlled comparisons of clomipramine and fluoxetine in the treatment of obsessive-compulsive disorder: Behavioral and biological results. *Archives of General Psychiatry, 47,* 926–932.

Pihl, R. O., Peterson, J., & Finn, P. (1990). Inherited predisposition to alcoholism: Characteristics of sons of male alcoholics. *Journal of Abnormal Psychology, 99,* 291–301.

Pike, K. M., & Rodin, J. (1991). Mothers, daughters, and disordered eating. *Journal of Abnormal Psychology, 101,* 198–204.

Pillard, R. C. (1990). The Kinsey Scale: Is it familial? In D. P. McWhirter, S. A. Sanders, & J. M. Reinisch (Eds.), *Homosexuality/heterosexuality: Concepts of sexual orientation* (pp. 88–100). New York: Oxford University Press.

Pillard, R. C., & Weinrich, J. D. (1986). Evidence of familial nature of male homosexuality. *Archives of Sexual Behavior, 43,* 808–812.

Pinderhughes, E. (1989). *Understanding race, ethnicity and power: The key to efficacy in clinical practice.* New York: Free Press.

Piran, N., Kennedy, S., Garfinkel, P. E., & Owens, M. (1985). Affective disturbance in eating disorders. *Journal of Nervous and Mental Disease, 173,* 395–400.

Pliszka, S. R. (1991). Antidepressants in the treatment of child and adolescent psychopathology. *Journal of Clinical Child Psychology, 3,* 313–320.

Plomin, R. (1989). Environment and genes: Determinants of behavior. *American Psychologist, 44,* 105–111.

Polcin, D. L. (1992). Issues in the treatment of dual diagnosis clients who have chronic mental illness. *Professional Psychology: Research and Practice, 23,* 30–37.

Polivy, J., & Herman, C. P. (1987). Diagnosis and treatment of normal eating. *Journal of Consulting and Clinical Psychology, 55,* 635–644.

Pomerleau, O. F., et al. (1986). Task Force 4: Nicotine and smoking relapse. National Working Conference on Smoking Relapse. *Health Psychology, 5 (Suppl.),* 41–51.

Pope, H. G., Hudson, J. I., Jonas, J. M., & Yurgelun-Todd, M. S. (1983). Bulimia treatment with imipramine: A placebo-controlled, double-blind study. *American Journal of Psychiatry, 140,* 554–558.

Pope, H. G., Jr., Jones, J. M., Hudson, J., Cohen, B. M., & Gunderson, J. G. (1983). The validity of DSM-III borderline personality disorder. *Archives of General Psychiatry, 40,* 23–30.

Pope, H. G., et al. (1984). Prevalence of anorexia nervosa and bulimia in three student populations. *International Journal of Eating Disorders, 3,* 45–51.

Popham, R. E., Schmidt, W., & Israelstam, S. (1984). Heavy alcohol consumption and physical health problems: A review of the epidemiologic evidence. In R. G. Smart et al. (Eds.), *Research advances in alcohol and drug problems* (Vol. 8). New York: Plenum.

Popper, K. (1985). Cited in Goleman (1985).

Powell, L. H., Friedman, M., Thoresen, C. E., Gill, J. J., & Ulmer, D. K. (1984). Can the Type A behavior pattern be altered after myocardial infarction? A second-year report from the Recurrent Coronary Prevention Project. *Psychosomatic Medicine, 46,* 293–313.

Prentky, R. A., & Knight, R. A. (1991). Identifying critical dimensions for discriminating among rapists. *Journal of Consulting and Clinical Psychology, 59,* 643–661.

Press, A., et al. (1985, March 18). The war against pornography. *Newsweek,* pp. 58–66.

Pressman, M. R. (1986). Sleep and sleep disorders: An introduction. *Clinical Psychology Review, 6,* 1–9.

Prichard, J. C. (1835). *Treatise on insanity.* London: Gilbert & Piper.

Prigatano, G. P. (1992). Personality disturbances associated with traumatic brain injury. *Journal of Consulting and Clinical Psychology, 60,* 360–368.

Prince, M. (1906). *The dissociation of a personality: A biographical study in abnormal psychology.* New York: Longmans, Green.

Prince, R., & Tcheng-Laroche, F. (1987). Culture-bound syndromes and international disease classification. *Culture, Medicine, and Psychiatry, 11,* 3–19.

Prior, M. R. (1984). Developing concepts of childhood autism: The influence of experimental cognitive research. *Journal of Consulting and Clinical Psychology, 52,* 4–16.

Pumariega, A. J. (1986). Acculturation and eating attitudes in adolescent girls: A comparative correlational study. *Journal of the American Academy of Child Psychiatry, 25,* 276–279.

Putnam, F. W., Guroff, J. J., Silberman, E. K., Barban, L., & Post, R. M. (1986). The clinical phenomenology of multiple personality disorder: Review of 100 recent cases. *Journal of Clinical Psychiatry, 47,* 285–293.

Pyle, R. L., Halvorson, P. A., & Goff, G. M. (1986). The increasing prevalence of bulimia in freshman college students. *International Journal of Eating Disorders, 5,* 631–647.

Pyszczynski, T., & Greenberg, G. (1985). Depression and preference for self-focusing stimuli after success and failure. *Journal of Personality and Social Psychology, 49,* 1066–1075.

Pyszczynski, T., & Greenberg, G. (1986). Evidence for a depressive self-focusing style. *Journal of Research in Personality, 20,* 95–106.

Pyszczynski, T., & Greenberg, J. (1987). Self-regulatory perseveration and the depressive self-focusing style: A self-awareness theory of reactive depression. *Psychological Bulletin, 102,* 122–138.

Quay, H. C. (1965). Psychopathic personality as pathological stimulation seeking. *American Journal of Psychiatry, 122,* 180–183.

Quinn, S. (1987). *A mind of her own: The life of Karen Horney.* New York: Summit.

Rabkin, J. G. (1980). Stressful life events and schizophrenia: A review of the literature. *Psychological Bulletin, 87,* 408–425.

Rabkin, J. G., & Zitrin, A. (1982). Antisocial behavior of discharged mental patients: Research findings and policy implications. In B. L. Bloom and S. J. Asher (Eds.), *Psychiatric patient's rights and patient advocacy.* New York: Human Sciences Press.

Rabkin, J. G., et al. (1991). Depression, distress, lymphocyte subsets, and human immunodeficiency virus symptoms on two occasions in HIV-positive homosexual men. *Archives of General Psychiatry, 48,* 111–119.

Rachman, S., & Bichard, S. (1988). The overprediction of fear. *Clinical Psychology Review, 8,* 303–312.

Rachman, S., & Levitt, K. (1985). Panics and their consequences. *Behaviour Research and Therapy, 23,* 600.

Rachman, S., Levitt, K., & Lopatka, C. (1988). Experimental analyses of panic: III. Claustrophobic subjects. *Behaviour Research and Therapy, 26,* 41–52.

Rachman, S., & Lopatka, C. (1986). Match and mismatch in the prediction of fear: I. *Behaviour Research and Therapy, 24,* 387–393.

Rachman, S., Lopatka, C., & Levitt, K. (1988). II. Experimental analyses of panic: Panic patients. *Behaviour Research and Therapy, 26,* 33–40.

Rachman, S. J., & Hodgson, R. J. (1974). Synchrony and desynchrony in fear and avoidance. *Behaviour Research and Therapy, 12,* 311–318.

Rachman, S. J., & Hodgson, R. J. (1980). *Obsessions and compulsions.* Englewood Cliffs, NJ: Prentice-Hall.

Rajfer, J., et al. (1992). Nitric oxide as a mediator of relaxation of the corpus cavernosum in response to nonadrenergic, noncholinergic neurotransmission. *New England Journal of Medicine, 326,* 90–94.

Rajput, A. H., Offord, K. P., Beard, C. M., & Kurland, L. T. (1984). Epidemiology of Parkisonism: Incidence, classification, and mortality. *Annals of Neurology, 16,* 278–282.

Ramirez, L. F., McCormick, R. A., Russo, A. M., & Taber, J. I. (1983). Patterns of substance abuse in pathological gamblers undergoing treatment. *Addictive Behaviors, 8,* 425–428.

Rao, S. M., Huber, S. J., & Bornstein, R. A. (1992). Emotional changes with multiple sclerosis and Parkinson's disease. *Journal of Consulting and Clinical Psychology, 60,* 369–378.

Rapee, R. M. (1985). Distinction between panic disorder and generalized anxiety disorder: Clinical presentation. *Australian and New Zealand Journal of Psychiatry, 19,* 227–232.

Rapee, R. M. (1987). The psychological treatment of panic attacks: Theoretical conceptualization and review of evidence. *Clinical Psychology Review, 7,* 427–438.

Rapee, R. M. (1990). Psychological mechanisms underlying the response to biological challenge procedures in panic disorder. In N. McNaughton & G. Andrews (Eds.), *Anxiety* (pp. 75–81). Dunedin, New Zealand: University of Otago Press.

Rapee, R. M. (1991). Generalized anxiety disorder: A review of clinical features and theoretical concepts. *Clinical Psychology Review, 11,* 419–440.

Rapee, R. M., Litwin, E. M., & Barlow, D. H. (1990). Impact of life events on subjects with panic disorder and on comparison subjects. *American Journal of Psychiatry, 147,* 640–644.

Rapee, R. M., et al. (1992). Response to hyperventilation and inhalation of 5.5% carbon dioxide-enriched air across the DSM-III-R anxiety disorders. *Journal of Abnormal Psychology, 101,* 538–552.

Rapp, S. R., Parisi, S. A., & Walsh, D. A. (1988). Psychological dysfunction and physical health among elderly medical inpatients. *Journal of Consulting and Clinical Psychology, 56,* 851–855.

Raps, C. S., Peterson, C., Reinhard, K. E., Abramson, L. Y., & Seligman, M. E. P. (1982). Attributional style among depressed patients. *Journal of Abnormal Psychology, 91,* 102–108.

Rasmussen, T., & Milner, B. (1975). Clinical and surgical studies of the cerebral speech areas in man. In K. J. Zulch, O. Creutzfeldt, & G. C.

Galbraith (Eds.), *Cerebral localization.* Berlin: Springer-Verlag.

Rathus, S. A. (1978). Treatment of recalcitrant ejaculatory incompetence. *Behavior Therapy, 9,* 962.

Rathus, S. A. (1993). *Psychology* (5th ed.). Fort Worth TX: Harcourt Brace Jovanovich.

Rathus, S. A., & Fichner-Rathus, L. (1994). *Making the most of college* (2nd ed.). Englewood Cliffs, NJ: Prentice Hall.

Rathus, S. A., & Nevid, J. S. (1977). *Behavior therapy.* Garden City, NY: Doubleday.

Rathus, S. A., Nevid, J. S., & Fichner-Rathus, L. (1993). *Human sexuality in a world of diversity.* Boston: Allyn & Bacon.

Rathus, S. A., Senna, J., & Siegel, L. (1974). Delinquent behavior and academic investment among suburban youth. *Adolescence, 9,* 481–494.

Ravussin, E., et al. (1988). Reduced rate of energy expenditure as a risk factor for body-weight gain. *New England Journal of Medicine, 318,* 467–472.

Raz, N., & Raz, S. (1990). Structural brain abnormalities in the major psychoses: A quantitative review of the evidence from computerized imaging. *Psychological Bulletin, 108,* 93–108.

Razin, A. M., Swencionis, C., & Zohman, L. R. (1986). Reduction of physiological, behavioral, and self-report responses in Type A behavior: A preliminary report. *International Journal of Psychiatry in Medicine, 16,* 31–47.

Redd, W. H., et al. (1987). Cognitive/attentional distraction in the control of conditioned nausea in pediatric cancer patients receiving chemotherapy. *Journal of Consulting and Clinical Psychology, 55,* 391–395.

Reich, J. (1987). Prevalence of DSM-III-R self-defeating (masochistic) personality disorder in normal and outpatient populations. *Journal of Nervous and Mental Diseases, 175,* 52–54.

Reich, J., & Noyes, R. (1986). Letters to the editor: Differentiating schizoid and avoidant personality disorders. *American Journal of Psychiatry, 143,* 1061–1063.

Reich, J., & Yates, W. (1988). A pilot study of treatment of social phobia with alprazolam. *American Journal of Psychiatry, 145,* 590–594.

Reid, W. H., & Balis, G. U. (1987). Evaluation of the violent patient. In R. E. Hales and A. J. Frances (Eds.), *American Psychiatric Association Annual Review* (Vol. 6,). Washington, DC: American Psychiatric Press.

Reid, W. J. (1986). Antisocial personality. In R. Michels and J. O. Cavenar, Jr. (Eds.), *Psychiatry* (Vol. 1,). New York: Basic.

Reinisch, J. M. (1990). *The Kinsey Institute new report on sex: What you must know to be sexually literate.* New York: St. Martin's Press.

Reisberg, B., et al. (1986). Assessment of presenting symptoms. In L. W. Poon (Ed.), *Handbook for clinical memory assessment of older adults* (pp. 108–128). Washington, DC: American Psychological Association.

Reisberg, B., Ferris, S. H., DeLeon, M. J., & Crook, T. (1982). The Global Deterioration Scale for Assessment of Primary Degenerative Dementia. *American Journal of Psychiatry, 139,* 1136–1139.

Reiss, B. F. (1980). Psychological tests in homosexuality. In J. Marmor (Ed.), *Homosexual behavior* (pp. 296–311). New York: Basic.

Reiss, S. (1987). Theoretical perspectives on the fear of anxiety. *Clinical Psychology Review, 7,* 585–596.

Reiss, S., Peterson, R. A., Gursky, D. M., & McNally, R. J. (1986). Anxiety sensitivity, anxiety frequency and the predictions of fearfulness. *Behaviour Research and Therapy, 24,* 1–8.

Rennie v. Klein, 720 F. 2d. 266 (1983).

Resick, P. A., & Schnicke, M. K. (1990). Treating symptoms in adult victims of sexual assault. *Journal of Interpersonal Violence, 5,* 488–506.

Resnick, M., et al. (1992, March 24). *Journal of the American Medical Association.* Cited in Young Indians prone to suicide, study finds. *New York Times,* March 25, 1992, p. D24.

Review Panel. (1981). Coronary-prone behavior and coronary heart disease: A critical review. *Circulation, 63,* 1199–1215.

Rey, J. M., Stuart, G. W., Platt, J. M., Bashir, M. R., & Richards, I. M. (1988). DSM-III Axis IV revisited. *American Journal of Psychiatry, 145,* 286–292.

Rhodewalt, F., & Agustsdottir, S. (1984). On the relationship of hardiness to the Type A behavior pattern: Perception of life events versus coping with life events. *Journal of Research in Personality, 18,* 212–223.

Rice, M. E., Harris, G. T., & Quinsey, V. L. (1990). A follow-up of rapists assessed in a maximum-security psychiatric facility. *Journal of Interpersonal Violence, 5,* 435–448.

Rice, M. E., Quinsey, V. L., & Harris, G. T. (1991). Sexual recidivism among child molesters released from a maximum security psychiatric institution. *Journal of Consulting and Clinical Psychology, 59,* 381–386.

Rich, C. L., Fowler, R. C., Fogarty, L. A., & Young, D. (1988). San Diego Suicide Study: III. Relationships between diagnoses and stressors. *Archives of General Psychiatry, 45,* 589–592.

Rich, C. L., Ricketts, J. E., Thaler, R. C., & Young, D. (1988). Some differences between men and women who commit suicide. *American Journal of Psychiatry, 145,* 718–722.

Ridley, C. R. (1984). Clinical treatment of the nondisclosing black client: A therapeutic paradox. *American Psychologist, 39,* 1234–1244.

Riese, W. (1954). Auto-observation of aphasia: Reported by an eminent 19th century medical scientist. *Bulletin of the History of Medicine, 28,* 237–242.

Riether, A. M., & Stoudemire, A. (1988). Psychogenic fugue states: A review. *Southern Medical Journal, 81,* 568–571.

Riley, V. (1981). Psychoneuroendocrine influences on immunocompetence and neoplasia. *Science, 212,* 1100–1109.

Rimland, B. (1977). Comparative effects of treatment on child's behavior (drugs, therapies, schooling and several non-treatment events). *Institute for Child Behavior Research,* Publication 34.

Rimland, B. (1978). The savant capabilities of autistic children and their cognitive implications. In G. Serban (Ed.), *Cognitive defects in the development of mental illness.* New York: Brunner/Mazel.

Ritvo, E. R. (1976). Autism: From adjective to noun. In E. R. Ritvo (Ed.), *Autism: Diagnosis, current research and management* (pp. 3–6). New York: Spectrum Publications.

Ritvo, E. R., et al. (1989a). The UCLA-University of Utah epidemiologic survey of autism: Prevalence. *American Journal of Psychiatry, 146,* 194–199.

Ritvo, E. R., et al. (1989b). The UCLA-University of Utah epidemiologic survey of autism: Recurrence risk estimates and genetic counseling. *American Journal of Psychiatry, 146,* 1032–1036.

Ritvo, E. R., & Ritvo, R. (1992). The UCLA-University of Utah epidemiologic survey of autism: The etiologic role of rare diseases: Reply. *American Journal of Psychiatry, 149,* 146–147.

Robey, A. (1978). Guilty but mentally ill. *Bulletin of the American Academy of Psychiatry and the Law, 6,* 376.

Robins, L. N., Helzer, J. E., Croughan, J., & Ratcliff, K. S. (1981). National Institute of Mental Health: Diagnostic Interview Schedule. *Archives of General Psychiatry, 41,* 949–958.

Robins, L. N., et al. (1984). Lifetime prevalence of specific psychiatric disorders in three sites. *Archives of General Psychiatry, 41,* 949–958.

Robins, L. N., Locke, B. Z., & Reiger, D. A. (1991). An overview of psychiatric disorders in America. In L. N. Robins & D. A. Regier (Eds.), *Psychiatric disorders in America: The Epidemiologic Catchment Area Study* (pp. 328–366). New York: The Free Press.

Robins, L. N., & Regier, D. A. (1991). *Psychiatric disorders in America: The epidemiological catchment area.* New York: The Free Press.

Robins, L. N., Tipp, J., & Przybeck, T. (1991). Antisocial personality. In L. N. Robins & D. A. Regier (eds.), *Psychiatric disorders in America: The Epidemiologic Catchment Area Study* (pp. 258–290). New York: The Free Press.

Robinson, L. A., Berman, J. S., & Neimeyer, R. A. (1990). Psychotherapy for the treatment of depression: A comprehensive review of controlled outcome research. *Psychological Bulletin, 108,* 30–49.

Rodin, J., Bartoshuk, L., Peterson, C., & Schank, D. (1990). Bulimia and taste: Possible interactions. *Journal of Abnormal Psychology, 99,* 32–39.

Rodin, J., & Slochower, J. (1976). Externality in the nonobese: The effects of environmental responsiveness on weight. *Journal of Personality and Social Psychology, 33,* 338–344.

Roehl, J. E., & Gray, D. (1984). The crisis of rape: A guide to counseling victims of rape. *Crisis Intervention, 13,* 67–77.

Rogan, A. (1986, Fall). Recovery from alcoholism: Issues for black and Native American alcoholics. *Alcohol Health and Research World, 10,* 42–44.

Rogers, C. R. (1951). *Client-centered therapy.* Boston: Houghton Mifflin.

Rogers, J. L., Bloom, J. D., Manson, S. I., et al. (1983). Oregon's insanity defense system: A review of the first five years, 1978–1983. *Bulletin of the American Academy of Psychiatry and Law, 12,* 383–402.

Rogers, R., et al. (1990). The clinical presentation of command hallucinations in a forensic population. *American Journal of Psychiatry, 147,* 1304–1307.

Rogler, L. H., Cortes, D. E., & Malgady, R. G. (1991). Acculturation and mental health status among Hispanics: Convergence and new directions for research. *American Psychologist, 46,* 584–597.

Rohan, W. P. (1982). The concept of alcoholism: Assumptions and issues. In E. M. Pattison & E. Kaufman (Eds.), *Encyclopedic handbook of alcoholism* (pp. 31–39). New York: Gardner Press.

Rohde, P., Lewinsohn, P. M., & Seeley, J. R. (1991). Comorbidity of unipolar depression: II. Comorbidity with other mental disorders in adolescents and adults. *Journal of Abnormal Psychology, 101,* 214–222.

Rohsenow, D. J. (1983). Drinking habits and expectancies about alcohol's effects for self versus others. *Journal of Consulting and Clinical Psychology, 51,* 752–756.

Romanczyk, R. G., et al. (1975). Increasing isolate and social play in severely disturbed children: Intervention and postintervention effectiveness. *Journal of Autism and Childhood Schizophrenia, 5,* 730–739.

Rook, K. S., & Dooley, D. (1985). Applying social support research: Theoretical problems and future directions. *Journal of Social Issues, 41,* 5–28.

Room, R. (1984). Alcohol and ethnography: A case of problem deflation? *Current Anthropology, 25* (2), 169–191.

Rosebush, P. (1986). Double-blind, placebo controlled studies of bulimic patients. *American Journal of Psychiatry, 144,* 1197–1198.

Rosen, J. C., Gross, J., & Vara, L. (1987). Psychological adjustment of adolescents attempting to lose or gain weight. *Journal of Consulting and Clinical Psychology, 55,* 742–747.

Rosen, J. C., & Leitenberg, H. (1982). Bulimia nervosa: Treatment with exposure and response prevention. *Behavior Therapy, 13,* 117–124.

Rosen, L. A., et al. (1988). Effects of sugar (sucrose) on children's behavior. *Journal of Consulting and Clinical Psychology, 56,* 583–589.

Rosen, W. G., et al. (1984). Positive and negative symptoms in schizophrenia. *Psychiatry Research, 13,* 277–284.

Rosenman, R. H., Brand, R. J., Jenkins, C. D., Friedman, M., Straus, R., & Wurm, M. (1975). Coronary heart disease in the Western Collaborative Group Study: Final follow up experience of 8 1/2 years. *Journal of the American Medical Association, 233,* 872–877.

Rosenstein, M. J., Milazzo-Sayre, L. J., & Manderscheid, R. W. (1989). Care of persons with schizophrenia: A statistical profile. *Schizophrenia Bulletin, 15,* 45–58.

Rosenthal, D. (1970). *Genetic theory and abnormal behavior.* New York: McGraw-Hill.

Rosenthal, D., et al. (1968). Schizophrenics' offspring reared in adoptive homes. In D. Rosenthal & S. S. Kety (Eds.), *The transmission of schizophrenia.* Oxford, England: Pergamon Press.

Rosenthal, D., et al. (1975). Parent–child relationships and psychopathological disorder in the child. *Archives of General Psychiatry, 32,* 466–476.

Rosenthal, E. (1991, July 10). Technique for early prenatal test comes under question in studies. *New York Times,* p. C11.

Rosenthal, N. E., et al. (1984). Seasonal affective disorder: A description of the syndrome and preliminary findings with light therapy. *Archives of General Psychiatry, 41,* 72–80.

Rosenthal, N. E., et al. (1985). Seasonal affective disorder and phototherapy. *New York Academy of Sciences Annals, 453,* 260–269.

Roskies, E., et al. (1979). Generalizability and durability of treatment effects in an intervention program for coronary-prone (Type A) managers. *Journal of Behavioral Medicine, 2,* 195–207.

Roskies, E., et al. (1986). The Montreal Type A intervention project: Major findings. *Health Psychology, 5,* 45–69.

Rosman, B. L., Minuchin, S., & Liebman, R. (1976). Input and outcome of family therapy of anorexia nervosa. In J. L. Claghorn (Ed.), *Successful psychotherapy.* New York: Brunner/Mazel.

Ross, C. A., Norton, G. R., & Wozney, K. (1989). Multiple personality disorder: An analysis of 236 cases. *Canadian Journal of Psychiatry, 34,* 413–418.

Ross, C. A., et al. (1990). Structured interview data on 102 cases of multiple personality disorder from four centers. *American Journal of Psychiatry, 147,* 596–601.

Ross, C. A., et al. (1991). The frequency of multiple personality disorder among psychiatric inpatients. *American Journal of Psychiatry, 148,* 1717–1720.

Rossi, P. H. (1990). The old homeless and the new homelessness in historical perspective. *American Psychologist, 45,* 954–959.

Roth, L., & Meisel, A. (1977). Dangerousness, confidentiality, and the duty to warn. *American Journal of Psychiatry, 134,* 508–511.

Rothblum, E. (1983). Sex role stereotypes and depression in women. In V. Franks & E. Rothblum (Eds.), *The stereotyping of women: Its effects on mental health* (pp. 83–111). New York: Springer.

Rotheram-Borus, M. J., Trautman, P. D., Dopkins, S. C., & Shrout, P. E. (1990). Cognitive style and pleasant activities among female adolescent suicide attempters. *Journal of Consulting and Clinical Psychology, 58,* 554–561.

Rotter, J. B. (1972). Beliefs, social attitudes, and behavior: A social learning analysis. In J. B. Rotter, J. E. Chance, & E. J. Phares (Eds.), *Applications of a social learning theory of personality.* New York: Holt, Rinehart and Winston.

Roueche, B. (1980). *The medical detectives.* New York: Truman Talley.

Rounsaville, B. J., et al. (1987). The relation between specific and general dimensions of the psychotherapy process in interpersonal psychotherapy of depression. *Journal of Consulting and Clinical Psychology, 55,* 379–384.

Rousseau, F., et al. (1991). Direct diagnosis by DNA analysis of the fragile X syndrome of mental retardation. *New England Journal of Medicine, 325,* 1673–1681.

Roy, A., et al. (1991). Suicide in twins. *Archives of General Psychiatry, 48,* 29–32.

Roy-Byrne, P. P., Geraci, M., & Uhde, T. W. (1986). Life events and the onset of panic disorder. *American Journal of Psychiatry, 143,* 1424–1427.

Rozin, P., & Fallon, A. (1988). Body image, attitudes to weight, and misperceptions of figure preferences of the opposite sex: A comparison of men and women in two generations. *Journal of Abnormal Psychology, 97,* 342–345.

Rubio-Stipec, M., et al. (1989). Symptom scales of the diagnostic interview schedule: Factor results in Hispanic and Anglo samples. *Psychological Assessment: A Journal of Consulting and Clinical Psychology, 1,* 30–34.

Rubonis, A. V., & Bickman, L. (1991). Psychological impairment in the wake of disaster: The disaster-psychopathology relationship. *Psychological Bulletin, 109,* 384–399.

Ruderman, A. J., Belzer, L. J., & Halperin, A. (1985). Restraint, anticipated consumption, and overeating. *Journal of Abnormal Psychology, 94,* 547–555.

Ruderman, A. J., & Besbeas, M. (1992). Psychological characteristics of dieters and bulimics. *Journal of Abnormal Psychology, 101,* 383–390.

Ruiz, R. A. (1981). Cultural and historical perspectives in counseling Hispanics. In D. W. Sue (Ed.), *Counseling the culturally different: Theory and practice* (pp. 186–215). New York: Wiley.

Rush, A. J., & Weissenberger, J. (1986). Do thinking patterns predict depressive symptoms? *Cognitive Therapy and Research, 10,* 225–236.

Russo, N. F. (1990). Overview: Forging research priorities for women's mental health. *American Psychologist, 45,* 368–373.

Rutter, M. (1983). Cognitive deficits in the pathogenesis of autism. *Journal of Child Psychology & Psychiatry, 24,* 513–531.

Rutter, M., & Garmezy, N. (1983). Developmental psychopathology. In P. H. Mussen (Ed.), *Handbook of child psychology: Vol. 4, Socialization, Personality, and Social Development* (pp. 776–911). New York: John Wiley and Sons.

Rutter, M., Tizard, J., & Whitmore, K. (Eds.) (1981). *Education, health, and behavior.* Huntington, NY: Krieger.

Ryan, N. D., et al. (1987). The clinical picture of major depression in children and adolescents. *Archives of General Psychiatry, 44,* 854–861.

Sachdev, P., Hay, P. H., & Cumming, S. (1992). Psychosurgical treatment of obsessive-compulsive disorder. *Archives of General Psychiatry, 49,* 582–583.

Sackheim, H. A., Prudic, J., & Devanand, D. P. (1990). Treatment of medication-resistant depression with electroconvulsive therapy. In A. Tasman et al., (Eds., *Review of psychiatry,* Vol. 9. Washington, DC: American Psychiatric Press.

Sacks, O. (1985). *The man who mistook his wife for a hat and other clinical tales.* New York: Summit.

Sacks, O. (1985, February 20). The twins. *New York Review of Books,* pp. 16–20.

Sadker, M., & Sadker, D. (1985). Sexism in the schoolroom of the 1980s. *Psychology Today,* pp. 54–57.

Sagarin, E. (1977). Incest: Problems of definition and frequency. *Journal of Sex Research, 13,* 126–135.

Sajjad, S. H. A. (1991). Classification of koro. *American Journal of Psychiatry, 148,* 1279.

Sakheim, D. K. (1987). Distinguishing between organogenic and psychogenic erectile dysfunction. *Behaviour Research and Therapy 25,* 379–390.

Sales, E., Baum, M., & Shore, B. (1984). Victim readjustment following assault. *Journal of Social Issues, 40,* 117–136.

Salgado de Snyder, V. N. (1987). Factors associated with acculturative stress and depressive symptomatology among married Mexican immigrant women. *Psychology of Women Quarterly, 11,* 475–488.

Salgado de Snyder, V. N., Cervantes, R. C., & Padilla, A. M. (1990). Gender and ethnic differences in psychosocial stress and generalized distress among Hispanics. *Sex Roles, 22,* 441–453.

Salkovskis, P. M., Clark, D. M., & Hackmann, A. (1991). Treatment of panic attacks using cognitive therapy without exposure or breathing retraining. *Behaviour Research and Therapy, 29,* 161–166.

Salkovskis, P. M., & Warwick, H. M. (1986). Morbid preoccupations, health anxiety, and reassurance: A cognitive-behavioral approach to hypochondriasis. *Behaviour Research and Therapy, 24,* 597–602.

Salkovskis, P. M., Warwick, H. M. C., Clark, D. M., & Wessels, D. J. (1986). A demonstration of acute hyperventilation during naturally occurring panic attacks. *Behaviour Research and Therapy, 24,* 91–94.

Salzman, C., & Gutfreund, M. J. (1986). Clinical techniques and research strategies for studying depression and memory. In L. W. Poon (Ed.), *Handbook for clinical memory assessment of older adults* (pp. 257–267). Washington, DC: American Psychological Association.

Sameroff, A., Seifer, R., Zax, M., & Barocas, R. (1987). Early indicators of developmental risk: Rochester Longitudinal Study. *Schizophrenia Bulletin, 13,* 383–394.

Sanchez, E. G., & Mohl, P. C. (1992). Psychotherapy with Mexican-American patients. *American Journal of Psychiatry, 149,* 626–630.

Sanchez-Craig, M., Annis, H. M., Bornet, A. R., & MacDonald, K. R. (1984). Random assignment to abstinence or controlled drinking: Evaluation of a cognitive-behavioral program for problem drinkers. *Journal of Consulting and Clinical Psychology, 52,* 390–403.

Sanchez-Craig, M., & Wilkinson, D. A. (1986/1987) Treating problem drinkers who are not severely dependent on alcohol. *Drugs and Society, 1,* 39–67.

Sanders, J. (1974, September). *An autistic child in residential treatment.* Paper presented at American Psychological Association meeting, New Orleans.

Sanders, S. A., Reinisch, J. M., & McWhirter, D. P. (1990). Homosexuality/heterosexuality: An overview. In D. P. McWhirter, S. A. Sanders, & J. M. Reinisch (Eds.), *Homosexuality/heterosexuality: Concepts of sexual orientation* (pp. xix–xxvii). New York: Oxford University Press.

Sanderson, W. C., & Barlow, D. H. (1990). A description of patients diagnosed with DSM-III-R generalized anxiety disorder *Journal of Nervous & Mental Disease, 178,* 588–591.

Santiago, J. M., McCall-Perez, F., Gorcery, M., &

Beigel, A. (1985). Long-term psychological effects of rape in 35 rape victims. *American Journal of Psychiatry, 142,* 1338–1340.

Sass, L. (1982, August 22). The borderline personality. *New York Times Magazine,* pp. 12–15, 66–67.

Sateia, M. J. (1987). Behavioral modification in the treatment of smoking. *Psychiatric Medicine, 5,* 375–387.

Satel, S. L., Southwick, S., M., & Gawin, F. H. (1991). Clinical features of cocaine-induced paranoia. *American Journal of Psychiatry, 148,* 495–498.

Satir, V. (1967). *Conjoint family therapy* (rev. ed.). Palo Alto, CA: Science and Behavior.

Sattler, J. M. (1988). *Assessment of children.* San Diego: Jerome M. Sattler.

Sauter, A. W., & Nevid, J. S. (1991). Work skills training with chronic schizophrenic sheltered workers. *Rehabilitation Psychology, 36,* 255–264.

Saypol, D. C., Peterson, G. A., Howards, S. S., & Yanzel, J. J. (1983). Impotence: Are the newer diagnostic methods a necessity? *Journal of Urology, 130,* 260–262.

Scarr, S. (1981). Testing *for* children: Assessment and the many determinants of intellectual competence. *American Psychologist, 36,* 1159–1166.

Schachter, S., & Latané, B. (1964). Crime, cognition, and the autonomic nervous system. In D. Levine (Ed.), *Nebraska symposium on motivation* (Vol. 12, pp. 221–273). Lincoln: University of Nebraska Press.

Schaefer, C. E. (1979). *Childhood encopresis and enuresis.* New York: Van Nostrand.

Schaeffer, J., Andrysiak, T., & Ungerleider, J. T. (1981). Cognition and long-term use of ganja (cannabis). *Science, 213,* 465–466.

Schafer, D. W. (1986). Recognizing multiple personality patients. *American Journal of Psychotherapy, 40,* 500–510.

Schafer, J., & Brown, S. (1991). Marijuana and cocaine effect expectancies and drug use patterns. *Journal of Consulting and Clinical Psychology, 59,* 558–565.

Schechter, M., et al. (1984, June 9). Changes in sexual behavior and fear of AIDS. *Lancet,* p. 1293.

Scheff, T. J. (1966). *Being mentally ill: A sociological theory.* Chicago: Aldine.

Scheier, M. F., & Carver, C. S. (1985). Optimism, coping, and health: Assessment and implications of generalized outcome expectancies. *Health Psychology, 4,* 219–247.

Scheier, M. F., et al. (1989). Dispositional optimism and recovery from coronary artery bypass surgery: The beneficial effects on physical and psychological well-being. *Journal of Personality and Social Psychology, 57,* 1024–1040.

Schepis, M. R., Reid, D. H., & Fitzgerald, J. R. (1987). Group instruction with profoundly retarded persons: Acquisition, generalization, and maintenance of a remunerative work skill. *Journal of Applied Behavior Analysis, 20,* 97–105.

Schiavi, R. C. (1990). Chronic alcoholism and male sexual dysfunction. *Journal of Sex and Marital Therapy, 16,* 23–33.

Scheier, M. F., & Carver, C. S. (1985). Optimism, coping, and health: Assessment and implications of generalized outcome expectancies. *Health Psychology, 4,* 219–247.

Schildkraut, J. J. (1965). The catecholamine hypothesis of affective disorders: A review of the supporting evidence. *American Journal of Psychiatry, 122,* 509–522.

Schlinger, H. D., Jr. (1992). Theory in behavior analysis: An application to child development. *American Psychologist, 47,* 1396–1410.

Schmahl, D. P., Lichtenstein, E., & Harris, D. E. (1972). Successful treatment of habitual smokers with warm, smoky air and rapid smoking. *Journal of Consulting and Clinical Psychology, 38,* 105–111.

Schmauk, F. J. (1970). Punishment, arousal, and avoidance learning in sociopaths. *Journal of Abnormal Psychology, 76,* 443–453.

Schmeck, H., Jr. (1988, November 15). Depression and anxiety seen as cause of much addiction. *New York Times,* p. C3.

Schneider, B. H., & Byrne, B. M. (1987). Individualizing social skills training for behavior-disordered children. *Journal of Consulting and Clinical Psychology, 55,* 444–445.

Schneider, K. (1957). Primäre und sekundäre symptome bei der schizophrenia. *Fortschritte der Neurologie Psychiatrie, 25,* 487–490.

Schneider, N. G. (1987). Nicotine gum in smoking cessation: Rationale, efficacy, and proper use. *Comprehensive Therapy, 13,* 32–37.

Schoenfeld, H., Margolin, J., & Baum, S. (1987). Münchausen syndrome as a suicide equivalent: Abolition of syndrome by psychotherapy. *American Journal of Psychotherapy, 41,* 604–612.

Schoenman, T. J. (1984). The mentally ill witch in textbooks of abnormal psychology: Current status and implications of a fallacy. *Professional Psychiatry, 15,* 299–314.

Schopler, E., & Mesibov, G. B. (Eds.) (1984). *The effects of autism on the family.* New York: Plenum Press.

Schork, K. (1990, August 19). The despair of Pakistan's women: Not even Benazir Bhutto could stop the repression. *Washington Post.*

Schott, E. D. E., & Stunkard, A. J. (1987). Bulimia vs. bulimic behaviors on a college campus. *Journal of American Medical Association, 258,* 1213–1215.

Schotte, D. E., & Clum, G. A. (1982). Suicide ideation in a college population: A test of a model. *Journal of Consulting and Clinical Psychology, 50,* 690–696.

Schotte, D. E., & Clum, G. A. (1987). Problem-solving skills in suicidal psychiatric patients. *Journal of Consulting and Clinical Psychology, 55,* 49–54.

Schotte, D. E., Cools, J., & Payvar, S. (1990). Problem-solving deficits in suicidal patients: Trait vulnerability or state phenomenon? *Journal of Consulting and Clinical Psychology, 58,* 562–564.

Schreiner-Engel, P., et al. (1989). Low sexual desire in women: The role of reproductive hormones. *Hormones and Behavior, 23,* 221–234.

Schretlen, D. J. (1988). The use of psychological tests to identify malingered symptoms of mental disorder. *Clinical Psychology Review, 8,* 451–476.

Schuckit, M. A. (1983). Subjective responses to alcohol in sons of alcoholics and controls. *Archives of General Psychiatry, 41,* 879–884.

Schuckit, M. A. (1987). Biological vulnerability to alcoholism. *Journal of Consulting and Clinical Psychology, 55,* 301–309.

Schuckit, M. A., & Rayses, U. (1979). Ethanol ingestion: Differences in blood acetaldehyde concentrations in relatives of alcoholics. *Science, 203,* 54–55.

Schulsinger, F. (1972). Psychopathy: Heredity and environment. *International Journal of Mental Health, 1,* 190–206.

Schulsinger, H. (1976). A ten year follow-up of children of schizophrenic mothers: A clinical assessment. *Acta Psychiatrica Scandinavica, 53,* 371–386.

Schwab, J. J., Bialow, M. R., & Holzer, C. E. (1967). A comparison of two rating scales for depression. *Journal of Clinical Psychology, 23,* 94–96.

Schwartz, J. L. (1987). *Review and evaluation of smoking cessation methods: The United States and Canada, 1978–1985.* Published by the Division of Cancer Prevention and Control, National Cancer Institute, U.S. Department of Health and Human Services, Public Health Service, National Institutes of Health (NIH Publication No. 87–2940). Washington DC: U.S. Government Printing Office.

Schwartz, M. F., & Masters, W. H. (1984). The Masters and Johnson treatment program for dissatisfied homosexual men. *American Journal of Psychiatry, 141,* 173–181.

Schwartz, R. M. (1986). The internal dialogue: On the asymmetry between positive and negative thoughts. *Cognitive Therapy and Research, 10,* 591–605.

Schwartz, R. M., & Michelson, L. (1987). States-of-mind model: Cognitive balance in the treatment of agoraphobia. *Journal of Consulting and Clinical Psychology, 55,* 557–565.

Schwitzgebel, R. L., & Schwitzgebel, R. K. (1980). *Law and psychological practice.* New York: Wiley.

Scott, J. E., & Schwalm, L. A. (1988). Rape rates and the circulation rates of adult magazines. *Journal of Sex Research, 24,* 241–250.

Scovern, A. W., & Kilmann, P. R. (1980). Status of electroconvulsive therapy: Review of the outcome literature. *Psychological Bulletin, 87,* 260–303.

Sears, R. R., Maccoby, E. E., & Levin, H. (1957). *Patterns of child rearing.* New York: Harper & Row.

Segal, J. H. (1989). Erotomania revisited: From Kraepelin to DSM-III-R. *American Journal of Psychiatry, 146,* 1261–1266.

Segal, Z. V., et al. (1992). Cognitive and life stress predictors of relapse in remitted unipolar depressed patients: Test of the congruency hypothesis. *Journal of Abnormal Psychology, 101,* 26–36.

Segraves, R. (1988). Drugs and desire. In S. Leiblum & R. Rosen (Eds.), *Sexual desire disorders.* New York: Guilford Press.

Seidenberg, M., & Berent, S. (1992). Childhood epilepsy and the role of psychology. *American Psychologist, 47,* 1130–1133.

Seligman, M. E. P. (1973). Fall into helplessness. *Psychology Today, 7,* 43–48.

Seligman, M. E. P. (1975). *Helplessness: On depression, development, and death.* San Francisco: Freeman.

Seligman, M. E. P., & Maier, S. F. (1967). Failure to escape traumatic shock. *Journal of Experimental Psychology, 74,* 1–9.

Seligman, M. E. P., & Rosenhan, D. L. (1984). *Abnormal psychology.* New York: Norton.

Seligman, M. E. P., et al. (1988). Explanatory style change during cognitive therapy for unipolar depression. *Journal of Abnormal Psychology, 97,* 13–18.

Seligman, M. E. P., et al. (1984). Attributional style and depressive symptoms among children. *Journal of Abnormal Psychology, 93,* 235–238.

Selkoe, D. J. (1992). Aging brain, aging mind. *Scientific American, 267* (3), 134–142.

Selye, H. (1976). *The stress of life* (rev. ed.). New York: McGraw-Hill.

Semans, J. (1956). Premature ejaculation: A new approach. *Southern Medical Journal, 49,* 353–358.

Shadish, W. R., Jr., Lurigio, A. J., & Lewis, D. A. (1989). After deinstitutionalization: The present and future of mental health long-term care policy. *Journal of Social Issues, 45,* 1–15.

Shafi, I. (1986). Dr. Shafi replies. *American Journal of Psychiatry, 143,* 1193–1194.

Shagass, C., Straumanis, J. J., Roemer, R. A., & Amadeo, M. (1979). Temporal variability of somatosensory, visual, and auditory evoked potentials in schizophrenia. *Archives of General Psychiatry, 36,* 1341–1351.

Shapiro, D., & Goldstein, I. B. (1982). Behavioral perspectives on hypertension. *Journal of Consulting and Clinical Psychology, 50,* 841–859.

Shapiro, D. A., & Shapiro, D. (1982). Meta-analysis of comparative therapy outcome studies: A replication and refinement. *Psychological Bulletin, 92,* 581–594.

Shapiro, E. (1992, August 22). Fear returns to sidewalks of West 96th Street. *New York Times,* pp. B3–B4.

Shaw, J. (1989). The unnecessary penile implant. *Archives of Sexual Behavior, 18,* 455–460.

Shaw, E. D., Stokes, P. E., Mann, J. J., & Manevitz, A. Z. A. (1987). Effects of lithium carbonate on the memory and motor speed of bipolar patients. *Journal of Abnormal Psychology, 96,* 64–69.

Shaw, R., Cohen, F., Doyle, B., & Palesky, J. (1985). The impact of denial and repressive style on information gain and rehabilitation outcomes in myocardial infarction patients. *Psychosomatic Medicine, 47,* 262–273.

Shaywitz, S., Cohen, D., & Shaywitz, B. (1980). Behavior and learning difficulties in children of normal intelligence born to alcoholic mothers. *The Journal of Pediatrics, 96,* 978–982.

Shea, S., et al. (1992). Predisposing factors for severe, uncontrolled hypertension in an inner-city minority population. *New England Journal of Medicine, 327,* 776–781.

Sheingold, K., & Tenney, Y. J. (1982). Memory for a salient childhood event. In U. Niesser (Ed.), *Memory observed: Remembering in natural contexts.* San Francisco: Freeman.

Shekelle, R. B., Gale, M., & Norusis, M. (1985). Type A score (Jenkins Activity Survey) and risk of recurrent coronary heart disease in the Aspirin Myocardial Infarction Study. *American Journal of Cardiology, 56,* 221–225.

Shelton, R. C., & Weinberger, D. R. (1986). X-ray computed tomography studies in schizophrenia: A review and synthesis. In H. A. Nasrallah & D. R. Weinberger (Eds.), *The neurology of schizophrenia* (pp. 207–250). Amsterdam: Elsevier Science.

Shelton, R. C., et al. (1991). Biological and psychological aspects of depression. *Behavior Therapy, 22,* 201–228.

Shenon, P. (1990, September 2). Cocaine epidemic may have peaked. *New York Times.*

Sheridan, C. L., & Radmacher, S. A. (1992). *Health psychology: Challenging the biomedical model.* New York: Wiley.

Sherwin, B., Gelfand, M., & Brender, W. (1985). Androgen enhances sexual motivation in females: A prospective crossover study of sex steroid administration in the surgical menopause. *Psychosomatic Medicine, 47,* 339–351.

Shilts, R. (1988). *And the band played on: Politics, people, and the AIDS epidemic.* New York: Penguin Books.

Shneidman, E. S. (1985). *Definition of suicide.* New York: Wiley.

Shore, J. H., Tatum, E. L., & Vollmer, W. M. (1986). The Mount St. Helen's stress response syndrome. In J. H. Shore (Ed.), *Disaster stress studies: New methods and findings* (pp. 77–98). Washington, DC: American Psychiatric Press.

Shuchman, M. (1990, November 15). Depression hidden in deadly disease. *New York Times,* p. B17.

Shumaker, S. A., & Hill, D. R. (1991). Gender differences in social support and physical health. *Health Psychology, 10,* 102–11.

Shweder, R. (1985). Cross-cultural study of emotions. In A. Kleinman & B. Good (Eds.), *Culture and depression.* Berkeley: University of California Press.

Siegel, D. (1973). *The rights of mental patients.* New York: Avon.

Siegel, J. M., & Kuykendall, D. H. (1990). Loss, widowhood, and psychological distress among the elderly. *Journal of Consulting and Clinical Psychology, 58,* 519–524.

Siegel, K., et al. (1988). Patterns of change in sexual behavior among gay men in New York City. *Archives of Sexual Behavior, 17,* 481–497.

Siegel, L. J. (1992). *Criminology* (4th ed.). St. Paul: West.

Siever, L. J., Benstein, D. P., & Silverman, J. M. (1991). Schizotypal personality disorder: A review of its current status. *Journal of Personality Disorders, 5,* 4–16.

Siever, L. J., et al. (1990b). Increased morbid risk for schizophrenia-related disorders in relatives of schizotypal personality disordered patients. *Archives of General Psychiatry, 47,* 634–640.

Silverman, K., Evans, S. M., Strain, E. C., & Griffiths, R. R. (1992). Withdrawal syndrome after the double-blind cessation of coffee consumption. *New England Journal of Medicine, 327,* 1109–1114.

Silverman, L. H. (1984). Beyond insight: An additional necessary step in redressing intrapsychic conflict. *Psychoanalytic Psychology, 1,* 215–234.

Silverton, L., Finell, K. M., Mednick, S. A., & Schulsinger, F. (1985). Low birth weight and ventricular enlargement in a high-risk sample. *Journal of Abnormal Psychology, 94,* 405–409.

Simmons, J. Q., & Lovaas, O. L. (1969). Use of pain and punishment as treatment techniques with childhood schizophrenia. *American Journal of Psychotherapy, 23,* 23–36.

Singh, G. (1985). Dhat syndrome revisited. *Indian Journal of Psychiatry, 27,* 119–122.

Sintchak, J., & Geer, J. (1975). A vaginal plethysmograph system. *Psychophysiology, 12,* 113–115.

Sirles, E. A., & Franke, P. J. (1989). Factors influencing mother's reactions to intrafamily sexual abuse. *Child Abuse and Neglect, 13,* 131–139.

Skinner, B. F. (1938). *The behavior of organisms: An experimental analysis.* New York: Appleton.

Skinner, B. F. (1983). Intellectual self-management in old age. *American Psychologist, 38,* 239–244.

Slater, D., & Hans, V. P. (1984). Public opinion of forensic psychiatry following the Hinckley verdict. *American Journal of Psychiatry, 141,* 675–679.

Slater, J. F., & Depue, R. A. (1981). The contribution of environmental events and social support to serious suicide attempts in primary depressive disorder. *Journal of Abnormal Psychology, 90,* 275–285.

Sloane, R. B., Staples, F. R., Yorkston, N. J., Whipple, K., & Cristol, A. H. (1975). *Short-term analytically oriented psychotherapy versus behavior therapy.* Cambridge, MA: Harvard University Press.

Smith, D. (1982). Trends in counseling and psychotherapy. *American Psychologist, 37,* 802–809.

Smith, G. A., & Hall, J. A. (1982). Evaluating Michigan's guilty but mentally ill verdict: An empirical study. *University of Michigan Journal of Law Reform, 16,* 77.

Smith, J. N., & Baldessarini, R. J. (1980). Changes in prevalence, severity, and recovery in tardive dyskinesia with age. *Archives of General Psychiatry, 37,* 1368–1373.

Smith, M. E., & Fremouw, W. J. (1987). A realistic approach to treating obesity. *Clinical Psychology Review, 7,* 449–465.

Smith, M. L., & Glass, G. V. (1977). Meta-analysis of psychotherapy outcome studies. *American Psychologist, 32,* 752–760.

Smith, M. L., Glass, G. V., & Miller, T. I. (1980). *The benefits of psychotherapy.* Baltimore: Johns Hopkins University Press.

Smith, R. E., & Winokur, G. (1983). Affective disorders. In R. E. Tarter (Ed.), *The child at psychiatric risk.* New York: Oxford University Press.

Smith, R. J. (1978). *The psychopath in society.* New York: Academic Press.

Smith, S. C. (1983). *The great mental calculators.* New York: Columbia University Press.

Smith, S. S., & Newman, J. P. (1990). Alcohol and drug abuse-dependence disorders in psychopathic and nonpsychopathic criminal offenders. *Journal of Abnormal Psychology, 99,* 430–439.

Smith, T. W., Snyder, C. R., & Perkins, S. C. (1983). The self-serving function of hypochondriacal complaints: Physical symptoms as self-handicapping strategies. *Journal of Personality and Social Psychology, 44,* 787–797.

Smoking declines at a faster pace. (1992, May 22). *New York Times,* A17.

Snyder, S. H. (1977). Opiate receptors and internal opiates. *Scientific American, 236,* 44–56.

Snyder, S. H. (1980). *Biological aspects of mental disorder.* New York: Oxford University Press.

Snyder, S. H. (1984). Drug and neurotransmitter receptors in the brain. *Science, 224,* 22–31.

Sobell, M. B., & Sobell, L. C. (1973). Alcoholics treated by individualized behavior therapy: One year treatment outcome. *Behaviour Research and Therapy, 11,* 599–618.

Sobell, M. B., & Sobell, L. C. (1976). Second year treatment outcome of alcoholics treated by individualized behavior therapy: Results. *Behaviour Research and Therapy, 14,* 195–215.

Sobell, M. B., & Sobell, L. C. (1984). The aftermath of heresy: A response to Pendery et al.'s critique of "Individualized behavior therapy for alcoholics." *Behaviour Research and Therapy, 22,* 413–440.

Sobell, L. C., Toneatoo, A., & Sobell, M. B. (1990). Behavior therapy. In A. S. Bellack & M. Hersen (Eds.), *Comparative treatment for adult disorders.* (pp. 479–505). New York: Wiley.

Solomon, Z., Weisenberg, M., Schwarzwald, J., & Mikulincer, M. (1987). Posttraumatic stress disorder among frontline soldiers with combat stress reaction: The 1982 Israeli experience. *American Journal of Psychiatry, 144,* 448–454.

Somers, A. R. (1979). Marital status, health and use of health services. *Journal of the American Medical Association, 241,* 1818–1822.

Somervell, P. D., et al. (1989). The prevalence of major depression in black and white adults in five United States communities. *American Journal of Epidemiology, 130,* 725–735.

Sorenson, S. B., & Golding, J. M. (1988). Suicide ideation and attempts in Hispanics and non-Hispanic Whites: Demographic and psychiatric disorder issues. *Suicide and Life-Threatening Behavior, 18,* 205–218.

Sorenson, S. B., & Rutter, C. M. (1991). Transgenerational patterns of suicide attempt. *Journal of Consulting and Clinical Psychology, 59,* 861–866.

Sorenson, S. B., Rutter, C. M., & Aneshensel, C. S. (1991). Depression in the community: An investigation into age of onset. *Journal of Consulting and Clinical Psychology, 59,* 541–546.

Spanos, N. P. (1978). Witchcraft in histories of psychiatry: A critical analysis and an alternative conceptualization. *Psychological Bulletin, 85,* 417–439.

Spanos, N. P., Weekes, J. R., & Bertrand, L. D. (1985). Multiple personality: A social psychological perspective. *Journal of Abnormal Psychology, 94,* 362–376.

Spark, R. F. (1991). *Male sexual health: A couple's guide.* Mount Vernon, NY: Consumer Reports.

Spector, I. P., & Carey, M. P. (1990). Incidence and prevalence of the sexual dysfunctions: A critical review of the empirical literature. *Archives of Sexual Behavior, 19,* 389–408.

Speigel, D., & Cardena, E. (1991). Disintegrated experience: The dissociative disorders revisited. *Journal of Abnormal Psychology, 100,* 366–378.

Spencer, D. D., et al. (1992). Unilateral transplantation of human fetal mesencephalic tissue into the caudate nucleus of patients with Parkinson's disease. *New England Journal of Medicine, 327,* 1541–1548.

Spencer, D. J. (1983). Psychiatric dilemmas in Australian aborigines. *International Journal of Social Psychiatry, 29* (3), 208–214.

Spiegel, D., et al. (1989, October 14). Effect of psychosocial treatment on survival of patients with metastatic breast cancer. *Lancet*, pp. 888–891.

Spiegel, D. S., & Wissler, T. (1986). Family environment as a predictor of psychiatric rehospitalization. *American Journal of Psychiatry, 143,* 56–60.

Spiker, D., & Ricks, M. (1984). Visual self-recognition in autistic children: Developmental relationships. *Child Development, 55,* 214–225.

Spitzer, R. L. (1991). An outsider-insider's views about revising the DSMs. *Journal of Abnormal Psychology, 100,* 294–296.

Spitzer, R. L., Forman, J. B., & Nee, J. (1979). DSM-III field trials: I. Initial inter-rater diagnostic reliability. *American Journal of Psychiatry, 136,* 815–817.

Spitzer, R. L., & Forman, J. B. (1979). DSM-III field trials: II. Initial experience with the multiaxial system. *American Journal of Psychiatry, 136,* 818–820.

Spitzer, R. L., Gibbon, M., Skodol, A. E., Williams, J. B. W., & First, M. B. (1989). *DSM-III-R casebook.* Washington, DC: American Psychiatric Press.

Spitzer, R. L., et al. (1991). Results of a survey of forensic psychiatrists. *American Journal of Psychiatry, 148,* 875–879.

Spitzer, R. L., et al. (1992b). Now is the time to retire the term "organic mental disorders." *American Journal of Psychiatry, 149,* 240–244.

Spitzer, R. L., et al. (1992c). The Structured Clinical Interview for DSM-III-R (SCID). I: History, rationale, and description. *Archives of General Psychiatry, 49,* 624–629.

Spivak, G., Marcus, J., & Swift, M. (1986). Early classroom behaviors and later misconduct. *Developmental Psychology, 22,* 124–131.

Spivack, G., Platt, J. J., & Shure, M. B. (1976). *The problem-solving approach to adjustment.* San Francisco: Jossey-Bass.

Spohn, H. E., et al. (1986). Episodic and residual thought pathology in chronic schizophrenics: Effects of neuroleptics. *Schizophrenia Bulletin, 12,* 394–407.

Spreen, O. (1988). Prognosis of learning disability. *Journal of Consulting and Clinical Psychology, 56,* 836–842.

Squire, L. R. (1982). Neuropsychological effects of ECT. In W. B. Essman & R. Abrams (Eds.), *Electroconvulsive therapy.* New York: SP Medical and Scientific Books.

Squire, L. R., & Slater, P. C. (1983). Electroconvulsive therapy and complaints of memory dysfunction—A prospective 3 year follow-up study. *British Journal of Psychiatry, 142,* 1–8.

Squire, L. R., & Zouzounis, J. A. (1986). ECT and memory: Brief pulse versus sine wave. *American Journal of Psychiatry, 143,* 596–601.

Stamler, J. (1985a). Coronary heart disease: Doing the "right things." *New England Journal of Medicine, 312,* 1053–1055.

Stamler, J. (1985b). The marked decline in coronary heart disease mortality rates in the United States, 1968–1981: Summary of findings and possible explanations. *Cardiology, 72,* 11–12.

Stamler, J., et al. (1986). Is the relationship between serum cholesterol and risk of premature death from coronary heart disease continuous and graded? Findings in 356,222 primary screenees of the Multiple Risk Factor Intervention Trial (MRFIT). *Journal of the American Medical Association, 256,* 2823–2828.

Stampfer, M., & Hennekens, C. (1988). Alcohol consumption and cardiovascular disease in women. *New England Journal of Medicine, 319,* 267–273.

Stanton, A. H., et al. (1984). Effects of psy-

chotherapy in schizophrenia: I. Design and implementation of a controlled study. *Schizophrenia Bulletin, 10,* 520–563.

Steadman, H. J. (1979). *Beating a rap: Defendants found incompetent to stand trial.* Chicago: University of Chicago Press.

Steele, C. M., & Southwick, L. (1985). Alcohol and social behavior: I. The psychology of drunken excess. *Journal of Personality and Social Psychology, 48,* 18–34.

Stefanek, M. E., Ollendick, T. H., Baldock, W. P., Francis, G., & Yaeger, N. J. (1987). Self-statements in aggressive, withdrawn, and popular children. *Cognitive Therapy and Research, 11,* 229–239.

Stein, L. I., & Tess, A. A. (Eds.). (1978). *Alternatives to mental hospital treatment.* New York: Plenum.

Steinberg, L., Dornbusch, S. M., & Brown, B. B. (1992). Ethnic differences in adolescent achievement: An ecological perspective. *American Psychologist, 47,* 723–729.

Steinberg, M. (1991). The spectrum of depersonalization: Assessment and treatment. *Annual Review of Psychiatry, 10,* 223–247.

Steketee, G., & Foa, E. B. (1985). Obsessive-compulsive disorder. In D. H. Barlow (Ed.), *Clinical handbook of psychological disorders* (pp. 69–144). New York: Guilford Press.

Steptoe, A., Melville, D., & Ross, A. (1984). Behavioral response demands, cardiovascular reactivity, and essential hypertension. *Psychosomatic Medicine, 46,* 33–48.

Stern, J. S., & Lowney, P. (1986). Obesity: The role of physical activity. In K. Brownell & J. Fereyt (Eds.), *Handbook of eating disorders.* New York: Basic.

Stevenson, H. W., et al. (1985). Cognitive performance and academic achievement of Japanese, Chinese, and American children. *Child Development, 56,* 718–734.

Stevenson, H. W., Lee, S. Y., & Stigler, J. W. (1986). Mathematics achievement of Chinese, Japanese, and American children. *Science, 231,* 693–699.

Stiles, W. B., Shapiro, D. A., & Elliott, R. (1986). "Are all psychotherapies equivalent?" *American Psychologist, 41,* 165–180.

Stock, W. E. (1991). Feminist explanations: Male power, hostility, and sexual coercion. In E. Grauerholz & M. A. Koralewski (Eds.), *Sexual coercion: A sourcebook on its nature, causes, and prevention* (pp. 61–73). Lexington, MA: Lexington Books.

Stokols, D. (1992). Establishing and maintaining healthy environments: Toward a social ecology of health promotion. *American Psychologist, 47,* 6–22.

Stoller, R. J. (1969). Parental influences in male transexualism. In R. Green & J. Money (Eds.), *Transexualism and sex reassignment.* Baltimore: Johns Hopkins University Press.

Stone, A. (1976). The *Tarasoff* decisions: Suing psychotherapists to safeguard society. *Harvard Law Review, 90,* 358–378.

Stone, A. (1984). *Law, psychiatry and morality.* Washington, DC: American Psychiatric Press.

Stone, A., & Neale, J. M. (1984). Effects of severe daily events on mood. *Journal of Personality and Social Psychology, 46,* 137–144.

Stone, M. H. (1980). *The borderline syndromes: Constitution, personality, and adaptation.* New York: McGraw-Hill.

Storandt, M. (1983). Psychology's response to the graying of America. *American Psychologist, 38,* 323–326.

Strachan, A. M. (1986). Family intervention for the rehabilitation of schizophrenia: Toward protection and coping. *Schizophrenia Bulletin, 12,* 678–698.

Straube, E. (1979). On the meaning of electrodermal nonresponding in schizophrenia. *Journal of Nervous and Mental Disease, 167,* 601–611.

Strauss, J., & Ryan, R. M. (1987). Autonomy dis-

turbances in subtypes of anorexia nervosa. *Journal of Abnormal Psychology, 96,* 254–258.

Streissguth, A. P., Barr, H. M., Sampson, P. D., Darby, B. L., & Martin, D. C. (1989). IQ at age 4 in relation to maternal alcohol use and smoking during pregnancy. *Developmental Psychology, 25,* 3–11.

Streissguth, A. P., et al. (1984). Interuterine alcohol and nicotine exposure: Attention and reaction time in 4-year-old children. *Developmental Psychology, 20,* 533–541.

Stretch, R. H. (1985). Posttraumatic stress disorder among U.S. Army Reserve Vietnam and Vietnam-era veterans. *Journal of Consulting and Clinical Psychology, 53,* 935–936.

Stretch, R. H. (1987). Posttraumatic stress disorder among U.S. Army reservists: Reply to Nezu and Carnevale. *Journal of Consulting and Clinical Psychology, 55,* 272–273.

Strickler, D. P., Bigelow, G., Lawrence, C., & Liebson, I. (1976). Moderate drinking as an alternative to alcohol abuse: A nonaversive procedure. *Behaviour Research and Therapy, 14,* 279–288.

Strober, M. (1986). Psychopathology of adolescence revisited. *Clinical Psychology Review, 6,* 199–209.

Strober, M., & Humphrey, L. L. (1987). Familial contributions to the etiology and course of anorexia nervosa and bulimia. *Journal of Consulting and Clinical Psychology, 55,* 654–659.

Strunk, R. C., Mrazek, D. A., Fuhrman, A. S. W., & LaBrecque, J. F. (1985). Physiologic and psychological characteristics associated with deaths due to asthma in childhood: A case-controlled study. *Journal of the American Medical Association, 254,* 1193–1198.

Strupp, H. H. (1992). The future of psychodynamic psychotherapy. *Psychotherapy, 29,* 21–27.

Stuart, F., Hammond, C., & Pett, M. (1987). Inhibited sexual desire in women. *Archives of Sexual Behavior, 16,* 91–106.

Stubbs, E. G., Ritvo, E. R., & Mason-Brothers, A. (1985). Autism and shared parental HLA antigens. *Journal of Child Psychiatry, 24,* 182–185.

Study finds severe effects from childhood abuse. (1991, February 18). *New York Times,* p. 11.

Stunkard, A. J., & Wadden, T. A. (1992). Psychological aspects of severe obesity. *American Journal of Clinical Nutrition, 55* (Suppl.), 524S–432S.

Stunkard, A. J., et al. (1986). An adoption study of human obesity. *New England Journal of Medicine, 314,* 193, 198.

Stunkard, A. J., et al. (1990). A separated twin study of the body mass index. *New England Journal of Medicine, 322,* 1483–1487.

Stuss, D. T., Gow, C. A., & Hetherington, C. R. (1992). "No longer Gage." Frontal lobe dysfunction and emotional changes. *Journal of Consulting and Clinical Psychology, 60,* 349–359.

Suddath, R. L., Christison, G. W., Torrey, E. F., Casanova, M. F., & Weinberger, D. R. (1990). Anatomical abnormalities in the brains of monozygotic twins discordant for schizophrenia. *New England Journal of Medicine, 322,* 789–794.

Sue, S. (1988). Psychotherapeutic services for ethnic minorities: Two decades of research findings. *American Psychologist, 43,* 301–308.

Sue, S., & Okazaki, S. (1990). Asian-American educational achievements. *American Psychologist, 45,* 913–920.

Sue, S., et al. (1976). Conceptions of mental illness among Asian and Caucasian American students. *Psychological Reports, 38,* 703–708.

Sue, S., et al. (1991). Community mental health services for ethnic minority groups: A test of the cultural responsiveness hypothesis. *Journal of Consulting and Clinical Psychology, 59,* 533–540.

Sullivan, H. S. (1962). *Schizophrenia as a human process.* New York: Norton.

Surgeon General's Report. (1989). *Reducing the health consequences of smoking: 25 years of progress.* Atlanta: Centers for Disease Control.

Susser, E. S., Lin, S. P., & Conover, S. A. (1991). Risk factors for homelessness among patients admitted to a state mental hospital. *American Journal of Psychiatry, 148,* 1659–1664.

Susser, E. S., Struening, E. L., & Conover, S. (1989). Psychiatric problems in homeless men. *Archives of General Psychiatry, 46,* 845–850.

Sutherland, A. J., & Rodin, G. M. (1990). Factitious disorders in a general hospital setting: Clinical features and a review of the literature. *Psychosomatics, 31,* 392–399.

Sutherland, G. R., et al. (1991). Prenatal diagnosis of Fragile X syndrome by direct detection of the unstable DNA sequence. *New England Journal of Medicine, 325,* 1720–1722.

Sutker, P. B., Uddo-Crane, M., & Allain, A. N., Jr. (1991). Clinical and research assessment of posttraumatic stress disorder: A conceptual overview. *Psychological Assessment, 3,* 520–530.

Suzdak, P. D., Glowa, J. R., Crawley, J. N., & Schwartz, R. D. (1986). A selective imidazobenzodiazepine antagonist of ethanol in the rat. *Science, 225,* 1243–1247.

Swaim, R. C., Oetting, E. R., Edwards, R. W., & Beauvais, F. (1989). Links from emotional distress to adolescent drug use: A path model. *Journal of Consulting and Clinical Psychology, 57,* 227–231.

Swartz, M., et al. (1991). Somatization disorder. In L. N. Robins & D. A. Regier (Eds.), *Psychiatric disorders in America: The Epidemiologic Catchment Area Study* (pp. 220–257). New York: The Free Press.

Swayze, V. W., et al. (1990). Structural brain abnormalities in bipolar affective disorder; Ventricular enlargement and focal signal hyperintensities. *American Journal of Psychiatry, 47,* 1054–1059.

Sweeney, P. D., Anderson, K., & Bailey, S. (1986). Attributional style in depression: A meta-analytic review. *Journal of Personality and Social Psychology, 50,* 974–991.

Sweet, J. J., Newman, P., & Bell, B. (1992). Significance of depression in clinical neuropsychological assessment. *Clinical Psychology Review, 12,* 21–45.

Syndulko, K. (1978). Electrocortical investigations of sociopathy. In R. D. Hare and D. Schalling (Eds.), *Psychopathic behavior: Approaches to research* (pp. 145–156). Chichester, England: Wiley.

Szasz, G., et al. (1987). Induction of penile erection by intracavernosal injection: A double-blind comparison of phenoxybenzamine versus papaverine-phentolamine versus saline. *Archives of Sexual Behavior, 16,* 371–378.

Szasz, T. S. (1963). *Law, liberty and psychiatry.* New York: Macmillan.

Szasz, T. S. (1970a). *Ideology and insanity: Essays on the psychiatric dehumanization of man.* New York: Doubleday Anchor.

Szasz, T. S. (1984). *The therapeutic state: Psychiatry in the mirror of current events.* Buffalo: Prometheus.

Szymanski, S., Kane, J. M., & Lieberman, J. A. (1991). A selective review of biological markers in schizophrenia. *Schizophrenia Bulletin, 17,* 99–111.

Taber, G. I., McCormick, R. A., Russo, A. N., Adkins, B. J., & Ramirez, L. F. (1987). Follow-up of pathological gamblers after treatment. *American Journal of Psychiatry, 144,* 757–761.

Talbott, E., et al. (1985). Occupational noise exposure, noise-induced hearing loss, and the epidemiology of high blood pressure. *American Journal of Epidemiology, 121,* 501–514.

Talbott, J. A. (1981). *The chronic mentally ill: Treatment, programs, systems.* New York: Human Sciences Press.

Tannahill, R. (1980). *Sex in history.* New York: Stein and Day.

Tarasoff v. Regents of the University of California, 131 Cal Rptr. 14, 551 P. 2d 344 (1976).

Tarter, R., & Edwards, K. (1986). Antecedents to alcoholism: Implications for prevention and treatment. *Behavior Therapy, 17,* 346–361.

Tarter, R., Hegedus, A. M., Winsten, N. E., & Alterman, A. I. (1984). Neuropsychological, personality, and family characteristics of physically abused delinquents. *Journal of the American Academy of Child Psychiatry, 23,* 668–674.

Task Force Report, American Psychiatric Association. (1980). Effects of antipsychotic drugs: Tardive dyskinesia. *American Journal of Psychiatry, 37,* 1163–1171.

Taylor, C. B., Killen, J. D., and the Editors of Consumer Reports Books. (1991). *The facts about smoking.* Yonkers, NY: Consumer Reports.

Telch, C. F., & Telch, M. J. (1986). Group coping skills instruction and supportive group therapy for cancer patients: A comparison of strategies. *Journal of Consulting and Clinical Psychology, 54,* 802–808.

Tellegen, A., et al. (1988). Personality similarity in twins reared apart and together. *Journal of Personality and Social Psychology, 54,* 1031–1039.

Teng, E. L., Chui, H. C., Schneider, L. S., & Metzger, L. E. (1987). Alzheimer's dementia: Performance on the Mini-Mental State Examination. *Journal of Consulting and Clinical Psychology, 55,* 96–100.

Teri, L. (1992, November). Clinical problems in older adults. *Clinician's Research Digest* (Supplemental Bulletin No. 9).

Teri, L., & Wagner, A. (1992). Alzheimer's disease and depression. *Journal of Consulting and Clinical Psychology, 60,* 379–391.

Terr, L. C. (1991). Childhood traumas: An outline and overview. *American Journal of Psychiatry, 148,* 10–20.

Tessler, R. C., & Dennis, D. L. (1989). *Synthesis of NIHM-funded research concerning persons who are homeless and mentally ill.* Rockville, MD: National Institute of Mental Health.

Tharp, R. G. (1991). Cultural diversity and treatment of children. *Journal of Consulting and Clinical Psychology, 59,* 799–812.

Thase, M. E., et al. (1991). Cognitive behavior therapy of endogenous depression: I. An outpatient clinical replication series. *Behavior Therapy, 22,* 457–467.

Thigpen, C. H., & Cleckley, H. M. (1984). On the incidence of multiple personality disorder. *International Journal of Clinical and Experimental Hypnosis, 32,* 63–66.

Thoits, P. A. (1983). Dimensions of life events as influences upon the genesis of psychological distress and associated conditions: An evaluation and synthesis of the literature. In H. B. Kaplan (Ed.), *Psychosocial stress: Trends in theory and research.* New York: Academic Press.

Thompson, L. (1991, January 15). Health status of Hispanics: Nation's fastest-growing minority lacks access to medical care. *Washington Post.*

Thoreson, C. E., & Mahoney, M. J. (1974). *Behavioral self-control.* New York: Holt, Rinehart, and Winston.

Thoresen, C. E., & Powell, L. H. (1992). Type A behavior pattern: New Perspectives on theory, assessment, and intervention. *Journal of Consulting and Clinical Psychology, 60,* 560, 594–604.

Thurman, C. W. (1985a). Effectiveness of cognitive-behavioral treatments in reducing Type A behavior among university faculty. *Journal of Counseling Psychology, 32,* 74–83.

Thurman, C. W. (1985b). Effectiveness of cognitive-behavioral treatments in reducing Type A behavior among university faculty—one year later. *Journal of Counseling Psychology, 32,* 445–448.

Tienari, P., et al. (1987). Genetic and psychosocial factors in schizophrenia: The Finnish Adoptive Family Study. *Schizophrenia Bulletin, 13,* 477–484.

Tienari, P., et al. (1990). Adopted-away offspring of schizophrenics and controls: The Finnish adoptive family study of schizophrenia. In L. Robins & M. Rutter (Eds.), *Straight and devious pathways from childhood to adulthood.* New York: Cambridge University Press.

Tiihonen, J., et al. (1992). Modified activity of the human auditory cortex during auditory hallucinations. *American Journal of Psychiatry, 149,* 255–257.

Timpson, J., et al. (1988). Depression in a Native Canadian in Northwestern Ontario: Sadness, grief or spiritual illness? *Canada's Mental Health, 36* (2–3), 5–8.

Tobin, D. L., Johnson, C. L., & Dennis, A. B. (1992). Divergent forms of purging behavior in bulimia nervosa patients. *International Journal of Eating Disorders, 11,* 17–24.

Tolchin, M. (1989, July 19). When long life is too much: Suicide rises among elderly. *New York Times,* pp. A1, A15.

Tomlinson, B. E., Blessed, G., & Roth, M. (1970). Observations on the brains of demented old people. *Journal of the Neurological Sciences, 11,* 205–242.

Tonnesen, P., Norregaard, J., Simonsen, K., & Sawe, U. (1991). A double-blind trial of a 16-hour transdermal nicotine patch in smoking cessation. *New England Journal of Medicine, 325,* 311–315.

Torgersen, S. (1983). Genetic factors in anxiety disorders. *Archives of General Psychiatry, 40,* 1085–1089.

Torgersen, S. (1986). Genetic factors in moderately severe and mild affective disorder. *Archives of General Psychiatry, 43,* 222–226.

Toro, P. A., & Wall, D. D. (1991). Research on homeless persons: Diagnostic comparisons and practice implications. *Professional Psychology: Research and Practice, 22,* 479–488.

Toubiana, Y. H., Milgram, N. A., Strich, Y., & Edelstein, A. (1988). Crisis intervention in a school-community disaster: Principles and practice. *Journal of Community Psychology, 16,* 228–240.

Touchette, N. (1991). Bad rap for Prozac? *Journal of NIH Research, 3,* 42–47.

Tradgold, A. F. (1914). *Mental deficiency.* New York: Wainwood.

Transdermal Nicotine Study Group. (1991). Transdermal nicotine for smoking cessation: Six-month results from two multicenter, controlled clinical trials. *Journal of the American Medical Association, 266,* 3133–3138.

Treaster, J. B. (1991a, January 25). Drop in youth's cocaine use may reflect a societal shift. *New York Times,* p. A18.

Treaster, J. B. (1991b, October 29). Costly and scarce, marijuana is a high more are rejecting. *New York Times,* p. A1.

Treaster, J. B. (1991c, November 17). Fearing AIDS, users of heroin shift to inhaling. *New York Times,* p. L34.

Treatment of panic disorder, the. (1988, November). *Psychiatric Times* (Suppl.).

Treffert, D. A. (1988). The idiot savant: A review of the syndrome. *American Journal of Psychiatry, 145,* 563–572.

Tremblay, R. E., et al. (1992). Early disruptive behavior, poor school achievement, delinquent behavior, and delinquent personality: Longitudinal analyses. *Journal of Consulting and Clinical Psychology, 60,* 64–72.

Trimble, J. E. (1991). The mental health service and training needs of American Indians. In H. F. Myers et al. (Eds.), *Ethnic minority perspectives on clinical training and services in psychology* (pp. 43–48). Washington, DC: American Psychological Association.

Tross, S., & Hirsch, D. A. (1988). Psychological distress and neuropsychological complications of HIV infection and AIDS. *American Psychologist, 43,* 929–934.

Tseng, W., et al. (1992). Koro epidemics in Guangdong, China: A questionnaire survey. *Journal of Nervous and Mental Disease, 180,* 117–123.

Turkington, C. (1983). Drugs found to block dopamine receptors. *APA Monitor, 14,* 11.

Turner, R. J., & Wagonfield, M. O. (1967). Occupational mobility and schizophrenia. *American Sociological Review, 32,* 104–113.

Turner, S. M. (1992, December). Behavioral treatment of anxiety disorders in African-Americans. Paper presented at a symposium *Anxiety Disorders in African Americans,* presented by the State University of New York Health Science Center at Brooklyn, NY.

Turner, S. M., & Beidel, D. C. (1989). Social phobia: Clinical syndrome, diagnosis, and comorbidity. *Clinical Psychology Review, 9,* 3–18.

Turner, S. M., Beidel, D. C., & Costello, A. (1987). Psychopathology in the offspring of anxiety disorder patients. *Journal of Consulting and Clinical Psychology, 55,* 229–235.

Turner, S. M., Beidel, D. C., Dancu, C. V., & Keys, D. J. (1986). Psychopathology of social phobia and comparison to avoidant personality disorder. *Journal of Abnormal Psychology, 95,* 389–394.

Turner, S. M., Beidel, D. C., & Townsley, R. M. (1990). Social phobia: Relationship to shyness. *Behaviour Research and Therapy, 28,* 497–505.

Turner, S. M., Beidel, D. C., & Townsley, R. M. (1992). Social phobia: A comparison of specific and generalized subtypes and avoidant personality disorder. *Journal of Abnormal Psychology, 101,* 326–331.

Turner, S. M., & Luber, R. F. (1980). The token economy in day hospital settings: Contingency management or information feedback. *Journal of Behavior Therapy and Experimental Psychiatry, 11,* 89–94.

Turner, S. M., McCann, B. S., Beidel, D. C., & Mezzich, J. E. (1986). DSM-III classification of the anxiety disorders: A psychometric study. *Journal of Abnormal Psychology, 95,* 168–172.

Uebersax, J. S. (1987). ECT results and meta-analysis. *American Journal of Psychiatry, 144,* 255–256.

Ullmann, L. P., & Krasner, L. (1975). *A psychological approach to abnormal behavior* (2nd ed.). Englewood Cliffs, NJ: Prentice-Hall.

United States Bureau of the Census. (1989). *Statistical abstract of the United States: 1989* (109th ed.). Washington, DC: U.S. Government Printing Office.

USDHHS (United States Department of Health and Human Services). (1982). *The health consequences of smoking: Cardiovascular disease.* (DHHS Publication No. PHS 84-50204). Rockville, MD: Author.

USDHHS (United States Department of Health and Human Services). (1991). *Healthy people 2000: National health promotion and disease prevention objectives.* Washington, DC: U.S. Government Printing Office.

U.S. Department of Justice. (1986). *Attorney general's commission on pornography: Final report.* Washington, DC: U.S. Government Printing Office.

U.S. Department of Justice, Federal Bureau of Investigation. (1990). *Uniform Crime Reports. (1990). Rape statistics.* Washington, DC: U.S. Government Printing Office.

Unsettling Report on an Epidemic of Rape. *Time Magazine,* May 4, 1992, p. 15.

Vaillant, G. E. (1983). *The natural history of alcoholism.* Cambridge: Harvard University Press.

Vaillant, G. E., & Milofsky, E. S. (1982). The etiology of alcoholism. *American Psychologist, 37,* 494–503.

Van den Hout, M., Emmelkamp, P., Kraaykamp, H., & Griez, E. (1988). Behavioral treatment of obsessive-compulsives: Inpatient vs. outpatient. *Behaviour Research and Therapy, 26,* 331–332.

Van den Hout, M. A., Van der Molen, M., Griez, E., Lousberg, H., & Nansen, A. (1987). Reduction of CO_2-induced anxiety in panic attacks after repeated CO_2 exposure. *American Journal of Psychiatry, 144,* 788–791.

van der Molen, G. M., Van den Hout, M. A., Vroemen, J., Loustberg, H., et al. (1986). Cognitive determinants of lactate-induced anxiety. *Behaviour Research and Therapy, 24,* 677–680.

Van Dyke, C., & Byck, R. (1982). Cocaine. *Scientific American, 44* (3), 128–141.

Van Italie, T. B. (1985). Health implications of overweight and obesity in the United States. *Annals of Internal Medicine, 103,* 983–988.

van Kammen, D. P. (1977). Y-Aminobutyric acid (GABA) and the dopamine hypothesis of schizophrenia. *American Journal of Psychiatry, 134,* 138–143.

van Kammen, D. P., van Kammen, W. B., Mann, L. L., Seppala, T., & Linnoila, M. (1986). Dopamine metabolism in the cerebrospinal fluid of drug-free schizophrenic patients with and without cortical atrophy. *Archives of General Psychiatry, 43,* 978–983.

van Praag, H. M. (1988). Editorial: Biological psychiatry audited. *Journal of Nervous and Mental Disease, 176,* 195–199.

Vandenberg, S. G., Singer, S. M., & Daub, D. L. (1986). *The heredity of behavior disorders in adults and children.* New York: Plenum.

van Son, M. J. M., Mulder, G., & Londen, A. V. (1990). The effectiveness of dry bed training for nocturnal enuresis in adults. *Behaviour Research and Therapy, 28,* 347–349.

Van Wyk, P. H., & Geist, C. S. (1984). Psychosocial development of heterosexual, bisexual, and homosexual behavior. *Archives of Sexual Behavior, 13,* 505–544.

Vaughn, C. E., & Leff, J. P. (1976). The influence of family and social factors on the course of psychiatric illness. A comparison of schizophrenic and depressed neurotic patients. *British Journal of Psychiatry, 129,* 125–137.

Vaughn, C. E., & Leff, J. P. (1981). Patterns of emotional response in relatives of schizophrenic patients. *Schizophrenia Bulletin, 7,* 43–44.

Victor, M., Adams, R., & Collins, G. (1971). *The Wernicke-Korsakoff syndrome.* Philadelphia: Davis.

Vincent, K. R., & Harman, M. J. (1991). The Exner Rorschach: An analysis of its clinical validity. *Journal of Clinical Psychology, 47,* 596–599.

Visintainer, M. A., Volpicelli, J. R., & Seligman, M. E. P. (1982). Tumor rejection in rats after inescapable or escapable shock. *Science, 216,* 437–439.

Vogler, R. E., Compton, J. V., & Weissbach, T. A. (1975). Integrated behavior change techniques for alcoholics. *Journal of Consulting and Clinical Psychology, 43,* 233–243.

Vogler, G. P., DeFries, J. C., & Decker, S. N. (1985). Family history as an indicator of risk for reading disability. *Journal of Learning Disabilities, 18,* 419–421.

Volberding, P. A., et al. (1990). Zidovudine in asymptomatic human immunodeficiency virus infection. *New England Journal of Medicine, 322,* 941–949.

Volberg, R. A., & Steadman, H. J. (1988). Refining prevalence estimates of pathological gambling. *American Journal of Psychiatry, 145,* 502–505.

Wachtel, P. L. (1982). What can dynamic therapies contribute to behavior therapy? *Behavior Therapy, 13,* 594–609.

Wachtel, P. L. (1991). Toward a more seamless psychotherapeutic integration. *Journal of Psychotherapy Integration, 1,* 43–54.

Wagner, R. K., & Torgesen, J. K. (1987). The nature of phonological processing and its causal role in the acquisition of reading skills. *Psychological Bulletin, 101,* 192–212.

Walker, C. E., Hedberg, A., Clement, P. W., & Wright, L. (1981). *Clinical procedures for behavior therapy.* Englewood Cliffs, NJ: Prentice-Hall.

Wallace, C. J., & Liberman, R. P. (1985). Social skills training for patients with schizophrenia: A controlled clinical trial. *Psychiatry Research, 15,* 239–247.

Wallace, J. (1985). The alcoholism controversy. *American Psychologist, 40,* 372–373.

Wallace, J., & O'Hara, M. W. (1992). Increases in depressive symptomatology in the rural elderly: Results from a cross-sectional and longitudinal study. *Journal of Abnormal Psychology, 101,* 398–404.

Warheit, G. J., Vega, W. A., Auth, J., & Meinhardt, K. (1985). Psychiatric symptoms and dysfunctions among Anglos and Mexican Americans: An epidemiological study. In J. R. Greenley (Ed.), *Research in community and mental health* (pp. 3–32). London: JAI Press.

Warner, R. (1989). Deinstitutionalization: How did we get where we are? *Journal of Social Issues, 45,* 17–30.

Waterman, J. (1986). Family dynamics of incest with young children. In K. MacFarlane et al. (Eds.), *Sexual abuse of young children: Evaluation and treatment* (pp. 204–219). New York: Guilford.

Waterman, J., et al. (1986). Challenges for the future. In K. MacFarlane, et al. (Eds.), *Sexual abuse of young children: Evaluation and treatment* (pp. 315–332). New York: Guilford.

Waterman, J., & Lusk, R. (1986). Scope of the problem. In K. MacFarlane et al. (Eds.), *Sexual abuse of young children* (pp. 3–14). New York: Guilford Press.

Watson, J. B., & Rayner, R. (1920). Conditioned emotional reactions. *Journal of Experimental Psychology, 3,* 1–14.

Watson, J. D., & Crick, F. H. C. (1953). Molecular structure of nucleic acids: A structure for deoxyribose nucleic acid. *Nature, 171,* 737–738.

Watson, S. J., et al. (1978). Effects of naloxone on schizophrenia: Reductions in hallucinations in a subpopulation of subjects. *Science, 201,* 73–76.

Watt, D. C. (1982). The search for genetic linkage in schizophrenia. *British Journal of Psychiatry, 140,* 532–537.

Watters, W. W. (1986). Supra-biological factors in the assessment of males seeking penile prostheses. *Canadian Journal of Psychiatry, 31,* 25–31.

Wechsler, D. (1945). A standardized memory scale for clinical use. *Journal of Psychology, 19,* 87–95.

Wechsler, D. (1975). Intelligence defined and undefined: A relativistic appraisal. *American Psychologist, 30,* 135–139.

Wehr, T. A., Skwerrer, R. G., Jacobsen, F. M., Sack, D. A., & Rosenthal, N. E. (1987). Eye versus skin phototherapy of seasonal affective disorder. *American Journal of Psychiatry, 144,* 753–757.

Weinberger, D. R., et al. (1980). Cerebral ventricular enlargement in chronic schizophrenia: An association with poor response to treatment. *Archives of General Psychiatry, 37,* 11–13.

Weinberger, D. R., Cannon-Spoor, E., Potkin, S. G., & Wyatt, R. J. (1980). Poor premorbid adjustment and CT scan abnormalities in chronic schizophrenia. *American Journal of Psychiatry, 137,* 1410–1413.

Weinberger, D. R., Wagner, R. L., & Wyatt, R. J. (1983). Neuropathological studies of schizophrenia. A selective review. *Schizophrenia Bulletin, 9,* 193–212.

Weinberger, D. R., & Wyatt, R. J. (1982). Cerebral ventricular size: A biological marker for subtyping chronic schizophrenia. In E. Usdin and I. T. Hanin (Eds.), *Biological markers in psychiatry and neurology* (pp. 505–512). New York: Pergamon Press.

Weiner, B. A. (1985). The insanity defense: Historical development and present status. *Behavioral Sciences and the Law, 3,* 3–35.

Weiner, M. (1988). A crisis as a challenge. In M. K. Aronson (Ed.), *Understanding Alzheimer's disease.* New York: Scribner's.

Weiner, M. (1989, November 26). Evidence points to aluminum's link with Alzheimer's disease. *New York Times,* p. E12.

Weintraub, S. (1987). Risk factors in schizophrenia: The Stony Brook High-Risk Project. *Schizophrenia Bulletin, 13,* 439–450.

Weintraub, S., & Neale, J. M. (1984). Social behavior of children at risk for schizophrenia. In N. Watt, E. J. Anthony, L. C. Winne, & J. E. Rolf (Eds.), *Children at risk for schizophrenia: A longitudinal perspective* (pp. 279–285). New York: Cambridge University Press.

Weisman, A., & Worden, W. (1976). The existential plight in cancer: Significance of the first 100 days. *International Journal of Psychiatry and Medicine, 7,* 1–15.

Weiss, D., Plomin, R., & Mavis-Hetherington, E. (1991). Genetics and psychiatry: An unheralded window on the environment. *American Journal of Psychiatry, 148,* 283–291.

Weiss, G. (1985). Follow-up studies on outcome of hyperactive children. *Psychopharmacology Bulletin, 21,* 169–177.

Weiss, G., Minde, K., Werry, J. S., Douglas, V., & Nemeth, E. (1971). Studies on the hyperactive child: V. Five-year follow-up. *Archives of General Psychiatry, 24,* 409–414.

Weiss, R. (1992, April 8). Update on nicotine patches: With help, they help some. *New York Times,* p. C15.

Weiss, R. D. & Mirin, S. M. (1987). *Cocaine.* Washington, DC: American Psychiatric Press.

Weissman, A. N., & Beck, A. T. (1978, November). *Development and validation of the Dysfunctional Attitudes Scale: A preliminary investigation.* Paper presented at the meeting of the American Educational Research Association, Toronto, Canada.

Weissman, M. (1986). The relationship between panic disorder and agoraphobia: An epidemiologic perspective. *Psychopharmacology Bulletin, 22,* 787–791.

Weissman, M. (1987). Epidemiology of depression: Frequency, risk groups and risk factors. In *Perspectives on depressive disorders.* Rockville, MD: National Institute of Mental Health.

Weissman, M., et al. (1981). Depressed outpatients. Results one year after treatment with drugs and/or interpersonal psychotherapy. *Archives of General Psychology, 18,* 51–55.

Weissman, M. M. et al. (1989). Suicidal ideation and suicide attempts in panic disorder and attacks. *The New England Journal of Medicine, 321,* 1209–1214.

Weissman, M. M., et al. (1991). Affective disorders. In L. N. Robins & D. A. Regier (Eds.), *Psychiatric disorders in America: The Epidemiologic Catchment Area Study* (pp. 53–80). New York: The Free Press.

Weisz, J. R., et al. (1987). Epidemiology of behavioral and emotional problems among Thai and American children: Parent reports for ages 6 to 11. *Journal of the American Academy of Child and Adolescent Psychiatry, 26,* 890–897.

Weisz, J. R., et al. (1988). Thai and American perspective on over-and undercontrolled child behavior problems: Exploring the threshold model among parents, teachers, and psychologists. *Journal of Consulting and Clinical Psychology, 56,* 601–609.

Wenar, C. (1983). *Psychopathology from infancy through adolescence: A developmental approach.* New York: Random House.

Wender, P. H., Rosenthal, D., Kety, S. S., Schulsinger, F., & Welner, J. (1974). Cross-fostering: A research strategy for clarifying the role of genetic and experiential factors in the etiology of schizophrenia. *Archives of General Psychiatry, 30,* 121–128.

Wenzlaff, R. M., & Grozier, S. A. (1988). Depression and the magnification of failure. *Journal of Abnormal Psychology, 97,* 90–93.

Wertlieb, D., Weigel, C., & Feldstein, M. (1987). Stress, social support, and behavior symptoms in middle childhood. *Journal of Clinical Child Psychology, 16,* 204–211.

West, M. A. (1985). Meditation and somatic arousal reduction. *American Psychologist, 40,* 717–719.

Westermeyer, J. (1984). The role of ethnicity in substance abuse. In B. Stimmel (Ed.), *Cultural and sociological aspects of alcoholism and substance abuse* (pp. 9–18). New York: Haworth Press.

Wexler, B. E., & Cicchetti, D. V. (1992). The outpatient treatment of depression: Implications of outcome research for clinical practice. *Journal of Nervous and Mental Disease, 180,* 277–286.

Whalen, C. K., & Henker, B. (1985). The social worlds of hyperactive (ADDH) children. *Clinical Psychology Review, 5,* 447–478.

Whalen, C. K., & Henker, B. (1991). Therapies for hyperactive children: Comparisons, combinations, and compromises. *Journal of Consulting and Clinical Psychology, 59,* 126–137.

Whalen, C. K., et al. (1987). Natural social behaviors in hyperactive children: Dose effects of methylphenidate. *Journal of Consulting and Clinical Psychology, 55,* 187–193.

Whiffen, V. E. (1988). Vulnerability to postpartum depression: A prospective multivariate study. *Journal of Abnormal Psychology, 97,* 467–474.

Whiffen, V. E. (1992). Is postpartum depression a distinct diagnosis? *Clinical Psychology Review, 12,* 485–508.

Whitehead, W. E., & Bosmajian, L. S. (1982). Behavioral medicine approaches to gastrointestinal disorders. *Journal of Consulting and Clinical Psychology, 50,* 972–983.

Whitehouse, P. J., et al. (1982). Alzheimer's disease and senile dementia: Loss of neurons in the basal forebrain. *Science, 215,* 1237–1239.

Whitlock, F. A. (1967). The aetiology of hysteria. *Acta Psychiatric Scandinavia, 43,* 144–162.

Whybrow, P. C., & Prange, A. J. (1981). A hypothesis of thyroid-catecholamine-receptor interaction. *Archives of General Psychiatry, 38,* 106–113.

Wickenhaver, J. (1992, September 8). After the "Wild Man": Can an insane system be cured? *Manhattan Spirit,* pp. 13, 28.

Widiger, T. A. (1991). DSM-IV reviews of the personality disorders: Introduction to special series. *Journal of Personality Disorder, 5,* 122–134.

Widiger, T. A. (1992). Generalized social phobia versus avoidant personality disorder: A commentary on three studies. *Journal of Abnormal Psychology, 101,* 340–343.

Widiger, T. A., et al. (1991). Toward an empirical classification for the *DSM-IV. Journal of Abnormal Psychology, 100,* 280–288.

Widner, H., et al. (1992). Bilateral fetal mesencephalic grafting in two patients with Parkinsonism induced by 1-methyl-4-phenyl-1,2,

3,6-tetrahydropyridine (MPTP). *New England Journal of Medicine, 327,* 1556–1563.

Widom, C. S. (1989). Child abuse, neglect, and adult behavior: Research design and findings on criminality, violence, and child abuse. *American Journal of Orthopsychiatry, 59,* 355–367.

Wiens, A. N., & Menustik, C. E. (1983). Treatment outcome and patient characteristics in an aversion therapy program for alcoholism. *American Psychologist, 38,* 1089–1096.

Wig, N. N., et al. (1987). Distribution of expressed emotion components among relatives of schizophrenic patients in Aarhus and Chandigarh. *British Journal of Psychiatry, 151,* 160–165.

Wilbur, C. B. (1986). Psychoanalysis and multiple personality disorder. In B. G. Braun (Ed.), *Treatment of multiple personality disorder.* Washington, DC: American Psychiatric Press.

Wilkerson, I. (1992, September 4). Hurricane haunts children long after winds have died. *New York Times,* pp. A1, A10.

Wille, R., & Beier, K. M. (1989). Castration in Germany. *Annals of Sex Research, 2,* 103–133.

Willet, W. C., et al. (1990). Relation of meat, fat, and fiber intake to the risk of colon cancer in a prospective study among women. *The New England Journal of Medicine, 323,* 1664–1672.

Williams, D. H. (1986). The epidemiology of mental illness in Afro-Americans. *Hospital and Community Psychiatry, 37,* 42–49.

Williams, J. B. W. (1985). The Multiaxial system of DSM III: Where did it come from and where should it go? Its origins and critics. *Archives of General Psychiatry, 42,* 175–180.

Williams, J. B., et al. (1991). Multidisciplinary baseline assessment of homosexual men with and without human immunodeficiency virus infection: II. Standardized clinical assessment of current and lifetime psychopathology. *Archives of General Psychiatry, 48,* 124–130.

Williams, J. B., et al. (1992). The Structured Clinical Interview for DSM-III-(SCID): II. Multisite test-retest reliability. *Archives of General Psychiatry, 49,* 630–636.

Williams, J. M. (1984). *The psychological treatment of depression: A guide to the theory and practice of cognitive-behavior therapy.* New York: Free Press.

Williams, J. M., Little, M. M., Scates, S., & Blockman, N. (1987). Memory complaints and abilities among depressed older adults. *Journal of Consulting and Clinical Psychology, 55,* 595–598.

Williams, L. (1989, November 22). Psychotherapy gaining favor among blacks. *New York Times,* pp. A1, C7.

Williams, M. (1985). Alcohol and ethnic minorities: Black Americans—an update. *Alcohol Health and Research World, 9,* 52–54.

Williamson, D. F., Kahn, H. S., Remington, P. L., & Anda, R. F. (1990). The 10-year incidence of overweight and major weight gain in U.S. adults. *Archives of Internal Medicine, 150,* 665–672.

Wilson, G. T. (1978). Cognitive-behavior therapy: Paradigm shift or passing phase. In J. P. Foreyt and D. P. Rathjen (Eds.), *Cognitive-behavior therapy: Research and application* (pp. 7–33). New York: Plenum.

Wilson, G. T. (1982). Psychotherapy process and procedure: The behavioral mandate. *Behavior Therapy, 13,* 291–312.

Wilson, G. T. (1987). Chemical aversion conditioning treatment for alcoholism: A re-analysis. *Behaviour Research and Therapy, 25,* 503–516.

Wilson, G. T. (1991). Chemical aversion conditioning in the treatment of alcoholism: Further comments: *Behaviour Research and Therapy, 29,* 415–419.

Wilson, G. T., Rossiter, E., Kleifield, E. I., & Lindholm, L. (1986). Cognitive-behavioral treatment of bulimia nervosa: A controlled evaluation. *Behavior Research and Therapy, 24,* 277–288.

Wilson, G. T., & Walsh, T. (1991). Eating disorders in the *DSM-IV. Journal of Abnormal Psychology, 100,* 362–365.

Wilson, G. T., et al. (1991). Cognitive-behavioral treatment with and without response prevention for bulimia. *Behaviour Research and Therapy, 29,* 575–583.

Wilson, K. G., et al. (1992). Panic attacks in the nonclinical population: An empirical approach to case identification. *Journal of Abnormal Psychology, 101,* 460–468.

Wilson, J. P. (1978). *Ideology and crisis: The Vietnam veteran in transition, Part II.* Final report to the Disabled Veterans Association. Cleveland: Cleveland State University.

Wilson, R. S., & Kaszniak, A. W. (1986). Longitudinal changes: Progressive idiopathic dementia. In L. W. Poon (Ed.), *Handbook for clinical memory assessment of older adults* (pp. 285–294). Washington, DC: American Psychological Association.

Windle, M. (1990). A longitudinal study of antisocial behaviors in early adolescence as predictors of later adolescent substance use: Gender and ethnic group differences. *Journal of Abnormal Psychology, 99,* 86–91.

Winerip, M. (1991, December 18). Soldier in battle for the retarded. *New York Times,* pp. B1, B6.

Winfield, I., et al. (1990). Sexual assault and psychiatric disorders among a community sample of women. *American Journal of Psychiatry, 147,* 335–341.

Wing, J., & Nixon, J. (1975). Discriminating symptoms in schizophrenia. *Archives of General Psychiatry, 32,* 853–859.

Winston, A., et al. (1991). Brief psychotherapy of personality disorders. *Journal of Nervous and Mental Disease, 179,* 188–193.

Wirtz, P. W., & Harrell, A. V. (1987a). Effects of postassault exposure to attack-similar stimuli on long-term recovery of victims. *Journal of Consulting and Clinical Psychology, 55,* 10–16.

Wirtz, P. W., & Harrell, A. V. (1987b). Victim and crime characteristics, coping responses, and short-and long-term recovery from victimization. *Journal of Consulting and Clinical Psychology, 55,* 866–871.

Wise, E. H., & Barnes, D. R. (1986). The relationship among life events, dysfunctional attitudes, and depression. *Cognitive Therapy and Research, 10,* 257–266.

Wise, R. A. (1988). The neurobiology of craving. *Journal of Abnormal Psychology, 97,* 118–132.

Wise, T. P. (1978). Where the public peril begins: A survey of psychotherapists to determine the effects of *Tarasoff. Stanford Law Review, 135,* 165–190.

Witkin, H. A., et al. (1976). XYY and XXY men: Criminality and aggression. *Science, 193,* 547–555.

Wlazlo, Z., et al. (1990). Exposure in vivo vs. social skills training for social phobia: Longterm outcome and differential effects. *Behaviour Research and Therapy, 28,* 181–193.

Wolchick, S. A., et al. (1980). The effects of emotional arousal on subsequent sexual arousal in men. *Journal of Abnormal Psychology, 89,* 595–598.

Wolf, L., & Goldberg, B. (1986). Autistic children group: An 8- to 24-year follow-up study. *Canadian Journal of Psychiatry, 31,* 550–556.

Wolfe, B. E., & Goldfried, M. R. (1988). Research on psychotherapy integration: Recommendations and conclusions from an NIMH workshop. *Journal of Consulting and Clinical Psychology, 56,* 448–451.

Wolfe, V. V. (1990). Sexual abuse of children. In A. S. Bellack, M. Hersen, & A. E. Kazdin (1990). *International handbook of behavior modification and therapy.* (2nd ed.) (pp. 707–730). New York: Plenum Press.

Wolinsky, J. (1982). Responsibility can delay aging. *APA Monitor, 13,* 14, 41.

Wolpe, J. (1958). *Psychotherapy by reciprocal inhibition.* Stanford, CA: Stanford University Press.

Wolpe, J. (1973). *The practice of behavior therapy.* New York: Pergamon Press.

Wolpe, J. (1985). Existential problems and behavior therapy. *The Behavior Therapist, 8,* 126–127.

Wolpe, J., & Lazarus, A. A. (1966). *Behavior therapy techniques.* New York: Pergamon Press.

Wolpe, J., & Rachman, S. (1960). Psychoanalytic "evidence": A critique based on Freud's case of Little Hans. *Journal of Nervous and Mental Disease, 131,* 135–147.

Wolraich, M. L., et al. (1990). Stimulant medication use by primary care physicians in the treatment of attention-deficit hyperactivity disorder. *Pediatrics, 86,* 95–101.

Women under assault. (1990, July 16). *Newsweek,* p. 23.

Wood, J. M., et al. (1992). Effects of 1989 San Francisco earthquake on frequency and content of nightmares. *Journal of Abnormal Psychology, 101,* 219–234.

Wong, B. Y. L. (1986). Problems and issues in the definition of learning disabilities. In J. K. Torgeson & B. Y. L. Wong (Eds.), *Psychological and educational perspectives on learning disabilities* (pp. 3–26). Orlando, FL: Academic Press.

Wong, S. E., Massel, H. K., Mosk, M. D., & Liberman, R. P. (1986). Behavioral approaches to the treatment of schizophrenia. In G. D. Burrows, T. R. Norman, & G. Rubenstein (Eds.), *Handbook of studies on schizophrenia* (pp. 79–100). New York: Elsevier.

Woodruff, R. A., Clayton, P. J., & Guze, S. B. (1975). Is everyone depressed? *American Journal of Psychiatry, 132,* 627–628.

Woody, G. E., McLellan, A. T., Luborsky, L., & O'Brien, C. P. (1987). Twelve-month followup of psychotherapy for opiate dependence. *American Psychologist, 144,* 590–596.

Wurtman, R. J., & Wurtman, J. J. (1984). Nutrients, neurotransmitter synthesis, and the control of food intake. In J. A. Stunkard & E. Stellar (Eds.), *Eating and its disorders* (pp. 77–86). New York: Raven Press.

Wyatt v. Stickney, 334 F. Supp. 1341 (1971).

Wyatt, G. E. (1990). The aftermath of child sexual abuse of African American and white American women: The victim's experience. *Journal of Family Violence, 5,* 61–81.

Wyer, R. S., Jr., Bodenhausen, G. V., & Gorman, T. F. (1985). Cognitive mediators of reactions to rape. *Journal of Personality and Social Psychology, 48,* 324–338.

Wynne, L. C., Cole, R. E., & Perkins, P. (1987). University of Rochester Child and Family Study: Risk research in progress. *Schizophrenia Bulletin, 13,* 463–476.

Yamaguchi, F., Meyer, J. S., Yamamoto, M., Sakai, F., & Shaw, T. (1980). Noninvasive regional cerebral blood flow measurements in dementia. *Archives of Neurology, 37,* 410–418.

Yehuda, R., et al. (1992). Exposure to atrocities and severity of chronic posttraumatic stress disorder in Vietnam combat veterans. *American Journal of Psychiatry, 149,* 333–336.

Ying, Y. (1988). Depressive symptomatology among Chinese-Americans as measured by the CES-D. *Journal of Clinical Psychology, 44,* 739–746.

Yirmiya, N., & Sigman, M. (1991). High functioning individuals with autism: Diagnosis, empirical findings, and theoretical issues. *Clinical Psychology Review, 11,* 669–683.

Young, A. (1992). Cited in Blakeslee, S. (1992, October 27). Unusual clues help in long fight to solve Huntington's disease. *New York Times,* p. C3.

Youngberg v. Romeo, 102 S. Ct. 2452, 2463 (1982).

Zaiden, J. (1982). Psychodynamic therapy: Clinical applications. In A. J. Rush (Ed.), *Short-term psychotherapies for depression.* New York: Guilford Press.

Zalewski, C., & Arrcher, R. P. (1991). Assessment of borderline personality disorder: A review of MMPI and Rorschach findings. *Journal of Nervous & Mental Disease, 179,* 338–345.

Zane, N., & Sue, S. (1991). Culturally responsive mental health services for Asian Americans: Treatment and training issues. In H. F. Myers et al. (Eds.), *Ethnic minority perspectives on clinical training and services in psychology* (pp. 49–58). Washington, DC: American Psychological Association.

Zeiss, A. M., & Lewinsohn, P. M. (1986). Adapting behavioral treatment for depression to meet the needs of the elderly. *The Clinical Psychologist, 98,* 100.

Zigler, E., Taussig, C., & Black, K. (1992). Early childhood intervention: A promising preventative for juvenile delinquency. *American Psychologist, 47,* 997–1006.

Zilbergeld, B., & Evans, M. (1980,). The inadequacy of Masters & Johnson. *Psychology Today,* pp. 29–34, 47–53.

Zilbovicius, et al. (1992). Regional cerebral blood flow in childhood autism: A SPECT study. *American Journal of Psychiatry, 149,* 924–930.

Zillmann, D. (1989). Effects of prolonged consumption of pornography. In D. Zillmann & J. Bryant (Eds.), *Pornography: Research advances and policy considerations* (pp. 127–157). Hillsdale, NJ: Erlbaum.

Zillmann, D., & Weaver, J. B. (1989). Pornography and men's sexual callousness toward women. In D. Zillmann & J. Bryant (Eds.), *Pornography: Research advances and policy considerations* (pp. 95–125). Hillsdale, NJ: Lawrence Erlbaum Associates.

Zisook, S., & Shuchter, S. R. (1991). Depression through the first year after the death of a spouse. *American Journal of Psychiatry, 148,* 1346–1352.

Zorumski, C. F., & Isenberg, K. E. (1991). Insights into the structure and function of GABA-benzodiazepine receptors: Ion channels and psychiatry. *American Journal of Psychiatry, 148,* 162–172.

Zotter, D. L., & Crowther, J. H. (1991). The role of cognitions in bulimia nervosa. *Cognitive Therapy and Research, 15,* 413–426.

Zubin, J., & Spring, B. (1977). Vulnerability—new view of schizophrenia. *Journal of Abnormal Psychology, 86,* 103–126.

Zucker, K. J., & Green, R. (1992). Psychosexual disorders in children and adolescents. *Journal of Child Psychology and Psychiatry, 33,* 107–151.

Zuckerman, M. (1974). The sensation-seeking motive. In B. Maher (Ed.), *Progress in experimental personality research,* Vol. 7. New York: Academic Press.

Zuckerman, M. (1980). Sensation seeking. In H. London & J. Exner (Eds.), *Dimensions of personality.* New York: Wiley.

Zweig-Frank, H., & Paris, J. (1991). Parents' emotional neglect and overprotection according to the recollections of patients with borderline personality disorder. *American Journal of Psychiatry, 148,* 648–651.

Zweigenhaft, R., & Domhoff, G. W. (1991). *Blacks in the white establishment: A study of race and class in America.* New Haven, CT: Yale University Press.

Photo Acknowledgments

CHAPTER 1 Page 3, Bob Daemmrich/Stock Boston; p. 3, Steve Goldberg/Monkmeyer Press; p. 7, AP/Wide World Photos; p. 9, Alan Oddie/Photoedit; p. 9, Bob Daemmrich/Stock Boston; p. 9, Richard Hutchings/Photo Researchers; p. 11, The American Museum of Natural History, NY; p. 12, Granger Collection; p. 13, Granger Collection; p. 14, Granger Collection; p. 15, Bettmann; p. 17, Granger Collection; p. 18, Granger Collection; p. 19, Granger Collection; p. 20, Archives of The History of American Psychology-Univ. of Akron; p. 20, Carl Rogers Memorial Library; p. 20, Brooks/Cole Publishing Company, Pacific Grove, CA; p. 26, Jodi Buren/Woodfin Camp & Associates.

CHAPTER 2 Page 42, Michael Newman/Photoedit;. p. 44, Lew Merrim/Monkmeyer Press; p. 45, Frank Siteman/Stock Boston; p. 46, Archive/Bettmann; p. 47, Archive/Bettmann; p. 48, The Margaret S. Mahler Psychiatric Research Foundation; p. 52, Granger Collection; p. 54, Ken Heyman; p. 55, W. Hill, Jr./The Image Works; p. 55, Lawrence Migdale/Stock Boston; p. 57, Reuters/Bettmann; p. 60, Brandeis University; p. 61, Richard Hutchings/Photo Researchers; p. 62, Aaron T. Beck; p. 64, Margaret Bourke-White/Life Magazine © Time Warner Inc.; p. 65, Tracey Saar; p. 67, Gabor Demjen/Stock Boston; p. 70, Peter Southwick/Stock Boston; p. 71, Mark Richards/Photoedit; p. 73, J. & L. Weber/Peter Arnold; p. 80, Bob Daemmrich/Stock Boston.

CHAPTER 3 Page 84, Harvard University Press; p. 89, Judy Canty/Stock Boston; p. 93, Laima Druskis; p. 93, Brian Brake/Photo Researchers; p. 96, Bettmann; p. 97, Herbert Migdoll/Rainbow; p. 102, Honeywell, Inc.; p. 116, Dan Mc Coy/Rainbow; p. 120, Stacy Pick/Stock Boston; p. 120, Brookhaven National Laboratory; p. 121, George Zimbel/ Monkmeyer Press; p. 121, Alexander Tsiaras/Science Source/ Photo Researchers; p. 121, Archive of General Psychiatry.

CHAPTER 4 Page 127, Phyllis Picardi/Stock Boston; p. 128, Dr. D.J. Mc Laren/Science Photo Library/Photo Researchers; p. 129, Jim Howard/Toni Stone Worldwide/Chicago; p. 129, Myrleen Ferguson/Photoedit; p. 130, Karen Kasmauski/Woodfin Camp & Associates; p. 130, Alan Oddie/Photoedit; p. 136, Bob Daemmrich/Stock Boston; p. 139, Charles Gatewood; p. 141, Vanessa Vick/Photo Researchers; p. 144, Joel Gordon; p. 146, W. Marc Bernsau/The Image Works; p. 147, Joel Gordon; p. 150, Pedrick/The Image Works; p. 152, B. Grunzweig/Photo Researchers; p. 152; p. 156, Joel Gordon; p. 159, Mary Kate Denny/Photoedit; p. 165, AP/World Wide Photos; p. 165, Pool J.O. Barcelone/Gamma-Liaison.

CHAPTER 5 Page 175, David E. Dempster/Offshoot Stock; p. 179, Billy E. Barnes/Stock Boston; p. 179, David E. Dempster/Offshoot Stock; p. 184, Tony Stone Worldwide/Chicago; p. 187, UPI/Bettmann; p. 189, TJ Florian; p. 193, Focus on Sports; p. 200, Van Bucher/Photo Researchers; p. 202, James Wilson/Woodfin Camp & Associates; p. 202, Thomas S. England/Photo Researchers.

CHAPTER 6 Page 213, AP/Wide World Photos; p. 215 , Film Stills Archive/Museum of Modern Art; p. 219, Werner H. Muller/Peter Arnold; p. 223, Michael Weisbrot/Stock Boston; p. 224, AP/Wide World Photos; p. 228, Ray Ellis/Science Source/Photo Researchers; p. 230, Carl Purcell/Photo Researchers; p. 233, UPI/Bettmann; p. 235, Granger Collection.

CHAPTER 7 Page 241, Joel Gordon; p. 243, Paul Conklin/Monkmeyer Press; p. 244, Charles Harbutt/Actuality,

661

Inc.; p. 244, Joan Liftin/Actuality, Inc.; p. 245, Doug Goodman/Monkmeyer Press; p. 246, George Bellerose/Stock Boston; p. 252, Karen Preuss/The Image Works; p. 254, C. Seghers/Photo Researchers; p. 256, Grant LeDuc/Monkmeyer Press; p. 256, Hugh Rogers/Monkmeyer Press; p. 259, Superstock; p. 264, Willie L. Hill, Jr./Stock Boston; p. 266, Michal Heron/Monkmeyer Press; p. 273, James Wilson/Woodfin Camp & Associates; p. 279, Sybil Shackman/Monkmeyer Press.

CHAPTER 8 Page 286, Savino/The Image Works; p. 288, UPI/Bettmann; p. 288, Photofest; p. 292, Photofest; p. 292, Granger Collection; p. 294, Bettmann; p. 294, Joel Gordon; p. 296, Erika Stone; p. 298, Laurie Simmons/Metro Pictures; p. 300, Chuck Koelsch/Stock Boston; p. 300, Bill Gallery/Stock Boston; p. 304, Alon Reininger/Contact Press Images/Woodfin Camp & Associates; p. 308, Stock Boston; p. 311, Jan Halaska/Photo Researchers.

CHAPTER 9 Page 322, Starr/Stock Boston; p. 322, Lawrence Migdale/Tony Stone Worldwide/Chicago; p. 324, Joel Gordon; p. 326, Arnold Hinton/Monkmeyer Press; p. 326, Bill Aron/Photo Researchers; p. 326, Lawrence Migdale/Photo Researchers; p. 334, Dan Mc Coy/Rainbow; p. 336, Bettmann; p. 336, Granger Collection; p. 337, Joel Gordon; p. 340, Nick Koudis/American Cancer Society; p. 343, Rousseau/The ImageJWorks; p. 350, John Spragens, Jr./Photo Researchers; p. 354, Joel Gordon; p. 355, H. Kanus/Photo Researchers; p. 357, Jay Wiley/Monkmeyer Press.

CHAPTER 10 Page 367, George Holton/Photo Researchers; p. 367, Lee Snyder/Photo Researchers; p. 368, Girdaudon/Art Resource; p. 371, Ben Barnhart/Offshoot; p. 375, AP/Wide World Photos; p. 375, AP/Wide World Photos; p. 378, Time Magazine; p. 382, Rhoda Sidney; p. 384, Randy Matusow/Monkmeyer Press; p. 388, Michael Newman/Photoedit; p. 389, Custom Medical Stock Photo; p. 392, Frank Siteman/Stock Boston; p. 395, Didier De Fays/Tony Stone Worldwide/Chicago; p. 403, G. Thomas Bishop/Custom Medical Stock Photo.

CHAPTER 11 Page 409, Granger Collection; p. 409, Granger Collection; p. 411, Sandy Skoglund/Janet Borden, Inc.; p. 413, Dion Ogust/The Image Works; p. 417, Peter Ginter/The Image Bank; p. 419, American Association of Psychology; p. 421, Benyas-Kaufman Photographers, Inc.; p. 422, Grunnitis/Monkmeyer Press; p. 423, Mitchell Funk/The Image Bank; p. 425, Bettmann; p. 431, Laima Druskis; p. 433, George Zimbel/Monkmeyer Press; p. 435, Nancy C. Andreason/University of Iowa; p. 435, Nancy C. Andreason/University of Iowa; p. 449, Kip Rano/Gamma-Liaison; p. 449, Gorman/Gamma-Liaison.

CHAPTER 12 Page 455, Frank Siteman/Stock Boston; p. 459, Steve Weber/Tony Stone Images; p. 463, Robert P. Friedland/Case Western Reserve University; p. 463, AP/World Wide Photos; p. 469, Ch. Petit/Photo Researchers; p. 470, David Leah/Science Photo Library/Photo Researchers; p. 472, Bettmann; p. 473, Simon Fraser/Science Photo Library/Photo Researchers; p. 474, David Sams/Stock Boston; p. 476, Jeff Persons/Stock Boston; p. 476, Dennis Budd Gray/Stock Boston; p. 478, Granger Collection; p. 478, Louis Caravaque/Granger Collection.

CHAPTER 13 Page 486, Tony Freeman/Photoedit; p. 488, Erika Stone; p. 492, Mimi Forsyth/Monkmeyer Press; p. 495, John Mac Pherson/Monkmeyer Press; p. 498, Alexander Tsiaras/Science Source/Photo Researchers; p. 499, Susan Lapides/Design Conceptions; p. 500, Photofest; p. 503, Will and Deni Mc Intyre/Photo Researchers; p. 513, Charles Harbutt/Actuality, Inc.; p. 513, Bob Daemmrich/The Image Works; p. 515, Jean Claude LeJeune/Stock Boston; p. 516, Lawrence Migdale/Photo Researchers; p. 519, Steve Shapiro/Sygma; p. 525, Reuters/Bettmann.

CHAPTER 14 Page 536, Erich Hartmann/Magnum Photos; p. 539, Deke Simon/The Real People Press; p. 543, Susan Rosenberg/Photo Researchers; p. 546, Dan Mc Coy/Rainbow; p. 549, Jim Pickerell/Tony Stone Worldwide/Chicago; p. 550, Susan Lapides/Design Conceptions; p. 557, Michael Newman/Photoedit; p. 560, Stacy Pickerell/Tony Stone Worldwide/Chicago; p. 561, Harry J. Przeken, Jr./Medichrome/Stock Shop; p. 564, Will and Deni Mc Intyre/Photo Researchers; p. 568, Barbara Rios/Photo Researchers; p. 570, Lionel J.M. Delevingne/Stock Boston.

CHAPTER 15 Page 577, AP/Wide World Photos; p. 578, AP/Wide World Photos; p. 579, Peter Southwick/Stock Boston; p. 579, Tom Mc Carthy/Picture Cube; p. 582, Photofest; p. 584, AP/Wide World Photos; p. 586, Bettmann; p. 586, Schapiro/Gamma-Liaison; p. 593, AP/Wide World Photos; p. 595, Ellis Herwig/Stock Boston;p. 599, E. Crews/The Image Works; p. 599, Jean Claude LeJeune/Stock Boston; p. 599, Bob Daemmrich/Stock Boston.

Author Index

Subject Index

DSM-IV DRAFT CRITERIA (1993)
COMPARED TO DSM-III-R (1987)

American Psychiatric Association

AXIS I: CLINICAL SYNDROMES AND OTHER CONDITIONS THAT MAY BE A FOCUS OF CLINICAL ATTENTION

DISORDERS USUALLY FIRST DIAGNOSED IN INFANCY, CHILDHOOD, OR ADOLESCENCE (in DSM-III-R, category labeled: DISORDERS USUALLY FIRST *EVIDENT* IN INFANCY, CHILDHOOD, OR ADOLESCENCE)

Mental Retardation (In DSM-III-R, coded on Axis II)

Mild Mental Retardation

Moderate Mental Retardation

Severe Mental Retardation

Profound Mental Retardation

Learning Disorders (In DSM-III-R, labeled Academic Skills Disorder and coded on Axis II)

Reading Disorder (Developmental Reading Disorder)

Mathematics Disorder (Developmental Arithmetic Disorder)

Disorder of Written Expression (Developmental Expressive Writing Disorder)

Motor Skills Disorder (In DSM-III-R, coded on Axis II)

Developmental Coordination Disorder

Pervasive Developmental Disorders (In DSM-III-R, coded on Axis II)

Autistic Disorder

Rett's Disorder

Childhood Disintegrative Disorder

Asperger's Disorder

Disruptive Behavior and Attention-deficit Disorders (In DSM-III-R, labeled Disruptive Behavior Disorders)

Attention-deficit/Hyperactivity Disorder

Oppositional Defiant Disorder

Conduct Disorder

Feeding and Eating Disorders of Infancy or Early Childhood (In DSM-III-R, category was labeled Eating Disorders and included Anorexia Nervosa and Bulimia Nervosa, which are now given their own category)

Pica

Rumination Disorder

Feeding Disorder of Infancy or Early Childhood

Tic Disorders

Tourette's Disorder

Chronic Motor or Vocal Tic Disorder

Transient Tic Disorder

Communication Disorders (In DSM-III-R, labeled language and Speech Disorders and coded on Axis II)

Expressive Language Disorder (In DSM-III-R, labeled Developmental Expressive Language Disorder)

Mixed Receptive/Expressive Language Disorder (In DSM-III-R, labeled Developmental Receptive Language Disorder)

Phonological Disorder (In DSM-III-R, labeled Developmental Articulation Disorder)

Stuttering (In DSM-III-R, categorized as a Speech Disorder Not Elsewhere Classified)

Elimination Disorders

Encopresis (In DSM-III-R, labeled Functional Encopresis)

Enuresis (In DSM-III-R, labeled Functional Enuresis)

Other Disorders of Infancy, Childhood, or Adolescence

Separation Anxiety Disorder

Selective Mutism (In DSM-III-R, labeled Elective Mutism)

Reactive Attachment Disorder of Infancy or Early Childhood

Stereotypic Movement Disorder (In DSM-III-R, labeled Stereotypy/Habit Disorder)

(Note: Avoidant Disorder of Childhood or Adolescence, Identity Disorder, and Cluttering which were present in DSM-III-R, are not included in DSM-IV)

DELIRIUM, DEMENTIA, AMNESIC AND OTHER COGNITIVE DISORDERS (IN DSM-III-R, CATEGORY LABELED: ORGANIC MENTAL SYNDROME AND DISORDERS)

Deliria

Delirium due to a General Medical Condition

Substance-Induced Delirium

Delirium due to Multiple Etiologies

Dementias

Dementia of the Alzheimer's Type (In DSM-III-R, labeled Primary Degenerative Dementia of the Alzheimer's Type)

Vascular Dementia

Dementias due to Other General Medical Conditions

Dementia due to HIV Disease
Dementia due to Head Trauma
Dementia due to Parkinson's Disease
Dementia due to Huntington's Disease
Dementia due to Pick's Disease
Dementia due to Creutzfeldt-Jakob Disease
Dementia due to Other General Medical Condition

Substance-Induced Persisting Dementia

Dementia due to Multiple Etiologies

Amnestic Disorders

Amnestic Disorder due to a General Medical Condition

Substance-Induced Persisting Amnestic Disorder

MENTAL DISORDERS DUE TO A GENERAL MEDICAL CONDITION NOT ELSEWHERE CLASSIFIED

Catatonic Disorder due to a General Medical Condition

Personality Change due to a General Medical Condition

SUBSTANCE-RELATED DISORDERS (IN DSM-III-R, CATEGORY LABELED: PSYCHOACTIVE SUBSTANCE USE DISORDERS)

Alcohol Use Disorders

Alcohol Dependence

Alcohol Abuse

Alcohol Intoxication (In DSM-III-R, classified as an organic mental disorder)

Alcohol Withdrawal (In DSM-III-R, labeled Uncomplicated Alcohol Withdrawal and classified as an organic mental disorder)

Amphetamine (or Related Substance) Use Disorders

Caffeine Use Disorders

Cannabis Use Disorders

Cocaine Use Disorders

Hallucinogen Use Disorders

Inhalant Use Disorders

Nicotine Use Disorders

Opioid Use Disorders

Phencyclidine Use Disorders

Sedative, Hypnotic, or Anxiolytic Substance Use Disorders

Polysubstance Use Disorder

Other (or Unknown) Substance Use Disorders

SCHIZOPHRENIA AND OTHER PSYCHOTIC DISORDERS (IN DSM-III-R, CATEGORY LABELED: SCHIZOPHRENIA)

Schizophrenia

Paranoid Type

Disorganized Type

Catatonic Type

Undifferentiated Type

Residual Type

Schizophreniform Disorder (In DSM-III-R, classified within category of Psychotic Disorders Not Elsewhere Classified)

Schizoaffective Disorder (In DSM-III-R, classfied within category of Psychotic Disorders Not Elsewhere Classified)

Delusional Disorder (In DSM-III-R, labeled Delusional [Paranoid] Disorder, a major Axis I category)

Brief Psychotic Disorder (Replaces DSM-III-R category of Brief Reactive Psychosis, and is no longer necessarily reactive)

Shared Psychotic Disorder (also labeled Folie a Deux) (Replaces DSM-III-R category of Induced Psychotic Disorder)

Psychotic Disorder due to a General Medical Condition

Substance-Induced Psychotic Disorder

MOOD DISORDERS

Depressive Disorders

Major Depressive Disorder (In DSM-III-R, labeled